ATLAS OF THE WORLD

Cartographic Editor
Harold Fullard M.Sc.

Contents

Map Contents

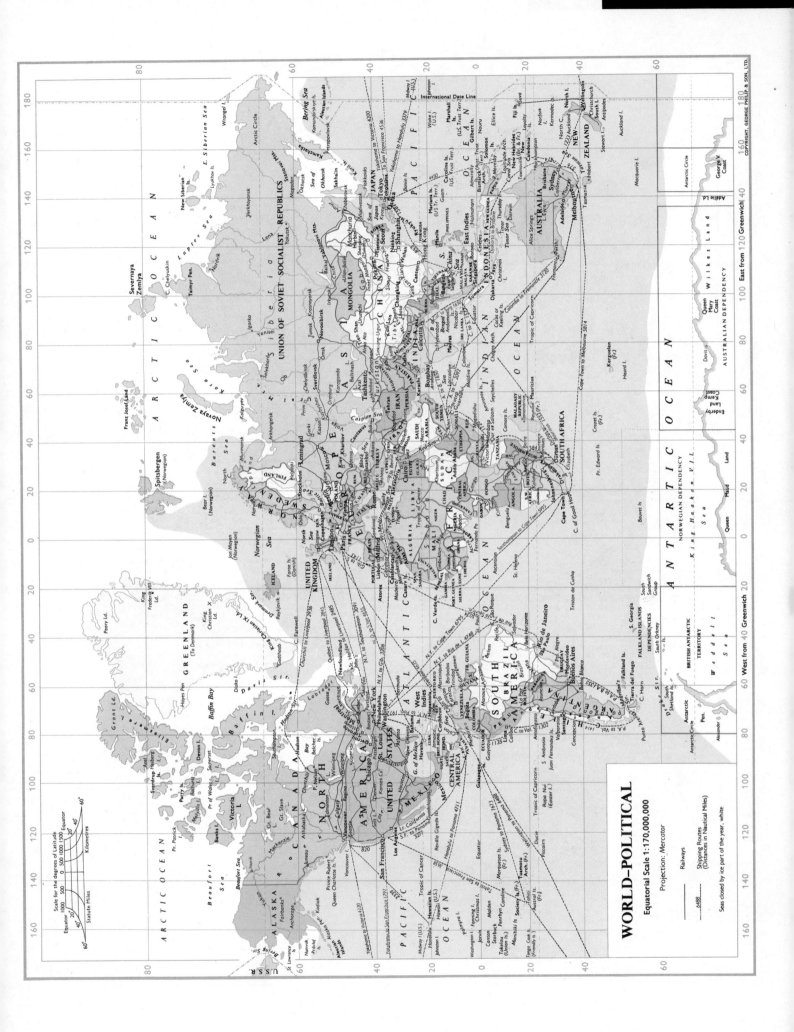

WORLD—POLITICAL

Equatorial Scale 1:170,000,000

Projection: Mercator

Railways

6488 ······ Shipping Routes
(Distances in Nautical Miles)

Seas closed by ice part of the year, white

COPYRIGHT, GEORGE PHILIP & SON, LTD.

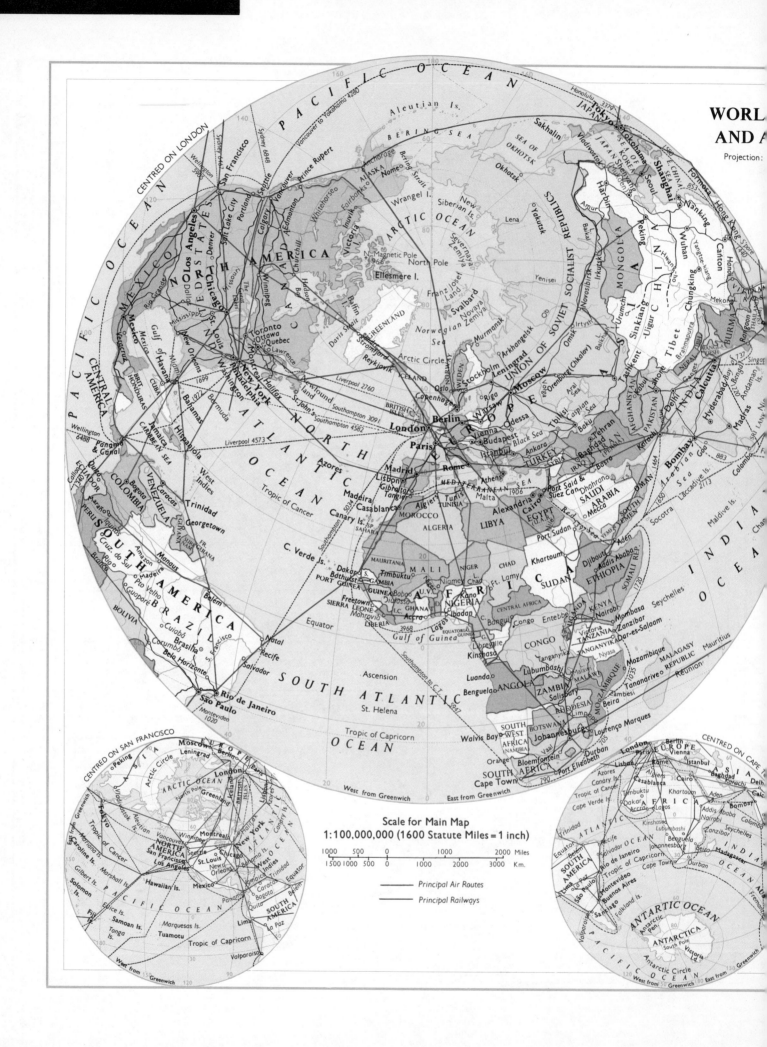

WORL
AND A

Projection:

Scale for Main Map
1:100,000,000 (1600 Statute Miles = 1 inch)

1000   500   0   1000   2000 Miles
1500 1000 500 0   1000   2000   3000 Km.

—————— Principal Air Routes
—————— Principal Railways

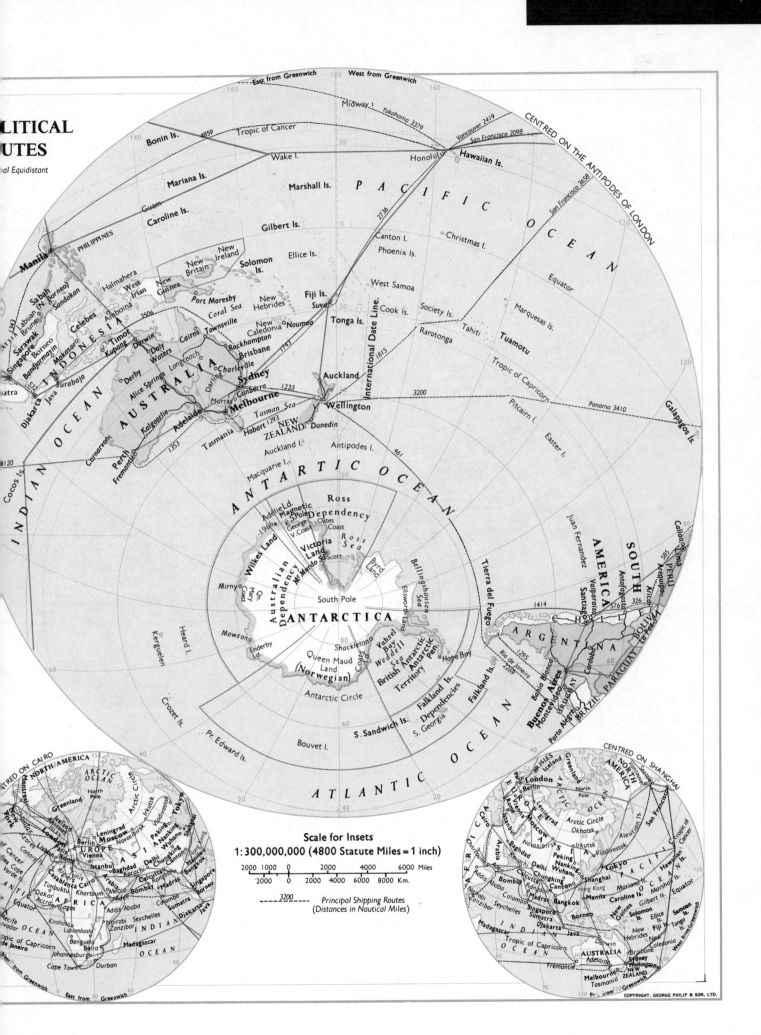

POLITICAL
ROUTES

al Equidistant

CENTRED ON THE ANTIPODES OF LONDON

CENTRED ON CAIRO

CENTRED ON SHANGHAI

Scale for Insets
1 : 300,000,000 (4800 Statute Miles = 1 inch)

2000 1000 0   2000   4000   6000 Miles

2000   0   2000   4000   6000   8000 Km.

— — — 3200 — — —   *Principal Shipping Routes*
(Distances in Nautical Miles)

COPYRIGHT, GEORGE PHILIP & SON, LTD.

ARCTIC OCEAN

ICELAND

Reykjavik   Husavik   Akureyri

Jan Mayen

Faroe Is.
(Dan.)

UNITED
KINGDOM

Montreal to Glasgow 2693
New York to Glasgow 2959

Liverpool to Montreal 2760   Quebec 2872
Liverpool to New York 3043
New York to Southampton 3091   Cherbourg 3065

ATLANTIC OCEAN

Shetland
Is.

Orkney
Is.

NORTH
SEA

NORWAY
SWEDEN
FINLAND

Hammerfest   North C.
Tromsö
Narvik
Kiruna
Gällivare
Luleå

White
Sea

Kolguyev

Pechenga
Murmansk

Liverpool to Murmansk 1713 Archangelsk 2104
Glasgow to Archangelsk 2036

Mezen
Arkhangelsk

Kristiansund
Trondheim
Östersund   Vaasa
Sundsvall   Tampere
Gävle
Bergen   Sogne Fd.
Galdhöpiggen
8097
Lillehammer

Hebrides

Glasgow   Inverness   Aberdeen
Ben   Dundee   Leith to G. 508   C. 610
Nevis
4406   Edinburgh
Londonderry   N.I.   Carlisle

Belfast   Isle of
Man

Galway   IRELAND   Manchester   Leeds
Limerick   Dublin   Liverpool   York
Cork   C. Clear

Oslo
Drammen
Stavanger

Skagerrak
Göteborg
DENMARK
Aalborg   Kattegat
Aarhus   Jönköping
Esbjerg   Copenhagen
Malmö
Flensburg   Kiel
Rostock
Hamburg

L. Vaner
L. Vatter
Stockholm
Uppsala
Örebro
Eskilstuna
Norrköping

Sundsvall

Östersund

Helsinki
Kronstadt

Tallinn
ESTONIA
Pskov

Kuopio

L. Onega

Vyborg   L.
Ladoga
Leningrad

Novgorod   Rybinsk
Res.
Chudskoye   Yaroslavl

LATVIA
Liepaja   Riga

MOSCOW

Swansea   WALES   Birmingham   Norwich
Cardiff   Leeds
Bristol   LONDON
Southampton   Portsmouth   Dover
Plymouth   Scilly Is.

English Channel   Calais
Cherbourg   Le Havre   Rouen   Lille
Brest   Caen   Reims
Rennes   PARIS
Le Mans
Nantes   Orléans   Metz
Tours   Strasbourg
FRANCE   Dijon   Mulhouse
Limoges   Clermont
Ferrand   Geneva
BAY OF BISCAY   Lyons 15,780
St. Etienne   Mt. Blanc
Central   Grenoble
Bordeaux   Massif
Garonne   Cevennes
Toulouse   Avignon
Maladetta   Perpignan   Sète
11,170   Marseilles
Pyrenees   Andorra   Toulon

Amsterdam   Groningen
The Hague
Rotterdam   NETH.
Antwerp
BELGIUM   Brussels
LUX.
Cologne   Halle   Leipzig
Dortmund   Essen   Magdeburg
Wiesbaden   Frankfurt   Dresden
Mainz   KarlMarxstadt
Würzburg   (Chemnitz)
Freiburg   Nürnberg   Plzeň
Stuttgart
Munich   Linz
Basel   SWITZERLAND   Salzburg
Bern   Zürich   Innsbruck   AUSTRIA
Milan   Trento   VIENNA
Brescia   Graz
Turin   Venice   Trieste
Genoa   Bologna   Ljubljana   Zagreb
Spezia   Ravenna   Rijeka
Florence   San Marino   Ancona
Leghorn   ADRIATIC

GERMANY
Bremen   Erfurt
Hanover
Magdeburg   BERLIN
Halle   Leipzig
Dresden   Wrocław   Katowice   Kraków
Prague   CZECHOSLOVAKIA
Bohemian   Brno   Ostrava   Košice
Danube   Bratislava   Miskolc
BUDAPEST   Debrecen
HUNGARY
Szeged   Cluj
Pécs   RUMANIA
Timişoara   Braşov
Belgrade   Transylvanian Alps   Ploesti
Novi Sad   Galaţi
YUGOSLAVIA   Bucharest
Sarajevo   Dinaric Alps   Danube
Split   Niš   Constanţa
Dubrovnik   Pleven   Varna
Sofia   Balkans   Sliven   Burgas
Skopje   BULGARIA
Tirane   Plovdiv   Edirne
ALBANIA   Rhodope   Istanbul   Üsküdar
Thessaloniki   Pindus   Bursa
Kerkira   GREECE   Balikesir
Patrai   Piraievs   Athens
Izmir
Aydin

POLAND
Gdynia   Gdańsk   Kaliningrad
Szczecin   Bydgoszcz   Warsaw
Poznań   Wisła
Łódź   Lublin
Częstochowa   Brest
Wrocław   Breslau
Katowice   Kraków   Lvov

LITHUANIA
Klaipeda
Kaunas   Vilnius
Daugavpils
W. Dvina   Vitebsk
Minsk   Smolensk
WHITE RUSSIA
Białystok
Pripyat   Chernigov   Gomel
Zhitomir   Kiev   Orel
Berdichev   UNION
Lvov   Dnepr
Kirovograd   Poltava
Chernovtsy   Kharkov
MOLDA   Nikolayev
Kishinev   Odessa
Dnepropetrovsk

BLACK

Sevastopol

SPAIN
C. Finisterre   Oviedo   Santander   San Sebastian
Vigo   Cantabrian Mts.   Bayonne
Porto   Valladolid   Ebro
Douro   Zaragoza
Coimbra   Duero
PORTUGAL   MADRID   Barcelona
Lisbon   Tagus   Valencia   Balearic Is.
Guadiana   Toledo   Menorca
Badajoz   Sierra Morena   Palma   Mallorca
Córdoba   (Majorca)
Sevilla   Murcia   Alicante
Guadalquivir   Granada   Cartagena
Málaga   Sa. Nevada   Almería
Cádiz   Str. of Gibraltar   Gibraltar

Ushant

Corsica
Ajaccio

Sardinia

Tyrrhenian Sea

Cagliari

ROME
Naples
Vesuvius
3891

Palermo   Messina
Reggio
Sicily   Etna
10,378
Catania

Ionian Sea

MEDITERRANEAN SEA

Rabat   Fez
Casablanca   Meknes
Marrakech   MOROCCO
Great Atlas
Saharan Atlas

Oran   Algiers
Tlemcen   Blida
ALGERIA   Constantine
Biskra

TUNIS
TUNISIA
Sousse
Sfax

Tripoli

Benghazi

LIBYA

Cyprus

NAT

TU

Ankara

Konya

Antalya

Crete

Al Iskandariya
(Alexandria)

Cairo
(AlQahirah)   Suez

EGYPT

West   5   from Greenwich   0   5   East from 10 Greenwich   15   20   25   30

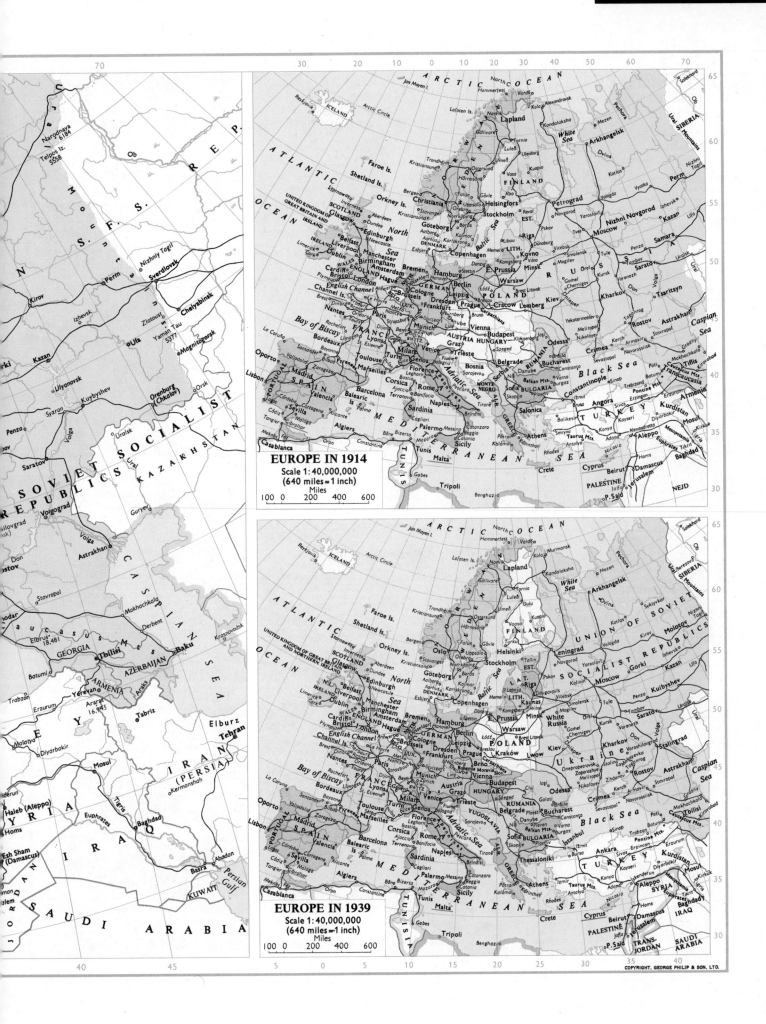

EUROPE IN 1914

Scale 1:40,000,000
(640 miles=1 inch)

Miles

100 0 200 400 600

EUROPE IN 1939

Scale 1:40,000,000
(640 miles=1 inch)

Miles

100 0 200 400 600

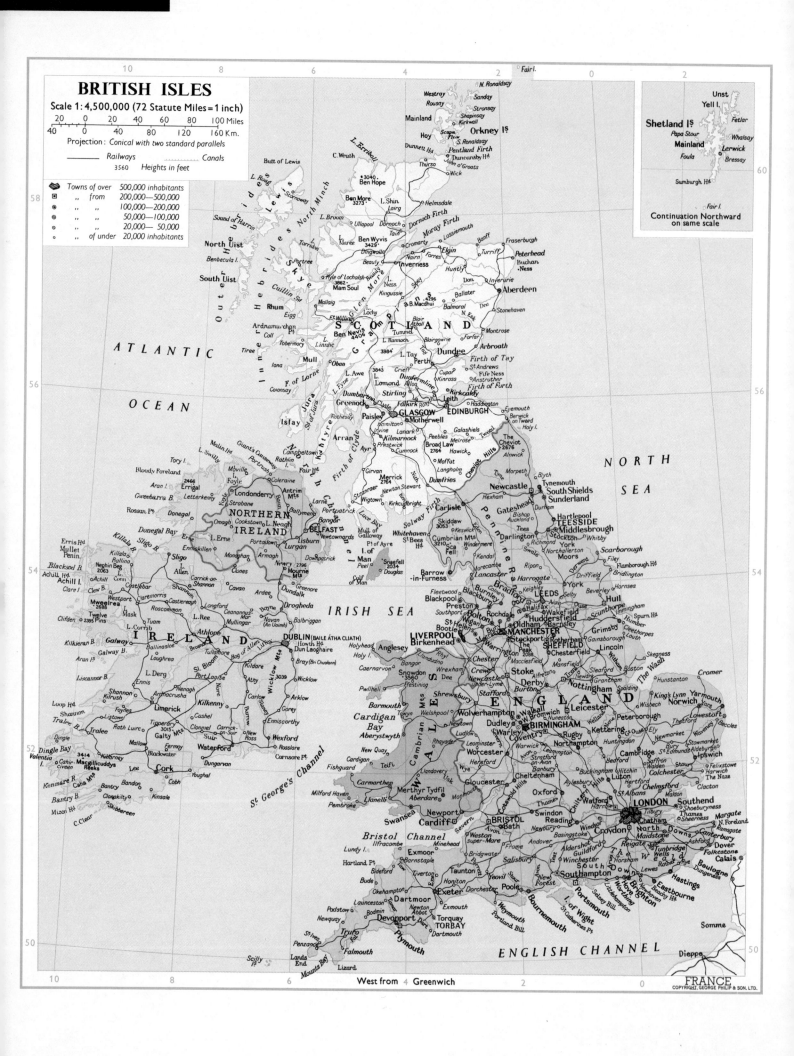

BRITISH ISLES

Scale 1 : 4,500,000 (72 Statute Miles = 1 inch)

Projection : Conical with two standard parallels

——— Railways .... Canals
3560 Heights in feet

	Towns of over	500,000 inhabitants
	,, from	200,000—500,000
	,, ,,	100,000—200,000
	,, ,,	50,000—100,000
	,, ,,	20,000— 50,000
	,, of under	20,000 inhabitants

Shetland Is
Unst
Yell I.
Fetlar
Papa Stour
Whalsay
Mainland
Lerwick
Foula
Bressay
Sumburgh Hd
Fair I.
Continuation Northward
on same scale

ATLANTIC
OCEAN

SCOTLAND

NORTHERN
IRELAND

IRELAND

ENGLAND

WALES

NORTH
SEA

IRISH SEA

St George's Channel

Bristol
Channel

ENGLISH CHANNEL

FRANCE
COPYRIGHT. GEORGE PHILIP & SON. LTD.

West from Greenwich

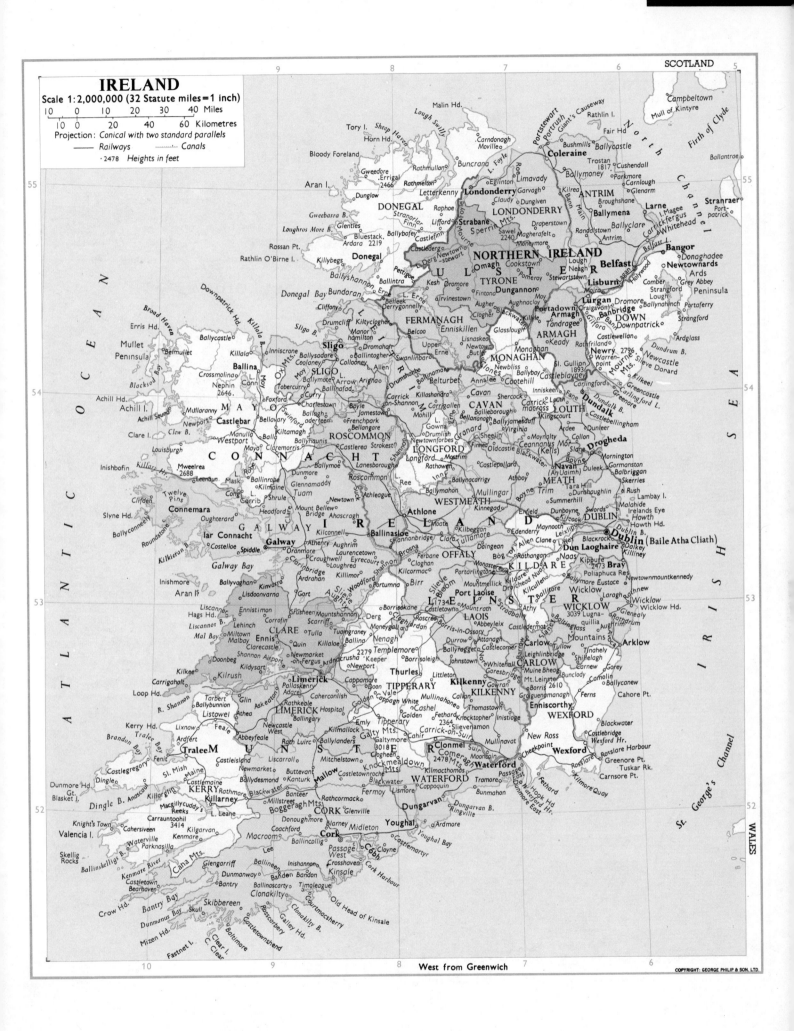

IRELAND

Scale 1:2,000,000 (32 Statute miles=1 inch)

10   0   10   20   30   40 Miles
10 0   20   40   60 Kilometres
Projection: Conical with two standard parallels
———— Railways   ········· Canals
·2478 Heights in feet

West from Greenwich

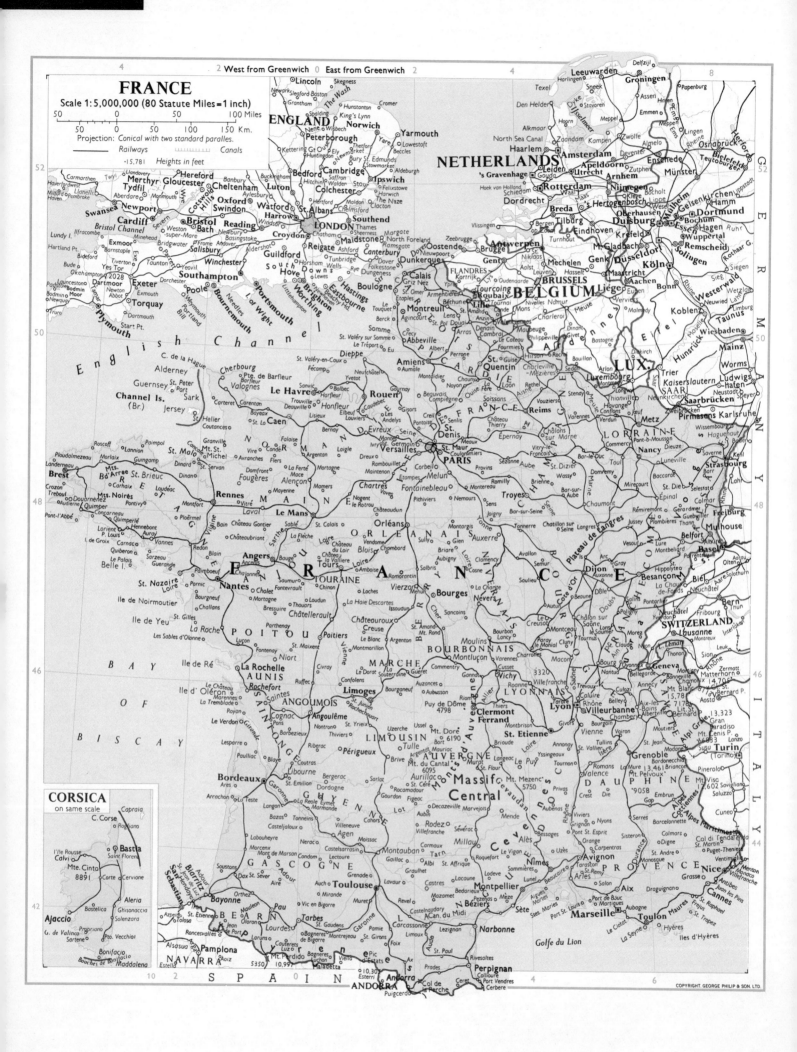

FRANCE

Scale 1:5,000,000 (80 Statute Miles = 1 inch)

50   0   50   100 Miles
50 0 50 100 150 Km.

Projection: Conical with two standard paralles.

——— Railways   Canals

·15,781   Heights in feet

CORSICA

on same scale

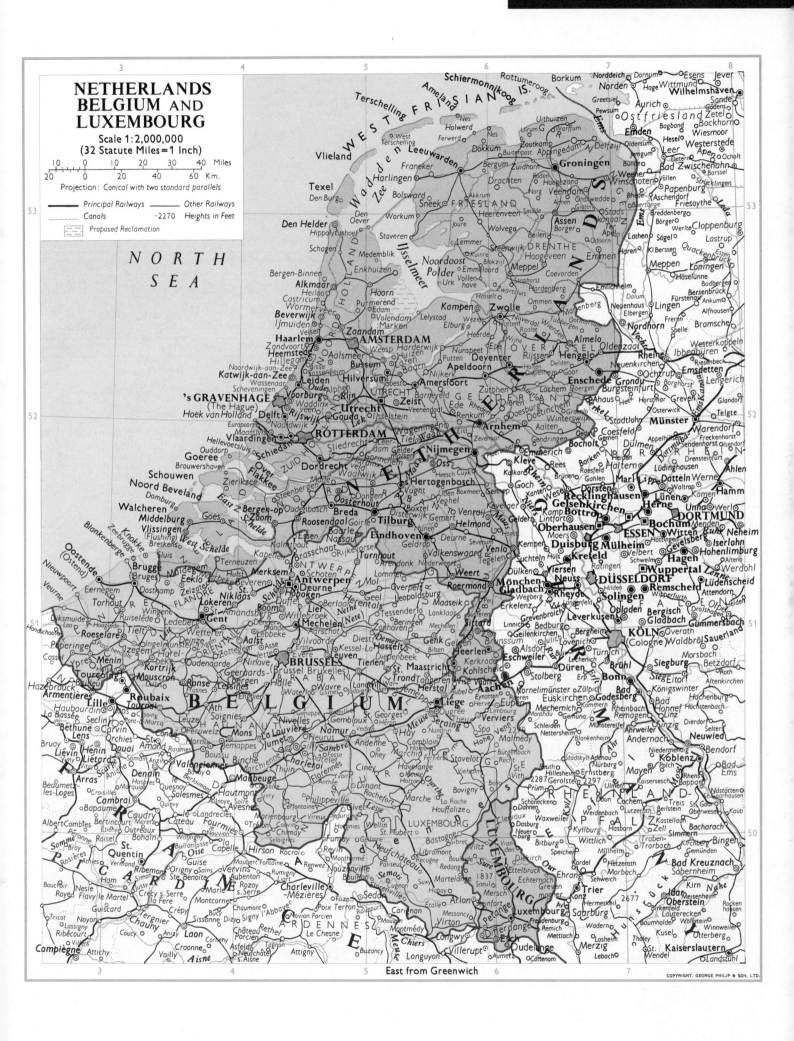

NETHERLANDS BELGIUM AND LUXEMBOURG

Scale 1:2,000,000
(32 Statute Miles=1 Inch)

10   0   10   20   30   40 Miles
20   0   20   40   60 Km.

Projection: Conical with two standard parallels

Principal Railways ——— Other Railways
Canals ·2270 Heights in Feet
Proposed Reclamation

NORTH SEA

COPYRIGHT. GEORGE PHILIP & SON, LTD.

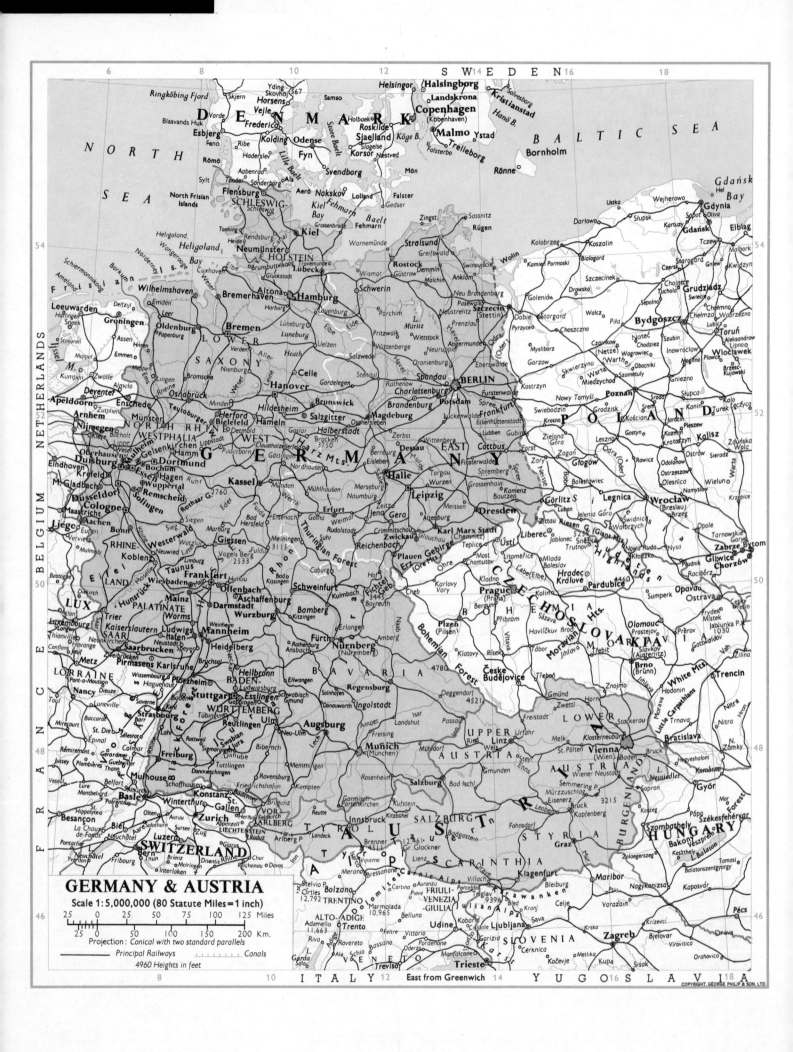

GERMANY & AUSTRIA

Scale 1:5,000,000 (80 Statute Miles=1 inch)

25 0   25   50   75   100   125 Miles

25   0   50   100   150   200 Km.

Projection: Conical with two standard parallels

——— Principal Railways   ·········· Canals

4960 Heights in feet

COPYRIGHT. GEORGE PHILIP & SON. LTD.

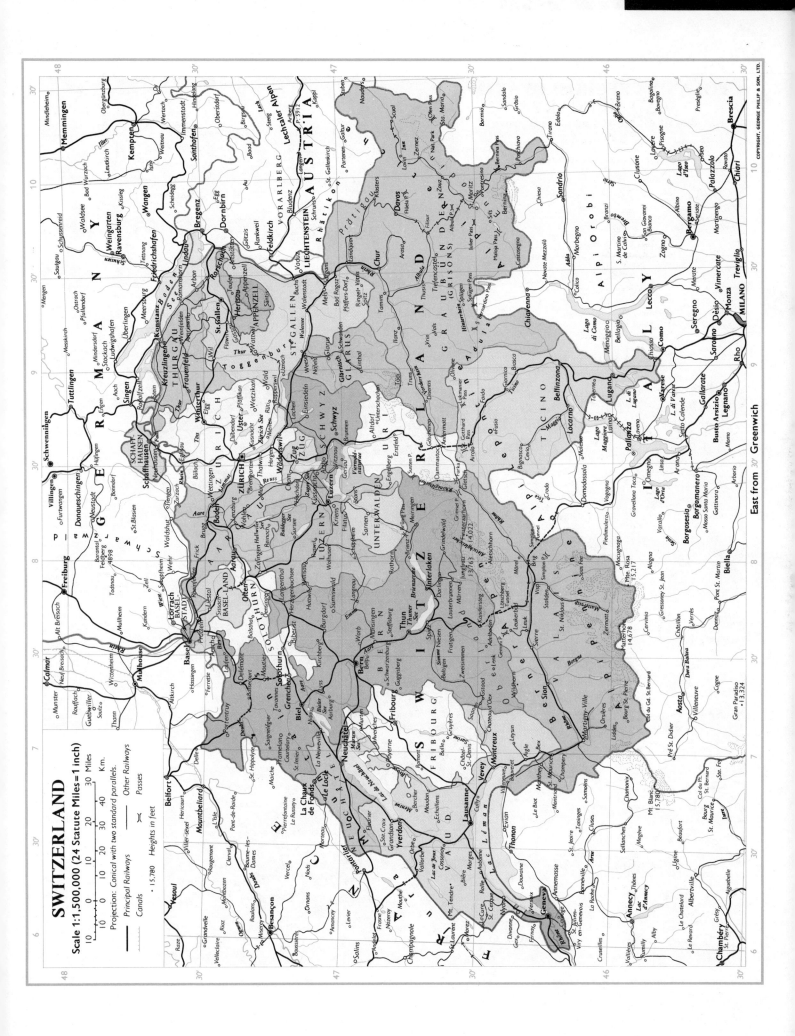

SWITZERLAND

Scale 1:1,500,000 (24 Statute Miles=1 inch)

Projection: Conical with two standard parallels.

— Principal Railways
— Other Railways
—— Canals
—<— Passes
• 15,780   Heights in feet

East from 30' Greenwich

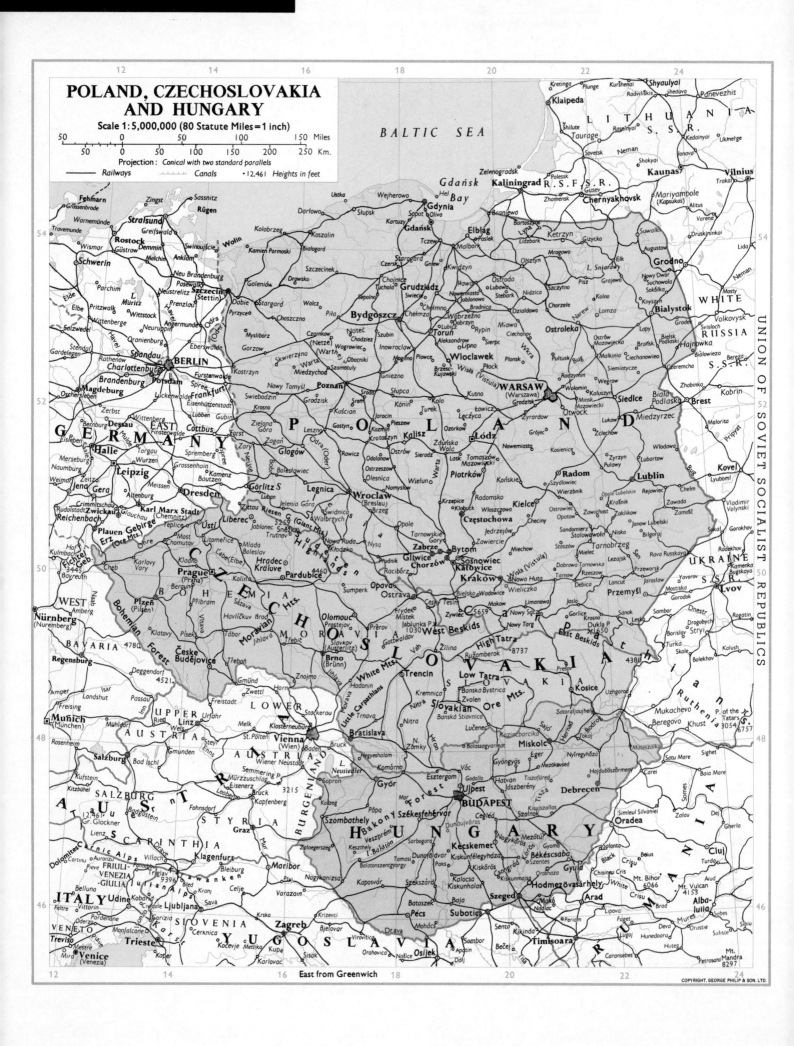

POLAND, CZECHOSLOVAKIA AND HUNGARY

Scale 1:5,000,000 (80 Statute Miles=1 inch)

50   0   50   100   150 Miles

50   0   50   100   150   200   250 Km.

Projection : Conical with two standard parallels

—— Railways   ········ Canals   •12,461 Heights in feet

BALTIC SEA

East from Greenwich

COPYRIGHT. GEORGE PHILIP & SON. LTD.

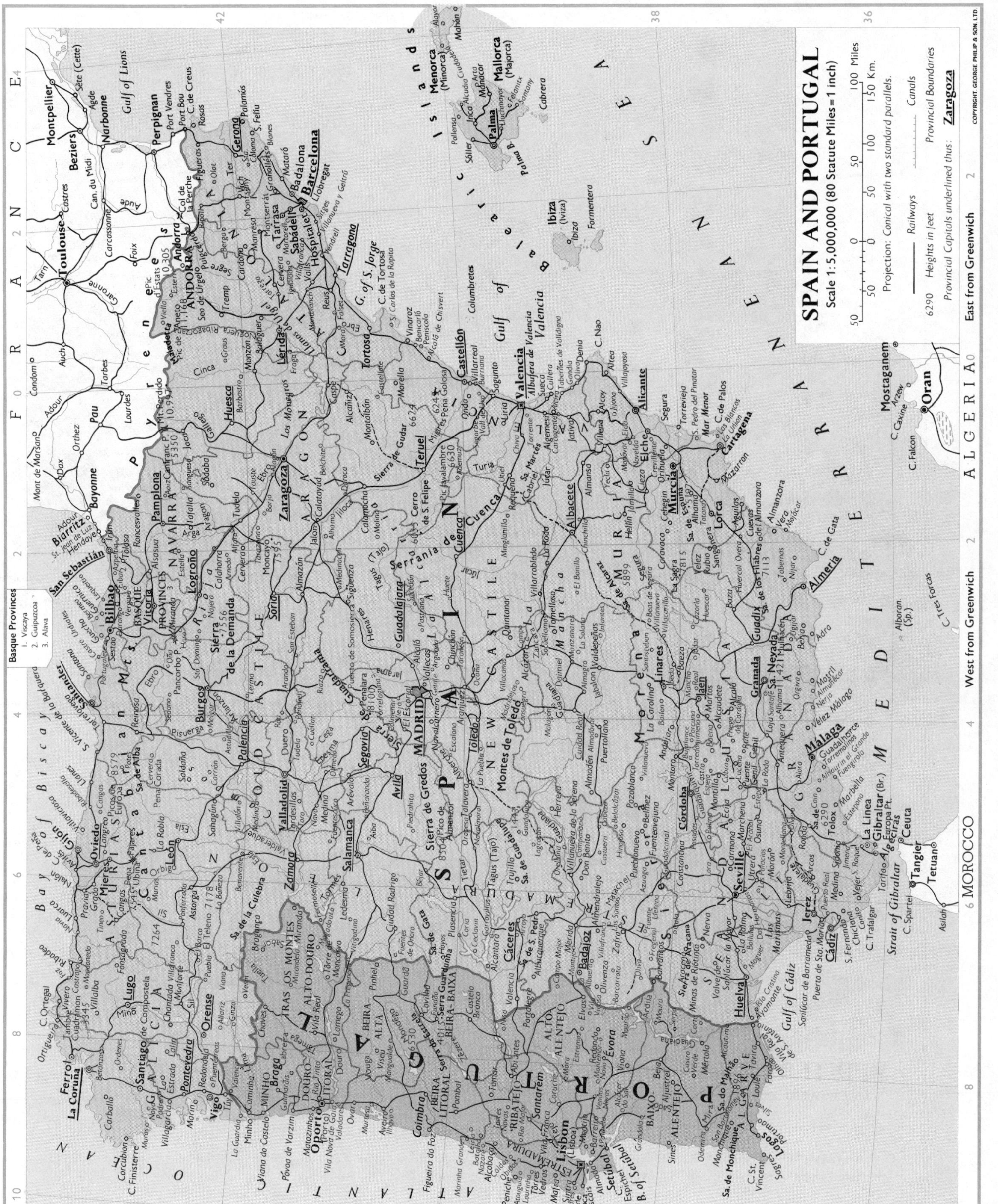

SPAIN AND PORTUGAL

Scale 1:5,000,000 (80 Statute Miles=1 inch)

Projection: Conical with two standard parallels.

50 0 50 100 100 Miles

0 50 100 150 Km.

—— Heights in feet Railways Canals

6290 Provincial Boundaries

Provincial Capitals underlined thus: <u>Zaragoza</u>

COPYRIGHT. GEORGE PHILIP & SON, LTD.

Basque Provinces
1. Viscaya
2. Guipuzcoa
3. Alava

East from Greenwich

West from Greenwich

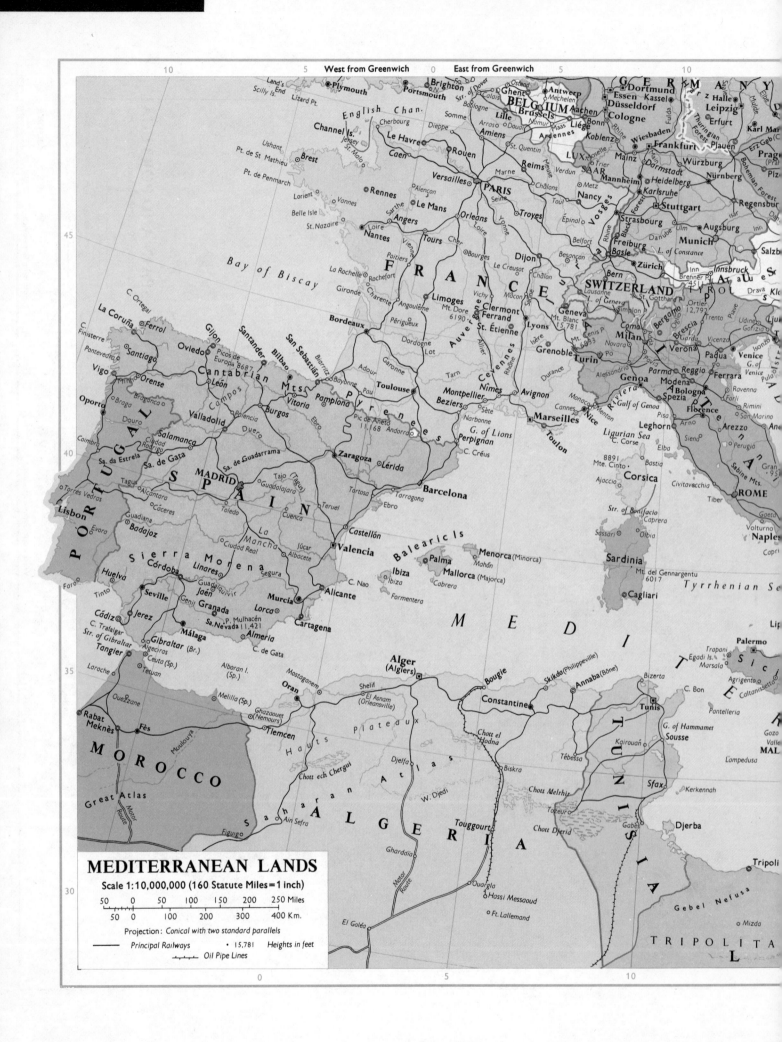

MEDITERRANEAN LANDS

Scale 1:10,000,000 (160 Statute Miles=1 inch)

50 0   50   100   150   200   250 Miles
50 0   100   200   300   400 Km.

Projection: Conical with two standard parallels

—————— Principal Railways   • 15,781 Heights in feet
⊢⊢⊢⊢⊢ Oil Pipe Lines

ITALY AND THE BALKAN STATES

Scale 1:5,000,000 (80 Statute Miles=1 inch)

Projection: Conical with two standard parallels.

——— Railways   ····· Canals   6017 Heights in feet

CRETE
on same scale

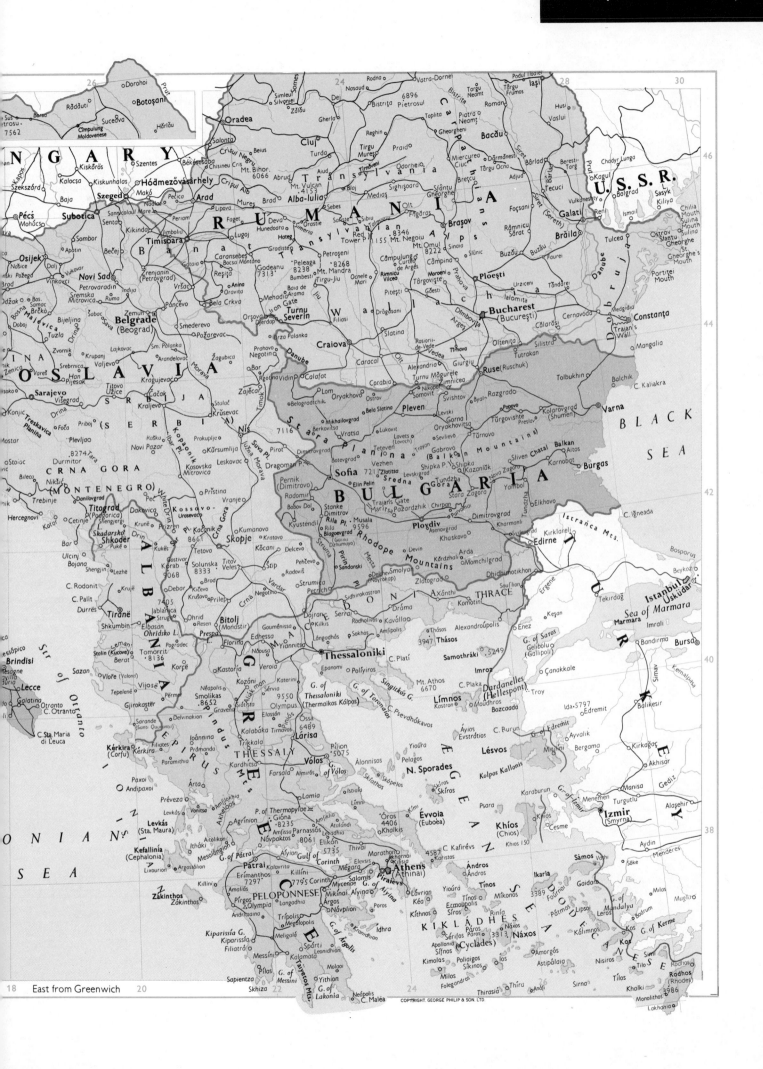

COPYRIGHT. GEORGE PHILIP & SON. LTD.

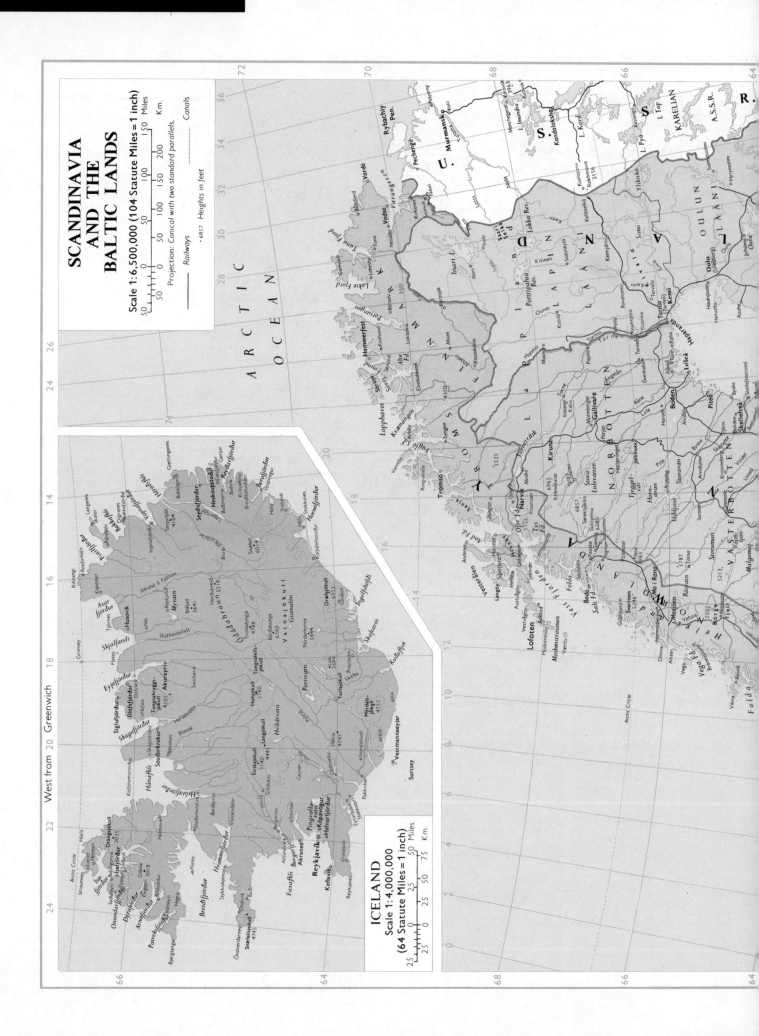

SCANDINAVIA
AND THE
BALTIC LANDS

Scale 1:6,500,000 (104 Statute Miles = 1 inch)

Projection: Conical with two standard parallels.

Railways ——— Heights in feet · 6857

Canals

ARCTIC OCEAN

ICELAND
Scale 1:4,000,000
(64 Statute Miles = 1 inch)

West from 20 Greenwich

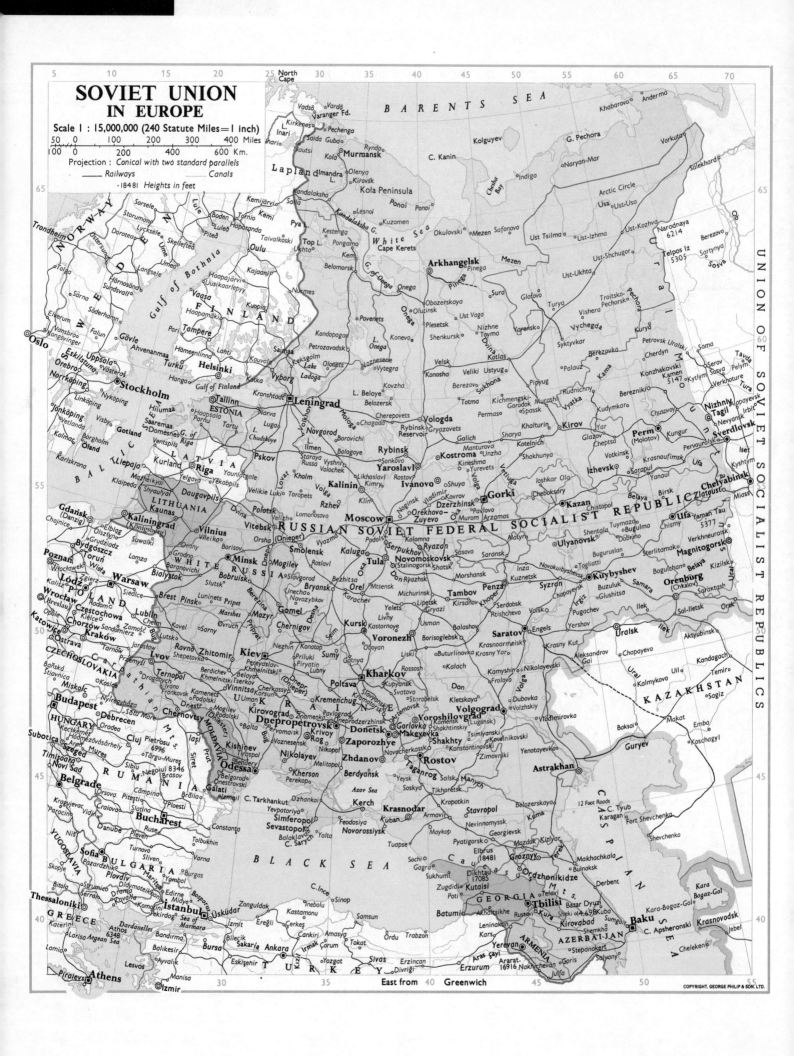

SOVIET UNION
IN EUROPE

Scale 1 : 15,000,000 (240 Statute Miles = 1 inch)

50 0   100   200   300   400 Miles
100 0   200   400   600 Km.

Projection : Conical with two standard parallels
——— Railways   .... Canals
· 18481 Heights in feet

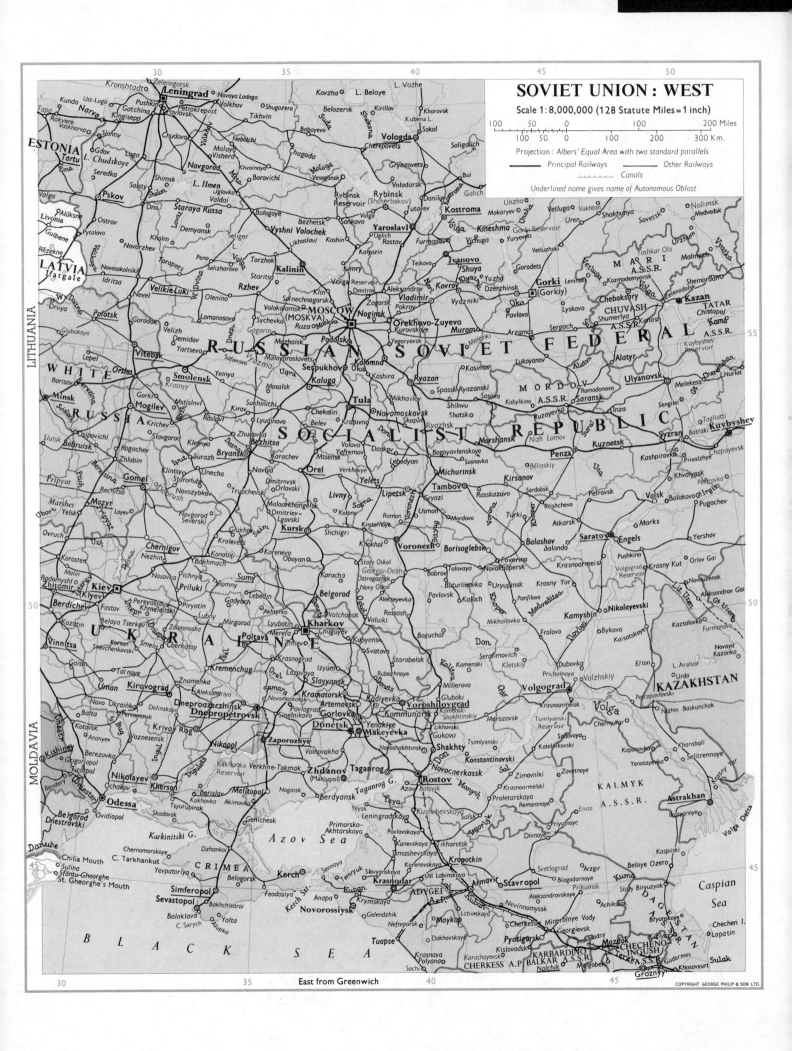

SOVIET UNION : WEST

Scale 1:8,000,000 (128 Statute Miles = 1 inch)

100   50   0   100   200 Miles
100 50 0   100   200   300 Km.

Projection: Albers' Equal Area with two standard parallels

Principal Railways ———   ——— Other Railways

········· Canals ·········

Underlined name gives name of Autonomous Oblast

East from Greenwich

COPYRIGHT GEORGE PHILIP & SON LTD.

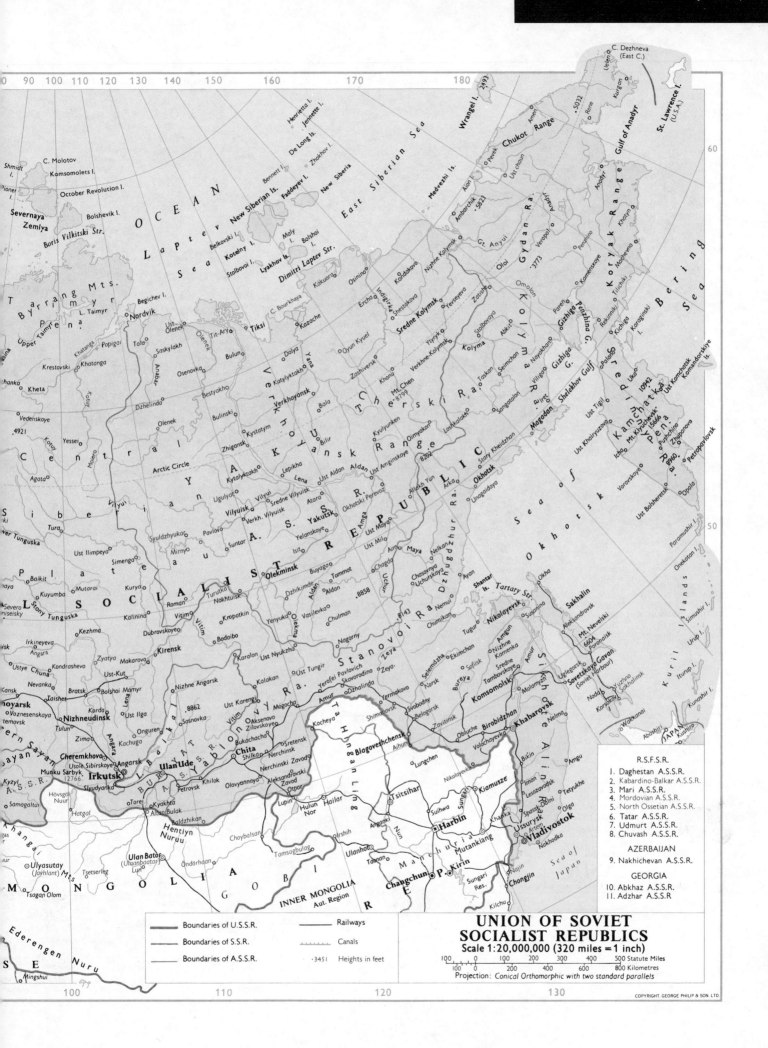

UNION OF SOVIET
SOCIALIST REPUBLICS
Scale 1:20,000,000 (320 miles = 1 inch)
Projection: Conical Orthomorphic with two standard parallels

Boundaries of U.S.S.R.
Boundaries of S.S.R.
Boundaries of A.S.S.R.
Railways
Canals
·3451 Heights in feet

R.S.F.S.R.
1. Daghestan A.S.S.R.
2. Kabardino-Balkar A.S.S.R.
3. Mari A.S.S.R.
4. Mordovian A.S.S.R.
5. North Ossetian A.S.S.R.
6. Tatar A.S.S.R.
7. Udmurt A.S.S.R.
8. Chuvash A.S.S.R.

AZERBAIJAN
9. Nakhichevan A.S.S.R.

GEORGIA
10. Abkhaz A.S.S.R.
11. Adzhar A.S.S.R.

COPYRIGHT. GEORGE PHILIP & SON. LTD

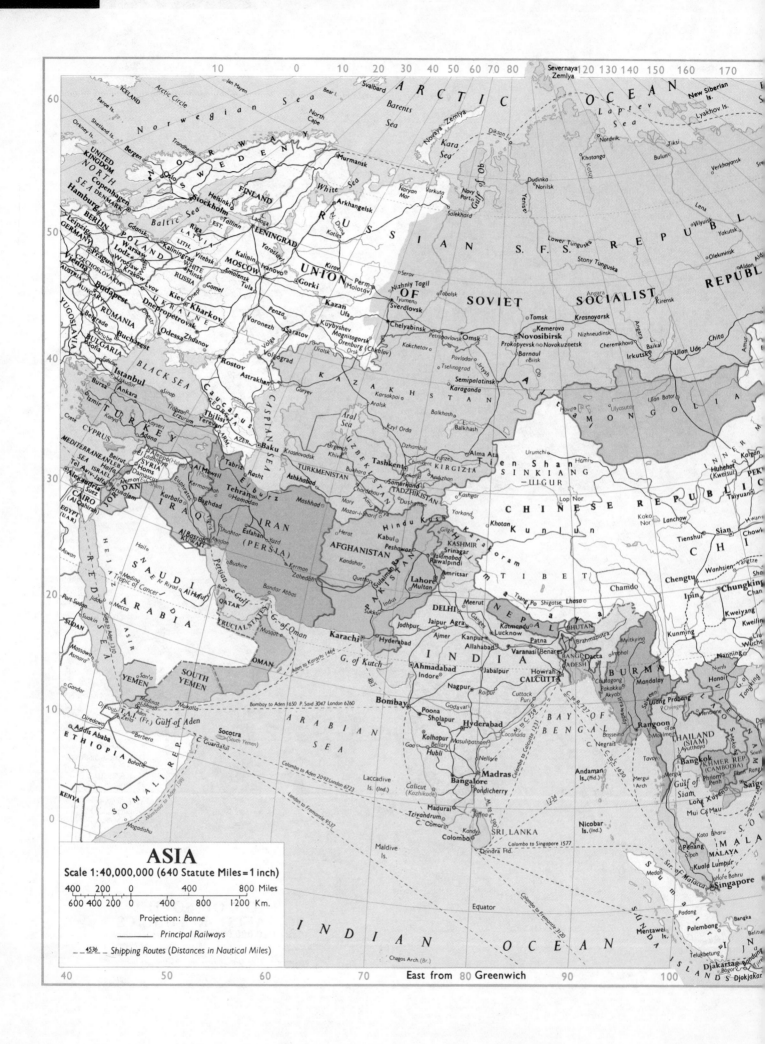

ARCTIC OCEAN

Arctic Circle

Norwegian Sea

Barents Sea

Kara Sea

Laptev Sea

RUSSIAN S.F.S.R.

SOVIET SOCIALIST REPUBLIC

UNION OF

Moscow

Leningrad

FINLAND

SWEDEN

NORWAY

UNITED KINGDOM

GERMANY

POLAND

RUSSIA

UKRAINE

KAZAKHSTAN

MONGOLIA

CHINESE REPUBLIC

SINKIANG – UIGUR

TIBET

BLACK SEA

TURKEY

SYRIA

IRAQ

IRAN (PERSIA)

AFGHANISTAN

PAKISTAN

KASHMIR

NEPAL

BHUTAN

INDIA

BURMA

SAUDI ARABIA

YEMEN

SOUTH YEMEN

CASPIAN SEA

ARABIAN SEA

BAY OF BENGAL

SRI LANKA

MEDITERRANEAN SEA

RED SEA

Gulf of Aden

ETHIOPIA

SOMALI REP.

KENYA

CALCUTTA

BOMBAY

Madras

Bangalore

Karachi

DELHI

THAILAND (SIAM)

BANGKOK

KHMER REP. (CAMBODIA)

MALAYA

Singapore

INDIAN OCEAN

Equator

ASIA
Scale 1:40,000,000 (640 Statute Miles=1 inch)

400 200 0   400   800 Miles
600 400 200 0   400   800   1200 Km.

Projection: Bonne

——— Principal Railways

– –4536– – Shipping Routes (Distances in Nautical Miles)

East from Greenwich

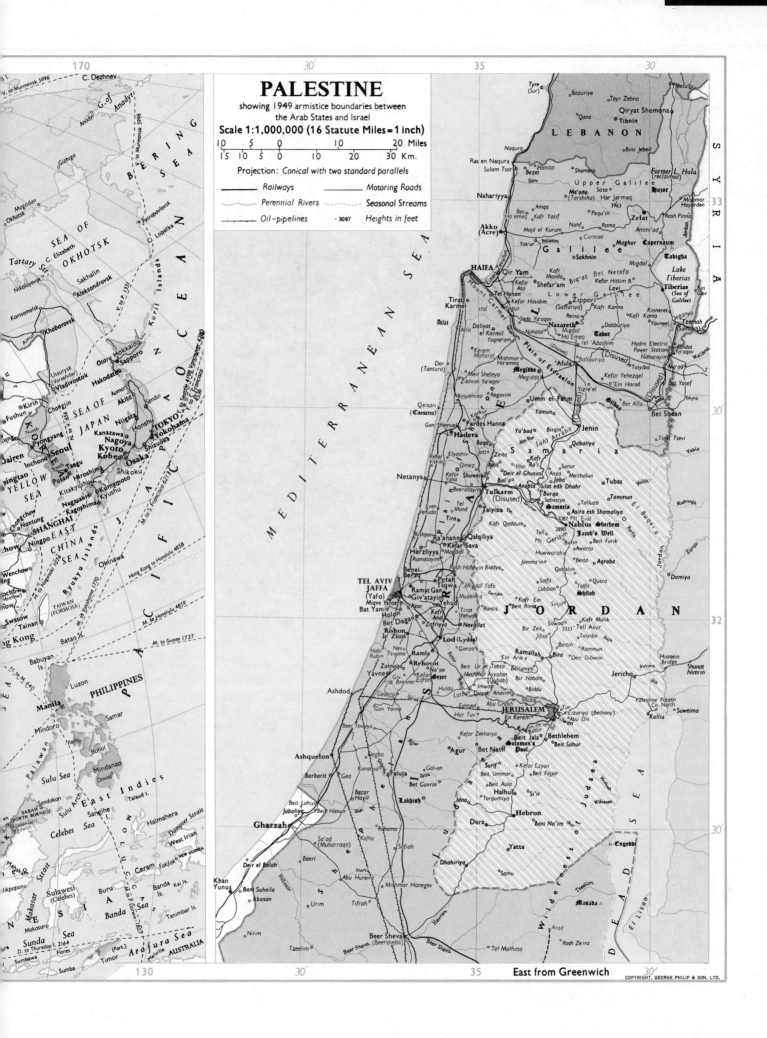

PALESTINE

showing 1949 armistice boundaries between
the Arab States and Israel

Scale 1:1,000,000 (16 Statute Miles=1 inch)

10   5   0   10   20 Miles
15 10 5 0   10   20   30 Km.

Projection: *Conical with two standard parallels*

———— Railways   ———— Motoring Roads
———— Perennial Rivers   -------- Seasonal Streams
———— Oil-pipelines   · 3087 Heights in feet

COPYRIGHT, GEORGE PHILIP & SON, LTD.

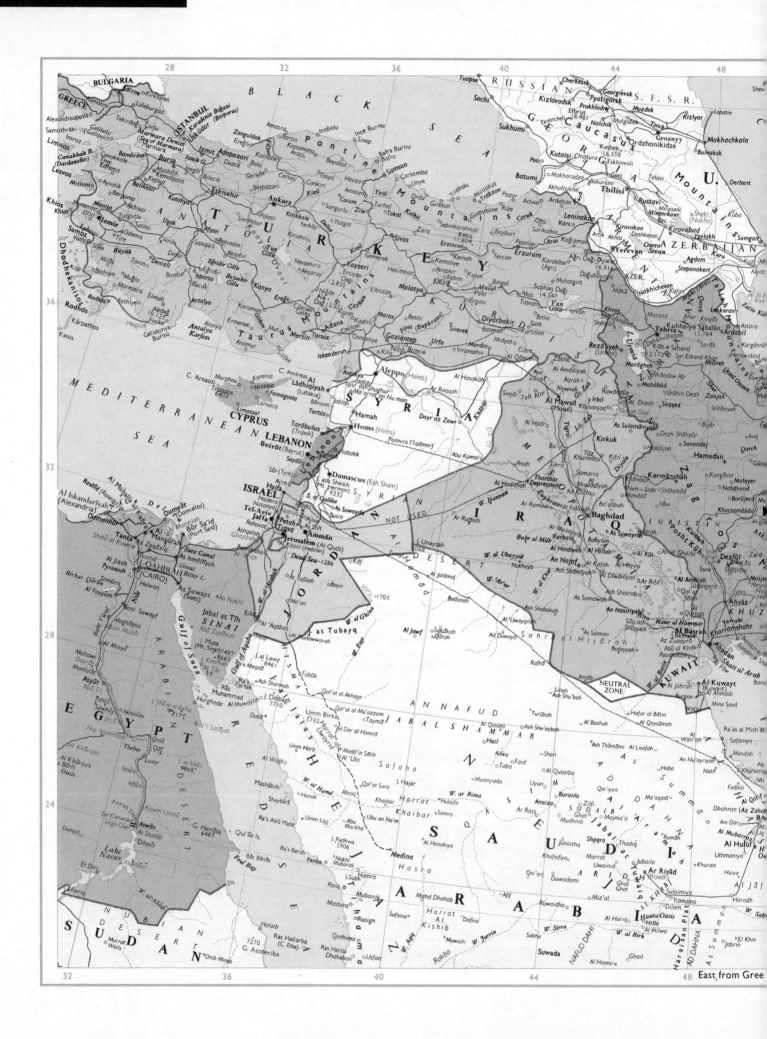

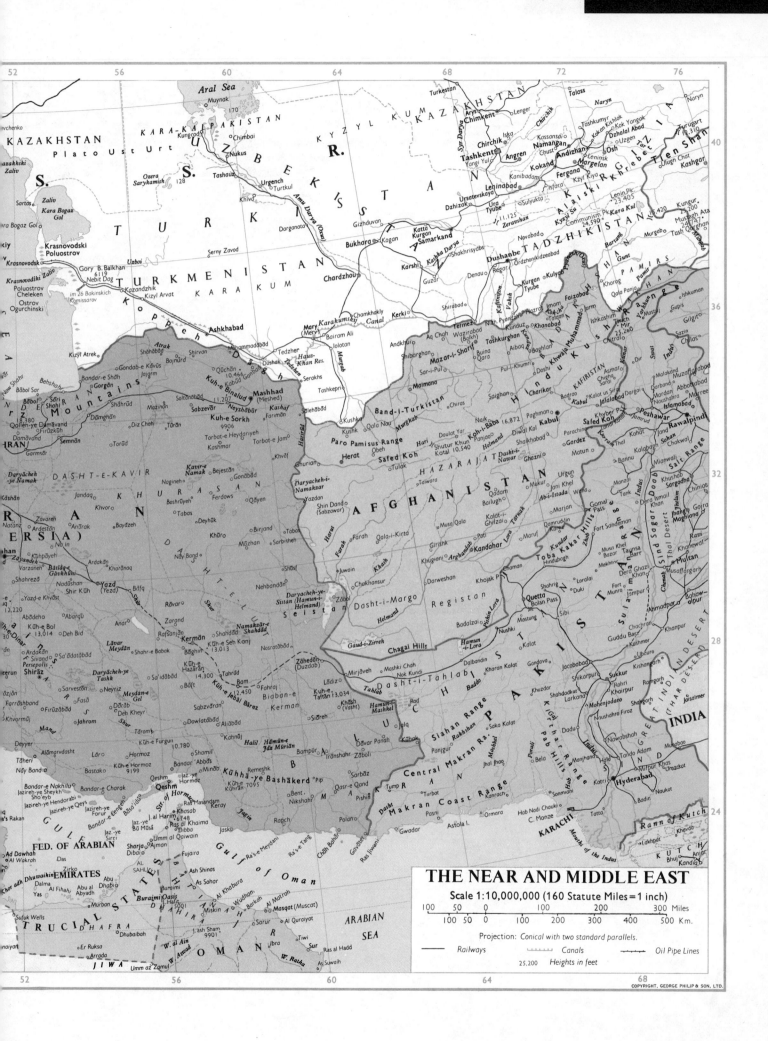

THE NEAR AND MIDDLE EAST
Scale 1:10,000,000 (160 Statute Miles = 1 inch)

| 100 | 50 | 0 | | 100 | | 200 | | 300 Miles |

| 100 | 50 | 0 | | 100 | 200 | 300 | 400 | 500 Km. |

Projection: Conical with two standard parallels.

———— Railways ·········· Canals ——·——· Oil Pipe Lines

25,200 Heights in feet

Continuation southwards
on same scale

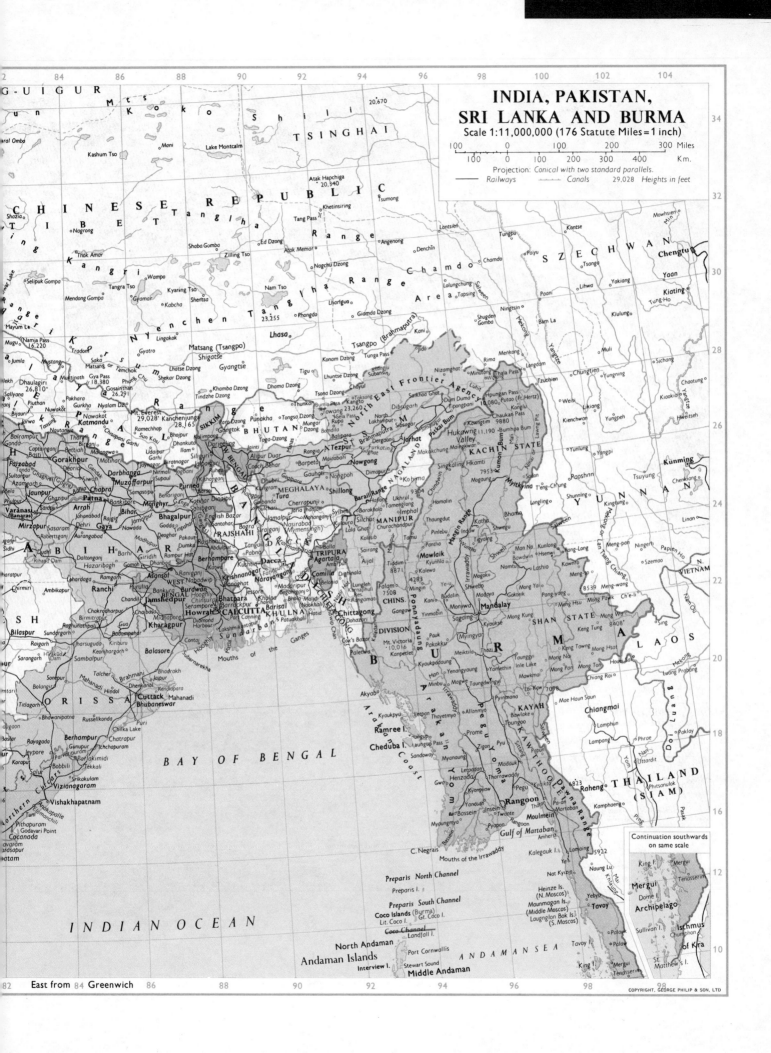

INDIA, PAKISTAN, SRI LANKA AND BURMA
Scale 1:11,000,000 (176 Statute Miles = 1 inch)

100   0   100   200   300 Miles
100   0   100   200   300   400   Km.

Projection: *Conical with two standard parallels.*
———— Railways   +++++ Canals   29,028 *Heights in feet*

COPYRIGHT, GEORGE PHILIP & SON, LTD

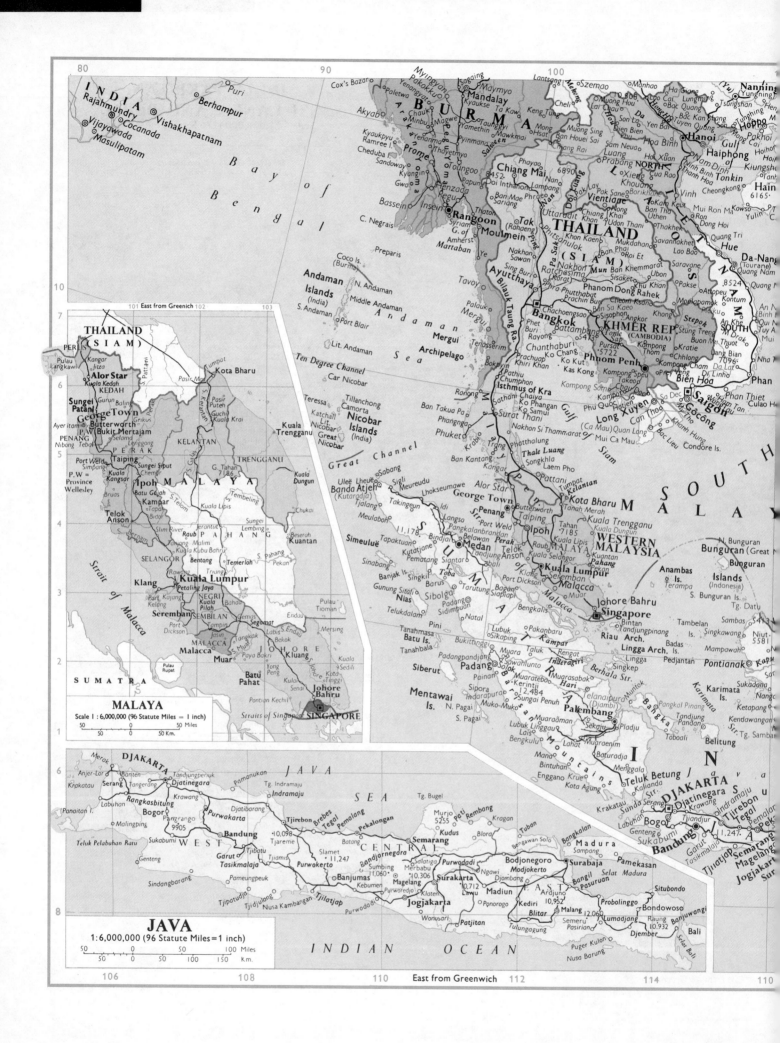

MALAYA

Scale 1 : 6,000,000 (96 Statute Miles = 1 inch)

JAVA

1:6,000,000 (96 Statute Miles = 1 inch)

East from Greenwich

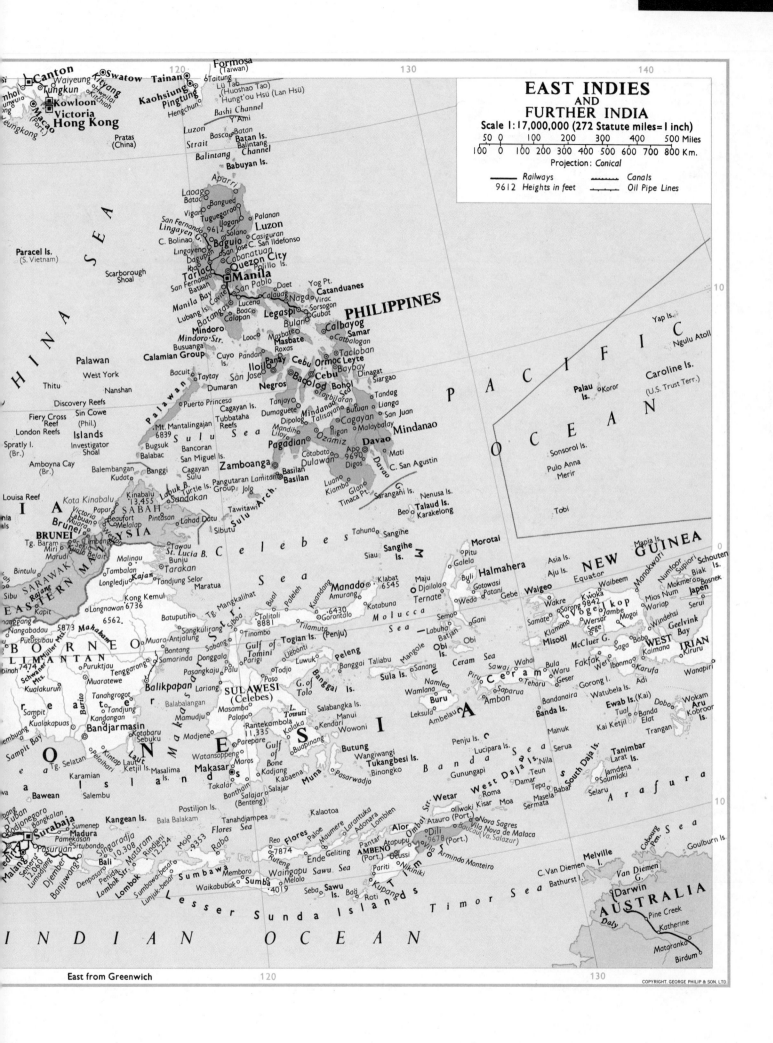

EAST INDIES
AND
FURTHER INDIA
Scale 1:17,000,000 (272 Statute miles=1 inch)

50 0   100   200   300   400   500 Miles

100 0   100 200 300 400 500 600 700 800 Km.

Projection: *Conical*

———— Railways   .... Canals

9612 *Heights in feet*   ⌐⌐⌐⌐ Oil Pipe Lines

East from Greenwich

COPYRIGHT. GEORGE PHILIP & SON. LTD

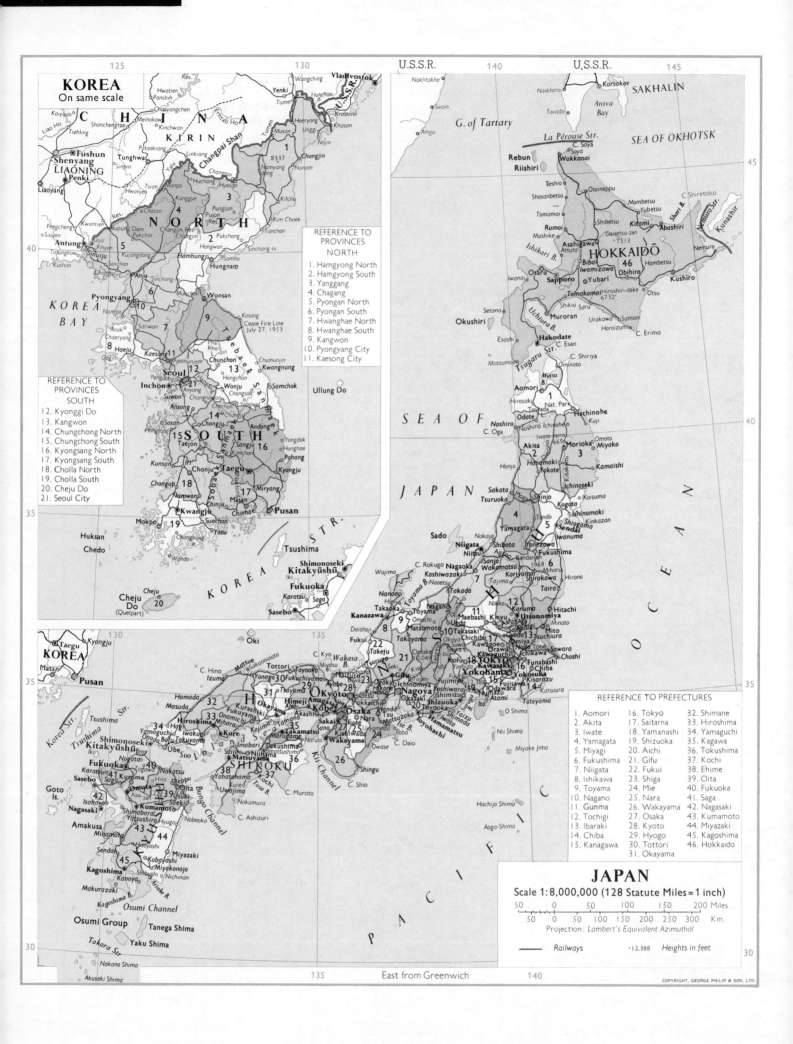

KOREA
On same scale

REFERENCE TO PROVINCES
NORTH
1. Hamgyong North
2. Hamgyong South
3. Yanggang
4. Chagang
5. Pyongan North
6. Pyongan South
7. Hwanghae North
8. Hwanghae South
9. Kangwon
10. Pyongyang City
11. Kaesong City

REFERENCE TO PROVINCES
SOUTH
12. Kyonggi Do
13. Kangwon
14. Chungchong North
15. Chungchong South
16. Kyongsang North
17. Kyongsang South
18. Cholla North
19. Cholla South
20. Cheju Do
21. Seoul City

REFERENCE TO PREFECTURES

1. Aomori	16. Tokyo	32. Shimane
2. Akita	17. Saitama	33. Hiroshima
3. Iwate	18. Yamanashi	34. Yamaguchi
4. Yamagata	19. Shizuoka	35. Kagawa
5. Miyagi	20. Aichi	36. Tokushima
6. Fukushima	21. Gifu	37. Kochi
7. Niigata	22. Fukui	38. Ehime
8. Ishikawa	23. Shiga	39. Oita
9. Toyama	24. Mie	40. Fukuoka
10. Nagano	25. Nara	41. Saga
11. Gunma	26. Wakayama	42. Nagasaki
12. Tochigi	27. Osaka	43. Kumamoto
13. Ibaraki	28. Kyoto	44. Miyazaki
14. Chiba	29. Hyogo	45. Kagoshima
15. Kanagawa	30. Tottori	46. Hokkaido
	31. Okayama	

JAPAN
Scale 1:8,000,000 (128 Statute Miles=1 inch)

50   0   50   100   150   200 Miles
50   0 50 100 150 200 250 300 Km.
Projection: Lambert's Equivalent Azimuthal

——— Railways   ·12,388 Heights in feet

East from Greenwich

COPYRIGHT, GEORGE PHILIP & SON, LTD.

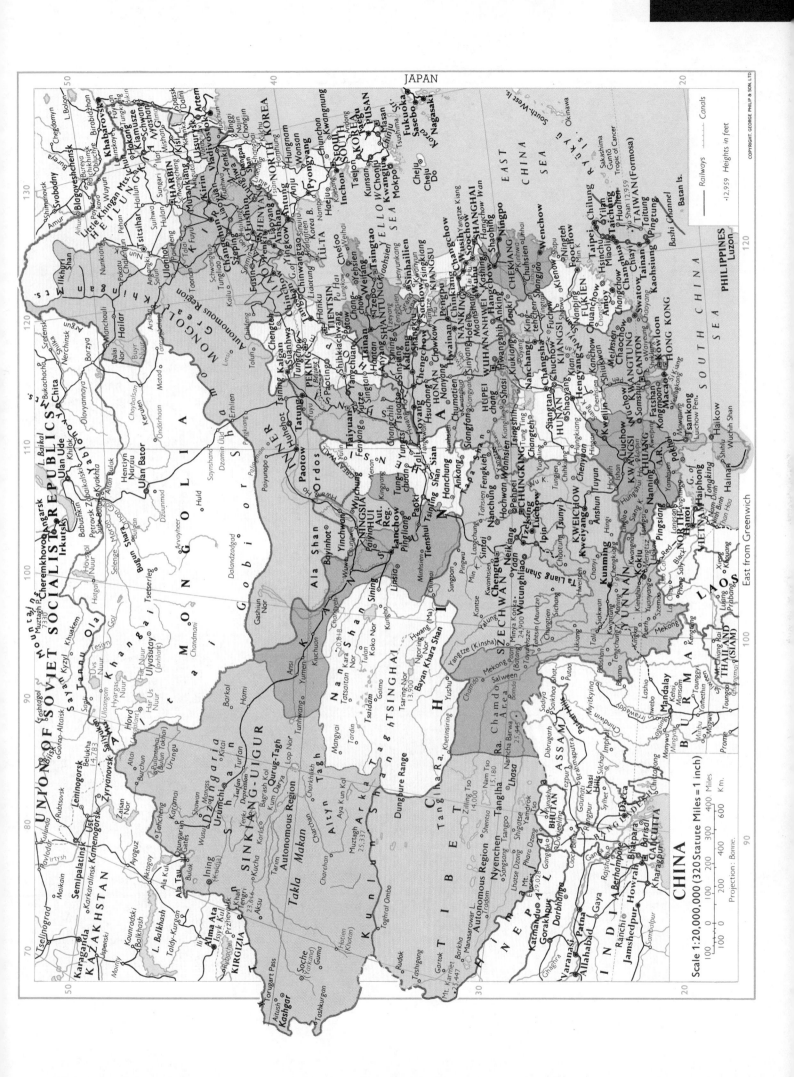

JAPAN

CHINA

Scale 1:20,000,000 (320 Statute Miles = 1 inch)

Projection: Bonne.

East from Greenwich

COPYRIGHT. GEORGE PHILIP & SON, LTD.

Railways
Canals
·12,959 Heights in feet

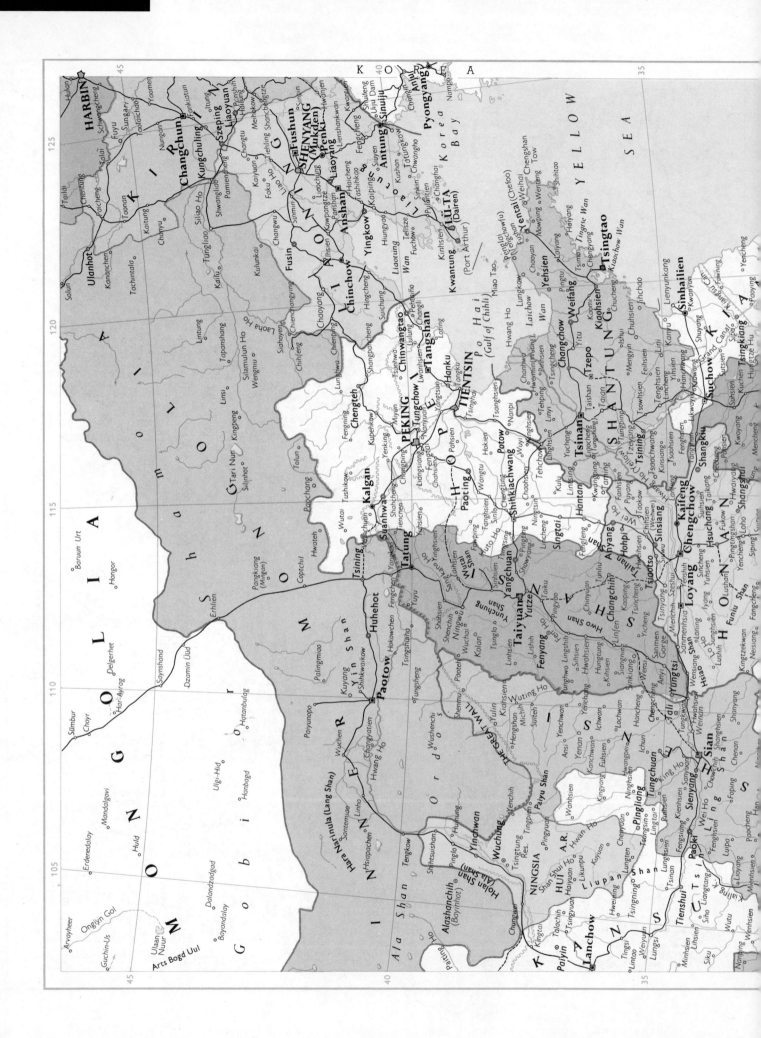

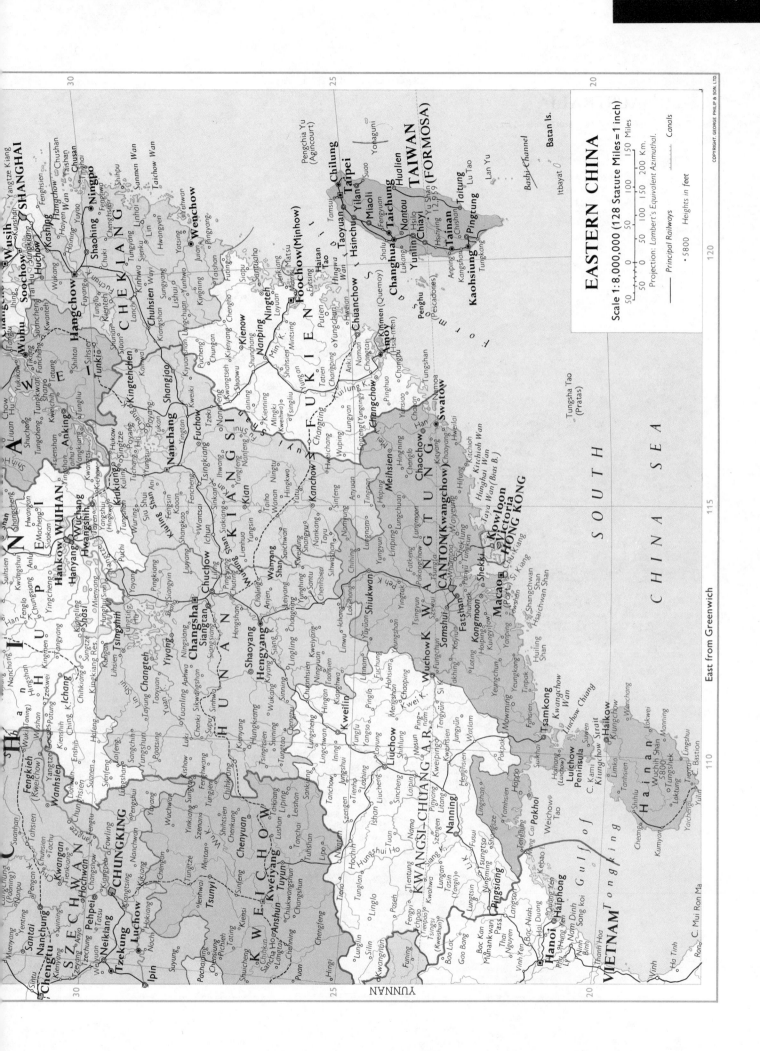

EASTERN CHINA

Scale 1:8,000,000 (128 Statute Miles = 1 inch)

Projection: Lambert's Equivalent Azimuthal.

—— Principal Railways   Canals

•5800 Heights in feet

COPYRIGHT GEORGE PHILIP & SON, LTD.

East from Greenwich

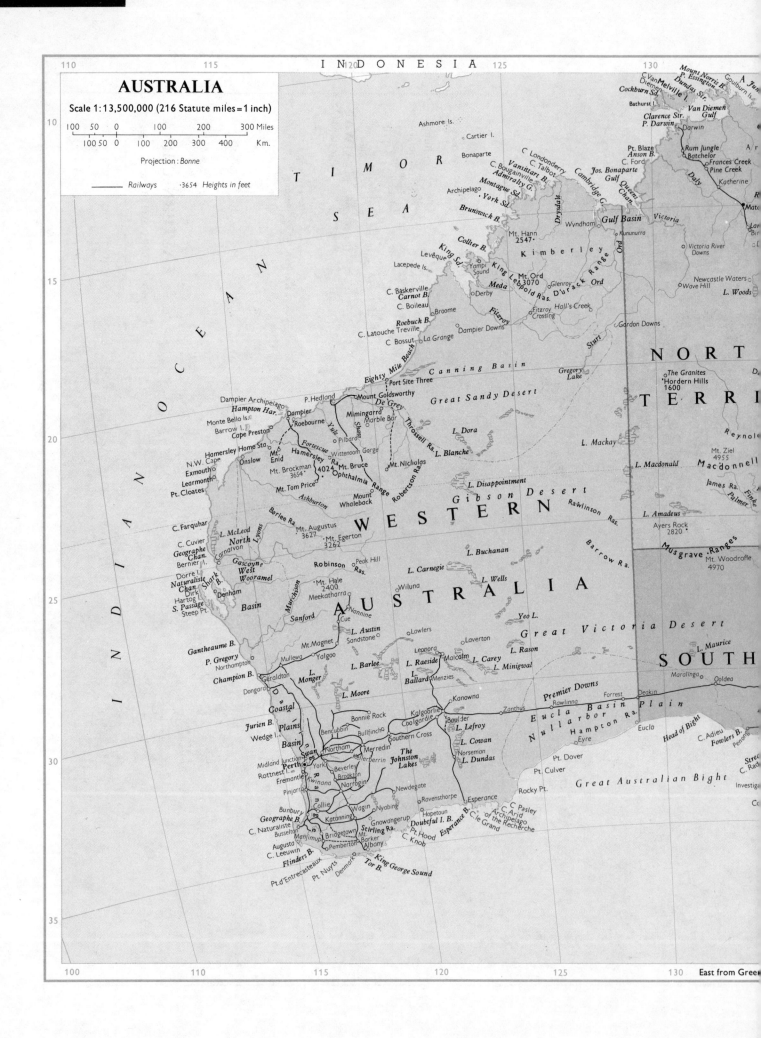

AUSTRALIA

Scale 1:13,500,000 (216 Statute miles=1 inch)

100 50 0   100   200   300 Miles
100 50 0   100   200   300   400   Km.

Projection : *Bonne*

——— Railways   ·3654 *Heights in feet*

I N D O N E S I A

T I M O R   S E A

I N D I A N   O C E A N

Ashmore Is.

Cartier I.

Bonaparte

C. Londonderry
C. Talbot
Vansittart B.
C. Bougainville
Admiralty G.
Montague Sd.
York Sd.

Cambridge G.
Jos. Bonaparte
Gulf
Queens
Chan.

Mount Norris B.
P. Essington
Dundas Str.
Van Diemen
Gulf
Melville I.
Bathurst I.
Cockburn Sd.
Clarence Str.
P. Darwin   Darwin
Pt. Blaze
Anson B.
C. Ford
Rum Jungle
Batchelor
Frances Creek
Pine Creek
Katherine

Daly

Brunswick B.

Collier B.
Levêque
King Sd.
King Leopold Ras.
Lacepede Is.
Yampi
Sound
Meda
Derby
C. Baskerville
Carnot B.
C. Boileau
Broome
Roebuck B.
C. Latouche Treville
C. Bossut   La Grange

Mt. Hann
2547

K i m b e r l e y

Mt. Ord
3070
Glenroy
Fitzroy
Crossing   Hall's Creek

D'urack Range
Ord
Ord

Wyndham   Gulf Basin   Victoria
Kununurra

Victoria River
Downs

Newcastle Waters
Wave Hill   L. Woods

Gordon Downs

Dampier Downs

Fitzroy

Sturt

N O R T
T E R R I

Eighty   Mile   Beach
Port Site Three
Mount Goldsworthy
De Grey
Mimingarra
Marble Bar

C a n n i n g   B a s i n
G r e a t   S a n d y   D e s e r t

Gregory
Lake

The Granites
Hordern Hills
1600

R e y n o l e
Mt. Ziel
4955
M a c d o n n e l l
James Ra.
Palmer

Dampier Archipelago
Hampton Har.
Monte Bello Is.
Barrow I.
Cape Preston
P. Hedland
Dampier
Roebourne
Ytale
Pilbara
Shaw
Throssell Ra.
Mt. Nicholas
L. Dora
L. Blanche

L. Mackay
L. Macdonald

N.W. Cape
Exmouth
Learmonth
Pt. Cloates
Hamersley Home Sta.
Onslow
Mt.
Enid
Mt. Brockman
3654
Fortescue
Hamersley Ra.
Wittenoom Gorge
4024
Mt. Bruce
Ophthalmia
Range
Robertson Ras.
L. Disappointment

G i b s o n   D e s e r t
Rawlinson
Ras.

L. Amadeus
Ayers Rock
2820

C. Farquhar
Mt. Tom Price
Ashburton
Mount
Whaleback

C. Cuvier
Geographe
Chan.
Bernier I.
L. McLeod
North
Cornarvon
Berlee Ra.
Lyons
Mt. Augustus
3627
·Mt. Egerton
3262

W E S T E R N

L. Buchanan
Barrow Ra.
M u s g r a v e · R a n g e s
Mt. Woodroffe
4970

Dorre I.
Naturaliste
Chan.
Dirk
Hartog I.
S. Passage
Steep Pt.
Denham
Shark
B.
Gascoyne
West
Wooramel
Basin
Murchison
Robinson
Ras.
Peak Hill
Mt. Hale
2400
Meekatharra

L. Carnegie
L. Wells

Wiluna

G r e a t   V i c t o r i a   D e s e r t

L. Maurice

S O U T H

Gantheaume B.
P. Gregory
Northampton
Champion B.
Geraldton
Dongara
Mullewa
Yalgoo
Sanford
Nannine
Cue
Mt. Magnet
Sandstone
L. Austin
Lawlers
L. Carey
Yeo L.
L. Rason

Maralinga   Ooldea

Leonora
Malcolm
L. Raeside
L.
Ballard
Menzies
L. Minigwal

Premier Downs
Forrest
Rawlinna   Deakin
Zanthus
Eucla Basin
N u l l a r b o r   P l a i n
Hampton Ra.
Eucla
Mundrabilla

Coastal
Plains
Basin
Jurien B.
Wedge I.
L.
Monger
L. Moore
Bonnie Rock
Bencubbin
Bullfinch
Kanowna
Kalgoorlie
Coolgardie
Boulder
L. Lefroy
L. Cowan
Norseman
L. Dundas

Pt. Dover
Pt. Culver
Eyre
Head of Bight
C. Adieu
Fowlers B.
Great Australian Bight

Midland Junction
Perth
Rottnest I.
Fremantle
Swan
Northam
York
Beverley
Brookton
Merredin
Kellerberrin
Southern Cross
The
Johnston
Lakes
Newdegate
Pinjarra
Swinana
Narrogin

Rocky Pt.
Esperance

C. Pasley
C. Arid
Archipelago
of the Recherche

Bunbury
Collie
Wagin   Nyabing
Katanning
Gnowangerup
Geographe B.
C. Naturaliste
Busselton
Augusta
C. Leeuwin
Manjimup
Bridgetown
Pemberton
Stirling Ra.
Mt.
Barker
Albany
Hopetoun
Ravensthorpe
Doubtful I. B.
Esperance B.
Pt. Hood
C. le Grand
C. Knob

Flinders B.
Pt. d'Entrecasteaux   Pt. Nuyts   Denmark
Tor B.
King George Sound

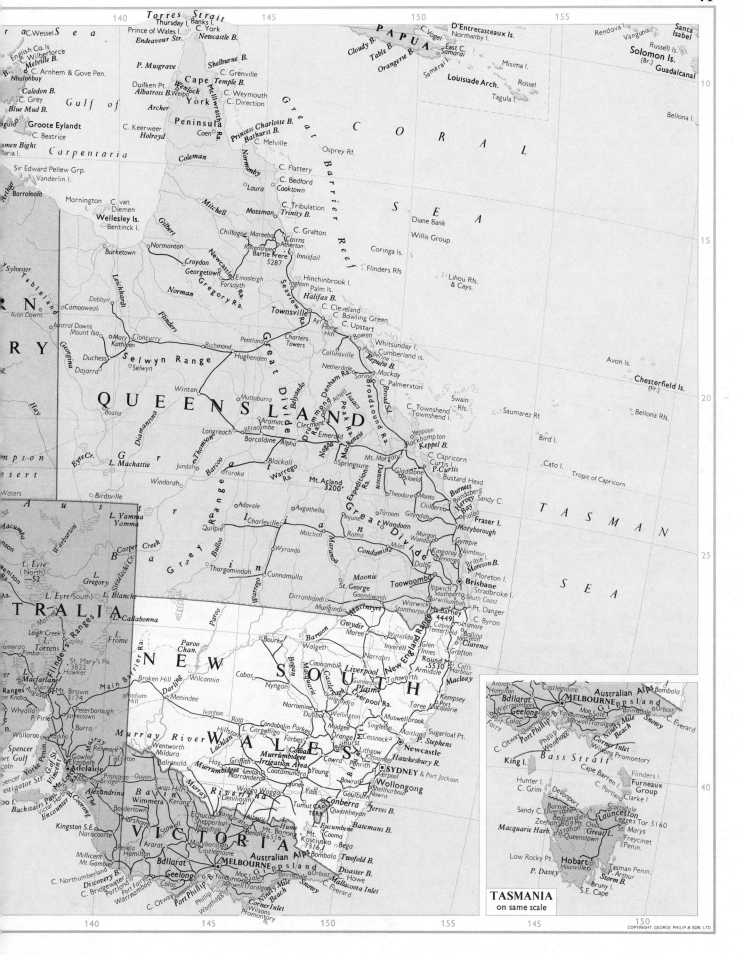

TASMANIA
on same scale

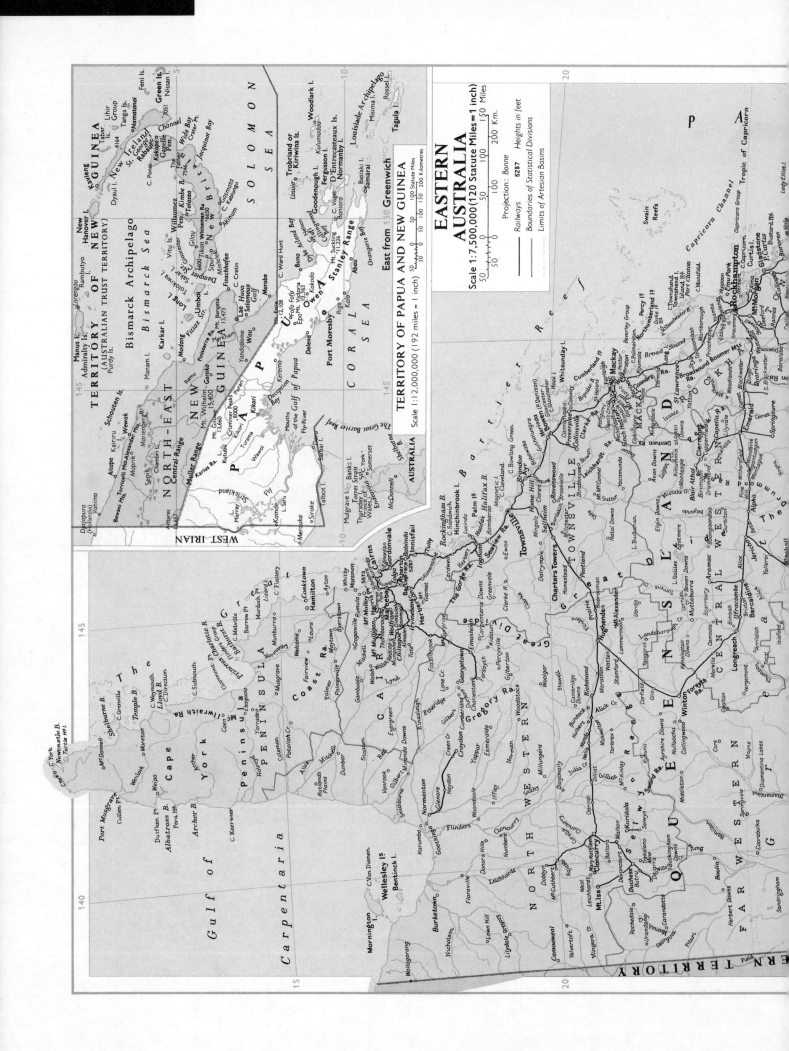

TERRITORY OF PAPUA AND NEW GUINEA

Scale 1:12,000,000 (192 miles = 1 inch)

East from 150 Greenwich

EASTERN AUSTRALIA

Scale 1:7,500,000 (120 Statute Miles = 1 inch)

Projection: Bonne   5287 Heights in feet

———— Railways
—·—·— Boundaries of Statistical Divisions
········ Limits of Artesian Basins

50   0   50   100   150   200 Km.
50   0   50   100 Statute Miles

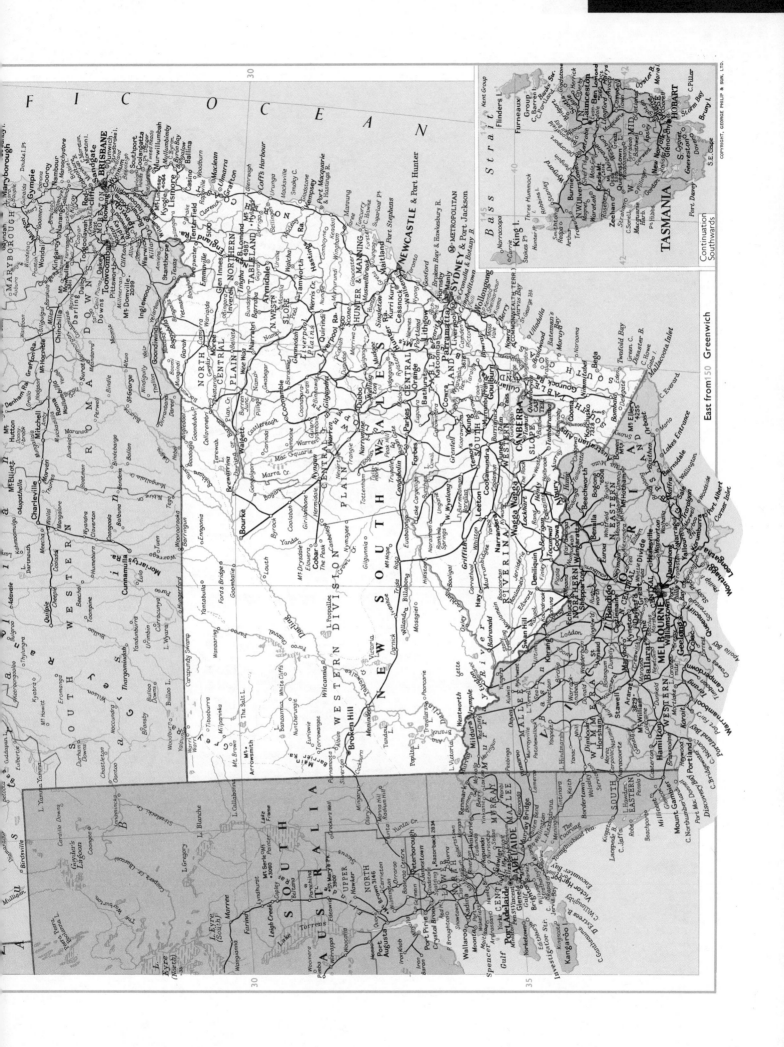

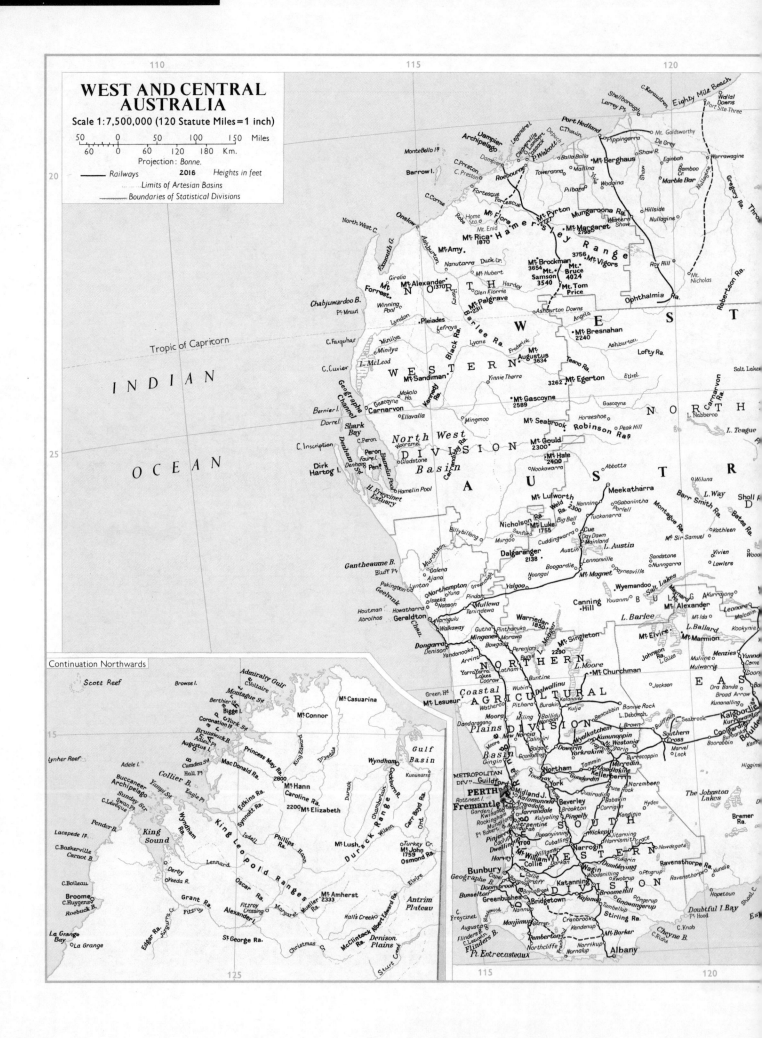

WEST AND CENTRAL AUSTRALIA

Scale 1:7,500,000 (120 Statute Miles=1 inch)

50   0   50   100   150 Miles
60   0   60   120   180 Km.

Projection: Bonne.

——— Railways   2016   Heights in feet
········· Limits of Artesian Basins
━━━━━ Boundaries of Statistical Divisions

Continuation Northwards

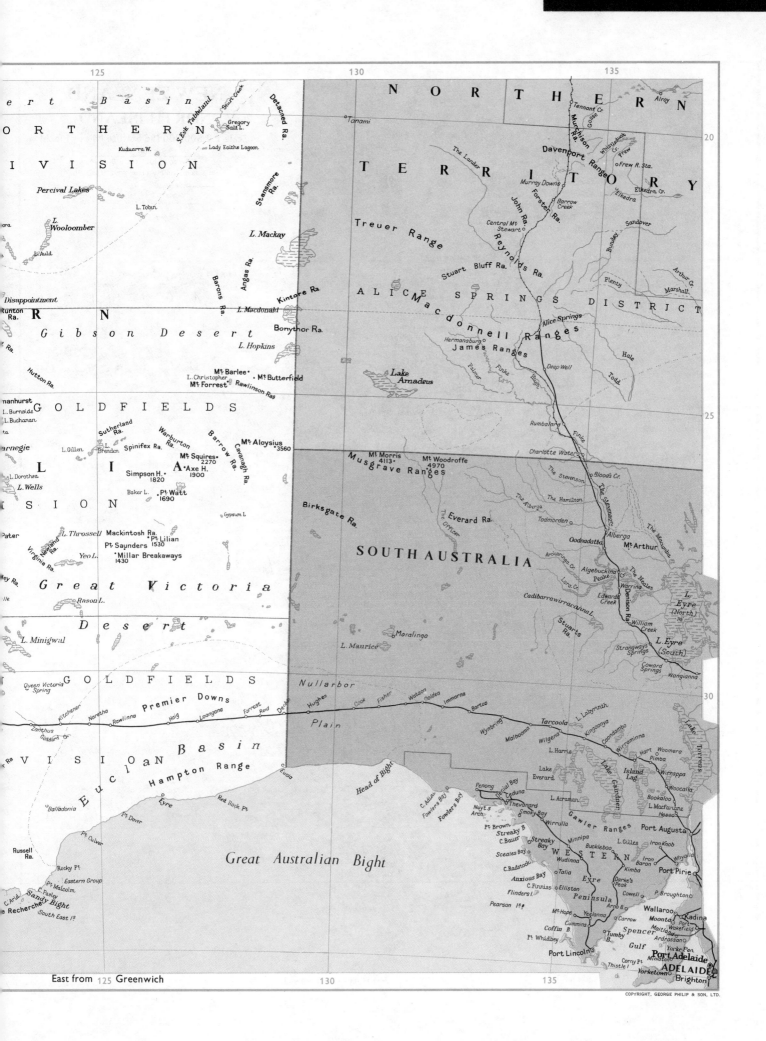

ert Basin

ORTHERN

DIVISION

Percival Lakes

Kuduarra W.

L. Wooloomber

L. Auld

Disappointment

Runton Ra.

Gibson Desert

Hutton Ra.

manhurst

L. Burnside

L. Buchanan

arnegie

L. Gillen

L. Brenden

Spinifex Ra.

L. Dorothea

L. Wells

GOLDFIELDS

Sutherland Ra.

Warburton Ra.

Barrow Ra.

Mt Aloysius *3560

Mt Squires* 2270

Simpson H.* 1820

A Axe H. 1900

Baker L. Pt Watt 1690

Gypsum L.

L. Throssell Mackintosh Ra.

Newland Ra.

Virginia Ra.

Yeo L.

Pt Lilian 1530

Pt Saunders 1530

Millar Breakaways 1430

ey Ra.

Pater

Great Victoria

Rason L.

L. Minigwal

D e s e r t

Queen Victoria Spring

GOLDFIELDS

Kitchener

Narstha

Rawlinna

Premier Downs

Haig

Loongana

Forrest

Reid

Deakin

Zanthus

Goddard Cr.

VISION

Euclan Basin

Hampton Range

Balladonia

Pt Dover

Eyre

Eucla

Red Rock Pt.

Head of Bight

Russell Ra.

Rocky Pt.

Pt Culver

Eastern Group

Pt Malcolm

C. Arid

C. Pasley

e Recherche

Sandy Bight

South East I.

Great Australian Bight

S. Esk Tabbland

Scott Creek

Gregory Salt L.

Lady Eaiths Lagoon

Stansmore Ra.

L. Tobin

L. Mackay

Angas Ra.

Barons Ra.

Kintore Ra.

L. Macdonald

Bonython Ra.

L. Hopkins

Mt Barlee* *Mt Butterfield

L. Christopher

Mt Forrest Rawlinson Ras.

Detached Ra.

Tanami

NORTHERN

T E R R I T O R Y

The Lander

Davenport Range

Murray Downs

Central Mt Stewart

John Ra.

Forster Ra.

Barrow Creek

Treuer Range

Stuart Bluff Ra.

Reynolds Ra.

A L I C E M c S P R I N G S D I S T R I C T

Macdonnell Ranges

Alice Springs

Hermansburg

James Ranges

Palmer

Finke

Deep Well

Hale

Todd

Lake Amadeus

Mt Morris 4113*

Mt Woodroffe 4970

Musgrave Ranges

Birksgate Ra.

Everard Ra.

The Officer

SOUTH AUSTRALIA

Rumbalara

Finke

Charlotte Waters

The Stevenson

Blood's Cr.

The Hamilton

The Alberga

Todmorden

Alberga

Oodnadatta

Mt Arthur

Arckaringa Cr.

Algebuckina Peake

The Neales

Edwards Creek

Denison Ra.

Warrina

L. Eyre (North) 35

Cadibarrawirracannal.

Moralinga

L. Maurice

Stuarts Ra.

Lora Cr.

Strangways Springs

Coward Springs

William Creek

L. Eyre (South)

Wangianna

Nullarbor

Hughes

Cook

Fisher

Watson

Ooldea

Immarna

Barton

Plain

Wynbring

Tarcoola

L. Labyrinth

Kingoonya

Coondambo

Wirraminna

Malbooma

Wilgena

Penong

Denial Bay

Ceduna

C. Adieu

Fowlers Bay

Fowlers Bay

Nuyts Arch.

Pt Brown

Streaky B.

C. Bauer

Scseales Bay

C. Radstock

Anxious Bay

C. Finniss

Flinders I.

Pearson Is.

Smoky Bay

Wirrulla

Streaky Bay

Wudinna

Talia

Elliston

Mt Hope

Coffin B.

Pt Whidbey

Pt Lincoln

Thevenard

L. Acraman

Lake Everard

L. Harris

Lake Gairdner

Island Lag.

Gawler Ranges

Minnipa

L. Gilles

Buckleboo

W E S T E R N

Yeelanna

Cummins

Jumby B.

Corny Pt

Thistle I.

Pimba

Hart

Woomera

Wirrappa

Woocalla

Bookaloo

L. Macfarlane

Hesso

Port Augusta

Iron Knob

Iron Baron

Kimba

Darke's Peak

E y r e

Darke's Peak

Cowell

Arno B.

Carrow

Spencer

Maitland

Gulf

Yorketown

Yorke Pen.

Minlaton

Whyalla

Port Pirie

P. Broughton

Wallaroo

Moonta

Kadina

Port Wakefield

Ardrossan

Port Adelaide

ADELAIDE

Brighton

Peninsula

L. Eyre

Torrens

Lake Torrens

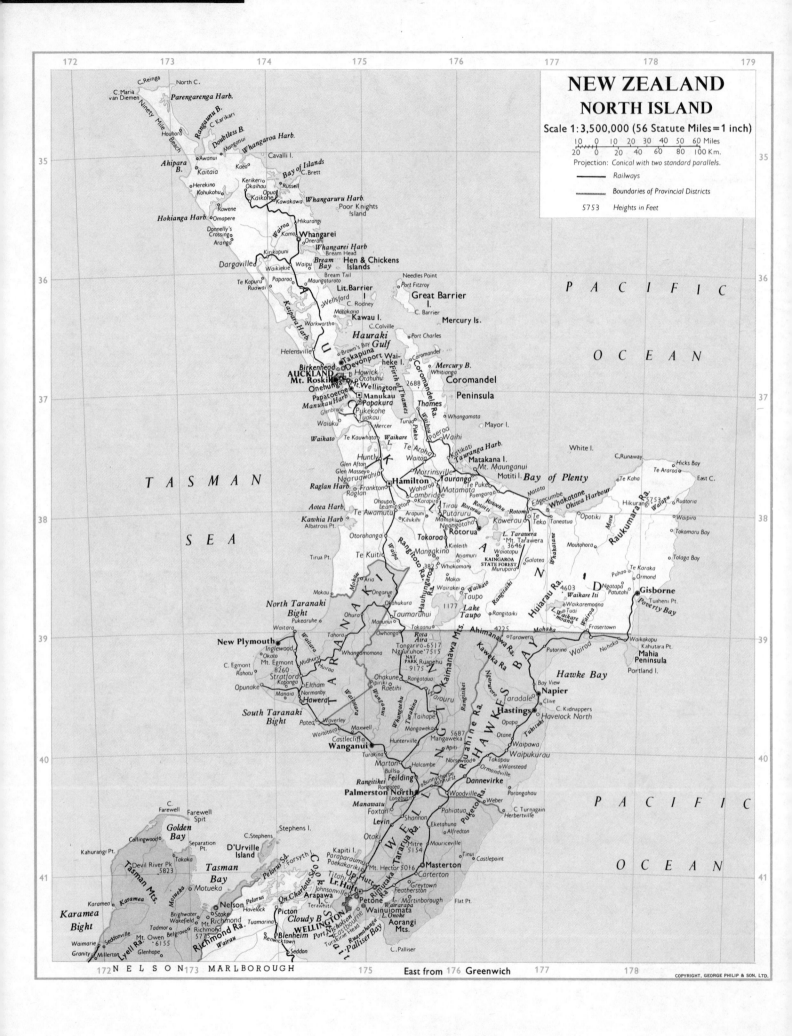

NEW ZEALAND
NORTH ISLAND
Scale 1:3,500,000 (56 Statute Miles=1 inch)

10 0 10 20 30 40 50 60 Miles
20 0   20   40 60   80 100 Km.

Projection: Conical with two standard parallels.
———— Railways
———— Boundaries of Provincial Districts
5753   Heights in Feet

COPYRIGHT, GEORGE PHILIP & SON, LTD.

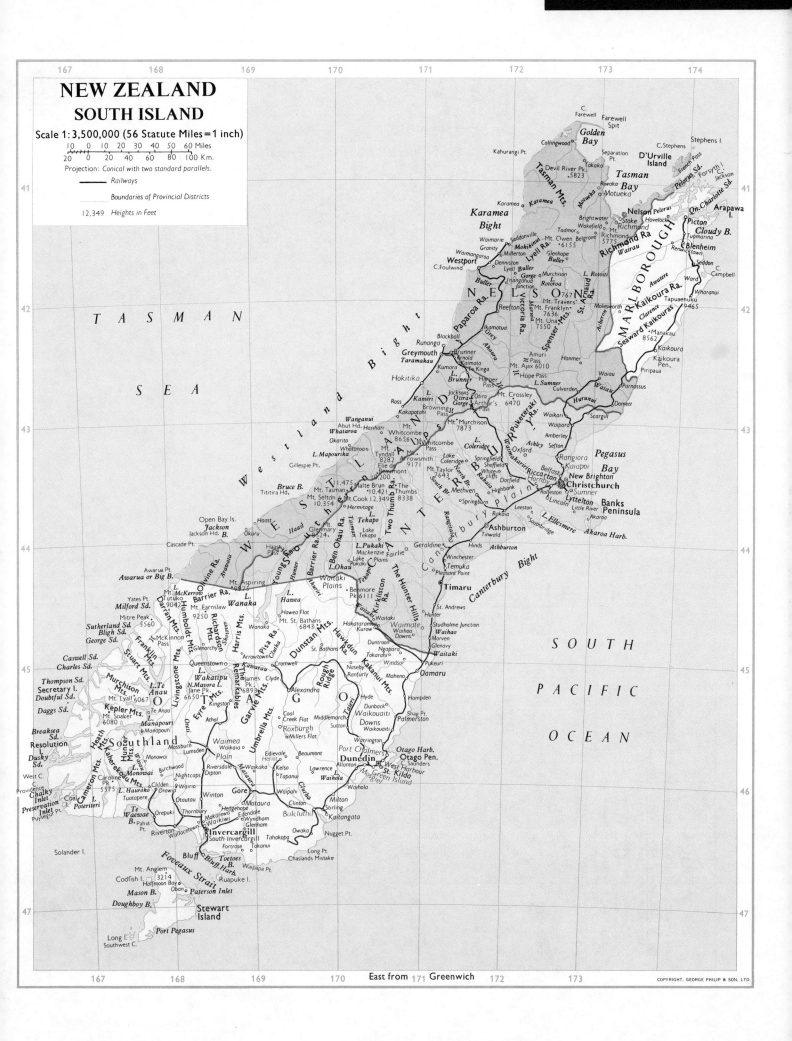

NEW ZEALAND
SOUTH ISLAND

Scale 1:3,500,000 (56 Statute Miles = 1 inch)

10 0 10 20 30 40 50 60 Miles
20 0 20 40 60 80 100 Km.

Projection: Conical with two standard parallels.

————— Railways

············· Boundaries of Provincial Districts

12,349 *Heights in Feet*

TASMAN

SEA

SOUTH

PACIFIC

OCEAN

C. Farewell
Farewell
Spit
Golden
Bay
Collingwood
C. Stephens
Stephens I.
Kahurangi Pt.
Takaka
Separation
Pt.
D'Urville
Island
Devil River Pk.
5823
Riwaka
Motueka
Tasman
Bay
Pelorus Sd.
French Sd.
Forsyth I.
C. Jackson
Arapawa
I.

Karamea
Karamea
Mts.
Tasman
Mts.
Brightwater
Wakefield
Motueka
Richmond
Stoke
Nelson Pelorus
Havelock
Richmond Ra
Picton
Cloudy B.
On Charlotte Sd.
Tuamarina
Blenheim
Renwicktown

Karamea
Bight
Waimarie
Granity
Millerton
Seddonville
Mokihinui
Mt. Owen Belgrove
6155
Denniston
Glenhope
Buller
Richmond
5775
Wairau
Seddon
C. Campbell
Ward
Wharanui

Westport
C.Foulwind
Lyell
Gorge
Inangahua
Junction
Buller
L.
Rotoroa
Murchison
L.
Rotoiti
St. Arnaud Ra.
Molesworth
Tapuaenuku
9465
MARLBOROUGH
Awatere
Seaward Kaikouras

N E L S O N
767
Mt. Travers
Mt. Franklyn
7636
Spenser Mts.
Mt. Una
7550
Amuri
Pass
Mt. Ajax 6010
Hanmer
Hmner
Clarence
Seaward Kaikouras
8562
Kaikoura
Kaikoura
Pen.

Reefton
Blackball
Victoria Ra.
Maruia
Hope Pass

Runanga
Grey
Ikamatua
Ahaura
Culverden
Waiau
Parnassus
Piripaua

Greymouth
Taramakau
Brunner
Arnold
Kaimata
Te Kinga
L.
Brunner
Harper
Pass
L. Sumner
Hurunui
Waikari
Waipara
Scargill
Domett

Hokitika
Kumara
Jacksons
Otira
Gorge
Otira
Arthur's
Pass
Mt. Crossley
6470
Waiau
Amberley
Sefton

Ross
L.
Kanieri
Browning
Kakapotahi
Pass
Whitcombe
Pass
Mt. Murchison
7873
Oxford
White-
cliffs
Ashley
Rangiora
Kaiapoi
Pegasus
Bay

Wanganui
Abut Hd.
Harihari
Mt.
Whitcombe
8656
L.
Coleridge
Springfield
Sheffield
Darfield
Belfast
Riccarton
Hornby
New Brighton
Christchurch

Whataroa
Okarito
Whataroa
L. Mapourika
Tyndall
8282
Mt. Taylor
7643
North Br.
Methven
Rolleston
Highbank
Lincoln
Sumner
Lyttelton
Banks
Peninsula

Gillespie Pt.
Arrowsmith
9171
Mt.
Coleridge
South Br.
Rakaia
Leeston
L. Ellesmere
Akaroa Harb.
Little River
Akaroa

Bruce B.
Tititira Hd.
Elie de
Beaumont
10,200
The
Thumbs
8338
Springburn
Rakaia
Southbridge

Mt. Tasman
11,475
Malte Brun
10,421
Mt. Cook 12,349
Mt. Sefton
10,354
Hermitage
Two Thumb Ra.
Rakaia
Geraldine
Hinds
Ashburton
Canterbury Bight

Open Bay Is.
Jackson
Jackson Hd. B.
Haast
Okuru
Mt.
Glenmary
8524
L.
Tekapo
Lake
Tekapo
L.Pukaki
Mackenzie
Plains
Fairlie
Winchester
Temuka
Pleasant Point

Cascade Pt.
Haast
Pass
Ben Ohau Ra.
L.Ohau
Waitaki
Plains
Benmore
Pk. 6111
Timaru
St. Andrews
Hunter

Awarua Pt.
Awarua or Big B.
Mt. Aspiring
9975
Young Ra.
South Ra.
Hunter
Barrier Ra.
Ahuriri
The Hunter Hills
Studholme Junction
Waihao

Yates Pt.
Milford Sd.
Mt.
McKerrow
L.
Tutoko
9042
Olivine Ra.
L.
Wanaka
Mt. Earnslaw
9250
L.
Hawea
Hawea Flat
Waitaki
Kurow
Hakataramea
Waihao
Downs
Morven
Glenavy

Mitre Peak 5560
McKinnon
Pass
Darran Mts.
Humboldt Mts.
Mt. St. Bathans
6843
Duntroon
Ngapara
Waihao
Waitaki

Sutherland Sd.
Bligh Sd.
George Sd.
Franklin Mts.
Richardson Mts.
Harris Mts.
Wanaka
Cromwell
St. Bathans
Tokarahi
Oamaru

Caswell Sd.
Charles Sd.
Stuart Mts.
Glenorchy
Pisa Ra.
Clutha
Naseby
Takanui Mts.
Maheno

Thompson Sd.
Secretary I.
Doubtful Sd.
Murchison Mts.
Mt. Lyall 6067
Queenstown
L.
Wakatipu
James Pk.
6893
The Remarkables
Kawarau
Clyde
Alexandra
Ranfurly
Hyde
Hampden

Daggs Sd.
Kepler Mts.
Mt. Soaker
6080
N. Mavora L.
Jane Pk.
6650
Eyre Mts.
Garvie Mts.
Clyde
Roxburgh
Middlemarch
Dunback
Waikouaiti
Downs
Shag Pt.
Palmerston

Breaksea
Sd.
Resolution
Heath Mts.
L.Te
Anau
Kingston
Umbrella Mts.
Coal
Creek Flat
Millers Flat
Sutton
Waikouaiti

Dusky
Sd.
Hunter Mts.
Te Anau
Mossburn
Waimea
Waikaia
Plain
Beaumont
Taieri
Warrington

West C.
Providence
Chalky
Inlet
Cameron Mts.
Caroline
Pk.
5575
L.
Monowai
L.
Manapouri
Manapouri
Lumsden
Waikaia
Edievale
Heriot
Lawrence
Waipori
Port Chalmers
Allanton
Otago Harb.
Saunders
Otago Pen.
West Harbour

Preservation
Inlet
Puysegur Pt.
Kaherekoau Mts.
L. Hauroko
Clifden
Birchwood
Nightcaps
Wairio
Riversdale
Dipton
Kelso
Tapanui
Dunedin
St. Kilda
Green Island

O T A G O

S o u t h l a n d

Coal
I.
Poteriti
Tuatapere
Orawia
Otautau
Thornbury
Winton
Gore
Mataura
Clinton
Milton
Mosgiel
Waihola

Solander I.
Te
Waewae
B.
Pahia
Pt.
Orepuki
Riverton
Wallacetown
Waikiwi
Invercargill
South Invercargill
Fortrose
Hedgehope
Edendale
Wyndham
Gleniam
Mataura
Waipahi
Clutha
Waihola
Balclutha
Stirling
Kaitangata
Owaka
Nugget Pt.
Long Pt.
Chaslands Mistake
Tahakopa

Mt. Anglem
3214
Codfish I.
Halfmoon Bay
Oban
Paterson Inlet
Bluff
Bluff Hart.
Toetoes
B.
Waipapa Pt.
Ruapuke I.
Takanui
Foveaux Strait

Mason B.
Doughboy B.
Stewart
Island

Long I.
Southwest C.
Port Pegasus

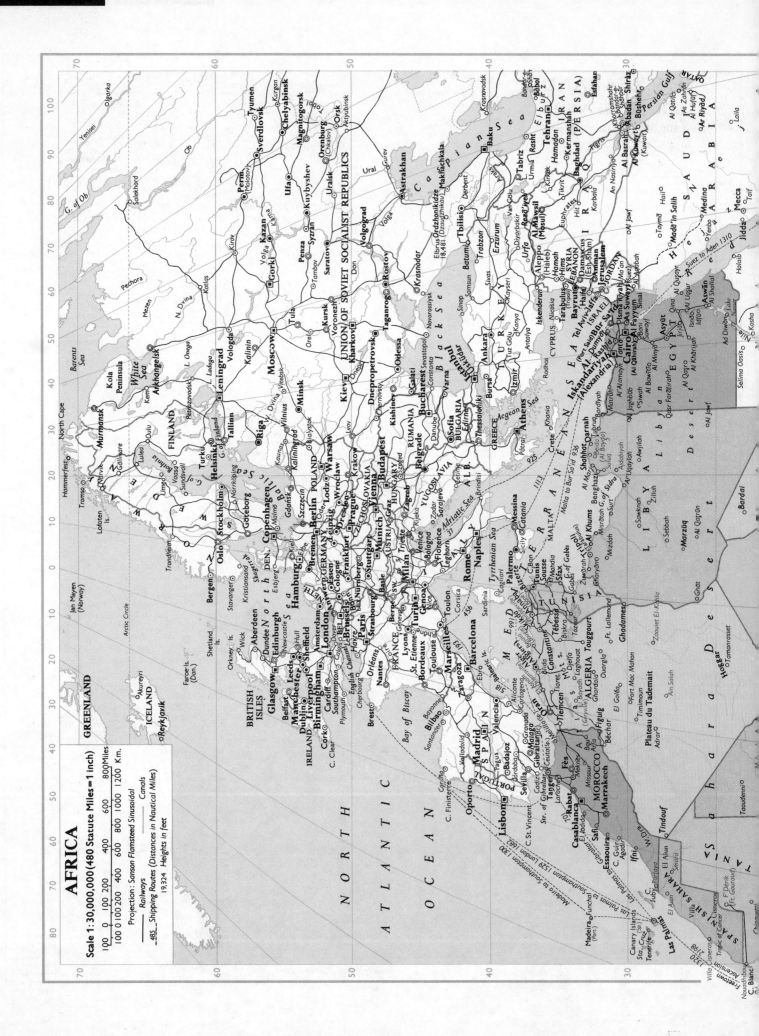

AFRICA

Scale 1:30,000,000 (480 Statute Miles=1 inch)

100 0 100 200 400 600 800 Miles
100 0 100 200 400 600 800 1000 1200 Km.

Projection: Sanson Flamsteed Sinusoidal

Railways
485 Shipping Routes (Distances in Nautical Miles)
Canals
19,324 Heights in feet

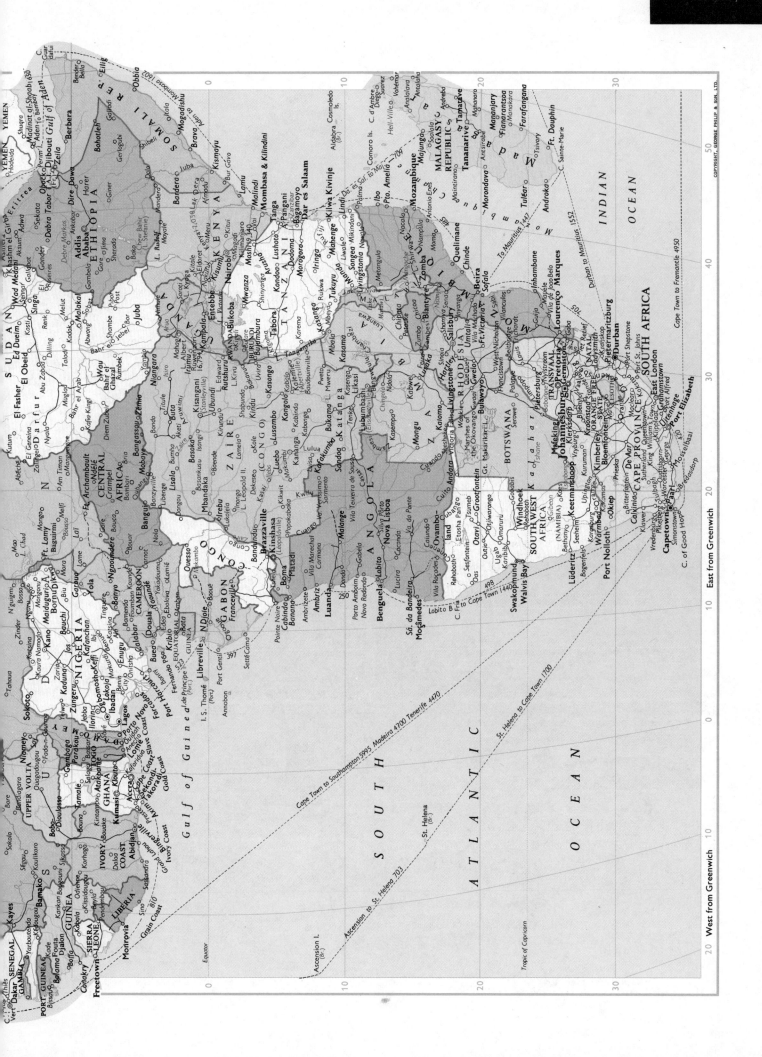

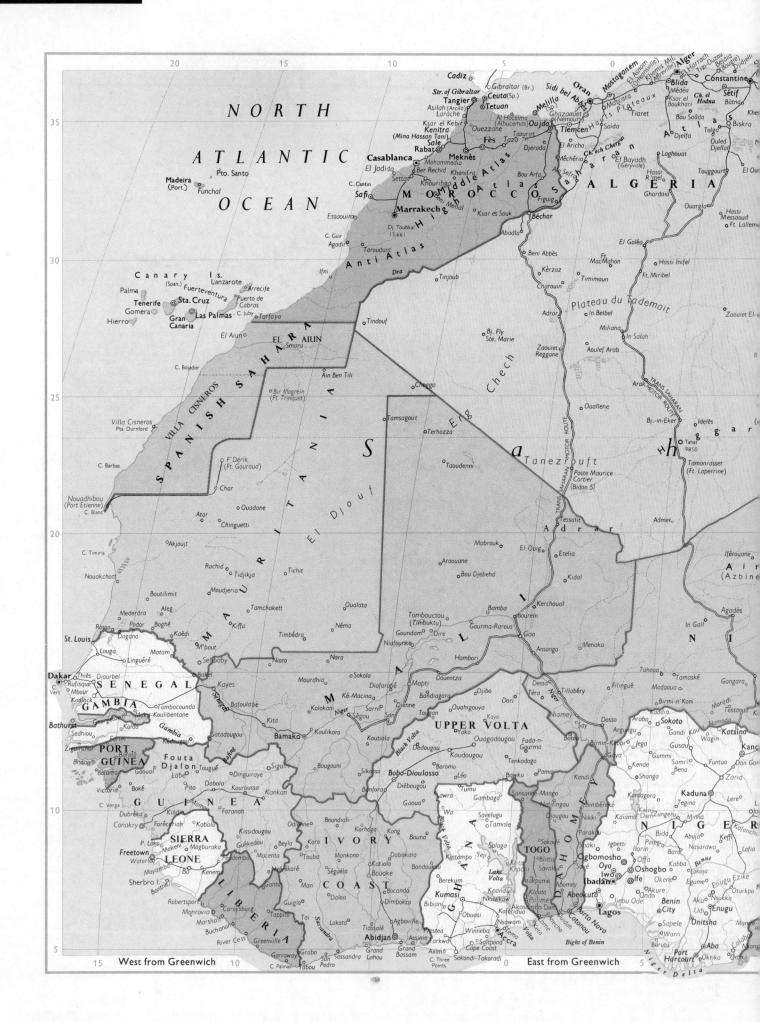

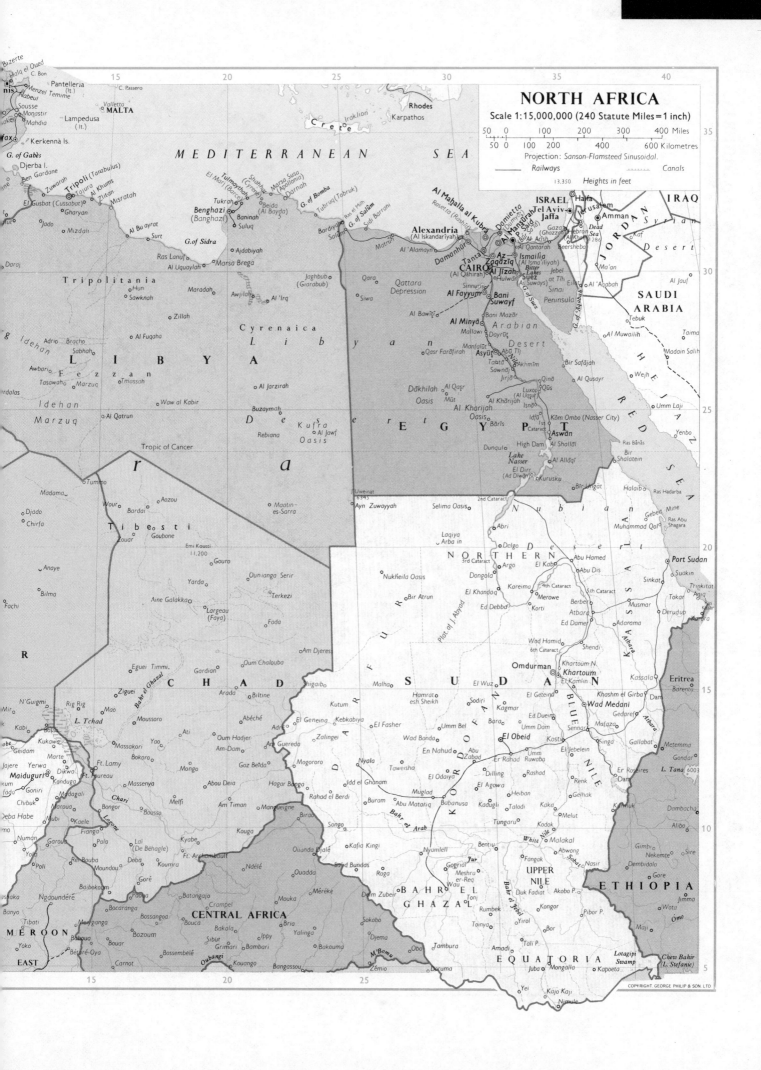

NORTH AFRICA

Scale 1:15,000,000 (240 Statute Miles=1 inch)

| 50 | 0 | 100 | 200 | 300 | 400 Miles |

| 50 | 0 | 100 | 200 | 400 | 600 Kilometres |

Projection: Sanson-Flamsteed Sinusoidal.

——— Railways ········ Canals

13,350 Heights in feet

MEDITERRANEAN SEA

MALTA

Crete

Rhodes

Karpathos

Pantelleria (It.)

C. Passero

Lampedusa (It.)

Bizerte
Hala el Oued
C. Bon
Menzel Temime
Nabeul
Sousse
Monastir
Mahdia
Kerkenna Is.
G. of Gabès
Djerba I.
Ben Gardane
Zuwarah
Tripoli (Tarabulus)
Tajura
Al Khums
Zlitan
Misratah
El Gusbat (Cussabat)
Gharyan
Al Bu ayrat
Surt
G.of Sidra
Ras Lanuf
Al Uquaylah
Marsa Brega
Ajdabiyah
El Magrun
Tulmaythah (Ptolemais)
Shahhat
Marsa Susa (Apollonia)
Darnah
G. of Bomba
Tukrah
Benghazi (Banghazi)
Baninah
Beida (Al Bayda)
Suluq
Tubruq (Tobruk)
G. of Salum
Rue el Milh
Bardiyah
Sidi Barrani
Salum
Matruh
Al 'Alamayn
Damanhur
Rosetta (Rashid)

Alexandria (Al Iskandariyah)

ISRAEL
Tel Aviv
Jaffa
Haifa
Jerusalem
IRAQ
Amman
JORDAN
Syrian
Desert

Al Mahalla al Kubra
Damietta
Dumyat
Port Said
Al Mansurah
Gaza (Ghazzah)
Hebron
Dead Sea 286
Beersheba
Az Zaqaziq
Ismailia (Al Isma'iliyah)
CAIRO (Al Qahirah)
Al Jizah
Hulwan
Bitter Lakes
Suez (As Suways)
Jebel at Tih
Sinai Peninsula
Ma'an
Al 'Aqabah
SAUDI ARABIA
Tebuk
Al Jauf

Tanta

Daraj

Tripolitania

Hun
Sawknah

Maradah
Awjilah
Al 'Irq

Jaghbub (Giarabub)

Qara
Siwa

Qattara Depression

Al Fayyum
Bani Suwayf

Sinnuris
Al Bawiti

Al Minya
Mallawi
Dayrut

Arabian

Manfalut
Qasr Farafirah
Abu Tij
Asyut
Tahta
Sawnaj
Akhmim

Desert

Bani Mazar

Al Muwailih
Madain Salih
Taima

Zillah

Cyrenaica

Libya

Al Fuqaha

Al Jazirah

L i b y a n

Jirja
Qina
Bir Safajah

Fezzan

Adiro
Bracha
Sabhah
Tasawah
Marzuq
Tmassah

Waw al Kabir

Idehan

Buzaymah

De

Kufra
Al Jawf
Oasis

Rebiana

Dakhila
Oasis
Al Qasr
Mut

s

e

Luxor (Al Uqsur)
Esna

r t

Al Kharijah
Baris

a

E G Y P T

Idfu
Kom Ombo (Nasser City)
Aswan
High Dam
Al Shallal
1st Cataract

RED SEA

Al Qusayr

Wejh

Umm Laji

Yenbo

HEJAZ

Ras Banas

Dungul

Lake Nasser

El Dirr (Ad Diwan)
Al Allaqi

Kuruku

Bir Shalatein

Tropic of Cancer

Al Qatrun

Tummo

Tibesti

Madama
Wour
Bardai
Aozou

Emi Koussi 11,200
Goubone

Zouar

Djado
Chirfa
Anaye
Bilma
Fachi

Ayn Zuwayyah
Uweinat 6345

Selima Oasis

2nd Cataract

N u b i a n

Gebeit Mine

Muhammad Qol

Ras Abu Shagara

Halaib
Ras Hadarba

Laqiya Arba in

Abri

D e s e r t

Delgo

Abu Hamed

Port Sudan

Suakin

Nukheila Oasis
Bir Atrun

3rd Cataract

Dongola

Argo
El Kab

Abu Dis

Sinkat

Trinkitat

Aozou

Yarda

Ounianga Serir

Terkezi

Largeau (Faya)

Fada

Am Djeress

Oum Chalouba

Gordian

Eguei Timmi

Ziguei

Bahr el Ghazal

CHAD

Arada

Biltine

Malha

Kutum

Hamrat esh Sheikh

El Wuz

S U D A N

El Khandaq

Ed Debba

Kareima
Merowe
Korti

4th Cataract

Berber

5th Cataract

Atbara
Ed Damer

Musmar

Tokar

Derudeb

El Geteina

Khashm el Girba

Dam

Eritrea

Barentu

Plat. of J. Abyad

6th Cataract

Wad Hamid

Shendi

Khartoum N.

Omdurman
Khartoum
El Kamlin

NORTHERN

Maatin-es-Sarra

N'Guigmi
Rig Rig
Mao
L. Tchad
Moussoro
Yao
Massakori
Bokoro
Ati
Oum Hadjer
Am-Dam
Abéché
Adré
Am Gureda
Zalingei

El Geneina
Kebkabiya
El Fasher
Wad Bonda

Sodiri

Bara

Kagmar

Um Dueim

Kaka

DARFUR

KORDOFAN

Umm Bel

En Nahud

Abu Zabad

El Obeid

Kosti

Ed Dueim

El Jebelein

Kassala

Wad Medani

Gedaref

Matana

Sennar

Er Roseires Dam

L. Tana 6003

Gallabat

Metemma

Gondar

Kukawa
Marte
Maiduguri
Dikwa
Ft. Foureau
Massenya
Mongo
Abou Deia
Melfi
Goz Beida
Mogororo
Nyala
Idd el Ghanam
Buram
Abu Matariq
Muglad
Bubanusa

Kadugli
Talodi
Heiban
Rashad
El Agowa

Renk
Gelhak

Dambacha

Dambacha

Jajere
Yerwa
Chari
Bongor
Bousso
Kélo
Lai (De Béhagle)
Kyabé
Am Timan
Mangueigne
Birao

Kouga

Ouanda Djalé

Kafia Kingi

Songo

Bahr el Arab

Nyumilell

Tungaru

Kodok

Melut

Gimbi
Nekemte

Gore

Sire

Maroua
Kaele
Mubi
Deba Habe
Numan
Garoua
Rey Bouba
Poli
Yola
Ngaoundéré
Tibati
Banyo
CAMEROON
EAST
Bétaré-Oya

Pala
Doba
Moundou
Goré
Baibokoum
Bossangoa
Bozoum
Bouar
Bossembélé
Batangafo
Bouca
Crampel
Bakala
Grimari
Bambari
Ippy
Yalinga
Bria
Djema

Bozoum

CENTRAL AFRICA

Ndélé

Ouadda

Mouka

Méréke

Delm Zubeir

BAHR EL GHAZAL

Wau
Tonj
Rumbek

Gogrial
Meshra er-Req

Duk Fadiat

UPPER NILE

White Nile
Malakal
Abwong
Fangok

Bentiu

Kongor

Pibor P.

Wota

Maji

ETHIOPIA

Jimma

Gore

Dembidolo

Nasir

Sobat

Bahr el Jebel

EQUATORIA

Amadi
Tali P.
Tombura
Yambio
Obo
Doruma
Zémio
Bangassou
Kouango
Carnot
Kounango
Oubangi
M'Bomu
Bakouma

Juba
Mongalla
Kapoeta
Yei
Kajo Kaji
Nimule

Lotagipi Swamp

Chew Bahir (L. Stefanie)

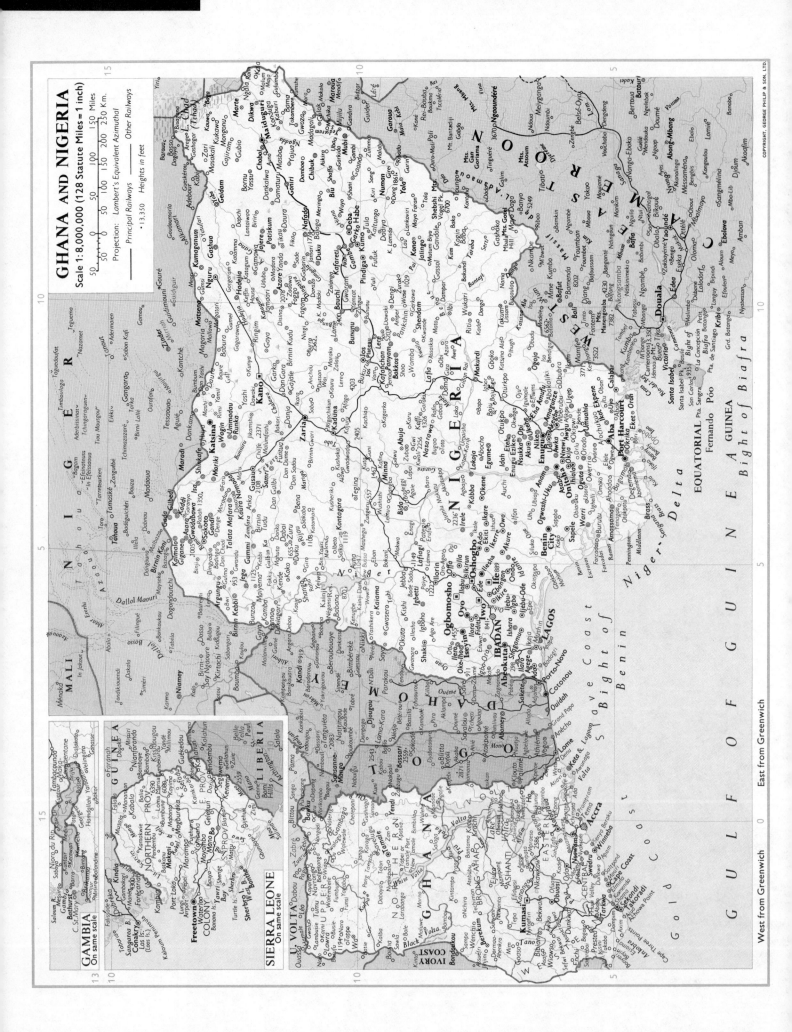

GHANA AND NIGERIA

Scale 1:8,000,000 (128 Statute Miles = 1 inch)

Projection: Lambert's Equivalent Azimuthal

——— Principal Railways ——— Other Railways

• 13,350   Heights in feet

50   0   50   100   150   200   250 Km.

50   0   50   100   150 Miles

GAMBIA
On same scale

SIERRA LEONE
On same scale

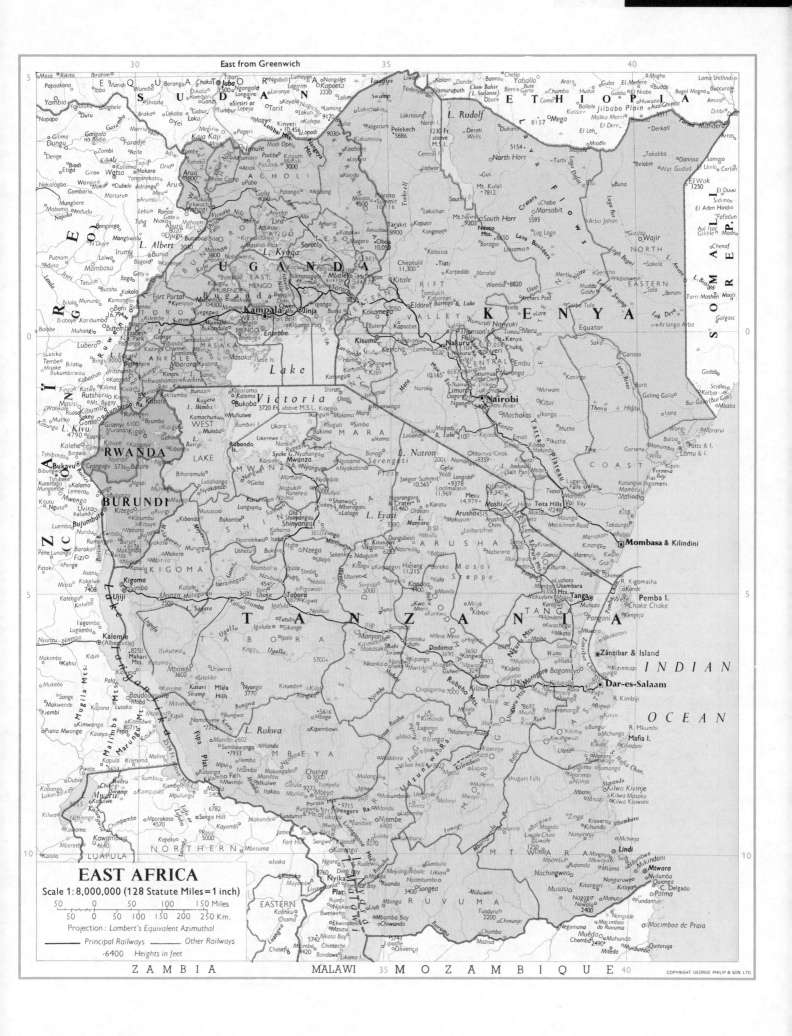

EAST AFRICA

Scale 1:8,000,000 (128 Statute Miles = 1 inch)

50   0   50   100   150 Miles
50   0   50 100 150 200 250 Km.

Projection: Lambert's Equivalent Azimuthal

—— Principal Railways   —— Other Railways
·6400   Heights in feet

AFRICA
CENTRAL AND SOUTH

Scale 1:15,000,000 (240 Statute Miles=1 inch)

Projection: Sanson-Flamsteed Sinusoidal.

Railways

Heights in feet

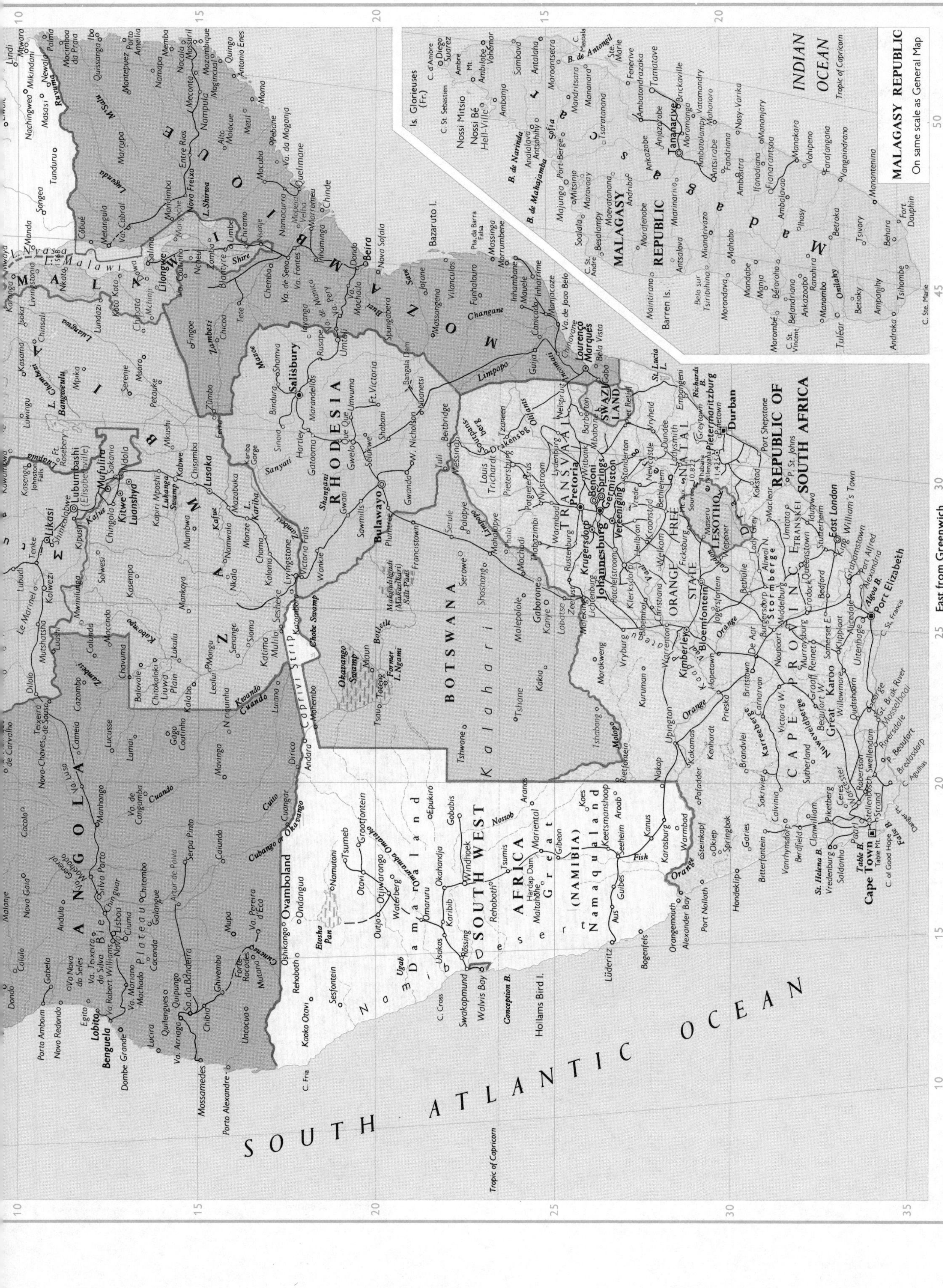

SOUTH ATLANTIC OCEAN

INDIAN OCEAN

ANGOLA

Planalto Plateau

Bié

ZAMBIA

MALAWI

L. Malawi
L. Nyasa

RHODESIA

Salisbury
Bulawayo

BOTSWANA

Kalahari

Okavango Swamp

Caprivi Strip

SOUTH WEST AFRICA
(NAMIBIA)

Damaraland

Great Namaqualand

Windhoek

TRANSVAAL
Pretoria
Johannesburg
Germiston
Springs
Benoni
Krugersdorp
Vereeniging

ORANGE FREE STATE
Bloemfontein
Kimberley

SWAZI LAND

LESOTHO

NATAL
Durban
Pietermaritzburg

REPUBLIC OF SOUTH AFRICA

CAPE PROVINCE
Great Karoo
Port Elizabeth
East London
Cape Town
C. of Good Hope
Table Mt.

TRANSKEI

Lourenço Marques
Beira

MOZAMBIQUE

Limpopo
Zambezi

Lubumbashi
(Elisabethville)
Kitwe
Lusaka
Luanshya

Victoria Falls
Livingstone

MALAGASY REPUBLIC
On same scale as General Map

Tananarive

Tropic of Capricorn

East from Greenwich

COPYRIGHT. GEORGE PHILIP & SON, LTD.

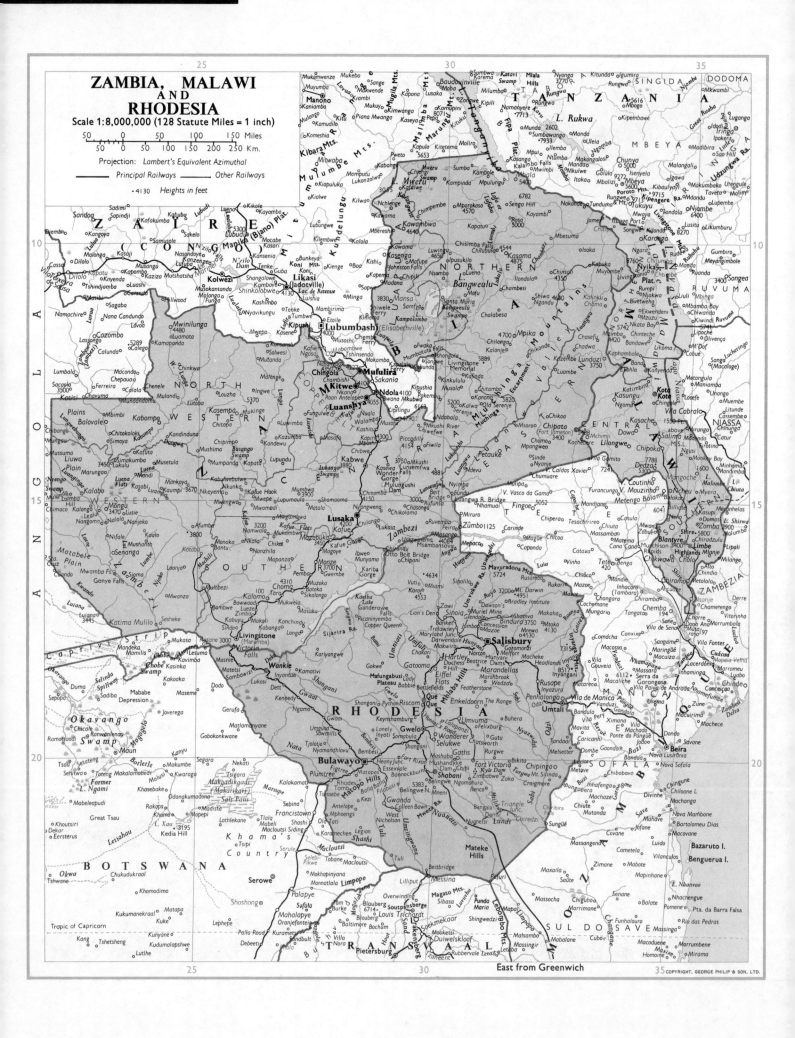

ZAMBIA, MALAWI AND RHODESIA

Scale 1:8,000,000 (128 Statute Miles = 1 inch)

50   0   50   100   150 Miles
50   0   50   100   150   200   250 Km.

Projection: Lambert's Equivalent Azimuthal

———— Principal Railways ———— Other Railways

· 4130   Heights in feet

East from Greenwich

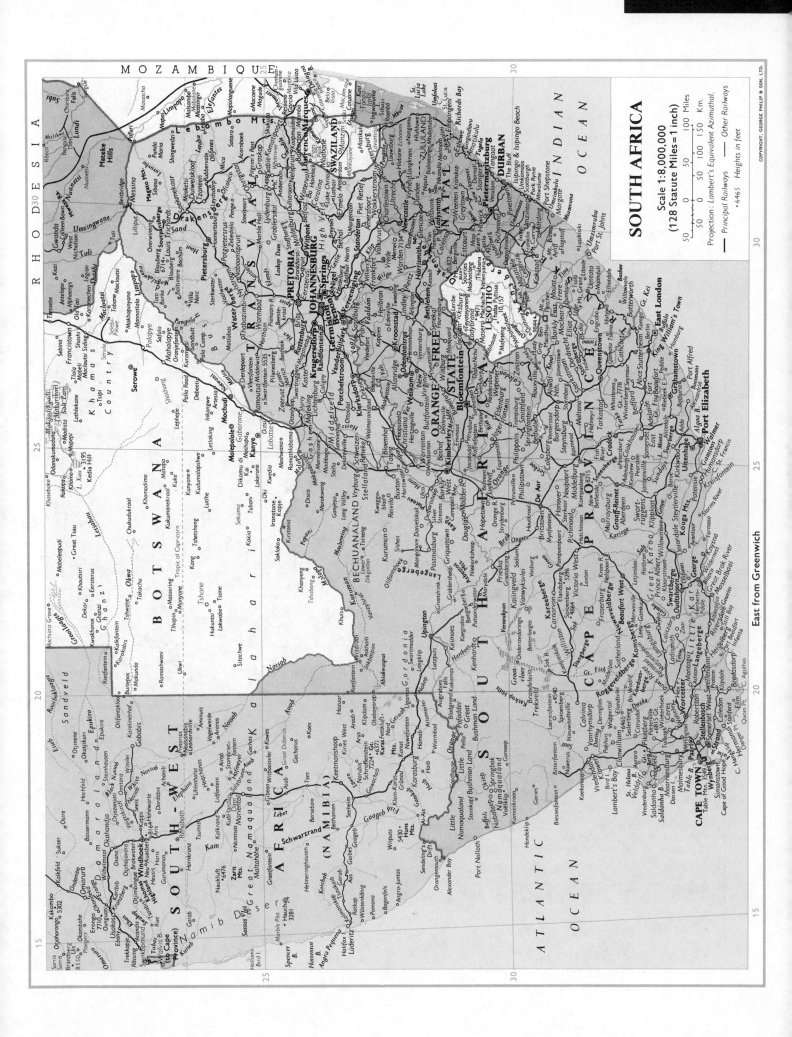

SOUTH AFRICA

Scale 1:8,000,000
(128 Statute Miles=1 inch)

Projection: Lambert's Equivalent Azimuthal.

—— Principal Railways   —— Other Railways

•6465 · Heights in feet

East from Greenwich

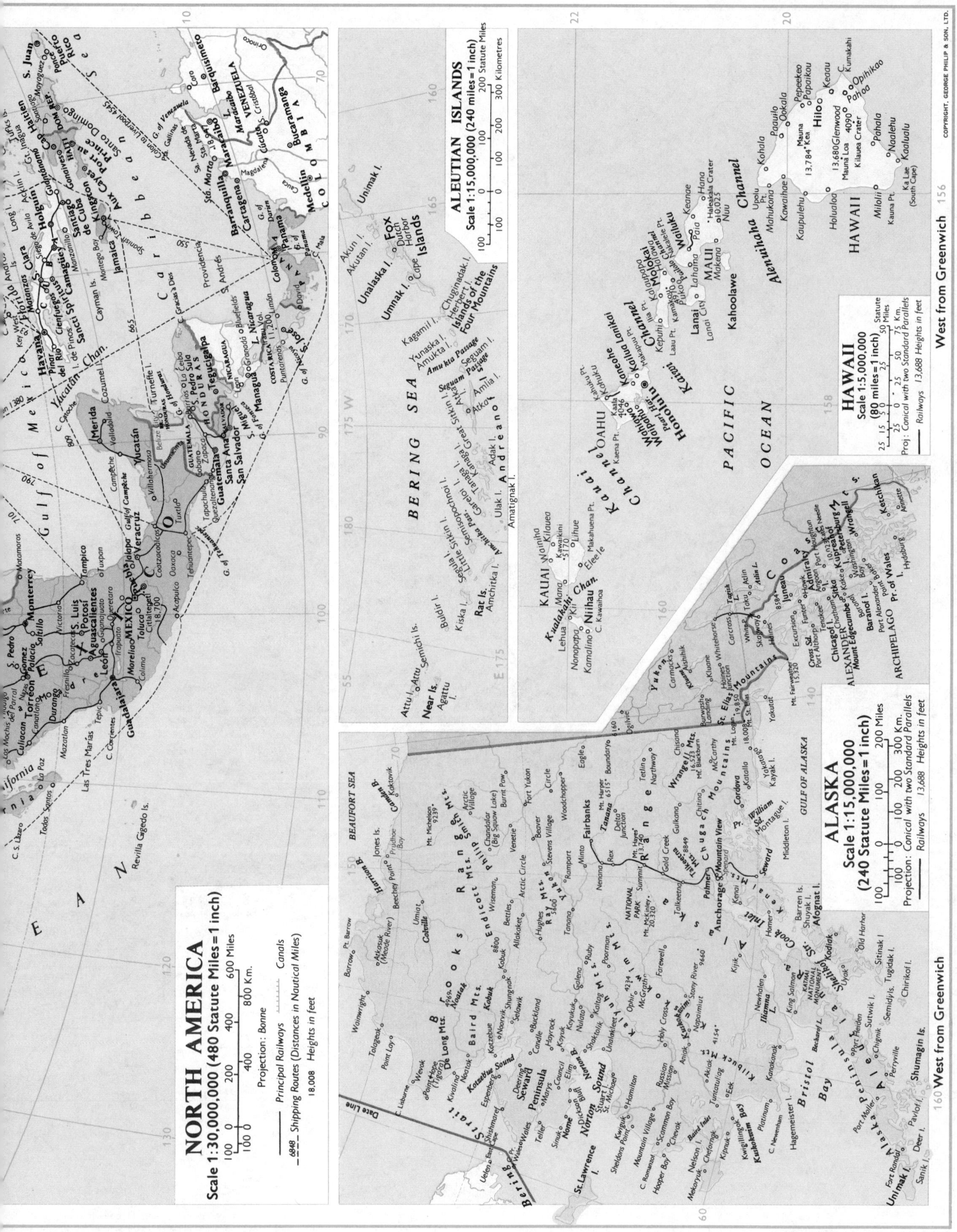

NORTH AMERICA

Scale 1:30,000,000 (480 Statute Miles=1 inch)

100 0   200   400   600 Miles
100 0   400   800 Km.

Projection: Bonne

Principal Railways   Canals
6848 Shipping Routes (Distances in Nautical Miles)
18,008 Heights in feet

ALEUTIAN ISLANDS

Scale 1:15,000,000 (240 miles=1 inch)

100   0   100   200   300 Statute Miles
100   0   100   200   300 Kilometres

HAWAII

Scale 1:5,000,000
(80 miles=1 inch)
25 15 0   25   50   75 Statute Miles
25 0   25   50   75 Km.
Proj: Conical with two Standard Parallels
Railways 13,688 Heights in feet

ALASKA

Scale 1:15,000,000
(240 Statute Miles=1 inch)

100   0   100   200   300 Km.
100   0   100   200 Miles
Projection: Conical with two Standard Parallels
Railways 13,688 Heights in feet

BERING SEA

PACIFIC OCEAN

BEAUFORT SEA

GULF OF ALASKA

COLOMBIA

VENEZUELA

MEXICO

160 West from Greenwich

West from Greenwich 156

COPYRIGHT. GEORGE PHILIP & SON, LTD.

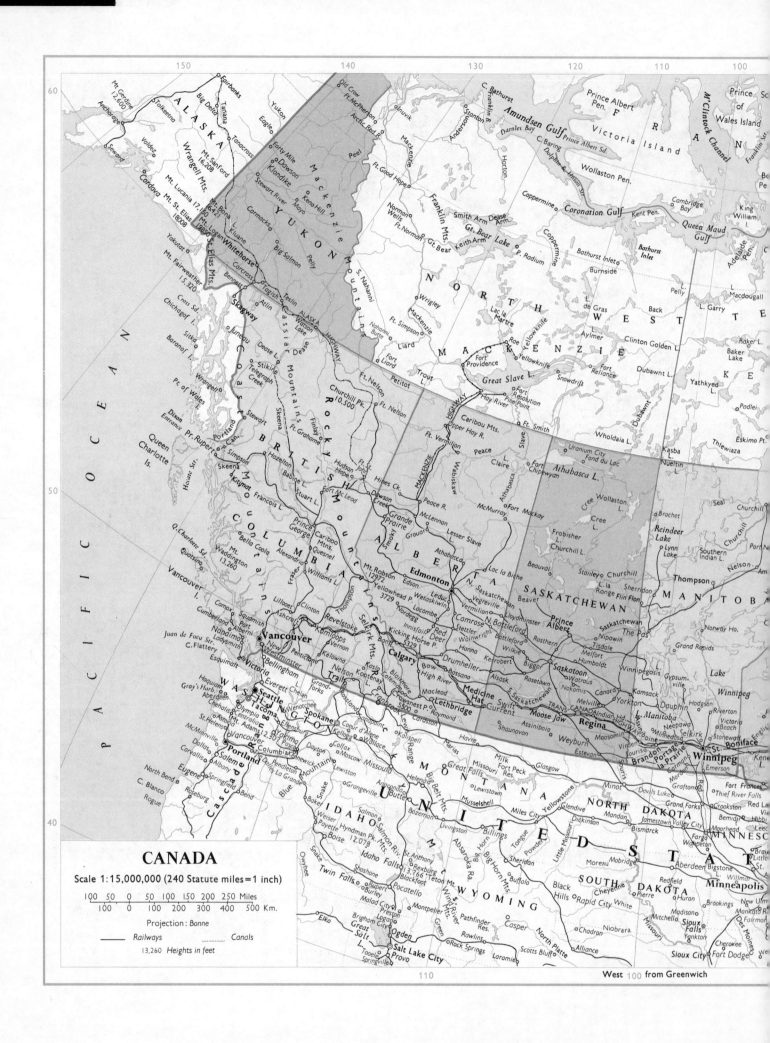

CANADA

Scale 1:15,000,000 (240 Statute miles=1 inch)

100 50 0 50 100 150 200 250 Miles
100 0 100 200 300 400 500 Km.

Projection: Bonne

——— Railways   Canals
13,260   Heights in feet

West 100 from Greenwich

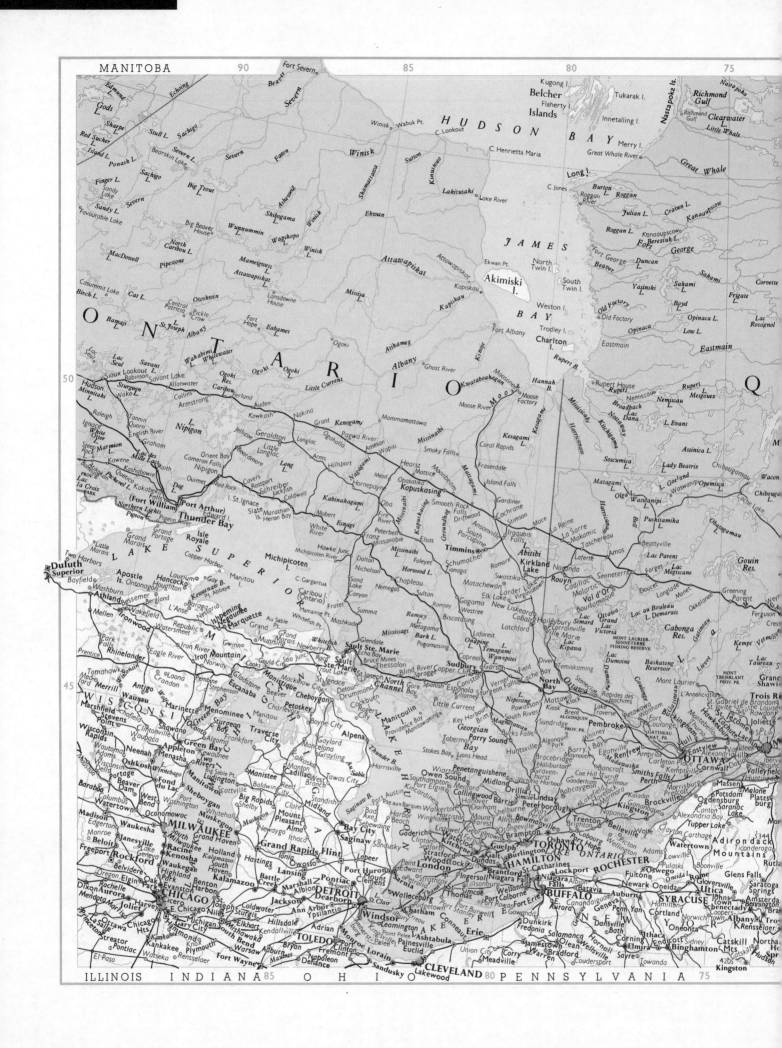

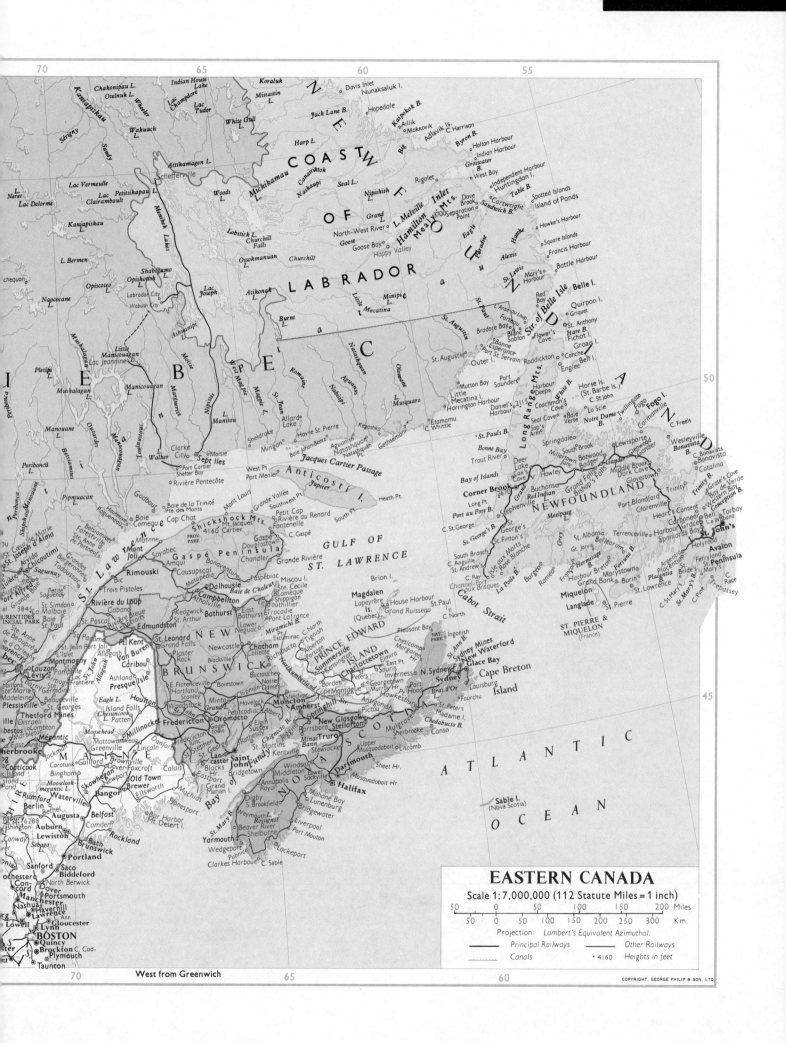

70   65   60   55

COAST

OF

Kaniapiskau

Chakonipau L.
Otelnuk L.
Indian House Lake
Wheeler
Lac Champdoré
Lac Tudor
Koraluk
White Gull

Mistastin L.
Davis Inlet
Nunaksaluk I.
Jack Lane B.
Hopedale
Makkovik
Aillik
Adlavik Is.
C. Harrison

Strigny
Sandy
Wakuach
Schefferville
Attikamagen L.
Harp L.
Big
Byron B.
Holton Harbour
Indian Harbour
Groswater B.
West Bay

L. Neret
Lac Delorme
Lac Vermeulle
Lac Petitsikapau
Lac Clairambault
Menihek Lakes
Michikamau L.
Canairiktok
Naskaupi L.
Seal L.
Nipishish
Rigolet
Dove Brook
Cartwright
Sandwich B.
Separation Point
Spotted Islands
Island of Ponds
Independent Harbour
Huntingdon I.
Table B.

L. Bermen
Opiscoteo
Shabogamo L.
Opiskotish
Grand L.
North-West River
Goose
Goose Bay
Happy Valley
L A B R A D O R
Mealy Mts.
3700
Eagle
Paradise
Hawke's Harbour
Square Islands
Francis Harbour

Kaniapiskau
Labrador City
Wabush City
Lac Joseph
Ashuanipi
Ossokmanuan
Churchill
Churchill Falls
Lobstick L.
Alexis
Battle Harbour

chequon
Naocacane
L. Bienville
Little Manicouagan
Lac Jeannine
Burnt
Little Mecatina
Minipie
St. Lewis
Red Bay
Str. of Belle Isle
Belle I.
Quirpon I.
Griquet

QUEBEC
NEWFOUNDLAND

Pletipi
Mushalagan
Manicouagan
Maisie
Romaine
St. Augustin
L'Anse au Loup
Forteau
Bradore Bay
Blanc Sablon
Bonne Esperance
Port St. Servain
Outer I.
St. Augustin
Roddickton
Conche
Englee
Bell I.
St. Anthony
Hare B.
Fichot I.
Groais I.

Manouane
West Magpie
Magpie L.
St. Jean
Allardo Lake
Aguanus
Natashipi
Musquaro
Olomane
Mutton Bay
Port Saunders
Little Mecatina I.
Harrington Harbour
Daniel's Harbour
Long Range Mts.
Harbour Deepe
Coachman's Cove
White B.
Horse Is.
(St. Barbe Is.)
C. St. John
La Scie
Baie Verte
Notre Dame B.
Twillingate
Fogo
Fogo I.
C. Freels

Peribonca
Clarke City
Sept Iles
Shelter Bay
Rivière Pentecôte
Sheldrake
Mingan
Havre St. Pierre
Aguanish
Natashquan
Natashquan Pt.
Kegashka
Gethsémani
Etamamu
C. Whittle
St. Pauls B.
Seal Cove
Sop's Arm
Springdale
Botwood
Badger
South Brook
Middle Brook
Gander
Dark Cove
Glenwood
Wesleyville
Bonavista
Catalina

Pipmuacan
Godbout
Baie de la Trinité
Pte. des Monts
Cap Chat
Mont Louis
Grande Vallée
Southwest Pt.
Petit Cap
Rivière au Renard
Fontenelle
C. Gaspé
Heath Pt.
Bonne Bay
Trout River
Deer Lake
Cox's
Millertown Jc.
Bishop's Falls
Grand Falls
Jc.
Gambo
Gloverton
Trinity
Grate's Cove
Bay de Verde
Western Bay

Peribonca L.
Manouane L.
Betsiamites
Forestville
Ste. Anne de Portneuf
Baie Comeau
Les Escoumins
Shickshock Mts.
4160
PROV. PARK.
Cartier
St. Jacques
East
Douglastown
Chandler
Grande Rivière
GULF OF
ST. LAWRENCE
Anticosti I.
Jupiter
South Pt.
Bay of Islands
Corner Brook
2670
Buchans
Red Indian
Howley
Grand L.
Bishop's Falls
Long Pt.
Stephenville
Meelpaeg
Conception B.
Port Blandford
Clarenville
Heart's Content
Carbonear
Bell I.
Torbay
Spaniard's Bay
St. John's
Holyrood

St. Laz
Mont Joli
Sayabec
Gaspé Peninsula
Rimouski
Bic
Trois Pistoles
Amqui
Causapscal
Matapédia
Bonaventure
Pospébiac
Miscou I.
Brion I.
Magdalen Is.
Lapeyrère
(Quebec)
House Harbour
Grand Ruisseau
St. Paul
C. Ray
C. St. George's B.
George's
St. Fintan's
St. George's
Burgeo
Ramea
Hermitage
François
Harbour Breton
Marystown
Grand Bank
Burin
Placentia
St. Mary's
Argentia
Placentia B.
Bride's
St. Mary's
Trepassey
Race
Avalon Peninsula

Rivière du Loup
Cabano
Lac Bleu
Trois Eroits
Edmundston
Ft. Kent
Van Buren
Caribou
Dalhousie
Campbellton
Atholville
Baie de Chaleur
Kedgwick
St. Arthur
Bathurst
East Bathurst
Tracadie
Shippigan
Lameque
Pont Lafrance
Lower Neguac
Miramichi B.
Escuminac
C. North
Tignish
Alberton
Pleasant Bay
Cheticamp
Margaree
NAT. PARK.
Ingonish
St. Ann's
Sydney Mines
New Waterford
Glace Bay
Cape Breton Island
C. North
Channel-Port aux Basques
Isle aux Morts
Rose Blanche
La Poile B.
Gt. Jervis
Belleoram
St. Albans
Terrenceville
Fortune B.
St. Lawrence
St. Pierre
Langlade
ST. PIERRE & MIQUELON
(France)
Miquelon

NEW BRUNSWICK
St. Leonard
Grand Falls
Plaster Rock
Newcastle
Collette
Chatham
Richibucto
Buctouche
Blackville
Chipman
Notre Dame
Cape Tormentine
Borden
Summerside
Kensington
PRINCE EDWARD ISLAND
Charlottetown
Montague
Souris
East Pt.
Georgetown
Murray
Port Hood
Inverness
N. Sydney
Sydney
Louisburg
Fourchu
Bras d'Or
Madame I.

E. Florenceville
Hartland
Woodstock
Stanley
Ashland
Presque Isle
Houlton
Island Falls
Patten
Chesuncook L.
Minto
Havelock
Petitcodiac
Alberton
Shediac
Moncton
Amherst
Springhill
Parrsboro
Minas Basin
Truro
Upper Musquodoboit
Liscomb
Antigonish
Mulgrave
Canso
Chedabucto B.
St. Peters
Pictou
New Glasgow
Stellarton
Sherbrooke

Eagle L.
Island Falls
Millinocket
Woodstock
Fredericton
Oromocto
Gagetown
Sussex
Elgin
Moosehead
Mattawamkeag
Greenville
Lincoln
Danforth
Fredericton Jc.
Rothesay
Chipman
Jemseg
St. Martins
Kentville
Windsor
Lower Stewiacke
Sackville
Musquodoboit Hr.
Sheet Hr.

MAINE
Jackman
East Anguc
Caratunk
Guilford
Dover-Foxcroft
Brownville
Greenville
Bingham
Newport
Old Town
Brewer
Bangor
Ellsworth
Skowhegan
Machias
Jonesport
Bar Harbor
Mt. Desert I.
Lincoln
Blacks Hr.
Bridgewater
Eastport
Grand Manan I.
St. Stephen
Saint John
Lancaster
Fundy Bay
Digby
Annapolis Royal
Bridgetown
Middleton
Kentville
Halifax
Dartmouth
Musquodoboit Hr.
Mahone Bay
Lunenburg
Bridgewater
Liverpool
Port Mouton
Yarmouth
Wedgeport
Pubnico
Clarkes Harbour
C. Sable
Lockeport
Shelburne
Beaver River
Rossignol L.
Weymouth
Meteghan
S. Brookfield
St. Mary B.

NOVA SCOTIA

ATLANTIC
OCEAN

Sable I.
(Nova Scotia)

Sherbrooke
Thetford Mines
Disraeli
Asbestos
East Angus
Mégantic
Sherbrooke
Lac Mégantic
Coaticook
Island Pond
Rangeley
Mooselookmeguntic L.
Rumford
Berlin
Bethel
Waterville
Augusta
Belfast
Camden
Rockland
Bath
Brunswick
Portland
Saco
Biddeford
Sanford
Rochester
Dover
Somersworth
Portsmouth
Manchester
Nashua
Haverhill
Lawrence
Lowell
Lynn
BOSTON
Quincy
Brockton
C. Cod
Plymouth
Taunton
Concord
Berwick
North Berwick
Gloucester
Ann

St. Joseph d'Alma
Chicoutimi
Grandes Bergeronnes
Tadoussac
St. Siméon
La Malbaie
St. Paul
Baie St. Paul
Saguenay
St. Cœur de Marie
Arvida
LAURENTIDES
PROVINCIAL PARK
Ste. Anne de Beaupré
L'Islet
Montmagny
Lauzon
Lévis
Quebec
3845
Pampille
Ste. Marie
Beauceville
St. Georges
Plessisville
Victoriaville
Drummondville
La Tuque

West from Greenwich

70   65   60

EASTERN CANADA

Scale 1:7,000,000 (112 Statute Miles = 1 inch)

50   0   50   100   150   200 Miles

50   0   50   100   150   200   250   300 Km.

Projection: *Lambert's Equivalent Azimuthal.*

———— *Principal Railways*   ———— *Other Railways*

‒‒‒‒‒ *Canals*   •4160 *Heights in feet*

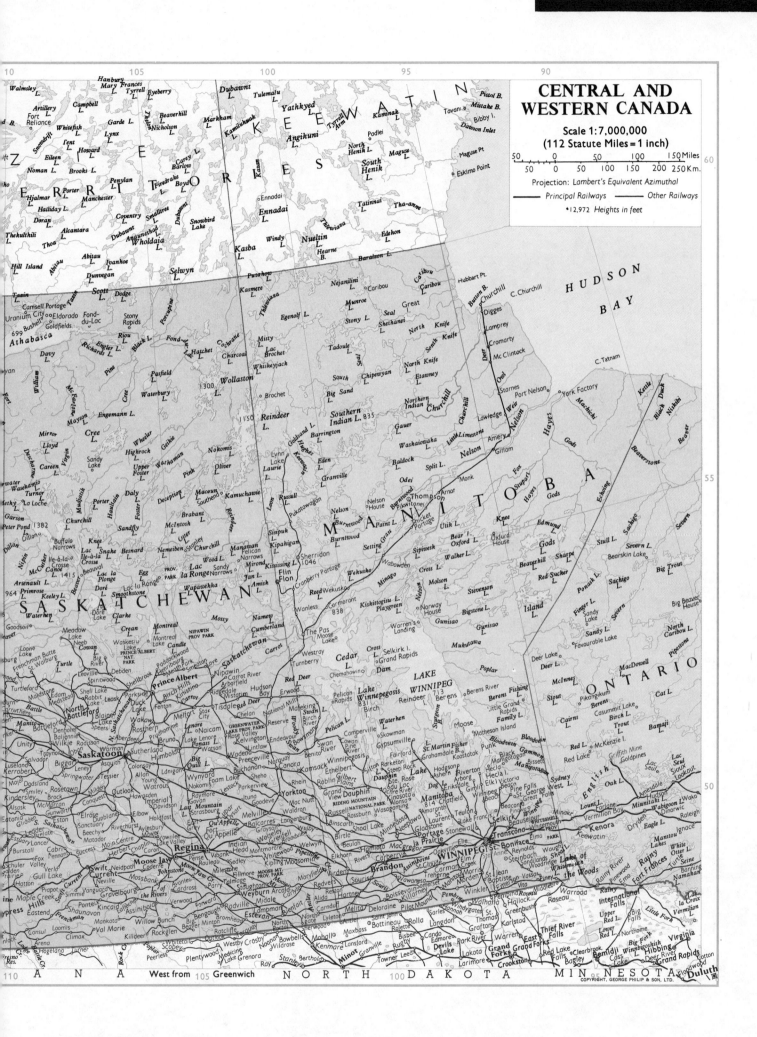

CENTRAL AND WESTERN CANADA

Scale 1:7,000,000
(112 Statute Miles = 1 inch)

50   0   50   100   150 Miles
50   0   50   100   150   200 250 Km.

Projection: Lambert's Equivalent Azimuthal

——— Principal Railways   ——— Other Railways

•12,972 Heights in feet

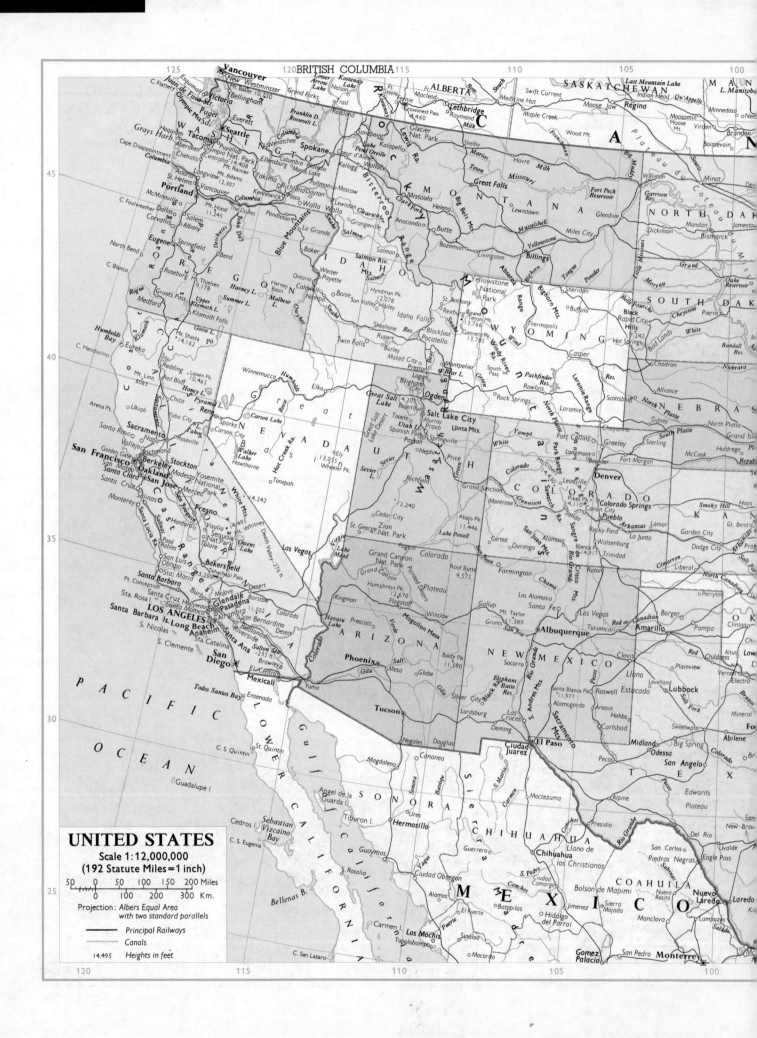

UNITED STATES
Scale 1:12,000,000
(192 Statute Miles = 1 inch)

50 0 50 100 150 200 Miles
0 100 200 300 Km.

Projection: *Albers Equal Area*
with two standard parallels

———— Principal Railways

·········· Canals

14,495 Heights in feet

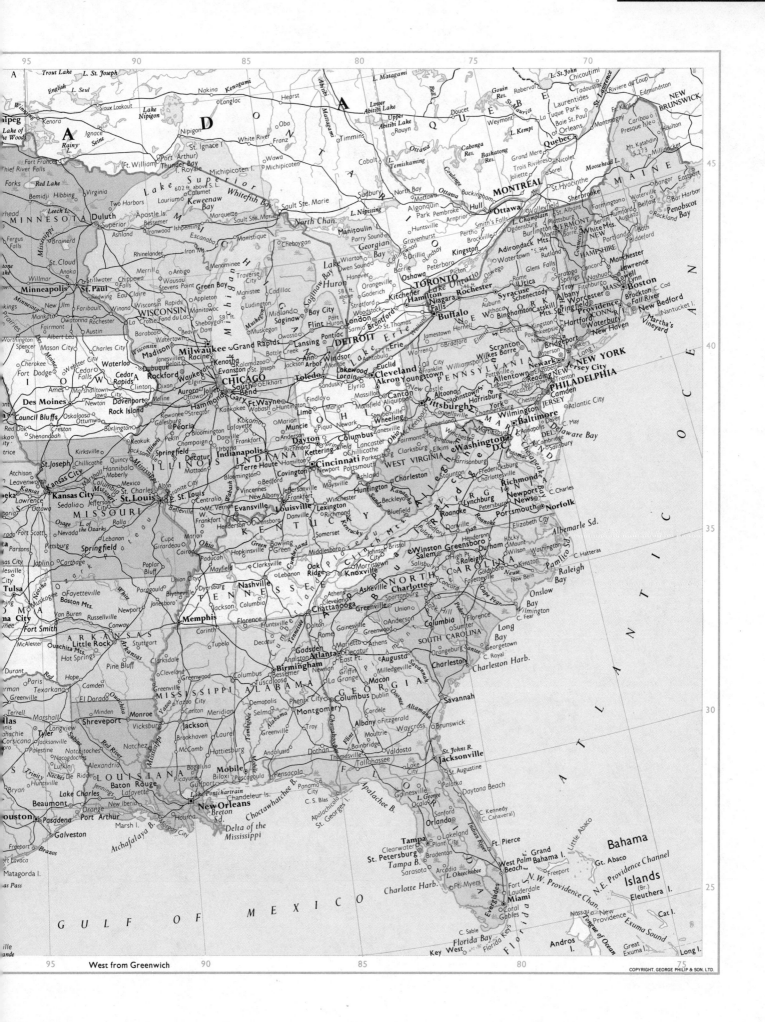

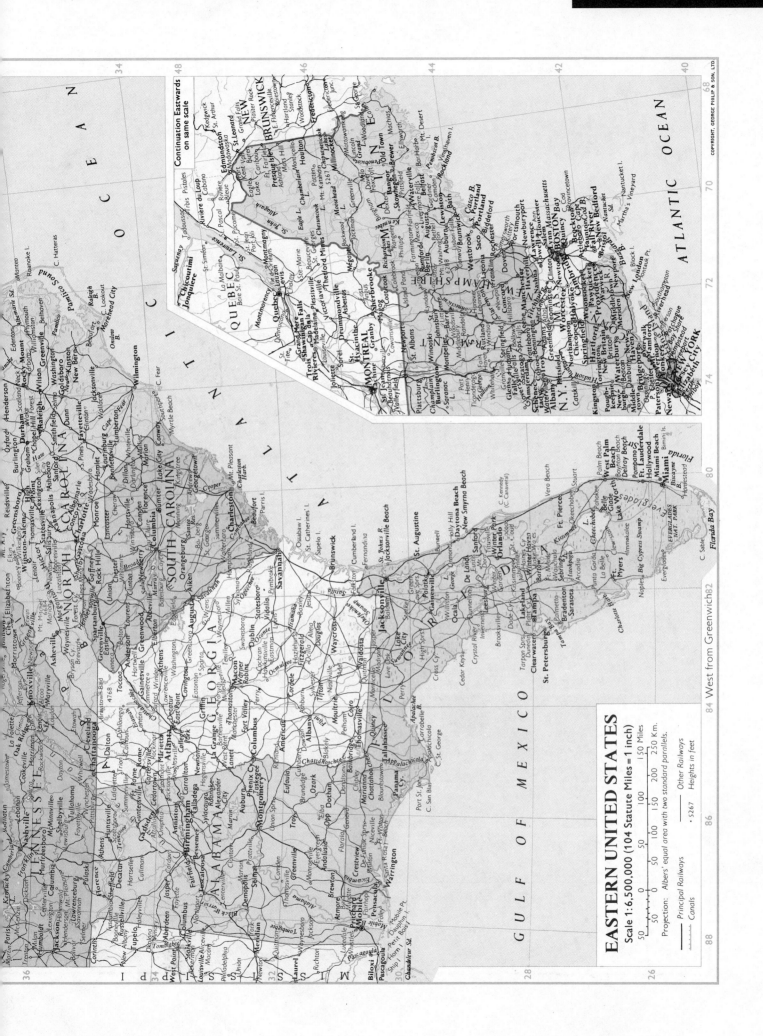

EASTERN UNITED STATES

Scale 1:6,500,000 (104 Statute Miles=1 inch)

Projection: Albers' equal area with two standard parallels.

50   0   50   100   150   200   250 Km.

50   0   50   100   150 Miles

Principal Railways   Other Railways

Canals   •5267 Heights in feet

Continuation Eastwards on same scale

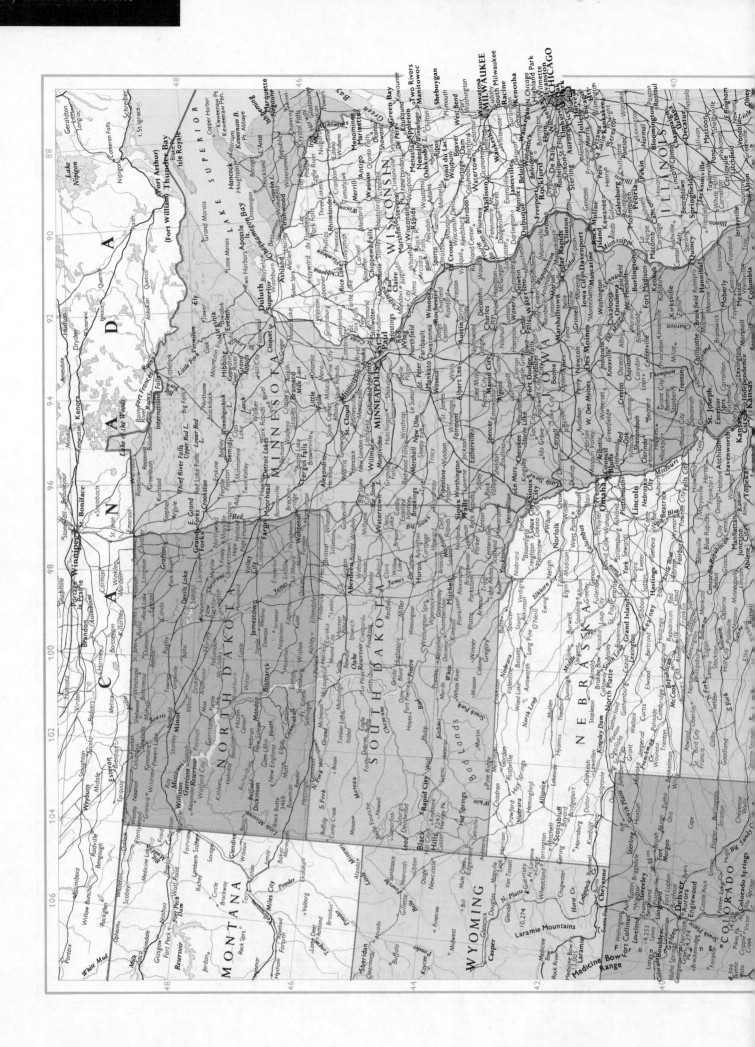

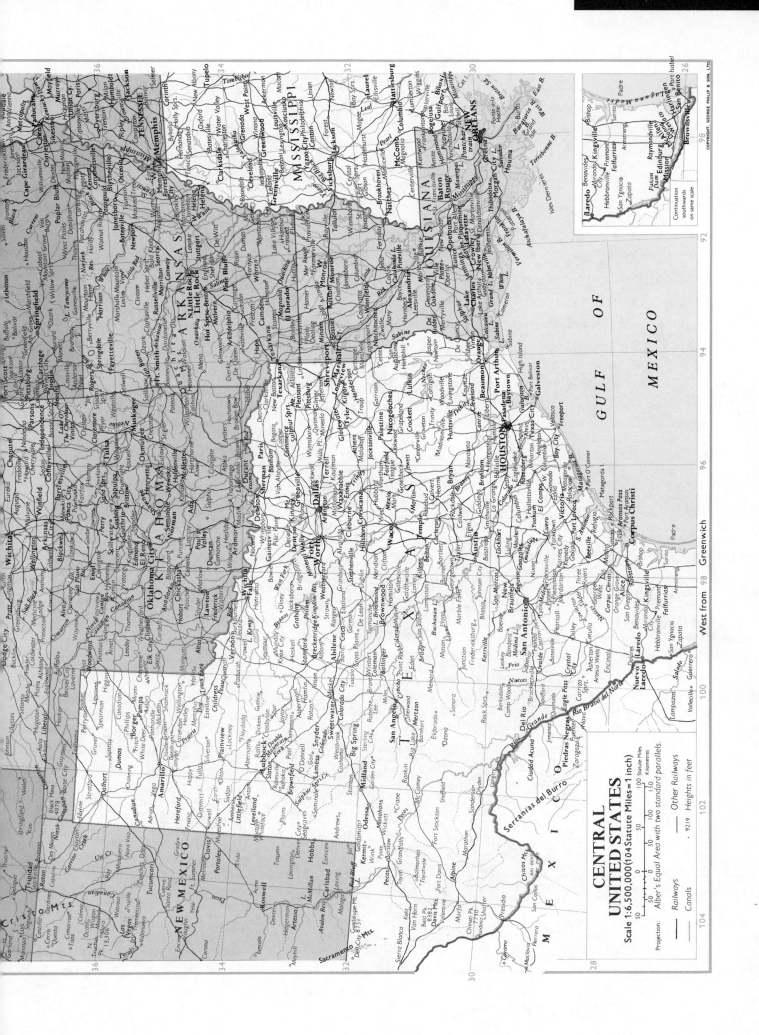

CENTRAL
UNITED STATES

Scale 1:6,500,000(104 Statute Miles=1 inch)

Projection: Alber's Equal Area with two standard parallels.

—— Railways	—— Other Railways
········· Canals	· 9219 Heights in feet

GULF OF

MEXICO

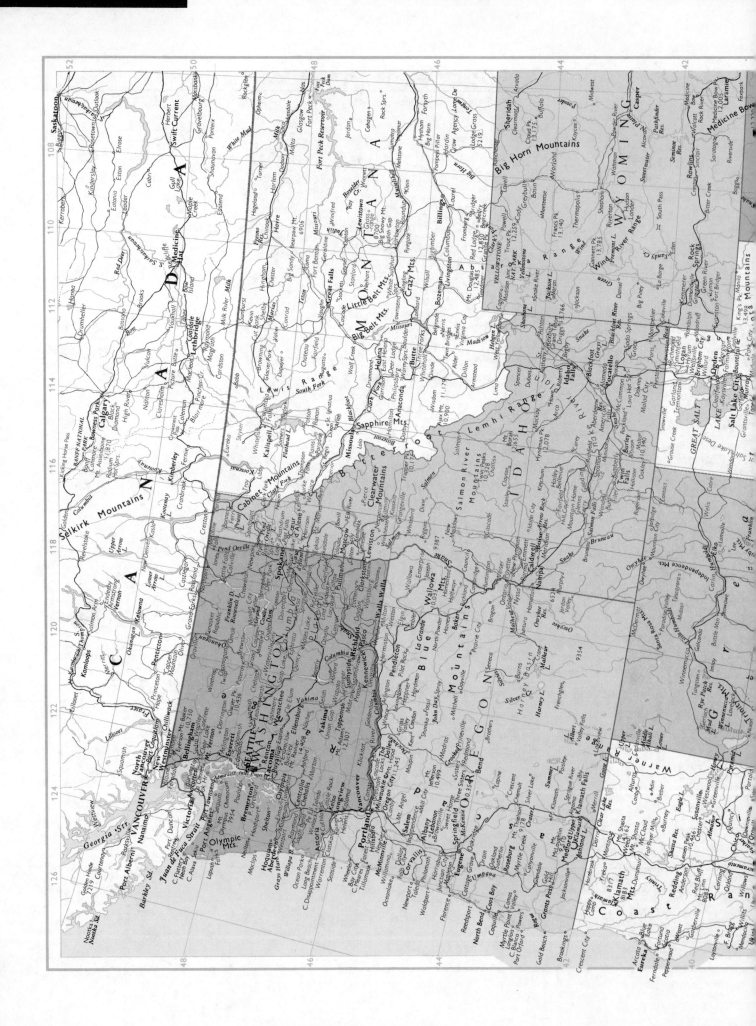

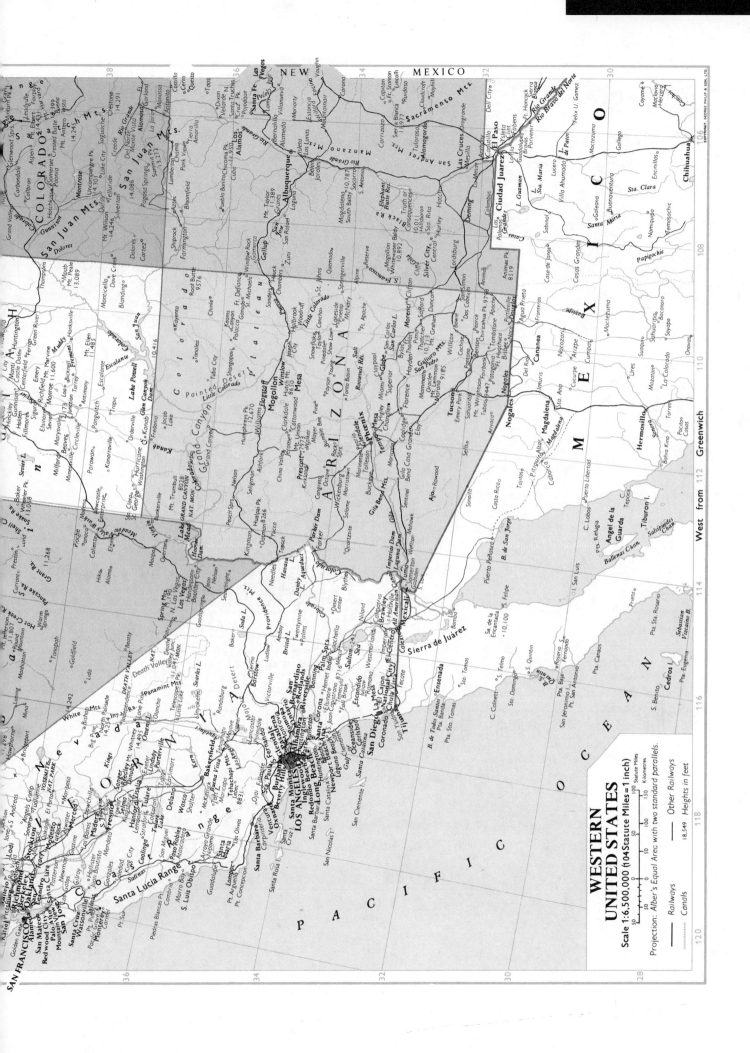

PACIFIC OCEAN

**WESTERN
UNITED STATES**

Scale 1:6,500,000 (104 Statute Miles=1 inch)

Projection: Alber's Equal Area with two standard parallels.

| | 50 | 100 Statute Miles |
| 50 | 100 | 150 Kilometres |

— Railways ···· Other Railways

---- Canals   18,549 Heights in feet

COPYRIGHT GEORGE PHILIP & SON, LTD.

West from Greenwich

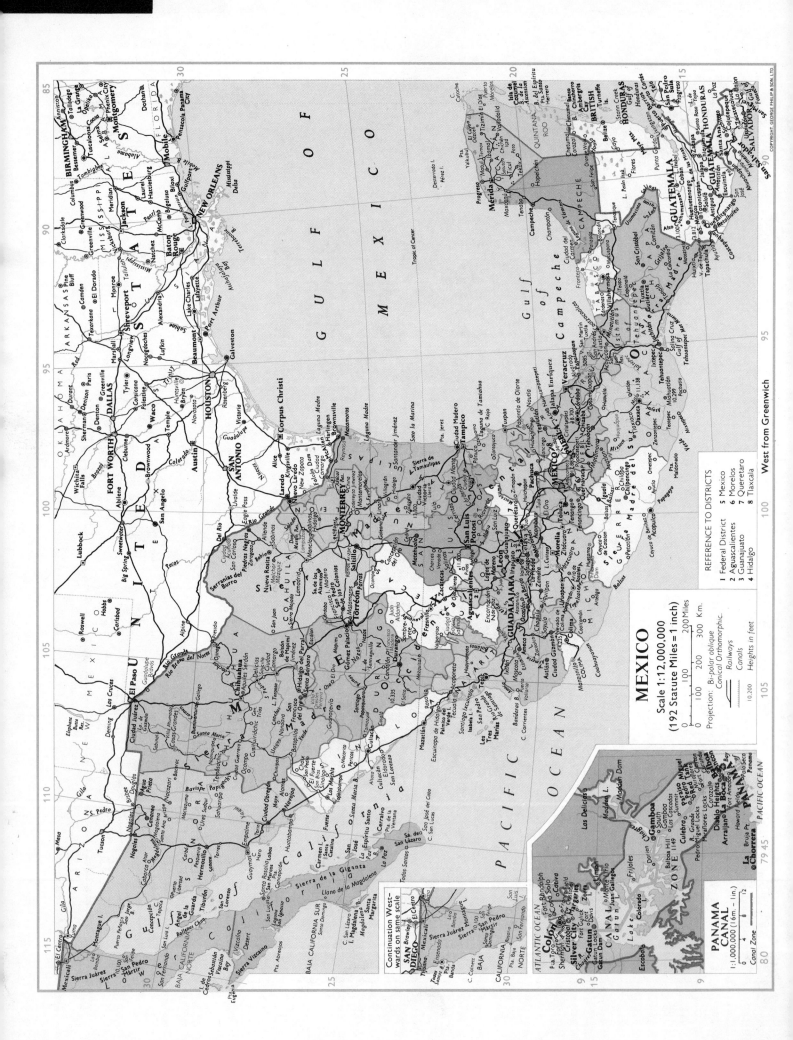

MEXICO

Scale 1:12,000,000
(192 Statute Miles = 1 inch)

Projection: Bi-polar oblique
Conical Orthomorphic.

| 0 | 100 | 200 | 300 Km. |

| 0 | 100 | 200 Miles |

Railways
Canals
10,200 △ Heights in feet

REFERENCE TO DISTRICTS

1 Federal District 5 Mexico
2 Aguascalientes 6 Morelos
3 Guanajuato 7 Queretaro
4 Hidalgo 8 Tlaxcala

West from Greenwich

Continuation West-wards on same scale

PANAMA CANAL

1:1,000,000 (16m.=1 in.)

| 0 | 4 | 8 | 12 |

Canal Zone

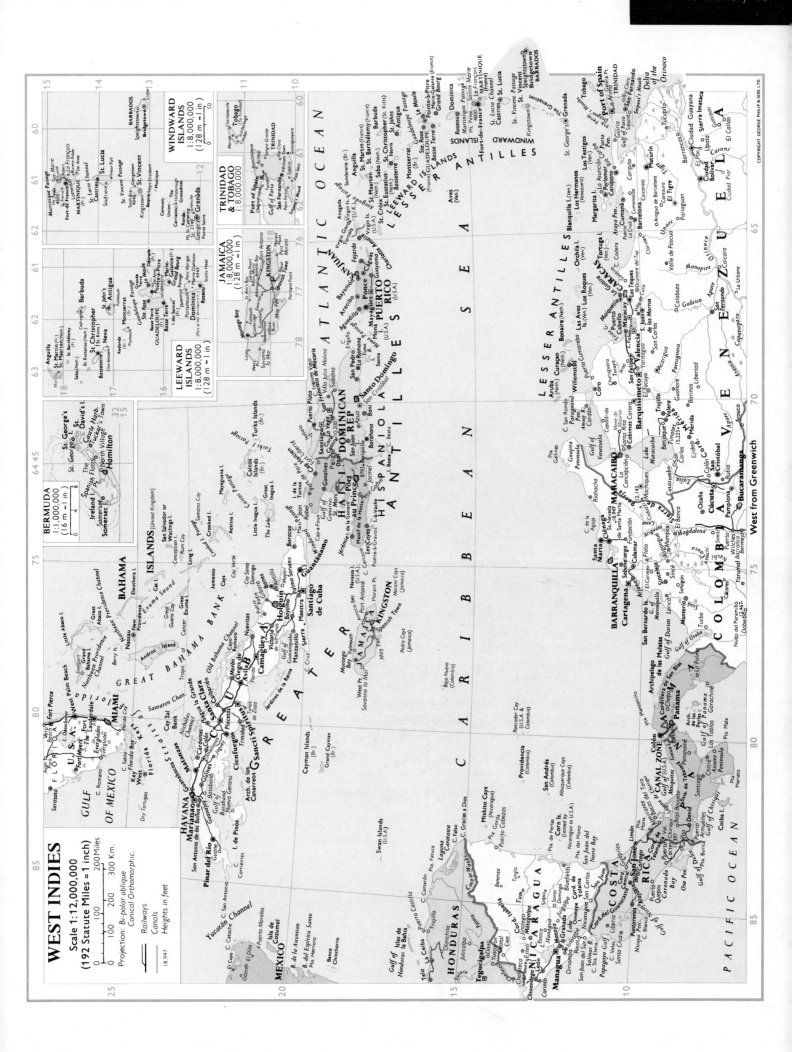

WEST INDIES

Scale 1:12,000,000
(192 Statute Miles = 1 inch)

Projection: Bi-polar oblique
Conical Orthomorphic.

Railways
Canals
Heights in feet

BERMUDA
1:1,000,000
(16 m. = 1 in.)

WINDWARD ISLANDS
1:8,000,000
(128 m. = 1 in.)

TRINIDAD & TOBAGO
1:8,000,000

JAMAICA
1:8,000,000
(128 m. = 1 in.)

LEEWARD ISLANDS
1:8,000,000
(128 m. = 1 in.)

COPYRIGHT GEORGE PHILIP & SON LTD

ATLANTIC OCEAN

PACIFIC OCEAN

GULF OF MEXICO

CARIBBEAN SEA

GREATER ANTILLES

LESSER ANTILLES

BAHAMA ISLANDS

GREAT BAHAMA BANK

HISPANIOLA

MEXICO
U.S.A.
FLORIDA
CUBA
JAMAICA
HAITI
DOMINICAN REP.
PUERTO RICO
HONDURAS
NICARAGUA
COSTA RICA
PANAMA
CANAL ZONE
COLOMBIA
VENEZUELA

HAVANA
MIAMI
KINGSTON
Santo Domingo
Port au Prince
SAN JUAN
MARACAIBO
CARACAS
BARRANQUILLA
Port of Spain

SOUTH AMERICA

Scale 1 : 30,000,000 (480 Statute Miles = 1 inch)

100   0   100   200   300   400   500   600 Miles
100   0   200   400   600   800 Kilometres

Projection : Bonne

——— Railways   5034 — — Shipping Routes
                      (Distances in Nautical Miles)
        23,081 Heights in feet

COPYRIGHT: GEORGE PHILIP & SON. LTD.

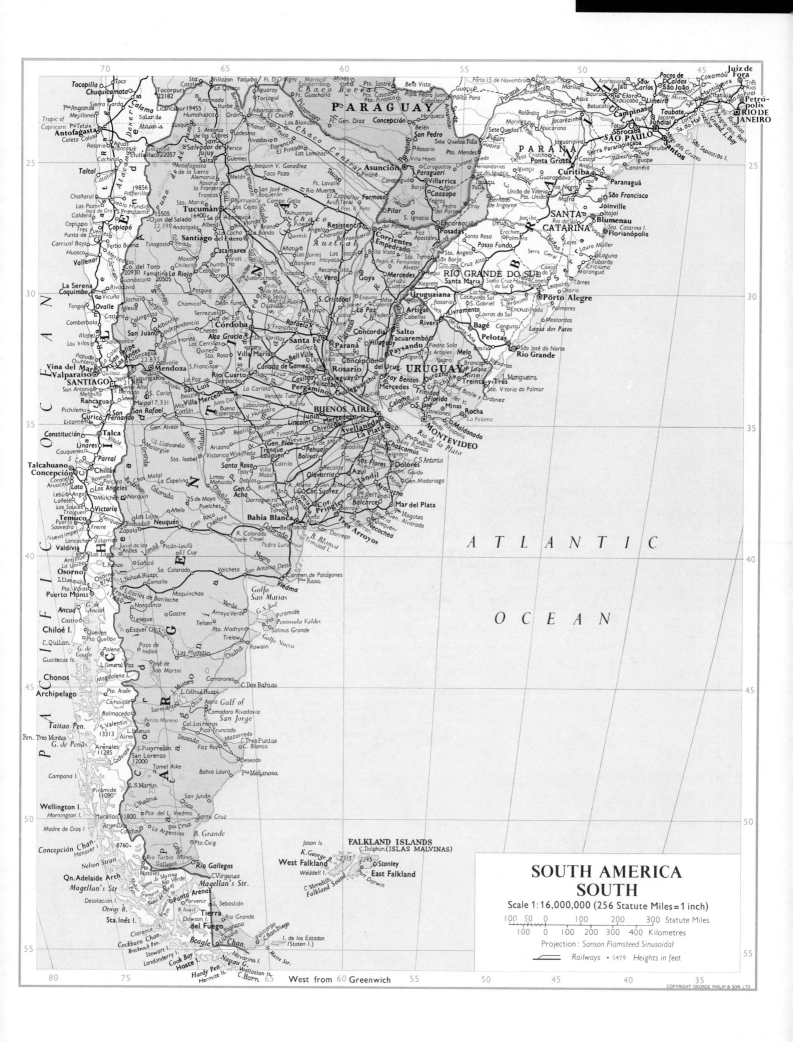

ATLANTIC

OCEAN

PACIFIC OCEAN

PARAGUAY

URUGUAY

RIO GRANDE DO SUL

SANTA CATARINA

PARANÁ

ARGENTINA

CHILE

RIO DE JANEIRO

SÃO PAULO

BUENOS AIRES

MONTEVIDEO

FALKLAND ISLANDS (ISLAS MALVINAS)
West Falkland   East Falkland
Stanley

West from 60 Greenwich

**SOUTH AMERICA
SOUTH**

Scale 1:16,000,000 (256 Statute Miles=1 inch)

100 50 0   100   200   300   Statute Miles
     100   0   100   200   300   400   Kilometres

Projection : Sanson Flamsteed Sinusoidal

Railways   • 5479 Heights in feet

COPYRIGHT GEORGE PHILIP & SON LTD

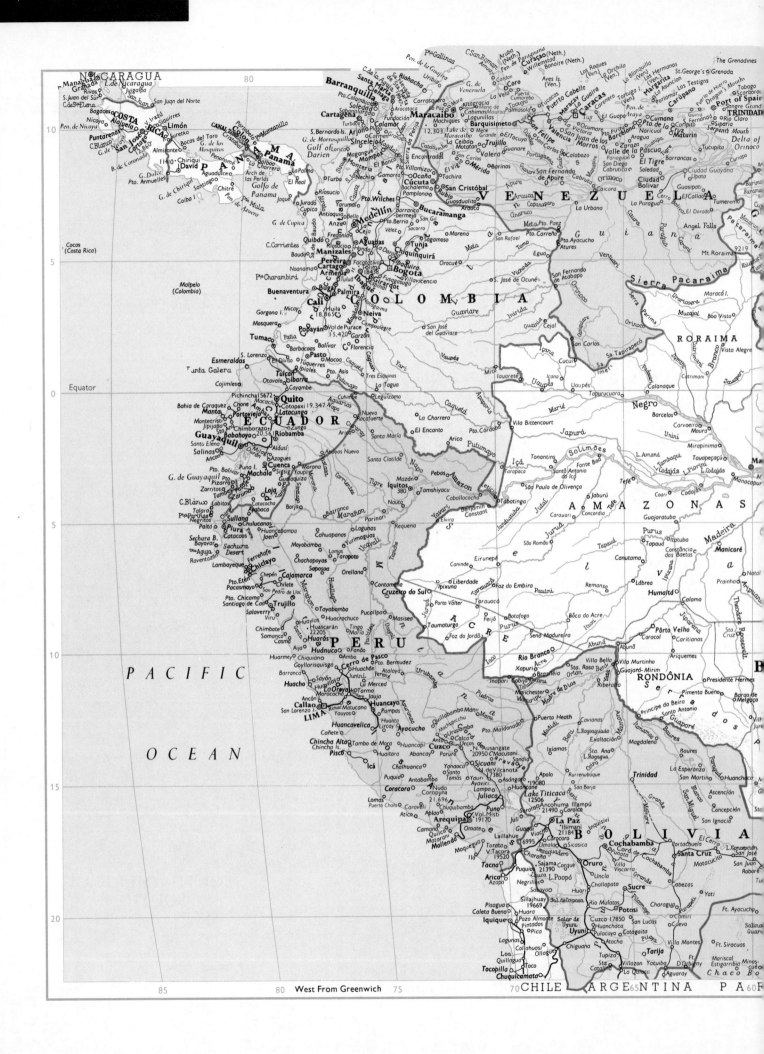

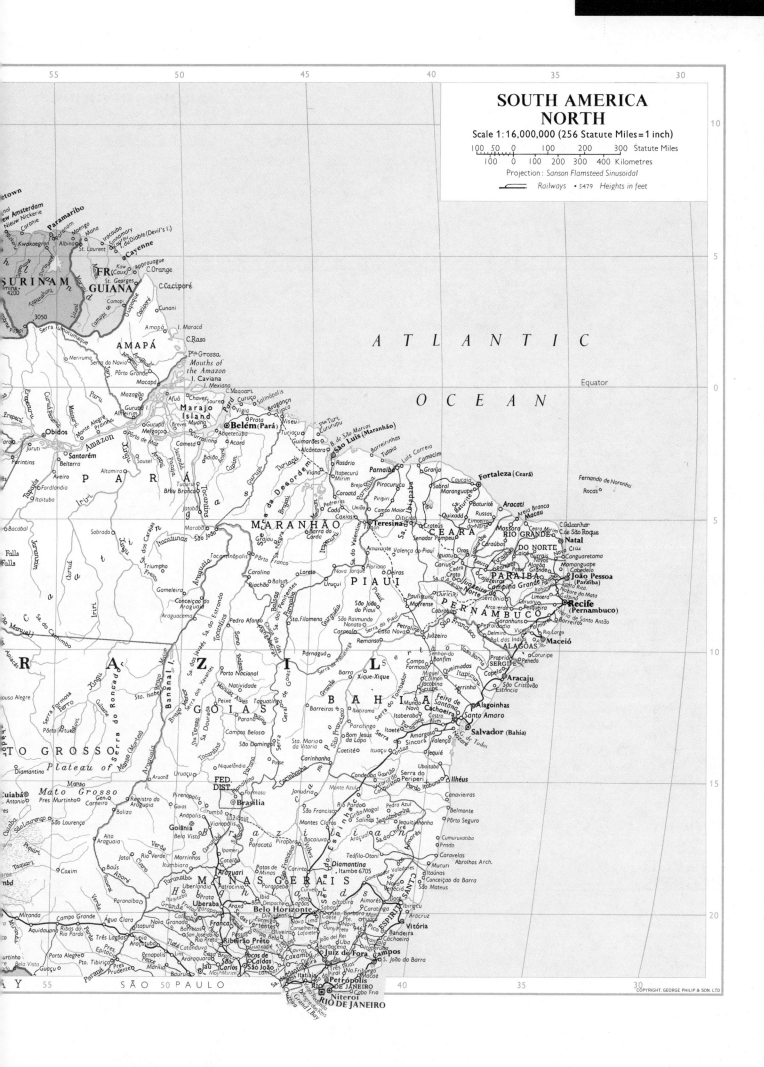

SOUTH AMERICA
NORTH
Scale 1:16,000,000 (256 Statute Miles=1 inch)

100 50 0   100   200   300   Statute Miles
100   0   100   200   300   400   Kilometres
Projection: Sanson Flamsteed Sinusoidal

Railways   • 5479   Heights in feet

A T L A N T I C

O C E A N

Equator

COPYRIGHT. GEORGE PHILIP & SON. LTD

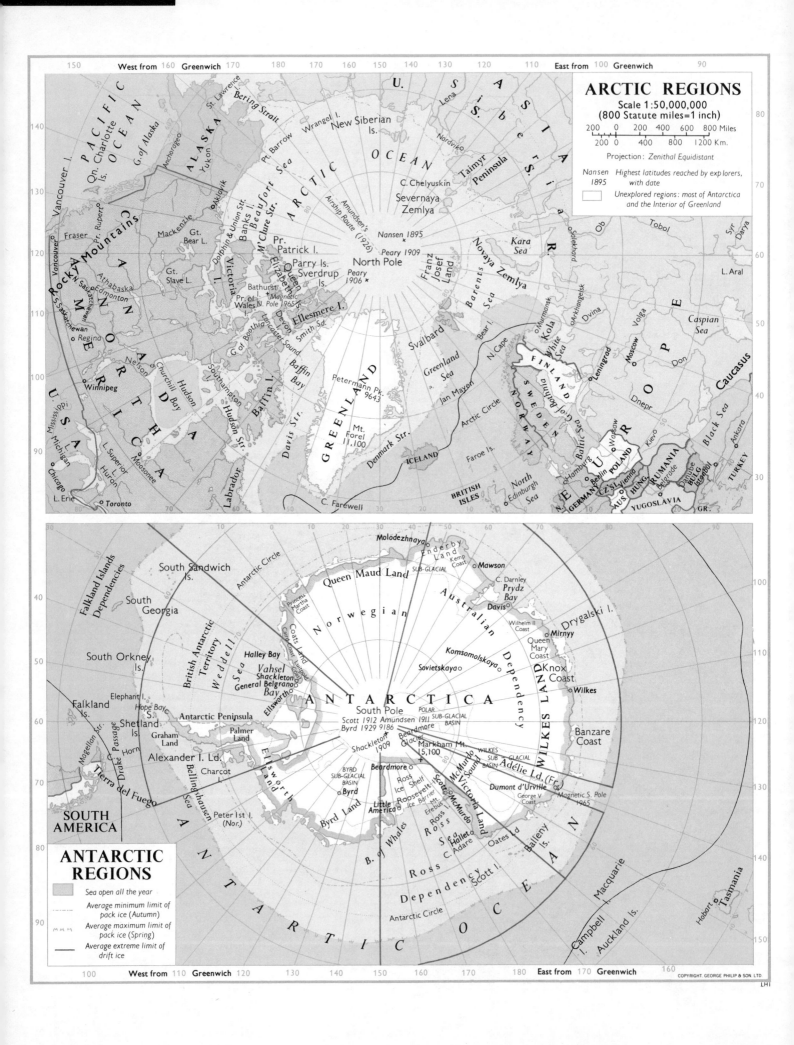

ARCTIC REGIONS
Scale 1:50,000,000
(800 Statute miles=1 inch)

200 0   200 400 600 800 Miles
200 0   400   800   1200 Km.

Projection: Zenithal Equidistant

Nansen 1895   Highest latitudes reached by explorers,
with date

Unexplored regions: most of Antarctica
and the Interior of Greenland

ANTARCTIC REGIONS

Sea open all the year

Average minimum limit of
pack ice (Autumn)

Average maximum limit of
pack ice (Spring)

Average extreme limit of
drift ice

INDEX

The latitudes and longitudes given below are primarily intended as a guide to finding the places on the maps and in some cases are only approximate.

ABBREVIATIONS

Afghan. . . . .*Afghanistan*
Afr. . . . . . .*Africa*
Ala. . . . . . .*Alabama*
Alas. . . . . .*Alaska*
Alb. . . . . . .*Albania*
Alg. . . . . . .*Algeria*
Alta. . . . . .*Alberta*
Amaz. . . . .*Amazonas*
Amer. . . . . .*America*
Ang. . . . . . .*Angola*
Ant. . . . . . .*Antarctica*
Arch. . . . . .*Archipelago*
Arg. . . . . . .*Argentina*
Ariz. . . . . .*Arizona*
Ark. . . . . . .*Arkansas*
A.S.S.R. . . .*Autonomous Soviet Socialist Republic*
Atlan. . . . . .*Atlantic*
Aust. . . . . .*Austria*
Austral. . . .*Australia*

B. . . . .*Bay, Bight (Baie, Baia)*
B. (Iran.) . .*Bandar*
B.C. . . . . . .*British Columbia*
Ban. . . . . .*Bangladesh*
Beds. . . . . .*Bedfordshire*
Belg. . . . . .*Belgium*
Berks. . . . . .*Berkshire*
Bg. . . . . . .*Berg*
Bol. . . . . . .*Bolivia*
Bot. . . . . . .*Botswana*
Braz. . . . . .*Brazil*
Br., Brit. . .*British*
Bri. . . . . . .*Bridge*
Bucks. . . . .*Buckinghamshire*
Bulg. . . . . .*Bulgaria*

C. . . . .*Cape (Cabo)*
Calif. . . . . .*California*
Cam. . . . . .*Cameroon*
Cambs. . . . .*Cambridgeshire & I. of Ely*
Can. . . . . .*Canada, Canal*
Cant. . . . . .*Canton*
Cards. . . . . .*Cardiganshire*
Cas. . . . . . .*Castle*
Cat. . . . . . .*Cataract*
Cent. . . . . .*Central*
Chan. . . . . .*Channel*
Ches. . . . . .*Cheshire*
Chih. . . . . .*Chihuahua*
Co. . . . . . .*County*
Col. . . . . . .*Colombia, Colony*
Colo. . . . . .*Colorado*
Conn. . . . . .*Connecticut*
Cont. . . . . .*Continent*
C. Prov. . . .*Cape Province*
Cr. . . . .*Creek*
Cumb. . . . . .*Cumberland*
Cy. . . . .*City*
Cz. . . . .*Czechoslovakia*

D.C. . . . . .*District of Columbia*
Del. . . . . . .*Delaware*
Den. . . . . . .*Denmark*
Des. . . . . . .*Desert*
Dist. . . . . . .*District*
Div. . . . . . .*Division*
Dom. Rep. .*Dominican Republic*

E. . . . .*East*
Ec. . . . .*Ecuador*
Eg. . . . .*Egypt*
EG. . . . . . .*Equatorial Guinea*
Eng. . . . . . .*England*
Est. . . . . . .*Estuary*
Eur. . . . . . .*Europe*

Fd. . . . . . .*Fjord, Fiord*
Fed. . . . . . .*Federal, Federation*
Fin. . . . . . .*Finland*
Fla. . . . . . .*Florida*
For. . . . . . .*Forest*

Fr. . . . .*France, French*
Fs. . . . .*Falls*
Ft. . . . .*Fort*

G. . . . .*Gulf, Gebel*
Ga. . . . . . .*Georgia*
Ger. . . . . . .*Germany*
Glos. . . . . .*Gloucestershire*
Gr. . . . . . .*Greece*
Green. . . . . .*Greenland*
Grp. . . . . . .*Group*
Gt. . . . . . .*Great*
Guat. . . . . .*Guatemala*
Gui. . . . . . .*Guiana*
Guy. . . . . .*Guyana*

Hants. . . . . .*Hampshire*
Harb. . . . . .*Harbour, Harbor*
Hd. . . . . . .*Head*
Here. . . . . .*Herefordshire*
Herts. . . . . .*Hertfordshire*
Ho. . . . . . .*House*
Hond. . . . . .*Honduras*
Hs. . . . . . .*Hills*
Hts. . . . . . .*Heights*
Hung. . . . . .*Hungary*
Hunt. . . . .*Huntingdon & Peterborough*

I(s). . . . . . .*Island(s) (Iles, Ile)*
Ice. . . . . . .*Iceland*
Ill. . . . .*Illinois*
Ind. . . . . . .*Indiana*
Indon. . . . . .*Indonesia*
I. of M. . . .*Isle of Man*
I. of W. . . .*Isle of Wight*
Ire. . . . . . .*Ireland*
Isr. . . . . . .*Israel*
Isth. . . . . .*Isthmus*
It. . . . .*Italy*

J. . . . .*Jebel, Jabal*
Jap. . . . . . .*Japan*
Jc., Junc. . .*Junction*

Kan. . . . . .*Kansas*
Ken. . . . . .*Kenya*
King. . . . . .*Kingdom*
Ky. . . . . . .*Kentucky*

L. . . . .*Lake, Loch, Lough, Lago*
La. . . . . . .*Louisiana*
Lab. . . . . .*Labrador*
Lag. . . . . . .*Lagoa, Lagoon, Laguna*
Lancs. . . . .*Lancashire*
Ld. . . . .*Land*
Leics. . . . . .*Leicestershire*
Les. . . . . . .*Lesotho*
Lib. . . . . . .*Liberia*
Lim. . . . . . .*Limerick*
Lr. . . . .*Lower*
Lux. . . . . . .*Luxembourg*

Mack . . . . .*Mackenzie*
Madag. . . . .*Malagasy Rep.*
Mal. . . . . . .*Malawi*
Man. . . . . .*Manitoba*
Mass. . . . . .*Massachusetts*
Maur. . . . . .*Mauritania*
Md. . . . . . .*Maryland*
Me. . . . . . .*Maine*
Medit. . . . . .*Mediterranean*
Mex. . . . . .*Mexico*
M. Grosso .*Mato Grosso*
Mich.
  (U.S.A.) .*Michigan*
Mich.
  (Mexico) *Michoacan*
Mid. . . . . .*Middle*

Minn. . . . .*Minnesota*
Miss. . . . . .*Mississippi*
Mo. . . . . . .*Missouri*
Mong. . . . . .*Mongolia*
Mon. . . . . .*Monmouthshire*
Mont. . . . . .*Montana*
Mor. . . . . . .*Morocco*
Mozam. . . .*Mozambique*
Mt. . . . . . .*Mountain, Mount*
Mte. . . . . . .*Monte*
Mth. . . . . .*Mouth*
Mti. . . . . . .*Monti*
Mts. . . . . .*Mountains, Monts*

N. . . . .*North, Northern*
Natl. Pk. . .*(N.P.), National Park*
N.B. . . . . . .*New Brunswick*
N.C. . . . . . .*North Carolina*
N.D. . . . . . .*North Dakota*
Neb. . . . . . .*Nebraska*
Neth. . . . . .*Netherlands*
Neth. Gui. .*Netherlands Guiana*
Nev. . . . . . .*Nevada*
Newf. . . . . .*Newfoundland*
N. Guin. . . .*New Guinea*
N.H. . . . . . .*New Hampshire*
Nic. . . . . . .*Nigeria*
N.J. . . . . . .*New Jersey*
N. Mex. . . .*New Mexico*
Nor. . . . . . .*Norway*
Northants. .*Northamptonshire*
Northumb. *Northumberland*
Notts. . . . .*Nottinghamshire*
N.S. . . . . . .*Nova Scotia*
N.S.W. . . . .*New South Wales*
N. Terr. . . .*Northern Territory, Australia*
N.W. Terr. .*North-West Territories, Canada*
N.Y. . . . . . .*New York*
N.Z. . . . . . .*New Zealand*

O. . . . .*Oasis*
Oc. . . . . . .*Ocean*
O.F.S. . . . . .*Orange Free State*
Okla. . . . . .*Oklahoma*
Ont. . . . . . .*Ontario*
Ore. . . . . . .*Oregon*

P. . . . .*Pass*
Pa. . . . .*Pennsylvania*
Pac. . . . . . .*Pacific*
Pak. . . . . . .*Pakistan*
Pan. . . . . . .*Panama*
Par. . . . . . .*Paraguay*
Pass. . . . . . .*Passage*
P.E.I. . . . . .*Prince Edward Island*
Pen. . . . . . .*Peninsula*
Phil. . . . . . .*Philippines*
Pk. . . . .*Peak, Park*
Plat. . . . . . .*Plateau*
Pl. . . . .*Plain, Planina*
Pol. . . . . . .*Poland*
Port. . . . . . .*Portugal, Portugese*
Préf. . . . . . .*Préfecture*
Prom. . . . . .*Promontory*
Prot. . . . . . .*Protectorate*
Prov. . . . . .*Province, Provincial*
Pt., Pte. . . .*Point, Pointe*
Pta. . . . . . .*Punta*
Pto. . . . . . .*Porto, Puerto (Port)*

Que. . . . . .*Quebec*
Queens. . . .*Queensland*

R. . . . .*River, Rio*
Ra. . . . . . .*Range*
Raj. . . . . . .*Rajasthan*
Rd. . . . . . .*Road*
Reg. . . . . . .*Region*
Rep. . . . . . .*Republic*
Res. . . . . . .*Reservoir, Reserve*
Rf. . . . .*Reef*

R.I. . . . . . .*Rhode Island*
Rhod. . . . .*Rhodesia*
Rks. . . . . . .*Rocks*
R.S.F.S.R. .*Russian Soviet Federal Socialist Republic*
Rum. . . . . .*Rumania*

S. . . . .*South, Sea*
Sa. . . . .*Sierra, Serra*
Salop. . . . . .*Shropshire*
Sask. . . . . .*Saskatchewan*
S. Austral. .*South Australia*
Sax. . . . . . .*Saxony*
S.C. . . . . . .*South Carolina*
Scot. . . . . . .*Scotland*
S.D. . . . . . .*South Dakota*
Sd. . . . . . .*Sound*
S.—Holst. .*Schleswig-Holstein*
Si. Arabia .*Saudi Arabia*
S. Leone . .*Sierra Leone*
S.L. Potosi *San Luis Potosi*
Sp., Span. .*Spain, Spanish*
S.S.R. . . . .*Soviet Socialist Republic*
st. . . . .*State*
St., Ste. . . .*Saint, Sainte*
Stn. . . . . . .*Station*
Staffs. . . . .*Staffordshire*
Str. . . . . . .*Strait*
Sud. . . . . . .*Sudan*
Sur. . . . . . .*Surinan*
S.W. Africa *South-West Africa*
Swed. . . . .*Sweden*
Switz. . . . .*Switzerland*

Tan. . . . . .*Tanzania*
Tas. . . . . . .*Tasmania*
Tenn. . . . . .*Tennessee*
Terr. . . . . .*Territory*
Tex. . . . . . .*Texas*
Tia. . . . . . .*Thialand*
Tipp. . . . . .*Tipperary*
tn. . . . .*Town*
Trans. . . . .*Transvaal*
Tr. 'Oman .*Trucial 'Oman*
Tur. . . . . . .*Turkey*

U. . . . .*Union*
U.A.R. . . . .*United Arab Republic*
Ugan. . . . . .*Uganda*
Ukr., S.S.R.*Ukrainian Soviet Socialist Republic*
Ut.P. . . . . .*Uttar Pradesh*
Up. . . . . . .*Upper*
Urug. . . . . .*Uruguay*
U.S.A. . . . .*United States of America*
U.S.S.R. . .*Union of Soviet Socialist Republic*

Va. . . . . . .*Virginia*
Ven. . . . . . .*Venezuela*
Vic. . . . . . .*Victoria*
Vol. . . . . . .*Volcano*
Vt. . . . . . .*Vermont*

W. . . . .*West, Western, wadi, wady*
War. . . . . . .*Warwickshire*
Wash. . . . .*Washington*
W.I. . . . . . .*West Indies*
Wick. . . . . .*Wicklow*
Wilts. . . . . .*Wiltshire*
W. Ind. . . .*West Indies*
Wind. Is. . .*Windward Islands*
Wis. . . . . . .*Wisconsin*
Worcs. . . . .*Worcestershire*
W. Va. . . . .*West Virginia*
Wyo. . . . . .*Wyoming*

Yorks. . . . .*Yorkshire*
Y.slav . . . .*Yugoslavia*

Zam. . . . . .*Zambia*

A

	MAP		
Aachen, Germany	14	50 47N	6 4 E
Aalsmeer, Netherlands	13	52 17N	4 43 E
Aalst, Belgium	13	50 56N	4 3 E
Äänekoski, Finland	23	62 38N	25 40 E
Aarau & Canton, Switz.	15	47 23N	8 2 E
Aare R., Switzerland	15	46 43N	8 8 E
Aarschot, Belgium	13	50 59N	4 49 E
Aba, Congo	53	3 52N	30 17 E
Aba, Nigeria	52	5 10N	7 19 E
Aba, Paraguay	71	26 0S	55 50W
Abacaxis, Brazil	78	3 50S	58 35W
Abacaxis R., Brazil	78	5 0S	58 35W
Abadan, Iran	30	30 22N	48 20 E
Abadeh, Iran	31	31 8N	52 40 E
Abadla, Algeria	50	31 0N	2 25W
Abaetetuba, Brazil	79	1 45S	48 59W
Abak, Nigeria	52	4 33N	7 52 E
Abakaliki, Nigeria	52	6 22N	8 2 E
Abakan, U.S.S.R.	26	53 40N	91 10 E
Abala, Mali	52	14 59N	3 4 E
Abancay, Peru	78	13 50S	72 50W
Abarqu, Persia	30	31 10N	53 20 E
Abasan, Egypt	29	31 19N	34 21 E
Abashiri, Japan	36	44 0N	144 15 E
Abau, Papua	42	10 1S	148 42 E
Abaya L., Ethiopia	54	6 30N	37 50 E
Abbaye, Pt., U.S.A.	68	46 58N	88 4W
Abbeville, France	12	50 6N	1 50 E
Abbeville, La., U.S.A.	71	30 0N	92 5W
Abbeville, S.C., U.S.A.	69	34 12N	82 23W
Abbeyleix, Ireland	11	52 55N	7 20W
Abbotsford, Canada	64	49 0N	122 10W
Abbotsford, U.S.A.	68	44 55N	90 20W
Abbottabad, Pakistan	32	34 10N	73 15 E
Abbotts, W. Australia	44	26 20S	118 19 E
Abdulpur, E. Pakistan	33	24 15N	89 0 E
Abéché, Chad.	51	13 50N	20 35 E
Åbenrå, Denmark	23	55 4N	9 26 E
Abeokuta, Nigeria	52	7 3N	3 19 E
Aberdare, Wales	10	51 43N	3 27W
Aberdare Ra., Kenya	53	0 25S	36 35 E
Aberdeen, Canada	65	52 25N	106 15W
Aberdeen, Idaho, U.S.A.	72	43 1N	112 47W
Aberdeen, Miss., U.S.A.	69	33 45N	88 44W
Aberdeen, Scotland	10	57 9N	2 6W
Aberdeen, S.D., U.S.A.	70	45 31N	98 28W
Aberdeen, S.D., U.S.A.	66	45 30N	98 30W
Aberdeen, Wash., U.S.A.	72	47 0N	123 50W
Abernathy, U.S.A.	71	33 47N	101 47W
Aberystwyth, Wales	10	52 25N	4 6W
Ab-i-Istada L., Afghan.	31	32 30N	68 0 E
Abidjan, Ivory Coast	50	5 16N	3 58W
Abiekwasput L., C. Prov.	57	27 30S	20 5 E
Abilene, Kans., U.S.A.	70	39 0N	97 16W
Abilene, Texas, U.S.A.	71	32 22N	99 40W
Abingdon, U.S.A.	70	40 51N	90 24W
Ab-i-Panja R., Afghan.	31	36 45N	71 33 E
Abisko, Sweden	22	68 21N	18 50 E
Abitau L., Canada	65	60 30N	107 0W
Abitau R., Canada	65	60 20N	108 20W
Abitibi L., Canada	62	48 40N	79 40W
Abkhaz, A.S.S.R., U.S.S.R.	26	43 0N	41 30 E
Abkit, U.S.S.R.	27	64 10N	157 10 E
Åbo. *See* Turku.	23		
Abocho, Nigeria	52	7 34N	6 56 E
Abohar, India	32	30 10N	74 10 E
Abolo, Congo (Fr.)	54	0 10N	14 10 E
Aboméy, Dahomey	52	7 10N	2 5 E
Abong-Mbang, Cam.	52	4 0N	13 8 E
Abonnema, Nigeria	52	4 30N	6 48 E
Aboso, Ghana	52	5 18N	1 55W
Abou Deia, Chad.	51	11 20N	19 20 E
Abqaiq, Saudi Arabia	30	26 0N	49 45 E
Abrantes, Portugal	17	39 24N	8 7W
Abraq, Saudi Arabia	30	25 49N	38 39 E
Abreojos Pt., Mexico	74	26 50N	113 40W
Abri, Sudan	51	20 47N	30 27 E
Abrolhos Arch., Brazil	79	18 0S	38 30W
Abrud, Rumania	21	46 19N	23 5 E
Abruzzi and Molise, reg., Italy	20	42 15N	14 0 E
Absaroka Ra., U.S.A.	72	44 40N	110 0W
Abu, dist., Jordan	29	31 47N	35 14 E
Abu al Abyadh I., Persian Gulf	31	24 10N	53 46 E
Abu al Khasib, Iraq	30	30 27N	47 59 E
Abu Ali I., Saudi Arabia	30	27 20N	49 27 E
Abu Dhabi, Tr. 'Oman	31	24 28N	54 23 E
Abu Dis, Sudan	51	19 12N	33 38 E
Abu Ghosh, Israel	29	31 48N	35 6 E
Abu Hamed, Sudan	51	19 32N	33 13 E
Abu Hureira, Israel	29	31 22N	34 37 E
Abu Kamal, Syria	30	34 27N	40 55 E
Abu Markha, Arabia	30	25 4N	38 22 E
Abu Matariq, Sudan	51	11 0N	26 10 E
Abu Nar, R., Jordan	29	32 25N	35 8 E
Abu Tij, Egypt	51	27 4N	31 15 E
Abu Zabad, Sudan	51	12 25N	29 10 E
Abuja, Nigeria	52	9 16N	7 2 E
Abunã, Brazil	78	9 40S	65 20W
Aburo, mt., Congo	53	20 1N	30 50 E
Abut Head, N.Z.	47	43 6S	170 16 E
Abwong, Sudan	51	9 2N	32 14 E
Acajutla, Salvador	74	13 40N	89 50W
Acambaro, Mexico	74	20 0N	100 40W
Acaponeta, Mexico	74	22 30N	105 20W

	MAP		
Acapulco, Mexico	74	16 51N	99 56W
Acara, Brazil	79	2 11S	48 20W
Acarigua, Venezuela	75	9 35N	69 12 E
Acatecas, dist., Mexico	74	23 15N	107 30W
Acatlan, Mexico	74	18 10N	98 3W
Acayucan, Mexico	74	17 59N	94 58W
Accomac, U.S.A.	68	37 43N	75 40W
Accra, Ghana	52	5 35N	0 15W
Acheron R., N.Z.	47	42 15S	173 5 E
Achikulak, U.S.S.R.	25	44 40N	44 47 E
Achill Sound, Ireland	11	53 53N	9 55W
Achill Hd., Ireland	11	53 59N	10 15W
Achill I., Ireland	11	53 58N	10 5W
Achimota, Ghana	52	5 35N	0 15W
Achinsk, U.S.S.R.	26	56 20N	90 20 E
Acholi, dist., Uganda	53	3 0N	33 0 E
Achowa, Pt., Ghana	52	4 25N	2 2W
Achuanipi L., Canada	63	52 30N	66 0W
Acireale, Italy	20	37 37N	15 9 E
Ackerman, U.S.A.	69	33 20N	89 8W
Acklin's I., Bahamas	75	22 30N	74 0W
Acme, Canada	64	51 30N	113 35W
Acme, U.S.A.	71	33 36N	104 14W
Aconcagua Mt., Arg.	77	32 50S	70 0W
Aconquija, Sierra de, Argentina	77	27 0S	66 0W
Acornhoek, Transvaal	57	24 31S	31 2 E
Acqui, Italy	20	44 40N	8 28 E
Acraman, L., S. Austral.	45	32 3S	135 25 E
Acre. *See* Akko	29		
Acre R., Brazil	78	10 45S	68 25W
Acre, Prov., Brazil	78	9 0S	71 0W
Acri, Italy	20	39 29N	16 23 E
Ad Dahna Des. Arabia	30	26 15N	46 30 E
Ad Dammām, Si. Arabia	30	26 22N	50 2 E
Ad Dar al Hamrā, Saudi Arabia	30	27 22N	37 42 E
Ad Dawhah, Qatar	31	25 19N	51 30 E
Ad Diwan. *See* El Dirr, Egypt	51		
Ad Duwayd, Si. Arabia	30	30 16N	42 13 E
Ad Khālis, Iraq	30	33 58N	44 32 E
Ada, Ghana	52	5 44N	0 40 E
Ada, Minn., U.S.A.	70	47 27N	96 30W
Ada, Okla., U.S.A.	71	34 50N	96 45W
Adak, I., Aleutian I.	59	52 30N	176 30W
Adamaou, Massif de L', Cameroon	52	7 20N	12 20 E
Adamello, Mt., Italy	20	46 10N	10 34 E
Adaminaby, N.S.W.	43	36 0S	148 45 E
Adams, Mass., U.S.A.	68	42 45N	73 5W
Adams Bridge, Sri Lanka	32	9 15N	79 40 E
Adams L., Canada	64	51 20N	119 40W
Adams Mt., Alaska	59	55 58N	130 35W
Adams Mt., U.S.A.	72	46 10N	121 28W
Adam's Pk., Sri Lanka	32	6 55N	80 45 E
Adana, Turkey	30	37 0N	35 16 E
Adapazari, Turkey	30	40 48N	30 25 E
Adarama, Sudan	51	17 0N	34 58 E
Adare, Ireland	11	52 34N	8 48W
Adare C., Antarctica	80	71 0S	171 0 E
Adavale, Queensland	43	25 52S	144 32 E
Adda R., Italy	20	45 25N	9 30 E
Addington C., Alaska	64	55 30N	133 40W
Addis Ababa, Ethiopia	54	9 2N	38 42 E
Addo, Cape Province	57	33 32S	25 44 E
Adebour, Niger	52	12 24N	12 5 E
Adel, U.S.A.	69	31 10N	83 28W
Adelaide, Cape Province	57	32 42S	26 20 E
Adelaide, S. Australia	43	34 55S	138 32 E
Adelaide Pen., Canada	60	67 60N	98 0W
Adelboden, Switzerland	15	46 29N	7 35 E
Adélie Land, Antarctica	80	67 0S	140 0 E
Ademuz, Spain	17	40 5N	1 13W
Aden, South Arabia	28	12 50N	45 0 E
Aden, G. of, Asia	49	13 0N	50 0 E
Adendorp, C. Prov.	57	31 16S	24 32 E
Aderbissinat, Niger	52	15 34N	7 54 E
Adermaien, Niger	52	14 58N	9 20 E
Adh Dharma, Arabia	31	24 30N	46 10 E
Adi, Congo	53	3 26N	30 48 E
Adi I., Indonesia	35	4 15S	133 30 E
Adieu, C., S. Australia	45	32 0S	132 10 E
Adige, R., Italy	20	45 9N	11 50 E
Adilabad, India	32	19 33N	78 35 E
Adilang, Uganda	53	2 44N	33 28 E
Adili, Ethiopia	53	4 2N	39 20 E
Adin, U.S.A.	72	41 11N	121 0W
Adirondack Mts., U.S.A.	68	44 0N	74 0W
Adjohon, Dahomey	52	6 41N	2 32 E
Adjud, Rumania	21	46 7N	27 10 E
Adjumani, Uganda	53	3 20N	31 50 E
Adlavik Is., Canada	63	55 2N	58 45W
Admer, Algeria	50	20 23N	5 20 E
Admiralty Inlet, U.S.A.	72	48 0N	122 35W
Admiralty I., Alaska	64	57 40N	134 35W
Admiralty Is., Territory of New Guinea	42	2 5S	146 15 E
Ado, Nigeria	52	6 36N	2 56 E
Adonara I., Indonesia	35	8 15S	123 5 E
Adoni, India	32	15 33N	77 18W
Adour R., France	12	43 48N	0 50W
Adra, Spain	17	36 43N	3 3W
Adranga, Congo	53	2 58N	30 25 E
Adrano, Italy	20	37 40N	14 49 E
Adrar, Algeria	50	27 57N	0 12W
Adré, Chad.	51	13 40N	22 20 E
Adri, Libya	51	27 40N	12 35 E

	MAP		
Adria, Italy	20	45 4N	12 3 E
Adrian, Mich., U.S.A.	68	41 55N	84 0W
Adrian, Tex., U.S.A.	71	35 17N	102 35W
Adriatic Sea, Europe	20	43 0N	16 0 E
Aduku, Uganda	53	2 3N	32 45 E
Adula Alps, Switz.	15	46 30N	9 0 E
Adwa, Ethiopia	54	14 11N	38 58 E
Adwa, Saudi Arabia	30	27 17N	42 34 E
Adzhar, A.S.S.R., U.S.S.R.	26	42 0N	42 0 E
Adzugopi, Uganda	53	3 20N	31 50 E
Æbeltoft, Denmark	23	56 12N	10 41 E
Ægean Sea, Europe	21	37 0N	25 0 E
Aeraman L., Australia	42	32 0S	135 30 E
Aerö I., Denmark	14	54 53N	10 20 E
Aesch, Switzerland	15	47 29N	7 32 E
Affreville, Algeria	50	36 11N	2 14 E
Afghanistan, St., Asia	31	33 0N	65 0 E
Afikpo, Nigeria	52	5 56N	7 54 E
Afmadu, Somali Rep.	49	0 35N	41 58 E
Afognak I., Alaska	59	58 15N	152 30W
Afragola, Italy	20	40 54N	14 15 E
Afram R., Ghana	52	6 35N	0 15W
Africa, cont.	48-49	37 0N to 35 0S	30 0W to 51 30 E
Afuá, Brazil	79	0 15S	50 10W
Afula, Israel	29	32 37N	35 17 E
Afumba, Zambia	56	15 35S	25 54 E
Afyon, Turkey	30	38 20N	30 15 E
Agades, Niger	50	16 58N	8 10 E
Agadir, Morocco	50	30 36N	9 42W
Agaie, Nigeria	52	9 2N	6 32 E
Agano, R., Japan	36	37 50N	139 30 E
Agartala, India	33	23 50N	91 23 E
Agashi, India	32	19 30N	72 50 E
Agassiz, Canada	64	49 14N	121 52W
Agata, U.S.S.R.	27	66 50N	98 10 E
Agate, Canada	62	48 30N	83 0 E
Agattu I., Aleutian Is.	59	52 30N	173 30 E
Agawa, Canada	62	47 35N	84 30W
Agbabu, Nigeria	52	6 35N	4 48 E
Agbelouvé, Togoland	52	6 34N	1 11 E
Agbor, Nigeria	52	6 19N	6 10 E
Agboville, Ivory Coast	50	5 56N	4 16W
Agege, Nigeria	52	6 35N	3 9 E
Agen, France	12	44 12N	0 38 E
Aghā-Jāri, Iran	30	30 49N	49 47 E
Agincourt, France	12	50 35N	2 2 E
Ago Are, Nigeria	52	8 30N	6 30 E
Agogo, Ghana	52	6 50N	1 10W
Agouna, Dahomey	52	8 19N	2 1 E
Agra, India	32	27 17N	78 13 E
Agri, Denmark	20	56 14N	10 32 E
Agri. *See* Karaköse, Turkey.	30		
Aǧri Daǧi (Ararat), Turkey	30	39 40N	44 24 E
Agrigento, Italy	20	37 19N	13 33 E
Agrinion, Greece	21	38 37N	21 27 E
Agua Clara, Brazil	79	20 25S	52 45W
Agua Prieta, Mexico	74	31 20N	109 32W
Aguadas, Colombia	78	5 40N	75 38W
Aguadilla, Puerto Rico	75	18 27N	67 10W
Aguadulce, Panama	59	8 17N	80 31W
Aguanaval R., Mexico	74	24 30N	103 0W
Aguanish, Canada	63	50 14N	62 2W
Aguanus R., Canada	63	51 0N	62 0W
Aguarico R., Ecuador	78	0 20S	76 0W
Aguaray, Argentina	77	22 14S	63 45W
Aguas Blancas, Chile	77	24 15S	69 55W
Aguascalientes, tn. & st., Mexico	74	22 0N	102 12W
Aguie, Niger	52	13 31N	7 46 E
Aguilas, Spain	17	37 23N	1 35W
Aguja, C. de la, Col.	78	11 30N	74 15W
Aguja Pta., Peru	78	6 0S	81 0W
Agulhas C., C. Prov.	57	34 25S	20 0 E
Agur, Israel	29	31 42N	34 55 E
Ahamansu, Ghana	52	7 38N	0 35 E
Ahar, Iran	30	38 35N	47 0 E
Ahascragh, Ireland	11	53 24N	8 20W
Ahaura, New Zealand	47	42 21S	171 34 E
Ahimanawa Ra., N.Z.	46	39 5S	176 30 E
Ahipara B., N.Z.	46	35 5S	173 5 E
Ahiri, India	32	19 30N	80 0 E
Ahmadabad, India	32	23 0N	72 40 E
Ahmadpur, W. Pak.	31	29 10N	71 18 E
Ahmadnagar, India	32	19 7N	74 46 E
Ahoada, Nigeria	52	5 8N	6 36 E
Ahousat, Canada	64	49 20N	126 0W
Ahuachapan, Salvador	74	13 54N	89 52W
Ahuriri R., N.Z.	47	44 27S	169 45 E
Ahvenanmaa (Åland) Is., Finland	23	60 15N	20 0 E
Ahwa, India	32	20 45N	73 40 E
Ahvāz, Persia	30	31 20N	48 40 E
Ai-Ais, S.W. Africa	57	28 20S	12 30 E
Aibaq, Afghanistan	31	36 18N	68 4 E
Ai Owuno. *See* Otukpa.	52		
Aichi, pref., Japan	36	35 0N	137 15 E
Aigle, Switzerland	15	46 18N	6 58 E
Aigues Mortes, France	12	43 35N	4 12 E
Aihsien, China	39	18 30N	109 12 E
Aihun, China	37	49 55N	127 20 E
Aija, Peru	78	9 50S	77 45W
Aijal, India	33	23 40N	93 30 E
Aiken, U.S.A.	69	33 34N	81 50W
Aillik, Canada	63	55 30N	59 3W
Aim, U.S.S.R.	27	59 0N	133 55 E

	MAP		
Aimores, Minas Gerais, Brazil	79	19 30S	41 10W
Aimorés, Sa dos, Brazil	79	19 0S	40 30W
Ain, W. al, R., Muscat & Oman	31	23 44N	56 0 E
Ain R., France	12	46 7N	5 22 E
Ain Beida, Algeria	50	35 50N	7 29 E
Ain Ben Tili, Maur.	50	25 59N	9 27W
Ain Dar, Saudi Arabia	30	25 45N	49 10 E
Ain Salah, Algeria	50	27 10N	2 32 E
Ain Sefra, Algeria	50	32 47N	0 37W
Ainaži, U.S.S.R.	23	57 52N	24 28 E
Aine Galakka, Chad.	51	18 10N	18 30 E
Ainsworth, U.S.A.	70	42 36N	99 49W
Aiol, Japan	36	34 52N	134 28 E
Aion, I., U.S.S.R.	27	69 50N	169 0 E
Air (Azbine), dist., Niger	50	18 30N	8 0 E
Airob, S.W. Africa	57	24 10S	21 30 E
Airolo, Switzerland	15	46 31N	8 38 E
Aishihik, Yukon	59	61 34N	137 31W
Aisne R., France	12	49 12N	4 47 E
Aitape, N.E. New Guinea	42	3 0S	142 5 E
Aitkin, U.S.A.	70	46 30N	93 37W
Aitos, Bulgaria	21	42 47N	27 16 E
Aitolikon, Greece	21	38 26N	21 21 E
Aiud, Rumania	21	46 19N	23 55 E
Aix-en-Provence, Fr.	12	43 32N	5 27 E
Aix-les-Bains, France	12	45 41N	5 53 E
Aiyina & G, Greece	21	37 45N	23 26 E
Aiyansh, Canada	64	55 15N	129 0W
Aiyion, Greece	21	38 15N	22 5 E
Aizpute, U.S.S.R.	23	56 54N	21 37 E
Ajaccio, Corsica, Fr.	12	41 55N	8 40 E
Ajano, W. Australia	44	27 56S	114 35 E
Ajanta Range, India	32	20 28N	75 50 E
Ajax, mt., U.S.A.	72	45 30N	113 30W
Ajdabiyah, Libya	51	30 50N	20 10 E
Ajedabya, Libya	51	30 45N	20 15 E
Ajena, Ghana	52	6 22N	0 9W
Ajiur R., Israel	29	31 42N	34 49 E
Ajlun, Jordan	30	32 20N	35 48 E
Ajman, Trucial 'Oman	31	25 25N	55 30 E
Ajmer, India	32	26 28N	74 37 E
Ajo, U.S.A.	73	32 53N	112 57W
Aju Is., Indonesia	35	0 35N	131 5 E
Ajua, Ghana	52	4 50N	1 55W
Ak Dag Mt., Turkey	30	36 35N	29 35 E
Akaba, Togoland	52	8 10N	1 2 E
Akaroa, New Zealand	47	43 49S	172 59 E
Akaroa Harbour, N.Z.	47	43 53S	172 58 E
Akashi, Japan	36	34 45N	135 0 E
Akcaabat, Turkey	30	41 01N	39 34 E
Akegbe, Nigeria	52	6 17N	7 28 E
Akershus, prov., Nor.	23	60 10N	11 15 E
Aketi, Congo	54	2 38N	23 47 E
Akhaltsikhe, U.S.S.R.	24	41 40N	43 0 E
Akharnai, Greece	21	38 5N	23 44 E
Akheloos, R., Greece	21	39 5N	21 25 E
Akhisar, Turkey	30	38 56N	27 48 E
Akhmin, Egypt	51	26 31N	31 47 E
Akhtyrka, U.S.S.R.	25	50 25N	35 0 E
Akiak, Alaska	59	60 40N	160 40W
Akimiski I., Canada	62	52 50N	81 30W
Akimovka, U.S.S.R.	25	46 44N	35 0 E
Akita, Japan	36	39 45N	140 0 E
Akita, pref., Japan	36	39 40N	140 30 E
Akjoujt, Mauritania	50	19 45N	15 15W
Akko (Acre), Israel	29	32 35N	35 4 E
Aklampa, Mali	52	8 15N	2 10 E
Aklavik, Canada	60	68 5N	135 40W
Ako, N. Reg., Nigeria	52	10 19N	10 48 E
Akoafim, Cameroon	52	2 20N	12 50 E
Akobo R., Ethiopia	54	7 10N	34 25 E
Akola, India	32	20 42N	77 2 E
Akonolinga, Cameroon	52	3 40N	12 15 E
Akosombo Dam, Ghana	50	6 20N	0 5 E
Akot, India	32	21 10N	77 10 E
Akpatok I., Canada	61	60 30N	68 0W
Akranes, Iceland	22	64 18N	21 53W
Akron, Colo., U.S.A.	70	40 11N	103 15W
Akron, Ohio, U.S.A.	68	41 7N	81 31W
Aksaray, Turkey	30	38 25N	34 2 E
Aksehir, Turkey	30	38 30N	31 30 E
Aksenovo Zilovskoye, U.S.S.R.	27	53 20N	117 40 E
Aksu, China	37	41 30N	82 30 E
Aksum, Ethiopia	54	14 5N	38 40 E
Aktyubinsk, U.S.S.R.	24	50 20N	57 0 E
Aku, Nigeria	52	6 40N	7 18 E
Akulurak, Alaska	59	62 35N	164 32W
Akun I., Aleutian Is.	59	54 30N	166 0W
Akure, Nigeria	52	7 15N	5 5 E
Akureyri, Iceland	22	65 37N	18 3W
Akuseki Shima, Japan	36	29 26N	129 30 E
Akutan I., Aleutian Is.	59	54 20N	167 0W
Akyab, Burma	33	20 15N	93 0 E
Al Ahmandi, Kuwait	30	29 11N	48 9 E
Al 'Alamayn, Egypt	51	30 48N	28 58 E
Al Allāqi, Egypt	51	23 32N	33 0 E
Al Amādiyah, Iraq	30	37 6N	43 29 E
Al 'Aqabah, Jordan	30	29 37N	35 0 E
Al 'Aramah, Si. Arabia	30	26 0N	46 30 E
Al 'Arish, Egypt	51	31 8N	33 50 E
Al Bashuk, Si. Arabia	30	28 10N	44 41 E
Al Basrah (Basra), Iraq	30	30 30N	47 47 E
Al Batin, Iraq	30	30 20N	47 0 E
Al Bayda, Libya	51	32 30N	21 30 E
Al Buayrat, Libya	51	31 30N	5 55 E

	MAP		
Al Diwaniyah, Iraq	30	32 0N	45 0 E
Al Fuqaha, Libya	51	27 40N	15 10 E
Al Fallujah, Iraq	30	33 20N	43 46 E
Al Fayyum, Egypt	51	29 17N	30 50 E
Al Hadithah, Iraq	30	34 9N	42 16 E
Al Hadr, Iraq	30	35 35N	42 44 E
Al Hamād, Si. Arabia	30	31 40N	39 0 E
Al Hamar, Si. Arabia	66	22 23N	46 6 E
Al Hamdr, Si. Arabia	30	22 20N	46 0 E
Al Hanakiya, Si. Arabia	30	24 58N	40 55 E
Al Hariq, Saudi Arabia	30	23 29N	46 27 E
Al Hasakah, Syria	30	36 34N	40 40 E
Al Hayy, Iraq	30	32 10N	46 03 E
Al Hillah, Iraq	30	32 29N	42 25 E
Al Hilwa, Saudi Arabia	30	23 24N	46 48 E
Al Hindiyah, Iraq	30	32 32N	44 13 E
Alhuarin el Grande, Sp.	17	36 41N	4 42W
Al-Hoceima, Morocco	50	35 20N	4 0W
Ali al Gharbi, Iraq	30	32 27N	46 41 E
Al Hufuf, Si. Arabia	30	25 24N	49 37 E
Al Hisma, Saudi Arabia	30	29 0N	35 45 E
Al Irq, Libya	51	29 0N	21 40 E
Al Iskandariyah (Alexandria), Egypt	51	31 10N	29 55 E
Al Ismā'ilyah. *See* Ismailia.	51		
Al Jāfurah, Si. Arabia	30	24 30N	50 0 E
Al Jahrah, Kuwait	30	29 30N	47 42 E
Al Jalāmid, Si. Arabia	30	31 26N	39 47 E
Al Jarzirah, Libya	51	26 10N	42 25 E
Al Jawf, Saudi Arabia	30	29 55N	39 37 E
Al Jizah, Egypt	51	30 5N	31 10 E
Al Jubayl, Si. Arabia	30	26 55N	49 40 E
Al Kafah, Iraq	30	32 1N	44 24 E
Al Khalil. *See* Hebron, Egypt.	51		
Al Khari, Si. Arabia	30	24 0N	47 0 E
Al Kharijah, Egypt	51	25 30N	30 30 E
Al Khums, Libya	51	32 30N	12 50 E
Al Kut, Iraq	30	32 30N	45 49 E
Al Kuwayt (Kuwait), Kuwait	30	29 28N	48 0 E
Al Lādhiqiyah (Latakia), Syria	30	35 34N	35 42 E
Al Lisafah, Si. Arabia	30	27 38N	46 48 E
Al Mahalla al Kubra, Egypt	51	31 10N	31 0 E
Al Manşurah, Egypt	51	31 5N	31 25 E
Al Matrah, Muscat & 'Oman	31	23 40N	58 29 E
Al Mawsil, Iraq	30	36 20N	43 08 E
Al Migdādiyah, Iraq	30	34 6N	45 1 E
Al Minyā, Egypt	51	28 7N	33 33 E
Al Mubarraz, Si. Arabia	30	25 30N	49 36 E
Al Mudawwarah, Jordan	30	29 22N	35 39 E
Al Musayyib, Iraq	30	32 47N	44 19 E
Al Muwailih, Si. Arabia	30	27 40N	35 30 E
Al Qāhirah (Cairo), Eg.	51	30 2N	31 12 E
Al Qamishli, Turkey	30	37 6N	41 9 E
Al Qasara, Si. Arabia	30	27 49N	42 24 E
Al Qaşr, Egypt	51	25 44N	28 42 E
Al Qatrun, Libya	51	24 59N	14 55 E
Al Qaysumah, Si. Arabia	30	28 17N	46 19 E
Al Quraiyat, 'Oman	31	23 17N	58 53 E
Al Qurnah, Iraq	30	31 1N	47 25 E
Al Qusaiba, Si. Arabia	30	27 0N	43 43 E
Al Qusayr, Egypt	51	26 14N	34 9 E
Al Shallāl, Egypt	51	24 2N	32 52 E
Al 'Ula, Saudi Arabia	30	26 35N	38 0 E
Al Uqayr, Si. Arabia	30	25 40N	50 7 E
Al Uqsur. *See* Luxor, Egypt.	51		
Al Uquaylah, Libya	51	30 12N	19 10 E
Al Uwayqilah, Saudi Arabia	30	30 32N	42 7 E
Al Wajh, Saudi Arabia	30	26 16N	36 27 E
Al Waqrah, Qatar	31	25 10N	51 35 E
Al Wari'ah, Si. Arabia	30	27 51N	47 26 E
Ala, Italy	20	45 46N	11 0 E
Ala Dagh, Mt., Turkey	30	37 50N	35 13 E
Ala Shan, China	38	38 30N	105 50 E
Alabama City, U.S.A.	69	34 0N	86 0W
Alabama R., U.S.A.	69	32 0N	87 0W
Alabama, st., U.S.A.	69	33 0N	86 30W
Alagir, U.S.S.R.	26	43 10N	44 20 E
Alagôa Grande, Brazil	79	7 3S	35 35W
Alagôas, st., Brazil	79	9 40S	35 50W
Alagoinhas, Brazil	79	12 0S	38 20W
Alagon, Spain	17	41 46N	1 12W
Alajuela, Costa Rica	78	10 2N	84 8W
Alamagordo, U.S.A.	73	32 57N	105 59W
Alamarvdasht, Iran	31	27 38N	52 56 E
Alameda, Calif., U.S.A	73	37 47N	122 10W
Alameda, Canada	65	49 15N	102 20W
Alameda, Idaho, U.S.A.	72	43 1N	112 29W
Alameda, N. Mex., U.S.A.	73	35 12N	106 8W
Alamo, U.S.A.	73	37 52N	115 10W
Alamos, Mexico	74	27 0N	109 0W
Alamosa, U.S.A.	73	37 30N	106 0W
Åland, *See* Ahvenanmaa Is.	23		
Åland Str., Baltic Sea	23	60 0N	19 20 E
Alanga Arba, Kenya	53	0 6N	40 25 E
Alanya, Turkey	30	36 36N	32 0 E
Alapayevsk, U.S.S.R.	24	57 55N	62 0 E
Alaro, Spain	17	39 40N	2 45 E
Alaska, st., U.S.A.	59	65 0N	150 0W
Alaska, G. of, Alaska	59	58 0N	145 0W
Alaska Highway, Alas.	59	62 30N	141 0W
Alaska Pen., Alaska	59	56 0N	160 0W
Alaska Ra., Alaska	59	63 0N	151 0W
Alassio, Italy	20	44 1N	8 10 E
Alatri, Italy	20	41 44N	13 21 E
Alatyr, U.S.S.R.	25	54 45N	46 35 E
Alatyr R., U.S.S.R.	25	54 45N	45 30 E
Alava C., U.S.A.	72	48 12N	124 43W
Alausi, Ecuador	78	2 0S	78 50W
Alawa, Nigeria	52	10 25N	6 30 E
Alayor, Spain	17	39 57N	4 8 E
Alba, Italy	20	44 41N	8 1 E
Alba, Spain	17	40 50N	5 32W
Alba-Iulia, Rumania	21	46 8N	23 39 E
Albacete, Spain	17	39 0N	1 50W
Albanel, L., Canada	62	51 0N	73 20W
Albania, rep., Europe	21	41 0N	20 0 E
Albano, Italy	20	45 20N	11 48 E
Albany, Canada	63	44 50N	65 2W
Albany, Ga., U.S.A.	69	31 40N	84 10W
Albany, Jamaica	75	18 12N	76 50W
Albany, Minn., U.S.A.	70	45 38N	94 32W
Albany, N.Y., U.S.A.	68	42 40N	73 47W
Albany, Oreg., U.S.A.	72	44 30N	123 0W
Albany, Texas, U.S.A.	71	32 47N	99 16W
Albany, W. Australia	44	35 1S	117 58 E
Albany R., Canada	62	51 30N	87 0W
Albardon, Argentina	77	31 20S	68 30W
Albatross B., Queens.	42	12 45S	141 30 E
Albatross Pt., N.Z.	46	38 7S	174 44 E
Albemarle, U.S.A.	69	35 27N	80 15W
Albemarle Sd., U.S.A.	69	36 5N	76 0W
Albenga, Italy	20	44 3N	8 12 E
Alberche R., Spain	17	40 10N	4 30W
Alberdi, Argentina	77	27 30S	65 40W
Alberga, S. Australia	45	27 10S	135 30 E
Alberni, Canada	64	49 20N	124 50W
Albert, Canada	62	45 51N	64 38W
Albert, France	12	50 0N	2 38 E
Albert L., E. Africa	53	1 30N	31 0 E
Albert L., U.S.A.	72	42 40N	120 10W
Albert Canyon, Canada	64	51 0N	121 55W
Albert Lea, U.S.A.	68	43 37N	94 23W
Albert Nile, R., Ugan.	53	3 20N	31 30 E
Alberta, prov., Can.	64-65	54 40N	115 0W
Albertinia, C. Prov.	57	34 11S	21 34 E
Alberton, Canada	63	46 50N	64 0W
Albertville, Congo	54	5 55S	29 9 E
Albi, France	12	43 56N	2 9 E
Albia, U.S.A.	68	41 0N	92 50W
Albina, Surinam	79	5 45N	54 15W
Albion, Idaho, U.S.A.	72	42 24N	113 32W
Albion, Ill., U.S.A.	68	38 20N	88 0W
Albion, Mich., U.S.A.	68	42 15N	84 45W
Albion, Neb., U.S.A.	70	41 45N	98 0W
Albion, N.S.W.	43	31 41S	141 31 E
Ålborg, Denmark	23	57 3N	9 52 E
Albreda, Canada	64	52 35N	119 10W
Albula P., Switzerland	15	46 35N	9 32 E
Albula R., Switzerland	15	46 28N	9 38 E
Albuquerque, U.S.A.	73	35 0N	106 40W
Albuquerque Cays, Col.	75	12 10N	81 50W
Alburquerque, Spain	17	39 15N	7 1W
Albury, N.S.W.	43	36 0S	146 50 E
Alcacer do Sal, Port.	17	38 22N	8 33W
Alcala, Spain	17	40 27N	3 23W
Alcalá de Chisvert, Sp.	17	40 18N	0 14 E
Alcamo, Italy	20	37 59N	12 55 E
Alcaniz, Spain	17	41 2N	0 8W
Alcântara, Brazil	79	2 20S	44 30W
Alcantara, Spain	17	39 41N	6 57W
Alcantara L., Canada	65	61 0N	107 10W
Alcazar, Spain	17	39 24N	3 15W
Alcira, Spain	17	39 9N	0 30W
Alcoa, U.S.A.	69	35 50N	84 0W
Alcobaca, Portugal	17	39 32N	9 0W
Alcoutim, Portugal	17	37 25N	7 28W
Alcova, U.S.A.	72	42 35N	106 47W
Alcoy, Spain	17	38 43N	0 30W
Alcudia, Spain	17	39 51N	3 9 E
Aldabra Is., Seychelles	49	9 22S	46 28W
Aldama, Mexico	74	22 50N	98 10W
Aldamas, Mexico	74	26 0N	99 20W
Aldan, U.S.S.R.	27	58 40N	125 30 E
Aldan R., U.S.S.R.	27	62 30N	135 30 E
Aldeburgh, England	10	52 9N	1 35 E
Alder, U.S.A.	72	43 27N	112 2W
Alderney I., Chan. I.	12	49 42N	2 12W
Aldershot, England	10	51 15N	0 43W
Aldersyde, Canada	64	50 40N	113 53W
Alédjo, Dahomey	52	9 20N	1 30 E
Aledo, U.S.A.	70	41 10N	90 16W
Aleg, Mali	50	17 15N	13 50W
Alegrete, Brazil	77	29 40S	56 0W
Aleisk, U.S.S.R.	26	52 40N	83 0 E
Aleksandriya, U.S.S.R.	25	48 42N	33 3 E
Aleksandrov, U.S.S.R.	25	56 28N	38 50 E
Aleksandrov Gai, U.S.S.R.	25	50 30N	48 10 E
Aleksandrovsk, U.S.S.R.	27	50 50N	142 10 E
Aleksandrovski Zavod, U.S.S.R.	27	50 40N	117 50 E
Aleksandrovskoye, U.S.S.R.	26	60 35N	77 50 E
Aleksandrovskoye, U.S.S.R.	25	44 44N	43 12 E
Aleksandrow, Poland	16	52 50N	18 47 E
Alekseyevka, U.S.S.R.	25	50 43N	38 40 E
Alemania, Argentina	77	25 40S	65 30W
Alençon, France	12	48 27N	0 4 E
Alentejo Alto & Baixo, provs., Portugal	17	38 55N	7 40W
Alenuihaha Chan., Hawaii	59	20 10N	156 0W
Aleppo. *See* Halab.	30		
Aleria, France	12	42 7N	9 33 E
Alert B., Canada	64	50 30N	127 35W
Alés, France	12	44 9N	4 5 E
Alessandria, Italy	20	44 54N	8 37 E
Ålesund, Norway	23	62 28N	6 5 E
Aletschgletscher, glacier, Switzerland	15	46 24N	7 58 E
Aletschhorn, Switz.	15	46 28N	8 0 E
Aleutian Islands, Pac.Oc.	59	50 0N	163 0W to 17 20 E
Aleutian Range, Alaska	59	58 0N	155 0W
Alexander, U.S.A.	70	47 48N	103 23W
Alexander Arch., Alaska	59	57 0N	135 0W
Alexander Bay, C. Prov.	57	28 40S	16 30 E
Alexander I. Land, Antarctica	50	69 0S	70 0W
Alexander City, U.S.A.	69	32 58N	85 57W
Alexander Mts., New Guinea	42	3 50S	143 30 E
Alexander Mt., Queens.	42	21 13S	144 25W
Alexander Mt., W. Australia	44	22 40S	115 27 E
Alexandra, N.Z.	47	45 14S	169 25 E
Alexandra, Victoria	43	37 8S	145 40 E
Alexandra Falls, Canada	64	60 25N	116 30W
Alexandretta (Iskenderun), Turkey	30	36 32N	36 10 E
Alexandria, (A Iskandariyah), Egypt	51	31 10N	29 55 E
Alexandria, B.C., Can.	64	52 35N	122 20W
Alexandria, Ont., Can.	62	45 19N	74 38W
Alexandria, C. Prov.	57	33 38S	26 28 E
Alexandria, Rumania	21	43 57N	25 24 E
Alexandria, Ind., U.S.A.	68	40 15N	85 40W
Alexandria, La., U.S.A.	71	31 15N	92 30W
Alexandria, Minn., U.S.A.	70	45 51N	95 23W
Alexandria, S.D., U.S.A.	70	43 42N	97 46W
Alexandria, Va., U.S.A.	68	38 47N	77 1 E
Alexandria B., U.S.A.	68	44 20N	75 52W
Alexandrina L., S. Australia	43	35 30S	139 15 E
Alexandroúpolis, Gr.	21	40 50N	25 54 E
Alexis Creek, Canada	64	52 0N	123 20W
Alexis R., Canada	63	52 30N	57 10W
Alfaro, Spain	17	42 10N	1 50W
Alfredton, N.Z.	46	40 41S	175 54 E
Alfreton, England	10	53 6N	1 22W
Alftanes, Iceland	22	64 29N	22 10W
Algarve, prov., Port.	17	37 15N	8 10W
Algebuckina, S. Austral.	45	27 58S	135 55 E
Algeciras, Spain	17	36 9N	5 28W
Alger (Algiers), Algeria	50	36 42N	3 8 E
Algeria, Africa	50	32 50N	3 0 E
Alghero, Italy	20	40 34N	8 20 E
Algiers. *See* Alger.	50		
Algoa B., C. Prov.	57	35 50S	25 45 E
Algoma, Oreg., U.S.A.	72	42 23N	121 50W
Algoma, Wis., U.S.A.	68	44 35N	87 27W
Algona, U.S.A.	70	43 3N	94 10W
Algonquin Park, Can.	62	45 35N	78 35W
Algonquin Prov. Pk., Canada	62	45 50N	78 30W
Algorta, Uruguay	77	32 25S	57 25W
Alhama, Spain	17	41 18N	1 55W
Alhama, Spain	17	37 2N	3 58W
Alhama, Spain	17	37 51N	1 27W
Alhuampa, Argentina	77	27 10S	62 30W
Alhuarin el Grande, Sp.	17	36 41N	4 42W
Ali al Gharbi, Iraq	30	32 27N	46 41 E
Aliabād, Iran	31	28 11N	57 33 E
Aliakmon, R., Greece	21	40 10N	22 0 E
Alibag, India	32	18 38N	72 56 E
Alibo, Ethiopia	54	10 0N	37 0 E
Alibori R., Dahomey	52	11 30N	2 47 E
Alicante, Spain	17	38 23N	0 30W
Alice, Cape Province	57	32 48S	26 55 E
Alice, Queensland	42	23 36S	145 43 E
Alice, U.S.A.	71	27 45N	98 2W
Alice R., Queensland	42	23 40S	145 0 E
Alice Arm, Canada	64	55 29N	129 23W
Alice Springs, N. Terr.	45	23 36S	133 53 E
Alice Springs, dist., N. Territory	45	23 5S	133 56 E
Alicedale, C. Prov.	57	33 15S	26 4 E
Aliceville, U.S.A.	69	33 9N	88 10W
Alick Creek, Queens.	42	21 0S	142 50 E
Alicudi I., Italy	20	38 33N	14 20 E
Alida, Canada	65	49 25N	101 55W
Aligarh, India	32	27 55N	78 10 E
Aligudarz, Iran	30	33 32N	49 40 E
Alingsås, Sweden	23	57 57N	12 36 E
Alipur, Pakistan	32	29 25N	70 55 E
Alipur Duar, India	33	26 30N	89 35 E
Aliquippa, U.S.A.	68	40 38N	80 18W
Aliwal, N., C. Prov.	57	30 45S	26 45 E
Alix, Canada	64	52 25N	113 15W
Aljustrel, Portugal	17	37 55N	8 10W
Alkamari, Niger	52	13 28N	11 9 E
Alkmaar, Netherlands	13	52 37N	4 45 E
Allada, Dahomey	52	6 41N	2 9 E
Allagash R., U.S.A.	69	47 0N	69 20W
Allahabad, India	33	25 25N	81 58 E
Allakaket, Alaska	59	66 28N	153 20W
Allakh Yun, U.S.S.R.	27	60 50N	137 5 E
Allan, Canada	65	51 50N	106 0W
Allanmyo, Burma	33	19 25N	95 13 E
Allanridge, O.F.S.	57	27 40S	26 40 E
Allanton, New Zealand	47	45 55S	170 15 E
Allanwater, Canada	62	50 14N	90 10W
Allard Lake, Canada	62	50 31N	63 31W
Allariz, Spain	17	42 11N	7 50W
Allas Str., Indonesia	35	9 0S	116 40 E
Allegan, U.S.A.	68	42 32N	85 52W
Allegany, U.S.A.	68	42 6N	78 30W
Allegheny Mts., U.S.A.	68	38 0N	80 0W
Allegheny R., U.S.A.	68	41 30N	79 20W
Allen, Bog of, Ireland	11	53 15N	7 0W
Allen, Lough, Ireland	11	53 15N	7 0W
Allende, Mexico	74	28 20N	100 50W
Alleppey, India	32	9 30N	76 28 E
Aller R., Germany	14	52 39N	9 49 E
Alliance, Nebr., U.S.A.	70	42 0N	103 0W
Alliance, Ohio, U.S.A.	68	41 0N	81 0W
Allier R., France	12	46 40N	3 10 E
Alliston, Canada	62	44 15N	79 55W
Alloa, Scotland	10	56 7N	3 49W
Allora, Queensland	43	28 2S	152 0 E
Alltentown, U.S.A.	68	40 36N	75 30W
Alma Ata, U.S.S.R.	26	43 20N	76 50 E
Alma, Ga., U.S.A.	69	31 35N	82 30W
Alma, Kansas, U.S.A.	70	39 1N	96 19W
Alma, Mich., U.S.A.	68	43 25N	84 40W
Alma, Neb., U.S.A.	70	40 8N	99 20W
Alma, Wis., U.S.A.	70	44 18N	91 55W
Almada, Portugal	17	38 41N	9 10W
Almaden, Queensland	42	17 22S	144 40 E
Almaden, Spain	17	38 49N	4 52W
Almagro, Spain	17	38 50N	3 45W
Almanor L., U.S.A.	72	40 15N	121 12W
Almansa, Spain	17	38 51N	1 5W
Almanzor, Pl. de, Spain	17	40 5N	5 20W
Almanzora, Spain	17	37 10N	1 55W
Almazan, Spain	17	41 30N	2 30W
Alméirim, Brazil	79	1 10S	52 0W
Almelo, Netherlands	13	52 22N	6 42 E
Almendralejo, Spain	17	38 41N	6 26W
Almeria, tn. & prov., Spain	17	36 52N	2 32W
Almirante, Chile	78	29 33S	71 15W
Almirante, Panama	75	9 10N	82 30W
Almiros, Greece	21	39 11N	22 45 E
Almodovo, Spain	17	38 44N	4 13W
Almora, India	32	29 38N	79 42 E
Almuñécar, Spain	17	36 43N	3 41W
Alnwick, England	10	55 25N	1 42W
Aloi, Uganda	53	2 17N	33 10 E
Alonsa, Canada	65	50 50N	99 0W
Alor Is., Indonesia	35	8 10S	124 30 E
Alor Star, Malaya	34	6 7N	100 22 E
Alora, Spain	17	36 49N	4 46W
Alouef Arab, Algeria	50	27 10N	1 20 E
Aloum, Cameroon	52	2 50N	10 48 E
Aloysius Mt., W. Australia	45	26 1S	128 50 E
Alpes Cottiennes, Fr.	12	44 43N	6 59 E
Alpes Maritimes, Fr.	12	43 55N	7 10 E
Alpi Grande, France	12	45 30N	7 10 E
Alpena, U.S.A.	68	45 6N	83 25W
Alpine, U.S.A.	71	30 35N	103 35W
Alps, mts., Europe	8	46 0N to 47 0N	6 0 E to 10 0 E
Alroy, N. Territory	45	19 16S	135 58 E
Als, Denmark	23	57 24N	10 17 E
Alsace, reg., France	12	48 15N	7 25 E
Alsask, Canada	65	51 25N	110 0W
Alsasua, Spain	17	42 53N	2 11W
Alsina, Argentina	77	34 40S	58 25W
Alsten, I., Norway	22	65 55N	12 30 E
Alta Gracia, Argentina	77	31 40S	64 30W
Alta Lake, Canada	64	50 10N	123 0W
Altaelv, R., Norway	22	69 0N	23 30 E
Altagracia, Venezuela	78	10 45N	71 30W
Altai, dist., China	65	46 50N	89 0 E
Altai Mts., Asia	27	48 0N	90 0 E
Altamaha R., U.S.A.	69	31 50N	82 0W
Altamira, Brazil	79	3 0S	52 50W
Altamura, Italy	20	40 50N	16 33 E
Altan Bulak, Mongolia	65	50 20N	106 25 E
Altar, Mexico	74	30 40N	111 50W
Altata, Mexico	74	24 30N	108 0W
Altavista, U.S.A.	68	37 9N	79 22W
Altdorf, Switzerland	15	46 52N	8 36 E
Altea, Spain	17	38 38N	0 2W
Alte Fjord, Norway	22	70 10N	23 0 E
Altenburg, Germany	14	50 59N	12 25 E
Altkirch, France	12	47 37N	7 15 E
Alto Araguaia, Brazil	79	17 15S	53 20W
Alto Chindio, Mozam.	56	16 14S	35 18 E
Alto Cuchumatanes, Guat.	74	15 30N	91 10W
Alto Molocue, Mozam.	55	15 38S	37 42 E
Alton, Queensland	43	28 0S	149 21 E
Alton, U.S.A.	70	43 15N	90 5W
Altona, Germany	14	53 32N	9 56 E
Altoona, U.S.A.	68	40 32N	78 24W
Altos do Parana, Par.	79	25 0S	55 0W
Altstätten, Switzerland	15	47 22N	9 33 E
Alturas, U.S.A.	72	41 30N	120 32W
Altus, U.S.A.	71	34 30N	99 25W
Altyn Tagh, Tibet	65	38 50N	89 0 E
Aluksne, U.S.S.R.	25	57 30N	27 0 E

	Map	Lat.	Long.
Alupka, U.S.S.R.	25	44 23N	34 2 E
Alva, U.S.A.	71	36 50N	98 50W
Alvarado, Mexico	74	18 40N	95 50W
Alvarado, U.S.A.	71	32 28N	97 14W
Alvear, Argentina	77	29 5S	57 40W
Alvesta, Sweden	23	56 54N	14 35 E
Alvin, U.S.A.	71	29 27N	95 15W
Alvkarleby, Sweden	23	60 32N	17 40 E
Alvsborg, co., Sweden	23	58 30N	12 30 E
Alvsby, Sweden	22	65 42N	20 52 E
Alwar, India	32	27 38N	76 34 E
Alzada, U.S.A.	70	45 5N	104 25W
Am-Dam, Chad.	51	12 40N	20 35 E
Am Djeress, Chad.	51	16 15N	22 50 E
Am Guereda, Chad.	51	12 53N	21 14 E
Am Timan, Chad.	51	11 0N	20 10 E
Amadeus L., Australia	45	24 54S	131 0 E
Amadi, Sudan	54	5 30N	30 24 E
Amadjuak, Canada	61	64 0N	72 40W
Amadjuak L., Canada	61	65 0N	71 0W
Amagunze, Nigeria	52	6 18N	7 35 E
Amakusa B., Japan	36	32 30N	130 0 E
Amakusu I., Japan	36	32 15N	130 10 E
Amal, Sweden	23	59 2N	12 40 E
Amalias, Greece	21	37 47N	21 22 E
Amalner, India	32	21 5N	75 5 E
Amambai, Sa de., Braz.	77	23 0S	55 30W
Amana L., Brazil	78	2 35N	64 30W
Amandola, Italy	20	42 59N	13 21 E
Amangeldy, U.S.S.R.	26	50 10N	65 10 E
Amantea, Italy	20	39 8N	16 3 E
Amapá, Brazil	79	2 5N	50 50W
Amapá, st., Brazil	79	1 40N	52 0W
Amarah, Iraq	30	31 57N	47 12 E
Amarante, Brazil	79	6 15S	42 50W
Amaranth, Canada	65	50 36N	98 43W
Amargosa, Brazil	79	13 0S	39 50W
Amarillo, U.S.A.	65	35 14N	101 46W
Amaro, Mte., Italy	20	42 5N	14 6 E
Amarpur, India	33	23 30N	91 45 E
Amasra, Turkey	30	41 48N	32 25 E
Amassama, Nigeria	52	5 1N	6 2 E
Amasya, Turkey	30	40 40N	35 50 E
Amatari, Brazil	78	3 0S	59 0W
Amatignak I., Aleutian Is.	59	51 19N	179 10W
Amatikulu, Natal	57	29 3S	31 33 E
Amatitlan, Guatemala	74	14 29N	90 38W
Amazon R., S. America	79	2 0S	53 30W
Amazon, Mouths of, Brazil	78	0 30N	49 30W
Amazonas, st., Brazil	78	4 20S	64 0W
Ambala, India	32	30 23N	76 56 E
Ambalangoda, Sri Lanka	32	6 15N	80 5 E
Amban, Cameroon	52	2 20N	11 15 E
Ambarchik, U.S.S.R.	27	69 40N	162 20 E
Ambasamudram, India	32	8 45N	77 27 E
Ambata, Ecuador	78	1 5S	78 42W
Ambelau I., Indonesia	35	3 50S	127 15 E
Ambeno, Port. Timor	35	9 20S	124 30 E
Amberg, Germany	14	49 25N	11 52 E
Ambergris Cay, Br. Hond.	74	18 0S	88 0W
Amberley, N.Z.	47	43 9S	172 44 E
Ambikapur, India	33	23 15N	83 15 E
Ambo, Peru	78	10 5S	76 10W
Amboise, France	12	47 24N	1 0 E
Ambon, Indonesia	35	3 45S	128 5 E
Amboseli L., Kenya	53	2 35S	37 8 E
Amboy, Col., U.S.A.	73	34 35N	115 47W
Amboy, Ill., U.S.A.	68	41 43N	89 21W
Amboyna Cay, I., S. China Sea	35	7 50N	112 55 E
Ambre, C. d', Malag Rep.	55	11 58S	49 14 E
Ambriz, Angola	54	7 48S	13 8 E
Ambrizète, Angola	54	7 10S	12 52 E
Amby, Queensland	43	26 30S	148 11 E
Amchitka I., Aleutian Is.	59	51 30N	179 0 E
Amchitka Pass, Aleutian Is.	59	51 50N	180 0
Amderma, U.S.S.R.	26	69 45N	61 30 E
Ameca, & R., Mexico	74	20 30N	104 0W
Amecameca, Mexico	74	19 10N	89 57W
Amedzofe, Ghana	52	6 50N	0 30 E
Ameland I., Neth.	13	53 27N	5 45 E
Amen, U.S.S.R.	27	68 50N	179 40W
American Falls, U.S.A.	72	43 0N	112 40W
Americus, U.S.A.	69	32 0N	84 10W
Amersfoort, Transvaal	57	26 59S	29 53 E
Amery, Canada	65	56 35N	94 5W
Ames, U.S.A.	70	42 0N	93 40W
Amesdale, Canada	65	50 2N	92 55W
Ameson, Canada	62	49 50N	84 35W
Amfiklia, Greece	21	38 38N	22 35 E
Amfilokhia, Greece	21	38 52N	21 9 E
Amfipolis, Greece	21	40 48N	23 52 E
Amfissa, Greece	21	38 32N	22 22 E
Amgu, U.S.S.R.	27	45 45N	137 15 E
Amguid, Algeria	50	26 28N	5 25 E
Amgun R., U.S.S.R.	27	52 50N	138 0 E
Amherst, Burma	34	16 10N	97 0 E
Amherst, Canada	63	45 48N	64 8W
Amherst, U.S.A.	71	33 58N	102 26W
Amherst, Mt., W. Australia	44	17 58S	126 42 E
Amherstburg, Canada	62	42 10N	83 0W
Amiata Mt., Italy	20	42 50N	11 40 E
Amiens, France	12	49 54N	2 16 E
Amiens, Queensland	43	28 34S	151 49 E
Aminuis, S.W. Africa	57	23 43S	19 21 E
Amirante Is., Indian Oc.	5	6 0S	53 0 E
Amisk L., Canada	65	54 35N	102 15W
Amite, U.S.A.	71	30 45N	90 31W
Amla, India	32	21 55N	78 10 E
Amlia, I., Aleutian Is.	59	52 5N	173 30W
Amman, Jordan	30	32 0N	35 52 E
Ammi'ad, Israel	29	32 55N	35 32 E
Amorgos I, Greece	21	36 50N	25 57 E
Amory, U.S.A.	69	33 59N	88 30W
Amos, Canada	62	48 35N	78 5W
Amoy, China	39	24 30N	118 5 E
Amper, Nigeria	52	9 25N	9 40 E
Amper R., W. Germany	14	48 30N	12 30 E
Amqa, Israel	29	32 59N	35 10 E
Amqui, Canada	63	48 28N	67 27W
Amraoti (Amravati), India	32	20 58N	77 56 E
Amreli, India	32	21 35N	71 17 E
Amriswil, Switz.	15	47 33N	9 18 E
Amritsar, India	32	31 35N	74 57 E
Amroha, India	32	28 53N	78 30 E
Amrunyasi, Ghana	52	6 8N	1 45W
Amsterdam, Neth.	13	52 23N	4 45 E
Amsterdam, S. Africa	57	26 38S	30 40 E
Amsterdam, U.S.A.	68	42 58N	74 10W
Amuay, Venezuela	78	11 50N	70 10W
Amuay, B., Venezuela	75	11 50N	70 10W
Amuda, Uganda	53	1 58N	34 56 E
Amukta I., Aleutian Is.	59	52 29N	171 18W
Amukta Passage	59	52 29N	172 0W
Amundsen Gulf, Canada	60	70 30N	123 0W
Amur R., U.S.S.R.	27	53 30N	122 30 E
Amurang, Indonesia	35	1 5N	124 40 E
Amuri Pass, N.Z.	47	42 31S	172 11 E
Amuria, Uganda	53	2 4N	33 38 E
Amy Mt., W. Australia	44	22 14S	115 49 E
Amyot, Canada	62	48 25N	84 55W
An Khe, Viet Nam	34	14 0N	108 20 E
An Nafud, Desert, Arabia	30	28 15N	41 0 E
An Najaf, Iraq	30	32 3N	44 15 E
An Nasiriyah, Iraq	30	31 0N	46 15 E
An Nhon, Viet Nam	34	13 55N	109 7 E
An Nu'ayriyah, Saudi Arabia	30	27 30N	48 29 E
An Uaimh (Navan), Ire.	11	53 39N	6 40W
Ana Branch R., N.S.W.	43	33 30S	141 43 E
'Anabta, Jordan	29	32 19N	35 7 E
Anaconda, U.S.A.	72	46 7N	113 0W
Anacortes, U.S.A.	72	48 30N	122 40W
Anadar R., U.S.S.R.	27	72 0N	114 0 E
Anadarko, U.S.A.	71	35 2N	98 15W
Anadyr, U.S.S.R.	27	64 40N	177 10 E
Anadyr, R., U.S.S.R.	27	66 30N	170 0 E
Anadyr, G. of, U.S.S.R.	27	64 0N	180 0 E
Anah, Iraq	30	34 28N	41 58 E
Anai Mudi, Mt., India	32	10 12N	77 20 E
Anaiza, Saudi Arabia	30	26 4N	44 8 E
Anak, N. Korea	36	38 30N	125 50 E
Anakapalle, India	33	17 44N	83 3 E
Analalava, Malagasy Rep.	55	14 35S	48 0 E
Anam, Nigeria	52	6 19N	6 41 E
Anambas Is., Indonesia	34	3 20N	106 30 E
Anamoose, U.S.A.	70	47 54N	100 15W
Anamosa, U.S.A.	70	42 8N	91 28W
Anamur, Turkey	30	36 8N	32 58 E
Anamurburnu C., Tur.	30	36 5N	32 50 E
Anantapur, India	32	14 39N	77 42 E
Anantnag, Kashmir	32	33 45N	75 10 E
Anapa, U.S.S.R.	25	44 55N	37 25 E
Anapolis, Brazil	79	16 15S	48 50W
Anapu R., Brazil	79	3 5S	51 30W
Anar, Iran	31	30 55N	55 13 E
Anārak, Iran	31	33 30N	53 34 E
Anascaul, Ireland	11	52 10N	10 3W
Anatolia, reg., Asia	30	38 0N	29 0 E
Anatone, U.S.A.	72	46 8N	117 10W
Anatuya, Argentina	77	28 20S	62 50W
Anaunethad L., Canada	65	61 0N	105 0 E
Anaye, Niger	51	19 15N	12 50 E
Anayev, U.S.S.R.	25	47 40N	30 0 E
Ancenis, France	12	47 21N	1 10W
Anchau, Nigeria	52	11 0N	8 10 E
Anchorage, Alaska	59	61 32N	149 50W
Ancohuma Illampu Mt., Bolivia	78	16 0S	68 50W
Ancon, Ecuador	78	2 25S	80 45W
Ancon, Panama Canal Zone	74	8 57N	79 33W
Ancona, Italy	20	43 37N	13 30 E
Ancuaze, Mozambique	56	16 49S	34 31 E
Ancud, Chile	77	42 0S	73 50W
Ancud, G. of, Chile	77	42 0S	73 0W
And Fd., Norway	22	69 0N	16 30 E
Andalgala, Argentina	77	27 35N	66 30 E
Andalsnes, Norway	23	62 35N	7 43 E
Andalusia, U.S.A.	69	31 20N	86 30W
Andalusia, prov., Spain	17	37 35N	5 0W
Andaman Is., India	28	12 30N	92 30 E
Andaman Strait, India	33	12 30N	92 30 E
Andara, S.W. Africa	55	18 2S	21 9 E
Andenes, Norway	22	69 18N	16 10 E
Anderanbukane, Niger	52	15 28N	2 58 E
Andermatt, Switzerland	15	46 38N	8 35 E
Anderson, Cal., U.S.A.	72	40 30N	122 21W
Anderson, Ind., U.S.A.	68	40 5N	85 40W
Anderson, Mo., U.S.A.	71	36 42N	94 30W
Andes, Cordillera de las, mts., South America	77	7 0N to 53 0S	65 0W to 80 0W
Andhra Pradesh, st., India	32	15 0N	80 0 E
Andikithira, Greece	20	38 22N	22 38 E
Andipaxoi, I., Greece	21	39 9N	20 13 E
Andizhan, U.S.S.R.	26	41 10N	72 0 E
Andkhui, Afghanistan	31	36 52N	65 8 E
Andoas Nuevo, Ec.	78	2 20S	76 50W
Andong, Korea	36	36 35N	128 30 E
Andorra, rep. & tn., Eur.	8	42 30N	1 30 E
Andover, England	10	51 13N	1 29W
Andreanof Is., Aleutian Is.	59	51 0N	178 0W
Andreas C., Cyprus	30	35 43N	34 32 E
Andreba, Malagasy Rep.	55	17 30S	48 32 E
Andrews, S.C., U.S.A.	69	33 29N	79 30W
Andrews, Texas, U.S.A.	71	32 16N	102 31W
Andria, Italy	20	41 13N	16 17 E
Andritsaina, Greece	21	37 29N	21 52 E
Androka, Malagasy Rep.	55	24 58S	44 2 E
Andros, & I., Greece	21	37 50N	24 58 E
Andros I., Bahama Is.	75	24 30N	78 0W
Andudu, Zaire	53	2 29N	28 31 E
Andujar, Spain	17	38 3N	4 5W
Andulo, Angola	55	11 25S	16 45 E
Anécho, Togo	52	6 12N	1 36 E
Anegada, I., Virgin Is.	75	18 45N	64 20W
Anegada Passage, W.I.	75	18 40N	64 30W
Anekho, Togo	52	6 12N	1 34 E
Añelo, Argentina	77	38 15S	68 40W
Aneto, Pic de, Spain	17	42 38N	0 38W
Angamos, Pta., Chile	77	23 10S	70 27W
Angangki, China	37	47 13N	123 46 E
Angara R., U.S.S.R.	27	54 20N	103 0 E
Ånge, Sweden	23	62 31N	15 35 E
Angel Falls, Venezuela	78	5 57N	62 30W
Angel de la Guarda I., Mexico	74	29 30N	113 30W
Angela R., W. Austral.	44	23 37S	118 0 E
Ängelholm, Sweden	23	56 15N	12 58 E
Angels Camp, U.S.A.	73	38 5N	120 31W
Ångerman, R., Sweden	23	64 0N	17 20 E
Angermünde, Germany	14	53 1N	14 0 E
Angers, France	12	47 30N	0 35W
Ängersån R., Sweden	22	66 50N	22 15 E
Angikuni L., Canada	65	62 10N	99 40W
Angkor, Cambodia	34	13 10N	104 0 E
Angledool, N.S.W.	43	29 5S	147 53 E
Anglem Mt., N.Z.	47	46 45N	167 53 E
Anglesey I., co., Wales	10	53 17N	4 20W
Angleton, U.S.A.	71	29 13N	95 22W
Angliers, Canada	62	47 30N	79 20W
Ango, Zaire	54	4 10N	26 5 E
Angol, Chile	77	37 56S	72 45W
Angola, U.S.A.	68	41 40N	85 0W
Angola, Port. terr., Afr.	55	12 0S	18 0 E
Angoon, Alaska	59	57 30N	134 40W
Angostura II, Salto de, Cat., Colombia	78	2 37N	72 57W
Angostura III, Salto de, Cat., Colombia	78	2 45N	70 57W
Angoulême, France	12	45 39N	0 10 E
Angoumois, prov., Fr.	12	45 30N	0 25 E
Angra dos Reis, Brazil	77	23 0S	44 10W
Angra Juntas, S.W. Afr.	57	26 40S	15 40 E
Angra Pequena B., S.W. Africa	57	26 38S	15 10 E
Anguilla I., W. Indies	75	23 30N	79 40W
Anguille C., Canada	63	47 54N	59 28W
Angus, Canada	62	44 20N	79 50W
Angwa R., Rhodesia	56	16 15S	30 15 E
Anholt I., Denmark	23	56 43N	11 35 E
Anhsien, China	39	31 38N	104 30 E
Anhwa, China	39	28 18N	111 25 E
Anhwei, China	39	31 10N	117 39 E
Ani, China	39	28 51N	115 29 E
Aniak, Alaska	59	61 33N	160 10W
Anié, Togo	52	7 46N	1 14 E
Animas, U.S.A.	73	31 58N	108 53W
Anina, Rumania	21	45 5N	21 50 E
Anjen, China	39	26 45N	113 10 E
Anjer-Lor, Indonesia	34	6 6S	105 56 E
Anjidiv I., India	32	14 40N	74 10 E
Anjou, prov., France	12	47 20N	0 30W
Anju, Korea	36	39 30N	125 30 E
Anka, Nigeria	52	12 13N	5 58 E
Ankang, China	38	32 30N	109 27 E
Ankara, Turkey	30	40 0N	32 54 E
Anki, China	39	25 1N	118 15 E
Anking, China	39	30 32N	117 10 E
Anklam, Germany	14	53 50N	13 42 E
Ankobar, Ethiopia	49	9 35N	39 40 E
Ankobra R., Ghana	52	5 15N	2 14W
Ankolé, King. of, Uganda	53	0 30S	30 30 E
Ankoro, Zaire	54	6 45S	26 49 E
Anlu, China	39	31 28N	114 35 E
Ann C., U.S.A.	69	42 37N	70 37W
Ann Arbor, U.S.A.	68	42 17N	83 45W
Anna, U.S.A.	68	37 28N	89 10W
Annaba, Algeria	50	36 47N	7 38 E
Annal, British Guiana	78	4 0N	59 0W
Annalee, Ireland	11	54 3N	7 15W
Annandale, Queens.	42	21 58S	148 20 E
Annandale, Queens.	43	25 22S	138 36 E
Annapolis, U.S.A.	68	39 0N	76 30W
Annapolis Royal, Can.	63	44 44N	65 32W
Annecy, France	12	45 55N	6 8 E
Annenkovo, U.S.S.R.	25	54 5N	47 20 E
Annette, Alaska	59	55 2N	131 36W
Anning, China	37	24 50N	102 25 E
Anniston, U.S.A.	69	33 45N	85 50W
Annobón I, Sp. Guinea	49	1 35S	5 35 E
Annonay, France	12	45 15N	4 40 E
Annotto Bay, Jamaica	75	18 17N	77 3W
Ano Viánnos, Greece	20	35 2N	25 21 E
Anoka, U.S.A.	70	45 30N	93 26W
Anping, China	39	23 10N	120 10 E
Ansāb, Saudi Arabia	30	29 22N	44 45 E
Ansbach, Germany	14	49 17N	10 34 E
Anshan, China	38	41 10N	123 0 E
Anshun, China	39	26 13N	106 8 E
Ansi Kansu, China	38	40 30N	95 50 E
Ansi Shensi, China	38	36 57N	109 6 E
Anson, U.S.A.	71	32 47N	99 50W
Ansong, S. Korea	36	36 80N	127 30 E
Ansonville, Canada	62	48 46N	80 43W
Ansley, U.S.A.	70	41 20N	99 24W
Anstruther, Scotland	10	56 14N	2 40W
Anta, Peru	78	13 15S	72 10W
Antabamba, Peru	78	14 40S	73 0W
Antakya, Turkey	30	36 14N	36 10 E
Antalaha, Malagasy Rep.	55	14 57S	50 20 E
Antalya, Turkey	30	36 52N	30 45 E
Antalya Körfezi, B., Turkey	30	36 15N	31 30 E
Antarctic Pen., Ant.	80	70 0S	65 0W
Antarctica, cont.	80	90 0S	
Antelope, Rhodesia	56	21 2S	28 31 E
Antequera, Spain	17	37 5N	4 33W
Antero, mt., U.S.A.	73	38 39N	106 38W
Anthony, Kan., U.S.A.	71	37 8N	98 2W
Anthony, N. Mex., U.S.A.	73	32 0N	106 36W
Anti Atlas Mts., Mor.	50	30 30N	6 30W
Antibes, France	12	43 34N	7 6 E
Anticosti I., Canada	63	49 20N	62 40W
Antigo, U.S.A.	68	45 8N	89 10W
Antigonish, Canada	63	45 38N	61 58W
Antigua, Guatemala	74	14 34N	90 41W
Antigua I., West Indies	75	17 0N	61 50W
Antilhue, Chile	77	40 0S	73 15W
Antilla, Cuba	75	20 40N	75 50W
Antilles, Greater, W. Indies	75	18 0N	75 0W
Antilles, Lesser, W. Indies	75	12 40N	65 0W
Antimony, U.S.A.	73	38 7N	112 0W
Antioch, U.S.A.	73	38 2N	121 48W
Antioquia, Colombia	78	6 40N	75 55W
Antipodes Is., N.Z.	80	49 45S	178 40 E
Antler, U.S.A.	70	49 0N	100 16W
Antler, R., Canada	65	49 10N	102 0W
Antlers, U.S.A.	71	34 9N	95 35W
Antofagasta, Chile	77	23 50S	70 20W
Antofagasta de la Sierra, Argentina	77	25 0S	67 15W
Anton, U.S.A.	71	33 46N	102 4W
Antonina, Brazil	77	25 26S	48 42W
Antonio Enez, Mozam.	55	16 20S	40 0 E
Antonito, U.S.A.	73	37 4N	106 1W
Antrim, N. Ireland	11	54 43N	6 13W
Antrim, co., N. Ireland	11	54 58N	6 20W
Antrim Plateau, W. Australia	44	18 0S	128 40 E
Antsirabe, Malagasy Rep.	55	19 55S	47 2 E
Antung, China	38	40 10N	124 20 E
Antwerp, Belgium	13	51 13N	4 25 E
Antwerp, prov., Belg.	13	51 15N	4 40 E
Anuktuvuk Plat., Alas.	59	69 30N	150 0W
Anupgarh, India	32	29 10N	73 10 E
Anuppur, India	33	23 5N	81 45 E
Anuradhapura, Iran	32	8 22N	80 28 E
Anvik, Alaska	59	62 43N	160 20W
Anxious B., S. Austral.	45	33 23S	134 45 E
Anyang, China	38	36 0N	114 27 E
Anyi, China	38	35 0N	110 44 E
Anyang, S. Korea	36	37 40N	127 10 E
Anyeke, Uganda	53	2 25N	32 40 E
Anyo, China	39	30 5N	105 20 E
Anyuan, China	39	24 55N	115 9 E
Anza, Colombia	78	6 30N	75 55W
Anza, Jordan	29	32 22N	35 12 E
Anzhero-Sudzhensk, U.S.S.R.	26	56 10N	85 40 E
Anzin, France	12	50 22N	3 30 E
Anzio, Italy	20	41 28N	12 37 E
Aomori, Japan	36	40 45N	140 45 E
Aomori, pref., Japan	36	40 45N	140 40 E
Aorangi Mts., N.Z.	46	41 30S	175 25 E
Aosta, Italy	20	45 43N	7 20 E
Aotea Harbour, N.Z.	46	38 1S	174 51 E
Aozou, Chad.	51	21 40N	17 25 E
Apache, Ariz., U.S.A.	73	31 45N	109 6W
Apache, Okla., U.S.A.	71	34 49N	98 25W
Apalachee B., U.S.A.	69	30 0N	84 0W
Apalachicola, U.S.A.	69	29 40N	85 0W
Apam, Ghana	52	5 25N	0 50W
Apapa, Nigeria	52	6 25N	3 25 E
Apaporis R., Col.	78	0 30S	70 30W
Aparri, Philippines	35	18 15N	121 55 E
Apatin, Yugoslavia	21	45 40N	19 0 E
Apatzingan, Mexico	74	19 0N	102 20W
Apeldoorn, Neth.	13	52 13N	5 57 E
Apennines, Mts., Italy	20	44 20N	10 20 E

Place	Map	Lat.	Long.
Apiacas, Serra dos, Brazil	79	10 0s	57 0W
Apies, R., Transvaal	57	25 44s	28 12 E
Apiskigamish L., Can.	62	55 20N	73 20W
Apiti, New Zealand	46	39 58s	175 54 E
Apizaco, Mexico	74	19 26N	98 9W
Aplao, Peru	78	16 0s	72 40W
Apo, Mt., Philippines	35	6 53N	125 14 E
Apollo Bay, Victoria	43	38 46s	143 38 E
Apollonia, Greece	21	36 58N	24 43 E
Apollonia (Marsa Susa), Libya	51	32 52N	21 59 E
Apolo, Bolivia	78	14 30s	68 30W
Apore R., Brazil	79	18 50s	52 0W
Aporima R., N.Z.	47	46 9s	168 2 E
Apostle Is., U.S.A.	70	47 0N	91 0W
Apostoles, Argentina	77	28 0s	56 0W
Apoteri, Guyana	78	4 5N	58 20W
Appalachian Mts., U.S.A.	69	38 0N	80 0W
Appalachicola, R., U.S.A.	69	30 0N	85 0W
Appenzell, Switz.	15	47 20N	9 24 E
Appenzell, can., Switz.	15	47 20N	9 20 E
Appleton, U.S.A.	68	44 17N	88 25W
Approuague, Fr. Gui.	79	4 20N	52 0W
Apsheronski C., U.S.S.R.	24	40 10N	50 15 E
Apsley, Tasmania	43	42 24s	147 5 E
Apucarana, Brazil	77	23 45s	51 50W
Apulia, reg., Italy	20	41 5N	16 20 E
Apure R., Venezuela	78	8 0N	69 20W
Apurimac R., Peru	78	12 10s	73 30W
Aq Chah, Afghanistan	31	37 0N	66 0 E
Aqaba, Jordan	30	29 31N	35 0 E
Aqaba, G. of, Jordan	30	28 15N	33 20 E
Aqiq, W., Si. Arabia	30	23 30N	40 54 E
'Aqrah, Iraq	30	36 46N	43 45 E
Aquidaunana, Brazil	79	20 30s	55 50W
Aquiles Serdan, Mexico	74	27 37N	105 54W
Ar Ramadi, Iraq	30	33 30N	43 14 E
Ar Raqqah, Syria	30	35 59N	39 0 E
Ar Rass, Si. Arabia	30	25 52N	41 41 E
Ar Rifa, Iraq	30	31 46N	46 5 E
Ar Riyud (Riyadh) Si. Arabia	30	24 44N	46 43 E
Ar Rutbah, Iraq	30	33 2N	40 17 E
'Ar'ar, W., Iraq	30	31 23N	42 26 E
'Arab, Wadi el, Jordan	29	32 37N	35 39 E
Araba, Nigeria	52	13 7N	5 0 E
Arabia, Asia	28	15 0N to 30 0 N	35 0E to 59 0 E
Arabian Desert, Egypt	51	27 40N	32 0 E
Arabian Sea, Indian Ocean	30	21 0N	63 0 E
Araç, Turkey	30	41 20N	33 20 E
Aracajú, Brazil	79	11 0s	37 0W
Aracataca, Colombia	78	10 50N	75 15W
Aracati, Brazil	79	4 30s	37 45W
Araçatuba, Brazil	79	21 10s	50 30W
Aracena, Spain	17	37 53N	6 38W
Aracruz, Brazil	79	20 0s	40 10W
Araçuai, Brazil	79	17 0s	42 0W
Arad, Rumania	21	46 10N	21 20 E
Arada, Chad.	51	15 0N	20 20 E
Arafura Sea, Australia	35	10 0s	135 0 E
Aragon, prov., Spain	17	41 25N	1 0W
Aragua, Venezuela	78	9 35N	64 50W
Aragua de Barcelona, Venezuela	75	9 25N	64 52W
Araguacema, Brazil	79	8 50s	49 20W
Araguaia, Brazil	79	14 10s	51 5W
Araguaiana, Brazil	79	15 0s	56 10W
Araguari, Brazil	79	18 40s	48 10W
Araguari R., Brazil	79	1 0N	51 40W
Arak, Algeria	50	25 35N	3 45 E
Arak, Persia	30	34 8N	49 50 E
Arakan Coast, Burma	33	19 0N	94 0 E
Arakan Yoma, mts., Burma	33	20 0N	94 30 E
Aral, Sea of, Central Asia	26	44 30N	60 0 E
Aralsk, U.S.S.R.	26	46 50N	61 20 E
Aralsor L., U.S.S.R.	25	49 5N	48 30 E
Araluen, N.S.W.	43	35 36s	149 49 E
Aramac, Queensland	42	22 58s	145 14 E
Aran I., Ireland	11	55 0N	8 30W
Aran Is., Ireland	11	53 5N	9 42W
Aranci, Italy	20	41 0N	9 35 E
Aranda, Spain	17	41 39N	3 42W
Arandis, S.W. Africa	57	22 24s	15 0 E
Arandjelovac, Y.slav.	21	44 18N	20 37 E
Aranga, New Zealand	46	35 44s	173 40 E
Aranjuez, Spain	17	40 1N	3 40W
Aranos, S.W. Africa	57	24 9s	19 7 E
Aransas Pass, U.S.A.	71	28 0N	97 0W
Araouane, Mali	50	18 55N	3 30W
Arapahoe, U.S.A.	70	40 23N	99 54W
Arapawa, I. N. Zealand	46	41 12s	174 20 E
Arapkir, Turkey	30	39 0N	38 30 E
Arapuni, New Zealand	46	38 4s	175 40 E
Araq, Iran	31	34 0N	49 40 E
Ararangua, Brazil	77	29 0s	49 30W
Araraquara, Brazil	77	21 50s	48 0W
Ararat, Australia	43	37 16s	143 0 E
Ararat, Mt. *See* Ağri Daği	30		
Araro, Ethiopia	54	4 57N	38 50 E
Aras R., Turkey	30	40 10N	42 30 E
Arauca, Chile	78	37 10s	73 30W
Arauca, Colombia	75	7 0N	70 40W
Arauca, R., Venezuela	75	7 30N	69 0W
Arauco, Chile	77	37 16s	73 25W
Araunã, Brazil	79	16 0s	51 10W
Arawata R., N.Z.	47	44 13s	168 40 E
Araxa, Brazil	79	19 45s	47 0W
Arba Jahan, Kenya	53	2 5N	39 5N
Arbai-Here, Mongolia	37	46 25N	102 45 E
Arbatax, Italy	20	39 57N	9 42 E
Arbaty, U.S.S.R.	26	52 50N	90 30 E
Arbon, Switzerland	15	47 31N	9 26 E
Arborfield, Canada	65	53 0N	103 0W
Arborg, Canada	65	51 0N	97 20W
Arbroath, Scotland	10	56 34N	2 35W
Arbuckle, U.S.A.	72	39 3N	124 6W
Arc, France	12	47 28N	5 34 E
Arcachon, France	12	44 40N	1 10W
Arcadia, Fla., U.S.A.	69	27 5N	82 0W
Arcadia, La., U.S.A.	71	32 33N	92 58W
Arcadia, Neb., U.S.A.	70	41 29N	99 3W
Arcadia, Wis., U.S.A.	68	44 13N	91 29W
Arcata, U.S.A.	72	40 57N	124 9W
Archer B., Queensland	42	13 20s	141 30 E
Archer R., Queensland	42	13 20s	142 25 E
Archers Post, Kenya	53	0 35N	37 35 E
Arco, U.S.A.	72	43 38N	113 17W
Arcola, Canada	65	49 40N	102 30W
Arcos, Spain	17	36 45N	5 45W
Arcot, India	32	12 53N	79 20 E
Arcoverde, Brazil	79	8 28s	37 15W
Arctic Red River, Can.	60	67 15N	134 0W
Arctic Village, Alaska	59	68 5N	145 47W
Arda R., Bulgaria	21	41 40N	25 40 E
Ardabil, Iran	30	38 20N	48 21 E
Ardakān, Iran	31	30 22N	52 3 E
Ardakan, Iran	31	32 20N	54 0 E
Årdal, Norway	23	61 15N	7 45 E
Ardara, Ireland	11	54 47N	8 25W
Ardee, Ireland	11	53 51N	6 32W
Ardennes, Belgium–France	13	49 30N	5 10 E
Ardfert, Ireland	11	52 20N	9 47W
Ardglass, N. Ireland	11	54 16N	5 38W
Ardila R., Spain	17	38 10N	7 20W
Ardistan, Iran	31	33 22N	52 24 E
Ardjuno Mt., Indonesia	34	7 49s	112 39 E
Ardmore, Ireland	11	51 58N	7 43W
Ardmore, Okla., U.S.A.	71	34 10N	97 0W
Ardmore, S.D., U.S.A.	70	43 4N	103 38W
Ardnacrusha, Ireland	11	52 43N	8 38W
Ardnamurchan, Pt., Scotland	10	56 44N	6 14W
Ardrahan, Ireland	11	53 10N	8 50W
Ardrossan, S. Australia	42	34 22s	137 53 E
Ards Pen., N. Ireland	11	54 30N	5 30W
Arecibo, Puerto Rico	75	18 29N	66 42W
Arege, Nigeria	52	13 29N	13 19 E
Areia Branca, Brazil	79	5 0s	37 0W
Arena, Canada	65	49 10N	109 5W
Arenales Mt., Chile	79	47 5s	73 40W
Arendal, Norway	23	58 28N	8 46 E
Arequipa, Peru	78	16 20s	71 30W
Arès, France	12	44 47N	1 8W
Arevalo, Spain	17	41 3N	4 43W
Arezzo, Italy	20	43 28N	11 50 E
Arganda, Spain	17	40 20N	3 25W
Argens R., France	12	43 28N	6 8 E
Argenta, Canada	64	50 20N	116 55W
Argenta, Italy	20	44 37N	11 50 E
Argentan, France	12	48 45N	0 1W
Argentario, Mt., Italy	20	42 23N	11 10 E
Argentat, France	12	45 6N	1 56 E
Argentina, rep., S. Amer.	77	35 0s	66 0W
Argentino L., Arg.	77	50 10s	73 0W
Argenton, France	12	46 36N	1 30 E
Arges R., Rumania	21	44 30N	25 50 E
Arghandab R., Afghan.	31	31 30N	65 30 E
Argolis, Canada	62	48 45N	83 30W
Argolis, G. of, Greece	21	37 10N	23 0 E
Argos, Greece	21	37 37N	22 43 E
Argostolion, Greece	21	38 12N	20 33 E
Argungu, Nigeria	52	12 40N	4 31 E
Argyle, U.S.A.	70	48 24N	96 46W
Århus, Denmark	23	56 7N	10 11 E
Aria, New Zealand	46	38 33s	175 0 E
Ariamsvlei, S.W. Africa	57	28 8s	19 50 E
Ariano, Italy	20	41 9N	15 6 E
Arica, Chile	78	18 32s	70 20W
Arica, Colombia	78	2 0s	71 50W
Arica, Peru	78	1 30s	75 30W
Arid, C., W. Australia	45	33 58s	123 18 E
Arigna, Ireland	11	54 5N	8 8W
Ariguani R., Colombia	75	9 30N	74 0W
Arima, Trinidad	75	10 38N	61 17W
Arinos R., Brazil	79	11 15s	57 0W
Ario de Rosales, Mex.	74	19 10N	101 50W
Aripuana R., Brazil	78	7 30s	60 0W
Ariquemes, Brazil	78	9 58s	63 3W
Aris, S.W. Africa	57	22 48s	17 10 E
Aristazabal I., Canada	64	52 40N	129 10W
Arivaca, U.S.A.	73	31 34N	111 21W
Arizona, Argentina	77	35 45s	65 25W
Arizona, st., U.S.A.	73	34 20N	111 30W
Arizpe, Mexico	74	30 20N	110 11W
Arjeplog, Sweden	22	66 3N	18 2 E
Arjona, Colombia	78	10 14N	75 22W
Arka, U.S.S.R.	27	60 15N	142 0 E
Arka Tagh, China	37	36 20N	91 0 E
Arkadelphia, U.S.A.	71	34 0N	93 0W
Arkansas, st., U.S.A.	71	35 0N	92 0W
Arkansas R., U.S.A.	71	38 0N	98 0W
Arkansas City, U.S.A.	71	37 0N	97 0W
Arkhangelsk, U.S.S.R.	24	64 40N	41 0 E
Arklow, Ireland	11	52 48N	6 10W
Arkonam, India	32	13 7N	79 43 E
Arlberg, Switzerland	14	47 8N	10 18 E
Arlberg Pass, Switz.	14	47 8N	10 15 E
Arlee, U.S.A.	72	47 13N	114 6W
Arles, France	12	43 41N	4 40 E
Arlington, O.F.S.	57	28 1s	27 53 E
Arlington, Oreg., U.S.A.	72	45 45N	120 14W
Arlington, S.D., U.S.A.	70	44 25N	97 2W
Arlington, Tex., U.S.A.	71	32 45N	97 4W
Arlington, Wash., U.S.A.	72	48 12N	122 9W
Armadale, W. Australia	44	32 12s	116 0 E
Armagh, Canada	63	46 41N	70 32W
Armagh, N. Ireland	11	54 22N	6 40W
Armagh, co., N. Ireland	11	54 16N	6 35W
Armarkantak, Mt., India	68	22 45N	82 0 E
Armavir, U.S.S.R.	24	45 2N	41 7 E
Armenia, Colombia	78	4 35N	75 45W
Armenia, Salvador	74	13 46N	89 32W
Armenia, S.S.R., U.S.S.R.	24	40 0N	41 0 E
Armentières, France	12	50 40N	2 50 E
Armeria, R., Mexico	74	20 5N	104 5W
Armidale, N.S.W.	43	30 36s	151 40 E
Armour, U.S.A.	70	43 21N	98 24W
Arms, Canada	62	49 34N	86 3W
Armstead, U.S.A.	72	45 1N	112 50W
Armstrong, B.C., Can.	64	50 25N	119 10W
Armstrong, Ont., Can.	62	50 20N	98 0W
Armstrong, U.S.A.	71	27 0N	97 47W
Arnar Fd., Iceland	22	65 45N	23 40W
Arnauti C., Cyprus	30	35 5N	32 20 E
Arnedo, Spain	17	42 12N	2 5W
Arnett, U.S.A.	71	36 5N	99 43W
Arnhem, Netherlands	13	51 58N	5 55 E
Arnhem Ld., N. Terr.	40	13 15s	133 30 E
Arno, Italy	20	43 40N	10 55 E
Arno Bay, S. Australia	45	33 58s	136 35 E
Arnold, New Zealand	47	42 30s	171 22 E
Arnold, U.S.A.	70	41 30N	100 12W
Arnot, Canada	65	55 46N	96 42W
Arnöy, I., Norway	22	70 5N	20 30 E
Arnprior, Canada	62	54 23N	76 25W
Arntfield, Canada	62	48 10N	79 25W
Aroa, Venezuela	75	10 30N	69 0W
Aroab, S.W. Africa	57	26 41s	19 39 E
Arochukuo, Nigeria	52	5 25N	7 50 E
Arona, Italy	20	45 45N	8 32 E
Aros B., Indonesia	34	4 15N	98 22 E
Arosa, Switzerland	15	46 47N	9 41 E
Arrada, Trucial 'Oman	31	22 52N	53 44 E
Arrah, India	33	25 35N	84 32 E
Arraijan, Panama	74	8 56N	79 36W
Arran I., Scotland	10	55 34N	5 12W
Arrandale, Canada	64	54 57N	130 0W
Arras, France	12	50 17N	2 46 E
Arrecife, Canary Is.	50	28 59N	13 40W
Arrée, Mts. d', France	12	48 26N	3 55W
Arriaga, Mexico	74	21 55N	101 23W
Arrilalah, Queensland	42	23 46s	143 49 E
Arrino, W. Australia	44	29 25s	115 33 E
Arrow L., Ireland	11	54 3N	8 20W
Arrow Rock Res., U.S.A.	72	43 40N	115 45W
Arrowhead, Canada	64	50 40N	117 55W
Arrowsmith Mt., N.S.W.	43	30 7s	141 38 E
Arrowsmith, Mt., N.Z.	47	43 18s	170 56 E
Arrowtown, N.Z.	47	44 57s	168 50 E
Arroyo, Spain	17	39 28N	6 38W
Arroyo Grande, U.S.A.	73	35 5N	120 2W
Arroyo Verde, Arg.	77	42 5s	65 10W
Arsenault, L., Canada	65	55 5N	108 50W
Arshan, Mongolia	37	47 10N	120 5 E
Arsikere, India	32	13 15N	76 15 E
Arta, Greece	21	39 8N	21 2 E
Arta, Spain	17	39 40N	3 20 E
Arteaga, Mexico	74	18 50N	102 20W
Artemovsk, U.S.S.R.	25	48 35N	37 55 E
Artemovsk, U.S.S.R.	27	54 45N	93 35 E
Artesia, Bechuanaland	57	24 2s	26 19 E
Artesia, U.S.A.	71	32 48N	104 27W
Artesian, U.S.A.	70	44 2N	97 56W
Artesian Wells, U.S.A.	71	28 16N	99 16W
Arth, Switzerland	15	47 3N	8 32 E
Arthington, Libya	52	6 35N	10 45W
Arthur, Canada	62	43 55N	80 40W
Arthur, Mt., S.Austral.	45	27 25s	136 2 E
Arthur R., Tasmania	43	41 8s	144 45 E
Arthur's P., N.Z.	47	42 54s	171 35 E
Artigas, Uruguay	77	30 20s	56 30W
Artois, reg., France	12	50 20N	2 30 E
Artsa Bogdo, Mongolia	38	44 25N	102 45 E
Artvin, Turkey	30	41 14N	41 44 E
Aru Is., Indonesia	35	6 0s	134 30 E
Arua, Uganda	54	3 1N	30 58 E
Aruba I., Neth. W. Indies	78	12 30N	70 0W
Arumbi, Zaire	53	2 34N	30 2 E
Arun R., England	10	50 48N	0 33W
Arupuni Falls, N.Z.	46	38 24s	176 9 E
Arus, S.W. Africa	57	27 2s	19 5 E
Arusha, Tanzania	53	3 20s	36 40 E
Arusha, prov., Tan.	53	4 0s	36 30 E
Arusha Chini, Tan.	53	38 30s	37 10 E
Aruwimi R., Zaire	54	1 30N	25 0 E
Arvada, U.S.A.	72	44 42N	106 11W
Arvidsjaur, Sweden	22	65 35N	19 10 E
Arvika, Sweden	23	59 42N	12 42 E
Arys, U.S.S.R.	26	42 20N	68 30 E
Arzamas, U.S.S.R.	25	55 27N	43 55 E
Arzgir, U.S.S.R.	25	45 18N	44 23 E
As Salman, Iraq	30	30 30N	44 30 E
As Salt, Jordan	30	32 1N	35 47 E
As Samawah, Iraq	30	31 18N	45 17 E
As Sohar, 'Oman	31	24 20N	56 40 E
As Sulamāniyah, Iraq	30	35 38N	45 28 E
As Sulman, Iraq	31	30 30N	44 30 E
As Summan, Si. Arabia	30	23 0N	48 30 E
As Summan Des., Saudi Arabia	30	27 0N	47 0 E
As Suwaih, 'Oman	31	22 10N	59 33 E
As Suwayda, Syria	30	32 42N	36 33 E
As Suwayrah, Iraq	30	32 55N	44 47 E
As Suways. *See* Suez, Egypt.	51		
Asa, Nigeria	52	4 59N	7 20 E
Asab, Ethiopia	57	13 0N	42 40 E
Asaba, Nigeria	52	6 12N	6 38 E
Asafo, Ghana	52	6 20N	2 40W
Asahi Dake, Japan	36	43 40N	143 0 E
Asahigawa, Japan	36	43 45N	142 30 E
Asamankese, Ghana	52	5 50N	0 40W
Asangaro, Peru	78	14 55s	70 10W
Asani, Congo	53	4 35s	28 59 E
Asankrangwa, Ghana	52	5 45N	2 30W
Asansol, India	33	23 40N	87 1 E
Asara, Nigeria	52	13 30N	5 10 E
Asbestos, Canada	63	45 47N	71 58W
Asbestos Mts., C. Prov.	57	29 0s	23 0 E
Ascención, Bolivia	78	15 30s	61 40W
Ascension, B. de la, Mexico	74	20 20N	87 20W
Ascension I., Atlantic Ocean	5	8 0s	14 15W
Aschaffenburg, Ger.	14	49 58N	9 8 E
Ascoli Piceno, Italy	20	42 51N	13 34 E
Ascope, Peru	78	7 50s	79 0W
Asela, Ethiopia	54	8 0N	39 0 E
Asenovgrad, Bulgaria	21	42 1N	24 51 E
Ash Grove, U.S.A.	71	37 19N	93 34W
Ash Shabakah, Iraq	30	30 49N	43 39 E
Ash Shāmiyah, Iraq	30	31 57N	44 36 E
Ash Sharmah, Saudi Arabia	30	28 4N	35 13 E
Ash Shatrah, Iraq	30	31 25N	46 10 E
Ash Shinas, 'Oman	31	24 40N	56 29 E
Ash Shu 'aybah, Saudi Arabia	30	27 55N	43 0 E
Ashaira, Saudi Arabia	30	21 40N	40 40 E
Ashanti, Ghana	52	7 30N	2 0W
Ashburn, U.S.A.	69	31 42N	83 40W
Ashburton, N.Z.	47	43 53s	171 48 E
Ashburton Downs, W. Australia	44	23 28s	117 18 E
Ashburton R., N.Z.	47	44 3s	171 50 E
Ashburton, R., W. Australia	44	22 5s	115 0 E
Ashcroft, Canada	64	50 40N	121 20W
Ashdod, Israel	29	31 46N	34 39 E
Ashdot Ya'aqov, Israel	29	32 39N	35 35 E
Asheboro, U.S.A.	69	35 43N	79 46W
Ashern, Canada	65	51 40N	98 25W
Asherton, U.S.A.	71	28 26N	99 14W
Asheville, U.S.A.	69	35 30N	82 30W
Asheweig R., Canada	62	54 0N	88 0W
Ashford, England	10	51 8N	0 53 E
Ashford, U.S.A.	72	46 45N	122 3W
Ashfork, U.S.A.	73	35 15N	112 31W
Ashhurst, New Zealand	46	40 17s	175 45 E
Ashikaga, Japan	36	36 28N	139 29 E
Asilah, Morocco	50	35 29N	6 0W
Ashizuri C., Japan	36	32 40N	133 0 E
Ashkhabad, U.S.S.R.	26	38 0N	57 50 E
Ashland, Kan., U.S.A.	71	37 10N	99 45W
Ashland, Ky, U.S.A.	68	38 25N	82 40W
Ashland, Neb., U.S.A.	70	41 8N	96 24W
Ashland, Ohio, U.S.A.	68	40 52N	82 20W
Ashland, Oreg., U.S.A.	72	42 11N	122 40W
Ashland, Wis., U.S.A.	70	46 40N	90 52W
Ashley, U.S.A.	70	46 4N	99 23W
Ashley R., N.Z.	47	43 8s	172 14 E
Ashmont, Canada	64	54 7N	111 29W
Ashqelon, Israel	29	31 40N	34 35 E
Ashtabula, U.S.A.	68	41 52N	80 50W
Ashti, India	32	18 50N	75 15 E
Ashton, Cape Province	57	33 50s	20 5 E
Ashton, U.S.A.	72	44 2N	111 29W
Ashuapmuchuan R., Can	62	49 0N	73 10W
Asia Is., Indonesia	35	1 0N	131 13 E
Asifabad, India	32	19 25N	79 25 E
Asikuma, Ghana	52	6 30N	0 12 E
Asinara, G. of, Italy	20	41 0N	8 30 E
Asinara I., Italy	20	41 5N	8 15 E
Asino, U.S.S.R.	26	57 0N	86 0 E
Asir, Saudi Arabia	48	18 40N	42 30 E
Asira esh Shamaliya, Jordan	29	32 15N	35 16 E
Askeaton, Ireland	11	52 37N	8 58W
Askersund, Sweden	23	58 58N	14 8 E

	MAP		
Askham, England	57	54 37N	2 45W
Askim, Norway	23	59 33N	11 10 E
Askira, Nigeria	52	10 43N	13 1 E
Asmar, Afghanistan	31	35 10N	71 27 E
Aso, Japan	36	32 0N	132 0 E
Aspen, U.S.A.	73	39 13N	106 48W
Aspermont, U.S.A.	71	33 8N	100 14W
Aspiring Mt., N.Z.	47	44 23N	168 46 E
Asquith, Canada	65	52 20N	107 10W
Assaikio, Nigeria	52	8 34N	8 55 E
Assam, st., India	33	25 45N	92 30 E
Asse, Belgium	13	50 54N	4 12 E
Assen, Netherlands	13	53 0N	6 35 E
Assens, Denmark	23	55 16N	9 52 E
Assiniboia, Canada	65	49 40N	106 0W
Assiniboine Mt., Can.	64	50 50N	115 45W
Assiniboine R., Canada	65	49 45N	99 0W
Assinica, L., Canada	62	50 30N	75 20W
Assinie, Ivory Coast	50	5 9N	3 17W
Assinika L., Canada	62	50 30N	75 20W
Assis, Brazil	77	22 40S	50 20W
Assisi, Italy	20	43 4N	12 36 E
Astara, U.S.S.R.	30	38 30N	48 50 E
Asti, Italy	20	44 54N	8 11 E
Astipalaia I., Greece	21	36 32N	26 22 E
Astola, I., W. Pakistan	31	25 9N	63 47 E
Astorga, Spain	17	42 29N	6 8W
Astoria, U.S.A.	72	46 16N	123 50W
Astra, Argentina	77	45 40S	67 35W
Astrakhan, U.S.S.R.	25	46 25N	48 5 E
Astudillo, Spain	17	42 12N	4 22W
Asturias, Spain	17	43 50N	6 0W
Asunción, Paraguay	77	25 11S	57 30W
Aswa, R., Uganda	53	2 10N	30 20 E
Aswan, Egypt	51	24 4N	32 57 E
Aswan Dam, Egypt	51	24 5N	32 54 E
Asyut, Egypt	51	27 11N	31 4 E
At Tafilah, Jordan	30	30 49N	35 33 E
Atacama Desert, Chile	77	24 0S	69 20W
Atakpame, Togo	52	7 31N	1 13 E
Atalandi, Greece	21	38 39N	22 58 E
Atalaya, Peru	78	10 45S	73 50W
Atami, Japan	36	35 6N	139 0W
Atapupu, Indonesia	35	9 5S	124 55 E
Atar, Mauritania	50	20 30N	13 5W
Atara, U.S.S.R.	27	63 10N	129 10 E
Atascadero, U.S.A.	73	35 30N	120 40W
Atasuski, U.S.S.R.	26	48 20N	71 0 E
Atauro I., Port. Timor	35	8 10S	125 30 E
Atbara, Sudan	51	17 50N	34 3 E
Atbara R., Sudan	51	16 30N	35 20 E
Ath Thamami, Saudi Arabia	30	27 43N	45 1 E
Atbasar, U.S.S.R.	26	51 50N	68 25 E
Atchafalaya B., U.S.A.	71	29 30N	91 20W
Atchison, U.S.A.	70	39 40N	95 0W
Atebubu, Ghana	52	7 47N	1 0W
Athabaska, Canada	64	54 45N	113 20W
Athabaska L., Canada	65	59 10N	109 30W
Athabaska R., Canada	64	55 50N	112 40W
Athboy, Ireland	11	53 37N	6 55W
Athea, Ireland	11	52 27N	9 18W
Athenai. *See* Athens.	21		
Athenry, Ireland	11	53 18N	8 45W
Athens, Greece	21	37 58N	23 46 E
Athens, Ala., U.S.A.	69	34 49N	86 58W
Athens, Ga., U.S.A.	69	34 0N	83 30W
Athens, Ohio, U.S.A.	68	39 22N	82 6W
Athens, Tex., U.S.A.	71	32 12N	95 47W
Atherton, Queensland	42	17 17S	145 30 E
Athi, R., Kenya	53	2 15S	38 0 E
Athieme, Dahomey	52	6 37N	1 40 E
Athleague, Ireland	11	53 34N	8 17W
Athlone, Ireland	11	53 26N	7 57W
Athol, New Zealand	47	45 30S	168 35 E
Athol, U.S.A.	69	42 37N	72 12W
Atholville, Canada	63	48 5N	67 5W
Athos, Mt., Greece	21	40 9N	24 22 E
Athy, Ireland	11	53 0N	7 0W
Ati, Sudan	51	13 5N	29 2 E
Atiak, Uganda	53	3 25N	32 5 E
Atiavi, Ghana	52	6 50N	0 50 E
Atico, Peru	78	16 20S	73 42W
Atikokan, Canada	62	48 40N	91 40W
Atikonak, L., Canada	63	53 45N	64 30W
Atiumuri, New Zealand	46	38 24S	176 5 E
Atka, Aleutian Is.	59	52 14N	174 15W
Atka I., Aleutian Is.	59	52 5N	174 40W
Atkarsk, U.S.S.R.	25	51 55N	45 2 E
Atkasuk (Meade R.), Alaska	59	70 30N	157 20W
Atkinson, U.S.A.	70	42 33N	98 59W
Atlanta, Ark., U.S.A.	71	33 6N	94 13W
Atlanta, Ga., U.S.A.	69	33 50N	84 15W
Atlantic, U.S.A.	70	41 23N	95 0W
Atlantic City, U.S.A.	68	39 25N	74 25W
Atlantic Ocean	6	0 0	20 0W
Atlin, Canada	64	59 40N	133 40W
Atlin L., Canada	64	59 30N	133 50W
Atlit, Israel	29	32 42N	34 56 E
Atlit (site), Israel	29	32 42N	34 55 E
Atmore, U.S.A.	69	31 2N	87 30W
Atnarko, Canada	64	52 25N	126 0W
Atocha, Bolivia	78	21 0S	66 10W
Atoka, U.S.A.	71	34 21N	96 8W
Atotonilco, Mexico	74	20 20N	98 40W
Atouguia, Portugal	17	39 21N	9 17W
Atoyac, Mexico	74	17 10N	100 30W
Atrak R., Persia	31	38 0N	56 0 E
Atrato R., Colombia	78	7 10N	76 50W
Atsoum, Mts., Cam.	52	7 0N	12 30 E
Atsuta, Japan	36	43 39N	141 30 E
Attalla, U.S.A.	69	34 2N	86 5W
Attanagh, Ireland	11	52 50N	7 19W
Attawapiskat L., Can.	62	52 20N	88 0W
Attawapiskat Town & R., Canada	62	53 10N	85 30W
Attica, U.S.A.	68	40 20N	87 15W
Attikamagen L., Can.	63	54 54N	66 25W
Attil, Jordan	29	32 23N	35 4 E
Attleboro, U.S.A.	69	41 56N	71 18W
Attock, Pakistan	32	33 52N	72 20 E
Attopeu, Laos	34	14 56N	106 50 E
Attu, Aleutian Is.	59	52 55N	173 11 E
Attu I., Aleutian Is.	59	52 55N	173 0 E
Attur, India	32	11 35N	78 30 E
Atuel R., Argentina	77	35 30S	67 30W
Atures, Venezuela	78	5 30N	68 5W
Atvidaberg, Sweden	23	58 13N	16 5 E
Atwater, U.S.A.	73	37 24N	120 35W
Atwood, U.S.A.	70	39 51N	101 1W
Au Sable, R., U.S.A.	68	44 45N	84 0W
Aual Ghinda, Ethiopia	53	4 15N	40 15 E
Auasberg, mt., S.W. Afr.	57	23 0S	17 20 E
Aubagne, France	12	43 17N	5 37 E
Aubel R., and dept., Fr.	12	48 34N	4 0 E
Aubenas, France	12	44 37N	4 24 E
Aubigny, France	12	47 30N	2 24 E
Aubin, France	12	44 33N	2 15 E
Auburn, Queensland	43	25 58S	150 35 E
Auburn, Cal., U.S.A.	73	38 57N	121 5W
Auburn, Ind., U.S.A.	68	41 20N	85 0W
Auburn, Nebr., U.S.A.	70	40 25N	95 50W
Auburn, N.Y., U.S.A.	69	42 57N	76 39W
Auburndale, U.S.A.	69	28 5N	81 45W
Aubusson, France	12	45 57N	2 11 E
Auch, France	12	43 39N	0 36 E
Auchi, Nigeria	52	7 6N	6 13 E
Auckland, N.Z.	46	36 52S	174 46 E
Auckland, prov., N.Z.	46	38 0S	176 0 E
Auckland Is., S. Ocean	5	51 0S	166 0 E
Aude R., France	12	42 47N	2 9 E
Auden, Canada	62	50 17N	87 54W
Audierne, France	12	48 1N	4 34W
Audubon, U.S.A.	70	41 40N	94 59W
Augathella, Queens.	43	26 2S	146 29 E
Augher, N. Ireland	11	54 25N	7 10W
Aughnacloy, N. Ireland	11	54 25N	7 0W
Aughrim, Clare, Ire.	11	53 0N	8 57W
Aughrim, Wicklow, Ire.	11	52 52N	6 20W
Augrabies Falls, Cape Province	57	28 35S	20 20 E
Augsburg, Germany	14	48 22N	10 54 E
Augusta, Italy	20	37 14N	15 12 E
Augusta, Ark., U.S.A.	71	35 15N	91 28W
Augusta, Ga., U.S.A.	69	33 29N	81 59W
Augusta, Kan., U.S.A.	71	37 39N	97 0W
Augusta, Mont., U.S.A.	72	47 30N	112 28W
Augusta, S.C., U.S.A.	69	33 35N	82 0W
Augusta, Wis., U.S.A.	70	44 38N	91 5W
Augusta L., Australia	45	26 44S	122 32 E
Augustow, Poland	16	53 52N	23 2 E
Augustus, I., W. Australia	44	15 15S	124 28 E
Augustus, Mt., W. Australia	44	24 14S	116 48 E
Auja R., Jordan	29	31 58N	35 22 E
Auld, L., W. Australia	45	22 30S	123 43 E
Aul Isac Gilible, Somali Republic	53	2 0N	42 0 E
Ault, U.S.A.	70	40 40N	104 46W
Aumale, France	12	49 45N	1 42 E
Auna, Nigeria	52	10 9N	4 42 E
Aunis, France	12	46 0N	0 50W
Auob, R., S.W. Africa	57	26 0S	19 55 E
Auraiya, India	32	26 27N	79 31 E
Aurangabad, Bihar, India	33	24 45N	84 18 E
Aurangabad, Maharashtra, India	32	19 50N	75 23 E
Auray, France	12	47 40N	3 0W
Aurillac, France	12	44 45N	2 26 E
Auronza, Italy	20	46 33N	12 27 E
Aurora, Canada	68	44 0N	79 30W
Aurora, C. Prov.	57	32 40S	18 29 E
Aurora, Colo., U.S.A.	70	39 47N	104 56W
Aurora, Ill., U.S.A.	70	41 44N	88 25W
Aurora, Minn., U.S.A.	70	40 54N	98 0W
Aurora, Mo., U.S.A.	71	36 59N	93 45W
Aus, S.W. Africa	57	26 35S	16 12 E
Ausangate, Nevada, mt., Peru	78	13 49N	71 15 E
Aust-Agder, Norway	23	58 45N	8 30 E
Austin, Minn., U.S.A.	70	43 51N	92 58W
Austin, Texas, U.S.A.	71	30 20N	97 45W
Austin, W. Australia	44	27 40S	117 50 E
Austin, L., W. Australia	44	27 40S	118 0 E
Austral Downs, N. Terr.	41	20 32S	137 33 E
Austral Is., Pacific Oc.	6	23 25S	148 30W
Australia, Commonwealth of	40–41	10 35S to 43 38S	114 0 E to 153 40 E
Australian Alps	43	36 30S	148 8 E
Australian Cap. Terr.	42	35 15S	149 8 E
Austria, rep., Europe	14	46 28N to 49 0N	9 32 E to 17 10 E
Austvågöy, I., Norway	22	68 25N	14 45 E
Autlan, Mexico	74	19 40N	104 30W
Autun, France	12	46 58N	4 17 E
Auvergne, Monts d', Fr.	12	45 0N	3 0 E
Auxerre, France	12	47 48N	3 32 E
Auxonne, France	12	47 10N	5 20 E
Auzances, France	12	46 2N	2 30 E
Avakubi, Zaire	54	1 16N	27 30 E
Avallon, France	12	47 30N	3 53 E
Avalon Pen., Canada	63	47 0N	53 20W
Avalon Res., U.S.A.	68	32 28N	103 14W
Aveiro, Brazil	79	3 10S	55 5W
Aveiro, Portugal	17	40 37N	8 38W
Avej, Iran	30	35 40N	49 15 E
Avellaneda, Argentina	77	34 50S	58 10W
Avellino, Italy	20	40 54N	14 46 E
Avenches, Switzerland	15	46 53N	7 3 E
Aversa, Italy	20	40 58N	14 11 E
Avery, U.S.A.	72	47 19N	115 50W
Aves I., Leeward Is.	75	15 40N	63 40W
Aves Is., Venezuela	78	12 0N	67 40W
Avesta, Sweden	23	60 9N	16 8 E
Avezzano, Italy	20	42 2N	13 24 E
Aviá Terai, Argentina	77	26 45S	60 50W
Avigliano, Italy	20	40 44N	15 41 E
Avignon, France	12	43 57N	4 50 E
Avila, Spain	17	40 39N	4 43W
Aviles, Spain	17	43 35N	5 57W
Avoca, Tasmania	43	41 53S	148 0 E
Avoca, R., Ireland	11	52 50N	6 10W
Avoca, R., Victoria	43	35 50S	143 30 E
Ávola, Canada	64	51 45N	119 30W
Avola, Italy	20	36 56N	15 7 E
Avon, U.S.A.	70	43 1N	98 3W
Avon, R., Hants., Eng.	10	50 57N	1 45W
Avon R., War., Eng.	10	52 23N	1 30W
Avon, R., Wilts., Eng.	10	51 22N	2 20W
Avon, R., Worcs., Eng.	10	52 8N	1 53W
Avon, R., W. Australia	44	32 0S	116 55 E
Avon Downs, Queens.	42	21 50S	137 16 E
Avon Downs, N. Terr.	41	19 59S	137 28 E
Avonlea, Canada	65	50 0N	105 0W
Avontuur, C. Prov.	57	33 43S	23 9 E
Avranches, France	12	48 40N	1 20W
Awarta, Jordan	29	32 10N	35 17 E
Awaro, Lak, Wadi, Ken.	53	1 6N	40 50 E
Awarua Pt., N.Z.	47	44 15S	168 5 E
Awash, Ethiopia	54	9 8N	40 7 E
Awaso, Ghana	52	6 15N	2 22W
Awatere, R., N.Z.	47	41 55S	173 35 E
Awbari, Libya	51	26 55N	12 50 E
Awe, Nigeria	52	8 10N	9 8 E
Awe, L., Scotland	10	56 15N	5 15W
Awgu, Nigeria	52	6 4N	7 24 E
Awjilah, Libya	51	29 8N	21 7 E
Awka, Nigeria	52	6 12N	7 5 E
Awunaga, Ghana	52	5 41N	0 53 E
Ax, France	12	42 43N	1 50 E
Axar Fd., Iceland	22	66 20N	16 45W
Axe Hill, W. Australia	45	26 25N	126 44 E
Axel Heiberg I., Can.	58	80 0N	90 0W
Axim, Ghana	52	4 51N	2 15W
Ay, France	12	49 3N	4 0 E
Ayabe, Japan	36	35 27N	135 20 E
Ayacucho, Argentina	78	37 5S	58 20W
Ayacucho, Peru	77	13 0S	74 0W
Ayaguz, U.S.S.R.	26	48 10N	80 0 E
Ayamonte, Spain	17	37 12N	7 24W
Ayan, U.S.S.R.	27	56 30N	138 16 E
Ayaviri, Peru	78	14 50S	70 35W
Ayeritam, Malaya	34	5 24N	100 18 E
Ayios Evstratios I., Gr.	21	39 34N	24 58 E
Aylesbury, Canada	65	50 57N	105 51W
Aylesbury, England	10	51 48N	0 49W
Aylmer L., Canada	60	64 0N	109 0W
Ayn' Zuwayyah, Libya	51	21 30N	24 58 E
Ayos, Cameroon	52	3 58N	12 30 E
Ayr, Queensland	42	19 35S	147 25 E
Ayr, Scotland	10	55 28N	4 37W
Ayre, Pt. of, Isle of Man	10	54 27N	4 21W
Ayrshire Downs, Queensland	42	22 0S	142 41 E
Ayton, Queensland	42	15 45S	145 25 E
Ayun, Saudi Arabia	31	26 30N	43 50 E
Ayutla, Mexico	74	16 58N	99 17W
Ayutthaya, Siam	34	14 25N	100 30 E
Ayvalik, Turkey	30	39 20N	26 46 E
Az Zagazig, Egypt	51	30 40N	31 12 E
Az Zahrān, Si. Arabia	30	26 15N	50 7 E
Az Zubayr, Iraq	30	30 22N	47 43 E
Azamgarh, India	33	26 35N	83 13 E
Azaouak, Sudan	52	15 56N	3 25 E
Azapa, Chile	78	18 40S	17 15W
Azara, Nigeria	52	8 25N	9 9 E
Azare, Nigeria	52	11 55N	10 10 E
Azerbaijan, Iran	30	38 0N	46 30 E
Azerbaijan S.S.R., U.S.S.R.	24	40 20N	48 0 E
Azile, Zaire	53	3 32N	29 53 E
Azogues, Ecuador	78	2 35S	78 0W
Azor, Israel	29	32 2N	34 48 E
Azores Is., N. Atlantic	5	38 44N	29 0W
Azov, U.S.S.R.	25	47 3N	39 25 E
Azov, Sea of, U.S.S.R.	25	46 0N	36 30 E
Azovy, U.S.S.R.	26	64 55N	64 35 E
Azpeitia, Spain	17	43 12N	2 19W
Aztec, U.S.A.	73	36 51N	107 59W
Azua, Dom. Rep.	75	18 25N	70 44W
Azuaga, Spain	17	38 16N	5 39W
Azuero Pen., Panama	73	7 30N	80 30W
Azul, Argentina	77	36 42S	59 43W

B

	MAP		
Ba Labakk, Lebanon	30	34 10N	13 13 E
Baa, Indonesia	35	10 50S	123 0 E
Baalbek, Lebanon	30	34 2N	36 14 E
Baarle Nassau, Belgium	13	51 27N	4 56 E
Baarn, Netherlands	13	52 12N	5 17 E
Bab el Mandeb Str., Red Sea	30	12 35N	43 25 E
Babac I., Indonesia	35	7 50S	129 45 E
Babahoyo, Ecuador	78	1 40S	79 30W
Babakin, W. Australia	44	32 11S	117 52 E
Babana, Nigeria	52	10 31N	5 9 E
Babanango, Natal	57	28 21S	31 3 E
Babanusa, Sudan	54	12 0N	27 50 E
Babati, Tanzania	53	4 11S	35 46 E
Babayevo, U.S.S.R.	25	59 24N	35 55 E
Babb, U.S.A.	72	48 57N	113 29W
Babimbi, Cameroon	52	4 27N	10 55 E
Babinda, Queensland	42	17 27S	146 0 E
Babine L. & R., Can.	64	54 40N	126 10W
Babo, Indonesia	35	2 30S	133 30 E
Babol, Iran	31	36 45N	52 40 E
Babol Sar, Iran	31	36 50N	52 40 E
Baboma, Zaire	53	2 30N	27 30 E
Babura, Nigeria	52	12 51N	8 59 E
Babuyan Is., Phil.	35	19 20N	121 25 E
Babylon, site of, Iraq	30	32 40N	44 30 E
Bac Kan, Viet Nam	34	22 13N	105 55 E
Bac Lieu, Viet Nam	34	9 5N	105 10 E
Bac Ninh, Viet Nam	39	21 19N	105 53 E
Bac Quang, Viet Nam	34	22 15N	105 10 E
Bacabel, Brazil	79	5 20S	56 45W
Bacău, Rumania	21	46 35N	26 55 E
Baccarat, France	12	48 28N	6 42 E
Bacchus Marsh, Vic.	43	37 38S	144 25 E
Bacerac, Mexico	74	30 20N	109 0W
Bachelina, U.S.S.R.	26	57 45N	67 20 E
Back R., Canada	60	65 10N	104 0W
Baclieu, Viet Nam	34	9 20N	105 45 E
Bacolod, Philippines	35	10 50N	123 0 E
Bacuit, Philippines	35	11 20N	119 20 E
Bad R., U.S.A.	70	44 10N	100 50W
Bad Axe, U.S.A.	68	43 48N	82 59W
Bad Hersfeld, Germany	14	50 53N	9 43 E
Bad Ischl, Austria	14	47 43N	13 38 E
Bad Kissingen, Ger.	14	50 12N	10 5 E
Bad Lands, U.S.A.	70	43 40N	102 30W
Bad Ragaz, Switzerland	15	47 1N	9 30 E
Badagara, India	32	11 35N	75 40 E
Badagri, Nigeria	52	6 11N	3 1 E
Badajoz, Spain	17	38 50N	6 59W
Badalona, Spain	17	41 26N	2 15 E
Badalzai, Afghanistan	31	29 59N	65 36 E
Badampahar, India	33	22 10N	86 15 E
Badanah, Saudi Arabia	30	30 58N	41 30 E
Badas Is., Indonesia	34	0 45N	107 5 E
Baddo R., Pakistan	32	28 15N	65 0 E
Badeggi, Nigeria	52	9 1N	6 8W
Baden, Austria	14	48 1N	16 13 E
Baden, Germany	14	48 45N	8 17 E
Baden, Switzerland	15	47 28N	8 18 E
Baden Wurttemberg, land, Germany	14	48 33N	9 0 E
Badgastein, Austria	14	47 8N	13 8 E
Badger, Canada	63	49 0N	56 4W
Badin, Pakistan	32	24 38N	68 54 E
Badnera, India	32	20 50N	77 47 E
Badrah, Iraq	30	33 8N	45 55 E
Badrao, Afghanistan	31	34 49N	69 41 E
Badrinath, India	32	30 45N	79 30 E
Badulla, Sri Lanka	32	7 1N	81 7 E
Baena, Spain	17	37 37N	4 20W
Baeza, Spain	17	37 57N	3 25W
Bafang, Cameroon	51	5 10N	10 5 E
Bafata, Port. Guinea	50	12 8N	15 20 E
Baffin Bay, Canada	61	72 0N	65 0W
Baffin I., Canada	61	68 0N	77 0W
Bafia, Cameroon	52	4 40N	11 10 E
Bafilo, Togo	52	9 22N	1 22 E
Bafing, R., Guinea	50	12 0N	10 30W
Bafoulabe, Sudan	50	13 50N	10 55W
Bafoussam, Cameroon	52	5 31N	10 25 E
Bafq, Iran	31	31 40N	55 20 E
Bafra, Turkey	30	41 34N	35 56 E
Bafra-burnu C., Turkey	30	41 40N	36 0 E
Baft, Iran	31	29 15N	56 38 E
Bafut, W. Cam.	52	6 6N	10 2 E
Bafwasende, Zaire	54	1 20N	27 0 E
Bagaces, Costa Rica	78	10 31N	85 18W
Bagalkot, India	32	16 10N	75 40 E
Bagam, Cameroon	52	5 42N	10 18 E
Bagam, Niger	52	15 38N	6 31 E
Bagam Siapiapi, Indon.	34	2 15N	101 0 E
Bagamoyo, Tan.	53	6 30N	38 57 E
Bagbele, Zaire	53	4 22N	29 18 E
Bagé, Brazil	77	31 22N	54 6W
Baggs, U.S.A.	72	41 2N	107 45W
Baghdad, Iraq	30	33 20N	44 30 E
Bagheria, Italy	20	38 5N	13 30 E
Baghin, Iran	31	30 12N	56 45 E
Baghlan, Afghanistan	31	36 12N	69 0 E
Bagley, U.S.A.	70	47 32N	95 27W
Baglintang I., Phil.	35	19 50N	122 10 E
Bagnères de Bigorre, Fr.	12	43 5N	0 9 E
Bagnères Luchon, Fr.	12	42 47N	0 38 E
Bagotville, Canada	63	48 22N	70 54W
Bagrash Kol, China	37	42 0N	87 0 E

Place	Map	Lat.	Long.
Baguio, Philippines	35	16 26N	120 34 E
Bahama Is., W. Indies	75	24 40N	74 0W
Bahan, Malaya	34	2 48N	102 26 E
Bahawalnagar, Pak.	32	30 0N	73 15 E
Bahawalpur, Pak.	32	29 37N	71 40 E
Bahia, Is. de la, Hond.	75	16 45N	86 15W
Bahia. *See* Salvador, Brazil	79		
Bahia, st., Brazil	79	12 0S	42 0 E
Bahia Blanca, Arg.	77	38 35S	62 13W
Bahia Laura, Arg.	77	48 10S	66 30W
Bahia Negra, Paraguay	79	20 5S	58 5W
Bahias, C. dos, Arg.	77	45 0S	65 40W
Bahr al Milb L., Iraq	30	32 40N	43 40 E
Bahr el 'Arab, Sudan	51	10 0N	26 0 E
Bahr el Ghazal (Soro) W., Chad.	54	15 0N	17 10 E
Bahr el Jebel R., Sud.	54	7 30N	30 30 E
Bahraich, India	33	27 38N	81 50 E
Bahrain I., Persian Gulf	31	26 0N	50 35 E
Bahramabad, Iran	31	30 28N	56 2 E
Bahu Solo, Indonesia	35	3 15S	122 10 E
Baia-de-Arama, Rum.	21	44 59N	22 48 E
Baia-Mare, Rumania	20	47 40N	23 37 E
Baião, Brazil	79	2 50S	49 15W
Baie Comeau, Canada	63	49 12N	68 10W
Baie de la Trinité, Can.	63	49 25N	67 20W
Baie Johan Beetz, Can.	63	50 18N	62 50W
Baie Verte, Canada	63	49 55N	56 12W
Baiji, Iraq	30	35 0N	43 30 E
Baikal L., U.S.S.R.	27	53 0N	108 0 E
Baikit, U.S.S.R.	27	61 50N	95 50 E
Baikonur, U.S.S.R.	26	47 48N	65 50 E
Baile Atha Cliath (Dublin)	11	53 20N	6 18W
Bailen, Spain	17	38 8N	3 48W
Bailey Ra., W. Austral.	45	28 18S	123 0 E
Bailieborough, Ireland	11	53 55N	7 0W
Bailugh, Afghanistan	31	32 47N	66 59 E
Bainbridge, Ga., U.S.A.	69	31 0N	84 40W
Bainville, U.S.A.	70	48 7N	104 6W
Baird, U.S.A.	71	32 27N	99 25W
Baird Inlet, Alaska	59	61 0N	164 0W
Baird Mts., Alaska	59	67 40N	160 0W
Bairnsdale, Victoria	43	37 43S	147 35 E
Baise R., France	12	43 37N	0 23 E
Baitadi, Nepal	32	29 35N	80 25 E
Baixo Alentejo, prov., Portugal	17	38 0N	8 0W
Baja, Hungary	16	46 12N	18 59 E
Baja Pta., Mexico	74	29 50N	116 0W
Baja California Norte, Mexico	74	30 0N	117 0W
Baja California Sur, Mexico	74	25 45N	113 30W
Bajo Boquete, Panama	75	8 50N	82 30W
Bajo Nuevo I., Car. Sea	75	15 45N	78 40W
Bajoga, Nigeria	52	10 57N	11 12 E
Bakel, Central Africa	50	14 56N	12 20W
Baker, Calif., U.S.A.	73	35 15N	116 2W
Baker, Mont., U.S.A.	70	46 27N	104 15W
Baker, Nev., U.S.A.	73	38 58N	114 7W
Baker, Oreg., U.S.A.	72	44 45N	117 51W
Baker, L., Canada	60	64 0N	97 0W
Baker Lake, Canada	60	64 35N	97 10W
Baker L., W. Austral.	45	26 52S	126 9 E
Baker, Mt., U.S.A.	72	48 50N	121 0W
Bakersfield, U.S.A.	73	35 27N	119 0W
Bakhchisarai, U.S.S.R.	25	44 40N	33 45 E
Bakhmach, U.S.S.R.	25	51 10N	32 45 E
Bakkaflói, B., Iceland	22	66 10N	15 0W
Bakkagerdi, Iceland	22	65 33N	13 58W
Bakkalfjördur, Iceland	22	66 5N	15 10W
Bakony For., Hungary	16	47 20N	17 40 E
Bakor, Gambia	52	12 59N	10 15W
Bakori, Nigeria	52	11 34N	7 25 E
Baksai, U.S.S.R.	24	47 40N	51 20 E
Baku, U.S.S.R.	24	40 25N	49 45 E
Bakundi, Nigeria	52	8 2N	10 42 E
Bal'a, Jordan	29	32 20N	35 6 E
Bala, U.S.S.R.	27	66 45N	133 0 E
Balabac I., Philippines	35	8 0N	117 0 E
Balabalangan I., Indon.	35	7 5S	118 15 E
Balaghat, India	32	21 49N	80 12 E
Balaghat Ra., India	32	18 50N	76 30 E
Balaguer, Spain	17	41 50N	0 50 E
Balaka, Malawi	56	14 57S	34 55 E
Balaklava, S. Austral.	43	34 7S	138 22 E
Balaklava, U.S.S.R.	25	44 30N	33 30 E
Balakovo, U.S.S.R.	25	52 4N	47 55 E
Balambangan I., Sabah	35	7 17N	116 57 E
Balancan, Mexico	74	17 49N	91 32W
Balanda, U.S.S.R.	25	51 30N	44 40 E
Balangan I., Indonesia	35	2 20S	117 30 E
Balashov, U.S.S.R.	25	51 30N	43 10 E
Balasore, India	33	21 35N	87 3 E
Balassagyarmat, Hung.	16	48 4N	19 15 E
Balate, Mozambique	56	22 50S	34 29 E
Balaton, L., Hungary	16	46 50N	17 40 E
Balatonszentgyörgy, Hungary	16	46 41N	17 19 E
Balboa, Panama	74	9 0N	79 30W
Balboa Hill, Panama Canal Zone	74	9 6N	79 44W
Balbriggan, Ireland	11	53 35N	6 10W
Balbuna, Queensland	43	27 56S	146 20 E
Balcarce, Argentina	77	38 0S	58 10W
Balcarres, Canada	65	50 50N	103 35W

Place	Map	Lat.	Long.
Balchik, Bulgaria	21	43 28N	28 11 E
Balclutha, N.Z.	47	46 15S	169 45 E
Bald Knob, U.S.A.	71	35 17N	91 32W
Bald Pk., U.S.A.	71	30 45N	104 15W
Baldegger See, Switz.	15	47 13N	8 16 E
Baldock, L., Canada	65	50 30N	102 25W
Baldwin, Fla., U.S.A.	69	30 15N	82 10W
Baldwin, Mich., U.S.A.	68	43 54N	85 53W
Baldwin, N.Y., U.S.A.	68	43 48N	73 28W
Baldwinsville, U.S.A.	68	43 10N	76 19W
Baldzhikan, U.S.S.R.	27	49 20N	110 30 E
Balearic Is., Spain	17	39 30N	3 0 E
Balfouriya, Israel	29	32 38N	35 18 E
Bali, W. Cam.	52	5 54N	10 0 E
Bali I., Indonesia	7	8 20S	115 0 E
Bali, Selat, str., Indon.	34	8 30S	114 25 E
Balia, Sierra Leone	52	9 22N	11 1W
Balikesir, Turkey	30	39 35N	27 58 E
Balikpapan, Indonesia	35	1 10S	116 55 E
Baling, Malaya	34	5 41N	100 55 E
Balintang Chan., Phil.	35	19 50N	122 0 E
Balipara, India	33	26 50N	92 45 E
Balisa, Brazil	79	16 0S	52 20W
Baljennie, Canada	65	52 33N	107 54W
Balkan Mts. (Stara Planina), Bulgaria	21	42 40N	25 0 E
Balkan Pen.	21	44 0N to 36 0N	
		18 0 E to 28 0 E	
Balkh (Wazirabad), Afghanistan	31	36 44N	66 47 E
Balkhash, U.S.S.R.	26	46 50N	74 50 E
Balkhash, L., U.S.S.R.	26	46 0N	74 50 E
Balla, Ireland	11	53 47N	9 8W
Balla Balla, Rhod.	56	20 28S	29 2 E
Balla Balla, W. Austral.	44	20 40S	117 45 E
Balladonia, W. Australia	45	32 20S	123 45 E
Ballaghaderreen, Ire.	11	53 55N	8 35W
Ballale, Ethiopia	53	4 33N	38 55 E
Ballanagare, Ireland	11	53 56N	8 22W
Ballara, Queensland	42	20 57S	139 58 E
Ballarat, Victoria	43	37 33S	143 50 E
Ballard, L., W. Austral.	44	29 20S	120 10 E
Ballater, Scotland	10	57 2N	3 2W
Ballenas Chan., Mexico	74	29 10N	113 45W
Balleny Is., S. Ocean	80	66 30S	163 0 E
Ballia, India	33	25 46N	84 12 E
Ballidu, W. Australia	43	30 33S	116 38 E
Ballina, Mayo, Ireland	11	54 7N	9 10W
Ballina, Tipp., Ireland	11	52 49N	8 27W
Ballina, N.S.W.	43	28 50S	153 31 E
Ballinafad, Ireland	11	54 2N	8 20W
Ballinamore, Ireland	11	54 3N	7 48W
Ballinascarthy, Ireland	11	51 40N	8 52W
Ballinasloe, Ireland	11	53 20N	8 12W
Ballincollig, Ireland	11	51 52N	8 35W
Ballineen, Ireland	11	51 43N	8 57W
Ballingarry, Limerick, Ireland	11	52 29N	8 50W
Ballinger, U.S.A.	71	31 44N	99 58W
Ballinrobe, Ireland	11	53 36N	9 13W
Ballinskelligs B., Ire.	11	51 50N	10 17W
Ballintogher, Ireland	11	54 11N	8 21W
Ballintra, Ireland	11	54 35N	8 9W
Ballitore, Ireland	11	53 1N	6 49W
Ballybay, Ireland	11	54 8N	6 52W
Ballybofey, Ireland	11	54 48N	7 47W
Ballybunion, Ireland	11	52 30N	9 40W
Ballycanew, Ireland	11	52 37N	6 18W
Ballycastle, Ireland	11	54 17N	9 24W
Ballycastle, N. Ireland	11	55 12N	6 15W
Ballycastle B., N. Ire.	11	55 12N	6 15W
Ballyclare, Ireland	11	53 40N	8 0W
Ballyclare, N. Ireland	11	54 46N	6 0W
Ballydesmond, Ireland	11	52 11N	9 15W
Ballyhaunis, Ireland	11	53 47N	8 47W
Ballyjamesduff, Ireland	11	53 52N	7 11W
Ballylanders, Ireland	11	52 25N	8 21W
Ballymahon, Ireland	11	53 35N	7 45W
Ballymena, N. Ireland	11	54 53N	6 18W
Ballymoe, Ireland	11	53 41N	8 28W
Ballymoney, N. Ireland	11	55 5N	6 30W
Ballymore, Ireland	11	53 30N	7 40W
Ballymote, Ireland	11	54 5N	8 30W
Ballynacarrigy, Ireland	11	53 35N	7 32W
Ballynahinch, N. Ire.	11	54 24N	5 55W
Ballyragget, Ireland	11	52 47N	7 20W
Ballysadare, Ireland	11	54 12N	8 30W
Ballyshannon, Ireland	11	54 30N	8 10W
Ballyvaughan, Ireland	11	53 7N	9 10W
Balmaceda, Chile	77	46 0S	71 50W
Balmoral, Scotland	10	57 3N	3 13W
Balmorhea, U.S.A.	71	30 59N	103 41W
Balobe, Zaire	53	0 5N	32 0 E
Balonne R., Queens.	43	28 10S	148 40 E
Balovale, Zambia	56	13 30S	23 15 E
Balrampur, India	33	27 30N	82 20 E
Balranald, N.S.W.	43	34 32S	143 34 E
Balsas, Brazil	79	7 25S	46 50W
Balsas, Mexico	74	17 40N	99 30W
Balsas R., Brazil	79	10 50S	47 30W
Balsas R., Mexico	74	18 30N	101 20W
Balstad, Norway	22	68 2N	13 40 E
Balsthal, Switzerland	15	47 19N	7 42 E
Balta, U.S.A.	70	48 13N	100 3W
Balta, U.S.S.R.	25	48 2N	29 45 E
Baltia, Kenya	53	8 0S	40 40 E
Baltic Sea, Europe	23	56 0N	20 0 E
Baltiisk, U.S.S.R.	23	54 38N	19 55 E
Baltimore, Canada	57	44 2N	78 10W

Place	Map	Lat.	Long.
Baltimore, Ireland	11	51 28N	9 21W
Baltimore, Transvaal	56	23 15S	28 20 E
Baltimore, U.S.A.	68	39 18N	76 37W
Baltinglass, Ireland	11	52 57N	6 42W
Baluchistan, Pakistan	32	27 30N	65 0 E
Bam, Iran	31	29 7N	58 14 E
Bama, Nigeria	52	11 33N	13 33 E
Bamako, Sudan	50	12 34N	7 55W
Bamba, Sudan	50	17 5N	1 0W
Bambari, Central Afr.	54	5 40N	20 35 E
Bambaroo, Queensland	42	18 57S	146 15 E
Bambaya, Guinea	52	9 10N	10 5W
Bambaye, Guinea	52	9 15N	10 40W
Bamberg, Germany	14	49 54N	10 53 E
Bamberg, U.S.A.	69	33 19N	81 1W
Bambili, Zaire	54	3 48N	26 8 E
Bamboi, Ghana	52	1 84N	2 15W
Bamboo Cr., Australia	44	20 55S	120 12 E
Bamenda, W. Cam.	52	5 57N	10 11 E
Bamfield, Canada	64	48 45N	125 10W
Bamian, Afg.	32	34 50N	67 50 E
Bamian, prov., Afg.	32	35 0N	67 15 E
Bamkin, Cameroon	52	6 3N	11 27 E
Bampur, Iran	31	27 15N	60 21 E
Bampur R., Iran	31	27 20N	59 30 E
Ban Hovei San, Laos	34	20 22N	100 32 E
Ban Kadan, Thailand	34	14 32N	105 4 E
Ban Khemmarat, Thai.	34	16 3N	105 13 E
Ban Mae Sariang, Thai.	34	17 45N	97 59 E
Ban Rhai, Thailand	34	16 0N	102 50 E
Ban Sa Kaeo, Thailand	34	13 38N	102 30 E
Ban Takua Pa, Thailand	34	8 55N	98 25 E
Ban Tha Uthen, Thai.	34	17 10N	104 40 E
Bana, Malawi	56	12 23S	34 2 E
Banagi, Tanzania	53	2 16S	34 51 E
Banalia, Zaire	54	2 40N	25 20 E
Banana, Zaire	54	6 0S	12 20 E
Banana, Queensland	42	24 32S	150 12 E
Banana Is., S. Leone	52	8 10N	13 16W
Bananal I., Brazil	79	11 30S	50 30W
Banaras (Varanasi), India	33	25 22N	83 8 E
Banat, dist., Rumania	21	45 30N	21 20 E
Banbridge, N. Ireland	11	54 21N	6 16W
Banbury, England	10	52 4N	1 21W
Bancannia L., N.S.W.	43	30 44S	141 53 E
Banco Chinchorro Is., Mexico	74	18 20N	88 0W
Bancoran I., Phil.	35	7 50N	118 45 E
Bancroft, Canada	62	45 10N	77 50W
Banda, Madhya Pradesh, India	32	24 5N	79 0 E
Banda, Uttar Pradesh, India	32	25 30N	80 26 E
Banda, Pta., Mexico	74	31 47N	116 50W
Banda Elat, Indonesia	35	5 30S	133 0 E
Banda Is., Indonesia	35	4 37S	129 50 E
Banda Sea, Indonesia	35	6 0S	130 0 E
Bandaisan Mt., Japan	36	37 40N	140 15 E
Bandanaira, Indonesia	35	4 35S	129 50 E
Bandar Abbas, Iran	31	27 15N	56 15 E
Bandar Atjeh, Indonesia	34	5 35N	95 20 E
Banar-e-Charak, Iran	31	26 41N	54 17 E
Bandar-e-Lengeh, Iran	31	26 33N	54 53 E
Bandar-e-Mashur, Iran	30	30 38N	49 6 E
Bandar-e-Nakhilu, Iran	31	26 57N	53 29 E
Bandar-e-Pahlavi, Iran	30	37 33N	49 21 E
Bandar-e-Rig, Iran	30	29 33N	50 38 E
Bandar-e-Shah, Iran	31	37 0N	54 5 E
Bandar-e-Shahpur, Iran	30	30 25N	49 5 E
Bandar Maharani (Muar), Malaya	34	2 3N	102 34 E
Bandar Peggaram (Batu Pahat), Malaya	34	1 50N	102 56 E
Bandawe, Malawi	56	11 58S	34 5 E
Bandera, Argentina	77	28 55S	62 20W
Bandera, U.S.A.	71	29 42N	99 0W
Banderas B., Mexico	74	20 40N	105 30W
Bandiagara, Sudan	50	14 12N	3 29W
Bandikui, India	32	27 2N	76 35 E
Bandjarmasin, Indon.	34	3 20S	114 25 E
Bandjarnegara, Indon.	34	7 24S	109 42 E
Bandjrma, Turkey	30	40 20N	28 0 E
Bandon, Ireland	11	51 44N	8 45W
Bandon R., Ireland	11	51 43N	9 0W
Bandula, Mozambique	56	19 0S	33 7 E
Bandundu, Zaire	54	3 15S	17 22 E
Bannockburn, Scotland	10	56 5N	3 55W
Bandung, Indonesia	34	6 36S	107 48 E
Banes, Cuba	75	21 0N	75 38W
Banff, Canada	64	51 20N	115 40W
Banff, Scotland	10	57 40N	2 32W
Banff National Park, Canada	64	51 30N	116 0W
Banfora, Volta	50	10 40N	4 40W
Banga, Nigeria	52	12 32N	6 25 E
Bangala Dam, Rhod.	56	21 7S	31 25 E
Bangalore, India	32	12 59N	77 40 E
Bangalow, N.S.W.	43	28 41S	153 30 E
Banganté, Cameroon	52	5 10N	10 40 E
Bangassou, Central African Republic	54	4 55N	23 55 E
Bangeta, Mt., New Guinea	42	6 10S	147 0 E
Banggai, Indonesia	35	1 40S	123 30 E

Place	Map	Lat.	Long.
Banggi I., Indonesia	35	7 25S	117 20 E
Banghazi (Benghazi), Libya	51	31 11N	20 3 E
Bangil, Indonesia	34	7 36S	112 50 E
Bangka I., Indonesia	34	2 0S	105 50 E
Bangkalan, Indonesia	34	7 2S	112 46 E
Bangkok, Thailand	34	13 45N	100 35 E
Bangor, N. Ireland	11	54 40N	5 40W
Bangor, U.S.A.	69	44 48N	68 42W
Bangor, Wales	10	53 13N	4 9W
Bangued, Philippines	35	17 40N	120 37 E
Bangui, Central African Republic	54	4 23N	18 35 E
Bangweulu L., Zambia	56	11 0S	29 45 E
Bangweulu Swamps, Zambia	56	11 0S	29 45 E
Bani, Dom. Rep.	75	18 16N	70 22W
Bani Mazâr, Egypt	51	28 32N	30 44 E
Bani Na'im, Jordan	29	31 31N	35 10 E
Bani Suheila, Israel	29	31 21N	34 20 E
Bani Suwayf, Egypt	51	29 9N	31 5 E
Baniara, Papua	42	9 44S	149 54 E
Banissa, Ethiopia	53	4 5N	40 10 E
Baniyas, Syria	31	35 10N	36 0 E
Banilouara, Dahomey	52	11 21N	2 30 E
Baniyas, Syria	30	35 10N	36 0 E
Banjak I., Indonesia	34	2 10N	97 10 E
Banja Luka, Yugoslavia	20	44 49N	17 24 E
Banjumas, Indonesia	34	7 32S	109 18 E
Banjuwangi, Indonesia	34	8 13S	114 21 E
Banket, S. Rhodesia	56	17 25S	30 28 E
Bankipore, India	33	25 35N	85 10 E
Banks I., Canada	64	73 30N	120 0W
Banks I., Queensland	42	10 10S	142 5 E
Banks Peninsula, N.Z.	47	43 45S	173 15 E
Banks Str., Tasmania	43	40 40S	148 10 E
Bankura, India	33	23 11N	87 18 E
Bann, R., Ireland	11	52 40N	6 25W
Bann, R., N. Ireland	11	54 24N	6 23W
Banning, Canada	65	44 41N	77 31W
Banning, U.S.A.	73	33 0N	116 59W
Bannockburn, Rhod.	56	20 17S	29 48 E
Bannu, Pakistan	32	33 0N	70 38 E
Banobo, Cameroon	52	3 1N	14 5 E
Banská Bystrica, C.Slov.	16	48 46N	19 54 E
Banská Stiavnica, C.Slov.	16	48 25N	18 55 E
Banswara, India	32	23 32N	74 24 E
Bantadiji, Mt., Cam.	52	8 20N	13 30 E
Bantem, Indonesia	34	6 2S	106 9 E
Bantama, Ghana	52	7 30N	0 40W
Banteer, Ireland	11	52 8N	8 53W
Banthain, Indonesia	35	5 30S	119 55 E
Bantry, Ireland	11	51 40N	9 28W
Bantry B., Ireland	11	51 35N	9 50W
Bantva, India	32	21 31N	70 9 E
Bantval, India	32	12 54N	75 0 E
Banu, Afghanistan	31	35 40N	69 10 E
Banyo, Cameroon	52	6 50N	11 40 E
Banza, C., Zaire	53	4 2S	29 14 E
Banzare Coast, Ant.	80	66 30S	125 0 E
Banzyville, Zaire	54	4 15N	21 8 E
Bao Lac, China	39	23 1N	105 43 E
Bapatla, India	32	15 55N	80 30 E
Baqa, Israel	29	32 25N	35 2 E
Ba'qubah, Iraq	30	33 45N	44 50 E
Bar, Yugoslavia	21	42 8N	19 8 E
Bar-le-Duc, France	12	48 47N	5 10 E
Bar-sur-Aube, France	12	48 14N	4 40 E
Bar-sur-Seine, France	12	48 7N	4 20 E
Bar Harbor, U.S.A.	69	44 15N	68 20W
Bara, Sudan	51	13 50N	30 57 E
Barabinsk, U.S.S.R.	26	55 20N	78 20 E
Baraboo, U.S.A.	70	43 28N	89 46W
Baracoa, Cuba	75	20 20N	74 30W
Baradine, N.S.W.	43	30 58S	149 4 E
Baraga, U.S.A.	70	46 48N	88 31W
Baragol, Kenya	53	1 44N	36 50 E
Barahona, Dom. Rep.	75	18 13N	71 7W
Barail Range, India	33	25 15N	93 20 E
Baraka, Zaire	53	4 10S	29 1 E
Barakhola, India	33	25 0N	92 45 E
Barakula, Queensland	43	26 30S	150 33 E
Baralaba, Queensland	42	24 13S	149 50 E
Baralzon, L., Canada	65	59 40N	97 45W
Baram Point, Sarawak	35	4 45N	114 5 E
Barama, R., Guyana	78	7 40N	60 0W
Baramati, India	32	18 12N	74 39 E
Baramula, Kashmir	32	34 15N	74 20 E
Baran, India	32	25 9N	76 40 E
Baranof, Alaska	59	57 10N	135 30W
Baranof I., Alaska	59	57 0N	135 10W
Baranovichi, U.S.S.R.	23	53 10N	26 0 E
Barao de Melgaço, Brazil	78	11 50S	60 45W
Barataria B., U.S.A.	71	29 23N	89 50W
Barbacoas, Colombia	78	1 0N	75 38W
Barbacena, Brazil	79	21 15S	43 56W
Barbados I., W. Indies	75	13 0N	59 30W
Barbarit, Israel	29	31 38N	34 35 E
Barbas C., Sp. Sahara	50	22 26N	16 42W
Barbastro, Spain	17	42 2N	0 5 E
Barberton, Transvaal	57	25 42S	31 2 E
Barberton, U.S.A.	68	41 0N	81 40 E
Barbezieux, France	12	45 28N	0 10W
Barbourville, U.S.A.	69	36 55N	83 55W
Barbuda and Redonda Is., Leeward Islands	75	17 30N	61 40W

	MAP		
Barcaldine, Queens.	42	23 33 s	145 13 E
Barcarrota, Spain	17	38 31N	6 55W
Barce (El Marj), Libya	51	32 30N	20 50 E
Barcellona, Italy	20	38 9N	15 11 E
Barcelona, Spain	17	41 21N	2 10 E
Barcelona, Venezuela	78	10 10N	64 40W
Barcelonnette, France	12	44 23N	6 40 E
Barcelos, Brazil	78	0 59 s	62 58W
Barcoo, R., Queens.	42	24 33 s	145 30 E
Barcs, Hungary	16	45 58N	17 28 E
Bárdábunga, mt., Ice.	22	64 38N	17 34W
Bardai, Chad.	51	21 25N	17 0 E
Bardera, Somali Rep.	49	2 20N	42 27 E
Bardiyah, Libya	51	31 45N	25 0 E
Bardoc, W. Australia	44	30 18 s	121 12 E
Bardstown, U.S.A.	68	37 50N	85 29W
Bareilly, India	32	28 22N	79 27 E
Barellan, N.S.W.	43	34 1 s	146 30 E
Barenthal, Germany	54	47 52N	8 4 E
Barents Sea, Arctic Oc.	5	73 0N	39 0 E
Barfleur, France	12	49 40N	1 17W
Barfleur, Pte. de, Fr.	12	49 42N	1 17W
Barhi, India	33	24 15N	85 25 E
Barhok, Malaya	34	6 8N	102 22 E
Bari, Italy	20	41 6N	16 52 E
Bari Doab, Pakistan	32	30 20N	73 0 E
Bari Sadri, India	32	24 20N	74 30 E
Barima, R., Guyana	78	7 55N	60 0W
Barinas, Venezuela	75	8 36N	70 15W
Baringo, Kenya	53	0 47N	36 16 E
Baringo L., Kenya	53	0 40N	36 10 E
Bârîs, Egypt	51	24 39N	30 35 E
Barisal, Bangladesh	33	22 50N	90 32 E
Barisan Mts., Indonesia	34	3 30 s	102 15 E
Barito, R., Indonesia	35	2 50 s	114 50 E
Bark L., Ont., Canada	62	46 58N	82 25W
Barkah, 'Oman	31	23 40N	57 58 E
Barkha, China	65	31 0N	81 10 E
Barkley Sound, Canada	64	48 50N	125 10W
Barkly East, C. Prov.	57	30 58 s	27 33 E
Barkly Tableland, Australia	41	19 50 s	138 40 E
Barkly West, C. Prov.	57	28 5 s	24 31 E
Barkol, China	37	43 30N	92 50 E
Barksdale, U.S.A.	71	29 45N	100 0W
Bârlad, Rumania	21	46 15N	27 38 E
Bârlad, R., Rumania	21	46 0N	27 40 E
Barlee, L., W. Austral.	44	29 15 s	119 30 E
Barlee Ra., W. Austral.	44	23 30 s	116 0 E
Barletta, Italy	20	41 20N	16 17 E
Barlow L., Canada	65	61 50N	103 0W
Barmedman, N.S.W.	43	34 9 s	147 21 E
Barmer, India	32	25 45N	71 20 E
Barmera, S. Australia	43	34 16 s	140 29 E
Barmouth, Wales	10	52 44N	4 3W
Barnala, India	32	30 25N	75 30 E
Barnaul, U.S.S.R.	26	53 20N	83 40 E
Barnesville, U.S.A.	69	33 6N	84 9W
Barnesville, U.S.A.	70	46 44N	96 27W
Barneveld, Netherlands	13	52 7N	5 36 E
Barnhart, U.S.A.	71	31 7N	101 4W
Barnsley, England	10	53 33N	1 29W
Barnstaple, England	10	51 5N	4 3W
Baro, Nigeria	52	8 35N	6 18 E
Baroda, India	32	22 20N	73 10 E
Baroe, Cape Province	57	33 13 s	24 32 E
Barotse, Province Zambia	56	15 0 s	23 0 E
Baroua, Nigeria	52	13 52N	13 9 E
Barpeta, India	33	26 20N	91 10 E
Barques, Pte. aux, U.S.A.	68	44 5N	82 55W
Barquisimeto, Venezuela	78	9 58N	69 13W
Barr, France	12	48 25N	7 28 E
Barr Smith Ra., W. Australia	44	27 0 s	120 30 E
Barra, Brazil	79	11 0 s	43 10W
Barra, Gambia	52	13 21N	16 36W
Barra do Corda, Brazil	79	5 30 s	45 10W
Barra Falsa, Pta. da, Mozam.	56	22 55 s	35 36 E
Barraba, N.S.W.	43	30 21 s	150 35 E
Barrackpore (Barrackpur), India	33	22 44N	88 30 E
Barranca, Lima, Peru	78	10 45 s	77 50W
Barranca, Loreto, Peru	78	4 50 s	76 50W
Barranca-Bermeja, Col.	78	7 0N	73 50W
Barrancas, Venezuela	78	8 55N	62 5W
Barranco Branco, Braz.	79	21 0 s	57 50W
Barrancos, Portugal	17	38 10N	7 1W
Barranquilla, Colombia	78	11 0N	74 50W
Barras, Brazil	79	4 15 s	42 10W
Barre, U.S.A.	69	44 15N	72 30W
Barreiras, Brazil	79	12 0 s	45 0W
Barreirinhas, Brazil	79	2 30 s	42 50W
Barreiro, Portugal	17	38 40N	9 4W
Barreiros, Brazil	79	8 50 s	35 15W
Barren Is., Malagasy Rep.	55	18 30 s	44 0 E
Barren Junc., N.S.W.	42	30 5 s	149 0 E
Barretos, Brazil	79	20 30 s	48 35W
Barrhead, Canada	64	54 10N	114 30W
Barrie, Canada	62	44 25N	79 45W
Barrie I., Canada	62	45 55N	82 40W
Barrier Ra., N.Z.	47	44 30 s	168 30 E
Barrier Reef, Gt., Australia	41	19 0 s	149 0 E
Barrier, C., N.Z.	46	36 21 s	175 33 E
Barrier Mts., N.Z.	47	44 35 s	168 15 E
Barriere, Canada	64	51 20N	120 10W
Barrington, U.S.A.	68	42 8N	88 5W
Barrington, L., Canada	65	56 55N	100 15W
Barringun, N.S.W.	43	29 1 s	145 41 E
Barron R., Queensland	42	17 0 s	145 29 E
Barrow, Alaska	59	71 14N	156 16W
Barrow, Argentina	77	38 10 s	60 10W
Barrow I., W. Austral.	44	20 45 s	115 20 E
Barrow Pt., Alaska	59	71 28N	156 0W
Barrow Pt., Queens.	42	14 25 s	144 40 E
Barrow R., W. Austral.	45	26 0 s	127 40 E
Barrow, R., Ireland	11	52 46N	7 0W
Barrow-in-Furness, Eng.	10	54 8N	3 15W
Barry's Bay, Canada	62	45 30N	77 40W
Barsi, India	32	18 10N	75 50 E
Barsoi, India	33	25 40N	88 0 E
Barstow, Calif., U.S.A.	73	34 54N	117 3W
Barstow, Tex., U.S.A.	71	31 29N	103 45W
Bartica, Guyana	78	6 25N	58 40W
Bartin, Turkey	30	41 40N	32 25 E
Bartle Frère Mt., Queensland	42	17 27 s	145 50 E
Bartlesville, U.S.A.	71	36 50N	95 58W
Bartlett, U.S.A.	71	30 47N	97 28W
Bartlett, L., Canada	64	62 50N	118 20W
Bartolomeu Dias, Mozambique	56	21 10 s	35 8 E
Bartoszyce, Poland	16	54 15N	20 55 E
Bartow, U.S.A.	69	27 53N	81 49W
Barun Urta, Mongolia	38	46 38N	113 10 E
Barus, Indonesia	34	2 10N	98 20 E
Barwon (Darling), R., N.S.W.	43	29 10 s	148 47 E
Bāsa'idū, Iran	31	26 33N	55 18 E
Basco I., Philippines	35	20 30N	122 0 E
Basel (Basle), Switz.	15	47 35N	7 35 E
Basel, canton, Switz.	15	47 45N	7 45 E
Basento, R., Italy	20	40 35N	16 10 E
Bashee, R., C. Prov.	57	32 14 s	28 55 E
Bashi Channel, Phil.	35	21 20N	121 0 E
Basiaki, I., Papua	42	10 15 s	151 0 E
Basidu, Iran	31	26 35N	55 16 E
Basilan I., Philippines	35	6 35N	122 0 E
Basilicata (Lucania), reg., Italy	20	40 30N	16 0 E
Basilio, Brazil	77	32 0 s	53 20W
Basim, India	32	20 12N	77 13 E
Basin, U.S.A.	72	44 22N	108 0W
Basingstoke, England	10	51 15N	1 5W
Baskatong Res., Can.	62	46 46N	75 50W
Basoka, Zaire	54	1 16N	23 40 E
Basongo, Zaire	54	4 15 s	20 20 E
Basque Prov., Spain	17	41 55N	2 40W
Basra (Al Basra), Iraq	30	30 30N	47 50 E
Bass Strait, Australia	43	40 0 s	146 0 E
Bassano, Canada	64	50 45N	112 30W
Bassano, Italy	20	45 45N	11 45 E
Bassari, Togo	52	9 19N	0 57 E
Bassas da India, I., Mozambique Chan.	49	39 30 s	22 30 E
Basse, Gambia	52	13 13N	14 15W
Basse Terre, Guadeloupe I.	75	16 0N	61 40W
Basse Terr, dist., Guadeloupe	75	16 10N	61 40W
Bassein, Burma	33	16 0N	94 30 E
Bassein, R., Burma	33	16 0N	94 30 E
Bassermann, S.W. Afr	57	21 33 s	17 2 E
Basseterre, St. Kitts, W. Indies	75	17 17N	62 43W
Bassett, U.S.A.	69	36 47N	79 58W
Basset, U.S.A.	70	42 40N	99 30W
Bassila, Dahomey	52	9 0N	1 44 E
Bastak, Iran	31	27 15N	54 22 E
Bastar, India	33	19 25N	81 40 E
Bastelica, France	12	42 0N	9 3 E
Basti, India	33	26 52N	82 55 E
Bastia, Corsica	12	42 40N	9 30 E
Bastion C., China	39	18 5N	109 35 E
Bastrop, U.S.A.	71	30 5N	97 17W
Bastutrask, Sweden	22	64 47N	20 0 E
Bata, Rio Muni	54	1 57N	9 50 E
Bataan, Pen., Phil.	35	14 40N	120 25 E
Batabano, Cuba	75	22 40N	82 20W
Batabano, G. of, Cuba	75	22 30N	82 30W
Batac, Philippines	35	18 5N	120 25 E
Bataisk (Bataysk), U.S.S.R.	25	47 3N	39 45 E
Batalha, Portugal	17	39 38N	8 56W
Batan, Philippines	35	20 22N	122 0 E
Batan Is., Philippines	35	21 0N	121 56 E
Batang, Java, Indon.	34	7 0 s	109 38 E
Batangas, Philippines	35	13 53N	121 9 E
Bátaszék, Hungary	16	46 14N	18 41 E
Batavia, U.S.A.	69	43 0N	78 10W
Bataysk (Bataisk), U.S.S.R.	25	47 3N	39 45 E
Bateman's B., Australia	43	35 40 s	150 12 E
Bates Ra., W. Austral.	44	27 22 s	121 0 E
Batesburg, U.S.A.	69	33 54N	81 32W
Batesville, Ark., U.S.A.	71	35 47N	91 41W
Batesville, Miss., U.S.A.	71	34 21N	89 58W
Batesville, Tex., U.S.A.	71	28 58N	99 33W
Bath, Canada	62	44 12N	76 45W
Bath, England	10	51 22N	2 22W
Bath, U.S.A.	69	42 20N	77 17W
Bathurst, Canada	63	47 37N	65 43W
Bathurst, C. Prov.	57	33 30 s	26 55 E
Bathurst, Gambia	50	13 28N	16 40W
Bathurst, N.S.W.	43	33 25 s	149 31 E
Bathurst B., Queens.	42	14 16 s	144 25 E
Bathurst C., Canada	60	70 30N	128 30W
Bathurst I., N. Terr.	58	76 30N	130 10W
Bathurst Inlet, Canada	60	67 15N	108 30W
Batie, Volta	52	9 55N	7 20 E
Batinah, dist., Muscat & Oman	31	24 0N	57 0 E
Batjan I., Indonesia	35	0 50 s	130 27 E
Batlāq-e-Gāvkhuni, Iran	31	32 20N	53 0 E
Batlow, N.S.W.	43	35 31 s	148 15 E
Batman, Turkey	30	37 55N	41 0 E
Batna, Algeria	50	35 34N	6 15 E
Batoka, Zambia	56	16 45 s	27 15 E
Baton Rouge, U.S.A.	71	30 30N	91 5W
Batopilas, Mexico	74	27 48N	107 54 E
Batouri, Cameroon	54	4 30N	14 25 E
Batovi, R., Brazil	79	15 50N	53 12W
Batrak, U.S.S.R.	25	53 16N	48 47 E
Båtsfjord, Norway	22	70 35N	29 45 E
Battambang, Cambodia	34	13 7N	103 12 E
Batticaloa, Sri Lanka	32	7 43N	81 45 E
Battir, Jordan	29	31 44N	35 8 E
Battle Creek, U.S.A.	68	42 20N	85 10W
Battle Harbour, Can.	63	52 13N	55 42W
Battle Lake, U.S.A.	70	46 49N	95 12W
Battle Mt., U.S.A.	72	40 38N	116 58W
Battle R., Canada	64	52 30N	111 30W
Battlefields Rhod.	56	18 37 s	29 47 E
Battleford, Canada	65	52 45N	108 15W
Batu, Ethiopia	54	6 55N	39 49 E
Batu Anam, Malaya	34	2 35N	102 43 E
Batu Gajah, Malaya	34	4 28N	101 3 E
Batu Is., Indonesia	34	0 30 s	98 25 E
Batu Pahat (Bandar Peggaram), Malaya	34	1 50N	102 56 E
Batumi, U.S.S.R.	24	41 30N	41 30 E
Batuputih, Indonesia	35	1 20N	118 40 E
Baturadja, Indonesia	34	4 15 s	104 15 E
Baturité, Brazil	79	4 28 s	38 45W
Bat Yam, Israel	29	32 2N	34 42 E
Baucan, Port. Timor			
Bauchi, Nigeria	52	10 22N	9 48 E
Baudette, U.S.A.	70	48 47N	94 32W
Baudo, Colombia	78	5 10N	77 20W
Baudo, Sa. de, Col.	78	5 10N	77 0W
Baudouinville, Zaire	54	7 0 s	29 48 E
Bauple, Queensland	43	25 50 s	152 33 E
Baura, Nigeria	52	12 53N	8 44 E
Baures, Bolivia	78	14 0 s	62 55W
Baures, R., Bolivia	78	13 0 s	63 0W
Baurú, Brazil	77	22 10 s	49 0W
Baús, Brazil	79	18 30 s	52 58W
Bauska, U.S.S.R.	23	56 25N	25 15 E
Bautzen, Germany	14	51 11N	14 25 E
Bauya, Sierra Leone	52	8 15N	12 38W
Båvands Huk, Den.	23	55 30N	8 0 E
Bavaria, Germany	14	49 8N	11 30 E
Bavispe Papigochic, R., Mexico	74	30 30N	109 0W
Bawdwin, Burma	33	23 9N	97 18 E
Bawean I., Indonesia	34	5 46 s	112 35 E
Bawku, Ghana	52	11 3N	0 19W
Bawlake, Burma	33	19 0N	97 30 E
Baxley, U.S.A.	69	31 43N	82 23W
Baxter Springs, U.S.A.	71	37 4N	94 47W
Bay City, Mich., U.S.A.	68	43 35N	83 51W
Bay City Oreg. U.S.A.	72	45 32N	123 53W
Bay City, Tex., U.S.A.	71	29 0N	95 58W
Bay de Verde, Newf.	63	48 4N	52 55W
Bay Minette, U.S.A.	69	30 52N	87 46W
Bay of Islands, N.Z.	46	35 15 s	174 6 E
Bay, St. Louis, U.S.A.	71	30 48N	89 27W
Bay Shore, U.S.A.	68	40 40N	73 25W
Bay Springs, U.S.A.	71	31 58N	89 16W
Bay View, N.Z.	46	39 27 s	176 52 E
Bayamo, Cuba	75	20 20N	76 40W
Bayamón, Puerto Rico	75	18 24N	66 10W
Bayan Aul, U.S.S.R.	26	50 45N	75 45 E
Bayan Dalai, Mongolia	38	43 29N	103 29 E
Bayan Khara Shan, China	37	34 30N	96 45W
Bayanga, Central Afr.	54	2 52N	16 23 E
Bayard, U.S.A.	70	41 50N	103 25W
Bayāzeh, Iran	31	33 23N	55 0 E
Baybay, Philippines	35	10 40N	124 55 E
Bayburt, Turkey	30	40 15N	40 20 E
Bayeux, France	12	49 17N	0 42W
Bayfield, U.S.A.	70	46 48N	90 47W
Bayinhot, China	38	39 55N	105 35 E
Bayir, Jordan	30	30 47N	36 53 E
Bayonne, France	12	43 30N	1 28W
Bayovar, Peru	78	5 50 s	81 0W
Bayreuth, Germany	14	49 56N	11 35 E
Bayrut. *See* Beirut, Lebanon	30		
Baytown, U.S.A.	71	29 42N	94 59W
Baza, Spain	17	37 30N	2 47W
Bazar Dyuzi, U.S.S.R.	24	41 12N	48 10 E
Bazaruto I., Mozam.	56	21 40 s	35 28 E
Bazas, France	12	44 27N	0 13W
Bazuriye, Lebanon	29	33 15N	35 16 E
Beach, U.S.A.	70	47 0N	104 0W
Beachport, S. Australia	43	37 29 s	140 0 E
Beachy Hd., England	10	50 44N	0 16 E
Beacon, U.S.A.	68	41 32N	73 58W
Beaconsfield, Tasmania	43	41 8 s	146 50 E
Beal Ra., Queensland	43	25 30 s	141 30 E
Bear Creek, U.S.A.	72	45 13N	109 7W
Bear I., Arctic Ocean	5	74 30N	19 0 E
Bear L. and R., U.S.A.	72	42 0N	111 20W
Bearamore, Canada	62	49 36N	87 59W
Beardmore, Ant.	80	83 10 s	177 0 E
Beardmore Glacier, Ant.	80	84 30 s	170 0 E
Beardstown, U.S.A.	70	40 0N	90 27W
Beas de Segura, Spain	17	38 15N	2 53W
Beata C., Dom. Rep.	75	17 40N	71 30W
Beata I., Dom. Rep.	75	17 40N	71 31W
Beatrice, Rhodesia	56	18 13 s	30 47 E
Beatrice, U.S.A.	70	40 20N	96 40W
Beattock, Scotland	10	55 18N	3 28W
Beatton R., Canada	64	56 30N	120 50W
Beatty, U.S.A.	73	36 57N	116 47W
Beattyville, Can.	62	48 50N	77 8W
Beaucaire, France	12	43 48N	4 39 E
Beauceville, Canada	63	46 13N	70 46W
Beaudesert, Queensland	43	28 0 s	152 48 E
Beaufort, Sabah	35	5 30N	115 40 E
Beaufort, N.C., U.S.A.	69	34 50N	76 45W
Beaufort, S.C., U.S.A.	69	32 25N	80 40W
Beaufort Sea, Alaska	59	70 30N	146 0W
Beaufort West, C Prov.	57	32 18 s	22 36 E
Beauharnois, Canada	62	45 20N	73 20W
Beaulieu R., Canada	64	62 30N	113 0W
Beauly, Scotland	10	57 29N	4 27W
Beauly R., Scotland	10	57 26N	4 36W
Beaumont, N.Z.	47	45 50 s	169 33 E
Beaumont, U.S.A.	71	30 5N	94 8W
Beaune, Cote-d'Or, Fr.	12	47 2N	4 50 E
Beausejour, Canada	65	50 5N	96 35 E
Beauvais, France	12	49 25N	2 8 E
Beauval, Canada	65	55 9N	107 35W
Beaver, Alaska, U.S.A.	59	66 28N	147 28W
Beaver, Alberta, Can.	64	51 40N	117 30W
Beaver, Utah, U.S.A.	73	38 20N	112 35W
Beaver R., Lab., Can.	63	53 36N	62 0W
Beaver R., Sask., Can.	65	54 20N	108 40W
Beaver R., Yukon, Can.	64	60 20N	125 30W
Beaver, R., U.S.A.	67	41 0N	80 30W
Beaver City, Nebraska, U.S.A.	70	40 11N	99 48W
Beaver City, Texas, U.S.A.	71	36 48N	100 31W
Beaver Dam, U.S.A.	70	43 28N	88 50W
Beaver Lodge, Canada	64	55 11N	119 29W
Beaverhill L., Canada	64	53 30N	133 0W
Beaverhill L., Man., Canada	65	54 5N	94 50W
Beaverhill L., N. Terr., Canada	65	62 40N	104 20W
Beaverstone R., Canada	65	55 40N	90 30W
Beawar, India	32	26 3N	74 18 E
Beazley, Argentina	77	33 50 s	66 30W
Beccles, England	10	52 27N	1 33 E
Bečej, Yugoslavia	21	45 36N	20 4 E
Becharof L., Alaska	59	58 0N	156 30W
Beckley, U.S.A.	68	37 50N	81 8W
Bedang, Malaya	34	5 45N	100 30 E
Bédarieux, France	12	43 37N	3 10 E
Bedford, Canada	62	45 8N	72 58W
Bedford, C. Prov.	57	32 40 s	26 10 E
Bedford, England	10	52 8N	0 29W
Bedford, Ind., U.S.A.	68	38 50N	86 30W
Bedford, Ohio, U.S.A.	69	41 23N	81 32W
Bedford, Va., U.S.A.	69	37 22N	79 41W
Bedford, U.S.A.	70	40 37N	94 43W
Bednesti, Canada	64	53 50N	123 10W
Bedourie, Queensland	42	24 18 s	139 23 E
Beechal, Queensland	34	27 10 s	145 3 E
Beech-Grove, U.S.A.	68	39 40N	86 5W
Beechworth, Victoria	43	36 20 s	146 38 E
Beechy, Canada	64	50 53N	107 24W
Beechy Point, Alaska	59	70 48N	149 18W
Beenleigh, Queensland	43	27 45 s	153 0 E
Beer Sheva (Beersheba), Israel	29	31 14N	34 47 E
Beer Toviyya, Israel	29	31 44N	34 42 E
Beeri, Israel	29	31 25N	34 30 E
Beerot Yits-Haq, Israel	29	31 27N	34 29 E
Beerotayim, Israel	29	32 19N	34 59 E
Beersheba (Beer Sheva), Israel	29	31 15N	34 48 E
Beestekraal, Transvaal	57	25 21 s	27 32 E
Beeville, U.S.A.	71	28 28N	97 45W
Befale, Zaire	54	0 25N	20 45 E
Bega, New South Wales	43	36 38 s	149 48 E
Begamganj, Bangladesh	33	23 0N	91 5 E
Begichev I., U.S.S.R.	27	74 20N	112 30 E
Begoro, Ghana	52	6 26N	0 24W
Behariganj, India	33	25 45N	87 5 E
Behm Can., Alaska	64	55 50N	130 10W
Behshahr, Iran	31	36 48N	53 30 E
Beilen, Netherlands	13	52 49N	6 30 E
Beira, Mozambique	56	19 50 s	34 52 E
Beira Alta, prov., Port.	17	40 35N	7 35W
Beira Baixa, prov., Port.	17	39 50N	7 35W
Beira Litoral, prov., Portugal	17	40 5N	8 30W
Beirut (Bayrut), Lebanon	30	33 53N	35 31 E
Beit Aula, Jordan	29	31 33N	35 2 E
Beit Bridge, Zambia	56	14 59 s	30 2 E
Beit Fajjar, Jordan	29	31 38N	35 9 E
Beit Furik, Jordan	29	32 11N	35 20 E
Beit Hanun, Egypt	29	31 32N	34 32 E
Beit Jala, Jordan	29	31 43N	35 11 E

	MAP		
Beit Lahiya, Egypt	29	31 32N	34 30 E
Beit Rima, Jordan	29	32 2N	35 6 E
Beit Sahur, Jordan	29	31 42N	35 13 E
Beit Ummar, Jordan	29	31 38N	35 7 E
Beit' Ur et Tahta, Jord.	29	31 54N	35 5 E
Beita, Jordan	29	32 9N	35 18 E
Beitbridge, Rhod.	56	22 12 S	30 0 E
Beius, Rumania	21	46 40N	22 23 E
Beitin, Jordan	29	31 56N	35 14 E
Beituniya, Jordan	29	31 54N	35 10 E
Beja, Portugal	17	38 2N	7 53W
Béja, Tunisia	51	36 43N	9 6 E
Bejar, Spain	17	40 21N	5 45W
Bejestān, Iran	31	34 36N	58 0 E
Békéscsaba, Hungary	16	46 40N	21 10 E
Bekok, Malaya	34	2 18N	103 8 E
Bekwai, Ghana	52	6 30N	1 34W
Bela, India	33	25 50N	82 0 E
Bela, Pakistan	32	26 12N	66 20 E
Bela Crkva, Yugoslavia	21	44 55N	21 27 E
Bela Slatina, Bulgaria	21	43 27N	23 55 E
Bela Vista, Brazil	77	17 0 S	49 0W
Belalcázar, Spain	17	38 36N	5 12W
Bela Vista, Paraguay	77	22 10 S	56 20W
Belawan, Indonesia	34	3 33N	98 32 E
Belaya Tserkov, U.S.S.R.	25	49 40N	30 10 E
Belaya R., U.S.S.R.	24	55 40N	54 0 E
Belcher Is., Canada	62	56 20N	79 20W
Belchite, Spain	17	41 18N	0 43W
Belcoo, Ireland	11	54 18N	7 52W
Belém (Pará), Brazil	79	1 20 S	48 30W
Belen, Argentina	77	1 20 S	48 30W
Belen, U.S.A.	73	34 40N	106 50W
Belev, U.S.S.R.	25	53 50N	36 5 E
Belfast, New Zealand	47	43 27 S	172 39 E
Belfast, N. Ireland	11	54 35N	5 56W
Belfast, Transvaal	57	25 42 S	30 2 E
Belfast L., N. Ireland	11	54 40N	5 50W
Belfield, U.S.A.	70	46 55N	102 51W
Belfodio, Ethiopia	51	10 40N	34 20 E
Belfort, France	12	47 38N	6 50 E
Belfry, U.S.A.	72	45 12N	109 0W
Belgaum, India	32	15 55N	74 35 E
Belgium, King., Europe	13	51 30N	5 0 E
Belgorod, U.S.S.R.	24	50 35N	36 35 E
Belgorod Dnestrovski, U.S.S.R.	24	46 11N	30 23 E
Belgrade, U.S.A.	72	45 47N	111 7W
Belgrade (Beograd), Yugoslavia	21	44 50N	20 37 E
Belgrano, Argentina	77	38 50 S	62 0W
Belgrove, N.Z.	47	41 27 S	172 59 E
Belhaven, U.S.A.	69	35 34N	76 35W
Belingwe, Rhodesia	56	20 29 S	29 57 E
Belingue N. Mt., Rhodesia	56	20 32 S	29 57 E
Belitung I., Indonesia	34	3 10 S	107 50 E
Belize, Brit. Hond.	74	17 25N	88 0W
Belkovski I., U.S.S.R.	27	75 40N	135 10 E
Bell, Queensland	43	26 54 S	151 29 E
Bell Bay, Tasmania	43	41 2 S	146 58 E
Bell I., Canada	63	50 46N	55 35W
Bell Island Hot Springs, Alaska	64	55 57N	131 29W
Bell R., Canada	62	49 20N	77 10W
Bell Irving R., Canada	64	56 30N	129 30W
Bell Ville, Argentina	77	32 40 S	62 40W
Bella Bella I., Canada	64	52 10N	128 10W
Bella Coola, Canada	64	52 25N	126 40W
Bella Vista, Argentina	77	28 33 S	59 0W
Bellaire, U.S.A.	68	45 1N	85 0W
Bellananagh, Ireland	11	53 55N	7 25W
Bellary, India	32	15 10N	76 56 E
Bellata, N.S.W.	43	29 53 S	149 46 E
Bellaugh, Ireland	11	52 25N	7 58W
Bellavary, Ireland	11	53 54N	9 10W
Belle I., France	12	47 20N	3 10W
Belle Glade, U.S.A.	69	26 93N	80 38W
Belle Isle, Canada	63	51 57N	55 25W
Belle Isle. Str. of, Can.	63	51 30N	56 30W
Belleek, N. Ireland	11	54 30N	8 6W
Bellefontaine, U.S.A.	68	40 20N	83 45W
Bellefonte, U.S.A.	68	40 56N	77 45W
Bellfourche, U.S.A.	70	44 45N	103 55W
Bellfourche R., U.S.A.	70	44 30N	104 50W
Bellegarde, Ain, France	12	46 6N	5 49 E
Belleoram, Newf. can.	63	47 20N	55 15W
Belle Plaine, Iowa, U.S.A.	70	41 50N	92 17W
Belle Plaine, Minn., U.S.A.	70	44 37N	93 46W
Bellerive, Tasmania	43	42 49 S	147 25 E
Belleville, Canada	62	44 15N	77 37W
Belleville, Kan., U.S.A.	70	39 51N	97 38W
Belleville, Ill., U.S.A.	70	38 30N	90 0W
Bellevue, Canada	62	46 35N	84 10W
Bellevue, U.S.A.	72	43 30N	114 18W
Belley, France	12	45 46N	5 41 E
Bellingen, N.S.W.	43	30 25 S	152 50 E
Bellingham, U.S.A.	72	48 45N	122 27W
Bellinghausen Sea, S. Ocean, Antarctica	80	66 0 S	80 0W
Bellinzona, Switzerland	15	46 11N	9 1 E
Bello, Colombia	78	6 40N	75 55W
Bellows Falls, U.S.A.	69	43 10N	72 30W
Belluno, Italy	20	46 8N	12 6 E
Bellville, U.S.A.	71	29 56N	96 17W
Belogorsk, U.S.S.R.	27	51 15N	128 25 E
Belmez, Spain	17	38 17N	5 17W
Belmont, C.Prov.	57	29 28 S	24 22 E
Belmonte, Bahia, Brazil	79	16 0 S	39 0W
Belmullet, Ireland	11	54 13N	9 58W
Belo Horizonte, Brazil	79	20 0 S	44 0W
Beloble, Kenya	53	3 18N	40 3 E
Belogorsk, U.S.S.R.	25	45 3N	34 35 E
Belogradtchik, Bulgaria	21	43 37N	22 40 E
Beloit, Kansas, U.S.A.	70	39 30N	98 8W
Beloit, S., U.S.A.	68	42 30N	89 0W
Beloit, Wis., U.S.A.	70	42 35N	89 0W
Belomorsk, U.S.S.R.	24	64 35N	34 30 E
Belonia, India	33	23 15N	91 30 E
Belovo, U.S.S.R.	26	54 30N	86 0 E
Beloye L., U.S.S.R.	25	60 10N	37 35 E
Beloye Ozero, U.S.S.R.	25	45 15N	46 50 E
Belozersk, U.S.S.R.	25	60 0N	37 30 E
Belsé-Oya, Cameroon	52	5 40N	14 30 E
Beltana, S. Australia	43	30 48 S	138 25 E
Belterra, Brazil	79	2 45 S	55 0W
Belton, U.S.A.	71	31 4N	97 30W
Belturbet, Ireland	11	54 6N	7 28W
Belukha Mt., U.S.S.R.	26	49 50N	86 50 E
Belvidere, U.S.A.	70	42 15N	88 55W
Bely, I., U.S.S.R.	26	73 20N	71 0 E
Belyando R., Queens.	42	22 45 S	146 37 E
Belzoni, U.S.A.	71	33 9N	90 30W
Bembesi, Rhodesia	56	20 0 S	28 58 E
Bemidji, U.S.A.	70	47 30N	94 50W
Ben Gardane, Tunisia	51	33 11N	11 11 E
Ben Hope, Scotland	10	58 24N	4 36W
Ben Lomond, N.S.W.	43	30 0 S	151 37 E
Ben Lomond, Tasmania	43	41 32 S	147 45 E
Ben More Assynt, Scot.	10	58 7N	4 51W
Ben Nevis, Scotland	10	56 48N	5 0W
Ben Ohau Ra., N.Z.	41	44 1 S	170 4 E
Ben Wyvis, Scotland	10	57 40N	4 35W
Bena, Nigeria	52	11 20N	5 50 E
Benalla, Victoria	43	36 30 S	146 0 E
Benanee, N.S.W.	43	34 26 S	142 56 E
Benani, Kenya	53	0 42N	40 33 E
Benares. *See* Varanasi.			
Benavente, Spain	17	42 2N	5 43W
Benavides, U.S.A.	71	27 34N	98 26W
Benbecula I., Scotland	10	57 26N	7 20W
Bencubbin, W. Austral.	44	30 45 S	117 48 E
Bend, U.S.A.	72	44 0N	121 10W
Bende, Nigeria	52	5 31N	7 30 E
Bendena, Queensland	43	27 50 S	146 51 E
Bender Beila, Somali Rep.	49	9 30N	50 48 E
Bendery, U.S.S.R.	25	46 50N	29 50 E
Bendigo, Victoria	43	36 40 S	144 15 E
Bene Beraq, Israel	29	32 6N	34 49 E
Benevento, Italy	20	41 7N	14 45 E
Benga, Mozambique	56	16 7 S	33 30 E
Bengal. *See* E. and W. Bengal.			
Bengal, Bay of, Asia	33	17 0N	89 0 E
Bengalla, N.S.W.	43	28 33 S	150 42 E
Bengawan Solo R., Indonesia	34	7 5 S	112 25 E
Benghazi (Banghazi), Libya	51	32 10N	20 3 E
Bengkalis, Indonesia	34	1 30N	102 10 E
Bengkulu, Sumatra	34	3 50 S	102 20 E
Bengough, Canada	65	49 25N	105 10W
Benguela, Angola	55	12 37 S	13 25 E
Benguerual, Mozam.	56	21 58 S	35 28 E
Beni, Zaire	53	0 30N	29 27 E
Beni Abbes, Algeria	50	30 10N	2 5W
Beni R., Bolivia	78	10 30 S	96 0W
Beni Mellal, Morocco	50	32 18N	6 31W
Beniah L., Canada	64	63 25N	112 40W
Benicarló, Spain	17	40 23N	0 23 E
Benin, Bight of, W. Afr.	52	5 0N	3 0 E
Benin City, Nigeria	52	6 20N	5 31 E
Benin, R., Nigeria	52	5 45N	5 2 E
Benito, Canada	65	52 0N	101 30W
Benjamim Constant, Brazil	78	4 40 S	70 15W
Benkelman, U.S.A.	70	40 6N	101 31W
Bennett, Canada	64	59 50N	135 0W
Bennett I., U.S.S.R.	27	76 44N	150 0 E
Bennettsville, U.S.A.	69	34 38N	79 39W
Bennington, U.S.A.	68	42 52N	73 12W
Benoni, Transvaal	57	26 11 S	28 18 E
Benson, U.S.A.	73	31 50N	110 5W
Bent, Iran	31	26 22N	59 25 E
Bentinck I., Queensland	42	17 3 S	139 35 E
Bentiu, Sudan	54	9 14N	29 49 E
Benton, Ark., U.S.A.	71	34 31N	92 35W
Benton, Ill., U.S.A.	71	38 0N	88 57W
Benton Harbor, U.S.A.	68	42 10N	86 28W
Bentong, Malaya	34	3 31N	101 55 E
Benue R., Nigeria	52	7 50N	6 30 E
Beo, Indonesia	35	4 25N	126 50 E
Beograd (Belgrade), Yugoslavia	21	44 50N	20 30 E
Beppu, Japan	36	33 10N	126 0 E
Bequia, I., West Indies	75	13 0N	61 15W
Ber Rechid, Morocco	50	33 18N	7 36W
Berat, Albania	21	40 43N	19 59 E
Berber, Sudan	51	18 0N	34 0 E
Berbera, Somali. Rep.	49	10 30N	45 2 E
Berbéra, Chad	51	10 33N	16 35 E
Berberati, Cent. Africa	54	4 15N	15 40 E
Berbice R., Guyana	79	5 20N	58 10W
Berdichev (Ossipevsk), U.S.S.R.	25	49 57N	28 30 E
Berdyansk, U.S.S.R.	25	46 45N	36 50 E
Berea, U.S.A.	68	37 35N	84 18W
Berek, France	12	50 24N	1 35 E
Bereka, Tanzania	53	4 27 S	35 45 E
Berekum, Ghana	52	7 29N	2 34W
Berens I., Canada	65	52 20N	97 20W
Berens R., Canada	65	51 50N	93 30W
Berens River, Canada	65	52 25N	97 0W
Beresti-Jarg, Rumania	21	46 5N	27 53 E
Bereza, White Russia, U.S.S.R.	23	52 30N	25 0 E
Berezina R., U.S.S.R.	25	54 10N	28 10 E
Bereziuk L., Canada	62	54 0N	76 30W
Berezniki, U.S.S.R.	24	59 25N	56 5 E
Berezov, U.S.S.R.	24	60 20N	44 0 E
Berezov, U.S.S.R.	24	64 0N	65 0 E
Berezovka, U.S.S.R.	25	47 25N	30 55 E
Berezovka, U.S.S.R.	24	60 55N	53 0 E
Berga, Spain	17	42 6N	1 48 E
Bergamo, Italy	20	45 42N	9 40 E
Bergen-Binnen, Neth.	13	52 40N	4 41 E
Bergen, Norway	23	60 23N	5 27 E
Bergen-op-Zoom, Neth.	13	51 30N	4 18 E
Berghaus, mt. W. Australia	44	20 45 S	118 20 E
Bergsjo, Sweden	23	61 59N	17 9 E
Bergville, Natal	57	28 44 S	29 26 E
Berhala Str., Indonesia	34	1 0 S	104 15 E
Berhampore, India	33	24 2N	88 27 E
Berhampur, India	33	19 15N	84 54 E
Berikwa, Tanzania	53	9 33 S	38 0 E
Bering Sea, U.S.S.R.	5	58 0N	167 0 E
Bering Str.	59	66 0N	170 0W
Beringen, Belgium	13	51 4N	5 13 E
Berislav, U.S.S.R.	25	46 50N	33 30 E
Berja, Spain	17	36 50N	2 56W
Berkeley, U.S.A.	73	38 0N	122 20W
Berkeley Spr., U.S.A.	69	39 39N	78 14W
Berkovitsa, Bulgaria	21	43 15N	23 05 E
Berland R., Canada	64	54 0N	117 30W
Berlevåg, Norway	22	70 43N	29 20 E
Berlin, Cape Province	57	32 52 S	27 33 E
Berlin, Germany	14	52 32N	13 24 E
Berlin, Md., U.S.A.	69	38 19N	75 12W
Berlin, Wis., U.S.A.	70	43 57N	88 58W
Bermejo R., Argentina	77	22 30 S	64 30W
Bermejo R., Argentina	77	22 30 S	68 0W
Bermejo Teuco, R., Arg.	77	23 30 S	63 0W
Bermen L., Canada	63	53 40N	69 0W
Bermeo, Spain	17	43 25N	2 47W
Bermuda, Atlantic Oc.	5	32 45N	65 0W
Bernam R., Malaya	34	3 47N	101 5 E
Bern, Switzerland	15	46 57N	7 28 E
Bern, canton, Switz.	15	46 51N	7 35 E
Bernado de Irigoyen, Brazil	77	26 20 S	53 50W
Bernalillo, U.S.A.	73	35 20N	106 31W
Bernay, France	12	50 16N	1 44 E
Bernburg, Germany	14	51 47N	11 42 E
Berner Alpen, Switz.	15	46 30N	9 50 E
Bernese Oberland, mts., Switzerland	15	46 20N	7 20 E
Bernier I., W. Australia	44	24 50 S	113 12 E
Bernina Mts., Switz.	15	46 23N	9 50 E
Bernina P., Switzerland	15	46 24N	10 2 E
Beror Hayil, Israel	29	31 34N	34 38 E
Beroun, Czechoslovakia	16	49 57N	14 5 E
Berozovy Yar., U.S.S.R.	26	76 45 E	58 50N
Berri, S. Australia	43	34 14 S	140 35 E
Berrigan, N.S.W.	43	35 38 S	145 49 E
Berry, N.S.W.	43	34 46 S	150 43 E
Berry Is., Bahamas	75	25 30N	77 45W
Berryville, U.S.A.	71	36 26N	93 33W
Berseba, S.W. Africa	57	26 0 S	17 46 E
Berthaund, U.S.A.	70	40 23N	105 2W
Berthold, U.S.A.	70	48 17N	101 45W
Bertoua, Cameroon	52	4 30N	13 45 E
Bertrand, U.S.A.	70	40 34N	99 34W
Berufjördhur, Iceland	22	64 48N	14 25W
Berwick, U.S.A.	68	41 4N	76 13W
Berwick-upon-Tweed, England	10	55 47N	2 0W
Besançon, France	12	47 15N	6 0 E
Beserah, Malaya	34	3 48N	103 20 E
Besnard L., Canada	65	55 30N	106 0W
Besni, Turkey	31	37 45N	37 52 E
Bessages, France	12	44 18N	4 8 E
Bessemer, Alas, U.S.A.	69	33 22N	87 0W
Bessemer, Mich., U.S.A.	70	46 26N	90 0W
Bestyakh, U.S.S.R.	27	69 30N	124 30 E
Bet Alfa, Israel	29	32 31N	35 25 E
Bet Dagan, Israel	29	32 1N	34 39 E
Bet Guvrin, Israel	29	31 37N	34 54 E
Bet Ha'emeq, Israel	29	32 58N	35 8 E
Bet Natif, Israel	29	31 42N	35 0 E
Bet Shean, Israel	29	32 30N	35 30 E
Bet Yosef, Israel	29	32 34N	35 33 E
Beta, Queensland	42	23 42 S	146 23 E
Betanzos, Spain	17	43 15N	8 12W
Bete, Nigeria	52	7 1N	9 43 E
Bethal, Transvaal	57	26 27 S	29 28 E
Bethanien, S.W. Africa	57	26 32 S	17 11 E
Bethany, Jordan	29	31 47N	35 15 E
Bethany, O.F.S., S. Afr.	57	29 34 S	25 59 E
Bethany, U.S.A.	70	40 14N	94 0W
Bethel, Me., U.S.A.	69	44 22N	70 46W
Bethlehem, Jordan	29	31 43N	35 12 E
Bethlehem, O.F.S., S. Africa	57	28 14 S	28 18 E
Bethlehem, Pa., U.S.A.	68	40 39N	75 24W
Bethnal, Canada	62	47 40N	81 40W
Bethulie, O.F.S., S. Afr.	57	30 31 S	25 59 E
Béthune, France	12	50 30N	2 38 E
Betoota, Queensland	43	25 40 S	140 42 E
Betsiamites, Canada	63	48 56N	68 40W
Betsiamites, R., Can.	63	50 0N	70 0W
Bettiah, India	33	26 48N	84 33 E
Bettles, Alaska	59	66 44N	152 10W
Betul, India	32	21 48N	77 59 E
Betuwe, Netherlands	13	51 55N	5 35 E
Beulah, Canada	65	50 16N	101 2W
Beulah, U.S.A.	70	47 18N	101 51W
Beverley, England	10	53 52N	0 26W
Beverley, W. Australia	44	32 9 S	116 56 E
Beverly, Canada	64	53 36N	113 21W
Beverly, U.S.A.	72	46 52N	119 59W
Beverley Group, Queens.	42	21 22 S	150 15 E
Beverly Hills, U.S.A.	73	34 6N	118 29W
Beverwijk, Neth.	13	52 28N	4 38 E
Bewani Mts., N. Guinea	42	3 15 S	141 30 E
Beyin, Ghana	52	5 1N	2 41W
Beyla, Guinea	50	8 38N	8 38W
Beypazari, Turkey	30	40 10N	31 48 E
Beysehir gölü, L., Tur.	30	37 45N	31 30 E
Bezet, Israel	29	33 4N	35 8 E
Bezhetsk, U.S.S.R.	25	57 50N	36 45 E
Bezhitsa, U.S.S.R.	25	53 25N	34 18 E
Béziers, France	12	43 20N	3 12 E
Bezwada, India. *See* Vijayavada.			
Bhachau, India	32	23 20N	70 15 E
Bhadarwah, Kashmir	32	33 5N	75 40 E
Bhadrakh, India	33	21 10N	86 30 E
Bhadravati, India	32	13 49N	76 15 E
Bhagalpur, India	33	25 10N	87 0 E
Bhaisa, India	32	19 08N	77 59 E
Bhakkar, W. Pakistan	32	31 40N	71 5 E
Bhākra Dam, India	32	31 20N	76 35 E
Bhamo, Burma	33	24 15N	97 15 E
Bhamragarh, India	32	19 30N	80 40 E
Bhandara, India	32	21 5N	79 42 E
Bhanrer Ra., India	32	23 40N	79 45 E
Bharat, (Indian Union), rep., Asia	32	22 0N	78 0 E
Bharatpur, Madhya Pradesh, India	33	23 45N	81 45 E
Bharatpur, Raj., India	32	27 15N	77 30 E
Bhatinda, India	32	30 15N	74 57 E
Bhatkal, India	32	14 2N	74 35 E
Bhatpara, India	33	22 50N	88 25 E
Bhaun, Pakistan	32	32 55N	72 40 E
Bhavnagar (Bhaunagar), India	32	21 45N	72 10 E
Bhawanipatna, India	33	19 55N	83 30 E
Bhera, W. Pak.	32	32 28N	72 58 E
Bhilsa, India	32	23 28N	77 53 E
Bhilwara, India	32	25 25N	74 38 E
Bhima R., India	32	17 20N	76 30 E
Bhimavaram, India	33	16 34N	81 35 E
Bhind, India	32	26 33N	78 47 E
Bhir (Bir), India	32	18 58N	75 52 E
Bhiwandi, India	32	19 15N	73 0 E
Bhiwani, India	32	28 50N	76 9 E
Bhojpur, Nepal	33	27 15N	87 10 E
Bhola, Bangladesh	33	22 45N	90 45 E
Bhopal, India	32	23 20N	77 50 E
Bhor, India	32	18 12N	73 53 E
Bhubaneswar, India	33	20 15N	85 50 E
Bhuj, India	32	23 15N	69 49 E
Bhusawal, India	32	21 1N	75 56 E
Bhutan, st., Asia	33	27 25N	89 50 E
Biaboye, Zaire	53	0 18N	28 35 E
Biafra, Bight of, Cam.	52	3 30N	9 20 E
Biak I., Indonesia	35	1 0 S	136 0 E
Biala Podlaska, Poland	16	52 3N	23 5 E
Bialogard, Poland	16	54 2N	15 58 E
Bjalowiez, Poland	16	52 41N	23 50 E
Bialystok, Poland	16	53 10N	23 10 E
Biano (Manika) Plat., Zaire	56	10 0N	26 0 E
Biarritz, France	12	43 29N	1 33W
Bias B. *See* Taya Wan	39		
Biasca, Switzerland	15	46 22N	8 58 E
Bibai, Japan	36	43 24N	141 59 E
Bibby I., Canada	65	61 55N	93 0W
Biberach, Germany	14	48 5N	9 49 E
Biberist, Switz.	15	47 11N	7 34 E
Bibiani, Ghana	52	6 30N	2 8W
Biboohra, Queensland	42	16 35 S	145 27 E
Bibungwa, Zaire	53	2 40 S	28 10 E
Bic, Canada	63	48 20N	68 41W
Bicknell, U.S.A.	73	38 21N	111 32W
Bida, Nigeria	52	9 3N	5 58 E
Bidar, India	32	17 55N	77 35 E
Bidassoa R., Spain	17	43 10N	1 41W
Biddya, Jordan	29	32 7N	35 4 E
Bideford, England	10	51 1N	4 12W
Bidon 5 (poste Maurice Cortier), Algeria	50	22 14N	1 2 E
Bidor, Malaya	34	4 6N	101 15 E
Bidzar, Cameroon	52	10 0N	14 3 E
Bié Plateau, Angola	55	12 0 S	16 0 E
Bieber, U.S.A.	72	41 5N	121 6W
Biel, Switzerland	15	47 8N	7 14 E
Bielefeld, Germany	14	52 2N	8 31 E
Bieler See, Switz.	15	47 6N	7 5 E

	MAP		
Biella, Italy	20	45 33N	8 3 E
Bielsk Podlaski, Poland	16	52 47N	23 11 E
Bielsko, Poland	16	49 55N	19 5 E
Biên Hoa, S. Viet Nam	34	11 3N	106 53 E
Bienfait, Canada	65	49 10N	102 50W
Biesiesfontein, C. Prov.	57	30 57S	17 58 E
Big B., New Zealand	47	44 18S	168 5 E
Big Beaver, Canada	65	49 10N	105 10W
Big Beaver House, Can.	62	52 59N	89 50W
Big Bell, W. Australia	44	27 12S	117 45 E
Big Belt Mts., U.S.A.	72	46 40N	111 30W
Big Black R., U.S.A.	71	32 40N	90 27W
Big Blue R., U.S.A.	70	40 15N	96 35W
Big Cypress Swamp, U.S.A.	69	26 12N	81 10W
Big Delta, Alaska, U.S.A.	60	64 15N	145 0W
Big Falls, U.S.A.	70	48 10N	93 47W
Big Fork R., U.S.A.	70	48 25N	93 49W
Big Horn, U.S.A.	72	46 10N	107 25W
Big Horn Mts., U.S.A.	72	44 10N	107 0W
Big Horn R., U.S.A.	72	45 40N	107 50W
Big Lake, U.S.A.	71	31 9N	101 27W
Big Muddy River, U.S.A.	70	48 40N	104 30W
Big Pine, U.S.A.	73	37 13N	118 21W
Big Piney, U.S.A.	72	42 32N	110 7W
Big Quill L., Canada	65	51 48N	105 40W
Big Rapids, U.S.A.	68	43 42N	85 27W
Big River, Canada	65	53 50N	107 0W
Big Sable Pt., U.S.A.	68	44 5N	86 30W
Big Salmon, Canada	60	61 50N	136 0W
Big Sandy, U.S.A.	72	48 11N	110 5W
Big Sandy Creek, U.S.A.	70	38 50N	103 15W
Big Snowy Mt., U.S.A.	72	46 45N	109 15W
Big Spring, U.S.A.	71	32 10N	101 25W
Big Springs, U.S.A.	70	41 07N	102 06W
Big Squaw Lake (Chandeler)	59	67 32N	148 35W
Big Stone City, U.S.A.	70	45 19N	96 29W
Big Stone Gap, U.S.A.	69	36 52N	82 45W
Big Stone Lake, U.S.A.	70	45 2N	96 0W
Big Trout Lake, Can.	62	53 40N	90 0W
Bigfork, U.S.A.	72	48 3N	114 3W
Biggar, Canada	65	52 10N	108 0W
Bigge, I., W. Australia	44	14 35S	125 10 E
Bigge Ra., Queensland	42	24 50S	149 25 E
Biggenden, Queensland	43	25 31S	152 4 E
Bigstone L., Canada	65	53 40N	95 50W
Bigtimber, U.S.A.	72	45 50N	109 59W
Bigwa, Tanzania	53	7 12S	39 9 E
Bihac, Yugoslavia	20	44 49N	15 47 E
Bihar, tn. and st., India	33	25 5N	85 40 E
Biharamulo, Tan.	53	2 34S	31 20 E
Bihor, Mt., Rumania	21	46 29N	22 47 E
Biisk, U.S.S.R.	26	52 40N	85 0 E
Bijapur, Madhya Pradesh, India	32	18 50N	80 50 E
Bijapur, Mysore, India	32	16 50N	75 55 E
Bijauri, Nepal	33	28 5N	82 20 E
Bijeljina, Yugoslavia	21	44 46N	19 17 E
Bijnor, India	32	29 27N	78 11 E
Bikaner, India	32	28 2N	73 18 E
Bikin, U.S.S.R.	27	46 50N	134 15 E
Bikita, Rhodesia	56	20 6S	31 41 E
Bikoro, Zaire	54	0 48S	18 15 E
Bikoué, Cameroon	52	4 5N	11 50 E
Bilara, India	32	26 14N	73 53 E
Bilaspur, India	33	22 2N	82 15 E
Bilati, Zaire	53	0 34S	28 49 E
Bilauk Taung Ra., Thai.	34	13 30N	99 15 E
Bilbao, Spain	17	43 16N	2 56W
Bildudalur, Iceland	22	65 40N	23 40W
Bileca, Jugoslavia	21	42 53N	18 27 E
Bilecik, Turkey	31	40 10N	30 5 E
Bilgoraj, Poland	16	50 35N	22 42 E
Bilir, U.S.S.R.	27	65 40N	131 20 E
Bill, U.S.A.	70	43 18N	105 16W
Billa, Nigeria	52	8 54N	12 19 E
Billiate, Malawi	56	15 0S	34 33 E
Billings, U.S.A.	72	45 43N	108 29W
Billybillong, Australia	44	27 20S	115 20 E
Bilma, Niger	51	18 50N	13 30 E
Biloela, Queensland	42	24 23S	150 40 E
Bilolo, Zaire	53	0 40N	28 40 E
Biloxi, U.S.A.	69	30 30N	89 0W
Bilpamorea Claypan, Queens.	43	25 0S	140 0 E
Biltine, Chad.	51	14 40N	20 50 E
Bimbéreké, Dahomey	52	10 11N	2 43 E
Bimbila, Ghana	52	8 54N	0 5 E
Bin Yauri, Nigeria	52	10 50N	4 50 E
Bina-Etawah, India	32	24 9N	78 10 E
Bindebango, Queens.	43	27 44S	147 23 E
Bindjai, Indonesia	34	3 50N	98 30 E
Bindle, Queensland	43	27 40S	148 52 E
Bindum, Cameroon	52	2 33N	12 52 E
Bindura, Rhodesia	56	17 18S	31 18 E
Binduri, Ghana	52	10 59N	0 21W
Bingara, N.S.W.	43	29 45S	15 30 E
Bingerville, Ivory Coast	50	5 18N	3 49W
Bingham, U.S.A.	69	45 5N	69 50W
Bingham Canyon, U.S.A.	72	40 32N	112 9W
Binghampton, U.S.A.	68	42 9N	75 54W
Bingi, Zaire	53	0 20S	29 0 E
Bingöl, Turkey	30	39 20N	41 0 E
Binji, Nigeria	52	13 15N	4 58 E

	MAP		
Binnaway, N.S.W.	43	31 28S	149 24 E
Binongko I., Indonesia	35	5 55S	123 55 E
Binscarth, Canada	65	50 40N	101 20W
Bint Jebeil, Lebanon	29	33 8N	35 25 E
Bintan I., Indonesia	34	1 0N	104 0 E
Bintang, Gambia	52		Inset
Bintuhan, Indonesia	34	4 50S	103 25 E
Bintulu, Sarawak	35	3 3N	113 8 E
Binyamina, Israel	29	32 32N	34 56 E
Biodi, Zaire	53	3 15N	28 30 E
Biologard, Poland	23	54 0N	16 0 E
Bipindi, Cameroon	52	3 6N	10 21 E
Biq'at Bet Netofa, Is.	29	32 49N	34 22 E
Bir, India	32	18 58N	75 52 E
Bir Nabada, Jordan	29	31 52N	35 12 E
Bi'r Safajah, Egypt	51	26 48N	33 55 E
Bîr Shalatein, Egypt	51	23 5N	35 25 E
Bîr Ungât, Egypt	51	22 0N	34 0 E
Bir Zeit, Jordan	29	31 59N	35 11 E
Bira, Jordan	29	31 55N	35 12 E
Birao, Central Africa	51	10 20N	22 40 E
Biratnagar, Nepal	33	26 30N	87 15 E
Birch Hills, Canada	65	53 10N	105 10W
Birch I., Canada	65	52 25N	99 50W
Birch Mts., Canada	64	58 0N	113 0W
Birch R., Canada	64	58 20N	113 20W
Birch River, Canada	65	52 30N	101 10W
Birchwood, N.Z.	47	45 54S	167 51 E
Birchip, Victoria	43	35 52S	143 0 E
Bird City, U.S.A.	71	39 47N	101 31W
Bird I., Cape Province	57	32 3S	18 17 E
Birdsville, Queensland	43	25 51S	139 20 E
Birdum, N. Territory	40	15 50S	133 0 E
Birecik, Turkey	30	37 0N	38 0 E
Birganj, Nepal	33	27 5N	85 0 E
Birimgan, Queensland	42	22 41S	147 25 E
Biriri, Nigeria	52	12 8N	11 48 E
Birjand, Iran	31	32 57N	59 10 E
Birkenhead, England	10	53 24N	3 1W
Birkenhead, N.Z.	46	36 49S	174 46 E
Birmingham, England	10	52 30N	1 55W
Birmingham, U.S.A.	69	33 40N	86 50W
Birmitrapur, India	33	22 30N	84 5 E
Birnin Gwari, Nigeria	52	11 0N	6 45 E
Birnin Kebbi, Nigeria	52	12 32N	4 12 E
Birnin Koni, Niger	52	13 55N	5 15 E
Birnin Kudu, Nigeria	52	11 30N	9 29 E
Birnin Tudu, Nigeria	52	12 9N	5 24 E
Birobidzhan, U.S.S.R.	27	48 50N	132 50 E
Birquin, Jordan	29	32 23N	35 15 E
Birr, Ireland	11	53 7N	7 55W
Birrie R., N.S.W.	43	29 5S	147 20 E
Birs, R., Switz.	15	47 27N	7 33 E
Birsk, U.S.S.R.	24	55 25N	55 30 E
Birtle, Canada	65	50 30N	101 5W
Biscayne B., U.S.A.	69	25 40N	80 12W
Bisceglie, Italy	20	41 14N	16 30 E
Biscotasing, Canada	62	47 19N	82 8W
Biševo I., Yugoslavia	20	42 57N	16 3 E
Bishee, U.S.A.	73	31 29N	109 58W
Bishop, Calif., U.S.A.	73	37 54N	118 28W
Bishop, Texas, U.S.A.	71	27 33N	97 47W
Bishop Auckland, Eng.	10	54 40N	1 40W
Bishop's Falls, Canada	63	49 2N	55 24W
Biskra, Algeria	50	34 50N	5 52 E
Bismarck, U.S.A.	69	46 49N	100 49W
Bismarck Arch., Terr. of, New Guinea	42	3 30S	148 30 E
Bismarck Sea, New Guinea	42	4 0S	148 0 E
Biso, Uganda	53	1 99N	31 26 E
Bison, U.S.A.	70	45 34N	102 30W
Bissagos Is., Port. Guin.	50	11 30N	16 30W
Bissau, Port. Guinea	50	11 45N	15 45W
Bissett, Canada	65	46 14N	78 4W
Bistcho L., Canada	64	59 45N	119 20W
Bistriţa, Rumania	21	47 9N	24 35 E
Bistriţa, R., Rumania	21	47 0N	26 0 E
Bitlis, Turkey	30	38 20N	42 3 E
Bitolj (Monastir), Y.slav.	21	41 5N	21 21 E
Bitonto, Italy	20	41 7N	16 40 E
Bitter Creek, U.S.A.	72	41 32N	108 30W
Bitterfontein, C.Prov.	57	31 3N	18 16 E
Bitterroot Mts., U.S.A.	72	47 0N	115 0W
Bitterroot, R., U.S.A.	72	46 20N	114 15W
Bittou, Volta	52	11 17N	0 18W
Bitumount, Canada	64	57 26N	112 40W
Bityug R., U.S.S.R.	25	51 45N	40 30 E
Biu, Nigeria	52	10 40N	12 3 E
Biwa L., Japan	36	35 15N	135 45 E
Biwabik, U.S.A.	70	47 32N	92 26W
Bizana, Cape Province	57	30 50S	29 52 E
Bizerte, Tunisia	51	37 15N	9 50 E
Bjargtangar C., Iceland	22	65 30N	24 30W
Bjelovar, Yugoslavia	20	45 56N	16 49 E
Björneborg. *See* Pori.	23		
Blaavands Huk, pt., Denmark	23	55 30N	8 0 E
Black B., Canada	62	48 40N	88 30W
Black Butte Mt., U.S.A.	70	46 30N	103 30W
Black Diamond, Can.	64	50 45N	114 22W
Black Duck R., Canada	65	56 0N	91 0W
Black Forest, Germany	14	48 0N	8 0 E
Black Hills, U.S.A.	70	44 0N	103 50W
Black I., Canada	65	51 20N	96 40W
Black L., Sask., Can.	65	59 20N	105 30W
Black Mesa, mt., U.S.A.	71	36 50N	102 45W
Black Ra., U.S.A.	73	33 30N	107 45W
Black Ra., W. Austral.	44	24 0N	115 30 E

	MAP		
Black, R., Ark., U.S.A.	71	36 15N	90 45W
Black, R., Mo., U.S.A.	71	37 32N	91 0W
Black, R., N. Viet Nam	37	21 40N	104 0 E
Black R. Falls, U.S.A.	70	44 17N	90 52W
Black Sea, Europe	24	43 30N	35 0 E
Black Volta R., Ghana	52	9 0N	2 40W
Black Warrior R., U.S.A.	69	33 0N	87 45W
Blackall, Queensland	42	24 26S	145 27 E
Blackball, N.Z.	47	42 22S	171 26 E
Blackburn, England	10	53 44N	2 30W
Blackburn, Mt., Alaska	59	61 50N	143 20W
Blackbutt, Queensland	43	26 51S	152 6 E
Blackduck, U.S.A.	70	47 43N	94 31W
Blackfoot, U.S.A.	72	43 10N	112 20W
Blackfoot, R., U.S.A.	72	47 0N	113 30W
Blackfoot River Res., U.S.A.	72	42 50N	111 30W
Blackpool, England	10	53 48N	3 3W
Blackrock, Dublin, Ire.	11	53 18N	6 11W
Blacks Harbour, Can.	63	45 3N	66 49W
Blacksburg, U.S.A.	68	37 17N	80 23W
Blacksod B., Ireland	11	54 6N	10 0W
Blackstone, U.S.A.	68	37 6N	78 0W
Blackstone R., Canada	64	61 0N	122 30W
Blackville, Canada	63	46 50N	65 49W
Blackwater, Ireland	11	52 27N	6 20W
Blackwater, Queens.	42	23 35S	149 0 E
Blackwater R., Ireland	11	52 27N	9 40W
Blackwater R., Ireland	11	53 46N	7 0W
Blackwater R., N. Ire.	11	54 25N	7 0W
Blackwell, U.S.A.	71	36 55N	97 20W
Blackwood R., W. Australia	44	34 8S	115 10 E
Bladgrond, C. Prov.	57	28 52S	19 57 E
Blagodarnoye, U.S.S.R.	25	45 7N	43 37 E
Blagoevgrad (Gorna Dzhumayo), Bulgaria	21	42 1N	23 5 E
Blagoveschensk, U.S.S.R.	27	50 20N	127 30 E
Blagoveshchensk, U.S.S.R.	24	59 40N	42 10 E
Blain, France	12	47 30N	1 45W
Blaine, Canada	64	52 50N	106 50W
Blaine, Wash., U.S.A.	72	48 59N	122 43W
Blaine Lake, Canada	65	52 51N	106 52W
Blair, U.S.A.	70	41 37N	96 6W
Blair Atholl, Queens.	42	22 42S	147 31 E
Blair Atholl, Scotland	10	56 46N	3 50W
Blairgowrie, Scotland	10	56 36N	3 21W
Blairmore, Canada	64	49 40N	114 25W
Blaj, Rumania	21	46 10N	23 57 E
Blake Pt., U.S.A.	70	48 10N	88 30W
Blakely, Ga., U.S.A.	69	31 22N	85 0W
Blakely, Pa., U.S.A.	69	41 28N	75 35W
Blama, Sierra Leone	52	7 58N	11 26W
Blanc C., Mauritania	50	20 50N	17 0W
Blanc, Mt., Italy–Fr.	12	45 50N	6 52 E
Blanc Sablon, Canada	63	51 24N	57 8W
Blanca Bay, Argentina	77	39 10S	61 30W
Blanchard, U.S.A.	71	35 7N	97 42W
Blanche L., S. Austral.	43	29 15S	139 40 E
Blanche, L., W. Australia	45	22 30S	123 21 E
Blanchisseuse, Trinidad, West Indies	75	10 40N	62 20W
Blanco, C. Prov.	57	23 56S	22 25 E
Blanco, U.S.A.	71	30 5N	98 29W
Blanco C., Argentina	78	47 10S	65 50W
Blanco C., Costa Rica	75	9 34N	85 8W
Blanco C., Peru	78	4 10S	81 10W
Blanco C., U.S.A.	72	42 50N	124 40W
Blandá R., Iceland	22	65 25N	19 35W
Blanding, U.S.A.	73	37 37N	109 26W
Blanes, Spain	17	41 40N	2 48 E
Blankenberghe, Belgium	13	51 20N	3 9 E
Blanquilla I., Ven.	75	12 0N	64 40W
Blantyre, Malawi	56	15 45S	35 0 E
Blarney, Ireland	11	51 57N	8 35W
Blaye, France	12	45 8N	0 40W
Bled, Yugoslavia	20	46 27N	14 7 E
Blednaya Mt., U.S.S.R.	26	65 50N	65 30 E
Bleiburg. Austria	14	46 43N	14 46 E
Blekinge, co., Sweden	23	56 15N	15 15 E
Blenheim, N.Z.	47	41 38S	174 5 E
Blida, Algeria	50	36 30N	2 49 E
Bligh Sd., N.Z.	47	44 46S	167 31 E
Blind River, Canada	62	46 15N	83 0W
Bliss Landing, Canada	64	50 0N	130 0W
Blitar, Indonesia	34	8 5S	112 11 E
Blitta, Togoland	52	8 23N	1 6 E
Block I., U.S.A.	58	41 13N	71 35W
Bloemfontein, O.F.S.	57	29 6S	26 14 E
Bloemhof, Transvaal	57	27 38S	25 32 E
Blois, France	12	47 35N	1 20 E
Blonduós, Iceland	22	65 40N	20 12W
Bloods Cr., S. Australia	45	26 10S	135 7 E
Bloodvein R., Canada	65	51 40N	96 30W
Bloody Foreland, Ire.	11	55 10N	8 18W
Bloomer, U.S.A.	70	45 6N	91 30W
Bloomfield, Iowa, U.S.A.	70	40 42N	92 27W
Bloomfield, Neb. U.S.A.	70	42 37N	97 35W
Bloomfield, N. Mex., U.S.A.	73	36 46N	107 59W
Bloomington, Ill., U.S.A.	68	40 25N	89 0W
Bloomington, Ind., U.S.A.	68	39 10N	86 30W

	MAP		
Bloomsburg, U.S.A.	68	41 0N	76 30W
Blora, Indonesia	34	6 57S	111 25 E
Blouberg, Transvaal	57	23 8S	29 0 E
Blouberg, mt., Trans.	57	23 8S	29 0 E
Blountstown, U.S.A.	69	30 28N	85 5W
Blue I., U.S.A.	70	41 40N	87 45W
Blue Lake, U.S.A.	72	40 56N	124 0W
Blue Mts., Oreg., U.S.A.	72	45 30N	118 10W
Blue Mts., Pa., U.S.A.	68	40 35N	76 30W
Blue Mountains, N.S.W.	43	33 30S	150 0 E
Blue Nile, prov., Sudan	51	12 30N	34 30 E
Blue Nile R. (Bahr El Azrak), Sudan	54	10 30N	35 0 E
Blue Rapids, U.S.A.	70	39 40N	96 37W
Blue Ridge, Canada	69	54 5N	115 20W
Blueberry R., Canada	64	56 40N	121 40W
Bluefield, U.S.A.	68	37 18N	18 14W
Bluefields, Nicaragua	75	12 0N	83 50W
Bluestack Mts., Ireland	11	54 46N	8 5W
Bluff, Alaska	59	64 50N	164 48W
Bluff, New Zealand	47	46 36S	168 19 E
Bluff Harbour, N.Z.	47	46 36S	168 21 E
Bluff, Pt., W. Austral.	44	27 47S	117 11 E
Bluffton, U.S.A.	68	40 43N	85 9W
Blumenau, Brazil	77	27 0S	49 0W
Blunt, U.S.A.	70	44 34N	100 0W
Bly, U.S.A.	72	42 23N	121 0W
Blyth, Northumb., Eng.	10	55 8N	1 32W
Blythe, U.S.A.	73	33 38N	114 37W
Blytheville, U.S.A.	71	35 58N	89 55W
Bo, Sierra Leone	52	7 55N	11 50W
Boa, Malawi	56	12 36S	34 10 E
Boa Vista, Brazil	79	2 48N	60 30W
Boac, Philippines	35	13 20N	122 0 E
Boaco, Nicaragua	75	12 29N	85 35W
Boatman, Queensland	43	27 40S	146 54 E
Bobadilla, Spain	17	37 2N	4 44W
Bobawaba, Queensland	42	19 46S	147 33 E
Bobbili, India	33	18 35N	83 30 E
Bobbio, Italy	20	44 57N	9 22 E
Bobcaygeon, Canada	62	44 33N	78 33W
Bobéna, Dahomey	52	10 55N	3 38 E
Bobo Dioulasso, Ivory Coast	50	11 8N	4 13W
Bobov Dol, Bulgaria	21	42 20N	23 0 E
Bóbr R., Poland	16	51 25N	15 30 E
Bobrov, U.S.S.R.	25	51 5N	40 2 E
Bobruisk, U.S.S.R.	25	53 10N	29 15 E
Boca do Acre, Brazil	78	8 50S	66 27W
Bocaiuva, Brazil	79	17 10S	43 50W
Bocanda, Ivory Coast	50	7 5N	4 31W
Bocas del Toro, Panama	75	9 15N	82 20W
Bochalema, Colombia	78	7 40N	72 30W
Bocholt, Germany	14	51 50N	6 35 E
Bochum, Germany	14	51 28N	7 12 E
Boda, Central Africa	54	4 19N	17 26 E
Bodaibo, U.S.S.R.	27	57 50N	114 0 E
Boden, Sweden	22	65 50N	21 42 E
Bodensee, L., Ger.–Switzerland	15	47 40N	9 30 E
Bodhan, India	32	18 40N	77 55 E
Bodinga, Nigeria	52	12 58N	5 10 E
Bodjonegoro, Indon.	34	7 11S	111 54 E
Bodmin, England	10	50 28N	4 44W
Bodö, Norway	22	67 17N	14 27 E
Bodo, Canada	65	52 11N	110 4W
Bodrog R., Hungary	16	48 15N	21 35 E
Bodrum, Turkey	30	37 5N	27 30 E
Boerne, U.S.A.	71	29 47N	98 13W
Bofu, Japan	36	34 8N	131 40 E
Boga, Zaire	53	1 0N	29 58 E
Bogan Gate, N.S.W.	43	33 6S	147 44 E
Bogan R., N.S.W.	43	32 23S	147 40 E
Bogantungan, Queens.	42	23 41S	147 17 E
Bogata, U.S.A.	71	33 28N	95 15W
Bogelusa, U.S.A.	71	30 47N	89 50W
Bogenfels, S.W. Africa	51	27 25S	15 25 E
Boggabilla, N.S.W.	43	28 36S	150 24 E
Boggeragh Mts.. Ire.	11	52 2N	8 55W
Boghari, Algeria	50	35 51N	2 52 E
Boghé, Mauritania	50	16 45N	14 10W
Bogol Magno, Ethiopia	53	4 25N	41 30 E
Bogong Mt., Victoria	43	36 40S	147 15 E
Bogor, Indonesia	34	6 36S	106 48 E
Bogoro, Zaire	53	1 55N	30 17 E
Bogoro, Nigeria	52	9 37N	9 29 E
Bogotá, Colombia	78	4 34N	74 0W
Bogotol, U.S.S.R.	26	56 15N	89 50 E
Bogou, Togo	52	10 40N	0 12 E
Bogoyavlenskoye, U.S.S.R.	25	53 20N	40 10 E
Bogra, Bangladesh	33	24 46N	89 22 E
Boguchar, U.S.S.R.	25	49 55N	40 30 E
Bogulchan, U.S.S.R.	24	53 0N	56 20 E
Bohemia, C.Slov.	16	50 0N	14 0 E
Bohemian Forest, mts., Czechoslovakia	16	49 20N	13 0 E
Bohol I., Philippines	35	9 58N	124 20 E
Bohotlen, Somali Rep.	49	8 20N	46 25 E
Boi, Nigeria	52	9 35N	9 27 E
Boiestown, Canada	63	46 27N	66 26W
Boise, U.S.A.	72	43 54N	116 20W
Boise City, U.S.A.	71	36 45N	102 30W
Boissevain, Canada	65	49 15N	100 0W
Bojana, R., Albania–Yugoslavia	21	42 0N	25 25 E
Boju, Nigeria	52	7 18N	7 52 E
Boju Ega, Nigeria	52	7 18N	7 55 E
Bokani, Nigeria	52	9 28N	5 9 E

Place	MAP	Lat.	Long.
Boké, Guinea	50	10 56N	14 17w
Bokhara R., N.S.W.	43	29 25s	147 8 E
Bokkos, Nigeria	52	9 16N	8 56 E
Bokna Fd., Norway	23	59 12N	5 30 E
Bokoro, Chad.	51	12 25N	17 14 E
Bokote, Zaïre	54	0 12s	21 8 E
Bokpyin, Burma	34	11 10N	98 10 E
Bokungu, Zaïre	54	0 35s	22 50 E
Bolama, Port. Guinea	50	11 30N	15 30w
Bolangum, Victoria	43	36 50s	142 55 E
Bolanos, R., Mexico	74	22 0N	104 10w
Bolbec, France	12	49 30N	0 30 E
Bole, Ghana	52	9 0N	2 28w
Boleslawiec, Poland	16	51 17N	15 37 E
Bolgart, W. Australia	44	31 15s	116 22 E
Bolgatahga, Ghana	52	10 44N	0 53w
Bolgu I., Papua	44	9 13s	142 17 E
Boliden, Sweden	22	64 50N	20 20 E
Bolinao C., Philippines	35	16 30N	119 55 E
Bolivar, Argentina	77	36 2s	60 53w
Bolivar, Colombia	78	2 0N	77 0w
Bolivar, Mo., U.S.A.	71	37 46N	93 29w
Bolivar, Tenn., U.S.A.	71	35 15N	89 0w
Bolivar, Tenn., U.S.A.	69	35 14N	89 0w
Bolivia, rep., S. Amer.	78	17 6s	64 0w
Böllnäs, Sweden	23	61 22N	16 28 E
Bollon, Queensland	43	28 1s	147 30 E
Bollulos, Spain	17	37 22N	6 32w
Bolbo, Zaïre	54	2 6s	16 20 E
Bologna, Italy	20	44 30N	11 20 E
Bologoye, U.S.S.R.	25	57 55N	34 0 E
Bolomba, Zaïre	54	0 35N	19 0 E
Bolsena, L., Italy	20	42 35N	11 55 E
Bolshevik I., U.S.S.R.	27	78 30N	102 0 E
Bolshoi Altym, U.S.S.R.	26	62 25N	66 50 E
Bolshoi I., U.S.S.R.	27	73 30N	142 0 E
Bolshoi Mamyr, U.S.S.R.	27	56 20N	102 55 E
Bolsón de Mapimi, reg., Mexico	74	27 10N	104 10w
Bolsward, Netherlands	13	53 3N	5 32 E
Bolton, England	10	53 35N	2 26w
Bolu, Turkey	30	40 45N	31 35 E
Bolúngarvik, Iceland	22	66 12N	23 15w
Bolvadin, Turkey	30	38 42N	31 4 E
Bolzano, Italy	20	46 30N	11 20 E
Bom Despacho, Brazil	79	19 40s	46 27w
Bom Jardim, Brazil	79	12 20s	38 45w
Bom Jesus da Lapa, Brazil	79	13 10s	43 30w
Boma, Zaïre	54	5 50s	13 4 E
Bomba, G. of, Libya	51	32 20N	23 15 E
Bombala, N.S.W.	43	36 56s	149 15 E
Bombay, India	32	18 55N	72 50 E
Bombo, Uganda	53	0 36N	32 31 E
Bomboma, Zaïre	54	2 14N	19 6 E
Bombwe, Zambia	56	17 14s	25 21 E
Bomdila, India	33	27 15N	92 10 E
Bomi Hills, Liberia	52	7 1N	10 38 E
Bomili, Zaïre	54	1 45N	27 8 E
Bömlo, I., Norway	23	59 45N	5 10 E
Bomongo, Zaïre	54	1 21N	18 18 E
Bompata, Ghana	52	1 40N	1 0w
Bon C., Tunisia	51	37 1N	11 2 E
Bona Mt., Canada	60	61 20N	140 0w
Bonaire I., Neth. W. Indies	78	12 10N	68 15w
Bonaparte Archipelago, W. Australia	40	15 0s	124 30 E
Bonaparte, R., Canada	64	51 20N	121 0w
Bonar Bridge, Scotland	10	57 53N	4 20w
Bonaventure, Canada	63	48 5N	63 32w
Bonavista, Canada	63	48 40N	53 5w
Bonavista, B., Canada	63	48 58N	53 25w
Bonavista C., Canada	63	48 41N	53 5w
Bondeno, Italy	20	44 53N	11 25 E
Bondo, Zaïre	54	3 55N	23 53 E
Bondoukou, Ivory Coast	52	8 0N	2 49w
Bondowoso, Indonesia	34	7 56s	113 49 E
Bone, Gulf of, Indon.	35	4 10s	120 50 E
Bo'ness, Scotland	10	56 0N	3 38w
Bongandanga, Zaïre	54	1 28N	21 3 E
Bongongo, Zaïre	53	2 10N	29 35 E
Bongor, Chad.	51	10 35N	15 20 E
Bonham, U.S.A.	71	33 30N	96 0w
Bonifacio, Corsica	20	41 24N	9 10 E
Bonifacio, Str. of, Cors.	20	41 25N	9 0 E
Bonin Is., Pacific Ocean	5	27 0N	142 0 E
Bonkoukou, Niger	52	14 0N	3 14 E
Bonn, Germany	14	50 43N	7 6 E
Bonne B., Canada	63	40 31N	58 0w
Bonne Espérance, Can.	63	51 24N	57 40w
Bonne Terre, U.S.A.	71	37 58N	90 34w
Bonners Ferry, U.S.A.	72	48 47N	116 51w
Bonneville, France	12	46 5N	6 24 E
Bonnie Rock, W. Australia	44	30 29s	118 22 E
Bonny, Nigeria	52	4 25N	7 13 E
Bonny, R., Nigeria	52	4 20N	7 14 E
Bonnyville, Canada	65	54 20N	110 45w
Bonshaw, N.S.W.	43	29 0s	151 14 E
Bontang, Indonesia	35	0 10N	117 30 E
Bonthe, Sierra Leone	52	7 30N	12 33w
Bonyeri, Ghana	52	4 58N	2 45w
Bonython Ra., W. Australia	45	23 40s	128 45 E
Boogardie, W. Austral.	44	28 0s	117 40 E
Bookaloo, S. Australia	45	31 57s	137 20 E
Booker, U.S.A.	71	36 28N	100 30w
Boolboonda, Queens.	43	25 3s	151 44 E
Booleroo Centre, S. Australia	43	32 50s	138 18 E
Booligal, N.S.W.	43	33 58s	144 53 E
Boom, Belgium	13	51 6N	4 20 E
Boomer Mts., Queens.	42	23 15s	149 45 E
Boomi, N.S.W.	43	28 40s	149 30 E
Boonah, Queens.	43	28 0s	152 35 E
Boone, U.S.A.	70	42 3N	93 49w
Boone, N.C., U.S.A.	69	36 14N	81 43w
Booneville, Ark., U.S.A.	71	35 8N	93 58w
Booneville, Miss., U.S.A.	69	34 39N	88 34w
Boongoondoo, Queens.	42	22 55s	145 55 E
Boonmoo, Queensland	42	17 15s	145 5 E
Boonville, Ind., U.S.A.	68	38 3N	87 18w
Boonville, Mo., U.S.A.	68	39 0N	92 40w
Boorabbin, W. Austral.	44	31 12s	120 18 E
Boorooman, Queens.	42	20 51s	144 50 E
Booroorban, N.S.W.	42	34 53s	144 46 E
Boothia Gulf, Canada	61	70 0N	90 0w
Boothia Pen., Canada	60	70 30N	95 0w
Booué, Gabon	54	0 5s	11 55 E
Bopo, Nigeria	52	7 33N	7 50 E
Bor, Sudan	54	6 10N	31 36 E
Bor, Yugoslavia	21	44 8N	22 7 E
Borang, Sudan	53	4 50N	30 59 E
Borås, Sweden	23	57 42N	13 1 E
Borazjan, Iran	31	29 22N	51 10 E
Borba, Brazil	78	4 39s	59 35w
Bordeaux, France	12	44 50N	0 36w
Borden, Canada	63	46 18N	63 47w
Bordertown, S. Austral.	43	36 21s	140 44 E
Bordeyri, Iceland	22	65 12N	21 8w
Bordighera, Italy	20	43 47N	7 40 E
Bordj Fly Ste. Marie, Algeria	50	27 15N	3 10w
Bordj-in-Eker, Algeria	50	24 5N	5 10 E
Bore, Ethiopia	53	4 40N	37 35 E
Borganes, Iceland	22	64 33N	21 55w
Börgefjell, mts., Nor.	22	65 20N	13 30 E
Borger, U.S.A.	71	35 40N	101 20w
Borgholm, Sweden	23	56 54N	16 48 E
Borgne R., Switz.	15	46 10N	7 25 E
Borgo San Lorenzo, It.	20	43 57N	11 21 E
Borgosesia, Italy	20	45 43N	8 9 E
Bori, Dahomey	52	9 46N	2 29 E
Borikane, Laos	34	18 37N	103 37 E
Borinage, Belgium	13	50 22N	3 50 E
Boris Vilkitski Strait, U.S.S.R.	27	77 40N	105 0 E
Borisoglebsk, U.S.S.R.	25	51 27N	42 5 E
Borisov, U.S.S.R.	25	54 17N	28 28 E
Borja, Paraguay	77	25 35s	56 40w
Borja, Peru	78	4 20s	77 40w
Borja, Spain	17	41 48N	1 34w
Borkum I., Germany	14	53 35N	6 40 E
Borlange, Sweden	23	60 28N	15 25 E
Bormio, Italy	20	46 28N	10 22 E
Borneo, I., East Indies	35	1 0N	115 0 E
Borneo, N. (Sabah), Malaysia	35	5 0N	117 0 E
Bornholm I., Denmark	23	55 8N	14 55 E
Bornu, prov., Nigeria	52	12 0N	12 0 E
Bornu Yassu, Nigeria	52	12 14N	12 25 E
Boromo, Ivory Coast	50	11 45N	2 58w
Bororen, Queensland	42	24 13s	151 33 E
Borovichi, U.S.S.R.	25	58 30N	33 50 E
Borris, Ireland	11	52 36N	6 57w
Borris-in-Ossory, Ire.	11	52 57N	7 40w
Borrisokane, Ireland	11	53 0N	8 8w
Borrisoleigh, Ireland	11	52 48N	7 58w
Börselv, Norway	22	70 20N	25 30 E
Bort, France	12	45 24N	2 29 E
Borujerd, Iran	30	34 0N	48 45 E
Bosa, Sardinia	20	40 18N	8 30 E
Bosanska Gradiska, Yugoslavia	20	45 15N	17 18 E
Bosanska Petrovac, Yugoslavia	20	44 35N	16 21 E
Bosanski Novi, Y. slav.	20	45 2N	16 22 E
Boshoek, S. Africa	57	25 30s	27 9 E
Boshof, O.F.S.	57	28 31s	25 13 E
Boshruyeh, Iran	31	34 1N	57 25 E
Bosna R., Yugoslavia	21	44 50N	18 10 E
Bosnek, Indonesia	35	1 5s	136 10 E
Bosnia and Hercegovina, Yugoslavia	20	44 40N	17 0 E
Bosobolo, Zaïre	54	4 11N	19 55 E
Bosoti, S. Rhodesia	56	20 57s	27 33 E
Bosporus. See Karadeniz Bogazi, Turkey	30		
Bossembelé, Cent. Afr.	54	5 25N	17 40 E
Bossier City, U.S.A.	71	32 32N	93 15w
Bosso, Niger	52	13 40N	13 15 E
Bostan, W. Pakistan	32	30 23N	67 00 E
Boston, England	10	52 59N	0 2w
Boston, U.S.A.	69	42 20N	71 0w
Boston Bar, Canada	64	49 52N	121 22w
Boswell, Canada	64	49 50N	117 0w
Boswell, U.S.A.	71	34 1N	95 55w
Botad, India	32	22 15N	71 40 E
Botafogo, Brazil	78	8 40s	69 40w
Botany B., N.S.W.	43	34 2s	151 6 E
Botevgrad, Bulgaria	21	42 55N	23 47 E
Bothaville, O.F.S.	57	27 23s	26 34 E
Bothnia, G. of, Europe	23	63 0N	21 0 E
Bothwell, Tasmania	43	42 20s	146 58 E
Botletle, R., Botswana	56	20 10s	24 20 E
Botosani, Rumania	21	47 42N	26 41 E
Botou, Niger	52	12 45N	2 5 E
Botswana, Africa	57	23 0s	24 0 E
Botterleegte, C. Prov.	57	30 33s	21 22 E
Bottineau, U.S.A.	70	48 49N	100 28w
Botucatu, Brazil	77	22 55s	48 30w
Botwood, Canada	63	49 6N	55 23w
Bou Arfa, Morocco	50	33 0N	2 0w
Bou Djebeha, Sudan	50	18 33N	2 50w
Bou Saâda, Algeria	50	35 9N	4 8 E
Bouaké, Ivory Coast	50	7 40N	4 55w
Boudi, Ethiopia	53	4 5N	40 10 E
Bougie, Algeria	50	36 42N	5 2 E
Bougouni, Sudan	50	11 30N	7 20w
Bouillon, Belgium	13	49 44N	5 3 E
Boukma, Cameroon	52	8 30N	13 50w
Boukoumbé, Dahomey	52	10 12N	1 0 E
Boulder, Colo., U.S.A.	70	40 0N	105 0w
Boulder, Mont., U.S.A.	72	46 14N	112 5w
Boulder, W. Australia	44	30 55s	121 28 E
Boulder City, U.S.A.	73	36 1N	114 56w
Boulia, Queensland	42	22 52s	139 51 E
Boulogne-sur-Mer, Fr.	12	50 42N	1 36 E
Boumba, Niger	52	12 23N	2 52 E
Bouna, Ivory Coast	52	9 10N	3 0w
Boundary, Yukon	59	64 37N	140 53w
Boundiali, Ivory Coast	50	9 30N	6 20w
Bountiful, U.S.A.	72	40 26N	111 56w
Bourbon Lancy, France	12	46 37N	3 45 E
Bourbonnais, prov., Fr.	12	46 28N	3 0 E
Bourem, Sudan	50	17 6N	0 10w
Boureyni, Niger	52	12 54s	3 51 E
Bourganeuf, France	12	45 57N	1 45 E
Bourges, France	12	47 5N	2 22 E
Bourgneuf, France	12	47 2N	1 58w
Bourgogne, reg., Fr.	12	47 0N	4 30 E
Bourgoin, France	12	45 36N	5 17 E
Bourke, N.S.W.	43	30 8s	145 55 E
Bourlamaque, Canada	62	48 5N	77 56w
Bournemouth, England	10	50 43N	1 53w
Boutilimit, Mauritania	50	17 45N	14 40w
Bouvet I., S. Atlan. Oc.	5	55 0s	3 30 E
Bouza, Niger	52	4 30N	6 0 E
Bovigny, Belgium	13	50 12N	5 55 E
Bovill, U.S.A.	72	46 50N	116 25w
Bovino, Italy	20	41 15N	15 20 E
Bow R., Canada	64	51 10N	115 0w
Bowbells, U.S.A.	70	48 40N	102 15w
Bowdle, U.S.A.	70	45 30N	99 38w
Bowen (Port Denison), Queensland	42	20 0s	148 16 E
Bowen Downs, Queens.	42	22 30s	145 0 E
Bowen Mts., Victoria	43	37 0s	148 0 E
Bowen R., Queensland	42	20 42s	147 45 E
Bowgada, W. Australia	44	29 19s	116 19 E
Bowie, Ariz., U.S.A.	73	32 20N	109 31w
Bowie, Okla., U.S.A.	71	33 32N	97 54w
Bowling Green, Ky., U.S.A.	68	37 0N	86 25w
Bowling Green, Ohio, U.S.A.	68	41 22N	83 40w
Bowling Green C., Queensland	42	19 20s	147 28 E
Bowman, U.S.A.	71	46 11N	103 25w
Bowmanville, Canada	62	43 55N	78 40w
Bowness Park, Canada	64	50 51N	114 25w
Bowral, N.S.W.	43	34 26s	150 27 E
Bowron R., Canada	64	53 30N	122 0w
Bowser L., Canada	64	56 30N	130 0w
Bowsman, Canada	65	52 25N	101 20w
Bowwood, Zambia	56	17 5s	26 20 E
Boxtel, Netherlands	13	51 36N	5 9 E
Boyabat, Turkey	30	41 28N	34 47 E
Boyanup, W. Australia	44	33 39s	115 38 E
Boyce, U.S.A.	71	31 27N	92 37w
Boyd L., Canada	65	51 30N	103 20w
Boyd L., Canada	62	52 40N	76 10w
Boyer R., Canada	64	58 20N	116 50w
Boyle, Ireland	11	53 58N	8 19w
Boyne City, U.S.A.	68	45 12N	84 55w
Boyne, R., Ireland	11	53 43N	6 15w
Boyne R., Queensland	43	26 0s	151 20 E
Boynton Beach, U.S.A.	69	26 31N	80 3w
Boyup Brook, W. Australia	44	33 47s	116 40 E
Bozca Ada, Turkey	30	39 49N	26 3 E
Bozeman, U.S.A.	72	45 40N	111 0w
Brabant L., Canada	65	56 0N	104 10w
Brabant, prov., Belgium	13	49 15N	5 20 E
Brac I., Yugoslavia	20	43 20N	16 40 E
Bracciano L., Italy	20	42 8N	12 12 E
Bracebridge, Canada	62	45 5N	79 20w
Bracebridge, England	9	53 13N	0 33w
Brach, Libya	51	27 31N	14 20 E
Bräcke, Sweden	23	62 42N	15 32 E
Bracketville, U.S.A.	71	29 22N	100 19w
Braço Maior R., Brazil	79	10 45s	50 50w
Braço Menor R., Brazil	79	12 0s	50 0w
Brad, Rumania	21	46 10N	22 50 E
Bradenton, U.S.A.	69	27 25N	82 35w
Bradford, England	10	53 47N	1 45w
Bradford, Pa., U.S.A.	68	41 58N	78 41w
Bradley, U.S.A.	71	33 4N	93 42w
Bradley Institute, S. Rhodesia	56	17 7s	31 25 E
Bradore Bay, Canada	63	51 27N	57 18w
Brady, U.S.A.	71	31 0N	99 25w
Braeburn, Canada	64	61 25N	135 30w
Braemar, Scotland	10	57 2N	3 20w
Bragança, Brazil	79	1 0s	47 2w
Brahmanbaria, Ban.	33	23 50N	91 15 E
Brahmani R., India	33	21 0N	85 15 E
Brahmaputra R., India	33	26 30N	93 30 E
Brahmaur, India	32	32 25N	76 35 E
Braidwood, N.S.W.	43	35 27s	149 49 E
Braila, Rumania	21	45 19N	27 59 E
Brainerd, U.S.A.	70	46 20N	94 10w
Brajau, R., Brazil	79	4 40s	46 0w
Brak R., C. Prov.	57	29 50s	23 10 E
Brakwater, S.W. Africa	57	22 24s	17 6 E
Bralorne, Canada	64	50 50N	123 15w
Bramhapuri, India	32	20 40N	79 55 E
Brampton, Canada	62	43 45N	79 45w
Bramsche, Germany	14	52 27N	7 57 E
Branco R., Brazil	78	1 30N	61 15w
Brandberg, mt., S.W. Africa	57	21 10s	14 33 E
Brandenburg, Germany	14	52 24N	12 33 E
Brandfort, O.F.S.	57	28 40s	26 30 E
Brandon, Canada	65	49 50N	100 0w
Brandon, Queensland	42	19 31s	147 14 E
Brandon B., Ireland	11	52 17N	10 8w
Brandvlei, C. Prov.	57	30 25s	20 30 E
Braniewo, Poland	23	54 25N	19 50 E
Bransby, Queensland	43	28 10s	142 0 E
Bransk, Poland	16	52 47N	22 50 E
Branson, Ark., U.S.A.	71	36 39N	93 17w
Branson, Colo., U.S.A.	71	37 1N	103 57w
Brantford, Canada	62	43 15N	80 15w
Branxholme, Victoria	43	37 52s	141 49 E
Brasiléia, Brazil	78	10 9s	68 35w
Brasilia, fed. dist., Brazil	79	15 30s	47 30w
Braşov, Rumania	21	45 39N	25 35 E
Brass, Nigeria	52	4 15N	6 14 E
Brass R., Nigeria	52	4 15N	6 13 E
Brasschaat, Belgium	13	51 19N	4 27 E
Brassey Ra., W. Austral.	44	25 8s	122 15 E
Brasstown Bald, mt., U.S.A.	69	34 54N	83 45w
Bratislava, C.Slov.	16	48 10N	17 7 E
Bratsk, U.S.S.R.	27	56 10N	101 30 E
Brattleboro, U.S.A.	69	42 53N	72 37w
Brava, Somali Rep.	49	1 20N	44 8 E
Brawley, U.S.A.	73	33 0N	115 40w
Bray, France	11	49 57N	2 40 E
Bray-sur-Seine, France	12	48 24N	3 12 E
Brazeau, Canada	64	52 30N	116 10w
Brazil, rep., S. Amer.	79	5 0N to 34 0s	35 0w to 74 0w
Brazil, U.S.A.	68	39 30N	87 8w
Brazilian Highlands, Brazil	79	18 0s	46 30w
Brazos, R., U.S.A.	71	30 30N	96 40w
Brazzaville, Congo (Fr.)	54	4 9s	15 12 E
Breaden, L., W. Austral.	45	25 51s	125 28 E
Breaksea Sd., N.Z.	47	45 35s	166 39 E
Bream Bay, N.Z.	46	35 56s	174 35 E
Bream Head, N.Z.	46	35 51s	174 35 E
Bream Tail, N.Z.	46	36 3N	174 36 E
Brebes, Indonesia	34	6 52s	109 3 E
Breckenridge, Colo., U.S.A.	70	38 28N	105 18w
Breckenridge, Minn., U.S.A.	70	46 21N	96 32w
Breckenridge, Texas, U.S.A.	71	32 49N	98 51w
Brecknock Pen., Chile	77	54 50s	73 30w
Břeclav, C.Slov.	16	48 46N	16 53 E
Breda, Netherlands	13	51 35N	4 45 E
Bredasdorp, C. Prov.	57	34 33s	20 2 E
Bregenz, Austria	14	47 30N	9 45 E
Breid Bay, Antarctica	80	71 25s	25 0 E
Breidifjördur, Iceland	22	65 15N	24 0w
Brejo, Brazil	79	34 40s	73 5w
Bremen, Germany	14	53 4N	8 47 E
Bremen, land, Germany	23	53 6N	8 46 E
Bremerhaven, Germany	14	53 34N	8 35 E
Bremersdorp, (Manzini), Swaziland	57	26 30s	31 25 E
Bremerton, U.S.A.	72	47 30N	122 40w
Bremgarten. Switz.	15	47 21N	8 20 E
Brenham, U.S.A.	71	30 5N	96 15w
Brenner Pass, Alps	20	47 0N	11 30 E
Brent, Canada	62	46 0N	78 30w
Brescia, Italy	20	45 33N	10 13 E
Breskens, Netherlands	13	51 23N	3 33 E
Breslau. See Wroclaw.	16		
Bresnahan, Mt., W. Australia	44	23 45s	117 55 E
Bressanone. Italy	20	46 43N	11 39 E
Bressay I., Scotland	10	60 10N	1 5w
Bressuire, France	12	46 51N	0 30w
Brest, France	12	48 24N	4 31w
Brest, U.S.S.R.	24	52 10N	23 40 E
Bretagne, prov., Fr.	12	48 0N	3 0w
Bretcu, Rumania	21	46 7N	26 18 E
Breton, Canada	64	53 0N	114 30w
Breton Sd., U.S.A.	71	29 30N	89 0w
Brett, C., New Zealand	46	35 11s	174 21 E
Breu Branco, Brazil	79	4 0s	49 30w
Brevard, U.S.A.	69	35 19N	82 42w
Breves, Brazil	79	1 30s	50 0w
Brevik, Norway	23	59 6N	9 45 E
Brewarrina, N.S.W.	43	30 0s	146 51 E
Brewer, U.S.A.	63	44 43N	68 50w
Brewster, U.S.A.	72	48 7N	119 46w
Brewster C. Greenland	58	70 0N	25 0w
Brewton, U.S.A.	69	31 9N	87 2w

Place	MAP	Lat.	Long.
Breyten, Transvaal	57	26 16 S	30 0 E
Briagolong, Victoria	43	37 45 S	147 0 E
Briançon, France	12	44 54 N	6 39 E
Briare, France	12	47 38 N	2 45 E
Bribie I., Queensland	43	27 0 S	152 58 E
Bridge R., Canada	64	50 50 N	122 40 W
Bridgeport, Calif., U.S.A.	73	38 16 N	119 15 W
Bridgeport, Conn., U.S.A.	68	41 12 N	73 12 W
Bridgeport, Neb., U.S.A.	70	14 42 N	103 8 W
Bridgeport, Texas, U.S.A.	71	33 12 N	97 47 W
Bridges, U.S.A.	72	45 19 N	108 55 W
Bridgeton, U.S.A.	68	39 29 N	75 10 W
Bridgetown, Canada	63	44 55 N	65 12 W
Bridgetown, Barbados	75	13 0 N	59 30 W
Bridgetown, W. Austral.	44	33 58 S	116 7 E
Bridgewater, Canada	63	44 25 N	64 31 W
Bridgewater C., Victoria	43	38 12 S	141 28 E
Bridgewater, U.S.A.	70	43 34 N	90 30 W
Bridgwater, England	10	51 7 N	3 0 W
Bridlington, England	10	54 6 N	0 11 W
Bridport, Tasmania	43	41 0 S	147 25 E
Brienne, France	12	48 24 N	4 30 E
Brienz, Switzerland	15	46 46 N	8 2 E
Brienzer See, Switz.	15	46 44 N	7 53 E
Brifu, Gambia	52	13 30 N	14 0 E
Brig, Switzerland	15	46 18 N	7 59 E
Briggsdale, U.S.A.	70	40 35 N	103 58 W
Brigham City, U.S.A.	72	41 30 N	112 2 W
Bright, Victoria	43	36 42 S	146 56 E
Brighton, Canada	62	44 3 N	77 44 W
Brighton, England	10	50 50 N	0 9 W
Brighton, S. Australia	43	35 1 S	138 30 E
Brighton, Tasmania	43	42 40 S	147 14 E
Brighton, U.S.A.	70	39 59 N	104 48 W
Brightwater, N.Z.	47	41 22 S	173 9 E
Brikama, Gambia	52	13 15 N	16 45 W
Brilliant, Canada	64	49 19 N	117 55 W
Brindisi, Italy	21	40 39 N	17 55 E
Brinkley, U.S.A.	71	34 50 N	91 14 W
Brion I., Canada	63	47 46 N	61 26 W
Brioude, France	12	45 18 N	3 22 E
Brisbane, Queensland	43	27 25 S	152 54 E
Brisbane R., Queens.	43	27 0 S	152 25 E
Bristol, Canada	69	45 33 N	76 30 W
Bristol, England	10	51 26 N	2 35 W
Bristol, Conn., U.S.A.	69	41 44 N	72 37 W
Bristol, S.D., U.S.A.	70	45 25 N	97 32 W
Bristol B., Alaska	59	58 30 N	158 0 W
Bristol Channel, Eng.	10	51 18 N	3 30 W
Bristow, U.S.A.	71	35 49 N	96 27 W
British Antarctic Terr.	80	67 0 S	40 0 W
British Columbia, prov., Canada	64	55 0 N	125 15 W
British Honduras, col., Central America	74	17 0 N	88 30 W
British Isles, Europe	10	50 0 N to 60 0 N	10 0 W to 2 0 E
Brits, Transvaal	57	25 37 S	27 48 E
Britstown, C. Prov.	57	30 37 S	23 30 E
Britt, Canada	62	45 46 N	80 35 W
Britton, U.S.A.	70	45 40 N	97 48 W
Brive, France	12	45 10 N	1 32 E
Brixton, Queensland	42	23 32 S	144 52 E
Brno (Brünn), C.Slov.	16	49 10 N	16 35 E
Broach, India	32	21 47 N	73 0 E
Broad Arrow, W. Australia	44	30 23 S	121 15 E
Broad Haven, Ireland	11	54 20 N	9 55 W
Broad R., U.S.A.	69	34 30 N	81 26 W
Broad Sd., Queensland	42	22 0 S	149 45 E
Broadback R., Canada	62	51 20 N	78 0 W
Broadlaw, mt., Scot.	10	55 30 N	3 22 W
Broadus, U.S.A.	70	45 30 N	105 26 W
Broadview, Canada	65	50 25 N	102 35 E
Brochet, Canada	62	47 12 N	72 42 W
Brochet, Canada	65	57 55 N	101 40 W
Brock, Canada	65	51 30 N	108 35 W
Brocken, mt., Germany	14	51 48 N	10 40 E
Brockman Mt., W. Australia	44	22 25 S	117 15 E
Brockport, U.S.A.	68	43 3 N	77 57 W
Brockton, U.S.A.	69	42 8 N	71 2 W
Brockville, Canada	62	44 37 N	75 38 W
Brockway, U.S.A.	70	47 25 N	105 44 W
Brod, Croatia, Y.slav.	21	45 10 N	18 2 E
Brod, Macedonia, Yugoslavia	21	41 35 N	21 17 E
Brodnica, Poland	16	53 15 N	19 25 E
Brogan, U.S.A.	72	44 17 N	117 30 W
Broken B., N.S.W.	43	33 30 S	151 15 E
Broken Bow, Neb. U.S.A.	70	41 26 N	99 33 W
Broken Bow, Okla., U.S.A.	71	34 1 N	94 46 W
Broken Hill, N.S.W.	43	31 58 S	141 29 E
Bromhead, Canada	65	49 18 N	103 40 W
Brönderslev, Denmark	23	57 17 N	9 55 E
Bronkhorstspruit, Trans.	57	25 46 S	28 45 E
Brönnöysund, Norway	22	65 27 N	12 25 E
Bronte, Italy	20	37 48 N	14 49 E
Bronte, U.S.A.	71	31 52 N	100 16 W
Brookfield, U.S.A.	70	39 48 N	92 46 W
Brookhaven, U.S.A.	71	31 40 N	90 25 W
Brookings, N. Dak., U.S.A.	70	44 20 N	97 0 W
Brookings, Oreg., U.S.A.	72	42 5 N	124 18 W
Brookmere, Canada	64	49 52 N	120 53 W
Brooks, Canada	64	50 35 N	111 55 W
Brooks B., Canada	64	50 20 N	127 50 W
Brooks Ra., Alaska	59	68 40 N	147 0 W
Brooksville, U.S.A.	69	41 11 N	79 7 W
Brookton, W. Austral.	44	32 22 S	116 57 E
Brookville, Queensland	42	20 9 S	146 57 E
Brookville, U.S.A.	68	39 25 N	85 0 W
Brooloo, Queensland	43	26 30 S	152 36 E
Broom, L., Scotland	10	57 55 N	5 15 W
Broome, W. Australia	44	18 0 S	122 15 E
Broome Hill, W. Australia	44	33 40 S	117 36 E
Brosna R., Ireland	11	53 8 N	8 0 W
Brothers, U.S.A.	72	43 56 N	120 33 W
Broughshane, N. Ire.	11	54 54 N	6 12 W
Brouwershaven, Neth.	13	51 45 N	3 55 E
Browerville, U.S.A.	70	46 5 N	94 52 W
Brown Mt., S. Austral.	43	32 30 N	138 0 E
Brownfield, U.S.A.	71	33 7 N	102 15 W
Browning, U.S.A.	72	48 32 N	113 0 W
Browning Pass, N.Z.	47	42 57 S	171 21 E
Brownlee, Canada	65	50 43 N	105 59 W
Brown's Bay, N.Z.	46	36 42 S	174 44 E
Brownsville, Oreg., U.S.A.	72	44 28 N	123 0 W
Brownsville, Tenn., U.S.A.	71	35 33 N	89 15 W
Brownsville, Texas, U.S.A.	71	26 0 N	97 25 W
Brownwood, U.S.A.	71	31 45 N	99 0 W
Brownwood L., U.S.A.	71	31 50 N	99 0 W
Broye, R., Switz.	15	46 52 N	7 00 E
Bru, Iceland	22	65 5 N	15 25 W
Bruas, Malaya	34	4 31 N	100 46 E
Bruce B., New Zealand	47	43 35 S	169 35 E
Bruce Mt., W. Austral.	44	22 31 S	118 6 E
Bruce Mines, Canada	62	46 20 N	83 45 W
Bruce Rock, W.Austral.	44	31 51 S	118 2 E
Bruchsal, Germany	14	49 9 N	8 39 E
Bruck, Lower Austria	14	48 1 N	16 47 E
Bruck, Styria, Austria	14	47 24 N	15 16 E
Bruges (Brugge), Belg.	13	51 13 N	3 13 E
Brugg, Switzerland	15	47 29 N	8 11 E
Brundidge, U.S.A.	69	31 43 N	85 45 W
Bruneau, U.S.A.	72	42 57 N	115 50 W
Bruneau, R., U.S.A.	72	42 40 N	115 45 W
Brunei, Borneo	35	4 52 N	115 0 E
Brunei, prot., Borneo	35	4 52 N	115 0 E
Brunig P., Switzerland	15	46 46 N	8 8 E
Brunnen, Switzerland	15	46 59 N	8 37 E
Brunner, New Zealand	47	42 27 S	171 20 E
Brunner, L., N.Z.	47	42 38 S	171 30 E
Bruno, Canada	65	52 20 N	105 30 W
Brunsbüttelkoog, Ger.	14	53 55 N	9 10 E
Brunswick, Canada	63	45 20 N	67 7 W
Brunswick, Germany	14	52 15 N	10 30 W
Brunswick, Ga., U.S.A.	67	31 10 N	81 30 W
Brunswick, Me., U.S.A.	69	43 53 N	69 50 W
Brunswick, Md., U.S.A.	69	39 20 N	77 38 W
Brunswick, Miss., U.S.A.	68	39 27 N	93 7 W
Brunswick, Mo., U.S.A.	68	39 26 N	93 10 W
Brunswick, Va., U.S.A.	69	36 40 N	77 52 W
Brunswick Pen., Chile	77	53 30 S	71 30 W
Bruny I., Tasmania	43	43 20 S	147 15 E
Brush, U.S.A.	70	40 18 N	103 36 W
Brusque, Brazil	77	27 5 S	49 0 W
Brussel. *See* Brussels.	13		
Brussels (Bruxelles), Belgium	13	50 51 N	4 21 E
Bruthen, Victoria	43	38 30 S	146 50 E
Bruxelles. *See* Brussels.	13		
Bryan, Ohio, U.S.A.	68	41 30 N	84 30 W
Bryan, Texas, U.S.A.	71	30 45 N	96 0 W
Bryansk, U.S.S.R.	25	53 15 N	34 20 E
Bryanskoye, U.S.S.R.	25	44 9 N	47 10 E
Bryant, U.S.A.	70	44 40 N	97 27 W
Bryne, Norway	23	58 45 N	5 36 E
Bryson City, U.S.A.	69	35 28 N	83 25 W
Brza Palanka, Y.slav.	21	44 28 N	22 37 E
Brzeg, Poland	16	50 52 N	17 27 E
Buapinang, Indonesia	35	4 40 S	121 30 E
Bubanza, Burundi	53	3 6 S	29 22 E
Bubu R., Tanzania	53	5 35 S	35 27 E
Bucak, Turkey	30	37 27 N	30 38 E
Bucaramanga, Col.	78	7 0 N	73 0 W
Buccarale, Ethiopia	53	4 32 N	42 0 E
Buchan Ness, Scotland	10	57 29 N	1 48 W
Buchanan, Canada	65	51 40 N	102 45 W
Buchanan, Liberia	50	5 57 N	10 2 W
Buchanan L., Queens.	42	21 33 S	145 50 E
Buchanan L., U.S.A.	71	30 55 N	98 28 W
Buchanan L., W. Australia	45	25 30 S	123 0 E
Buchans, Canada	63	49 0 N	57 2 W
Buchardo, Argentina	77	34 40 S	63 30 W
Bucharest (Bucuresti), Rumania	21	44 27 N	26 10 E
Buchs, Switzerland	15	47 9 N	9 28 E
Buckeye, U.S.A.	73	33 27 N	112 39 W
Buckhannon, U.S.A.	68	39 2 N	80 10 W
Buckingham, Canada	62	45 37 N	75 24 W
Buckingham, England	10	52 0 N	0 59 W
Buckingham B., N.Terr.	40	12 0 S	136 2 E
Buckingham Downs, Queensland	42	22 1 S	139 42 E
Buckland, Alaska	59	65 59 N	161 19 W
Buckleboo, S.Australia	45	32 55 S	136 15 E
Buckley, U.S.A.	72	47 8 N	122 2 W
Bucklin, U.S.A.	71	37 36 N	99 32 W
Buctouche, Canada	63	46 30 N	64 45 W
Bucyrus, U.S.A.	68	40 48 N	83 0 W
Budalin, Burma	33	22 20 N	95 10 E
Budapest, Hungary	16	47 29 N	19 5 E
Budareyri, Iceland	22	65 0 N	14 10 W
Budaun, India	32	28 5 N	79 10 E
Budde, Ethiopia	53	4 30 N	40 30 E
Buddenovsk, U.S.S.R.	25	44 50 N	44 15 E
Bude, England	10	50 49 N	4 33 W
Budir, Iceland	22	64 48 N	23 21 W
Budjala, Zaire	54	2 50 N	19 40 E
Budrio, Italy	20	44 31 N	11 31 E
Budslav, U.S.S.R.	23	54 47 N	27 23 E
Buea, W. Cameroon	52	4 10 N	9 9 E
Buena Esperanza, Arg.	77	34 45 S	65 22 W
Buena Vista, Calif., U.S.A.	73	35 12 N	119 18 W
Buena Vista, Col., U.S.A.	73	38 51 N	106 6 W
Buena Vista, Va., U.S.A.	68	37 47 N	79 23 W
Buenaventura, Chihuahua Mexico	74	33 40 S	69 0 W
Buenaventura, Col.	78	4 0 N	77 0 W
Buenos Aires, Arg.	77	34 30 S	58 20 W
Buenos Aires, prov., Argentina	77	35 0 S	58 0 W
Buffalo, Minn., U.S.A.	68	45 10 N	93 58 W
Buffalo, Mo., U.S.A.	68	37 40 N	93 5 W
Buffalo, N.Y., U.S.A.	69	42 55 N	78 50 W
Buffalo, Okla., U.S.A.	71	36 51 N	99 41 W
Buffalo, S.D., U.S.A.	70	45 39 N	103 32 W
Buffalo L., Canada	64	60 20 N	115 30 W
Buffalo Narrows, Can.	65	55 52 N	108 28 W
Buffalo R., Canada	64	60 30 N	115 0 W
Buffalo R., S. Africa	57	28 0 S	31 0 E
Buffalo Head Hills, Canada	64	58 0 N	116 20 W
Buffels R., C.Prov.	57	29 36 S	17 15 E
Buford, U.S.A.	69	34 5 N	84 0 W
Bug R., Poland	16	51 20 N	23 40 E
Bug R., U.S.S.R.	25	48 0 N	31 0 E
Buga, Colombia	78	4 0 N	77 0 W
Buga, Nigeria	52	8 1 N	7 16 E
Buganda King. & Prov., Uganda	53	0 0 N	31 30 E
Buganga, Uganda	53	0 25 N	32 0 E
Bugel, Tg., C., Indon.	34	6 28 S	111 2 E
Bugisu, dist., E. Prov., Uganda	53	1 20 N	34 20 E
Bugojno, Yugoslavia	20	44 2 N	17 25 E
Bugrino, U.S.S.R.	26	69 0 N	49 20 E
Bugsak, I., Philippines	35	8 15 N	117 15 E
Bugulma, U.S.S.R.	24	54 38 N	52 40 E
Buguma, Nigeria	52	4 42 N	6 55 E
Bugun Shara, Mon.	37	48 40 N	103 00 E
Buguruslan, U.S.S.R.	24	53 42 N	52 15 E
Buhera, Rhodesia	56	19 20 S	31 35 E
Buhl, U.S.A.	72	42 38 N	114 50 W
Bui, U.S.S.R.	25	58 30 N	41 30 E
Buina Qara, Afghan.	31	36 23 N	66 53 E
Buina Qara, Afghan.	31	36 23 N	66 53 E
Buinaksk, U.S.S.R.	24	42 52 N	47 0 E
Bujagali, Uganda	53	0 30 N	33 12 E
Bujalance, Spain	17	37 53 N	4 23 W
Bujnurd, Iran	31	37 35 N	57 15 E
Bujumbura (Usumbra), Burundi	53	3 16 S	29 18 E
Bukachacha, U.S.S.R.	27	52 55 N	116 50 E
Bukama, Zaire	55	9 10 S	25 50 E
Bukandula, Uganda	53	0 13 N	31 50 E
Bukavu, Zaire	53	2 20 S	28 52 E
Bukedi, dist., E. Prov., Uganda	53	1 0 N	34 0 E
Bukene, Tanzania	53	4 15 S	32 48 E
Bukhara, U.S.S.R.	26	39 50 N	64 10 E
Bukima, Tanzania	53	1 50 S	33 25 E
Bukit Mertajam, Malaya	34	5 22 N	100 28 E
Bukittingi, Indonesia	34	0 20 S	100 20 E
Bukombe, Tanzania	53	3 32 S	32 4 E
Bukumbirwa, Zaire	53	0 50 S	28 55 E
Bukuru, Nigeria	52	9 42 N	8 48 E
Bukuya, Uganda	53	0 42 N	31 52 E
Bula, Indonesia	35	3 10 S	130 20 E
Bülach, Switzerland	15	47 32 N	8 32 E
Bulagan, Mongolia	37	48 34 N	103 12 E
Bulan, Philippines	35	12 45 N	124 0 E
Bulandshahr, India	32	28 28 N	77 58 E
Bulangan, Indonesia	35	2 45 N	117 25 E
Bulawayo, Rhodesia	56	20 7 S	28 32 E
Buldana, India	32	20 30 N	76 18 E
Buldir, I., Aleutian Is.	59	52 20 N	175 55 E
Bulgaria, rep., Europe	21	42 35 N	34 30 E
Bulgroo, Queensland	43	25 47 S	143 58 E
Buli, Indonesia	35	1 5 N	128 25 E
Bulinski, U.S.S.R.	27	68 10 N	123 5 E
Bulkley R., Canada	64	55 0 N	127 25 W
Bulle, Switzerland	15	46 37 N	7 3 E
Buller Gorge, N.Z.	47	41 40 S	172 10 E
Buller R., New Zealand	47	41 45 S	172 25 E
Bullfinch, W. Australia	44	30 58 S	119 3 E
Bulli, New South Wales	43	34 15 S	150 57 E
Bulloo L., Queensland	43	28 43 S	142 25 E
Bulloo R., Queensland	43	27 20 S	144 0 E
Bulloo Downs, Queens.	43	28 28 S	143 0 E
Bulls, New Zealand	46	40 10 S	175 24 E
Bulong, W. Australia	44	30 42 S	121 42 E
Bulsar, India	32	20 40 N	72 58 E
Bultfontein, O.F.S.	57	28 18 S	26 10 E
Bulun, U.S.S.R.	27	70 37 N	127 30 E
Bulun Takhai (Puluntohai), Sinkiang	37	47 4 N	87 20 E
Bulung I., Indonesia	35	4 45 S	122 10 E
Bumba, Zaire	54	2 13 N	22 30 E
Bumbesti, Rumania	21	45 13 N	23 22 E
Bumbiri I., Tanzania	53	1 40 S	31 52 E
Bumble Bee, U.S.A.	73	34 8 N	112 18 W
Bumbum, Nigeria	52	14 10 N	8 10 E
Bumbuna, Sierra Leone	52	9 4 N	11 44 W
Bumhpa Bum, mt., Burma	33	26 40 N	97 20 E
Bumi R., Rhodesia	56	17 30 S	28 30 E
Bumla Pass, India-Tibet	33	27 50 N	91 55 E
Buna, Kenya	53	2 58 N	39 30 E
Buna, Papua	42	8 31 S	148 30 E
Bunazi, Tanzania	53	1 13 S	31 24 E
Bunbury, W. Australia	44	33 20 S	115 35 E
Bunclody, Ireland	11	52 40 N	6 40 W
Buncrana, Ireland	11	55 8 N	7 28 W
Bundaberg, Queens.	42	24 54 S	152 22 E
Bundarra, N.S.W.	43	30 9 S	151 3 E
Bundi, India	32	25 30 N	75 35 E
Bundock, Queensland	42	20 39 S	142 53 E
Bundoran, Ireland	11	54 24 N	8 17 W
Bunga R., Nigeria	52	10 50 N	9 45 E
Bungendore, N.S.W.	43	35 14 S	149 30 E
Bungil Cr., Queensland	43	27 0 S	149 0 E
Bungu, Tanzania	53	7 35 S	39 3 E
Bunguran I., Indonesia	34	4 0 N	108 0 E
Bunia, Zaire	53	1 35 N	30 20 E
Bunji, Kashmir	32	35 45 N	74 40 E
Bunjil, W. Australia	44	29 38 S	116 20 E
Bunju I., Indonesia	35	3 35 N	117 50 E
Bunkerville, U.S.A.	73	36 47 N	114 6 W
Bunkeya, Zaire	56	10 22 S	27 1 E
Bunkie, U.S.A.	71	31 0 N	92 9 W
Bunmahor, Ireland	11	52 8 N	7 22 W
Bunnell, U.S.A.	69	29 28 N	81 12 W
Bunnythorpe, N.Z.	46	40 16 S	175 39 E
Bunsuru R., Nigeria	52	13 0 N	6 35 E
Buntine, W. Australia	44	29 56 S	116 28 E
Bununu, Nigeria	52	10 6 N	9 25 E
Bununu, Nigeria	52	9 51 N	9 32 E
Bunyoro, King. of, Uganda	53	1 30 N	31 30 E
Bunza, Nigeria	52	12 8 N	4 0 E
Buol, Indonesia	35	1 15 N	121 30 E
Buon Ma Thuot, Viet Nam	34	12 50 N	108 5 E
Bur Acaba, Somali Rep.	53	3 12 N	44 20 E
Bur Gavo (Bur Gao), Somali Rep.	53	1 10 S	41 50 E
Bur Sa'id, *See* Port Said, Egypt	51		
Bura, Kenya	53	1 5 S	40 5 E
Buraida, Saudi Arabia	30	26 20 N	44 8 E
Buraimi Oasis, 'Oman	31	24 15 N	55 43 E
Burakin, W. Australia	44	30 28 S	117 17 E
Buram, Sudan	51	10 50 N	25 5 E
Buras, U.S.A.	71	29 19 N	89 31 W
Burbank, U.S.A.	73	34 9 N	118 23 W
Burbanks, W. Australia	44	31 1 S	121 1 E
Burcher, N.S.W.	43	33 30 S	147 12 E
Burchun, China	37	47 44 N	86 55 E
Burdekin R., Queens.	42	19 50 S	147 15 E
Burdett, Canada	64	49 50 N	111 30 W
Burdur, Turkey	30	37 45 N	30 22 E
Burdwan, India	33	23 16 N	87 54 E
Bureå, Sweden	22	64 36 N	21 15 E
Bureya R., U.S.S.R.	27	51 30 N	133 0 E
Burg, Germany	14	52 16 N	11 50 E
Burg, Netherlands	13	53 3 N	4 50 E
Burgan, Kuwait, Arabia	30	29 0 N	47 57 E
Burgas, Bulgaria	21	42 33 N	27 29 E
Burgdorf, Switzerland	15	47 3 N	7 37 E
Burgeo, Newfoundland	63	47 37 N	57 38 W
Burgersdorp, C. Prov.	57	31 0 S	26 20 E
Burgos, Spain	17	42 21 N	3 42 W
Burgsvik, Sweden	23	57 3 N	18 19 E
Burhanpur, India	32	21 18 N	76 20 E
Burigi, L., Tanzania	53	2 2 S	31 22 E
Burin, Canada	63	47 1 N	55 14 W
Burin, Jordan	29	32 11 N	35 15 E
Burji, Ethiopia	54	5 29 N	37 51 E
Burkburnett, U.S.A.	71	34 4 N	98 32 W
Burke, U.S.A.	72	47 31 N	115 51 W
Burke R., Queensland	42	22 35 N	140 5 E
Burketown, Queensland	42	17 45 S	139 33 E
Burks Falls, Canada	62	45 37 N	79 10 W
Burleigh Heads, Queens.	43	28 0 S	153 20 E
Burley, U.S.A.	72	42 30 N	113 45 W
Burlington, Ont., Can.	62	43 20 N	79 50 E
Burlington, Col., U.S.A.	70	39 21 N	102 19 W
Burlington, Iowa, U.S.A.	70	40 48 N	91 10 W
Burlington, Kan., U.S.A.	71	38 12 N	95 48 W
Burlington, N.C., U.S.A.	69	36 7 N	79 27 W
Burlington, N.J., U.S.A.	68	40 5 N	74 50 W
Burlington, Vt., U.S.A.	68	44 27 N	73 14 W
Burlington, Wash., U.S.A.	72	48 30 N	122 25 W
Burlington, Wis., U.S.A.	68	42 41 N	88 18 W
Burlyu Tobe, U.S.S.R.	26	46 30 N	79 10 E
Burma, Union of, rep., Asia	33	21 0 N	96 30 E
Burnaby I., Canada	64	52 25 N	131 10 W

	MAP		
Burnett, U.S.A.	71	30 43N	98 12W
Burnett Hds., Queens.	42	24 46 S	152 22 E
Burnett R., Queens.	43	25 30 S	151 30 E
Burney, U.S.A.	72	40 55N	121 43W
Burnie, Tasmania	43	41 4 S	145 56 E
Burnley, England	10	53 47N	2 15W
Burns, Oreg., U.S.A.	72	43 37N	119 5W
Burns, Wyo., U.S.A.	70	41 13N	104 36W
Burns L., Canada	64	54 20N	125 54W
Burnside, L., Australia	45	25 25 S	123 0 E
Burnside R., Canada	60	66 20N	110 0W
Burnt L., Canada	63	52 25N	63 40W
Burnt Creek, Canada	63	54 50N	66 40W
Burnt Paw, Alaska	59	67 2N	142 43W
Burntwood L., Canada	65	55 35N	99 40W
Burntwood R., Canada	65	55 45N	98 0W
Burqa, Jordan	29	32 18N	35 11 E
Burra, Nigeria	52	11 0N	8 57 E
Burra, S. Australia	43	33 40 S	138 55 E
Burracoppin, Australia	44	31 23 S	118 25 E
Burrinjuck Dam, N.S.W.	43	34 50 S	148 45 E
Burruyacu, Argentina	77	26 20 S	64 50W
Bursa, Turkey	30	40 15N	29 5 E
Burstall, Canada	65	50 30N	109 50W
Burton, Westmorland, England	7	54 12N	2 43W
Burton B., Congo	53	4 14 S	29 10 E
Burton L., Canada	62	54 45N	78 20W
Burtville, W. Australia	45	28 42 S	122 33 E
Buru I., Indonesia	35	3 30 S	126 30 E
Burufu, Ghana	52	10 25N	2 50W
Burullics, L., Egypt	30	31 28N	30 48 E
Burundi, st., Africa	53	3 0 S	30 0 E
Bururi, Congo	53	3 58 S	29 35 E
Burutu, Nigeria	52	5 20N	5 29 E
Burwash Landing, Yukon	59	61 21N	139 1W
Burwell, U.S.A.	70	41 50N	99 5W
Bury St. Edmunds, Eng.	10	52 15N	0 42 E
Buryat A.S.S.R. U.S.S.R.	27	52 0N	107 0 E
Busa, Nigeria	52	10 16N	4 32 E
Busanga Swamp, Zambia	56	14 15 S	25 45 E
Busayyah, Iraq	30	30 7N	46 8 E
Busby, Canada	64	53 55N	114 0W
Bushehr (Bushire), Iran	31	29 0N	50 49 E
Bushell, Canada	65	59 35N	108 35W
Bushenyi, Uganda	53	0 32 S	30 12 E
Bushire (Bushehr), Iran	31	28 57N	50 55 E
Bushman Land, dist., Cape Province	57	29 30 S	19 30 E
Bushmans R., S. Africa	57	33 14 S	26 1 E
Bushmills, N. Ireland	11	55 14N	6 32W
Bushnell, Ill., U.S.A.	70	40 30N	90 30W
Bushnell, Neb., U.S.A.	70	41 17N	103 55W
Bushveld, reg., Trans.	57	23 30 S	27 30 E
Busie, Ghana	52	10 29N	2 22W
Businga, Congo	54	3 30N	20 50 E
Buskerud, Norway	23	60 20N	8 45 E
Busla, Uganda	53	0 20N	34 5 E
Busoga, terr., E. prov., Uganda	53	0 20N	33 30 E
Busra, Syria	30	32 30N	36 25 E
Bussa, Nigeria	52	10 11N	4 32 E
Busselton, W. Australia	44	33 42 S	115 15 E
Bustard, Hd., Queens.	42	24 0 S	151 45 E
Busu Djanoa, Congo	54	1 50N	21 5 E
Busuanga, Philippines	35	12 10N	120 0 E
Buta, Congo	54	2 50N	24 53 E
Butare, Rwanda	53	2 31 S	29 52 E
Bute Garta, Ethiopia	53	4 30N	37 30 E
Bute Inlet, Canada	64	50 40N	124 50W
Butedale, Canada	64	53 10N	128 40W
Butemba, Uganda	53	1 11N	31 36 E
Butembo, Congo	54	0 9N	29 16 E
Butere, Kenya	53	0 14N	34 30 E
Butiaba, Uganda	53	1 50N	31 20 E
Butler, Mo., U.S.A.	71	38 19N	94 24W
Butler, Pa., U.S.A.	68	40 52N	79 52W
Butsha, Zaire	53	0 50N	29 15 E
Butte, U.S.A.	72	46 0N	112 35W
Butte, U.S.A.	70	42 58N	98 54W
Butterworth, C. Prov.	57	32 20 S	28 11 E
Butterworth, Malaya	34	5 24N	100 23 E
Buttevant, Ireland	11	52 14N	8 40W
Button, B., Canada	65	54 40N	99 0W
Butuan, Philippines	35	8 52N	125 36 E
Buturlinovka, U.S.S.R.	25	50 50N	40 35 E
Buyaga, U.S.S.R.	27	59 50N	127 0 E
Buyonga, Tanzania	53	4 38 S	29 52 E
Buyr Nor, Mongolia	37	47 50N	117 30 E
Büyük R., Turkey	30	37 50N	28 0 E
Buzau, Rumania	21	45 10N	26 57 E
Buzau R., Rumania	21	45 10N	27 20 E
Buzaymah, Libya	51	24 35N	22 0 E
Buzi R., Mozambique	55	19 52 S	34 30 E
Buzuluk, U.S.S.R.	24	52 48N	52 12 E
Buzzards B., U.S.A.	69	41 30N	70 50W
Bwana Mkubwa, Zambia	56	13 8 S	28 38 E
Betweha, Malawi	56	11 15 S	34 13 E
Bwi, Nigeria	52	12 32N	4 3 E
Byala, Bulgaria	21	43 28N	25 44 E
Bydgoszcz, Poland	16	53 10N	18 0 E
Byelorussia. *See* White Russia.	24		

	MAP		
Byemoor, Canada	64	52 0N	112 17W
Byers, U.S.A.	70	39 47N	104 14W
Byerstown, Queensland	42	16 0 S	144 32 E
Byglands, Norway	23	58 50N	7 50 E
Byhalia, U.S.A.	71	34 50N	89 43W
Bykle, Norway	23	59 21N	7 20 E
Bykovo, U.S.S.R.	25	49 50N	45 25 E
Bylas, U.S.A.	73	33 9N	110 10W
Byrd, Antarctica	80	80 0 S	120 0W
Byrd Land, Ant.	47	80 0 S	145 0W
Byrd Sub-Glacial Basin, Ant.	80	82 0 S	120 0W
Byrock, N.S.W.	43	30 40 S	146 27 E
Byron B., Canada	63	54 42N	57 40W
Byron C., N.S.W.	43	28 34 S	153 37 E
Byrrang Mts., U.S.S.R.	27	75 0N	100 0 E
Byske, Sweden	22	64 59N	21 17 E
Byske, R., Sweden	22	65 20N	20 0 E
Bytom, Poland	16	50 25N	19 0 E
Byumba, Rwanda	53	1 40 S	29 59 E

C

	MAP		
Ca Mau, Viet Nam. *See* Quan Long	34		
Caamano Sd., Canada	64	52 50N	129 0W
Caatingås, reg., Brazil	79	17 7 S	45 55W
Caazapa, Paraguay	77	26 8 S	56 19W
Caballococha, Peru	75	4 0 S	70 35W
Cabanatuan, Philippines	35	15 30N	121 5 E
Cabano, Canada	63	47 40N	68 56 E
Cabedelo, Brazil	79	7 0 S	34 50W
Cabellos, Uruguay	77	31 0 S	57 15W
Cabeza, Spain	17	38 43N	5 17W
Cabezas, Bolivia	78	18 45 S	63 25W
Cabimas, Venezuela	75	10 30N	71 25W
Cabinda, Angola	54	5 40 S	12 11 E
Cabinet Mts., U.S.A.	72	48 15N	115 45W
Cabo Fria, Brazil	79	22 51 S	42 3W
Cabonga Res., Canada	62	47 35N	76 40W
Cabool, U.S.A.	68	37 10N	92 10W
Caboolture, Queens.	43	27 5 S	152 47 E
Cabot Str., Canada	63	47 0N	59 30W
Cabra, Spain	17	37 30N	4 28W
Cabreira Mts., Portugal	17	41 35N	8 18W
Cabrera I., Spain	17	39 6N	2 59 E
Cabri, Canada	65	50 35N	108 25W
Cabriel R., Spain	17	39 20N	1 20W
Cabrobo, Brazil	79	8 30 S	39 20W
Cabrutas, Venezuela	78	7 40N	66 16W
Čačak, Yugoslavia	21	43 54N	20 22 E
Cacares, Colombia	75	7 30N	75 26W
Cacequi, Brazil	77	29 49 S	54 50W
Caceres, Brazil	79	16 5 S	57 40W
Cáceres, Spain	17	39 26N	6 23W
Cache B., Canada	62	46 26N	80 1W
Cache Lake, tn., Can.	62	49 50N	74 30W
Cachimbo, Sa. do, Braz.	79	9 0 S	55 30W
Cachinal, Chile	77	25 0 S	69 30W
Cachoeira, Brazil	79	12 30 S	39 0W
Cachoeiro, Brazil	79	21 0 S	41 10W
Cachoeira do Sul, Brazil	77	30 0 S	53 0W
Caciporé, C., Brazil	79	3 50N	51 10W
Caciporé, R., Brazil	79	3 0N	51 30W
Cacolo, Angola	55	10 10 S	19 20 E
Caconda, Angola	55	13 48 S	15 8 E
Caddo, U.S.A.	71	34 8N	96 16W
Cadereyta Jimenez, Mexico	74	25 40N	100 0W
Cadibarrawirracanna, L., S. Australia	45	29 0 S	135 30 E
Cadillac, Canada	62	49 45N	108 0W
Cadillac, U.S.A.	68	44 16N	85 23W
Cadiz, Spain	17	36 30N	6 20W
Cadiz, G. of, Spain	17	36 35N	6 20W
Cadomin, Canada	64	52 59N	117 28W
Cadotte R., Canada	64	56 35N	117 0W
Caen, France	12	49 10N	0 22W
Caernarvon, Wales	10	53 8N	4 17W
Caeté, Brazil	79	20 0 S	43 40W
Caetité, Brazil	79	13 50 S	42 50W
Cagayan, Philippines	35	8 30N	124 40 E
Cagayan R., Phil.	35	17 30N	121 42 E
Cagayan Sula I., Phil.	35	7 5N	118 30 E
Cagayanes Is., Phil.	35	9 40N	121 18 E
Cagli, Italy	20	43 32N	12 38 E
Cagliari, Italy	20	39 15N	9 6 E
Cagliari, G. of, Italy	20	39 8N	9 10 E
Cagua Mt., Philippines	35	18 20N	122 12 E
Caguan R., Colombia	78	1 0N	74 40W
Caguas, Mexico	75	18 15N	65 58W
Caha Mts., Ireland	11	51 45N	9 40W
Caherconlish, Ireland	11	52 36N	8 30W
Cahersiveen, Ireland	11	51 57N	10 13W
Cahir, Ireland	11	52 22N	7 55W
Cahore Pt., Ireland	11	52 34N	6 11W
Cahors, France	12	44 27N	1 27 E
Cahuapanas, Peru	78	5 15 S	77 0W
Caianda, Angola	56	11 29 S	23 29 E
Caicara, Venezuela	78	7 50N	66 10W
Caicó, Brazil	79	6 20 S	37 0W
Caicos Is., W. Indies	75	21 40N	71 40W
Caicos Passage, W. Ind.	75	22 45N	72 45W
Caihaique, Chile	77	45 30 S	71 45W
Caird Coast, Antarctica	80	75 0 S	20 0W
Cairns, Queensland	42	16 55 S	145 51 E
Cairns Div., Queens	42	16 33 S	144 0 E

	MAP		
Cairo. *See* Al Qâhirah.	51		
Cairo, Ga., U.S.A.	69	30 52N	84 12W
Cairo, Ill., U.S.A.	71	37 1N	89 9W
Caiundo, Angola	55	15 50 S	17 52 E
Cajamarca, Peru	78	7 5 S	78 28W
Cajazeiras, Brazil	79	7 0 S	38 30W
Cala, Cape Province	57	31 30 S	27 42 E
Cala, Spain	17	37 59N	6 21W
Calabar, Nigeria	52	4 57N	8 20 E
Calabozo, Venezuela	75	9 0N	67 20W
Calabria, reg., Italy	20	39 4N	16 30 E
Calafat, Rumania	21	43 58N	22 59 E
Calaforte, Argentina	77	50 25 S	72 25W
Calais. France	12	50 57N	1 56 E
Calais, Maine, U.S.A.	69	45 5N	67 20W
Calala, Angola	56	12 44 S	23 41 E
Calama, Brazil	78	8 0 S	62 50W
Calama, Chile	77	22 30 S	68 55W
Calamar, Colombia	78	10 15N	74 55W
Calamian Group, Phil.	35	11 50N	119 55 E
Calamocha, Spain	17	40 50N	1 17W
Calanaque, Brazil	78	0 5 S	64 0W
Calapan, Philippines	35	13 25N	121 7 E
Calarasi, Rumania	21	44 14N	27 23 E
Calatayud, Spain	17	41 20N	1 40W
Calauag, Philippines	35	13 55N	122 15 E
Calbayog, Philippines	35	12 7N	124 37 E
Calca, Peru	78	13 10 S	72 0W
Calcasieu, L., U.S.A.	71	30 0N	93 15W
Calcutta, India	33	22 36N	88 24 E
Caldas, Portugal	17	39 24N	9 10W
Caldera, Chile	77	27 5 S	70 55W
Caldwell, Idaho, U.S.A.	72	43 40N	116 30W
Caldwell, Kan., U.S.A.	71	37 3N	97 36W
Caldwell Tex., U.S.A.	71	30 30N	98 44W
Caledon, C. Prov.	57	34 14 S	19 23 E
Caledon, R., S. Africa	57	30 0 S	26 46 E
Caledonian Can., Scot.	10	57 27N	4 18W
Calego, Angola	56	12 12 S	23 43 E
Caleta Buena, Chile	78	19 55 S	70 5W
Caleta Coloso, Chile	77	23 55 S	70 30W
Calexico, U.S.A.	73	32 38N	115 32W
Calf of Man, I., I. of M.	10	54 4N	4 48W
Calgary, Canada	64	51 0N	114 10W
Calhoun, U.S.A.	69	37 35N	87 18W
Cali, Colombia	78	3 25N	76 35W
Calice, Italy	20	44 15N	9 50 E
Calicut. *See* Kozhikode.	32		
Caliente, U.S.A.	73	37 40N	114 32W
California, U.S.A.	70	38 36N	92 30W
California, st., U.S.A.	73	37 0N	120 0W
California, Gulf of, Mex.	74	27 0N	111 0W
Calingasta, Argentina	77	31 15 S	69 30W
Calingiri, W. Australia	44	31 5 S	116 40 E
Calipatria, U.S.A.	73	33 4N	115 30W
Calistoga, U.S.A.	73	38 36N	122 33W
Calitzdorp, C. Prov.	57	33 32 S	21 14 E
Callabonna L., S. Australia	43	29 40 S	140 0 E
Callan, Ireland	11	52 33N	7 25W
Callao, Peru	78	12 0 S	77 0W
Callaway, U.S.A.	70	41 22N	99 57W
Callide, Queensland	42	24 23 S	150 33 E
Calling L., Canada	64	55 20N	113 20W
Calliope, Queensland	42	24 0 S	151 16 E
Calmar, U.S.A.	68	43 10N	91 53W
Caloundra, Queens.	43	26 45 S	153 10 E
Caltagirone, Italy	20	37 13N	14 30 E
Caltanissetta, Italy	20	37 30N	14 3 E
Caluire-et-Claire, Fr.	12	45 49N	4 51 E
Calulo, Angola	55	10 2 S	14 55 E
Calunda, Angola	56	12 12 S	23 42 E
Calvert, U.S.A.	71	30 59N	96 44W
Calvert I., Canada	64	51 30N	128 0W
Calvert Ra., mts., W. Australia	45	24 10 S	123 0 E
Calvi, Corsica	20	42 34N	8 43 E
Calvinia, C. Prov.	57	31 28 S	19 45 E
Camabatela, Angola	34	8 20 S	15 26 E
Camagüey, Cuba	75	21 20N	78 0W
Camaiore, Italy	20	43 57N	10 18 E
Camana, Peru	78	16 30 S	72 50W
Camarón C., Honduras	75	16 0N	85 0W
Camarones, Argentina	78	44 50 S	66 0W
Camas, U.S.A.	72	45 40N	122 29W
Camas Valley, U.S.A.	72	43 0N	123 42W
Cambay, India	32	22 23N	72 33 E
Cambay, G. of, India	32	20 45N	72 30 E
Cambodia, st., Asia	34	12 15N	105 0 E
Camboon, Queensland	43	25 3 S	150 28 E
Cambrai, France	12	50 11N	3 14 E
Cambria, U.S.A.	73	35 36N	121 3W
Cambridge, England	10	52 13N	0 8 E
Cambridge, Jamaica	75	Inset	
Cambridge, N.Z.	46	37 54 S	175 29 E
Cambridge, Idaho, U.S.A.	72	44 33N	116 54W
Cambridge, Mass., U.S.A.	69	42 20N	71 2W
Cambridge, Md., U.S.A.	69	38 33N	76 4W
Cambridge, Minn., U.S.A.	70	45 32N	93 15W
Cambridge, Neb., U.S.A.	70	40 19N	100 10W
Cambridge, B., Canada	60	69 10N	105 0W
Cambridge Downs, Queensland	42	20 27 S	142 58 E

	MAP		
Camden, N.S.W.	43	34 5 S	150 38 E
Camden, Ark., U.S.A.	71	33 30N	92 50W
Camden, N.C., U.S.A.	69	36 19N	76 10W
Camden, N.J., U.S.A.	69	39 58N	75 1W
Camden, N.Y., U.S.A.	69	43 22N	75 46W
Camden, Tenn., U.S.A.	68	36 8N	88 10W
Camden B., Alaska	59	71 0N	145 0W
Camdenton, U.S.A.	71	37 59N	92 48W
Cameia, Angola	55	11 34 S	20 55 E
Camerino, Italy	20	43 10N	13 4 E
Cameron, La., U.S.A.	71	29 48N	93 17W
Cameron, Mo., U.S.A.	70	39 43N	94 15W
Cameron, Tex., U.S.A.	71	31 0N	97 0W
Cameron Falls, Canada	62	48 8N	88 20W
Cameron Hills, Canada	64	60 20N	118 0W
Cameron Mts., N.Z.	41	46 1 S	167 0 E
Cameroon, Rep., Africa	54	5 0N	12 30 E
Cameroons Mt., W. Cameroon	52	4 45N	8 55 E
Cameroun, R., Cam.	52	4 0N	9 25 E
Cametá, Brazil	79	2 0 S	49 30W
Caminha, Portugal	17	41 50N	8 50W
Camino, U.S.A.	73	38 46N	120 43W
Camiri, Bolivia	78	20 0 S	63 26W
Camo, Ethiopia	53	4 30N	38 20 E
Camocim, Brazil	79	2 55 S	40 50W
Camolin, Ireland	11	52 37N	6 26W
Camoola, Queensland	42	23 0 S	144 24 E
Camooweal, Queens.	42	19 56 S	138 7 E
Camopi, Fr. Guiana	79	3 10N	52 25W
Camopi R., French Guiana	79	2 30N	53 30W
Camp Cook, U.S.A.	70	45 36N	104 0W
Camp Wood, U.S.A.	71	29 41N	99 59W
Campagna, dist., Italy	20	41 58N	12 20 E
Campana I, Chile	77	48 20 S	75 10W
Campanario, Spain	17	38 52N	5 38W
Campania, reg., Italy	20	40 50N	14 45 E
Campbell, C. Prov.	57	28 49 S	23 44 E
Campbell, C., N.Z.	47	41 44 S	174 19 E
Campbell I., S. Ocean	80	52 30 S	169 0 E
Campbell L., Canada	65	63 15N	106 25W
Campbell R., Canada	64	50 5N	125 20W
Campbell Town, Tas.	43	41 52 S	147 30 E
Campbellpore, Pakistan	32	33 45N	72 20 E
Campbellsville, U.S.A.	68	37 20N	85 21W
Campbellton, Canada	63	47 57N	66 43W
Campbelltown, N.S.W.	43	34 5 S	150 48 E
Campbeltown, Scotland	10	55 25N	5 36W
Campeche, Mexico	74	19 50N	90 32W
Campeche, G. of, Mex.	74	19 30N	93 0W
Campeche, st., Mexico	74	19 50N	90 32W
Camperdown, Victoria	43	38 4 S	143 12 E
Camperville, Canada	65	52 0N	100 15W
Campina, Rumania	21	45 10N	25 45 E
Campina Grande, Bra.	79	17 20 S	35 57W
Campinas, Brazil	77	22 50 S	47 0W
Campo, Gabon	54	2 22N	9 50 E
Campo, Spain	17	39 23N	3 7W
Campo Beló, Brazil	79	21 0 S	45 30W
Campo Formoso, Braz.	79	10 30 S	40 20W
Campo Gallo, Arg.	79	26 30 S	63 0W
Campo Grande, Brazil	79	20 25 S	54 40W
Campo Maior, Brazil	79	4 50 S	42 30W
Campo Major, Portugal	17	38 59N	7 7W
Campoalegré, Colombia	78	2 50N	75 20W
Campobasso, Italy	20	41 34N	14 40 E
Campos, Brazil	79	21 50 S	41 20W
Campos Belos, Brazil	79	13 10 S	46 45W
Câmpulung, Rumania	21	45 17N	25 3 E
Camrose, Canada	64	53 0N	112 50W
Camsell, L., Canada	65	62 55N	111 20W
Camsell Portage, Can.	65	59 39N	109 12W
Camurra, N.S.W.	43	29 21 S	149 52 E
Can Tho, Viet Nam	34	10 3N	105 40 E
Canada, st., N. Amer.	58	60 0N	100 0W
Canada de Gomez, Arg.	77	32 55 S	61 30W
Cañada Honda, Arg.	77	32 0 S	68 25W
Canadian, U.S.A.	71	36 0N	100 25W
Canadian R., U.S.A.	71	36 0N	100 40W
Canakkale, B. (Dardanelles), Tur.	30	40 15N	26 25 E
Canal du Midi, France	12	43 20N	2 50 E
Canal Flat, Canada	64	50 10N	115 55W
Canal Zone, Panama	74	9 0N	79 45W
Canandaigua, U.S.A.	68	42 55N	77 18W
Cananea, Mexico	74	31 0N	110 20W
Cananéia, Brazil	77	25 0 S	47 50W
Canarreos, Arch. de los, Cuba	75	21 35N	81 40W
Canary Is., Atlan. Oc.	50	29 30N	17 0W
Canaveral, C. (C. Kennedy), U.S.A.	69	28 25N	80 40W
Canavieiras, Brazil	79	15 45 S	39 0W
Canbelego, N.S.W.	43	31 32 S	146 18 E
Canberra, Cap. Terr., Australia	43	35 15 S	149 8 E
Canby, Calif., U.S.A.	72	41 28N	120 58W
Canby, Minn., U.S.A.	70	44 44N	96 15W
Canby, Oregon, U.S.A.	72	45 30N	122 45W
Cancale, France	12	48 40N	1 50W
Candia. *See* Iráklion.	20		
Candle, Alaska	59	65 57N	161 50W
Candle L., Canada	65	53 45N	105 20W
Cando, N.D., U.S.A.	70	48 35N	99 11W
Candoa, Philippines	35	17 1N	120 30 E
Canela, Brazil	77	29 20 S	50 50W
Canelones, Uruguay	77	34 32 S	56 10W
Canéte, Chile	77	37 50 S	73 10W

	MAP		
Cañete, Peru	78	13 0s	76 30w
Canfrac P., Spain	17	42 44N	0 32w
Cangas, Spain	17	43 10N	6 33w
Canguaretama, Brazil	79	6 20s	35 5w
Cangussu, Brazil	77	31 22s	52 43w
Canicado, Mozambique	55	24 31s	33 2 E
Canicatti, Italy	20	37 21N	13 50 E
Caninde, Brazil	78	6 45s	71 0w
Canim L., Canada	64	51 45N	120 50w
Cankiri, Turkey	30	40 40N	33 30 E
Canmore, Canada	64	51 7N	115 18w
Canna I., Scotland	10	57 3N	6 33w
Cannamore, India	32	11 53N	72 27 E
Cannes, France	12	43 32N	7 0 E
Canning Hill, W. Australia	44	28 44s	117 45 E
Cannon Ball R., U.S.A.	70	46 10N	102 0w
Cannonvale, Queens.	42	20 16s	148 45 E
Canoe L., Sask., Can.	65	55 10N	108 15w
Canon City, U.S.A.	70	38 32N	105 20w
Canora, Canada	65	51 40N	102 30w
Canouan, Windward Is.	75		Inset
Canowindra, N.S.W.	43	33 35s	148 38 E
Cantabrian, Mts., Spain	17	43 0N	5 10w
Cantal, Mts. du, Fr.	12	45 10N	2 35 E
Cantaura, Venezuela	75	9 22N	64 24w
Canterbury, England	10	51 17N	1 5 E
Canterbury, Queens.	43	25 22s	141 49 E
Canterbury, dist., N.Z.	47	43 45s	171 19 E
Canterbury Bight, N.Z.	47	44 16s	171 55 E
Canterbury Plains, N.Z.	47	43 55s	171 22 E
Cantin C., Morocco	50	33 35N	9 23w
Canton (Kwangchow), China	39	23 15N	113 15 E
Canton, Ga., U.S.A.	69	34 13N	84 29w
Canton, Ill., U.S.A.	70	40 31N	90 1w
Canton, Miss., U.S.A.	67	32 32N	90 1w
Canton, Mo., U.S.A.	70	40 8N	91 31w
Canton, N.Y., U.S.A.	68	44 32N	75 9w
Canton, Ohio, U.S.A.	68	40 47N	81 22w
Canton, S.D., U.S.A.	70	43 18N	96 33w
Canton Res., U.S.A.	71	36 8N	98 35w
Cantu, Italy	20	45 44N	9 8 E
Canudos, Brazil	79	7 25s	53 15w
Canumã R., Brazil	78	6 25s	58 50w
Canutama, Brazil	78	6 30s	64 20w
Canutillo, U.S.A.	73	31 56N	106 35w
Canxixe, Mozambique	56	17 35s	34 19 E
Canyon, Canada	62	47 25N	84 30w
Canyon, U.S.A.	73	35 0N	101 57w
Canyonville, U.S.A.	72	42 57N	123 17w
Cap Haitien, Haiti	75	19 40N	72 20w
Capaia, Angola	55	8 40s	20 12 E
Canakçur, Turkey	31	38 53N	40 30 E
Capanaparo, R., Ven.	75	7 0N	68 0w
Capatáride, Venezuela	75	11 15N	70 22w
Cape Barren I., Tas.	43	40 25s	148 15 E
Cape Breton I., Canada	63	46 0N	61 0w
Cape Coast, Ghana	52	5 5N	1 45w
Cape Girardeau, U.S.A.	71	37 20N	89 30w
Cape Kennedy, U.S.A. *See* Kennedy, C.	67		
Cape Prov., prov., Rep. of S.A.	57	32 0s	23 0 E
Cape R., Queensland	42	20 46s	146 38 E
Cape Town, C. Prov.	57	33 56s	18 28 E
Cape Verde Is., Atlantic Ocean	5	17 10N	25 20w
Cape York Pen., Queensland	42	13 30s	142 30 E
Capel, W. Australia	44	33 35s	115 35 E
Capela, Brazil	79	10 15N	37 0w
Capella, Queensland	42	23 2s	148 1 E
Capernaum (site), Israel	29	32 54N	35 32 E
Capesterre, Guadeloupe	75		Inset
Capim R., Brazil	79	3 0s	48 0w
Capis, Philippines	35	11 36N	122 49 E
Capital Terr., Australia	43	35 17s	149 8 E
Capitan, U.S.A.	73	33 38N	105 36w
Capoche, R., Mozam.	56	15 0s	32 35 E
Capoeiras Falls, Brazil	79	7 0s	57 45w
Caponda, Mozambique	56	16 0s	31 29 E
Caporatto (Kobarid), Yugoslavia	20	46 16N	13 35 E
Cappamore, Ireland	11	52 38N	8 20w
Cappawhite, Ireland	11	52 35N	8 10w
Cappoquin, Ireland	11	52 9N	7 46w
Capraia I., Italy	20	42 2N	9 50 E
Capreol, Canada	62	46 40N	80 50w
Caprera I., Italy	20	41 12N	9 28 E
Capri I., Italy	20	40 34N	14 15 E
Capricorn C., Queens.	42	23 30s	151 17 E
Capricorn Chan., Queensland	42	23 0s	152 30 E
Capricorn Gp., Queens.	42	23 30s	152 0 E
Caprino, Italy	20	45 37N	10 46 E
Caprivi Strip, S.W. Afr.	55	17 50s	23 0 E
Captainganj, India	33	26 55N	83 45 E
Capulin, U.S.A.	71	36 46N	104 0w
Caquetá, R., Colombia	78	1 0N	75 30w
Caracal, Rumania	21	44 8N	24 22 E
Caracas, Venezuela	78	10 30N	66 50w
Caracol, Guaporé, Braz.	78	9 15s	64 20w
Caracol, Piaui, Brazil	78	9 15s	43 45w
Caraga, Philippines	35	7 18N	126 33 E

	MAP		
Caraguatay, Paraguay	77	25 10s	56 51w
Carajou, Canada	64	57 45N	117 0w
Carangola, Brazil	79	20 50s	42 5w
Caransebes, Rumania	21	45 28N	22 18 E
Carapeguá, Paraguay	76	25 40s	57 0w
Carapundy Swamp, N.S.W.	43	29 5s	143 28 E
Caraquez, B. de, Ecu.	78	0 30s	80 30w
Caratasca Lag., Hond.	75	15 30N	83 40w
Caratinga, Brazil	79	19 50s	42 10w
Carauari, Brazil	78	4 48s	66 47w
Caraúbas, Brazil	79	5 50s	37 25w
Caravaca, Spain	17	38 8N	1 52w
Caravelas, Brazil	79	17 50s	39 20w
Caraveli, Peru	78	15 45s	73 25w
Carballo, Spain	17	43 14N	8 42w
Carberry, Canada	65	49 50N	99 25w
Carbon, Canada	64	51 30N	113 20w
Carbonara, C., Italy	20	39 8N	9 30 E
Carbondale, Ill., U.S.A.	71	37 45N	89 10w
Carbondale, Pa., U.S.A.	68	41 37N	75 30w
Carbonia, Italy	20	39 10N	8 30 E
Carcagente, Spain	17	39 7N	0 27w
Carcasse, C., Haiti	75	18 30N	74 28w
Carcassonne, France	12	43 13N	2 20 E
Carcross, Canada	64	60 20N	134 40w
Cardamom Hills, India	32	9 30N	77 15 E
Cardenas, Cuba	75	23 0N	81 30w
Cárdenas, S.L. Potosi, Mexico	74	22 0N	99 41w
Cárdenas, Tabasco, Mexico	74	17 59N	93 21w
Cardiff, Wales	10	51 28N	3 11w
Cardigan, Wales	10	52 6N	4 41w
Cardigan B., Wales	10	52 30N	4 30w
Cardillo Downs, Queensland	43	26 39s	140 35 E
Cardon, Venezuela	75	11 37N	70 13w
Cardona, Spain	17	41 56N	1 40 E
Cardross, Canada	65	49 50N	105 40w
Cardston, Canada	64	49 15N	113 20w
Cardwell, Queensland	42	18 14s	146 2 E
Carei, Rumania	20	47 40N	22 28 E
Carenero, Venezuela	78	10 40N	66 5w
Carentan, France	12	49 19N	1 15w
Carey, U.S.A.	68	41 0N	83 20w
Carey, U.S.A.	72	43 18N	113 58w
Carey L., Canada	65	62 20N	103 0w
Carey, L., W. Austral.	45	29 0s	122 15 E
Careysburg, Liberia	50	6 34N	10 30w
Cargados Garajos Is.	7	16 30s	59 37 E
Carhaix, France	12	48 18N	3 36w
Caribbean Sea, W.I.	75	15 0N	75 0w
Cariboo Mts., Canada	64	53 0N	121 0w
Caribou, Canada	65	59 20N	97 50w
Caribou, U.S.A.	69	46 55N	68 0w
Caribou I., Canada	62	47 23N	85 48w
Caribou Is., Canada	64	61 50N	113 20w
Caribou, L. & R., Can.	65	58 50N	96 0w
Caribou Mts., Canada	64	58 50N	115 40w
Caribou, R., Canada	64	61 10N	126 0w
Caricanhi, Mozam.	56	19 20s	33 40 E
Carinda, N.S.W.	43	30 30s	147 37 E
Carinde, Mozambique	56	15 35s	31 11 E
Carinhanha, Brazil	79	14 15s	44 0w
Carinhanha R., Brazil	79	14 50s	45 30w
Carini, Italy	20	38 9N	13 10 E
Caripito, Venezuela	75	10 2N	63 0w
Caritanas, Brazil	78	9 20s	63 0w
Carius, Brazil	79	6 35s	39 30w
Carleton Place, Can.	62	45 8N	76 11w
Carlin, U.S.A.	72	40 46N	116 5w
Carlingford L., Ireland	11	54 0N	6 5w
Carlinville, U.S.A.	72	39 16N	89 55w
Carlisle, England	10	54 54N	2 55w
Carlisle, U.S.A.	68	40 12N	77 10w
Carloforte, Italy	20	39 10N	8 18 E
Carlow, Ireland	11	52 50N	6 58w
Carlow, co., Ireland	11	52 43N	6 50w
Carlsbad, U.S.A.	71	32 20N	104 0w
Carlsbad, U.S.A.	73	33 13N	117 25w
Carlyle, Canada	65	49 40N	102 20w
Carlyle, U.S.A.	70	38 34N	89 24w
Carmacks, Canada	59	62 0N	136 0w
Carman, Canada	65	49 40N	98 0w
Carmangay, Canada	64	50 10N	113 10w
Carmarthen, Wales	10	51 15N	4 20w
Carmaux, France	12	44 3N	2 10 E
Carmel, U.S.A.	73	36 32N	121 56w
Carmel Mt., Israel	64	32 45N	35 3 E
Carmelo, Uruguay	77	34 0s	58 20w
Carmen, Colombia	78	9 45N	75 7w
Carmen I., Mexico	74	26 0N	111 20w
Carmen, R., Chile	77	29 0s	70 30w
Carmen, R., Mexico	74	30 30N	107 0w
Carmen de Patagones, Argentina	77	40 50s	63 0w
Carmi, Canada	64	49 30N	119 0w
Carmi, U.S.A.	68	38 6N	88 10w
Carmila, Queensland	42	21 53s	149 25 E
Carmona, Spain	17	37 28N	5 42w
Carnac, France	12	47 35N	3 5w
Carnarvon, Australia	44	24 51s	113 42 E
Carnarvon, S. Africa	57	30 56s	22 8 E
Carnarvon Ra., Queens.	43	25 15s	148 30 E
Carnarvon Ra., W. Australia	44	25 0s	120 45 E
Carnatic, dist., India	32	12 0N	79 0 E

	MAP		
Cardonagh, Ireland	11	55 15N	7 16w
Carnduff, Canada	65	49 10N	101 50w
Carnegie L., Australia	45	26 5s	122 30 E
Carnew, Ireland	11	52 43N	6 30w
Carnic Alps, Italy	20	46 36N	12 45 E
Carnlough, N. Ireland	11	55 0N	6 0w
Carnsore Pt., Ireland	11	52 10N	6 20w
Caro, U.S.A.	68	43 28N	83 25w
Carolina, Brazil	79	7 10s	47 30w
Carolina, Transvaal	57	26 5s	30 6 E
Caroline, Queensland	43	25 31s	146 44 E
Caroline Is., Pacific Oc.	5	8 0N	150 0 E
Caroline Ra., W. Australia	44	16 15s	126 20 E
Carolside, Canada	64	51 20N	111 40w
Caromandel, N.Z.	46	36 46s	175 31 E
Caron, Canada	65	50 30N	105 50w
Caroni R., Venezuela	75	4 50N	62 20w
Carora, Venezuela	75	10 12N	70 7w
Carpathians, Mts., Europe	16	49 0N	23 0 E
Carpentaria, G., N. Australia	41	14 0s	139 0 E
Carpentaria Downs, Queensland	42	18 44s	144 20 E
Carpentras, France	12	44 3N	5 2 E
Carpi, Italy	20	44 47N	10 52 E
Carpiná, Brazil	79	7 40s	35 25w
Carpinteria, U.S.A.	73	34 28N	119 32w
Carrabelle, U.S.A.	69	29 52N	84 40w
Carrandibby Ra., W. Australia	44	26 0s	115 20 E
Carrandotte, Queens.	42	21 55s	138 31 E
Carrantuohill Mt., Ire.	11	52 0N	9 44w
Carrara, Italy	20	44 5N	10 7 E
Carrasquero, Venezuela	78	10 55N	72 0w
Carrathool, N.S.W.	43	34 22s	145 30 E
Carrick Ra., N.Z.	47	45 15s	169 8 E
Carrick-on-Shannon, Ireland	11	53 57N	8 7w
Carrick-on-Suir, Ire.	11	52 22N	7 30w
Carrickfergus, N. Ire.	11	54 43N	5 50w
Carrickmacross, Ire.	11	54 0N	6 43w
Carrieton, S. Australia	43	32 37s	138 27 E
Carrigaholt, Ireland	11	52 37N	9 42w
Carrigallen, Ireland	11	53 59N	7 40w
Carrington, U.S.A.	70	47 30N	99 6w
Carrión, Spain	17	42 23N	4 41w
Carrizal Bajo, Chile	77	28 5s	71 20w
Carrizo Cr., R., U.S.A.	71	36 25N	103 45w
Carrizo Springs, U.S.A.	71	28 30N	99 47w
Carrizozo, U.S.A.	73	33 37N	105 57w
Carroll, U.S.A.	70	42 2N	94 55w
Carrollton, Ill., U.S.A.	70	39 20N	90 25w
Carrollton, Ky., U.S.A.	68	38 40N	85 10w
Carrollton, Mo., U.S.A.	70	39 18N	93 30w
Carrot R., Canada	65	53 25N	103 0w
Carrow., S. Australia	45	34 6s	136 22 E
Carruthers, Canada	65	52 54N	109 15w
Carsamba, Turkey	31	41 15N	36 45 E
Carson, U.S.A.	70	46 29N	101 30w
Carson, L., U.S.A.	66	39 50N	118 40w
Carson City, U.S.A.	66	39 0N	119 40w
Carson Sink, U.S.A.	66	39 40N	117 40w
Carsonville, U.S.A.	68	43 25N	82 39w
Cartagena, Spain	17	37 38N	0 59w
Cartago, Colombia	78	4 24N	76 13w
Cartaret, France	12	49 23N	1 47w
Cartersville, U.S.A.	69	34 11N	84 48w
Carterton, N.Z.	46	41 2s	175 31 E
Carthage, Ark., U.S.A.	71	34 2N	92 32w
Carthage, Ill., U.S.A.	70	40 24N	91 4w
Carthage, Mo., U.S.A.	71	37 10N	94 10w
Carthage, N.Y., U.S.A.	68	43 59N	73 57w
Carthage, S.D., U.S.A.	70	44 13N	97 40w
Carthage, Tex., U.S.A.	71	32 7N	94 25w
Cartwright, Canada	63	53 41N	56 58w
Caruaru, Brazil	79	8 20s	36 0w
Carúpano, Venezuela	78	10 45N	63 15w
Caruthersville, U.S.A.	68	36 10N	89 40w
Carvoeiro, Brazil	78	1 15s	62 0w
Carwell, Queensland	42	24 46s	146 43 E
Casa Branca, Brazil	79	21 50s	47 0w
Casa Grande, U.S.A.	73	32 50N	111 46w
Casa Nova, Brazil	79	9 10s	41 5w
Casablanca, Morocco	50	33 30N	7 37w
Casale, Italy	20	45 57N	8 23 E
Casalmaggiore, Italy	20	44 59N	10 25 E
Casas Grandes, Mex.	74	30 22N	108 0w
Cascade, Idaho, U.S.A.	72	44 30N	116 3w
Cascade, Wash., U.S.A.	72	47 17N	117 45w
Cascade Locks, U.S.A.	72	45 42N	121 56w
Cascade Pt., N.Z.	47	44 1s	168 20 E
Cascade Ra., U.S.A.	72	46 0N	121 30w
Casco B., U.S.A.	69	43 45N	70 0w
Cascoes, Portugal	17	38 40N	9 25w
Caserta, Italy	20	41 5N	14 20 E
Cashel, Ireland	11	52 31N	7 53w
Cashmere, U.S.A.	72	47 31N	120 34w
Casiguran, Philippines	35	16 15N	122 15 E
Casilda, Argentina	77	33 10s	61 10w
Casino, N.S.W.	43	28 52s	153 3 E
Casiquiare R., Ven.	78	3 0N	67 0w
Casma, Peru	78	9 30s	78 20w
Caspe, Spain	17	41 14N	0 1w
Casper, U.S.A.	72	42 50N	106 20w
Caspian Sea, U.S.S.R.	26	43 0N	50 0 E
Cass Lake, U.S.A.	70	47 25N	94 33w

	MAP		
Cass City, U.S.A.	68	43 35N	83 12w
Cassai, Angola	56	10 36s	22 3 E
Cassano allónio, Italy	20	39 48N	16 20 E
Casselton, U.S.A.	70	47 0N	97 20w
Cassembe, Mozam.	56	13 25s	36 11 E
Cassiar Mts., Canada	64	39 30N	130 30w
Cassino, Italy	20	41 30N	13 50 E
Cassora, Angola	56	11 20s	24 0 E
Cassville, U.S.A.	71	36 43N	94 0w
Castano, Argentina	77	31 0s	69 55w
Castelbuono, Italy	20	37 56N	14 4 E
Casteljaloux, France	12	44 19N	0 6 E
Castellammare, Sicily, Italy	20	38 2N	12 51 E
Castellammare, G. of, It.	20	35 5N	12 55 E
Castelloe, Ireland	12	53 17N	9 33w
Castellón, Spain	17	39 58N	0 3w
Castellote, Spain	17	40 48N	0 15w
Castelnaudary, France	12	43 20N	1 58 E
Castelo Branco, Port.	17	39 50N	7 31w
Castelsarrasin, France	12	44 4N	1 5 E
Castelvetrano, Italy	20	37 40N	12 46 E
Casterton, Victoria	43	37 30s	141 30 E
Castiglione, Italy	20	42 47N	10 52 E
Castile, Old and New, Spain	17	41 30N	4 0w
Castle Dale, U.S.A.	73	39 10N	111 2w
Castle Harbour, Berm.	75	32 17N	64 44w
Castle Rock, Cal., U.S.A.	71	39 26N	104 51w
Castle Rock, Wash., U.S.A.	72	46 19N	122 54w
Castlebar, Ireland	11	53 52N	9 20w
Castlebellingham, Ire.	11	53 53N	6 22w
Castleblayney, Ireland	11	54 7N	6 44w
Castlebridge, Ireland	11	52 23N	6 28w
Castlecliff, N.Z.	46	39 55s	175 0 E
Castlecomer, Ireland	11	52 49N	7 13w
Castlederg, N. Ireland	11	54 43N	7 35w
Castledermot, Ireland	11	52 55N	6 50w
Castlefinn, Ireland	11	54 47N	7 35w
Castlegar, Canada	64	49 20N	117 40w
Castlegate, U.S.A.	73	39 43N	110 52w
Castlegregory, Ireland	11	52 16N	10 0w
Castleisland, Ireland	11	52 14N	9 28w
Castlemaine, Ireland	11	52 10N	9 42w
Castlemaine, Victoria	43	37 2s	144 12 E
Castlemartyr, Ireland	11	51 54N	8 3w
Castlepoint, N.Z.	46	40 53s	176 12 E
Castlepollard, Ireland	11	53 40N	7 20w
Castlereagh R., N.S.W.	43	30 30s	148 14 E
Castletown, Berehaven, Ireland	11	51 40N	9 54w
Castletown, Westmeath, Ireland	11	53 27N	7 30w
Castletownroche, Ire.	11	52 10N	8 28w
Castletownsend, Ire.	11	51 31N	9 11w
Castlewellan, N. Ire.	11	54 16N	5 57w
Castlewood, U.S.A.	69	36 54N	82 16w
Castor, Canada	64	52 15N	111 50w
Castres, France	12	43 37N	2 13 E
Castries, St. Lucia, West Indies	75	14 0N	60 50w
Castro, Brazil	77	24 45s	50 0w
Castro, Chile	77	42 30s	73 50w
Castro, Spain	17	37 44N	4 29w
Castro Alves, Brazil	79	12 55s	39 40w
Castro Urdiales, Spain	17	43 23N	3 19w
Castro Verde, Portugal	17	37 41N	8 4w
Castropol, Spain	17	43 32N	7 0w
Castrovillari, Italy	20	39 49N	16 11 E
Castroville, U.S.A.	71	29 17N	98 49w
Castuera, Spain	17	38 43N	5 37w
Casuarina, Mt., W. Australia	44	14 28s	127 34 E
Casula, Mozambique	56	51 28s	33 40 E
Caswell Sd., N.Z.	47	44 58s	167 9 E
Cat I., Bahamas	75	24 30N	75 30w
Cat, I., U.S.A.	71	30 15N	89 5w
Cat, L., Canada	62	51 40N	91 50w
Catacaos, Peru	78	5 20s	80 45w
Catacocha, Ecuador	78	5 58s	79 40w
Catahoula, L., U.S.A.	68	31 30N	92 7 E
Catala, Angola	56	12 10s	13 30 E
Catalão, Brazil	79	18 5s	47 52w
Catalina, Canada	63	48 31N	53 4w
Catalina, Chile	77	25 20s	69 54w
Catalonia, prov., Spain	17	41 40N	1 15 E
Catamarca, Argentina	77	28 30s	65 50w
Catamarca, prov. Arg.	77	28 30s	65 50w
Catanduanes Is., Phil.	35	13 50N	124 20 E
Catanduva, Brazil	79	21 20s	49 10w
Catania, Sicily, Italy	20	37 31N	15 4 E
Catania, G. of, Italy	20	37 25N	15 8 E
Catanzaro, Italy	20	38 54N	16 38 E
Catatumbo R., Ven.	78	9 10N	72 30w
Cataxa, Mozambique	56	15 59s	33 11 E
Catbalogan, Philippines	35	11 45N	124 55 E
Catembe, Mozambique	57	26 00s	32 32 E
Cathcart, C. Prov.	57	32 18s	27 10 E
Cathlamet, U.S.A.	71	46 15N	123 29w
Cativa, Panama	74	9 21N	79 49w
Catlellsburg, U.S.A.	68	38 23N	82 38w
Catoche C., Mexico	74	21 40N	87 0w
Catrilo, Argentina	77	36 25s	63 30w
Catrimane, R., Brazil	77	1 30N	62 15w
Catrimani, Brazil	78	0 40N	62 40w
Catskill, U.S.A.	68	42 14N	73 52w

	MAP		
Catskill Mts., U.S.A.	68	42 10N	74 38W
Catuane, Mozambique	57	26 48S	32 18E
Catur, Mozambique	56	13 42S	35 34E
Cauca R., Colombia	78	7 30N	75 30W
Caucaia, Brazil	79	3 40S	38 50W
Caucasus Ra., U.S.S.R.	24	43 0N	44 0E
Caudebec, France	12	49 20N	1 1E
Caungula, Angola	54	8 15S	18 50E
Cauquenes, Chile	77	36 0S	72 30W
Caura R., Venezuela	78	6 50N	64 35W
Causapscal, Canada	63	48 19N	67 12W
Causses, Mts., France	12	44 15N	3 15E
Cauterets, France	12	42 52N	0 8W
Cauvery R., India	32	12 0N	77 45E
Cava, Campagna, Italy	20	40 43N	14 41E
Cavalli, I., N.Z.	46	35 0S	173 58E
Cavalier, U.S.A.	70	48 49N	97 34W
Cavan, Ireland	11	54 0N	7 22W
Cavan, co., Ireland	11	53 58N	7 10W
Cavarzere, Italy	20	45 8N	12 4E
Cave City, U.S.A.	68	37 13N	85 57W
Cavers, Canada	62	48 55N	87 41W
Caviana I., Brazil	79	0 15N	50 0W
Cavianas, Bolivia	78	12 40S	67 0W
Cavite, Philippines	35	14 30N	120 55E
Cawnpore. *See* Kanpur.	33		
Caxambú, Brazil	77	22 0S	45 0W
Caxias, Maranhao, Brazil	79	5 0S	43 27W
Caxias do Sul, Brazil	77	29 20S	51 10W
Caxito, Angola	54	8 30S	13 30E
Cay Sal Bank, Bah.	75	23 30N	80 0W
Cay Santo Domingo, I., Bahamas	75	22 0N	75 40W
Cay Verde, I., Bah.	75	22 15N	75 12W
Cayambe, Ecuador	78	0 5N	78 10W
Cayce, U.S.A.	69	33 59N	81 2W
Cayenne, Fr. Guiana	79	5 0N	52 18W
Cayman Is., Caribbean Sea	75	19 40N	79 50W
Cayo, Brit. Honduras	74	17 10N	89 0W
Cayo Romano Is., Cuba	75	22 10N	78 10W
Cayuga L., U.S.A.	68	42 50N	76 30W
Cazin, Yugoslavia	20	44 57N	15 57E
Cazombo, Angola	55	12 0S	22 48E
Cazorla, Spain	17	37 55N	3 1W
Ceanannus Mor, Ire.	11	53 42N	6 53W
Ceará, st., Brazil	79	5 0S	40 0W
Ceara Mirim, Brazil	79	5 35S	35 25W
Cebollar, Argentina	77	29 10S	66 35W
Cebu, Philippines	35	10 30N	124 0E
Cebu, I., Philippines	35	10 23N	123 58E
Cecil Plains, Queens.	43	27 30S	151 11E
Cecina, Italy	20	43 19N	10 33E
Ceclavin, Spain	17	39 50N	6 45W
Cedar L., Ont., Can.	65	46 3N	78 25W
Cedar Falls, U.S.A.	70	42 39N	92 29W
Cedar Keys, U.S.A.	69	29 9N	83 5W
Cedar Rapids, U.S.A.	70	41 55N	91 38W
Cedar R., U.S.A.	70	41 50N	91 50W
Cedarburg, U.S.A.	70	43 18N	87 58W
Cedartown, U.S.A.	69	34 5N	85 0W
Cedarvale, Canada	64	54 55N	128 25W
Cedarville, C. Prov.	57	30 23S	29 3E
Cedarville, U.S.A.	72	41 32N	120 15W
Cedral, Mexico	74	23 50N	100 42W
Cedro, Brazil	79	6 45S	39 8W
Cedros I., Mexico	74	28 10N	115 20W
Ceduna, S. Australia	45	32 7S	133 46E
Ceepeecee, Canada	64	49 52N	126 42W
Cefalù, Italy	20	38 3N	14 1E
Cega R., Spain	17	41 17N	4 10W
Cegléd, Hungary	16	47 10N	19 47E
Ceglie Messapico, Italy	21	40 39N	17 31E
Cehegin, Spain	17	38 6N	1 47W
Cejal, Colombia	78	2 47N	68 2W
Celaya, Mexico	74	20 30N	100 37W
Celebes (Sulawesi) I., Indonesia	35	2 0S	120 0E
Celebes Sea, Indonesia	35	3 0N	123 0E
Celina, U.S.A.	68	40 32N	84 31W
Celje, Yugoslavia	20	46 16N	15 18E
Celle, Germany	14	52 37N	10 4E
Cement, U.S.A.	71	34 51N	98 6W
Cenis, Mt. Pass, Fr.	12	45 15N	6 56E
Ceno R., Italy	20	44 40N	9 52E
Center, N.D., U.S.A.	70	47 10N	101 18W
Center, Texas, U.S.A.	71	31 47N	94 13W
Center City, U.S.A.	68	45 22N	92 55W
Centerfield, U.S.A.	73	39 6N	111 50W
Centerville, Ala., U.S.A.	69	32 55N	87 7W
Centerville, Iowa., U.S.A.	70	40 39N	92 55W
Centerville, Miss., U.S.A.	71	31 5N	91 2W
Centerville, S.D., U.S.A.	70	43 11N	96 57W
Centerville, Tenn., U.S.A.	69	35 46N	87 29W
Centerville, Tex., U.S.A.	71	31 13N	95 58W
Cento, Italy	20	44 43N	11 16E
Central, dist., S. Austral.	43	34 30S	138 15E
Central, dist., Victoria	43	37 30S	145 0E
Central, U.S.A.	73	32 45N	108 11W
Central Africa, Rep., Africa	54	7 0N	20 0E
Central America	59	7 0N to 18 30N	77 0W to 94 30W

	MAP		
Central City, U.S.A.	70	41 8N	98 0W
Central I., Kenya	53	3 30N	36 0E
Central Java, Indon.	34	7 10S	110 0E
Central Makran Ra., West Pakistan	32	26 40N	64 20E
Central Mt. Stewart, N. Territory	45	22 50S	132 30E
Central Patricia, Can.	62	51 20N	90 10W
Central Plain Div., N.S.W.	43	31 37S	147 28E
Central Province, Kenya	53	0 45S	36 45E
Central Province, Zambia	56	15 50N	29 0E
Central Range, New Guinea	42	5 0S	143 0E
Central Region, Ghana	52	5 35N	1 30W
Central Siberian Plat., U.S.S.R.	27	65 0N	105 0E
CentralSouthernRegion, China	39	30 0N	113 0E
Central Tableland, dist., N.S.W.	43	33 30S	149 30E
Central Western Div., Queensland	42	23 5S	145 21E
Central Western Slope, dist., N.S.W.	43	32 30S	148 40E
Centralia, Ill., U.S.A.	70	38 32N	89 5W
Centralia, Mo., U.S.A.	70	39 12N	92 6W
Cephalonia I. (Kefallinia I.)	21	38 20N	20 40E
Ceram I., Indonesia	35	3 10S	129 0E
Ceram Sea, Indonesia	35	2 30S	128 30E
Cerbère, France	12	42 26N	3 10E
Ceres, Argentina	77	29 55S	61 55W
Ceres, Cape Province	57	33 21S	19 18E
Cerignola, Italy	20	41 17N	15 53E
Cerigo (Kithica), I.,	20	36 20N	22 40E
Cerkes, Turkey	30	40 50N	32 55E
Cerknica, Yugoslavia	20	45 48N	14 21E
Cernavodă, Rumania	21	44 22N	28 3E
Cerralvo, I., Mexico	74	24 20N	109 45E
Cerreto, Italy	20	41 17N	14 32E
Cerritos, Mexico	74	22 20N	100 20W
Cerro, U.S.A.	71	36 45N	105 31W
Cerro Bolivar, Ven.	78	7 35N	62 45W
Cerro de San Felipe, Sp.	17	40 35N	1 45W
Cervera, Catalonia, Sp.	17	41 40N	1 16E
Cervera, Navarra, Sp.	17	42 3N	1 59W
Cervera, Old Castile, Spain	17	42 54N	4 35W
Cervione, France	12	42 20N	9 31E
Cesar, R., Colombia	78	10 0N	73 45W
Cesena, Italy	20	44 9N	12 13E
Cēsis, U.S.S.R.	23	57 18N	25 28E
Céske Budéjovice, Czechoslovakia	16	48 55N	14 25E
Cėsky Krumlov, C.Slov.	16	48 43N	14 21E
Cesky Tesin (Těšin), Czechoslovakia	16	49 45N	18 39E
Cessnock, N.S.W.	42	33 0S	151 15E
Cestos R., Liberia	50	5 30N	9 30W
Cetinje, Yugoslavia	21	42 23N	18 59E
Ceuta (Sp.), Morocco	50	25 52N	5 26W
Ceva, Italy	20	44 23N	8 0E
Ceyhan, Turkey	30	37 4N	35 47E
Ceyhan, R., Turkey	30	36 45N	35 42E
Ceylon. *See* Sri Lanka			
Chabjuwardoo B., W. Australia	44	23 0S	113 30E
Chachapoyas, Peru	78	6 15S	77 50W
Chachran, Pakistan	32	29 0N	70 30E
Chachran, Pakistan	31	21 0N	70 30E
Chachoengsao, Thailand	34	13 45N	101 12E
Chachro, Pakistan	32	25 5N	70 15E
Chaco Boreal, Paraguay	77	22 30S	60 10W
Chaco Central, Arg.	77	24 0S	61 0W
Chacon C., Alaska	64	54 40N	132 0W
Chacorão Falls, Brazil	79	6 45S	57 45W
Chad L. (Tchad), Chad	51	13 30N	13 30E
Chad (Tchad), Rep., Africa	51	12 0N	17 0E
Chade, Mozambique	53	12 0S	40 5E
Chadileo R., Argentina	77	37 30S	66 0W
Chadron, U.S.A.	70	42 50N	103 0W
Chadwa, Zambia	56	12 5S	32 35E
Chaeryong, N. Korea	36	38 20N	125 37E
Chafe, Nigeria	52	11 59N	6 52E
Chagai Hills, Afghan.	31	29 30N	63 0E
Chagang, prov., N. Korea	36	41 0N	126 0E
Chagda, U.S.S.R.	27	58 45N	130 30E
Chagoda, U.S.S.R.	25	59 10N	35 25E
Chagos Arch., Indian Oc.	5	6 0S	72 0E
Chargres, R., Pan. Canal Zone	74	9 5N	79 40W
Chaguaramas, Trinidad	75	10 46N	61 43W
Chāh Bahār, Iran	31	25 19N	60 41E
Chaibasa, India	33	22 30N	85 55E
Chaka, Sudan	53	4 58N	31 30E
Chakansur, Afghan.	31	31 14N	62 0E
Chakari, Rhodesia	56	18 5S	29 51E
Chake Chake, Tanzania	53	5 15S	39 45E
Chakonipau L., Canada	63	56 10N	67 45W
Chakradharpur, India	33	22 45N	85 40E
Chakrata, India	32	30 43N	77 58E
Chakwal, Pakistan	32	32 50N	72 45E
Chalabesa, Zambia	56	11 30S	30 55E
Chalawa, R., Nigeria	52	11 54N	8 0E

	MAP		
Chaleur, Baie de, Can.	63	47 55N	65 30W
Chalhuanca, Peru	78	14 15S	73 5W
Chaling, China	39	26 55N	113 30E
Chalisgaon, India	32	20 30N	75 10E
Chalky Inlet, N.Z.	47	46 3S	166 31E
Challans, France	12	46 50N	2 0W
Challapata, Bolivia	78	19 0S	66 50W
Challis, U.S.A.	72	44 32N	114 27W
Chalna, Bangladesh	33	22 38N	89 31E
Chalon-sur-Saône, Fr.	12	46 48N	4 50E
Chalonnes, France	12	47 20N	0 45W
Châlons-sur-Marne, Fr.	12	48 58N	4 20E
Cham, Switzerland	15	47 11N	8 28E
Chama, Zambia	56	11 10S	33 20E
Chama, U.S.A.	73	36 58N	106 34W
Chaman, Pakistan	32	30 58N	66 25E
Chamba, Cameroon	53	8 40N	12 48E
Chamba, India	32	32 35N	76 10E
Chambal R., India	32	26 0N	76 55E
Chamberlain, U.S.A.	70	43 59N	99 55W
Chamberlain, L., U.S.A.	69	46 15N	69 10W
Chamberlaine, R., W. Australia	44	16 20S	127 50E
Chambers, U.S.A.	73	35 14N	109 29W
Chambersburg, U.S.A.	69	39 53N	77 41W
Chambery, France	12	45 34N	5 55E
Chambesi, Zambia	56	10 58S	31 5E
Chambezi, R., Zambia	56	10 20S	31 58E
Chambishi, Zambia	56	12 39N	28 1E
Chambord, Canada	63	48 25N	72 6W
Chambord, France	12	47 37N	1 30E
Chambri, L., N. Guinea	42	4 12S	143 5E
Ch'amdo, China	37	31 10N	97 35E
Chametengo, Mozam.	56	17 1S	35 24E
Chamical, Argentina	77	30 25S	66 20W
Chamonix, France	12	45 55N	6 51E
Champagne, prov., Fr.	13	49 0N	4 40E
Champaign, U.S.A.	70	40 8N	88 12W
Champdoré, Lac, Can.	63	56 0N	66 0W
Champery, Swit.	15	46 11N	6 52E
Champion, Canada	64	50 20N	133 10W
Champlain, Canada	63	64 27N	72 24W
Champlain, L., U.S.A.	68	44 30N	73 20W
Champoton, Mexico	74	19 20N	90 50W
Chamrajnagar, India	32	11 50N	76 55E
Chañaral, Chile	77	26 15S	70 50W
Chanda, India	32	19 57N	79 25E
Chandalar (Big Squaw Lake), Alaska	59	67 35N	148 20W
Chandarun, India	32	26 55N	74 20E
Chandeleur Is., U.S.A.	67	29 50N	88 50W
Chandeleur Sd., U.S.A.	69	29 58N	88 40W
Chandigarh, India	32	30 30N	76 58E
Chandil, India	33	23 0N	86 5E
Chandler, Canada	63	48 18N	64 46W
Chandler, Ariz., U.S.A.	73	33 20N	111 52W
Chandler, Okla., U.S.A.	71	35 40N	97 15W
Chandpur, Bangladesh	33	23 8N	90 42E
Changhowon, S. Korea	36	37 10N	127 37E
Changhung, S. Korea	36	34 40N	126 53E
Changjin, tn. & res., N. Korea	36	40 30N	127 18E
Changshu, China	39	31 39N	120 45E
Changshun, China	39	25 55N	106 20E
Changtai, China	39	24 40N	117 45E
Chanteh, China	39	29 0N	111 25E
Changting, China	39	25 40N	116 20E
Changtu, China	38	42 50N	124 0E
Changwu, China	38	42 20N	122 50E
Changyatien, Inner Mongolia	38	38 58N	100 30E
Changyeh, China	37	38 58N	100 30E
Chanhwa, China	38	37 37N	117 38E
Chankiang (Tsamkong), China	39	21 5N	110 20E
Channapatna, India	32	12 40N	77 15E
Channel Is., Br. Isles	12	49 30N	2 40W
Channing, Mich., U.S.A.	70	46 9N	88 3W
Channing, Tex., U.S.A.	71	35 41N	102 23W
Chantada, Spain	17	42 37N	7 48W
Chanthaburi, Siam	34	12 38N	102 12E
Chantrey Inlet, Canada	60	67 30N	96 0W
Chanute, U.S.A.	71	37 44N	95 30W
Chanyi, China	37	25 37N	103 50W
Chaoan, China	39	23 47N	117 8E
Chaochow, China	39	23 40N	116 30E
Chaohsien, China	38	37 10N	114 50E
Chaohwa, China	38	32 20N	105 45E
Chaotung, China	37	27 22N	103 30E
Chang Kiang, R., China	39	29 10N	117 0E
Changane, R., Mozam.	56	23 30S	34 0E
Changara, Mozam.	56	16 50S	33 17E
Changchih, China	39	36 7N	113 0E
Changchow, Fukien, China	39	24 32N	117 34E
Changchow, Kiangsu, China	39	31 50N	120 0E
Changchow, Shantung, China	38	30 57N	118 0E
Changchun (Hsinking), China	38	43 50N	125 15E
Changai, China	38	39 13N	122 26E
Changhua, Taiwan	39	24 0N	120 31E
Changli, China	38	39 45N	119 15E
Changlo, China	39	24 1N	115 33E
Chagning, China	39	26 18N	112 17E
Changpai, China	37	41 29N	128 12E
Changpai Shan, China —N. Korea	37	42 0N	128 0E

	MAP		
Changping, China	38	40 15N	116 15E
Changping, China	39	25 21N	117 28E
Changpu, China	39	24 8N	117 36E
Changsan-got, Korea	36	38 10N	124 35E
Changsha, China	39	28 10N	113 5E
Changshow, China	39	29 50N	107 0E
Chaoyan, China	38	37 26N	120 16E
Chaoyang, China	39	23 17N	116 33E
Chaoyang, China	38	41 45N	120 18E
Chaoyangchen, China	36	42 35N	126 0E
Chap Kuduk, U.S.S.R.	26	48 45N	55 5E
Chapayevo, U.S.S.R.	26	50 25N	51 10E
Chapel Hill, U.S.A.	69	35 53N	79 3W
Chapleau, Canada	62	47 45N	83 30W
Chaplin, Canada	65	50 29N	106 40W
Chapra, India	33	25 48N	84 50E
Char, Niger	50	21 40N	12 45W
Charadai, Argentina	77	27 35S	60 0W
Charagua, Bolivia	78	19 45S	63 10W
Charambirá Pt., Col.	78	4 20N	77 30W
Charaña, Bolivia	78	17 30S	69 35W
Charcas, Mexico	74	23 10N	101 20W
Charchan, China	37	38 8N	85 33E
Charchan, R., China	37	38 50N	87 0E
Charcot I., Antarctica	80	70 0S	75 0W
Chardzhou, U.S.S.R.	26	39 0N	63 20E
Chari, R., Chad.	51	10 55N	16 15E
Charikar, Afghanistan	31	35 0N	69 10E
Chariton R., U.S.A.	70	40 10N	92 45W
Charkhari, India	32	25 24N	79 45E
Charkhlikh, China	37	39 2N	88 2E
Charleroi, Belgium	13	50 24N	4 27E
Charles, C., U.S.A.	68	37 18N	76 0W
Charles City, U.S.A.	70	43 2N	92 41W
Charles L., Canada	65	59 45N	110 40W
Charles Sd., N.Z.	47	45 2S	167 6E
Charles Town, U.S.A.	68	39 17N	77 52W
Charleston, Queens.	42	18 33S	143 35E
Charleston, Miss., U.S.A.	71	34 0N	90 8W
Charleston, S.C., U.S.A.	67	32 55N	80 0W
Charleston, W. Va., U.S.A.	68	38 20N	81 36W
Charleston, Mo., U.S.A.	71	36 58N	89 27W
Charleston Harb., U.S.A.	69	32 40N	80 0W
Charlestown, Ireland	11	53 58N	8 48W
Charlestown, Natal	57	27 26S	29 53E
Charlesville, Zaire	54	5 27S	20 59E
Charleville, France	12	49 44N	4 40E
Charleville, Queens.	43	26 24S	146 15E
Charlevoix, U.S.A.	68	45 19N	86 17W
Charlotte, Mich., U.S A.	68	84 48N	42 36W
Charlotte, N.C., U.S.A.	69	35 16N	80 46W
Charlotte Amalie, Virgin Is.	75	18 22N	64 56W
Charlotte Harb., U.S.A.	69	26 40N	82 10W
Charlotte L., Canada	64	52 11N	125 19W
Charlotte Waters, N. Territory	45	25 56S	134 54E
Charlottenburg, Ger.	14	52 30N	13 21E
Charlottesville, U.S.A.	68	38 1N	78 30W
Charlottetown, Canada	63	46 19N	63 3W
Charlotteville, Tobago	75		Inset
Charlton, Canada	62	47 45N	80 0W
Charlton, U.S.A.	70	40 59N	93 17W
Charlton I., Canada	62	52 0N	79 20W
Charny, Canada	63	46 43N	71 15W
Charolles, France	12	46 27N	4 16E
Charouin, Algeria	50	29 10N	0 15W
Charre, Mozambique	56	17 19S	35 10E
Charters Towers, Queensland	42	20 5S	146 13E
Chartres, France	12	48 29N	1 30E
Chascomus, Argentina	77	35 30S	58 0W
Chasefu, Zambia	56	11 55N	32 58E
Chaslands Mistake, New Zealand	47	46 38S	169 22E
Chasonga, Zambia	56	15 14S	29 9E
Chasovnya Uchurskaya, U.S.S.R.	27	57 10N	133 15E
Chastleton, Queens.	43	27 30S	141 35E
Chatal Balkan, Bulg.	21	42 45N	25 50E
Château d'Oex, Switz.	15	46 28N	7 7E
Château du Loir, Fr.	12	47 40N	0 25E
Château Gontier, Fr.	12	47 50N	0 42W
Château la Vallière, Fr.	12	47 30N	0 20E
Château Thierry, Fr.	12	49 3N	3 20E
Châteaubriant, France	12	47 43N	1 23W
Châteaudun, Fr.	12	48 3N	1 20E
Chateauroux, France	12	46 50N	1 40E
Châtel St. Denis, Switz.	15	46 32N	6 54E
Châtellerault, France	12	46 50N	0 30E
Chatfield, U.S.A.	70	43 49N	92 16W
Chatham, & Str., Alas.	64	57 30N	135 0W
Chatham, Alaska	59	57 30N	135 0W
Chatham, N.B., Can.	63	47 2N	65 28W
Chatham, Ont., Can.	62	42 23N	82 15W
Chatham, England	10	51 22N	0 32E
Chatham, U.S.A.	71	32 24N	92 29W
Châtillon-sur-Seine, Fr.	12	47 50N	4 33E
Chatrapur, India	33	19 22N	85 2E
Chatsworth, Rhod.	56	19 39S	30 50E
Chattahoochee, U.S.A.	69	30 43N	84 51W
Chattahoochee R., U.S.A.	69	31 20N	85 0W
Chattanooga, U.S.A.	69	35 0N	85 20W
Chau Do, Viet Nam	34	10 4N	105 10E

	MAP		
Chau L., N.Z.	47	44 15 S	169 51 E
Chauk, Burma	34	21 0N	94 58 E
Chaukan Pass, Burma	33	27 0N	97 15 E
Chaumont, Fr.	12	48 7N	5 8 E
Chauny, France	12	49 37N	3 12 E
Chauru, Dahomey	52	8 54N	2 35 E
Chauvin, Canada	65	52 45N	110 10W
Chaux-de-Fonds. La, Switzerland	15	47 1N	6 43 E
Chaves, Brazil	79	0 15 S	49 55W
Chaves, Portugal	17	41 45N	7 32W
Chavuma, Zambia	56	13 10 S	22 55 E
Cheb, Czechoslovakia	16	50 9N	12 20 E
Cheboksary, U S.S.R.	25	56 8N	47 30 E
Cheboygan, U.S.A.	68	45 40N	84 30W
Chechon, S. Korea	36	37 5N	128 9 E
Checiny, Poland	16	50 46N	20 37 E
Checotah, U.S.A.	71	35 30N	95 30W
Chedabucto B., Can.	63	45 25N	61 0W
Cheduba I., Burma	33	18 45N	93 40 E
Cheekpoint, Ireland	11	52 16N	7 0W
Cheepie, Queensland	43	26 43 S	144 59 E
Chefoo, China	38	37 30N	121 25 E
Chefornak, Alaska	59	60 12N	164 18W
Chegga, Algeria	50	34 25N	5 55 E
Chegga, Mauritania	50	25 15N	5 40W
Chehalis, U.S.A.	72	46 40N	123 0W
Cheju, S. Korea	36	33 31N	126 29 E
Cheju Do, I., S. Korea	36	33 30N	126 30 E
Chekalin, U.S.S.R.	25	54 10N	36 10 E
Chekiang, prov. China	39	29 20N	120 0 E
Chelan, U.S.A.	72	47 51N	119 59W
Chelan L., U.S.A.	66	48 0N	120 20W
Cheleken, U.S.S.R.	24	39 30N	53 0 E
Cheli, China	34	22 5N	100 40 E
Chelkar, U.S.S.R.	26	47 40N	59 32 E
Chelkar Tengiz, L., U.S.S.R.	26	48 0N	63 10 E
Chelm (Kholm), Poland	16	51 8N	23 30 E
Chelmno, Poland	16	53 20N	18 30 E
Chelmsford, England	10	51 44N	0 29 E
Chelmza, Poland	16	53 10N	18 39 E
Chelsea, U.S.A.	71	36 33N	95 29W
Cheltenham, England	10	51 53N	2 7W
Chelyabinsk, U.S.S.R.	24	55 10N	61 35 E
Chemahawin, Canda.	65	53 8N	99 40W
Chemainus, Canada	64	48 54N	123 42W
Chemba, Mozambique	56	17 11 S	34 53 E
Chembar, U.S.S.R.	25	53 0N	43 25 E
Chembe Ferry, Zaire	56	11 40 S	28 30 E
Chemnitz. *See* Karl Marx Stadt.	14		
Chemong, Canada	65	53 20N	102 0W
Chemor, Malaya	34	4 45N	101 9 E
Chemult, U.S.A.	72	43 15N	121 50W
Chen, Mt., U.S.S.R.	27	65 10N	141 20 E
Chenab R., W. Pak.	32	30 40N	71 30W
Chenaf, Somali Rep.	53	1 50N	41 40 E
Chenele, Angola	56	17 0N	24 0 E
Cheney, U.S.A.	72	47 30N	117 31W
Chengan, China	39	28 30N	107 30 E
Chengcheng, China	38	35 10N	109 50 E
Chengchow, China	38	34 45N	113 45 E
Chengfeng, China	39	25 15N	105 45 E
Chengho, China	39	27 30N	118 45 E
Chenghsien, China	39	29 30N	120 40 E
Chengkiang, China	37	24 39N	102 50 E
Chengpuh, China	39	26 15N	110 10 E
Chengshan Tow, Pen., China	38	37 27N	122 30 E
Chengteh, China	38	41 0N	117 55 E
Chengting, China	38	38 5N	113 33 E
Chengtu, China	39	30 40N	104 12 E
Chengu, China	38	33 1N	107 29 E
Chengyang, China	38	36 25N	120 25 E
Chengyang, China	38	32 31N	114 27 E
Chengyangkwan, China	39	32 30N	116 35 E
Chenhsien, China	39	25 34N	112 57 E
Chenki, China	39	27 59N	110 0 E
Chenkung, China	39	27 9N	108 29 E
Chenning, China	39	26 0N	105 50 E
Chensiung, China	39	27 21N	104 58 E
Chentung, China	38	45 52N	123 10 E
Chenyuan, China	39	27 0N	108 20 E
Chenyuan, China	38	35 33N	107 30 E
Cheong, China	39	19 17N	108 39 E
Chéom Ksan, Cambodia	34	14 15N	104 50 E
Chepaua, Angola	56	12 42 S	23 45 E
Chepen, Peru	78	7 10 S	79 30W
Chepes, Argentina	77	31 20 S	66 35W
Chepo, Panama	75	9 10N	76 6W
Cheptsa, U.S.S.R.	24	57 58N	53 0 E
Cheptulil, Mt., Kenya	53	1 25N	35 35 E
Chequamegon Bay, U.S.A.	70	46 45N	90 45W
Cher R., France	12	47 10N	2 10 E
Cheraw, U.S.A.	69	34 42N	79 54W
Cherbourg, France	12	49 39N	1 40W
Cherdyn, U.S.S.R.	24	60 20N	56 20 E
Cheremkhovo, U.S.S.R.	27	53 32N	102 40 E
Cheremshan R., U.S.S.R.	25	54 30N	50 30 E
Cherepanovo, U.S.S.R.	26	54 15N	83 30 E
Chereponi, Ghana	52	10 9N	1 39W
Cherepovets, U.S.S.R.	25	59 5N	37 55 E
Cherkassy, U.S.S.R.	25	49 30N	32 0 E
Cherkessk, U.S.S.R.	25	44 25N	42 10 E
Cherlak, U.S.S.R.	26	54 15N	74 55 E
Chernaya, U.S.S.R.	27	70 30N	89 10 E
Chernigov, U.S.S.R.	25	51 28N	31 20 E
Chernogorsk, U.S.S.R.	26	54 5N	91 10 E
Chernomorskoye, U.S.S.R.	25	45 31N	32 46 E
Chernovtsy, U.S.S.R.	24	48 0N	26 0 E
Cherny Yar, U.S.S.R.	25	48 6N	45 55 E
Chernyakovsk, U.S.S.R.	23	54 29N	21 48 E
Cherokee, Iowa., U.S.A.	70	42 50N	95 30W
Cherokee, Okla., U.S.A.	71	36 45N	98 25W
Cherquenco, Chile	77	38 35 S	72 0W
Cherrapunji, India	33	25 17N	91 47 E
Cherry Creek, U.S.A.	72	39 56N	114 57W
Cherryvale, U.S.A.	71	37 17N	95 33W
Cherski Ra., U.S.S.R.	27	64 0N	145 0 E
Chesapeake B., U.S.A.	68	38 10N	76 15W
Chesha B., U.S.S.R.	24	67 20N	47 0 E
Chester, Canada	63	44 35N	64 12W
Chester, England	10	53 12N	2 53W
Chester, Calif., U.S.A.	72	40 21N	121 15W
Chester, Ill., U.S.A.	71	37 58N	89 47W
Chester, Mont., U.S.A.	72	48 31N	110 59W
Chester, Pa., U.S.A.	68	39 51N	75 21W
Chester, S.C., U.S.A.	69	34 40N	81 0W
Chesterfield, Canada	61	63 0N	91 0W
Chesterfield, England	10	53 14N	1 26W
Chesterfield Inlet, Can.	60	63 30N	91 0W
Chesterfield Is., Tasman Sea	41	19 52 S	158 15 E
Chesuncook L., U.S.A.	69	46 0N	69 10W
Chetek, U.S.A.	68	45 38N	91 39W
Cheticamp, Canada	63	46 37N	60 59W
Chetumal, Mexico	74	18 30N	88 20W
Chevak, Alaska	59	61 33N	165 36W
Cheviot, The, mt., Eng.	10	55 28N	2 8W
Cheviot Hills, Scotland	10	55 28N	2 8W
Cheviot Ra., Queens.	43	25 20 S	143 45 E
Chew-Bahir L., Ethiopia	53	4 40N	30 50 E
Chewelah, U.S.A.	72	48 21N	117 47W
Cheyenne, U.S.A.	70	41 9N	104 49W
Cheyenne, U.S.A.	71	35 36N	99 37W
Cheyenne R., Big, U.S.A.	70	44 40N	101 0W
Cheyenne Wells, U.S.A.	70	38 52N	102 24W
Cheyne Bay, Australia	44	34 30 S	118 45 E
Chhatarpur, India	32	24 55N	79 43 E
Chhindwara, India	32	22 2N	78 59 E
Chhlong, Cambodia	34	12 11N	106 2 E
Chiang Khan, Thailand	34	18 0N	102 2 E
Chiang Rai, Thailand	34	19 52N	99 50 E
Chiapas, st., Mexico	74	17 0N	92 45W
Chiasso, Italy	15	45 51N	9 02 E
Chiavari, Italy	20	44 20N	9 20 E
Chiavenna, Italy	20	46 18N	9 23 E
Chiba, Japan	36	35 30N	140 7 E
Chiba, pref., Japan	36	35 25N	140 15 E
Chibabava, Mozam.	56	20 13 S	33 38 E
Chibango, Angola	56	13 38 S	21 55 E
Chibi, Rhodesia	56	20 17 S	30 30 E
Chibia, Angola	55	15 10 S	13 50 E
Chibougamau L., Can.	62	49 50N	74 20W
Chibougamau R., Can.	62	49 50N	75 40W
Chibuk, Nigeria	52	10 52N	12 50 E
Chibwe, Zambia	56	14 12 S	28 32 E
Chicacole. *See* Srikakulam.	32		
Chicago, U.S.A.	70	41 56N	87 50W
Chicago Heights, U.S.A.	70	41 30N	87 40W
Chicago & I., Alaska	59	58 0N	136 0W
Chicale, Botswana	56	19 37 S	22 27 E
Chichen Itzá, Mexico	74	20 40N	88 32W
Chichibu, Japan	36	36 7N	139 6 E
Chickasha, U.S.A.	71	35 0N	98 0W
Chiclana, Spain	17	36 27N	6 9W
Chiclayo, Peru	78	6 42 S	79 50W
Chico, U.S.A.	72	39 45N	122 0W
Chico R., Argentina	77	44 0 S	67 0W
Chico R., Argentina	77	49 30 S	69 30W
Chicoa, Mozambique	56	15 35 S	32 20 E
Chicoma Pk., U.S.A.	73	35 57N	106 40W
Chicopee, U.S.A.	69	42 6N	72 37W
Chicoutimi, Canada	63	48 28N	71 5W
Chidambaram, India	32	11 20N	79 45 E
Chidley, C., Canada	61	60 30N	64 15W
Chienchangying, Inner Mongolia	38	42 15N	119 20 E
Chiengi, Zambia	56	8 38 S	9 10 E
Chiengmai, Thailand	34	18 55N	98 55 E
Chienping, China	38	41 30N	119 35 E
Chiese, R., Italy	20	45 20N	10 25 E
Chieti, Italy	20	42 22N	14 10 E
Chifeng, China	38	42 30N	118 35 E
Chifre, Sa. do, Brazil	79	17 0 S	41 0W
Chigha Sarai, Afghan.	31	35 1N	71 7 E
Chignecto B., Canada	63	45 33N	64 50W
Chignik, Alaska	59	56 18N	158 27W
Chiguana, Bolivia	78	21 0 S	67 50W
Chigubo, Mozambique	56	22 50 S	33 34 E
Chihing, China	39	24 57N	114 0 E
Chihkiang, China	39	27 27N	109 0 E
Chihkiang, China	39	30 18N	111 35 E
Chihkin, China	39	26 35N	105 17 E
Chihsien (Weihwei), China	38	35 35N	114 15 E
Chihuaha, Mexico	74	28 40N	106 3W
Chihuahua, st., Mexico	74	28 40N	106 3W
Chik Ballapur, India	32	13 25N	77 45 E
Chikishlyar, U.S.S.R.	31	37 55N	54 0 E
Chikmagalur, India	32	13 15N	75 45 E
Chiko, Zambia	56	15 55 S	26 35 E
Chikoa, Zambia	56	13 24 S	32 7 E
Chikolama, Zambia	56	15 8 S	28 40 E
Chikwawa, Malawi	56	16 2 S	34 50 E
Chilako R., Canada	64	53 40N	123 10W
Chilanga, Zambia	56	15 33 S	28 16 E
Chilapa, Mexico	74	17 40N	99 20W
Chilas, Kashmir	32	35 25N	74 5 E
Chilaw, Sri Lanka	32	7 30N	79 50 E
Chilcotin R., Canada	64	52 25N	124 10W
Childers, Queensland	43	25 15 S	152 17 E
Childress, U.S.A.	71	34 26N	100 13W
Chile, rep., S. America	77	17 30 S to 55 0 S	71 15W
Chilecito, Argentina	77	29 0 S	67 40W
Chilete, Peru	78	7 10 S	78 50W
Chili, Gulf of (Po Hai), China	38	38 30N	119 0 E
Chili, U.S.S.R.	26	44 10N	66 55 E
Chilia Mouth, Rumania	21	45 20N	29 35 E
Chililabombwe, Zaire	56	12 18 S	27 33 E
Chilka L., India	33	19 40N	85 25 E
Chilkat P., Canada	64	59 50N	136 30W
Chilko, L. & R., Can.	64	51 20N	124 10W
Chilkoot P., Canada	64	59 40N	134 0W
Chillagoe, Queensland	42	17 14 S	144 33 E
Chillan, mt., Chile	77	37 0 S	70 0W
Chillicothe, Ill., U.S.A.	70	40 55N	89 30W
Chillicothe, Miss., U.S.A.	70	39 47N	93 31W
Chillicothe, Ohio, U.S.A.	68	39 51N	82 58W
Chilliwack, Canada	64	49 10N	122 0W
Chiloane, I., Mozam.	56	20 40 S	34 35 E
Chiloé I., Chile	77	42 50 S	73 45W
Chilonga, Zambia	56	12 2 S	31 17 E
Chilpancingo, Mexico	74	17 30N	99 40W
Chiltern Hills, England	10	51 44N	0 42W
Chilton, U.S.A.	70	44 1N	88 12W
Chilubula, Zambia	56	10 14 S	30 51 E
Chilung, China	39	25 5N	121 40 E
Chimaco, Angola	56	15 14 S	22 1 E
Chimacum, U.S.A.	72	48 2N	122 48W
Chimai, China	37	33 49N	100 6 E
Chimay, Belgium	13	50 3N	4 20 E
Chimborazo, mt., Ec.	78	1 20 S	78 55W
Chimbote, Peru	78	9 0 S	78 35W
Chimkent, U.S.S.R.	26	42 40N	69 25 E
Chimpembe, Zambia	56	9 31 S	29 33 E
China, rep., Asia	29	55 0N to 18 30N and	70 0 E to 133 0 E
China, Mexico	74	25 40N	99 20W
Chinati Pk., U.S.A.	71	30 0N	104 15W
Chinavane, Mozam.	55	25 2 S	32 47 E
Chincha Is., Peru	78	13 35 S	76 20W
Chincha Alta, Peru	78	13 20 S	76 0W
Chinchaga R., Canada	64	58 30N	118 20W
Chinchilla, Queensland	43	26 45 S	150 38 E
Chinchilla, Spain	17	38 53N	1 40W
Chinchon, Spain	17	38 53N	3 26W
Chinchow. (Chinhsien), China	38	41 10N	121 10 E
Chincoteague, U.S.A.	68	37 58N	75 21W
Chindamani, Mongolia	37	45 20N	97 59 E
Chinde, Mozambique	56	18 45 S	36 30 E
Chindwin R., Burma	33	22 30N	95 0 E
Ching K., China	39	30 25N	110 15 E
Chingleput, India	32	12 42N	79 58 E
Chingola, Zambia	56	13 0 S	27 30 E
Chingole, Malawi	56	13 4 S	34 17 E
Chinguar, Angola	55	12 18 S	16 45 E
Chinguetti, Niger	50	20 25N	12 15W
Chingune, Mozambique	56	20 33 S	35 0 E
Chinhae, S. Korea	36	35 8N	128 52 E
Chiniot, Pakistan	32	31 45N	73 0 E
Chinipas, Mexico	74	27 30N	108 20W
Chinju, Korea	36	35 15N	128 0 E
Chinkiang, China	39	32 15N	119 30 E
Chinkolobwe (Shinkolobwe), Zaire	56	11 10 S	26 40 E
Chinkwa, Zambia	56	12 45 S	24 30 E
Chinle, U.S.A.	73	36 13N	109 33W
Chino Valley, U.S.A.	73	34 50N	112 30W
Chinon, France	12	47 10N	0 15 E
Chinook, U.S.A.	72	48 37N	109 10W
Chins Division, Burma	33	22 0N	93 0 E
Chinsali, Zambia	56	10 30 S	32 2 E
Chinsura, India	33	22 53N	88 25 E
Chinteche, Malawi	56	11 50 S	34 5 E
Chinunga, Mozambique	56	13 31 S	35 55 E
Chinunje, Tanzania	53	11 9 S	37 19 E
Chinwangtao, China	38	40 0N	119 35 E
Chinyuan, China	38	36 31N	111 10 E
Chiôco, Mozambique	56	16 28 S	33 15 E
Chioggia, Italy	20	45 13N	12 15 E
Chios (Khios), I., Gr.	21	38 25N	25 55 E
Chip Lake, Canada	64	53 35N	115 35W
Chipani, Rhodesia	56	16 10 S	29 11 E
Chipata, Zambia	56	13 38 S	32 38 E
Chipera, Mozambique	56	15 22 S	32 35 E
Chipewyan, L., Canada	65	58 0N	98 40W
Chipili, Zambia	56	10 45 S	29 4 E
Chipimp, Zambia	56	14 0 S	25 40 E
Chipinga, Rhodesia	56	20 13 S	32 36 E
Chipley, U.S.A.	69	30 45N	85 32W
Chipman, Canada	63	46 6N	65 53W
Chipogoro, Tanzania	53	6 52 S	36 3 E
Chipoka, Malawi	56	13 57 S	34 28 E
Chippewa Falls, U.S.A.	70	44 55N	91 22W
Chippewa R., U.S.A.	70	44 45N	91 45W
Chiquian, Peru	78	10 10 S	77 0W
Chiquibamba, Peru	78	15 45 S	72 45W
Chiquimula, Guatemala	74	14 51N	89 37W
Chiquinquira, Colombia	78	5 40N	74 0W
Chir R., U.S.S.R.	25	48 45N	42 10 E
Chira R., Peru	78	4 50 S	80 45W
Chiradzula, Malawi	56	15 40 S	35 11 E
Chirala, India	32	15 50N	80 20 E
Chiramba, Mozam.	56	16 55 S	34 39 E
Chiras, Afghanistan	31	35 14N	65 40 E
Chirfa, Niger	51	20 55N	12 5 E
Chiribira Falls, Rhod.	56	20 5 S	32 15 E
Chiricahu, Pk., U.S.A.	73	31 50N	109 15W
Chirikof, Alaska	59	55 45N	155 40W
Chiriqui, G. of, Pan.	75	8 0N	82 10W
Chiriqui, Lag. de, Pan.	75	9 10N	82 0W
Chiriqui Mt., Panama	78	8 55N	82 35W
Chirmiri, India	33	23 15N	82 20 E
Chiromo, Malawi	56	16 30 S	35 7 E
Chirpan, Bulgaria	21	42 10N	25 19 E
Chirundu, Rhodesia	56	16 0 S	28 59 E
Chisamba, Zambia	56	14 55 S	28 20 E
Chisan, China	39	22 50N	120 30 E
Chisana, Alaska	59	62 3N	142 8W
Chisapani Garhi, Nepal	33	27 35N	85 15 E
Chisholm, Canada	64	54 50N	114 15W
Chishtian, Pakistan	32	29 45N	72 45 E
Chisimba Falls, Zambia	56	14 55 S	28 20 E
Chişinău Criş, Rumania	21	46 32N	21 37 E
Chismy, U.S.S.R.	24	54 40N	55 15 E
Chistopol, U.S.S.R.	25	55 25N	50 38 E
Chita, U.S.S.R.	27	52 0N	113 25 E
Chitaldrug (Chitadurga) India	32	14 15N	76 28 E
Chitamba, Zambia	56	12 50 S	30 45 E
Chitapa, Zambia	56	13 20 S	25 50 E
Chitek L., Canada	65	52 30N	99 30W
Chitembo, Angola	56	13 30 S	16 50 E
Chitina, Alaska	59	61 38N	144 45W
Chitokeloki, Zambia	56	13 55 S	23 25 E
Chitorgarh, India	32	24 52N	74 43 E
Chitradurga, India	32	14 15N	76 28 E
Chitral, W. Pakistan	32	35 50N	71 56 E
Chitré, Panama	75	7 59N	80 27W
Chittagong, Bangladesh	32	22 19N	91 55 E
Chittagong, terr., Bangladesh	33	23 30N	91 5 E
Chittoor, India	32	13 15N	79 5 E
Chittur, India	32	10 40N	74 45 E
Chiukwangshun, China	39	26 4N	106 13 E
Chiusi, Italy	20	43 2N	11 57 E
Chiuta, Mozambique	56	15 29 S	33 20 E
Chiuta, L., Mozam.	56	14 30 S	35 50 E
Chiute, Mozambique	56	20 40 S	33 10 E
Chiva, Spain	17	39 27N	0 41W
Chivasso, Italy	20	45 10N	7 52 E
Chivilcoy, Argentina	77	35 0 S	60 0W
Chiwanda, Tanzania	53	11 21 S	34 55 E
Chiwefwe, Zambia	56	13 37 S	29 31 E
Choba, Kenya	53	2 27N	38 3 E
Chobe, R. (Linyanti, R.) Botswana	56	18 10 S	24 10 E
Chobe Swamp, Botswana	56	18 30 S	23 40 E
Chobol, Nigeria	52	12 12N	12 30 E
Chodziez, Poland	16	52 58N	17 0 E
Choele Choel, Arg.	77	39 11 S	65 40W
Chohsien, China	38	39 30N	116 0 E
Choibalsan, Mongolia	37	48 0N	114 40 E
Choiren, Mongolia	37	46 12N	108 36 E
Choix, Mexico	74	26 40N	108 10W
Chojnice, Poland	16	53 42N	17 40 E
Cholet, France	12	47 4N	0 52W
Chola North, Prov., S. Korea	36	35 50N	127 10 E
Cholla South, Prov., S. Korea	36	35 0N	127 0 E
Cholo, Malawi	56	16 7 S	35 5 E
Cholon, Viet Nam	34	10 56N	106 32 E
Choluteca & R., Hond.	75	13 20N	87 14W
Choma, Zambia	56	16 57 S	26 58 E
Chomba, Mozambique	53	11 35 S	39 15 E
Chomo, Zambia	56	13 30 S	32 10 E
Chomutov, C.Slov.	16	50 28N	13 23 E
Chone, Ecuador	78	0 40 S	80 0W
Chongjin, Korea	36	41 40N	129 40 E
Chöngju, Korea	36	39 15N	125 0 E
Chongson, S. Korea	36	37 26N	128 38 E
Chongup, S. Korea	36	35 35N	126 50 E
Chonos Arch., Chile	77	45 0 S	75 0W
Chorzele, Poland	16	53 15N	21 2 E
Chorzów, Poland	16	50 18N	19 0 E
Chos Malal, Argentina	77	37 15N	70 5W
Chosan, N. Korea	36	40 50N	125 45 E
Choshi, Japan	36	35 45N	140 45 E
Choszczno, Poland	16	53 7N	15 25 E
Chota Udaipur, India	32	22 20N	74 0 E
Choteau, U.S.A.	72	47 51N	112 11W
Chotila, India	32	22 30N	71 15 E
Chott Djerid, Tunisia	50	34 10N	8 0 E
Chott ech Chergui, Alg.	50	34 10N	0 30 E
Chott el Hodna, Alg.	50	35 30N	4 30 E
Chow Hu, China	39	31 35N	117 30 E
Chowan R., U.S.A.	69	36 35N	77 10W

Place	Map	Lat.	Long.
Chowchilla, U.S.A.	73	37 8N	120 10W
Chowehin, China	38	34 10N	108 12 E
Chowkow, China	38	33 32N	114 31 E
Christchurch, N.Z.	47	43 33 S	172 39 E
Christian Sd., Alaska	64	56 10N	134 30W
Christiana, Transvaal	57	27 52 S	25 8 E
Christie B., Canada	64	62 40N	110 30W
Christina R., Canada	65	56 20N	110 30W
Christmas I., Indian Oc.	5	10 0 S	105 40 E
Christmas I., Pac. Oc.	5	1 58N	157 27W
Chroma B., U.S.S.R.	28	72 0N	145 0 E
Chu Chu, Canada	64	51 30N	120 10W
Chu Kiang, China	39	31 0N	107 0 E
Chu Kiang, China	39	22 15N	113 45 E
Chuanchow, China	39	24 50N	118 35 E
Chuanhsien, China	39	25 50N	111 12 E
Chubut R., Argentina	77	43 0 S	70 0W
Chucheng, China	38	36 0N	119 20 E
Chuchow, China	38	35 30N	118 40 E
Chucul, Argentina	77	33 0 S	64 0W
Chudovo, U.S.S.R.	25	59 10N	31 30 E
Chudskoye L., U.S.S.R.	23	58 13N	27 30 E
Chugach, Mts., Alaska	59	61 0N	146 0W
Chuginadak I., Aleut. I.	59	53 0N	169 50W
Chuguyev, U.S.S.R.	25	49 55N	36 45 E
Chugwater, U.S.A.	70	41 50N	104 51W
Chuhsien, China	39	30 51N	106 52 E
Chuhsien, China	39	28 50N	118 50 E
Chuhsien, China	38	35 30N	118 35 E
Chuka, Kenya	53	0 20 S	37 38 E
Chukai, Malaya	34	4 13N	103 25 E
Chuki, China	39	29 43N	120 12 E
Chuki, China	39	32 20N	110 0 E
Chukot Ra., U.S.S.R.	27	68 0N	176 0 E
Chukudukraal, Botswana	56	22 27 S	23 28 E
Chula Vista, U.S.A.	73	32 38N	117 6W
Chulman, U.S.S.R.	27	57 5N	124 50 E
Chulucanas, Peru	78	5 0 S	80 0W
Chulym R., U.S.S.R.	26	57 20N	88 30 E
Chumatien, China	38	32 59N	114 1 E
Chumba, Ethiopia	53	4 35N	38 17 E
Chumbicha, Argentina	77	29 0 S	66 10W
Chumikan, U.S.S.R.	27	54 40N	135 10 E
Chumphon, Thailand	34	10 35N	99 14 E
Chumuare, Mozam.	56	14 20 S	31 40 E
Chumunjin, S. Korea	36	37 55N	127 44 E
Chunchon, Korea	36	37 55N	127 30 E
Chungchong N., prov., Korea	36	36 45N	126 30 E
Chungchong S., prov., Korea	36	36 45N	127 30 E
Chungan, China	39	27 45N	117 58 E
Chungchong North, Prov., S. Korea	36	36 52N	127 15 E
Chungchong South, Prov., S. Korea	36	36 30N	126 45 E
Chunghsien, China	39	30 20N	107 12 E
Chungju, S. Korea	36	36 58N	127 59 E
Chungking, China	39	29 35N	106 50 E
Chungsiang, China	39	31 18N	112 44 E
Chungtien, China	37	27 46N	99 45 E
Chunya, Tanzania	53	8 31 S	33 28 E
Chuquicamata, Chile	77	22 15 S	69 0W
Chur, Switzerland	15	46 52N	9 32 E
Churachandpuri, India	33	24 20N	93 40 E
Church House, Canada	64	50 20N	125 10W
Churchill C., Canada	65	58 50N	93 10W
Churchill L., Canada	65	56 0N	108 20W
Churchill Pk., Canada	64	58 10N	125 10W
Churchill R., Canada	65	57 5N	96 30W
Churchman, Mt., W. Australia	44	29 55 S	117 50 E
Churu, India	32	28 20N	75 0 E
Churuguara, Ven.	75	10 52N	69 35W
Chusan I., China	39	30 0N	122 20 E
Chushan, China	39	32 12N	110 20 E
Chushul, Kashmir	32	33 40N	78 40 E
Chusovoy, U.S.S.R.	24	58 15N	57 40 E
Chuting, China	39	27 30N	113 0 E
Chuvash, A.S.S.R., U.S.S.R.	26	55 30N	48 0 E
Chwaka, Tanzania	53	6 8 S	39 28 E
Chwangho, China	38	39 40N	123 0 E
Cicero, U.S.A.	70	41 48N	87 48W
Ciechanov, Poland	16	52 52N	20 38 E
Ciechanowiec, Poland	16	52 32N	22 30 E
Ciego de Avila, Cuba	75	21 50N	78 50W
Ciénaga, Colombia	78	11 0N	74 10W
Cienfuegos, Cuba	75	22 10N	80 30W
Cieza, Spain	17	38 17N	1 23W
Cilician Gates Pass, Turkey	30	37 20N	34 52 E
Cilician Taurus Mt., Turkey	30	36 40N	34 0 E
Cimarron, U.S.A.	71	36 30N	104 47W
Cimarron, R., U.S.A.	71	37 10N	102 10W
Cimone Mte., Italy	20	44 9N	10 53 E
Cîmpulung Moldovenese, Rumania	21	47 30N	25 36 E
Cinaruco R., Ven.	78	6 45N	69 0W
Cinch, R., U.S.A.	69	36 0N	84 15W
Cincinnati, U.S.A.	68	39 8N	84 25W
Cinto, Mte., France	12	42 24N	8 54 E
Circle, Alaska	59	65 50N	144 30W
Circle, U.S.A.	70	47 28N	105 32W
Circleville, Ohio, U.S.A.	68	39 35N	83 0W
Circleville, Utah, U.S.A.	73	38 11N	112 22W
Ciriciuma, Brazil	77	28 45 S	49 28W
Cirpan, Bulgaria	21	42 10N	25 19 E
Cisco, U.S.A.	71	32 25N	99 0W
Citlaltepetl, Mt., Mex.	74	18 0N	97 20W
Citrusdal, C. Prov.	57	32 35 S	19 0 E
Citta della Pieve, Italy	20	42 57N	12 0 E
Citta di Castello, Italy	20	43 28N	12 16 E
Ciudad Acuna, Mexico	74	29 20N	101 10 E
Ciudad Bolivar, Ven.	78	8 5N	63 30W
Ciudad Camargo, Mex.	74	27 41N	105 10W
Ciudad de Valles, Mex.	74	22 0N	98 30W
Ciudad del Carmen, Mexico	74	18 20N	97 50W
Ciudad Garcia Salinas, Mexico	74	22 55N	103 10W
Ciudad Guayana, Ven.	78	8 23N	62 40W
Ciudad Guerrero, Mex.	74	28 33N	107 28W
Ciudad Guzmán, Mex.	74	19 40N	103 30W
Ciudad Juárez, Mexico	74	31 42N	106 29W
Ciudad Madero, Mexico	74	22 19N	97 50W
Ciudad Mante, Mexico	74	22 50N	99 0W
Ciudad Obregon, Mex.	74	27 28N	109 59W
Ciudad Real, Spain	17	38 59N	3 55W
Ciudad Rodrigo, Spain	17	40 35N	6 32W
Ciudad Victoria, Mex.	74	23 41N	99 9W
Ciudadela, Spain	17	40 0N	3 50 E
Ciuma, Angola	55	13 0 S	15 45 E
Cividale, Italy	20	46 5N	13 25 E
Civita Castellana, Italy	20	42 18N	12 24 E
Civitanova, Italy	20	43 20N	13 40 E
Civitavecchia, Italy	20	42 6N	11 46 E
Civray, France	12	46 10N	0 17 E
Civril, Turkey	30	38 20N	29 16 E
Cizre, Turkey	30	37 19N	42 10 E
Clacton-on-Sea, Eng.	10	51 47N	1 10 E
Clairambault, Lac, Can.	63	54 30N	69 0W
Claire L., Canada	64	58 30N	112 0W
Clairemont, U.S.A.	71	33 6N	100 39W
Clamecy, France	12	47 28N	3 30 E
Clane, Ireland	11	53 18N	6 40W
Clanton, U.S.A.	69	32 48N	86 36W
Clanwilliam, C. Prov.	57	32 11 S	18 52 E
Clara, Ireland	11	53 20N	7 38W
Clare, co., Ireland	11	52 52N	8 55W
Clare, Queensland	42	19 47 S	147 9 E
Clare, S. Australia	43	38 51 S	138 36 E
Clare, U.S.A.	68	43 49N	84 45W
Clare I., Ireland	11	53 48N	10 0W
Clare R., Ireland	11	53 20N	9 0W
Clarecastle, Ireland	11	52 49N	8 57W
Claredon, Ark., U.S.A.	71	34 41N	91 19W
Claredon, Tex., U.S.A.	71	34 58N	100 49W
Claremont, U.S.A.	69	43 23N	72 20W
Claremont Pt., Queens.	42	14 0 S	143 38 E
Claremore, U.S.A.	71	36 22N	95 40W
Claremorris, Ireland	11	53 45N	9 0W
Clarence I., Chile	77	54 0 S	72 0W
Clarence R., N.S.W.	43	29 20 S	152 40 E
Clarence R., N.Z.	47	42 17 S	173 15 E
Clarence Str., Alaska	64	55 40N	132 10W
Clarenville, Canada	63	48 10N	54 1W
Claresholm, Canada	64	50 0N	113 45W
Clarinbridge, Ireland	11	53 13N	8 55W
Clarinda, U.S.A.	70	40 45N	95 1W
Clarines, Venezuela	75	9 56N	65 11W
Clarion, U.S.A.	70	42 41N	93 45W
Clark, U.S.A.	70	44 57N	97 44W
Clark Fork, U.S.A.	72	48 9N	116 10W
Clark Fork, R., U.S.A.	72	47 0N	114 0W
Clarkdale, U.S.A.	73	34 50N	112 6W
Clarke City, Canada	63	50 12N	66 38W
Clarke, L., Canada	65	54 25N	107 0W
Clarke Ra., Queens.	42	20 45 S	148 20 E
Clarke R., Queensland	42	19 13 S	145 27 E
Clarkes Harbour, Canada	63	43 25N	65 38W
Clarksburg, U.S.A.	68	39 18N	80 21W
Clarksdale, U.S.A.	71	34 5N	90 45W
Clarkston, U.S.A.	72	46 25N	117 3W
Clarksville, Ark., U.S.A.	71	35 29N	93 29W
Clarksville, Tenn., U.S.A.	69	36 32N	87 20W
Clarksville, Tex., U.S.A.	71	33 35N	95 0W
Claro, R. Brazil	79	18 10 S	51 10W
Clatskanie, U.S.A.	72	46 10N	123 48W
Claude, U.S.A.	71	35 5N	101 24W
Claudy, N. Ireland	11	54 55N	7 10W
Clausthalzellerfeld, Ger.	14	51 40N	10 25 E
Claverton, Queensland	43	27 27 S	145 52 E
Clay, U.S.A.	69	38 29N	81 9W
Clay Center, U.S.A.	70	39 30N	97 10W
Claypool, U.S.A.	73	33 28N	110 50W
Clayton, N. Mex., U.S.A.	71	36 30N	103 10W
Clayton, U.S.A.	72	44 17N	114 29W
Clayton, N.Y., U.S.A.	68	44 16N	76 2W
Cle Elum, U.S.A.	72	47 13N	120 51W
Clear C., Ireland	11	51 26N	9 30W
Clear I., Ireland	11	51 26N	9 30W
Clear L., Calif., U.S.A.	72	39 0N	122 45W
Clear Lake, S.D., U.S.A.	70	44 48N	96 41W
Clear Lake, Wash., U.S.A.	72	48 29N	122 18W
Clear Lake Res., U.S.A.	72	41 56N	121 10W
Clearfield, Penn., U.S.A.	68	41 0N	78 27W
Clearfield, Utah, U.S.A.	72	41 8N	112 0W
Clearmont, U.S.A.	72	44 41N	106 25W
Clearwater, Sta., Can	64	51 40N	120 0W
Clearwater, Mts., U.S.A.	72	46 20N	115 20W
Clearwater, U.S.A.	69	28 0N	82 50W
Clearwater L., Canada	62	56 10N	75 0W
Clearwater R., Canada	64	51 50N	115 50W
Clearwater R., Canada	65	56 40N	109 30W
Cleaverville, Australia	44	20 39 S	117 0 E
Cleburne, U.S.A.	71	32 18N	97 25W
Cleethorpes, England	10	53 33N	0 2W
Clermont, Queensland	42	22 46 S	147 38 E
Clermont-Ferrand, Fr.	12	45 46N	3 4 E
Clervaux, Luxembourg	13	50 3N	6 1 E
Cleveland, Queensland	43	27 31 S	153 3 E
Cleveland, Miss., U.S.A.	71	33 43N	90 44W
Cleveland, Ohio, U.S.A.	68	41 28N	81 43W
Cleveland, Okla., U.S.A.	71	36 18N	96 31W
Cleveland, Tenn., U.S.A.	69	35 10N	84 45W
Cleveland, Texas, U.S.A.	71	30 16N	95 2W
Cleveland C., Queens.	42	19 12 S	147 0 E
Cleveland, Mt., U.S.A.	64	48 55N	113 50W
Clew Bay, Ireland	11	53 54N	9 50W
Clewiston, U.S.A.	69	26 44N	80 50W
Clifden, Ireland	11	53 30N	10 2W
Clifden, New Zealand	47	46 1 S	167 42 E
Cliff, U.S.A.	73	32 58N	108 39W
Cliffony, Ireland	11	54 25N	8 28W
Clifton, Queensland	43	27 59 S	151 53 E
Clifton, Ariz., U.S.A.	73	33 0N	109 10W
Clifton, U.S.A.	71	31 45N	97 34W
Clifton Forge, U.S.A.	68	37 49N	79 50W
Climax, Canada	65	49 10N	108 20W
Clinch R., U.S.A.	68	36 40N	83 0W
Clint, U.S.A.	73	31 37N	106 13W
Clinton, B.C., Canada	64	51 0N	121 40W
Clinton, Ont., Canada	62	43 38N	81 33W
Clinton, New Zealand	47	46 12 S	169 23 E
Clinton, Ark., U.S.A.	71	35 35N	92 30W
Clinton, Ill., U.S.A.	70	40 8N	88 59W
Clinton, Ind., U.S.A.	68	39 40N	87 22W
Clinton, Iowa, U.S.A.	70	41 50N	90 18W
Clinton, Mass., U.S.A.	68	42 26N	71 40W
Clinton, Mo., U.S.A.	71	38 30N	93 40W
Clinton, N.C., U.S.A.	69	35 5N	78 15W
Clinton, N.Y., U.S.A.	68	43 3N	75 22W
Clinton, Okla., U.S.A.	71	35 30N	99 0W
Clinton, S.C., U.S.A.	69	34 30N	81 54W
Clinton, Tenn., U.S.A.	69	36 8N	84 10W
Clinton Colden L., Can.	60	64 0N	107 0W
Clintonville, U.S.A.	70	44 35N	88 46W
Clive, New Zealand	46	39 36 S	176 58 E
Clive, L., Canada	64	63 15N	118 55W
Clocolan, O.F.S.	57	28 55 S	27 34 E
Clogan, W'meath, Ire.	11	53 33N	7 15W
Clogheen, Ireland	11	52 17N	8 0W
Clogher, Louth, Ireland	11	53 47N	6 15W
Clogher, Roscommon, Ireland	11	53 55N	8 2W
Clogher, N. Ireland	11	54 25N	7 10W
Clogher Hd., Ireland	11	53 48N	6 15W
Cloghjordan, Ireland	11	52 57N	8 2W
Clonakilty, Ireland	11	51 37N	8 53W
Clonakilty B., Ireland	11	51 33N	8 50W
Cloncurry, Queens.	42	20 40 S	140 28 E
Cloncurry R., Queens.	42	20 15 S	140 35 E
Clones, Ireland	11	54 10N	7 13W
Clonmel, Ireland	11	52 22N	7 42W
Clo-oose, Canada	64	48 40N	124 45W
Cloquet, U.S.A.	70	46 50N	92 30W
Cloudy B., N.Z.	47	41 25 S	174 10 E
Cloudcroft, U.S.A.	73	33 0N	105 45W
Cloverdale, Canada	64	49 5N	122 50W
Cloverdale, U.S.A.	72	38 50N	123 2W
Clovis, U.S.A.	71	34 20N	103 10W
Clows, U.S.A.	73	36 15N	119 40W
Cloyne, Ireland	11	51 52N	8 7W
Cluj, Rumania	21	46 47N	23 38 E
Cluny, France	12	46 26N	4 38 E
Clutha R., N.Z.	47	45 39 S	169 25 E
Clyde, Canada	64	54 10N	113 40W
Clyde, New Zealand	47	45 12 S	169 20 E
Clyde, U.S.A.	69	43 8N	76 52W
Clyde, Firth of, Scot.	10	55 20N	5 0W
Clyde, R., Scotland	10	55 46N	3 58W
Coachella, U.S.A.	73	33 44N	116 13W
Coachford, Ireland	11	51 54N	8 48W
Coahoma, U.S.A.	71	32 12N	101 17W
Coahuila, st., Mexico	74	27 0N	112 30W
Coal, I., N.Z.	47	46 9 S	166 40 E
Coal Creek Flat, N.Z.	47	45 29 S	169 19 E
Coal R., Canada	64	60 30N	127 10W
Coalcoman, Mexico	74	18 40N	103 10W
Coalgate, U.S.A.	71	34 31N	96 15W
Coalinga, U.S.A.	73	36 9N	120 24W
Coalspur, Canada	64	53 15N	117 0W
Coalville, U.S.A.	72	40 58N	111 27W
Coari, Brazil	78	63 20 S	3 50W
Coast Mts., Canada	64	52 0N	126 0W
Coast Prov., Kenya	53	2 30 S	39 30W
Coast Prov., Tan.	53	7 10 S	39 0 E
Coast Range, Chile	59	30 0 S	71 0W
Coast Range, N. Amer.	72	40 0N	124 0W
Coast Range, U.S.A.	73	36 0N	121 0W
Coastal Plains Basin, W. Australia	44	30 45 S	115 30 E
Coatepeque, Guat.	74	14 46N	91 55W
Coatesville, U.S.A.	68	39 59N	75 30W
Coaticook, Canada	63	45 10N	71 46W
Coats I., Canada	61	62 30N	82 0W
Coats Land, Ant.	80	76 0 S	18 0W
Coatzacoalcos, Mexico	74	18 7N	94 35W
Cobalt, Canada	62	47 25N	79 42W
Coban, Guatemala	74	15 30N	90 21W
Cobar, N.S.W.	43	31 27 S	145 48 E
Cobb, Mt., N.Z.	47	41 2 S	172 30 E
Cobh, Ireland	11	51 50N	8 18W
Cobija, Bolivia	78	11 0 S	68 50W
Cobleskill, U.S.A.	68	42 40N	74 30W
Cobre, U.S.A.	72	41 8N	114 27W
Cóbué, Mozambique	56	12 0 S	34 58 E
Coburg, Germany	14	50 16N	10 55 E
Cocagne, Canada	63	46 20N	64 36W
Cocanada, India	33	16 55N	82 20 E
Cochabamba, Bolivia	78	17 15 S	66 20W
Cochemane, Mozam.	56	16 58 S	32 48 E
Cochin, India	32	9 55N	76 22 E
Cochise, U.S.A.	73	32 7N	109 58W
Cochran, U.S.A.	69	32 25N	83 23W
Cochrane, Alta., Can.	64	51 20N	114 30W
Cochrane, Ont., Can.	62	49 0N	81 0W
Cochrane L., Chile	77	47 10 S	72 0W
Cochrane R., Canada	65	58 10N	101 20W
Cockburn, S. Australia	43	32 5 S	141 50 E
Cockburn Chan., Chile	77	54 30 S	72 0W
Cockburn I., Canada	62	45 55N	83 20W
Coco Chan., India	33	13 40N	93 0 E
Coco Is., India	33	12 0 S	96 0 E
Coco R. (Wanks), Central America	75	14 10N	85 0W
Coco Solito, Pan. Can. Zone	74	9 22N	79 53W
Cocoa, U.S.A.	69	28 22N	80 40W
Cocobeach, Gabon	54	0 59N	9 34 E
Cocos-Keeling Is., Indian Ocean	5	12 12 S	96 54 E
Cocula, Mexico	74	20 20N	104 0W
Cod, C., U.S.A.	69	42 5N	70 30W
Codájas, Brazil	78	3 40 S	62 0W
Codajas L., Brazil	78	3 10 S	61 55W
Codajás R., Brazil	78	3 0 S	63 30W
Codazzi, Colombia	75	10 17N	73 10W
Coderre, Canada	65	50 11N	106 31W
Codfish, I., N.Z.	47	46 48 S	167 40 E
Codó, Brazil	79	4 30 S	43 55W
Cody, U.S.A.	72	44 32N	108 59W
Coe Hill, Canada	62	44 53N	77 44W
Coen, Queensland	42	13 52 S	143 12 E
Coeroeni, R., Surinam	79	3 0N	57 20W
Cœur d'Alene, U.S.A.	72	47 35N	116 47W
Coevorden, Neth.	13	52 40N	6 44 E
Coffeyville, U.S.A.	71	37 0N	95 40W
Coffin B., S. Australia	45	34 20 S	135 26 E
Coff's Harb., N.S.W.	43	30 16 S	153 5 E
Coghinas R., Sardinia, It.	20	40 52N	8 52 E
Cognac, France	12	45 41N	0 20W
Cohagen, U.S.A.	72	47 4N	106 33W
Cohoes, U.S.A.	68	42 47N	73 42W
Cohuna, Victoria	43	35 45 S	144 15 E
Coiba I., Panama	75	7 30N	81 40W
Coig, R., Argentina	77	51 20 S	70 30W
Coimbatore, India	32	11 2N	76 59 E
Coiro R., Bolivia	78	14 20 S	66 30W
Cojedes R., Venezuela	78	9 40N	68 50W
Cojimies, Ecuador	78	0 20N	80 0W
Cojutepequé, Salvador	74	13 41N	88 54W
Cokeville, U.S.A.	72	42 4N	110 58W
Colac, Victoria	43	38 10 S	143 30 E
Colby, U.S.A.	70	39 28N	101 0W
Colchester, England	10	51 54N	0 55 E
Cold L., Canada	65	54 30N	110 0W
Coldwater, U.S.A.	71	37 14N	99 21W
Coldwell, Canada	62	48 45N	86 30W
Colebrook, U.S.A.	69	44 52N	71 30W
Coleman, Canada	64	49 40N	114 30W
Coleman, U.S.A.	71	31 50N	99 28W
Coleman R., Queens.	42	14 57 S	142 30 E
Cölemerik, Turkey	31	37 35N	43 45 E
Colenso, Natal	57	28 44 S	29 50 E
Coleraine, N. Ireland	11	55 8N	6 40 E
Coleraine, Victoria	43	37 36 S	141 40 E
Coleridge L., N.Z.	47	43 17 S	171 30 E
Colesberg, C. Prov.	57	30 35 S	25 5 E
Colfax, La., U.S.A.	71	31 32N	92 44W
Colfax, Wash., U.S.A.	72	46 57N	117 28W
Colhué Huapi L., Arg.	77	45 30 S	69 0W
Coligny, Transvaal	57	26 17 S	26 18 E
Colima, Mexico	74	19 10N	103 40W
Colima, st., Mexico	74	19 10N	103 40W
Coll I., Scotland	10	56 40N	6 35W
Collahuasi, Chile	78	21 5 S	68 45W
Collarenebri, N.S.W.	43	29 30 S	148 30 E
Collares, Portugal	17	38 43N	9 28W
Collbran, U.S.A.	73	39 15N	107 58W
Colleen Bawn, Rhodesia	56	21 5 S	29 15 E
College Park, U.S.A.	69	33 42N	84 27W
Collette, Canada	63	46 40N	65 30W
Collie, W. Australia	44	33 25 S	116 30 E
Collie Cardiff, W. Australia	44	33 19 S	116 2 E
Collingwood, Canada	62	44 30N	80 20W
Collingwood, N.Z.	47	40 42 S	172 40 E
Collingwood, Queens.	42	22 20 S	142 31 E
Collingwood, B., Papua	42	9 25 S	149 12 E
Collins, Canada	62	50 20N	89 30W
Collinsville, Queens.	42	20 30 S	147 56 E
Collioume, France	12	42 32N	3 5 E

	MAP		
Collon, Ireland	11	53 46N	6 29w
Collooney, Ireland	11	54 11N	8 28w
Colmar, France	12	48 5N	7 20 E
Colmars, France	12	44 11N	6 39w
Colmenar Viego, Spain	17	40 39N	3 47w
Colmor, U.S.A.	71	36 15N	104 36w
Colne, England	10	53 51N	2 11w
Colnett, C., Mexico	74	30 58N	116 20w
Cologne, (Köln), Ger.	14	50 56N	6 57 E
Colomb Béchar, Algiers	50	31 38N	2 18w
Colombia, Mexico	74	27 40N	99 50w
Colombia, rep., S. America	78	3 45N	73 0w
Colombo, Sri Lanka	32	6 56N	79 58 E
Colome, U.S.A.	70	43 19N	99 43w
Colon, Cuba	75	22 42N	80 54w
Colón, Panama Rep.	75	9 20N	80 0w
Colon, Venezuela	75	8 2N	72 17w
Colonia, Uruguay	77	34 25 S	57 50w
Colonia Las Heras, Arg.	77	46 30 S	69 0w
Colonial Hts., U.S.A.	68	37 17N	77 25w
Colonsay, Canada	65	51 59N	105 52w
Colonsay I., Scotland	10	56 4N	6 12w
Colorado, st., U.S.A.	73	37 40N	106 0w
Colorado Des., U.S.A.	66	34 20N	116 0w
Colorado I., Pan. Can. Zone	74	9 12N	79 50w
Colorado Plat., U.S.A.	73	35 0N	112 0w
Colorado R., Argentina	77	37 30 S	69 0w
Colorado R., Argentina	77	28 0 S	67 20w
Colorado R., U.S.A.	73	33 30N	114 30w
Colorado R., Lit., U.S.A.	73	36 0N	111 20w
Colorado Springs, U.S.A.	70	38 50N	104 50w
Colorado, st., U.S.A.	70	39 5N	104 45w
Colotlan, Mexico	74	22 20N	103 20w
Colton, U.S.A.	72	44 34N	74 58w
Columbia, Miss., U.S.A.	71	31 30N	89 48w
Columbia, Mo., U.S.A.	70	38 58N	92 20w
Columbia, N.C., U.S.A.	69	35 55N	76 14w
Columbia, S.C., U.S.A.	67	34 0N	81 0w
Columbia, District of, U.S.A.	69	38 55N	77 0w
Columbia C., Canada	58	83 0N	70 0w
Columbia City, U.S.A.	68	41 8N	85 30w
Columbia Falls, U.S.A.	72	48 25N	114 12w
Columbia Hts., U.S.A.	70	45 4N	93 15w
Columbia Mt., Canada	64	52 20N	117 30w
Columbia Plat., U.S.A.	72	47 0N	119 0w
Columbia R., N. Amer.	72	51 50N	118 0w
Columbo, Angola	55	9 10 S	13 28 E
Columbretes Is., Spain	17	39 50N	0 50 E
Columbus, Ga., U.S.A.	69	32 30N	85 0w
Columbus, Ind., U.S.A.	68	39 12N	85 55w
Columbus, Mo., U.S.A.	69	33 30N	88 30w
Columbus, Mont., U.S.A.	72	45 39N	109 14w
Columbus, N.D., U.S.A.	70	48 54N	102 44w
Columbus, Nebr., U.S.A.	70	41 30N	97 25w
Columbus, New Mex., U.S.A.	73	31 50N	107 40w
Columbus, Ohio, U.S.A.	68	40 0N	83 0w
Columbus, Wis., U.S.A.	70	43 51N	89 4w
Colusa, U.S.A.	72	39 15N	124 3w
Colville, U.S.A.	72	48 32N	117 57w
Colville, C., N.Z.	46	36 29 S	175 21 E
Colville R., Alaska	59	69 10N	153 0w
Comacchio, Italy	20	44 41N	12 10 E
Comacha, Mozambique	56	17 45 S	33 14 E
Comallo, Argentina	77	41 0 S	70 5w
Comanche, Oklahoma, U.S.A.	71	34 28N	97 59w
Comanche, Tex., U.S.A.	71	31 52N	98 32w
Combahee, R., U.S.A.	69	32 45N	80 50w
Combarbala, Chile	77	31 10 S	71 0w
Comber, N. Ireland	11	54 33N	5 45w
Comblain, Belgium	13	50 29N	5 35 E
Comboyne, N.S.W.	43	31 30 S	152 28 E
Comeragh Mts., Ireland	11	52 17N	7 35w
Comet, Queensland	42	23 36 S	148 38 E
Comet R., Queensland	42	23 58 S	148 30 E
Comet Vale, Australia	44	29 55 S	121 4 E
Cometela, Mozam.	56	21 51 S	34 29 E
Comilla, Bangladesh	33	23 22N	91 18 E
Comiso, Italy	20	36 57N	14 35 E
Comitan, Mexico	74	16 18N	92 9w
Commentry, France	12	46 20N	2 46 E
Commerce, U.S.A.	69	34 10N	83 25w
Commercy, France	12	48 46N	5 34 E
Committee B., Canada	61	68 0N	87 0w
Communism Pk., U.S.S.R	26	39 0N	73 0 E
Como, Italy	20	45 48N	9 5 E
Como, L. of, Italy	20	46 5N	9 17 E
Comodoro Rivadavia, Argentina	77	45 50 S	67 40w
Comorin, C., India	32	8 3N	77 40 E
Comoro Is., Mozam. Chan.	49	12 0 S	44 0 E
Comox, Canada	64	49 42N	125 0w
Compiègne, France	12	49 24N	2 50 E
Compostela, Mexico	74	21 20N	105 0w
Conakry, Guinea	52	9 29N	13 49w
Concarneau, France	12	47 52N	3 56w
Conceição, Mozam.	56	18 47 S	36 8 E
Conceiçao de Barra, Brazil	79	18 50 S	39 50w
Conceiçao do Araguaia, Brazil	79	8 0 S	49 2w
Concepción, Bolivia	77	15 50 S	61 40w
Concepción, Chile	77	36 50 S	73 0w
Concepción, Paraguay	78	23 30 S	57 20w
Concepcion, U.S.A.	73	34 28N	120 30w
Concepcion B., Mexico	74	26 50N	112 0w
Concepcion C., U.S.A.	78	34 30N	120 30w
Concepción, Chan., Chile	77	50 50 S	75 0w
Concepción L., Bolivia	78	17 20 S	61 10w
Concepción R., Mexico	74	30 40N	113 0w
Concepcion del Oro, Mexico	74	24 40N	101 30w
Concepción del Urug., Argentina	77	32 35 S	58 20w
Conception B., Canada	63	47 45N	53 10w
Conception I., Bahamas	75	23 52N	75 9w
Concession, Rhod.	56	17 27 S	30 56 E
Conchas Dam, U.S.A.	71	35 24N	104 12w
Conche, Canada	63	50 48N	57 0w
Concho, U.S.A.	73	34 29N	109 40w
Concho R., U.S.A.	71	31 30N	100 0w
Conchos R., Mexico	74	29 20N	104 50w
Conchos R., Mexico	74	25 0N	98 50w
Concord, N.H., U.S.A.	69	43 5N	71 30w
Concord, N.C., U.S.A.	69	35 25N	80 35w
Concordia, Argentina	77	31 20 S	58 2w
Concordia, Brazil	78	4 35 S	66 40w
Concordia, U.S.A.	70	39 35N	97 38w
Concrete, U.S.A.	64	48 31N	121 49w
Condamine R., Queens.	43	26 55 S	150 15 E
Condé, France	12	50 26N	3 34 E
Conde, U.S.A.	70	45 15N	97 45w
Condeuba, Brazil	79	15 0 S	42 0w
Condobolin, N.S.W.	43	33 4 S	147 6 E
Condom, France	12	43 57N	0 22 E
Condon, U.S.A.	72	45 15N	120 12w
Condore Is., Viet Nam	34	8 10N	7 0 E
Condroz, Belgium	13	50 25N	5 20 E
Conflans, Haute Saône, France	12	47 50N	6 22w
Conflans, Meurthe et Moselle, France	12	49 10N	5 52 E
Confolens, France	12	46 2N	0 40 E
Cong, Ireland	11	53 33N	9 18w
Congo Central, prov. Congo	54	5 15 S	13 30 E
Congo, Rep., Africa	54	3 0 S	22 0 E
Congo, Rep. Fr. Community, Africa	54	2 0 S	16 0 E
Congress, U.S.A.	73	34 11N	112 52w
Conicarit, Mexico	74	27 20N	109 20w
Conil, Spain	17	36 17N	6 10w
Coniston, Canada	62	45 32N	80 51w
Conjeeveram. (Kancheepuram)	32	12 50N	79 42 E
Conklin, Canada	64	53 35N	111 0w
Conn L., Ireland	11	54 3N	9 15w
Conna, Ireland	11	52 5N	8 8w
Connacht, prov., Ireland	11	53 45N	9 0w
Conneaut, U.S.A.	68	41 55N	80 32w
Connecticut, R., U.S.A.	69	44 50N	71 34w
Connecticut, st., U.S.A.	68	41 40N	72 40w
Connell, U.S.A.	72	46 43N	118 57w
Connelsville, U.S.A.	68	40 5N	79 32w
Connemara, dist., Ire.	11	53 29N	9 45w
Connersville, U.S.A.	68	39 40N	85 10w
Connor, Mt., W. Australia	44	14 38 S	126 10 E
Connors Ra., Queens.	42	21 45 S	149 15 E
Conquest, Canada	65	53 35N	107 0w
Conrad, U.S.A.	64	48 11N	112 0w
Conselheiro Lafaite, Brazil	79	20 50 S	44 0w
Consort, Canada	65	52 0N	110 47w
Constance, L., of, Switzerland	15	47 39N	9 11 E
Constância dos Baetas, Brazil	78	6 5 S	62 20w
Constanta, Rumania	21	44 14N	28 38 E
Constantina, Spain	17	37 51N	5 40w
Constantine, Algeria	50	36 25N	6 30 E
Constitucion, Chile	77	35 20 S	72 30w
Consuegra, Spain	17	39 28N	3 30w
Consul, Canada	65	49 20N	109 30w
Contai, India	33	21 54N	87 55 E
Contact, U.S.A.	72	41 51N	114 50w
Contamana, Peru	78	7 10 S	74 55w
Contas R., Brazil	79	13 55 S	41 0w
Content, U.S.A.	65	47 57N	107 33w
Conway, Queensland	42	20 22N	148 42 E
Conway, Ark., U.S.A.	71	35 0N	92 25w
Conway, N.H., U.S.A.	68	43 48N	71 8w
Conway, S.C., U.S.A.	69	33 49N	79 2w
Cooch Behar, India	33	26 22N	89 29 E
Cook, S. Australia	45	30 35 S	130 25 E
Cook, U.S.A.	70	47 48N	92 41w
Cook Bay, Chile	77	55 10 S	70 0w
Cook Inlet, Alaska	59	60 0N	152 0w
Cook Is., Pacific Ocean	5	22 0 S	157 0w
Cook, Mount, N.Z.	47	43 36 S	170 9 E
Cook Strait, N.Z.	46	41 15 S	174 29 E
Cookeville, U.S.A.	69	36 10N	85 30w
Cookhouse, C. Prov.	57	32 44 S	25 47 E
Cookstown, N. Ireland	11	54 40N	6 43w
Cooktown, Queens.	42	15 30 S	145 16 E
Coolabah, N.S.W.	43	31 0 S	146 15 E
Cooladdi, Queensland	43	26 37 S	145 23 E
Coolah, N.S.W.	43	31 48 S	149 41 E
Coolamon, N.S.W.	43	34 46 S	147 8 E
Coolaney, Ireland	11	54 10N	8 36w
Coolangatta, Queens.	43	28 11 S	153 29 E
Coolgardie, W. Austral.	44	30 59 S	121 5 E
Coolidge, U.S.A.	73	32 59N	111 32w
Coolup, W. Australia	44	32 43 S	115 48 E
Cooma, N.S.W.	43	36 12N	149 8 E
Coonabarabran, N.S.W.	43	31 14 S	149 18 E
Coonamble, N.S.W.	43	30 56 S	148 27 E
Coondambo, S. Austral.	45	31 4 S	135 58 E
Coondapoor, India	32	13 42N	74 40 E
Coongee, Queensland	43	27 9 S	140 8 E
Cooper, Mt., Canada	64	50 10N	117 11w
Coongoola, Queensland	43	27 43 S	145 47 E
Cooper, U.S.A.	71	33 19N	95 44w
Cooper Mt., Canada	64	50 10N	117 11w
Cooper, R., U.S.A.	69	33 0N	79 55w
Cooper's Creek (Barcoo R.), S. Australia	43	27 30 S	139 17 E
Cooperstown, U.S.A.	68	42 42N	74 57w
Cooperstown, U.S.A.	70	47 30N	98 12w
Coorabulka, Queensland	42	23 41 S	139 53 E
Coorong, The, S. Australia	43	35 50 S	139 20 E
Coorow, W. Australia	44	29 50 S	115 59 E
Cooroy, Queensland	43	26 22 S	152 54 E
Coos Bay, U.S.A.	72	43 22N	124 16w
Cootamundra, N.S.W.	43	34 36 S	148 1 E
Cootehill, Ireland	11	54 5N	7 5w
Cooyar, Queensland	43	26 59 S	151 51 E
Copainata, Mexico	74	17 8N	93 11w
Cope, U.S.A.	70	39 45N	103 0w
Copenhagen, Denmark (Kobenhavn)	23	55 35N	12 30 E
Copiapó, Chile	77	27 15 S	70 20w
Copiapo R., Chile	77	27 15 S	71 0w
Copley, S. Australia	43	30 31 S	138 25 E
Copp, L., Canada	64	60 12N	114 50w
Coppell, Canada	62	49 30N	83 50w
Coppename R., Surinam	79	4 30N	56 30w
Copper Cliff, Canada	62	46 30N	81 4w
Copper Harbour, U.S.A.	70	47 31N	87 55w
Copper Mt., Canada	64	49 20N	120 30w
Copper Queen, Rhod.	56	17 29 S	29 18 E
Copperfield, Queens.	42	22 50 S	147 38 E
Coppermine, Canada	60	68 0N	116 0w
Coppermine R., Can.	60	66 30N	115 30w
Coptchil, Mongolia	38	42 10N	112 40 E
Coquihalla, Canada	64	49 35N	121 0w
Coquille, U.S.A.	72	43 13N	124 12w
Coquimbo, Chile	77	30 0 S	71 20w
Corabia, Rumania	21	43 48N	24 30 E
Coracora, Peru	78	15 5 S	73 45w
Corada P., mt., Spain	17	42 53N	4 50w
Coral Rapids, Canada	62	50 20N	81 40w
Coral Sea, Pac. Oc.	5	15 0 S	150 0 E
Corangamite, L., Vic.	43	38 0 S	143 30 E
Corato, Italy	20	41 12N	16 22 E
Corbeil-Essomes, France	12	48 37N	2 30 E
Corbin, U.S.A.	69	37 0N	84 0w
Corcoran, U.S.A.	73	36 6N	119 31w
Corcubion, Spain	17	42 58N	9 11w
Cordalba, Queensland	43	25 12 S	152 10 E
Cordele, U.S.A.	69	32 0N	83 50w
Cordell, U.S.A.	71	35 16N	99 0w
Cordillera de los Andes, South America	78	5 0 S	78 0w
Cordillera Central, Col.	75	6 0N	75 0w
Cordillera Central, Costa Rica	78	10 15N	84 0w
Cord. de Caravaya, Peru	78	14 0 S	70 30w
Cord. di Cochabamba, Bolivia	78	17 20 S	66 20w
Cord. Occidental, Col.	78	5 0N	76 30w
Cordoba, Mexico	74	18 50N	97 0w
Cordoba, Spain	17	37 50N	4 50w
Cordoba, prov., Arg.	77	31 22 S	64 15w
Cordoba, Sierra de, Arg.	77	31 10 S	64 25w
Cordobo, Mexico	74	26 20N	103 30w
Cordova, U.S.A.	69	33 45N	87 12w
Cordova Mines, Can.	59	44 34N	77 47w
Corella R., Queensland	42	20 15 S	140 30 E
Corfield, Queensland	42	21 40 S	143 21 E
Corfon, Somali. Rep.	53	3 12N	42 15 E
Corfu (Kerkira), Greece	21	39 40N	19 40 E
Coria, Spain	17	40 0N	6 33w
Corigliano, Italy	20	39 37N	16 32 E
Corinth, Greece	21	37 56N	23 0 E
Corinth, Miss., U.S.A.	69	35 0N	88 30w
Corinth, G. of, Greece	21	38 10N	22 40 E
Corinto, Brazil	75	18 20 S	44 30w
Corinto, Nicaragua	79	12 30N	87 10w
Cork, Ireland	11	51 54N	8 30w
Cork, co., Ireland	11	52 0N	8 30w
Cork, Queensland	42	23 2 S	142 3 E
Cork Harb., Ireland	11	51 46N	8 16w
Corleone, Italy	20	37 48N	13 16 E
Corlu, Turkey	21	41 9N	27 48 E
Cormontibo, Fr. Guiana	79	3 40N	54 10w
Cormorant, Canada	65	54 5N	100 45w
Corn Is., Cent. Amer.	75	12 0N	83 0w
Cornell, U.S.A.	70	45 9N	91 7w
Corner Brook, Canada	63	49 0N	58 0w
Corner Inlet, Victoria	43	38 40 S	146 30 E
Cornie C., W. Austral.	44	21 20 S	115 30 E
Corning, Ark., U.S.A.	71	36 28N	90 35w
Corning, Calif., U.S.A.	72	39 56N	122 11w
Corning, Iowa, U.S.A.	70	40 59N	94 41w
Corning, N.Y., U.S.A.	68	42 10N	77 3w
Cornish Cr., Queens.	42	22 29 S	144 50 E
Cornwall, Canada	62	45 5N	74 45w
Cornwall, N.Y., U.S.A.	69	41 28N	74 3w
Cornwallis Is., Canada	58	75 0N	95 0w
Corny Pt., S. Australia	45	34 51 S	137 0 E
Coro, Venezuela	78	11 30N	69 45w
Coroatá, Brazil	79	4 20 S	44 0w
Corocoro, Bolivia	78	17 15 S	69 19w
Coroico, Bolivia	78	16 0 S	67 50w
Coromandel Coast, India	32	12 30N	81 0 E
Coromandel Ra., N.Z.	46	36 55 S	175 40 E
Corona, Calif., U.S.A.	73	33 48N	117 32w
Corona, New Mexico, U.S.A.	73	34 20N	105 32w
Coronado, U.S.A.	73	32 42N	117 13w
Coronado B., Costa Rica	78	9 0N	83 40w
Coronation, Canada	64	52 10N	111 30w
Coronation Gulf, Can.	60	68 0N	114 0w
Coronation I., Alaska	64	55 52N	134 20w
Coronation Is., W. Australia	44	15 0 S	124 58 E
Coronel, Chile	77	37 0 S	73 10w
Coronel Oviedo, Par.	77	25 15 S	55 20w
Coronie, Surinam	79	5 55N	56 25w
Corowa, N.S.W.	43	35 58 S	146 21 E
Corozal, Br. Hond.	74	18 30N	88 30w
Corozal, Pan. Can. Zone	74	8 59N	79 34w
Corpus Christi, U.S.A.	71	27 50N	97 28w
Corpus Christie L, U.S.A.	71	28 4N	97 56w
Corque, Bolivia	78	18 10 S	67 50w
Corrib, L., Ireland	11	53 25N	9 10w
Corrientes, Argentina	27	27 30 S	58 45w
Corrientes C., Colombia	75	5 30N	77 30w
Corrientes C., Mexico	74	20 20N	105 40w
Corrientes R., Peru	78	3 30 S	75 40w
Corrigan, U.S.A.	71	30 59N	94 49w
Corrigin, W. Australia	44	32 18 S	117 45 E
Corrofin, Ireland	11	53 27N	8 50w
Corry, U.S.A.	68	41 55N	79 39w
Corse C., Corsica	20	43 0N	9 21 E
Corsica I., Medit. Sea, dept. of France	20	42 0N	9 0 E
Corsicana, U.S.A.	71	32 5N	96 30w
Corte, France	12	42 19N	9 11 E
Corte, Portugal	17	37 44N	7 29w
Cortez, U.S.A.	73	37 23N	108 32w
Cortina, Italy	20	46 33N	12 8 E
Cortland, U.S.A.	68	42 35N	76 11w
Cortona, Italy	20	43 16N	12 0 E
Coruche, Portugal	17	38 57N	8 30w
Coruh, R., Turkey	30	40 40N	40 50 E
Corum, Turkey	30	40 30N	35 5 E
Corumbá, Brazil	79	16 0 S	48 50w
Corumba, Brazil	79	19 0 S	57 30w
Corumbá R., Brazil	79	17 25 S	48 30w
Coruripe, Brazil	79	10 5 S	36 10w
Corvallis, U.S.A.	72	44 30N	123 15w
Corvette L., Canada	62	53 25N	73 55w
Corydon, U.S.A.	70	40 43N	93 24w
Cosalá, Mexico	74	24 20N	106 50w
Cosamaloapan, Mexico	74	18 23N	95 50w
Cosenza, Italy	20	39 17N	16 14 E
Coshocton, U.S.A.	68	40 17N	81 51w
Cosmeledo, Islands Seychelles	49	9 45 S	47 0 E
Cosne, France	12	47 24N	2 54 E
Cossack, W. Australia	44	20 38 S	117 12 E
Cossonay, Switzerland	15	46 36N	6 31 E
Costa Rica, rep., Cent. America	75	10 0N	84 0w
Costilla, U.S.A.	71	37 0N	105 29w
Cotabato, Philippines	35	7 8N	124 13 E
Cotagaita, Bolivia	78	20 45 S	65 30w
Coteau des Prairies, U.S.A.	67	44 30N	97 0w
Cotonou, Dahomey	52	6 20N	2 25 E
Cotopaxi, vol., Ec.	78	0 30 S	78 30w
Cotswold Hills, Eng.	10	51 42N	2 10w
Cottage Grove, U.S.A.	72	43 48N	123 4w
Cottbus, Germany	14	51 44N	14 20 E
Cottonwood, Canada	64	53 5N	121 50 E
Cottonwood, U.S.A.	73	34 57N	112 2w
Cotulla, U.S.A.	71	28 28N	99 14w
Coudersport, U.S.A.	68	41 45N	78 1w
Coulee City, U.S.A.	72	47 39N	119 15w
Coutommiers, France	12	48 50N	3 3 E
Coulonge R., Canada	62	46 50N	77 20w
Council, Alaska	59	64 55N	163 44w
Council, Idaho, U.S.A.	72	44 45N	116 29w
Council Bluffs, U.S.A.	70	41 15N	95 50w
Council Grove, U.S.A.	70	38 37N	96 30w
Courantyne R., S. Amer.	79	5 0N	57 45w
Courtelary, Switzerland	15	47 11N	7 2 E
Courtenay, Canada	64	49 45N	125 0w
Courtmacsherry, Ire.	11	51 37N	8 37w
Coushatta, U.S.A.	71	32 1 S	93 21w
Coutances, France	12	49 3N	1 28w
Coutinho, Mozam.	56	16 5 S	31 35 E

	MAP		
Coutras, France	12	45 3N	0 8W
Coutts, Canada	64	49 0N	112 0W
Covane, Mozambique	56	21 25S	33 55E
Coventry, England	10	52 25N	1 31W
Coventry L., Canada	65	61 15N	106 15W
Covilhã, Portugal	17	40 17N	7 31W
Covington, Ga., U.S.A.	69	33 36N	83 50W
Covington, Ky., U.S.A.	68	39 0N	84 35W
Covington, Okla., U.S.A.	71	36 18N	97 35W
Covington, Tenn., U.S.A.	71	35 31N	89 42W
Covodas, Sa. das, Brazil	79	8 30S	47 0W
Cowal L., N.S.W.	43	33 40S	147 25E
Cowan, Canada	65	52 5N	100 45W
Cowan L., Canada	65	54 0N	107 20W
Cowan, L., W. Austral.	44	31 45S	121 45E
Cowansville, Canada	62	45 14N	72 46W
Coward Springs, S. Australia	45	29 25S	127 1E
Cowell, S. Australia	45	33 40S	136 5E
Cowra, N.S.W.	43	33 49S	148 42E
Cox's Bazar, Bangladesh	33	21 25N	92 3E
Cox's Cove, Canada	63	49 7N	58 5W
Coyuca de Benitez, Mex.	74	17 1N	100 8W
Coyuca de Catalan, Mex.	74	18 20N	100 50W
Cozad, U.S.A.	70	40 56N	99 58W
Cozumel, I. de, Mexico	74	20 30N	86 40W
Cracow, Queensland	43	25 14S	150 24E
Cradle Mt., Tasmania	43	41 40S	146 0E
Cradock, C. Prov.	57	32 8S	25 36E
Craig, Alaska	64	55 30N	133 0W
Craig, U.S.A.	72	40 30N	107 31W
Craigmore, Rhod.	56	20 28S	32 30E
Craigs Ra., Queens.	43	26 30S	151 10E
Craiguenamanagh, Ire.	11	52 33N	6 57W
Craiova, Rumania	21	44 21N	23 48E
Cranberry Lake, Can.	64	49 48N	125 20W
Cranbery Portage, Can.	65	54 36N	101 22W
Cranbrook, Canada	64	49 30N	115 55W
Cranbrook, W. Austral.	44	34 20S	117 35E
Crandon, U.S.A.	79	45 32N	88 55W
Crane, Barbados	75	Inset	
Crane, U.S.A.	71	31 25N	102 28W
Crane, U.S.A.	72	43 28N	118 35W
Crater L., U.S.A.	72	42 57N	122 2W
Crater Pt., New Guinea	42	5 12S	152 5E
Crateus, Brazil	79	5 10S	40 50W
Crato, Brazil	79	7 10S	39 25W
Crawford, U.S.A.	70	42 40N	103 20W
Crawfordsville, U.S.A.	68	40 0N	86 55W
Crazy Mts., U.S.A.	72	46 12N	110 30W
Crean L., Canada	65	54 5N	91 15W
Cree L., Canada	65	57 30N	107 0W
Cree R., Canada	65	58 0N	106 20W
Creighton, U.S.A.	70	42 31N	97 54W
Creil, France	12	49 15N	2 34E
Crema, Italy	20	45 21N	9 40E
Cremona, Italy	20	45 8N	10 2E
Cres I., Yugoslavia	20	44 50N	14 25E
Cresbard, U.S.A.	70	45 12N	98 57W
Crescent, Okla., U.S.A.	71	35 38N	97 35W
Crescent, Oreg., U.S.A.	72	43 29N	121 40W
Crescent City, U.S.A.	72	41 47N	124 14W
Cresciuma, Brazil	77	28 50S	49 25W
Cressman, Canada	62	47 40N	72 55W
Cressy, Victoria	43	38 10S	143 38E
Crest, France	12	44 44N	5 2E
Crested Butte, U.S.A.	73	38 53N	106 58W
Creston, Canada	64	49 10N	116 40W
Creston, Iowa., U.S.A.	70	41 0N	94 30W
Creston, Wash., U.S.A.	72	47 45N	118 32W
Creston, Wyo., U.S.A.	72	41 45N	107 42W
Crestview, U.S.A.	69	30 45N	86 35W
Creswick, Victoria	43	37 19S	143 50E
Crete, U.S.A.	70	40 42N	96 58W
Crete, I., Greece	20	35 15N	25 0E
Cretin, C., New Guinea	42	6 40S	147 57E
Créus, C., Spain	17	42 20N	3 19E
Creuse R., France	12	46 25N	9 40E
Crevillente, Spain	17	38 12N	0 48W
Crewe, England	10	53 6N	2 28W
Crieff, Scotland	10	56 22N	3 50W
Crillon, Mt., Alaska	64	50 39N	137 14W
Crimea, Pen., U.S.S.R.	25	45 0N	34 0E
Crimmitschau, Ger.	14	50 49N	12 21E
Cripple Creek, U.S.A.	70	38 49N	105 14W
Cristobal, Panama	74	9 10N	80 0W
Crisul Negru, R., Rum.	21	46 40N	22 0E
Crisul Alb, R., Rum.	21	46 20N	22 0E
Crna, R., Yugoslavia	21	41 20N	22 15E
Crna Gora, Mts. Y.slav.	21	42 12N	21 30E
Crna Gora (Monte-negro), prov., Y.slav.	21	43 0N	19 30E
Croagh Patrick, mt., Ireland	11	53 46N	9 40W
Croatia, fed.unit, Y.slav.	20	45 40N	17 0E
Crockers Well, S. Australia	43	31 35S	139 40E
Crockett, U.S.A.	71	31 20N	95 30W
Crocodile Is., N. Terr.	40	12 0S	134 59E
Crocodile R., Trans.	57	24 30S	27 10E
Cromarty, Canada	65	58 5N	94 10W
Cromarty, Scotland	10	57 40N	4 2W
Cromer, England	10	52 56N	1 18E
Cromwell, N.Z.	47	45 3S	169 14E
Cronulla, N.S.W.	43	34 3S	151 8E
Crooked I., Bahamas	75	22 50N	74 10W
Crooked I. Pass., Bah.	75	23 0N	74 0W
Crooked River, Canada	64	52 50N	103 45W
Crooked, R., U.S.A.	72	44 28N	121 0W
Crookston, U.S.A.	70	47 50N	96 40W
Crookston, Neb., U.S.A.	70	42 58N	100 45W
Crooksville, U.S.A	68	39 45N	82 5W
Crookwell, N.S.W.	43	34 28S	149 24E
Crosby, U.S.A.	70	46 30N	93 56W
Crosbyton, U.S.A.	71	33 33N	101 13W
Cross C., S.W. Africa	55	21 55S	13 57E
Cross City, U.S.A.	69	29 35N	83 5W
Cross, L., Canada	65	54 20N	97 50W
Cross Plains, U.S.A.	71	32 6N	99 3W
Cross R., Nigeria	52	4 46N	8 20E
Cross Sound, Alaska	59	58 20N	136 30W
Crossett, U.S.A.	71	33 7N	91 58W
Crossfield, Canada	64	51 25N	114 0W
Crosshaven, Ireland	11	51 48N	8 19W
Crossmolina, Ireland	11	54 6N	9 21W
Crotone, Italy	20	39 5N	17 6E
Crow Agency, U.S.A	72	45 35N	107 30W
Crow Hd., Ireland	11	51 34N	10 9W
Crowell, U.S.A.	71	33 58N	99 45W
Crowes, Victoria	43	38 43S	143 24E
Crowl Cr., N.S.W.	43	32 5S	145 30E
Crowley, U.S.A.	71	30 10N	92 18W
Crown Point, U.S.A.	68	41 24N	87 23W
Crown Princess Martha Land, Antarctica	80	71 0S	10 0W
Crow's Nest, Queens.	43	27 14S	152 2E
Crowsnest Pass, Canada	64	49 40N	114 40W
Croydon, London., Eng.	10	51 22N	0 5W
Croydon, Queensland	42	18 15S	142 14E
Crozon, France	12	48 15N	4 30W
Crusheen, Ireland	11	52 57N	8 52W
Cruz, C., Cuba	75	19 50N	77 50W
Cruz Alta, Argentina	77	33 0S	61 50W
Cruz Alta, Brazil	77	28 40S	53 32W
Cruz del Eje, Arg.	77	30 45S	64 50W
Cruzeiro, Brazil	77	22 50S	45 0W
Cruzeiro do Sul, Brazil	78	7 35S	72 35W
Cry L., Canada	64	58 45N	129 0W
Crystal Brook, S. Australia	43	33 20S	138 7E
Crystal City, Mo., U.S.A.	71	38 14N	90 23W
Crystal City, Texas, U.S.A.	71	29 0N	99 50W
Crystal Falls, U.S.A.	68	46 7N	88 21W
Crystal River, U.S.A.	69	28 54N	82 35W
Crystal Springs, U.S.A.	70	46 9N	88 14W
Crystalbrook, Queens.	43	25 31S	147 59E
Csongrad, Hungary	16	46 43N	20 12E
Cua Rao, Viet Nam	34	19 15N	104 30E
Cuácua, R., Mozam.	56	18 0S	36 0E
Cuadramon Mt., Spain	17	43 27N	7 33W
Cuando, R., Angola	55	14 0S	19 30E
Cuangar, Angola	55	17 34S	18 39E
Cuarto, R.,	77	33 10S	63 50W
Cuba, U.S.A.	73	36 0N	106 59W
Cuba, rep. W. Indies	75	22 0N	79 0W
Cuballing, W. Australia	44	32 48S	117 4E
Cubango, R. (Okavango R.), Angola	55	17 0S	18 0E
Cubo, Mozambique	56	23 22S	33 40E
Cucui, Brazil	78	1 10N	66 50W
Cúcuta, Colombia	78	8 0N	72 30W
Cudahy, U.S.A.	68	42 54N	87 52W
Cuddalore, India	32	11 46N	79 45E
Cuddapah, India	32	14 30N	78 47E
Cuddapan L., Queens.	43	25 40S	141 22E
Cuddingwarra, Western Australia	44	2 18S	117 47E
Cudgegong, N.S.W.	43	32 42S	149 44E
Cudgewa, Victoria	43	36 10S	147 42E
Cue, W. Australia	44	27 20S	117 55E
Cuéllar, Spain	17	41 23N	4 21E
Cuenca, Ecuador	78	2 50S	79 9W
Cuenca, Spain	16	40 5N	2 10W
Cuernavaca, Mexico	74	18 50N	99 20W
Cuero, U.S.A.	71	29 7N	97 17W
Cuervo, U.S.A.	71	35 2N	104 27W
Cuevas de Vera, Spain	17	37 13N	1 59W
Cuevas del Amanzora, Spain	17	37 19N	1 53W
Cuevo, Bolivia	78	20 25S	63 30W
Cuhimbe, Peru	78	0 5S	75 25W
Cuiabá, Brazil	79	15 30S	56 0W
Cuiaba R., Brazil	79	16 50S	56 0W
Cuillin Sd., Scotland	10	57 4N	6 20W
Cuito R., Angola	55	17 20S	19 40E
Cuitzeo, L., Mexico	74	20 0N	101 20E
Culbertson, U.S.A.	70	48 8N	104 30W
Culebra, Pan. Can. Zone		Inset	
Culgoa R., Queensland	43	28 40S	147 45E
Culiacán, Mexico	74	24 50N	107 40W
Cullarin Ra., N.S.W.	43	34 50S	149 20E
Cullen Pt., Queensland	42	11 50S	141 57E
Cullera, Spain	17	39 9N	0 17W
Cullman, U.S.A.	69	34 13N	86 50W
Cully, Switzerland	15	46 29N	6 44E
Culoz, France	12	45 47N	5 46E
Culpeper, U.S.A.	68	38 29N	77 59W
Culver Pt., W. Austral.	45	32 51S	124 4E
Culverden, N.Z.	47	42 47S	172 49E
Cumaná, Venezuela	75	10 30N	64 5W
Cumanacoa, Venezuela	75	10 17N	63 58W
Cumberland, Canada	64	49 40N	125 0W
Cumberland, Queens.	42	18 26S	143 17E
Cumberland, U.S.A.	70	45 30N	92 2W
Cumberland I., U.S.A.	69	30 52N	81 30W
Cumberland Is., Queens.	42	20 45S	149 25E
Cumberland L., Canada	65	54 10N	102 55W
Cumberland Pen., Can.	61	67 0N	65 0W
Cumberland Plat., U.S.A.	69	36 0N	85 0W
Cumberland R., U.S.A.	69	36 20N	85 50W
Cumberland Sd., Can.	61	65 30N	66 0W
Cumbrian Mts., Eng.	10	54 30N	3 5W
Cumbum, India	32	15 40N	79 10E
Cummins, S. Australia	45	34 12S	135 50E
Cumnock, Scotland	10	55 27N	4 18W
Cumuruxatiba, Brazil	79	17 20S	39 25W
Cunani, Brazil	79	3 0N	51 5W
Cunene R., Angola	55	17 0S	15 0E
Cuneo, Italy	20	44 23N	7 31E
Cunnamulla, Queens.	43	28 2S	145 38E
Cupar, Canada	65	51 0N	104 10W
Cupar, Scotland	10	56 20N	3 0W
Cupica, Colombia	78	6 50N	77 30W
Cupica, G. de, Col.	78	6 25N	77 30W
Curaçao, I., Neth. W. Indies	75	12 10N	69 0W
Curaray R., Peru	78	1 15S	75 30W
Curicó, Chile	77	34 55S	71 20W
Curitiba, Brazil	77	25 20S	49 10W
Curracunya, Queens.	43	28 29S	144 9E
Currais Novos, Brazil	79	6 15S	36 20W
Curralinho, Brazil	79	1 35S	49 30W
Currant, U.S.A.	73	38 49N	115 30W
Current, R., U.S.A.	71	37 15N	91 15W
Currie, Tasmania	43	39 45S	143 55E
Currie, U.S.A.	72	40 15N	114 44W
Currituck Sd., U.S.A.	69	36 27N	75 55W
Curry, Ireland	11	54 0N	8 47W
Curtea-de-Arges, Rum.	21	45 12N	24 42E
Curtis, U.S.A.	70	40 40N	100 30W
Curtis I., Queensland	42	23 40S	151 15E
Curuá Panema R., Braz.	79	0 30S	55 20W
Curuca, Brazil	79	0 35S	47 50W
Curundu, Pan. Can. Zone	74	8 59N	79 38W
Cururupa, Brazil	79	1 47S	44 51W
Curuzú Cuatia, Arg.	77	29 50S	58 5W
Curvelo, Brazil	79	19 0S	44 35W
Cushendall, N. Ireland	11	55 5N	6 3W
Cushing, U.S.A.	71	35 57N	96 46W
Cusihuiriachie, Mexico	74	28 10N	106 50W
Cussabat (El Gusbat), Libya	51	32 25N	14 2E
Cusset, France	12	46 8N	3 28E
Custer, U.S.A.	70	43 47N	103 36W
Cut Bank, U.S.A.	72	48 40N	112 21W
Cuthbert, U.S.A.	69	31 47N	84 47E
Cuttack, India	33	20 25N	85 57E
Cuvette Centrale, prov. Zaire	54	1 10S	20 50E
Cuvier, C., W. Austral.	44	24 10S	113 20E
Cuxhaven, Germany	14	53 51N	8 41E
Cuyahoga Falls, U.S.A.	68	41 8N	81 30W
Cuyo Is., Philippines	35	11 0N	121 0E
Cuyuni R., Guyana	78	7 0N	59 30W
Cuzco, Peru	78	13 32S	72 0W
Cuzco Mt., Bolivia	78	20 0S	66 50W
Cyangugu, Rwanda	53	2 30S	28 57E
Cyclades (Kikladhes), Is., Greece	21	37 30N	25 25E
Cygnet, Tasmania	43	43 8S	147 1E
Cynthiana, U.S.A.	68	38 20N	84 18W
Cypress Hs., Canada	65	49 40N	109 30W
Cyprus I., E. Medit. Sea	30	35 0N	33 0E
Cyrenaica, reg., Libya	51	27 30N	22 30E
Cyrene (Shahhat), Libya	51	32 52N	21 35E
Czar, Canada	65	52 28N	110 48W
Czarnków, Poland	16	52 55N	16 38E
Czechoslovakia, rep., Europe	16	49 0N	17 0E
Czeremcha, Poland	16	52 32N	23 20E
Czersk, Poland	16	53 46N	17 58E
Czestochowa, Poland	16	50 49N	19 5E

D

Da R., Viet Nam	34	21 45N	103 45E
Da Lat, Viet Nam	34	12 3N	108 32E
Da-Nang (Tourane) Viet Nam	34	16 10N	108 7E
Dabai, Nigeria	52	11 25N	5 15E
Dabakala, Ivory Coast	50	8 15N	4 20W
Dabburiya, Israel	29	32 42N	35 22E
Dabhoi, India	32	22 10N	73 20E
Dabie, Poland	16	53 27N	14 45E
Dabnou, Niger	52	14 9N	5 21E
Dabola, Guinea	50	10 50N	11 5W
Dabou, Volta	52	11 19N	1 51W
Daboya, Ghana	52	9 30N	1 20W
Dabra Tabor, Ethiopia	54	11 50N	37 58E
Dabrowa Tarnowska, Poland	16	50 12N	20 59E
Dacca, tn. & terr., Bangladesh	33	23 43N	90 26E
Dachstein, Mt., Austria	14	47 29N	90 26E
Dadanawa, Guyana	78	2 50N	59 29W
Dade City, U.S.A.	69	28 20N	82 12W
Dadiya, Nigeria	52	9 35N	11 24E
Dadu, Pakistan	32	26 45N	67 45E
Daet, Philippines	35	14 10N	123 14E
Dafina, Saudi Arabia	30	23 11N	42 0E
Dagana, Senegal	50	16 30N	15 20W
Dagaya, Niger	52	13 51N	13 1E
Daggs Sd., N.Z.	47	45 23S	166 45E
Daghestan A.S.S.R., U.S.S.R.	26	42 30N	47 0E
Dagoreti, Kenya	53	1 18S	36 42E
Dagupan, Philippines	35	16 3N	120 33E
Dahlak Kebir, I., Ethiopia	54	15 50N	40 10E
Dahlonega, U.S.A.	69	34 35N	83 59W
Dahomey, rep., W. Afr.	52	8 0N	2 0E
Dailekh, Nepal	33	28 50N	81 42E
Daimiel, Spain	17	39 5N	3 35W
Daingean, Ireland	11	53 18N	7 15W
Daio, C., Japan	36	34 15N	136 45E
Dairen, China	38	39 0N	121 35E
Daisetsu-zan, mt., Japan	36	43 47N	142 40E
Dayrut, Egypt	51	27 34N	30 43E
Daishoji, Japan	36	36 20N	136 15E
Dajarra, Queensland	42	21 42S	139 30E
Dakala, Niger	52	14 27N	2 27E
Dakar, Senegal	50	14 34N	17 29W
Dakaraoua, Gora, Niger	52	14 2N	7 0E
Dakhlah Oasis, Egypt	51	25 30N	27 50E
Dakhovskaya, U.S.S.R.	25	44 7N	39 55E
Dakingari, Nigeria	52	11 37N	4 1E
Dakota City, U.S.A.	70	42 28N	96 26W
Dakovica, Y.slav.	21	42 22N	20 26E
Dal, R., Sweden	23	60 20N	17 0E
Dalai Nor, Inner Mongolia, China	37	49 0N	117 40E
Dalan Dzadagad, Mongolia	38	43 10N	103 30E
Dalarö, Sweden	23	59 8N	18 25E
Dalbandin, Pakistan	32	29 0N	64 23E
Dalby, Queensland	43	27 10S	151 17E
Dalfsen, Netherlands	13	52 31N	6 15E
Dalgaranger, mt., W. Australia	44	27 15S	117 2E
Dalgonally, Queensland	42	20 8S	141 20E
Dalhart, U.S.A.	71	36 0N	102 30W
Dalhousie, Canada	63	48 0N	66 26W
Daliyat el Karmil, Is.	29	32 42N	35 3E
Dalj, Yugoslavia	21	45 28N	18 58E
Dalkey, Ireland	11	53 16N	6 7W
Dall I., Alaska	64	54 59N	133 25W
Dallarnil, Queensland	43	25 19S	152 2E
Dallas, Oreg., U.S.A.	72	45 0N	123 15W
Dallas, Tex., U.S.A.	71	32 50N	96 50W
Dallol Bosso, Niger	52	14 14N	3 15E
Dallol Mauri, Niger	52	13 45N	4 0E
Dalma Al Fihahi, I., Truc. Oman	31	24 24N	52 18E
Dalmatia, Yugoslavia	20	43 20N	17 0E
Dalny, Canada	65	49 10N	101 0W
Daloa, Ivory Coast	50	7 0N	6 30W
Dalrymple, Queens.	43	19 50S	146 10E
Dalton, Ga., U.S.A.	69	34 45N	85 0W
Dalton, Neb., U.S.A.	70	41 29N	103 0W
Dalton Post, Canada	64	66 42N	137 0W
Daltonganj, India	33	24 0N	84 4E
Dalvik, Iceland	22	66 2N	18 20W
Dalwallinu, W. Austral.	44	30 12S	116 33E
Daly L., Canada	65	56 35N	105 40W
Daly, R., N. Territory	40	14 0S	131 12E
Daly Waters, N. Terr.	40	16 15S	133 25E
Dam, Surinam	79	4 45N	55 0W
Daman, India	32	20 25N	72 57E
Damana, Niger	52	13 52N	3 13E
Damanhûr, Egypt	51	31 0N	30 30E
Damar, I., Indonesia	35	7 15S	128 30E
Damaraland, dist., S.W. Africa	57	21 0S	17 0E
Damaro, Niger	52	13 1N	2 19E
Damascus, *See* Esh Sham.	30		
Damaturu, Nigeria	52	11 45N	11 55E
Damāvand, tn. & mt., Iran	31	35 47N	52 3E
Damba, Angola	54	6 44S	15 29E
Dambacha, Ethiopia	54	10 35N	37 30E
Damboa, Nigeria	52	11 9N	13 2E
Dâmbovita R., Rum.	21	44 40N	26 0E
Damchok, Kashmir	32	32 40N	79 20E
Damghan, Iran	31	36 10N	54 17E
Damietta (Dumyat), Egypt	51	31 30N	31 0E
Damiya, Jordan	29	32 6N	35 34E
Dammastock, Mt., Switzerland	15	46 38N	8 26E
Damoh, India	32	23 50N	79 28E
Dampar, Nigeria	52	7 19N	10 3E
Dampier, W. Australia	40	20 35S	117 0E
Dampier Arch., W. Australia	44	20 38S	116 32E
Dampier Str., New Guinea	42	5 50S	148 10E
Dan Chadi, Nigeria	52	12 47N	5 17E
Dan Dume, Nigeria	52	11 28N	7 8E
Dan Gora, Nigeria	52	11 30N	8 7E
Dan Gulbi, Nigeria	52	11 40N	6 15E

Place	Map	Lat.	Long.
Dan Sadau, Nigeria	52	11 25N	6 20 E
Dan Yashi, Nigeria	52	14 3N	8 22 E
Dana, Lac, Canada	62	50 50N	76 50W
Danbury, Conn., U.S.A.	68	41 23N	73 29W
Dandaragan, W.Austral.	44	30 40S	115 40 E
Dande, Ethiopia	53	4 50N	36 18 E
Dandeldhura, Nepal	32	29 20N	80 35 E
Dandeli, India	32	15 10N	74 35 E
Dandenong, Victoria	43	37 52S	145 12 E
Danger Pt., C. Prov.	57	34 21S	19 18 E
Danger Pt., N.S.W.	43	28 8S	153 36 E
Danguno, Nigeria	52	10 1N	7 0 E
Daniel, U.S.A.	72	42 50N	110 3W
Daniel's Harbour, Can.	63	50 13N	57 35W
Danielskuil, C. Prov.	57	28 11S	23 33 E
Danilov, U.S.S.R.	25	58 16N	40 13 E
Danilovgrad, Y.slav.	21	42 38N	19 9 E
Danissa, Kenya	53	3 19N	40 54 E
Danja, Nigeria	52	11 29N	7 30 E
Dankalwa, Nigeria	52	11 52N	12 12 E
Dankama, Nigeria	52	13 20N	7 44 E
Dankhar Gompa, India	32	32 8N	78 12 E
Dankov, U.S.S.R.	25	53 20N	39 5 E
Danli, Honduras	75	14 4N	86 35W
Dannemora, Sweden	23	60 11N	17 53 E
Dannemora, U.S.A.	68	44 41N	73 44W
Dannevirke, N.Z.	46	40 12S	176 8 E
Dannhauser, Natal	57	27 0S	30 3 E
Dansville, U.S.A.	68	42 32N	77 41W
Danube, R., Europe	21	45 0N	28 20 E
Danville, Ill., U.S.A.	68	40 10N	87 40W
Danville, Ky., U.S.A.	68	37 40N	84 45W
Danville, Va., U.S.A.	69	36 38N	79 21W
Dapchi, Nigeria	52	12 32N	11 31 E
Dapong, Togoland	52	10 55N	0 16W
Dar al Hamra, Saudi Arabia	30	27 22N	37 43 E
Darab, Iran	31	28 50N	54 30 E
Daraj, Libya	51	30 10N	10 22 E
Darazo, Nigeria	52	10 57N	10 26 E
Darband, Pakistan	32	34 30N	72 50 E
Darbhanga, India	33	26 15N	86 3 E
Darby, U.S.A.	72	46 2N	114 14W
D'Arcy, Canada	64	50 35N	122 30W
Dardanelle, U.S.A.	71	35 11N	93 12W
Dardanelles, str., Tur. *See* Canakkale.	30		
Dareel, Queensland	43	28 53S	148 54 E
Dar-es-Salaam, Tan.	53	6 50S	39 12 E
Darfield, New Zealand	47	43 29S	172 7 E
Darfur, prov., Sudan	51	12 35N	25 0 E
Dargai, Pakistan	32	34 25N	71 45 E
Dargan Ata, U.S.S.R.	26	40 40N	62 20 E
Dargaville, N.Z.	46	35 57S	173 52 E
Darien, Pan. Canal Zone	74	9 7N	79 46W
Darien, G. of, Col.	78	9 0N	77 0W
Darjeeling, India	33	27 3N	88 18 E
Dark Cove, Canada	63	49 54N	54 5W
Darkan, W. Australia	44	33 19S	116 37 E
Darke's Peak, S. Australia	45	33 29S	136 18 E
Darling Downs, Queensland	43	27 20S	150 30 E
Darling Ra., W. Australia	44	32 30S	116 0 E
Darling R., N.S.W.	43	31 0S	144 30 E
Darlington, England	10	54 33N	1 33W
Darlington, S.C., U.S.A.	69	34 18N	79 50W
Darlington, Wis., U.S.A.	70	42 40N	90 5W
Darlot, L., W. Austral.	44	27 45S	121 30 E
Darlowo, Poland	16	54 25N	16 25 E
Dârmănesti, Rumania	21	46 21N	26 33 E
Darmstadt, Germany	14	49 51N	8 40 E
Darnah, Libya	51	32 45N	22 39 E
Darnall, S. Africa	57	29 16S	31 23 E
Darnick, N.S.W.	43	32 48S	143 38 E
Darnley B., Canada	60	69 30N	124 0W
Darnley, C., Ant.	80	78 0S	70 0 E
Daroca, Spain	17	41 9N	1 25W
Darragueira, Arg.	77	37 40S	63 10W
Darran Mts., N.Z.	47	44 37S	167 59 E
Darrington, U.S.A.	72	48 14N	122 35W
Dart R., England	10	50 34N	3 56W
Dartmoor, England	10	50 36N	4 0W
Dartmouth, Canada	63	44 40N	63 30W
Dartmouth, England	10	50 21N	3 35W
Dartmouth L., Queens.	43	26 5S	145 15 E
Daru, Papua	42	8 53S	143 22 E
Daru, Sierra Leone	52	8 0N	10 52W
Darvel, Scotland	10	55 37N	4 20W
Darwen, England	7	53 42N	2 29W
Darwendale, Rhod.	56	17 41S	30 33 E
Datweshan, Afghan.	31	31 5N	64 7 E
Darwha, India	32	20 15N	77 45 E
Darwin, N. Territory	40	12 20S	130 50 E
Darwin Mt., Rhod.	56	16 45S	31 33 E
Daryācheh-ye Namak, Iran	31	34 45N	51 45 E
Daryacheh-i-Namakzar L., Iran	31	34 0N	60 30 E
Daryacheh-ye-Sistan (Hamun-i-Helmand), Iran	31	31 0N	61 10 E
Daryacheh-ye Tashk, Iran	31	29 30N	54 0 E
Das I., Persian Gulf	31	25 3N	52 59 E
Dasht R., Pakistan	32	25 40N	62 20 E
Dasht-e-Kavir, des., Iran	31	34 30N	55 0 E
Dasht-e-Lut., des., Iran	30	31 30N	58 0 E
Dasht-i-Margo, des., Afghanistan	31	30 40N	62 30 E
Dasht-i-Nawar, des., Afghanistan	31	33 45N	67 45 E
Dasht-i-Tahlab, Reg., W. Pakistan	31	28 37N	62 45 E
Dassa Zume, Dahomey	52	7 46N	2 14 E
Dassari, Chad	52	11 0N	16 7 E
Dassen I., C. Prov.	57	33 27S	18 3 E
Datia, India	32	25 41N	78 28 E
Datu C., Sarawak	34	2 7N	109 45 E
Daugavpils, U.S.S.R.	23	55 53N	26 32 E
Daukara, U.S.S.R.	26	45 55S	59 30 E
Daulalbeg Oldi, Kashmir	32	35 22N	77 45 E
Daulat Yar, Afghan.	31	34 30N	65 45 E
Daulatabad, Iran	31	28 22N	56 38 E
Dauphin, Canada	65	51 15N	100 5W
Dauphin I., U.S.A.	69	30 16N	88 10W
Dauphiné, prov., Fr.	12	45 15N	5 25 E
Daura, Iraq	31	33 15N	44 30 E
Daura, N. Reg., Nig.	52	11 31N	11 24 E
Daura, N. Reg., Nig.	52	13 2N	8 21 E
Davangere, India	32	14 25N	75 50 E
Davao, Philippines	35	7 0N	125 40 E
Davao, G. of, Philip.	35	6 30N	125 48 E
Dāvar Panah, Iran	31	27 22N	62 14 E
Davenport, Iowa, U.S.A.	70	41 30N	90 34W
Davenport, Wash., U.S.A.	72	47 39N	118 9W
David, Panama	75	8 30N	82 30W
David, Panama	78	8 26N	82 26W
David City, U.S.A.	70	41 18N	97 12W
Davidson, Sask., Can.	65	51 20N	106 0W
Davis, Antarctica	80	69 50S	95 0 E
Davis, U.S.A.	73	38 32N	121 46W
Davis Inlet, Canada	63	55 50N	60 45W
Davis Mts., U.S.A.	71	30 40N	104 15W
Davis Str., Canada	61	67 0N	58 0W
Davos, Switzerland	15	46 48N	9 49 E
Dawaki, Nigeria	52	9 25N	9 33 E
Dawna Range, Burma	33	16 30N	98 30 E
Dawson, Canada	60	64 10N	139 30W
Dawson Inlet, Canada	65	61 40N	93 30W
Dawson I., Chile	77	53 50S	70 50W
Dawson R., Queens.	43	25 35S	149 10 E
Dawson Creek, Canada	64	55 45N	120 15W
Dawson's, Rhodesia	56	17 0S	30 57 E
Day Dawn, W. Australia	44	27 29S	117 50 E
Daylesfield, Victoria	43	37 15S	144 5 E
Dayr az Zawr, Syria	30	35 22N	40 6 E
Dayrut, Egypt	51	27 34N	30 43 E
Dayshan I., China	39	30 20N	122 10 E
Daysland, Canada	64	52 50N	112 20W
Dayton, Ohio, U.S.A.	68	39 45N	84 10W
Dayton, Wash., U.S.A.	72	46 20N	118 0W
Dayul-gompa, China	37	29 10N	98 0 E
Dayville, U.S.A.	72	44 30N	119 32W
De Aar, Cape Province	57	30 39S	24 0 E
De Behagle, Chad	54	9 25N	16 30 E
De Funiak Springs, U.S.A.	69	30 42N	86 10W
de Gras, L., Canada	60	65 0N	110 30W
De Grey, R., W. Austral.	44	20 30S	120 0 E
Déhane, Cameroon	52	3 30N	10 8 E
De Kalb, U.S.A.	68	41 55N	88 45W
De Land, U.S.A.	69	29 1N	81 19W
De Leon, U.S.A.	71	32 7N	98 34W
De Long Is., U.S.S.R.	27	77 0N	159 0 E
de Peel, Netherlands	13	51 25N	5 45 E
De Pere, U.S.A.	68	44 28N	88 1W
De Queen, U.S.A.	71	34 1N	94 24W
De Quincy, U.S.A.	71	30 30N	93 28W
De Ridder, U.S.A.	71	30 48N	93 15W
De Soto, U.S.A.	71	38 5N	90 30W
De Witt, U.S.A.	71	34 17N	91 17W
Dead Sea, Jordan—Israel	29	31 30N	35 30 E
Deadwood, U.S.A.	70	44 26N	103 44W
Dealesville, O.F.S.	57	28 41S	25 44 E
Dean R., Canada	64	52 50N	126 0W
Deán Funes, Argentina	77	30 20S	64 20W
Dease Arm, Canada	60	66 45N	120 6W
Dease L., Canada	64	58 40N	130 5W
Dease R., Canada	64	59 10N	129 50W
Death R., Canada	63	55 40N	69 20W
Death Valley, U.S.A.	73	36 0N	116 40W
Death Valley Junction, U.S.A.	73	36 18N	116 29W
Death Valley National Monument, U.S.A.	73	36 30N	116 35W
Deauville, France	12	49 23N	0 2 E
Deba Habe, Nigeria	52	10 14N	11 20 E
Debar, Yugoslavia	21	41 21N	20 37 E
Debden, Canada	65	53 30N	106 50W
Debeeti, Botswana	57	23 45S	26 29 E
Debica, Poland	16	50 2N	21 25 E
Debolt, Canada	64	55 12N	118 25W
Debre Markos, Ethiopia	54	10 20N	37 40 E
Debrecen, Hungary	16	47 33N	21 42 E
Decatur, Ga., U.S.A.	69	33 47N	84 17W
Decatur, Ill., U.S.A.	68	39 50N	89 0W
Decatur, Ind., U.S.A.	68	40 52N	85 28W
Decatur, Tex., U.S.A.	71	33 14N	97 35W
Decazeville, France	12	44 34N	2 15 E
Deccan, plat., India	32	14 0N	77 0 E
Deception Bay, Papua	42	7 50S	144 35 E
Decorah, U.S.A.	70	43 16N	91 47W
Dedougou, Volta	50	12 30N	3 35W
Dedza, Malawi	56	14 20S	34 20 E
Dee, R., Scotland	10	57 4N	3 7W
Dee, R., Wales	10	53 15N	3 7W
Deeford, Queensland	42	23 55S	150 12 E
Deep B., Canada	65	56 25N	103 10W
Deep B., China	39	21 45N	112 0 E
Deep Bay, Malawi	56	10 28S	34 12 E
Deep Well, N. Terr.	45	24 22S	134 0 E
Deepwater, N.S.W.	43	29 8S	152 2 E
Deer, I., Alaska	59	54 55N	162 20W
Deer L., Canada	65	52 40N	94 0W
Deer R., Canada	65	57 40N	94 30W
Deer Lodge, U.S.A.	72	46 25N	112 40W
Deer Park, U.S.A.	72	47 59N	117 29W
Deer River, U.S.A.	70	47 20N	93 46W
Deering, Alaska	59	66 4N	162 50W
Deesa, India	32	24 18N	72 10 E
Defferrari, Argentina	77	38 15S	59 30W
Defiance, U.S.A.	68	41 20N	84 20W
Deganya, Israel	29	32 43N	35 34 E
Degema, Nigeria	52	4 50N	6 48 E
Degerfors, Sweden	23	64 16N	19 6 E
Degerhamn, Sweden	23	56 21N	16 28 E
Deggendorf, Germany	14	48 50N	12 58 E
Deh Bid, Iran	31	30 39N	53 11 E
Deh Kheyr, Iran	31	28 44N	54 41 E
Dehane, Cameroon	52	3 31N	10 3 E
Dehkhvāreqan, I., Iran	30	37 50N	45 52 E
Dehibat, Tunisia	51	32 6N	10 37 E
Dehiwala, Sri Lanka	32	6 52N	79 52 E
Dehra Dun, India	32	30 20N	78 4 E
Dehri, India	33	24 50N	84 15 E
Deim Zubeir, Sudan	51	7 43N	26 16 E
Deinze, Belgium	13	50 59N	3 33 E
Deir Dibwan, Jordan	29	31 55N	35 15 E
Deir el Balah, Israel	29	31 26N	34 21 E
Deir el Ghusun, Jordan	29	32 21N	35 4 E
Dej, Rumania	21	47 10N	23 52 E
Deka R., Rhodesia	56	18 0S	26 30 E
Dekar, Botswana	56	21 30S	23 10 E
Dekese, Zaire	54	3 24S	21 24 E
Del Norte, U.S.A.	73	37 44N	106 24W
Del Rio, U.S.A.	71	29 15N	100 50W
Delagoa B., Mozam.	57	25 58S	32 35 E
Delano, U.S.A.	73	35 49N	119 15W
Delagua, U.S.A.	71	37 26N	104 36W
Delareyville, Transvaal	57	26 41S	25 26 E
Delavan, Ill., U.S.A.	68	40 20N	89 35W
Delavan, Wis., U.S.A.	70	42 35N	88 36W
Delaware, U.S.A.	68	40 20N	83 0W
Delaware, st., U.S.A.	69	39 0N	75 40W
Delaware R., U.S.A.	69	41 50N	75 15W
Delaware City, U.S.A.	69	39 34N	75 37W
Delegate, N.S.W.	43	37 4S	149 0 E
Delémont, Switzerland	15	47 22N	7 20 E
Delena, Terr. of Papua	42	9 0S	146 35 E
Delft, Netherlands	13	52 1N	4 22 E
Delfzijl, Netherlands	13	53 20N	6 55 E
Delgado C., Mozam.	53	10 45S	40 40 E
Delger Het, Mongolia	38	45 43N	110 29 E
Delgir-Khangai, Mon.	37	45 40N	104 50 E
Delgo, Sudan	51	20 6N	30 40 E
Delhi, India	32	28 38N	77 17 E
Delia, Canada	64	51 25N	112 30W
Delice R., Turkey	30	39 45N	34 15 E
Delicias, Mexico	74	28 10N	105 30W
Dell City, U.S.A.	73	31 57N	105 15W
Dell Rapids, U.S.A.	70	43 54N	96 44W
Delmiro, Brazil	79	9 30S	38 8W
Deloraine, Canada	65	49 15N	101 0W
Deloraine, Tasmania	43	41 30S	146 40 E
Delphi, U.S.A.	68	40 37N	86 40W
Delphos, U.S.A.	68	40 51N	84 17W
Delportshoop, C. Prov.	57	28 22S	24 20 E
Delray Beach, U.S.A.	69	26 27N	80 4W
Delta, U.S.A.	73	39 25N	112 32W
Delvada, India	32	20 45N	71 0 E
Delvinakion, Greece	21	39 57N	20 32 E
Demba, Zaire	54	5 28S	22 15 E
Demer R., Belgium	13	51 0N	5 0 E
Demerara R., Br. Gui.	78	7 0N	58 0W
Demibidolo, Ethiopia	54	8 56N	34 53 E
Demidov, U.S.S.R.	25	55 10N	31 30 E
Deming, U.S.A.	73	32 10N	107 50W
Demini R., Brazil	78	1 0N	62 55W
Demmin, Germany	14	53 54N	13 2 E
Demmit, Canada	64	55 20N	119 50W
Demopolis, U.S.A.	69	32 30N	87 48W
Demyansk, U.S.S.R.	25	57 30N	32 27 E
Den Helder, Neth.	13	52 57N	44 5 E
Den Oever, Netherlands	13	52 56N	5 2 E
Denain, France	12	50 20N	3 22 E
Dengdeng, Cameroon	52	5 16N	13 31 E
Denge, Zaire	53	3 40N	28 0 E
Denge, Nigeria	52	12 52N	5 21 E
Dengi, Nigeria	52	9 25N	9 55 E
Denham, W. Australia	44	25 56S	113 31 E
Denham Ra., Queens.	42	26 0S	148 45 E
Denham Ra., Queens.	43	22 0S	148 0 E
Denham Sd., W. Austral.	44	25 45S	113 15 E
Denholm, Canada	65	52 40N	108 0W
Denia, Spain	17	38 49N	0 8 E
Denial B., S. Australia	45	32 7S	133 40 E
Deniliquin, N.S.W.	43	35 30S	144 58 E
Denison, Iowa, U.S.A.	70	42 1N	95 18W
Denison, Texas, U.S.A.	71	33 50N	96 40W
Denison, W. Australia	44	29 15S	114 58 E
Denison Ra., S. Austral.	45	28 30S	136 0 E
Denizli, Turkey	30	37 42N	29 2 E
Denmark, king., Eur.	23	55 30N	9 0 E
Denmark Str.	55	65 0N	30 0W
Denniston, N.Z.	47	41 45S	171 49 E
Denny, Scotland	10	56 1N	3 55W
Denpasar, Indonesia	35	8 45S	115 5 E
Denton, Mont., U.S.A.	72	47 19N	109 50W
Denton, Texas, U.S.A.	71	33 10N	97 8W
D'Entrecasteaux Is., Papua	42	9 0S	151 0 E
Denu, Ghana	52	6 4N	1 8 E
Denver, U.S.A.	70	39 48N	105 0W
Denver City, U.S.A.	71	32 58N	102 46W
Deo R., Cameroon	52	8 20N	12 20 E
Deoghar, India	33	24 30N	86 59 E
Deolali, India	32	19 50N	73 50 E
Deoli, India	32	25 50N	75 50 E
Deoria, India	33	28 31N	83 48 E
Deosai Mts., Kashmir	32	36 30N	74 30 E
Dera Ghazi Khan, Pak.	32	30 5N	70 43 E
Dera Ismail Khan, W. Pakistan	32	31 51N	70 53 E
Dera Ismail Khan, Terr., W. Pakistan	32	32 30N	70 0 E
Deraa, Syria	31	32 38N	36 10 E
Derati Wells, Kenya	53	3 52N	36 33 E
Derbent, U.S.S.R.	24	42 5N	48 15 E
Derby, England	10	52 55N	1 28W
Derby, Tasmania	43	41 9S	147 48 E
Derby, W. Australia	44	17 18S	123 40 E
Derdepoort, Transvaal	57	24 39S	26 25 E
Derg, Lough, Ireland	11	53 0N	8 20W
Derg, L., Ireland	11	54 37N	7 53W
Dergaon, India	33	26 45N	94 0 E
Derkali, Kenya	53	3 55N	40 18 E
Derre, Mozambique	56	17 0S	36 10 E
Derrygonnelly, N. Ire.	11	54 25N	7 50W
Derudub, Sudan	51	17 31N	36 7 E
Derwent, Canada	65	53 41N	111 0W
Derwent, R., Yorks., England	10	54 10N	0 45W
Derwent R., Tasmania	42	42 20S	146 30 E
Des Milles Lacs, Ls., Canada	62	48 45N	90 35W
Des Moines, Iowa, U.S.A.	68	41 35N	93 37W
Des Moines, New Mexico, U.S.A.	71	36 47N	103 50W
Des Moines, R., U.S.A.	68	41 15N	93 0W
Desaguadero R., Bol.	78	17 30S	68 0W
Deschaillons, Canada	63	46 34N	72 7W
Deschutes, R., U.S.A.	72	45 15N	121 10W
Deseado, Argentina	77	47 45S	66 0W
Deseado R., Argentina	77	40 0S	69 0W
Desert Basin, W. Australia	45	19 50S	125 0 E
Desert Center, U.S.A.	73	33 46N	115 29W
Deshnef C., U.S.S.R.	29	66 0N	170 0W
Désirade, I., Leeward Islands Inset	75	16 17N	61 5W
Desna R., U.S.S.R.	25	51 0N	30 50 E
Desolación I., Chile	77	53 0S	74 0W
Desordem, Sa. da, Brazil	77	5 0S	47 0W
Despeñaperros, Puerto de, Spain	17	38 27N	3 30W
Dessa, Niger	50	14 34N	1 3 E
Dessau, Germany	14	51 49N	12 15 E
D'Estrees B., S. Australia	43	35 48S	137 45 E
Detached Ra., W. Australia	45	20 0S	128 40 E
Detmold, Germany	14	51 55N	8 50 E
Detour, U.S.A.	68	45 49N	83 56W
Detour Pt., U.S.A.	68	45 37N	86 35W
Detroit, Mich., U.S.A.	68	42 20N	83 10W
Detroit, Texas U.S.A.	71	33 38N	95 14W
Detroit Lakes, U.S.A.	70	46 48N	95 49W
Dett, Rhodesia	56	18 32S	26 57 E
Deurne, Belgium	13	51 12N	4 24 E
Deurne, Netherlands	13	51 27N	5 49 E
Deva, Rumania	21	45 53N	22 55 E
Deva, Spain	17	43 17N	2 21W
Devakottai, India	32	9 55N	78 45 E
Deventer, Netherlands	13	52 15N	6 10 E
Deveron R., Scotland	10	57 22N	3 0W
Devils Lake, U.S.A.	70	48 5N	98 50W
Devil's I. (I. du Diable), Fr. Guiana	79	5 16N	52 34W
Devils Paw, mt., N. Amer.	64	58 45N	133 59W
Devin, Bulgaria	21	41 44N	24 24 E
Devon, Canada	64	53 24N	113 26W
Devon I., Canada	58	75 0N	86 0W
Devoncourt, Queens.	42	21 8S	140 12 E
Devonport, England	10	50 23N	4 11W
Devonport, N.Z.	46	36 49S	174 49 E
Devonport, Tasmania	43	41 12S	146 28 E
Dewas, India	32	22 59N	76 3 E
Dewetsdorp, O.F.S.	57	29 33S	26 39 E

	MAP		
Drakensberg, Mts., South Africa	57	31 0s	25 0 E
Drama, Greece	21	41 9N	24 10 E
Drammen, Norway	23	59 42N	10 12 E
Dranga Jökull, Mt., Iceland	22	66 12N	22 15w
Draperstown, N. Ire.	11	54 48N	6 47 E
Drava R., Yugoslavia	21	45 50N	18 0w
Drawsko, Poland	16	53 35N	15 50 E
Drayacheh-i-Namakzar, L., Iran-Afghan.	31	34 0N	60 30w
Drayton Valley, Can.	64	53 25N	114 58w
Drenthe, prov., Neth.	13	52 52N	6 40 E
Dresden, Germany	14	51 2N	13 45 E
Dreux, France	12	48 44N	1 23 E
Driftwood, Canada	62	49 8N	81 23w
Driggs, U.S.A.	72	43 45N	111 40w
Drimmond, U.S.A.	72	46 41N	113 9w
Drin R., Albania	21	42 20N	20 0 E
Drina R., Yugoslavia	21	44 30N	19 10 E
Drissa, U.S.S.R.	23	55 55N	27 50 E
Dröbak, Norway	23	59 39N	10 48 E
Drogheda, Ireland	11	53 45N	6 20w
Drogobych, U.S.S.R.	24	49 20N	23 30 E
Droichead Nua, Ireland	11	53 11N	6 50w
Dromahair, Ireland	11	54 13N	8 18w
Dromocto, Canada	63	45 51N	66 32w
Dromore, Ireland	11	51 51N	9 42w
Dromore, N. Ireland	11	54 31N	7 28w
Drouplé, Mt., Ivory Coast	50	2 30N	7 30w
Drug, India	33	21 15N	81 22 E
Drumcliff, Ireland	11	54 20N	8 30w
Drumheller, Canada	64	51 25N	112 40w
Drumlish, Ireland	11	53 50N	7 47w
Drummond, Queens.	42	22 51 s	147 31 E
Drummond I., U.S.A.	68	46 0N	83 40w
Drummond Ra., Queens.	42	23 45 s	147 10 E
Drummondville, Can.	63	45 55N	72 25w
Drumright, U.S.A.	71	35 59N	96 37w
Drumshambo, Ireland	11	54 2N	8 4w
Druya, U.S.S.R.	25	55 45N	27 15 E
Dry Tortugas Is., U.S.A.	75	24 35N	83 0w
Dryden, Canada	65	49 50N	92 50w
Dryden, U.S.A.	71	30 1N	102 2w
Drygalski I., Ant.	80	66 0s	92 0 E
Du, Ghana	52	10 26N	1 34w
Du Bois, U.S.A.	68	41 8N	78 45w
Du Quoin, U.S.A.	68	38 0N	89 10w
Duaringa, Queensland	42	23 42 s	149 42 E
Dubai, Trucial 'Oman	31	25 15N	55 17 E
Dubawnt, L., Canada	65	63 0N	102 0w
Dubawnt, R., Canada	65	61 10N	103 40w
Dubbo, N.S.W.	43	32 11 s	148 35 E
Dübendorf, Switz.	15	47 28N	8 37 E
Dubica, Yugoslavia	20	45 17N	16 48 E
Dublin (Baile Atha Cliath), Ireland	11	53 20N	6 18w
Dublin, co., Ireland	11	53 25N	6 20w
Dublin, Ga., U.S.A.	69	32 30N	83 0w
Dublin, Tex., U.S.A.	71	32 0N	98 20w
Dublin B., Ireland	11	53 20N	6 0w
Dubois, U.S.A.	72	44 10N	112 14w
Dubovka, U.S.S.R.	25	49 5N	44 50 E
Dubréka, Guinea	52	9 46N	13 31w
Dubrovnik, Y.slav.	21	42 39N	18 6 E
Dubrovskoye, U.S.S.R.	27	58 55N	111 0 E
Dubuque, U.S.A.	70	42 30N	90 41w
Duchess, Queensland	42	21 20 s	139 50 E
Duchess Hill, Rhod.	56	18 18 s	30 13 E
Ducie I., Pacific Ocean	5	24 47 s	124 50w
Duck Cr., W. Australia	44	22 30 s	116 30 E
Duck I., Canada	62	55 50N	77 15w
Duck L., Canada	65	52 50N	106 0w
Dudhi, India	33	24 15N	83 15 E
Dudinka, U.S.S.R.	26	69 30N	86 0 E
Dudley, England	10	52 30N	2 5w
Dugi Otok, I. Yugoslavia	20	44 0N	15 5 E
Dugonti, Mongolia	38	45 58N	105 30 E
Duifken Pt., Queens.	42	12 31 s	141 30 E
Duisburg, Germany	14	51 27N	6 42 E
Duiwelskloof, Trans.	56	23 42 s	30 10 E
Duk Fadiat, Sudan	54	7 49N	31 31 E
Dukana, Kenya	53	4 0N	37 0 E
Duke I., Alaska	64	54 50N	131 20w
Duke Is., Queensland	42	21 55 s	150 15 E
Dukhan, Qatar	31	25 25N	50 50 E
Duki, Pakistan	32	30 15N	68 30 E
Dukkum, Neth.	13	53 20N	6 1 E
Dukla, P., Pol.-C.Slov.	16	49 25N	21 40 E
Duku, Nigeria	52	10 43N	10 43 E
Duku, Nigeria	52	11 11N	4 55 E
Dulawan, Philippines	35	7 5N	124 20 E
Dulce, G. of, Costa Rica	75	8 40N	83 20w
Dulce R., Argentina	77	29 30 s	63 0w
Duleek, Ireland	11	53 40N	6 24w
Dullstroom, Transvaal	57	25 24 s	30 7 E
Duluth, Minn., U.S.A.	70	46 48N	92 10w
Dum Duma, India	33	27 40N	95 40 E
Dumaguete, Phil.	35	9 17N	123 15 E
Dumaran I., Phil.	35	10 40N	119 55 E
Dumaresq R., N.S.W.	43	28 45 s	151 12 E
Dumas, U.S.A.	71	35 45N	101 58w
Dumas, U.S.A.	71	33 52N	91 30w
Dumbarton, Scotland	10	55 58N	4 35w
Dumbleyung, W. Australia	44	33 17 s	117 42 E

	MAP		
Dumbulah, Queens.	42	17 11 s	145 7 E
Dumfries, Scotland	10	55 4N	3 37w
Dumka, India	33	24 0N	87 22 E
Dumoine, Lac, Canada	62	46 55N	77 55w
Dumoine R., Canada	62	46 40N	77 50w
Dumont d'Urville, Ant.	80	67 10 s	141 0 E
Dumyat. *See* Damietta	51		
Dun Laoghaire, Ire.	11	53 17N	6 9w
Dunafoldvár, Hungary	16	46 50N	18 57 E
Dunback, N.Z.	47	45 23 s	170 36 E
Dunbar, Queensland	42	16 0s	142 22 E
Dunblane, Canada	65	51 20N	106 55w
Dunboyne, Ireland	11	53 25N	6 30w
Duncan, Canada	64	48 45N	123 40w
Duncan, U.S.A.	71	34 25N	98 0w
Duncan, U.S.A.	73	32 43N	109 9w
Duncan L., Quebec, Canada	64	53 35N	77 55w
Duncan L., N.W. Terr., Canada	64	62 54N	113 59w
Duncansby Hd., Scot.	10	58 39N	3 0w
Dundalk & B., Ireland	11	53 55N	6 45w
Dundas, Canada	62	43 17N	79 59w
Dundas, W. Australia	44	32 28 s	121 42 E
Dundas I., Canada	64	54 30N	130 50w
Dundas L., W. Australia	43	32 28 s	121 45 E
Dundee, Natal	57	28 11N	30 15 E
Dundee, Scotland	10	56 29N	3 0w
Dundrum, Ireland	11	53 17N	6 15w
Dundrum B., N. Ire.	11	54 12N	5 40w
Dunedin, New Zealand	47	45 50 s	170 33 E
Dunedin, U.S.A.	69	28 1N	82 45w
Dunedoo, N.S.W.	43	32 0s	149 22 E
Dunfermline, Scotland	10	56 5N	3 28w
Dungannon, N. Ireland	11	54 30N	6 47w
Dungarpur, India	32	23 52N	73 45 E
Dungarvan, Ireland	11	52 6N	7 40w
Dungarvan B., Ireland	11	52 5N	7 35w
Dungbure Range, China	37	35 0N	90 0 E
Dungeness, England	10	50 54N	0 59 E
Dungiven, N. Ireland	11	54 55N	6 56w
Dunglow, Ireland	11	54 57N	8 20w
Dungog, N.S.W.	43	32 22 s	151 40 E
Dungu, Zaire	53	3 48N	28 37 E
Dungu, Zaire	54	3 40N	28 32 E
Dunkassa, Dahomey	52	10 22N	3 14 E
Dunkeld, Queensland	43	26 58 s	148 2 E
Dunkeld, Victoria	43	37 40 s	142 22 E
Dunkerque, France	12	51 2N	2 20 E
Dunkirk, U.S.A.	68	42 30N	79 18w
Dunkwa, Ghana	52	6 0N	1 47w
Dunkwa, Ghana	52	5 23N	1 1w
Dunlop, U.S.A.	70	41 50N	95 31w
Dunleer, Ireland	11	53 50N	6 23w
Dunmanus B., Ireland	11	51 31N	9 50w
Dunmanway, Ireland	11	51 43N	9 8w
Dunmore, Ireland	11	53 37N	8 44w
Dunmore, U.S.A.	68	41 27N	75 38w
Dunmore East, Ireland	11	52 9N	7 0w
Dunmore Hd., Ireland	11	52 34N	9 52w
Dunn, U.S.A.	69	35 18N	78 36w
Dunnellon, U.S.A.	69	29 4N	82 28w
Dunnet Hd., Scotland	10	58 38N	3 22w
Dunning, U.S.A.	70	41 53N	100 4w
Dunolly, Victoria	43	36 46 s	143 44 E
Dunqul, Oasis, Egypt	51	23 40N	31 10 E
Dunseith, U.S.A.	70	48 47N	100 1w
Dunshaughlin, Ireland	11	53 31N	6 32w
Dunsmuir, U.S.A.	72	41 0N	122 10w
Dunstan Mts., N.Z.	47	44 53 s	169 35 E
Dunster, Canada	64	53 8N	119 50w
Duntroon, New Zealand	47	44 51 s	170 40 E
Dunvegan L., Canada	65	60 12N	105 58w
Dunwich, Queensland	43	27 30 s	153 26 E
Dupree, U.S.A.	70	45 3N	101 36w
Dupuyer, U.S.A.	72	48 13N	112 30w
Durack Ra., W. Austral.	44	16 40 s	127 40 E
Durán, Ecuador	78	2 0s	79 50w
Durance, R., France	12	44 0N	6 0 E
Durand, U.S.A.	68	42 54N	83 58w
Durango, Mexico	74	24 3N	104 39w
Durango, st., Mexico	74	25 0N	105 0w
Durango, Spain	17	43 13N	2 40w
Durant, U.S.A.	71	34 0N	96 25w
Durazno, Uruguay	77	33 25 s	56 38w
Durban, Natal	57	29 49 s	31 1 E
Durge Nur, Mongolia	37	47 45N	93 30 E
Durham, Canada	62	44 16N	80 48w
Durham, England	10	54 47N	1 34w
Durham, Queensland	42	18 15 s	143 28 E
Durham, U.S.A.	69	36 0N	78 52w
Durham Downs, Queens.	43	27 0s	141 49 E
Durian Tipus, Malaya	34	3 6N	102 16 E
Durmitor Mt., Y.slav.	21	43 18N	19 0 E
Durnford Pta., Spanish Sahara	50	23 51N	15 58w
Durrës, Albania	21	41 19N	19 28 E
Durrow, Ireland	11	52 51N	7 23w
Duru, Zaire	53	4 10N	29 59 E
D'Urville Island, N.Z.	47	40 50 s	173 55 E
Dushak, U.S.S.R.	26	37 20N	60 10 E
Dushanbe (Stalinabad), U.S.S.R.	26	38 50N	68 50 E
Dusky Sd., N.Z.	47	45 47 s	166 29 E
Düsseldorf, Germany	14	51 15N	6 46 E
Dutch Harb., Aleu. Is.	59	53 40N	166 30w
Dutsan Wai, Nigeria	52	10 50N	8 10 E

	MAP		
Dutulun Mts., Mongolia	37	48 30N	111 30 E
Duwadami, S. Arabia	30	24 35N	44 15 E
Duye, Zaire	53	1 50N	28 57 E
Düzce, Turkey	30	40 48N	31 12 E
Duzdab. *See* Zāhedān, Persia	31		
Dvina R. (N.), U.S.S.R.	24	61 40N	45 30 E
Dwarka, India	32	22 18N	69 8 E
Dweka, R., C. Prov.	57	32 30 s	19 20 E
Dwellingup, Australia	44	32 38 s	115 58 E
Dwight, U.S.A.	68	41 5N	88 25w
Dwyka, Cape Province	57	33 4 s	12 33 E
Dyaul, I., N. Guinea	42	3 0s	150 57 E
Dyer, C., Canada	61	67 0N	61 0w
Dyersburg, U.S.A.	71	36 3N	89 27w
Dyke Acland B., Papua	42	9 0s	148 40 E
Dyle R., Belgium	13	51 0N	4 35 E
Dyrafjördur, Iceland	22	65 50N	23 30w
Dysart, Canada	65	50 57N	104 1w
Dzamyn Ude, Mongolia	38	44 30N	110 58 E
Dzerzhinsk, U.S.S.R.	25	56 15N	43 15 E
Dzhailma, U.S.S.R.	26	51 30N	61 50 E
Dzhalal Abad, U.S.S.R.	26	41 0N	73 0 E
Dzhalinda, U.S.S.R.	27	53 40N	124 0 E
Dzhambul, U.S.S.R.	26	43 10N	71 0 E
Dzhankoi, U.S.S.R.	25	45 40N	34 30 E
Dzhargalantu, Mongolia	37	48 0N	91 20 E
Dzhelinda, U.S.S.R.	27	70 0N	114 10 E
Dzhetygara, U.S.S.R.	26	52 10N	61 0 E
Dzhezkazgan, U.S.S.R.	26	47 10N	67 40 E
Dzhikimde, U.S.S.R.	27	59 5N	121 55 E
Dzhizak, U.S.S.R.	26	40 20N	68 0 E
Dzhugdzhur Ra., U.S.S.R.	27	57 30N	138 0 E
Dzialdowo, Poland	16	53 15N	20 15 E
Dzigbe, Ghana	52	1 54N	0 20 E
Dzun Bulak, Mongolia	37	47 30N	113 30 E
Dzun Mod, China	37	36 18N	97 20 E
Dzungaria, dist., China	37	44 0N	89 0 E
Dzungarian Gates, China	37	45 0N	82 20 E

E

	MAP		
Eabamet L., Canada	62	51 30N	88 0w
Eads, U.S.A.	70	38 33N	102 49w
Eagle, Alaska	59	64 44N	141 29w
Eagle, U.S.A.	70	39 40N	106 47w
Eagle L., Canada	65	49 54N	93 20w
Eagle L., Calif., U.S.A.	72	40 35N	120 50w
Eagle L., Me., U.S.A.	69	46 23N	69 22w
Eagle Butte, U.S.A.	70	45 2N	101 15w
Eagle Grove, U.S.A.	70	42 37N	93 53w
Eagle Lake, U.S.A.	71	29 36N	96 24w
Eagle Pass, U.S.A.	71	28 45N	100 35w
Eagle River, Mich., U.S.A.	63	47 26N	88 20w
Eagle River, Wis., U.S.A.	68	45 55N	89 17w
Earl Grey, Canada	65	50 57N	104 43w
Earle, U.S.A.	71	35 15N	90 30w
Earlimart, U.S.A.	73	35 57N	119 17w
Earlton Junc., Canada	62	47 45N	79 55w
Earnslaw Mt., N.Z.	47	44 39 s	168 31 E
Earth, U.S.A.	71	34 15N	102 29w
Easley, U.S.A.	69	34 52N	82 35w
East B., U.S.A.	71	29 0N	89 30w
East C., N.Z.	46	37 42 s	178 35 E
East C. (C. Dezhneva), U.S.S.R.	59	66 0N	170 0w
East Angus, Canada	63	45 30N	71 40w
East Bathurst, Canada	63	47 35N	65 40w
East Beskids Mts., C.Slov.	16	49 10N	22 0 E
East Cameroon, Cameroon	54	5 0N	12 0 E
East Chicago, U.S.A.	68	41 40N	87 30w
East China Sea, Asia	37	27 0N	125 0 E
East Cleveland, U.S.A.	68	41 32N	81 33w
East Coulee, Canada	64	51 23N	112 27w
East Florenceville, Can.	63	46 26N	67 36w
East Germany, Europe	14	50 0N to 55 0N	
East Grand Forks, U.S.A.	70	48 0N	97 0w
East Indies, Asia	34–35	0 0	120 0 E
East Java, Prov., Indon.	34	7 40 s	112 36 E
East Jordan, U.S.A.	68	45 10N	85 7w
East London, C. Prov.	57	33 0 s	27 55 E
East Orange, U.S.A.	68	40 45N	74 15w
East Pakistan, Asia	33	24 0N	90 0 E
East Pine, Canada	64	55 48N	120 5w
East Point, Ga., U.S.A.	63	33 40N	84 28w
East St. Louis, Ill., U.S.A.	70	38 36N	90 10w
East Schelde R., Neth.	13	51 38N	3 40 E
East Siberian Sea, U.S.S.R.	27	73 0N	160 0 E
East Tawas, U.S.A.	68	44 17N	83 31w
Eastbourne, England	10	50 46N	0 18 E
Eastbourne, N.Z.	46	41 19 s	174 55 E
Eastend, Canada	65	49 32N	108 50w
Easter I. *See* Rapa Nui.	5		
Eastern Ghats Mts., India	32	15 0N	80 0 E
Eastern Goldfields Div., W. Australia	45	30 10 s	125 35 E
Eastern Group, Is., W. Australia	45	33 48 s	124 4 E

	MAP		
Eastern Prov., Kenya	53	1 0N	38 30 E
Eastern Prov., Zambia	56	13 50 s	32 0 E
Eastern Prov., Tanzania	53	7 30 s	38 0 E
Eastern Prov., Uganda	53	2 10N	34 0 E
Eastern Region, China	38	33 0N	120 0 E
Eastern Region, Ghana	52	6 30N	0 25w
Eastern Sayan Mt., U.S.S.R.	27	54 0N	96 0 E
Eastland, U.S.A.	71	32 28N	98 45w
Eastmain, Canada	62	52 20N	78 30w
Eastmain R., Canada	62	52 27N	72 26w
Eastman, Canada	69	45 18N	72 19w
Eastmere, Queensland	42	22 28 s	145 59 E
Easton, Md., U.S.A.	68	38 47N	76 7w
Easton, Pa., U.S.A.	68	40 41N	75 15w
Easton, Wash., U.S.A.	72	47 15N	121 9w
Eastview, Canada	62	45 27N	75 40w
Eaton, U.S.A.	70	40 38N	104 38w
Eatonia, Canada	65	51 20N	109 25w
Eatonton, U.S.A.	69	33 29N	83 24w
Eau Claire, S.C., U.S.A.	69	34 5N	81 2w
Eau Claire, Wis., U.S.A.	70	44 46N	91 30w
Ebagoola, Queens.	42	14 15 s	143 12 E
Ebal, Cameroon	52	3 22N	13 52 E
Eban, Nigeria	52	9 40N	4 50 E
Eberswalde, Germany	14	42 49N	13 50 E
Ebi Nor, China	37	45 0N	82 20 E
Eboli, Italy	20	40 39N	15 2 E
Ebolova, Cameroon	52	2 57N	11 11 E
Ebony, S.W. Africa	57	22 5N	15 15 E
Ebro, R., Spain	17	41 49N	1 15w
Echallens, Switzerland	15	46 41N	6 39 E
Echaneni, Natal	57	27 37 s	32 3 E
Echo Bay, Canada	62	46 29N	84 4w
Echternach, Luxem.	13	49 49N	6 3 E
Echuca, Victoria	43	36 3 s	144 46 E
Ecija, Spain	17	37 30N	5 10w
Ecuador, rep., S. America	78	0 0 to 5 0s	
	74	0w to 81 0w	
Ed Damer, Sudan	51	17 27N	34 0 E
Ed Debba, Sudan	51	18 0N	30 51 E
Ed Dueim, Sudan	51	14 0N	32 10 E
Edam, Canada	65	53 20N	108 40w
Edam, Netherlands	13	52 31N	5 3 E
Ede, Netherlands	13	52 4N	5 40 E
Ede, Nigeria	52	7 45N	4 29 E
Edea, Cameroon	52	3 51N	10 9 E
Edehon L., Canada	65	60 25N	97 5w
Eden, New South Wales	43	37 3 s	149 55 E
Eden, Texas, U.S.A.	71	31 15N	99 50w
Eden, Wyo., U.S.A.	72	42 3N	109 29w
Eden L., Canada	65	56 50N	100 0w
Edenburg, O.F.S.	57	29 43 s	25 58 E
Edendale, N.Z.	47	46 19 s	168 48 E
Edenderry, Ireland	11	53 21N	7 3 E
Edenton, U.S.A.	69	36 5N	76 36w
Edenville, O.F.S.	57	27 33 s	27 42 E
Edeowie, S. Australia	43	31 26 s	138 23 E
Eder R., Germany	14	51 3N	8 20 E
Edgar, U.S.A.	70	40 25N	98 0w
Edgecumbe, N.Z.	46	37 58 s	176 46 E
Edgefield, U.S.A.	69	33 43N	81 59w
Edgeley, U.S.A.	70	46 28N	98 40w
Edgemont, U.S.A.	70	43 18N	103 0 E
Edhessa, Greece	21	40 48N	22 3 E
Edievale, New Zealand	47	45 48 s	169 22 E
Edina, U.S.A.	70	40 7N	92 53w
Edinburgh, Scotland	10	55 57N	3 12w
Edinburgh, U.S.A.	71	26 19N	98 7w
Edirne, Turkey	30	41 40N	26 45 E
Edithburgh, S. Austral.	43	35 5 s	137 38 E
Edmond, U.S.A.	71	35 38N	97 30w
Edmonds, U.S.A.	72	47 52N	122 25w
Edmonton, Canada	64	53 30N	113 30w
Edmund L., Canada	62	54 40N	93 0w
Edmundston, Canada	63	47 23N	68 20w
Edna, U.S.A.	71	29 0N	98 43w
Edna Bay, Alaska	64	55 55N	133 40w
Edouard, Lac, Canada	63	47 40N	72 16w
Edremit, Turkey	30	39 40N	27 0 E
Edremit, G. of, Turkey	21	39 27N	26 35 E
Edsbyn, Sweden	23	61 22N	15 45 E
Edson, Canada	64	53 40N	116 28w
Edward I., Canada	62	48 25N	88 37w
Edward L., Africa	53	0 20s	29 40 E
Edward, R., N.S.W.	43	35 15 s	144 50 E
Edwards Creek, S. Australia	45	28 20 s	135 58 E
Eek, Alaska	59	60 13N	162 2w
Eeklo, Belgium	13	51 11N	3 33 E
Eersterus, Botswana	56	21 30 s	22 50 E
Efeinateuss, Niger	52	15 30N	6 25 E
Effingham, U.S.A.	70	39 8N	88 30w
Effiums, Nigeria	52	6 55N	8 0 E
Efiduasi, Ghana	52	6 45N	1 25w
Efoulen, Cameroon	52	2 51N	10 33 E
Egadi Is., Italy	20	38 0N	12 10 E
Eganville, Canada	62	45 32N	77 5w
Egeland, U.S.A.	70	48 39N	99 2w
Egenolf L., Canada	65	58 50N	100 0w
Eger, Hungary	16	47 53N	20 27 E
Egersund, Norway	23	58 26N	5 59 E
Egerton, Mt., W. Australia	44	24 42 s	117 44 E
Egg L., Canada	65	54 30N	73 0w

	MAP		
Egido, Venezuela	75	8 34N	71 15W
Eginbah, W. Australia	44	20 49S	119 46E
Egito, Angola	55	12 0S	13 50E
Eglinton, N. Ireland	11	55 3N	7 10W
Eglisau, Switzerland	15	47 35N	8 32E
Egmont, C., N.Z.	46	39 16S	174 5E
Egmont, Mt., N.Z.	46	39 17S	174 5E
Egridir, Turkey	30	37 53N	30 50E
EgridirGölü, Turkey	30	38 0N	30 50E
Egua, Colombia	78	5 5N	68 0W
Eguei Timmi, Chad	51	15 35N	16 25E
Egume, Nigeria	52	7 30N	7 14E
Egypt, st., U.A.R.	51	25 0N	30 0E
Eha Amufu, Nigeria	52	6 30N	7 40E
Ehime, pref., Japan	36	33 30N	132 40E
Eidsvold, Queensland	43	25 25S	151 12E
Eidsvoll, Norway	23	60 19N	11 17E
Eifel, mts., Germany	14	50 10N	6 45E
Eiffel Flats, Rhodesia	56	18 15S	30 0E
Eigg, I., Scotland	10	56 54N	6 10W
Eighty Mile Beach, W. Australia	44	19 30S	120 40E
Eil L., Scotland	10	56 50N	5 15W
Eilat, Israel	51	29 30N	34 56E
Eildon, L. Australia	43	37 10S	146 0E
Eileen L., Canada	65	62 18N	107 40W
Ein Gev, Israel	29	32 47N	35 37E
Ein Harod, Israel	29	32 33N	35 22E
Einasleigh, Queens.	42	18 32S	144 5E
Einasleigh R., Queens.	42	17 33S	143 0E
Eindhoven, Netherlands	13	51 26N	5 30E
Einsiedeln, Switzerland	15	47 7N	8 46E
Eiriksjökull, mt., Ice.	22	64 46N	20 23W
Eirunepé, Brazil	78	6 35S	70 0W
Eisenach, Germany	14	50 58N	10 18E
Eisenhüttenstadt (Stalinstadt), E. Germany	16	52 9N	14 41E
Eisenkappel, Austria	24	46 29N	14 36E
Eisleben, Germany	14	51 31N	11 31E
'Eizariya, Jordan	29	31 47N	35 15E
Ejura, Ghana	52	7 25N	1 25W
Ekalaka, U.S.A.	70	45 57N	104 30W
Eket, Nigeria	52	4 38N	7 56E
Eketahuna, N.Z.	46	40 38S	175 43E
Ekimchan, U.S.S.R.	27	53 0N	133 0E
Ekiti, Nigeria	52	7 20N	5 14E
Ekohlo, Malawi	56	12 14S	33 32E
Eksjö, Sweden	23	57 37N	15 0E
Ekwan, R., Canada	62	53 30N	85 30W
Ekwan Pt., Canada	62	53 15N	82 10W
Ekwendeni, Malawi	56	11 29S	33 49E
El Aden Hindi, Somali Rep.	53	2 20N	42 10E
El Agowa, Sudan	54	11 10N	29 0E
El Aiun, Sp. Sahara	50	27 10N	8 0W
El Aium, terr., Sp. Sahara	50	27 0N	12 0W
El Arahal, Spain	17	37 16N	5 31W
El Aricha, Algeria	50	34 12N	1 23W
El Azucar, Res., Mex.	74	26 10N	98 15W
El Banco, Colombia	78	9 0N	74 0W
El Barco, Spain	17	42 23N	7 0W
El Bawiti, Egypt	51	28 25N	28 45E
El Bonillo, Spain	17	38 57N	2 35W
El Buqei'a, Jordan	29	32 15N	35 30E
El Cajon, U.S.A.	73	32 47N	117 1W
El Callao, Venezuela	78	7 25N	61 50W
El Campo, U.S.A.	71	29 12N	96 25W
El Centro, U.S.A.	73	32 50N	115 40W
El Cerro, Bolivia	78	17 30S	61 40W
El Chorro, Argentina	77	23 5S	62 10W
El Cuy, Argentina	77	39 55S	68 25W
El Cuyo, Mexico	74	21 30N	87 40E
El Diaz, Mexico	74	21 0N	87 15W
El Dirr (Ad Diwān), Egypt	51	22 30N	32 10E
El Diviso, Colombia	78	1 20N	78 5W
El Djouf, Mauritania	50	20 0N	9 0W
El Dorado, Ark., U.S.A.	71	33 10N	92 40W
El Dorado, Kan., U.S.A.	71	37 51N	96 56W
El Dorado, Venezuela	78	6 55N	61 30W
El Dorado Springs, U.S.A.	71	37 51N	94 0W
El Dudu, Somali Rep.	53	2 38N	41 47E
El Encanto, Colombia	78	1 30S	73 15W
El Escorial, Spain	17	40 32N	4 10W
El Fasher, Sudan	51	13 33N	25 26E
El Fuerte, Mexico	74	26 30N	108 40W
El Geteina, Sudan	54	14 50N	32 27E
El Goléa, oasis, Algeria	50	30 30N	2 50E
El Guapo, Venezuela	78	10 20N	65 55W
El Gusbat (Cussabat), Libya	51	32 25N	14 2E
El Jadida, Morocco	50	33 11N	8 17W
El Jebelein, Sudan	54	12 40N	32 55E
El Kab, Sudan	51	19 27N	32 46E
El Kamlin, Sudan	54	15 3N	33 11E
El Khandaq, Sudan	51	18 30N	30 30E
El Khin, Si. Arabia	30	23 15N	49 11E
El Leh, Ethiopia	53	4 0N	39 20E
El Lisan, Jordan	29	31 18N	35 28E
El Mahalla el Kubra, (Al Mahalla al Kubra) Egypt	51	31 10N	31 0E
El Marj (Barce), Libya	51	32 25N	20 40E
El Niabo, Ethiopia	54	4 39N	39 56E
El Obeid, Sudan	54	13 8N	30 10E
El Odaiya, Sudan	51	12 0N	28 13E
El Oro, Mexico	74	25 50N	105 20W
El Oued, Algeria	50	33 20N	6 40E
El Ouig, Mali	50	19 25N	0 25E
El Paso, Tex., U.S.A.	73	31 50N	106 30W
El Pintado, Arg.	77	24 30S	61 45W
El Portal, U.S.A.	73	37 44N	119 46W
El Progreso, Honduras	59	15 26N	87 51W
El Qantara, Egypt	51	30 51N	32 20E
El Quseir, Syria	31	34 30N	36 44E
El Real, Panama	78	8 6N	77 42W
El Reno, U.S.A.	71	35 30N	98 0W
El Salto, Mexico	74	23 47N	105 22W
El Sauce, Nicaragua	75	13 0N	86 40W
El Sciama, Somali Rep.	53	2 30N	41 2E
El Tigre, Venezuela	78	8 55N	64 24W
El Tocuyo, Venezuela	78	9 50N	69 50W
El Uinle, Somali Rep.	53	2 40S	41 50E
El Vigia, Venezuela	78	8 55N	71 30W
El Wak, Kenya	53	2 55N	40 55E
El Wuz, Sudan	54	15 5N	13 10E
El Zappallar, Argentina	77	26 25S	59 25W
Elamanchili, India	33	17 28N	82 53E
Elands R., Transvaal	57	25 10S	29 10E
Elandsberg, C. Prov.	57	32 17S	21 0E
Elandsvlei, C. Prov.	57	32 19S	19 31E
El Asnam, Algeria	50	36 10N	1 19E
Elassa, I., Crete	20	35 16N	26 20E
Elassón, Greece	21	39 53N	22 12E
Elâzig, Turkey	30	38 37N	39 22E
Elba I., Italy	20	42 48N	10 15E
Elbar, Spain	17	43 12N	2 28W
Elbasan, Albania	21	41 7N	20 5E
Elbe R., Germany	14	53 25N	10 7E
Elberfeld-Barmen (Wuppertal), W. Ger.	14	51 15N	7 10E
Elbert, Mt., Colo., U.S.A.	73	39 12N	106 36W
Elberta, U.S.A.	68	44 35N	86 14W
Elberton, U.S.A.	69	34 7N	82 51W
Elbeuf, France	12	49 17N	1 2E
Elbistan, Turkey	30	38 14N	37 14E
Elblag, Poland	16	54 10N	19 25E
Elbow, Canada	65	51 10N	106 30W
Elbrus, Mt., U.S.S.R.	24	43 30N	42 30E
Elburg, Netherlands	13	52 26N	5 50E
Elche, Spain	17	38 15N	0 42W
Elda, Spain	17	38 29N	0 47W
Elde R., Germany	14	53 26N	11 40E
Eldon, U.S.A.	71	38 21N	92 34W
Eldora, U.S.A.	70	42 19N	93 5W
Eldorado, Canada	65	59 35N	108 30W
Eldorado, Mexico	74	24 0N	107 30W
Eldorado, Ill., U.S.A.	68	37 50N	88 25W
Eldorado, Tex., U.S.A.	71	30 47N	100 32W
Eldoret, Kenya	53	0 30N	35 25E
Electra, U.S.A.	71	34 0N	99 0W
Eleele, Hawaiian Is.	59	21 55N	159 36W
Eleki, Niger	52	14 55N	7 50E
Elele, Nigeria	52	4 59N	6 48E
Elephant Butte Res., U.S.A.	73	33 45N	107 30W
Elephant I., British Antarctic Territory	80	61 0S	55 0W
Elephant Pass, Sri Lanka	32	9 35N	80 25E
Eleuthera I., Bahamas	75	25 0N	76 20W
Elevsis, Greece	21	38 4N	23 36E
Elgin, Canada	63	45 48N	65 10W
Elgin, Scotland	10	57 39N	3 20W
Elgin, Ill., U.S.A.	70	42 0N	88 20W
Elgin, Neb., U.S.A.	70	41 59N	98 3W
Elgin, Nev., U.S.A.	73	37 24N	114 33W
Elgin, N.D., U.S.A.	70	46 28N	101 48W
Elgin, Oregon, U.S.A.	72	46 43W	118 27W
Elgin, Texas, U.S.A.	71	30 24N	97 23W
Elgin Downs, Queens.	42	22 0S	146 55E
Elgon, Mt., Kenya–Uganda	53	1 20N	34 30E
Elida, U.S.A.	71	33 51N	103 13W
Elie, Canada	65	49 48N	97 52W
Elie de Beaumont, mt., N.Z.	47	43 28S	170 29E
Elikon, mts., Greece	21	38 20N	22 50E
Elila R., Congo	54	3 0S	26 30E
Elim, Cape Province	57	34 36S	19 45E
Elim, Alaska	59	64 35N	162 20W
Elin Pelin, Bulgaria	21	42 41N	23 35E
Elista, U.S.S R.	24	46 25N	44 17E
Elizabeth, S. Australia	43	34 45S	38 35E
Elizabeth, U.S.A.	68	40 37N	74 18W
Elizabeth City, U.S.A.	69	36 18N	76 16W
Elizabethton, U.S.A.	69	36 20N	82 13W
Elizabethtown, Ky., U.S.A.	68	37 40N	85 54W
Elk, Poland	23	53 50N	22 20E
Elk City, U.S.A.	71	35 27N	99 26W
Elk I., Canada	65	51 0N	96 20W
Elk L., Canada	62	47 40N	80 25W
Elk Point, Canada	65	54 10N	110 55W
Elk River, Idaho, U.S.A.	72	46 47N	116 12W
Elk River, Minn. U.S.A.	70	45 17N	93 34W
Elkhart, Ind., U.S.A.	68	41 42N	85 55W
Elkhart, Kansas, U.S.A.	71	87 1N	101 56W
Elkhorn, Canada	65	50 0N	101 11W
Elkhorn R.. U.S.A.	70	42 0N	97 30W
Elkhovo, Bulgaria	21	42 10N	26 40E
Elkin, U.S.A.	69	36 17N	80 50W
Elkins, U.S.A.	68	38 53N	79 53W
Elko, Canada	64	49 20N	115 10W
Elko, U.S.A.	72	40 50N	115 50W
Ellavalla, W. Australia	44	25 4S	114 20E
Ellen, mt., U.S.A.	73	38 3N	110 54W
Ellendale, U.S.A.	70	46 3N	95 30W
Ellensburg, U.S.A.	72	47 0N	120 30W
Ellenville, U.S.A.	68	41 42N	74 23W
Ellery, Mt., Victoria	43	37 20S	148 44E
Ellesmere I., Canada	58	79 30N	80 0W
Ellesmere Ld., Canada	58	78 0N	98 0W
Ellesmere L., N.Z.	47	43 46S	172 27E
Ellice Is., Pac. Oc.	5	8 0S	176 0E
Ellichpur, India	32	21 22N	77 32E
Ellig, Somali Rep.	49	7 47N	49 45E
Ellinwood, U.S.A.	71	38 25N	98 30W
Elliot, Cape Province	57	31 18S	27 50E
Elliotdale, C. Prov.	57	31 58S	28 43E
Elliott Mt., Queens.	43	25 58S	147 29E
Ellis, U.S.A.	70	39 0N	99 36W
Elliston, S. Australia	45	33 39S	134 59E
Ellisville, U.S.A.	71	31 34N	89 16W
Ellore (Eluru), India	32	16 43N	81 4E
Ellsworth, Antarctica	80	78 10S	44 0W
Ellsworth, Kan., U.S.A.	70	38 46N	98 15W
Ellsworth, Maine, U.S.A.	69	44 34N	68 24W
Ellsworth Land, Ant.	80	75 0S	90 0W
Ellwangen, W. Germany	14	48 58N	10 10E
Ellwood City, U.S.A.	68	40 52N	80 19W
Elm Creek, Canada	65	49 45N	98 0W
Elma, Canada	65	49 50N	96 0W
Elma, U.S.A.	72	47 2N	122 58W
Elmali, Turkey	30	36 20N	30 0E
Elmhurst, U.S.A.	70	41 52N	87 58W
Elmina, Ghana	52	5 5N	1 21W
Elmira, Canada	63	46 30N	61 59W
Elmira, U.S.A.	68	42 8N	76 55W
Elouera, N.S.W.	43	31 21S	145 48E
Eloy, U.S.A.	73	32 45N	111 40W
Elphinstone, Queens.	42	21 30S	148 17E
Elrose, Canada	65	51 20N	108 0W
Elsas, Canada	62	48 32N	82 55W
Elsberry, U.S.A.	68	39 10N	90 45W
Elsinore, Calif., U.S.A.	73	33 40N	117 20W
Elsinore, Utah, U.S.A.	73	38 43N	112 8W
Eltham, New Zealand	46	39 26S	174 19E
El'ton, U.S.S.R.	25	49 5N	46 52E
Eluru (Ellore) Indian Union	32	16 48N	81 8E
Elvas, Portugal	17	38 50N	7 17W
Elvebakken, Norway	22	69 58N	23 20E
Elverum, Norway	23	60 55N	11 34E
Elvira, Brazil	78	5 0S	72 45W
Elwood, U.S.A.	68	40 20N	85 50W
Elwood, U.S.A.	70	40 39N	99 52W
Ely, England	10	52 24N	0 16E
Ely, Minn., U.S.A.	70	47 56N	91 49W
Ely, Nev., U.S.A.	73	39 10N	114 50W
Elyashiv, Israel	29	32 23N	34 55E
Elyria, U.S.A.	68	41 22N	82 8W
Ema R., U.S.S.R.	25	58 25N	27 0E
Emali, Kenya	53	2 1S	37 30E
Emba, U.S.S.R.	24	47 0N	55 30E
Embarcación, Arg.	77	23 10S	64 0W
Embarras Portage, Can.	64	58 27N	111 29W
Embrun, France	12	44 34N	6 30E
Embu, Kenya	53	0 30S	37 30E
Emden, Germany	14	53 22N	7 12E
Emeq Zevulun, Israel	29	32 50N	35 4E
Emerald, Queensland	42	23 30S	148 11E
Emerson, Canada	65	49 0N	97 10W
Emery Park, U.S.A.	73	32 12N	111 0W
Emi Koussi Mt., Chad	51	20 0N	18 55E
Emly, Ireland	11	52 28N	8 20W
Emmaus, O.F.S.	57	29 2S	25 15E
Emmaville, N.S.W.	43	29 24S	151 31E
Emmeloord, Neth.	13	52 44N	5 46E
Emmen, Netherlands	13	52 48N	6 57E
Emmental, val., Switz.	15	47 0N	7 35E
Emmetsburg, U.S.A.	70	43 5N	94 38W
Emmett, U.S.A.	72	43 51N	116 31W
Emo, U.S.A.	70	48 42N	93 51W
Empalme, Mexico	74	28 1N	110 49W
Empangeni, Natal	57	28 43S	31 52E
Empedrado, Argentina	77	28 0S	58 46W
Empoli, Italy	20	43 43N	10 57E
Emporia, Kans., U.S.A.	70	38 25N	96 16W
Emporia, Va., U.S.A.	69	36 41N	77 32W
Emporium, U.S.A.	68	41 30N	78 17W
Empress, Canada	65	51 0N	110 0W
Ems, Germany	14	50 20N	7 43E
Ems R., Germany	14	52 37N	7 16E
Emu Park, Queensland	42	23 13S	150 50E
En Kerem, Israel	29	31 47N	35 6E
Enaerlin, U.S.A.	70	46 44N	97 41W
Enagi, Nigeria	52	9 2N	5 36E
Encarnacion de Diaz, Mexico	74	21 30N	102 20W
Encarnación, Paraguay	77	27 15S	56 0W
Enchant, Canada	64	50 14N	112 22W
Enchi, Ghana	52	5 53N	2 48W
Encinal, U.S.A.	71	28 0N	99 18W
Encino, U.S.A.	73	34 40N	105 28W
Encontrados, Venezuela	78	9 10N	72 34W
Encounter B., S. Australia	43	34 45S	138 45E
Encruzilhada, Brazil	77	30 30S	52 35W
Endau, Malaya	34	2 40N	103 38E
Endau R., Malaya	34	2 30N	103 30E
Ende, Indonesia	35	8 45S	121 30E
Endeavour, Canada	65	52 20N	102 45W
Endeavour Str., Queens.	42	10 45S	142 0E
Enderby, Canada	64	50 35N	119 10W
Enderby Land, Ant.	80	66 0S	53 0E
Endicott, N.Y., U.S.A.	68	42 6N	76 2W
Endicott, Wash, U.S.A.	72	46 57N	117 43W
Endicott Mts., Alaska	59	68 0N	152 0W
Enesma R., Spain	17	41 10N	4 30W
Enfield, Ireland	11	53 25N	6 50W
Engadin, valley, Switz.	15	46 30N	9 55E
Engaña C., Dom. Rep.	75	18 30N	68 20W
Engcobo, C. Prov.	57	31 39S	28 1E
Engelberg, Swit.	15	46 48N	8 26E
Engels, U.S.S.R	25	51 28N	46 6E
Engemann L., Canada	65	57 55N	107 0W
Enggano I., Indonesia	34	5 20S	102 40E
Enghien, Belgium	13	50 41N	4 2E
England, st., Europe	10	50 0N to 55 45N	14 0E to 5 40W
England, U.S.A.	71	34 30N	92 0W
Englee, Canada	63	50 45N	56 5W
Engler L., Canada	65	59 0N	106 40W
Englewood, Colorado, U.S.A.	70	39 41N	104 59W
Englewood, Kan., U.S.A.	71	37 3N	99 58W
English Co's Is., N. Territory	41	11 58S	136 20E
English R., Canada	65	50 30N	93 50W
English Bazar, India	33	24 58N	88 21E
English Chan., Europe	10	50 0N	2 0W
English River, Canada	62	49 14N	90 58W
Engteng (Yungting), China	39	24 48N	116 47E
Enid, U.S.A.	71	36 26N	97 52W
Enkeldoorn, Rhod.	56	19 2S	30 52E
Enkhuizen, Neth.	13	52 42N	5 17E
Enna, Italy	20	37 34N	14 15E
Ennadai & L., Canada	65	61 0N	101 0W
Enngonia, N.S.W.	43	29 21S	145 50E
Ennis, Ireland	11	52 51N	8 59W
Ennis, Mont., U.S.A.	72	45 24N	111 44W
Ennis, Texas, U.S.A.	71	32 25N	96 43W
Enniscorthy, Ireland	11	52 30N	6 35W
Enniskillen, N. Ire.	11	54 20N	7 40W
Ennistimon, Ireland	11	52 57N	9 18W
Enns, R., Austria	14	48 8N	14 27E
Enriquillo L., Dom. Republic	75	18 20N	72 5W
Enschede, Neth.	13	52 13N	6 53E
Ensenada, Mexico	74	31 50N	116 50W
Enshih, China	39	30 18N	109 27E
Ensuiko, China	39	23 25N	120 10E
Entebbe, Uganda	53	0 3N	32 30E
Enterprise, Oregon, U.S.A.	72	45 27N	117 16W
Enterprise, Utah, U.S.A.	73	37 33N	113 45W
Entrance, Canada	64	53 25N	117 50W
Entrance Island, Alaska	64	57 18N	133 40W
Entre Rios, prov., Arg.	55	30 30S	58 30W
Entrecasteaux, Pt., W. Australia	44	34 50S	115 57E
Entwistle, Canada	64	53 30N	115 0W
Enugu, Nigeria	52	6 30N	7 30E
Enugu Ezike, Nigeria	52	7 0N	7 29E
Enumclaw, U.S.A.	72	47 12N	122 0W
Epa, Papua	42	8 30S	146 55E
Epanome, Greece	21	40 25N	22 59E
Epe, Netherlands	13	52 21N	5 59E
Epe, Nigeria	52	6 36N	3 59E
Epernay, France	12	49 3N	3 56E
Ephesus, ancient city, Turkey	30	38 0N	27 30E
Ephraim, U.S.A.	73	39 27N	111 33W
Ephrata, U.S.A.	72	47 21N	119 32W
Epinal, France	12	48 19N	6 27E
Epirus, prov., Greece	21	39 40N	20 40E
Eport L., Scotland	24	57 33N	7 10W
Epukiro, S.W. Africa	57	21 30S	19 0E
Epukiro, R., S.W. Afr.	57	21 30S	19 20E
Equatorial Guinea	54	1 30N	10 0E
Er Roseires, Sudan	51	11 55N	34 30E
Er Ruksa, Trucial Oman	31	23 5N	53 27E
Erciyas dag, Mt., Turk.	30	38 30N	35 30E
Erden-Dalai, Mongolia	38	46 2N	104 59E
Erebus, Mt., Ant.	80	77 35S	167 0E
Eregli, Turkey	30	41 15N	31 30E
Erechim, Brazil	77	27 40S	52 5W
Erepecú L., Brazil	79	1 30S	56 30W
Erepecuru R., Brazil	79	0 30S	56 0W
Erfurt, Germany	14	50 58N	11 2E
Erg Chech, reg., N.Afr.	50	25 0N	2 30W
Erg Idehan, dist., Libya	51	27 0N	11 0E
Ergani, Turkey	30	38 26N	39 49E
Erhlien, Mongolia	38	43 50N	112 0E
Erice, Italy	20	38 4N	12 34E
Erie, U.S.A.	68	42 7N	80 2W
Erie, L., Canada–U.S.A.	68	42 30N	82 0W
Erieau, Canada	62	42 16N	81 57W
Eriksdale, Canada	65	50 52N	98 7W
Erimanthos, mt., Gr.	21	37 50N	21 55E
Erith, Canada	64	53 25N	116 46W

	MAP		
Eritrea, prov., Ethiopia	49	14 0N	41 0 E
Erlangen, Germany	14	49 35N	11 0 E
Erlistoun, W. Australia	45	27 51 S	122 16 E
Ermelo, Transvaal	57	26 31 S	29 59 E
Ermenek, Turkey	30	36 44N	33 0 E
Ermoupolis, Greece	21	37 26N	24 55 E
Ernakulam, India	32	9 59N	76 19 E
Erne, Lough, N. Ire.	11	54 14N	7 30W
Erne R., Ireland	11	54 30N	8 16W
Erode, India	32	11 24N	77 45 E
Eromanga, Queens.	43	26 40 S	143 11 E
Erongo, S.W. Africa	57	21 45 S	15 45 E
Erongo, mt., S.W. Afr.	57	21 37 S	15 30 E
Er Rahad, Sudan	54	12 42N	30 33 E
Erramala Hills, India	32	15 30N	78 15 E
Erriboll L., Scotland	10	58 30N	4 40W
Errigal Mt., Ireland	11	55 2N	8 8W
Erris Hd., Ireland	11	54 19N	10 0W
Erskine, U.S.A.	70	47 13N	95 59W
Erufu, Nigeria	52	8 39N	5 43 E
Eruwa, Nigeria	52	7 33N	3 26 E
Erwin, U.S.A.	69	36 10N	82 28W
Erwood, Canada	65	52 51N	102 10W
Erz Gebirge, mts., Germany & C. Slov.	16	50 25N	13 0 E
Erzincan, Turkey	30	39 46N	39 30 E
Erzurum, Turkey	30	39 57N	41 15 E
Esamen, Cameroon	52	2 53N	13 16 E
Esan C., Japan	36	41 40N	141 10 E
Esashi, Japan	36	41 53N	140 10 E
Esbjerg, Denmark	23	55 29N	8 29 E
Escalante, U.S.A.	73	37 49N	111 36W
Escalante, R., U.S.A.	73	37 35N	111 0W
Escalon, Mexico	74	26 40N	104 20W
Escalona, Spain	17	40 9N	4 29W
Escambia R., U.S.A.	69	30 45N	87 15W
Escanaba, U.S.A.	69	30 45N	87 15W
Esch-sur-Alzette, Luxembourg	13	49 32N	6 0 E
Escobal, Panama	74	9 6N	80 1W
Escondido, U.S.A.	73	33 10N	117 3W
Escravos R., Nigeria	52	5 35N	5 15 E
Escuintla, Guatemala	74	14 20N	90 48W
Escuminac, Pt., Canada	63	47 4N	64 49W
Esfahan, Iran	31	32 43N	51 33 E
Esdraelon, pl., Israel	29	32 37N	35 12 E
Eseka, Cameroon	52	3 41N	10 44 E
Esh Sham (Damascus), Syria	30	33 30N	36 18 E
Eshowe, Natal	57	28 50 S	31 30 E
Eshtaol, Israel	29	31 47N	35 0 E
Esiama, Ghana	52	4 48N	2 25W
Esino R., Italy	20	43 28N	13 8 E
Esk, Queensland	43	27 15 S	152 22 E
Eska, Alaska	59	61 55N	148 50W
Eskifjördur, Iceland	22	65 3N	13 55W
Eskilstuna, Sweden	23	59 22N	16 32 E
Eskimo Pt., Canada	65	61 20N	94 0W
Eskisehir, Turkey	30	39 50N	30 35 E
Esla R., Spain	17	41 45N	5 50W
Esmeralda, Queens.	42	18 50 S	142 36 E
Esmeraldas, Ecuador	78	1 0N	79 40W
Esnagi L., Canada	62	48 30N	84 22W
Espanola, Canada	62	46 15N	81 46W
Esparta, Costa Rica	59	9 59N	84 46W
Espe, U.S.S.R.	26	44 0N	74 5 E
Espejo, Spain	17	37 40N	4 35W
Espenberg, Alaska	59	66 28N	164 0W
Esperance, co., W. Australia	44	33 28 S	121 40 E
Esperance B., W. Australia	44	33 48 S	121 55 E
Esperanza, Argentina	77	31 29 S	61 3W
Espichel C., Portugal	17	38 22N	9 16W
Espinal, Colombia	78	4 10N	75 0W
Espinhaco, Serra do, Brazil	79	17 0 S	43 50W
Espirito Santo, st., Brazil	79	17 30 S	40 30W
Espiritu Santo, B. del, Mexico	75	19 15N	79 40W
Espiritu Santo, I., Mex.	74	24 12N	110 30W
Esquel, Argentina	77	42 40 S	71 20W
Esquina, Argentina	77	30 0 S	59 30W
Esquinapa de Hidalgo, Mexico	74	22 50N	105 50W
Essaouira, Mor.	50	31 32N	9 42W
Essen, Belgium	13	51 27N	4 26 E
Essen, Germany	14	51 28N	6 59 E
Essequibo R., Guyana	78	5 45N	58 50W
Essexvale, S. Rhod.	56	20 18 S	29 0 E
Essie, Mt., Papua	42	8 4 S	147 2 E
Esslingen, Germany	14	48 43N	9 19 E
Estados, I. de los (Staten I.), Arg.	77	54 50 S	64 30W
Estância, Brazil	79	11 15 S	37 30W
Estancia, U.S.A.	73	34 48N	106 2W
Estcourt, Natal	57	28 58 S	29 53 E
Este, Italy	20	45 12N	11 40 E
Esteli, Nicaragua	75	13 9N	86 22W
Estelline, S.D., U.S.A.	70	44 38N	96 52W
Estelline, Tex., U.S.A.	71	34 31N	100 27W
Estepa, Spain	17	37 4N	4 52W
Estepona, Spain	17	36 24N	5 7W
Estevan, Canada	65	49 10N	103 0W
Estevan Is., Canada	64	53 10N	129 30W
Esther, Canada	65	51 40N	110 18W
Estherville, U.S.A.	70	43 29N	94 51W

	MAP		
Eston, Canada	65	51 8N	108 40W
Estonia S.S.R., U.S.S.R.	23	58 30N	25 30 E
Estrela, Serra da, Port.	17	40 25N	7 30W
Estremadura, prov., Portugal	17	39 0N	8 40W
Estremadura, old prov., Spain	17	39 0N	6 10W
Estremoz, Portugal	17	38 51N	7 39W
Estrondo, Sa. do, Braz.	79	9 0 S	49 0W
Estuary, Canada	65	50 57N	109 52W
Esztergom, Hungary	16	47 47N	18 44 E
Etah, India	32	27 35N	78 40 E
Etamamu, Canada	63	50 18N	59 59W
Étampes, France	12	48 26N	2 10 E
Étaples, France	12	50 30N	1 39 E
Etawah, India	32	26 48N	79 6 E
Etawney L., Canada	65	58 10N	97 50W
Eteh, Nigeria	52	7 2N	7 28 E
Etelia, Mali	50	19 10N	0 55 E
Ethel R., W. Australia	44	24 44 S	119 0 E
Ethelbert, Canada	65	51 32N	100 25W
Etheridge R., Queens.	42	17 45 S	143 15 E
Ethiopia, st., Africa	54	8 0N	40 0 E
Etna Mt., Italy	20	37 45N	15 0 E
Etoile, Zaire	56	11 37 S	27 33 E
Etolin I., Alaska	64	56 5N	132 20W
Eton, Queensland	42	21 16 S	149 3 E
Etosha Pan, S.W. Afr.	55	18 40 S	16 30 E
Etzatlan, Mexico	74	20 48N	104 5W
Etzikom Coulee, R., Canada	64	49 8N	112 0W
Eu, France	12	50 3N	1 26 E
Euabalong, N.S.W.	43	33 6 S	146 29 E
Euboea (Evvoia) I., Gr.	21	38 30N	23 45 E
Euchu L., Canada	64	53 25N	125 20W
Eucla Basin, W. Australia	45	31 19 S	126 9 E
Euclid, U.S.A.	68	41 32N	81 31W
Eucumbene, L., New South Wales	41	36 2 S	148 40 E
Eudora, U.S.A.	71	33 4N	91 15W
Eudunda, S. Australia	43	34 8 S	139 1 E
Eufaula, U.S.A.	71	35 19N	95 33W
Eugene, U.S.A.	72	44 0N	123 8W
Eugenia, Pta., Mexico	74	27 50N	115 5W
Eugowra, N.S.W.	43	33 22 S	148 24 E
Eulbertie, Queensland	43	25 53 S	141 51 E
Eulo, Queensland	43	28 10 S	145 0 E
Eunice, La., U.S.A.	71	30 31N	92 27W
Eunice, N. Mex., U.S.A.	71	32 29N	103 6W
Eupen, Belgium	13	50 37N	6 3 E
Euphrates (Firat), R., Iraq, Syria & Turkey	30	33 30N	43 0 E
Eureka, Calif., U.S.A.	72	40 50N	124 0W
Eureka, Ill., U.S.A.	68	40 42N	89 18W
Eureka, Kan., U.S.A.	71	37 50N	96 25W
Eureka, Mont., U.S.A.	72	48 53N	115 6W
Eureka, Nev., U.S.A.	73	39 32N	116 2W
Eureka, S.D., U.S.A.	70	45 49N	99 34W
Eureka, Utah, U.S.A.	73	40 0N	112 0W
Euriowi, N.S.W.	43	31 18 S	141 38 E
Euroa, Victoria	43	36 38 S	145 35 E
Europa, I., Mozam.	49	22 30 S	40 30 E
Europa Pt., Gibraltar	17	36 3N	5 21W
Europe, cont.	8-9	36 0N to 71 0N	9 30W to 66 0 E
Europoort, Neth.	13	51 59N	4 10 E
Eustis, U.S.A.	69	24 54N	81 36W
Euston, N.S.W.	43	34 30 S	142 46 E
Eutsuk L., Canada	64	53 20N	126 40W
Eval Mt., Jordan	29	32 15N	35 15 E
Evandale, Tasmania	43	41 32 S	147 15 E
Evans, U.S.A.	70	40 28N	104 45W
Evans L., Canada	62	50 50N	77 0W
Evans Pass, U.S.A.	70	41 0N	105 35W
Evanston, Ill., U.S.A.	70	42 0N	87 40W
Evanston, Wy., U.S.A.	72	41 10N	111 0W
Evansville, Ind., U.S.A.	68	38 0N	87 35W
Evansville, Wis., U.S.A.	68	42 47N	89 18W
Eveleth, U.S.A.	70	47 29N	92 31W
Even Yahuda, Israel	29	32 16N	34 53 E
Everard, C., Victoria	43	37 45 S	149 16 E
Everard Ra., S. Austral.	45	27 5 S	132 40 E
Everard, L., S. Austral.	45	31 30 S	135 0 E
Everest, Mt., Nepal–China	33	28 5N	86 58 E
Everett, U.S.A.	72	47 59N	122 14W
Everglades, U.S.A.	69	26 0N	80 40W
Everglades Nat. Park, U.S.A.	69	25 0N	80 50W
Evergreen, Queensland	42	17 5 S	142 38 E
Evergreen, U.S.A.	69	31 28N	86 55W
Everson, U.S.A.	72	48 56N	122 26W
Evora, Portugal	17	38 33N	7 57W
Évreux, France	12	49 0N	1 8 E
Evriks Jökull, Mt., Ice.	22	64 47N	20 21W
Evvoia (Eubœa) I., Gr.	21	38 30N	24 0 E
Ewab Is., Indonesia	35	5 10 S	132 10 E
Ewan, Queensland	42	19 15 S	145 55 E
Ewarton, Jamaica	75		Inset
Ewing, U.S.A.	70	42 20N	98 19W
Ewo, Congo	54	0 48 S	14 45 E
Exaltación, Bolivia	78	13 10 S	65 20W
Excelsior Spr., U.S.A.	70	39 21N	94 10W
Exe R., England	10	50 38N	3 30W
Exeter, England	10	50 43N	3 31W
Exeter, Calif., U.S.A.	73	36 20N	119 7W

	MAP		
Exeter, Neb., U.S.A.	70	40 40N	97 29W
Exmoor, England	10	51 10N	3 55W
Exmouth, England	10	50 37N	3 24W
Exmouth G., W. Australia	44	22 15 S	114 15 E
Expedition Range, Queensland	42	24 30 S	149 12 E
Exstew, Canada	64	54 25N	129 10W
Exuma Sd., W. Indies	75	24 30N	76 20W
Eyasi L., Tanzania	53	4 40 S	35 0 E
Eyeberry L., Canada	65	63 9N	104 40W
Eyemouth, Scotland	10	55 53N	2 5W
Eyjafjördur, Iceland	22	66 0N	18 15W
Eymet, France	12	44 40N	0 25 E
Eyrarbakki, Iceland	22	65 50N	21 1W
Eyre, W. Australia	45	32 17 S	126 25 E
Eyre Cr., Queensland	42	24 42 S	139 0 E
Eyre L., S. Australia	41	28 30 S	136 45 E
Eyre Mts., N.Z.	47	45 25 S	168 25 E
Eyre Pen., S. Australia	45	33 30 S	137 17 E
Eyrecourt, Ireland	11	53 12N	8 8W

F

	MAP		
Fabens, U.S.A.	73	31 32N	106 9W
Fabriano, Italy	20	43 20N	12 52 E
Facatativa, Colombia	78	4 48N	74 32W
Fachi, Niger	51	18 5N	11 30 E
Fada, Chad	51	17 13N	21 30 E
Fada-n-Gourma, Volta	50	12 10N	0 30 E
Faddeyev, I., U.S.S R.	27	75 40N	144 0 E
Faenza, Italy	20	44 17N	11 53 E
Fagam, Nigeria	52	11 1N	10 1 E
Făgăras, Rumania	21	45 48N	24 58 E
Fagernes, Norway	23	61 0N	9 16 E
Fagersta, Sweden	23	60 1N	15 46 E
Fǎget, Rumania	21	45 52N	22 10 E
Fagnano L., Argentina	77	54 30 S	68 0W
Fagnes, Belgium	13	50 7N	4 30 E
Fahrej, Iran	31	29 1N	58 54 E
Fadhili, Saudi Arabia	30	26 54N	49 7 E
Fahsien, China	39	21 30N	110 34 E
Faid, Saudi Arabia	30	27 1N	42 52 E
Faido, Switzerland	15	46 28N	8 48 E
Fair Haven, U.S.A.	69	43 38N	73 14W
Fair Haven, U.S.A.	68	43 35N	73 16W
Fair Hd., N. Ireland	11	55 14N	6 10W
Fair I., Scotland	10	59 30N	1 40W
Fairbank, U.S.A.	73	31 45N	110 15W
Fairbanks, Alaska	59	64 59N	147 40W
Fairbury, U.S.A.	70	40 5N	97 5W
Fairfax, U.S.A.	71	36 34N	96 47W
Fairfield, Rhodesia	56	19 20 S	30 42 E
Fairfield, Ala., U.S.A.	69	33 30N	87 0W
Fairfield, Calif., U.S.A.	73	38 14N	122 2W
Fairfield, Idaho, U.S.A.	72	43 23N	114 46W
Fairfield, Ill., U.S.A.	70	38 20N	88 20W
Fairfield, Me., U.S.A.	69	44 38N	69 39W
Fairfield, Mont., U.S.A.	72	47 40N	112 0W
Fairfield, Texas, U.S.A.	71	31 40N	95 45W
Fairford, Canada	65	51 40N	98 45W
Fairhope, U.S.A.	69	30 35N	87 50W
Fairlie, New Zealand	47	44 5 S	170 49 E
Fairmont, Minn., U.S.A.	70	43 37N	94 30W
Fairmont, W.Va., U.S.A.	68	39 29N	80 60W
Fairmont Hot Springs, Canada	64	50 20N	115 56W
Fairplay, U.S.A.	73	38 15N	106 0W
Fairport, U.S.A.	68	43 8N	77 29W
Fairview, Canada	64	56 5N	118 25W
Fairview, Queensland	42	15 31 S	144 17 E
Fairview, N.D., U.S.A.	70	47 49N	104 7W
Fairview, Okla., U.S.A.	71	36 15N	98 30W
Fairview, Utah, U.S.A.	73	39 43N	111 29W
Fairweather, Mt., Alas.	59	59 0N	137 42W
Faith, U.S.A.	70	45 2N	102 5W
Faizabad, Afghanistan	31	37 7N	70 33 E
Faizabad, India	33	26 45N	82 10 E
Fajardo, Puerto Rico	75	18 20N	65 42W
Fajr Wadi, Si. Arabia	30	30 6N	38 18 E
Fakfak, Indon.	35	3 0 S	132 15 E
Faku, China	38	42 30N	123 35 E
Fal R., England	10	50 17N	4 55W
Falaba, Sierra Leone	52	9 50N	11 25W
Falaise, France	12	48 54N	0 12W
Falam, Burma	33	23 0N	93 45 E
Falcon Dam, U.S.A.	74	26 50N	99 20W
Falcone, C., Italy	20	41 0N	8 10 E
Falfurrias, U.S.A.	71	27 11N	98 9W
Falher, Canada	64	55 50N	117 15W
Falkenberg, Sweden	23	56 56N	12 30 E
Falkirk, Scotland	10	56 0N	3 47W
Falkland Is. (Islas Malvinas), Atlan. Oc.	77	51 30 S	58 30W
Falkland Islands Dependency, Antarctica	80	55 0 S	45 0W
Falköping, Sweden	23	58 12N	13 33 E
Fall Brook, U.S.A.	73	33 27N	117 15W
Fall River, U.S.A.	69	41 45N	71 5W
Fall River Mills, U.S.A.	72	41 0N	121 29W
Fallon, Mont., U.S.A.	70	46 47N	105 4W
Fallon, Nev., U.S.A.	72	39 30N	118 46W
Falls City, U.S.A.	70	40 0N	95 40W
Falls City, U.S.A.	72	44 53N	123 30W
Falmouth, Antigua	75		Inset
Falmouth, England	10	50 9N	5 5W
Falmouth, Jamaica	75	18 30N	77 40W

	MAP		
Falmouth, Ky., U.S.A.	68	38 40N	84 20W
False B., C. Prov.	57	35 15 S	18 40 E
False Divi Pt., India	33	15 35N	80 50 E
Falset, Spain	17	41 7N	0 50 E
Falso, C., Honduras	75	15 10N	85 20W
Falster I., Denmark	23	54 49N	12 0 E
Falsterbo, Sweden	23	55 23N	12 50 E
Faluja, Israel	29	31 48N	31 37 E
Falun, Sweden	23	60 32N	15 39 E
Famagusta, Cyprus	30	35 8N	33 55 E
Famatina, Mt., Arg.	77	29 5 S	68 0W
Family L., Canada	65	51 50N	95 35W
Fancheng, China	39	32 15N	112 0 E
Fancheng, China	39	31 10N	118 10 E
Fane R., Ireland	11	53 59N	6 32W
Fangak, Sudan	54	9 0N	30 50 E
Fanghsien, China	39	32 0N	111 0 E
Fanhsien, China	38	35 50N	115 35 E
Fankiatun, China	38	43 44N	125 5 E
Fanna, Nigeria	52	11 39N	3 51 E
Fanning I., Pac. Oc.	5	3 51N	159 22W
Fanny Bay, Canada	64	49 27N	124 58W
Fano, Italy	20	43 50N	13 0 E
Fanö I., Denmark	14	55 25N	8 25 E
Fanshaw, Alaska	64	57 11N	133 30W
Faotan Ho, China	39	21 50N	110 30 E
Far Western Div., Queensland	42	23 16 S	140 21W
Faradje, Zaire	53	3 50N	29 40 E
Farafangana, Madag.	55	22 58 S	47 57 E
Farah, Afghanistan	31	32 20N	61 21 E
Farah R., Afghanistan	31	32 20N	62 0 E
Faranah, Guinea	52	10 3N	10 45W
Farewell, Alaska	59	62 30N	154 0W
Farewell C., Greenland	61	59 40N	43 40W
Farewell C., N.Z.	47	40 29 S	172 43 E
Fargo, U.S.A.	70	47 0N	97 0W
Fari'a R., Jordan	29	32 12N	35 27 E
Faribault, U.S.A.	70	44 15N	93 19W
Faridkot, India	32	30 44N	74 45 E
Faridpur, Bangladesh	33	23 33N	89 51 E
Farim, Port. Guinea	50	12 27N	15 17W
Farimān, Iran	31	35 44N	59 58 E
Farina, S. Australia	43	29 55 S	138 12 E
Farkwa, Tanzania	53	5 27 S	35 43 E
Farlane, Canada	65	50 0N	94 10W
Farleigh, Queensland	42	21 5 S	149 6 E
Farmerville, U.S.A.	71	32 47N	92 28W
Farmington, N. Mex. U.S.A.	73	36 45N	108 13W
Farmington, Utah, U.S.A.	72	41 0N	111 56W
Farmville, U.S.A.	68	37 19N	78 22W
Farnham Mt., Canada	64	50 25N	116 30W
Faro, Brazil	79	2 0 S	56 45W
Faro, Portugal	17	37 2N	7 55W
Fårö I., Sweden	23	57 58N	19 15 E
Farquhar, C., Australia	44	23 50 S	113 36 E
Farrar R., Scotland	10	57 24N	4 50W
Farrars Cr, Queens.	42	24 30 S	141 40 E
Farrashband, Iran	31	28 55N	52 6 E
Farrell, Pa., U.S.A.	68	41 13N	80 29W
Farsala, Greece	21	39 17N	22 23W
Farsund, Norway	23	58 3N	6 42 E
Fartak, Ra's, Si. Arab.	30	28 0N	35 7 E
Faru, Nigeria	52	12 37N	6 14 E
Farwell, U.S.A.	71	34 25N	103 0W
Farwell Spit, N.Z.	47	40 32 S	173 0 E
Fasa, Iran	31	29 0N	53 32 E
Fasano, Italy	20	40 50N	17 20 E
Fastnet, I., Ireland	11	51 24N	9 35W
Fastov, U.S.S.R.	25	50 7N	29 57 E
Fataki, Zaire	53	4 33 S	28 5 E
Fatehgarh, India	32	27 25N	79 35 E
Fatehpur, Rajasthan, India	32	28 0N	75 4 E
Fatehpur, Uttar Pradesh, India	39	25 56N	80 56 E
Father, The, Mt., Terr. of New Guinea	42	5 2 S	151 20 E
Fati, China	39	23 10N	113 10 E
Fatkeng, China	39	23 53N	113 31 E
Fatshan, China	39	23 0N	113 4 E
Faulkton, U.S.A.	70	45 3N	99 5W
Faure I., W. Australia	44	25 52 S	113 50 E
Fǎurei, Rumania	21	45 6N	27 19 E
Fauresmith, O.F.S.	57	29 44 S	25 17 E
Fauske, Norway	22	67 17N	15 25 E
Favara, Italy	20	37 19N	13 39 E
Favignana, I., Italy	20	37 56N	12 18 E
Favourable Lake, Can.	62	52 40N	98 0W
Fawangchen, China	38	35 15N	113 45 E
Fawn R., Canada	62	54 20N	89 0W
Faxaflói, B., Iceland	22	64 25N	23 0W
Faya (Largeau), Chad	51	17 58N	19 6 E
Fayette, Mo., U.S.A.	70	39 10N	92 40W
Fayetteville, Arkansas, U.S.A.	71	36 0N	94 5W
Fayetteville, N.C., U.S.A.	69	35 3N	78 53W
Fayetteville, Tenn., U.S.A.	69	35 0N	86 30W
Fazilka, India	32	30 27N	74 2 E
Feale R., Ireland	11	52 26N	9 28W
Fear, C., U.S.A.	69	33 45N	78 0W
Feather R., U.S.A.	72	39 30N	121 20W
Featherstone, N.Z.	46	41 6 S	175 20 E
Featherstone, Rhod.	56	18 44 S	30 45 E

	Map		
Fécamp, France	12	49 45N	0 22E
Federal District, Mex.	74	24 30N	99 10W
Fehmarn Belt, Den.	14	54 35N	11 20E
Fehmarn I., Germany	14	54 26N	11 10E
Feihsien, China	38	35 10N	118 0E
Feijo, Brazil	78	8 30S	70 30W
Feilding, N.Z.	46	40 13S	175 35E
Feira, Zambia	56	15 35S	30 18E
Feira de Santana, Brazil	79	12 20S	39 0W
Felanitx, Spain	17	39 27N	3 7E
Feldkirch, Austria	14	47 15N	9 37E
Felipe, Cerro de, Spain	17	40 20N	1 30W
Felixburg, Rhodesia	56	19 29S	30 51E
Felixstowe, England	10	51 58N	1 22W
Feltre, Italy	20	46 1N	11 55E
Femunden L., Norway	23	62 5N	11 55E
Fen Ho, China	38	37 20N	111 50E
Fencheng, Kiangsi, China	39	28 8N	115 42E
Fencheng, Liaoning, China	38	40 27N	124 2E
Fengchen, Mongolia	38	40 27N	112 8E
Fengfeng, China	38	36 34N	114 19E
Fenghsien, Kiangsu, China	38	34 40N	116 40E
Fenghsien, Kiangsu, China	39	30 55N	121 27E
Fenghsien, Shensi, China	38	33 50N	106 35E
Fenghwang, China	39	27 48N	109 25E
Fengkieh (Kweichow), China	39	31 6N	109 30E
Fenglo, China	39	31 35N	112 25E
Fengning, China	38	41 20N	117 10E
Fengsiang, China	38	34 28N	106 30E
Fengsin, China	39	28 50N	115 15E
Fengtai, China	38	39 50N	116 26E
Fengtu, China	39	29 58N	107 45E
Fengyi, China	39	23 46N	106 49E
Fengyuan, Taiwan	39	24 15N	120 42E
Fenit, Ireland	11	52 17N	9 51W
Fennimore, U.S.A.	70	42 59N	90 40W
Fenton, Canada	65	53 0N	105 35W
Fenyang, Anhwei, China	38	32 50N	117 27E
Fenyang, Shansi, China	38	37 25N	111 45E
Feodosiya, U.S.S.R.	25	45 2N	35 28E
Ferbane, Ireland	11	53 17N	7 50W
Ferdows, Iran	31	34 5N	58 0E
Ferentino, Italy	20	41 42N	13 14E
Fergana, U.S.S.R.	26	40 50N	71 50E
Fergus, Canada	62	43 43N	80 24W
Fergus Falls, U.S.A.	70	46 25N	96 0W
Ferguson, Canada	62	47 50N	73 30W
Fergusson I., Papua	42	9 30S	150 40E
Ferla, Italy	20	37 7N	14 55E
Ferland, Canada	62	50 19N	88 27W
Fermanagh, co., N. Ire.	11	54 21N	7 40W
Fermo, Italy	20	43 10N	13 42E
Fermoselle, Spain	17	41 19N	6 27W
Fermoy, Ireland	11	52 4N	8 18W
Fernandina, U.S.A.	69	30 40N	81 30W
Fernando Póo, I., Afr.	52	3 30N	8 40E
Ferndale, Calif., U.S.A.	72	40 32N	124 20W
Ferndale, Wash., U.S.A.	72	48 52N	122 35W
Fernie, Canada	64	49 30N	115 5W
Fernley, U.S.A.	72	39 36N	119 16W
Ferns, Ireland	11	52 35N	6 30W
Ferozepore, India	32	30 55N	74 40E
Ferrara, Italy	20	44 50N	11 36E
Ferreira, Zaire	56	12 50S	23 0E
Ferreñafe, Peru	79	6 35S	79 50W
Ferriday, U.S.A.	71	31 39N	91 32W
Ferro, R., Brazil	79	14 30S	54 30W
Ferrol, Spain	17	43 29N	8 15W
Ferron, U.S.A.	73	39 3N	111 6W
Fertile, U.S.A.	70	47 37N	96 17W
Fès, Morocco	50	34 5N	4 55W
Feshi, Zaire	54	6 0S	18 10E
Fessenden, U.S.A.	70	47 39N	99 31W
Fethard, Tipperary, Ire.	11	52 29N	7 42W
Fethard, Wexford, Ire.	11	52 12N	6 51W
Fethiye, Turkey	30	36 36N	29 10E
Fetlar I., Scotland	10	60 36N	0 52W
Fettluft-Nord, S.W. Afr.	57	27 34S	19 23E
Fezzan, dist., Libya	51	26 30N	15 0E
Ffestiniog, Wales	10	52 58N	3 56W
Fianarantsoa, Madag.	55	21 30S	47 0E
Fianga, Chad	51	9 55N	15 20E
Fichot I., Canada	63	51 12N	55 40W
Fichtel Geb., mt., E. Germany	14	50 26N	12 55E
Ficksburg, O.F.S.	57	28 51S	27 53E
Fiditi, Nigeria	52	7 45N	3 53E
Field, B.C., Canada	64	51 25N	116 30W
Field, Ont., Canada	62	46 32N	80 1W
Fife Ness, Scotland	10	56 17N	2 35W
Fifth Cataract, Sudan	51	18 15N	33 50E
Figeac, France	12	44 37N	2 2E
Figtree, Rhodesia	56	20 22S	28 20E
Figueira, Brazil	79	18 50S	42 5W
Figueira da Foz, Port.	17	40 7N	8 54W
Figueras, Spain	17	42 18N	2 58E
Figuig, Morocco	50	32 5N	1 5W
Fiji Is., Pac. Oc.	5	17 20S	179 0E
Fika, Nigeria	52	11 15N	11 13'E
Filabusi, Rhodesia	56	20 30S	29 15E
Filer, U.S.A.	72	42 35N	114 38W
Filey, England	10	54 13N	0 18W

	Map		
Filiasi, Rumania	21	44 32N	23 31E
Filiates, Greece	21	39 38N	20 16E
Filiatrá, Greece	21	37 9N	21 35E
Filicudi I., Italy	20	38 35N	14 33E
Filingué, Niger	52	14 19N	3 21E
Filipstad, Sweden	23	59 42N	14 5E
Fillmore, Canada	65	49 50N	103 25W
Fillmore, Calif., U.S.A.	73	34 28N	118 58W
Fillmore, Utah, U.S.A.	73	38 59N	112 17W
Finale, Italy	20	44 50N	8 16E
Finch Hatton, Queens.	42	21 10S	148 40E
Findlay, U.S.A.	68	41 0N	83 41W
Finger L., Canada	62	53 15N	93 35W
Fingoé, Mozambique	56	14 55S	32 10E
Finike, Turkey	30	36 21N	30 10E
Finisterre, C., Spain	17	42 50N	9 19W
Finisterre Ra., Terr. of New Guinea	42	5 58S	146 10E
Finke, R., N. Terr.	45	24 30S	133 5E
Finland, rep., Europe	23	70 0N	27 0E
Finland, G. of, Europe	23	60 0N	26 0E
Finlay Forks, Canada	64	56 0N	123 50W
Finlay R., Canada	64	57 10N	125 30W
Finley, N.S.W.	43	35 50S	145 40E
Finley, U.S.A.	70	47 35N	97 49W
Finmoore, Canada	64	54 0N	123 30W
Finn R., Ireland	11	54 50N	7 55W
Finnegan, Canada	64	51 11N	112 8W
Finmark, prov., Norway	22	69 30N	25 0E
Finschafen, Terr. of New Guinea	42	6 32S	147 55E
Finsteraarhorn Mt., Switzerland	15	46 31N	8 10E
Finsterwalde, Germany	14	51 37N	13 42E
Fintona, N. Ireland	11	54 30N	7 20W
Fipa Plateau, Tan.	53	8 0S	31 20E
Firat R. (Euphrates), Iraq	30	33 30N	43 0E
Fire River, Canada	62	48 47N	83 36W
Firebag R., Canada	65	57 40N	111 0W
Firedrake L., Canada	65	61 25N	104 40W
Firenze (Florence), Italy	20	43 47N	11 15E
Firotino, Somali Rep.	56	14 0S	35 8E
Firozabad, India	32	27 10N	78 25E
Firuzabad, Iran	31	28 52N	52 35E
Firuzkuh, Iran	31	35 50N	52 40E
Firuza, U.S.S.R.	26	38 0N	57 50E
Firuzd, U.S.S.R.	31	38 0N	57 55E
Fish R., C. Prov.	57	31 51S	25 25E
Fish R., S.W. Africa	57	27 45S	17 32E
Fisher, S. Australia	45	30 30S	130 58E
Fisher B., Canada	65	51 40N	97 20W
Fishguard, Wales	10	51 59N	4 59W
Fishing L., Canada	65	52 10N	95 30W
Fiskenaesset, Greenland	61	63 0N	51 0W
Fitchburg, U.S.A.	69	42 35N	71 47W
Fitz Roy, Argentina	77	47 10S	67 0W
Fitzgerald, U.S.A.	69	31 45N	83 10W
Fitzpatrick, Canada	62	47 29N	72 46W
Fitzroy R., Queens.	42	23 10S	150 10E
Fitzroy Crossing, W. Australia	44	18 9S	125 38E
Fiwila, Zambia	56	13 58S	29 33E
Fizi, Zaire	53	4 20S	28 48E
Flagler, U.S.A.	70	39 20N	103 3W
Flagstaff, C. Prov.	57	31 3S	29 31E
Flagstaff, U.S.A.	73	35 10N	111 40W
Flagstone, Canada	64	49 4N	115 10W
Flaherty I., Canada	62	56 0N	79 55W
Flakstad, Norway	22	68 3N	13 25E
Flåm, Norway	23	60 50N	7 8E
Flambeau, U.S.A.	70	45 40N	90 55W
Flamborough Hd., Eng.	10	54 8N	0 4E
Flandre Occid., prov., Belgium	13	51 0N	3 0E
Flandre Orientale, prov., Belgium	13	51 0N	4 0E
Flandreau, U.S.A.	70	44 5N	96 33W
Flåsjön L., Sweden	22	64 11N	16 5E
Flat Pt., N.Z.	46	41 15S	175 59E
Flat R., Canada	64	61 30N	126 40W
Flat River, U.S.A.	71	37 50N	90 32W
Flatey I., Iceland	22	65 23N	22 50W
Flatey I., Iceland	22	66 12N	17 50W
Flateyri, Iceland	22	66 3N	23 30W
Flathead L., U.S.A.	72	47 50N	114 0W
Flattery C., Queens.	42	14 58S	145 25E
Flattery, C., U.S.A.	72	48 21N	124 42W
Flawil, Switzerland	15	47 25N	9 12E
Flaxton, U.S.A.	70	48 56N	102 27W
Fleetwood, England	10	53 55N	3 1W
Flekkefjord, Norway	23	58 22N	6 43E
Flensburg, Germany	14	54 46N	9 28E
Flers, France	12	48 47N	0 33W
Fleurier, Switzerland	15	46 54N	6 35E
Flinders B., W. Australia	44	34 19S	115 9E
Flinders Grp., Queens.	42	14 28S	144 17E
Flinders I., S. Austral.	45	33 49S	134 30E
Flinders I., Tasmania	43	40 0S	148 0E
Flinders Ranges, S. Australia	43	31 25S	138 35E
Flinders R., Queens	42	18 15S	140 45E
Flinflon, Canada	65	54 50N	102 0W
Flint, U.S.A.	68	43 0N	83 40W
Flint R., U.S.A.	69	31 20N	84 10W
Floodwood, U.S.A.	70	46 58N	92 56W

	Map		
Flora, U.S.A.	70	38 40N	88 30W
Flora, Mt., W. Austral.	44	21 47S	116 45E
Florala, U.S.A.	69	31 0N	86 20W
Floraville Queensland	42	18 8S	139 56E
Florence (Firenze), Italy	20	43 47N	11 15E
Florence, Ala., U.S.A.	69	34 50N	87 50W
Florence, Ariz., U.S.A.	73	33 0N	111 25W
Florence, Colo., U.S.A.	70	38 28N	105 0W
Florence, Ore., U.S.A.	72	44 1N	124 4W
Florence, S.C., U.S.A.	69	34 5N	79 50W
Florence Bay, Malawi	56	10 35S	34 15E
Florencia, Colombia	78	1 50N	75 50W
Florennes, Belgium	13	50 15N	4 35E
Florenville, Belgium	13	49 40N	5 19E
Flores, Guatemala	74	16 50N	89 40W
Flores I., Canada	64	49 20N	126 10W
Flores I., Indonesia	35	8 35S	121 0E
Flores Sea, Indonesia	35	6 30S	124 0E
Floresville, U.S.A.	71	29 8N	98 7W
Floriano, Brazil	79	6 50S	43 0W
Florianopolis, Brazil	77	27 30S	48 30W
Florida, Uruguay	77	34 7S	56 10W
Florida, st., U.S.A.	69	28 30N	82 0W
Florida B., U.S.A.	69	25 0N	81 20W
Florida Str., U.S.A.	75	25 0N	80 0W
Florina, Greece	21	40 48N	21 26E
Floro, Norway	23	61 36N	5 0E
Flower's Cove, Canada	63	51 14N	56 46W
Floydada, U.S.A.	71	33 58N	101 16W
Flüela P., Switzerland	15	46 46N	9 18E
Flushing, Netherlands	13	51 26N	3 34E
Fly R., Papua	42	7 50S	141 20E
Foam Lake, Canada	65	51 40N	103 15W
Foça, Turkey	30	38 40N	26 50E
Foča, Yugoslavia	21	43 31N	18 47E
Focsani, Rumania	21	45 41N	27 15E
Fofha, Israel	29	31 29N	34 40E
Fofo Fofo, Papua	42	8 20S	147 0E
Foggia, Italy	20	41 28N	15 31E
Foggo, Nigeria	52	11 21N	9 57E
Fogo, & I., Canada	63	49 40N	54 5W
Fohnsdorf, Austria	14	47 12N	14 41E
Foix, France	12	42 58N	1 38E
Foix, dist., France	12	42 59N	1 35E
Fokku, Nigeria	52	11 36N	4 32E
Folda, Norway	22	67 27N	15 35E
Folda, B., Norway	22	67 30N	15 5E
Folégandros, I., Greece	21	36 40N	24 55E
Foley, U.S.A.	69	30 24N	87 41W
Foleyet, Canada	62	48 15N	82 25W
Folgefonni, mts., Nor.	23	60 23N	6 34E
Foligno, Italy	20	42 58N	12 40E
Folkestone, England	10	51 5N	1 11E
Folkston, U.S.A.	69	30 55N	102 0W
Follett, U.S.A.	71	36 28N	100 8W
Follonica, Italy	20	42 55N	10 45E
Folsom, U.S.A.	73	38 39N	121 14W
Fond du lac, Canada	65	59 20N	107 10W
Fond Du Lac, U.S.A.	70	43 46N	88 26W
Fond du lac R., Canada	65	58 55N	104 50W
Fondi, Italy	20	41 21N	13 25E
Fonsagrada, Spain	17	43 11N	7 7W
Fonseca, G. of, Central America	74	13 10N	87 40W
Fontainebleau, France	12	48 24N	2 40E
Fontas R., Canada	64	58 20N	121 30W
Fonte Boa, Brazil	78	2 25S	66 0W
Fontem, W. Cameroon	52	5 32N	9 52E
Fontenelle, Canada	63	48 54N	64 33W
Fontevrault, France	12	47 11N	0 3E
Foochow (Minhow), China	39	26 9N	119 17E
Foping, China	38	33 35N	107 58E
Forakungo, Mozam.	56	14 55S	33 20E
Forbes, N.S.W.	43	33 22S	148 0E
Forbes Mt., Canada	64	51 50N	117 0W
Forbesganj, India	33	26 18N	87 16E
Forcados, Nigeria	52	5 26N	5 26E
Forcados R., Nigeria	52	5 25N	5 20E
Fordlandia, Brazil	79	3 50S	55 30W
Fords Bridge, N.S.W.	43	29 41S	145 29E
Fordyce, U.S.A.	71	33 50N	92 20W
Forécariah, Guinea	52	9 20N	13 10W
Forel Mt., Greenland	58	67 0N	36 0W
Foremost, Canada	64	49 26N	112 41W
Forest, U.S.A.	71	32 25N	89 29W
Forest Cy., Iowa, U.S.A.	70	43 13N	93 36W
Forest Cy., N.C. U.S.A.	69	35 18N	81 53W
Forest Gro, U.S.A.	72	45 30N	123 6W
Forest Lawn, Canada	64	51 4N	114 0W
Forestburg, Canada	64	52 35N	112 1W
Forestville, Canada	63	42 44N	80 25W
Forestville, U.S.A.	68	44 41N	87 29W
Forfar, Scotland	10	56 40N	2 53W
Forget, Canada	62	49 40N	102 50W
Forks, U.S.A.	72	47 59N	124 30W
Forli, Italy	20	44 14N	12 2E
Forman, U.S.A.	70	46 12N	97 36W
Formentera I., Spain	17	38 40N	1 30E
Formiga, Brazil	79	20 20S	45 35W
Formosa, Argentina	77	26 15S	58 10W
Formosa, Bahia, Brazil	79	11 0S	45 0W
Formosa, C. Prov.	57	33 52S	23 41E
Formosa, Goiaz, Brazil	79	15 25S	47 20W
Formosa, I., China. *See* **Taiwan.**	37		
Formosa, Serra, Brazil	79	12 30S	55 25W
Formosa Str., China	39	24 30N	120 0E

	Map		
Fornovo, Italy	20	44 41N	10 6E
Forres, Scotland	10	57 37N	3 38W
Forrest, Victoria	43	38 22S	143 40E
Forrest, W. Australia	45	30 55S	128 12E
Forrest City, U.S.A.	71	35 0N	90 47W
Forrest Mt., W. Australia	44	22 55S	114 46E
Forrester I., Alaska	64	54 50N	133 30W
Forsayth, Queensland	42	18 33S	143 34E
Forse, Sweden	23	63 8N	17 1E
Forssa, Finland	23	60 47N	23 35E
Forst, Germany	16	51 43N	14 37E
Forster N.S.W.	43	32 12S	152 31E
Forster, Ra., N. Terr.	45	21 28S	133 56E
Forsyth, U.S.A.	69	46 18N	87 22W
Forsyth, U.S.A.	72	46 15N	106 37W
Forsyth, I., N.Z.	47	40 58S	174 6E
Forsyth Range, Queens.	42	22 40S	143 10E
Fort Abbas, Pakistan	32	29 15N	72 55E
Fort Albany, Canada	62	52 15N	81 35W
Fort Amador, Pan. Can. Zone	74	8 56N	79 32W
Fort Apache, U.S.A.	73	33 50N	110 0W
Fort Archambault, Chad	54	9 5N	18 23E
Fort Assiniboine, Can.	64	54 20N	114 45W
Fort Babine, Canada	64	55 22N	126 37W
Fort Beaufort, C. Prov.	57	32 46S	26 40E
Fort Benton, U.S.A.	72	47 51N	110 36W
Fort Bragg, U.S.A.	72	39 27N	123 23W
Fort Bretonnet, Chad	51	10 34N	16 52E
Fort Bridger, U.S.A.	72	41 23N	110 20W
Fort Charlet (Djanet), Algeria	50	24 25N	9 25E
Fort Chimo, Canada	61	58 10N	68 18W
Fort Chipewyan, Can.	65	58 46N	111 9W
Fort Clayton, Pan. Can. Zone	74	9 0N	79 35W
Fort Collins, U.S.A.	70	40 30N	105 4W
Fort Coulonge, Canada	62	45 50N	76 45W
Fort Crampel, Cen. Afr. Republic	54	7 8N	19 18E
Fort Dauphin, Madag.	55	25 0S	46 57E
Fort Davis, U.S.A.	71	30 34N	103 55W
Fort Davis, Pan. Can. Zone	74	9 17N	79 56W
Fort de France, Mart.	75	14 36N	61 2W
Fort de Polignac, Algeria	50	26 45N	8 55E
Fort Defiance, U.S.A.	73	35 46N	109 2W
Fort Dodge, U.S.A.	70	42 29N	94 10W
Fort D'Orbigny, Bolivia	77	22 0S	62 50W
Fort Erie, Canada	62	42 55N	78 56W
Fort Fairfield, U.S.A.	69	46 45N	67 50W
Fort Fitzgerald, Canada	64	59 51N	111 41W
Fort Flatters, Algeria	50	27 10N	6 40E
Fort Foureua, Cam.	51	12 0N	14 55E
Fort Frances, Ont., Can.	65	48 35N	93 25W
Fort Garland, U.S.A.	71	37 29N	105 27W
Fort Gen. Diaz, Par.	77	23 35S	60 40W
Fort George, Canada	62	53 40N	79 0W
Fort George R., Canada	62	53 50N	77 0W
Fort Good Hope, Can.	60	66 14N	128 40W
Fort Gouraud (Idjil), Mauritania	50	22 40N	12 45W
Fort Grahame, Canada	64	56 30N	124 35W
Fort Guachalla, Par.	77	22 20S	62 15W
Fort Gulick, Pan. Can. Zone	74	Inset	
Fort Hancock, U.S.A.	73	31 22N	105 53W
Fort Hetz (Putao), Burma	33	27 28N	97 30E
Fort Hill, Malawi	56	9 42S	33 17E
Fort Hope, Canada	62	51 30N	88 10W
Fort Huachuca, U.S.A.	73	31 33N	110 30W
Fort Johnston, Malawi	56	14 25S	35 16E
Fort Kent, U.S.A.	69	47 12N	68 30W
Fort Klamath, U.S.A.	72	42 42N	121 59W
Fort Lallemand, Algeria	50	31 13N	6 17E
Fort Lamy, Chad	51	12 4N	15 8E
Fort Laperrine (Tamanrasset), Alg.	50	22 40N	5 40E
Fort Laramie, U.S.A.	70	42 15N	104 30W
Fort Lauderdale, U.S.A.	69	26 10N	80 5W
Fort Lavalle, Argentina	77	25 40S	60 10W
Fort Liard, Canada	64	60 20N	123 30W
Fort Liberté, Haiti	74	19 42N	71 51W
Fort Lupton, U.S.A.	70	40 0N	104 50W
Fort Mackay, Canada	64	57 12N	111 41W
Fort Madison, U.S.A.	70	40 37N	91 24W
Fort McMahon, Algeria	50	29 43N	1 34E
Fort Meade, U.S.A.	69	27 45N	81 45W
Fort Miribel, Algeria	50	29 31N	2 55W
Fort Morgan, U.S.A.	70	40 16N	103 50E
Fort Munro, Pakistan	32	29 51N	70 2W
Fort Myers, U.S.A.	69	26 30N	82 0E
Fort Nelson, Canada	64	58 50N	122 30W
Fort Nelson R., Can.	69	59 20N	123 30W
Fort Norman, Canada	60	64 57N	125 30W
Fort Payne, U.S.A.	69	34 25N	85 44W
Fort Peck, U.S.A.	72	48 2N	106 28W
Fort Peck Dam, U.S.A.	72	48 0N	106 20W
Fort Peck Res., U.S.A.	72	47 40N	107 0W
Fort Pierce, U.S.A.	69	27 29N	80 19W
Fort Pierre, U.S.A.	70	44 27N	100 25W
Fort Plain, U.S.A.	69	42 56N	74 39W
Fort Portal, Uganda	53	0 45N	30 15E
Fort Providence, Can.	64	61 20N	117 30W
Fort Qu'Appelle, Can.	65	50 45N	103 50W
Fort Randell, Alaska	59	55 10N	162 40W

	Map		
Fort Randolph, Pan. Canal Zone	74	9 23N	79 53W
Fort Reliance, Canada	65	62 40N	109 0W
Fort Resolution, Can.	64	61 10N	114 40W
Fort Rixon, S. Rhod.	56	20 2s	29 25 E
Fort Rocades, Angola	55	16 27s	15 2 E
Fort Rousset, Congo	54	0 35s	16 5 E
Fort St. James, Canada	64	54 30N	124 10W
Fort St. John, Canada	64	56 15N	120 50W
Fort Sandeman, Pak.	32	31 20N	69 25 E
Fort Scott, U.S.A.	71	38 0N	94 40W
Fort Selkirk, Canada	60	62 52N	137 25W
Fort Severn, Canada	62	56 0N	87 40W
Fort Sherman, Pan. Can. Zone	74	9 22N	79 56W
Fort Shevchenko, U.S.S.R.	24	44 30N	50 10 E
Fort Sibut, Central African Republic	54	5 52N	19 10 E
Fort Simpson, Canada	64	61 45N	121 30W
Fort Siracuas, Par.	78	21 63s	61 46W
Fort Smith, Canada	64	60 0N	112 0W
Fort Smith, U.S.A.	71	35 25N	94 25W
Fort Stanton, U.S.A.	73	33 31N	105 36W
Fort Stockton, U.S.A.	71	30 45N	103 0W
Fort Sumner, U.S.A.	71	34 30N	104 14W
Fort Thomas, U.S.A.	73	33 3N	109 59W
Fort Trinquet, Maur.	50	25 10N	11 25W
Fort Valley, U.S.A.	69	32 33N	83 52W
Fort Vermillion, Can.	64	58 20N	116 0W
Fort Victoria, Rhod.	56	20 8s	30 55 E
Fort Walton Beach, U.S.A.	69	30 25N	86 40W
Fort Wayne, U.S.A.	68	41 5N	85 10W
Fort William, Canada	62	48 20N	89 10W
Fort William, Scotland	10	56 48N	5 8W
Fort Worth, U.S.A.	71	32 45N	97 25W
Fort Yates, U.S.A.	70	46 8N	100 42W
Fort Yukon, Alaska	59	66 35N	145 12W
Fortaleza (Ceará), Braz.	79	3 35s	38 35W
Fortaleza, Brazil	79	16 0s	41 20W
Forte Rocades, Angola	55	16 38s	15 22 E
Forteau, Canada	63	51 28N	57 1W
Fortescue, W. Australia	44	21 4s	116 4 E
Fortescue R., W. Australia	44	21 20s	116 45 E
Forth, Firth of, Scot.	10	56 5N	2 55W
Fortin Ayacucho, Par.	78	23 28s	60 14W
Fortin Corrales, Par.	78	22 21s	60 35W
Fortore R., Italy	20	41 40N	15 0 E
Fortrose, New Zealand	47	46 38s	168 45 E
Fortuna, Calif., U.S.A.	72	40 35N	124 12W
Fortuna, N.D., U.S.A.	70	48 57N	103 45W
Fortune Bay, Canada	63	47 30N	55 22W
Fortymile, Canada	60	64 20N	140 30W
Foso, Ghana	52	5 45N	1 19W
Fossano, Italy	20	44 39N	7 40 E
Fossil, U.S.A.	72	44 59N	120 15W
Fossilbrook, Queens.	42	17 47s	144 29 E
Fosston, U.S.A.	70	47 34N	95 39W
Foster R., Canada	65	56 10N	105 45W
Fostoria, Ohio, U.S.A.	68	41 8N	83 25W
Fougères, France	12	48 21N	1 14W
Foul Pt., Sri Lanka	32	8 35N	81 25 E
Foula I., Scotland	10	60 10N	2 5W
Foulwind Cape, N.Z.	47	41 45s	171 29 E
Foumban, Cameroon	52	5 45N	10 50 E
Foumbot, Cameroon	52	5 45N	10 40 E
Fountain, U.S.A.	70	38 44N	104 43W
Fountain Green, U.S.A.	73	39 40N	111 38W
Fourchu, Canada	63	45 43N	60 17W
Fouriesburg, O.F.S.	57	28 38s	28 14 E
Fourmies, France	12	50 1N	4 2 E
Foúrnoi, I., Greece	21	37 37N	27 0 E
Fourth Cataract, Sudan	51	18 47N	32 5 E
Fouta Djalon, Guinea	50	11 20N	12 10W
Foveaux St., N.Z.	47	46 42s	168 10 E
Fowing, China	38	33 46N	119 43 E
Fowler, Calif., U.S.A.	73	36 40N	119 43W
Fowler, Kansas, U.S.A.	71	37 27N	100 12W
Fowlers Bay, & tn. S. Australia	45	32 0s	132 29 E
Fowlerton, U.S.A.	71	28 29N	98 47W
Fowling, China	39	29 35N	107 30 E
Fowman, Iran	30	37 18N	49 16 E
Fowping, China	38	38 50N	111 27 E
Fowyang, China	38	33 0N	116 0 E
Fox Is., Aleutain Is.	59	53 30N	168 0W
Fox R., Canada	65	55 20N	95 40W
Fox Valley, Canada	65	50 30N	109 25W
Foxe Basin, Canada	61	68 30N	77 0W
Foxe Channel, Canada	61	66 0N	80 0W
Foxe Pen., Canada	61	65 0N	76 0W
Foxford, Ireland	11	54 0N	9 7W
Foxpark, U.S.A.	72	41 3N	106 10W
Foxton, New Zealand	46	40 29s	175 18 E
Foxwarren, Canada	65	50 30N	101 15W
Foyle, Lough, N. Ire.	11	55 6N	7 8W
Foyle R., N. Ireland	11	54 58N	7 22W
Foynes, Ireland	11	52 37N	9 5W
Foz, Spain	17	43 33N	7 20W
Foz do Embira, Brazil	78	7 29s	70 14W
Foz do Iguaçu, Brazil	77	25 33s	54 31W
Foz do Jordão, Brazil	78	9 40s	20 12W
Fraga, Spain	17	41 32N	0 23 E
Franca, Brazil	79	20 25s	47 30W
Francavilla, Italy	21	42 25N	14 18 E
France, rep., Europe	12	47 0N	3 0 E
Frances L., Canada	64	61 30N	129 20W
Frances R., Canada	64	60 30N	129 10W
Frances Viejo C., Dom. Republic	74	19 44N	69 65W
Franceville, Gabon	54	1 40s	13 32 E
Franche Comté, prov., France	12	46 30N	5 50 E
Francis C., Canada	63	47 50N	52 46W
Francis Harbour, Can.	63	52 34N	55 44W
Francisco I Madero, Durango, Mexico	74	24 25N	104 20W
Franciso I. Madero, Coahuila, Mexico	74	25 50N	103 12W
Francistown, Botswana	57	21 7s	27 33 E
François, Canada	63	47 34N	56 45W
Francois L., Canada	64	54 0N	125 30W
Frances Pk., U.S.A.	72	43 50N	109 5W
Franeker, Neth.	13	53 12N	5 33 E
Frankfield, Jamaica	75	18 8N	77 22W
Frankfort, O.F.S.	57	27 16s	28 30 E
Frankfort, Ind., U.S.A.	68	40 20N	86 33W
Frankfort, Kan., U.S.A.	70	39 40N	96 28W
Frankfort, Ky., U.S.A.	68	38 12N	84 55W
Frankfort, Mich., U.S.A.	68	44 38N	86 14W
Frankfurt-on-Main, Ger.	14	50 7N	8 40 E
Frankfurt-on-Oder, Ger	16	52 20N	14 31 E
Franklin, terr., Canada	60	71 0N	99 0W
Franklin, C. Prov.	57	30 18s	29 30 E
Franklin, Ky., U.S.A.	68	36 40N	86 30W
Franklin, La., U.S.A.	71	29 47N	91 29W
Franklin, Neb., U.S.A.	70	40 7N	98 55W
Franklin, N.H., U.S.A.	69	43 28N	71 39W
Franklin, N.J., U.S.A.	69	41 9N	74 38W
Franklin, Pa., U.S.A.	69	41 22N	79 45W
Franklin, Tenn., U.S.A.	68	35 54N	86 53W
Franklin, Va., U.S.A.	69	36 40N	76 58W
Franklin, W.Va., U.S.A.	69	38 38N	79 21W
Franklin B., Canada	60	70 0N	126 0W
Franklin, L., U.S.A.	72	40 20N	115 25W
Franklin Mts., Canada	60	66 0N	125 0W
Franklin Mts., N.Z.	47	44 55s	167 45 E
Franklin Str., Canada	60	72 0N	96 0W
Franklin D. Roosevelt L., U.S.A.	72	48 28N	118 14W
Franklinton, U.S.A.	71	30 50N	90 13W
Franklyn Mt., N.Z.	47	42 4s	172 42 E
Frankston, Victoria	43	38 8s	145 8 E
Frankton, N.Z.	46	37 47s	175 16 E
Franz, Canada	62	48 25N	84 30W
Franz Josef Land, U.S.S.R.	80	80 0N	52 0 E
Frascati, Italy	20	41 48N	12 41 E
Fraser L., Canada	64	54 0N	124 50W
Fraser or Gt. Sandy I., Queensland	43	25 15s	153 0 E
Fraser R., Canada	64	53 30N	120 40W
Fraser Ra., W. Australia	45	31 40s	122 50 E
Fraserburg, C. Prov.	57	31 55s	21 30 E
Fraserburgh, Scotland	10	57 41N	2 0W
Fraserdale, Canada	62	49 55N	81 30W
Frasertown, N.Z.	46	38 58s	177 28 E
Frater, Canada	62	47 20N	84 25W
Frauenfeld, Switz.	15	47 34N	8 54 E
Fray Bentos, Uruguay	77	33 10s	58 15W
Fredericia, Denmark	23	55 34N	9 43 E
Frederick, Md., U.S.A.	68	39 25N	77 23W
Frederick, Okla., U.S.A.	71	34 27N	99 0W
Frederick, S.D., U.S.A.	70	45 56N	98 28W
Frederick R., W. Australia	44	24 0s	117 0W
Frederick Sd., Alaska	64	57 10N	134 0 E
Fredericksberg, U.S.A.	68	36 18N	77 29W
Fredericksburg, U.S.A.	71	30 14N	98 53W
Fredericton, Canada	63	45 57N	66 40W
Fredericton Junc., Can.	63	45 41N	66 40W
Frederikshaab, Green.	61	62 0N	49 30W
Frederikshavn, Den.	23	57 28N	10 31 E
Fredonia, Colombia	78	6 0N	75 45W
Fredonia, Ariz., U.S.A.	73	36 59N	112 32W
Fredonia, Kan., U.S.A.	71	37 33N	95 51W
Fredonia, N.Y., U.S.A.	68	42 26N	79 20W
Fredericktown, U.S.A.	71	37 4N	90 32W
Fredrikstad, Norway	23	59 12N	10 59 E
Freels, C., Canada	63	49 16N	53 30W
Freeman, U.S.A.	70	43 29N	97 28W
Freeport, Ill., U.S.A.	70	42 15N	89 39W
Freeport, Tex., U.S.A.	71	28 27N	95 18W
Freeport, N.Y., U.S.A.	69	40 39N	73 35W
Freetown, Sierra Leone	52	8 30N	13 10W
Fregenal, Spain	17	38 12N	6 40W
Freiburg, Germany	14	48 0N	7 52 E
Freire, Chile	77	39 0s	72 50W
Freising, Germany	14	48 24N	11 47 E
Freistadt, Austria	14	48 30N	14 30 E
Fréjus, France	12	43 25N	6 44 E
Fremantle, W. Austral.	44	32 1s	115 47 E
Fremont, Mich., U.S.A.	68	43 29N	85 59W
Fremont, Nebr., U.S.A.	70	41 30N	96 30W
Fremont, Ohio, U.S.A.	68	41 20N	83 5W
Fremont L., Canada	63	54 10N	63 20W
Fremont R., U.S.A.	73	38 15N	110 20W
French R., U.S.A.	68	41 42N	80 15W
French Guiana, Fr. Overseas Department, South America	76	4 0N	53 0W
French Pass, N.Z.	47	40 53s	173 56 E
Frenchglen, U.S.A.	72	42 58N	118 59W
Frenchman Cr., U.S.A.	70	40 30N	101 35W
Frenchman R., Canada	65	49 20N	108 0W
Frenchman Butte, Can.	65	53 36N	109 36W
Frenchpark, Ireland	11	53 53N	8 25W
Fresco, R., Brazil	79	7 10s	51 45W
Freshwater, Canada	63	47 18N	53 58W
Freshwater L., U.S.A.	65	48 13N	98 57W
Fresnillo, Mexico	74	23 10N	103 0W
Fresno, U.S.A.	73	36 47N	119 50W
Fresno Res., U.S.A.	72	48 45N	110 0W
Freswick, Scotland	10	58 35N	3 5W
Frew R., Sta., N. Terr.	45	20 36s	135 8 E
Freycinet, C., W. Australia	44	34 9s	115 0 E
Freycinet Pen., Tas.	41	42 10s	148 15 E
Fria C., S.W. Africa	55	18 0s	13 2 E
Frias, Argentina	77	28 40s	65 5W
Fribourg, Switzerland	15	46 49N	7 9 E
Fribourg, can., Switz.	15	45 40N	7 0 E
Frick, Switzerland	15	47 31N	8 2 E
Friedrichshafen, Ger.	14	47 39N	9 29 E
Friesland, prov., Neth.	13	53 5N	5 50 E
Frijoles, Pan. Can. Zone	74	9 11N	79 48W
Frio, R., U.S.A.	71	29 35N	99 43W
Friockheim, Scotland	10	56 39N	2 40W
Friona, U.S.A.	71	34 37N	102 43W
Frisian Is., Neth., Ger.	13	53 30N	6 0 E
Fritch, U.S.A.	71	35 37N	101 32W
Friuli-Venezia Giulia, reg., Italy	20	46 0N	13 0 E
Froan, I., Norway	23	63 55N	8 45 E
Frobisher B., Canada	61	63 0N	67 0W
Frobisher Sd., Canada	61	62 30N	66 0W
Frohavet, str., Norway	23	63 52N	9 0 E
Froid, U.S.A.	70	48 16N	104 29W
Frolovo, U.S.S.R.	25	49 45N	43 30 E
Fromberg, U.S.A.	72	45 24N	108 55W
Frome, England	10	51 16N	2 17W
Frome, L., S. Australia	43	30 45s	139 45 E
Fromosa Bay, Kenya	53	2 50s	40 30 E
Front Range Mts., U.S.A.	70	40 0N	105 10W
Front Royal, U.S.A.	68	38 55N	78 10W
Frontera, Mexico	74	18 32N	92 38W
Frosinone, Italy	20	41 38N	13 20 E
Frostburg, U.S.A.	68	39 43N	78 57W
Frostisen, mt., Norway	22	68 17N	17 5 E
Fröya I., Norway	23	63 45N	8 45 E
Frunze, U.S.S.R.	26	42 40N	74 50 E
Frutal, Brazil	79	20 0s	49 0W
Frutigen, Switzerland	15	46 35N	7 38 E
Fu Shui, China	39	27 15N	116 30 E
Fuchow, China	38	39 45N	121 45 E
Fuchow, China	39	28 0N	116 15 E
Fuchun Kiang, R., China	39	30 0N	120 0 E
Fuchung, China	39	24 30N	111 26 E
Fuengirola, Spain	17	36 32N	4 41W
Fuente, Spain	17	38 17N	6 19W
Fuente-Alamo, Spain	17	38 44N	1 24W
Fuenteovejuna, Spain	17	38 16N	5 24W
Fuenterabia, Spain	17	43 22N	1 53W
Fuentes de Onoro, Spain	17	40 33N	6 52W
Fuentesauco, Spain	17	41 15N	5 30W
Fuerteventura I, Canary Islands	50	28 30N	14 0W
Fuglo Sd., Norway	22	14 0N	20 0 E
Fuhsien, China	38	36 10N	109 10 E
Fujaira, Trucial 'Oman	31	25 7N	56 18 E
Fujisawa, Japan	36	35 25N	139 27 E
Fuji San, Mt., (Fujiyama) Japan	36	35 20N	138 30 E
Fukai I., Japan	36	32 30N	128 45 E
Fukien, prov., China	39	25 50N	118 0 E
Fukow, China	38	34 2N	114 15 E
Fukuchiyama, Japan	36	35 25N	135 9 E
Fukui, Japan	36	36 0N	136 10 E
Fukuoka, Japan	36	33 30N	130 30 E
Fukuoka, pref., Japan	36	33 30N	131 0 E
Fukushima, Japan	36	37 45N	140 25 E
Fukushima, pref., Japan	36	37 30N	140 15 E
Fulda, Germany	14	50 32N	9 41 E
Fulda R., Germany	14	50 55N	9 45 E
Fullerton, Calif., U.S.A.	73	33 52N	117 58W
Fullerton, Nebr., U.S.A.	70	41 25N	97 56W
Fulton, Ill., U.S.A.	68	41 50N	90 5W
Fulton, Mo., U.S.A.	70	38 50N	91 55W
Fulton, N.Y., U.S.A.	69	43 20N	76 22W
Fumbusi, Ghana	52	10 25N	1 20W
Funabashi, Japan	36	35 45N	140 0 E
Funchal, Madeira	50	32 45N	16 55W
Fundación, Colombia	75	10 35N	74 10W
Fundão, Portugal	17	40 9N	7 30W
Fundu, Zambia	56	14 57s	30 14 E
Fundy, B. of, Canada	63	45 0N	66 0W
Fungchun, China	39	23 25N	111 35 E
Fungulwe, Zambia	56	13 28s	27 10 E
Funhalouro, Mozam.	56	22 55s	34 22 E
Funing, China	39	23 39N	105 39 E
Funiu Shan, China	38	33 40N	112 30 E
Funsi, Ghana	52	10 21N	1 54W
Funtua, Nigeria	52	11 35N	7 25 E
Furancungo, Mozam.	56	14 51s	33 39 E
Furka P., Switzerland	15	46 36N	8 27 E
Furkating, India	33	26 30N	94 0 E
Furmanov, U.S.S.R.	25	57 25N	41 3 E
Furmanovo, U.S.S.R.	25	49 42N	49 25 E
Furneaux Is., Tasmania	43	40 10s	147 50 E
Fürstenwalde, Germany	14	52 20N	14 3 E
Fürth, Germany	14	49 29N	11 0 E
Fury and Hecla Str., Canada	61	69 40N	81 0W
Fusa, Nigeria	52	9 48N	9 0 E
Fusagasuga, Colombia	78	4 30N	74 30W
Fuse, Japan	36	34 42N	135 36 E
Fushan, China	38	37 30N	121 5 E
Fushun, China	38	41 55N	123 55 E
Fusin, China	38	42 8N	121 39 E
Fusui, China	39	22 33N	107 58 E
Futsing, China	39	25 43N	119 21 E
Futuk, Nigeria	52	9 45N	10 56 E
Futung, China	39	27 21N	120 13 E
Fuyang, China	39	30 6N	119 55 E
Fuyu, China	38	45 15N	124 50 E
Fuyuan, China	37	48 32N	134 17 E
Fwaka, Zambia	56	12 5s	29 25 E
Fyn I., Denmark	23	55 18N	10 20 E
Fyne, L., Scotland	10	56 0N	5 20W

G

	Map		
Ga, Ghana	52	9 50N	2 11W
Gaanda, Nigeria	52	10 10N	12 27 E
Gabanintha, W. Austral.	44	26 53s	118 35 E
Gabarin, Nigeria	52	11 3N	10 28 E
Gabdo, Cameroon	52	7 57N	13 22 E
Gabela, Angola	55	11 0s	14 37 E
Gaberones, Botswana	57	24 45s	25 55 E
Gabes, Tunisia	51	33 53N	10 2 E
Gabes, G. of, Tunisia	51	34 0N	10 30 E
Gabo I., Victoria	43	37 33s	149 57 E
Gabon, rep. Africa	54	2 0s	12 0 E
Gabrovo, Bulgaria	21	42 52N	25 27 E
Gach Saran, Iran	31	30 15N	50 45 E
Gada, Nigeria	52	13 38N	5 36 E
Gadag, India	32	15 30N	75 45 E
Gadarwara, India	32	22 50N	78 50 E
Gaddede, Sweden	22	64 30N	14 15 E
Gadhada, India	32	22 0N	71 35 E
Gadsden, Ala., U.S.A.	69	34 1N	86 0W
Gadsden, Ariz., U.S.A.	73	32 32N	114 50W
Gadwal, India	32	16 10N	77 50 E
Gadyach, U.S.S.R.	25	50 25N	33 58 E
Găesti, Rumania	21	44 48N	25 19 E
Gaeta, Italy	20	41 12N	13 35 E
Gaffney, U.S.A.	69	35 10N	81 31W
Gafsa, Tunisia	50	34 19N	8 42 E
Gagarawa, Nigeria	52	12 27N	9 38 E
Gagarin, U.S.S.R.	25	55 30N	35 0 E
Gagetown, U.S.A.	63	43 39N	83 15W
Gagnon L., Canada	65	61 55N	110 40W
Gago Coutinho, Angola	55	14 18s	21 18 E
Gagra, U.S.S.R.	24	43 20N	40 10 E
Gahini, Rwanda	53	1 50s	30 30 E
Gaibanda, Bangladesh	33	25 21N	89 36 E
Gaillac, France	12	43 54N	1 54 E
Gainesville, Fla., U.S.A.	69	29 40N	82 20W
Gainesville, Ga., U.S.A.	69	34 20N	83 50W
Gainesville, Mo., U.S.A.	71	36 36N	92 30W
Gainesville, Tex., U.S.A.	71	33 40N	97 10W
Gainsborough, England	10	53 23N	0 46W
Gairdner L., S. Austral.	45	31 30s	136 0 E
Gairezi R., Mozam.	56	17 45s	33 0 E
Gaisin, U.S.S.R.	25	48 57N	29 25 E
Gajale, Nigeria	52	11 25N	8 10 E
Gajiram, Nigeria	52	12 29N	13 9 E
Gal Oya Dam, Sri Lanka	32	7 12N	81 16 E
Galadi, Ethiopia	52	6 59N	46 30 E
Galadima Kogo, Nigeria	52	10 2N	6 58 E
Galangue, Angola	55	13 48s	16 3 E
Galapagos Is., Pac. Oc.	5	0 0	89 0W
Galas R., Malaya	34	4 55N	101 57 E
Galashiels, Scotland	10	55 37N	2 50W
Galatea, New Zealand	46	38 24s	176 45 E
Galati, Rumania	21	45 27N	28 2 E
Galatina, Italy	21	40 10N	18 10 E
Galax, U.S.A.	69	36 40N	80 59W
Galcanhar C., Brazil	79	5 10s	35 15W
Galdhöpiggen, mt., Nor.	23	61 45N	8 40 E
Galeana, Mexico	74	24 40N	100 0W
Galela, Indonesia	35	1 50N	127 55 E
Galena, Alaska	59	66 0N	155 26W
Galena, W. Australia	44	27 48s	114 42 E
Galera Pt., Trinidad	75	10 49N	60 54W
Galera, Punta, Ecuador	78	1 50N	80 20W
Galesburg, U.S.A.	70	41 0N	90 20W
Galicia, old prov., Sp.	17	42 43N	8 0W
Galilee, dist., Israel	29	32 53N	35 18 E
Galilee, Lower, dist., Is.	29	32 47N	35 20 E
Galilee, Sea of, Israel	30	32 55N	35 30 E
Galilee, Upper, Israel	29	33 3N	35 25 N
Galilee L., Queensland	42	22 25s	145 45 E
Galim, Cameroon	52	7 5N	12 22 E
Galina Pt., Jamaica	75		Inset
Galiuro Mts., U.S.A.	73	32 40N	110 20W
Gall, U.S.A.	71	32 47N	101 28W
Gallabat, Sudan	54	12 55N	36 4 E
Gallatin, U.S.A.	69	36 25N	86 30W
Galle, Sri Lanka	32	6 5N	80 10 E
Gallego, Mexico	74	29 50N	106 23W
Gallegos R., Argentina	77	51 50s	71 0W
Galley Hd., Ireland	11	51 32N	8 56W
Gallinas, Pta., Col.	75	12 30N	71 40W
Gallipoli, Italy	21	40 8N	18 0 E

Place	Map	Lat.	Long.
Gallipoli, Turkey. *See* Gelibolu.	30		
Gallipolis, U.S.A.	68	38 50N	82 10W
Gällivare, Sweden	22	67 7N	20 32E
Galloway, Canada	64	53 30N	116 50W
Galloway, Mull of, Scot.	10	54 38N	4 50W
Gallup, U.S.A.	73	35 30N	108 40W
Galma Galla, Kenya	53	1 11S	40 49E
Gal-on, Israel	29	31 38N	34 51E
Galoya, Sri Lanka	32	8 5N	80 55E
Galt, Canada	62	43 21N	80 19W
Galty Mts., Ireland	11	52 22N	8 10W
Galtymore, mt., Ireland	11	52 22N	8 10W
Galula, Tanzania	53	8 40S	33 0E
Galveston, U.S.A.	71	29 10N	94 50W
Galveston B., U.S.A.	71	29 30N	94 45W
Galvez, Argentina	77	32 0S	61 20W
Galway, Ireland	11	53 16N	9 4W
Galway B., Ireland	11	53 10N	9 20W
Galway, co., Ireland	11	53 21N	9 0W
Galya, U.S.A.	70	41 8N	90 1W
Gam, Indonesia	35	0 45S	128 10E
Gamarra, Colombia	78	8 20N	73 45W
Gamawa, Nigeria	52	12 2N	10 32E
Gambaga, Ghana	52	10 30N	0 28W
Gambia, W. Africa	52	13 25N	16 0W
Gambia, R., W. Africa	52	13 20N	15 45W
Gamboa, Panama Canal Zone	74	9 8N	79 42W
Gamboma, Congo (Fr.)	54	1 55S	16 0E
Gamboola, Queensland	42	16 29S	143 43E
Gameleira, Brazil	79	7 50S	50 0W
Gamerco, U.S.A.	73	35 32N	108 49W
Gamka, R., C. Prov.	57	32 50S	22 25E
Gammon, R., Canada	65	51 12N	95 10W
Gamoep, C. Prov.	57	29 56S	18 25E
Gamtoos R., C. Prov.	57	33 45S	24 30E
Gamvik, Norway	22	71 0N	28 15E
Gan Goriama, Mts., Cameroon	52	7 45N	13 0E
Gan Shemuel, Israel	29	32 28N	34 56E
Gan Yavne, Israel	29	31 48N	34 42E
Gana, Nigeria	52	5 28N	5 47E
Gana, R., Nigeria	52	12 30N	11 10E
Ganado, Ariz., U.S.A.	73	35 43N	109 32W
Ganado, Tex., U.S.A.	71	29 2N	98 31W
Gananoque, Canada	62	44 25N	76 10W
Ganāveh, Iran	30	29 39N	50 31E
Gandak, R., India	33	27 0N	84 8E
Gandava, W. Pakistan	32	28 32N	67 32E
Gander, Canada	63	49 1N	54 33W
Gander L., Canada	63	48 58N	54 45W
Ganderowe Falls, Rhodesia	56	17 20S	29 10E
Gāndhi Sagar Dam, India	32	24 30N	75 30E
Gandi, Nigeria	52	12 56N	5 44E
Gandia, Spain	17	38 58N	0 9W
Gandole, Nigeria	52	8 28N	11 35E
Ganga R., India	32	25 30N	87 0E
Ganganagar, India	32	29 55N	73 55E
Gangalana na Bodio, Congo	53	3 55N	28 0E
Gangara, Niger	52	14 35N	8 40E
Gangaw, Burma	33	22 5N	94 15E
Ganges (Ganga), Mouths of the, India–Bangladesh	33	21 30N	89 0E
Ganges (Ganga), R., India	33	25 30N	82 0E
Gangtok, India	33	27 20N	88 40E
Gannatt, France	12	46 7N	3 11E
Gannett Pk., U.S.A.	72	43 15N	110 0W
Gannvalley, U.S.A.	70	44 2N	98 56W
Ganspan, C. Prov.	57	27 57S	24 47E
Ganta, Liberia	50	7 15N	8 59W
Gantheaume B., W. Australia	44	27 40S	114 10E
Gantheaume C., S. Australia	43	35 58S	137 27E
Ganyesa, Cape Province	57	26 35S	24 11E
Ganzi, Sudan	53	4 30N	31 15E
Gao, Mali	50	16 15N	0 5W
Gao Bang, China	39	22 43N	106 15E
Gaoua, Volta	50	10 20N	3 15W
Gaoual, Guinea	50	11 35N	13 25W
Gap, France	12	44 33N	6 5E
Garachiné, Panama	75	8 0N	78 12W
Garagoumsa, Niger	52	13 40N	8 30E
Garah, N.S.W.	43	29 2S	149 30E
Garamba R., Congo	53	4 0N	29 30E
Garanhuns, Brazil	79	8 50S	36 30W
Garba Tula, Kenya	53	0 33N	38 22E
Garber, U.S.A.	71	36 28N	97 33W
Garberville, U.S.A.	72	40 9N	123 50W
Garda Lake, Italy	20	45 40N	10 40E
Gardala, Ethiopia	54	5 40N	37 25E
Garde L., Canada	65	62 50N	106 15W
Garden City, Kan., U.S.A.	71	37 58N	100 46W
Garden City, Texas, U.S.A.	71	31 49N	101 28W
Garden I., W. Austral.	44	32 12S	115 38E
Gardez, Afghanistan	31	33 31N	68 59E
Gardian, Chad	51	15 45N	19 40E
Gardiner, Me., U.S.A.	69	44 11N	69 45W
Gardiner, Mont., U.S.A.	72	45 3N	119 48W
Gardiner, N. Mexico, U.S.A.	71	36 56N	104 29W
Gardner, U.S.A.	68	42 35N	72 0W
Gardner Canal, Canada	64	53 30N	128 30W
Gardnerville, U.S.A.	73	38 58N	119 44W
Gareloi, I., Aleutian Is.	59	51 49N	178 50W
Garfield, Utah, U.S.A.	72	40 45N	112 11W
Garfield, Wash., U.S.A.	72	47 1N	117 7W
Gargano, Mt., Italy	20	41 45N	15 50E
Gargantua C., Canada	62	47 35N	85 0W
Gargett, Queensland	42	21 13S	148 47E
Garhchiroli, India	32	20 15N	80 0E
Garian, Libya	51	32 10N	13 0E
Garibaldi, Canada	64	49 56N	123 15W
Garibaldi Prov. Pk., Canada	64	49 55N	122 50W
Garies, Cape Province	57	30 32S	17 59E
Garigliano R., Italy	20	41 13N	13 44E
Garissa, Kenya	53	0 36S	39 45E
Garkida, Nigeria	52	10 27N	12 36E
Garko, Nigeria	52	10 12N	11 6E
Garko, Nigeria	52	11 45N	8 53E
Garland, U.S.A.	72	41 47N	112 12W
Garmisch Partenkirchen, Germany	14	47 30N	11 6E
Garmsār, Iran	31	35 22N	52 17E
Garner, U.S.A.	70	43 4N	93 35W
Garnett, U.S.A.	71	38 21N	95 17W
Garonne R., France	12	44 45N	0 32W
Garoua, Cameroon	52	9 19N	13 21E
Garraway, Liberia	50	4 35N	8 0W
Garrison, Mont., U.S.A.	72	46 31N	112 50W
Garrison, N.D., U.S.A.	71	31 47N	94 30W
Garrison, Texas, U.S.A.	70	47 37N	101 27W
Garrison Reservoir, U.S.A.	70	47 50N	102 30W
Garrovillas, Spain	17	39 40N	6 33W
Garry L., Canada	60	65 40N	101 20W
Garsen, Kenya	54	2 20S	40 5E
Garson, Canada	62	50 5N	96 50W
Gartok, China	37	31 45N	80 31E
Garu, Niger	52	14 1N	1 40E
Garub, S.W. Africa	57	26 33S	16 0E
Garut, Indonesia	34	7 14S	107 53E
Garvagh, N. Ireland	11	55 0N	6 41W
Garvie Mts., N.Z.	47	45 27S	169 59E
Gary, U.S.A.	68	41 35N	87 20W
Garzon, Colombia	78	2 10N	75 40W
Gasan Kuli, U.S.S.R.	31	37 45N	54 15E
Gasconade R., U.S.A.	68	37 30N	92 20W
Gascone, prov., France	12	43 42N	0 20E
Gascoyne, Mt., W. Australia	44	24 50S	116 35E
Gascoyne R., W. Australia	44	25 15S	114 15E
Gashagar, Nigeria	52	13 23N	12 48E
Gashaka, Nigeria	52	7 20N	11 29E
Gashium Nor, China	37	42 20N	100 40E
Gashua, Nigeria	52	12 54N	11 0E
Gasmata, Terr. of New Guinea	42	6 15S	150 30E
Gaspé, Canada	63	48 52N	64 30W
Gaspé C., Canada	63	48 48N	64 7W
Gaspé Pen., Canada	63	48 45N	65 40W
Gassaway, U.S.A.	68	38 40N	80 45W
Gassol, Nigeria	52	8 34N	10 25E
Gastonia, U.S.A.	69	35 14N	81 5W
Gastre, Argentina	77	42 10S	69 15W
Gata, C. de, Spain	17	36 41N	2 13W
Gataga R., Canada	64	58 25N	123 30W
Gataia, Rumania	21	45 26N	21 30E
Gatchina, U.S.S.R.	23	59 35N	30 0E
Gate City, U.S.A.	68	36 40N	82 38W
Gateshead, England	10	54 57N	1 37W
Gatesville, U.S.A.	71	31 30N	97 46W
Gaths, Rhodesia	56	26 2S	30 30E
Gatineau R., Canada	62	46 20N	76 0W
Gatineau Nat. Park, Canada	62	45 50N	77 0W
Gatooma, Rhodesia	56	18 20S	29 52E
Gatton, Queensland	43	27 32S	152 14E
Gatun, Pan. Can. Zone	74	9 16N	79 55W
Gatun Dam, Pan. Canal	74	9 16N	79 55W
Gatun, L., Panama	74	9 7N	79 56W
Gatun Locks, Pan. Can.	74	9 16N	79 55W
Gaud-i-Zirreh, Afghan.	31	29 45N	62 0E
Gauer L., Canada	65	57 10N	97 30W
Gauhati, India	33	26 5N	91 55E
Gauja R., U.S.S.R.	23	57 0N	24 0E
Gaula, Norway	23	61 22N	5 42E
Gaula R., Norway	23	62 57N	11 0E
Gausta, mt., Norway	23	59 50N	8 27E
Gavarnie, France	12	42 44N	0 0
Gavāter, Iran	31	25 9N	61 23E
Gavellona Toce, Italy	20	45 56N	8 32E
Gavião, R., Brazil	77	14 50S	41 30W
Gavl Fd., Norway	22	69 0N	15 30E
Gävle, Sweden	23	60 41N	17 13E
Gävleborg, prov., Swed.	23	61 35N	61 0E
Gavrilovo, U.S.S.R.	22	69 8N	35 48E
Gawachab, S.W. Africa	57	27 3S	17 50E
Gawilgarh Hills, India	32	21 15N	76 45E
Gawler, S. Australia	43	34 30S	138 42E
Gawler Ranges, S. Australia	45	32 30S	135 45E
Gawu, Nigeria	52	9 14N	6 46E
Gaya, Niger	52	11 58N	3 28E
Gaya, India	33	24 47N	85 4E
Gaya, Nigeria	52	11 57N	9 0E
Gaylord, U.S.A.	68	45 1N	84 39W
Gayndah, Queensland	43	25 35S	151 39E
Gaza (Ghazzah), Egypt	51	31 30N	34 28E
Gazafa, Niger	52	13 30N	9 47E
Gazelle Pen., N. Guin.	42	4 40S	152 0E
Gazi, Kenya	53	4 25S	39 29E
Gaziantep, Turkey	30	37 6N	37 6N
Gbangba, Liberia	52	7 57N	9 31W
Gbekebo, Nigeria	52	6 26N	4 48E
Gboko, Nigeria	52	7 17N	9 4E
Gbongan, Nigeria	52	7 26N	4 18E
Gdansk Poland	16	54 22N	18 40E
Gdansk Bay, Poland	16	54 40N	19 0E
Gdov, U.S.S.R.	25	58 40N	27 55E
Gdynia, Poland	16	54 35N	18 33E
Gea, Israel	29	31 38N	34 37E
Gebe, I., Indonesia	35	0 5N	129 25E
Gebeit Mine, Sudan	51	21 3N	36 29E
Gedaref, Sudan	54	14 2N	35 28E
Gedera, Israel	29	31 49N	34 46E
Gedo, Ethiopia	34	8 59N	37 29E
Gedser, Denmark	14	54 35N	11 55E
Geelong, Victoria	43	38 2S	144 20E
Geelvink B., Indonesia	35	3 0S	135 20E
Geelvink Chan., W. Australia	44	28 30S	114 0E
Geeraardsbergen, Belg.	13	50 45N	3 53E
Geeveston, Tasmania	43	43 7S	146 53E
Geidam, Nigeria	52	12 57N	11 57E
Geikie R., Canada	65	57 20N	104 30W
Geiranger, Norway	23	62 2N	6 32E
Geita, Tanzania	53	2 40S	32 4E
Gela (Terranova), Italy	20	37 5N	14 13E
Gelahun, Liberia	52	7 55N	10 28W
Gelai Mt., Tanzania	53	2 35S	36 7E
Geldermalsen, Neth.	13	51 52N	5 17E
Geldrop, Netherlands	13	51 25N	5 32E
Gelehun, Sierra Leone	52	8 10N	10 30W
Gelendzhik, U.S.S.R.	25	44 33N	38 17E
Gelhak, Sudan	54	11 2N	32 42E
Gelibolu (Gallipoli), Tur.	30	40 28N	26 43E
Gelidonya burun, C., Turkey	30	36 14N	30 24E
Gelitung, Indonesia	35	8 40S	122 15E
Gelsenkirchen, Germany	14	51 30N	7 5E
Gemas, Malaya	34	2 35N	102 36E
Gembloux, Belgium	13	50 34N	4 43E
Gemena, Zaire	54	3 20N	19 40E
Gemerek, Turkey	30	39 11N	36 5E
Gemmi Pass, Switz.	15	46 26N	7 30E
Gendringen, Neth.	13	51 52N	6 21E
General Acha, Arg.	77	37 20S	64 38W
General Alvarado, Arg.	77	38 20S	57 50W
General Alvear, Arg.	77	36 0S	60 0W
General Alvear, Arg.	77	35 0S	67 40W
General Belgrano, Arg.	77	36 0S	58 30W
General Belgrano, Ant.	80	78 50S	38 0W
General Carneiro, Braz.	79	15 40S	52 50W
General Guido, Arg.	77	36 40S	57 50W
General La Madrid, Argentina	77	37 30S	61 10W
General Madariga, Arg.	77	37 0S	57 0W
General Paz, Argentina	77	27 50S	57 45W
General Paz L., Chile	77	44 0S	72 0W
General Pico, Argentina	77	35 45S	63 50W
General Pinedo, Arg.	77	27 15S	61 30W
General Roca, Arg.	77	39 0S	67 40W
General Trias, Mexico	74	28 20N	106 20W
General Villegas, Arg.	77	35 0S	63 0W
Genesee, Idaho, U.S.A.	72	46 31N	116 58W
Genesee, Ill., U.S.A.	70	41 26N	90 11W
Genesee, R., U.S.A.	68	42 30N	78 10W
Geneseo, U.S.A.	70	38 32N	98 7W
Geneva, Switzerland	15	46 12N	6 9E
Geneva, L., Switzerland	15	46 26N	6 30E
Geneva L., U.S.A.	70	42 34N	88 29W
Geneva, Ill., U.S.A.	68	41 55N	88 20W
Geneva, Neb., U.S.A.	70	40 34N	97 35W
Geneva, N.Y., U.S.A.	69	42 53N	77 0W
Geneva, Ohio, U.S.A.	67	41 49N	80 58W
Genichesk, U.S.S.R.	25	46 12N	34 50E
Genil R., Spain	17	37 12N	3 50W
Genk, Belgium	13	50 58N	5 32E
Gennargentu, Monti., It.	20	40 0N	9 20E
Genne, Liberia	52	7 15N	10 42W
Gennep, Netherlands	13	51 41N	5 59E
Genoa (Genova), Italy	20	44 24N	8 57E
Genoa, Ill., U.S.A.	68	42 5N	88 40W
Genoa, Neb., U.S.A.	70	41 30N	97 44W
Genoa, Gulf of, Italy	20	44 0N	9 0E
Genova. *See* Genoa	20		
Gent, Belgium	13	51 4N	3 44E
Genteng, Indonesia	34	7 22S	106 22E
Geographe B., W. Australia	44	33 30S	115 15E
Geographe Chan., W. Australia	44	24 30S	113 0E
George, Cape Province	57	33 58S	22 29E
George L., N.S.W.	43	35 10S	149 25E
George L., Uganda	54	0 5N	30 20E
George L., Fla., U.S.A.	67	29 15N	81 35W
George L., N.Y., U.S.A.	69	43 40N	73 30W
George R., Canada	61	58 40N	66 0W
George Sd., N.Z.	47	44 50S	167 24E
George V. Coast, Ant.	80	67 0S	148 0E
George West, U.S.A.	71	28 18N	98 6W
Georgetown, Australia	42	18 17S	143 33E
Georgetown, Guyana	79	6 50N	58 12W
Georgetown, Ont., Can.	62	43 40N	80 0W
Georgetown, Canada	63	46 13N	62 24W
Georgetown, Gambia	52	13 30N	14 47W
Georgetown, Malaya	34	5 25N	100 19E
Georgetown, Colorado, U.S.A.	73	39 47N	105 42W
Georgetown, Delaware, U.S.A.	69	38 44N	75 22W
Georgetown, Kentucky, U.S.A.	68	38 12N	84 35W
Georgetown, Ohio, U.S.A.	68	38 50N	83 50W
Georgetown, Texas, U.S.A.	71	30 36N	97 42W
Georgia, S.S.R., U.S.S.R.	24	41 0N	45 0E
Georgia, st., U.S.A.	69	32 0N	82 0W
Georgian B., Canada	62	45 20N	81 0W
Georgievsk, U.S.S.R.	25	44 12N	43 28E
Georgina R., Queens.	42	20 15S	138 0E
Gera, Germany	14	50 53N	12 5E
Geral, Serra, Brazil	77	28 30S	51 0W
Geral de Goias, Serra, Brazil	79	13 0S	46 25W
Geraldine, New Zealand	47	44 5S	171 15E
Geraldine, U.S.A.	72	47 40N	110 15W
Geraldton, W. Austral.	44	28 48S	114 32E
Gerardmer, France	12	48 3N	6 50E
Gerede, Turkey	30	40 48N	32 12E
Gering, U.S.A.	70	41 54N	103 42W
Gerizim Mt., Jordan	29	32 13N	35 15E
Gerlach, U.S.A.	72	40 38N	119 25W
Gerlogubi, Ethiopia	49	6 53N	45 3E
Germansen Landing, Canada	64	55 43N	124 40W
Germany, st., Europe	14	51 0N	10 0E
Germiston, Transvaal	57	26 11S	28 10E
Gerona, Spain	17	41 58N	2 46E
Gerpir C., Iceland	22	65 6N	13 32W
Gerrard, Canada	64	50 30N	117 20W
Gersau, Switzerland	15	47 0N	8 32E
Gerufa, Botswana	56	19 10N	26 0E
Géryville, Algeria	50	33 40N	0 55E
Geser, Indonesia	35	3 50N	130 35E
Gesthsémani, Canada	63	50 17N	60 28W
Getafe, Spain	17	40 21N	3 42W
Gettysburg, Pa., U.S.A.	68	39 47N	77 18W
Gettysburg, S.D., U.S.A.	70	45 4N	99 58W
Gety, Congo	53	1 10N	30 7E
Gevaudan, dist., Fr.	12	44 40N	3 40E
Geyser, Iceland	22	64 19N	20 19W
Geyser, U.S.A.	72	47 17N	110 30W
Gezer (site), Israel	29	31 51N	34 51E
Ghadames, Libya	51	30 11N	9 5E
Ghaghra (Gogra), R., India	33	26 30N	83 0E
Ghail, Saudi Arabia	30	21 40N	46 20E
Ghana, st., Africa	52	6 0N	1 0W
Ghazipur, India	33	25 38N	83 35E
Ghar R., Jordan	29	31 31N	35 17E
Ghardaia, Algeria	50	32 31N	3 37E
Gharyan, Libya	51	32 10N	13 0E
Ghat, Libya	51	24 55N	10 20E
Ghat, Saudi Arabia	30	26 0N	45 6E
Ghat Ghat, Saudi Arabia	30	24 26N	46 15E
Ghazal, B. el, Chad	54	15 0N	17 0E
Ghazaouet, Algeria	50	35 0N	2 0W
Ghaziabad, India	32	28 39N	77 26E
Ghazni, Afghanistan	31	33 30N	68 17E
Ghazza W., Israel	29	31 22N	34 27E
Ghazzah. *See* Gaza, Egypt.	51		
Ghent (Gent), Flanders	13	51 4N	3 43E
Gheorgheni, Rumania	21	46 43N	25 41E
Gherla, Rumania	21	47 0N	23 57E
Ghisonaccia, France	12	42 1N	9 26E
Ghivemba, Angola	55	15 48S	14 8E
Ghorat, Afghanistan	32	34 29N	65 10E
Ghorat, prov., Afg.	32	34 45N	65 5E
Ghost River, Canada	62	51 25N	83 20W
Ghotki, Pakistan	32	28 5N	69 30E
Ghugus, India	32	20 0N	79 0E
Ghurian, Afghanistan	31	34 17N	61 25E
Giannutri, I. di, Italy	20	42 15N	11 6E
Giant Mts. *See* Riesen G., Poland	16		
Giant's Castle, Mt., Natal	57	29 20S	29 30E
Giant's Causeway, N. Ireland	11	55 15N	6 30W
Giarabub (Jaghbub), Libya	51	29 42N	24 38E
Giari, Nigeria	52	11 52N	13 16E
Giarre, Italy	20	37 44N	15 10E
Giaveno, Italy	20	45 3N	7 20E
Gibara, Cuba	75	21 0N	76 20W
Gibbon, U.S.A.	70	40 36N	98 47W
Gibeon, S.W. Africa	57	25 8S	17 50E
Gibihi, Australia	42	24 38S	149 59E
Gibraltar, Europe	50	36 7N	5 22W
Gibraltar, Str. of, Mediterranean Sea	50	35 55N	5 40W
Gibson City, U.S.A.	68	40 22N	88 20W
Gibson Desert, W. Australia	45	24 0S	125 0E
Gibsons Landing, Can.	64	49 25N	123 40W
Giddings, U.S.A.	71	30 9N	96 58W

	MAP		
Gien, France	12	47 40N	2 36 E
Giessen, Germany	14	50 34N	8 40 E
Gifu, Japan	36	35 30N	136 45 E
Gigane, Nigeria	52	13 30N	5 15 E
Giglio I., Italy	20	42 20N	10 52 E
Gijón, Spain	17	43 32N	5 42W
Gil I., Canada	64	53 10N	129 15W
Gila R., U.S.A.	33	33 0N	113 30W
Gila Bend, U.S.A.	73	33 0N	112 46W
Gila Bend Mts., U.S.A.	73	33 15N	113 0W
Gilau, New Guinea	42	5 30S	149 3 E
Gilbedi, Nigeria	52	13 36N	5 46 E
Gilbert R., Queensland	42	17 10S	141 45 E
Gilbert Mt., Canada	64	50 50N	124 15W
Gilbert Plains, Canada	65	51 9N	100 28W
Gilbert Is., Pac. Ocean	5	1 0S	176 0 E
Gilberton, Queensland	42	19 16S	143 35 E
Gilboa, Israel	29	32 31N	35 25 E
Gilboa Mt., Israel	29	32 31N	35 24 E
Giles L., W. Australia	44	29 39S	119 43 E
Gilford, N. Ireland	11	54 23N	6 20W
Gilford I., Canada	64	50 40N	126 30W
Gilgandra, N.S.W.	43	31 38S	148 35 E
Gilgil, Kenya	53	0 29S	36 16 E
Gilgit, Kashmir	32	35 50N	74 15 E
Gilgunnia, N.S.W.	43	32 24S	145 59 E
Gilgulgul, Queensland	43	26 26S	150 0 E
Gilima, Zaire	53	3 51N	28 51 E
Gillam, Canada	65	56 20N	94 40W
Gilles, L., S. Australia	45	32 45S	136 53 E
Gillespie Pt., N.Z.	47	43 24S	169 49 E
Gillette, U.S.A.	70	44 19N	105 30W
Gilliat, Queensland	42	20 40S	141 28 E
Gilliat R., Queensland	42	21 0S	141 30 E
Gilmer, U.S.A.	71	32 45N	94 59W
Gilmour, Canada	62	44 48N	77 37W
Gilroy, U.S.A.	73	37 5N	121 36W
Gilsbakki, Iceland	22	64 44N	21 3W
Gimbi, Ethiopia	54	9 3N	35 42 E
Gimli, Canada	65	50 40N	97 10W
Gimzo, Israel	29	31 56N	34 56 E
Gin Gin, Queensland	43	25 0S	152 0 E
Giner, Ethiopia	49	7 12N	40 40 E
Gingin, W. Australia	44	31 22S	115 37 E
Gingindhlovu, Natal	57	29 0S	31 36 E
Ginzo, Spain	17	42 3N	7 47W
Gioia, Italy	20	40 49N	16 55 E
Giona, mt., Greece	21	38 42N	22 30 E
Giovi, P. de, Italy	20	44 30N	8 55 E
Gi-Paraná R., Brazil	78	8 30S	62 30W
Gippsland, Australia	43	37 45S	147 15 E
Giralia, W. Australia	44	22 31S	114 15 E
Girard, U.S.A.	71	37 31N	94 52W
Girardot, Colombia	78	4 20N	74 55W
Giresun, Turkey	30	40 58N	38 19 E
Giridih, India	33	24 10N	86 21 E
Giriftu, Kenya	53	1 52N	39 50 E
Girishk, Afghanistan	31	31 47N	64 24 E
Giro, Congo	53	3 10N	28 55 E
Giro, Nigeria	52	11 7N	4 42 E
Gironde, R., France	12	45 30N	1 0W
Girvan, Ayr, Scotland	10	55 15N	4 50W
Gisborne, New Zealand	46	38 39S	178 5 E
Gisenyi, Rwanda	53	1 41S	29 30 E
Gisors, France	12	49 15N	1 40 E
Guilianova, Italy	20	42 45N	13 58 E
Giurgin ,Rumania	21	43 52N	25 57 E
Giv'at Brenner, Israel	29	31 52N	34 47 E
Giv'atayim, Israel	29	32 3N	34 48 E
Givors, France	12	45 35N	4 45 E
Giza, see Al Jīzah, Egypt	51		
Gizhiga, U.S.S.R.	27	62 0N	150 27 E
Gizhiga G., U.S.S.R.	27	61 0N	158 0 E
Gizycko, Poland	16	54 2N	21 48 E
Gjinokastër, Albania	21	40 7N	20 16 E
Gjövik, Norway	23	60 47N	10 43 E
Glace Bay, Canada	63	46 11N	59 58W
Glacier, Canada	64	51 20N	117 40W
Glacier B., Alaska	64	58 40N	136 10W
Glacier Bay National Monument, Alaska	64	58 50N	136 30W
Glacier National Park, Canada	64	51 40N	118 0W
Glacier National Park, U.S.A.	72	48 50N	113 40W
Glacier Peak, U.S.A.	72	48 4N	121 2W
Gladewater, U.S.A.	71	32 32N	94 58W
Gladsheim Pk., mt., Canada	64	49 40N	117 35W
Gladstone, Canada	65	50 20N	99 0W
Gladstone, N.S.W.	43	31 0S	153 0 E
Gladstone, Otago, N.Z.	47	44 36S	169 20 E
Gladstone, Queensland	42	23 52S	151 16 E
Gladstone, S. Australia	43	33 15S	138 16 E
Gladstone, Tasmania	43	40 56S	148 0 E
Gladstone, U.S.A.	70	45 52N	87 1W
Gladstone, W. Austral.	44	25 53S	114 30 E
Gladwin, U.S.A.	68	43 59N	84 29W
Gladys L., Canada	64	59 50N	132 52W
Gláma, mt., Iceland	22	65 48N	22 58W
Glama R., Norway	23	60 30N	12 8 E
Glåmfjord, Norway	22	66 45N	14 0 E
Glan, Philippines	35	5 45N	125 20 E
Glärnisch, mt., Switz.	15	47 1N	9 0 E
Glarus, Switzerland	15	47 3N	9 4 E
Glarus, can., Switz.	15	47 2N	9 5 E
Glasco, U.S.A.	70	39 25N	97 21W
Glasgow, Scotland	10	55 52N	4 14W
Glasgow, Ky., U.S.A.	69	37 0N	85 55W
Glasgow, Mont., U.S.A.	72	48 10N	106 39W
Glasslough, Ireland	11	54 20N	6 53W
Glauchau, Germany	14	50 50N	12 33 E
Glazov, U.S.S.R.	24	58 0N	52 30 E
Gleichen, Canada	64	50 50N	113 0W
Glen Afton, N.Z.	46	37 46N	175 4 E
Glen Canyon Dam, U.S.A.	73	37 0N	111 12W
Glen Falls, U.S.A.	68	43 20N	73 40W
Glen Florrie, W. Australia	44	22 55S	115 59 E
Glen Innes, N.S.W.	43	29 40S	151 39 E
Glen More, Scotland	10	57 10N	4 50W
Glen Massey, N.Z.	46	37 41S	175 3 E
Glen Ullin, U.S.A.	70	46 50N	101 49W
Glenarm, N. Ireland	11	54 58N	5 58W
Glenavy, New Zealand	47	44 54S	171 7 E
Glencoe, Natal	57	28 11S	30 11 E
Glencoe, S. Australia	43	37 43S	140 31 E
Glencoe, U.S.A.	70	44 45N	94 8W
Glendale, Canada	62	46 45N	84 2W
Glendale, Rhodesia	56	17 16S	31 0 E
Glendale, Ariz., U.S.A.	73	33 35N	112 13W
Glendale, Calif., U.S.A.	73	34 12N	118 15W
Glendale, Ore., U.S.A.	72	42 45N	123 30W
Glendive, U.S.A.	70	47 0N	105 0W
Glendo, U.S.A.	70	42 35N	105 2W
Glenealy, Ireland	11	52 59N	6 10W
Glenelg, S. Australia	43	34 58S	138 30 E
Glenelg, R., Victoria	43	37 10S	141 30 E
Glengarriff, Ireland	11	51 45N	9 33W
Glenham, New Zealand	47	46 26S	168 52 E
Glenhaughton, Queens.	43	25 25S	149 18 E
Glenhope, N.Z.	47	41 40S	172 39 E
Glenmary, Mt., N Z.	47	43 59S	169 54 E
Glenmora, U.S.A.	71	31 0N	92 32W
Glenmorgan, Queens.	43	37 15S	149 30 E
Glennamaddy, Ireland	11	53 37N	8 33W
Glenns Ferry, U.S.A.	72	43 0N	115 19W
Glenorchy, N.Z.	47	44 51S	168 24 E
Glenorchy, Tasmania	43	42 51S	147 11 E
Glenore, Queensland	42	17 50S	141 12 E
Glenreagh, N.S.W.	43	30 2S	153 1 E
Glenties, Ireland	11	54 48N	8 18W
Glenville, Ireland	11	52 3N	8 27W
Glenville, U.S.A.	68	38 56N	80 50W
Glenwood, Canada	63	49 0N	54 56W
Glenwood, Ark., U.S.A.	71	34 18N	93 32W
Glenwood, Iowa, U.S.A.	70	41 7N	95 43W
Glenwood, Minn., U.S.A.	70	45 40N	95 26W
Glenwood Springs, U.S.A.	73	39 32N	107 15W
Gletsch, Switzerland	15	46 33N	8 22 E
Glettinganes, C., Ice.	22	65 30N	13 30W
Glidden, U.S.A.	65	46 10N	90 32W
Glin, Ireland	11	52 34N	9 17W
Gliwice (Gleiwitz), Pol.	16	50 22N	18 41 E
Globe, U.S.A.	73	33 22N	110 40W
Glogów, Poland	16	51 37N	16 5 E
Glotovo, U.S.S.R.	24	63 40N	49 30 E
Gloucester, England	10	51 52N	2 15W
Gloucester, N.S.W.	43	32 0S	151 59 E
Gloucester, U.S.A.	69	42 38N	70 39W
Gloucester, C., Terr. of New Guinea	42	5 30S	148 20 E
Gloucester I., Queens.	42	20 0S	148 30 E
Gloversville, U.S.A.	68	43 5N	74 18W
Glovertown, Canada	63	48 40N	54 3W
Gluboki, U.S.S.R.	25	48 35N	40 25 E
Glubokoye, U.S.S.R.	25	55 10N	27 45 E
Glückstadt, Germany	14	53 46N	9 28 E
Glukhov, U.S.S.R.	25	51 40N	33 50 E
Gmünd, Carinthia, Aust.	14	46 54N	13 31 E
Gmünd, Lower Austria	14	48 45N	15 0 E
Gmunden, Austria	14	47 55N	13 48 E
Gniew, Poland	16	53 50N	18 50 E
Gniezno (Gnesen), Pol.	16	52 33N	17 39 E
Gnowangerup, W. Australia	44	33 58S	117 59 E
Goa, India	32	15 33N	73 59 E
Goageb, S.W. Africa	57	26 45S	17 11 E
Goabeb R., S.W. Africa	57	27 45S	17 20 E
Goalpara, India	33	26 11N	90 40 E
Goaso, Ghana	52	6 48N	2 30W
Goba, Ethiopia	54	7 1S	40 0 E
Goba, Mozambique	57	26 10S	32 13 E
Gobabis, S.W. Africa	57	22 16S	19 0 E
Gobbo, Ethiopia	53	4 40N	39 40 E
Gobi (Shamo) Desert, Mongolia	65	43 40N	109 0 E
Gobokonkwane, Botswana	56	19 30S	25 40 E
Gochas, S.W. Africa	57	24 55S	18 55 E
Gocong, Vietnam	34	10 20N	107 0 E
Godavari Point, India	33	17 0N	82 20 E
Godavari R., India	32	19 5N	79 0 E
Godbout, Canada	63	49 20N	67 38W
Godda, India	33	24 50N	87 20 E
Goddard, Alaska	64	57 0N	135 30W
Goddard Cr., W. Australia	45	31 12S	123 40 E
Goderich, Canada	62	43 45N	81 41W
Godhra, India	32	22 49N	73 40 E
Godob, Somali Rep.	53	1 0S	41 55 E
Gödöllö, Hungary	16	47 35N	19 23 E
Gods L., Canada	62	54 40N	94 10W
Godthaab, Greenland	61	64 15N	51 0W
Goeland L., Canada	62	49 50N	76 40W
Goeree I., Netherlands	13	51 50N	4 0 E
Goes, Netherlands	13	51 30N	3 55 E
Gogama, Canada	62	47 35N	81 35W
Gogebic L., U.S.A.	70	46 30N	89 30W
Gogra, R., *see* Ghaghra	33		
Gogrial, Sudan	54	8 30N	28 0 E
Goiania, Brazil	79	16 35S	49 20W
Goias, Brazil	79	15 55S	50 10W
Goias, st., Brazil	79	12 10S	48 0W
Gojra, Pakistan	32	31 10N	72 40 E
Goksu R., Turkey	30	36 55N	33 0 E
Gokteik, Burma	33	22 26N	97 0 E
Gokwe, Rhodesia	56	18 2S	28 47 E
Gol, Norway	23	60 43N	8 56 E
Golconda, U.S.A.	72	40 57N	117 30W
Gold Beach, U.S.A.	72	42 27N	124 27W
Gold Creek, Alaska	59	62 45N	149 44W
Gold Hill, U.S.A.	72	42 29N	123 4W
Goldap, Poland	23	54 19N	22 19 E
Golden, Canada	64	51 20N	117 0W
Golden, Ireland	11	52 30N	8 0W
Golden, U.S.A.	70	39 49N	105 13W
Golden Bay, N.Z.	47	40 40S	172 50 E
Golden Gate, U.S.A.	73	37 40N	122 33W
Golden Prairie, Canada	65	50 13N	109 37W
Golden Ridge, W. Australia	44	30 50S	121 37 E
Golden Vale, Ireland	11	52 33N	8 17W
Goldendale, U.S.A.	72	45 50N	120 45W
Goldfield, U.S.A.	73	37 45N	117 0W
Goldfields, Canada	65	59 28N	108 31W
Goldpines, Canada	65	50 45N	93 5W
Goldsand L., Canada	65	57 0N	101 10W
Goldsboro, U.S.A.	69	35 20N	78 0W
Goldsmith, U.S.A.	71	31 58N	102 43W
Goldthwaite. U.S.A.	71	31 27N	98 30W
Goleniów, Poland	16	53 35N	14 50 E
Golfito, Costa Rica	75	8 41N	83 5W
Goliad, U.S.A.	71	28 41N	97 21W
Gollel, Swaziland	57	27 20S	31 55 E
Golmo, China	37	36 30N	95 10 E
Golosa, Peña, Spain	17	40 15N	0 19W
Golpayegan, Iran	30	33 22N	50 13 E
Goma, Zaire	54	1 40S	29 42 E
Gombari, Zaire	53	2 55N	28 56 E
Gombe, Nigeria	52	10 19N	11 2 E
Gombi, Nigeria	52	10 12N	12 45 E
Gomel, U.S.S.R.	25	52 28N	31 0 E
Gomera Is., Canary Is.	50	28 10N	17 5W
Gomez Palacio, Mexico	74	25 40N	104 40W
Gomoh, India	33	23 50N	86 15 E
Gonaïves, Haiti	75	19 20N	72 50W
Gonaïves, G. of, Haiti	75	19 29N	72 42W
Gonâve I., Haiti	75	18 40N	73 20W
Gonda, India	33	27 9N	81 58 E
Gondab-e kāvus, Iran	31	37 23N	55 20 E
Gondal, India	32	21 51N	70 52 E
Gonder, Ethiopia	54	12 32N	37 30 E
Gondia, India	32	21 30N	80 10 E
Gondola, Mozambique	56	19 2S	33 42 E
Gongola R., Nigeria	52	10 30N	10 22 E
Gongolgon, N.S.W.	43	30 22S	146 50 E
Goniri, Nigeria	52	11 28N	12 21 E
Gonja, Tanzania	53	4 15S	38 0 E
Gonye Falls, Zambia	56	16 38S	23 38 E
Gonzales, Calif., U.S.A.	73	36 31N	121 29W
Gonzales, Tex., U.S.A.	71	29 31N	97 28W
Good Hope, C. of, Cape Province	57	34 24S	18 30 E
Goodenough, I., Papua	42	9 20S	150 20 E
Gooderham, Canada	62	44 54N	78 21W
Goodeve, Canada	65	51 10N	103 10W
Goodhouse, C. Prov.	57	28 57S	18 13 E
Gooding, U.S.A.	72	43 0N	114 46W
Goodland, U.S.A.	70	39 15N	101 50W
Goodna, Queensland	43	27 38S	152 54 E
Goodnight, U.S.A.	71	35 1N	101 12W
Goodooga, N.S.W.	43	29 5S	147 25 E
Goodsir, Mt., Canada	64	51 10N	116 29W
Goodsoil, Canada	65	54 24N	109 12W
Goodsprings, U.S.A.	73	35 50N	115 29W
Goolwa, S. Australia	43	35 25S	138 52 E
Goomalling, W. Austral.	44	31 15S	116 42 E
Goombalie, N.S.W.	43	29 59S	145 26 E
Goomburra, Queens.	43	28 1S	152 8 E
Goomeri, Queensland	43	26 15S	152 6 E
Goondna, Mozambique	56	19 45S	33 49 E
Goondiwindi, Queens.	43	28 30S	150 21 E
Goondoon, Queensland	42	24 57S	151 7 E
Goondublui, N.S.W.	43	29 11S	148 31 E
Goongarrie, W. Austral.	44	30 12S	121 3 E
Goor, Netherlands	13	52 13N	6 33 E
Goose L., U.S.A.	72	41 0N	120 25W
Goose, R., Alberta, Can.	64	54 50N	117 0W
Goose, R., Quebec, Can.	63	53 30N	61 30W
Goose Bay, Canada	63	53 15N	60 20W
Goothinga, Queensland	42	17 36S	140 50 E
Gop, India	32	22 5N	69 50 E
Göppingen, Germany	14	48 42N	9 40 E
Gora, Niger	52	13 55N	6 30 E
Gorakhpur, India	33	26 47N	83 32 E
Gorda, Pta, Nicaragua	75	14 10N	83 10W
Gordon, U.S.A.	70	42 52N	102 6W
Gordon L., Alberta, Canada	65	56 35N	110 40W
Gordon L., N.W. Terr., Canada	64	63 0N	113 50W
Gordon R., Tasmania	43	42 30S	145 40 E
Gordonvale, Queens.	42	17 5S	145 50 E
Gore, Ethiopia	54	8 12N	35 32 E
Goré, Chad	54	7 59N	16 49 E
Gore, New Zealand	47	46 5S	168 58 E
Gore Bay, Canada	62	45 57N	82 20W
Goresbridge, Ireland	11	52 38N	7 0W
Gorey, Ireland	11	52 41N	6 18W
Gorgān, Iran	31	36 57N	54 26 E
Gorge, The, Ra., Queensland	42	18 27S	145 30 E
Gorgona I., Colombia	78	3 0N	78 10W
Gorgona I., Italy	20	43 27N	9 52 E
Gorgoram, Nigeria	52	12 40N	10 39 E
Gori R., Kenya	53	1 5S	34 45 E
Gorinchem, Netherlands	13	51 50N	4 59 E
Goris, U.S.S.R.	24	39 30N	46 5 E
Gorizia, Italy	20	45 56N	13 37 E
Gorkiy, U.S.S.R.	25	56 20N	44 0 E
Gorki, U.S.S.R.	25	54 12N	31 5 E
Gorki Res., U.S.S.R.	25	57 50N	43 50 E
Gorlice, Poland	16	49 35N	21 11 E
Görlitz, Germany	16	51 10N	14 59 E
Gorlovka, U.S.S.R.	25	48 25N	37 58 E
Gorman, U.S.A.	71	32 12N	98 44W
Gormanston, Ireland	11	53 38N	6 12W
Gorna Dzhumaya. *See* Blagoyevgad, Bulg.	21		
Gorna Oryakhovista, Bulgaria	21	43 8N	25 43 E
Gorno Filinskoye, U.S.S.R.	26	60 5N	70 0 E
Gorodets, U.S.S.R.	25	56 38N	43 28 E
Gorodok, U.S.S.R.	25	55 30N	30 3 E
Goroka, Terr. of N. Gui.	42	5 50S	145 30 E
Goromonzi, S. Rhod.	56	17 52S	31 22 E
Gorong I., Indonesia	35	4 5S	131 15 E
Gorongosa. Serra da, Mozambique	56	18 30S	34 0 E
Gorongose R., Mozam.	56	20 40S	34 30 E
Gorontalo, Indonesia	35	0 35N	123 13 E
Goronyo, Nigeria	52	13 29N	5 39 E
Gort, Ireland	11	53 4N	8 50W
Gorzów, Poland	16	51 1N	18 21 E
Göschenen, Switz.	15	46 41N	8 35 E
Gosford, N.S.W.	43	33 23S	151 18 E
Goshen, U.S.A.	68	41 36N	85 50W
Goshen, dist., C. Prov.	57	25 50S	25 0 E
Goslar, Germany	14	51 55N	10 23 E
Gospic, Yugoslavia	20	44 35N	15 23 E
Gossau, Switzerland	15	47 24N	9 14 E
Gosse, R., N. Terr.	45	19 55S	134 35 E
Gostivar, Yugoslavia	21	41 48N	20 57 E
Gostyń, Poland	16	51 50N	17 3 E
Göta Canal, Sweden	23	58 45N	14 15 E
Gotaland, reg., Sweden	23	58 5N	14 0 E
Gote, Zaire	53	2 15N	30 46 E
Göteborg, Sweden	23	57 43N	11 59 E
Göteborg and Bohus, prov., Sweden	23	58 25N	11 45 E
Gotel, Mts., Nigeria	52	7 10N	12 50 E
Gotha, Germany	14	50 56N	10 42 E
Gothenburg, U.S.A.	70	40 59N	100 5W
Gotland I., Sweden	23	58 15N	18 30 E
Goto Is., Japan	36	32 55N	129 10 E
Gotowasi, Indonesia	35	0 40N	128 30 E
Gotska Sandon I., Swed.	23	58 24N	19 15 E
Gott Pt., mt., Canada	64	50 18N	122 16W
Gottingen, Germany	14	51 31N	9 55 E
Gottwaldov, C.Slov.	16	49 10N	17 40 E
Goubone, Chad	51	20 45N	17 10 E
Gouda, Netherlands	13	52 1N	4 42 E
Goudoumarlia, Niger	52	13 40N	11 10 E
Goudreau, Canada	62	48 20N	84 30W
Gouin Res., Canada	62	48 35N	74 40W
Goulburn, Australia	43	34 45S	149 43 E
Goulburn R., Victoria	43	36 30S	145 20 E
Gould, Mt., Australia	44	25 46S	117 18 E
Goumenissa, Greece	21	40 56N	22 27 E
Goundam, Mali	50	16 25N	3 45W
Gourdon. France	12	44 44N	1 23 E
Gouré, Niger	52	14 0N	10 10 E
Gourits R., C. Prov.	57	34 15S	21 45 E
Gourma-Rarous, Mali	50	16 55N	2 5W
Gournay, France	12	49 29N	1 41 E
Gouro, Chad	51	19 30N	19 30 E
Gourock Ra., N.S.W.	43	36 0S	149 25 E
Gouverneur, U.S.A.	68	44 18N	75 30W
Govan, Canada	65	51 20N	105 0W
Govenlock, Canada	65	49 15N	109 50W
Gowan Ra., Queensland	42	24 50S	144 50 E
Gowanda, U.S.A.	68	42 29N	78 58W
Gowna, L., Ireland	11	53 52N	7 35W
Gowran, Ireland	11	52 38N	7 5W
Goya, Argentina	77	29 10S	59 10W
Goyllarisquisga, Peru	78	10 19S	76 31W
Goz Beida, Chad	51	12 20N	21 30 E
Gozo I., Malta	18	36 0N	14 13 E
Graaff-Reinet, C. Prov.	57	32 13S	24 32 E
Grabo, Ivory Coast	50	4 55N	7 25W
Gračac, Yugoslavia	20	44 18N	15 57 E
Grace, U.S.A.	72	42 32N	111 45W
Grace, L., W. Austral.	44	33 15S	118 15 E
Gracemere, Queensland	42	23 25S	150 29 E
Graceville, U.S.A.	70	45 36N	96 26W

MAP

Gracias à Dios, C., Central America 75 15 0N 83 20W
Gradaus, Serra dos, Brazil 79 8 0S 50 30W
Grădiste, Rumania 21 45 37N 23 11E
Grado, Spain 17 43 23N 6 6W
Grady, U.S.A. 71 34 47N 103 15W
Grænalón L., Iceland 22 64 10N 17 15W
Grafton, Australia 43 29 35S 153 0E
Grafton, U.S.A. 70 48 28N 97 25W
Grafton Ra., Queens. 43 26 15S 149 30E
Graham, Canada 62 49 20N 90 30W
Graham, U.S.A. 71 33 7N 98 34W
Graham I., Canada 64 53 40N 132 30W
Graham R., Canada 64 56 40N 123 15W
Graham Land, Ant. 80 67 0S 65 0W
Graham Bell, I., U.S.S.R. 26 80 50N 63 0E
Grahamdale, Canada 65 51 30N 98 34W
Grahamstown, C. Prov. 57 33 19S 26 31E
Grajaú, Brazil 79 5 50S 46 30W
Grajewo, Poland 16 53 39N 22 30E
Grampian Mts., Scot. 10 56 50N 4 0W
Gran Canaria, Canary Islands 50 27 55N 15 35W
Gran Paradiso, mt., It. 20 45 32N 7 15E
Gran Sasso, mt., Italy 20 42 25N 13 30E
Granada, Colombia 78 9 55N 74 35W
Granada, Nicaragua 75 11 58N 86 0W
Granada, Spain 17 37 10N 3 35W
Granada, U.S.A. 71 38 5N 102 17W
Granada, prov., Spain 17 37 0N 3 0W
Granard, Ireland 11 53 47N 7 30W
Granbury, U.S.A. 71 32 29N 97 50W
Granby, Canada 62 45 25N 72 45W
Grand L., Lab., Canada 63 53 40N 60 40W
Grand L., N.B., Canada 63 45 57N 66 7W
Grand L., Newf., Can. 63 48 45N 57 45W
Grand R., Michigan, U.S.A. 68 43 0N 85 30W
Grand R., Mo., U.S.A. 70 39 40N 93 22W
Grand R., S.D., U.S.A. 70 45 50N 101 0W
Grand Bahama I., Bahama Is. 75 26 5N 78 0W
Grand Bank, Canada 63 47 15N 56 0W
Grand Bassam, Ivory Coast 50 5 10N 3 49W
Grand Batanga, Cam. 52 2 50N 9 55E
Grand Blanc, U.S.A. 52 42 55N 83 39W
Grand Bourg, W. Indies 75 15 50N 61 20W
Grand Canal, China 38 35 0N 117 0E
Grand Canyon, U.S.A. 73 36 20N 113 30W
Grand Canyon Nat. Monument, U.S.A. 73 36 15N 113 30W
Grand Cayman I., W. Indies 75 19 20N 81 20W
Grand Coulee, U.S.A. 72 47 58N 119 0W
Grand Coulee Dam, U.S.A. 72 48 1N 118 58W
Grand Falls, N.B., Can. 63 47 2N 67 46W
Grand Falls, Newf., Can. 63 49 0N 55 43W
Grand Forks, Canada 64 49 0N 118 30W
Grand Forks, U.S.A. 70 48 0N 97 0W
Grand Haven, U.S.A. 68 43 2N 86 15W
Grand Island, U.S.A. 70 40 55N 98 19W
Grand Isle, U.S.A. 71 29 14N 89 59W
Grand L. Victoria, Can. 62 47 35N 77 35W
Grand Lahou, Ivory Coast 50 5 10N 5 0W
Grand Manan I., Can. 63 44 45N 66 52W
Grand Marais, U.S.A. 70 47 47N 90 26W
Grand Mère, Canada 62 46 36N 72 40W
Grand Popo, Dahomey 52 6 15N 1 44E
Grand Rapids, Mich., U.S.A. 68 42 55N 85 40W
Grand Rapids, Minn. U.S.A. 70 47 19N 93 29W
Grand Ruisseau Canada 63 47 24N 61 52W
Grand Valley U.S.A. 73 39 30N 108 1W
Grand View, Canada 65 51 11N 100 51W
Grande Baie, Canada 63 48 19N 70 52W
Grande B., Argentina 77 50 30S 68 20W
Grande R., Argentina 77 36 0S 69 30W
Grande R., Bolivia 78 15 35S 64 0W
Grande R., Bahia, Brazil 79 11 30S 44 30W
Grande R., Minas Gerais, Brazil 79 20 0S 50 0W
Grande, Serra, Brazil 79 5 0S 41 30W
Grande Prairie, Canada 64 55 15N 118 50W
Grande Rivière, Can. 63 48 26N 64 30W
Grande Terre, dist., Leeward Islands 75 Inset
Grande Vallée, Canada 63 49 13N 65 5W
Grandes Bergeronnes, Canada 63 48 16N 69 35W
Grandfalls, U.S.A. 71 31 17N 102 56W
Grandola, Portugal 17 38 12N 8 35W
Grandson, Switzerland 15 46 49N 6 39E
Grandview, U.S.A. 72 46 15N 119 58W
Granger, Wash., U.S.A. 72 46 21N 120 9W
Granger, Wyo., U.S.A. 72 41 38N 109 59W
Grängeberg, Sweden 23 60 6N 15 0E
Grangeville, U.S.A. 72 46 0N 116 10W
Granite City, U.S.A. 70 38 40N 90 15W
Granite Falls, U.S.A. 70 44 47N 95 32W
Granite Peak, U.S.A. 72 45 3N 109 45W
Granity, New Zealand 47 41 39S 171 51E
Granja, Brazil 79 3 17S 40 50W
Granna, Sweden 23 58 0N 14 33E
Granollers, Spain 17 41 39N 2 18E
Grant, U.S.A. 70 40 50N 101 50W
Grant B., Tanzania 53 2 0S 33 12E
Grant Ld., Canada 58 82 0N 80 0W
Grant, mt., Nev., U.S.A. 72 39 40N 117 50W
Grant, mt., Nev., U.S.A. 73 38 42N 118 50W
Grant Ra., U.S.A. 73 38 30N 115 30W
Grant City, U.S.A. 70 40 29N 94 28W
Grant Duff Ra., Austral. 44 27 16S 122 0E
Grantham, England 10 52 55N 0 39W
Grants, U.S.A. 73 35 12N 107 55W
Grant's Pass, U.S.A. 72 42 30N 123 15W
Grantsburg, U.S.A. 70 45 45N 92 13W
Grantsville, U.S.A. 72 40 36N 112 30W
Granville, France 12 48 50N 1 35W
Granville, N.Y., U.S.A. 68 43 25N 73 18W
Granville, N.D., U.S.A. 70 48 20N 100 47W
Granville L., Canada 65 56 20N 100 35W
Grão Mogol, Brazil 79 16 25S 42 35W
Grapeland, U.S.A. 71 31 29N 95 28W
Graskop, Transvaal 57 24 56S 30 49E
Grass R., Canada 65 55 18N 98 10W
Grass Range, U.S.A. 72 46 59N 108 59W
Grass Valley, Calif., U.S.A. 72 39 0N 121 0W
Grass Valley, Ore., U.S.A. 72 45 21N 120 47W
Grasse, France 12 43 38N 6 56E
Grate's Cove, Canada 63 48 8N 53 0W
Graubünden (Grisons), canton, Switzerland 15 46 45N 9 30E
Graulhet, France 12 43 45N 1 58E
Gravelbourg, Canada 65 49 50N 105 35W
Gravenhurst, Canada 63 44 52N 79 20W
Gravina di Puglia, Italy 20 40 50N 16 25E
Gray, France 12 47 27N 5 35E
Grayling, U.S.A. 68 44 40N 84 42W
Grayling R., Canada–U.S.A. 64 59 30N 126 0W
Grays Harb., U.S.A. 72 46 55N 124 5W
Grays L., U.S.A. 72 43 0N 111 30W
Grayson, Canada 65 50 45N 102 40W
Graz, Austria 14 47 4N 15 27E
Gready I., Canada 63 53 47N 56 19W
Greasy I., Canada 64 62 55N 122 17W
Great L., Tasmania 43 41 55S 146 46E
Great Abaco I., Bah. 75 26 30N 77 20W
Great Anyui, R., U.S.S.R. 27 67 10N 162 0E
Great Australian Bight, Australia 45 33 0S 130 0E
Great Bahama Bk., W. Indies 75 23 30N 78 0W
Great Barrier I., N.Z. 46 36 12S 175 25E
Great Barrier Reef, Australia 42 19 0S 149 0E
Great Bear L., Canada 60 65 0N 120 0W
Great Bear R., Canada 60 65 0N 124 0W
Great Bend, U.S.A. 70 38 25N 98 55W
Great Berg, R., C. Prov. 57 32 50S 18 20E
Great Blasket, I., Ire. 11 52 5N 10 32W
Great Britain, Europe 10 50 0N to 58 0N
Great Bushman Land, S. Africa 57 29 0S 19 0E
Great Central, Canada 64 49 20N 125 10W
Great Channel, Indon. 34 0 15N 98 0E
Great Coco I., India 33 14 10N 93 25E
Great Divide, Australia 42 23 0S 146 0E
Great Driffield, Eng. 10 54 0N 0 25W
Great Exuma I., Bah. 75 23 30N 75 50W
Great Falls, U.S.A. 72 47 29N 111 19W
Great Fish R., C. Prov. 57 31 30S 20 16E
Great Guana Cay, Is., Bahama Islands 75 23 50N 76 20W
Great Himalaya Ra., Asia 33 29 0N 84 0E
Great Inagua I., Bah. 75 21 0N 73 20W
Great Indian (Thar) Desert, India 32 27 40N 72 0E
Great Jarvis, Canada 63 47 39N 57 12W
Great Karas Mts., S.W. Africa 57 27 10S 18 45E
Great Karoo, S. Africa 57 32 30S 23 0E
Great Kei, R., C. Prov. 57 32 15S 27 45E
Great Khingan Mts., Mongolia 37 48 0N 121 0E
Great Lakes, Canada–U.S.A. 62 44 0N 82 0W
Great Long L., Canada 63 56 22N 71 0W
Great Namaqualand, S.W. Africa 57 26 0S 18 0E
Great Natuna I., Indon. 35 4 0N 108 5E
Great Ouse, R., Eng. 10 52 23N 0 10E
Great Ruaha R., Tan. 53 8 0S 34 30E
Great St. Bernard P., Switzerland 20 45 50N 7 10E
Great Salt Lake, U.S.A. 72 41 0N 112 30W
Great Salt Lake Depression, U.S.A. 72 40 45N 113 30W
Great Salt Lake Desert, U.S.A. 66 40 20N 113 50W
Great Salt Plains Res., U.S.A. 71 36 45N 98 12W
Great Scarcies, Sierra Leone 52 Inset
Great Sitkin, I., Aleu. Is. 59 50 0N 176 40W
Great Slave L., Canada 64 61 30N 114 20W
Great Tsau, mt., Botswana 57 21 15S 23 20E
Great Victoria Desert, Australia 45 28 30S 125 0E
Great Whale River, Can. 62 55 20N 75 30W
Great Winterhoek, mt., S. Africa 57 33 7S 19 10E
Greater Antilles, W. Indies 75 17 40N 74 0W
Greater Sunda Is., Indonesia 35 5 0N to 10 0S
95 0E to 125 0E
Gredos, Sa de, Spain 17 40 20N 5 0W
Greece, Europe 21 40 0N 23 0E
Greeley, U.S.A. 70 40 26N 104 44W
Green B., U.S.A. 70 45 0N 87 30W
Green Bay, U.S.A. 70 44 32N 88 0W
Green C., N.S.W. 43 37 13S 150 1E
Green Hd., W. Austral. 44 30 8S 114 55E
Green I., New Zealand 47 45 54S 170 27E
Green Is., New Guinea 42 4 30S 154 10E
Green L., Canada 64 51 26N 121 12W
Green R., Ky., U.S.A. 68 37 15N 86 30W
Green R., Wyo., U.S.A. 72 43 0N 110 0W
Green Cove Springs, U.S.A. 69 29 59N 81 40W
Green Creek, Queens. 42 18 10S 142 7E
Green River, Utah, U.S.A. 73 38 59N 110 13W
Green River, Wyo., U.S.A. 72 41 34N 109 27W
Greenbush, U.S.A. 70 48 47N 96 3W
Greenbushes, W. Australia 44 33 48S 116 0E
Greencastle, N. Ireland 11 54 2N 6 5W
Greencastle, U.S.A. 68 39 40N 86 50W
Greenfield, Iowa, U.S.A. 70 41 18N 94 29W
Greenfield, Mass., U.S.A. 69 42 38N 72 38W
Greenfield, Miss., U.S.A. 71 37 29N 93 44W
Greenfield, Tenn., U.S.A. 68 36 10N 88 48W
Greening, Canada 62 48 10N 74 55W
Greenland, N. America 58 66 0N 45 0W
Greenock, Scotland 10 55 57N 4 46W
Greenore, Ireland 11 54 2N 6 8W
Greenore Pt., Ireland 11 52 15N 6 20W
Greenough, R., W. Australia 44 28 10S 115 4E
Greensboro, N.C., U.S.A. 69 36 5N 79 47W
Greensburg, Kan., U.S.A. 71 37 35N 99 16W
Greensburg, Pa., U.S.A. 69 40 18N 79 31W
Greenvale, Queensland 42 19 0S 145 5E
Greenville, Liberia 50 5 7N 9 6W
Greenville, Alabama, U.S.A. 69 31 50N 86 40W
Greenville, Calif., U.S.A. 72 40 12N 120 59W
Greenville, Ill., U.S.A. 70 38 51N 89 25W
Greenville, Me., U.S.A. 69 45 30N 69 32W
Greenville, Michigan, U.S.A. 68 43 12N 85 14W
Greenville, Miss., U.S.A. 71 33 20N 91 0W
Greenville, N.C., U.S.A. 69 35 36N 77 23W
Greenville, Ohio, U.S.A. 68 40 6N 84 37W
Greenville, Penn., U.S.A. 68 41 23N 80 22W
Greenville, S.C., U.S.A. 69 34 53N 82 25W
Greenville, Tenn., U.S.A. 69 36 15N 82 50W
Greenville, Texas, U.S.A. 71 33 0N 96 0W
Greenville C., Queens. 42 11 57S 143 12E
Greenwater L., Prov. Park, Canada 65 52 30N 103 0W
Greenwood, Canada 64 49 10N 118 40W
Greenwood, Miss., U.S.A. 71 33 30N 90 0W
Greenwood, S.C., U.S.A. 69 34 11N 82 10W
Gregory, U.S.A. 70 43 14N 99 23W
Gregory, L., Australia 43 29 0S 139 0E
Gregory R., Queensland 42 18 58S 139 0E
Gregory Ra., Queens. 42 19 0S 143 10E
Gregory Ra., W. Australia 44 21 30S 121 15E
Griefswald, Germany 14 54 6N 13 23E
Grenå, Denmark 23 56 26N 10 51E
Grenada, U.S.A. 71 33 45N 89 50W
Grenada I., W. Indies 75 12 10N 61 40W
Grenade, France 12 43 47N 0 28W
Grenadines, The, Is., Windward Islands 75 12 40N 61 30W
Grenchen, Switzerland 15 47 12N 7 24E
Grenen, C., Denmark 23 57 45N 10 38E
Grenfell, Canada 65 50 30N 102 50W
Grenfell, N.S.W. 43 33 52S 148 8E
Grenoble, France 12 45 12N 5 42E
Grenora, U.S.A. 70 48 38N 103 57W
Grenville, Windward Is. 75 Inset
Grenville Chan., Canada 64 53 40N 129 40W
Gresham, U.S.A. 72 45 31N 122 30W
Greta, N.S.W. 43 32 38S 151 21E
Gretna, U.S.A. 71 29 55N 90 2W
Grey Abbey, N. Ireland 11 54 32N 5 35W
Grey Mt., Queensland 42 24 40S 144 37E
Grey Range, N.S.W. 43 29 30S 141 47E
Grey Range, Queens. 43 27 0S 143 30E
Grey R., Canada 63 48 0N 57 50W
Grey R., New Zealand 47 42 17S 171 35E
Greybull, U.S.A. 72 44 30N 108 1W
Greymouth, N.Z. 47 42 29S 171 13E
Greytown, Natal 57 29 1S 30 36E
Greytown, N.Z. 46 41 5S 175 29E
Gribbell I., Canada 64 53 20N 128 40W
Gridley, U.S.A. 72 39 23N 121 40W
Griffin, U.S.A. 69 33 10N 84 10W
Griffith, N.S.W. 43 34 14S 145 46E
Grignan, France 12 44 26N 4 56E
Grigoriopol, U.S.S.R. 25 47 10N 29 20E
Grijalva, R., Mexico 74 16 20N 92 20W
Grik, Malaya 34 5 25N 101 7E
Grimari, Cent. Afr. Republic 54 5 43N 20 0E
Grimsby, England 10 53 35N 0 5W
Grimsel P., Switzerland 15 46 34N 8 20E
Grimsey I., Iceland 22 66 30N 17 55W
Grimshaw, Canada 64 56 10N 117 40W
Grimstad, Norway 23 58 22N 8 35E
Grindavik, Iceland 22 63 50N 22 27W
Grindelwald, Switz. 15 46 38N 8 2E
Grinnell, U.S.A. 70 41 41N 92 48W
Griqualand West, dist., Cape Province 57 28 40S 23 30E
Griquet, Canada 63 51 30N 55 35W
Gris Nez, C., France 12 50 50N 1 35E
Groais I., Canada 63 50 55N 55 35W
Groblersdal, Transvaal 57 25 15S 29 25E
Grodek, Poland 16 53 46N 23 38E
Grodzisk, Poland 16 52 15N 16 22E
Gródzisk, Warsaw, Pol. 16 52 8N 20 40E
Groen, R., C. Prov. 57 30 47S 23 0E
Groenlo, Netherlands 13 52 2N 6 40E
Groesbeck, U.S.A. 71 31 31N 96 32W
Groganville, Queens. 42 16 20S 144 22E
Grójec, Poland 16 51 50N 20 58E
Grong, Norway 22 64 25N 12 8E
Groningen. Netherlands 13 53 15N 6 35E
Groningen, prov., Neth. 13 53 16N 6 40E
Groom, U.S.A. 71 35 8N 100 59W
Groot R., C. Prov. 57 33 10S 23 53E
Groot Marico, Trans. 57 25 34S 26 27E
Grootdrink, C. Prov. 57 28 31S 21 44E
Groote Eylandt, N. Terr., Australia 41 14 0S 136 50E
Grootfontein, S.W. Afr. 57 19 35S 18 6E
Grootlaagte R., Bot. 57 21 25S 21 0E
Grootvloer, C. Prov. 57 30 0S 20 40E
Gros Cap C., Canada 64 62 0N 113 20W
Gross Glockner, mt., Austria 14 47 5N 12 44E
Grossa Pta., Brazil 79 1 20N 50 0W
Grossenbrode, Germany 14 54 21N 11 4E
Grossenhain, Germany 14 51 17N 13 32E
Grosseto, Italy 20 42 45N 11 7E
Grosswater B., Canada 63 54 10N 57 0W
Groten, U.S.A. 70 45 30N 98 3W
Grottaglie, Italy 20 40 32N 17 25E
Grouard, Canada 64 55 30N 116 10W
Groundhog R., Canada 62 48 30N 82 0W
Grouse Creek, U.S.A. 72 41 46N 113 57W
Groveton, N.H., U.S.A. 68 44 34N 71 30W
Groveton, Texas, U.S.A. 71 31 2N 95 3W
Groznyy, U.S.S.R. 25 43 20N 45 45E
Grudziadz, Poland 16 53 30N 18 47E
Grumo, Italy 20 41 1N 16 41E
Grünau, S.W. Africa 57 27 47S 18 23E
Grundy Center, U.S.A. 70 42 20N 92 30W
Gruver, U.S.A. 71 36 15N 101 16W
Gruyères, Switzerland 15 46 35N 7 4E
Gryazi, U.S.S.R. 25 52 30N 39 58E
Gryazovets, U.S.S.R. 25 58 50N 40 20E
Gstaad, Switzerland 15 46 28N 7 18E
Gua, India 33 22 15N 85 25E
Guacanayabo, G. of, Cuba 75 20 40N 77 20W
Guacu, Brazil 77 22 10S 54 30W
Guadalajara, Mexico 74 20 40N 103 20W
Guadalajara, Spain 17 40 37N 3 12W
Guadalcanal, Spain 17 38 5N 5 52W
Guadalete R., Spain 17 36 45N 5 47W
Guadalhorce, Spain 17 36 52N 4 42W
Guadalquivir R., Spain 17 38 0N 4 0W
Guadalupe, Spain 17 39 27N 5 17W
Guadalupe, U.S.A. 73 34 58N 120 34W
Guadalupe Bravos, Mex. 74 31 23N 106 7W
Guadalupe Mt., U.S.A. 71 31 50N 104 45W
Guadalupe, R., U.S.A. 71 29 28N 97 30W
Guadeloupe I., Fr. W. Indies 75 16 20N 61 40W
Guadeloupe Pass, Leeward Islands 75 16 50N 68 15W
Guadiana R., Sp.–Port. 17 37 55N 7 39W
Guadix, Spain 17 37 18N 3 11W
Guafo, G. of, Chile 77 43 35S 74 0W
Guainia R., Colombia 78 2 30N 68 30W
Guaira, Brazil 77 24 5S 54 10W
Guaitecas Is., Chile 77 44 0S 74 30W
Guajará-Mirim, Brazil 78 10 50S 65 20W
Guajarat, St., India 32 23 0N 71 45E
Guajaratuba, Brazil 78 5 0S 63 0W
Guajira Pen., Colombia 75 12 20N 72 0W

Place	Map	Lat.	Long.
Gualaquiza, Ecuador	78	3 30s	78 30w
Gualeguay, Argentine	77	33 10s	59 20w
Gualeguaychu, Arg.	77	33 0s	58 30w
Guam I., Pacific Ocean	5	13 30N	144 45E
Guanabacoa, Cuba	75	23 8N	82 15w
Guanacaste, Cord. del, Costa Rica	75	10 40N	85 4w
Guanacevio, Mexico	74	25 40N	106 0w
Guanajayo, Cuba	75	22 56N	82 42w
Guanajuato, Mexico	74	21 0N	101 20w
Guanare, Venezuela	78	9 0N	69 50w
Guanare R., Venezuela	78	8 30N	68 50w
Guane, Cuba	75	22 10N	84 0w
Guanipa R., Venezuela	78	9 30N	64 0w
Guanta, Venezuela	78	10 15N	64 38w
Guantanamo, Cuba	75	20 10N	75 20w
Guaporé R., Brazil	78	13 0s	63 0w
Guaqui, Bolivia	78	16 41s	68 54w
Guarapuava, Brazil	77	25 20s	51 30w
Guarda, Portugal	17	40 32N	7 20w
Guardafui, Somali Rep.	49	11 55N	51 10E
Guardiagrele, Italy	20	42 11N	14 11E
Guarico, Venezuela	78	9 0N	67 30w
Guarico, R., Ven.	78	8 0N	67 10w
Guasdualito, Ven.	78	7 20N	70 45w
Guasipati, Venezuela	78	7 40N	61 55w
Guastalla, Italy	20	44 55N	10 40E
Guatemala, rep., Cen. America	75	15 40N	90 30w
Guatemala, Guatemala	75	14 40N	90 30w
Guatiare, Venezuela	75	10 31N	66 31w
Guavire R., Colombia	78	3 30N	71 0w
Guaxupé, Brazil	79	21 10s	47 5w
Guayaguayare, Trinidad	75	Inset	
Guayama, Puerto Rico	75	18 0N	66 10w
Guayaquil, Ecuador	78	2 15N	79 52w
Guayaquil, G. of, Ec.	78	3 10s	81 0w
Guaymas, Mexico	74	27 50N	111 0w
Guba, Ethiopia	53	4 52N	39 18E
Guba, Congo	56	10 38s	26 27E
Gubat, Philippines	35	12 50N	124 5E
Gubbio, Italy	20	43 20N	12 34E
Gubin, E. Germany	14	51 59N	14 42E
Gubio, Nigeria	52	12 30N	12 42E
Guchil, Malaya	34	5 35N	102 10E
Guchin, Mongolia	38	45 32N	102 28E
Gudbrandsdal, R., Nor.	23	61 40N	9 30E
Guddu Barr, W. Pak.	31	28 40N	69 36E
Gudermes, U.S.S.R.	25	43 24N	46 20E
Gudivada, India	32	16 30N	81 15E
Gudur, India	32	14 12N	79 55E
Gudvangen, Norway	23	60 53N	6 50E
Guebwiller, France	12	47 55N	7 12E
Guecho, Spain	17	43 21N	2 59w
Guekedou, Guinea	52	8 40N	10 5w
Guélé Mendouka, Cam.	52	4 26N	12 52E
Guelma, Algeria	50	36 25N	6 35E
Guelph, Canada	62	43 35N	80 20w
Güemes, Argentina	77	24 50s	65 0w
Guéné, Dahomey	52	11 44N	3 16E
Guérande, France	12	47 20N	2 26w
Guéret, France	12	46 11N	1 51E
Guernsey, U.S.A.	70	42 20N	104 45w
Guernsey I., Channel Is.	12	49 30N	2 35w
Guerrero, Mexico	74	28 20N	100 30w
Gueskérou, Niger	52	13 39N	13 1E
Guessou, Dahomey	52	10 0N	2 58E
Gueydon, U.S.A.	71	30 1N	92 28w
Guibes, S.W. Africa	57	26 42s	16 50E
Guider, Cameroon	52	9 55N	13 59E
Guidigri, Niger	52	13 45N	9 58E
Guidimouni, Niger	52	13 42N	9 31E
Guiglo, Ivory Coast	50	6 45N	7 30w
Guija, Mozambique	55	24 31s	32 59E
Guildford, England	10	51 14N	0 34w
Guildford, W. Australia	44	31 48s	115 55E
Guimarëis, Portugal	17	41 28N	8 24w
Guimarães, Brazil	79	2 9s	44 35E
Guinea, Port., W. Afr.	50	12 0N	15 0w
Guinea, st., W. Africa	50	10 20N	10 0w
Guines, Cuba	75	22 50N	82 0w
Guingamp, France	12	48 34N	3 10w
Guir, C., Morocco	50	30 40N	9 50E
Guiria, Venezuela	78	10 34N	62 18w
Guise, France	12	49 52N	3 35E
Gujranwala, Pakistan	32	32 10N	74 12E
Gujrat, Pakistan	32	32 40N	74 2E
Gukovo, U.S.S.R.	25	47 50N	40 15E
Gulak, Nigeria	52	10 50N	13 30E
Gulargambone, N.S.W.	43	31 18s	145 22E
Gulbarga, India	32	17 20N	76 50E
Gulbene, U.S.S.R.	25	57 10N	26 50E
Gulbin Ka R., Nigeria	52	10 45N	6 8E
Gulf Basin, N. Terr.	40	15 20s	128 30E
Gulf Basin, W. Austral.	44	15 20s	128 30E
Gulfport, U.S.A.	71	30 25N	89 0w
Gulgong, N.S.W.	43	32 30s	149 30E
Gulkana, Alaska	59	62 15N	145 30w
Gull Lake, Canada	65	50 10N	108 55w
Gulma, Nigeria	52	12 40N	4 23E
Gulu, Uganda	53	2 50N	32 22E
Gulwe, Tanzania	53	6 28s	36 29E
Guma, Sinkiang	37	37 30N	78 20E
Gumbiro, Tanzania	53	10 1s	35 20E
Gumel, Nigeria	52	12 39N	9 22E
Gummi, Nigeria	52	12 4N	5 9E
Gumsi, Nigeria	52	13 13N	10 15E
Gümüsane, Turkey	30	40 30N	39 30E
Guna, India	32	24 40N	77 19E
Gunabad, Iran	31	34 22N	58 40E
Gunalda, Queensland	43	26 2s	152 30E
Gundagai, N.S.W.	43	35 3s	148 6E
Gungu, Zaire	54	5 43s	19 20E
Gungura, Nigeria	52	10 40N	10 20E
Gunisao L., Canada	65	53 30N	96 20w
Gunisao R., Canada	65	53 35N	97 20w
Gunma, pref., Japan	36	36 35N	139 0E
Gunn, Canada	64	43 30N	114 2w
Gunnbjorns Mts., Green.	58	69 45N	29 50w
Gunnedah, N.S.W.	43	30 59s	150 15E
Gunnison, U.S.A.	73	39 10N	111 50w
Gunnison R., U.S.A.	73	38 50N	108 30w
Gunog Tahan, Mt., Malaya	34	4 45N	102 25E
Guntakal, India	32	15 11N	77 27E
Guntersville, U.S.A.	69	34 18N	86 16w
Guntur, India	32	16 23N	80 30E
Gunung Sitoli, Indon.	34	1 15N	97 30E
Gunung Sugi, Indonesia	34	4 55s	105 10E
Gunungapi I., Indon.	35	6 45s	126 30E
Gunupur, India	33	19 5N	83 50E
Gunworth, Canada	65	51 20N	108 10w
Gupis, Kashmir	32	36 15N	73 20E
Gurar R., Nigeria	52	8 30N	6 46E
Gurchān, Iran	30	34 58N	49 20E
Gurdaspur, India	32	32 3N	75 25E
Gurdon, U.S.A.	71	33 57N	93 12w
Gurgaon, India	32	28 33N	77 10E
Gurgueia R., Brazil	79	8 30s	44 0w
Gurin, Nigeria	52	9 6N	12 48E
Gurkha, Nepal	33	28 5N	84 40E
Gurumanas, S.W. Africa	57	23 2s	16 49E
Gurun, Malaya	34	5 48N	100 28E
Gurupá, Brazil	79	1 25s	51 36w
Gurupa, I., Brazil	79	1 0s	51 40E
Gurupi R., Brazil	79	3 20s	47 20w
Guryev, U.S.S.R.	24	47 5N	52 0E
Gus, Kenya	53	2 45N	37 20E
Gusau, Nigeria	52	12 18N	6 31E
Gustavus, Alaska	64	58 25N	135 50w
Gustine, U.S.A.	73	37 18N	121 0w
Güstrow, Germany	14	53 47N	12 12E
Gutha, W. Australia	44	28 58s	115 55E
Guthalungra, Queens.	42	19 52s	147 50E
Guthrie, Okla., U.S.A.	71	35 51N	97 28w
Guthrie, Texas, U.S.A.	71	33 37N	100 17w
Guttenberg, U.S.A.	70	42 46N	91 9w
Guyana South America	78	5 0N	59 0w
Gutu, Rhodesia	56	19 34s	31 8E
Guyenne, prov., France	12	44 30N	0 40E
Guymon, U.S.A.	71	36 41N	101 29w
Guyra, N.S.W.	43	30 15s	151 40E
Guzman, L. de, Mexico	74	19 40N	103 40w
Gwa, Burma	34	17 30N	94 40E
Gwaai, Rhodesia	56	19 15s	27 45E
Gwaai R., Rhodesia	56	19 15s	27 40E
Gwabegar, N.S.W.	43	30 31s	149 0E
Gwadabawa, Nigeria	52	13 20N	5 15E
Gwadar, Pakistan	32	25 10N	62 18E
Gwadwada, Nigeria	52	10 15N	7 15E
Gwalior, India	32	26 12N	78 10E
Gwanara, Nigeria	52	18 55N	3 10E
Gwanda, Rhodesia	56	20 55s	29 0E
Gwaram, Nigeria	52	11 15N	9 51E
Gwarzo, Nigeria	52	12 20N	8 55E
Gwasero, Nigeria	52	9 30N	8 30E
Gweebarra B., Ireland	11	54 52N	8 21w
Gweedore, Ireland	11	55 4N	8 15w
Gwelo, Rhodesia	56	19 28s	29 45E
Gwelo, R., Rhodesia	56	18 50s	29 0E
Gwembe, Zambia	56	16 30N	27 40E
Gwi, Nigeria	52	9 0N	7 10E
Gwinn, U.S.A.	70	46 15N	87 29w
Gwio Kura, Nigeria	52	12 40N	11 2E
Gwolu, Ghana	52	10 59N	1 59w
Gwoza, Nigeria	52	11 12N	13 40E
Gwydir R., N.S.W.	43	29 30s	149 20E
Gydan Ra., U.S.S.R.	27	66 0N	166 0E
Gympie, Queensland	43	26 11s	152 38E
Gyoda, Japan	36	36 17N	139 30E
Gyoma, Hungary	16	46 56N	20 58E
Gyöngyös, Hungary	16	47 48N	20 15E
Györ, Hungary	16	47 41N	17 40E
Gypsum, L., W. Austral.	45	27 15s	127 36E
Gypsum Pt., Canada	64	61 45N	114 40w
Gypsumville, Canada	65	51 45N	98 40w
Gyula, Hungary	16	46 38N	21 17E

H

Place	Map	Lat.	Long.
Ha Giang, N. Vietnam	34	22 50N	104 58E
Haapamäkj, Finland	23	62 18N	24 28E
Haapsalu, U.S.S.R.	23	58 55N	23 30E
Haarlem, Netherlands	13	52 23N	4 39E
Haast, New Zealand	47	43 51s	169 1E
Haast P., New Zealand	47	44 6s	169 21E
Haast R., New Zealand	47	43 58s	169 25E
Hab Nadi Chauki, Pak.	32	25 0N	66 50E
Hab R., Pakistan	32	25 15N	67 8E
Haba, Saudi Arabia	30	27 11N	47 0E
Habaswein, Kenya	53	1 20N	39 25E
Habay, Canada	64	55 43N	124 40w
Habbaniya, L., Iraq	31	33 15N	43 30E
Hadsund, Denmark	23	56 44N	10 8E
Haeju, Korea	36	38 5N	125 30E
Haenertsburg, Transvaal	57	23 53s	29 58E
Hafar al Batin, Si. Arabia	30	28 25N	56 50E
Hafizabad, Pakistan	32	32 5N	73 40E
Haflong, India	33	25 10N	93 5E
Hafnarfjördur, Iceland	22	64 3N	21 55w
Haft-Kel, Iran	30	31 30N	49 32E
Hagar Banga, Sudan	51	10 40N	22 45E
Hagemeister I., Alaska	59	58 40N	161 0w
Hagen, Germany	14	51 21N	7 29E
Hagenau, France	12	48 50N	7 40E
Hagerman, U.S.A.	71	33 3N	104 24w
Hagerstown, U.S.A.	68	39 39N	77 46w
Hachado Pino, Arg.	77	38 45s	71 0w
Hachijo Shima, Japan	36	30 0N	139 45E
Hachinohe, Japan	36	40 30N	141 29E
Hackett, Canada	64	52 9N	112 28w
Haddington, Scotland	6	55 57N	2 48w
Hadeija, Nigeria	52	12 30N	9 59E
Hadeija R., Nigeria	52	12 20N	9 30E
Haden, Queensland	43	27 15s	151 53E
Hadera, Israel	29	32 27N	34 55E
Haderslev, Denmark	23	55 17N	9 30E
Hadhal, Mongolia	37	50 27N	100 12E
Hadhramaut, Arabia	28	15 30N	49 30E
Hadjene, Indonesia	35	3 30s	118 50E
Hagfors, Sweden	23	60 3N	13 45E
Hagi, Iceland	22	65 28N	23 25w
Hagi, Japan	36	34 30N	131 30E
Hags Hd., Ireland	11	52 57N	9 30w
Hague, C. de la, France	12	49 45N	2 0w
Hague, The ('s Gravenhage), Neth.	13	52 7N	4 17E
Haicheng, China	38	40 55N	122 45E
Haifa, Israel	29	32 48N	35 0E
Haig, W. Australia	45	30 55s	126 23E
Hail, Saudi Arabia	30	27 28N	42 2E
Hailar, China	37	49 10N	119 50E
Hailey, U.S.A.	72	43 30N	114 15w
Haileybury, Canada	62	47 30N	79 38w
Hailun, China	37	47 10N	127 10E
Hailung, China	38	42 50N	126 0E
Hailuoto, R., Finland	22	65 0N	24 50E
Haimen, China	39	31 53N	121 10E
Hainan I., China	39	19 10N	109 30E
Hainaut, prov., Belg.	13	50 30N	4 0E
Haines, Alaska	64	59 20N	135 30w
Haines, U.S.A.	72	44 55N	117 58w
Haines City, U.S.A.	69	28 6N	81 35w
Haines Junction, Can.	64	60 45N	137 21w
Haining, China	39	30 30N	120 35E
Haiphong, Viet Nam	34	21 2N	106 45E
Haitan Tao, I., China	39	25 30N	119 45E
Haiti, rep., Hispaniola	75	19 0N	72 30w
Haiyaniya, Si. Arabia	31	28 49N	42 30E
Haiyen, China	39	30 33N	120 57E
Haiyong, China	38	36 46N	121 15E
Haiyuan, China	38	36 38N	105 45E
Hajdúböszörmény, Hung.	16	47 40N	21 30E
Hajnówka, Poland	16	52 45N	23 40E
Hajr, dist., 'Oman	31	24 0N	56 34E
Hakataramea, N.Z.	47	44 30s	170 30E
Hakataramea R., N.Z.	47	44 35s	170 40E
Hakodate, Japan	36	41 45N	140 44E
Hakowchen, Mongolia	38	41 25N	111 5E
Hala, Pakistan	32	25 50N	68 20E
Halab (Aleppo), Syria	30	36 12N	37 13E
Halabjah, Iraq	30	35 10N	45 58E
Halaib, Sudan	51	22 5N	36 30E
Halawa, Hawaiian Is.,	59	21 10N	156 43w
Halberstadt, Germany	14	51 53N	11 2E
Halcombe, N.Z.	46	40 8s	175 30E
Halden, Norway	23	59 7N	11 30E
Haldwani (Kathgodam), India	32	29 25N	79 30E
Hale, Mt., W. Austral.	44	26 0s	117 16E
Haleakala Crater, Hawaian Is.	59	20 43N	156 10w
Haleyville, U.S.A.	69	34 15N	87 40w
Half Assini, Ghana	52	5 1N	2 50w
Halfway, U.S.A.	72	44 55N	117 11w
Halfway R., Canada	64	56 40N	122 30w
Halbul, Jordan	29	31 35N	35 7E
Haliburton, Canada	62	45 0N	78 30w
Halifax, Canada	63	44 38N	63 35w
Halifax, England	10	53 43N	1 51w
Halifax, Queensland	42	18 35s	146 20E
Halifax B., Queensland	42	18 50s	147 0E
Halil, Iran	31	27 49N	58 20E
Halland, prov., Sweden	23	57 0N	12 30E
Halle, Belgium	13	50 44N	4 13w
Halle, Germany	14	51 29N	12 0E
Hällefors, Sweden	23	59 46N	14 30E
Hallett, Antarctica	80	72 10s	170 0E
Hallettsville, U.S.A.	71	29 28N	96 58w
Halley Bay, Antarctica	80	75 30s	26 0w
Halliday, U.S.A.	70	47 25N	102 26w
Halliday L., Canada	65	61 22N	108 55w
Hallingdall, R., Norway	23	60 34N	9 42E
Hällnäs, Sweden	22	64 18N	19 40E
Hallsberg, Sweden	23	59 5N	15 0E
Hallwiler See, Switz.	15	47 17N	8 14E
Halmahera I., Indon.	35	0 40N	128 0E
Halmstead, Sweden	23	56 37N	12 56E
Hals Fd., Norway	23	62 53N	8 30E
Hälsingborg, Sweden	23	56 3N	12 42E
Halstead, U.S.A.	70	47 20N	97 15w
Halstead, U.S.A.	71	38 0N	97 29w
Halvad, India	32	23 0N	71 10E
Ham Tan, Viet Nam	34	10 39N	107 47E
Hamak, Syria	30	35 10N	36 40E
Hamada, Japan	36	34 50N	132 10E
Hamadan, Iran	30	34 52N	48 32E
Hamale, Ghana	52	10 56N	2 15w
Hamamatsu, Japan	36	34 45N	137 45E
Hamar, Norway	23	60 48N	11 7E
Hamaroy, Norway	22	68 8N	15 47E
Hambantota, Sri Lanka	32	6 10N	81 10E
Hamber Prov. Park, Canada	64	52 10N	118 0w
Hamburg, Germany	14	53 32N	9 59E
Hamburg, Ark., U.S.A.	71	33 13N	91 46w
Hamburg, Iowa, U.S.A.	70	40 36N	95 36w
Hamburg, N.Y., U.S.A.	57	42 44N	78 50w
Hamd, W.al, Si. Arabia	30	25 45N	37 30E
Hämeen Lääni, Finland	23	62 0N	24 0E
Hämeenlinna, Finland	23	61 3N	24 26E
Hamelin Pool, W. Australia	44	26 22s	114 20E
Hameln, W. Germany	14	52 6N	6 10E
Hamersley Ra., W. Australia	44	22 0s	117 45E
Hamgyong North, prov., N. Korea	36	41 45N	129 30E
Hamgong South, prov., N. Korea	36	40 30N	128 0E
Hamhung, N. Korea	37	39 54N	127 35E
Hami, China	37	42 50N	93 28E
Hamilton, Alaska	59	66 55N	164 0w
Hamilton, Bermuda	75	Inset	
Hamilton, Canada	62	43 20N	79 50w
Hamilton, New Zealand	46	37 47s	175 19E
Hamilton, Queensland	42	15 31s	145 8E
Hamilton, Scotland	10	55 47N	4 2w
Hamilton, Mo., U.S.A.	70	39 44N	94 0w
Hamilton, Mon., U.S.A.	72	46 16N	114 10w
Hamilton, N.Y., U.S.A.	68	42 50N	75 33w
Hamilton, Ohio, U.S.A.	68	39 20N	84 35w
Hamilton, Tex., U.S.A.	71	31 39N	98 4w
Hamilton, Victoria	43	37 37s	142 0E
Hamilton Inlet, Canada	63	54 20N	57 30w
Hamilton R., Canada	63	53 10N	6 30w
Hamilton R., Queens.	42	22 55s	140 25E
Hamiota, Canada	65	50 11N	100 38w
Hamirpur, India	32	25 57N	80 10E
Hamlet, U.S.A.	69	34 56N	79 40w
Hamley Bridge, S. Australia	43	34 17s	138 35E
Hamlin, U.S.A.	71	32 57N	100 4w
Hamm, Germany	14	51 40N	7 48E
Hammar, Hor al, L., Iraq	31	30 45N	47 15E
Hammenton, U.S.A.	68	39 40N	74 47w
Hammerfest, Norway	22	70 33N	23 50E
Hammond, Ind., U.S.A.	68	41 40N	87 30w
Hammond, La., U.S.A.	71	30 31N	90 29w
Hammond Downs, Queensland	43	25 27s	142 46E
Hammondsport, U.S.A.	70	42 25N	77 14w
Hampden, N.Z.	47	45 18s	170 50E
Hampton, Ark., U.S.A.	71	33 31N	92 30w
Hampton, Iowa, U.S.A.	68	42 42N	93 12w
Hampton, Va., U.S.A.	68	37 4N	76 18w
Hampton Ra., W. Australia	45	31 50s	126 45E
Hamra, Si. Arabia	30	24 2N	38 55E
Hamrat esh Sheikh, Sudan	51	14 45N	27 55E
Hāmun-e Jaz Murian, Iran	31	27 30N	59 0E
Hamun-i-Helmand, L. *See* Daryacheh-ye-Sistan, Iran	31		
Hamun-i-Lora, Pak.	32	29 38N	64 58E
Hamun-i-Mashkel, Pak.	32	28 30N	63 0E
Han Kiang, Hupei, China	39	31 30N	112 25E
Han Kiang, Kwangtung, China	39	23 45N	116 30E
Han Bojdo, Mongolia	38	43 20N	107 10E
Han-Pijesak, Y.slav.	21	44 8N	18 57E
Hana, Hawaian Is.,	59	20 45N	156 0w
Hanak, Saudi Arabia	30	25 32N	37 0E
Hanamaki, Japan	36	39 23N	141 10E
Hanang Mt., Tanzania	53	4 28s	35 25E
Hanau, Germany	14	50 8N	8 56E
Hancheng, China	38	35 27N	110 28E
Hanchung (Nancheng), China	38	33 0N	107 10E
Hancock, Mich., U.S.A.	68	47 10N	88 35w
Hancock, Minn., U.S.A.	70	45 29N	95 47w
Handa, Japan	36	35 0N	137 0E
Handeni, Tanzania	53	5 25s	38 2E
Haney, Canada	64	49 12N	122 40w
Hanford, U.S.A.	73	36 25N	119 45w
Hangang, R., S. Korea	36	37 20N	127 40E
Hangchow, China	39	30 20N	120 5E
Hangchow Wan, China	39	30 40N	122 0E
Hangklip, C., C. Prov.	57	34 26s	18 48E
Hanita, Israel	29	33 5N	35 10E
Hankiang, China	39	24 45N	118 40E
Hankinson, U.S.A.	70	46 10N	96 27w
Hanko, Finland	23	59 50N	23 2E
Hankow, China	39	30 45N	114 15E

	MAP		
Hanksville, U.S.A.	73	38 22N	110 43W
Hanle, Kashmir	32	32 45N	79 1E
Hanmer, New Zealand	47	42 32S	172 50E
Hann, Mt., W. Austral.	44	15 55S	125 56E
Hanna, Canada	64	51 40N	112 0W
Hannaford, U.S.A.	70	47 25N	98 16W
Hannah, U.S.A.	70	49 0N	98 34W
Hannah B., Canada	62	51 20N	80 0W
Hannibal, U.S.A.	70	39 10N	91 24W
Hannover, Germany	14	52 23N	9 43E
Hanoi, Viet Nam	34	21 5N	105 40E
Hanover, Canada	62	44 9N	81 2W
Hanover, C. Prov.	57	31 4S	24 29E
Hanover, Germany. *See* **Hannover.**	14		
Hanover, Conn., U.S.A.	69	41 39N	72 4W
Hanover, Pa., U.S.A.	68	39 46N	76 59W
Hanover I., Chile	77	51 0S	74 50W
Hansi, India	32	29 10N	75 55E
Hanton, China	38	36 34N	114 28E
Hanyang, China	39	30 35N	114 10E
Hanyin, China	38	32 40N	108 31E
Haparanda, Sweden-Finland	22	65 52N	24 8E
Happy, U.S.A.	71	34 45N	101 47W
Happy Camp, U.S.A.	72	41 47N	123 29W
Hapur, India	32	28 45N	77 45E
Haqal, Saudi Arabia	30	29 10N	35 0E
Har Jarmaq, Israel	29	32 59N	35 24E
Har Tuv, Israel	29	31 46N	35 0E
Hara-Airag, Mongolia	38	46 40N	109 15E
Hara Narinula, Inner Mongolia	38	41 30N	106 30E
Haradh, Saudi Arabia	31	24 5N	49 0E
Harads, Sweden	22	66 3N	21 10E
Haraisan Plateau, Saudi Arabia	30	23 0N	47 50E
Harer, Ethiopia	49	9 20N	42 8E
Harut, R., Afghan.	31	32 20N	62 0E
Harbin, China	37	45 45N	126 41E
Harbor Beach, U.S.A.	68	43 50N	82 38W
Harbor Springs, U.S.A.	68	45 28N	85 0W
Harbour Breton, Can.	63	47 29N	55 50W
Harbour Deep, Canada	63	50 25N	56 30W
Harbour Grace, Canada	63	47 40N	53 22W
Harburg, Nieder Sachsen, Germany	14	53 27N	9 58E
Harda, India	32	22 22N	77 8E
Hardanger Fd., Nor.	23	60 15N	6 0E
Hardap Dam, S.W. Africa	55	24 32S	17 50E
Hardenberg, Neth.	13	52 34N	6 37E
Harderwijk, Neth.	13	52 21N	5 39E
Hardey R., W. Austral.	44	23 0S	116 30E
Hardin, U.S.A.	72	45 50N	107 35W
Harding, Natal	57	30 32S	29 55E
Hardisty, Canada	64	52 40N	111 25W
Hardman, U.S.A.	72	45 12N	119 45W
Hardoi, India	32	27 26N	80 15E
Hardwar, India	32	29 58N	78 16E
Hardy, U.S.A.	71	36 18N	91 30W
Hardy Pen., Chile	77	55 30S	68 20W
Hare B., Canada	63	51 17N	56 0W
Harfleur, France	12	49 30N	0 10E
Hargshamn, Sweden	23	60 12N	18 30E
Harhari, N.Z.	47	43 8S	170 30E
Hari R., Indonesia	34	1 10S	101 50E
Harima Sea, Japan	36	34 40N	134 30E
Haringvliet, Neth.	13	51 51N	4 0E
Harirud, R., Afghan.	31	35 0N	61 4E
Haris, S.W. Africa	57	22 48S	16 52E
Harlan, Iowa, U.S.A.	70	41 37N	95 20W
Harlan, Ky., U.S.A.	69	36 58N	83 20W
Hârlău, Rumania	21	47 23N	27 0E
Harlem, U.S.A.	72	48 32N	108 45W
Harlingen, Netherlands	13	53 11N	5 25E
Harlingen, U.S.A.	71	26 30N	97 50W
Harlowton, U.S.A.	72	46 29N	109 50W
Harney Basin, U.S.A.	72	43 30N	119 0W
Harney L., U.S.A.	72	43 0N	119 0W
Harney Pk., U.S.A.	70	43 45N	103 30W
Harnösand, Sweden	23	62 38N	18 5E
Haro, Spain	17	42 35N	2 55W
Haro C., Mexico	74	27 50N	111 0W
Harp L., Canada	63	55 10N	61 40W
Harper, Mt., Alaska	59	64 14N	143 55W
Harpers Pass, N.Z.	47	41 43S	171 55E
Harrat Al Kishib, Mts., Saudi Arabia	30	23 0N	41 30E
Harrat al Uwairyd, Saudi Arabia	30	26 50N	38 0E
Harrat Khaibar, Mts., Saudi Arabia	30	25 45N	40 0E
Harricanaw R. Canada	62	50 30N	79 10W
Harriman, U.S.A.	69	36 0N	84 35W
Harrington Harbour, Canada	62	50 31N	59 30W
Harris, L., S. Australia	45	31 5S	135 5E
Harris Mts., N.Z.	47	44 49S	168 49E
Harris Pk., Queens.	42	16 35S	145 29E
Harris, Sd. of, Scotland	10	57 44N	7 6W
Harrisburg, Ill., U.S.A.	68	37 42N	88 30W
Harrisburg, Nebraska, U.S.A.	70	41 36N	103 45W
Harrisburg, Ore., U.S.A.	72	44 17N	123 10W
Harrisburg, Pa., U.S.A.	68	40 18N	76 52W
Harrismith, O.F.S.	57	28 15S	29 8E
Harrismith, W. Austral.	44	32 57S	117 47E
Harrison, Ark., U.S.A.	71	36 10N	93 4W
Harrison, Idaho, U.S.A.	72	47 29N	116 46W
Harrison, Neb., U.S.A.	70	42 43N	103 56W
Harrison B., Alaska	59	70 25N	151 0W
Harrison C., Canada	63	54 55N	57 50W
Harrison L., Canada	64	49 40N	122 0W
Harrisonburg, U.S.A.	68	38 28N	78 52W
Harrisonville, U.S.A.	70	38 37N	94 23W
Harriston, Canada	62	43 57N	80 53W
Harrisville, U.S.A.	68	44 40N	83 19W
Harrogate, England	10	53 59N	1 32W
Harrow, London, Eng.	10	51 35N	0 15W
Harsprånget, Sweden	22	66 26N	19 40E
Harstad, Norway	22	68 48N	16 30E
Hart, U.S.A.	68	43 42N	86 21W
Hartford, Conn., U.S.A.	68	41 47N	72 41W
Hartford, Ky., U.S.A.	68	37 26N	86 50W
Hartford, S.D., U.S.A.	70	43 41N	96 58N
Hartford, Wis., U.S.A.	70	43 18N	88 23W
Hartford City, U.S.A.	68	40 22N	85 20W
Hartland, Canada	63	46 20N	67 32W
Hartland Pt., England	10	51 2N	4 32W
Hartley, Rhodesia	56	18 10S	30 7E
Hartley Bay, Canada	64	53 27N	129 18W
Hartney, Canada	65	49 30N	100 35W
Harts R., Transvaal	57	27 15S	25 12E
Hartselle, U.S.A.	69	34 26N	86 58W
Hartshorne, U.S.A.	71	34 48N	95 32W
Hartsville, U.S.A.	69	34 23N	80 2W
Hartswater, C. Prov.	57	27 46S	24 49E
Hartwell, U.S.A.	69	34 21N	82 52W
Harvey, Ill., U.S.A.	68	41 40N	87 40W
Harvey, N.D., U.S.A.	70	47 47N	99 58W
Harvey, W. Australia	44	33 4S	115 48E
Harwich, England	10	51 56N	1 18E
Harz Mts., Germany	14	51 40N	10 40E
Hasa, Saudi Arabia	30	26 0N	49 0E
Hasa Oasis, S. Arabia	30	25 15N	49 30E
Hasan dag, Turkey	30	38 10N	34 10E
Hasan Kuli, U.S.S.R.	31	37 32N	53 59E
Hasasa, W., Jordan	29	31 34N	35 24E
Haskell, Okla., U.S.A.	71	35 49N	95 41W
Haskell, Tex., U.S.A.	71	33 8N	99 44W
Hasra, reg., Si. Arabia	30	24 12N	40 30E
Hassan, India	32	13 0N	76 5E
Hasselt, Belgium	13	50 56N	5 21E
Hassi Inifel, Algeria	50	29 50N	3 30E
Hassi R'mel, Algeria	50	32 57N	3 7E
Hässleholm, Sweden	23	56 8N	13 50E
Hastings, England	10	50 51N	0 36E
Hastings, New Zealand	46	39 39S	176 52E
Hastings, Mich., U.S.A.	68	42 40N	85 20W
Hastings, Minn., U.S.A.	70	44 41N	92 51W
Hastings, Neb., U.S.A.	70	40 34N	98 22W
Hastings R., N.S.W.	43	31 24S	152 50E
Hastings Ra., N.S.W.	43	31 14S	152 0E
Hatan Bulak, Mongolia	38	43 15N	109 0E
Hatay, Turkey	31	36 30N	36 15E
Hatch, U.S.A.	73	32 41N	107 10W
Hatchet L., Canada	65	58 35N	103 50W
Hateg, Rumania	21	45 36N	23 0E
Hathras, India	32	27 36N	78 6E
Hatia, Bangladesh	33	22 30N	91 10E
Hatien, Cambodia	34	10 24N	104 30E
Hatteras, C., U.S.A.	69	35 10N	75 30W
Hattiesburg, U.S.A.	71	31 20N	89 20W
Hatton, Canada	65	50 2N	109 50W
Hatvan, Hungary	16	47 40N	19 45E
Haugesund, Norway	23	59 23N	5 13E
Hauhangaroa Ra., N.Z.	46	38 42S	175 40E
Haukipuda, Finland	22	65 12N	25 20E
Haukivesi, L., Finland	23	62 15N	28 30E
Haultain R., Canada	65	56 20N	106 40W
Hauraki Gulf, N.Z.	46	36 35S	175 5E
Hauran Wadi, Syria	31	33 30N	41 0E
Hauroko L., N.Z.	47	45 59S	167 21E
Haut Congo, prov., Zaire	54	1 40N	24 20E
Haut Uele, reg., Zaire	53	3 0N	28 30E
Hauta Oasis, S. Arabia	30	23 39N	47 0E
Haute Volta, W. Africa	50	13 0N	2 0W
Hauterive, Canada	63	49 10N	68 20W
Hauts Plateaux, mts., Algeria	50	35 0N	2 0E
Havana, Cuba	75	23 0N	82 30W
Havana, U.S.A.	70	40 17N	90 3W
Havasu L., U.S.A.	73	34 40N	114 0W
Havel, R., E. Germany	14	53 10N	13 10E
Havel, R., E. Germany	14	52 45N	12 10E
Havelange, Belgium	13	50 23N	5 15E
Havelock, Canada	63	46 2N	65 24W
Havelock, Canada	62	44 26N	77 53W
Havelock, N.Z.	47	41 17S	173 48E
Havelock, Swaziland	57	25 58S	31 8E
Havelock N., N.Z.	46	39 42S	176 53E
Haverhill, U.S.A.	69	42 50N	71 2W
Havlíčkův Brod, C. Slov.	16	49 36N	15 33E
Havre, U.S.A.	72	48 40N	109 34W
Havre St. Pierre, Can.	63	50 18N	63 33W
Havza, Turkey	30	41 0N	35 35E
Haw, R., U.S.A.	69	37 43N	80 52W
Hawaii, st., U.S.A., Pacific Ocean	59	20 0N	155 0W
Hawaiian Is., Pac. Oc.	59	20 0N	158 0W
Hawarden, Canada	65	51 25N	106 30W
Hawarden, U.S.A.	70	43 3N	96 28W
Hawdon L., S. Australia	43	37 0S	140 0E
Hawea Flat, N.Z.	47	44 40S	169 19E
Hawea L., N.Z.	47	44 28S	169 19E
Hawera, New Zealand	46	39 35S	174 19E
Hawick, Scotland	10	55 25N	2 48W
Hawk, Alaska	59	58 6N	134 44W
Hawkdun Ra., N.Z.	47	44 53S	170 5E
Hawke B., N.Z.	46	39 25S	177 20E
Hawke C., N.S.W.	43	32 12S	152 32E
Hawke Junc., Canada	62	48 0N	84 30W
Hawke R., Canada	63	53 6N	56 30W
Hawker, S. Australia	43	31 59S	138 22E
Hawke's Bay, N.Z.	46	39 45S	176 35E
Hawke's Harbour, Can.	63	53 2N	55 50W
Hawkesbury, Canada	62	45 35N	74 40W
Hawkesbury R., N.S.W.	43	33 30S	151 10E
Hawkinsville, U.S.A.	69	32 17N	83 30W
Hawley, U.S.A.	70	46 59N	96 18W
Hawr al Hammar, Iraq	30	30 40N	47 00E
Hawthorne, U.S.A.	73	38 32N	119 24W
Haxton, U.S.A.	70	40 40N	102 37W
Hay, Australia	43	34 30S	144 51E
Hay, Wales	10	52 4N	3 9W
Hay L., Canada	64	58 50N	119 0W
Hay Lakes, Canada	64	53 12N	113 2W
Hay R., Canada	64	53 50N	118 0W
Hay R., Canada	64	59 0N	117 40W
Hay Springs, U.S.A.	70	42 41N	102 39W
Hayange, France	12	49 20N	6 2E
Haycock, Alaska	59	65 11N	161 19W
Hayden, Ariz., U.S.A.	73	33 0N	110 49W
Hayden, Colo., U.S.A.	72	40 30N	107 15W
Haydon, Queensland	42	18 0S	141 30E
Hayes, U.S.A.	70	44 25N	101 0W
Hayes Mt., Alaska	59	63 40N	146 35W
Hayes R., Canada	65	56 0N	93 20W
Haynesville, U.S.A.	71	33 0N	93 14W
Hays, Canada	64	50 6N	111 49W
Hays, U.S.A.	70	38 53N	99 20W
Haysport, Canada	64	54 12N	130 10W
Hayward, U.S.A.	70	46 2N	91 30W
Hazarajat, dist., Afghanistan	31	34 0N	66 0E
Hazard, U.S.A.	68	37 18N	83 10W
Hazaribagh, India	33	23 58N	85 26E
Hazelhurst, U.S.A.	71	31 54N	90 28W
Hazen, Nev., U.S.A.	72	39 32N	119 0W
Hazen, N.D., U.S.A.	70	47 19N	101 35W
Hazleton, Canada	64	55 20N	127 42W
Hazleton, N.D., U.S.A.	70	46 32N	100 16W
Hazleton, Pa., U.S.A.	68	40 58N	76 0W
Hazor (site), Israel	29	33 2N	35 2E
Hazrat Imam, Afghan.	31	37 18N	68 47E
Hazuur, S.W. Africa	57	26 40S	19 52E
Head of Bight B., S. Australia	40	31 35S	131 15E
Headford, Ireland	11	53 28N	9 6W
Headlands, Rhodesia	56	18 15S	32 2E
Healdton, U.S.A.	71	34 12N	97 32W
Healesville, Victoria	43	37 35S	145 30E
Heany Junction, S. Rhodesia	56	20 5S	28 40E
Heard I., S. Indian Oc.	5	53 0S	74 0E
Hearne, U.S.A.	71	30 54N	96 35W
Hearne L., Canada	64	2 20N	113 30W
Hearst, Canada	62	49 40N	83 41W
Heart, R., U.S.A.	70	46 40N	101 30W
Heart's Content, Can.	63	47 54N	53 27W
Heath Mt., N.Z.	47	45 39S	167 9E
Heath Pt., Canada	63	49 8N	61 40W
Heavener, U.S.A.	71	34 50N	94 6W
Hebbronville, U.S.A.	71	27 17N	98 34W
Hebel, Queensland	43	28 59S	147 44E
Heber Springs, U.S.A.	71	35 29N	92 0W
Hébertville, Canada	63	48 25N	71 44W
Hebgen, L., U.S.A.	72	44 45N	111 15W
Hebrides, Is., Inner, Scotland	10	57 20N	6 40W
Hebrides, Is., Outer, Scotland	10	57 50N	7 25W
Hebron, Canada	61	58 10N	62 50W
Hebron, Jordan	29	31 32N	35 6E
Hebron, N.D., U.S.A.	70	46 57N	102 2W
Hebron, Neb., U.S.A.	70	40 12N	97 33W
Hecate Str., Canada	64	53 10N	130 30W
Heceta I., Alaska	64	55 46N	133 40W
Hecla, U.S.A.	70	45 58N	98 7W
Hecla I., Canada	65	51 10N	96 50W
Hector, Queensland	42	21 16S	149 20E
Hector Mt., N.Z.	46	40 56S	175 18E
Hedaru, Tanzania	53	4 30S	37 45E
Hede, Sweden	23	62 23N	13 43E
Hedemark, prov., Nor.	23	61 0N	12 0E
Hedemora, Sweden	23	60 18N	15 58E
Hedgehope, N.Z.	47	46 12S	168 34E
Hedley, U.S.A.	71	34 50N	100 37W
Heemstede, Neth.	13	52 19N	4 37E
Heerde, Netherlands	13	52 24N	6 2E
Heerenveen, Neth.	13	52 57N	5 55E
Heerlen, Netherlands	13	50 55N	6 0E
Hegyeshalom, Hungary	16	47 53N	17 19E
Heiban, Sudan	54	11 10N	30 25E
Heide, Germany	14	54 10N	9 7E
Heidelberg, C. Prov.	57	34 6S	20 50E
Heidelberg, Germany	14	49 23N	8 41E
Heidelberg, Transvaal	57	26 30S	28 23E
Heilbron, O.F.S.	57	27 16S	27 59E
Heilbronn, W. Germany	14	49 8N	9 14E
Heilungkiang, prov., China	37	47 0N	129 0E
Heinfung, Mt., Korea	36	40 25N	127 45E
Heinola, Finland	23	61 13N	26 10E
Heinsburg, Canada	65	53 50N	110 30W
Heinze (N. Moscos), Is., Burma	33	14 0N	97 30E
Hejaz, Saudi Arabia	30	26 0N	37 30E
Hekimhan, Turkey	30	38 50N	38 0E
Hekla, Mt., Iceland	22	63 56N	19 35W
Hel, Poland	16	54 38N	18 50E
Helena, Ark., U.S.A.	71	34 30N	90 35W
Helena, Mont., U.S.A.	72	46 40N	112 0W
Helensville, N.Z.	46	36 41S	174 29E
Helgeland, dist., Nor.	22	66 20N	13 30E
Helidon, Queensland	43	27 31S	152 6E
Heligoland, I., North Sea	14	54 10N	7 51E
Heligoland B., Germany	14	54 0N	8 0E
Hellevoetsluis, Neth.	13	51 50N	4 8E
Hellin, Spain	17	38 31N	1 40W
Hellville, Madagascar	55	13 20S	48 12E
Helmand R., Afghan.	31	34 0N	67 0E
Helmeringhausen, S.W. Africa	57	25 53S	16 50E
Helmond, Netherlands	13	51 29N	5 41E
Helmsdale, Scotland	10	58 7N	3 40W
Helper, U.S.A.	73	39 42N	110 50W
Helsingfors. *See* **Helsinki.**	23		
Helsingör, Denmark	23	56 2N	12 35E
Helsinki, Finland	23	60 15N	25 3E
Hemet, U.S.A.	73	33 45N	117 0W
Hemingbad, U.S.A.	70	42 21N	103 2W
Hemnesberget, Norway	22	66 14N	13 40E
Hemphill, U.S.A.	71	31 49N	93 46W
Hempstead, U.S.A.	71	40 42N	73 34W
Hemse, Sweden	23	57 15N	18 20E
Hen & Chicken Is., New Zealand	46	35 55S	174 45E
Henares R., Spain	17	40 55N	3 0W
Hendaye, France	12	43 23N	1 47W
Henderson, Ky., U.S.A.	68	37 50N	87 38W
Henderson, Minn., U.S.A.	68	44 29N	93 54W
Henderson, N.C., U.S.A.	69	36 18N	78 23W
Henderson, Nevada, U.S.A.	73	36 2N	115 0W
Henderson, Texas, U.S.A.	71	32 8N	94 49W
Hendersonville. U.S.A.	69	35 21N	82 28W
Hengelo, Netherlands	13	52 15N	6 48E
Henghsien, China	39	22 32N	109 15E
Hengshan, China	38	38 0N	108 56E
Hengyang, China	39	26 58N	112 25E
Henjam, I., Pers. G.	31	26 50N	55 58E
Henlopen C., U.S.A.	68	38 48N	75 5W
Hennebont, France	12	47 49N	3 19W
Hennenman, O.F.S.	57	27 59S	27 1E
Hennessy, U.S.A.	71	36 7N	97 58W
Henribourg, Canada	65	53 25N	105 38W
Henrietta, U.S.A.	71	33 48N	98 14W
Henrietta, I., U.S.S.R.	27	77 30N	157 0E
Henrietta Maria C., Canada	62	55 10N	82 30W
Henry, U.S.A.	70	41 5N	89 20W
Henry Freycinet Est., W. Australia	44	26 20S	113 45E
Henry R., W. Australia	44	23 0S	115 40E
Henryette, U.S.A.	71	35 29N	96 1W
Hentein Nuru, mts., Mongolia	37	48 50N	109 0E
Henty, N.S.W.	43	35 30S	147 0E
Henzada, Burma	34	17 38N	95 35E
Heppen, U.S.A.	72	45 24N	119 31W
Héradsflói, fjord, Ice.	22	65 47N	14 0W
Heradsvötn, R., Iceland	22	65 35N	19 18W
Herat, Afghanistan	31	34 20N	62 7E
Herbert, Canada	65	50 30N	107 10W
Herbert, Queensland	42	23 29S	150 48E
Herbert Downs, Queens.	42	23 0S	139 11E
Herbert I., Aleutian Is.	59	53 50N	170 0W
Herbert R., Queensland	42	18 33S	146 0E
Herberton, Queensland	42	17 28S	145 25E
Herbertsdale, C. Prov.	57	34 0S	21 45E
Herbertville, N.Z.	46	40 29S	176 34E
Hercegnovi, Y.slav.	21	42 30N	18 33E
Herdubreid, mt., Ice.	22	65 10N	16 22W
Heredia, Costa Rica	78	10 0N	84 8W
Hereford, England	10	52 4N	2 42W
Hereford, U.S.A.	71	34 48N	102 27W
Herekino, New Zealand	46	35 16S	173 11E
Herentals, Belgium	13	51 12N	4 51E
Herford, Germany	14	52 7N	8 39E
Herington, U.S.A.	70	38 42N	97 0W
Herisau, Switzerland	15	47 22N	9 17E
Herjehognä, mt., Nor.	23	61 45N	12 6E
Herkimer, U.S.A.	68	43 0N	74 59W
Herman, U.S.A.	70	45 49N	76 4W
Hermann, U.S.A.	70	38 40N	91 28W
Hermannsburg, Austral.	45	20 0S	132 45E
Hermanus, C. Prov.	57	34 27S	19 12E
Hermidale, N.S.W.	43	31 30S	146 42E
Hermiston, U.S.A.	72	45 50N	119 16W
Hermitage, N.Z.	47	43 44S	170 5E
Hermitage B., Canada	63	47 33N	56 10W
Hermite Is., Chile	77	55 50S	68 0W
Hermon, mt., Syria. *See* **Jabal ash Sheik**	30		
Hermosillo, Mexico	74	29 10N	111 0W

	MAP		
Hernad R., Hungary	16	48 20N	21 15 E
Hernanarias, Brazil	77	25 10 S	55 20W
Hernando, U.S.A.	71	34 43N	90 0W
Herning, Denmark	23	56 8N	9 0 E
Heron Bay, Canada	62	48 40N	85 25W
Herowabad, Iran	30	37 44N	48 38 E
Herreid, U.S.A.	70	45 50N	100 5W
Herrera, Spain	17	39 12N	5 3W
Herrero, Pla., Mexico	74	19 0N	87 30W
Herrick, Tasmania	43	41 5 S	147 55 E
Herrin, U.S.A.	71	37 50N	89 0W
Herschal, C. Prov.	57	30 37 S	27 10 E
Herstal, Belgium	13	50 41N	5 39 E
Hertford, England	10	51 47N	0 4W
's Hertogenbosch, Neth.	13	51 42N	5 18 E
Hertzogville, O.F.S.	57	28 9 S	25 30 E
Hervey B., Queens.	43	25 0 S	152 45 E
Hervey Is., Pacific Oc.	5	19 30 S	159 0W
Hervey Junc., Canada	62	46 50N	72 29W
Herzliyya, Israel	29	32 10N	34 50 E
Herzogenbuchsee, Switz.	15	47 12N	7 43 E
Hesbaye, dist., Belgium	13	50 40N	5 5 E
Hesteyri, Iceland	22	64 11N	22 59W
Hesso, S. Australia	43	32 8 S	137 24 E
Het Loo, Netherlands	13	42 15N	5 57 E
Hettingen, U.S.A.	70	46 3N	102 38W
Hewett, C., Canada	61	70 10N	68 10W
Hex River Mts., C. Prov.	57	33 20 S	19 48 E
Hexham, England	10	54 58N	2 7W
Heywood, Victoria	43	38 8 S	141 37 E
Hiawatha, Kan., U.S.A.	70	39 55N	95 34W
Hiawatha, Utah, U.S.A.	73	39 27N	111 15W
Hibbard, Canada	62	47 50N	74 5W
Hibbing, U.S.A.	70	47 30N	93 0W
Hibbs Pt., Tasmania	43	42 35 S	145 20 E
Hickman, U.S.A.	71	36 35N	89 8W
Hickory, U.S.A.	69	35 46N	81 17W
Hidalgo, Mexico	74	27 50N	99 50W
Hidalgo, st., Mexico	74	20 30N	99 10W
Hidalgo del Parral, Mex.	74	26 10N	104 50W
Hierro, I., Canary I.	50	27 57N	17 56W
Hifung, China	39	23 0N	115 14 E
Higgins, U.S.A.	71	36 5N	100 0W
Higginsville, W. Austral.	44	31 42 S	121 38 E
High Dam, Egypt	51	24 5N	32 53 E
High I., U.S.A.	71	29 32N	94 27W
High Point, U.S.A.	69	35 57N	79 58W
High Prairie, Canada	64	55 30N	116 30W
High River, Canada	64	50 30N	113 50W
High Springs, U.S.A.	69	29 50N	82 40W
High Tatra Mts., C.Slov.	16	49 20N	20 0 E
Highbank, N.Z.	47	43 37 S	171 48 E
Highland Park, Ill., U.S.A.	70	42 10N	87 50W
Highland Park, Mich.,	68	42 25N	83 0W
Highmore, U.S.A.	70	44 34N	99 26W
Highrock, L., Canada	65	57 15N	105 30W
Higley, U.S.A.	73	33 19N	111 14W
Hiiumaa I., U.S.S.R.	23	58 50N	22 45 E
Hiko, U.S.A.	73	37 30N	115 15W
Hikone, Japan	36	35 15N	136 10 E
Hikurangi, N.Z.	46	37 54 S	178 5 E
Hildesheim, Germany	14	42 9N	9 55 E
Hill City, Idaho, U.S.A.	72	43 22N	115 1W
Hill City, Kan., U.S.A.	70	39 25N	99 51W
Hill City, Minn., U.S.A.	70	46 58N	93 33W
Hill City, S.D., U.S.A.	70	44 0N	103 35W
Hill Island L., Canada	65	60 30N	109 50W
Hilla, Saudi Arabia	30	23 32N	46 48 E
Hillman, U.S.A.	68	45 5N	83 52W
Hillmond, Canada	65	53 26N	109 41W
Hillsboro, Kan., U.S.A.	70	38 26N	87 12W
Hillsboro, N.C., U.S.A.	69	36 7N	79 7W
Hillsboro, N.D., U.S.A.	70	47 30N	97 1W
Hillsboro, N. Mexico, U.S.A.	73	32 59N	107 33W
Hillsboro, Ore., U.S.A.	72	45 30N	123 0W
Hillsboro, Tex., U.S.A.	71	32 0N	97 10W
Hillsborough, Carriacou, Windward Islands	75		Inset
Hillside, W. Australia	44	21 44 S	119 17 E
Hillsport, Canada	62	49 27N	85 34W
Hillston, N.S.W.	43	33 30 S	145 31 E
Hilo, Hawaiian Islands	59	19 42N	155 4W
Hilversum, Netherlands	13	52 14N	5 10 E
Himachal Pradesh, st., India	33	31 30N	77 0 E
Himalayas, mts., Asia	28	30 0N	80 0 E
Himeji, Japan	36	34 50N	134 40 E
Himi, Japan	36	36 50N	137 0 E
Himo, Tanzania	53	3 26 S	37 34 E
Hims (Homs), Syria	30	34 49N	36 45 E
Hinchinbrook I., Queens.	42	18 20 S	146 15 E
Hinde Rapids, Zaire	54	5 25 S	27 3 E
Hindian, Iran	30	29 5N	49 40 E
Hindian R., Iran	30	30 20N	50 20 E
Hindmarsh L., Victoria	43	35 50 S	141 55 E
Hinds, New Zealand	47	43 59 S	171 36 E
Hindubagh, W. Pakistan	31	30 52N	67 47 E
Hindupur, India	32	13 49N	77 32 E
Hines Creek, Canada	64	56 20N	118 40W
Hingan, China	39	25 34N	110 35 E
Hinganghat, India	32	20 30N	78 59 E
Hingchen, China	38	40 45N	120 45 E
Hingham, U.S.A.	72	48 33N	110 29W
Hingi, China	39	25 10N	105 35 E
Hingkwo, China	39	26 20N	115 10 E

	MAP		
Hingning, China	39	24 5N	115 47 E
Hingoli, India	32	19 41N	77 15 E
Hingshan, China	39	31 15N	100 49 E
Hingwa Nan, China	39	25 15N	119 15 E
Hingwo, China	39	26 25N	115 10 E
Hinna, Nigeria	52	10 25N	11 28 E
Hinnoy, I., Norway	22	68 40N	16 28 E
Hino, C., Japan	36	35 28N	132 45 E
Hinojosa, Spain	17	38 30N	5 17W
Hinsdale, U.S.A.	68	48 23N	106 47W
Hinterrhein, R., Switz.	15	46 40N	9 25 E
Hinton, U.S.A.	69	37 40N	80 51W
Hippolitushoef, Neth.	13	52 56N	45 9 E
Hirākud Dam, India	33	21 35N	83 35 E
Hirono, Japan	36	37 15N	141 0 E
Hirosaki, Japan	36	40 32N	140 30 E
Hiroshima, Japan	36	34 30N	132 30 E
Hiroshima, pref., Japan	36	34 40N	133 0 E
Hiroshiri-dake, mt., Japan	36	42 40N	142 52 E
Hirson, France	12	49 55N	4 4 E
Hirtshals, Denmark	23	57 36N	9 55 E
Hispaniola I., W. Indies	75	19 0N	71 0W
Hissar, India	32	29 12N	75 45 E
Hit, Iraq	30	33 38N	42 46 E
Hita, Japan	36	33 19N	131 3 E
Hitachi, Japan	36	36 48N	140 43 E
Hitchin, England	10	51 57N	0 16W
Hitoyoshi, Japan	36	32 13N	130 45 E
Hitra I., Norway	23	63 30N	8 45 E
Hiungyao, China	38	40 15N	122 10 E
Hiwasa, Japan	36	33 40N	134 30 E
Hjalmar L., Canada	65	61 35N	109 15W
Hjalmaren L., Sweden	23	59 18N	15 40 E
Hjörring, Denmark	23	57 29N	9 59 E
Hlatikulu, Swaziland	57	26 59 S	31 22 E
Hlobane, Natal	57	27 42 S	31 0 E
Hluhluwe, Natal	57	28 5 S	32 20 E
Ho, Ghana	52	6 37N	0 27 E
Hoa Binh, N. Viet Nam	34	20 52N	105 12 E
Hoachanas, S.W. Afr.	57	23 55 S	18 4 E
Hoadley, Canada	64	52 45N	114 30W
Hoare B., Canada	61	65 30N	62 30W
Hobart, Tasmania	43	42 50 S	147 21 E
Hobart, U.S.A.	71	35 0N	99 2W
Hobbs, U.S.A.	66	32 40N	103 3W
Hobhouse, O.F.S.	57	29 30 S	27 10 E
Hoboken, Belgium	13	51 11N	4 21 E
Hobro, Denmark	23	56 39N	9 46 E
Höbsögöl, Mongolia	37	43 36N	109 40 E
Hoburg I., Sweden	23	56 55N	18 5 E
Hochatown, U.S.A.	71	34 8N	94 39W
Hochdorf, Switzerland	15	47 10N	8 18 E
Hochstetter, Mt., N.Z.	47	42 31 S	172 1 E
Hochstetter Dome, N.Z.	47	43 38 S	170 28 E
Hochwan, China	39	30 0N	106 15 E
Hodeida, Yemen	49	14 50N	43 0 E
Hodgson, Canada	65	51 20N	97 40W
Hodgson, Queensland	43	26 25 S	148 35 E
Hódmezovásárhely, Hungary	16	46 28N	20 22 E
Hodonin, C.Slov.	16	48 50N	17 0 E
Hoeryong, N. Korea	36	42 28N	129 40 E
Hof, Germany	14	50 18N	11 55 E
Hof, Iceland	22	64 33N	14 30W
Hofei, China	39	31 48N	117 15 E
Hofengchow, China	39	29 55N	110 5 E
Hofmeyr, C. Prov.	57	31 39 S	25 50 E
Höfn, Iceland	22	64 16N	15 10W
Hofors, Sweden	23	60 35N	16 15 E
Hofsjökull, Ice-field, Ice.	22	64 50N	18 50W
Hofsos, Iceland	22	65 53N	19 18W
Hogansville, U.S.A.	69	33 14N	84 50W
Hoggar, Algeria	50	23 30N	6 30 E
Hogeland, U.S.A.	68	48 54N	108 40W
Hogoro, Tanzania	53	5 56 S	36 25 E
Hohe Venn Mts., Belg.	13	50 32N	6 10 E
Hohenwald, U.S.A.	69	35 33N	87 31W
Hohoe, Ghana	52	7 8N	0 32 E
Hohpi, China	38	35 50N	114 10 E
Hohsien, China	39	24 15N	111 25 E
Hoihong, China	39	20 58N	110 8 E
Hoihow, China	39	20 0N	110 20 E
Hoima, Uganda	53	1 25N	31 25 E
Hoiping, China	39	22 30N	112 30 E
Hoisington, U.S.A.	70	38 33N	98 48W
Hoi-xuan, N. Viet Nam	34	20 22N	105 9 E
Hokang, China	37	47 0N	130 10 E
Hokianga Harb., N.Z.	46	35 31 S	173 22 E
Hokianghsien, China	39	28 50N	105 50 E
Hokien, China	38	38 30N	116 1 E
Hokitika, N.Z.	47	42 42 S	171 0 E
Hokkaido, I., Japan	36	43 30N	143 0 E
Hokow, China	39	22 30N	103 54 E
Hokow, China	39	40 25N	111 10 E
Hola, Kenya	53	1 30 S	40 3 E
Holan Shan, China	38	38 30N	105 30 E
Holboek, co., Denmark	14	55 43N	11 41 E
Holbrook, N.S.W.	43	35 42 S	147 18 E
Holbrook, U.S.A.	73	35 0N	110 0W
Holden, Canada	64	53 13N	112 11W
Holdenville, U.S.A.	73	35 4N	96 28W
Holdfast, Canada	65	51 0N	105 25W
Holdrege, U.S.A.	70	40 25N	99 30W
Hole Narsipur, India	32	12 46N	76 14 E
Holguin, Cuba	75	20 50N	76 20W
Hollams Bird I., S.W. Africa	57	24 40 S	14 30 E

	MAP		
Holland, Mich., U.S.A.	68	42 47N	86 0W
Hollidaysburg, U.S.A.	68	40 26N	78 25W
Hollis, U.S.A.	71	34 42N	99 57W
Hollister, Calif., U.S.A.	73	36 52N	121 26W
Hollister, Idaho, U.S.A.	72	42 21N	114 36W
Holly, U.S.A.	71	36 6N	162 12W
Holly Hill, U.S.A.	69	29 15N	81 3W
Holly Springs, U.S.A.	71	34 45N	89 28W
Hollywood, Cal., U.S.A.	66	34 0N	118 20W
Hollywood, Florida, U.S.A.	69	26 1N	80 9W
Holmavik, Iceland	22	65 42N	21 40W
Holmsund, Sweden	23	63 41N	20 20 E
Holon, Israel	29	32 2N	34 47 E
Holroyd R., Queens.	42	14 25 S	142 15 E
Holstebro, Denmark	23	56 22N	8 33 E
Holsteinborg, Green.	61	67 0N	53 20W
Holt, Iceland	22	63 35N	19 38W
Holton, U.S.A.	70	39 30N	95 46W
Holton Harbour, Can.	63	54 50N	57 0W
Holtville, U.S.A.	73	32 49N	115 24W
Holvaloa, Hawaiian Is.,	59	19 37N	155 57W
Holwerd, Netherlands	13	53 23N	5 5 E
Holy I., England	10	55 42N	1 48W
Holy I., Wales	10	53 17N	4 37W
Holy Land	29	33 0N	35 0 E
Holy Cross, Alaska	59	62 17N	160 0W
Holyhead, Wales	10	53 18N	4 38W
Holyoke, U.S.A.	68	42 14N	72 37W
Holyrood, Canada	63	47 27N	53 8W
Holywood, N. Ireland	11	54 38N	5 50W
Homa, Kenya	53	0 31 S	34 30 E
Homalin, Burma	33	24 55N	95 0 E
Hombori, Mali	50	15 20N	1 38W
Homedale, U.S.A.	72	43 40N	116 58W
Home Hill, Queensland	42	19 43 S	147 25 E
Homer, U.S.A.	59	42 38N	76 11W
Homer, U.S.A.	71	32 48N	93 5W
Homestead, Queens.	42	20 20 S	145 40 E
Homestead, U.S.A.	69	25 29N	80 27W
Homestead, U.S.A.	72	45 2N	116 57W
Hominy, U.S.A.	71	36 27N	96 28W
Homnabad, India	32	17 45N	77 5 E
Homoine, Mozambique	56	23 55 S	35 10 E
Homs (Hims), Syria	30	34 40N	36 45 E
Hon Gay, Viet Nam	35	21 2N	107 5 E
Honan, prov., China	38	33 45N	113 20 E
Honda, Colombia	78	5 15N	74 40W
Hondeklip, C. Prov.	57	30 19 S	17 17 E
Hondo, U.S.A.	71	29 18N	99 2W
Hondo, R., Brit. Hond.	74	17 48N	89 0W
Honduras, rep., Cent. America	74	14 40N	86 30W
Honduras, G. of, Cent. America	74	16 50N	87 0W
Hönefoss, Norway	23	60 10N	10 12 E
Honey, L., U.S.A.	72	40 13N	120 14W
Honfleur, France	12	49 25N	0 10 E
Hong Ha, R., Viet Nam	34	21 45N	104 30 E
Hong Kong, China	39	22 25N	114 15 E
Hongchon, S. Korea	36	37 44N	127 53 E
Hongor, Mongolia	38	45 43N	112 41 E
Hongsong, S. Korea	36	36 37N	126 38 E
Hongwon, N. Korea	36	40 0N	127 56 E
Honiton, England	10	50 48N	3 11W
Honjo, Japan	36	39 25N	140 0 E
Honku, China	38	39 15N	116 45 E
Honolulu, Pacific Ocean	59	21 25N	157 55W
Honolulu I., Pacific Oc.	6	21 50N	157 50W
Honshu, I., Japan	36	36 0N	138 0 E
Hood Mt., U.S.A.	72	45 15N	122 0W
Hood Pt., W. Australia	44	34 21 S	119 31 E
Hood R., U.S.A.	72	45 44N	121 31W
Hoodsport, U.S.A.	72	47 26N	123 10W
Hoogeveen, Neth.	13	52 44N	6 27 E
Hoogezand, Neth.	13	53 11N	6 45 E
Hooghly, R., India	33	21 59N	88 10 E
Hook Hd., Ireland	11	58 8N	6 57W
Hook I., Queensland	42	20 4 S	149 0 E
Hook of Holland, Neth.	13	51 59N	4 5 E
Hooker, U.S.A.	71	36 56N	101 11W
Hoonah, Alaska	64	58 10N	135 30W
Hooper Bay, Alaska	59	61 30N	166 0W
Hoopeston, U.S.A.	68	40 30N	87 40W
Hoopstad, O.F.S.	57	27 50 S	25 55 E
Hoorn, Netherlands	13	52 38N	5 4 E
Hoover Dam, U.S.A.	73	36 0N	114 45W
Hope, Alaska	59	60 57N	149 57W
Hope, Canada	64	49 25N	121 25W
Hope, U.S.A.	70	47 23N	97 41W
Hope, U.S.A.	71	33 40N	93 30W
Hope Pass, N.Z.	47	42 37 S	172 6 E
Hope, Pt., Alaska	59	68 20N	166 40W
Hopedale, Canada	63	55 27N	60 22W
Hopefield, C. Prov.	57	33 3 S	18 22 E
Hopeh, prov., China	38	38 40N	115 40 E
Hopelchén, Mexico	74	19 46N	89 50W
Hopetoun, Victoria	43	35 48 S	142 25 E
Hopetoun, W. Australia	44	33 54 S	120 6 E
Hopetown, C. Prov.	57	29 34 S	24 3 E
Hoping, China	39	24 28N	114 59 E
Hopkins, U.S.A.	70	40 30N	94 49W
Hopkinsville, U.S.A.	69	36 52N	87 26W
Hopland, U.S.A.	72	39 0N	123 6W
Hoppo, China	39	21 35N	109 12 E
Hoquiam, U.S.A.	72	47 0N	123 55W
Hor Sanniya, L., Iraq	30	31 45N	47 0 E
Hordaland, co., Norway	23	60 25N	6 45 E

	MAP		
Horgen, Switzerland	15	47 15N	8 35 E
Hormoz, Iran	31	27 36N	55 0 E
Hormuz Str., Persian G.	31	26 30N	56 30 E
Horn, Austria	14	48 39N	15 40 E
Horn, C., Chile	77	55 50 S	67 30W
Horn C., Iceland	22	65 7N	13 25W
Horn C., Iceland	22	66 27N	22 25W
Horn Head, Ireland	11	55 13N	8 0W
Horn, I., U.S.A.	69	30 17N	88 40W
Horn Mts., Canada	64	62 0N	119 0W
Horn R., Canada	64	61 40N	117 40W
Hornafjördur, fiord, Ice.	22	64 12N	15 0W
Hornavan L., Sweden	22	66 7N	17 10 E
Hornbeck, U.S.A.	71	31 24N	93 27W
Hornbrook, U.S.A.	72	41 58N	122 35W
Hornby, New Zealand	47	43 33 S	172 33 E
Hornell, U.S.A.	68	42 23N	77 41W
Hornepayne, Canada	62	49 14N	84 48W
Hornsby, N.S.W.	43	33 42 S	151 2 E
Hornsea, England	10	53 55N	0 10W
Horoizumi, Japan	36	42 0N	143 10 E
Horqueta, Paraguay	77	23 15 S	56 55W
Horrible Mt., Queens.	43	26 22 S	149 40 E
Horse Creek, U.S.A.	70	41 30N	104 45W
Horse Is. (St. Barbe Is.), Canada	63	50 15N	55 0W
Horsefly, Canada	64	52 25N	121 30 E
Horsens, Denmark	23	55 52N	9 50 E
Horseshoe. W. Austral.	44	25 27 S	118 32W
Horsham, England	10	51 4N	0 20W
Horsham, Victoria	43	36 44 S	142 13 E
Horten, Norway	23	59 25N	10 32 E
Horton, U.S.A.	70	39 41N	95 31W
Horton R., Canada	60	69 0N	124 0W
Horwood L., Canada	62	48 1N	82 55W
Hoshangabad, India	32	22 45N	77 45 E
Hoshiarpur, India	32	31 30N	75 58 E
Hosmer, U.S.A.	70	45 36N	99 26W
Hospet, India	32	15 15N	76 20 E
Hospital. Ireland	11	52 30N	8 28W
Hospitalet, Spain	17	41 21N	2 6 E
Hoste I., Chile	77	55 0 S	69 0W
Hot Creek Ra., U.S.A.	73	39 0N	116 0W
Hot Springs, Alaska	59	65 2N	150 45W
Hot Springs, Ark., U.S.A.	71	34 30N	93 0W
Hot Springs, S.D., U.S.A.	70	43 30N	103 30W
Hotagen, Sweden	23	63 50N	14 30 E
Hotagen, L., Sweden	23	63 50N	14 30 E
Hotchkiss, U.S.A.	70	38 48N	107 38W
Hoting, Sweden	23	64 8N	16 15 E
Hotte, Massif de la, Mts., Haiti	75	18 25N	74 0W
Hottentot B., S.W. Afr.	57	26 8 S	14 59 E
Hou, R., Laos	34	21 30N	102 15 E
Houck, U.S.A.	73	35 16N	109 10W
Houd, Mongolia	37	48 2N	91 20 E
Houffalize, Belgium	13	50 8N	5 48 E
Houghton, U.S.A.	70	47 9N	88 39W
Houghton L., U.S.A.	68	44 20N	84 40W
Houhora, New Zealand	46	34 49 S	173 9 E
Houlton, U.S.A.	69	46 5N	68 0W
Houma, U.S.A.	71	29 35N	90 50W
Hourtin et de Carcans, L., France	12	45 10N	1 4W
Houston, Canada	64	54 25N	126 30W
Houston, Mo., U.S.A.	71	37 25N	91 59W
Houston, Tex., U.S.A.	71	29 50N	95 20W
Hout R., Transvaal	57	23 30 S	29 27 E
Houtkraal, C. Prov.	57	30 23 S	24 5 E
Houtman Is., W. Australia	44	28 28 S	113 40 E
Hove, England	10	50 50N	0 10W
Howard, Queensland	43	25 16 S	152 32 E
Howard, Kan., U.S.A.	71	37 30N	96 17W
Howard, S.D., U.S.A.	70	44 2N	97 30W
Howatharra, W. Australia	44	28 29 S	114 33 E
Howe, U.S.A.	72	43 46N	113 0W
Howe C., N.S.W.	43	37 30 S	150 0 E
Howell, U.S.A.	68	42 38N	84 0W
Howick, Natal	57	29 28 S	30 14 E
Howick, New Zealand	46	36 54 S	174 48 E
Howley, Canada	63	49 12N	57 2W
Howrah, India	33	22 37N	88 27 E
Howth, Ireland	11	53 23N	6 3W
Howth Hd., Ireland	11	53 21N	6 0W
Hoyanger, Norway	23	61 25N	6 50 E
Hoyos, Spain	17	40 9N	6 45W
Hpungan Pass, Burma	33	27 30N	96 55 E
Hrádek, Czechoslovakia	16	48 46N	16 16 E
Hron R., C.Slov.	16	48 0N	18 4 E
Hrvtafjördúr, Iceland	22	65 30N	21 10W
Hsaichwan Shan, China	39	21 35N	112 32 E
Hsenwi, Burma	33	23 22N	97 55 E
Hsiao Shan, China	38	34 15N	110 45 E
Hsiapachen, Inner Mongolia	38	40 43N	106 35 E
Hsilo R., Formosa	39	23 35N	120 35 E
Hsinchu, Taiwan	39	24 48N	120 59 E
Hsinying, China	39	23 20N	120 15 E
Hsüchang, China	38	34 2N	114 0 E
Huacho, Peru	78	10 35 S	76 0W
Huachon, Peru	78	11 10 S	77 35W
Huacrachuco, Peru	78	8 35 S	76 50W
Huailas, Peru	78	8 50 S	78 0W

	MAP		
Huaillay Peru	78	11 0s	76 25w
Huaitara, Peru	78	13 50s	75 0w
Huajuapan, Mexico	74	17 50N	98 0w
Hualien, Formosa	39	23 59N	121 28 E
Huallaga R., Peru	78	7 30s	76 10w
Huancabamba, Peru	78	5 10s	79 15w
Huancane, Peru	78	15 10s	69 50w
Huancapi, Peru	78	13 25s	74 0w
Huancavelica, Peru	78	12 50s	75 5w
Huancayo, Peru	78	12 5s	75 0w
Huanchaca, Bolivia	78	20 20s	66 45w
Huanchaca, Bolivia	78	14 50s	61 10w
Huanta, Peru	78	12 20s	74 2w
Huánuco, Peru	78	9 55s	76 15w
Huara, Chile	78	19 55s	69 50w
Huaras, Peru	78	9 30s	77 32w
Huari, Bolivia	78	19 0s	66 50w
Huascaran Mt., Peru	78	9 0s	77 30w
Huasco, Chile	77	28 24s	71 15w
Huatabampo, Mexico	74	26 50N	109 50w
Huauchinango, Mexico	74	20 11N	98 4w
Huaynamota, Mexico	74	22 0N	104 35w
Hubbard, U.S.A.	71	31 49N	96 47w
Hubbart Pt., Canada	65	59 10N	94 55w
Hubli, India	32	15 22N	75 15 E
Huchang, Korea	36	41 30N	126 35 E
Huchow, China	39	30 55N	120 5 E
Huchuetenango, Guatemala	59	15 25N	91 30w
Huddersfield, England	10	53 38N	1 49w
Hudat, Ethiopia	53	4 40N	39 10 E
Hudiksvall, Sweden	23	61 43N	17 10 E
Hudson, Canada	62	50 6N	92 9w
Hudson, Mich., U.S.A.	68	41 50N	84 20w
Hudson, N.Y., U.S.A.	72	42 15N	73 46w
Hudson, Wis., U.S.A.	70	44 57N	92 45w
Hudson Bay, Canada	61	60 0N	86 0w
Hudson Bay Junc., Can.	65	52 50N	102 30w
Hudson Falls, U.S.A.	68	43 18N	73 34w
Hudson Hope, Canada	64	56 0N	121 54w
Hudson Str., Canada	61	62 0N	70 0w
Hudson R., U.S.A.	68	42 0N	73 52w
Hué, Viet Nam	34	16 30N	107 35 E
Huelva, Spain	17	37 18N	6 57w
Huercal Overa, Spain	17	37 23N	2 3w
Huesca, Spain	17	42 8N	0 25w
Huescar, Spain	17	37 44N	2 35w
Huetamo, Mexico	74	18 36N	100 54w
Huetuetenango, Guat.	74	15 18N	91 53w
Huete, Spain	17	40 10N	2 43w
Hughenden, Queens.	42	20 52s	144 10 E
Hugh, R., N. Terr.	45	24 30s	133 55 E
Hughes, Alaska	59	65 59N	154 5w
Hughes, S. Australia	45	30 40s	129 30 E
Hughes, R., Canada	65	56 0N	100 30w
Hugo, Col., U.S.A.	70	39 12N	103 29w
Hugo, Okla., U.S.A.	71	34 0N	95 30w
Hugoton, U.S.A.	71	37 14N	101 19w
Huhehot, China	38	40 50N	111 50 E
Huiarau Ra., N.Z.	46	38 45s	176 55 E
Huichapan, Mexico	74	20 24N	99 40w
Huila Mt., Colombia	78	3 0N	76 0w
Huiling-Shan I., China	39	21 40N	111 50 E
Huinung, China	38	39 4N	106 37 E
Huiroa, New Zealand	46	39 15s	174 30 E
Huisne R., France	12	48 13N	0 45 E
Huixtla, Mexico	74	15 9N	92 30w
Huiya, Saudi Arabia	30	24 44N	49 12 E
Huka Falls, N.Z.	46	38 39s	176 6 E
Hukawng Valley, Burma	33	26 30N	96 30 E
Huksan Chedo, I., S. Korea	36	34 22N	125 13 E
Hukuntsi, Botswana	57	24 2s	21 48 E
Hula, Ethiopia	54	6 33N	38 30 E
Hula L., Israel (reclaimed)	29	33 5N	35 8 E
Hulaifa, Saudi Arabia	30	26 0N	40 58 E
Hulan, China	38	46 2N	126 50 E
Hulbert, Queensland	42	20 38s	142 35 E
Hulda, Israel	29	31 50N	34 51 E
Huldo, Mongolia	37	45 10N	105 35 E
Hull, Canada	62	45 20N	75 40w
Hull R., England	10	53 55N	0 23w
Hulst, Netherlands	13	51 17N	4 2 E
Humahuaca, Argentina	77	23 10s	65 25w
Humaitá, Amazonas, Brazil	78	7 35s	62 40w
Humansdorp, C. Prov.	57	34 2s	24 46 E
Humber R., England	10	53 42N	0 20w
Humble, U.S.A.	71	29 58N	95 14w
Humboldt, Canada	65	52 15N	105 9w
Humboldt, Tenn., U.S.A.	71	35 50N	88 55w
Humboldt, Iowa, U.S.A.	70	42 44N	94 13w
Humboldt Bay, U.S.A.	66	41 0N	124 0w
Humboldt Gl., Green.	58	79 30N	63 0w
Humboldt Mts., N.Z.	47	44 40s	168 11 E
Humboldt R., U.S.A.	72	40 55N	116 0w
Hume, L. Victoria	43	36 0s	147 0 E
Humeburn, Queensland	43	27 26s	145 10 E
Humphreys Pk., U.S.A.	73	35 25N	111 40w
Hun, Libya	51	29 25N	16 5 E
Huna Floi, Iceland	22	65 50N	21 0w
Húnafloi, B., Iceland	22	65 50N	21 0w
Hunan, prov., China	39	27 35N	111 20 E
Hunchun, China	39	42 55N	130 28 E
Hundred Mile Ho., Can.	64	51 40N	121 20w

	MAP		
Hunedoara, Rumania	21	45 40N	22 50 E
Hung Ho, R., China	38	33 10N	115 30 E
Hungary, st., Europe	16	47 20N	19 20 E
Hungerford, Queens.	43	28 58s	144 25 E
Hunghae, S. Korea	36	36 5N	129 22 E
Hunghai Wan, China	39	22 40N	115 30 E
Hunghu (Sinti), China	39	29 53N	113 18 E
Hungkiang, China	39	27 0N	109 51 E
Hungnam, Korea	36	40 0N	127 30 E
Hungshui K., China	39	24 20N	107 20 E
Hungshui K., R., China	39	24 20N	107 10 E
Hungtze Hu, China	38	33 20N	118 35 E
Hungund, India	32	16 0N	76 0 E
Hung Yen, N. Viet Nam	39	20 38N	106 5 E
Huni, Ghana	52	5 30N	1 53w
Huns Mts., S.W. Africa	57	27 25s	17 9 E
Hunsrück Mts., Ger.	14	50 0N	7 30 E
Hunstanton, Eng.	10	52 57N	0 30 E
Hunsur, India	32	12 20N	76 19 E
Hunter, New Zealand	47	44 36s	171 2 E
Hunter, U.S.A.	70	47 15N	97 15w
Hunter and Manning, dist., N.S.W.	43	32 15s	151 15 E
Hunter I., Canada	64	51 55N	128 0w
Hunter Is., Tasmania	43	40 30s	144 46 E
Hunter Mts., N.Z.	47	45 43s	167 25 E
Hunter R., N.S.W.	43	32 25s	150 50 E
Hunter R., N.Z.	47	44 15s	169 29 E
Hunter Ra., N.S.W.	43	32 45s	150 15 E
Hunters Hill, The, N.Z.	47	44 26s	170 46 E
Hunter's Road, S. Rhod.	56	19 10s	29 43 E
Hunterville, N. Z.	46	39 56s	175 35 E
Huntingdon, Canada	62	45 10N	74 10w
Huntingdon, England	10	52 20N	0 11w
Huntingdon, Pa., U.S.A.	68	40 28N	78 1w
Huntingdon, Tenn., U.S.A.	68	36 0N	82 25w
Huntingdon I., Canada	63	53 48N	56 45w
Huntington, Calif., U.S.A.	73	33 59N	118 17w
Huntington, Ind., U.S.A.	68	40 52N	85 30w
Huntington, Ore., U.S.A.	72	44 24N	117 20w
Huntington, Utah, U.S.A.	73	39 20N	111 1w
Huntington, W. Va., U.S.A.	68	38 20N	82 30w
Huntly, New Zealand	46	37 34s	175 11 E
Huntly, Scotland	10	57 27N	2 48w
Huntsville, Canada	62	45 25N	79 15w
Huntsville, Ala., U.S.A.	69	34 44N	86 33w
Huntsville, Tex., U.S.A.	71	30 50N	95 35w
Huntung, China	38	36 15N	111 34 E
Hunyani Dams, Rhodesia	56	18 0s	31 10 E
Hunyani R., Rhod.	56	16 15s	30 27 E
Hupei, prov., China	39	31 15N	113 0 E
Hurley, N. Mexico, U.S.A.	73	32 40N	108 7w
Hurley, Wis., U.S.A.	70	46 27N	90 13w
Huron L., Canada–U.S.A.	62	45 0N	83 0w
Hurricane, U.S.A.	73	37 10N	113 19w
Hurunui R., N.Z.	47	42 48s	172 25 E
Husavik, Iceland	22	66 3N	17 13w
Husi, Rumania	21	46 41N	28 7 E
Huskvarna, Sweden	23	57 47N	14 15 E
Hussar, Canada	64	51 10N	112 40w
Hussein Br., Jordan	29	31 53N	35 33 E
Husum, Sweden	23	63 21N	19 12 E
Hutch, mt., U.S.A.	73	34 50N	111 26w
Hutchinson, C. Prov.	57	31 30s	23 9 E
Hutchinson, Kan., U.S.A.	71	38 3N	97 59w
Hutchinson, Minn., U.S.A.	70	44 50N	94 26w
Huto Ho, China	38	38 30N	113 45 E
Huttig, U.S.A.	71	33 2N	92 12w
Hutton Mt., Queens.	43	25 52s	148 22 E
Hutton Ra., W. Austral.	45	24 45s	123 40 E
Huttwil, Switzerland	15	47 7N	7 50 E
Huwan, Egypt	51	29 50N	31 20 E
Huwunnh, Ethiopia	53	4 25N	40 2 E
Huwwara, Jordan	29	32 9N	35 15 E
Huy, Belgium	13	50 31N	5 51 E
Hvammsfjördur, Ice.	22	65 3N	22 30w
Hvar, Yugoslavia	20	43 10N	16 45 E
Hvita R., Iceland	22	64 50N	21 20w
Hvitárvatn, I., Iceland	22	64 35N	19 33w
Hwahsien, China	38	34 27N	109 33 E
Hwai Ho, China	39	32 20N	114 30 E
Hwainan, China	38	32 31N	116 58 E
Hwaiyang, China	38	33 40N	115 5 E
Hwaiyang Shan, China	39	32 0N	114 0 E
Hwan Ho, China	38	35 30N	107 50 E
Hwang Ho, R., China	38	37 15N	117 40 E
Hwangan, China	39	31 20N	114 42 E
Hwangchwan, China	39	32 12N	115 5 E
Hwanghae North, prov., N. Korea	36	38 28N	126 41 E
Hwanghae South, prov., N. Korea	36	38 15N	125 0 E
Hwangpei, China	38	35 42N	109 4 E
Hwangshih, China	39	30 8N	115 0 E
Hwangyenhsen, China	39	28 40N	121 10 E
Hwanjen, China	38	41 20N	125 20 E
Hwateh, Mongolia	38	41 50N	114 6 E
Hweianhsien, China	39	5 25N	118 50 E
Hweichanghsien, China	39	30 25N	115 40 E

	MAP		
Hweihsien, China	38	35 30N	113 50 E
Hweilaih, China	39	23 10N	116 18 E
Hweimin, China	38	37 30N	117 30 E
Hweining, China	38	36 45N	105 10 E
Hweitseh, China	37	31 0N	105 0 E
Hwo Shan, China	38	36 30N	112 0 E
Hwohsien, China	38	36 30N	111 38 E
Hwokiu, China	39	32 30N	116 15 E
Hyannis, U.S.A.	70	42 2N	101 46w
Hyattsville, U.S.A.	69	38 59N	76 55w
Hydaburg, Alaska	59	55 20N	132 40w
Hyde, New Zealand	47	45 18s	170 16 E
Hyden, W. Australia	44	32 24s	118 46 E
Hyderabad, India	32	17 10N	78 20 E
Hyderabad, Terr., W. Pakistan	32	25 0N	68 0 E
Hyderabad, W. Pak.	32	25 23N	68 36 E
Hyères, France	12	43 8N	6 9 E
Hyères, Is. de, France	12	43 0N	6 28 E
Hyesan, N. Korea	36	41 16N	128 7 E
Hyland Mt., N.S.W.	43	30 11s	152 25 E
Hyland Post, Canada	64	57 40N	128 10w
Hyland R., Canada	64	60 30N	128 20w
Hyndman Pk., U.S.A.	66	44 4N	114 0w
Hyndman Pk., U.S.A.	72	43 52N	114 2w
Hyogo, pref., Japan	36	35 15N	135 0 E
Hyrum, U.S.A.	72	41 38N	111 50w
Hyrynsalmi, Finland	22	64 40N	28 47 E
Hysham, U.S.A.	72	46 19N	107 11w
Hyuga, Japan	36	32 35N	131 40 E
Hyvinkää, Finland	22	60 38N	25 0 E

I

Iaco, R., Brazil	78	10 15s	69 30w
Iar Connacht, dist., Ireland	11	53 20N	9 25w
Iasi, Rumania	21	47 10N	27 40 E
Iauareté, Colombia	78	0 20N	69 5w
Iba, Philippines	35	15 22N	120 0 E
Ibadan, Nigeria	52	7 22N	3 58 E
Ibagué, Colombia	78	4 40N	75 20w
Ialomita, R., Rumania	21	44 37N	26 30 E
Ibar R., Yugoslavia	21	43 15N	20 40 E
Ibaraki, pref., Japan	36	36 10N	140 10 E
Ibarra, Ecuador	78	0 30N	78 0w
Ibba, Sudan	53	4 55N	29 2 E
Iberville, Canada	62	55 19N	73 17w
Ibi, Nigeria	52	8 15N	9 50 E
Ibiá, Brazil	79	19 30s	46 30w
Ibiapaba, Sa. da, Braz.	79	5 0s	42 0w
Ibicuy, Argentina	77	33 55s	59 10w
Ibiraçu, Brazil	79	19 50s	40 30w
Ibiri, Tanzania	53	4 56s	32 33 E
Ibiza (Iviza) I., Spain	17	39 0N	1 30 E
Ibo, Mozambique	55	12 21s	40 40 E
Ibonama, Indonesia	35	3 30s	133 35 E
Ibotirama, Brazil	79	12 17s	43 25w
Ibra, 'Oman	31	23 30N	58 29 E
Ibrahim, J., Si. Arabia	30	20 25N	41 5 E
Iburi, B., Japan	36	42 30N	140 30 E
Ibwe Munyama, Zambia	56	16 9s	28 34 E
Icá, Peru	78	14 0s	75 30w
Iça R., Brazil	78	2 55s	69 0w
Icaña. Argentina	78	28 50s	63 0w
Icaño, Argentina	77	28 53s	65 20w
Ice Barrier Mt., Ant.	80	79 0s	179 0w
Iceland I., N. Atlan. Oc.	22	65 0N	19 0w
Icha, U.S.S.R.	27	55 30N	156 0 E
Ichang, China	39	25 19N	112 52 E
Ichchapuram, India	33	19 10N	84 40 E
Ichikawa, Japan	36	35 55N	139 58 E
Ichinohe, Japan	36	40 10N	141 25 E
Ichinomiya, Japan	36	35 22N	136 55 E
Ichinoseki, Japan	36	39 0N	141 8 E
Ichnya, U.S.S.R.	25	50 50N	32 20 E
Ichun, Kiangsi, China	39	27 40N	114 18 E
Ichun, Shensi, China	38	35 18N	108 58 E
Ichwan, China	38	36 10N	110 0 E
Icy Str., Alaska	64	58 20N	135 30w
Ida Grove, U.S.A.	70	42 17N	95 28w
Idabel, U.S.A.	71	33 55N	94 55w
Idah, Nigeria	52	6 10N	6 40 E
Idaho, st., U.S.A.	74	44 10N	114 0w
Idaho City, U.S.A.	72	43 50N	115 47w
Idaho Falls, U.S.A.	74	43 30N	112 10w
Idaho Springs, U.S.A.	70	39 48N	105 30w
Idanre, Nigeria	52	7 8N	5 5 E
Idd el Ghanam, Sudan	51	11 30N	24 25 E
Idehan Marzuq, des., Libya	51	25 0N	13 20 E
Idelès, Algeria	50	23 58N	5 53 E
Idenau, W. Cameroon	52	4 12N	8 58 E
Idfu, Egypt	51	25 0N	32 49 E
Idhi, Mt., Crete	20	35 15N	24 45 E
Idhra, I., Greece	20	37 25N	23 30 E
Idi, Indonesia	34	4 55N	97 45 E
Idiofa, Zaire	54	4 55s	19 42 E
Idjil (Ft. Gourand), Mauritania	50	22 40N	12 45w
Idna, Jordan	29	31 34N	34 58 E
Idodi, Tanganyika	53	2 55s	35 8 E
Idritsa, U.S.S.R.	25	56 25N	28 57 E
Idutywa, C. Prov.	57	32 8s	28 18 E
Ienhwai, China	39	27 52N	106 21 E
Ieper (Ypres), Belgium	13	50 51N	2 53 E

	MAP		
Ierapetra, Crete	20	35 0N	25 44 E
Iesi, Italy	20	43 32N	13 12 E
Ierzu, Sardinia	20	39 48N	9 32 E
Iesi, Italy	20	43 32N	13 12 E
Ifakara, Tanzania	53	8 8s	36 41 E
Ife, Nigeria	52	7 30N	4 31 E
Iférouané, Niger	50	19 5N	8 35 E
Iferuan, Niger	50	19 2N	8 31 E
Iffley, Queensland	42	18 50s	141 10 E
Ifni, Span. Col., Africa	50	29 25N	10 10w
Ifoko, Nigeria	52	4 31N	8 0 E
Ifon, Nigeria	52	6 58N	5 40 E
Ifukutwa, Tanzania	53	6 7s	30 55 E
Igalula, Tanzania	53	5 13s	33 0 E
Iganga, Uganda	53	0 36N	33 28 E
Igarapava, Brazil	79	20 0s	48 0w
Igarka, U.S.S.R.	26	67 30N	87 20 E
Igatpuri, India	32	19 41N	73 38 E
Igawa, Tanzania	53	8 46s	34 23 E
Igbetti, Nigeria	52	8 44N	4 6 E
Igbo-ora, Nigeria	52	7 27N	3 17 E
Igboho, Nigeria	52	8 40N	3 50 E
Igbor, Nigeria	52	7 46N	8 34 E
Iğdir, Turkey	30	39 59N	44 0 E
Iggesund, Sweden	23	61 39N	17 10 E
Iglesia, Argentina	77	30 30s	69 10w
Ignace, Canada	62	49 30N	91 40w
Iguala, Mexico	74	18 20N	99 40w
Igualada, Spain	17	41 37N	1 37 E
Iguape, Brazil	77	24 44s	47 31w
Iguape R., Brazil	77	24 40s	48 0w
Iguaçú Falls, Arg.–Braz.	77	25 35s	54 22w
Iguaçú, R., Brazil	77	25 35s	52 20w
Iguatú, Brazil	79	6 20s	39 25w
Iguéla, Gabon	54	2 0s	9 16 E
Igumale, Nigeria	52	6 49N	7 55 E
Ihiala, Nigeria	52	5 40N	6 55 E
Ihing, China	39	31 30N	119 50 E
Ihsien, China	38	30 0N	118 0 E
Ihugh, Nigeria	52	7 1N	9 0 E
Ihwang, China	39	27 33N	116 6 E
Iida, Japan	36	35 35N	137 56 E
Iisalmi, Finland	23	63 38N	27 10 E
Ijara, Kenya	53	1 36s	40 32 E
Ijebu-Igbo, Nigeria	52	6 56N	4 1 E
Ijebu-ode, Nigeria	52	6 47N	3 52 E
IJmuiden, Netherlands	13	52 28N	4 35 E
IJsselmeer, Netherlands	13	52 45N	5 20 E
Ikamatua, New Zealand	47	42 15s	171 41 E
Ikang, Nigeria	52	4 49N	8 30 E
Ikanga, Kenya	53	1 42s	38 4 E
Ikara, Nigeria	52	11 13N	8 8 E
Ikare, Nigeria	52	7 18N	5 40 E
Ikeda, Japan	36	34 0N	133 50 E
Ikeja, Nigeria	52	6 28N	3 45 E
Ikela, Zaire	54	1 0s	23 35 E
Ikerre, Nigeria	52	7 25N	5 19 E
Iki, I., Japan	36	33 45N	129 42 E
Ikimba L., Tanzania	53	1 30s	31 20 E
Ikire, Nigeria	52	7 10N	4 15 E
Ikirun, Nigeria	52	7 57N	4 39 E
Ikole, Nigeria	52	7 40N	5 37 E
Ikom, Nigeria	52	6 0N	8 42 E
Ikoma, Tanzania	53	2 2s	34 36 E
Ikot Ekpene, Nigeria	52	5 12N	7 40 E
Ikrayanoye, U.S.S.R.	25	46 10N	47 52 E
Ikungu, Tanzania	53	1 34s	33 41 E
Ikutha, Kenya	53	2 5s	38 11 E
Ila, Nigeria	52	8 0N	4 51 E
Ilagan, Philippines	35	17 1N	121 50 E
Ilam, Nepal	33	26 55N	87 55 E
Ilām, Persia	30	33 44N	46 31 E
Illan, Taiwan	37	24 45N	121 42 E
Ile-à-la-Crosse, L., Can.	65	55 30N	108 0w
Ile de France, prov., Fr.	12	49 0N	2 20 E
Ile d'Oleron, France	12	45 58N	1 28w
Ile Rousse, Corsica	12	42 38N	8 55 E
Ilek, U.S.S.R.	24	51 40N	53 0 E
Ilek, R., U.S.S.R.	24	51 0N	51 10 E
Ilemba, Tanzania	53	8 16s	31 59 E
Ilero, Nigeria	52	8 0N	3 20 E
Ilesha, Northern Nig.	52	8 57N	3 28 E
Ilesha, Western Nig.	52	7 37N	4 40 E
Ilfracombe, England	10	51 13N	4 8w
Ilfracombe, Queens.	42	23 30s	144 30 E
Ilgan, Philippines	35	8 15N	124 25 E
Ilhavo, Portugal	17	40 33N	8 43w
Ilhéus, Brazil	79	15 0s	39 10w
Ili, U.S.S.R.	26	44 10N	77 20 E
Ili R., U.S.S.R.	26	44 30N	76 30 E
Iliamna, L., Alaska	59	59 30N	155 0w
Ilich, U.S.S.R.	26	41 0N	68 10 E
Iliff, U.S.A.	70	40 52N	103 2w
Iliodhromia I., Greece	21	39 12N	23 52 E
Ilion, U.S.A.	68	43 0N	75 3w
Ilkal, India	32	15 59N	76 11 E
Ilkhuri-Shan Mts., China	37	51 30N	124 0 E
Illampú Mt., Bolivia	78	16 0s	68 50w
Illapel, Chile	77	32 0s	71 10w
'Illar, Jordan	29	32 23N	35 7 E
Illela, Niger	52	14 29N	5 14 E
Iller, R., Germany	14	47 53N	10 10 E
Illimani Mt., Bolivia	78	16 30s	67 50w
Illinois, st., U.S.A.	70	40 15N	89 30w
Illinois R., U.S.A.	70	40 20N	90 0w
Illiwa R., Guyana	78	3 10N	58 55w
Ilmen L., U.S.S.R.	25	58 15N	31 10 E

Place	Map	Latitude	Longitude
Ilo, Peru	78	17 40 s	71 20w
Ilobu, Nigeria	52	7 45N	4 25 E
Iloilo, Philippines	35	10 45N	122 33 E
Ilondola, Zambia	56	10 42 s	31 47 E
Ilongero, Tanzania	53	4 41 s	34 50 E
Ilora, Nigeria	52	7 45N	3 50 E
Ilorin, Nigeria	52	8 30N	4 35 E
Ilovolyo R., U.S.S.R.	25	49 50N	44 45 E
Ilwaki, Indonesia	35	7 55 s	126 30 E
Imabari, Japan	36	34 4N	133 0 E
Imandra L., U.S.S.R.	22	67 45N	33 0 E
Imatra, Finland	23	61 10N	28 50 E
Imbler, U.S.A.	72	45 30N	117 59w
Imeri, Sa. Venezuela	70	0 40N	65 30w
Imlay, U.S.A.	72	40 40N	118 12w
Immarna, S. Australia	45	30 30 s	132 12 E
Immingham, England	10	53 37N	0 12w
Immokalee, U.S.A	69	26 25N	81 20w
Imo R., Nigeria	52	4 55N	7 15 E
Imola, Italy	20	44 20N	11 42 E
Imperia, Italy	20	43 52N	8 0 E
Imperial, Canada	65	51 21N	105 28w
Imperial, Calif., U.S.A.	73	32 48N	115 32w
Imperial, Neb., U.S.A.	70	40 39N	101 37w
Impfondo, Congo (Fr.)	54	1 40N	18 0 E
Imphal, India	33	24 15N	94 0 E
Imroz, Turkey	30	40 10N	26 0 E
'Imwas, Jordan	29	31 51N	34 59 E
In Belbel, Algeria	50	27 55N	1 12 E
In Gall, Niger	50	16 58N	6 57 E
In Jakout, Mali	52	15 28N	3 3 E
In Samia, Niger	52	14 45N	8 21 E
Ina, Japan	36	35 50N	138 0 E
Inangahua Junc., N.Z.	47	41 52 s	171 59 E
Inapari, Peru	78	11 0 s	69 40w
Inari, Finland	22	68 54N	27 5 E
Inari L., Finland	22	69 0N	28 0 E
Inca de Ora, Chile	77	26 48 s	70 0w
Inceburun C., Turkey	30	42 2N	35 0 E
Inchon, Korea	37	37 30N	126 30 E
Incomtai, R., Mozam.	55	23 15 s	32 26 E
Indals R., Sweden	23	62 55N	16 50 E
Indarapura, Indonesia	34	2 5 s	101 2 E
Indaw, Burma	33	24 15N	96 5 E
Independence, Calif., U.S.A.	73	36 50N	118 12w
Independence, Iowa, U.S.A.	70	42 27N	91 55w
Independence, Kansas, U.S.A.	71	37 10N	95 50w
Independence, Miss., U.S.A.	70	39 4N	94 24w
Independence, Oregon, U.S.A.	72	44 51N	123 12w
Independence Mts., U.S.A.	72	41 15N	116 10w
Independencia, Arg.	77	31 40 s	68 23w
Independent Harbour, Canada	63	58 49N	57 0w
Inderagiri R., Indonesia	34	0 30 s	102 30 E
India, subcontinent, Asia	28	23 0N	80 0 E
India, U.S.A.	73	33 46N	116 16w
Indian Harbour, Can.	63	54 28N	57 15w
India Head, Canada	65	50 30N	103 35w
Indian House, L., Can.	63	66 30N	65 0w
Indian Ocean	5	15 0N to 35 0 s	45 0 E to 112 0 E
Indian Union (Bharat), rep., Asia	32	22 0N	78 0 E
Indiana, U.S.A.	68	40 38N	79 9w
Indiana, st., U.S.A.	68	40 0N	86 0w
Indianapolis, U.S.A.	68	39 42N	86 10w
Indianola, Iowa, U.S.A.	70	41 18N	93 34w
Indianola, Miss., U.S.A.	71	33 28N	90 31w
Indiga, U.S.S.R.	24	67 50N	48 50 E
Indigirka R., U.S.S.R.	27	69 30N	147 30 E
Indija, Yugoslavia	21	45 6N	20 7 E
Indonesia, rep., Asia	35	5 0 s	115 0 E
Indooroopilly, Queens.	43	27 35 s	152 47 E
Indore, India	32	22 42N	75 53 E
Indramaju, Indonesia	34	6 21 s	108 20 E
Indramaju Tg., C., Indonesia	34	6 15 s	108 18 E
Indravati, R., India	32	19 0N	81 15 E
Indur, Israel	29	32 37N	35 23 E
Indus, R., W. Pakistan	32	28 40N	70 10 E
Indwe, Cape Province	57	31 27 s	27 22 E
Inebolu, Turkey	30	41 55N	33 40 E
Inegöl, Turkey	30	40 5N	29 31 E
Infanta, C., C. Prov.	57	34 27 s	20 51 E
Infantes, Spain	17	38 43N	3 1w
Ingende, Zaire	54	0 12 s	18 57 E
Ingersoll, Canada	62	43 4N	80 55w
Ingham, Queensland	42	18 43 s	146 10 E
Inglewood, N.Z.	46	39 9 s	174 14 E
Inglewood, Queens.	43	28 25 s	151 8 E
Inglewood, U.S.A.	73	33 59N	118 27w
Inglewood, Victoria	43	36 29 s	143 53 E
Ingolfshöfdi B., Iceland	22	63 48N	16 38w
Ingonish, Canada	63	46 42N	60 18w
Ingomar, U.S.A.	72	46 33N	107 17w
Ingul R., U.S.S.R.	25	47 30N	32 15 E
Ingulets R., U.S.S.R.	25	47 20N	33 20 E
Ingwavuma, Natal	57	27 8 s	32 2 E
Ingwe, Zambia	56	13 0 s	26 0 E
Inhaca, Mozambique	57	26 1 s	32 58 E
Inhacoro (Tambara), Mozambique	56	16 45 s	34 10 E
Inhafenga, Mozambique	56	20 35 s	33 55 E
Inhambane, Mozam.	55	23 51 s	35 29 E
Inhaminga, Mozam.	56	18 25 s	34 45 E
Inharrime, Mozam.	55	24 29 s	35 1 E
Ining, China	39	25 19N	110 0 E
Inirida R., Colombia	78	3 0N	69 0w
Inishbofin I., Ireland	11	53 35N	10 12w
Inishmore, I., Ireland	11	53 7N	9 45w
Inistioge, Ireland	11	52 30N	7 5w
Injidiv, I., India	32	14 42N	74 4 E
Injune, Queensland	43	25 46 s	148 32 E
Inklin & R., Canada	64	58 50N	132 30w
Inkom, U.S.A.	72	42 50N	112 14w
Inland Sea, Japan	36	34 30N	133 30 E
Inle Lake, Burma	33	20 30N	97 0 E
Inn, R., Austria–Ger.	14	46 45N	10 10 E
Innamincka, S. Austral.	43	27 44 s	140 46 E
Inner Mongolia, China	37	45 0N	120 0 E
Innetalling, I., Canada	62	55 50N	79 5w
Innisfail, Canada	64	52 0N	114 0w
Innisfail, Queensland	42	17 33 s	146 5 E
Innisfree, Canada	64	53 25N	111 40w
Innsbruck, Austria	14	47 16N	11 23 E
Inney, R., Ireland	11	51 56N	10 0w
Inongo, Zaire	54	1 55 s	18 30 E
Inowroclaw, Poland	16	52 50N	18 20 E
Inquisivi, Bolivia	78	16 50 s	66 45w
Inscription C., Austral.	44	25 29 s	113 0 E
Insein, Burma	33	16 46N	96 18 E
Interlaken, Switzerland	15	46 41N	7 50 E
Interior, U.S.A.	70	43 46N	102 0w
International Falls, U.S.A.	70	48 36N	93 27w
Interview I., India	33	13 0N	93 0 E
Intiyaco, Argentina	77	28 50 s	60 0w
Inutil B., Chile	77	53 30 s	70 15w
Invercargill, N.Z.	47	46 24 s	168 24 E
Invercargill, Sth., N.Z.	47	46 26 s	168 23 E
Inverell, N.S.W.	43	29 42 s	151 2 E
Invermere, Canada	64	50 51N	116 9w
Inverness, Canada	63	46 15N	61 19w
Inverness, Scotland	10	57 29N	4 12w
Inverness, U.S.A.	69	28 50N	82 20w
Inverurie, Scotland	10	57 15N	2 21w
Investigator Str., S. Australia	43	35 30 s	137 0 E
Inwood, Canada	65	42 48N	81 59w
Inya, U.S.S.R.	26	50 45N	86 45 E
Inyanga, tn., Rhodesia	56	18 13 s	32 46 E
Inyanga Mts., Rhodesia	56	18 0 s	32 46 E
Inyantue, Rhodesia	56	18 34 s	26 42 E
Inyati, Rhodesia	56	19 41 s	28 52 E
Inyazura, Rhodesia	56	18 43 s	32 10 E
Inyokern, U.S.A.	73	35 38N	117 50w
Inza, U.S.S.R.	25	53 55N	46 25 E
Ioánnina, Greece	21	39 39N	20 57 E
Iola, U.S.A.	71	38 0N	95 20w
Iona I., Scotland	10	56 20N	6 25w
Ione, U.S.A.	72	48 48N	117 29w
Ione, U.S.A.	73	38 24N	120 59w
Ionia, U.S.A.	68	42 59N	85 7w
Ionian Is., Greece	21	38 40N	20 0 E
Ionian Sea, Europe	21	37 30N	17 30 E
Ios, Is., Greece	21	36 41N	25 20 E
Ioshkar Ola, U.S.S.R.	25	56 49N	47 50 E
Iowa City, U.S.A.	70	41 37N	91 31w
Iowa Falls, U.S.A.	70	42 30N	93 15w
Iowa, st., U.S.A.	70	42 18N	93 30w
Ipala, Tanzania	53	4 30 s	32 53 E
Ipameri, Brazil	79	17 55 s	48 10w
Ipiales, Colombia	78	1 0N	77 45w
Ipin, China	39	28 48N	104 51 E
Ipixuna, Brazil	78	7 10 s	72 20w
Ipoh, Malaya	34	4 36N	101 4 E
Ipokera, Tanzania	53	8 3 s	35 41 E
Ipole, Tanzania	53	5 46 s	32 45 E
Ippy, Cent. Afr. Rep.	54	6 5N	21 7 E
Ipswich, England	10	52 4N	1 9 E
Ipswich, Queensland	43	27 38 s	152 37 E
Ipswich, U.S.A.	70	45 30N	99 0w
Ipúia, Brazil	79	4 20 s	40 45w
Ipusukilo, Zambia	56	10 22 s	29 52 E
Iput R., U.S.S.R.	25	53 0N	32 10 E
Iquique, Chile	78	20 19 s	70 5w
Iquitos, Peru	78	3 45 s	73 10w
Iracoubo, Fr. Guiana	79	5 30N	53 10w
Iraklion (Candia), Crete	20	35 10N	25 10 E
Iran, st., Asia	31	30 0N	55 0 E
Irānshahr, Iran	31	27 13N	60 36 E
Irapuato, Mexico	74	20 40N	101 40w
Iraq, rep., S.W. Asia	30	33 0N	44 0 E
Irazu Vol., Costa Rica	78	10 10N	84 20w
Irbid, Jordan	30	32 36N	35 50 E
Irbil, Iraq	30	36 20N	44 5 E
Irbit, U.S.S.R.	24	57 50N	63 0 E
Irebu, Congo	54	0 40 s	17 55 E
Ireland, rep., Europe	11	53 0N	8 0w
Ireland's Eye, Ireland	11	53 25N	6 4w
Ireland, I., Bermuda	75	32 20N	65 0w
Irele, Nigeria	52	7 40N	5 40 E
Ireng R., Guyana	78	4 20N	59 30w
Iret, U.S.S.R.	27	60 10N	154 5 E
Irgiz R., U.S.S.R.	25	52 10N	49 10 E
Iringa, Tanzania	53	7 46 s	35 38 E
Iringa Prov., Tanzania	53	8 0 s	35 30 E
Iriri, R., Brazil	79	4 20 s	54 0w
Irish Sea, British Isles	10	54 0N	5 0w
Irkineyeva, U.S.S.R.	27	58 45N	97 0 E
Irkutsk, U.S.S.R.	27	52 10N	104 20 E
Irma, Canada	64	53 0N	111 20w
Iron Baron, S. Austral.	43	33 3 s	137 11 E
Iron Gate, pass, Rum.–Yugoslavia	21	44 42N	22 30 E
Iron Knob, S. Australia	43	32 46 s	137 8 E
Iron Mountain, U.S.A.	70	45 49N	88 4w
Iron River, U.S.A.	70	46 6N	88 40w
Ironbridge, England	11	52 38N	2 29w
Ironton, Minn., U.S.A.	68	46 38N	93 58w
Ironton, Mo., U.S.A.	71	37 49N	90 42w
Ironwood, U.S.A.	70	46 30N	90 10w
Iroquois Falls, Canada	62	48 40N	80 40w
Irrawaddy, Mouths of the, Burma	33	15 35N	95 0 E
Irrawaddy R., Burma	33	19 30N	95 15 E
Irricana, Canada	64	51 20N	113 40w
Irtysh R., U.S.S.R.	28	53 36N	75 30 E
Irumu, Zaire	53	1 22N	29 55 E
Irvine, Canada	65	50 0N	110 20w
Irvine, Scotland	10	55 37N	4 40w
Irvine, U.S.A.	68	37 42N	83 58w
Irvinebank, Queensland	42	17 27 s	145 15 E
Irvinestown, N. Ireland	11	54 28N	7 38w
Irymple, Victoria	43	34 14 s	142 8 E
Isa, Nigeria	52	13 14N	6 24 E
Isaac, L., Canada	64	53 10N	120 40w
Isaacs R., Queensland	42	22 15 s	148 30 E
Isabel, U.S.A.	70	45 28N	101 27w
Isabela, I., Mexico	74	22 0N	106 0w
Isabella Cord., mts., Nicaragua	75	13 30N	85 25w
Isafjördur, Iceland	22	66 10N	23 15w
Isahaya, Japan	36	32 55N	130 2 E
Isaka, Tanzania	53	3 54 s	32 57 E
Isangi, Zaire	54	0 52N	24 10 E
Isanlu Makutu, Nigeria	52	8 20N	5 44 E
Isar R., Germany	14	48 36N	12 20 E
Isarco R., Italy	20	46 34N	11 30 E
Isbergues, France	13	50 40N	2 25w
Ischia I., Italy	20	40 45N	13 51 E
Ise Bay, Japan	36	34 45N	136 45 E
Isebania, Tanzania	53	1 15 s	34 28 E
Iseke, Tanzania	53	6 27 s	35 0 E
Isenyela, Tanzania	53	8 36 s	33 30 E
Iseo, Italy	20	45 40N	10 3 E
Iseramagazi, Tang.	53	4 40 s	32 9 E
Isère R., France	12	45 15N	5 30 E
Isernia, Italy	20	41 35N	14 12 E
Iset R., U.S.S.R.	24	56 40N	61 30 E
Iseyin, Nigeria	52	8 0N	3 36 E
Ishan, Kanusu, China	39	36 5N	106 43 E
Ishan, Kwangsi, China	39	24 25N	108 30 E
Ishango, Zaire	53	0 8 s	29 36 E
Ishara, Nigeria	52	6 40N	3 40 E
Ishikari, Bay, Japan	36	43 15N	141 0 E
Ishikawa, pref., Japan	36	36 30N	136 30 E
Ishim, U.S.S.R.	26	56 10N	69 18 E
Ishim R., U.S.S.R.	26	54 10N	67 30 E
Ishinomaki, Japan	36	38 30N	141 20 E
Ishkashim, Afghan.	31	36 40N	71 40 E
Ishkuman, Kashmir	32	36 40N	73 50 E
Ishpeming, U.S.A.	70	46 30N	87 40w
Ishua, Nigeria	52	7 15N	5 50 E
Ishui, China	38	35 46N	118 30 E
Isiro, Zaire	54	2 53N	27 58 E
Isipingo & Beach, Natal	57	30 0 s	30 57w
Isisford, Queensland	42	24 15 s	144 21 E
Isisi, Tanzania	53	7 19 s	35 53 E
Isit, U.S.S.R.	27	61 0N	125 0 E
Iskenderun (Alexandretta), Tur.	30	36 32N	36 10 E
Iskut River, Canada	64	57 25N	130 20w
Isla Cristina, Spain	17	37 14N	7 18w
Island Lagoon, S. Australia	45	31 30 s	136 50 E
Islamabad, Kashmir	32	33 44N	75 11 E
Island Falls, Canada	62	49 35N	81 20w
Island Hd., Queensland	42	22 20 s	150 45 E
Island L., Canada	65	53 40N	94 30w
Island Pond, U.S.A.	69	44 50N	71 50w
Islands, B. of, Canada	63	49 11N	58 15w
Islas Malvinas. *See* Falkland Is.	77		
Islay, I., Scotland	10	55 46N	6 10w
Isle aux Morts, Canada	63	47 35N	59 0w
Isle of Man, Brit. Is.	10	54 30N	4 40w
Isle of Wight, Eng.	10	50 40N	1 20w
Isle Royale, U.S.A.	70	48 0N	88 45w
Isles Dernieres, U.S.A.	71	29 5N	90 45w
Isleta, U.S.A.	73	34 53N	106 45w
Ismailia (Al Ismā'ilyah), Egypt	51	30 37N	32 18 E
Ismay, U.S.A.	70	46 35N	104 45w
Isna, Egypt	51	25 17N	32 30 E
Isoka, Zambia	56	10 4 s	32 42 E
Isole Ponziane, Italy	20	40 52N	13 0 E
Isonzo R., Italy–Y.slav.	20	46 0N	13 40 E
Isparta, Turkey	30	37 47N	30 30 E
Israel, st., Asia	29	32 30N	32 30 E
Isseka, W. Australia	44	28 22 s	114 35 E
Issoudun, France	12	46 57N	2 0 E
Issyk-Kul, L., U.S.S.R.	26	42 30N	77 30 E
Istiala, Greece	21	38 57N	23 9 E
Istanbul, Turkey	30	41 0N	29 0 E
Istokpoga, L., U.S.A.	69	27 22N	81 14w
Istra, dist., Y.slav.	20	45 20N	14 0 E
Itaberaba, Brazil	79	12 25 s	40 30w
Itabira, Brazil	79	19 29 s	43 23w
Itabaiana, Brazil	79	7 20 s	35 25w
Itabuna, Brazil	79	14 55 s	39 25w
Itacaiunas R., Brazil	79	5 50 s	50 50w
Itaeté, Brazil	79	13 0 s	41 5w
Itaituba, Brazil	79	4 10 s	55 50w
Itajai, Brazil	77	27 0 s	48 45w
Itaka, Tanzania	53	8 52 s	32 48 E
Itala, Somali Rep.	49	2 58N	46 27 E
Italy, rep., Europe	20	42 0N	13 0 E
Itambe Mt., Brazil	79	18 30 s	43 15w
Itapecurú, Brazil	79	3 20 s	44 15w
Itapecuru R., Brazil	79	5 5 s	44 30w
Itaperuna, Brazil	79	21 10 s	42 0w
Itapicurá R., Brazil	79	11 0 s	38 30w
Itapura, Brazil	79	20 30 s	51 30w
Itaqui, Brazil	77	29 0 s	56 30w
Itarsi, India	32	22 39N	77 48 E
Itatiaia, Brazil	77	22 10 s	44 30w
Itatuba, Brazil	78	5 40 s	63 20w
Itaunas, Brazil	79	18 30 s	39 50w
Itbayat I., Philippines	39	20 40N	121 30 E
Ithaca, Mich., U.S.A.	68	43 19N	84 38w
Ithaca, N.Y., U.S.A.	69	42 25N	76 30w
Ithaki I., Greece	21	38 25N	20 43 E
Itigi, Tanzania	53	5 40 s	34 34 E
Ito, Japan	36	35 0N	138 56 E
Itobo, Tanzania	53	4 11 s	33 0 E
Itu, Brazil	77	23 10 s	47 15w
Itu, Nigeria	52	5 2N	7 35 E
Ituiutaba, Brazil	79	4 20 s	48 5w
Itumbiara, Brazil	79	18 20 s	49 10w
Ituna, Canada	65	51 15N	103 25w
Itunge Port, Tanzania	57	9 35 s	33 55 E
Iturbe, Argentina	73	23 0 s	65 25w
Ituri, R., Zaire	53	1 10N	29 30 E
Ituxi R., Brazil	77	9 0 s	66 25w
Iulian, U.S.A.	73	33 6N	116 38w
Ivalo, Finland	22	68 38N	27 35 E
Ivalo R., Finland	22	68 27N	26 30 E
Ivanhoe, N.S.W.	43	32 56 s	144 20 E
Ivanhoe, W. Australia	44	15 40 s	128 39 E
Ivanhoe, U.S.A.	70	44 30N	96 17w
Ivanhoe L., Canada	65	60 25N	106 30w
Ivano Frankovsk (Stanislav), U.S.S.R.	24	49 0N	24 40 E
Ivanovo, U.S.S.R.	25	57 5N	41 0 E
Iviza I., Spain	17	39 0N	1 30 E
Ivory Coast, rep., Afr.	50	7 30N	5 0w
Ivrea, Italy	20	45 30N	7 52 E
Ivry, France	12	47 1N	4 35 E
Iwakuni, Japan	36	34 15N	132 8 E
Iwamizawa, Japan	36	43 10N	141 45 E
Iwanai, Japan	36	43 0N	140 30 E
Iwanizawa, Japan	36	43 12N	141 57 E
Iwanuma, Japan	36	38 5N	141 0 E
Iwata, Japan	36	34 49N	137 59 E
Iwate, pref., Japan	36	39 30N	141 30 E
Iwate-yama, mt., Japan	36	40 0N	141 0 E
Iwo, Nigeria	52	7 39N	4 9 E
Ixcuintla, Mexico	74	21 30N	105 30w
Ixopo, Natal	57	30 11 s	30 5 E
Ixtepec, Mexico	74	16 40N	95 10w
Ixtlán, Mexico	74	17 23N	96 28w
Ixtlán, Mexico	74	16 40N	95 10w
Iyang, China	38	34 3N	112 30 E
Izabal L., Guatemala	74	15 30N	89 10w
Izamal, Mexico	74	20 56N	89 1w
Izegem, Belgium	13	50 55N	3 12 E
Izhevsk, U.S.S.R.	24	56 50N	53 0 E
Izmail, U.S.S.R.	24	45 22N	28 46 E
Izmir (Smyrna), Turkey	30	38 25N	27 8 E
Izmit, Turkey	30	40 45N	29 50 E
Iznik Gölü, Turkey	30	40 20N	28 55 E
Izumo, Japan	36	35 27N	132 40 E
Izyum, U.S.S.R.	25	49 12N	37 28 E

J

Place	Map	Latitude	Longitude
Jaba', Jordan	29	32 20N	35 13 E
Jabal ash Sheikh (Mt. Hermon), Syria	30	33 20N	36 0 E
Jabal at Tubayq, Jordan	30	29 40N	37 10 E
Jabal at Tuwaiq Mts., Saudi Arabia	30	22 0N	46 0 E
Jabal Hafit, Mt., Muscat & 'Oman	31	24 0N	56 0 E
Jabal Hajar, Mt., Saudi Arabia	30	26 20N	40 0 E
Jabal Radhwa, Mt., Saudi Arabia	30	24 33N	38 12 E
Jabal Shammar, Mts., Saudi Arabia	30	27 42N	41 0 E
Jabal Unayzah, Iraq	30	32 12N	39 18 E
Jabaliya, Israel	29	31 32N	34 27 E
Jabalon R., Spain	17	38 45N	3 35w
Jabalpur, India	32	23 9N	79 58 E
Jablah, Syria	30	35 27N	35 58 E
Jablanica Mt., Albania	21	41 11N	20 38 E
Jablonec, C.Slov.	16	50 43N	15 10 E
Jablonowo, Poland	16	53 23N	19 10 E
Jablunka P., C.Slov.	16	49 30N	18 42 E
Jabrin, Saudi Arabia	30	23 7N	48 52 E

Name	Map	Lat.	Long.
Jaburú, Brazil	78	4 0S	66 25W
Jacarei, Brazil	77	23 20S	46 0W
Jacarezinho, Brazil	77	23 5S	50 0W
Jachal, Argentina	77	30 5S	69 0W
Jack Lane B., Canada	63	55 45N	60 35W
Jackfish, Canada	62	48 45N	87 0W
Jackman, U.S.A.	69	45 35N	70 17W
Jacksboro, U.S.A.	71	33 14N	98 15W
Jackson, Ala., U.S.A.	69	31 32N	87 53W
Jackson, Calif., U.S.A.	71	37 28N	89 44W
Jackson, Ill., U.S.A.	73	38 24N	120 47W
Jackson, Ky., U.S.A.	68	37 35N	83 22W
Jackson, Mich., U.S.A.	68	42 18N	84 25W
Jackson, Minn., U.S.A.	70	43 38N	95 30W
Jackson, Miss., U.S.A.	71	32 20N	90 10W
Jackson, Ohio, U.S.A.	68	39 0N	82 40W
Jackson, Tenn., U.S.A.	71	35 40N	88 50W
Jackson, Wyo., U.S.A.	72	43 30N	110 46W
Jackson, W. Australia	44	30 12S	119 5E
Jackson, C., N.Z.	47	40 59S	174 20E
Jackson, L., U.S.A.	72	43 58N	110 45W
Jackson Bay, Canada	64	50 32N	125 57W
Jacksons, New Zealand	47	42 45S	171 33E
Jacksons B., N.Z.	47	43 58S	168 42E
Jacksonville, N.Z.	46	41 13S	174 49E
Jacksonville, Ala., U.S.A.	69	33 49N	85 45W
Jacksonville, Fla., U.S.A.	69	30 15N	81 38W
Jacksonville, Ill., U.S.A.	70	39 45N	90 11W
Jacksonville, N.C., U.S.A.	69	34 50N	77 29W
Jacksonville, Ore., U.S.A.	71	42 16N	122 59W
Jacksonville, Tex., U.S.A.	71	31 58N	95 15W
Jacksonville Beach, U.S.A.	69	30 19N	81 26W
Jacmel, Haiti	75	18 20N	72 40W
Jacob Lake, U.S.A.	73	37 20N	112 37W
Jacobabad, W. Pak.	32	28 20N	68 29E
Jacobina, Brazil	79	11 0S	40 30W
Jacob's Well, Jordan	29	32 13N	35 13E
Jacobsdal, O.F.S.	57	29 10S	24 47E
Jacques Cartier, Mt., Canada	63	48 57N	66 0W
Jacques Cartier Pass, Canada	63	49 50N	62 30W
Jacui, R., Brazil	77	30 0S	52 30W
Jacquinot B., N. Guin.	42	5 35S	151 30E
Jacuipe R., Brazil	79	11 30S	39 45W
Jacundá R., Brazil	79	2 35S	50 10W
Jado, Libya	51	31 58N	12 1E
Jaeger Summit, mt., Tanzania	53	2 52S	35 47E
Jaen, Peru	78	5 25S	78 40W
Jaen, Spain	17	37 44N	3 43W
Jaffa C., S. Australia	43	36 49S	139 38E
Jaffa. *See* Tel-Aviv-Jaffa.	29		
Jaffna, Sri Lanka	32	9 45N	80 2E
Jagadhri, India	32	30 10N	77 20E
Jagdalpur, India	33	19 3N	82 6E
Jagersfontein, O.F.S.	57	29 44S	25 27E
Jaghbub (Giarabub), Libya	51	29 45N	24 10E
Jagin R., Iran	31	26 0N	58 0E
Jagraon, India	32	30 50N	75 25E
Jagtial, India	32	18 50N	79 0E
Jaguarao, Brazil	77	32 30S	53 30W
Jaguariaiva, Brazil	77	24 10S	49 50W
Jaguaribe R., Brazil	79	6 0S	38 30W
Jaguey, Cuba	75	22 35N	81 7W
Jahanabad, India	33	25 15N	85 0E
Jahrom, Iran	31	28 30N	53 31E
Jainti, India	33	26 45N	89 40E
Jaipur, India	32	26 54N	75 52E
Jajarm, Iran	31	37 5N	56 20E
Jajce, Yugoslavia	20	44 19N	17 17E
Jajere, Nigeria	52	11 58N	10 25E
Jajpur, India	33	20 51N	86 28E
Jal, U.S.A.	71	32 5N	103 7W
Jalalabad, Afghanistan	31	34 30N	70 29E
Jalapa Enriquez, Mexico	74	19 30N	96 50W
Jalgaon, India	32	21 0N	75 42E
Jalingo, Nigeria	52	8 57N	11 15E
Jalna, India	32	19 48N	75 57E
Jalor, India	32	25 20N	72 35E
Jalpaiguri, India	33	26 32N	88 46E
Jalq, Iran	31	27 35N	62 33E
Jaltepec, R., Mexico	74	17 25N	95 30W
Jalud R., Israel	29	32 31N	35 32E
Jamaari, Nigeria	52	11 44N	9 53E
Jamaica I., W. Indies	75	18 10N	77 30W
Jamalpur, Bangladesh	33	24 52N	90 2E
Jamari, Nigeria	52	11 1N	10 52E
Jambe, New Guinea	35	1 15S	132 10E
Jamdena I., Indonesia	35	7 45S	131 20E
James, Malawi	56	9 36S	33 4E
James B., Canada	62	53 30N	80 30W
James R., U.S.A.	70	43 50N	98 0W
Jamestown, C. Prov.	57	31 6S	26 45E
Jamestown, Ireland	11	53 57N	8 3W
Jamestown, S. Austral.	43	33 10S	138 32E
Jamestown, Ky., U.S.A.	68	37 0N	85 5W
Jamestown, N.D., U.S.A.	70	47 0N	98 30W
Jamestown, Tenn., U.S.A.	69	36 25N	85 0W

Name	Map	Lat.	Long.
Jamkhandi, India	32	16 30N	75 15E
Jamma'in, Jordan	29	32 8N	35 12E
Jammu, Jammu and Kashmir	32	32 47N	74 50E
Jammu and Kashmir, st., Asia	32	32 44N	74 54E
Jamnagar, India	32	22 30N	70 0E
Jamner, India	32	20 45N	75 45E
Jampur, W. Pakistan	32	29 39N	70 33E
Jamrud, W. Pakistan	32	34 1N	71 28E
Jamshedpur, India	33	22 44N	86 20E
Jämtland, co., Sweden	23	62 45N	14 30E
Jamundá R., Brazil	78	1 25S	58 0W
Jan L., Canada	65	54 50N	102 55W
Jan Mayen Is., Arctic Ocean	8	71 0N	11 0W
Jand, Pakistan	32	33 30N	72 0E
Jandaq, Iran	31	34 3N	54 22E
Jandiatuba R., Brazil	78	5 0S	69 30W
Jandowae, Queensland	43	26 45S	151 7E
Janesville, U.S.A.	70	42 39N	89 1W
Janga, Ghana	52	10 5N	1 0W
Jangero, Nigeria	52	12 53N	6 27E
Jangky, U.S.S.R.	28	69 50N	134 20E
Jani Khel, Afghan.	31	32 51N	68 23E
Janów, Lubelski, Poland	16	50 43N	22 30E
Jansenville, C. Prov.	57	32 57S	24 39E
Januária, Brazil	79	15 25S	44 25W
Jaora, India	32	23 40N	75 10E
Japan, king., Asia	36	36 0N	136 0E
Japan, Sea of, Asia	29	40 0N	135 0E
Japen I., Indonesia	35	1 50S	136 0E
Japurá R., Brazil	78	2 0S	68 0W
Jaque, Panama	78	7 27N	78 15W
Jarales, U.S.A.	73	34 39N	106 45W
Jarama R., Spain	17	40 20N	3 35W
Jaranwala, Pakistan	32	31 15N	73 20E
Jarbridge, U.S.A.	72	41 56N	115 26W
Jardines de la Reina Is., Cuba	75	20 50N	78 50W
Jari R., Brazil	79	0 30N	53 20W
Jaria Jhanjail, Ban.	33	25 0N	90 45E
Jarocin, Poland	16	51 59N	17 29E
Jaroslaw, Poland	16	50 2N	22 42E
Järpen, Sweden	23	63 20N	13 40E
Jarrahdale, W. Austral.	44	32 24S	116 5E
Jarrahi R., Iran	30	30 50N	49 0E
Jarrin, W., Si. Arabia	30	23 0N	43 0E
Järvenpäa, Finland	23	60 24N	25 3E
Jarvie, Canada	64	54 30N	114 0W
Jarvis I., Pacific Ocean	5	0 15S	159 55W
Jarwa, India	33	27 45N	82 30E
Jasikan, Ghana	52	7 28N	0 33E
Jasin, Malaya	34	2 20N	102 26E
Jask, Iran	31	25 38N	57 45E
Jaslo, Poland	16	49 45N	21 30E
Jasper, Canada	64	52 55N	118 0W
Jasper, Ala., U.S.A.	69	33 48N	87 16W
Jasper, Fla., U.S.A.	69	30 31N	82 58W
Jasper, La., U.S.A.	71	30 58N	94 0W
Jasper, S.D., U.S.A.	70	43 51N	96 25W
Jasper Nat. Park, Can.	64	52 50N	118 10W
Jasper Place, Canada	64	53 33N	113 25W
Jászbereny, Hungary	16	47 30N	19 55E
Jatai, Brazil	79	17 50S	51 45W
Jath, India	32	17 0N	75 15E
Jativa, Spain	17	39 0N	0 32W
Jatobá, Brazil	79	4 48S	49 45W
Jatt, Israel	29	32 24N	35 2E
Jau, Brazil	77	22 10S	48 30W
Jauja, Peru	78	11 45S	75 30W
Jaunjelgava, U.S.S.R.	23	56 35N	25 12E
Jaunpur, India	33	25 46N	82 44E
Java Sea, Indonesia	34	4 35S	107 15E
Java I., Indonesia	34	7 0S	110 0E
Javaés, Sa. dos, Brazil	79	10 30S	49 0W
Javalambre P., Spain	17	40 10N	1 0W
Jay, U.S.A.	71	36 30N	94 47W
Jaydot, Canada	65	49 15N	110 15W
Jaynagar, Nepal	33	26 35N	86 9E
Jayton, U.S.A.	71	33 15N	100 32W
Jaz. ye Bu Musá, I., Iran	31	25 50N	55 5E
Jazireh Sheykh Sho'eyb I., Iran	31	26 49N	53 12E
Jazireh-ye Forur I., Iran	31	26 11N	54 30E
Jazireh-ye Hendorabi I., Iran	31	26 38N	53 36E
Jazireh-ye Hormoz, I., Iran	31	27 0N	56 25E
Jazireh-ye Qeys, I., Iran	31	26 30N	54 0E
Jazireh-ye Sirri, I., Iran	30	25 50N	54 30E
Jean, U.S.A.	73	35 45N	115 51W
Jeanette, U.S.A.	71	29 56N	91 33W
Jean Rabel, Haiti	75	20 0N	73 30W
Jebel, U.S.S.R.	24	39 45N	54 0E
Jebel al Lawz., mt., Saudi Arabia	30	28 35N	35 22E
Jebel ash Sham, mt., Muscat & 'Oman	31	23 0N	57 0E
Jebel at Tin, Egypt	51	29 32N	33 26E
Jebel Uweinat, Libya	51	22 20N	24 58E
Jeble, Syria	30	35 25N	36 0E
Jedrzejów, Poland	16	50 35N	20 15E
Jefferson, Iowa, U.S.A.	70	42 3N	94 26W

Name	Map	Lat.	Long.
Jefferson, Tex., U.S.A.	71	32 44N	94 27W
Jefferson, Wis., U.S.A.	70	43 0N	88 49W
Jefferson, mt., Nev., U.S.A.	73	38 45N	116 58W
Jefferson, Mt., Oregon, U.S.A.	72	44 32N	121 50W
Jefferson City, U.S.A.	70	38 34N	92 14W
Jega, Nigeria	52	12 15N	4 23E
Jekabpils, U.S.S.R.	24	56 27N	25 53E
Jelenia Góra, Poland	16	50 50N	15 45E
Jelgava (Mitau), Latvia S.S.R., U.S.S.R.	23	56 40N	22 50W
Jellicoe, Canada	62	49 40N	87 30W
Jemaa, Ghana	52	7 58N	1 47W
Jemeppe, Belgium	13	50 37N	5 30E
Jena, Germany	14	50 56N	11 33E
Jena, U.S.A.	71	31 41N	92 5W
Jenin, Jordan	29	32 28N	35 18E
Jenkins, U.S.A.	68	37 13N	82 41W
Jenner, Canada	64	50 45N	111 12W
Jennette I., U.S.S.R.	27	77 10N	157 50E
Jennings, U.S.A.	71	30 10N	92 45W
Jennings R., Canada	64	59 35N	131 30W
Jequié, Brazil	79	13 55S	40 5W
Jequitinhonha, Brazil	79	16 30S	41 0W
Jequitinhonha R., Braz.	79	16 30S	41 30W
Jerablus, Syria	30	36 50N	37 59E
Jerantut, Malaya	34	3 56N	102 22E
Jérémie, Haiti	75	18 40N	74 10W
Jerez, Pta., Mexico	74	22 58N	97 40W
Jerez, Spain	17	36 41N	6 7W
Jericho, Jordan	30	31 52N	35 27E
Jericho, Queensland	42	23 38S	146 6E
Jerilderie, N.S.W.	43	35 20S	145 41E
Jerome, U.S.A.	73	34 50N	112 0W
Jersey, I., Channel Is.	12	49 13N	2 7W
Jersey City, U.S.A.	68	40 41N	74 8W
Jerseyville, U.S.A.	70	39 4N	90 17W
Jerusalem, Israel–Jord.	29	31 47N	35 10E
Jervis Bay, N.S.W.	43	35 8S	150 46E
Jervis C., S. Australia	43	35 33S	138 1E
Jessore, Bangladesh	33	23 10N	89 10E
Jesup, U.S.A.	69	31 30N	82 0W
Jetmore, U.S.A.	71	38 7N	99 58W
Jetpur, India	32	21 45N	70 10E
Jewett, U.S.A.	71	31 24N	96 7W
Jeypore, India	33	18 50N	82 38E
Jhabua, India	32	22 43N	74 32E
Jhal Jhao, Pakistan	32	26 20N	65 35E
Jhalawar, India	32	24 35N	76 10E
Jhang Maghiana, Pak.	32	31 15N	72 15E
Jhansi, India	32	25 30N	78 36E
Jharsuguda, India	33	21 52N	84 6E
Jhatpat, W. Pakistan	32	26 15N	74 45E
Jhelum, Pakistan	32	33 0N	73 45E
Jhelum R., Pakistan	32	31 50N	72 10E
Jhunjhunu, India	32	28 10N	75 20E
Jibabo Plain, Ethiopia	53	4 20N	40 0E
Jibiya, Nigeria	52	13 5N	7 12E
Jidda, Saudi Arabia	30	21 29N	39 16E
Jido, India	33	29 0N	95 0E
Jifna, Jordan	29	31 58N	35 13E
Jihchao, China	38	35 28N	119 25E
Jihlava, C.Slov.	16	49 28N	15 35E
Jihlava R., C.Slov.	16	49 16N	16 10E
Jijona, Spain	17	38 34N	0 30W
Jikamshi, Nigeria	52	12 12N	7 45E
Jilcoa R., Spain	17	41 0N	1 20W
Jima, Ethiopia	54	7 40N	36 55E
Jimbolia, Rumania	21	45 47N	20 57E
Jimena, Spain	17	36 27N	5 23W
Jiménez, Mexico	74	27 9N	104 54W
Jinja, Uganda	53	0 30N	33 15E
Jinjini, Ghana	52	7 20N	3 42E
Jinotega, Nicaragua	74	13 6N	85 59E
Jipijapa, Ecuador	78	1 0S	80 40W
Jiquilpan, Mexico	74	19 57N	102 42W
Jirja, Egypt	51	26 17N	31 55E
Jisr ash Shughur, Syria	30	35 49N	36 18E
Jitarning, W. Australia	44	32 48S	117 57E
Jitra, Malaya	34	6 16N	100 25E
Jiu, R., Rumania	21	44 50N	23 20E
Joaçiba, Brazil	77	27 10S	51 30W
João, Mozambique	56	19 42S	34 26E
João Pessoa (Paraiba), Brazil	79	7 10S	35 0W
Joaquin V. Gonzâlez, Argentina	77	25 10S	64 0W
Jodar, Spain	17	37 52N	3 23W
Jodhpur, India	32	26 23N	73 2E
Joensuu, Finland	23	62 37N	29 49E
Joeuf, France	12	49 12N	6 1E
Jofane, Mozambique	56	21 15S	34 18E
Joffre, Mt., Canada	64	50 35N	115 10W
Jogbani, India	33	26 23N	87 14E
Joggins, Canada	63	45 42N	64 27W
Jogjakarta, Java	34	6 9S	106 49E
Johannesburg, Trans.	57	26 10S	28 8E
John Day R., U.S.A.	72	45 0N	120 0W
John o' Groats, Scot.	10	58 39N	3 3W
John Ra., N. Terr.	45	21 40S	133 20E
Johnshaven, Scotland	10	56 48N	2 20W
Johnson, U.S.A.	71	37 35N	101 47W
Johnson City, N.Y., U.S.A.	68	42 9N	76 0W
Johnson City, Tenn., U.S.A.	69	36 18N	82 21W

Name	Map	Lat.	Long.
Johnson City, Texas, U.S.A.	71	30 14N	98 28W
Johnson Ra., W. Australia	44	29 40S	119 15E
Johnson's Crossing, Canada	64	60 30N	133 10W
Johnston Falls, Zambia	56	10 38S	28 48E
Johnston Ls., The, W. Australia	44	32 20S	120 45E
Johnstone L., Canada	65	50 5N	105 40W
Johnstone Str., Canada	64	50 35N	126 20W
Johnstown, Ireland	11	52 46N	7 34W
Johnstown, U.S.A.	68	43 1N	74 20W
Johore, st., Malaya	34	2 5N	103 20E
Johore R., Malaya	34	1 45N	103 47E
Johore Bahru, Malaya	34	1 28N	103 46E
Johreh, R., Iran	30	30 33N	50 0E
Joigny, France	12	48 0N	3 20E
Joinville, Brazil	77	26 15S	48 55E
Jokkmokk, Sweden	22	66 37N	19 50E
Jökuldalar, R., Iceland	22	65 10N	15 0W
Joliet, U.S.A.	70	41 30N	88 0W
Joliette, Canada	62	46 3N	73 24W
Jolo I., Philippines	35	6 0N	121 0E
Jones C., Canada	62	54 33N	79 35W
Jones Is., Alaska	59	70 30N	149 20W
Jones Sd., Canada	58	76 0N	85 0W
Jonesboro, Ark., U.S.A.	71	35 30N	90 41W
Jonesboro, Ill., U.S.A.	71	37 28N	89 17W
Jonesboro, La., U.S.A.	71	32 14N	92 44W
Jong & R., Sierra Leone	52	8 0N	12 10W
Jönköping, Sweden	23	57 45N	14 10E
Jönköping, co., Sweden	23	57 45N	14 15E
Jonquière, Canada	63	48 27N	71 14W
Jonzac, France	12	45 27N	0 28W
Joplin, U.S.A.	71	37 0N	94 25W
Jordan, U.S.A.	72	47 55N	106 54W
Jordan, king., Asia	30	31 0N	36 0E
Jordan R., Jordan–Is.	30	32 10N	35 32E
Jordan Valley, U.S.A.	72	43 0N	116 2W
Jorhat, India	33	26 45N	94 20E
Jörn, Sweden	22	65 5N	20 12E
Jos & R., Nigeria	52	9 53N	8 51E
José Batlley Ordoñez, Uruguay	77	33 20S	55 10W
José de San Martin, Argentina	77	44 2S	70 30W
Joseph, U.S.A.	72	45 55N	117 32W
Joseph Bonaparte Gulf, Australia	40	13 53S	128 45E
Joseph City, U.S.A.	73	34 56N	110 20W
Joseph Lac, Canada	63	52 40N	65 40W
Jostedals Bre, mts., Nor.	23	61 45N	7 0E
Jotunheimen, mts., Nor.	23	61 30N	9 0E
Jourdanton, U.S.A.	71	28 57N	98 0W
Joussard, Canada	64	55 52N	115 50W
Joutseno, Finland	23	61 0N	28 28E
Joux, L. de, Switz.	15	46 38N	6 20E
Jovellanos, Cuba	75	22 40N	81 10W
Joverga, Botswana	56	19 20S	24 20E
Jozani, Tanzania	53	6 16S	39 26E
Juan Aldama, Mexico	74	24 20N	103 23W
Juan Bautista, U.S.A.	73	36 50N	121 32W
Juan de Fuca Str., U.S.A. and Canada	72	48 15N	124 0W
Juan Fernandez Is., Pac. Oc.	5	33 50S	80 0W
Juan Gallegos, I., Panama Canal Zone	74	Inset	
Juan les Pins, France	12	43 35N	7 13E
Juarez, Argentina	77	37 40S	59 43W
Juarez, Mexico	74	19 0N	90 10W
Juarez, Mexico	74	27 40N	100 50W
Juazeiro, Brazil	79	9 30S	40 30W
Juazeiro do Norte, Brazil	79	7 30S	38 30W
Juba, Sudan	53	4 57N	31 35E
Juba R., Somali Rep.	49	1 30N	42 35E
Jubaila, Si. Arabia	30	24 55N	46 24E
Juby C., Sp. Sahara	50	28 0N	12 59W
Jucar R., Spain	17	39 10N	0 45E
Juchitán, Mexico	74	16 27N	95 5W
Judaea, dist., Israel	29	31 35N	34 47E
Judaea, Wilderness of, Jordan	29	31 30N	35 15E
Judith, R., U.S.A.	72	47 30N	109 32W
Judith Gap, U.S.A.	72	46 43N	109 40W
Juian, China	39	27 51N	120 39E
Juigalpa, Nicaragua	74	12 6N	85 26W
Juiz de Fora, Brazil	79	21 43S	43 19W
Jukao, China	39	32 20N	120 32E
Julesberg, U.S.A.	70	41 2N	102 18W
Julfa, U.S.S.R.	24	39 0N	45 30E
Juli, Peru	78	16 10S	69 25W
Julia R., Queensland	42	20 17S	141 40E
Juliaca, Peru	78	15 25S	70 10W
Julianehaab, Greenland	61	60 40N	45 40W
Julier P., Switzerland	15	46 28N	9 32E
Jullundur, India	32	31 20N	75 40E
Jumbo, Rhodesia	56	17 28S	30 47E
Jumento Cays, Is., W. Indies	75	23 40N	75 40W
Jumet, Belgium	13	50 27N	4 25E
Jumilla, Spain	17	38 30N	1 20W
Jumla, Nepal	33	29 15N	82 13E
Jumna (Yumuna), R., India	32	29 0N	77 18E

	MAP		
Junagadh, India	32	21 32N	70 32 E
Junaitha, Si. Arabia	30	25 22N	44 25 E
Junan, China	38	33 0N	114 23 E
Junction, Texas, U.S.A.	71	30 30N	99 45W
Junction, Utah, U.S.A.	73	38 15N	112 16W
Junction B., N. Terr.	40	11 50s	134 1 E
Junction City, Kansas, U.S.A.	70	39 2N	96 51W
Junction City, Oregon, U.S.A.	72	44 15N	123 14W
Jundah, Queensland	42	24 46s	143 2 E
Jundiai, Brazil	77	23 10s	47 0W
Juneau, U.S.A.	59	58 21N	134 20W
Junee, N.S.W.	43	34 49s	147 32 E
Jungfrau, mt., Switz.	15	46 32N	7 58 E
Jungshui, China	39	25 2N	109 9 E
Jungyün, China	39	22 57N	110 43 E
Junin, Argentina	77	34 33s	60 57W
Junin, L., Peru	78	11 2s	76 7W
Junin de los Andes, Arg.	77	39 45s	71 0W
Junnar, India	32	19 15N	73 58 E
Juntura, U.S.A.	72	43 44N	118 5W
Jupia, Brazil	79	20 55s	51 30W
Jupiter R., Canada	63	49 30N	63 10W
Juquiá, Brazil	77	24 20s	47 50W
Jur, R., Sudan	54	8 54N	29 0 E
Jura I., Scotland	10	56 0N	5 50W
Jura Mts., Fr–Switz.	15	46 35N	6 5 E
Jura, Sd. of, Scotland	10	56 0N	5 40W
Jurado, Colombia	78	7 10N	77 50W
Jurm, Afghanistan	31	36 50N	70 45 E
Juruá R., Brazil	78	5 20s	67 40W
Juruena, Brazil	78	13 0s	58 10W
Juruena, R., Brazil	78	8 0s	58 30W
Jurumento R., Arg.	77	25 30s	64 0W
Jussey, France	12	47 50N	5 55 E
Justo Daract, Arg.	77	34 50s	65 8W
Jutai R., Brazil	78	4 25s	68 10W
Juticalpa, Honduras	75	14 40N	85 50W
Juwain, Afghanistan	31	31 45N	61 30 E
Jylhämä, Finland	22	64 30N	26 45 E
Jylland (Jutland), Den.	23	56 25N	9 30 E
Jyväskylä, Finland	23	62 12N	25 47 E
K			
K2, Mt., Kashmir	32	36 0N	77 0 E
Kaabong, Uganda	53	3 33N	34 6 E
Kaap Plateau, C. Prov.	57	28 30s	24 0 E
Kaapmuiden, Transvaal	57	25 32s	31 22 E
Kabaena I., Indonesia	35	5 15s	122 0 E
Kabala, Sierra Leone	52	9 38N	11 37W
Kabale, Uganda	53	1 11s	30 0 E
Kabalo, Zaire	54	6 0s	27 0 E
Kabambare, Zaire	54	4 40s	27 45 E
Kabanga, Zambia	56	17 30s	26 55 E
Kabango, Zaire	56	8 41s	28 10 E
Kabarnet, Kenya	53	0 35N	35 50 E
Kabasha, Zaire	53	0 42s	29 11 E
Kabba, Nigeria	52	7 45N	6 45 E
Kabgaye, Rwanda	53	2 5s	29 44 E
Kabi, Niger	51	13 30N	12 35 E
Kabinakagami L., Can.	62	45 55N	84 12W
Kabinda, Congo	54	6 2s	24 14 E
Kabir R., Israel	29	31 55N	34 57 E
Kabobo, Zaire	53	5 1s	29 0 E
Kabompo, Zambia	56	13 15s	24 10 E
Kabompo R., Zambia	56	13 30s	24 20 E
Kabongo, Zaire	54	7 12s	25 43 E
Kabou, Togo	52	9 34N	0 57 E
Kabubu, Zaire	56	9 45s	24 45 E
Kabud Gonbad, Iran	31	37 8N	59 45 E
Kabul, Afghanistan	31	34 28N	69 18 E
Kabul, prov., Afg.	32	34 20N	68 45 E
Kabul R., Afghanistan	31	34 30N	70 0 E
Kabulwebulwe, Zambia	56	9 45s	25 55 E
Kabunda, Zambia	56	11 10s	28 50 E
Kabunga, Zaire	53	1 35s	28 0 E
Kabuyu, Zambia	56	16 31s	26 0 E
Kabwe, Zaire	56	14 27s	28 28 E
Kacanik, Yugoslavia	21	42 15N	21 12 E
Kachebere, Zambia	56	13 47s	32 49 E
Kachia, Nigeria	52	9 51N	7 52 E
Kachin, St., Burma	33	26 0N	97 0 E
Kachira, L., Uganda	53	0 35s	31 7 E
Kachiry, U.S.S.R.	26	53 10N	75 50 E
Kachuga, U.S.S.R.	27	54 5N	105 42 E
Kackar, Turkey	19	40 45N	41 30 E
Kada, Chad	51	19 20N	19 39 E
Kaddi, Nigeria	52	13 33N	5 41 E
Kade, Ghana	52	6 7N	0 56W
Kadei R., Cameroon	52	4 0N	15 0 E
Kadina, S. Australia	43	34 0s	137 43 E
Kadiri, India	32	14 12N	78 13 E
Kadirli, Turkey	30	37 23N	36 5 E
Kadiyevka, U.S.S.R.	25	48 35N	38 30 E
Kadjang, Indonesia	35	5 25s	10 20 E
Kadoka, U.S.A.	70	43 51N	101 30W
Kadugli, Sudan	51	10 58N	29 47 E
Kaduna, Nigeria	52	10 30N	7 21 E
Kaédi, Mauritania	50	16 20N	13 25W
Kaena Pt., Hawaiian Is.	59	20 54N	157 4W
Kaeo, New Zealand	46	35 6s	173 49 E
Kaesong, & prov., N. Korea	36	38 0N	126 35W
Kaf, Arabia	30	31 22N	37 25 E
Kafakumba, Zaire	56	9 38s	23 46 E
Kafanchan, Nigeria	52	9 40N	8 20 E
Kafareti, Nigeria	52	10 25N	11 4 E
Kafia Kingi, Sudan	54	9 20N	24 25 E
Kafinda, Zambia	56	12 39s	30 20 E
Kafirstan, U.S.S.R.	31	35 20N	71 0 E
Kafr Ana, Israel	29	32 2N	34 48 E
Kafr 'Ein, Jordan	29	32 3N	35 7 E
Kafr Kama, Israel	29	32 44N	35 26 E
Kafr Kanna, Israel	29	32 45N	35 20 E
Kafr Malik, Jordan	29	32 0N	35 18 E
Kafr Manda, Israel	29	32 49N	35 15 E
Kafr Qaddum, Jordan	29	32 14N	35 7 E
Kafr Ra'i, Jordan	29	32 23N	35 9 E
Kafr Yasif, Israel	29	32 58N	35 10 E
Kafu R. Uganda	53	1 15N	31 20 E
Kafue, Zambia	56	15 45s	28 4 E
Kafue Flats, Zambia	56	15 40s	27 25 E
Kafue Gorge, Zambia	56	15 47N	28 25 E
Kafue, R., Zambia	56	15 30s	25 50 E
Kafulwe, Zambia	56	9 2s	29 1 E
Kafuta, Gambia	52	13 13N	16 23W
Kagamil, I., Aleutian Is.	59	53 0N	169 40W
Kagan, U.S.S.R.	26	39 50N	64 45 E
Kagara, Niger	52	13 30N	12 52 E
Kagarko, Nigeria	52	9 28N	7 36 E
Kagawa, pref., Japan	36	34 10N	134 0 E
Kagera R., Tanzania	53	1 12s	31 15 E
Kagizman, Turkey	30	40 10N	43 10 E
Kagmar, Sudan	51	14 26N	30 28 E
Kagoshima, Japan	36	31 36N	130 40 E
Kagoshima, pref., Japan	36	31 45N	130 30 E
Kagoshima B., Japan	36	31 0N	130 40 E
Kagulu, Uganda	53	1 16N	33 18 E
Kahe, Tanzania	53	3 31s	37 27 E
Kahemba, Zaire	54	7 18s	18 55 E
Kaherekoau, Mts., N.Z.	47	45 50s	167 20 E
Kahia, Zaire	53	6 22s	28 21 E
Kahmoomulga, Queensland	43	26 5s	145 39 E
Kahnuj, Iran	31	27 58N	57 36 E
Kahoka, U.S.A.	70	40 24N	91 41W
Kahoolwe, I., Hawaiian Islands	59	20 30N	156 40W
Kahuku; Hawaiian Islands	59	21 40N	157 56W
Kahuku Pt., Hawaiian Islands	59	21 42N	158 0W
Kahutara Pt., N.Z.	46	39 6s	178 1 E
Kagmar, Sudan	54	14 26N	30 28 E
Kai Ketjil I., Indon.	35	5 55s	132 45 E
Kaiama, Nigeria	52	9 36N	4 1 E
Kaiapoi, N.Z.	47	43 24s	172 40 E
Kaieteur Falls, Guy.	78	5 20N	59 25W
Kaifeng, China	38	34 45N	114 30 E
Kaihwa, China	39	29 10N	118 17 E
Kaikohe, N.Z.	46	35 25s	173 49 E
Kaikoura, N.Z.	47	42 25s	173 43 E
Kaikoura Pen., N.Z.	47	42 25s	173 43 E
Kaikoura Ra., N.Z.	47	41 59s	173 41 E
Kailahun, Sierra Leone	52	8 18N	10 39W
Kailua Lanikai, Hawaiian Islands	59	21 33N	157 45W
Kaimana, Indonesia	35	3 30s	133 45 E
Kaimanawa Mts., N.Z.	46	39 15s	175 56 E
Kainkordu, Sierra Leone	52	Inset	
Kaipara Harbour, N.Z.	46	36 25s	174 14 E
Kaiping, China	38	40 30N	122 20 E
Kaipokok B., Canada	63	55 10N	50 40W
Kairouan, Tunisia	50	35 45N	10 5 E
Kaisatskoye, U.S.S.R.	25	49 47N	46 49 E
Kaiserlautern, Germany	14	49 30N	7 43 E
Kaisiadorys, U.S.S.R.	23	54 54N	24 30 E
Kaitaia, New Zealand	46	35 8s	173 17 E
Kaitangata, N.Z.	47	46 17s	169 51 E
Kaitung, China	38	44 50N	122 45 E
Kaiwi Channel, Hawaiian Islands	59	21 15N	157 30 E
Kaiyüan, China	38	42 40N	123 50 E
Kaiyuh, Mts., Alaska	59	64 0N	158 0W
Kajaani, Finland	23	64 17N	27 46 E
Kajabbi, Queensland	42	20 0s	140 1 E
Kajan R., Indonesia	35	2 40N	116 40 E
Kajang, Malaya	34	2 59N	101 48 E
Kajiado, Kenya	53	1 48s	36 48 E
Kajo Kaji, Sudan	53	3 58N	31 40 E
Kajuru, Nigeria	52	10 17N	7 33 E
Kaka, Sudan	51	10 41N	32 13 E
Kakabeka Falls, Can.	62	48 24N	89 37W
Kakamas, C. Prov.	51	28 45s	20 33 E
Kakamega, Kenya	53	0 25N	34 50 E
Kakanui Mts., N.Z.	47	45 10s	170 30 E
Kakapotahi, N.Z.	47	43 0s	170 42 E
Kake, Alaska	59	57 0N	134 0W
Kakelwe, Zaire	53	4 50s	29 0 E
Kakhovka, U.S.S.R.	25	46 50N	33 18 E
Kakia, Botswana	57	24 48s	23 22 E
Kakinada (Cocanada) India	33	16 55N	82 20 E
Kakisa L., Canada	64	61 0N	117 40W
Kakisa R., Canada	64	60 55N	117 30W
Kakitumba, Rwanda	53	1 55s	30 26 E
Kakoaka, Botswana	56	18 45s	24 18 E
Kakola, Zaire	53	0 44N	29 43 E
Kakombo, mt., Rhod.	57	15 6s	30 47 E
Kaktovik, Alaska	59	70 8N	143 50W
Kakumaa, Kenya	53	3 44N	34 53 E
Kakuora, U.S.S.R.	26	71 35N	144 50 E
Kakwa R., Canada	64	54 20N	119 20W
Kala Bar Panja, Afghan.	31	37 39N	71 25 E
Kalabagh, Pakistan	32	33 0N	71 35 E
Kalabáka, Greece	21	39 42N	21 39 E
Kalabo, Zambia	56	14 58s	22 33 E
Kalach, U.S.S.R.	25	50 22N	41 0 E
Kaladan R., Burma	33	21 30N	92 45 E
Kaladar, Canada	62	44 37N	77 5W
Kalahari Des., Africa	57	24 0s	22 0 E
Kalakamati, Guy.	56	20 39s	27 21 E
Kalam, Ethiopia	53	4 58N	35 57 E
Kalama, Kenya	53	1 35s	37 21 E
Kalama, U.S.A.	72	46 1N	122 47W
Kalamata, Greece	21	37 3N	22 10 E
Kalamazoo, U.S.A.	68	42 20N	85 40W
Kalamazoo R., U.S.A.	68	42 15N	86 0W
Kalambo Falls, Tan.	53	8 37s	31 15 E
Kalamunnda, W. Australia	44	32 0s	116 0 E
Kalan, Turkey	30	39 7N	39 32 E
Kalannie, W. Australia	44	30 12s	117 17 E
Kalaotoa I., Indonesia	35	7 20s	121 50 E
Kalat, W. Pakistan	32	29 8N	66 31 E
Kalat, Terr., W. Pak.	32	27 0N	66 0 E
Kalat-i-Ghilzai, Afghan.	31	32 15N	66 58 E
Kalat us Siraj, Afghan.	31	34 49N	70 12 E
Kalávrita, Greece	21	38 3N	22 8 E
Kalehe, Zaire	53	2 8s	28 57 E
Kalemie, France	12	45 40N	6 22 E
Kalewa, Burma	33	23 15N	94 20 E
Kalfafellsstadhur, Ice.	22	64 11N	15 45W
Kalfshamarsvik, Iceland	22	66 1N	20 26W
Kalgan, China	38	40 50N	114 50 E
Kalgoorlie, W. Austral.	44	30 40s	121 22 E
Kalianda, Indonesia	34	5 50s	105 45 E
Kaliduwarry, Queens.	44	25 3s	138 30 E
Kalima, Zaire	54	2 36s	26 34 E
Kalimantan, Prov., Indonesia	35	0 1s	115 0 E
Kalimnos I., Greece	21	37 0N	27 0 E
Kalimpong, India	33	27 4N	88 35 E
Kalinin, U.S.S.R.	25	56 55N	35 55 E
Kalinina, U.S.S.R.	27	60 0N	108 15 E
Kaliningrad (Königsberg), U.S.S.R.	24	54 42N	20 32 E
Kalinku, Zambia	56	11 15s	3 11 E
Kaliro, Uganda	53	0 53N	33 30 E
Kalispell, U.S.A.	72	48 14N	114 21W
Kalista, Tasmania	43	42 45s	146 35 E
Kalisz, Poland	16	51 45N	18 8 E
Kalitva R., U.S.S.R.	25	49 10N	40 45 E
Kaliua, Tanzania	53	5 3s	31 47 E
Kalix, Sweden	22	64 50N	23 5 E
Kalix R., Sweden	22	67 0N	22 0 E
Kalkaska, U.S.A.	68	44 45N	85 10W
Kalkfeld, S.W. Africa	57	20 53s	16 11 E
Kalkfontein, Botswana	57	22 8s	20 53 E
Kalkrand, S.W. Africa	57	24 3s	17 33 E
Kall L., Sweden	23	63 35N	13 10 E
Kallia, Jordan	29	31 46N	35 30 E
Kallonis, Kolpos, G., Greece	21	39 10N	26 10 E
Kalmalo, Nigeria	52	13 37N	5 15 E
Kalmar, Sweden	23	56 39N	16 22 E
Kalmar, co., Sweden	23	57 25N	16 30 E
Kalmunai, Sri Lanka	32	7 25N	81 55 E
Kalmyk, A.S.S.R., U.S.S.R.	26	46 0N	47 0 E
Kalmykovo, U.S.S.R.	24	49 0N	51 35 E
Kalni R., Bangladesh	33	24 30N	91 10 E
Kalo, Papua	42	10 0s	147 50 E
Kalocsa, Hungary	16	46 32N	19 0 E
Kalonga, Zambia	56	16 58s	26 30 E
Lalonga, Zambia	56	15 11s	22 50 E
Kalonje, Zambia	56	12 3s	31 15 E
Kalossia, Kenya	53	1 39N	35 46 E
Kaltag, Alaska	59	64 20N	158 58W
Kaltungo, Nigeria	52	9 48N	11 19 E
Kaluga, U.S.S.R.	25	54 35N	36 10 E
Kalungwisi R. Zambia	56	9 30s	29 30 E
Kaluszyn, Poland	16	52 15N	21 45 E
Kalutara, Sri Lanka	32	6 35N	80 0 E
Kalvarija, U.S.S.R.	23	54 23N	23 13 E
Kalwa, Zambia	56	13 13s	30 18 E
Kalyan, India	32	19 17N	73 11 E
Kalyani, India	32	17 53N	76 57 E
Kalyazin, U.S.S.R.	25	57 15N	37 45 E
Kam R., Nigeria	52	8 15N	11 0 E
Kam Keut, Laos	34	18 17N	104 45 E
Kama, Canada	62	49 0N	88 0W
Kama R., U.S.S.R.	24	60 0N	53 0 E
Kamachumu, Tanzania	53	1 39s	31 37 E
Kamaguenam, Niger	52	13 27N	10 25 E
Kamaishi, Japan	36	39 20N	142 0 E
Kamakou, mt., Hawaiian Islands	59	21 6N	156 52W
Kamalino, Hawaiian Is.	59	21 51N	160 14W
Kamango, Zaire	53	0 38N	29 54 E
Kamapanda, Zambia	56	12 1s	24 4 E
Kamara, New Zealand	47	42 27s	171 11 E
Kamaran I., Red Sea	49	15 28N	42 35 E
Kamba, Nigeria	52	11 45N	3 40 E
Kambalda, W. Australia	44	31 9s	121 35 E
Kambia, Sierra Leone	52	9 3N	12 53W
Kambole, Togo	52	8 43N	1 39 E
Kambole, Zambia	56	8 45s	30 45 E
Kambove, Zaire	56	10 50s	26 39 E
Kamchatka, pen., U.S.S.R.	29	57 0N	160 0 E
Kamde, Neth. N. Guin.	42	8 0s	141 0 E
Kamen, U.S.S.R.	26	53 50N	81 30 E
Kamenets Podolski, U.S.S.R.	24	48 40N	26 30 E
Kamensk, U.S.S.R.	26	56 25N	62 45 E
Kamensk, U.S.S.R.	25	49 26N	41 19 E
Kamensk Uralskiy, U.S.S.R.	26	56 52N	62 0 E
Kamensk-Shakhtinskiy, U.S.S.R.	25	48 23N	40 20 E
Kamenskoye, U.S.S.R.	27	62 45N	165 0 E
Kami, C., China	39	20 15N	109 50 E
Kamiah, U.S.A.	72	46 13N	116 2W
Kamień Pomorski, Pol.	16	53 57N	14 43 E
Kamieskroon, C. Prov.	57	30 18s	18 6 E
Kamilukuk L., Canada	65	62 40N	100 0W
Kamina, Zaire	55	8 46s	25 0 E
Kaminak L., Canada	65	62 0N	95 0W
Kamloops, Canada	64	50 40N	120 20W
Kamo, New Zealand	46	35 42s	174 20 E
Kampala, Uganda	53	0 20N	32 30 E
Kampar, Malaya	34	4 18N	101 9 E
Kampar R., Indonesia	34	0 30N	102 0 E
Kampen, Netherlands	13	52 33N	5 53 E
Kampinda, Zambia	56	3 49s	29 55 E
Kampolombo L., Zambia	56	11 32s	29 40 E
Kampot, Cambodia	34	10 37N	104 11 E
Kamsack, Canada	65	51 35N	101 50W
Kamuchawie L., Can.	65	56 10N	102 0W
Kamuli, Uganda	53	0 57N	33 3 E
Kamyshin, U.S.S.R.	25	50 10N	45 30 E
Kamyshlov, U.S.S.R.	24	56 55N	62 40 E
Kan K., China	39	27 50N	115 20 E
Kanaaupscow, Canada	62	54 0N	76 40W
Kanab, U.S.A.	73	37 6N	112 38W
Kanab Cr., U.S.A.	73	36 45N	112 40W
Kanaga I., Aleutian Is.	59	51 45N	177 20W
Kanagawa, pref., Japan	36	35 20N	139 20 E
Kanakanak, Alaska	59	59 0N	158 35W
Kanakwie, Sierra Leone	52	Inset	
Kananchen, Inner Mon.	38	46 35N	121 43 E
Kanarraville, U.S.A.	73	37 35N	113 16W
Kanash, U.S.S.R.	25	55 48N	47 32 E
Kanawha R., U.S.A.	68	38 37N	81 50W
Kanazawa, Japan	36	36 30N	136 38 E
Kancheepuram (Conjeeveram), India	32	12 52N	79 45 E
Kanchenjunga, Mt., Nepal	33	27 50N	88 10 E
Kachindu, Zambia	56	17 45s	27 15 E
Kanchow, China	39	25 43N	115 0 E
Kanchuan, China	38	36 27N	109 10 E
Kanda Kanda, Zaire	54	6 52s	23 48 E
Kandagach, U.S.S.R.	24	49 20N	57 15 E
Kandaghat, India	32	31 0N	77 10 E
Kandahar, Afghanistan	31	31 32N	65 30 E
Kandalaksha, U.S.S.R.	22	67 9N	32 30 E
Kandangan, Indonesia	35	2 50s	115 20 E
Kandersteg, Switzerland	15	46 28N	7 40 E
Kandewu, Zambia	56	13 58s	26 15 E
Kandi, Dahomey	52	11 7N	2 55 E
Kandira, Turkey	30	41 5N	30 10 E
Kandla, India	32	23 0N	70 10 E
Kandrach, Pakistan	32	25 30N	65 30 E
Kandukur, India	32	15 15N	79 47 E
Kandy, Sri Lanka	32	7 18N	80 43 E
Kane, U.S.A.	68	41 39N	78 53W
Kane Basin, Greenland	58	79 0N	70 0W
Kaneohe, Hawaiian Is.	59	21 25N	157 48W
Kanevskaya, U.S.S.R.	25	46 3N	39 3 E
Kang, Botswana	56	23 41s	22 50 E
Kangar, Malaya	34	6 27N	100 12 E
Kangaroo I., S. Austral.	43	35 45s	137 0 E
Kangavar, Iran	30	34 40N	48 0 E
Kangean Is., Indonesia	35	6 55s	115 23 E
Kangetet, Kenya	53	1 57N	36 4 E
Kanggye, Korea	36	41 0N	126 35 E
Kango, Gabon	54	0 11N	10 5 E
Kangotovo, U.S.S.R.	26	63 30N	87 40 E
Kangoya, Zaire	56	9 57s	22 47 E
Kangshan, China	37	22 50N	120 15 E
Kangto, Mt., India	33	27 50N	92 35 E
Kangwon, Prov., S. Korea	36	37 45N	128 0 E
Kangwon, Prov., N. Korea	36	38 45N	127 21 E
Kani, Burma	33	22 25N	95 0 E
Kaniamba, Zaire	56	7 27s	26 59 E
Kaniapiskau L., Can.	63	53 52N	69 20W
Kaniapiskau R., Can.	63	55 15N	68 40W
Kanieri L., N.Z.	47	42 59s	171 9 E
Kanin C., U.S.S.R.	24	68 45N	43 30 E
Kaningo, Kenya	53	0 48s	38 32 E
Kankakee, Ill., U.S.A.	70	41 10N	87 52W
Kankakee R., U.S.A.	68	41 16N	87 10W
Kankan, Guinea	50	10 30N	9 15W
Kanker, India	33	20 18N	81 33 E
Kannapolis, U.S.A.	69	35 32N	80 37W
Kannauj, India	32	27 1N	79 58 E
Kanniyakumari, India	32	8 5N	77 30 E
Kannod, India	32	22 40N	76 45 E
Kano, Nigeria	52	12 0N	8 30 E
Kanona, Zambia	56	13 9s	30 39 E
Kanowna, W. Australia	44	30 23s	121 31 E
Kanoya, Japan	36	31 29N	130 56 E

	MAP		
Kanpur (Cawnpur), India	32	26 35N	80 20 E
Kansanshi, Zambia	56	12 5 S	26 22 E
Kansas, st., U.S.A.	70	38 30N	98 0W
Kansas R., U.S.A.	70	39 5N	95 40W
Kansas City, Kansas, U.S.A.	70	39 0N	94 37W
Kansas City, Mo., U.S.A.	70	39 4N	94 31W
Kansenia, Zaire	56	10 18 S	26 4 E
Kansk, U.S.S.R.	27	56 20N	95 37 E
Kansong, Korea	36	38 45N	128 15 E
Kansu, prov., China	37	36 5N	105 30 E
Kantché, Niger	52	13 31N	8 30 E
Kantse, China	37	31 37N	100 0 E
Kanturk, Ireland	11	52 10N	8 55W
Kanuchuan Rapids, Canada	65	54 25N	94 45W
Kanuma, Japan	36	36 44N	139 42 E
Kanus, S.W. Africa	57	27 52 S	18 42 E
Kanyada, Kenya	53	0 41 S	34 25 E
Kanye, Botswana	57	24 59 S	25 19 E
Kanyenda, Malawi	56	12 20 S	34 3 E
Kanyiragwa, Tan.	53	1 1 S	31 50 E
Kanyu, China	38	34 58N	119 0 E
Kanzenze, Zaire	56	10 29 S	25 13 E
Kaoan, China	39	28 23N	115 15 E
Kaohsiung, China	39		
Kaoko Otavi, S.W. Afr.	55	18 17 S	13 43 E
Kaolack, Senegal	50	14 15N	16 8W
Kaomi, China	38	36 26N	119 43 E
Kaoping, China	38	35 46N	112 57 E
Kaoura Débé, Niger	52	12 15N	3 50 E
Kaoyu, China	38	32 46N	119 28 E
Kaoyu Hu, China	38	32 50N	119 15 E
Kapanga, Zaire	54	8 30 S	22 40 E
Kapatu, Zambia	56	9 42 S	30 42 E
Kapema, Zambia	56	9 16 S	29 18 E
Kapfenberg, Austria	14	47 27N	15 17 E
Kaphambale, Malawi	56	12 14 S	33 55 E
Kapiri Mposhi, Zambia	56	14 0 S	28 40 E
Kapiskau R., Canada	62	52 20N	83 40W
Kapit, Sarawak	35	2 0N	13 5 E
Kapiti I., New Zealand	46	40 50 S	174 56 E
Kapoeta, Sudan	53	4 50N	33 35 E
Kapombo, Zaire	56	10 40 S	23 30 E
Kapona, Zaire	53	7 11 S	29 9 E
Kaponga, New Zealand	46	39 29 S	174 9 E
Kaposvar, Hungary	16	46 25N	17 47 E
Kapsabet, Kenya	53	0 14N	35 5 E
Kapuas R., Indonesia	35	0 20N	111 40 E
Kapulo, Zaire	53	8 20 S	29 16 E
Kapunda, S. Australia	43	34 20 S	138 56 E
Kapuskasing, Canada	62	49 25N	82 30W
Kapuskasing R., Can.	62	49 0N	82 50W
Kaputir, Kenya	53	2 5N	35 30 E
Kara, U.S.S.R.	26	69 10N	65 25 E
Kara Kalpak, A.S.S.R., U.S.S.R.	26	43 0N	60 0 E
Kara Kum, U.S.S.R.	26	39 30N	60 0 E
Kara Nor, China	37	38 10N	97 30 E
Kara Sea, U.S.S.R.	26	75 0N	70 0 E
Kara-Bogaz-Gol, U.S.S.R.	24	41 0N	53 30 E
Karabük, Turkey	30	41 12N	32 37 E
Karachayevsk, U.S.S.R.	25	43 45N	41 57 E
Karachev, U.S.S.R.	25	53 10N	35 5 E
Karachi, Pakistan	32	24 53N	67 0 E
Karachi, dist., Pak.	32	25 30N	66 45 E
Karad, India	32	17 15N	74 10 E
Karadeniz Bogazi (Bosporus), Turkey	30	41 0N	29 0 E
Karaga, Ghana	52	9 58N	0 28W
Karaganda, U.S.S.R.	26	49 50N	73 0 E
Karaginski I., U.S.S.R.	27	58 45N	164 0 E
Karäikal (Karikal), India	32	10 59N	79 50 E
Karaikkudi, India	32	10 0N	78 45 E
Karaj, Iran	31	35 4N	51 0 E
Karakas, U.S.S.R.	26	48 20N	83 30 E
Karakelong I., Indon.	35	4 30N	126 45 E
Karakoram Ra., Kashmir	32	35 20N	78 0 E
Karakoram, P., Kashmir–Sinkiang	32	35 40N	78 0 E
Karaköse (Agri), Tur.	30	39 42N	43 0 E
Karalon, U.S.S.R.	27	57 5N	115 50 E
Karamai, China	37	45 48N	84 30 E
Karaman, Turkey	30	37 14N	33 13 E
Karamea, N.Z.	47	41 14 S	172 6 E
Karamea Bight, N.Z.	47	41 22 S	171 40 E
Karamea R., N.Z.	47	41 13 S	172 25 E
Karamechen, Bot.	56	21 3 S	27 29 E
Karamian I., Indon.	35	5 5 S	114 30 E
Karamoja, Uganda	53	2 45N	34 15 E
Karapiro, N.Z.	46	37 55 S	175 34 E
Karasburg, S.W. Africa	57	28 0 S	18 43 E
Karasino, U.S.S.R.	26	66 50N	86 50 E
Karasjok, Norway	22	69 27N	25 30 E
Karatiya, Israel	29	31 39N	34 43 E
Karatsu, Japan	36	33 30N	130 0 E
Karatu, Tanzania	53	3 20 S	35 40 E
Karauzyak, U.S.S.R.	26	43 30N	59 30 E
Karawanken Mts., Yugoslavia	20	46 30N	14 40 E
Karbala, Iraq	30	32 47N	44 3 E
Karditsa, Greece	21	39 23N	21 54 E
Kärdla, U.S.S.R.	23	58 48N	22 40 E
Kareeberge, mts., Cape Province	57	30 40 S	22 20 E
Kareima, Sudan	51	18 30N	31 49 E
Kareiri Lake, N.Z.	47	42 49 S	171 9 E
Karelian A.S.S.R., U.S.S.R.	26	63 0N	32 30 E
Karganrud, Iran	30	37 55N	49 0 E
Kargat, U.S.S.R.	26	55 10N	80 15 E
Kargil, Kashmir	32	34 32N	76 12 E
Kariba Gorge, Rhod.	56	16 25 S	28 47 E
Kariba, L., Rhodesia	56	16 40 S	28 20 E
Karibib, S.W. Africa	57	21 59 S	15 50 E
Karibumba, Zaire	53	0 9N	29 13 E
Kariega R., C. Prov.	57	32 45 S	23 35 E
Karikal (Karaikal), India	32	10 52N	79 50 E
Karikari, C., N.Z.	46	34 48 S	173 25 E
Karimata I., Indonesia	34	1 40 S	109 0 E
Karimata Str., Indon.	34	2 0 S	108 20 E
Karimnagar, India	32	18 26N	79 10 E
Karistos, Greece	21	38 1N	24 25 E
Karius Ra., Papua	42	6 0 S	142 40 E
Kariyangwe, Rhod.	56	18 0 S	27 38 E
Karjaa, Finland	23	60 5N	23 45 E
Karkaralinsk, U.S.S.R.	26	49 30N	75 37 E
Karkass, Niger	52	14 53N	3 50 E
Karkhch, R., Iran	30	33 0N	48 0 E
Karkinitski G., U.S.S.R.	25	45 55N	33 0 E
Karkur, Israel	29	32 29N	34 57 E
Karl-Marx Stadt (Chemnitz), & dist., Germany	14	50 50N	12 55 E
Karlovac, Yugoslavia	20	45 31N	15 36 E
Karlove (Levskigrad), Bulgaria	21	42 38N	24 49 E
Karlovy Vary, C.Slov.	16	50 13N	12 51 E
Karlsborg, Sweden	23	58 33N	14 33 E
Karlshamn, Sweden	23	56 13N	14 56 E
Karlskoga, Sweden	23	59 22N	14 33 E
Karlskrona, Sweden	23	56 12N	15 42 E
Karlsruhe, Germany	14	49 3N	8 23 E
Karlstad, Sweden	23	59 24N	13 35 E
Karlstad, U.S.A.	70	48 37N	96 30W
Karma, Niger	52	13 40N	1 51 E
Karnal, India	32	29 42N	77 2 E
Karnali R., Nepal	33	29 0N	82 0 E
Karnaphuli Res., Ban.	33	22 45N	92 15 E
Karnes City, U.S.A.	71	28 56N	97 57W
Karoi, Rhodesia	56	16 46 S	29 45 E
Karonie, W. Australia	45	30 52 S	122 28 E
Karonga, Malawi	56	9 57 S	33 55 E
Karoonda, S. Australia	43	35 1 S	139 59 E
Karora, Sudan	49	17 45N	38 20 E
Karoussa, Guinea	50	10 50N	9 48W
Karpathos I., Greece	21	35 47N	27 10 E
Karpeddo, Kenya	53	1 10N	36 4 E
Kars, Turkey	30	40 40N	43 5 E
Karsakpai, U.S.S.R.	26	47 55N	66 40 E
Karshi, U.S.S.R.	26	39 0N	65 55 E
Karst, plat., Yugoslavia	20	45 40N	14 0 E
Kartaly, U.S.S.R.	26	53 10N	60 50 E
Kartuzy, Poland	16	54 22N	18 10 E
Karu, Nigeria	52	9 0N	7 30 E
Karufa, Indonesia	35	3 50 S	133 20 E
Karumba, Queensland	42	17 31 S	140 50 E
Karumo, Tanzania	53	2 31 S	32 50 E
Karumwa, Tanzania	53	3 13 S	32 40 E
Karun, R., Iran	30	31 15N	48 30 E
Karungu, Kenya	53	0 50 S	34 10 E
Karur, India	32	10 59N	78 2 E
Karwar, India	32	14 48N	74 11 E
Kas Kong, Cambodia	34	11 29N	103 10 E
Kasache, Malawi	56	13 25 S	34 16 E
Kasai, prov., Zaire	54	5 0 S	21 0 E
Kasai R., Zaire	54	11 15 S	21 0 E
Kasaji, Zaire	56	10 22 S	23 29 E
Kasama, Zambia	56	10 12 S	31 12 E
Kasane, S.W. Africa	56	17 31 S	24 50 E
Kasanga, Tanzania	53	8 29 S	31 9 E
Kasangulu, Zaire	54	4 15 S	15 15 E
Kasba L., Canada	65	60 20N	102 10W
Kasempa, Zambia	56	13 30 S	25 48 E
Kasene, Zaire	56	11 48 S	26 55 E
Kasenga, Zambia	56	15 45 S	24 28 E
Kasenye, Zaire	53	1 25N	30 27 E
Kasese, Uganda	53	0 30N	30 10 E
Kasewa, Zambia	56	14 20 S	28 58 E
Kaseya, Zaire	56	7 38 S	29 28 E
Kashabowie, Canada	62	48 40N	90 26W
Kashaf Rud, Iran	31	36 0N	60 30 E
Kashan, Iran	31	34 5N	51 30 E
Kashgar, China	37	39 30N	76 10 E
Kashimbo, Zaire	56	11 11 S	26 22 E
Kashin, U.S.S.R.	25	57 32N	37 22 E
Kashing, China	39	30 50N	120 40 E
Kashipur, India	32	29 15N	79 0 E
Kashira, U.S.S.R.	25	54 45N	38 10 E
Kashitu, Zambia	56	13 37 S	28 38 E
Kashiwazaki, Japan	36	37 28N	138 40 E
Kashmir. *See* Jammu and Kashmir.	32		
Kashmor, W. Pakistan	32	28 28N	69 32 E
Kasimov, U.S.S.R.	25	54 55N	41 20 E
Kasinka, Botswana	56	18 13 S	24 22 E
Kasisi Plains, Zambia	56	13 5 S	24 58 E
Kaskaskia R., U.S.A.	70	38 30N	89 20W
Kaskinen, Finland	23	62 22N	21 13 E
Kaslo, Canada	64	49 55N	117 0W
Kasmere L., Canada	65	59 30N	101 25W
Kasongo, Zaire	54	4 18 S	26 40 E
Kasongo Lunda, Zaire	54	6 30 S	16 51 E
Kásos, I., Greece	20	35 20N	26 56 E
Kaspiiski, U.S.S.R.	25	45 22N	47 23 E
Kassala, Sudan	54	15 23N	36 26 E
Kassala, prov., Sudan	51	15 20N	36 26 E
Kassel, Germany	14	15 19N	9 32 E
Kastamonu, Turkey	30	41 25N	33 43 E
Kastelli, Crete	20	35 29N	23 38 E
Kastoria, Greece	21	40 30N	21 19 E
Kastornoye, U.S.S.R.	25	51 55N	38 2 E
Kástron, Greece	21	39 53N	25 8 E
Kasulu, Tanzania	54	4 30 S	30 0 E
Kasungu, Malawi	56	13 1 S	33 30 E
Kasupi, Malawi	56	15 10 S	35 20 E
Kasur, Pakistan	32	31 5N	74 25 E
Katagum, Nigeria	52	12 10N	10 15 E
Katagum R., Nigeria	52	12 31N	10 58 E
Katahdin Mt., U.S.A.	67	45 50N	68 50W
Katako Kombe, Zaire	54	3 27 S	24 21 E
Katale, Tanzania	53	4 52 S	31 7 E
Katalla, Alaska	59	60 11N	144 35W
Katamma, Nigeria	52	12 31N	10 58 E
Katanda, Zaire	53	0 50 S	29 21 E
Katanga, reg., Zaire	55	9 50 S	25 0 E
Katanga Orientale, prov., Zaire	55	10 30 S	27 20 E
Katangi, India	32	21 45N	79 50 E
Katanning, W. Austral.	44	33 40 S	117 33 E
Katavi Swamp, Tan.	53	6 53 S	31 8 E
Katenga, Zaire	53	5 1 S	28 49 E
Katerini, Greece	21	40 15N	22 30 E
Kate's Needles, mts., Canada	59	57 0N	132 0W
Katha, Burma	33	24 10N	96 30 E
Katherine, Australia	40	14 27 S	132 20 E
Kathgodam (Haldwani), India	32	29 15N	79 32 E
Kathleen, W. Australia	44	27 29 S	120 30 E
Kathua, Kashmir	32	32 25N	75 30 E
Katihar, India	33	25 34N	87 36 E
Katikar, New Zealand	46	37 23 S	178 58 E
Katima Mulilo, Zambia	56	17 20 S	24 15 E
Katimbira, Malawi	56	12 40 S	34 0 E
Katiola, Ivory Coast	50	8 10N	5 10W
Katker Hills, C. Prov.	57	30 0 S	20 0 E
Katmai Nat. Park, Alaska	59	58 28N	155 0W
Katmandu, Nepal	33	27 45N	85 12 E
Katompe, Zaire	54	6 5 S	26 15 E
Katonga R., Uganda	53	0 14N	31 15 E
Katoomba. *See* Blue Mts.	42		
Katowice, Poland	16	50 17N	19 5 E
Katrineholm, Sweden	23	59 3N	16 12 E
Katsina, Nigeria	52	7 10N	9 20 E
Katsina Ala, Nigeria	52	7 10N	9 30 E
Katsina Ala, R., W. Cameroon	52	6 45N	10 0 E
Katsuura, Japan	36	35 15N	140 20 E
Kattegat, Denmark	23	56 50N	11 20 E
Katuma, Tanzania	53	6 21 S	30 36 E
Katungu, Kenya	53	2 56 S	40 8 E
Katwa, India	33	23 30N	89 25 E
Katwe, Uganda	53	0 4 S	29 50 E
Katwijk, Netherlands	13	52 12N	4 24 E
Katylyktakh, U.S.S.R.	27	68 50N	134 5 E
Kauai I., Hawaiian Is.	59	22 0N	160 0W
Kauai Chan, Hawaiian Islands	59	21 50N	159 0W
Kaufman, U.S.A.	71	32 34N	96 25W
Kaukauna, U.S.A.	70	44 19N	88 15W
Kauliranta, Finland	22	66 26N	23 40 E
Kaunas, U.S.S.R.	23	54 54N	23 54 E
Kaunpi, Zambia	56	14 50 S	24 15 E
Kaura Namoda, Nigeria	52	12 37N	6 33 E
Kauru, Nigeria	52	10 32N	8 11 E
Kautokeino, Norway	22	69 0N	23 15 E
Kau Ur., Gambia	52		Inset
Kauwa, Nigeria	52	13 1N	13 35W
Kavali, India	32	14 55N	80 1 E
Kavála, Greece	21	40 57N	24 28 E
Kavieng, Terr. of New Guinea	42	2 30 S	150 48 E
Kavinba, Botswana	56	18 2 S	24 38 E
Kavir-e-Namak, Des., Iran	31	34 40N	57 30 E
Kavirondo, G., Kenya	53	0 25 S	34 40 E
Kavu R., Tanzania	53	7 30 S	31 45 E
Kaw (Caux), Guyana	79	4 40N	52 15W
Kawagoe, Japan	36	36 0N	139 30 E
Kawaguchi, Japan	36	35 40N	139 33 E
Kawaihoa, C., Hawaiian Islands	59	21 46N	160 12W
Kawaikini, mt., Hawaiian Islands	59	22 3N	159 30W
Kawakawa, N.Z.	46	35 23 S	174 6 E
Kawama, Zambia	56	10 10 S	28 49 E
Kawambwa, Zambia	56	9 45 S	29 10 E
Kawarau R., N.Z.	47	45 2 S	169 4 E
Kawardha, India	35	21 59N	81 15 E
Kawasaki, Japan	36	35 40N	139 45 E
Kawau I., N.Z.	46	36 25 S	174 52 E
Kaweka Range, N.Z.	46	39 15 S	176 24 E
Kawene, Canada	62	48 45N	91 15W
Kawhia Harbour N.Z.	46	38 5 S	174 50 E
Kawngtim, Burma	33	26 55N	96 15 E
Kaya, Volta	50	13 25N	1 10W
Kayak, I., Alaska	59	59 55N	144 30W
Kayambi, Zambia	56	9 28 S	31 59 E
Kaycee, U.S.A.	72	43 45N	106 38W
Kayenda, Zaire	56	10 48 S	23 6 E
Kayenta, U.S.A.	73	36 45N	110 20W
Kayes, Mali	50	14 25N	11 30W
Kayima, Sierra Leone	52	8 54N	11 14W
Kayombo, Zaire	56	9 31 S	26 10 E
Kayoro, Ghana	52	11 0N	1 15 E
Kayseri, Turkey	30	38 45N	35 30 E
Kaysville, U.S.A.	72	41 42N	111 58W
Kazache, U.S.S.R.	27	70 52N	135 58 E
Kazakhstan, U.S.S.R.	26	49 0N	50 0 E
Kazan, U.S.S.R.	25	55 48N	49 3 E
Kazan R., Canada	65	62 0N	100 50W
Kazanluk, Bulgaria	21	42 38N	25 35 E
Kazatin, U.S.S.R.	25	49 45N	28 50 E
Kazbek, Mt., U.S.S.R.	24	42 48N	44 29 E
Kazembe, Zambia	56	12 10 S	32 33 E
Kazerun, Iran	31	29 38N	5 140 E
Kazinga & Channel, Uganda	53	0 20 S	29 59 E
Kaziza, Zaire	56	10 40 S	23 52 E
Kaztalovka, U.S.S.R.	25	49 47N	48 43 E
Kazumba, Zaire	54	6 25 S	22 5 E
Kazumba, Zambia	56	13 58 S	26 2 E
Kazura, Nigeria	52	12 41N	10 0 E
Kazym R., U.S.S.R.	26	63 40N	68 30 E
Kea, Greece	21	37 38N	24 20 E
Keaau, Hawaiian Is.	59	19 36N	155 2W
Keady, N. Ireland	11	54 15N	6 42W
Keams Canyon, U.S.A.	73	35 50N	110 15W
Kebao, I., N. Viet Nam	39	21 10N	107 28 E
Kebbi, Nigeria	52	12 2N	4 42 E
Kebkabiya, Sudan	51	13 50N	24 0 E
Kebnekaise, Sweden	22	67 55N	18 35 E
Kebumen, Indonesia	34	7 42 S	109 40 E
Kechika R., Canada	64	59 10N	127 10W
Kecskemet, Hungary	16	46 57N	19 35 E
Kedah, st., Malaya	34	5 50N	100 40 E
Kedainiai, U.S.S.R.	23	55 15N	23 57 E
Kedgwick, Canada	63	47 40N	67 20W
Kedia Hill, Bot.	56	21 8 S	24 35 E
Kediri, Indonesia	34	7 51 S	112 1 E
Kedjebi, Togo	52	8 15N	0 31 E
Kedougou, Senegal	50	12 35N	12 10W
Keefers, Canada	64	50 0N	121 40W
Keeley L., Canada	65	54 50N	108 5W
Keeling (Cocos) Is., Indian Ocean	7	11 0 S	95 0 E
Keene, U.S.A.	69	42 57N	72 17W
Keeper, Mt., Ireland	11	52 46N	8 17W
Keeroongooloo, Queens.	43	25 54 S	142 41 E
Keerweer C., Queens.	42	13 57 S	141 25 E
Keetmanshoop, S.W. Africa	57	26 35 S	18 8 E
Keewatin, Canada	65	49 47N	94 30W
Keewatin, U.S.A.	70	47 24N	93 0W
Keewatin, terr., Canada	65	63 20N	94 40W
Kefar Eqron, Israel	29	31 52N	34 49 E
Kefar Ezyon, Jordan	29	31 39N	35 7 E
Kefar Hasidim, Israel	29	32 47N	35 5 E
Kefar Hittim B., Israel	29	32 48N	35 27 E
Kefar Sava, Israel	29	32 11N	34 54 E
Kefar Szold, Israel	29	33 11N	35 34 E
Kefar Vitkin, Israel	29	32 22N	34 53 E
Kefar Yehezqel, Israel	29	32 34N	35 22 E
Kefar Yona, Israel	29	32 20N	34 54 E
Kefar Zekharya, Israel	29	31 43N	34 56 E
Keffi, Nigeria	52	8 55N	7 43 E
Keffin Hausa, Nigeria	52	12 13N	9 59 E
Keflavik, Iceland	22	64 2N	22 35W
Keg River, Canada	64	57 45N	117 50W
Kegashka, Canada	63	50 14N	61 18W
Kehl, Germany	14	48 34N	7 50 E
Keighley, England	10	53 52N	1 54W
Keimoes, C. Prov.	57	28 41 S	21 0 E
Keith, S. Australia	43	36 0 S	140 25 E
Keith Arm, Canada	60	65 30N	122 0W
Kekri, India	32	26 0N	75 10 E
Kelantan, st., Malaya	34	5 10N	102 0 E
Kelantan R., Malaya	34	5 35N	102 8 E
Kelif, U.S.S.R.	31	37 23N	66 10 E
Kelkit Cayi R., Turkey	30	40 20N	37 40 E
Kelle, Congo (Fr.)	54	0 7 S	14 20 E
Keller, U.S.A.	72	48 2N	118 40W
Kellerberrin, W. Austral.	44	31 36 S	117 38 E
Kellet C., Canada	58	72 0N	125 40W
Kellogg, U.S.A.	72	47 30N	116 0W
Kelloselkä, Finland	22	66 56N	28 54 E
Kells, Ireland	11	52 0N	10 7W
Kelowna, Canada	64	49 50N	119 25W
Kelsey Bay, Canada	64	50 25N	126 0W
Kelso, New Zealand	47	45 54 S	169 15 E
Kelso, U.S.A.	72	46 10N	122 50W
Kelvington, Canada	65	52 20N	103 30W
Ké-Macina, Mali	50	14 5N	5 20W
Kem, U.S.S.R.	24	65 0N	34 38 E
Kemah, Turkey	30	39 32N	39 5 E
Kemaliye, Turkey	30	39 15N	38 30 E
Kemano, Canada	64	53 35N	128 0W
Kembongo, W. Cam.	52	5 39N	9 26 E
Kemerovo, U.S.S.R.	26	55 20N	85 50 E
Kemi, Finland	22	65 48N	24 43 E
Kemi R., Finland	22	67 30N	28 30 E

Place	Map	Lat.	Long.
Kemijärvi, Finland	22	66 42N	27 30E
Kemmercer, U.S.A.	72	41 50N	111 30W
Kemp Coast, Antarctica	80	68 0S	64 0E
Kemp L., U.S.A.	71	33 47N	99 0W
Kempsey, N.S.W.	43	31 1S	152 50E
Kempt L., Canada	62	47 25N	74 30W
Kempten, Germany	14	47 42N	10 18E
Kemptville, Canada	62	45 1N	75 39W
Ken, R., Scotland	10	55 8N	4 12W
Kenai, Alaska	59	60 35N	151 11W
Kenai, Mts., Alaska	59	60 20N	150 30W
Kenai Pen., Alaska	59	61 0N	150 0W
Kenda Wangan, Indon.	34	2 30S	110 10E
Kendal, England	10	54 19N	2 44W
Kendal, N.S.W.	43	31 35S	152 44E
Kendallville, U.S.A.	68	41 25N	85 15W
Kendari, Indonesia	35	3 50S	122 30E
Kende, Nigeria	52	11 30N	4 12E
Kendenup, W. Austral.	44	34 22S	117 1E
Kendrapara (Kentapara) India	33	20 35N	86 30E
Kendrew, C. Prov.	57	32 30S	24 30E
Kendrick, U.S.A.	72	46 38N	116 41W
Kenedy, U.S.A.	71	28 51N	97 51W
Kenema, Sierra Leone	52	7 55N	11 13W
Keng Tung, Burma	33	21 0N	99 30E
Kenge, Zaire	54	4 50S	16 55E
Kenegja, Tanzania	53	5 25S	39 44E
Kenhardt, C. Prov.	57	29 19S	21 12E
Kenitra (Mina Hassan Tani), Morocco	50	34 11N	6 30W
Kenmare, Ireland	11	51 52N	9 35W
Kenmare, U.S.A.	70	48 42N	102 2W
Kenmare R., Ireland	11	51 45N	10 0W
Kennebec, U.S.A.	70	43 56N	99 54W
Kennedy, Rhodesia	56	18 52S	27 10E
Kennedy, C. (C. Canaveral), U.S.A.	67	28 28N	80 31W
Kennedy Ra., W. Australia	44	24 45S	115 10E
Kennett, U.S.A.	71	36 12N	90 3W
Kennewick, U.S.A.	72	46 11N	119 2W
Kenney Dam, Canada	64	53 30N	125 0W
Keno Hill, Canada	60	64 0N	135 40W
Kenogami R., Canada	62	50 20N	85 20W
Kenora, Canada	65	49 50N	94 35W
Kenosha, U.S.A.	70	42 35N	87 50W
Kensington, Canada	63	46 28N	63 34W
Kensington Downs, Queensland	42	22 31S	144 10E
Kensington, U.S.A.	70	39 47N	9 90W
Kent, Ohio, U.S.A.	71	41 8N	81 20W
Kent, Ore., U.S.A.	72	45 10N	120 43W
Kent, Pen., Canada	60	68 30N	108 0W
Kent Group Is., Tas.	43	39 28S	147 15E
Kentapara (Kendrapara), India	33	20 35N	86 30E
Kentland, U.S.A.	68	40 45N	87 25W
Kenton, U.S.A.	68	40 40N	83 35W
Kentucky, st., U.S.A.	68	37 20N	85 0W
Kentucky Dam, U.S.A.	71	37 0N	88 38W
Kentucky, L., U.S.A.	69	36 0N	88 0W
Kentucky R., U.S.A.	68	38 30N	85 0W
Kentville, Canada	63	45 6N	64 29W
Kentwood, U.S.A.	71	30 59N	90 30W
Kenugbe, Nigeria	52	10 2N	3 42E
Kenya, st., Africa	53	0 5N	37 0E
Kenya Mt., Kenya	53	0 8S	37 17E
Keokuk, U.S.A.	70	40 20N	91 22W
Keonjhargarh, India	33	21 40N	85 40E
Kepler Mts., N.Z.	47	45 25S	167 20E
Kepsut, Turkey	30	39 41N	28 9E
Kerang, Victoria	43	35 40S	143 55E
Keray, Iran	31	26 10N	57 7E
Kerchoual, Mali	50	17 20N	0 20E
Kerema, Papua	42	7 50S	145 50E
Keren Maharel, Israel	29	32 39N	34 59E
Keren, Ethiopia	49	15 45N	38 28E
Kerets C., U.S.S.R.	24	65 30N	39 50E
Kerewan, Gambia	52	13 29N	16 10W
Kerguelen I., Indian Oc.	5	48 30S	69 40E
Kericho, Kenya	53	0 24S	35 14E
Kerikeri, New Zealand	46	35 12S	173 59E
Kerintji, Indonesia	34	2 5S	101 0E
Kerkenna Is., Tunisia	51	34 48N	11 13E
Kérkira, Greece	21	39 38N	19 50E
Kerkrade, Netherlands	13	50 53N	6 4E
Kérkyra (Corfu), Gr.	21	39 38N	19 50E
Kermadec Is., Pac. Oc.	5	31 8S	175 16W
Kerman, Iran	31	30 15N	57 1E
Kerman Des., Iran	31	28 45N	59 30E
Kermanshah, Iran	30	34 23N	47 0E
Kermit, U.S.A.	71	31 47N	103 2W
Kern R., U.S.A.	73	35 35N	118 40W
Kerrobert, Canada	65	52 0N	109 11W
Kerrville, U.S.A	71	30 0N	99 6W
Kerry, co., Ireland	11	52 7N	9 35W
Kerry Hd., Ireland	11	52 26N	9 56W
Kerulen R., Mongolia	37	48 0N	114 0E
Kerzaz, Algeria	50	29 30N	1 20W
Kesagami L., Canada	62	50 30N	80 10W
Kesagami R., Canada	62	50 40N	80 10W
Kesh, N. Ireland	11	54 31N	7 43W
Kesis Mt., Turkey	30	39 53N	39 45E
Keskisuomen Lääni, Finland	23	63 0N	25 0E
Kestell, O.F.S.	57	28 17S	28 42E
Kestenga, U.S.S.R.	22	66 0N	31 50E
Keswick, England	10	54 35N	3 9W
Keszthely, Hungary	16	46 50N	17 15E
Ket R., U.S.S.R.	26	58 20N	84 30E
Keta, Ghana	52	5 49N	1 0E
Keta Lagoon, Ghana	52	5 55N	1 0E
Ketapang, Indonesia	34	1 55S	110 0E
Ketchikan, Alaska	59	55 25N	131 42W
Ketchum, U.S.A.	72	43 14N	114 23W
Kete Krachi, Ghana	52	7 42N	0 3W
Ketrzyn, Poland	16	54 5N	21 24E
Kettering, England	10	52 24N	0 44W
Kettle Falls, U.S.A.	72	48 36N	118 2W
Kettle R., Canada	65	49 40N	118 45W
Kevin, U.S.A.	72	48 47N	111 58W
Kewanee, U.S.A.	70	41 18N	90 0W
Kewaunee, U.S.A.	70	44 27N	87 30W
Keweenaw B., U.S.A.	70	47 0N	88 0W
Keweenaw Pen., U.S.A.	70	47 15N	88 30W
Key Harbour, Canada	62	45 50N	80 45W
Keyala, Sudan	53	4 27N	32 35E
Keynshamburg, Rhod.	56	19 15S	29 40E
Keyser, U.S.A.	68	39 26N	79 0W
Keystone, S.D., U.S.A.	70	43 55N	103 28W
Keystone, W. Va.. U.S.A.	68	37 27N	81 29W
Kezhma, U.S.S.R.	27	59 15N	100 57E
Kezi, S. Rhodesia	56	18 5S	25 47E
Khabarovo, U.S.S.R.	24	69 30N	60 30E
Khabarovsk, U.S.S.R.	27	48 20N	135 0E
Khabur, R., Syria	30	35 50N	40 51E
Khaibar, Saudi Arabia	30	25 38N	39 28E
Khairagarh, India	32	21 27N	81 2E
Khairpur, tn. & terr., Pakistan	32	27 25N	69 45E
Khalki I., Greece	21	36 15N	27 35E
Khalkis, Greece	21	38 27N	23 42E
Khalmer-Sede, U.S.S.R.	26	67 30N	78 30E
Khalturin, U.S.S.R.	24	58 40N	48 50E
Khama's Country, reg., Botswana	57	21 40S	26 25E
Khan Tengri, Mt., China	37	42 20N	80 10E
Khanapur, India	32	18 40N	75 40E
Khanaquin, Iraq	30	34 23N	45 25E
Khandwa, India	32	21 49N	76 22E
Khanewal, Pakistan	32	30 20N	71 55E
Khangai Mts., Mon.	37	48 50N	96 0E
Khanh Hung, Viet Nam	34	9 30N	105 40E
Khania, Greece	20	35 33N	24 4E
Khanion B., Greece	20	35 33N	23 55E
Khanka L., U.S.S.R.	27	45 0N	132 30E
Khanpur, Pakistan	32	28 42N	70 35E
Khanty-Mansiisk, U.S.S.R.	26	61 0N	69 0E
Kharabali, U.S.S.R.	25	47 31N	47 18E
Kharagpur, India	33	22 20N	87 25E
Kharan Kalat, W. Pak.	32	28 32N	65 26E
Kharānaq, Iran	31	32 20N	54 35E
Kharda, India	32	18 40N	75 40E
Khârga Oasis, Egypt	51	25 0N	30 0E
Khargon, India	32	21 45N	75 40E
Kharkov, U.S.S.R.	25	49 58N	36 20E
Kharovsk, U.S.S.R.	25	59 56N	40 13E
Khartoum, Sudan	51	15 31N	32 35E
Khartoum North, Sudan	51	15 15N	32 35E
Kharmanli, Bulgaria	21	41 55N	25 55E
Khasavyurt, U.S.S.R.	25	43 30N	46 40E
Khasebake, Botswana	57	20 38S	24 20E
Khāsh (Vasht), Iran	31	28 16N	61 6E
Khash Rud R., Afghan.	31	31 30N	61 30E
Khashm el Girba, Sudan	51	14 52N	35 50E
Khaskovo, Bulgaria	21	41 56N	25 30E
Khatanga, U.S.S.R.	27	72 0N	102 20E
Khatanga R., U.S.S.R.	27	70 30N	103 0E
Khatyn, U.S.S.R.	27	62 4N	175 0E
Khavda, India	32	23 50N	69 45E
Khed, India	32	18 54N	73 56E
Khed Brahma, India	32	24 0N	73 5E
Khenchela, Algeria	50	35 22N	7 9E
Khenifra, Morocco	50	33 0N	5 46W
Khersan R., Iran	31	31 20N	51 20E
Kherson, U.S.S.R.	25	46 35N	32 35E
Kheta R., U.S.S.R.	27	70 50N	96 0E
Khetinsiring, China	37	32 54N	92 29E
Kibali-Ituri, prov., Zaire	54	4 30N	26 30E
Khiitola, U.S.S.R.	23	61 10N	29 50E
Khilok, U.S.S.R.	27	51 30N	110 45E
Khios, Greece	21	38 27N	26 9E
Khios I., Greece	21	38 23N	29 0E
Khiva, U.S.S.R.	26	41 30N	60 18E
Khiyav, Iran	30	38 30N	47 45E
Khmeinitsk, U.S.S.R.	24	49 30N	26 40E
Khojak P., Afghan.	32	30 55N	66 30E
Khokhol, U.S.S.R.	25	51 35N	38 50E
Kholm, U.S.S.R.	25	57 10N	31 15E
Khomayn, Iran	30	33 47N	50 1E
Khomo, Botswana	57	21 12S	24 40E
Khomodimo, Botswana	57	22 46S	23 58E
Khong, Laos	34	14 8N	105 50E
Khonu, U.S.S.R.	27	66 30N	143 25E
Khoper R., U.S.S.R.	24	52 0N	43 20E
Khor adh Dhuwaihin, Muscat & 'Oman	31	24 20N	51 28E
Khora Sphákion, Greece	20	35 15N	24 9E
Khorramābād, Iran	30	33 34N	48 20E
Khorramshahr, Iran	30	30 29N	48 15E
Khotan, China	37	37 10N	80 0E
Khouribga, Morocco	50	32 58N	6 50W
Khoutsiri, Botswana	57	21 5S	23 0E
Khufaifaya, Si. Arabia	30	24 50N	44 39E
Khugiani, Afghanistan	31	31 40N	64 54E
Khuis, Botswana	57	26 40S	21 49E
Khukhan, Thailand	34	15 7N	104 15E
Khulna, Bangladesh	33	22 45N	89 34E
Khulna, Terr., Ban.	33	22 47N	89 21E
Khumain, Iran	30	33 40N	50 8E
Khur, Iran	31	32 55N	58 18E
Khur, W. al, Iraq	30	31 26N	43 23E
Khurais, Si. Arabia	30	24 58N	48 3E
Khurasan, prov., Iran	31	34 0N	57 0E
Khurma, Saudi Arabia	30	21 30N	42 8E
Khurr, Wadi al, Iraq	31	31 30N	43 15E
Khushab, Pakistan	32	32 20N	72 20E
Khutor Mikhailovsk, U.S.S.R.	25	52 9N	33 49E
Khuzdar, Pakistan	32	27 52N	66 30E
Khvāf, Iran	31	34 45N	60 20E
Khvalynsk, U.S.S.R.	25	52 30N	48 2E
Khvoinaya, U.S.S.R.	25	58 49N	34 28E
Khyber Pass, Afghan.	32	34 10N	71 8E
Khvor, Iran	31	33 53N	55 0E
Khvormuj, Iran	31	28 42N	51 27E
Khvoy, Iran	30	38 33N	45 0E
Khwaja Muhammad, mt., Afghanistan	31	36 0N	70 0E
Kiansien, China	38	38 20N	110 32E
Kialwe, Zaire	56	9 3S	27 18E
Kiama, N.S.W.	43	34 40S	150 50E
Kiamba, Philippines	35	6 0N	124 40E
Kiambi, Zaire	54	7 12S	28 0E
Kiambu and dist., Kenya	53	1 10S	36 51E
Kiamusze, China	37	46 45N	130 30E
Kian, China	39	27 3N	114 50E
Kianchwa, China	39	25 14N	111 30E
Kiangling, China	39	30 28N	112 12E
Kiangpeh, China	39	29 27N	105 30E
Kiangshan, China	39	28 50N	118 35E
Kiangsi, prov., China	39	27 30N	115 0E
Kiangsu, prov., China	39	33 15N	119 30E
Kiangsu Canal, China	38	33 30N	119 12E
Kiangtsing, China	39	29 14N	106 20E
Kiangyin, China	39	32 0N	120 25E
Kiangyu, China	39	31 35N	104 35E
Kiaochow Wan, bay, China	38	36 10N	120 15E
Kiaohsien, China	38	36 20N	120 0E
Kiapuluka, Zaire	56	9 0S	27 21E
Kiawang, China	38	34 27N	117 26E
Kibali R., Zaire	53	3 30N	29 14E
Kibangou, Congo (Fr.)	54	3 18S	12 22E
Kibara, mts., Zaire	56	8 10S	27 20E
Kibaya, Tang.	53	5 10S	36 50E
Kiberege, Tanzania	53	7 56S	36 58E
Kibi, Ghana	53	6 14N	0 31W
Kibiti, Tanzania	53	7 40S	39 0E
Kiboga, Uganda	53	0 55N	31 46W
Kiboko, Kenya	53	2 14S	37 45E
Kibombo, Zaire	54	3 54S	25 54E
Kibondo and dist., Tanzania	53	3 35S	30 33E
Kibumba, Rwanda	53	1 30S	29 12E
Kibungu, Burundi	53	2 10S	30 31E
Kibuye, Burundi	53	3 40S	29 59E
Kibuye, Rwanda	53	2 9S	29 23E
Kibwesa, Tanzania	53	6 10S	30 0E
Kibwezi, Kenya	53	2 27S	37 57E
Kicevo, Yugoslavia	21	41 34N	20 59E
Kichiga, U.S.S.R.	27	59 50N	163 5E
Kicking Horse Pass, Canada	64	51 30N	116 25W
Kichmengski-Gorodok, U.S.S.R.	24	60 0N	46 0E
Kichow, China	39	30 1N	115 23E
Kidal, Mali	50	17 50N	2 22E
Kidepo R., Sudan	53	5 0N	33 10E
Kidete, Tanzania	53	6 38S	36 47E
Kidnappers, C., N.Z.	46	39 40S	177 6E
Kidougou, Niger	52	12 50N	3 23E
Kidston, Queensland	42	18 52S	144 8E
Kidugalle, Tanzania	53	6 50S	38 20E
Kiel, Germany	14	54 16N	10 8E
Kiel B., Germany	14	54 30N	10 30E
Kiel Canal, Germany	14	54 15N	9 40E
Kienge, Zaire	56	10 33S	27 35E
Kienhsien, China	38	34 30N	108 7E
Kienko, China	39	31 50N	105 30E
Kienning, China	39	26 46N	116 43E
Kiensi, China	39	26 59N	105 59E
Kienten, China	39	29 30N	119 28E
Kienyang, Fukien, China	39	27 30N	118 0E
Kienyang, Honan, China	39	27 10N	109 50E
Kienyang, Szechwan, China	39	30 22N	104 30E
Kiev (Kiyev), U.S.S.R.	25	50 30N	30 28E
Kiffa, Mauritania	50	16 50N	11 15W
Kifisia, Greece	21	38 4N	23 49E
Kigali, Rwanda	54	1 57S	29 58E
Kigarama, Tanzania	53	1 1S	31 50E
Kigezi, dist., Uganda	53	0 50S	29 45E
Kigoma, Tanzania	54	4 50S	29 44E
Kigoma, prov. Tanzania	53	4 30S	30 30E
Kigwa, Tanzania	53	5 10S	33 13E
Kihikihi, New Zealand	46	38 2S	175 22E
Kihsien, China	38	36 20N	110 35E
Kihundo, Tanzania	53	9 27S	39 5E
Kihurio, Tanzania	53	4 29S	38 3E
Kii, Hawaiian Islands	59	21 59N	160 4W
Kii Chan., Japan	36	33 40N	135 0E
Kijabe, Kenya	53	0 56S	36 33E
Kisik, Alaska	59	60 19N	154 19W
Kikagati, Uganda	53	1 2S	30 40E
Kikale, Tanzania	53	7 51S	39 13E
Kikiang, China	39	28 58N	106 44E
Kikinda, Yugoslavia	21	45 50N	20 30E
Kikladhes Is. (Cyclades), Greece	21	37 50N	25 0E
Kikole, Zaire	56	9 26S	25 55E
Kikori, Papua	42	7 13S	144 15E
Kikori R., Papua	42	7 0S	143 40E
Kikwit, Zaire	54	5 5S	18 45E
Kilauea, Hawaiian Is.	59	22 13N	159 26W
Kilauea Crater, Hawaiian Islands	59	19 24N	155 16W
Kilbeheny, Ireland	11	52 18N	8 13W
Kilbuck Mts., Alaska	59	60 50N	160 0W
Kilchoan, Scotland	10	56 42N	6 8W
Kilchu, Korea	37	41 0N	129 10E
Kilcock, Ireland	11	53 24N	6 40W
Kilconnell, Ireland	11	53 20N	8 25W
Kilcormac, Ireland	11	53 10N	7 43W
Kilcoy, Queensland	43	26 59S	152 30E
Kilcullen, Ireland	11	53 8N	6 45W
Kilcummin, Queensland	42	22 16S	147 37E
Kildare, Ireland	11	53 10N	6 55W
Kildare, co., Ireland	11	53 10N	6 50W
Kilembe, Uganda	54	0 20N	29 59E
Kilgarvan, Ireland	11	51 54N	9 28W
Kilgore, U.S.A.	71	32 20N	94 50W
Kilifi, Kenya	53	3 40S	39 48E
Kilima, Uganda	53	1 31N	34 32E
Kilimanjaro, mt., Tan.	53	3 4S	37 21E
Kiliminjaro, prov., Tanzania	53	4 50S	36 50E
Kilimatinde, Tanzania	53	5 55S	34 58E
Kilindini, Kenya	53	4 4S	39 40E
Kilindoni, Mafia I., 53 Tanzania	53	7 59S	39 38E
Kilis, Turkey	30	36 44N	37 5E
Kilkee, Ireland	11	52 41N	9 40W
Kilkenny, Ireland	11	52 40N	7 17W
Kilkenny, co., Ireland	11	52 35N	7 15W
Kilkieran B., Ireland	11	53 18N	9 45W
Kilkis, Greece	21	40 58N	22 57E
Killala, Ireland	11	54 13N	9 12W
Killala B., Ireland	11	54 16N	9 8W
Killaloe, Ireland	11	52 48N	8 28W
Killam, Canada	64	52 45N	112 0W
Killarney, Man., Can.	65	49 10N	99 40W
Killarney, Ont., Canada	62	45 55N	81 30W
Killarney, Ireland	11	52 2N	9 30W
Killarney, Queensland	43	28 19S	152 14E
Killary Harb., Ireland	11	53 38N	9 52W
Killashandra, Ireland	11	54 0N	7 32W
Killdeer, U.S.A.	70	47 22N	102 47W
Killeen, U.S.A.	71	31 5N	97 44W
Killimor, Ireland	11	53 10N	8 17W
Killiney, Ireland	11	53 15N	6 8W
Killini, Greece	21	37 55N	21 8E
Killini, Mt., Greece	21	37 52N	22 26E
Killorglin, Ireland	11	52 6N	9 48W
Killybegs, Ireland	11	54 38N	8 26W
Killylea, N. Ireland	11	54 20N	6 45W
Kilmacthomas, Ireland	11	52 13N	7 27W
Kilmaine, Ireland	11	53 35N	9 7W
Kilmallock, Ireland	11	52 22N	8 35W
Kilmarnock, Scotland	10	55 36N	4 30W
Kilmore Quay, Ireland	11	52 11N	6 35W
Kiloli, Tanzania	53	6 50S	33 22E
Kilombero R., Tan.	53	8 12S	37 4E
Kilondo, Tanzania	53	9 47S	34 22E
Kilosa, Tanzania	53	6 40S	37 2E
Kilrea, N. Ireland	11	54 58N	6 34W
Kilrush, Ireland	11	52 39N	9 30W
Kiltamagh, Ireland	11	53 51N	9 0W
Kilwa, Zaire	56	9 16S	28 23E
Kilwa I., Zambia	56	9 15S	28 43E
Kilwa Kisiwani I., Tanzania	53	8 58S	39 30E
Kilwa Kivinje, Tan.	53	8 45S	39 25E
Kilwa Masoko, Tan.	53	9 20S	33 45E
Kim, U.S.A.	71	37 14N	103 20W
Kim R., Cameroon	52	5 48N	11 45E
Kim Chaek, N. Korea	36	40 40N	129 5E
Kimande, Tanzania	53	7 21S	35 38E
Kimba, S. Australia	45	33 8S	136 23E
Kimball, Neb., U.S.A.	70	41 18N	103 38W
Kimball, S.D., U.S.A.	70	43 49N	98 57W
Kimbe, B., N. Guinea	42	5 10S	150 40E
Kimberley, Canada	64	49 40N	116 10W
Kimberley, C. Prov.	57	28 43S	24 46E
Kimberley, dist., W. Australia	40	16 20S	126 0E
Kimberly, U.S.A.	72	42 33N	114 27W
Kimchon, S. Korea	36	36 20N	127 55E
Kimi, Greece	21	38 38N	24 0E
Kimolos I., Greece	21	36 48N	24 37E
Kimry, U.S.S.R.	25	56 55N	37 15E
Kimsquit, Canada	64	52 45N	127 5W
Kimwanga, Zaire	53	7 35S	28 39E

	MAP		
Kinabalu, Mt., Sabah	35	6 0N	116 0 E
Kinango, Kenya	53	4 7s	39 18 E
Kincaid, Canada	65	49 40N	107 0w
Kincardine, Canada	62	44 10N	81 40w
Kindersley, Canada	65	51 30N	109 10w
Kindia, Guinea	52	10 3N	12 49w
Kindu-Port-Empain, Congo	54	2 53s	25 57 E
Kineshma, U.S.S.R.	25	57 30N	42 5 E
Kinesi, Tanzania	53	1 28s	33 54 E
King City, U.S.A.	73	36 15N	121 9w
King Christian IX Ld., Greenland	58	68 0N	35 0w
King Christian X Land, Greenland	58	73 0N	30 0w
King Frederick VI Coast, Greenland	61	63 0N	43 0w
King Frederick VIII Ld., Greenland	58	77 30N	25 0w
King George, Is , Can.	61	57 20N	78 30w
King George Sound, W. Australia	40	35 2s	117 58 E
King George V Coast, Antarctica	80	67 0s	148 0 E
King Ho, R., China	38	34 45N	108 30 E
King I., Burma	33	12 30N	98 20 E
King I., Canada	64	52 15N	123 15w
King I., Tasmania	43	39 40s	144 0 E
King Leopold Ranges, W. Australia	44	17 20s	124 20 E
King Salmon, Alaska	59	58 40N	156 40w
King William I., Can.	60	69 0N	98 0w
King William's Town, Cape Province	57	32 51s	27 22 E
Kingaroy, Queensland	43	26 32s	151 51 E
Kingfisher, U.S.A.	71	35 49N	97 58w
Kinghsien, China	38	37 39N	116 16 E
Kingisepp, U.S.S.R.	25	59 25N	28 40 E
Kingkiang Res., China	39	30 10N	112 10 E
Kingku, China	37	23 29N	100 19 E
Kingman, Ariz., U.S.A.	73	35 10N	114 0w
Kingman, Kan., U.S.A.	71	37 35N	98 10w
Kingmen, China	39	31 10N	112 15 E
Kingning, China	39	27 55N	119 30 E
Kingoonya, S. Australia	45	30 59s	135 22 E
Kingpeng, China	38	43 10N	117 25 E
King's Lynn, England	10	52 45N	0 25 E
Kings Mountain, U.S.A.	69	37 0N	81 25w
Kings Pk, U.S.A.	72	40 58N	110 28w
Kings R., U.S.A.	73	36 55N	119 0w
Kingsburg, U.S.A.	73	36 32N	119 32w
Kingscote, S. Australia	43	35 33s	137 31 E
Kingscourt, Ireland	11	53 55N	6 48w
Kingsley, U.S.A.	70	42 34N	95 52w
Kingsley Dam, U.S.A.	70	41 15N	101 42w
Kingston, Canada	62	44 20N	76 30w
Kingston, Jamaica	75	18 0N	76 50w
Kingston, New Zealand	47	45 20s	168 43 E
Kingston, S. Australia	43	36 51s	139 55 E
Kingston, N.Y., U.S.A.	68	41 55N	74 0w
Kingston, Pa., U.S.A.	68	41 19N	75 58w
Kingstown, St. Vincent	75	13 10N	61 10w
Kingstree, U.S.A.	69	33 40N	79 48w
Kingsvale, Canada	64	49 55N	120 50w
Kingsville, Canada	62	42 3N	82 45w
Kingsville, U.S.A.	71	27 40N	98 0w
Kingtenchen, China	39	29 18N	117 9 E
Kingtzekwan, China	38	33 25N	111 10 E
Kingussie, Scotland	10	57 4N	4 2w
Kingyang, China	38	36 0N	107 45 E
Kinhsien, China	38	39 4N	121 45 E
Kinhwa, China	39	29 5N	119 32 E
Kiniama, Zaire	56	11 29s	28 25 E
Kinistino, Canada	65	53 0N	105 0w
Kinkala, Congo (Fr.)	54	4 18s	14 49 E
Kinkazan, I., Japan	36	38 27N	141 35 E
Kinkululu, Zambia	56	12 33s	29 58 E
Kinleith, New Zealand	46	38 20s	175 56 E
Kinloch, New Zealand	47	44 50s	168 20 E
Kinmen (Quemoy) I., China	39	24 26N	118 20 E
Kinnaird, Canada	64	49 13N	117 41w
Kinnegad, Ireland	11	53 28N	7 8w
Kinneret, Israel	29	32 44N	35 34 E
Kinoje R., Canada	62	52 0N	82 20w
Kinoni, Uganda	53	0 38s	30 29 E
Kinosota, Canada	65	50 52N	98 57w
Kinross, Scotland	10	56 13N	3 25w
Kinsale, Ireland	11	51 42N	8 31w
Kinsha (Yangtze), R., China	37	32 0N	97 2 E
Kinshasa, Zaire	54	4 20s	15 15 E
Kinsiang, China	38	35 10N	116 25 E
Kinsley, U.S.A.	71	35 57N	99 25w
Kinston, U.S.A.	69	35 10N	77 40w
Kinta, Ivory Coast	52	8 57N	2 41w
Kintampo, Ghana	52	8 5N	1 41w
Kintai, China	38	37 18N	104 10 E
Kintap, Indonesia	35	3 50s	115 20 E
Kintinku, Tanzania	53	5 58s	35 14 E
Kintyre, dist., Scotland	10	55 32N	5 35w
Kinuso, Canada	64	55 25N	115 25w
Kinvara, Ireland	11	53 8N	8 57w
Kinyangi, Tanzania	53	4 26s	34 38 E
Kinyeti, Mt., Sudan	53	3 56N	32 52 E
Kiosk, Canada	62	46 6N	78 53w

	MAP		
Kioshan, China	38	32 40N	114 0 E
Kiowa, Kan., U.S.A.	71	37 1N	98 30w
Kiowa, Okla., U.S.A.	71	34 45N	95 51w
Kipahigan, L., Canada	65	55 25N	101 58w
Kipanga, Zaire	53	9 25s	27 25 E
Kiparissia, Greece	21	37 15N	21 40 E
Kiparissia, G., Greece	21	37 30N	21 30 E
Kipatimu, Tanzania	53	8 22s	38 54 E
Kipawa L., Canada	62	46 50N	79 0w
Kipembawe, Tan.	53	7 41s	33 28 E
Kipengere Ra., Tan.	53	9 20s	34 20 E
Kipili, Tanzania	53	7 25s	30 40 E
Kipilingu, Zaire	56	13 4s	29 3 E
Kipling, Canada	65	50 10N	102 30w
Kipushi, Zaire	56	11 46s	27 15 E
Kipushia, Zaire	56	12 55s	29 35 E
Kirchberg, Switzerland	15	47 25N	9 4 E
Kirensk, U.S.S.R.	27	57 50N	107 55 E
Kirgizia, S.S.R., U.S.S.R.	26	42 0N	75 0 E
Kiri, Nigeria	52	9 40N	11 59 E
Kiriburu, India	33	22 0N	85 5 E
Kirikkale, Turkey	30	39 50N	33 31 E
Kirikopuni, N.Z.	46	35 50s	174 1 E
Kirillov, U.S.S.R.	25	59 51N	38 14 E
Kirin, China	37	43 50N	126 38 E
Kiriwina Is., Papua	42	8 30s	151 5 E
Kirkcaldy, Scotland	10	56 7N	3 10w
Kirkcudbright, Scotland	10	54 50N	4 3w
Kirkee, India	32	18 34N	73 56 E
Kirkenes, Norway	22	69 40N	30 5 E
Kirkjubol, Iceland	22	64 46N	13 58w
Kirkland, U.S.A.	73	34 28N	112 44w
Kirkland Lake, Canada	62	48 15N	80 0w
Kirklareli, Turkey	30	41 44N	27 12 E
Kirkliston Ra., N.Z.	47	44 25s	170 34 E
Kirksville, U.S.A.	70	40 21N	92 32w
Kirkuk, Iraq	30	35 30N	44 21 E
Kirkwall, Scotland	10	58 59N	2 59w
Kirkwood, C. Prov.	57	33 22s	25 15 E
Kirov, U.S.S.R.	24	58 25N	49 40 E
Kirov, U.S.S.R.	25	54 3N	34 12 E
Kirovabad (Elizavetpol), U.S.S.R.	24	40 45N	46 10 E
Kirovograd, U.S.S.R.	25	48 35N	32 20 E
Kirovsk, U.S.S.R.	24	67 48N	33 50 E
Kirovsk, mt., U.S.S.R.	22	67 48N	33 40 E
Kirriemuir, Canada	65	51 56N	110 20w
Kirsanov, U.S.S.R.	25	52 35N	42 40 E
Kirsehir, Turkey	30	39 14N	34 5 E
Kirtachi, Niger	52	12 52N	2 30 E
Kirthar Range, Pak.	32	27 0N	67 0 E
Kiruna, Sweden	22	67 50N	20 20 E
Kirundu, Zaire	54	0 50s	25 35 E
Kiruru, Indonesia	35	3 55s	134 55 E
Kiryandongo, Uganda	53	1 50N	32 0 E
Kiryu, Japan	36	36 34N	139 12 E
Kisaga, Tanzania	53	4 24s	34 18 E
Kisaki, Tanzania	53	7 28s	37 40 E
Kisangani, Zaire	54	0 41N	25 11 E
Kisar I., Indonesia	35	8 5s	127 10 E
Kisaraw, & R., Tan.	53	6 55s	39 8 E
Kisarazu, Japan	36	35 25N	139 59 E
Kishanganj, India	33	26 3N	88 14 E
Kishangarh, India	32	27 50N	70 30 E
Kishi, Zaire	56	10 32s	28 52 E
Kishi, Nigeria	52	9 6N	3 56 E
Kishinev, U.S.S.R.	24	47 1N	28 50 E
Kishiwada, Japan	36	34 27N	135 15 E
Kishow, China	39	28 8N	109 30 E
Kishtwar, Kashmir	32	33 20N	75 48 E
Kisi, China	37	45 17N	131 0 E
Kisii, Kenya	53	0 42s	34 44 E
Kisiju, Tanzania	53	7 23s	39 19 E
Kisizi, Uganda	53	1 0s	29 58 E
Kiska I., Aleutian Is.	59	52 0N	178 0 E
Kiskatinaw R., Canada	64	55 30N	120 30w
Kiskittogisu L., Canada	65	54 0N	98 0w
Kiskörös, Hungary	16	46 37N	19 20 E
Kiskunfelegyháza, Hungary	16	46 42N	19 53 E
Kiskunhalas, Hungary	16	46 28N	19 37 E
Kiskunmajsa, Hungary	16	46 30N	19 48 E
Kisoro, Uganda	53	1 17s	29 42 E
Kislovodsk, U.S.S.R.	25	43 50N	42 45 E
Kismayu, Somali Rep.	49	0 20s	42 30 E
Kiso R., Japan	36	35 20N	137 0 E
Kissidougou, Guinea	52	9 5N	10 0w
Kissimmee, U.S.A.	69	28 18N	81 22w
Kissimmee R., U.S.A.	69	27 20N	81 0w
Kississing L., Canada	65	55 15N	101 30w
Kistna (Krishna) R., India	32	16 30N	77 0 E
Kisújszállas, Hungary	16	47 12N	20 50 E
Kisumu, Kenya	53	0 3s	34 57 E
Kisuzi, Tanzania	53	4 10s	30 10 E
Kiswani, Tanzania	53	4 9s	38 0 E
Kiswere, Tanzania	53	9 30s	39 30 E
Kit Carsen, U.S.A.	70	38 37N	102 46w
Kita, Mali	50	13 5N	9 25w
Kitab, U.S.S.R.	26	39 15N	67 0 E
Kitai, China	37	44 2N	89 33 E
Kitakyushu, Japan	36	33 50N	130 50 E
Kitale, Kenya	53	1 0N	35 12 E
Kitambi, Tanzania	53	8 38s	38 48 E
Kitami, Japan	36	43 58N	143 59 E
Katangari, Tanzania	53	10 39s	39 20 E
Kitangiri, L., Tan.	53	4 5s	34 50 E

	MAP		
Kitaya, Tanzania	53	10 39s	40 10 E
Kitchener, Canada	62	43 30N	80 30w
Kitchener, W. Australia	45	30 55s	124 8 E
Kitchigama, R., Canada	62	50 35N	78 5w
Kitchioh, China	39	22 55N	116 0 E
Kitchion Wan, China	39	22 50N	115 40 E
Kitega, Burundi	53	3 30s	29 58 E
Kitetema, Zaire	53	8 43s	29 57 E
Kitgum, Uganda	53	3 23N	32 55 E
Kithira, Greece	20	36 10N	22 59 E
Kithira (Cerigo) I., Gr.	20	36 18N	23 0 E
Kithnos, Greece	21	37 25N	24 25 E
Kitimat, Canada	64	53 55N	129 0w
Kitinen R., Finland	22	67 50N	26 45 E
Kittanning, U.S.A.	68	40 49N	79 39w
Kittery, U.S.A.	69	43 7N	70 42w
Kittilä, Finland	22	67 38N	25 0 E
Kitu, Zaire	56	7 36s	27 41 E
Kitui, Kenya	53	1 20s	38 0 E
Kituku, Zaire	53	7 33s	30 19 E
Kitunda, Tanzania	53	6 50s	33 12 E
Kitutu, Tanzania	53	0 36s	34 51 E
Kitwe, Zambia	56	12 50s	28 0 E
Kitwe, Uganda	53	0 5s	30 28 E
Kityang, China	39	26 35N	111 51 E
Kitzbühel, Austria	14	47 27N	12 24 E
Kitzingen, Germany	14	49 44N	10 9 E
Kiuchuan, China	37	39 50N	99 34 E
Kiukiang, China	39	29 45N	116 5 E
Kiulung Shan, China	39	29 20N	114 30 E
Kiungchow, China	39	19 58N	110 14 E
Kiungchow Strait, China	39	20 10N	110 0 E
Kivalina, Alaska	59	67 45N	164 40w
Kivalo, mts., Finland	22	66 18N	26 0 E
Kivindi, Tanzania	53	11 32s	35 0 E
Kivu L., Zaire	53	2 0s	29 5 E
Kiyang, China	39	26 30N	111 45 E
Kiyev. *See* Kiev, U.S.S.R.	26		
Kiyuanshan, China	39	28 8N	117 43 E
Kiziguru, Rwanda	53	1 46s	30 24 E
Kizil, R., Turkey	30	39 10N	36 0 E
Kizilsk, U.S.S.R.	24	52 40N	58 40 E
Kizimkazi, Tanzania	53	6 31s	39 27 E
Kizyl-Atrek, U.S.S.R.	31	38 2N	55 15 E
Kizyl Kiya, U.S.S.R.	26	40 20N	72 35 E
Klaarstroom, C. Prov.	57	33 16s	22 30 E
Klabat Mt., Indonesia	35	1 45N	125 15 E
Kladno, Czechoslovakia	16	50 10N	14 7 E
Klagenfurt, Austria	14	46 38N	14 20 E
Klamath, R., U.S.A.	72	41 20N	123 20w
Klamath Falls, U.S.A.	72	42 20N	123 47w
Klamath Mts., U.S.A.	72	41 20N	123 10w
Klamono, Indonesia	35	1 10s	131 30 E
Klang, Malaya	34	3 3N	101 27 E
Klappan, R., Canada	64	57 50N	129 20w
Klar, R., Sweden	23	60 45N	13 30 E
Klaten, Indonesia	34	7 43s	110 36 E
Klatovy, C.Slov.	16	49 23N	13 18 E
Klawak, Alaska	64	55 35N	133 0w
Klawer, Cape Province	57	31 44s	18 36 E
Kleena Kleene, Canada	64	52 0N	124 50w
Klein, U.S.A.	72	46 26N	108 30w
Klein-karas, S.W. Afr.	57	27 33s	18 3 E
Klemtu, Canada	64	52 35N	128 55w
Klerksdorp, Transvaal	57	26 51s	26 38 E
Kletnya, U.S.S.R.	25	53 30N	33 2 E
Kletskaya, U.S.S.R.	25	49 20N	43 0 E
Kleve, Germany	14	51 46N	6 10 E
Klickitat, U.S.A.	72	45 50N	21 5w
Klin, U.S.S.R.	25	56 28N	36 48 E
Klinaklini R., Canada	64	51 30N	125 40w
Klintsy, U.S.S.R.	25	52 50N	32 10 E
Klip, R., O.F.S.	57	27 0s	29 0 E
Klipdale, C. Prov.	57	34 17s	19 58 E
Klipdam, Cape Province	57	28 18s	24 40 E
Klipplaat, C. Prov.	57	33 0s	24 22 E
Klobuck, Poland	16	50 55N	19 5 E
Klock, Canada	62	46 17N	78 30w
Klodzko, Poland	16	50 28N	16 40 E
Klondike, dist., Canada	60	64 0N	139 40w
Klosterneuburg, Austria	14	48 18N	16 19 E
Klosters, Switzerland	15	46 52N	9 52 E
Klouto, Togo	52	6 57N	1 44 E
Kluane, Canada	59	60 59N	138 22w
Kluane L., Canada	60	61 20N	138 40w
Kluang, Malaya	34	2 1N	103 20 E
Klukwan, Alaska	64	59 30N	136 0w
Klyazma R., U.S.S.R.	25	56 30N	42 0 E
Klyuchevsk, Mt., U.S.S.R.	27	55 50N	160 30 E
Knee L., Canada	65	55 0N	95 0w
Knight Inlet, Canada	64	50 50N	125 30w
Knights Town, Ireland	11	51 55N	10 18w
Knob, C., W. Australia	44	34 30s	119 30 E
Knobby Ra., N.Z.	47	45 25s	169 31 E
Knockmealdown Mts., Ireland	11	52 16N	8 0w
Knocktopher, Ireland	11	52 29N	7 14w
Knokke, Belgium	13	51 20N	3 17 E
Knossos, Crete	20	39 18N	25 10 E
Knox, U.S.A.	68	41 18N	86 36w
Knox C., Canada	64	54 15N	133 0w
Knox Coast, Antarctica	80	66 30s	108 0 E
Knox City, U.S.A.	71	33 24N	99 47w
Knoxville, Iowa, U.S.A.	70	41 17N	93 6w
Knoxville, Tenn., U.S.A.	69	36 0N	83 57w
Knysna, Cape Province	57	34 2s	23 2 E
Knyszyn, Poland	16	53 20N	22 56 E

	MAP		
Ko Chang I., Thailand	34	12 0N	102 20 E
Ko Kut, I., Thailand	34	11 50N	102 30 E
Ko Phangan I., Thai.	34	9 45N	100 10 E
Ko Samui I., Thailand	34	9 30N	100 0 E
Kobarid (Caporetto), Yugoslavia	20	46 15N	13 30 E
Kobayashi, Japan	36	31 56N	130 59 E
Kobe, Japan	36	34 45N	135 10 E
Koblenz, Germany	14	50 21N	7 36 E
Koboko, Uganda	53	3 23N	31 0 E
Kobroor I., Indonesia	35	6 10s	134 30 E
Kobuk, Alaska	59	67 15N	159 0w
Kobuk, R., Alaska	59	67 10N	159 0w
Kobylkino, U.S.S.R.	25	54 8N	43 46 E
Kočani, Yugoslavia	21	41 55N	22 25 E
Kočevje, Yugoslavia	20	45 39N	14 50 E
Kocheya, U.S.S.R.	27	52 30N	120 25 E
Kochi, Japan	36	33 30N	133 35 E
Kochi, pref., Japan	36	33 30N	133 15 E
Kodiak, Alaska	59	57 47N	152 25w
Kodiak I., Alaska	59	57 30N	153 30w
Kodinar, India	32	20 44N	70 46 E
Kodok, Sudan	51	9 57N	32 4 E
Koedoesberge, C. Prov.	57	32 40s	20 12 E
Koegrabie, C. Prov.	57	29 2s	21 43 E
Keokenaap, C. Prov.	57	31 30s	18 18 E
Koes, S. W. Africa	57	26 0s	19 15 E
Koffiefontein, O.F.S.	57	29 22s	24 58 E
Koforidua, Ghana	52	6 3N	0 17w
Kofu, Japan	36	35 40N	138 30 E
Koga, Tanzania	53	6 7s	32 20 E
Köge, Denmark	23	55 27N	12 10 E
Köge B., Denmark	14	55 30N	12 25 E
Kogin Baba, Nigeria	52	7 55N	11 35 E
Kogota, Japan	36	38 30N	141 5 E
Koh-i-Baba, Mt., Afghanistan	31	34 40N	67 35 E
Koh-i-Sangan Mt., Afghanistan	30	33 35N	64 50 E
Kohala, Hawaiian Is.	59	20 14N	155 48w
Kohat, Pakistan	32	33 40N	71 29 E
Kohima, India	33	25 35N	94 10 E
Kohukohu, N.Z.	46	35 21s	173 38 E
Kojima, Japan	36	34 40N	133 53 E
Kokand, U.S.S.R.	26	41 0N	71 10 E
Kokanee Glacier Prov. Park, Canada	64	49 40N	117 0w
Kokcha R., Afghanistan	31	37 0N	70 0 E
Kokchetav, U.S.S.R.	26	53 20N	69 10 E
Kokemäen, R., Finland	23	61 29N	21 10 E
Kokhtla Yarve, U.S.S.R.	23	59 28N	27 28 E
Kokiu, China	37	23 25N	103 5 E
Kokkala, Finland	23	63 50N	23 8 E
Koko, Nigeria	52	11 28N	4 29 E
Koko, Nigeria	52	6 5N	5 28 E
Kokoda, Papua	42	8 0s	148 0 E
Kokomo, Ind., U.S.A.	68	40 28N	86 8w
Koko Nor, L., Mon.	37	37 0N	100 0 E
Kokopo, N.E. New Guinea	42	4 25s	152 10 E
Komatsushima, Japan	36	34 3N	134 39 E
Kokstad, Cape Province	57	30 32s	29 29 E
Kokwarole, mt., Kenya	53	0 40N	36 7 E
Kola, U.S.S.R.	24	68 45N	33 8 E
Kola Pen., U.S.S.R.	24	67 30N	38 0 E
Kolahun, Liberia	52	8 15N	10 4w
Kolan, China	38	38 47N	111 35 E
Kolan, Queensland	42	24 43s	152 12 E
Kolar, India	32	13 12N	78 15 E
Kolarovgrad (Shumen), Bulgaria	21	43 27N	26 42 E
Kolayat (Srikolaytji), India	32	27 50N	73 0 E
Kolbio, Kenya	53	1 9s	41 14 E
Kolda, Senegal	50	12 55N	14 50w
Kolding, Denmark	23	55 30N	9 29 E
Kole, Zaire	54	3 16s	22 42 E
Kolguyev I., U.S.S.R.	24	69 20N	48 30 E
Kolhapur, India	32	16 43N	74 15 E
Kolin, Czechoslovakia	16	50 2N	15 9 E
Kolmanskop, S.W. Afr.	57	26 40s	15 12 E
Köln. *See* Cologne.	14		
Kolno, Poland	16	53 22N	21 59 E
Kolo, Niger	52	13 16N	2 49 E
Kolo, Poland	16	52 12N	18 37 E
Kolo, Tanzania	53	4 45s	35 49 E
Kolobrzeg, Poland	16	54 10N	15 35 E
Kolokani, Mali	50	12 35N	7 45w
Kolomiya, U.S.S.R.	24	48 31N	25 2 E
Kolosib, India	32	24 15N	92 45 E
Kolpashevo, U.S.S.R.	26	58 20N	83 5 E
Kolpny, U.S.S.R.	25	52 12N	37 10 E
Kolwezi, Zaire	56	10 50s	25 20 E
Kolyma Ra., U.S.S.R.	27	63 0N	157 0 E
Kolyma R., U.S.S.R.	27	64 40N	153 0 E
Kôm Ombo (Nasser City), Egypt	51	24 30N	32 57 E
Komadugu Gana R., Nigeria	52	12 30N	11 30 E
Komadugu Yobe R., Nigeria	52	12 51N	11 30 E
Komandorskie Is., U.S.S.R.	5	55 0N	167 0 E
Komárno, C.Slov.	16	47 49N	18 5 E
Komati R., Transvaal	57	25 48s	31 50 E
Komatipoort, Transvaal	57	25 25s	31 57 E
Kombone, Nigeria	52	4 25N	9 22 E
Komenda, Ghana	52	5 4N	1 28w

Place	Map	Lat.	Long.
Komeshia, Zaire	56	8 1 s	27 4 E
Komga, Cape Province	57	32 37 s	27 56 E
Komi, A.S.S.R., U.S.S.R.	26	64 0 N	55 0 E
Kommunarsk, U.S.S.R.	25	48 28 N	38 40 E
Komodo, Indonesia	35	8 37 s	119 20 E
Komona, Congo (Fr.)	54	3 12 s	13 10 E
Komotini, Greece	21	41 6 N	25 25 E
Kompong Cham, Indo-China	34	11 54 N	105 30 E
Kompong Speu, Cambodia	34	11 25 N	104 32 E
Kompong Thom, Indo-China	34	12 35 N	104 51 E
Kompongou, Dahomey	52	11 28 N	1 58 E
Komsberge, C. Prov.	57	32 41 N	20 46 E
Komsomolets I., U.S.S.R.	27	80 30 N	95 0 E
Komsomolsk, U.S.S.R.	27	50 30 N	137 0 E
Komsomolskaya, Ant.	80	73 45 s	97 0 E
Konawa, U.S.A.	71	34 58 N	96 46 W
Kondagaon, India	33	19 35 N	81 35 E
Kondakovo, U.S.S.R.	27	69 50 N	151 50 E
Konde, Tanzania	53	4 58 s	39 40 E
Kondinin, W. Australia	44	32 34 s	118 8 E
Kondoa, Tanzania	53	5 0 s	36 0 E
Kondopoga, U.S.S.R.	24	62 10 N	34 30 E
Kondrashevo, U.S.S.R.	27	57 20 N	98 20 E
Konduga, Nigeria	52	11 35 N	13 26 E
Konevo, U.S.S.R.	24	62 10 N	39 15 E
Kong, Ivory Coast	50	8 54 N	4 36 W
Kong Kemul, Mt., Indonesia	35	2 0 N	116 20 E
Kongmoon, China	39	22 32 N	113 4 E
Kongolo, Zaire	54	5 14 s	26 55 E
Kongor, Sudan	54	7 9 N	31 21 E
Kongsberg, Norway	23	59 37 N	9 38 E
Kongsvinger, Norway	23	60 12 N	12 2 E
Kongwa, Tanzania	53	6 11 s	36 26 E
Koni, Zaire	56	10 41 s	27 14 E
Koni Mts., Zaire	56	10 36 s	27 10 E
Konin, Poland	16	52 12 N	18 15 E
Konjic, Yugoslavia	21	43 42 N	18 0 E
Konkobiri, Dahomey	52	11 8 N	1 44 E
Konongo, Ghana	52	6 40 N	1 15 W
Konosha, U.S.S.R.	24	61 0 N	40 5 E
Konotop, U.S.S.R.	25	51 12 N	33 7 E
Końskie, Poland	16	51 15 N	20 23 E
Konstabel, C. Prov.	57	33 13 s	20 15 E
Konstantinovski, U.S.S.R.	25	47 33 N	41 10 E
Konta, India	33	17 50 N	81 25 E
Kontagora, Nigeria	52	10 23 N	5 27 E
Kontcha, Cameroon	52	7 59 N	12 15 E
Kontum, S. Viet Nam	34	14 24 N	108 0 E
Konya, Turkey	30	37 52 N	32 35 E
Konya Ovasi, Des., Tur.	30	38 30 N	33 0 E
Konza, Kenya	53	1 45 s	37 0 E
Kookynie, W. Australia	44	29 17 s	121 22 E
Koondrook, Victoria	43	35 33 s	144 8 E
Koorawatha, N.S.W.	43	34 2 s	148 33 E
Kooskia, U.S.A.	72	46 6 N	116 0 W
Koostatak, Canada	65	51 26 N	97 26 W
Kootenai, R., U.S.A.	72	48 30 N	115 27 W
Kootenay L., Canada	64	49 30 N	117 0 W
Kootenay Nat. Pk., Canada	64	51 0 N	116 5 W
Kootenay, R., Canada	64	50 0 N	116 0 W
Kootjieskolk, S. Africa	57	31 12 s	20 21 E
Kopanovka, U.S.S.R.	25	47 31 N	46 38 E
Kopaonik, Planina, Yugoslavia	21	43 10 N	21 0 E
Kopasker, Iceland	22	66 18 N	16 25 W
Kópavogur, Iceland	22	64 10 N	21 50 W
Koper, Yugoslavia	20	45 31 N	13 44 E
Kopervik, Norway	23	59 17 N	5 20 E
Kopet Dag Mts., U.S.S.R.	26	38 50 N	56 20 E
Köping, Sweden	23	59 31 N	16 3 E
Koppang, Norway	23	61 32 N	11 3 E
Kopparberg, Sweden	23	59 55 N	15 0 E
Kopparberg, co., Swed.	23	61 20 N	14 15 E
Kopperå, Norway	23	63 24 N	11 52 E
Korab, Mt., Y.slav.	21	41 44 N	20 40 E
Koraluk, R., Canada	63	56 12 N	63 0 W
Koraput, India	33	18 50 N	82 40 E
Korçë, Albania	21	40 37 N	20 50 E
Korčula, I., Y.slav.	20	42 57 N	16 55 E
Korda, U.S.S.R.	27	55 5 N	103 15 E
Kordofan, prov., Sudan	51	13 0 N	29 0 E
Koré Meroua, Niger	52	13 36 N	3 52 E
Korea, pen., Asia	36	34 0 N to 43 0 N	124 E to 131 E
Korea Bay, Yellow Sea	36	39 30 N	123 30 E
Korea, North, rep., Asia	36	38 0 N to 43 0 N	124 E to 131 E
Korea, South, rep., Asia	36	34 0 N to 38 0 N	125 E to 128 E
Korea Str., Korea-Jap.	36	28 40 N	134 10 E
Koregaon, India	32	17 40 N	74 10 E
Korenevo, U.S.S.R.	25	51 27 N	34 55 E
Korenovskaya, U.S.S.R.	25	45 23 N	39 27 E
Korhogo, Ivory Coast	50	9 29 N	5 28 W
Kori Creek, India	32	23 45 N	68 30 E
Koriyama, Japan	36	37 25 N	140 25 E
Korla, China	37	41 48 N	86 10 E
Kornat I., Yugoslavia	20	43 50 N	15 20 E
Koro, Ivory Coast	50	8 40 N	7 30 W
Korocha, U.S.S.R.	25	50 55 N	37 30 E
Korogwe, Tanzania	53	5 5 s	38 25 E
Koroit, Victoria	43	38 18 s	142 24 E
Koror I., Carolines	35	7 30 N	134 35 E
Körös, R., Hungary	16	46 45 N	20 20 E
Korosten, U.S.S.R.	25	50 57 N	28 25 E
Korsakov, U.S.S.R.	27	46 30 N	142 42 E
Korsör, Denmark	23	55 20 N	11 9 E
Korsun, U.S.S.R.	25	49 30 N	31 10 E
Korsun Shevchenkovski, U.S.S.R.	25	49 24 N	31 14 E
Korsze, Poland	23	54 11 N	21 9 E
Korti, Sudan	51	18 0 N	31 40 E
Kortrijk, Belgium	13	50 50 N	3 17 E
Korumburra, Victoria	43	38 26 s	145 50 E
Koryak Ra., U.S.S.R.	27	62 0 N	170 0 E
Kos, Greece	21	36 52 N	27 19 E
Kos, I., Greece	21	36 50 N	27 10 E
Koscian, Poland	16	52 5 N	16 40 E
Kosciusko, U.S.A.	71	33 2 N	89 34 W
Kosciusko, I., Alaska	64	56 0 N	133 40 W
Kosciusko Mt., N.S.W.	43	36 27 s	148 16 E
Koshchagyl, U.S.S.R.	24	46 45 N	54 0 E
Kosi L., Natal	57	27 0 s	32 50 E
Košice, Czechoslovakia	16	48 42 N	21 15 E
Kosong, Korea	36	38 40 N	128 0 E
Kosovo-Metohija, Autonomous Reg., Yugoslavia	21	42 50 N	21 30 E
Kosovska Mitrovica, Yugoslavia	21	42 54 N	20 52 E
Kostajnica, Y.slav.	20	45 17 N	16 30 E
Koster, Transvaal	57	25 52 s	26 54 E
Kosti, Sudan	51	13 8 N	32 43 E
Kostroma, U.S.S.R.	25	57 50 N	41 0 E
Kostroma R., U.S.S.R.	25	58 15 N	41 0 E
Kostrzyń, Poland	16	52 24 N	14 38 E
Kosvenski Kamen Mt., U.S.S.R.	24	59 30 N	57 30 E
Koszalin, Poland	16	54 12 N	16 8 E
Köszeg, Hungary	16	47 23 N	16 33 E
Kot Addu, Pakistan	32	30 30 N	71 0 E
Kota, India	32	25 15 N	75 52 E
Kota Agung, Indonesia	34	5 30 s	104 40 E
Kota Bharu, Malaya	34	6 7 N	102 14 E
Kota Kinabalu, Sabah	35	6 0 N	116 12 E
Kota-Kota, Malawi	56	12 55 s	34 15 E
Kota Tinggi, Malaya	34	1 44 N	103 53 E
Kotabaru, Indonesia	35	3 20 s	116 20 E
Kotabua, Indonesia	35	0 55 N	124 40 E
Kotaneelee, R., Canada	64	60 30 N	124 0 W
Kotcha R., Afghan.	30	36 56 N	69 45 E
Kotcho L., Canada	64	59 10 N	121 20 W
Kotelnich, U.S.S.R.	24	58 20 N	48 10 E
Kotelnikovski, U.S.S.R.	25	47 45 N	43 15 E
Kotolny, I., U.S.S.R.	27	75 10 N	139 0 E
Kotido, Uganda	53	3 0 N	34 2 E
Kotka, Finland	23	60 29 N	27 0 E
Kotli, Kashmir	32	33 30 N	73 55 E
Koton-Karifi, Nigeria	42	8 4 N	6 44 E
Kotonkoro, Nigeria	52	11 3 N	5 88 E
Kotor, Yugoslavia	21	42 25 N	18 47 E
Kotovsk, U.S.S.R.	25	47 55 N	29 35 E
Kotri, Pakistan	32	25 22 N	68 22 E
Kottagudem, India	32	17 30 N	80 40 E
Kottayam, India	32	9 35 N	76 33 E
Kotturu, India	32	14 50 N	76 15 E
Kotuy R., U.S.S.R.	27	68 20 s	98 0 E
Kotzebue, Alaska	59	66 46 N	162 30 W
Kotzebue Sound, Alaska	59	66 40 N	163 30 W
Kouande, Dahomey	52	10 15 N	1 35 E
Kouango, Cent. African Republic	54	5 0 N	20 10 E
Koudougou, Volta	50	12 10 N	2 20 W
Kouga, Chad	51	9 55 N	21 0 E
Kouga Mts., S. Africa	57	33 40 s	23 55 E
Kouilou, R., Congo (Fr.)	54	4 10 s	12 5 E
Koula Moutou, Gabon	54	1 15 s	12 25 E
Koulikoro, Mali	50	12 40 N	7 50 W
Koulou, Niger	52	13 9 N	3 5 E
Koumala, Queensland	42	21 38 s	149 15 E
Koumra, Chad	54	8 50 N	17 35 E
Kounradski, U.S.S.R.	26	47 20 N	75 0 E
Kountze, U.S.A.	71	30 17 N	94 19 W
Kourou, French Guiana	79	5 15 N	52 55 W
Koutaiala, Mali	50	12 25 N	5 35 W
Kouvola, Finland	23	60 53 N	26 43 E
Kovd, L., U.S.S.R.	22	66 50 N	32 15 E
Kovel, U.S.S.R.	24	51 10 N	25 0 E
Kovilpatti, India	32	9 10 N	77 50 E
Kovrov, U.S.S.R.	25	56 25 N	41 55 E
Kovzha, U.S.S.R.	25	60 20 N	37 10 E
Kowes, S.W. Africa	57	25 8 N	18 59 E
Kowkash, Canada	62	50 20 N	87 20 W
Kowloon, Hong Kong Territory	39	22 25 N	114 10 E
Kowpangtze, China	38	41 20 N	121 50 E
Koyiu, China	39	23 5 N	112 35 E
Koyuk, Alaska	59	64 55 N	161 20 W
Koyukuk, R., Alaska	59	65 45 N	156 30 W
Kozan, Turkey	30	37 30 N	35 45 E
Kozáni, Greece	21	40 18 N	21 48 E
Kozhikode (Calicut), India	32	11 15 N	75 43 E
Kozienice, Poland	16	51 35 N	21 30 E
Kožmin, Poland	16	51 48 N	17 27 E
Kozmodemyansk, U.S.S.R.	25	56 25 N	46 35 E
Kpabia, Ghana	52	9 10 N	0 20 W
Kpandae, Ghana	52	8 30 N	0 2 W
Kpandu, Ghana	52	6 58 N	0 16 E
Kpong, Ghana	52	6 11 N	0 9 E
Kra, Isthmus of, Thai.	34	10 15 N	99 30 E
Kraai, R., S. Africa	57	31 0 s	27 0 E
Krabi, Thailand	34	8 2 N	98 52 E
Kragan, Indonesia	34	6 43 s	111 38 E
Kragerö, Norway	23	58 56 N	9 30 E
Kragujevac, Yugoslavia	21	44 2 N	20 56 E
Krakatau, Indonesia	34	6 10 s	105 20 E
Krakow, Poland	16	50 3 N	19 55 E
Kraljevo, Yugoslavia	21	43 43 N	20 40 E
Kramatorsk, U.S.S.R.	25	48 50 N	37 30 E
Kramer, U.S.A.	73	35 0 N	117 39 W
Kramfors, Sweden	23	62 55 N	17 48 E
Krangede Falls, Sweden	23	63 9 N	16 10 E
Kranidhion, Greece	21	37 23 N	23 9 E
Kranj, Yugoslavia	20	46 16 N	14 22 E
Kranskop, Natal, S. Afr.	57	28 57 s	30 57 E
Krapivna, U.S.S.R.	25	53 58 N	37 10 E
Krasnaya Polyana, U.S.S.R.	25	43 40 N	40 25 E
Krasnik, Poland	16	50 55 N	22 5 E
Krasnoarmeisk, U.S.S.R.	25	48 30 N	44 25 E
Krasnoarmeiski, U.S.S.R.	25	47 6 N	42 15 E
Krasnodar, U.S.S.R.	25	45 5 N	38 50 E
Krasnograd, U.S.S.R.	25	49 27 N	35 27 E
Krasnokamsk, U.S.S.R.	24	58 0 N	56 0 E
Krasnoselkupsk, U.S.S.R.	26	65 20 N	82 10 E
Krasnoufimsk, U.S.S.R.	24	56 30 N	57 37 E
Krasnouralsk, U.S.S.R.	26	58 0 N	60 0 E
Krasnovodsk, U.S.S.R.	24	40 0 N	52 52 E
Krasnoyarsk, U.S.S.R.	27	56 8 N	93 0 E
Krasnoye, U.S.S.R.	25	54 30 N	31 28 E
Krasny Kut, U.S.S.R.	25	50 50 N	47 0 E
Krasny Yar, U.S.S.R.	25	50 42 N	44 45 E
Krasny Yar, U.S.S.R.	25	46 43 N	48 23 E
Kratie, Cambodia	34	12 32 N	106 10 E
Kratovo, Yugoslavia	21	42 6 N	22 10 E
Krawang, Indonesia	34	6 19 s	107 18 E
Krefeld, Germany	14	51 20 N	6 22 E
Kremenchug, U.S.S.R.	25	49 5 N	33 25 E
Kremmling, U.S.A.	71	40 6 N	106 23 W
Kremnica, C.Slov.	16	48 45 N	18 50 E
Krestovski, U.S.S.R.	27	71 50 N	101 30 E
Kreuzlingen, Switz.	15	47 38 N	9 12 E
Kribi, Cameroon	52	2 57 N	9 56 E
Krichev, U.S.S.R.	25	53 45 N	31 50 E
Kriens, Switzerland	15	47 3 N	8 17 E
Krishna (Kistna) R., India	32	16 26 N	76 45 E
Krishnanagar, India	33	23 15 N	88 33 E
Kristiansand, Norway	23	58 5 N	7 50 E
Kristianstad, Sweden	23	56 5 N	14 7 E
Kristianstad, co., Swed.	23	53 12 N	13 50 E
Kristiansund, Norway	23	63 10 N	7 45 E
Kristineberg, Sweden	22	65 10 N	18 15 E
Kristinehamn, Sweden	23	59 18 N	14 13 E
Kristinestad. *See* Kristiinankaupunki.	23		
Kristiinankaupunki (Kristinestad), Fin.	23	62 18 N	21 25 E
Krivoy Rog, U.S.S.R.	25	47 51 N	33 20 E
Križevci, Yugoslavia	20	46 3 N	16 32 E
Krk, I., Yugoslavia	20	45 5 N	14 56 E
Krokom, Sweden	23	63 20 N	14 30 E
Krolevets, U.S.S.R.	25	51 35 N	33 20 E
Krom River, S. Africa	57	32 0 s	23 0 E
Kronoberg, co., Sweden	23	56 45 N	14 30 E
Kronshtadt, U.S.S.R.	24	60 5 N	29 35 E
Kroombif, Queensland	42	24 20 s	150 45 E
Kroonstad, O.F.S.	57	27 43 s	27 19 E
Kropotkin, U.S.S.R.	25	58 50 N	115 10 E
Krosno, Poland	16	49 35 N	21 56 E
Krotoszyn, Poland	16	51 42 N	17 23 E
Krsko, Yugoslavia	20	45 57 N	15 30 E
Krue, Indonesia	34	5 10 s	104 0 E
Krugersdorp, Transvaal	57	26 5 s	27 46 E
Kruisfontein, C. Prov.	57	34 0 s	24 44 E
Krujë, Albania	21	41 31 N	19 35 E
Krunë, Albania	21	42 12 N	20 24 E
Krupanj, Yugoslavia	21	44 25 N	19 22 E
Krušovo, Yugoslavia	21	41 20 N	21 17 E
Kruzof I., Alaska	64	57 10 N	135 40 W
Krylbo, Sweden	23	60 7 N	16 15 E
Krymskaya, U.S.S.R.	25	44 57 N	37 50 E
Krzepice, Poland	16	50 58 N	18 50 E
Ksar el Kebir, Mor.	50	35 2 N	6 0 W
Ksar es Souk, Morocco	50	31 58 N	4 28 W
Kuala Belait, Brunei	35	4 45 N	114 25 E
Kuala Dungun, Malaya	34	4 46 N	103 25 E
Kuala Kangsar, Malaya	34	4 49 N	100 57 E
Kuala Kedah, Malaya	34	6 2 N	100 20 E
Kuala Klawang, Malaya	34	2 56 N	102 4 E
Kuala Krai, Malaya	34	5 32 N	102 12 E
Kuala Kubu Bahru, Malaya	34	3 34 N	101 40 E
Kuala Lipis, Malaya	34	4 22 N	102 5 E
Kuala Lumpur, Malaya	34	3 9 N	101 41 E
Kuala Pilah, Malaya	34	2 45 N	102 14 E
Kuala Sedili, Malaya	34	1 50 N	104 8 E
Kuala Trengganu, Malaya	34	5 20 N	103 8 E
Kualakahi Chan., Hawaiian Islands	59	22 0 N	159 55 W
Kualakapuas, Indon.	35	2 55 s	114 20 E
Kualakurun, Indonesia	35	1 10 s	113 50 E
Kuantan, Malaya	34	3 49 N	103 20 E
Kub, S.W. Africa	57	24 17 s	17 32 E
Kuba, U.S.S.R.	24	41 21 N	48 32 E
Kuban R., U.S.S.R.	25	45 5 N	38 0 E
Kubena L., U.S.S.R.	25	59 40 N	39 25 E
Kucha, China	37	41 43 N	82 58 E
Kuchen, China	38	33 30 N	117 20 E
Kuching, Sarawak	35	1 33 N	110 25 E
Kucöve, Albania	21	40 49 N	19 56 E
Kuda, India	32	23 10 N	71 25 E
Kudat, Sabah	35	7 0 N	116 42 E
Kudhafljot B., Iceland	22	63 28 N	18 15 W
Kudumalapshwe, Bot.	56	23 52 s	24 57 E
Kudus, Indonesia	34	6 48 s	110 51 E
Kudymkar, U.S.S.R.	24	59 0 N	54 30 E
Kufra Oasis, Libya	51	25 30 N	22 30 E
Kufstein, Austria	14	47 35 N	12 11 E
Kugong I., Canada	56	56 25 N	80 0 W
Kuhak, Iran	31	27 12 N	63 10 E
Kuh-e Aijuy Mt., Iran	31	31 35 N	51 47 E
Kuh-e Binalud, Iran	31	36 30 N	58 45 E
Kun-e-Bol, mt., Iran	31	30 50 N	52 40 E
Kuh-e-Dinar, mt., Iran	31	30 40 N	51 0 E
Kuh-e-Furgun, mt., Iran	31	27 45 N	56 30 E
Kuh-e Hazārān Mt., Iran	31	29 37 N	57 15 E
Kuh-e Hormoz, Iran	31	27 27 N	55 12 E
Kuh-e Jebāl Bārez Mts., Iran	31	29 0 N	58 0 E
Kuh-e Kuhrān, Mt., Iran	31	26 44 N	58 6 E
Kuh-e-Sahand, Iran	30	37 46 N	46 10 E
Kuh-e Seh Konj, Mt., Iran	31	30 17 N	57 24 E
Kuh-e Sorkh, mt., Iran	31	35 40 N	58 45 E
Kuh-e-Taftān, mt., Iran	31	28 44 N	61 0 E
Kuhha-ye Bashākerd, mt., Iran	31	27 0 N	59 0 E
Kuhha-ye Sabalān, Mt., Iran	30	38 25 N	47 45 E
Kuhpayeh, Iran	31	32 44 N	52 20 E
Kuibyshev (Kuybyshev), U.S.S.R.	25	53 20 N	50 7 E
Kuiseb R., S.W. Africa	57	23 40 s	15 30 E
Kuiu I., Alaska	64	56 40 N	134 10 W
Kuji, Japan	36	40 15 N	141 50 E
Kujangdong, N. Korea	36	39 52 N	126 0 E
Kukawa, Nigeria	52	13 58 N	13 27 E
Kuke, Botswana	56	22 24 s	24 27 E
Kukerin, W. Australia	44	33 13 s	118 0 E
Kukës, Albania	21	42 5 N	20 24 E
Kukumanekraal, Bot.	56	23 10 s	24 13 E
Kula, Nigeria	52	4 24 N	6 43 E
Kulai, Malaya	34	1 42 N	103 32 E
Kulal Mt., Kenya	53	2 49 N	36 55 E
Kulasekharapattanam, India	32	8 20 N	78 0 E
Kulaura, Bangladesh	33	24 30 N	92 8 E
Kuldiga, U.S.S.R.	23	56 58 N	21 59 E
Kuldja, China	37	44 0 N	81 0 E
Kuling, China	39	29 33 N	115 51 E
Kulja, W. Australia	44	30 35 s	117 31 E
Kulm, U.S.A.	70	46 20 N	98 58 W
Kulmbach, Germany	14	50 6 N	11 27 E
Kulpawn, R., Ghana	52	9 50 N	1 45 W
Kulu, China	38	37 15 N	115 5 E
Kulu, India	32	32 0 N	77 5 E
Kulunda, U.S.S.R.	26	52 45 N	79 15 E
Kulunkai, Inner Mon.	38	41 43 N	121 32 E
Kulwin, Victoria	43	35 0 s	142 42 E
Kulyaling, W. Australia	44	32 27 s	116 58 E
Kum Tekei, U.S.S.R.	26	43 10 N	79 30 E
Kuma R., U.S.S.R.	25	45 0 N	45 30 E
Kumaganum, Nigeria	52	13 8 N	10 38 E
Kumai B., Indonesia	35	3 10 s	111 45 E
Kumakahi, C., Hawaiian Islands	59	19 30 N	154 50 W
Kumamoto, Japan	36	32 45 N	130 45 E
Kumamoto, pref., Japan	36	32 30 N	131 0 E
Kumanovo, Y.slav.	21	42 9 N	21 42 E
Kumasi, Ghana	52	6 41 N	1 38 W
Kumba, W. Cam.	52	4 40 N	9 28 E
Kumbher, Nepal	33	28 20 N	81 25 E
Kumi, Togo	53	9 45 N	0 41 E
Kumla, Sweden	23	59 8 N	15 10 E
Kumo, Nigeria	52	10 1 N	11 12 E
Kumon Bum, Mts., Burma	33	26 0 N	97 15 E
Kumshe, Nigeria	52	11 25 N	14 1 E
Kumta, India	32	14 29 N	74 32 E
Kumyan, China	39	18 51 N	108 37 E
Kunanalling, W. Australia	44	30 36 s	121 0 E
Kunar, R., Afghan.-W. Pakistan	31	35 20 N	71 30 E
Kunashir, U.S.S.R.	36	44 0 N	146 0 E
Kunch, India	32	26 0 N	79 10 E
Kunda, U.S.S.R.	23	59 30 N	26 34 E
Kundelunga, dist., Zaire	56	9 30 s	27 40 E
Kundi, W. Australia	44	33 43 s	120 11 E

	MAP		
Kunduz, Afghanistan	30	36 50N	69 0 E
Kungan, China	39	30 0N	112 0 E
Kungchuling, China	38	43 30N	124 30 E
Kunghit I., Canada	64	52 0N	131 0W
Kungho, China	37	36 20N	100 46 E
Kungrad, U.S.S.R.	26	43 0N	58 40 E
Kungsbacka, Sweden	23	57 30N	12 7 E
Kungur, U.S.S.R.	24	57 20N	56 40 E
Kungurri, Queensland	42	21 3 S	148 46 E
Kungyifow, China	39	22 25N	112 45 E
Kunhsien, China	38	32 30N	111 17 E
Kuni, Togo	52	9 46N	0 39 E
Kunlong, Burma	33	23 20N	98 50 E
Kunlun Shan, mts., China	37	36 0N	85 0 E
Kunming, China	37	25 0N	102 45 E
Kunsan, Korea	36	36 0N	126 40 E
Kunsan, S. Korea	37	35 57N	126 42 E
Kunshan, China	39	31 26N	121 0 E
Kuntair, Gambia	52	13 30N	16 15W
Kuntaur, Gambia	52		Inset
Kununoppin, W. Austral.	44	31 5 S	117 48 E
Kunya, Nigeria	52	12 14N	8 30 E
Kunyane, Bot.	57	23 33 S	24 35 E
Kuolayarvi, U.S.S.R.	22	66 52N	29 20 E
Kuopio, Finland	23	62 53N	27 35 E
Kuopion Lääni, Finland	23	62 53N	27 35 E
Kupang, Indonesia	35	10 19 S	123 39 E
Kupehkow, China	38	40 45N	117 0 E
Kupreanof I., Alaska	64	56 40N	133 30W
Kupyansk, U.S.S.R.	25	49 45N	37 35 E
Kura R., U.S.S.R.	30	41 20N	48 0 E
Kurametsi, Rhodesia	56	23 25 S	27 5 E
Kuranda, Queensland	42	16 45 S	145 37 E
Kurashiki, Japan	36	34 42N	133 44 E
Kurdistan, reg., S.W. Asia	30	37 30N	42 0 E
Kurduvadi, India	32	18 6N	75 31 E
Kûrdzhali, Bulgaria	21	41 38N	25 21 E
Kure, Japan	36	33 15N	133 15 E
Kuressaar, U.S.S.R.	23	58 17N	23 32 E
Kurgaldzhino, U.S.S.R.	26	50 35N	70 20 E
Kurgan, U.S.S.R.	26	55 30N	65 0 E
Kurgan, U.S.S.R.	27	65 0N	172 0W
Kuridala, Queensland	42	21 16 S	140 29 E
Kurigram, Bangladesh	33	25 50N	89 45 E
Kuril Is., U.S.S.R.	29	45 0N	150 0 E
Kurmuk, Sudan	51	10 33N	34 21 E
Kurnalpi, W. Australia	45	30 29 S	122 16 E
Kurnool, India	32	15 45N	78 0 E
Kurovskoye, U.S.S.R.	25	55 35N	38 55 E
Kurow, New Zealand	47	44 4 S	170 29 E
Kurrajong, W. Austral.	44	28 39 S	120 59 E
Kurrawang, Australia	44	30 46 S	121 17 E
Kurri Kurri, N.S.W.	43	32 50 S	151 28 E
Kursk, U.S.S.R.	25	51 42N	36 11 E
Kursumlija, Yugoslavia	21	43 9N	21 19 E
Kuruman, C. Prov.	57	27 28 S	23 28 E
Kurtalan, Turkey	30	37 57N	41 42 E
Kuruman R., C. Prov.	57	27 5 S	21 30 E
Kurume, Japan	36	33 15N	130 30 E
Kurunegala, Sri Lanka	32	7 30N	80 18 E
Kurusku, Egypt	51	22 37N	32 20 E
Kurya, U.S.S.R.	27	61 15N	108 10 E
Kurya, U.S.S.R.	24	61 42N	57 20 E
Kusawa L., Canada	64	60 25N	136 20W
Kushaka, Nigeria	52	10 32N	6 41 E
Kushan, China	38	39 52N	123 32 E
Kushchevaskaya, U.S.S.R.	25	46 33N	39 35 E
Kusheriki, Nigeria	52	10 31N	6 26 E
Kushevat, U.S.S.R.	26	65 10N	65 30 E
Kushih, China	39	32 10N	115 47 E
Kushiro, Japan	36	43 0N	144 30 E
Kushk, Afghanistan	31	35 15N	62 25 E
Kushka, U.S.S.R.	26	35 20N	62 18 E
Kushtia, Bangladesh	33	23 55N	89 5 E
Kuskokwim Bay, Alaska	59	50 40N	162 30W
Kuskokwim Mts., Alaska	59	61 0N	158 0W
Kuskokwim R., Alaska	59	61 30N	160 0W
Kussa, Ethiopia	53	4 24N	38 50 E
Küssnacht, Switzerland	15	47 5N	8 26 E
Kustanai, U.S.S.R.	26	53 20N	63 45 E
Kuta, Nigeria	52	9 50N	6 37 E
Kütahya, Turkey	30	39 30N	30 2 E
Kutaisi, U.S.S.R.	24	42 19N	42 40 E
Kutatjane, Indonesia	34	3 45N	97 50 E
Kutch, G. of, India	32	22 50N	69 15 E
Kutno, Poland	16	52 13N	19 20 E
Kutu, Zaire	54	2 40 S	18 11 E
Kutubu, L., Papua	42	6 23N	143 12 E
Kutum, Sudan	51	14 20N	24 10 E
Kuwait Persian Gulf	30	29 30N	47 30 E
Kuwait, (Al Kuwayt), tn., Kuwait	30	29 20N	48 0 E
Kuwana, Japan	36	35 0N	136 35 E
Kuyang, Mongolia	38	41 15N	110 0 E
Kuybyshev, (Kuibyshev) U.S.S.R.	25	53 20N	50 7 E
Kuybyshev Res., U.S.S.R.	25	55 2N	49 30 E
Kuysanjaq, Iraq	30	36 5N	44 38 E
Kuyumba, U.S.S.R.	27	61 0N	97 5 E
Kuyung, China	39	32 7N	119 6 E
Kuznetsk, U.S.S.R.	25	53 12N	46 40 E
Kuzomen, U.S.S.R.	24	66 22N	36 50 E
Kvaenangen, Norway	22	69 55N	21 15 E

	MAP		
Kvalsund, Norway	22	70 30N	24 10 E
Kvarken, Finland	23	62 38N	21 2 E
Kvarner, G., Yugoslavia	20	44 50N	14 0 E
Kvarnerić, G., Yugoslavia	20	44 40N	14 35 E
Kwa Mtoro, Tanzania	53	5 14 S	35 34 E
Kwachaga, Tanzania	53	5 38 S	38 8 E
Kwachow, China	39	32 15N	119 24 E
Kwadacha, R., Canada	64	57 45N	125 0 E
Kwaggablad, C. Prov.	57	27 29 S	24 13 E
Kwakhanai, Botswana	57	21 41 S	21 19 E
Kwakoegron, Surinam	79	5 25N	55 25W
Kwale, Kenya	53	4 10 S	39 30 E
Kwali, Nigeria	52	8 56N	7 0 E
Kwamouth, Zaire	54	3 9 S	16 20 E
Kwande, Nigeria	52	8 43N	9 19 E
Kwangan, China	39	30 31N	106 32 E
Kwangchow. *See* Canton, China	39		
Kwangchow Wan, B., China	39	21 20N	111 50 E
Kwanghua (Laohokow), China	39	32 25N	111 40 E
Kwangju, Korea	36	35 10N	126 45 E
Kwangju, S. Korea	37	35 7N	126 52 E
Kwangnan, China	39	24 10N	105 0 E
Kwangnung, S. Korea	36	37 50N	128 56 E
Kwango, prov., Zaire	54	7 50 S	18 20 E
Kwangping, China	38	36 40N	114 41 E
Kwangshui, China	39	31 45N	114 0 E
Kwangsi-Chuang A.R., China	39	23 0N	109 0 E
Kwangtseh, China	39	27 25N	117 12 E
Kwangtsi, China	39	30 5N	115 45 E
Kwangtung, China	39	25 8N	101 55 E
Kwangtung, prov., China	37	23 35N	114 0 E
Kwangwazi, Tanzania	53	7 46 S	38 15 E
Kwangyuan, China	38	32 30N	105 50 E
Kwanhsien, China	37	31 1N	103 40 E
Kwanteh, China	39	31 0N	118 42 E
Kwantien, China	38	40 45N	124 45 E
Kwanyun, China	38	34 28N	119 12 E
Kwataboahegan R., Canada	62	51 10N	82 30W
Kwedia, Bot.	57	25 15 S	24 33 E
Kwei K., China	39	23 50N	111 10 E
Kweichih, China	39	30 40N	117 30 E
Kweichow, prov., China	39	26 40N	107 0 E
Kweihwa. *See* Mingki, China	39		
Kweihsien, China	39	23 0N	109 30 E
Kweiki, China	39	28 13N	117 8 E
Kweilin, China	39	25 16N	110 15 E
Kweiping, China	39	23 26N	110 5 E
Kweitung, China	39	26 0N	113 37 E
Kweiyang, China	39	26 30N	106 35 E
Kweiyang, China	39	25 41N	112 26 E
Kwidzyn, Poland	16	54 5N	18 58 E
Kwiguk, Alaska	59	62 52N	164 28W
Kwilo R., Zaire	54	3 45N	19 30 E
Kwilu, prov., Zaire	54	5 0 S	19 20 E
Kwilu, R., Zaire	54	6 0 S	19 30 E
Kwinana, W. Australia	44	32 15 S	115 47 E
Kwinella, Gambia. Inset	52	13 20N	15 50W
Kwo Ho, China	38	33 20N	116 50 E
Kwobrup, W. Australia	44	33 37 S	117 53 E
Kwohwa, China	39	23 30N	107 17 E
Kwoka, Mt., N. Guin.	35	0 30 S	132 25 E
Kwolla, Nigeria	52	9 0N	9 20 E
Kwoyang, China	38	33 30N	116 2 E
Kyabe, Chad	54	9 30N	19 0 E
Kyabra, Queensland	43	26 22 S	143 8 E
Kyaikto, Burma	33	17 16N	97 1 E
Kyakhta, U.S.S.R.	27	50 30N	106 25 E
Kyangin, Burma	34	18 20N	95 20 E
Kyaukpadaung, Burma	33	20 50N	95 8 E
Kyaukpyu, Burma	33	19 28N	93 30 E
Kyaukse, Burma	33	21 32N	96 6 E
Kyegegwa, Uganda	53	0 30N	31 0 E
Kyenjojo, Uganda	53	0 38N	30 40 E
Kyle of Lochalsh, Scot.	10	57 17N	5 43W
Kymen Lääni, Finland	23	62 0N	27 0 E
Kymi, R., Finland	23	60 50N	26 50 E
Kyneton, Victoria	43	37 10 S	144 29 E
Kynuna, Queensland	42	21 37 S	141 51 E
Kyo C., Japan	36	35 45N	135 15 E
Kyoga, L., Uganda	53	1 30N	33 0 E
Kyogle, N.S.W.	43	28 40 S	153 0 E
Kyongju, S. Korea	36	35 52N	129 15 E
Kyonggi Do, prov., S. Korea	36	37 45N	127 30 E
Kyongsang, N., prov., Korea	36	36 10N	128 39 E
Kyongsang, S., prov., S. Korea	36	35 30N	128 37 E
Kyonpyaw, Burma	33	17 16N	95 12 E
Kyotera, Uganda	53	0 35 S	31 33 E
Kyoto, and pref., Japan	36	35 0N	135 45 E
Kyrenia, Cyprus	30	35 20N	33 20 E
Kyshtym, U.S.S.R.	24	55 50N	60 20 E
Kystatym, U.S.S.R.	27	67 20N	123 10 E
Kytalyktakh, U.S.S.R.	27	65 30N	123 40 E
Kytylm, U.S.S.R.	24	59 20N	59 0 E
Kyulyunken, U.S.S.R.	27	64 10N	137 5 E
Kyunhla, Burma	33	23 25N	95 15 E
Kyushu, Japan	36	32 30N	131 0 E

	MAP		
Kyuquot, Canada	64	50 3N	127 25W
Kyuquot Sd., Canada	64	49 50N	126 30W
Kyustendil, Bulgaria	21	42 25N	22 41 E
Kywong, N.S.W.	43	34 58 S	146 44 E
Kyzyl, U.S.S.R.	27	51 50N	94 30 E
Kyzyl-Kiya, U.S.S.R.	26	40 10N	72 0 E
Kyzyl Kum, Turkistan	26	42 0N	65 0 E
Kyzyl Rabat, U.S.S.R.	26	37 45N	74 55 E
Kzyl-Orda, U.S.S.R.	26	44 50N	65 10 E

L

L'Annonciation, Canada	62	46 24N	74 52W
L'Anse, U.S.A.	70	46 45N	88 30W
L'Anse du Loup, Can.	63	51 34N	56 44W
La Albuera, Spain	17	38 45N	6 49W
La Alcarria, dist., Spain	17	40 30N	2 10W
La Argentino, Argentina	77	50 20 S	71 50W
La Ascension, Mexico	74	31 0N	108 10W
La Asuncion, Venezuela	75	11 0N	63 50W
La Banda, Argentina	77	27 45 S	64 10W
La Bañeza, Spain	17	42 17N	5 43W
La Barca, Mexico	74	20 20N	102 40W
La Barge, U.S.A.	72	42 13N	110 10W
La Belle, U.S.A.	69	26 45N	81 22W
La Biche R., Canada	64	60 40N	124 40W
La Blanquilla, I., Ven.	78	11 51N	64 37W
La Boca, Pan. Can. Zone	74	9 0N	79 30W
La Bomba, Mexico	74	31 53N	115 2W
La Calera, Chile	77	32 50 S	71 10W
La Carlota, Argentina	77	33 30 S	63 20W
La Carolina, Spain	17	38 17N	3 38W
La Cega, Colombia	78	7 0N	75 25W
La Ceiba, Honduras	75	15 40N	86 50W
La Ceiba, Venezuela	78	9 30N	71 0W
La Charité, France	12	47 10N	3 0 E
La Chaux de Fonds, Switz.	15	47 7N	6 50 E
La Chorrera, Colombia	78	0 55 S	73 0W
La Chorrera, Panama	78	8 50N	79 50W
La Ciotat, France	12	43 12N	5 36 E
La Cocha, Argentina	77	27 50 S	65 40W
La Concepción, Fernando Póo	52	3 28N	84 0 E
La Concepción, Ven.	75	10 40N	71 55W
La Concordia, Mexico	74	16 8N	92 38W
La Conner, U.S.A.	72	48 27N	122 30W
La Copelina, Argentina	77	37 10 S	67 40W
La Coruña, Spain	17	43 20N	8 25W
La Croix, L., Canada	62	48 20N	92 0W
La Crosse, Kan., U.S.A.	70	38 33N	99 15W
La Crosse, Wis., U.S.A.	70	43 48N	91 13W
La Dorada, Colombia	78	5 30N	74 40W
La Esperanza, Bolivia	78	14 34 S	62 10W
La Fayette, U.S.A.	68	40 22N	86 52W
La Fère, France	12	49 40N	3 20 E
La Ferté Macé, France	12	48 35N	0 21W
La Flèche, France	12	47 42N	0 5W
La Florencia, Argentina	77	24 0 S	62 5W
La Folette, U.S.A.	69	36 23N	84 9W
La François, Martinique	75	14 36N	60 59W
La Fregeneda, Spain	17	40 58N	6 54W
La Goulette, Tunisia	51	36 53N	10 17 E
La Grande, U.S.A.	72	45 15N	118 0W
La Grange, Ga., U.S.A.	69	33 2N	85 2W
La Grange, Tex., U.S.A.	71	29 54N	96 52W
La Grange, Ky., U.S.A.	68	38 20N	85 20W
La Granja, Spain	17	40 54N	4 2W
La Guaira, Venezuela	75	10 40N	67 0W
La Guardia, Spain	17	41 55N	8 52W
La Güera, terr., Sp. Sahara	50	22 5N	14 30W
La Harpe, U.S.A.	70	40 31N	90 59W
La Jara, U.S.A.	73	37 18N	105 59W
La Junta, Mexico	74	28 30N	107 20W
La Junta, U.S.A.	71	38 0N	103 30W
La Linea, Spain	17	36 15N	5 23W
La Loche, Canada	65	56 31N	109 27W
La Louvière, Belgium	13	50 27N	4 10 E
La Malbaie, Canada	63	47 40N	70 10W
La Martre R., Canada	60	63 10N	117 0W
La Merced, Peru	78	11 0 S	75 20W
La Mesa, Calif., U.S.A.	73	32 47N	117 3W
La Mesa, N. Mex., U.S.A.	73	32 6N	106 44W
La Motte L., Canada	62	48 10N	77 50W
La Moure, U.S.A.	70	46 28N	98 15W
La Mure, Isère, France	12	44 55N	5 48 E
La Orchila, Venezuela	78	12 0N	66 0W
La Oroya, Peru	78	11 40 S	76 0W
La Palma, Panama	75	8 15N	78 0W
La Palma, Spain	17	37 21N	6 38W
La Paloma, Uruguay	77	34 40 S	54 20W
La Paragua, Venezuela	78	7 10N	63 30W
La Paz, Argentina	77	30 50 S	59 45W
La Paz, Argentina	77	33 30 S	67 20W
La Paz, Bolivia	78	16 20 S	68 10W
La Paz, Honduras	74	14 20N	87 47W
La Paz, Mexico	74	24 10N	110 20W
La Paz, Venezuela	78	10 41N	72 0W
La Paz B., Mexico	74	24 20N	110 40W
La Pérade, Canada	63	46 35N	72 12W
La Pérouse Str., Japan	36	45 40N	142 0 E
La Piedad Cabadas, Mexico	74	20 20N	102 0W
La Plant, U.S.A.	70	45 12N	100 39W

	MAP		
La Plata, Argentina	77	35 0 S	57 55W
La Poile B., Canada	63	47 0N	58 0W
La Porte, U.S.A.	68	41 40N	86 40W
La Puebla, Spain	17	39 50N	4 25W
La Quiaca, Argentina	77	22 5 S	65 35W
La Reine, Canada	62	48 50N	79 30W
La Réole, France	12	44 35N	0 1W
La Rioja, Argentina	77	29 20 S	67 0W
La Robla, Spain	17	42 50N	5 41W
La Roche, France	12	46 40N	1 25W
La Rochelle, France	12	46 10N	1 9W
La Roda, Andalusia, Spain	17	37 14N	4 46W
La Roda, New Castille, Spain	17	39 13N	2 15W
La Romana, Dom. Rep.	75	18 27N	68 57W
La Ronge L., Canada	65	55 10N	105 0W
La Rubia, Argentina	77	30 10 S	61 50W
La Rouge, Lac, Canada	65	55 5N	105 20W
La Sagra Mt., Spain	17	38 0N	2 35W
La Salle, U.S.A.	70	41 20N	89 5W
La Sarre, Canada	62	48 45N	79 15W
La Scie, Canada	63	49 58N	55 36W
La Serena, Chile	77	29 55 S	71 10W
La Seyne, France	12	43 11N	5 53 E
La Souterraine, France	12	46 14N	1 29 E
La Spezia, Italy	20	44 8N	9 48 E
La Tagua, Colombia	78	9 2N	74 40W
La Teste, France	12	44 34N	1 9W
La Tremblade, France	12	45 46N	1 8W
La Tuque, Canada	62	47 30N	72 50W
La Unión, Chile	77	40 10 S	73 0W
La Unión, Spain	17	37 38N	0 53W
La Urbana, Venezuela	78	7 10N	66 55W
La Vega, Dom. Rep.	75	19 20N	70 30W
La Vela, Venezuela	78	11 30N	69 30W
La Victoria, Venezuela	78	10 15N	67 25W
Laau Pt., Hawaiian Is.,	59	21 6N	157 19W
Laba R., U.S.S.R.	25	45 0N	40 30 E
Labé, Guinea	50	11 24N	12 16W
Labe, see Elbe R., Czechoslavakia	16	50 5N	15 20 E
Laberge, L., Canada	64	61 15N	135 0W
Labinsk, U.S.S.R.	25	44 35N	40 50 E
Labis, Malaya	34	2 22N	103 2 E
Labouheyre, France	12	44 13N	0 55W
Laboulaye, Argentina	77	34 10 S	63 30W
Labrador, Canada	61	53 20N	61 0W
Labrador City, Canada	63	52 51N	67 0W
Lábrea, Brazil	78	7 15 S	64 51W
Labuan I., Sabah	35	5 15N	115 38 E
Labuha, Indonesia	35	0 30 S	127 30 E
Labuhan, Indonesia	34	6 26 S	105 50 E
Labuk B., Sabah	35	6 10N	117 50 E
Labyrinth L., S. Austral.	45	30 40 S	135 10 E
Lac Bouchette, Canada	63	48 20N	72 5W
Lac de Flambeau, U.S.A.	70	46 0N	89 53W
Lac Ile á la Crosse, Can.	65	55 30N	107 50W
Lac Jeannine, Canada	63	51 52N	67 40W
Lac la Biche, Canada	64	54 45N	111 50W
Lac la Biche L., Canada	64	54 50N	112 10W
Lac la Martre, Canada	60	63 0N	120 0W
Lac Megiscane, Canada	62	48 30N	76 30W
Lac la Plonge, Canada	65	55 10N	107 20W
Lac Seul, Canada	62	50 28N	92 0W
Lacantum, R., Mexico	74	16 0N	91 0W
Lacaune, France	12	43 43N	2 40 E
Laccadive Is., Indian Oc.	5	10 0N	72 30 E
Lacepede B., S. Austral.	43	36 40 S	139 31 E
Lacerdonia, Mozam.	56	17 30 S	35 28 E
Lachen, Switzerland	15	47 12N	8 52 E
Lachhmangarh, India	32	27 48N	75 6 E
Lachine, Canada	62	45 30N	73 40W
Lachlan R., N.S.W.	43	34 0 S	144 45 E
Lachute, Canada	62	45 39N	74 21W
Lackawanna, U.S.A.	68	42 49N	78 50W
Lackish (site), Israel	29	31 34N	34 51 E
Lacombe, Canada	64	52 30N	113 50W
Laconia, U.S.A.	69	43 32N	71 30W
Lacrosse, U.S.A.	72	46 47N	117 56W
Ladakh Range, Kashmir	32	34 0N	78 0 E
Lādiz, Iran	31	28 56N	61 14 E
Ladismith, C. Prov.	57	33 28 S	21 15 E
Ladoga, L., U.S.S.R.	23	61 15N	30 30 E
Lady Babbie, Rhod.	56	18 30 S	29 20 E
Lady Beatrix L., Canada	62	50 20N	76 50W
Lady Elliot I., Queens.	42	24 13 S	152 43 E
Lady Grey, C. Prov.	57	30 43 S	27 13 E
Ladybrand, O.F.S.	57	29 0 S	27 29 E
Ladysmith, Canada	64	49 0N	124 0W
Ladysmith, Natal, S. Africa	57	28 32 S	29 46 E
Ladysmith, U.S.A.	70	45 26N	91 3W
Lae, Terr. of N. Guinea	42	6 48 S	146 53 E
Laerdalsöyri, Norway	23	60 58N	7 35 E
Laesö I., Denmark	23	57 15N	10 53 E
Lafayette, Colorado, U.S.A.	70	40 1N	105 0W
Lafayette, Ga., U.S.A.	69	34 44N	85 15W
Lafayette, La., U.S.A.	71	30 18N	92 0W
Lafayette, Tenn., U.S.A.	69	36 35N	86 0W
Laferte, Canada	62	48 37N	78 48W
Lafia, Nigeria	52	8 33N	8 27 E
Lafiagi, Nigeria	52	8 52N	5 20 E
Laflèche, Canada	65	49 45N	106 40W
Laforest, Canada	62	47 4N	81 12W
Lagan R., N. Ireland	11	54 35N	5 55W

	MAP		
Lagarfljót R., Iceland	22	56 20N	14 25W
Lågen R., Norway	23	61 29N	10 2 E
Laggan B., Scotland	10	55 40N	6 20W
Laggan L., Scotland	10	56 57N	4 30W
Laghouat, Algeria	50	33 50N	2 50 E
Lagôa Mirim, Uruguay	77	33 0 S	53 30W
Lagonegro, Italy	20	40 8N	15 45 E
Lagos, Nigeria	52	6 25N	3 27 E
Lagos, Portugal	17	37 5N	8 41W
Lagos de Moreno, Mex.	74	21 21N	101 55W
Laguna, Brazil	77	28 30 S	48 50W
Laguna, U.S.A.	73	35 2N	107 28W
Laguna Beach, U.S.A.	73	33 33N	117 47W
Laguna Dam, U.S.A.	73	32 50N	114 30W
Laguna, Madre, Mexico	74	24 30N	97 30W
Laguna Madre, U.S.A.	71	27 0N	97 20W
Laguna de Tamiahua, Mexico	74	21 30N	97 20W
Laguna de Terminos, Mexico	74	18 30N	91 30W
Lagunas, Chile	78	21 0 S	69 45W
Lagunas, Peru	78	5 10 S	75 35W
Lagunillas, Venezuela	78	10 30N	71 20W
Lahad Datu, Sabah	35	5 0N	118 30 E
Lahaina, Hawaiian Is.	59	20 23N	156 40W
Lahat, Indonesia	34	3 45 S	103 30 E
Lahijan, Iran	30	37 10N	50 6 E
Lahinch, Ireland	11	52 56N	9 20W
Lahn R., Germany	14	50 52N	8 35 E
Laholm, Sweden	23	56 30N	13 2 E
Lahontan Res., U.S.A.	72	39 25N	119 10W
Lahore, Pakistan	32	31 32N	74 22 E
Lahore, Terr., W. Pak.	32	32 0N	74 0 E
Lahr, Germany	14	48 20N	7 52 E
Lahti, Finland	23	60 59N	25 45 E
Lai Chau, N. Viet Nam	34	22 5N	103 3 E
Laichan, Viet Nam	37	22 5N	103 3 E
Laichow Wan (Gulf), China	38	37 30N	119 30 E
Laidley, Queensland	43	27 39 S	152 20 E
Laidon L., Scotland	10	56 40N	4 40W
Laifeng, China	39	29 33N	109 19 E
Laigle, France	12	48 46N	0 38 E
Laila, Saudi Arabia	30	22 10N	46 40 E
Laillahue, mt., Peru	78	17 0 S	69 30W
Laingsburg, C. Prov.	57	33 9 S	20 52 E
Laipin, China	39	23 45N	109 15 E
Lais, Indonesia	34	3 35 S	102 0 E
Laisamis, Kenya	53	1 30N	37 52 E
Laiyangal, China	38	30 0N	120 50 E
Laja, R., Mexico	74	20 30N	101 10W
Lajes, Brazil	77	27 48 S	50 20W
Lajkovac, Yugoslavia	21	44 27N	20 14 E
Lak Boggali ,R., Kenya	53	1 30N	39 30 E
Lak Bor, R., Kenya	53	2 10N	39 30 E
Lak Dafat, R., Kenya	53	3 10N	38 30 E
Lak Dera R., Kenya	53	0 45N	40 30 E
Lake, prov., Tanzania	53	2 50 S	33 0 E
Lake Andes, U.S.A.	70	43 11N	98 30W
Lake Arthur, U.S.A.	71	30 4N	92 36W
Lake Brown, W. Austral.	44	30 57 S	118 22 E
Lake Cargelligo, N.S.W.	43	33 18 S	146 18 E
Lake Charles, U.S.A.	71	30 10N	93 10W
Lake Chrissie, Transvaal	57	26 20 S	30 13 E
Lake City, Colo., U.S.A.	73	38 5N	107 21W
Lake City, Fla., U.S.A.	69	30 10N	82 40W
Lake City, Iowa, U.S.A.	70	42 11N	94 44W
Lake City, Mich., U.S.A.	68	44 20N	85 10W
Lake City, Minn., U.S.A.	70	44 29N	92 23W
Lake Geneva, U.S.A.	68	42 38N	88 30W
Lake Lenore, Canada	65	51 40N	104 58W
Lake Linden, U.S.A.	62	47 10N	88 26W
Lake Louise, Canada	64	51 30N	116 10W
Lake Mills, U.S.A.	70	43 24N	93 31W
Lake Providence, U.S.A.	71	32 49N	91 13W
Lake O'The Cherokees, U.S.A.	71	36 45N	94 45W
Lake of the Woods, Can.	67	49 0N	95 0W
Lake Traverse, Canada	62	45 56N	78 4W
Lake Valley, Canada	65	50 39N	106 0W
Lake Village, U.S.A.	71	33 18N	91 17W
Lake Wales, U.S.A.	69	27 55N	81 32W
Lake Worth, U.S.A.	69	26 36N	80 3W
Lakefield, Canada	62	44 30N	78 20W
Lakeland, U.S.A.	69	28 0N	82 0W
Lakeport, U.S.A.	72	39 2N	122 59W
Lakeren, Belgium	13	51 6N	3 59 E
Lakes Entrance, Victoria	43	37 50 S	148 0 E
Lakeside, Ariz., U.S.A.	73	34 13N	109 59W
Lakeside, Neb., U.S.A.	70	42 7N	102 28W
Lakeview, U.S.A.	72	42 12N	120 26W
Lakewood, U.S.A.	68	41 28N	81 50W
Lakhania, Greece	21	35 58N	27 52 E
Lakhpat, India	32	23 48N	68 47 E
Laki, Iceland	22	64 8N	18 8W
Laki, Mt., Iceland	22	64 7N	18 5W
Lakin, U.S.A.	71	37 58N	101 17W
Lakitusaki, R., Canada	62	54 20N	83 0W
Lakki, Pakistan	32	32 38N	70 50 E
Lakhimpur, India	32	27 52N	80 47 E
Lakonia, G. of, Greece	21	36 30N	22 45 E
Lakota, Ivory Coast	50	5 50N	5 30W
Lakota, U.S.A.	70	48 6N	98 17W
Lakse Fd., Norway	22	70 40N	27 0 E
Lakselv, Norway	22	69 56N	25 0 E
Lakshimikantapur, India	33	22 5N	88 20 E
Lala Ghat, India	33	24 30N	92 40 E
Lalaga, Tanzania	53	3 31 S	33 59 E
Lalapanzi, Rhodesia	56	19 20 S	30 15 E
Lali, Iran	30	32 15N	49 30 E
Lalitpur, India	32	24 45N	78 25 E
Lama Kara, Togo	52	9 30N	1 15 E
Lama Shillindi, Ethiopia	53	4 50N	42 6 E
Lamadrid, Mexico	74	27 5N	101 49W
Lamaing, Burma	33	15 30N	97 55 E
Lamar, Colo., U.S.A.	71	38 5N	102 20W
Lamar, Mo., U.S.A.	71	37 30N	94 32W
Lamas, Peru	78	6 15 S	76 40W
Lambaréné, Gabon	54	0 41 S	10 13 E
Lambari, Brazil	77	22 0 S	45 15W
Lambay I., Ireland	11	53 30N	6 0W
Lambayeque, Peru	78	6 45 S	79 55W
Lambert, U.S.A.	70	47 44N	104 36W
Lambert, C., W. Austra.	44	20 35 S	117 13 E
Lamberts Bay, C. Prov.	57	32 5 S	18 17 E
Lambton, Canada	63	45 50N	71 6W
Lame Deer, U.S.A.	72	45 38N	106 34W
Lamego, Portugal	17	41 5N	7 52W
Lamentin, Martinique	75	14 38N	61 0W
Lamèque, Canada	63	47 45N	64 38W
Lameroo, S. Australia	43	35 22 S	140 33 E
Lamesa, U.S.A.	71	32 44N	101 52W
Lamia, Greece	21	38 55N	22 41 E
Lamitan, Philippines	35	6 40N	122 10 E
Lammermoor, Queens.	42	21 17 S	144 31 E
Lammermuir Hills, Scot.	10	55 50N	2 40W
Lamoille, U.S.A.	72	40 48N	115 30W
Lamont, Canada	64	53 40N	112 50W
Lampa, Peru	78	15 10 S	70 30W
Lampang, Thailand	34	18 16N	99 30 E
Lampasas, U.S.A.	71	31 3N	98 5W
Lampasos, Mexico	74	27 0N	100 30W
Lampedusa I., Medit.	51	35 36N	12 40 E
Lampman, Canada	65	49 25N	102 50W
Lampoc, U.S.A.	73	34 10N	120 30W
Lamprey, Canada	65	58 20N	94 0W
Lamu, Kenya	53	2 10 S	40 58 E
Lamy, U.S.A.	73	35 32N	105 57W
Lan Yu I., Taiwan	39	22 5N	121 30 E
Lanai City, Hawaiian Is.	59	20 50N	156 56W
Lanai, I., Hawaiian Is.	59	20 50N	156 55W
Lanark, Scotland	10	55 40N	3 48W
Lanark, co., Scotland	10	55 37N	3 50W
Lancaster, Canada	63	45 15N	66 7W
Lancaster, England	10	54 3N	2 48W
Lancaster, Calif., U.S.A.	73	34 44N	118 8W
Lancaster, Ky., U.S.A.	68	37 40N	84 40W
Lancaster, N.H., U.S.A.	68	44 27N	71 33W
Lancaster, Pa., U.S.A.	68	40 4N	76 19W
Lancaster, Wis., U.S.A.	70	42 48N	90 44W
Lancaster Sd., Canada	58	74 0N	84 0W
Lancer, Canada	65	50 48N	108 52W
Lanchi, China	39	29 15N	119 30 E
Lanchow, China	38	36 0N	103 50 E
Lanciano, Italy	20	42 15N	14 22 E
Lancut, Poland	16	50 10N	22 20 E
Landana, Angola	54	5 11 S	12 5 E
Lande, The, R., N. Territory	45	20 50 S	132 10 E
Landeck, Austria	14	47 9N	10 34 E
Landen, Belgium	13	50 45N	5 3 E
Lander, U.S.A.	72	42 5N	108 45W
Landerneau, France	12	48 28N	4 17W
Landfall I., India	33	13 40N	93 0 E
Landquart, Switzerland	15	46 58N	9 32 E
Land's End, England	10	50 4N	5 43W
Landsborough Cr., Queensland	42	22 0 S	144 15 E
Landshut, Germany	14	48 31N	12 10 E
Landskröna, Sweden	23	56 55N	12 57 E
Lane Creek, Queensland	42	18 5 S	143 29 E
Lanesborough, Ireland	11	53 40N	8 0W
Lanett, U.S.A.	69	33 0N	85 15W
Lanfeng, China	38	34 49N	114 52 E
Lang Jökull, Mts., Ice.	22	64 40N	20 30W
Langadhas, Greece	21	40 45N	28 4 E
Langadhia, Greece	21	37 40N	22 1 E
Langanes, Iceland	22	66 40N	14 20W
Langara I., Canada	64	54 20N	133 0W
Langchung, (Paoning) China	39	31 30N	106 0 E
Langdon, U.S.A.	70	48 47N	98 17W
Langeac, France	12	45 7N	3 29 E
Langeberge, C. Prov.	57	33 55 S	21 20 E
Langeberge, Mts., Cape Province	57	28 0 S	22 30 E
Langenburg, Canada	65	50 50N	101 40W
Langenthal, Switzerland	15	47 13N	7 47 E
Langesund, Norway	23	59 0N	9 45 E
Langham, Canada	65	52 25N	107 0W
Langholm, Scotland	10	55 9N	2 59W
Langholt, Iceland	22	63 36N	13 8W
Langjökull, mt., Iceland	22	64 40N	20 30W
Langkawi Is., Malaya	34	6 20N	99 45W
Langklip, C. Prov.	57	28 12 S	20 20 E
Langkrans, Natal	57	27 50 S	31 1 E
Langlade, Canada	62	48 25N	76 0W
Langlade, I., Saint Pierre & Miquelon	63	46 45N	56 25W
Langlo Downs, Queens.	43	25 28 S	145 42 E
Langlo R., Queensland	43	25 45 S	145 35 E
Langnau, Switzerland	15	46 56N	7 47 E
Lango, dist., Uganda	53	2 10N	33 0 E
Langon, France	12	44 33N	0 16W
Langöy I., Norway	22	68 45N	15 10 E
Langres, France	12	47 52N	5 20 E
Langres Plateau, France	12	47 45N	5 20 E
Langsa, Indonesia	34	4 30N	97 57 E
Langson, Viet Nam	39	21 50N	106 45 E
Langtai, China	39	26 9N	105 15 E
Langtry, U.S.A.	71	29 46N	101 31W
Languedoc, prov., Fr.	12	43 58N	3 22 E
Lanigan, Canada	65	51 50N	105 0W
Lankoviri, Nigeria	52	9 0N	11 23 E
Lannion, France	12	48 46N	3 29W
Lansdowne House, Can.	62	52 5N	88 0W
L'Anse, U.S.A.	62	46 46N	88 28W
Lansing, Mich., U.S.A.	68	42 47N	84 32W
Lantaiwa, Nigeria	52	17 7N	11 48 E
Lantsang, China	34	22 56N	100 11 E
Lanusei, Italy	20	39 53N	9 31 E
Lanwa, Nigeria	52	8 46N	4 43 E
Lanzarote I., Canary Is.	50	29 0N	13 40W
Lanzo, Italy	20	45 17N	7 29 E
Lao Cai, Viet Nam	34	22 15N	104 0 E
Laoag, Philippines	35	17 7N	120 34 E
Laoha Ho, China	38	43 0N	120 0 E
Laois, co., Ireland	11	53 0N	7 20W
Laohokow. *See* Kwanghua, China	39		
Laokay, N. Viet Nam	37	22 40N	104 0 E
Laon, France	12	49 33N	3 35 E
Laona. U.S.A.	68	45 32N	88 41W
Laos, st., Asia	34	17 45N	105 0 E
Lapa, Brazil	77	26 48 S	49 55W
Lapai, Nigeria	52	9 2N	6 37 E
Lapeer, U.S.A.	68	43 3N	83 20W
Lapeyrère, Canada	63	47 27N	62 0W
Lapin Lääni, Finland	22	67 10N	26 30 E
Lapine, U.S.A.	72	43 42N	121 31W
Lapland (Lappland), Europe	22	68 0N	26 0 E
Lappeenranta, Finland	23	61 5N	28 13 E
Laptev Sea, U.S.S.R.	27	76 0N	125 0 E
Lapush, U.S.A.	72	47 57N	124 42W
Lapy, Poland	16	53 0N	22 50 E
Laqiya Arba'in, Sudan	51	19 50N	28 18 E
Lar, Iran	31	27 40N	54 14 E
Larabanga, Ghana	52	9 16N	1 56W
Larache, Morocco	50	35 10N	6 5W
Laragh, Ireland	11	53 0N	6 20W
Laramie, U.S.A.	72	41 15N	105 29W
Laramie, mts., U.S.A.	70	42 0N	105 30W
Larantuka, Indonesia	35	8 5 S	122 55 E
Larat I., Indonesia	35	7 0 S	132 0 E
L'Aquila, Italy	20	42 22N	13 24 E
Lärbro, Sweden	23	57 47N	18 50 E
Larder Lake, Canada	62	48 5N	79 40W
Lare, Kenya	53	0 20N	37 56 E
Laredo, U.S.A.	71	27 34N	99 29W
Laredo Sd., Canada	64	52 30N	128 50W
Largeau. *See* Faya.	51		
Lariang, Indonesia	35	1 35 S	119 25 E
Larimore, U.S.A.	70	47 57N	97 33W
Larino, Italy	20	41 48N	14 54 E
Larisa, Greece	21	39 38N	22 28 E
Larkana, W. Pak.	32	27 32N	68 18 E
Larnaca, Cyprus	30	35 0N	33 35 E
Larne, Ireland	11	54 52N	5 50W
Larned, U.S.A.	71	38 13N	99 4W
Larrey Pt., Australia	44	20 1 S	119 6 E
Larteh, Ghana	52	5 50N	0 5W
Laruns, France	12	43 0N	0 28W
Laryak, U.S.S.R.	26	61 15N	80 0 E
Las Animas, U.S.A.	71	38 4N	103 17W
Las Aves, Is., W. Ind.	75	11 30N	67 30W
Las Blancos, Spain	17	37 39N	0 48W
Las Cascadas, Panama Canal Zone	74	9 5N	79 41W
Las Cejas, Argentina	77	26 50 S	64 50W
Las Cruces, U.S.A.	73	32 25N	106 50W
Las Delicias, Panama	74	9 27N	79 35W
Las Flores, Argentina	77	36 0 S	59 0W
Las Juries, Argentina	77	28 30 S	62 10W
Las Lajas, Argentina	77	38 30 S	70 25W
Las Lomitas, Argentina	77	24 35 S	60 50W
Las Marismas, Spain	17	37 5N	6 20W
Las Palmas, Canary Is.	50	28 10N	15 28W
Las Pipinas, Argentina	77	35 30 S	57 25W
Las Plumas, Argentine	77	43 40 S	67 15W
Las Rosas, Argentina	77	32 30 S	61 40W
Las Tablas, Panama	75	7 49N	80 14W
Las Toscas, Argentina	77	28 20 S	59 20W
Las Tres Marias Is., Mexico	74	21 20N	106 30W
Las Varillas, Argentina	77	32 0 S	62 50W
Las Vegas, N. Mex., U.S.A.	71	35 35N	105 10W
Las Vegas, Nev., U.S.A.	73	36 10N	115 5W
Lashburn, Canada	65	53 10N	109 40W
Lashio, Burma	33	23 0N	98 0 E
Lashma, U.S.S.R.	25	54 55N	41 10 E
Lask, Poland	16	51 35N	19 15 E
Lassen Pk., U.S.A.	72	40 30N	121 30W
Lassongo, Angola	56	12 0 S	22 45 E
Last Mountain L., Can.	65	51 0N	105 10W
Lastourville, Gabon	54	0 52 S	12 48 E
Lastovo I., Yugoslavia	20	42 47N	16 53 E
Latacunga, Ecuador	78	0 50 S	78 35W
Latakia (El Ladhiqiya), Syria	30	35 35N	35 46 E
Latchford, Canada	62	47 20N	79 50W
Latgale, dist., U.S.S.R.	23	56 20N	27 25 E
Latham, W. Australia	44	29 44 S	116 20 E
Latina, Italy	20	41 26N	12 53 E
Latium, reg., Italy	20	42 0N	12 30 E
Latrar, Iceland	22	66 24N	23 1W
Latrobe, Tasmania	43	41 14 S	146 30 E
Latur, India	32	18 25N	76 40 E
Latvia, S.S.R., U.S.S.R.	23	56 45N	24 30 E
Lau, Nigeria	52	9 9N	11 12 E
Lauca R., Bolivia	78	18 30 S	68 50W
Lauenbrück, Germany	14	53 12N	9 32 E
Laufen, Germany	15	47 55N	12 56 E
Laugheed, Canada	64	52 40N	111 35W
Laugnglon Bok (South Moscos) Is., Burma	33	13 50N	97 40 E
Launceston, England	10	50 38N	4 21W
Launceston, Tasmania	43	41 24 S	147 8 E
Laura, Queensland	42	15 32 S	144 32 E
Laurel, Miss., U.S.A.	71	31 50N	89 0W
Laurel, Mont., U.S.A.	72	45 43N	108 45W
Laurencetown, Ireland	11	53 14N	8 10W
Laurens, U.S.A.	69	34 30N	82 8W
Laurentian Plateau, Can.	63	50 0N	70 0W
Laurentides Provincial Park, Canada	63	47 40N	71 30W
Lauria, Italy	20	40 3N	15 50 E
Laurie, L., Canada	65	56 25N	101 50W
Laurinburg, U.S.A.	69	34 50N	79 25W
Laurium, U.S.A.	70	47 13N	88 26W
Lauro Müller, Brazil	77	28 25 S	49 30W
Lausanne, Switzerland	15	46 32N	6 38 E
Laut I., Indonesia	35	3 40 S	116 10 E
Laut Ketjil Is., Indon.	35	4 30 S	115 55 E
Lauterbrunnen, Switz.	15	46 36N	7 54 E
Lauwer Zee, Neth.	13	53 22N	6 10 E
Lauzon, Canada	63	46 48N	71 4W
Lava Hot Springs, U.S.A.	72	42 38N	112 1W
Laval, France	12	48 4N	0 48W
Lavalle, Argentina	77	32 45 S	68 30W
Lavalleja, Uruguay	77	34 10 S	55 30W
Lavar Mēydān, Iran	31	30 20N	54 30 E
Lavardac, France	12	44 12N	0 20 E
Laverne, U.S.A.	71	36 42N	99 59W
Laverton, W. Australia	45	28 44 S	122 29 E
Lavi, Israel	29	32 47N	35 25 E
Lavras, Minas Gerais, Brazil	77	21 20 S	45 0W
Lavras, Rio Grande do Sul, Brazil	79	30 50 S	54 0W
Lávrion, Greece	21	37 40N	24 4 E
Lawgi, Queensland	42	24 50 S	151 0 E
Lawledge, Canada	65	57 0N	94 10W
Lawlers, W. Australia	44	28 5 S	120 29 E
Lawn Hill, Queensland	42	11 36 S	138 33 E
Lawng Pit (Nmai) R., Burma	33	26 0N	98 10 E
Lawra, Ghana	52	10 39N	2 51W
Lawrence, New Zealand	47	45 55 S	169 41 E
Lawrence, Kans., U.S.A.	70	39 0N	95 15W
Lawrence, Mass., U.S.A.	69	42 40N	71 9W
Lawrenceburg, Indiana, U.S.A.	68	39 5N	84 50W
Lawrenceburg, Tenn., U.S.A.	69	35 12N	87 19W
Lawton, U.S.A.	71	34 33N	98 25W
Lawu Mt., Indonesia	34	7 40 S	111 13 E
Laytonville, U.S.A.	72	39 42N	123 30W
Le Blanc, France	12	46 37N	1 3 E
Le Bouthillier, Canada	63	47 47N	64 55W
Le Cateau, France	12	50 6N	3 30 E
Le Château, France	12	45 52N	1 12W
Le Creusot, France	12	46 50N	4 24 E
Le Dorat, France	12	46 14N	1 5 E
Le Grand, C., Australia	44	33 59 S	122 6 E
Le Havre, France	12	49 30N	0 5 E
Le Kef, Tunisia	51	36 12N	8 47 E
Le Locle, Switzerland	15	47 3N	6 44 E
Le Madonie, mts., Sicily	20	37 40N	13 30 E
Le Maire Str., Argentina	77	54 45 S	65 0W
Le Mans, France	12	48 0N	0 12 E
Le Marinel, Zaire	56	10 25 S	25 25 E
Le Mars, U.S.A.	70	43 0N	96 0W
Le Moule, Guadeloupe	75	16 20N	61 22W
Le Palais, France	12	47 21N	3 10W
Le Puy, France	12	45 3N	3 52 E
Le Roy, U.S.A.	71	38 6N	95 45W
Le Steere Ra., Western Australia	44	25 32 S	122 15 E
Le Sueur, U.S.A.	70	44 28N	93 55W
Le Touquet, France	12	50 30N	1 36 E
Le Tréport, France	12	50 3N	1 20 E
Le Vigan, France	12	43 59N	3 24 E
Lead, U.S.A.	70	44 20N	103 40W
Leader, Canada	65	50 50N	109 30W
Leadhills, Scotland	10	55 25N	3 47W
Leadville, U.S.A.	73	39 17N	106 23W
Leaf, R., U.S.A.	71	31 45N	89 20W
Leakey, U.S.A.	71	29 43N	99 43W
Leaksville, U.S.A.	69	36 30N	79 49W
Lealui, Zambia	56	15 10 S	23 2 E
Leamington, Canada	62	42 10N	82 30W
Leamington, England	10	52 18N	1 32W
Leamington, N.Z.	46	37 55 S	175 29 E
Leamington, U.S.A.	73	39 32N	112 16W

	MAP		
Leane L., Ireland	11	52 2N	9 32W
Leask, Canada	65	53 5N	106 45W
Leavenworth, Mo., U.S.A.	70	39 25N	95 0W
Leavenworth, Wash., U.S.A.	72	47 40N	120 36W
Lebanon, st., Asia	30	34 0N	36 0E
Lebanon, Ind., U.S.A.	68	40 3N	86 55W
Lebanon, Kans., U.S.A.	70	39 52N	98 32W
Lebanon, Ky., U.S.A.	68	37 35N	85 15W
Lebanon, Mo., U.S.A.	71	37 40N	92 40W
Lebanon, N.H., U.S.A.	68	43 38N	72 15W
Lebanon, Ore., U.S.A.	72	44 32N	122 57W
Lebanon, Pa., U.S.A.	68	40 20N	76 28W
Lebanon, Tenn., U.S.A.	67	36 15N	86 20W
Lebanon Mts., Lebanon	30	34 0N	36 0E
Lebec, U.S.A.	73	34 52N	118 58W
Lebedin, U.S.S.R.	25	50 35N	34 30E
Lebedyan, U.S.S.R.	25	53 0N	39 10E
Lebesby, Norway	22	70 28N	27 3E
Lebombo Mts., Mozam.	56	24 0S	32 0E
Lebrija, Spain	17	36 53N	6 5W
Lebu, Zaire	53	2 20N	30 17E
Lebu, Chile	77	37 30S	73 47W
Lecce, Italy	21	40 20N	18 10E
Lecco, Italy	20	45 50N	9 27E
Lech, R., Austria	14	47 19N	10 27E
Lectoure, France	12	43 56N	0 38E
Leczyca, Poland	16	52 5N	19 15E
Ledesma, Argentina	77	23 50S	64 50W
Ledesma, Spain	17	41 6N	5 59W
Leduc, Canada	64	53 20N	113 30W
Lee, U.S.A.	72	40 36N	115 33W
Lee R., Ireland	11	51 51N	9 2W
Leech L., U.S.A.	70	47 15N	94 23W
Leedey, U.S.A.	71	35 49N	99 26W
Leeds, England	10	53 48N	1 34W
Leenaun, Ireland	11	53 36N	9 41W
Leer, Germany	14	53 15N	7 26E
Leesburg, U.S.A.	69	39 8N	77 35W
Leeston, New Zealand	47	43 45S	172 19E
Leesville, U.S.A.	71	31 8N	93 16W
Leeton, N.S.W.	43	34 23S	146 23E
Leeu-Gamka, Cape Province	57	32 43S	21 59E
Leeuwarden, Neth.	13	53 15N	5 48E
Leeuwin, C., Australia	44	34 20S	115 9E
Leeward Is., W. Indies	75	16 30N	63 30W
Lefors, U.S.A.	71	35 29N	100 45W
Lefroy L., W. Australia	44	31 21S	121 40E
Lefroys, W. Australia	44	23 37S	115 44E
Legal, Canada	64	53 55N	113 45W
Legaspi, Philippines	35	13 10N	123 46E
Legend, Canada	64	49 30N	111 35W
Legendre I., W. Austral.	44	20 20S	116 50E
Leghorn (Livorno), Italy	20	43 32N	10 18E
Legion, Rhodesia	56	21 25S	28 30E
Legnago, Italy	20	45 10N	11 19E
Legnano, Italy	20	45 35N	8 55E
Legnica, Poland	16	51 12N	16 10E
Leguízamo, Colombia	78	0 8S	74 50W
Leh, Kashmir	32	34 15N	77 35E
Lehi, U.S.A.	72	40 20N	112 0W
Lehua, Hawaiian Is.	59	22 1N	160 6W
Lehututu, Botswana	57	24 0S	22 0E
Leicester, England	10	52 39N	1 9W
Leichhardt Ra., Queens.	42	20 46S	147 40E
Leichhardt, R., Queens.	42	18 40S	139 49E
Leiden, Holland	13	52 9N	4 30E
Leie R., Belgium	13	50 55N	3 25E
Leigh Creek, S. Austral.	43	30 28S	138 24E
Leighlinbridge, Ireland	11	52 45N	6 59W
Leine, R., Germany	14	52 30N	9 33E
Leinster, Prov., Ireland	11	53 0N	7 10W
Leinster Mt., Ireland	11	52 38N	6 47W
Leipzig, Germany	14	51 20N	12 23E
Leiria, Portugal	17	39 46N	8 53W
Leirvik, Norway	23	59 47N	5 31E
Leishan, China	39	26 7N	108 24E
Leith, Scotland	10	55 59N	3 11W
Leitrim, co., Ireland	11	54 8N	8 0W
Leixlip, Ireland	11	53 22N	6 30W
Leiyang, China	39	26 20N	112 46E
Lek R., Netherlands	13	51 56N	4 50E
Leksula, Indonesia	35	3 50S	127 25E
Leland, U.S.A.	71	33 26N	90 54W
Leleque, Argentina	77	42 15S	71 0W
Lelystad, Netherlands	13	52 30N	5 25E
Lema, Nigeria	52	12 58N	4 13E
Léman, Lac, Switzerland	15	46 26N	6 30E
Lembeni, Tanzania	53	3 45S	37 37E
Lemera, Zaire	53	3 0S	28 59E
Lemhi, Ra., U.S.A.	72	44 30N	113 30W
Lemmer, Netherlands	13	52 50N	5 42E
Lemmon, U.S.A.	70	45 58N	102 8W
Lemmon, mt., U.S.A.	73	32 30N	110 50W
Lemoore, U.S.A.	73	36 19N	119 47W
Lemu, Nigeria	52	9 27N	6 0E
Lemvig, Denmark	23	56 33N	8 20E
Lena, R., Siberia	27	64 30N	127 0E
Lenda, R., Congo	53	1 0N	28 15E
Leney, Canada	65	52 3N	107 35W
Lenggong, Malaya	34	5 5N	100 57E
Leninabad, U.S.S.R.	26	40 10N	69 40E
Leninakan, U.S.S.R.	24	41 0N	42 50E
Leningrad, U.S.S.R.	25	59 55N	30 20E
Leningradskaya, U.S.S.R.	25	46 25N	39 25E

	MAP		
Leninogorsk U.S.S.R.	26	50 20N	83 30E
Leninsk, U.S.S.R.	25	56 38N	46 10E
Leninsk-Kuznetski, U.S.S.R.	26	55 10N	86 0E
Lenk, Switzerland	15	46 27N	7 28E
Lenkoran, U.S.S.R.	30	39 45N	48 50E
Lennard, R., W. Australia	44	17 20S	124 40E
Lennonville, W. Austral.	44	27 50S	117 49E
Lenoir, U.S.A.	69	35 55N	81 36W
Lenoir City, U.S.A.	69	35 40N	84 20W
Lenora, U.S.A.	70	39 38N	100 0W
Lenore, L., Canada	65	52 30N	105 0W
Lens, France	12	50 26N	2 50E
Lentini, Italy	20	37 18N	15 0E
Lenzburg, Switzerland	15	47 23N	8 10E
Léo, Volta	52	11 3N	2 2W
Leoben, Austria	14	47 22N	15 5E
Leola, U.S.A.	70	45 48N	98 58W
Leominster, England	10	52 15N	2 43W
Leominster, U.S.A.	69	42 30N	71 44W
Leon, Mexico	74	21 7N	101 30W
León, Nicaragua	75	12 20N	86 51W
Leon, Spain	17	42 38N	5 34W
Leon, U.S.A.	70	40 40N	93 45W
Leon, prov., Spain	17	41 40N	5 55W
Leonardtown, U.S.A.	68	38 19N	76 39W
Leongatha, Victoria	43	38 30S	145 58E
Leõnidion, Greece	21	37 9N	22 52E
Leonora, W. Australia	44	28 47S	121 15E
Leopold II L., Zaire	54	2 0S	18 0E
Leopoldsburg, Belgium	13	51 7N	5 13E
Leoti, U.S.A.	70	38 31N	101 17W
Leoville, Canada	65	53 39N	107 33W
Lephepe, Botswana	56	23 22S	25 50E
Lepikha, U.S.S.R.	27	64 45N	125 55E
Lepontine Alps, Italy	15	46 20N	8 20E
Lequeitio, Spain	17	43 20N	2 32W
Lercara, Italy	20	37 45N	13 35E
Lerdal, Sweden	23	60 52N	12 2E
Léré, Chad	52	9 41N	14 17E
Lere, Nigeria	52	10 22N	8 31E
Lere, Nigeria	52	9 42N	9 20E
Leribe, Lesotho	57	28 51S	28 3E
Lerida, Spain	17	41 37N	0 39E
Lerma, Mexico	74	19 40N	90 40W
Lerma, Spain	17	42 0N	3 47W
Léros I., Greece	21	37 15N	26 48E
Lerwick, Shetland Is., Scotland	10	60 10N	1 10W
Les Andelys, France	12	49 15N	1 25E
Les Cayes, Haiti	75	18 15N	73 46W
Les Etroits, Canada	63	47 24N	68 54W
Les Landes, dist., France	12	45 0N	1 20W
Les Sables d'Olonne, Fr.	12	46 30N	1 45W
Les Tres Marias, Is., Mexico	74	12 20N	106 30W
Lesina, L., di, Italy	20	41 45N	15 25E
Lesko, Poland	16	49 30N	22 23E
Leskovac, Yugoslavia	21	43 0N	21 58E
Leslie, Transvaal	57	26 16S	28 55E
Leslie, U.S.A.	71	34 49N	92 39W
Lesnoi, U.S.S.R.	24	66 50N	34 20E
Lesotho, South Africa	57	29 40S	28 0E
Lesozavodsk, U.S.S.R.	27	45 30N	133 20E
Lesparre, France	12	45 18N	0 57W
Lesse R., Belgium	13	50 10N	5 0E
Lesser Antilles, W. Ind.	75	12 30N	61 0W
Lesser Slave L., Canada	64	55 30N	115 10W
Lesser Sunda Is., Indon.	35	7 30S	120 0E
Lessines, Belgium	13	50 42N	3 50E
Lestock, Canada	65	51 25N	104 0W
Lesueur, Mt., Western Australia	44	30 12S	115 8E
Lésvos, I., Greece	21	26 0N	39 15E
Leszno, Poland	16	51 50N	16 30E
Letaba, Transvaal	57	23 55S	31 35E
Letaba R., Transvaal	57	23 42S	31 25E
Lethbridge, Canada	64	49 45N	112 45W
Letiahau, R., Bot.	57	21 40S	23 30E
Leticia, Colombia	78	4 0S	70 0W
Letjiesbos, C. Prov.	57	32 31S	22 16E
Letpadan, Burma	33	17 45N	96 0E
Lette, New South Wales	43	34 3S	143 4E
Letterkenny, Ireland	11	54 57N	7 42W
Leuk, Switzerland	15	46 19N	7 37E
Leukerbad, Switzerland	15	46 23N	7 38E
Leuven (Louvain), Belg.	13	50 52N	4 42E
Leuze, Belgium	13	50 36N	3 37E
Levadnia, Greece	21	38 27N	22 54E
Levanger, Norway	23	63 43N	11 12E
Levanto, Italy	20	44 10N	9 37E
Levelland, U.S.A.	71	33 35N	102 17W
Levin, New Zealand	46	40 37S	175 18E
Levis, Canada	63	46 48N	71 9W
Levis, L., Canada	64	62 20N	118 0W
Lévka Ori, mt., Crete	20	35 15N	24 0E
Levkàs, Greece	21	38 48N	20 43E
Levkâs I. (Sta Maura), Greece	21	38 40N	20 43E
Levoca, Czechoslovakia	16	48 59N	20 35E
Levski, Bulgaria	21	43 21N	25 10E
Levskigrad (Karlove), Bulgaria	21	42 38N	24 49E
Lewellen, U.S.A.	70	41 24N	102 6W
Lewes, England	10	50 53N	0 2W
Lewes, U.S.A.	68	38 45N	75 8W

	MAP		
Lewis Range, mts., U.S.A.	72	48 20N	114 0W
Lewis, Butt of, Scotland	10	58 30N	6 12W
Lewisburg, U.S.A.	69	40 57N	76 57W
Lewisporte, Canada	63	49 15N	55 3W
Lewiston, Idaho, U.S.A.	72	46 25N	117 0W
Lewiston, Me., U.S.A.	63	44 5N	70 10W
Lewiston, Utah, U.S.A.	72	42 0N	111 50W
Lewistown, Mont., U.S.A.	72	47 0N	109 25W
Lewistown, Pa., U.S.A.	69	40 37N	77 33W
Lexington, Ill., U.S.A.	68	40 37N	88 47W
Lexington, Ky., U.S.A.	68	38 6N	84 30W
Lexington, Ore., U.S.A.	72	45 29N	119 12W
Lexington, Miss., U.S.A.	71	33 6N	90 2W
Lexington, Mo., U.S.A.	70	39 8N	93 52W
Lexington, Neb., U.S.A.	70	40 51N	99 44W
Lexington, Va., U.S.A.	79	37 50N	79 29W
Leysin, Switzerland	15	46 21N	7 1E
Leyte I., Philippines	35	10 45N	125 5E
Lezajsk, Poland	16	50 18N	22 30E
Lezhë, Albania	21	41 46N	19 34E
Lezignan, France	12	43 13N	2 43E
Lhakseumawe, Indon.	34	5 20N	97 10E
Lhasa, China	37	29 40N	91 10E
Lhatse Dzong, China	37	29 10N	87 45E
Li K., China	39	22 30N	107 25E
Liandambia, Zambia	56	13 12S	23 30E
Lianga, Philippines	35	8 50N	126 0E
Liangsiang, China	38	39 45N	116 10E
Liangtang, China	38	33 55N	106 20E
Liao Ho R., China	38	42 20N	123 20E
Liaocheng, China	38	36 30N	115 58E
Liaochung, China	38	41 35N	122 45E
Liaotung, Mts., China	38	40 0N	122 33E
Liaoyang, China	38	41 15N	123 10E
Liaoyuan, China	38	42 51N	125 12E
Liard R., Canada	64	61 20N	122 30W
Libby, U.S.A.	72	48 25N	115 31W
Libenge, Congo	54	3 40N	18 55E
Liberal, Kan., U.S.A.	71	37 4N	101 0W
Liberal, Mo., U.S.A.	71	37 32N	94 32W
Liberdade, Brazil	78	7 15S	71 50W
Liberec, Czechoslovakia	16	50 47N	15 7E
Liberia, Costa Rica	75	10 40N	85 30W
Liberia, st., W. Africa	50	6 30N	9 30W
Libertad, Mexico	75	30 0N	112 50W
Liberty, Mo., U.S.A.	70	39 14N	94 26W
Liberty, N.Y., U.S.A.	69	41 48N	74 45W
Liberty, Tex., U.S.A.	71	30 2N	95 0W
Libode, Cape Province	57	31 31S	29 2E
Libourne, France	12	44 55N	0 15W
Libramont, Belgium	13	49 55N	5 23E
Libreville, Gabon	54	0 25N	9 26E
Libya, St., N. Africa	51	28 30N	17 30E
Libyan Des., N. Africa	51	27 35N	25 0E
Licanten, Chile	77	34 55S	72 0W
Licata, Italy	20	37 6N	13 35E
Lichtenburg, Transvaal	57	26 8S	26 8E
Lida, U.S.A.	73	37 30N	117 32W
Liddel Water, Scotland	10	55 10N	2 50W
Lidköping, Sweden	23	58 31N	13 14E
Lidzbark, Poland	16	54 7N	20 34E
Liechtenstein, principality, Europe	14	47 8N	9 35E
Liége, Belgium	13	50 38N	5 35E
Liége, prov., Belgium	13	50 32N	5 35E
Lieksa, Finland	23	63 20N	30 0E
Lienhua, China	39	27 12N	113 46E
Lienkiang, China	39	26 9N	119 30E
Lienshankwan, China	38	41 0N	123 50E
Lienyunkang, China	38	34 45N	119 25E
Lienz, Austria	14	46 40N	12 46E
Liepaja, U.S.S.R.	24	56 30N	21 0E
Lier, Belgium	13	51 7N	4 34E
Liestal, Switzerland	15	47 29N	7 42E
Lievre, R. du, Canada	62	45 40N	75 40W
Liffey R., Ireland	11	53 21N	6 20W
Lifford, Ireland	11	54 50N	7 30W
Liguria, reg., Italy	20	44 20N	8 30E
Ligurian Sea, Italy	20	43 20N	9 0E
Lihsien, Hunan, China	39	29 34N	111 43E
Lihsien, Kansu, China	38	34 10N	105 0E
Lihue, Hawaiian Is.	59	21 59N	159 23W
Likasi, Zaire	56	10 55S	26 48E
Likati, Zaire	54	3 20N	24 0E
Likati, R., Congo	54	3 2N	23 56E
Likhoslavl, U.S.S.R.	25	57 12N	35 30E
Likhovski, U.S.S.R.	25	48 10N	40 10E
Likiang, China	37	26 50N	100 15E
Likoma I., Malawi	56	12 3S	34 45E
Likumburu, Tanzania	53	9 40N	35 15E
Likunpu, China	38	36 33N	106 27E
Likuyu, Tanzania	53	10 30S	36 30E
Likwayi, China	38	34 33N	116 35E
Lilay, Philippines	35	8 0N	122 40E
Lilian Pt., W. Australia	45	27 40S	126 2E
Liling, China	39	27 42N	113 29E
Lille, France	12	50 38N	3 3E
Lillehammer, Norway	23	61 8N	10 30E
Lillesand, Norway	17	58 12N	8 23E
Lilleström, Norway	23	59 58N	11 5E
Lilliput, Transvaal	56	23 30S	29 55E
Lillooet, Canada	64	50 40N	122 0W
Lillooet R., Canada	64	50 40N	123 20W
Lilongwe, Malawi	56	14 0S	33 48E
Lilydale, Queensland	42	19 2S	138 40E
Lilyvale, Queensland	42	23 10S	148 22E

	MAP		
Lima, Peru	78	12 0S	77 0W
Lima, Mont., U.S.A.	72	44 42N	112 32W
Lima, Ohio, U.S.A.	68	40 42N	84 5W
Lima R., Portugal	17	41 50N	8 18W
Limanowa, Poland	16	49 42N	20 22E
Limassol, Cyprus	30	34 42N	33 1E
Limavady, N. Ireland	11	55 3N	6 58W
Limay R., Argentina	77	39 40S	69 45W
Limay Mahuida, Arg.	77	37 10S	66 45W
Limbdi, India	32	22 36N	71 45E
Limbe, Malawi	56	15 55S	35 2E
Limbourg, Belgium	13	50 37N	5 57E
Limbourg, prov., Belg.	13	51 2N	5 25E
Limburg, Germany	14	50 22N	8 4E
Limburg, prov., Neth.	13	51 20N	5 55E
Limeira, São Paulo, Brazil	77	22 35S	47 28W
Limerick, Ireland	11	52 40N	8 38W
Limerick, co., Ireland	11	52 30N	8 50W
Limfjorden, Denmark	23	56 37N	8 22E
Limko, China	39	19 57N	109 32E
Limmat R., Switzerland	15	47 25N	8 25E
Limni, Greece	21	38 46N	23 20E
Limnos, I., Greece	21	39 50N	25 15E
Limoera, Brazil	79	7 40S	35 35W
Limoeiro do Norte, Brazil	79	5 5S	38 0W
Limoges, France	12	45 50N	1 15E
Limón, Costa Rica	75	10 0N	83 2W
Limon, Panama	74	9 20N	79 45W
Limon, U.S.A.	70	39 19N	103 42W
Limon, B., Pan. Canal Zone	74	9 22N	79 56W
Limousin, prov., France	12	45 30N	1 40E
Limoux, France	12	43 4N	2 12E
Limpopo R., Mozam.	57	24 15S	32 45E
Limuru, Kenya	53	1 6S	36 38E
Lin, China	39	28 53N	120 45E
Lina R., Sweden	22	67 0N	21 30E
Linah Ash Shu'bah, Saudi Arabia	30	29 0N	43 42E
Linares, Chile	77	35 50S	71 40W
Linares, Mexico	74	24 50N	99 40W
Linares, Spain	17	38 10N	3 40W
Lincheng, China	38	37 49N	114 30E
Lincheng, China	38	35 0N	117 20E
Lincoln, Argentina	77	34 55N	61 30W
Lincoln, England	10	53 14N	0 32W
Lincoln, New Zealand	47	43 38S	172 30E
Lincoln, Ill., U.S.A.	70	40 10N	89 20W
Lincoln, Kan., U.S.A.	70	39 5N	98 6W
Lincoln, Maine, U.S.A.	63	45 27N	68 29W
Lincoln, Neb., U.S.A.	70	40 50N	96 42W
Lincolnton, U.S.A.	69	35 30N	81 15W
Lind, U.S.A.	72	47 0N	118 32W
Linden, W. Australia	45	29 15S	122 22E
Linden, U.S.A.	71	33 0N	94 26W
Lindesay Mt., N.S.W.	43	28 20S	153 0E
Lindesnes, Norway	23	57 58N	7 3E
Lindi, Tanzania	53	10 0S	39 35E
Lindley, O.F.S.	57	27 52S	27 56E
Lindsay, Canada	62	44 22N	78 45W
Lindsay, Calif., U.S.A.	73	36 15N	119 4W
Lindsay, Okla., U.S.A.	71	34 47N	97 37W
Lindsborg, U.S.A.	70	38 36N	97 41W
Linea, La. *See* La Linea	17		
Linfen, China	38	36 0N	111 30E
Lingayen, Philippines	35	16 8N	120 20E
Lingayen B., Philippines	35	16 20N	120 10E
Lingchwan, China	39	26 30N	110 20E
Lingen, Germany	14	52 32N	7 21E
Lingga Arch, Indonesia	34	0 10S	104 30E
Lingga I., Indonesia	34	0 10N	104 40E
Linghsien, China	38	37 20N	116 30E
Lingle, U.S.A.	70	42 20N	104 24W
Lingling, China	39	26 14N	111 30E
Linglo, China	39	24 30N	106 27E
Lingshan, China	39	22 25N	109 10E
Lingshih, China	38	37 0N	111 50E
Lingshui, China	39	18 32N	109 55E
Lingtai, China	38	34 55N	107 30E
Linguére, Senegal	50	15 25N	15 5W
Linhai, China	39	28 50N	121 8E
Linho, Inner Mongolia	38	40 46N	107 30E
Linhsien, Shansi, China	38	38 10N	111 0E
Linhwaikwan, China	38	32 52N	117 38E
Lini, China	38	35 2N	118 10E
Linkiang, China	37	47 40N	132 50E
Linköping, Sweden	23	58 28N	15 36E
Linn Mt., U.S.A.	73	40 0N	123 0W
Linnam, China	39	24 51N	111 51E
Linnhe, L., Scotland	10	56 37N	5 25W
Linping, China	39	24 25N	114 32E
Lins, Brazil	79	21 45S	49 55W
Linshui, China	39	29 15N	111 0E
Linsia, China	37	35 31N	108 8E
Linsi, China	38	43 30N	118 5E
Lintao, China	38	36 20N	103 45E
Linthal, Switzerland	15	46 54N	9 0E
Lintlaw, Canada	65	52 5N	103 15W
Linton, Ind., U.S.A.	68	39 0N	87 10W
Linton, N.Dak., U.S.A.	70	46 48N	100 14W
Lintsing, China	38	35 55N	115 40E
Lintung, Inner Mongolia	38	43 50N	119 20E
Linwuh, China	39	25 25N	112 10E
Linyanti (Chobe), R., Bech.	56	18 0S	24 20E

	MAP		
Linyi, China	38	37 10N	116 50 E
Linz, Austria	14	48 18N	14 18 E
Liohwan, China	39	30 20N	108 19 E
Lion, Golfe du, France	12	43 0N	4 0W
Lion's Den, Rhodesia	56	17 15S	30 5 E
Lion's Head, Canada	62	44 58N	81 15W
Lioyang, China	38	33 30N	106 0 E
Lipali, Mozambique	56	15 50S	35 53 E
Lipari I., Italy	20	38 30N	14 55 E
Lipari Is., Italy	20	38 40N	15 0 E
Lipetsk, U.S.S.R.	25	52 45N	39 35 E
Liping, China	39	26 12N	109 0 E
Lipno, Poland	16	52 49N	19 15 E
Lipo, China	39	25 33N	107 45 E
Lipoche, Mozambique	56	11 52S	35 0 E
Lipova, Rumania	21	46 8N	21 42 E
Lippe R., Germany	14	51 30N	7 10 E
Lippstadt, Germany	14	51 40N	8 19 E
Lipscombe, U.S.A.	71	36 12N	100 15W
Lipsoi I., Greece	21	37 19N	26 50 E
Lira, Uganda	53	2 15N	32 55 E
Lircay, Peru	78	13 0S	74 45W
Liria, Spain	17	39 37N	0 35W
Lisala, Congo	54	2 12N	21 38 E
Lisbon, Portugal	17	38 42N	9 10W
Lisbon, U.S.A.	70	46 31N	97 45W
Lisbon Falls, U.S.A.	69	44 0N	70 2W
Lisburn, N. Ireland	11	54 30N	6 2W
Lisburne, C., Alaska	59	68 50N	166 0W
Liscannor B., Ireland	11	52 56N	9 22W
Liscarroll, Ireland	11	52 15N	8 44W
Liscomb, Canada	63	45 2N	62 0W
Lisdoonvarna, Ireland	11	53 2N	9 18W
Lishin, China	38	37 57N	110 59 E
Lishui, China	39	28 20N	119 48 E
Lisieux, France	12	49 10N	0 12 E
Liski, U.S.S.R.	25	51 3N	39 20 E
L'Islet, Canada	63	47 4N	70 23W
Lismore, Australia	43	28 44S	153 21 E
Lismore, Ireland	11	52 8N	7 58W
Lisnaskea, N. Ireland	11	54 15N	7 27W
Lissam, Nigeria	52	7 9N	10 3 E
Lista, R., Norway	23	58 0N	6 25 E
Listowel, Canada	62	44 44N	80 58W
Listowel, Ireland	11	52 27N	9 30W
Listowel Downs, Queens.	43	25 10S	145 12 E
Litang, China	39	23 10N	109 5 E
Litani R., French Guiana	79	3 0N	54 15W
Litani R., Lebanon	30	33 30N	35 40 E
Litchfield, Ill., U.S.A.	70	39 8N	89 40W
Litchfield, Minn., U.S.A.	70	45 6N	94 32W
Lithgow, N.S.W.	43	33 25S	150 8 E
Lithuania S.S.R., U.S.S.R.	23	55 30N	24 0 E
Litoměrice, C. Slov.	16	50 33N	14 10 E
Litoo, Tanzania	53	9 52S	38 13 E
Little, R., U.S.A.	71	31 50N	92 30W
Little Abaco I., W. Ind.	75	26 50N	77 30W
Little America, Antarctica	80	79 10S	163 0W
Little Barrier I., N.Z.	46	36 12S	175 8 E
Little Belt, Mts., U.S.A.	72	46 45N	111 0W
Little Blue, R., U.S.A.	70	40 15N	97 45W
Little Bushman Land, C. Prov.	57	29 10S	18 10 E
Little Cadotte R., Can.	64	56 30N	116 30W
Little Carpathians Mts., C. Slov.	16	48 30N	17 20 E
Little Coco I., India	33	13 50N	93 0 E
Little Colorado R., U.S.A.	73	36 0N	111 30W
Little Current, Canada	62	45 55N	82 0W
Little Current R., Can.	62	50 40N	86 0W
Little Falls, Minn., U.S.A.	70	45 58N	95 19W
Little Falls, N.Y., U.S.A.	68	43 3N	74 50W
Little Fork, R., U.S.A.	70	48 0N	93 15W
Little Grand Rapids, Canada	65	52 0N	95 29W
Little Humboldt, R., U.S.A.	72	41 15N	117 27W
Little Inagua I., Bahamas	75	21 40N	73 50W
Little Karoo, C. Prov.	57	33 45S	21 30 E
Little Khingan Mts., China	37	50 0N	125 0 E
Little Lake, U.S.A.	73	35 58N	117 58W
Little Longlac, Canada	62	49 42N	86 58W
Little Manicouagan I., Canada	63	52 0N	68 0W
Little Marais, U.S.A.	70	47 27N	91 5W
Little Mecatina, I. & R., Canada	63	50 30N	59 25W
Little Missouri R., U.S.A.	70	46 40N	103 50W
Little Namaqualand, Cape Province	57	29 0S	17 9 E
Little Rancheria R., Can.	64	59 50N	130 0W
Little Red, R., U.S.A.	71	35 35N	92 0W
Little River, N.Z.	47	43 45S	172 49 E
Little Rock, U.S.A.	71	34 41N	92 10W
Little Ruaha R., Tan.	53	7 30S	35 30 E
Little Sable Pt., U.S.A.	68	43 40N	86 32W
Little St. Bernard Pass, France–Italy	20	45 40N	6 40 E

	MAP		
Little Scarcies R., Sierra Leone	52	9 30N	12 25W
Little Sioux, R., U.S.A.	70	42 15N	96 0W
Little Smoky R., Can.	64	55 30N	117 10W
Little Snake, R., U.S.A.	72	40 45N	108 15W
Little Wabash R., U.S.A.	68	38 40N	88 20W
Little Whale, R., Can.	62	55 50N	75 0W
Littlefield, U.S.A.	71	33 50N	102 15W
Littlefork, U.S.A.	70	48 55N	93 33W
Littlehampton, England	10	50 48N	0 32W
Littleton, Ireland	11	52 38N	7 44W
Littleton, U.S.A.	69	44 19N	71 47W
Litunde, Mozambique	56	13 19S	35 48 E
Liu K., China	39	25 35N	109 0 E
Liuan, China	39	31 50N	116 35 E
Liucheng, China	39	24 25N	109 0 E
Liuchow, China	39	24 10N	109 10 E
Liuchow Chiang, China	39	20 40N	110 40 E
Liuli, Tanzania	53	11 5S	34 40 E
Liuwa Plain, Zambia	56	14 20S	22 30 E
Liuyang, China	39	28 13N	113 30 E
Liv Glacier, Antarctica	80	85 0S	168 0W
Live Oak, U.S.A.	69	30 17N	83 0W
Livermore Falls, U.S.A	69	44 29N	70 8W
Liverpool, N.S., Canada	63	44 5N	64 41W
Liverpool, England	10	53 25N	3 0W
Liverpool, N.S.W.	43	33 55S	150 52 E
Liverpool Plains, N.S.W.	43	31 15S	150 0 E
Liverpool Ra., N.S.W.	43	31 42S	150 10 E
Livingston, U.S.A.	72	45 40N	110 40W
Livingston, Guatemala	74	15 50N	88 50W
Livingstone, Zambia	56	17 50N	25 50 E
Livingstone, U.S.A.	71	30 39N	94 57W
Livingstone Memorial, Zambia	56	12 20S	30 18 E
Livingstone Mts., N.Z.	47	45 15S	168 9 E
Livingstone Mts., Tang.	53	10 0S	34 30 E
Livingstonia, Malawi	56	10 38S	34 5 E
Livny, U.S.S.R.	25	52 30N	37 30 E
Livorno (Leghorn), Italy	20	43 32N	10 18 E
Livramento, Brazil	77	30 55S	55 30W
Liwale, Tanzania	53	9 40S	38 10 E
Liwale Chini, Tan.	53	9 40S	38 0 E
Liwan, Sudan	53	4 58N	35 34 E
Lixnaw, Ireland	11	52 24N	9 37W
Lixourion, Greece	21	38 14N	20 24 E
Lizard I., Queensland	42	14 42S	145 30 E
Lizard Town, England	10	49 57N	5 13W
Ljubljana, Yugoslavia	20	46 4N	14 33 E
Ljungan, Sweden	23	57 59N	13 4 E
Ljungan, R., Sweden	23	62 40N	13 30 E
Ljungby, Sweden	23	56 49N	13 55 E
Ljusdal, Sweden	23	61 46N	16 3 E
Ljusnan R., Sweden	23	62 10N	14 0 E
Ljusne, Sweden	23	61 15N	17 14 E
Llancanelo L., Argentina	77	35 40S	69 0W
Llandudno, Wales	10	53 19N	3 51W
Llandovery, Wales	10	51 59N	3 49W
Llaneii, Wales	10	51 41N	4 11W
Llanes, Spain	17	43 25N	4 50W
Llano, U.S.A.	71	30 45N	98 44W
Llano R., U.S.A.	71	30 50N	99 0W
Llano de la Magdalena, Mexico	74	25 0N	112 0W
Llano Estacado, U.S.A.	66	34 0N	103 0W
Llanos, Col. and Ven.	78	6 60N	69 0W
Llanos d'Urgel, Spain	17	41 35N	0 50 E
Llanquihue L., Chile	77	41 10S	73 0W
Llera, Mexico	74	23 20N	99 0W
Llerena, Spain	17	38 17N	6 0W
Llivia, Spain	17	42 29N	1 57 E
Llobregat, Spain	17	41 24N	2 7 E
Lloyd B., Queensland	42	12 45S	143 27 E
Lloyd L., Canada	65	57 23N	109 0W
Lloydminster, Canada	65	53 20N	110 0W
Llullaillaco Mt., Chile	77	24 30S	68 30W
Lo Ho, R., China	38	34 15N	111 10 E
Loa, U.S.A.	73	38 13N	111 40W
Loa R., Chile	78	21 30S	70 0W
Loango, Zaire	53	2 0S	28 55 E
Loanja, Zambia	56	16 20S	24 46 E
Lobatsi, Botswana	57	25 11S	25 40 E
Loberia, Argentina	77	38 10S	58 40W
Lobito, Angola	55	12 18S	13 35 E
Lobitos, Peru	78	4 20S	81 10W
Lobos, I., Mexico	74	27 20N	110 30W
Lobstick L., Canada	63	54 0N	65 12W
Locarno, Switzerland	15	46 10N	8 47 E
Lochem, Netherlands	13	52 9N	6 26 E
Loches, France	12	47 7N	1 0 E
Lochwan, China	38	35 55N	109 30 E
Lochy, L., Scotland	10	56 58N	4 55W
Lock Haven, U.S.A.	68	41 7N	77 31W
Lockeport, N.S., Canada	63	43 47N	65 4W
Lockeport, B.C., Canada	64	52 40N	132 0W
Lockhart, N.S.W.	43	35 14S	147 40 E
Lockhart, U.S.A.	71	29 50N	97 39W
Lockney, U.S.A.	71	34 4N	101 28W
Lockport, U.S.A.	68	43 12N	78 42W
Lod, Israel	29	31 57N	34 54 E
Loddon R., Victoria	43	36 0S	143 50 E
Lodève, France	12	43 44N	3 19 E
Lodge Grass, U.S.A.	72	45 20N	107 27W
Lodgepole, U.S.A.	70	41 13N	102 36W
Lodgepole Cr., U.S.A.	70	41 40N	104 30W
Lodhran, Pakistan	32	29 32N	71 30 E

	MAP		
Lodi, Italy	20	45 19N	9 30 E
Lodi, U.S.A.	73	38 10N	121 18W
Lödingen, Norway	22	68 25N	16 0 E
Lodja, Zaire	54	3 30S	23 23 E
Lodwar, Kenya	53	3 15N	35 28 E
Łódź, Poland	16	51 45N	19 27 E
Loeriesfontein, C. Prov.	57	30 56S	19 26 E
Lofoten Is., Norway	22	68 20N	14 0 E
Lofty Ra., W. Australia	44	24 15S	119 30 E
Log Logo, Kenya	53	2 0N	37 57 E
Logan, Kansas, U.S.A.	70	39 43N	99 32W
Logan, Ohio, U.S.A.	68	39 35N	82 22W
Logan, Utah, U.S.A.	72	41 54N	111 50W
Logan, W. Va., U.S.A.	68	37 51N	81 59W
Logan Cr., Queensland	42	22 10S	147 30 E
Logan Downs, Queensland	42	22 19S	148 0 E
Logan Mt., Canada	60	60 40N	140 0W
Logansport, La., U.S.A.	71	31 58N	94 0W
Logansport, Ind., U.S.A.	68	40 40N	86 20W
Logirim, Sudan	53	4 50N	33 20 E
Logone R., Cameroon-Chad	51	10 0N	15 45 E
Logrono, Spain	17	42 28N	2 32W
Logrosan, Spain	17	39 20N	5 32W
Lohardaga, India	33	23 27N	84 45 E
Lohja, Finland	23	60 12N	24 0 E
Loho, China	38	33 30N	114 0 E
Loi Kaw, Burma	13	19 40N	97 17 E
Loiborsirret, Tan.	53	3 54S	36 26 E
Loimaa, Finland	23	60 50N	23 5 E
Loir R., France	12	47 58N	1 14 E
Loire R., France	12	47 25N	0 20W
Loja, Ecuador	78	3 59S	79 16W
Loja, Spain	17	37 10N	4 10W
Loka, Sudan	53	4 13N	31 0 E
Lokchong, China	39	25 11N	113 16 E
Lokichar, Kenya	53	2 23N	35 40 E
Lokichokio, Kenya	53	4 19N	34 13 E
Lokitaung, Kenya	53	4 18N	35 45 E
Lökken, Denmark	23	57 22N	9 41 E
Lökken, Norway	23	63 8N	9 45 E
Loko, Nigeria	52	8 2N	7 42 E
Lokobo, Sudan	53	4 20N	30 33 E
Lokoja, Nigeria	52	7 47N	6 45 E
Lokolama, Zaire	54	2 20S	20 15 E
Loktung, China	39	18 43N	109 2 E
Lokuti, Sudan	53	4 18N	33 18 E
Lokwabe, Botswana	57	24 10S	21 50 E
Lokwei, China	39	19 12N	110 30 E
Lolibai Mts., Sudan	53	3 50N	33 50 E
Lolimi, Sudan	53	4 35N	34 0 E
Loliondo, Tanzania	53	2 3S	35 44 E
Lolland I., Denmark	23	54 45N	11 30 E
Lolo, U.S.A.	72	46 50N	114 10W
Lolodorf, Cameroon	52	3 16N	10 49 E
Lolwa, Zaire	53	1 26N	29 31 E
Lom, Bulgaria	21	43 48N	23 20 E
Lom R., Cameroon	52	5 30N	14 1 E
Loma, U.S.A.	72	47 58N	110 29W
Loma Mansa, Mt., Guinea	52		Inset
Lomani, prov., Zaire	54	5 50S	25 0 E
Lomami R., Zaire	54	0 30S	24 15 E
Lomas, Peru	78	15 25S	74 55W
Lombard, U.S.A.	72	46 7N	111 29W
Lombardy, prov., Italy	20	45 33N	9 40 E
Lomblen I., Indonesia	35	8 30S	123 32 E
Lombok I., Indonesia	35	8 35S	116 20 E
Lombok Str., Indonesia	35	8 30S	115 50 E
Lomé, Togo	52	6 9N	1 20 E
Lomela, Zaire	54	2 5S	23 52 E
Lomela R., Zaire	54	1 30S	22 50 E
Lometa, U.S.A.	71	31 15N	98 25W
Lomié, Cameroon	52	3 13N	13 38 E
Loming, Sudan	53	4 27N	33 40W
Lomond, Canada	64	50 24N	112 36W
Lomond, L., Scotland	10	56 8N	4 38W
Lomonosovo, U.S.S.R.	25	55 35N	32 25 E
Lomza, Poland	16	53 10N	22 2 E
Lonavli, India	32	18 45N	73 25 E
Loncoche, Chile	77	39 20S	72 50W
Londiana, Kenya	53	0 9S	35 42 E
London, Canada	62	43 0N	81 15W
London, England	10	51 30N	0 5W
London, Ky., U.S.A.	68	37 11N	84 5W
London, Ohio, U.S.A.	68	39 55N	83 26W
Londonderry, N. Ireland	11	55 0N	7 20W
Londonderry, co., N. Ireland	11	54 56N	6 55W
Londonderry I., Chile	77	55 0S	71 0W
Londrina, Brazil	77	23 20S	51 48W
Löndsdal, Norway	22	66 46N	15 26 E
Lone Pine, U.S.A.	73	36 38N	118 2W
Lonely, Rhodesia	56	19 30S	28 47 E
Lonely Is., U.S.S.R.	28	77 30N	80 0 E
Long Beach, Calif., U.S.A.	73	33 46N	118 12W
Long Beach, Wash., U.S.A.	72	46 20N	124 2W
Long Branch, U.S.A.	68	40 19N	74 0W
Long Eaton, England	9	52 54N	1 16W
Long I., Canada	63	44 23N	66 19W
Long I., Queensland	43	22 8S	149 53 E
Long I., U.S.A.	68	40 50N	73 20W
Long, I., New Guinea	42	5 15S	147 5 E
Long, I., New Zealand	47	47 16S	167 26 E
Long L., Ont., Canada	62	49 30N	86 50W

	MAP		
Long L., N.Y., U.S.A.	68	43 57N	74 25W
Long Pine, U.S.A.	70	42 34N	99 43W
Long Pt., Newf., Canada	63	48 45N	58 52W
Long Pt., New Zealand	47	46 34S	169 36 E
Long Range Mts., Can.	63	49 30N	57 30W
Long Str., U.S.S.R.	28	70 0N	175 0 E
Long Xuyen, S. Viet Nam	34	10 19N	105 28 E
Longairo, Sudan	53	4 34N	32 22 E
Longburn, New Zealand	46	40 23S	175 35 E
Longford, Ireland	11	53 43N	7 50W
Longford, Tasmania	43	41 32S	147 3 E
Longford, co., Ireland	11	53 42N	7 45W
Longido, Tanzania	53	2 48S	36 33 E
Longju, India	33	28 35N	93 30 E
Longlac, Canada	62	49 45N	86 25W
Longledju, Indonesia	35	2 55N	116 30 E
Longmont, U.S.A.	70	40 10N	105 4W
Longnawan, Indonesia	35	21 50N	114 55 E
Longo, Zambia	56	17 35S	27 13 E
Longreach, Queensland	42	23 28S	144 14 E
Longuy, Cameroon	52	3 10N	9 58 E
Longview, Canada	64	50 32N	114 10W
Longview, Tex., U.S.A.	71	32 30N	94 45W
Longview, Wash., U.S.A.	72	46 9N	122 59W
Longwy, France	12	49 32N	5 46 E
Loning, China	38	34 25N	111 32 E
Lonoke, U.S.A.	71	34 47N	91 58W
Lons-le-Saunier, France	12	46 40N	5 31 E
Looc, Philippines	35	12 20N	122 5 E
Lookout, C., Canada	62	55 20N	84 30W
Lookout, C., U.S.A.	69	34 30N	76 30W
Loolmalasin Mt., Tan.	53	3 1S	35 44 E
Loomis, Canada	65	49 15N	108 45W
Loon L., Canada	65	44 50N	77 15W
Loon R., Canada	64	56 50N	115 20W
Loongana, W. Australia	45	30 52S	127 5 E
Loop Hd., Ireland	11	52 34N	9 55W
Loos Is. (Los Is.), Guinea	52	9 30N	13 50W
Lop Nor, China	37	40 20N	90 10 E
Lopatin, U.S.S.R.	25	43 50N	47 35 E
Lopeja (Sirsiri), Sudan	53	4 42N	31 57 E
Lopez C., Gabon	54	0 47S	8 40 E
Lopodi, Sudan	53	3 48N	33 18 E
Lopphavet I., Norway	22	70 12N	22 30 E
Lora, Spain	17	37 38N	5 38W
Lora R., Afghanistan	31	30 0N	66 0 E
Loralai, Pakistan	32	30 29N	68 30 E
Lorca, Spain	17	37 41N	1 42W
Lordsburg, U.S.A.	73	32 15N	108 45W
Lorena, Brazil	77	22 44S	45 7W
Lorengau, Terr. of New Guinea	42	2 10S	147 23 E
Loreto, Brazil	79	7 5S	45 30W
Loreto, Marches, Italy	20	43 27N	13 36 E
Lorian Swamp, Kenya	53	1 20N	40 0 E
Lorica, Colombia	75	9 14N	75 50W
Lorient, France	12	47 45N	3 23W
Lorne, Firth of, Scot.	10	56 20N	5 40W
Loronyo, Sudan	53	4 40N	32 37 E
Lorraine, dist., France	12	49 0N	6 0 E
Lorrainville, Canada	62	47 21N	79 23W
Loruguma, Kenya	44	2 56N	35 14 E
Los Is. (Loos Is.), Guinea	52	9 30N	13 50W
Los Alamos, U.S.A.	73	35 57N	106 17W
Los Andes, Chile	77	32 50S	70 40W
Los Angeles, Chile	77	37 25S	70 32W
Los Angeles, U.S.A.	73	34 0N	118 10W
Los Banos, U.S.A.	73	37 3N	120 51W
Los Blancos, Argentina	77	23 45S	62 30W
Los Cerrillos, Argentina	77	32 0S	65 30W
Los Gatos, U.S.A.	73	37 18N	121 59W
Los Hermanos I., Ven.	78	11 50N	64 20W
Los Lagos, Chile	77	39 54S	39 55W
Los Lunas, U.S.A.	73	34 50N	106 45W
Los Mochis, Mexico	74	25 45N	109 5W
Los Monegros, Spain	17	41 30N	0 10W
Los Olivos, U.S.A.	73	34 41N	120 6W
Los Palacios, Spain	17	37 11N	5 55W
Los Pozos, Chile	77	26 40S	70 30W
Los Roques I., Venezuela	78	12 0N	66 50W
Los Santos, Spain	17	38 30N	6 25W
Los Sauces, Chile	77	38 0S	72 50W
Los Teques, Venezuela	75	10 30N	66 5W
Los Testigos I., Ven.	78	11 30N	63 0W
Los Vilos, Chile	77	32 0S	71 30W
Losefe, Mozambique	56	12 59S	34 57 E
Loshing, China	39	24 48N	109 0 E
Loshkalakh, U.S.S.R.	27	62 45N	147 20 E
Lošinj I., Yugoslavia	20	44 55N	14 45 E
Loskop Dam, Transvaal	57	25 23S	29 20 E
Lossiemouth, Scotland	10	57 43N	3 17W
Lota, Chile	77	37 5S	73 10W
Lotagipi Swamp, Kenya-Sudan	53	4 45N	35 0 E
Lothiar, Transvaal	57	26 26S	30 27 E
Lothlekane, Botswana	57	21 25S	25 35 E
Loting, Hopeh, China	38	39 30N	118 55 E
Loting, Kwangtung, China	39	22 40N	111 32 E
Loto, Zaire	54	2 18S	23 0 E
Lotsani R., Botswana	56	22 32S	27 30 E
Lötschberg Tunnel, Switzerland	15	46 25N	7 40 E
Lotta R., U.S.S.R.	22	68 30N	30 0 E
Loudéac, France	12	48 11N	2 47W

	MAP		
Loudon, U.S.A.	69	35 41N	84 22W
Loudun, France	12	47 0N	0 5 E
Louga, Senegal	50	15 45N	16 5W
Loughrea, Ireland	11	53 11N	8 33W
Loughros More B., Ire.	11	54 48N	8 30W
Louis Trichardt, Trans.	57	23 0S	29 55 E
Louisa, U.S.A.	68	38 5N	82 40W
Louisburg, Canada	63	45 55N	60 0W
Louisburgh, Ireland	11	53 46N	9 49W
Louise I., Canada	64	52 55N	131 40W
Louiesville, Canada	62	46 20N	73 0W
Louisiade Arch., Papua	42	10 50S	152 30 E
Louisiana, U.S.A.	70	39 28N	91 2W
Louisiana, st., Y.S.A.	71	30 50N	92 0W
Louisville, Ky., U.S.A.	68	38 15N	85 45W
Louisville, Miss., U.S.A.	71	33 7N	89 3W
Loulé, Portugal	17	37 10N	8 0W
Lount L., Canada	65	50 10N	94 20W
Loup City, U.S.A.	70	41 17N	98 57W
Lourdes, France	12	43 6N	0 3W
Lourenço Marques, Mozambique	55	25 57S	32 34 E
Lourinha, Portugal	17	39 15N	9 17W
Louth, England	10	53 23N	0 0W
Louth, New South Wales	43	30 30S	145 8 E
Louth, Ireland	11	53 57N	6 33W
Louth, co., Ireland	11	53 55N	6 30W
Louviers, France	12	49 12N	1 10 E
Louwsburg, Natal	57	27 33S	31 21 E
Luzha, Zambia	56	13 0S	25 12 E
Lovat R., U.S.S.R.	25	57 30N	31 20 E
Love, Canada	65	53 30N	104 12W
Lovech (Lovets), Bulg.	21	43 8N	24 45 E
Loveland, U.S.A.	70	40 29N	105 2W
Lovelock, U.S.A.	72	40 12N	118 30W
Lovell, U.S.A.	72	44 51N	108 20W
Lovets (Lovech), Bulg.	21	43 8N	24 45 E
Lovere, Italy	20	45 50N	10 4 E
Loviisa, Finland	23	60 31N	26 20 E
Loving, U.S.A.	71	32 15N	104 2W
Lovington, U.S.A.	71	32 59N	103 23W
Lóvoa, Angola	56	11 38S	23 52 E
Low L., Canada	62	52 20N	76 20W
Low Tatra Mts., C. Slov.	16	48 52N	19 40 E
Lowa, Zaire	54	1 22S	25 52 E
Lowell, U.S.A.	69	42 38N	71 19W
Lower Arrow L., Canada	64	49 40N	118 5W
Lower Austria	14	48 45N	15 50 E
Lower California, st., Mexico	74	28 0N	112 30W
Lower Dikgatlon, Cape Province	57	27 6S	22 56 E
Lower Hutt, N.Z.	46	41 10S	174 55 E
Lower Laberge, Canada	64	60 27N	135 15W
Lower Lake, U.S.A.	72	38 55N	122 35W
Lower Neguac, Canada	63	47 20N	65 10W
Lower North, dist., S. Australia	43	33 45S	138 30 E
Lower Post, Canada	64	60 0N	128 35W
Lower Red L., U.S.A.	70	48 0N	95 0W
Lower Sackville, Canada	63	45 45N	63 43W
Lower Saxony, land, Germany	14	52 47N	9 15 E
Lower Seal, L., Canada	62	56 30N	74 23W
Lower Tunguska R., U.S.S.R.	27	64 20N	93 0 E
Lowestoft, England	10	52 29N	1 44 E
Lowicz, Poland	16	52 6N	19 55 E
Lowmead, Queensland	42	24 33S	151 47 E
Lowville, U.S.A.	68	43 48N	75 30W
Loxton, C. Province	57	31 30S	22 22 E
Loxton, S. Australia	43	34 23S	140 36 E
Loyalty Is., Pac. Oc.	5	21 0S	167 30 E
Loyang, China	38	34 40N	112 28 E
Loyev, U.S.S.R.	25	57 7N	30 40 E
Loyoro, Uganda	53	3 21N	34 18 E
Loyuan, China	39	26 25N	119 35 E
Loyung, China	39	24 25N	109 25 E
Loz, Jebel al, Arabia	30	28 40N	35 20 E
Lozovaya, U.S.S.R.	25	49 0N	36 27 E
Luabo, Mozambique	56	18 30S	36 10 E
Lualaba, prov., Zaire	56	10 30S	25 45 E
Lualaba R., Zaire	56	11 30S	25 56 E
Lualua R., Mozambique	56	17 30S	36 0 E
Luama, R., Zaire	53	5 20S	28 30 E
Luamata, Zambia	56	11 58S	24 25 E
Luambe, Zambia	56	12 30S	32 13 E
Luampa R., Zambia	56	15 30S	24 40 E
Luan, Philippines	35	6 10N	124 25 E
Luanda, Angola	55	8 58S	13 9 E
Luang Prabang, Laos	34	19 45N	102 10 E
Luanginga R., Angola	56	13 45S	21 0 E
Luangwa R., Zambia	56	11 40S	32 40 E
Luangwa R. Bridge, Zambia	56	14 59S	30 9 E
Luangwa Valley, Zambia	56	14 10S	30 40 E
Luanshya, Zambia	56	13 20S	28 8 E
Luapula, prov., Zambia	56	11 20S	3 56 E
Luapula R., Zambia	56	12 0S	29 0 E
Luarca, Spain	17	43 32N	6 32W
Luashi, Zaire	56	11 3S	23 38 E
Lubalo, Angola	55	9 0S	19 12 E
Luban, Poland	16	51 8N	15 17 E
Lubang Is., Philippines	35	13 50N	120 12 E
Lubartow, Poland	16	51 28N	22 42 E
Lubawa, Poland	16	53 30N	19 48 E
Lubban, Jordan	29	32 9N	35 14 E

	MAP		
Lübben, Germany	14	51 56N	13 54 E
Lubbock, U.S.A.	71	33 40N	102 0W
Lübeck, Germany	14	53 52N	10 41 E
Lübeck, dist., Germany	23	54 5N	10 35 E
Lubefu, Zaire	54	4 43S	24 25 E
Lubero, Zaire	54	0 3S	29 2 E
Lubicon L., Canada	64	56 22N	115 45W
Lubicz, Poland	16	53 7N	18 51 E
Lublin, Poland	16	51 12N	22 38 E
Lubny, U.S.S.R.	25	50 3N	32 58 E
Lubudi, Zaire	55	9 57S	25 59 E
Lubudi R., Zaire	55	9 30S	25 0 E
Lubuk Linggau, Indon.	34	3 15S	102 55 E
Lubuk Sikaping, Indon.	34	0 10N	100 15 E
Lubumbashi, Zaire	56	11 32S	27 28 E
Lubungwe, Zaire	56	9 35S	27 25 E
Lubutu, Zaire	54	0 40S	26 55 E
Lucca, Italy	20	43 50N	10 30 E
Luce Bay, Scotland	10	54 45N	4 48W
Lucea, Jamaica	75		Inset
Lucedale, U.S.A.	69	30 55N	88 34W
Lucena, Philippines	35	13 55N	121 25 E
Lucena, Spain	17	37 27N	4 31W
Lučenec, C. Slov.	16	48 18N	19 42 E
Lucera, Italy	20	41 30N	15 20 E
Lucheringo, Mozam.	56	12 0S	36 0 E
Luchow, China	39	28 54N	105 17 E
Luchuringo R., Mozam.	55	12 0S	36 30 E
Lucinda, Queensland	42	18 32S	146 22 E
Lucipara Is., Indonesia	35	5 28S	127 20 E
Lucira, Angola	55	14 0S	12 35 E
Lucite R., Mozambique	56	20 0S	33 10 E
Luckenwalde, Germany	14	52 5N	13 11 E
Luckhoff, O.F.S.	57	29 45S	24 48 E
Lucknow, India	32	26 50N	81 0 E
Lucky Lake, Canada	65	51 0N	107 0W
Luçon, France	12	46 28N	1 10W
Lucusse, Angola	55	12 37S	20 46 E
Lüderitz, S.W. Africa	57	26 37S	15 9 E
Ludhiana, India	32	30 57N	75 56 E
Ludington, U.S.A.	68	43 58N	86 27W
Ludlow, England	10	52 23N	2 42W
Ludlow, U.S.A.	73	34 43N	116 14W
Ludvika, Sweden	23	60 8N	15 14 E
Ludwigsburg, Germany	14	48 53N	9 11 E
Ludwigshafen, Germany	14	49 27N	8 27 E
Luebo, Zaire	54	5 21S	21 17 E
Luemba, Zaire	53	3 42S	28 39 E
Luena, Zaire	56	9 28S	25 45 E
Luena, Zambia	56	10 35S	20 15 E
Luena Flats, Zambia	56	14 45S	23 0 E
Luena R., Zambia	56	14 25S	24 0 E
Luete R., Zambia	56	16 0S	22 30 E
Lueze, Zambia	56	17 15S	26 18 E
Lufira R., Zaire	55	9 30S	27 0 E
Lufkin, U.S.A.	71	31 25N	94 40W
Lufu (Lufubu) R., Zambia	56	9 10S	31 0 E
Lufubu (Lufu) R., Zambia	56	9 10S	31 0 E
Lufupa R., Zambia	56	14 15S	25 45 E
Luga, U.S.S.R.	25	58 40N	29 55 E
Luga, R., U.S.S.R.	23	59 5N	28 30 E
Lugamba, Zaire	53	5 32S	29 10 E
Luganga, Zaire	53	4 12S	28 10 E
Lugano, Switzerland	15	46 0N	8 57 E
Lugansk, U.S.S.R.	25	48 33N	39 15 E
Lugard's Falls, Kenya	53	3 6S	38 41 E
Lugenda, R., Mozam.	55	12 30S	36 40 E
Lugga Dafat R., Kenya	53	2 0N	39 5 E
Lugnaquillia Mt., Ire.	11	52 58N	6 28W
Lugo, Italy	20	44 25N	11 54 E
Lugo, Spain	17	43 2N	7 35W
Lugoj, Rumania	21	45 42N	21 57 E
Lugufu, Tanzania	53	4 59S	30 10 E
Lugumba, Zaire	53	5 38S	29 1 E
Lugovoi, U.S.S.R.	26	43 0N	72 20 E
Luhaiya, Yemen	30	15 43N	42 45 E
Luhit R., India	33	28 0N	96 60 E
Luia, R., Mozambique	56	16 15S	31 55 E
Luiana, Angola	56	17 16S	22 54 E
Luiana, R., Angola	56	17 25S	22 30W
Luichow Pen., China	39	20 30N	110 0 E
Luido, Mozambique	56	21 30S	34 40 E
Luimba Hill, Zambia	56	14 59S	22 30 E
Luino, Italy	20	46 0N	8 42 E
Luipa, China	38	33 32N	107 1 E
Luis Correia, Brazil	79	3 0S	41 35W
Luisa, Zaire	54	7 40S	22 30 E
Luishia, Zaire	56	11 12S	26 58 E
Luitpold Coast, Ant.	80	78 0S	29 0W
Lujan, Argentina	77	34 45S	59 5W
Lukaia, Zambia	56	15 32S	28 42 E
Lukanga Swamp, Zambia	56	14 15S	27 50 E
Luke, Mt., W. Australia	44	27 10S	116 50 E
Lukenie R., Zaire	54	3 0S	18 50 E
Luki, China	39	28 9N	109 58 E
Lukmanier P., Switz.	15	46 34N	8 48 E
Lukolela, Zaire	54	1 10S	17 12 E
Lukonzolwa, Zaire	56	8 50S	28 46 E
Lukosi, Rhodesia	56	18 30S	26 30 E
Lukovit, Bulgaria	21	43 13N	24 11 E
Łuków, Poland	16	51 55N	22 25 E
Lukoyanov, U.S.S.R.	25	55 2N	44 20 E
Lukuga R., Zaire	53	5 50S	28 30 E

	MAP		
Lukulu, Zambia	56	14 35S	23 25 E
Lukulu R., Zambia	56	10 30S	31 0 E
Lukushashi R., Zambia	56	14 0S	30 3 E
Lule, R., Sweden	22	66 20N	20 48 E
Luleå, Sweden	22	65 35N	22 10 E
Luleburgaz, Turkey	30	41 24N	27 21 E
Luling, U.S.A.	71	29 45N	97 40W
Lulonga R., Zaire	54	1 0N	19 0 E
Lulua R., Zaire	54	6 20S	22 40 E
Luluabourg, Zaire	54	5 55S	22 18 E
Luluabourg, prov., Zaire	54	4 30S	23 40 E
Lulung, China	38	39 40N	118 40 E
Lulworth Mt., Western Australia	44	26 42S	117 15 E
Lumadjang, Indonesia	34	8 8S	113 16 E
Lumai, Angola	55	13 20S	21 25 E
Lumbala, Angola	56	12 35S	22 30 E
Lumbe, R., Zambia	56	16 10S	24 0 E
Lumberton, Miss., U.S.A.	71	31 0N	89 29W
Lumberton, N. Mex., U.S.A.	73	36 58N	106 53W
Lumberton, N.C., U.S.A.	69	34 37N	79 3W
Lumbwe, Kenya	53	0 15S	35 30 E
Lumby, Canada	64	50 10N	118 50W
Lumeyen, Sudan	53	4 57N	33 28 E
Lumsden, Canada	65	50 40N	104 50W
Lumsden, New Zealand	47	45 44S	168 27 E
Lunanga, Congo	53	4 15S	28 13 E
Lunbang, Sarawak	35	4 50N	115 5 E
Lund, Sweden	23	55 41N	13 12 E
Lund, U.S.A.	73	38 52N	115 0W
Lundar, Canada	65	50 50N	98 10W
Lundazi, Zambia	56	12 30S	33 20 E
Lundi R., Rhodesia	56	21 0S	31 0 E
Lundy I., England	10	51 10N	4 41W
Lüneburg, Germany	14	53 15N	10 23 E
Lüneburg Heath, dist., Germany	14	53 0N	10 0 E
Lunel, France	12	43 39N	4 9 E
Lunenburg, Canada	63	44 22N	64 18W
Lunéville, France	12	48 36N	6 30 E
Lunga R., Zambia	56	12 30S	24 30 E
Lungan, China	39	23 10N	107 39 E
Lungchuan, Chekiang, China	39	28 9N	119 14 E
Lungchuan, Kwangtung, China	39	24 6N	115 9 E
Lunghsien, China	38	34 58N	106 59 E
Lunghwa, China	38	41 25N	117 45 E
Lungi Airport, S. Leone	52		Inset
Lungkow, China	38	37 40N	120 25 E
Lungleh, India	33	22 55N	92 45 E
Lunglin, China	39	24 43N	105 31 E
Lungmoon, China	39	23 47N	114 16 E
Lungnam, China	39	24 47N	114 43 E
Lungshan, China	39	29 27N	109 27 E
Lungsheng, China	39	25 40N	109 57 E
Lungsi, China	38	35 0N	104 35 E
Lungtien, China	38	35 28N	106 29 E
Lungtsin, China	39	22 20N	106 52 E
Lunguya, Tanzania	56	3 23S	32 25 E
Lungwebungu, R., Zambia	56	13 40S	22 35 E
Lungyan, China	39	25 13N	117 0 E
Luni, India	32	26 0N	73 6 E
Luni R., India	32	25 40N	72 20 E
Luninets, U.S.S.R.	24	52 15N	27 0 E
Luning, U.S.A.	73	38 31N	118 13W
Lunjuk-besar, Indonesia	35	8 55S	117 20 E
Lunsemfwa Falls, Zambia	56	14 30S	29 15 E
Lunsemfwa R., Zambia	56	14 50S	20 10 E
Luombi, R., Zambia	56	9 55S	30 48 E
Lupembe, Tanzania	53	9 11S	35 10 E
Lupiro, Tanzania	53	8 21S	36 39 E
Lupumaula, Zambia	56	15 5S	26 36 E
Lupundu, Zambia	56	14 18S	26 30 E
Luray, U.S.A.	68	38 39N	78 26W
Lure, France	12	47 40N	6 30 E
Lure, M. de, France	12	44 6N	5 46 E
Luremo, Angola	55	8 19S	17 55 E
Luristan, Iran	30	33 20N	47 0 E
Lusahanga, Tanzania	53	2 50S	31 14 E
Lusaka, Zambia	56	15 25S	28 15 E
Lusaka St. Jacques, Zaire	53	7 7S	29 29 E
Lusambo, Zaire	54	4 53S	23 14 E
Luseland, Canada	65	52 4N	109 26W
Lushan, China	38	33 40N	112 48 E
Lushan, China	39	26 29N	107 58 E
Lushih, China	38	34 0N	111 0 E
Lushoto, Tanzania	53	4 40S	38 12 E
Lushun. *See* Port Arthur	38		
Lusie, Zambia	56	15 20S	23 30 E
Lusika, Zaire	53	0 20S	28 15 E
Lusikisiki, C. Prov.	57	31 21S	29 36 E
Lusitu, Tanzania	53	9 38S	34 40 E
Lusk, U.S.A.	70	42 50N	104 28W
Luswishi R., Zambia	56	13 30S	27 17 E
Lutlhe, Botswana	57	24 8S	23 48 E
Lutoba, Zambia	56	13 9S	24 58 E
Luton, England	10	51 53N	0 24W
Lutsk, U.S.S.R.	24	50 50N	25 15 E
Luverne, U.S.A.	70	43 38N	96 14W
Luvua R., Zaire	54	6 50S	27 30 E

	MAP		
Luvuvhu R., Transvaal	57	22 40S	30 55 E
Luwegu R., Tanzania	53	9 30S	37 10 E
Luwimba, Zambia	56	13 38S	26 40 E
Luwingu, Zambia	56	10 15S	30 2 E
Luwuk, Indonesia	35	10 0S	122 40 E
Luxembourg, Luxem.	13	49 37N	6 9 E
Luxembourg, duchy, Europe	13	50 0N	6 0 E
Luxembourg, prov., Belgium	13	49 58N	5 30 E
Luxor (Al Uqsur), Egypt	51	25 41N	32 38 E
Luz, France	12	42 53N	0 1 E
Luzern (Lucerne), Switz.	15	47 3N	8 18 E
Luzern (Lucerne), canton, Switzerland	15	47 2N	7 55 E
Luziania, Brazil	79	16 20S	48 0W
Luzon I., Philippines	35	16 30N	121 30 E
Luzon Strait, Phil.	35	20 20N	120 0 E
Lvov, U.S.S.R.	24	49 40N	24 0 E
Lwanhsien, China	38	39 45N	118 45 E
Lyakhov Is., U.S.S.R.	27	73 40N	141 0 E
Lyallpur, Pakistan	32	31 30N	73 5 E
Lyantonde, Uganda	53	0 24S	31 7 E
Lycksele, Sweden	22	64 38N	18 40 E
Lydenburg, Transvaal	57	25 8S	30 26 E
Lyell, New Zealand	47	41 48S	172 4 E
Lyell I., Canada	64	52 40N	131 35W
Lyell Range, N.Z	47	41 38S	172 20 E
Lyleton, Canada	65	49 4N	101 10W
Lyman, U.S.A.	72	41 24N	110 15W
Lyna, R., Poland	16	54 8N	20 30 E
Lynchburg, U.S.A.	68	37 23N	79 10W
Lynd R., Queensland	42	17 10S	143 40 E
Lynden, U.S.A.	72	48 58N	122 29W
Lyndhurst, S. Australia	43	30 15S	138 18 E
Lyndon, U.S.A.	68	44 30N	71 59W
Lyndon R., W. Austral.	44	23 20S	114 30 E
Lyndonville, U.S.A.	69	44 32N	72 1W
Lyngen, Norway	22	69 35N	20 20 E
Lynn, U.S.A.	69	42 28N	71 0W
Lynn Canal, Alaska	64	58 50N	135 20W
Lynn L., Canada	65	56 30N	101 40W
Lynton, W. Australia	44	28 11S	114 16 E
Lynx L., Canada	65	62 30N	106 25W
Lyonnais, prov., France	12	45 45N	4 15 E
Lyons, Rhône, France	12	45 46N	4 50 E
Lyons, Colo., U.S.A.	70	40 13N	105 2W
Lyons, Ga., U.S.A.	69	32 12N	82 19W
Lyons, Kan., U.S.A.	70	38 24N	98 14W
Lyons, N.Y., U.S.A.	68	43 3N	77 0W
Lyons R., W. Australia	44	24 0S	116 0 E
Lyskovo, U.S.S.R.	25	56 0N	45 3 E
Lyss, Switzerland	15	47 4N	7 19 E
Lytle, U.S.A.	71	29 14N	98 45W
Lyttelton, New Zealand	47	43 35S	172 44 E
Lytton, Canada	64	50 13N	121 31W
Lyubotin, U.S.S.R.	25	50 0N	36 4 E
Lyudinovo, U.S.S.R.	25	53 55N	34 25 E

M

	MAP		
Ma'ad, Jordan	29	32 37N	35 36 E
Ma'an, Jordan	30	30 12N	35 44 E
Maanshan, China	39	31 50N	118 34 E
Ma' Aqaiā, Si. Arabia	30	26 33N	47 19 E
Maarianhamina (Mariehamn), Finland	23	60 5N	19 55 E
Ma'arrat an Nu man, Syria	30	35 39N	36 30 E
Maas R., Netherlands	13	51 48N	5 30 E
Maatin-es-Sarra, Libya	51	21 45N	22 0 E
Mababe Depression, Botswana	56	18 50S	23 58 E
Mabalane, Mozambique	56	23 37S	32 31 E
Mabel L., Canada	64	50 40N	118 40W
Mabeleapudi, Botswana	56	20 58S	22 36 E
Mabirou, Gabon	54	1 10S	15 48 E
Mabonto, Sierra Leone	52		Inset
Mabote, Mozambique	56	22 3S	34 9 E
Mabrouk, Mali	50	19 30N	1 14W
Mabton, U.S.A.	72	46 13N	120 2W
Mabuki, Tanzania	53	2 59S	33 12 E
Mac Kay R., Canada	64	57 0N	112 0W
Mac Kenzie Sea, Ant.	80	68 0S	75 0 E
Macaé, Brazil	79	22 20S	41 55W
Macaliche, Mozam.	56	18 20S	33 30 E
Macaloge. *See* Sanga Moz.	56		
Macao I., China	39	22 15N	113 35 E
Macapá, Brazil	79	0 5N	51 10W
Macau, Brazil	79	5 0S	36 40W
Macchachi, Ecuador	78	0 30S	78 35W
Macclesfield, England	10	53 16N	2 9W
McCook, U.S.A.	70	40 15N	100 34W
Macdonnell Ra., Australia	45	23 40S	133 0 E
Macdougall L., Canada	60	66 20N	98 30W
Mace, Canada	62	48 55N	80 0W
Macedonia, Yugoslavia	21	41 40N	21 40 E
Maceió, Brazil	79	9 40S	35 41W
Macenta, Guinea	50	8 35N	9 20W
Macerata, Italy	20	43 19N	13 28 E
Macfarlane L., South Australia	45	32 5S	136 45 E

	MAP		
Macgillycuddy's Reeks, Ireland	11	52 2N	9 45W
Macgregor, Canada	65	49 57N	98 48W
Mach, Pakistan	32	29 50N	67 20 E
Machache Mts., Lesotho	57	29 20 S	28 0 E
Machakos, Kenya	53	1 28 S	37 15 E
Machala, Ecuador	78	3 10 S	79 50W
Machanga, Mozam.	56	20 58 S	34 57 E
Machattie L., Queens.	42	24 45 S	139 45 E
Machaze, Mozambique	56	20 51 S	33 26 E
Machece, Mozambique	56	19 17 S	35 33 E
Macheke, Rhodesia	56	18 8 S	31 50 E
Macheng, China	39	31 13N	115 6 E
Macherla, India	32	16 30N	79 25 E
Machevna, U.S.S.R.	27	61 20N	172 0 E
Machias, U.S.A.	63	44 40N	67 34W
Machili R., Zambia	56	17 15 S	25 0 E
Machiques, Venezuela	75	10 5N	72 30W
Machupicchu, Peru	78	13 2 S	72 50W
Macintyre R., N.S.W.	43	28 30 S	150 0 E
Mackay, Queensland	42	21 10 S	149 15 E
Mackay, U.S.A.	72	43 58N	113 32W
Mackay Div., Queens.	42	21 36 S	148 39 E
Mackenzie, Guyana	79	5 58N	58 28W
Mackenzie, terr., Can.	64	61 30N	114 30W
Mackenzie R., Canada	64	67 0N	130 30W
Mackenzie, R., Queens.	42	23 0 S	149 0 E
Mackenzie Mts., Can.	64	63 0N	131 0W
Mackenzie Plains, N.Z.	47	44 10 S	170 25 E
Mackenzie Red L., Can.	65	51 0N	93 30W
Mackinac, Straits of, U.S.A.	68	45 50N	84 40W
Mackinaw City, U.S.A.	68	45 45N	84 41W
Mackinnon Road, Kenya	53	3 40 S	39 0 E
Mackintosh Ra., W. Australia	45	27 39 S	125 32 E
Macklin, Canada	65	52 25N	110 0W
Macksville, N.S.W.	43	30 40 S	152 56 E
Maclean, N.S.W.	43	29 26 S	153 16 E
Maclear, C. Province	57	31 2 S	28 23 E
Macleay R., N.S.W.	43	30 47 S	152 30 E
Macleod, Canada	64	49 45N	113 30W
Macloutsie, Botswana	56	2 0 S	28 27 E
Macloutsie R., Botswana	56	22 0 S	28 30 E
Macloutsi Siding, Botswana	56	21 25 S	27 25 E
Macoduene, Mozam.	56	23 50 S	35 6 E
Macomb, U.S.A.	68	40 25N	90 40W
Macomer, Italy	20	40 16N	8 48 E
Mâcon, France	12	46 19N	4 50 E
Macon, Ga., U.S.A.	69	32 50N	83 45W
Macon, Miss., U.S.A.	70	33 4N	88 31W
Macon, Mo., U.S.A.	69	39 40N	92 26W
Macondo, Angola	56	12 40 S	23 48 E
Macossa, Mozambique	56	17 52 S	33 56 E
Macovane, Mozam.	56	22 40 S	34 10 E
Macquarie Harb., Tas.	43	42 18 S	145 25 E
Macquarie I., S. Ocean	80	55 0 S	160 0 E
Macquarie R., N.S.W.	43	21 0 S	147 31 E
Macquarie R., Tas.	43	41 45 S	147 15 E
Macroom, Ireland	11	51 54N	8 57W
Macuirima, Mozam.	56	19 14 S	35 5 E
Macuiza, Mozambique	56	18 0 S	34 28 E
Macusani, Peru	78	14 0 S	70 30W
Macuspana, Mexico	74	18 46N	92 36W
Madagali, Nigeria	25	10 56N	13 33 E
Macuspana, Mexico	74	18 46N	92 36W
Madain Salih, Saudi Arabia	30	26 50N	38 0 E
Madama, Niger	51	21 55N	13 45 E
Madame I., Canada	63	45 30N	60 58W
Madang, New Guinea	42	5 0 S	145 46 E
Madaoua, Niger	52	14 5N	6 27 E
Madara, Nigeria	52	11 45N	10 35 E
Madaripur, Bangladesh	33	23 2N	90 15 E
Madawaska, U.S.A.	69	44 30N	74 25W
Madawaska R., Canada	62	45 20N	77 30W
Madaya, Burma	33	22 20N	96 10 E
Maddalena I., Italy	20	41 15N	9 23 E
Maddaloni, Italy	20	41 4N	14 23 E
Madden Dam, Panama Canal Zone	74	9 13N	79 37W
Madden L., Pan. Can. Zone	74	9 20N	79 37W
Madeira Is., Atlantic	50	32 50N	17 0W
Madeira R., Brazil	78	5 30 S	61 20W
Madenda, Malawi	56	13 55 S	35 1 E
Madera, Mexico	74	29 20N	108 0W
Madera, U.S.A.	73	36 59N	120 1W
Madhupur, India	33	24 17N	86 38 E
Madhya Pradesh, st., India	32	21 50N	81 0 E
Madi Opei, Uganda	53	3 40N	33 0 E
Madibira, Tanzania	53	8 15 S	34 46 E
Madibogo, C. Prov.	57	26 25 S	25 10 E
Madidi R., Bolivia	78	13 0 S	68 0W
Madill, U.S.A.	71	34 4N	96 49W
Madimba, Zaire	54	5 0 S	15 0 E
Madinat al-Shaab, South Yemen	28	13 0N	45 0 E
Madinare, Botswana	56	21 57 S	27 52 E
Madingou, Congo (Fr.)	54	4 10 S	13 33 E
Madison, Ind., U.S.A.	68	38 42N	85 20W
Madison, Neb., U.S.A.	70	41 54N	97 26W
Madison, S.D., U.S.A.	70	44 0N	97 0W
Madison, Wis., U.S.A.	68	43 5N	89 25W
Madison R., U.S.A.	72	45 0N	112 0W

	MAP		
Madison Junction, U.S.A.	72	44 42N	110 49W
Madisonville, Ky., U.S.A.	68	37 20N	87 30W
Madisonville, Texas, U.S.A.	71	30 55N	95 48W
Madista, Botswana	56	20 55 S	25 8 E
Madiun, Indonesia	34	7 38 S	111 32 E
Mado, Somali Rep.	53	1 52N	41 40 E
Madona, Zambia	56	10 48 S	28 33 E
Madona, U.S.S.R.	23	56 53N	26 22 E
Madraka, Ras al, 'Oman	30	19 0N	57 45 E
Madras, India	32	13 8N	80 19 E
Madras, U.S.A.	72	44 35N	121 7W
Madre de Dios I., Chile	77	50 20 S	75 10W
Madre de Dios R., Bolivia	78	11 30 S	67 30W
Madre Occidental, Sierra, Mexico	74	27 0N	107 0W
Madre Oriental, Sierra, Mexico	74	25 0N	100 0W
Madrid, Spain	17	40 25N	3 45W
Madridejos, Spain	17	39 28N	3 33W
Madura I., Indonesia	34	7 0 S	113 20 E
Madura Selat, str., Indonesia	34	7 30 S	113 30 E
Madurai, India	32	9 55N	78 10 E
Maebashi, Japan	36	36 30N	139 0 E
Mafaza, Sudan	51	13 38N	34 30 E
Mafeking, Canada	65	52 40N	101 10W
Mafeking, C. Prov.	57	25 50 S	25 38 E
Mafeteng, Lesotho	57	29 48 S	27 18 E
Maffra, Victoria	43	37 53 S	146 58 E
Mafia I., Tanzania	53	7 50 S	39 48 E
Mafra, Brazil	77	26 10N	50 0W
Mafra, Portugal	17	38 55N	9 20W
Mafrense, Brazil	79	8 10 S	41 10W
Mafungabusi Plat., Rhodesia	56	18 30 S	29 8 E
Mafupa, Zambia	56	10 80 S	29 15 E
Magadan, U.S.S.R.	27	59 30N	151 0 E
Magadi, Kenya	54	1 55 S	36 20 E
Magaliesburg, Trans.	57	26 1 S	27 32 E
Magangué, Colombia	78	9 15N	74 45W
Magaria, Niger	52	14 9N	8 15 E
Magaria, Niger	52	12 59N	8 56 E
Magato Hills, Trans.	56	22 38 S	30 30 E
Magburaka, Sierra Leone	52	8 47N	12 0W
Magdalen Is., Canada	63	47 30N	61 40W
Magdalena, Argentina	77	35 5 S	57 30W
Magdalena, Bolivia	78	13 20 S	63 50W
Magdalena, Mexico	74	30 40N	110 50W
Magdalena, U.S.A.	73	34 10N	107 52W
Magdalena B., Mexico	74	24 30N	112 10W
Magdalena R., Col.	78	9 0N	74 20 E
Magdalena R., Mexico	74	30 50N	112 0W
Magdeburg, Germany	14	52 8N	11 36 E
Magdiel, Israel	29	32 10N	34 54 E
Magee, U.S.A.	71	31 51N	89 46W
Magee I., N. Ireland	11	54 48N	5 44W
Magelang, Indonesia	34	7 29 S	110 13 E
Magellan's Str., Chile	77	57 40 S	75 0W
Maggia R., Switzerland	15	46 18N	8 36 E
Maggiore L., N. Italy–Switzerland	20	46 0N	8 35 E
Maghar, Israel	29	32 54N	35 24 E
Magherafelt, N. Ireland	11	54 44N	6 37W
Magiscatzin, Mexico	74	22 40N	98 50W
Magnet, Tasmania	43	41 26 S	145 22 E
Magnetawan R., Can.	62	80N	45 40W
Magnetic I., Queensland	42	19 8 S	146 43 E
Magnetic N. Pole (1960)	80	74 9N	101 0W
Magnetic S. Pole (1960)	80	67 1 S	142 7 E
Magnitogorsk, U.S.S.R.	24	53 20N	59 0 E
Magnolia, Miss., U.S.A.	71	31 13N	90 29W
Magnolia, Ark., U.S.A.	71	33 15N	93 16W
Magoari, C., Brazil	79	0 25 S	48 20W
Magog, Canada	63	45 18N	72 9W
Magoro, Uganda	53	1 43N	34 7 E
Magoye, Zambia	56	16 0 S	27 35 E
Magpie L., Canada	56	51 0N	64 40W
Magrath, Canada	64	49 25N	112 50W
Magude, Mozambique	57	25 2 S	32 40 E
Magüe, Mozambique	56	15 43 S	31 40 E
Maguse L., Canada	65	61 35N	95 20W
Maguse Pt., Canada	65	61 20N	94 20W
Magwe, Burma	33	20 10N	95 0 E
Magwe, Sudan	53	4 8N	32 19 E
Mahābād, Iran	30	36 48N	45 45 E
Mahabaleshwar, India	32	17 56N	73 43 E
Mahad, India	32	18 5N	73 29 E
Mahagi, Zaire	53	2 16N	31 5 E
Mahaji Port, Zaire	53	2 9N	31 14 E
Mahakam R., Indonesia	35	1 0N	114 40 E
Mahalapye, Botswana	56	23 0 S	26 48 E
Mahallat, Iran	31	33 55N	50 30 E
Mahanadi R., India	33	20 33N	85 0 E
Mahanoro, Madagascar	55	19 58 S	48 50 E
Maharashtra, st., India	32	19 30N	76 0 E
Mahari Mts., Tan.	53	61 2 S	29 50 E
Mahave, Mozambique	56	21 4 S	35 0 E
Mahbubnagar, India	32	16 45N	77 59 E
Mahd Dhahab, Si. Arab.	30	23 33N	40 53 E
Mahdia, Tunisia	51	35 28N	11 0 E
Mahenge, Iringa, Tan.	53	7 39 S	36 16 E

	MAP		
Mahenge, Morogoro, Tan.	53	8 45 S	36 35 E
Maheno, New Zealand	47	45 10 S	170 50 E
Mahia Pen., N.Z.	46	39 9 S	177 55 E
Mahin, Nigeria	52	6 5N	4 51 E
Mahnomen, U.S.A.	70	47 24N	95 58W
Maho, Sri Lanka	32	7 45N	80 20 E
Mahoba, India	32	25 15N	79 55 E
Mahon, Spain	17	39 50N	4 18 E
Mahone Bay, Canada	63	44 30N	64 20W
Mahunda, Mozambique	53	11 41 S	39 30 E
Mahuta, Nigeria	52	11 32N	4 58 E
Mahuta, Tanzania	53	10 52 S	39 24 E
Mahuva, India	32	21 3N	71 50 E
Maia, Tanganyika	53	1 28 S	34 30 E
Maiama, Zambia	56	11 0 S	33 2 E
Maiawi L., East Africa	56	12 0 S	34 30 E
Maicurú R., Brazil	79	1 0 S	54 30W
Maidi, Yemen	30	16 20N	42 45 E
Maidstone, England	10	51 16N	0 31 E
Maiduguri, Nigeria	52	12 0N	13 20 E
Maie, Zaire	53	2 51N	30 30 E
Maigatari, Nigeria	52	12 51N	9 30 E
Maijdi (Noakhali), Bangladesh	33	22 48N	91 10 E
Maijirgui, Niger	52	13 49N	8 10 E
Maikala Range, India	32	22 0N	81 0 E
Maikop (Maykop), U.S.S.R.	25	44 35N	40 15 E
Maimana, Afghanistan	31	35 53N	64 38 E
Main, R., Germany	14	50 13N	11 0 E
Main, R., N. Ireland	11	54 49N	6 20W
Main Barrier Ra., N.S.W.	43	31 15 S	141 20 E
Main Centre, Canada	65	50 38N	107 20W
Maindombe, prov., Zaire	54	2 10 S	19 25 E
Maine, prov., France	12	48 0N	0 0 E
Maine, st., U.S.A.	69	45 20N	69 0W
Maine R., Ireland	11	52 10N	9 40W
Maingkwan, Burma	33	26 15N	96 45 E
Mainland, Orkney	10	59 0N	3 10W
Mainland, Shetland	10	60 15N	1 22W
Mainland, W. Australia	44	27 31 S	117 35 E
Mainpuri, India	32	27 18N	79 4 E
Maintenon, France	12	48 35N	1 35 E
Maintirano, Madag.	55	18 3 S	44 5 E
Mainz, Germany	14	50 0N	8 17 E
Maipo, Vol., Arg.–Chile	77	34 10 S	69 52W
Maipú, Argentina	77	37 0 S	58 0W
Mairabari, India	33	26 30N	92 30 E
Maisi, C., Cuba	15	20 10N	74 10W
Maison Carrée, Algeria	50	36 45N	3 5 E
Maitland, N.S.W.	43	32 44 S	151 36 E
Maitland, S. Australia	43	34 23 S	137 40 E
Maituru, Zaire	53	2 43N	29 49 E
Maiyema, Nigeria	52	12 5N	4 25 E
Maizuru, Japan	36	35 30N	135 24 E
Majavatn, Norway	22	65 10N	13 20 E
Majd el Kurum, Israel	29	32 56N	35 15 E
Majevica Mts., Y.slav.	21	44 45N	18 50 E
Maji, Ethiopia	54	6 20N	35 30 E
Majmaa, Saudi Arabia	30	25 57N	45 22 E
Major, Canada	65	51 52N	109 33W
Majorca I. *See* Mallorca	17		
Majunga, Madagascar	55	15 40 S	46 25 E
Maka Koulibentane, Senegal	52	13 40N	14 13W
Makaha, Rhodesia	56	17 17 S	32 35 E
Makak, Cameroon	52	3 36N	11 0 E
Makamba, Burundi	53	4 8 S	29 49 E
Makamic, Canada	62	48 46N	79 2W
Makanya, Tanzania	53	4 21 S	37 49 E
Makapuu Pt., Hawaiian Islands	59	21 18N	157 40W
Makarev, U.S.S.R.	25	57 55N	43 38 E
Makarewa, N.Z.	47	46 20 S	168 21 E
Makarikari Saltpan, Bech. Prot.	56	20 40 S	25 30 E
Makarovo, U.S.S.R.	27	57 40N	107 45 E
Makarska, Yugoslavia	20	43 20N	17 2 E
Makasar, Indonesia	35	5 10 S	119 20 E
Makasar, Str. of, Indon.	35	1 0 S	118 20 E
Makasuko, Tan.	53	6 0 S	34 58 E
Makat, U.S.S.R.	24	47 40N	53 0 E
Makeni, Sierra Leone	52	8 55N	12 5W
Makere, Tanzania	53	4 17 S	30 32 E
Makeyevka, U.S.S.R.	25	48 0N	38 0 E
Makachkala, U.S.S.R.	24	43 0N	47 15 E
Makimbo, Zaire	53	6 21 S	28 3 E
Makindu, Kenya	53	2 7 S	37 40 E
Makovik, Canada	63	55 0N	59 10W
Makó, Hungary	16	46 14N	20 33 E
Makokou, Gabon	54	0 40N	12 50 E
Makoli, Zambia	56	17 28 S	26 5 E
Makongolosi, Tan.	53	8 25 S	33 19 E
Makoro, Zaire	53	3 7N	29 58 E
Makoua, Congo, (Fr.)	54	0 5 S	15 50 E
Maków, Poland	16	49 43N	19 45 E
Makrai, India	32	22 3N	78 10 E
Makran, dist., Iran	31	26 15N	61 30 E
Makran Coast Ra., W. Pakistan	32	25 30N	64 0 E
Maksimki Yar, U.S.S.R.	26	58 50N	86 50 E
Maktau, Kenya	53	3 27 S	37 58 E
Makuliro, Tanzania	53	9 36 S	37 33 E
Maku, Iran	31	39 15N	44 31 E

	MAP		
Makumbako, Tan.	53	8 49 S	34 47 E
Makumbi, Zaire	54	5 50 S	20 44 E
Makurdi, Nigeria	52	7 43N	8 28 E
Makuyuni, Tan.	53	5 0 S	38 20 E
Makwassie, Transvaal	57	27 17 S	26 0 E
Makwende, Zaire	53	7 8 S	28 5 E
Makwiro, Rhodesia	56	17 58 S	30 28 E
Mal B., Ireland	11	52 50N	9 30W
Mala Pta., Panama	75	7 30N	80 0W
Malabar Coast, India	32	11 0N	75 0 E
Malabu, Nigeria	52	9 29N	12 41 E
Malacca, Malaya	34	2 15N	102 15 E
Malacca Str., Indon.	34	3 0N	101 0 E
Malacoota Inlet, Vic.	42	37 35 S	149 64 E
Malad City, U.S.A.	72	42 10N	112 20W
Maladetta, mts., Spain	17	42 40N	0 30 E
Malaga, Spain	17	36 43N	4 23W
Malagarasi R., Tan.	53	5 0 S	30 52 E
Malagasy Rep. (Madag.) Africa	55	19 0S	46 0 E
Malagón, Spain	17	39 11N	3 51W
Malagu, U.S.A.	71	32 13N	104 1W
Malahide, Ireland	11	53 26N	6 10W
Malakal, Sudan	51	9 33N	31 50 E
Malakand, Pakistan	32	34 40N	71 55 E
Malakoff, U.S.A.	71	32 9N	95 58W
Malakwa, Canada	64	50 55N	118 50W
Malamyzh, U.S.S.R.	27	50 0N	136 50 E
Malan, Indonesia	34	1 55 S	110 10 E
Malang, Indonesia	34	7 59 S	112 35 E
Malangali, Tanzania	53	8 30 S	34 45 E
Malangwa, Nepal	33	26 55N	85 30 E
Malanje, Angola	35	9 30 S	16 20 E
Malanville, Dahomey	52	11 57N	3 25 E
Malaren, L., Sweden	23	59 30N	17 10 E
Malargüe, Argentina	77	35 40 S	69 30W
Malartic, Canada	62	48 9N	78 9W
Malatya, Turkey	30	38 25N	38 20 E
Malawi (Nyasaland), rep., E. Afr.	55	13 0 S	34 0 E
Malay Peninsula, S.E. Asia	34	7 0N	100 0 E
Malaya, S.E. Asia	34	4 0N	102 0 E
Malaya Vishera, U.S.S.R.	25	58 55N	32 25 E
Malaybalay, Philippines	35	8 5N	125 15 E
Malayer, Iran	30	28 22N	56 38 E
Malaysia, Federation of	34	5 23N	110 0 E
Malazgirt, Turkey	30	39 10N	42 33 E
Malbaza, Niger	52	13 58N	5 28 E
Malbon, Queensland	42	21 5 S	140 17 E
Malbork, Poland	16	54 3N	19 10 E
Malbooma, S. Australia	45	30 42 S	134 9 E
Malchin, Germany	14	53 43N	12 44 E
Malcolm Pt., Australia	45	33 45 S	123 42 E
Maldegem, Belgium	13	51 14N	3 26 E
Malden, U.S.A.	71	36 32N	89 59W
Malden I., Pacific Ocean	5	4 3N	155 1W
Maldive Is., Ind. Oc.	5	6 50N	73 0 E
Maldon, England	10	51 43N	0 41 E
Maldonado, Uruguay	77	35 0 S	55 0W
Maldonado, Pta., Mex.	74	16 19N	98 35W
Malea C., Greece	21	36 23N	23 17 E
Malegaon, India	32	20 30N	74 30 E
Malendo, R., Nigeria	52	10 50N	5 15 E
Malenge, Zambia	56	12 40 S	26 42 E
Malgobek, U.S.S.R.	25	43 30N	44 52 E
Malgomaj L., Sweden	22	64 40N	16 30 E
Malgorou, Niger	52	12 10N	3 38 E
Malha, Sudan	51	15 5N	26 10 E
Malheur, L., U.S.A.	72	43 19N	118 50W
Malheur, R., U.S.A.	72	43 50N	117 50W
Mali, Rep. of, Africa	50	17 0N	4 0W
Mali, R., Burma	33	26 30N	97 30 E
Malimba Mts., Zaire	53	7 46 S	29 40 E
Malin Hd., Ireland	11	55 23N	7 20W
Malin R., Jordan	29	32 20N	35 29 E
Malinau, Indonesia	35	3 35N	116 30 E
Malindi, Kenya	53	3 10 S	40 0 E
Malingping, Indonesia	34	6 45 S	106 2 E
Malinyi, Tanzania	53	8 55 S	36 0 E
Malka Morris, Ethiopia	53	4 23N	38 58 E
Malkinia, Poland	16	52 42N	21 58 E
Mallaha, Israel	29	33 6N	35 35 E
Mallaig, Scotland	10	57 0N	5 50W
Mallaranny, Ireland	11	53 55N	9 48W
Mallawa, Niger	52	13 0N	9 32 E
Mallawi, Egypt	51	27 44N	30 44 E
Mallee, dist., Victoria	43	35 10 S	142 20 E
Mallina, W. Australia	44	20 48 S	118 0 E
Mallorca I., Balearic Is.	17	39 30N	3 0 E
Mallow, Ireland	11	52 8N	8 40W
Malmberget, Sweden	22	67 11N	20 40 E
Malmédy, Belgium	13	50 25N	6 2 E
Malmesbury, C. Prov.	57	33 28 S	18 41 E
Malmö, Sweden	23	55 33N	13 8 E
Malmöhus, co., Sweden	23	55 45N	13 25 E
Malmyzh, U.S.S.R.	25	56 35N	50 30 E
Maloarkhangelsk, U.S.S.R.	25	52 28N	36 30 E
Maloja P., Switzerland	15	46 23N	9 40 E
Malolo, Mozambique	53	5 25 S	36 38 E
Malombe L., Malawi	56	14 50 S	35 30 E
Malone, U.S.A.	68	44 50N	74 19W
Malonga, Zaire	56	10 25 S	23 5 E
Malonga Funga, Zaire	56	11 5 S	25 30 E

	MAP		
Maloyaroslavets, U.S.S.R.	25	55 2N	36 20 E
Malpura, India	32	26 25N	75 30 E
Malsambo, Mozam.	56	23 25S	32 30 E
Malta, Idaho, U.S.A.	72	42 16N	113 25W
Malta, Mont., U.S.A.	72	48 20N	107 47W
Malta I., Mediterranean	18	35 50N	14 30 E
Maltahöhe, S.W. Africa	57	24 45S	17 2 E
Malte Brun, mt., N.Z.	47	43 36S	170 22 E
Malua, Indonesia	34	2 55N	110 55 E
Malum Maja, Nigeria	52	12 0N	14 6 E
Malumfashi, Nigeria	52	11 48N	7 39 E
Malung, Sweden	23	60 38N	13 50 E
Maluwe, Ghana	52	8 48N	2 15W
Malvan, India	32	16 2N	73 30 E
Malvern, U.S.A.	71	34 21N	92 49W
Malvern Hills, Queens.	42	24 30S	145 8 E
Maly I., U.S.S.R.	27	74 20N	140 30 E
Malya, Tanzania	53	3 5S	33 38 E
Mam Soul, Mt., Scot.	10	57 17N	5 11W
Mamainse Pt., Canada	62	47 4N	84 43W
Mamaku, New Zealand	46	38 5S	176 8 E
Mamanguape, Brazil	79	6 50S	35 4W
Mambali, Tanzania	53	4 30S	32 40 E
Mambasa, Zaire	53	1 24N	28 59 E
Mambirima, Zaire	56	11 27S	27 40 E
Mambrui, Kenya	53	3 8S	40 8 E
Mameigwess L., Canada	62	52 50N	88 0W
Mamers, France	12	48 21N	0 22 E
Mamfe, W. Cameroon	52	5 50N	9 15 E
Mamilis, S.W. Africa	56	18 2S	24 0 E
Mammamattawa, Can.	62	50 25N	84 23W
Mammoth, U.S.A.	73	32 44N	110 39W
Mamoi, China	39	26 0N	119 25 E
Mamoré R., Bolivia	78	12 30S	65 20W
Mamou, Guinea	50	10 15N	12 0W
Mampawah, Indonesia	34	0 30N	109 5 E
Mampong, Ghana	52	7 6N	1 26W
Mamrey, L., Poland	16	54 10W	21 40 E
Mamudju, Indonesia	35	2 50S	118 50 E
Man, Ivory Coast	50	7 30N	7 40W
Man, I. of, British Isles	10	54 15N	4 30W
Mana, French Guiana	79	5 45N	53 55W
Mana, Hawaiian Is.	59	22 3N	159 46W
Mana, Indonesia	34	4 25S	102 55 E
Mana R., Fr. Guiana	79	4 30N	53 30W
Mannar, G. of, India	32	8 20N	79 0 E
Manacapuru, Brazil	78	3 10S	60 50W
Manacor, Spain	17	39 32N	3 12 E
Manado, Indonesia	35	1 40N	124 45 E
Managua, Nicaragua	78	12 0N	86 20W
Manaia, New Zealand	46	39 33S	174 8 E
Manakara, Madagascar	55	22 5S	48 5 E
Manakau, N.Z.	46	37 1S	174 55 E
Manama, Bahrain I.	31	26 11N	50 35 E
Manamadurai, India	32	9 40N	78 25 E
Mañana, Panama	78	9 10N	78 0W
Manajary, Madagascar	55	21 10S	48 28 E
Manankon, Sierra Leone	52		Inset
Manapire R., Venezuela	78	8 35N	66 10W
Manapouri, N.Z.	47	45 34S	167 39 E
Manapouri., L., N.Z.	47	45 32S	167 32 E
Manas R., Bhutan	33	26 50N	91 0 E
Manass, China	37	3 0S	60 0W
Manassa, U.S.A.	73	37 14N	105 57W
Manawan L., Canada	65	55 35N	103 20W
Mancelona, U.S.A.	68	44 54N	85 5W
Mancha, dist., Spain	17	39 5N	2 40W
Mancha Real, Spain	17	37 48N	3 39W
Manchester, Bolivia	72	11 30S	68 10W
Manchester, England	10	53 30N	2 15W
Manchester, Conn., U.S.A.	68	41 47N	72 34W
Manchester, Iowa, U.S.A.	70	42 27N	91 28W
Manchester, Ky., U.S.A.	68	37 10N	83 45W
Manchester, N.H., U.S.A.	68	43 0N	71 25W
Manchester, L., Can.	65	61 35N	106 0W
Manchouli, China	65	49 40N	117 40 E
Mand R., Iran	31	28 20N	52 30 E
Manda, Mbeya, Tang.	53	7 58S	32 26 E
Manda, Mbeya, Tang.	53	8 33S	32 38 E
Manda, Iringa, Tang.	53	10 30S	34 40 E
Mandal, Norway	23	58 2N	7 25 E
Mandal Gobi, Mon.	66	45 40N	106 10 E
Mandalay, Burma	33	22 0N	96 10 E
Mandali, Iraq.	30	33 52N	45 28 E
Mandan, U.S.A.	70	46 50N	101 0W
Mandasor (Mandsauz) India	32	24 5N	75 5 E
Mandeka, S. W. Afr.	56	17 55S	23 42 E
Mandera, Tanzania	53	6 14S	38 28 E
Mandi, India	32	31 39N	76 58 E
Mandi, Zambia	56	14 30S	24 45 E
Mandi Dabwali, India	32	29 50N	74 35 E
Mandie, Mozambique	56	16 28S	33 31 E
Mandih, Philippines	35	8 10N	123 5 E
Mandimba, Mozam.	56	14 20S	35 40 E
Mandinga, Panama	78	9 30N	79 5W
Mandjane, Mozam.	56	15 8S	33 15 E
Mandla, India	32	22 39N	80 30 E
Mandra, W. Pakistan	32	33 24N	73 16 E
Mandra Mt., Rumania	21	45 20N	23 37 E
Mandsaur (Mandasor) India	32	24 5N	75 5 E
Mandurah, W. Austral.	44	32 36S	115 48 E
Manduria, Italy	21	40 25N	17 38 E
Mandvi, India	32	22 51N	69 22 E
Mandya, India	32	12 30N	77 0 E
Manengouba, Mts., W. Cameroon	52	5 0N	9 45 E
Maneromango, Tan.	53	7 10S	38 51 E
Manfalût, Egypt	51	27 20N	30 52 E
Manfredonia, Italy	20	41 40N	15 55 E
Manfredonia, G. of, Italy	20	41 30N	16 10 E
Mangabeiras, Chapa da das, Brazil	79	10 0S	46 30W
Mangakino, N.Z.	46	38 22S	175 46 E
Mangalia, Rumania	21	43 48N	28 36 E
Mangalore, India	33	12 55N	74 47 E
Mangalore, Queens.	43	26 40S	146 5 E
Mangaweka, N.Z.	46	39 50S	175 49 E
Mangaweka, mt., N.Z.	46	39 52S	176 0 E
Mangin Range, Mts., Burma	33	24 15N	95 45 E
Mangkalihat, C., Indonesia	35	1 0N	119 0 E
Mangla Dam, W. Pak.,	32	33 5N	73 40 E
Mangole I., Indonesia	35	1 50S	125 55 E
Mangonui, N.Z.	46	35 1S	173 32 E
Mangualde, Portugal	17	40 38N	7 48W
Mangueira, L., Brazil	77	33 0S	52 50W
Mangum, U.S.A.	71	34 50N	99 30W
Mangyai, China	37	37 52N	91 26 E
Mangyshlak Pen., U.S.S.R.	26	43 40N	52 30 E
Manhao, China	34	23 0N	103 20 E
Manhattan, Kans., U.S.A.	70	39 10N	96 40W
Manhattan, Nev., U.S.A.	73	38 32N	117 4W
Manhica, Mozambique	57	25 23S	32 49 E
Manhongo, Angola	55	12 10S	18 38 E
Manhauçu, Brazil	79	20 20S	42 10W
Maniamba, Mozam.	56	12 49S	35 0 E
Manica e Sofala, dist., Mozambique	56	19 0S	33 45 E
Manicoré, Brazil	78	6 0S	61 10W
Manicouagan L. & R., Canada	63	51 25N	68 15W
Maniema, prov., Zaire	54	3 40S	26 0 E
Manifah, Si. Arabia	30	27 33N	48 55 E
Manifold C., Queens.	42	22 40S	150 50 E
Manigotagan, Canada	65	51 7N	96 19W
Manigotagan R., Can.	65	51 0N	96 0W
Manihiki I., Pac. Oc.	5	10 24S	161 1W
Manika (Biano), Plat., Zaire	56	9 55S	26 24 E
Manikpur, India	33	25 4N	81 6 E
Manila, Philippines	35	14 40N	121 3 E
Manila, U.S.A.	72	41 0N	109 41W
Manila B., Philippines	35	14 0N	120 3 E
Manilla, N.S.W.	43	30 45S	150 40 E
Manipur R., Burma	33	23 45N	93 40 E
Manipur, st., India	33	24 30N	94 0 E
Maniquira, Colombia	78	6 0N	73 40W
Manisa, Turkey	30	38 38N	27 30 E
Manistique, U.S.A.	68	45 59N	86 18W
Manistree, U.S.A.	68	44 15N	86 20W
Manito L., Canada	65	52 40N	109 40W
Manitoba, prov., Can.	65	55 30N	97 0W
Manitoba L., Canada	65	50 40N	98 30W
Manitou, Canada	65	49 20N	98 40W
Manitou Is., U.S.A.	68	45 8N	86 0W
Manitou L., Canada	63	50 55N	65 17W
Manitou Springs, U.S.A.	70	38 54N	104 56W
Manitoulin I., Canada	62	45 40N	82 30W
Manitowaning B., Can.	62	45 50N	81 48W
Manitowoc, U.S.A.	68	44 8N	87 40W
Manizales, Columbia	78	5 10N	75 30W
Manjacaze, Mozam.	55	24 47S	33 50 E
Manjhand, Pakistan	32	25 50N	68 10 E
Manjil, Iran	30	36 46N	49 30 E
Manjimup, Australia	44	34 15S	116 6 E
Manjra, R., India	32	18 0N	77 40 E
Mankaiana, Swaziland	57	26 38S	31 6 E
Mankato, Kans., U.S.A.	70	39 49N	98 9W
Mankato, Minn., U.S.A.	68	44 8N	93 59W
Mankim, Cameroon	52	5 1N	12 2 E
Mankono, Ivory Coast	50	8 10N	6 10W
Mankota, Canada	65	49 25N	107 5W
Mankoya, Zambia	55	14 58S	24 57 E
Mankulam, Sri Lanka	32	9 5N	80 30 E
Manly, N.S.W.	43	33 46S	151 14 E
Manmad, India	32	20 18N	74 28 E
Manna Hill, S. Austral.	43	32 26S	139 58 E
Mannar, Sri Lanka	32	9 1N	79 54 E
Mannheim, Germany	14	49 28N	8 29 E
Manning, Canada	64	56 53N	117 39W
Manning, U.S.A.	69	33 42N	80 12W
Manning, China	39	18 45N	110 28 E
Manning Prov. Park, Canada	64	49 9N	120 50W
Manning R., N.S.W.	43	31 50S	152 40 E
Mannington, U.S.A.	68	39 35N	80 25W
Mannu (Samassi) R., Italy	20	39 20N	8 30 E
Mannum, S. Australia	43	34 50S	139 17 E
Mano, Sierra Leone	52		Inset
Mano R., Sierra Leone	52		Inset
Manoel Alves R., Brazil	79	11 30S	46 30W
Manokware, Indonesia	35	0 50S	134 5 E
Manono, Zaire	54	7 15S	27 20 E
Manorhamilton, Ireland	11	54 19N	8 10W
Manosque, France	12	43 49N	5 47 E
Manovane R. and L., Canada	63	50 45N	70 45W
Manpo, N. Korea	36	41 8N	126 21 E
Manresa, Spain	17	41 48N	1 50 E
Mansa, Zambia	56	11 10S	28 50 E
Mansel I., Canada	61	62 0N	80 0W
Mansfield, England	10	53 8N	1 12W
Mansfield, Ohio, U.S.A.	68	40 45N	82 30W
Mansfield, La., U.S.A.	71	32 1N	93 44W
Mansfield, Wash., U.S.A.	72	47 50N	119 40W
Mansfield, Victoria	43	37 0S	146 0 E
Manso (Mortes) R., Brazil	79	16 0S	52 30W
Manson, Cr., Canada	64	55 37N	124 25W
Manta, Ecuador	78	1 0S	80 40W
Mantalingajan, Mt., Philippines	35	8 55N	117 45 E
Mantare, Tanzania	53	2 41S	33 12 E
Mantaro R., Peru	78	11 45S	75 45W
Manteca, U.S.A.	73	37 48N	121 13W
Manteo, U.S.A.	69	35 55N	75 41W
Mantes, France	12	48 59N	1 43 E
Manthani, India	32	18 40N	79 40 E
Manti, U.S.A.	73	39 10N	111 40W
Mantiqueira, Sa da, Brazil	77	22 25S	45 0W
Manton, U.S.A.	68	44 23N	85 25W
Mantova (Mantua), Italy	20	45 9N	10 48 E
Mänttä, Finland	23	62 0N	24 40 E
Mantua (Mantova), Italy	20	45 9N	10 48 E
Manturova, U.S.S.R.	24	58 10N	44 30 E
Manu, Peru	78	12 10S	71 0W
Manu R., Peru	78	12 20S	70 40W
Manui I., Indonesia	35	3 35S	123 5 E
Manuk I., Indonesia	35	5 40S	130 20 E
Manukau Harbour, New Zealand	46	37 3S	174 45 E
Manulla, Ireland	11	53 50N	9 10W
Manunui, New Zealand	46	38 54S	175 21 E
Manus I., Terr. of New Guinea	42	2 10S	147 0 E
Manville, U.S.A.	70	42 49N	104 42W
Manwat, India	32	19 20N	76 32 E
Many, U.S.A.	71	31 34N	93 29W
Many Peaks, Queens.	42	24 32S	151 25 E
Manyani, Kenya	53	3 4S	38 30 E
Manyara L., Tanzania	53	3 30S	36 0 E
Manych R., U.S.S.R.	25	47 0N	41 15 E
Manyonga R., Tanzania	53	4 0S	34 0 E
Manyoni, Tanzania	54	5 50S	34 57 E
Manzai, Pakistan	32	32 20N	70 15 E
Manzanares, Spain	17	39 0N	32 2W
Manzanillo, Cuba	75	20 20N	77 10W
Manzanillo, Mexico	74	19 0N	104 20W
Manzanillo, Pta., Panama	75	9 30N	79 40W
Manzano Mts., U.S.A.	73	34 15N	106 35W
Manzini (Bremersdorp), Swaziland	57	26 30S	31 25 E
Mao, Chad	51	14 4N	15 19 E
Mapai, Mozambique	56	22 55S	31 50 E
Mapanza, Zambia	56	16 15S	26 56 E
Mapari, R., Brazil	79	1 10N	52 30W
Mapia Is., Indonesia	35	0 50N	134 20 E
Mapimi, Mexico	74	25 50N	103 31W
Mapinhane, Mozam.	56	22 19S	35 3 E
Maple Creek, Canada	65	49 50N	109 25W
Mapleton, U.S.A.	72	44 3N	123 58W
Maplewood, U.S.A.	70	38 34N	90 15W
Mapuera R., Brazil	78	0 30S	58 25W
Mapulanguene, Mozambique	57	24 29S	32 6 E
Maqna, Saudi Arabia	30	28 25N	34 50 E
Maquela do Zombo, Angola	54	6 0S	15 15 E
Maquinchao, Argentina	77	41 15S	68 50W
Maquoketa, U.S.A.	70	42 3N	90 4W
Mar Chiquita, L., Arg.	77	30 30S	62 30W
Mar del Plata, Arg.	77	38 0S	57 30W
Mar Menor L., Spain	17	37 40N	0 45W
Mar Muerto, Mexico	74	94 4N	16 10W
Mar, Sa. do, Brazil	77	27 0S	50 0W
Mara, Kenya	53	1 6S	35 13 E
Mara, prov., Tanzania	53	1 45S	34 10 E
Mara, Venezuela	78	10 52N	71 53W
Mara R., Tanzania	53	1 30S	34 30 E
Marabá, Brazil	79	5 20S	49 5W
Maracá I., Amapa, Brazil	79	2 10N	50 30W
Maraca I., Rio Branco, Brazil	78	3 30N	61 40W
Maracaibo, Venezuela	78	10 37N	71 45W
Maracaibo, L., Ven.	78	9 20N	71 30W
Maracay, Venezuela	78	10 20N	67 35W
Maradah, Libya	51	29 20N	19 22 E
Maradi, Niger	52	13 35N	8 10 E
Maradun, Nigeria	52	12 35N	6 18 E
Maragheh, Iran	30	37 30N	46 12 E
Marajo I., Brazil	79	1 0S	49 30W
Maraku, Nigeria	52	10 44N	8 43 E
Maralal, Kenya	53	1 0N	36 38 E
Maralinga, S. Austral.	45	29 10S	131 15 E
Marana, U.S.A.	73	32 30N	111 16W
Marand, Iran	30	38 30N	45 45 E
Marandellas, Rhod.	56	18 5S	31 42 E
Maranguape, Brazil	79	3 55S	38 50W
Maranhão. *See* São Luis	79		
Maranhão, st., Brazil	79	5 0S	46 0W
Maranoa R., Queens.	43	27 10S	148 5 E
Marañon R., Peru	79	4 50S	75 35W
Marampa, Sierra Leone	52		Inset
Mararui, Kenya	53	1 58S	41 20 E
Maras, Turkey	30	37 37N	36 53 E
Marathon, Canada	62	48 44N	86 23W
Marathon, Queensland	42	20 51S	143 32 E
Marathon, N.Y., U.S.A.	69	42 35N	76 3W
Marathon, Texas, U.S.A.	71	30 11N	103 13W
Maratua I., Indonesia	35	2 10N	118 35 E
Marbella, Spain	17	36 30N	4 57W
Marble Bar, Western Australia	44	21 9S	119 44 E
Marble Falls, U.S.A.	71	30 32N	98 15W
Marble Hall, Transvaal	57	24 59S	29 21 E
Marbleton, Canada	63	45 36N	71 35W
Marburg, Germany	14	50 49N	8 44 E
Marche, Belgium	13	50 14N	5 20 E
Marche, prov., France	12	46 0N	1 20 E
Marchena, Spain	17	37 18N	5 23W
Marches, reg., Italy	20	43 22N	13 10 E
Mardan, Pakistan	32	34 15N	72 0 E
Mardin, Turkey	30	37 20N	40 36 E
Maree L., Scotland	10	57 40N	5 30W
Mareeba, Queensland	42	16 59S	145 28 E
Mareetsane, C. Prov.	57	26 9S	25 25 E
Maremma, reg., Italy	20	43 0N	10 30 E
Marengo, U.S.A.	70	41 42N	92 5W
Marennes, France	12	45 49N	1 5W
Marenyi, Kenya	53	4 13S	39 0 E
Marettimo, I., Italy	20	37 58N	12 5 E
Marfa, U.S.A.	71	30 15N	104 0W
Margaree Harbour, Canada	63	46 26N	61 8W
Margaret, mt., Western Australia	44	21 58S	117 48 E
Margaret Bay, Canada	64	51 20N	127 20W
Margarita I., Venezuela	78	11 0N	64 0W
Margate, England	10	51 23N	1 24 E
Margate, Natal	57	30 50S	30 20 E
Marguerite, Canada	64	52 30N	122 15W
Marguerite R., Canada	63	51 0N	67 0W
Mari, A.S.S.R. U.S.S.R.,	26	56 30N	48 0 E
Maria, I., N. Terr.	41	14 50S	135 55 E
Maria I., Tasmania	43	42 35S	148 0 E
Maria Kani, Kenya	53	3 52S	39 29 E
Maria van Diemen, C., New Zealand	46	34 29S	172 40 E
Mariana, Brazil	79	20 20S	43 20W
Mariana Is., Pac. Oc.	5	17 0N	145 0 E
Marianna, Ark., U.S.A.	71	35 47N	904 7W
Marianna, Florida, U.S.A.	69	30 45N	85 15W
Marias, R., U.S.A.	72	48 15N	112 0W
Mariato, Pta., Panama	75	7 12N	80 52W
Maribo, Denmark	23	54 48N	11 30 E
Maribor, Yugoslavia	20	46 36N	15 40 E
Maricopa, Arizona U.S.A.	73	33 7N	112 4W
Maricopa, California U.S.A.	73	35 4N	119 27W
Marie R., Brazil	78	0 45S	67 30W
Marie Galante I., W. Indies	75	16 0N	61 20W
Mariehamn. *See* Maarianhamina	23		
Marienberg, Neth.	13	52 30N	6 35 E
Marienberg, Terr. of New Guinea	42	3 54S	144 10 E
Mariental, S.W. Afr.	57	24 35S	18 0 E
Mariestad, Sweden	23	58 42N	13 55 E
Marietta, Ga., U.S.A.	69	34 0N	84 30W
Marietta, Ohio, U.S.A.	68	39 27N	81 27W
Mariga R., Nigeria	52	10 9N	6 0 E
Marigot, Leeward Is.	75		Inset
Marilia, Brazil	77	22 0S	50 0W
Marin, Spain	17	42 23N	8 41W
Marine City, U.S.A.	68	42 45N	82 29W
Marinette, Ariz., U.S.A.	73	33 36N	112 18W
Marinette, Wis., U.S.A.	70	45 4N	87 40W
Maringa, Brazil	77	23 25S	52 8W
Maringüé, Mozam.	56	17 55S	34 24 E
Marinha Grande, Port.	17	39 46N	8 56W
Marion, Ala., U.S.A.	69	32 33N	87 20W
Marion, Ill., U.S.A.	71	37 45N	88 50W
Marion, Ind., U.S.A.	68	40 35N	85 40W
Marion, Iowa, U.S.A.	70	42 2N	92 5W
Marion, Kans., U.S.A.	70	38 25N	97 1W
Marion, Ky., U.S.A.	68	37 20N	88 0W
Marion, Mich., U.S.A.	68	44 7N	85 8W
Marion, N.C., U.S.A.	69	35 42N	82 0W
Marion, Ohio, U.S.A.	68	40 38N	83 8W
Marion, S.C., U.S.A.	69	34 11N	79 22W
Marion, Va., U.S.A.	69	36 51N	81 29W

	MAP		
Mariposa, U.S.A.	73	37 30N	119 59W
Mariscal Estigarribia, Paraguay	78	22 25S	60 40W
Maritsa, R., Bulgaria	21	42 10N	24 0E
Mariuia River, N.Z.	47	42 5N	172 14E
Marjan, Afghanistan	31	32 8N	68 20E
Marked Tree, U.S.A.	71	35 32N	90 28W
Marken, Netherlands	13	52 26N	5 6E
Markham L., Canada	65	62 30N	102 35W
Markham Mts., Ant.	80	83 0S	160 0E
Markham, R., N. Guin.	42	6 30S	146 25E
Marks, U.S.S.R.	25	51 45N	46 50E
Marksville, U.S.A.	71	31 7N	92 1W
Marlborough, Guyana	78	2 45N	58 26W
Marlborough, N.Z.	47	41 45S	173 33E
Marlborough, Queens.	42	22 46S	149 52E
Marlin, U.S.A.	71	31 25N	96 50W
Marlow, U.S.A.	71	34 39N	97 59W
Marmagao, Goa, India	32	15 25N	73 56E
Marmande, France	12	44 30N	0 10E
Marmara Denizi (Sea of Marmara), Turkey	30	40 40N	28 15E
Marmaris, Turkey	30	36 50N	28 14E
Marmarq I., Turkey	30	40 35N	27 50E
Marmath, U.S.A.	70	46 21N	103 52W
Marmion L., Canada	62	48 55N	91 30W
Marmion Mt., W. Australia	44	29 16S	119 50E
Marmoladá, Mte., Italy	20	46 25N	11 55E
Marmora, Canada	62	44 28N	77 41W
Maroni, R., Fr. Guiana	79	4 0N	52 0W
Maroochydore, Queens.	43	26 42S	153 5E
Maroona, Victoria	43	37 27S	142 54E
Maros, Indonesia	35	4 55S	114 30E
Maroua, Cameroon	52	10 40N	14 20E
Marquard, O.F.S.	57	28 40S	27 28E
Marquesas Is., Pac. Oc.	5	9 30S	140 0W
Marquette, U.S.A.	70	46 30N	87 30W
Marra Cr., N.S.W.	43	30 40S	147 12E
Marrakech, Morocco	50	31 40N	8 0W
Marrat, Saudi Arabia	30	23 6N	45 35E
Marree, S. Australia	43	29 39S	138 1E
Marrimane, Mozam.	56	22 57S	33 55E
Marromeu, Mozam.	55	18 40S	36 25E
Marrupa, Mozam.	55	13 10S	37 30E
Mars Hill, U.S.A.	69	46 32N	67 59W
Marsa Susa (Apollonia), Libya	51	32 50N	22 0E
Marsabit, Kenya	53	2 10N	37 50E
Marsala, Italy	20	37 48N	12 25E
Marsden, Canada	65	52 51N	109 50W
Marseilles, France	12	43 18N	5 23E
Marshall, Ark., U.S.A.	71	35 51N	92 40W
Marshall, Minn., U.S.A.	70	44 27N	95 47W
Marshall, Miss., U.S.A.	70	39 8N	93 15W
Marshall, Tex., U.S.A.	71	32 29N	94 20W
Marshall, Liberia	50	6 8N	10 22W
Marshall Is., Pac. Oc.	5	9 0N	171 0E
Marshalltown, U.S.A.	70	42 0N	93 0W
Marshbrook, Rhodesia	56	18 33S	31 9E
Marshfield, Mo., U.S.A.	71	37 24N	92 59W
Marshfield, Wis., U.S.A.	70	44 39N	90 6W
Marstrand, Sweden	23	57 53N	11 35E
Marsupe R., Botswana	56	20 45S	26 35E
Mart, U.S.A.	71	31 33N	96 48W
Martaban, Burma	33	16 30N	97 35E
Martaban, G. of, Burma	33	15 40N	96 30E
Marte, Nigeria	52	12 23N	13 46E
Martelange, Belgium	13	49 49N	5 43E
Martha's Vineyard, U.S.A.	69	41 25N	70 35W
Martigny-Ville, Switz.	15	46 6N	7 3E
Martigues, France	12	43 24N	5 4E
Martin, S.D., U.S.A.	70	43 14N	101 44W
Martin, Tenn., U.S.A.	71	36 23N	88 51W
Martin L., U.S.A.	69	32 45N	85 50W
Martina Franca, Italy	21	40 42N	17 20E
Martinborough, N.Z.	46	41 14S	175 29E
Martinique, I., Fr. W. Indies	75	14 40N	61 0W
Martinique Pass., W. Indies	75	15 15N	61 0W
Martins-Fy., U.S.A.	68	40 7N	80 45W
Martinsburg, U.S.A.	68	39 30N	77 57W
Martinsville, Ind., U.S.A.	68	39 29N	86 23W
Martinsville, Va., U.S.A.	69	36 41N	79 52W
Marton, New Zealand	46	40 4S	175 23E
Martorell, Spain	17	41 29N	1 56E
Mártos, Spain	17	37 44N	3 58W
Maru, Nigeria	52	12 22N	6 22E
Marudi, Sarawak	35	4 10N	114 25E
Maruf, Afghanistan	31	31 30N	67 0E
Marugame, Japan	36	34 25N	133 56E
Marunga, Zambia	56	14 30S	23 11E
Marungu, Mt., Zaire	53	7 55S	29 52E
Marvejols, France	12	44 33N	3 19E
Marvel Lock, W. Australia	44	31 23S	119 25E
Marvine, mt., U.S.A.	73	38 40N	111 31W
Marwar, India	32	25 45N	73 35E
Mary, U.S.S.R.	26	37 40N	61 50E
Mary R., Queensland	43	26 10S	152 28E
Mary Frances L., Can.	65	63 30N	106 20W
Mary Henry Mt., Can.	64	58 30N	124 30W
Mary Kathleen, Queensland	42	20 35S	139 48E
Maryborough, Queens.	43	25 31S	152 37E
Maryborough, Victoria	43	37 0S	143 44E
Maryborough Div., Queensland	43	25 47S	151 38E
Marydale, C. Prov.	57	29 23S	22 5E
Maryfield, Canada	65	49 50N	101 35W
Maryland, st., U.S.A.	68	39 10N	76 40W
Maryland Junc, Rhodesia	56	12 45S	30 31E
Mary's Harbour, Can.	63	52 18N	55 51W
Marystown, Can.	63	47 10N	55 10W
Marysvale, U.S.A.	73	38 28N	112 16W
Marysville, Calif., U.S.A.	72	39 0N	121 40W
Marysville, Kan.	70	39 53N	96 36W
Marysville, Ohio, U.S.A.	68	40 15N	83 20W
Marysville, Wash., U.S.A.	64	48 3N	122 15W
Maryville, U.S.A.	69	35 50N	84 0W
Masafa, Zambia	56	13 50S	27 23E
Masai Steppe, Tan.	53	4 0S	36 30E
Masaka, dist., Uganda	53	0 20S	31 23E
Masakali, Nigeria	52	13 2N	12 32E
Masalima I., Indonesia	35	4 50S	116 50E
Masamba, Indonesia	35	2 30S	120 15E
Masan, Korea	36	35 15N	128 30E
Masanga, Tanzania	53	3 8S	33 30E
Masango, Rhodesia	56	15 40S	29 54E
Masba, Nigeria	52	10 35N	13 1E
Masbate I., Philippines	35	12 20N	123 30E
Mascara, Algeria	50	35 26N	0 6E
Mascota, Mexico	74	20 30N	104 50W
Masela I., Indonesia	35	8 5S	129 50E
Maseme, Botswana	56	18 45S	25 7E
Maseru, Lesotho	57	29 18S	27 30E
Mashaba, Rhodesia	56	20 2S	30 29E
Mashabih I., Si. Arabia	30	25 35N	36 30E
Masham, England	75	4 15N	1 40W
Mashash, Wadi, Jordan	29	31 36N	35 23E
Mashegu, Nigeria	52	10 0N	5 34E
Mashhad (Meshed), Iran	31	36 18N	59 32E
Mashi, Nigeria	52	13 0N	7 54E
Mashike, Japan	36	43 31N	141 30E
Mashki Chah, Pakistan	32	29 5N	62 30E
Mashkode, Canada	62	47 0N	84 5W
Mashonaland, Rhod.	56	19 0S	31 45E
Mashowing, R., Cape Province	57	26 35S	23 0E
Masibi, Mozambique	56	23 0S	34 18E
Masi Manimba, Zaire	54	4 40S	18 5E
Masilipatam (Masulipatnam), India	33	16 12N	81 12E
Masindi, Uganda	53	1 40N	31 43E
Masindi Port, Uganda	53	1 40N	32 4E
Masira, G. of, 'Oman	30	19 30N	58 0E
Masisea, Peru	78	8 35S	74 15W
Masisi, Zaire	53	1 19S	28 35E
Masjed Soleyma, Iran	30	31 59N	49 20E
Mask, L., Ireland	11	53 36N	9 24W
Masnie, Rhodesia	56	18 2S	25 52E
Mason, S.D., U.S.A.	70	45 13N	103 28W
Mason, Tex., U.S.A.	71	30 45N	99 14W
Mason B., N.Z.	47	46 55S	167 45E
Mason City, Iowa, U.S.A.	70	43 6N	93 15W
Mason City, Wash., U.S.A.	72	48 0N	119 0W
Masqat (Muscat), Muscat & Oman	31	23 38N	58 31E
Massa, Tuscany, Italy	20	44 2N	10 7E
Massa Marittima, Italy	20	43 3N	10 52E
Massachusetts, st., U.S.A.	69	42 25N	72 0W
Massachusetts B., U.S.A.	69	42 20N	69 40W
Massakori, Chad	51	13 0N	15 49E
Massamba, Mozam.	56	15 34S	33 35E
Massangena, Mozam.	56	21 35S	33 5E
Massara, Mozam.	56	0 20S	34 5E
Massena, U.S.A.	68	44 52N	74 55W
Massenya, Chad	51	11 30N	16 25E
Massering, Botswana	57	23 15S	21 49E
Masset & Sd., Canada	64	54 0N	132 0W
Massif Central, mt., France	12	45 30N	2 21E
Massillon, U.S.A.	68	40 47N	81 30W
Massinga, Mozam.	55	25 15S	35 22E
Massingir, Mozam.	57	23 49S	31 59E
Massocha, Mozam.	57	22 42S	32 12E
Masterton, N.Z.	46	40 56S	175 39E
Mastuj, Pakistan	32	36 20N	72 36E
Mastung, Pakistan	32	29 50N	66 42E
Mastura, Saudi Arabia	30	23 7N	38 52E
Masuda, Japan	36	34 45N	132 0E
Masuku, Zambia	56	17 28S	27 2E
Maswa, Tanzania	53	2 40S	33 57E
Matabele Plain, Zambia	56	16 5S	22 30E
Matabeleland, dist., Rhodesia	56	19 20S	28 0E
Matachel R., Spain	17	38 32N	6 0W
Matachewan, Canada	62	47 50N	80 55W
Matad, Mongolia	37	47 12N	115 30E
Matadi, Zaire	54	5 52S	13 31E
Matagorda, U.S.A.	71	28 50N	96 0W
Matagorda B., U.S.A.	71	28 35N	96 12W
Matagami L., Canada	62	49 50N	77 40W
Matagami R., Canada	62	49 50N	82 0W
Matagorda I., U.S.A.	71	28 10N	96 30W
Matakana, N.Z.	46	36 22S	174 41E
Matakana I., N.Z.	46	37 35S	176 5E
Matala, Zambia	56	15 8S	27 12E
Matale, Sri Lanka	32	7 30N	80 44E
Matam, Senegal	50	15 34N	13 17W
Matamata, N.Z.	46	37 48S	175 47E
Matamma, Ethiopia	54	12 13N	36 25E
Matamoros, Mexico	74	25 50N	97 30W
Matana, Burundi	53	3 45S	29 40E
Matandu R., Tan.	53	9 0S	38 30E
Matane, Canada	63	48 50N	67 33W
Matanzas, Cuba	75	23 0N	81 40W
Matapa, Botswana	57	23 16S	24 34E
Matapedia, Canada	63	48 0N	66 59W
Matara, Sri Lanka	32	5 58N	80 30E
Mataram, Indonesia	35	8 41S	116 10E
Matarani, Peru	78	16 50S	72 10W
Matareca, Mozam.	56	18 32N	33 19E
Mataro, Spain	17	41 32N	2 29E
Matata, New Zealand	46	37 54S	176 48E
Matatiele, C. Prov.	57	30 20S	28 49E
Mataura, New Zealand	47	46 11S	168 51E
Mataura R., N.Z.	47	45 49S	168 44E
Matehuala, Mexico	74	23 40N	100 50W
Mateke Hills, Rhod.	56	21 48S	31 0E
Matema, Mozambique	56	15 42S	33 26E
Matera, Italy	20	40 40N	16 37E
Mátészalka, Hungary	16	47 58N	22 20E
Matetsi, Rhodesia	56	18 12S	26 0E
Matheson Island, Can.	65	51 45N	96 56W
Mathis, U.S.A.	71	28 3N	97 19W
Mathura, India	32	27 30N	77 48E
Mati, Philippines	35	6 55N	126 15E
Matjiesfontein, Cape Province	57	33 12S	20 32E
Matla R., India	33	21 45N	88 45E
Matlabas, Transvaal	57	24 12S	27 28E
Matlamanyane, Botswana	56	19 25S	25 55E
Matmata, Tunisia	51	33 30N	10 5E
Mato Grosso, Brazil	78	15 0S	60 0W
Mato Grosso, st., Brazil	79	14 0S	55 0W
Mato Grosso Plat., Brazil	79	15 0S	54 0W
Matochkin Shar, U.S.S.R.	26	73 10N	56 40E
Matopo Hills, Rhod.	56	20 36S	28 20E
Matopos, Rhodesia	56	20 20S	28 29E
Matozinhos, Portugal	17	41 12N	8 41W
Matru, Sierra Leone	52		Inset
Matruh, Egypt	51	31 19N	27 9E
Matsena, Nigeria	52	13 5N	10 5E
Matsu, China	39	26 10N	119 55E
Matsue, Japan	36	35 25N	133 10E
Matsumae, Japan	36	41 30N	140 0E
Matsumoto, Japan	36	36 15N	138 0E
Matsuyama, Japan	36	33 45N	132 45E
Matsuzaka, Japan	36	34 35N	136 36E
Mattancheri, India	32	9 50N	76 15E
Mattawa, Canada	62	46 20N	78 45W
Mattawamkeag, U.S.A.	69	45 30N	68 30W
Mattervisp R., Switz.	15	46 10N	7 93E
Matterhorn, Mt., Switzerland	15	45 58N	7 39E
Mattice, Canada	62	49 40N	83 20W
Mattoon, U.S.A.	70	39 30N	88 20W
Matucana, Peru	78	11 55S	76 15W
Matun, Afghanistan	31	33 22N	69 58E
Maturin, Venezuela	78	9 50N	63 10W
Matylka, U.S.S.R.	26	63 55N	82 0E
Mau Escarpment, Kenya	53	0 40S	36 2E
Mau Ranipur, India	32	25 15N	79 15E
Maubeuge, France	12	50 17N	3 57E
Mauchline, Scotland	10	55 31N	4 23W
Maud Pt., Australia	44	23 9S	113 40E
Mauele, Mozambique	55	24 21S	34 8E
Maués, Brazil	79	3 20S	57 45W
Mauganj, India	33	24 40N	81 55E
Maughold Hd., I. of Man	75	54 18N	4 17W
Maui, I., Hawaiian Is.	59	21 0N	156 30W
Maule R., Chile	77	35 30S	71 0W
Mauleon, France	12	43 54N	0 10W
Maumee, U.S.A.	68	41 35N	83 40W
Maumee R., U.S.A.	68	41 15N	84 40W
Maumere, Indonesia	35	8 38S	122 13E
Maun, Botswana	55	20 0S	23 40E
Mauna Kea, mt., Hawaiian Is.	59	19 50N	155 25W
Mauna Loa, mt., Hawaiian Is.	59	21 9N	157 12W
Maunganui, Mt., N.Z.	46	37 39S	176 14E
Maungaturoto, N.Z.	46	36 6S	174 23E
Maungu, Kenya	53	3 32S	38 42E
Maunmagan Is., (Middle Moscos Is.)	33	14 0N	97 50E
Maupin, U.S.A.	72	45 7N	121 9W
Maurepas, L., U.S.A.	71	30 16N	90 30W
Maures, mts., France	12	43 15N	6 15E
Mauriac, France	12	45 13N	2 19E
Maurice L., S. Austral.	45	29 30S	131 0E
Mauriceville, N.Z.	46	40 45S	175 35E
Mauritania, Rep., Afr.	50	20 0N	10 0W
Mauritius, Indian Oc.	5	20 0S	57 0E
Mauston, U.S.A.	70	43 46N	90 2W
Mavinga, Angola	55	15 50S	20 10E
Mavita, Mozambique	56	19 33S	33 10E
Mavli, India	32	24 45N	73 55E
Mavuradona Mts., Rhodesia	56	16 30S	31 30E
Mawer, Canada	65	50 46N	106 22W
Mawkmai, Burma	33	20 14N	97 50E
Mawlaik, Burma	33	23 32N	94 17E
Mawson, Antarctica	80	67 30N	62 30E
Max, U.S.A.	70	47 47N	101 17W
Maxaila, Mozam.	56	22 13S	32 54E
Maxcanu, Mexico	74	20 40N	90 10W
Maxhamish L., Canada	64	59 52N	123 20W
Maxixe, Mozambique	56	23 48S	35 21E
Maxwell, New Zealand	46	39 50S	174 51E
Maxwelton, Queensland	42	20 42S	142 42E
May Pen., Jamaica	75	17 58N	77 15W
Mayaguana I., Bahamas	75	21 30N	72 44W
Mayaguez, Puerto Rico	75	18 11N	67 8W
Mayari, Cuba	75	20 41N	75 42W
Mayasu, Japan	36	35 30N	135 0E
Mayavaram, India	32	11 1N	79 40E
Maybell, U.S.A.	72	40 30N	107 57W
Mayenne, France	12	48 20N	0 38W
Mayer, U.S.A.	73	34 28N	112 30W
Mayerthorpe, Canada	64	53 57N	115 15W
Mayfield, U.S.A.	71	36 45N	88 40W
Mayhill, U.S.A.	73	32 55N	105 30W
Maykop (Maikop), U.S.S.R.	25	44 35N	40 15E
Maymyo, Burma	34	22 0N	96 30E
Maynard Hills, W. Australia	44	28 44S	119 45E
Mayne R., Queensland	42	23 40S	141 50E
Maynooth, Canada	62	45 14N	77 56W
Maynooth, Ireland	11	53 22N	6 38W
Mayo, Ireland	11	53 45N	9 10W
Mayo, co., Ireland	11	53 47N	9 7W
Mayo Daga, Nigeria	52	6 59N	11 25E
Mayo Faran, Nigeria	52	8 57N	12 2E
Mayo Landing, Canada	60	63 30N	136 0W
Mayo Lope, Nigeria	52	9 24N	11 48E
Mayobamba, Peru	78	6 0S	77 0W
Mayor I., New Zealand	46	37 16S	176 17E
Mayoumba, Gabon	54	3 18S	10 48E
Mayse'ka, Niger	52	14 0N	4 42E
Mayson L., Canada	65	57 55N	107 10W
Maysville, U.S.A.	68	38 43N	84 16W
Maytown, Queensland	42	16 0S	144 25E
Mayville, U.S.A.	70	47 33N	97 23W
Mazabuka, Zambia	56	15 50S	27 45E
Mazagan, Morocco	50	33 11N	8 30W
Mazagao, Brazil	79	0 20S	51 50W
Mazama, Canada	64	49 43N	120 8W
Mazamet, France	12	43 30N	2 20E
Mazán, Argentina	77	28 40S	66 30W
Mazán, Peru	78	3 15S	73 0W
Mazande Ran, Iran	30	36 30N	53 0E
Mazar-i-Sharif, prov., Afghanistan	32	36 0N	67 30E
Mazara, Italy	20	37 40N	12 34E
Mazarredo, Argentina	77	47 10S	66 50W
Mazarron, Spain	17	37 38N	1 19W
Mazaruni R., Guyana	78	6 15N	60 0W
Mažatlan, Mexico	74	23 10N	106 30W
Maze, Norway	22	69 17N	23 47E
Māzhan, Iran	31	32 33N	59 0E
Mazheikyai, U.S.S.R.	24	56 20N	22 20E
Mazinan, Iran	31	36 25N	56 48E
Maziua, Mozambique	53	11 40S	36 55E
Mazoe, Mozambique	56	16 40S	33 30E
Mazoe, Rhodesia	56	17 28S	30 58E
Mazoe R., Mozam.	56	16 45S	32 30E
Mba-Lib., Cameroon	52	2 40N	11 48E
Mbaba, Somali Rep.	53	1 30S	41 40E
M'babane, Swaziland	57	26 18S	31 6E
Mbaiki, Congo (Fr.)	54	3 53N	18 1E
Mbala, Zambia	56	8 50S	31 25E
Mbala Hill, Nigeria	52	6 50N	11 13E
Mbale, Uganda	54	1 5N	33 57E
Mbalmayo, Cameroon	52	3 33N	11 33E
Mbam R., Cameroon	52	4 55N	11 10E
Mbandaka, Zaire	59	0 1S	18 18E
Mbang Mts., Cam.	52	7 40N	13 20E
Mbanga, Cameroon	52	4 30N	9 33E
Mbaragandu, R., Tan.	53	9 50S	36 50E
Mbaragani, Tan.	53	3 21S	33 54E
Mbarara, Uganda	54	0 35S	30 35E
Mbate, Tanzania	53	8 55S	39 10E
Mbemkuru R., Tan.	53	9 42S	39 6E
Mbemba, Tanzania	53	8 57S	39 1E
Mbershi, Zambia	56	9 45S	28 45E
Mberubu, Nigeria	52	6 10N	7 38E
Mbesuma, Zambia	56	0 2S	32 8E
Mbeya, Tanzania	35	8 50S	33 30E
Mbeya, prov., Tan.	53	8 10S	33 30E
Mbeya, mt., Tan.	53	8 50S	33 30E
Mbimbi, Zambia	56	13 25S	23 2E
Mbirira, Tanzania	53	4 20S	30 12E

	MAP		
Mbirizi, Uganda	53	0 24 s	31 28 E
Mbogo, Tanzania	53	7 26 s	33 26 E
M'Bomu R., Zaire	54	5 0N	26 30 E
M'bonge, Nigeria	52	4 33N	9 12 E
Mboua, Cameroon	52	5 40N	11 30 E
Mbour, Senegal	50	14 22N	16 54W
M'Bout, Mauritania	50	16 1N	12 38W
Mbuji Mayi, Zaire	54	3 51N	23 40 E
M'bwat, Cameroon	52	6 7N	10 43 E
M'Clintock Chan., Canada	60	72 0N	103 0W
McAlester, U.S.A.	71	35 0N	95 50W
McAllen, U.S.A.	71	26 20N	98 0W
McCamey, U.S.A.	71	31 4N	102 16W
McCamman, U.S.A.	72	42 36N	112 9W
McCarthy, Alaska	59	61 25N	142 59W
McCauley I., Canada	64	53 40N	130 15W
McClintock, Canada	65	56 40N	94 5W
McCloud, U.S.A.	72	41 15N	122 10W
McCluer G., Indonesia	35	2 20 s	133 0 E
McClusky, U.S.A.	70	47 30N	100 30W
McComb, U.S.A.	71	31 20N	90 30W
McConnell Creek, Can.	64	57 0N	126 35W
McCook, U.S.A.	70	40 15N	100 40W
McCrea R., Canada	64	63 20N	113 50W
McCulloch, Canada	64	49 45N	119 10W
McCusker R., Canada	65	55 20N	108 40W
McDame, Canada	64	59 15N	129 25W
McDermitt, U.S.A.	72	42 0N	117 42W
McDonnell, Queensland	42	11 35 s	142 25 E
McFarlane R., Canada	65	58 0N	107 50W
McGehee, U.S.A.	71	33 37N	91 27W
McGill, U.S.A.	73	39 30N	114 40W
McGrath, Alaska	59	62 58N	155 40W
McGregor, Iowa., U.S.A.	70	42 59N	91 13W
McGregor, Minn., U.S.A.	70	46 37N	93 16W
McGregor R., Canada	64	54 0N	121 0W
Mchinga, Tanzania	53	9 42 s	39 42 E
Mchungu, Tanzania	53	7 50 s	39 20 E
McIlwraith Ra., Queens.	42	13 30 s	143 15 E
McInnes L., Canada	65	52 0N	93 45W
McIntosh, U.S.A.	70	45 58N	101 17W
McIntosh L., Canada	65	55 55N	105 0W
McKeesport, U.S.A.	68	40 20N	79 50W
McKenzie, U.S.A.	69	36 10N	88 30W
McKenzie, R., U.S.A.	72	44 7N	112 30W
McKerrow L., N.Z.	47	44 25 s	168 5 E
McKerrow Mts., N.Z.	47	44 12 s	160 20 E
McKinlay, Queensland	42	21 16 s	141 16 E
McKinley, Mt., Alaska	59	63 11N	151 0W
McKinney, U.S.A.	71	33 10N	96 41W
McKinnon's P., N.Z.	47	44 49 s	167 48 E
McKittrick, U.S.A.	73	35 39N	119 37W
McLaughlin, U.S.A.	70	45 52N	100 53W
McLean, U.S.A.	71	35 15N	100 32W
McLeansboro, U.S.A.	71	38 4N	88 32W
McLennan, Canada	64	55 50N	117 0W
McLeod B., Canada	65	63 0N	110 0W
McLoughlin, Mt., U.S.A	72	42 24N	122 15W
McLure, Canada	64	51 0N	120 10W
McLure, Str., Canada	58	74 0N	115 0W
McMillan, L., U.S.A.	71	32 40N	104 17W
McMinnville, U.S.A.	72	54 10N	123 0W
McMorran, Canada	65	51 19N	108 42W
McMurdo, Antarctica	80	78 0 s	166 0 E
McMurray, Canada	64	56 45N	111 30W
McNary, U.S.A.	73	34 6N	109 49W
McPherson, Canada	60	67 25N	135 0W
McPherson, U.S.A.	71	38 22N	97 41W
McVille, U.S.A.	70	47 49N	90 11W
Mdandu, Tanzania	53	9 5 s	34 37 E
Mead L., U.S.A.	73	36 10N	114 20W
Mead, Canada	62	49 26N	83 51W
Meade, U.S.A.	71	37 21N	100 25W
Meade River (Atkasuk) Alaska	59	70 40N	157 0W
Meadow Lake, Canada	65	54 10N	108 10W
Meadow Valley Wash, R., U.S.A.	73	37 30N	114 30W
Meadville, U.S.A.	68	41 39N	80 9W
Meaford, Canada	62	44 40N	80 40W
Mealy Mts., Canada	63	53 30N	59 0W
Meandarra, Queens.	43	27 16 s	149 53 E
Meander River, Canada	64	59 3N	117 18W
Meares, C., U.S.A.	72	45 30N	123 59W
Mearim R., Brazil	79	4 35 s	45 0W
Meath, co., Ireland	11	53 32N	6 40W
Meath Park, Canada	65	53 27N	105 22W
Meaux, France	12	48 58N	2 50 E
Mecanhelas, Mozam.	56	15 10 s	35 50 E
Mecca, Saudi Arabia	30	21 30N	39 54 E
Mecca, U.S.A.	73	33 30N	116 27W
Mechelen (Malines), Belgium	13	51 2N	4 29 E
Méchéria, Algeria	50	33 35N	0 18W
Meconta, Mozam.	55	15 0 s	39 50 E
Medan, Indonesia	34	3 40N	98 38 E
Medanosa, Pta., Arg.	77	48 0 s	66 0W
Medawachiya, Sri Lanka	32	9 30N	80 30 E
Medea, Algeria	50	36 12N	2 50 E
Medellin, Colombia	78	6 20N	75 45W
Medemblik, Netherlands	13	52 46N	5 8 E
Medenine, Tunisia	51	33 15N	10 35 E
Mederdra, Mauritania	50	17 0N	15 35W
Medford, Ore., U.S.A.	72	42 20N	122 45W
Medford, Wis., U.S.A.	70	45 7N	90 25W
Medgidia, Rumania	21	44 15N	28 19 E
Medias, Rumania	21	46 9N	24 22 E
Medical Lake, U.S.A.	72	47 35N	117 40W
Medicine Bow, U.S.A.	72	41 57N	106 15W
Medicine Bow Pk., U.S.A.	72	41 27N	106 20W
Medicine Bow Ra., U.S.A.	72	41 0N	106 15W
Medicine Hat, Canada	65	50 0N	110 45W
Medicine Lake, U.S.A.	70	48 30N	104 30W
Medicine Lodge, U.S.A.	71	37 22N	98 33W
Medina, Saudi Arabia	30	24 35N	39 52 E
Medina, Spain	17	41 50N	5 5W
Medina, N.D., U.S.A.	70	46 58N	99 16W
Medina, N.Y., U.S.A.	68	43 15N	78 27W
Medina, Ohio, U.S.A.	68	41 0N	81 50W
Medina, L., U.S.A.	71	29 35N	98 57W
Medina, R., U.S.A.	71	29 10N	98 15W
Medina Sidonia, Spain	17	36 28N	5 57W
Medinaceli, Spain	17	41 12N	2 30W
Mediterranean Sea	18–19	35 0N	15 0 E
Medstead, Canada	65	53 19N	108 5W
Medvedaka, U.S.S.R.	25	57 28N	50 0 E
Medveditsa R., U.S.S.R.	25	50 30N	44 0 E
Medvezhi Is., U.S.S.R.	27	70 50N	161 0 E
Medway R., England	10	51 12N	0 23 E
Meecha, Queensland	43	26 27 s	146 4 E
Meekatharra, W.Austral.	44	26 32 s	118 29 E
Meeker, U.S.A.	73	40 2N	107 58W
Meelpaeg L., Canada	63	48 18N	56 35W
Meenen, Belgium	13	50 47N	3 7 E
Meerut, India	32	29 1N	77 50 E
Meesen, Belgium	13	50 46N	2 50 E
Meeteetse, U.S.A.	72	44 10N	108 52W
Mega, Ethiopia	54	3 57N	38 30 E
Megalópolis, Greece	21	37 25N	22 7 E
Mégantic, Canada	63	45 36N	70 56W
Megara, Greece	21	37 58N	23 22 E
Megiddo, Israel	29	32 36N	35 11 E
Megiri, Sudan	53	4 0N	31 37 E
Megiscane, L., Canada	62	48 30N	75 30W
Mehadia, Rumania	21	44 56N	22 23 E
Mehsana, India	32	23 39N	72 26 E
Méhun, France	12	47 10N	2 13 E
Mei K., China	39	24 25N	116 10 E
Meihokow, China	38	42 31N	125 15 E
Meihsien, China	39	24 20N	116 0 E
Meiktila, Burma	33	21 0N	96 0 E
Meilen, Switzerland	15	47 17N	8 39 E
Meiningen, Germany	14	50 32N	10 25 E
Meir Shefeya, Israel	29	32 35N	34 58 E
Meiringen, Switzerland	15	46 43N	8 12 E
Meishan Dam, China	39	31 55N	116 10 E
Meissen, Germany	14	51 10N	13 29 E
Meitan, China	39	27 45N	107 45 E
Meithalun, Jordan	29	32 21N	35 16 E
Meiyganga, Cameroon	52	6 20N	14 10 E
Mejillones, Chile	77	23 10 s	70 30W
Mekelle, Ethiopia	54	13 42N	39 30 E
Mekhtar, Pakistan	32	30 30N	69 15 E
Meknès, Morocco	50	33 57N	5 39W
Meko, Nigeria	52	7 29N	2 50 E
Mekohija, Yugoslavia	21	52 54N	20 47 E
Mekong R., Asia	34	18 0N	104 15 E
Mekoryok, Alaska	59	60 20N	166 20W
Mékrou R., Dahomey	52	11 45N	2 18 E
Melagiri Hills, India	32	12 20N	77 30 E
Melalan, Sabah	35	5 10N	116 5 E
Melbo, Norway	22	68 31N	14 50 E
Melbourne, Victoria	43	37 40 s	145 0 E
Melchar Muzquiz, Mexico	74	27 53N	101 31W
Melekess, U.S.S.R.	25	54 25N	49 33 E
Melenki, U.S.S.R.	25	55 20N	41 37 E
Melfi, Chad	51	11 0N	17 59 E
Melfi, Italy	20	41 0N	15 40 E
Melfort, Canada	65	52 50N	104 40W
Melfort, Rhodesia	56	18 0 s	31 25 E
Melgaço, Brazil	79	1 45 s	50 50W
Melgar, Spain	17	42 27N	4 17W
Meligalâ, Greece	21	37 15N	21 59 E
Melilla, Sp. town, N. Africa	50	35 15N	2 57W
Melipilla, Chile	77	33 45 s	71 40W
Melita, Canada	65	49 15N	101 5W
Melito, Italy	20	37 55N	15 47 E
Melk, Austria	14	48 13N	15 20 E
Mellansel, Sweden	23	63 25N	18 10 E
Mellen, U.S.A.	70	46 22N	90 37W
Mellerud, Sweden	23	58 41N	12 28 E
Mellette, U.S.A.	70	45 11N	98 29W
Melmoth, Natal	57	28 33 s	31 28 E
Melo, Uruguay	77	32 20 s	54 10W
Melolo, Indonesia	35	9 55 s	120 40 E
Melrose, Scotland	10	55 35N	2 44W
Melrose, U.S.A.	71	34 26N	103 33W
Mels, Switzerland	15	47 3N	9 21 E
Melsetter, Rhodesia	56	19 48 s	32 48 E
Melstone, U.S.A.	72	46 35N	108 0W
Melun, France	12	48 32N	2 39 E
Melut, Sudan	51	10 30N	32 20 E
Melville, Canada	65	51 0N	102 50W
Melville B., Greenland	58	75 30N	64 0W
Melville C., Queensland	42	14 11 s	144 32 E
Melville I., Canada	58	75 30N	111 0W
Melville I., N. Territory	40	11 30 s	131 0 E
Melville L., Canada	63	53 45N	59 40W
Melville Pen., Canada	61	68 0N	84 0W
Melvin R., Canada	64	58 50N	117 0W
Memboro, Indonesia	35	9 30 s	119 30 E
Memel, O.F.S.	57	27 38 s	29 36 E
Memmingen, Germany	14	47 59N	10 12 E
Memphis, Tenn., U.S.A.	71	35 7N	90 0W
Memphis, Texas, U.S.A.	71	34 43N	100 30W
Mena, U.S.A.	71	34 40N	94 15W
Ménaka, Mali	52	15 59N	2 18 E
Menard, U.S.A.	71	30 57N	99 45W
Menasha, U.S.A.	68	44 13N	88 27W
Mencheng, China	38	33 25N	116 45 E
Mencheong, China	39	19 45N	110 50 E
Mende, France	12	44 31N	3 30 E
Mendif, Cameroon	52	10 25N	14 23 E
Mendocin, U.S.A.	72	39 22N	123 48W
Mendocino C., U.S.A.	66	40 30N	124 20W
Mendota, Calif., U.S.A.	73	36 43N	120 22W
Mendota, Ill., U.S.A.	70	41 35N	89 5W
Mendoza, Argentina	77	32 50 s	68 52W
Mendoza R., Argentina	77	33 0 s	69 0W
Mene de Mauroa, Ven.	78	10 44N	71 0W
Mene Grande, Ven.	78	9 49N	70 56W
Menemen, Turkey	30	38 36N	27 4 E
Menfi, Italy	20	37 36N	12 57 E
Menggala, Indonesia	34	4 20 s	105 15 E
Mengo, dist., Uganda	53	1 3N	32 30 E
Mengshan, China	39	24 13N	110 33 E
Mengtsz, China	37	23 20N	103 20 E
Mengyin, China	38	35 40N	117 55 E
Menihek Lakes, Canada	63	54 0N	67 0W
Menin, Belgium	13	50 47N	3 7 E
Menindee, N.S.W.	43	32 20 s	142 25 E
Meningie, S. Australia	43	35 36 s	139 21 E
Menominee, U.S.A.	70	45 9N	87 39W
Menominee R., U.S.A.	70	45 30N	87 50W
Menomonie, U.S.A.	70	44 50N	91 55W
Menorca (Minorca) I., Balearic Is.	17	40 0N	4 0 E
Mentawei Is., Indonesia	34	2 0 s	99 0 E
Menton, France	12	43 50N	7 29 E
Mentz, L., C. Prov.	57	33 10 s	25 8 E
Menzel Temime, Tunisia	51	36 50N	11 0 E
Menzies, W. Australia	44	29 40 s	120 58 E
Meori, Nigeria	52	13 12N	10 27 E
Mepaco, Mozambique	56	15 55 s	31 0 E
Meppel, Netherlands	13	52 52N	6 12 E
Meppen, Germany	14	52 41N	7 20 E
Mer Rouge, U.S.A.	71	32 55N	91 45W
Merabélou, B., Greece	20	35 10N	25 50 E
Merak, Indonesia	34	5 55 s	106 1 E
Merano, Italy	20	46 40N	11 10 E
Merbabu Mt., Indon.	34	7 30 s	110 40 E
Mercara, India	32	12 30N	75 45 E
Mercato, Forli, Italy	53	43 57N	12 11 E
Merced, U.S.A.	73	37 15N	120 30W
Mercedes, Buenos Aires, Argentina	77	34 40 s	59 30W
Mercedes, Corrientes, Argentina	77	29 10 s	58 5W
Mercedes, Uruguay	77	33 12 s	58 0W
Merceditas, Chile	77	28 20 s	70 35W
Mercer, New Zealand	46	37 16 s	175 5 E
Mercury Bay, N.Z.	46	36 47 s	175 46 E
Mercury, I., N.Z.	46	36 26 s	175 50 E
Mercy C., Canada	61	65 0N	62 30W
Merefa, U.S.S.R.	25	49 56N	36 2 E
Méréke, Congo (Fr.)	54	7 35N	23 0 E
Mergui, Burma	34	12 30N	98 35 E
Mergui Arch., Burma	33	11 30N	97 30 E
Merida, Mexico	74	20 50N	89 40W
Merida, Spain	17	38 55N	6 25W
Mérida, Venezuela	78	8 33N	71 10W
Merida, Cord., mts., Venezuela	78	8 30N	71 0W
Meriden, U.S.A.	68	41 33N	72 47W
Meridian, Idaho, U.S.A.	72	43 37N	116 21W
Meredian, Miss., U.S.A.	69	32 20N	88 42W
Meridian, Texas, U.S.A.	71	31 52N	97 36W
Merinda, Queensland	42	19 59 s	148 9 E
Meringa, Nigeria	52	10 43N	11 59 E
Meringur, Victoria	43	34 20 s	141 19 E
Merir I., Carolines	35	4 25N	132 20 E
Meriruma, Brazil	79	1 5N	54 50W
Merkel, U.S.A.	71	32 30N	100 0W
Merksem, Belgium	13	51 16N	4 25 E
Merowe, Sudan	51	18 29N	31 46 E
Merredin, W. Australia	44	31 28 s	118 18 E
Merrick, mt., Scotland	10	55 8N	4 30W
Merrill, Ore., U.S.A.	72	42 0N	121 32W
Merrill, Wis., U.S.A.	70	45 11N	89 41W
Merriman, U.S.A.	70	42 57N	101 36W
Merritt, Canada	64	50 10N	120 45W
Merriwa, N.S.W.	43	32 6 s	150 22 E
Merry I., Canada	62	55 57N	77 40W
Merryville, U.S.A.	71	30 46N	93 31W
Merseburg, Germany	14	51 20N	12 0 E
Mersey R., England	10	53 20N	2 56W
Mersin, Turkey	30	36 51N	34 36 E
Mersing, Malaya	34	2 25N	103 50 E
Merthyr Tydfil, Wales	10	51 45N	3 23W
Merti, Kenya	53	1 0N	38 56 E
Mertola, Portugal	17	37 40N	7 40 E
Mertondale, W. Australia	44	28 38 s	121 28 E
Mertzon, U.S.A.	71	31 14N	100 49W
Meru, Kenya	54	0 2N	37 35 E
Meru Mt., Tanzania	53	3 14 s	36 44 E
Merweville, C. Prov.	57	32 37 s	21 31 E
Mesa, U.S.A.	73	33 20N	111 50W
Mesagne, Italy	21	40 34N	17 48 E
Mesewa, Ethiopia	49	15 35N	39 25 E
Mesgovez, L., Canada	62	51 20N	75 0W
Meshed (Mashhad), Iran	31	36 20N	59 32 E
Meshra-er-Req, Sudan	54	8 26N	29 18 E
Mesick, U.S.A.	68	44 24N	85 42W
Mesilinka, R., Canada	64	56 30N	125 30W
Mesilla, U.S.A.	73	37 17N	106 48W
Mesolóngion, Greece	21	38 27N	21 28 E
Mesopotamia, reg., Iraq	30	33 30N	44 0 E
Méssaména, Cameroon	52	3 48N	12 49 E
Messina, Italy	20	38 10N	15 32 E
Messina, Transvaal	57	22 20 s	30 12 E
Messina, Str. of, Italy	20	38 5N	15 35 E
Messini, Greece	21	37 3N	22 0 E
Messini, G. of, Greece	21	36 40N	22 20 E
Mesta R., Bulgaria	21	41 30N	24 0 E
Mestre, Italy	20	45 30N	12 13 E
Meta I., Indonesia	35	3 20N	106 15 E
Meta, R., Ven./Col.	78	6 0N	68 30W
Metagama, Canada	62	47 0N	81 55W
Metaline Falls, U.S.A.	72	48 54N	117 28W
Metán, Argentina	77	25 30 s	65 0W
Metangula, Mozam.	55	11 35 s	34 55 E
Metauro R., Italy	20	43 45N	12 59 E
Metchosin, Canada	64	48 15N	123 37W
Megengo Balame, Mozambique	56	14 49 s	34 34 E
Methven, New Zealand	47	43 38 s	171 40 E
Methy L., Canada	65	56 30N	69 50W
Meti, Mozambique	55	16 25N	39 0 E
Metković, Yugoslavia	21	43 6N	17 39 E
Metlakatla, Alaska	64	55 15N	131 30W
Metlika, Yugoslavia	20	45 40N	15 20 E
Metolola, Mozambique	56	16 36 s	35 44 E
Metove, Mozambique	56	20 9 s	33 1 E
Metropolis, U.S.A.	71	37 10N	88 47W
Metropolitan, dist., New South Wales	43	34 0 s	151 0 E
Mettur Dam, India	32	11 45N	77 45 E
Metulla, Israel	29	33 17N	35 34 E
Metz, France	12	49 8N	6 10 E
Meulaboh, Indonesia	34	4 11N	96 3 E
Meurcuda, Indonesia	34	5 20N	96 20 E
Meuse R., Belgium	13	50 32N	5 20 E
Mexia, U.S.A.	71	31 45N	96 25W
Mexiana I., Brazil	79	0 0N	49 30W
Mexicali, Mexico	74	32 40N	115 30W
Mexico City, Mexico	74	19 20N	99 10W
Mexico, Me., U.S.A.	69	44 35N	70 30W
Mexico, Mo., U.S.A.	70	39 10N	91 52W
Mexico, N.Y., U.S.A.	69	43 30N	76 19W
Mexico, Fed. dist., Mex.	74	19 20N	99 10W
Mexico, rep., America	74	15 0N to 32 30N	87 0W to 117 0W
Mexico, G. of, America	71	25 0N	90 0W
Meyanginibole, Tan.	53	10 17 s	35 30 E
Meydan-e Gel, Iran	31	29 15N	55 0 E
Meydān-e Naftun, Iran	30	31 55N	49 22 E
Meyo, Cameroon	52	2 48N	11 8 E
Mèze, France	12	43 27N	3 36 E
Mezen, U.S.S.R.	24	65 50N	44 20 E
Mezen R., U.S.S.R.	24	64 40N	47 30 E
Mézenc, Mt., France	12	44 54N	4 11 E
Mezières, Ardennes, Fr.	12	49 45N	4 42 E
Mezökovsed, Hungary	16	47 50N	20 37 E
Mezötúr, Hungary	16	47 0N	20 41 E
Mezquital, Mexico	74	23 30N	104 20W
Mgeta, Tan.	53	8 22 s	36 6 E
Mhlaba Hills, Rhodesia	56	18 30 s	30 30 E
Mhow, India	32	22 33N	75 50 E
Miahuatlán, Mexico	74	16 21N	96 36W
Miami, Rhodesia	56	16 40 s	29 49 E
Miami, Ariz., U.S.A.	74	33 25N	111 0W
Miami, Fla., U.S.A.	69	25 52N	80 5W
Miami, Texas, U.S.A.	71	35 41N	100 34W
Miami R., U.S.A.	68	39 20N	84 40W
Miami Beach, U.S.A.	69	25 49N	80 6W
Miamisburg, U.S.A.	68	39 40N	84 18W
Miāndow Ab, Iran	30	37 1N	46 22 E
Mianwali, Pakistan	32	32 38N	71 28 E
Miao Tao Is., China	38	38 10N	120 50 E
Miaoli, China	39	24 35N	120 53W
Miass, U.S.S.R.	24	55 0N	60 5 E
Mica, Transvaal	57	24 9 s	30 46 E
Micay, Colombia	78	3 0N	77 40W
Michelson, Mt., Alaska	59	69 19N	144 30W
Michen, China	38	37 59N	110 0 E
Michigan, st., U.S.A.	67	44 40N	85 40W
Michigan, L., U.S.A.	68	44 0N	87 0W
Michigan City, Ind., U.S.A.	68	41 42N	86 56W
Michika, Nigeria	52	10 36N	13 23 E
Michikamau, L., Can.	63	54 0N	64 0W
Michipicoten, River Canada	62	47 55N	84 55W
Michipicoten I., Canada	62	47 40N	85 50W
Michoacan, st., Mexico	74	19 0N	102 0W
Michurinsk, U.S.S.R.	25	52 58N	40 27 E
Mid-Western Region, Nigeria	52	5 50N	5 40 E
Midale, Canada	65	49 25N	103 20W

	MAP		
Midas, U.S.A.	72	41 14N	116 50W
Middelburg, Neth.	13	51 30N	3 36 E
Middelburg, Transvaal	57	25 46 S	29 28 E
Middelfart, Denmark	23	55 30N	9 43 E
Middelpos, C. Prov.	57	31 55 S	20 13 E
Middelwit, Transvaal	57	24 48 S	27 8 E
Middle Alkali, L., U.S.A.	72	41 30N	120 0 E
Middle Andaman, I., Indian Ocean	33	12 40N	93 0 E
Middle Atlas, mts., Morocco	50	33 0N	5 0W
Middle Brook, Canada	63	48 40N	54 20W
Middel Loup, R., U.S.A.	70	41 45N	99 30W
Middle Moscos (Maunmayan), Is.,	33	14 10N	97 45 E
Middleburg, C. Prov.	55	31 29 S	25 0 E
Middlebury, U.S.A.	69	44 0N	73 9W
Middelmarch, N.Z.	47	45 30 S	170 9 E
Middleport, U.S.A.	68	39 0N	82 5W
Middlesboro, U,.S.A.	69	36 40N	83 40W
Middlesbrough, Eng.	10	54 34N	1 13W
Middleton I., Alaska	59	59 22N	145 50W
Middleton, Canada	63	44 57N	65 4W
Middleton, Queensland	42	22 21 S	141 30 E
Middleton, Conn., U.S.A.	68	41 37N	72 40W
Middleton, N.Y., U.S.A.	68	41 28N	74 28W
Middleton, Ohio, U.S.A.	68	39 29N	84 24W
Middleton R., Nigeria	52	4 30N	5 40 E
Midhurst, New Zealand	46	39 17 S	174 18 E
Midland, Canada	62	44 45N	79 50W
Midland, Mich., U.S.A.	68	43 37N	84 17W
Midland, Tex., U.S.A.	71	32 0N	102 10W
Midland Junc, W. Australia	44	31 50 S	115 58 E
Midlands Region, Tas.	43	42 5 S	147 0 E
Midleton, Ireland	11	51 52N	8 12W
Midlothian, U.S.A.	71	32 30N	97 0W
Midnapore, India	33	22 25N	87 21 E
Midvale, U.S.A.	72	40 42N	111 53W
Midway I., Pac. Oc.	5	28 0N	178 0W
Midwest, U.S.A.	72	43 27N	106 16W
Midyat, Turkey	30	37 25N	41 23 E
Mie, pref. Japan	36	34 20N	136 20 E
Miechów, Poland	16	50 21N	20 5 E
Miedzychod, Poland	16	52 35N	15 53 E
Miedzyrzecz, Poland	16	52 26N	15 35 E
Mielec, Poland	16	50 20N	21 28 E
Mielelek, N. Guinea	42	6 0 S	148 59 E
Mienchih, China	38	34 50N	111 50 E
Mienhsien, China	38	33 15N	106 33 E
Mienyang, China	39	30 10N	113 20 E
Mier, Mexico	74	26 20N	99 20W
Miercurea Civc, Rum.	21	46 21N	25 48 E
Mieres, Spain	17	43 18N	5 48W
Miette, Canada	64	53 0N	117 51W
Migdal, Israel	29	32 51N	35 30 E
Migdal Ha' Emeq, Is.	29	32 41N	35 15 E
Migdal Yafo, Israel	29	32 5N	34 58 E
Miguel Alves, Brazil	79	4 11 S	42 55W
Miguel Calmon, Brazil	79	11 5 S	40 45W
Mihara, Japan	36	34 30N	133 10 E
Miharu, Japan	36	37 25N	140 30 E
Mijares R., Spain	17	40 15N	0 50W
Mijilu, Nigeria	52	10 22N	13 19 E
Mikese, Tanzania	53	6 49 S	38 0 E
Mikhailov, U.S.S.R.	25	54 20N	39 0 E
Mikhailovgrad, Bulgaria	21	43 27N	23 16 E
Mikhailovka, U.S.S.R.	25	50 3N	43 5 E
Mikindani, Tanzania	53	10 15 S	40 2 E
Mikinduri, Kenya	53	0 8N	37 58 E
Mikkeli, Finland	23	61 43N	27 25 E
Mikkelin Laani, Finland	23	61 50N	26 30 E
Mikkwa R., Canada	64	57 40N	114 30W
Mikonos, I., Greece	21	37 50N	25 20 E
Mikumi, Tanzania	53	7 26 S	37 9 E
Milaca, U.S.A.	70	45 45N	93 37W
Milagio, Ecuador	78	2 0 S	79 30W
Milan, Italy	20	45 28N	9 10 E
Milan, Mo., U.S.A.	70	40 10N	93 5W
Milan, Tenn., U.S.A.	71	35 55N	88 45W
Milang, S. Australia	43	35 20 S	138 55 E
Milange, Mozambique	56	16 9 S	35 44 E
Milas, Turkey	30	37 20N	27 50 E
Milazzo, Italy	20	38 13N	15 13 E
Milbank, U.S.A.	70	45 16N	96 34W
Milbanke Sd., Canada	64	52 25N	128 30W
Milden, Canada	65	51 29N	107 32W
Mildura, Victoria	43	34 8 S	142 7 E
Miles, Queensland	43	26 37 S	150 10 E
Miles, U.S.A.	71	31 37N	100 13W
Miles City, U.S.A.	70	46 20N	105 50W
Milestone, Canada	65	50 0N	104 30W
Milford, Del., U.S.A.	68	38 52N	75 27W
Milford, Utah, U.S.A.	73	38 27N	113 1W
Milford, Pa., U.S.A.	68	41 20N	74 47W
Milford Haven, Wales	10	51 43N	5 2W
Milford Sd., N.Z.	47	44 34 S	167 47 E
Miling, W. Australia	44	30 30 S	116 17 E
Militello, Italy	20	37 16N	14 46 E
Milk, R., Canada	64	49 9N	111 25W
Milk, R., U.S.A.	72	48 30N	107 15W
Milk River, Canada	64	49 10N	111 30W
Mill City, U.S.A.	72	44 45N	122 28W
Millar Breakaways, mt., W. Australia	45	28 0 S	125 20 E
Millau, France	12	44 8N	3 4 E
Millchester, Queensland	42	20 15 S	146 16 E
Mille Lacs, L., U.S.A.	70	46 10N	93 30W
Milledgeville, U.S.A.	69	33 7N	85 15W
Millen, U.S.A.	69	32 50N	81 57W
Miller, U.S.A.	70	44 34N	99 0W
Millerovo, U.S.S.R.	25	48 57N	40 28 E
Miller's Flat, N.Z.	47	45 39 S	169 23 E
Millerton, New Zealand	47	41 39 S	171 54 E
Millertown Junction, Canada	63	48 49N	56 28W
Millet, Canada	64	53 10N	113 30W
Millicent, S. Australia	43	37 34 S	140 21 E
Millinocket, U.S.A.	68	45 45N	68 45W
Millmerran, Queens.	43	27 53 S	151 16 E
Mills L., Canada	64	61 30N	118 20W
Millstreet, Ireland	11	52 4N	9 5W
Millungera, Queensland	42	19 47 S	141 35 E
Millville, U.S.A.	68	39 22N	75 0W
Milnor, U.S.A.	70	46 18N	97 28W
Milo, Canada	64	50 35N	112 50W
Milos & I., Greece	21	36 44N	24 25 E
Milparinka, N.S.W.	43	29 40 S	141 52 E
Milton, New Zealand	47	46 7 S	169 59 E
Milton, Fla., U.S.A.	69	30 38N	87 0W
Milton, Ore, U.S.A.	72	45 58N	118 28W
Milton, Pa., U.S.A.	68	41 0N	76 53W
Miltown Malbay, Ireland	11	52 51N	9 25W
Milumba, Tanzania	53	7 5 S	31 4 E
Milwaukee, U.S.A.	68	43 9N	87 58W
Milwaukie, U.S.A.	72	45 29N	122 40W
Mim, Ghana	52	6 57N	2 33W
Min K., China	37	26 30N	118 30 E
Mina, U.S.A.	73	38 24N	118 8W
Mina Hassan Tani (Kenitra), Morocco	50	34 20N	6 40W
Mina Saud, Neutral Zone, Arabia	30	28 47N	48 18 E
Minab, Iran	31	27 10N	57 1 E
Minamata, Japan	36	32 15N	130 27 E
Minago R., Canada	65	54 20N	98 50W
Minaki, Canada	65	50 0N	94 40W
Minas, Uruguay	77	34 25 S	55 20W
Minas Basin, Canada	63	45 20N	64 12W
Minas de Riotinto, Spain	17	37 41N	6 37W
Minas Gerais, st., Brazil	79	18 50 S	46 0W
Minas-cué, Paraguay	77	22 0 S	59 45W
Minatitlan, Mexico	74	17 58N	94 35W
Minato, Japan	36	36 25N	140 35 E
Minbu, Burma	33	20 10N	95 0 E
Mindanao, Philippines	35	8 0N	125 0 E
Mindanao Sea, Phil.	35	8 50N	123 0 E
Minden, Germany	14	52 18N	8 54 E
Minden, U.S.A.	71	32 40N	93 10W
Mindoro, I., Philippines	35	13 0N	121 0 E
Mindoro Strait, Phil.	35	12 30N	119 30 E
Mindouli, Congo (Fr.)	54	4 12 S	14 28 E
Minehead, England	10	51 12N	3 29W
Mineola, U.S.A.	71	32 41N	84 59W
Mineral Wells, U.S.A.	71	32 50N	98 5W
Mineralnye Vody, U.S.S.R.	25	44 18N	43 15 E
Minersville, U.S.A.	73	38 30N	112 58W
Minervino Murge, Italy	20	41 6N	16 5 E
Mingan, Canada	63	50 20N	64 0W
Mingan. *See* Pangkiang	38		
Mingan Is., Canada	63	50 14N	63 20W
Mingary, S. Australia	43	32 7 S	140 43 E
Mingela, Queensland	42	19 42 S	146 42 E
Mingenew, W. Austral.	44	29 12 S	115 21 E
Mingera Cr., Queens.	42	20 34 S	138 20 E
Mingin, Burma	33	22 50N	94 30 E
Mingki (Kweihwa), China	39	26 22N	117 9 E
Minglanilla, Spain	17	39 34N	1 38W
Mingmoo, W. Australia	44	25 14 S	115 38 E
Mingoyo, Tanzania	53	10 9 S	39 29 E
Mingulay I., Scotland	10	56 50N	7 40W
Minho, prov., Portugal	17	41 43N	8 25W
Minhomar, Mozambique	56	14 15 S	36 13 E
Minhsien, China	37	34 27N	104 0 E
Minidoka, U.S.A.	72	42 46N	113 32W
Minigwal L., W. Australia	45	29 31 S	123 14 E
Minilya, W. Australia	44	23 55 S	114 0 E
Minilya R., W. Australia	44	23 45 S	114 0 E
Minipi L., Canada	63	52 25N	61 0W
Mink L., Canada	62	61 12N	117 40W
Minkiang, China	67	32 30N	114 10 E
Minna, Nigeria	52	9 37N	6 30 E
Minneapolis, Kan., U.S.A.	70	39 9N	97 43W
Minneapolis, Minn., U.S.A.	70	44 58N	93 20W
Minnedosa, Canada	65	50 20N	99 50W
Minnesota, St., U.S.A.	70	46 0N	94 30W
Minnesota R., U.S.A.	67	44 30N	95 0W
Minnipa, S. Australia	45	32 56 S	135 8 E
Minnitaki L., Canada	62	50 0N	92 0W
Mino R., Spain	17	43 0N	7 38W
Minorca I. *See* Menorca	17		
Minot, N.D., U.S.A.	69	48 10N	101 30W
Minsk Mazowiecki, Poland	16	52 10N	21 33 E
Minto, Canada	59	62 34N	136 50W
Minton, Canada	65	49 10N	104 10W
Mintsing, China	39	26 15N	118 50 E
Minturn, U.S.A.	73	39 36N	106 23W
Minusinsk, U.S.S.R.	26	53 50N	91 20 E
Minutang, India	33	28 15N	96 30 E
Minya Konka, Mt., China	37	29 47N	101 53 E
Mio, U.S.A.	68	44 38N	84 8W
Mioale, Ethiopia	53	3 42N	39 0 E
Mios Num I., Indon.	35	1 30 S	135 10 E
Miquelon I., St. Pierre and Miquelon, N. Amer.	63	47 10N	56 50W
Miqve Ysrael, Israel	29	32 2N	34 46 E
Mir Ali Khel, Pakistan	32	31 45N	69 35 E
Mira, Italy	20	45 26N	12 9 E
Mira R., Portugal	17	37 30N	8 30W
Miraflores, Mexico	74	23 20N	109 45W
Miraflores Locks, Panama Canal Zone	74	8 59N	79 30W
Miraj, India	32	16 50N	74 45 E
Miram Shah, Pakistan	32	33 2N	70 5 E
Mirama, Mozambique	56	23 52 S	35 37 E
Miramichi B., Canada	63	47 15N	65 0W
Mirand L., Canada	65	55 10N	103 0W
Miranda, Brazil	79	20 10 S	56 15W
Miranda, Spain	17	42 40N	3 0W
Miranda do Douro, Portugal	17	41 32N	6 20W
Miranda Downs, Queensland	42	17 23 S	141 50 E
Miranda R., Brazil	79	20 30 S	56 30W
Mirande, France	12	43 32N	0 24 E
Mirandella, Portugal	17	41 32N	7 16W
Mirando City, U.S.A.	71	27 27N	98 54W
Mirandola, Italy	20	44 52N	11 51 E
Mirango, Malawi	56	13 38 S	34 57 E
Mirani, Queensland	42	21 12 S	148 59 E
Mirboo N., Victoria	43	38 15 S	146 7 E
Mirecourt, France	12	48 20N	6 10 E
Mirgorod, U.S.S.R.	25	49 58N	33 50 E
Miri, Sarawak	35	4 18N	114 0 E
Miriam Vale, Queens.	42	24 20 S	151 39 E
Mitjaveh, Iran	31	29 6N	61 24 E
Mirjawa, Iran	31	29 10N	61 20 E
Mirny, U.S.S.R.	27	62 40N	114 0 E
Mirny, Antarctica	80	67 50 S	46 0 E
Mirond L., Canada	65	55 5N	102 35W
Mirpur, Kashmir	32	33 15N	73 45 E
Mirpur Khas, Pakistan	32	25 30N	69 0 E
Mirror, Canada	64	52 30N	113 0W
Mirror R., Canada	65	57 20N	108 30W
Miruro, Mozambique	56	15 21 S	30 28 E
Mirwari, Kenya	53	1 10 S	38 1 E
Miryang, S. Korea	36	35 34N	128 52 E
Mirzapur, India	32	25 10N	82 45 E
Misantla, Mexico	74	19 50N	96 50W
Miscou I., Canada	63	47 57N	64 31W
Mishan, China	37	45 33N	131 57 E
Mishawaka, U.S.A.	68	41 40N	86 0W
Mishwar Ayyalon, Israel	29	31 52N	34 57 E
Mishmar Ha'emeq, Israel	29	32 37N	35 7 E
Mishmar Hanegev, Israel	29	31 32N	34 48 E
Mishmar Hayarden, Israel	29	33 0N	35 36 E
Misima, I., Papua	42	10 40 S	152 48 E
Misira, Gambia	52		Inset
Misisi, Zaire	53	4 45 S	28 39 E
Miskin, Muscat, Oman	31	23 44N	56 52 E
Miskolc, Hungary	16	48 7N	20 50 E
Misoke, Zaire	53	0 42 S	28 6 E
Misool I., Indon.	53	2 0 S	130 0 E
Misratah, Libya	51	32 18N	15 3 E
Missarabie, Canada	62	48 20N	86 6W
Missinaibi L., Canada	62	48 14N	83 15W
Missinaibi R., Canada	62	50 30N	82 40W
Mission, S.D., U.S.A.	70	43 23N	100 35W
Mission, Texas, U.S.A.	71	26 14N	98 22W
Missisia L., Canada	62	52 20N	85 7W
Missisicabi R., Canada	62	51 10N	79 0W
Mississagi R., Canada	62	46 45N	83 25W
Mississippi, st., U.S.A.	71	33 0N	90 0W
Mississippi, Delta of, U.S.A.	67	29 0N	89 0W
Mississippi R., U.S.A.	70	41 0N	91 0W
Missoula, U.S.A.	72	46 54N	114 0W
Missouri, st., U.S.A.	70	38 25N	92 15W
Missouri R., U.S.A.	70	38 40N	91 45W
Missouri Valley, U.S.A.	70	41 33N	95 52W
Mistake, B., Canada	65	68 8N	93 0W
Mistake Cr., Queens.	42	22 15 S	147 0 E
Mistassibi R., Canada	62	50 0N	72 8W
Mistassini R., Canada	62	49 30N	72 45W
Mistastin L., Canada	63	55 58N	63 40W
Mistatim, Canada	65	52 50N	103 20W
Misti Vol., Peru	78	16 10 S	71 10W
Mistretta, Italy	20	37 56N	14 20 E
Misumi, Japan	36	32 30N	130 32 E
Mitau. *See* Jelgava	23		
Mitchell, Queensland	43	26 29 S	147 58 E
Mitchell, Ind., U.S.A.	68	38 42N	86 25W
Mitchell, Neb., U.S.A.	70	41 59N	103 47W
Mitchell, Ore., U.S.A.	72	44 30N	120 14W
Mitchell, S.D., U.S.A.	70	43 40N	98 0W
Mitchell R., Queens.	42	16 27 S	144 15 E
Mitchelstown, Ireland	11	52 16N	8 18W
Miteda, Mozambique	53	11 49 S	39 40 E
Mitilini, Greece	21	39 6N	26 34 E
Mitkof I., Alaska	64	56 40N	132 50W
Mitla, Mexico	74	16 56N	96 19W
Mito, Japan	36	36 20N	140 30 E
Mitre, mt., N.Z.	46	40 48 S	175 29 E
Mitta Mitta R., Victoria	43	36 45 S	147 36 E
Mitu, Colombia	78	1 0N	70 0W
Mitumba, Tanzania	87	7 8 S	31 2 E
Mitumba Mts., Zaire	56	10 0 S	26 20 E
Mitwaba, Zaire	55	8 30 S	27 25 E
Mityana, Uganda	53	0 25N	32 4 E
Mitzick, Gabon	54	0 45N	11 40 E
Miyake-jima, Japan	36	34 0N	139 30 E
Miyakonojo, Japan	36	31 32N	131 5 E
Miyasu, Japan	36	35 35N	135 10 E
Mixtepec, Mexico	74	16 2N	97 0W
Miyako, Japan	36	39 49N	141 59 E
Miyau, Japan	36	33 0N	131 10 E
Miyazaki, Japan	36	32 0N	131 30 E
Miyazaki, pref., Japan	36	32 10N	132 0 E
Miz'al, Saudi Arabia	30	24 0N	45 18 E
Mizdah, Libya	51	31 23N	12 50 E
Mizen Hd., Ireland	11	51 27N	9 50W
Mjanji, Uganda	53	0 16N	34 0 E
Mjölby, Sweden	23	58 19N	15 10 E
Mjösa, L., Norway	23	60 45N	11 0 E
Mjosa, R., Norway	23	60 40N	11 0 E
Mkalama, Tanzania	53	4 2 S	34 45 E
Mkamba's, Tanzania	53	8 1 S	37 52 E
Mkata, Tanzania	53	6 44 S	37 28 E
Mkere, Tanzania	53	4 58 S	30 0 E
Mkoani, Tanzania	53	5 24 S	39 41 E
Mkokotoni, Tanzania	53	5 55 S	39 16 E
Mkonumbi, Kenya	53	2 22 S	40 44 E
Mkosi, Mozambique	53	11 22 S	38 25 E
Mkpanak, Nigeria	52	4 38N	7 57 E
Mkpot, Nigeria	52	5 40N	8 40 E
Mkula, Tanzania	53	11 1 S	39 30 E
Mkulwa, Tanzania	53	8 31 S	32 30 E
Mkulwe, Tanzania	53	8 33 S	32 19 E
Mkumbi, Ras., Tan.	53	7 30 S	39 47 E
Mkunduchi, Tanzania	53	6 28 S	39 36 E
Mkushi, Zambia	56	14 20 S	29 20 E
Mkushi R., Zambia	56	13 38 S	29 27 E
Mkuu, Tanzania	53	3 12 S	37 39 E
Mkuze R., Natal	57	27 45 S	32 30 E
Mkwaja, Tanzania	53	5 45 S	38 48 E
Mkwaya, Tanzania	53	6 17 S	35 0 E
Mkwuera, Tanzania	53	10 30 S	35 30 E
Mladá Boleslav, C.-Slov.	16	50 27N	14 53 E
Mlagarasi R., Tanzania	53	4 0 S	30 30 E
Mlala Hills, Tanzania	53	7 0 S	31 30 E
Mlali, Tanzania	53	6 59 S	37 38 E
Mlanje, Malawi	55	16 2 S	35 30 E
Mlawa, Poland	16	53 9N	20 25 E
Mlazo, Tanzania	53	6 59 S	35 40 E
Mlele, Tanzania	53	5 25 S	38 12 E
Mlembo R., Zambia	56	13 45 S	30 0 E
Mlewa, Tanzania	53	7 36 S	34 20 E
Mlewera, Tanzania	53	7 20 S	35 29 E
Mloa, Tanzania	53	6 29 S	35 49 E
Mme, W. Cameroon	52	6 18N	10 14 E
Mnazi, Tanzania	53	8 57 S	39 1 E
Mneni, Rhod.	56	20 38 S	30 2 E
Mnyuzi, Tanzania	53	5 13 S	38 34 E
Mo R., Togo	52	9 0N	0 40 E
Mo i Rana, Norway	22	66 15N	14 7 E
Moa, Tanzania	53	4 46 S	39 8 E
Moa I., Indonesia	35	8 15 S	128 0 E
Moa Sulima, S. Leone	52		Inset
Moab, U.S.A.	73	38 35N	109 30W
Moama, N.S.W.	43	36 3 S	144 45 E
Moamba, Mozambique	57	25 34 S	32 16 E
Moapa, U.S.A.	73	36 43N	114 40W
Moate, Ireland	11	53 25N	7 43W
Moba, Zaire	53	7 4 S	29 45 E
Mobaye, Congo (Fr.)	54	4 25N	21 5 E
Moberly, U.S.A.	70	39 25N	92 25W
Moberly R., Canada	64	56 5N	122 0W
Mobert, Canada	62	48 41N	85 40W
Mobile, U.S.A.	69	30 41N	88 3W
Mobile B., U.S.A.	69	30 45N	88 0W
Mobile Pt., U.S.A.	69	30 15N	88 0W
Mobridge, U.S.A.	70	45 6N	100 21W
Mocabe Kasari, Zaire	56	9 58 S	26 16 E
Mocha, Yemen	30	13 18N	43 15 E
Mochudi, Botswana	57	24 28 S	26 5 E
Mocimboa da Praia, Mozam.	53	11 20 S	40 23 E
Mocimboa do Ruvuma, Mozam.	53	11 25 S	39 20 E
Moclips, U.S.A.	72	47 20N	124 12W
Mocoa, Colombia	78	1 15N	76 45W
Mócorito, Mexico	74	25 20N	108 0W
Mocoro, Brazil	79	5 10 S	37 15W
Moctezuma, Chih., Mex.	74	30 10N	109 30W
Moctezuma, S. Luis Potosi, Mexico	74	22 40N	101 10W
Moctezuma R., Mexico	74	21 20N	99 0W
Mocuba, Mozambique	55	16 52 S	36 57 E
Modane, France	12	45 12N	6 40 E
Modasa, India	32	23 28N	73 20 E
Modder R., S. Africa	57	29 1 S	24 39 E
Modele, W. Cameroon	52	6 30N	9 59 E
Modena, Italy	20	44 39N	10 55 E
Modena, U.S.A.	73	37 52N	113 52W
Modesto, U.S.A.	73	37 30N	121 0W
Modica, Italy	20	36 52N	14 45 E
Modjokerto, Indonesia	34	7 29 S	112 25 E
Modu R., Nigeria	52	8 15N	8 5 E

Name	Map	Lat.	Long.
Moengo, Guyana	79	5 45N	54 20W
Moeri, Zaire	53	3 57N	30 22 E
Moeskroen, Belgium	13	50 45N	3 11 E
Moffat, Scotland	10	55 20N	3 27W
Mofu, I., Zambia	56	11 4 S	30 20 E
Mofwe L., Zambia	56	9 40 S	28 40 E
Mogadoura, Portugal	17	41 22N	6 47W
Mogadishu, Somali Rep.	49	2 2N	45 21 E
Mogalakwena R., Trans.	51	23 0 S	28 40 E
Mogami R., Japan	36	38 45N	140 0 E
Mogaung, Burma	33	25 20N	97 0 E
Mogho, Ethiopia	53	4 58N	40 20 E
Mogi das Cruzes, Brazil	77	23 45 S	46 20W
Mogilev, U.S.S.R.	25	53 55N	30 18 E
Mogilev Podolski, U.S.S.R.	24	48 20N	27 40 E
Mogilno, Poland	16	52 39N	17 55 E
Mogincual, Mozam.	55	15 33 S	40 29 E
Mogocha, U.S.S.R.	27	53 40N	119 50 E
Mogogelo R., Botswana	56	19 30 S	23 45 E
Mogoi, Indonesia	35	1 55 S	133 10 E
Mogôk, Burma	33	23 0N	96 40 E
Mogollon, U.S.A.	73	53 27N	108 47W
Mogollon Mesa Mts., U.S.A.	73	34 40N	111 0W
Mogororo, Sudan	51	12 21N	22 24 E
Mogotes Pt., Argentina	77	38 10 S	57 30W
Moguer, Spain	17	37 15N	6 52W
Moha, Canada	64	50 55N	122 25W
Mohács, Hungary	16	46 0N	18 43 E
Mohaka R., N.Z.	46	39 13 S	176 39 E
Mohaleshoek, Lesotho	57	30 9 S	27 29 E
Mohall, U.S.A.	70	48 47N	101 29W
Mohanganj, Bangladesh	33	24 50N	91 5 E
Mohawk, U.S.A.	73	32 45N	113 47W
Mohembo, S.W. Africa	56	18 15 S	21 43 E
Mohenjodaro, W. Pak.	31	27 20N	68 0 E
Mohill, Ireland	11	53 57N	7 52W
Mohoro, Tanzania	53	8 2 S	39 12 E
Moia, Sudan	53	5 1N	28 2 E
Moiero R., U.S.S.R.	27	67 30N	104 20 E
Mointy, U.S.S.R.	26	47 40N	73 45 E
Moisakula, U.S.S.R.	23	58 2N	25 12 E
Moisie, R., Canada	63	51 50N	66 34W
Moissac, France	12	44 7N	1 5 E
Mojácar, Spain	17	37 6N	1 55W
Mojave, U.S.A.	73	35 5N	118 10W
Mojave Desert, U.S.A.	73	35 0N	117 30W
Moji, Japan	36	33 50N	131 0 E
Mojib, Wadi el, Jordan	29	31 27N	35 35 E
Mojo I., Indonesia	35	8 10 S	117 40 E
Mokai, New Zealand	46	38 32 S	175 56 E
Mokambo, Zaire	56	12 26 S	28 22 E
Mokau, New Zealand	46	38 42 S	174 39 E
Mokau R., New Zealand	46	38 35 S	174 55 E
Mokhapinyana, Botswana	56	22 15 S	27 20 E
Mokhotlong, Les.	57	29 15 S	29 8 E
Mokihinui, R., N.Z.	47	41 35 S	172 10 E
Mokmor, Indonesia	35	1 5 S	136 0 E
Mokokchung, India.	33	26 15N	94 30 E
Mokola, Cameroon	52	10 47N	13 48 E
Mokolo Ho., W. Australia	44	24 45 S	114 17 E
Mokpo, Korea	36	34 50N	126 30 E
Moku, Zaire	53	3 0N	29 20 E
Mokwa, Nigeria	52	9 19N	5 3 E
Mol, Belgium	13	51 11N	5 7 E
Mola, Italy	20	41 3N	17 5 E
Moláoi, Greece	21	36 49N	22 56 E
Molchanovo, U.S.S.R.	26	57 40N	83 50 E
Moldavia S.S.R., U.S.S.R.	24	47 0N	28 0 E
Molde, Norway	23	62 43N	7 2W
Mole Cr., Tasmania	43	41 31 S	146 25 E
Molepolole, Botswana	57	24 28 S	25 28 E
Molesworth, N.Z.	47	42 5 S	173 16 E
Molfetta, Italy	20	41 12N	16 35 E
Molina, Spain	17	40 46N	1 52W
Moline, U.S.A.	70	41 30N	90 30W
Moliro, Zaire	54	8 5 S	30 30 E
Mollendo, Peru	78	17 0 S	72 0W
Mölndal, Sweden	23	57 40N	11 59 E
Moledechno, U.S.S.R.	23	54 20N	26 50 E
Molodezhnaya, Ant.	80	67 50 S	46 0 E
Molokai, I., Hawaii	59	21 10N	157 0W
Molong, N.S.W.	43	33 5 S	148 54 E
Molopo R., Botswana	57	25 40 S	24 30 E
Molotov C., U.S.S.R.	27	81 10N	95 0 E
Moloundou, Cameroon	54	2 5N	15 15 E
Molson L., Canada	65	54 20N	96 50W
Molteno, Cape Province	57	31 22 S	26 22 E
Molucca Is., Indonesia	25	1 0 S	127 0 E
Molucca Sea, Indonesia	35	4 0 S	124 0 E
Molusi, Botswana	56	20 19 S	24 22 E
Moma, Mozambique	55	16 46 S	39 10 E
Momba R., Tanzania	53	8 30 S	32 16 E
Mombasa, Kenya	53	4 0 S	39 35 E
Mombetsu, Japan	36	44 12N	143 20 E
Momchilgrad, Bulgaria	21	41 33N	25 23 E
Momence, U.S.A.	68	41 10N	87 40W
Mominabad, India	32	18 44N	76 23 E
Mompós, Colombia	75	9 19N	74 28W
Momputu, Zaire	56	8 35 S	28 7 E
Mon, R., Burma	33	20 30N	94 30 E

Name	Map	Lat.	Long.
Mön I., Denmark	23	54 51N	12 15 E
Mona, Puerto Rico	75	17 58N	67 48W
Mona Pass., W. Indies	75	18 0N	67 40W
Mona, Pta., Costa Rica	75	9 25N	82 30W
Monaco, principality, Europe	12	43 3	72 3 E
Monaghan, Ireland	11	54 15N	6 58W
Monaghan, co., Ireland	11	54 10N	7 0W
Monahans, U.S.A.	71	31 34N	102 47W
Monaka Bantu, Zambia	56	15 56 S	25 19 E
Monarch Mt., Canada	64	51 55N	125 57W
Monashee Mts., Canada	64	50 0N	118 20W
Monasterevan, Ireland	11	53 10N	7 5W
Monastir (Bitolj), Y.slav.	21	41 0N	21 17 E
Monastir, Tunisia	51	35 42N	10 49 E
Monawatu R., N.Z.	46	40 28 S	175 15 E
Moncay, Spain	17	41 43N	1 51 E
Moncay, N. Viet Nam	39	21 31N	108 0 E
Monchegorsk, U.S.S.R.	22	67 40N	33 15 E
Monchique, Portugal	17	37 19N	8 38W
Monclova, Mexico	74	26 50N	101 30W
Moncton, Canada	63	46 7N	64 51W
Mondego R., Portugal	17	40 28N	8 0W
Mondo, Tanzania	53	4 59 S	36 2 E
Mondonedo, Spain	17	43 25N	7 23W
Mondovi, Italy	20	44 23N	7 56 E
Mondovi, U.S.A.	68	44 37N	91 40W
Monessen, Pa., U.S.A.	68	40 9N	79 50W
Monet, Canada	62	48 10N	75 40W
Monett, U.S.A.	71	36 56N	93 58W
Moneygall, Ireland	11	52 54N	7 59W
Moneymore, Ireland	11	54 42N	6 40W
Monfalcone, Italy	20	45 49N	13 32 E
Monforte, Spain	17	42 31N	7 33W
Mong Hsat, Burma	33	20 15N	99 30 E
Möng Hsu, Burma	33	21 54N	98 30 E
Möng Kung, Burma	33	21 35N	97 35 E
Mong Noi, Burma	33	20 32N	97 51 E
Möng Pan, Burma	33	20 28N	98 30 E
Mong Pawk, Burma	33	21 59N	99 16 E
Mong Ton, Burma	33	20 17N	98 54 E
Mong Yai, Burma	33	22 21N	98 2 E
Mongalla, Sudan	54	5 8N	31 55 E
Mongar Dzong, Bhutan	33	27 15N	91 20 E
Mongbwalu, Zaire	53	1 56N	30 3 E
Monger L., Australia	44	29 0 S	117 15 E
Monghyr, India	33	25 23N	86 30 E
Mongo, Chad.	51	12 14N	18 43 E
Mongo R., Sierra Leone Inset	52	46 48N	12 7 E
Mongolia, rep., Asia	37	47 0N	103 0 E
Mongonu, Nigeria	52	12 40N	13 32 E
Mongo, Zambia	56	15 16 S	23 12 E
Monk, Canada	65	47 7N	69 59W
Monkey Bay, Malawi	56	14 3 S	35 4 E
Monkira, Queensland	42	24 46 S	140 30 E
Monkoto, Zaire	54	1 38 S	20 35 E
Monmouth, England	10	51 48N	2 43W
Monmouth, U.S.A.	68	40 50N	90 40W
Monmouth, Mt., Canada	64	51 1N	123 43W
Monnatlala, Bot.	56	22 35 S	27 25 E
Mono, Pta del, Nic.	75	12 0N	83 30W
Mono R., Dahomey	52	6 30N	1 43 E
Monolithos, Rhodes	21	36 3N	27 45 E
Monongahela R., U.S.A.	69	39 15N	80 30W
Monopoli, Italy	20	40 57N	17 18 E
Monovar, Spain	17	38 28N	0 53W
Monowai L., N.Z.	47	45 53 S	167 25 E
Monreale, Italy	20	38 6N	13 16 E
Monroe, La., U.S.A.	71	32 45N	92 4W
Monroe, Mich., U.S.A.	67	41 55N	83 20W
Monroe, N.C., U.S.A.	69	35 2N	80 37W
Monroe, Utah, U.S.A.	73	38 43N	112 4W
Monroe, Wash., U.S.A.	68	47 50N	121 58W
Monroe, Wis., U.S.A.	70	42 33N	89 36W
Monroe City, U.S.A.	68	39 40N	91 40W
Monroeville, U.S.A.	69	31 33N	87 15W
Monrovia, Liberia	50	6 18N	10 47W
Monrovia, U.S.A.	73	34 10N	118 1W
Mons, Belgium	13	50 27N	3 58 E
Monserrat, Spain	17	41 49N	1 48 E
Monsterås, Sweden	23	57 3N	16 33 E
Mont Bugoy, Zaire	53	1 23 S	29 0 E
Mont Blanc, mt., France–Italy	12	45 48N	6 50 E
Mont de Marsan, France	12	43 54N	0 31W
Mont Joli, Canada	63	48 37N	68 10W
Mont Laurier, Canada	62	46 35N	75 30W
Mont Laurier Senneterre, Fishing Reserve, Canada	62	47 30N	77 20W
Mont-Louis, Canada	63	49 14N	65 40W
Mont St. Michel, France	12	48 40N	1 30W
Mont Tremblant Prov. Park, Canada	62	46 30N	74 30W
Montagu, C. Prov.	57	33 45 S	20 8 E
Montague, Canada	63	46 10N	62 39W
Montague, Queensland	42	23 42 S	147 13 E
Montague, U.S.A.	72	41 45N	122 32W
Montague I., Alaska	59	60 0N	147 30W
Montague I., Mexico	74	31 40N	144 40W
Montague Ra., W. Australia	44	27 15 S	119 45 E
Montalban, Spain	17	40 50N	0 45W
Montalcino, Italy	20	43 4N	11 30 E
Montalto, Italy	25	42 20N	11 36 E

Name	Map	Lat.	Long.
Montana, st., U.S.A.	72	47 0N	110 0W
Montargis, France	12	48 0N	2 43 E
Montauban, France	12	44 0N	1 21 E
Montauk Pt., U.S.A.	68	41 5N	71 51W
Montbéliard, France	12	47 31N	6 48 E
Montblanch, Spain	17	41 23N	1 4 E
Montbrison, France	12	45 36N	4 3 E
Montceau, France	12	46 40N	4 23 E
Montdidier, France	12	49 38N	2 35 E
Monte Alegre, Brazil	79	2 0 S	54 0W
Monte Bello Is., W. Australia	44	20 22 S	115 30 E
Monte Caseros, Uruguay	77	30 10 S	57 50W
Monte Coman, Arg.	77	34 40 S	68 0W
Monte Lirio, Panama Canal Zone	74	Inset	
Monte Morelos, Mexico	74	25 10N	99 50W
Monto S. Angelo, Italy	20	41 43N	15 58 E
Monte Santu C., Italy	20	40 5N	9 42 E
Monte Verde, Angola	55	8 43 S	16 50 E
Monte Vista, U.S.A.	73	37 39N	106 8W
Monteagle, Queensland	42	22 25 S	147 5 E
Montebello, Canada	62	45 40N	74 55W
Montecristi, Ecuador	78	1 0 S	80 40W
Montecristo I., Italy	20	42 20N	10 20 E
Montego B., Jamaica	75	18 30N	78 0W
Montellana, Spain	17	36 59N	5 34W
Montello, U.S.A.	70	34 49N	89 21W
Montemorelos, Mexico	74	25 11N	99 42W
Montemor-o-Novo, Portugal	17	38 39N	8 14W
Montenegro (Crna Gora) Prov., Yugoslavia	21	42 40N	19 20 E
Montepuez, Mozam.	55	13 9 S	39 0 E
Montereau, France	12	48 22N	2 57 E
Monterey, Calif., U.S.A.	73	36 30N	122 0W
Monterey, Va., U.S.A.	69	38 26N	79 37W
Monteria, Colombia	75	8 45N	75 54W
Monterrey, Mexico	74	25 40N	100 30W
Montes Claros, Brazil	79	16 30 S	43 50W
Montesano, U.S.A.	72	47 0N	123 33W
Montevideo, Uruguay	77	34 50 S	56 11W
Montezuma, U.S.A.	70	41 33N	92 32W
Montfort-sur-Meu, Fr.	12	48 8N	1 58W
Montgomery, Pakistan	32	30 45N	73 8 E
Montgomery, Ala., U.S.A.	69	32 20N	85 20W
Montgomery, W. Va., U.S.A.	68	38 9N	81 21W
Monticello, Ark., U.S.A.	71	33 36N	91 49W
Monticello, Fla., U.S.A.	69	30 35N	83 50W
Monticello, Ind., U.S.A.	68	40 40N	86 45W
Monticello, Iowa, U.S.A.	70	42 11N	91 13W
Monticello, Ky., U.S.A.	69	36 52N	84 50W
Monticello, Me., U.S.A.	69	46 19N	67 51W
Monticello, Minn., U.S.A.	70	45 16N	93 46W
Monticello, Miss., U.S.A.	71	31 32N	90 7W
Monticello, Utah, U.S.A.	73	37 52N	109 51W
Montijo, Portugal	17	38 41N	8 57W
Montilla, Spain	17	37 36N	4 40W
Montivideo, U.S.A.	70	44 56N	95 39W
Montlucon, France	12	46 22N	2 36 E
Montmagny, Canada	63	46 58N	70 34W
Montmartre, Canada	65	50 20N	103 15W
Montmédy, France	12	49 30N	5 20 E
Montmorency, Canada	63	46 53N	71 11W
Montmorillon, France	12	46 26N	0 50 E
Monto, Queensland	42	24 52 S	151 12 E
Montoro, Spain	17	38 1N	4 27W
Montpelier, Idaho, U.S.A.	72	42 15N	111 10W
Montpelier, Ohio, U.S.A.	68	41 53N	84 40W
Montpelier, Vt., U.S.A.	69	44 15N	72 38W
Montpellier, France	12	43 37N	3 52 E
Montreal, Canada	62	45 31N	73 34W
Montreal Lake, Canada	65	54 18N	106 0W
Montreal L., Canada	65	54 20N	105 45W
Montréjeau, France	12	43 6N	0 35 E
Montreuil, France	12	50 27N	1 45 E
Montreux, Switzerland	15	46 26N	6 55 E
Montrose, Scotland	10	56 43N	2 28W
Montrose, U.S.A.	73	38 30N	107 52W
Monts, Pte des, Canada	63	49 27N	67 12W
Montseny, Spain	17	41 50N	2 21 E
Montserrat I., Leeward Islands	75	16 40N	62 10W
Monveda, Zaire	54	3 0N	21 35 E
Mônywa, Burma	33	22 7N	95 11 E
Monze, Zambia	56	16 25 S	27 30 E
Monze C., Pakistan	32	24 47N	66 37 E
Monzon, Spain	17	41 52N	0 10 E
Mooi River, Natal	57	29 13 S	29 50 E
Mooketsi, Transvaal	57	23 40 S	30 9 E
Moonah Cr., Queens.	42	21 45 S	138 30 E
Moonbeam, Canada	62	49 20N	82 10W
Mooncoin, Ireland	11	52 18N	7 17W
Moonie R., Queensland	43	27 46 S	150 0 E
Moonta, S. Australia	43	34 6 S	137 32 E
Moora, W. Australia	44	30 37 S	115 58 E
Mooraberree, Queens.	43	25 13 S	140 54 E
Moorcroft, U.S.A.	70	44 17N	104 26W

Name	Map	Lat.	Long.
Moore, L., W. Austral.	44	29 30 S	117 30 E
Moore, R., W. Austral.	44	31 5 S	115 25 E
Moorefield, U.S.A.	68	39 5N	78 59W
Mooresville, U.S.A.	69	35 36N	80 45W
Moorhead, U.S.A.	70	47 0N	96 45W
Moorreesburg, C. Prov.	57	33 6 S	18 38 E
Moose Factory, Canada	62	52 20N	80 40W
Moose I., Canada	65	51 35N	97 0W
Moose Jaw, Canada	65	50 30N	105 30W
Moose Jaw Cr., Canada	65	50 0N	105 0W
Moose Lake, Canada	65	53 30N	100 15W
Moose Lake, U.S.A.	70	46 29N	92 45W
Moose L., Canada	65	53 40N	100 0W
Moose Mt., R., Canada	65	49 40N	102 40W
Moose Mt., Prov. Park	65	49 45N	102 40W
Moose River, Canada	62	51 0N	81 20W
Moose R., Canada	62	51 0N	81 10W
Moosehead L., U.S.A.	69	45 40N	69 40W
Moosomin, Canada	65	50 9N	101 40W
Moosonee, Canada	62	51 20N	80 40W
Mooti, Somali Rep.	53	0 34N	41 37 E
Mopeia, Mozambique	55	17 30 S	35 40 E
Mopepi, Botswana	57	21 13 S	24 52 E
Mopti, Mali	50	14 30N	4 0W
Moquegua, Peru	78	17 15 S	70 46W
Mór, Hungary	16	47 25N	18 12 E
Mor Matamoros, Mex.	74	18 30N	98 30W
Mora, Cameroon	52	11 3N	14 6 E
Mora, Portugal	17	38 55N	8 10W
Mora, Tarragona, Spain	17	41 6N	0 39 E
Mora, Sweden,	23	60 57N	14 38 E
Mora, Minn., U.S.A.	70	45 53N	93 16W
Mora, N. Mex., U.S.A.	71	35 53N	105 15W
Moradabad, India	32	28 50N	78 50 E
Moran, Kan., U.S.A.	71	37 58N	95 14W
Moran, Wyo., U.S.A.	72	43 53N	110 33W
Morant Cays, Is., Jamaica	75	17 30N	76 0W
Morant Pt., Jamaica	75	17 55N	76 12W
Moratuwa, Sri Lanka	32	6 45N	79 55 E
Morava R., C.Slov.	16	49 50N	16 50 E
Morava R., Yugoslavia	21	44 10N	21 10 E
Moravia, Reg., Europe	16	49 7N	15 57 E
Moravian Heights, mts.	16	49 15N	15 0W
Moravid, U.S.A.	70	40 52N	92 47W
Morawa, W. Australia	44	29 13 S	116 0 E
Morawhanna, Guy.	78	8 30N	59 40W
Moray Firth, Scotland	10	57 50N	3 30W
Morcenx, France	12	44 0N	0 55W
Morden, Canada	65	49 15N	98 10W
Mordovo, U.S.S.R.	25	52 13N	40 50 E
Möre and Romsdal, prov., Norway	23	62 30N	8 0 E
Morea (Carpolac), Vic.	43	36 33 S	141 14 E
Moreau R., U.S.A.	70	45 5N	103 0W
Morecambe, England	10	54 5N	2 52W
Moree, N.S.W.	43	29 28 S	149 48 E
Morehead, U.S.A.	68	38 12N	83 32W
Morehead City, U.S.A.	69	34 46N	76 44W
Morelia, Mexico	74	19 40N	101 11W
Morella, Queensland	42	23 0 S	143 47 E
Morella, Spain	17	40 35N	0 2W
Morelos, st., Mexico	74	18 40N	99 10W
Morena, India	32	26 35N	78 0 E
Morena, Sierra, Spain	17	38 20N	4 0W
Morenci, U.S.A.	73	33 5N	109 26W
Moreno, Colombia	78	6 0N	71 50W
Moresby I., Canada	64	52 30N	131 40W
Moresnet, Belgium	13	40 44N	5 59 E
Moreton, Queensland	43	12 22 S	142 30 E
Moreton B., Queensland	43	27 13 S	152 54 E
Moreton C., Queensland	43	27 2 S	153 12 E
Moreton, Div., Queensland	43	27 25 S	152 30 E
Moreton I., Queensland	43	27 10 S	153 10 E
Morez, France	12	46 31N	6 2 E
Morgan, S. Australia	43	34 0 S	139 35 E
Morgan, U.S.A.	72	41 4N	111 43W
Morgan City, U.S.A.	71	29 40N	91 15W
Morganfield, U.S.A.	68	37 40N	87 55W
Morgans, W. Australia	44	28 40 S	122 0 E
Morganton, U.S.A.	69	35 46N	81 48W
Morgantown, U.S.A.	68	39 39N	79 58W
Morganville, Queens.	43	25 10 S	152 0 E
Morgenzon, Transvaal	57	26 45 S	29 36 E
Morges, Switzerland	15	46 31N	6 29 E
Moriah, Tobago	75	Inset	
Moriarty's Ra., Queens.	43	28 10 S	145 20 E
Moriaty, U.S.A.	73	35 3N	106 2W
Morice L., Canada	64	53 50N	127 40W
Moriki, Nigeria	52	12 52N	6 30 E
Morinville, Canada	64	53 49N	113 41W
Morioka, Japan	36	39 45N	141 8 E
Morjärv, Sweden	22	66 6N	22 58 E
Morkalla, Victoria	43	34 18 S	141 4 E
Morlaix, France	12	48 36N	3 52W
Morne Diablotin, mt., Leeward Is.	75	Inset	
Morney, Queensland	43	25 22 S	141 23 E
Mornington, Ireland	11	53 42N	6 17W
Mornington, Victoria	43	38 8 S	145 5 E
Mornington I., Chile	77	49 50 S	75 30W
Mornington I., Queens.	42	16 30 S	139 30 E
Morno, Ghana	52	8 45N	1 45W
Moro, R., Sierra Leone	52	Inset	
Morobe, Terr. of New Guinea	42	7 49 S	147 38 E
Morocco, st., N. Africa	50	32 0N	5 0W

	MAP		
Morococha, Peru	78	11 40s	76 5w
Moroeni, Rumania	21	45 1N	25 40E
Morogoro, Tanzania	53	6 45s	37 45E
Morogoro, prov., Tan.	53	8 0s	37 30E
Morokweng, C. Prov.	57	26 8s	23 45E
Moroleón, Mexico	74	20 8N	101 32w
Morón, Cuba	75	22 0N	78 30w
Morón, Spain	17	37 6N	5 28w
Morona, Ecuador	78	2 40s	77 35w
Morona R., Peru and Ecuador	78	3 30s	77 10w
Morondava, Madag.	55	20 25s	44 30E
Morotai I., Indonesia	35	2 10N	128 30E
Moroto, Uganda	53	2 28N	34 42E
Moroto Summit, mt., Uganda	53	2 27N	34 46E
Morozovsk, U.S.S.R.	25	48 25N	41 40E
Morpeth, England	10	55 11N	1 41w
Morphou, Cyprus	30	35 13N	33 0E
Morrilton, U.S.A.	71	35 5N	92 46w
Morrinhos, Brazil	79	17 45s	49 10w
Morrinsville, N.Z.	46	37 40s	175 32E
Morris, Canada	65	49 25N	97 30w
Morris, Ill., U.S.A.	70	41 20N	88 20w
Morris, Minn., U.S.A.	70	45 35N	95 55w
Morrisburg, Canada	62	44 55N	75 7w
Morrison, U.S.A.	70	41 47N	89 58w
Morristown, Ariz., U.S.A.	73	33 51N	112 39w
Morristown, S.D., U.S.A.	70	45 58N	101 44w
Morristown, Tenn., U.S.A.	68	36 18N	83 20w
Morro B., U.S.A.	73	35 27N	120 52w
Morrosquillo, G. of, Colombia	78	9 40N	75 50w
Morrumbala, Mozam.	56	17 18s	35 39E
Morrumbene, Mozam.	56	23 38s	35 20E
Morshansk, U.S.S.R.	25	53 28N	41 50E
Mortagne, Charente Maritime, France	12	45 28N	0 49w
Mortagne, Orne, France	12	48 30N	0 32E
Mortagne, Vendée, Fr.	12	46 59N	0 50w
Morteros, Argentina	77	30 50s	62 2w
Mortes (Manso) R., Brazil	79	13 30s	51 50w
Mortlake, Victoria	43	38 5s	142 50E
Morton, Texas, U.S.A.	71	33 43N	102 56w
Morton, Wash., U.S.A.	72	46 35N	122 16w
Moruchak, U.S.S.R.	31	35 50N	63 6E
Moruya, N.S.W.	43	35 58N	150 3E
Morven, New Zealand	47	44 50s	171 6E
Morven, Queensland	43	26 25s	147 3E
Morvi, India	32	22 50N	70 52E
Morwell, Victoria	43	38 10s	146 22E
Mosalsk, U.S.S.R.	25	54 30N	34 55E
Moscow, U.S.A.	72	46 39N	116 59w
Moscow (Moskva), U.S.S.R.	25	55 45N	37 35E
Moselle R., France	14	49 15N	6 10E
Moses Lake, U.S.A.	72	47 8N	119 19w
Mosgiel, New Zealand	47	45 53s	170 21E
Moshi, Tanzania	53	3 18s	37 27E
Mosjöen, Norway	22	65 52N	13 20E
Moskenesöy, L., Nor.	22	67 38N	13 0E
Moskenstraumen, str., Norway	22	67 45N	13 0E
Mosquera, Colombia	78	2 35N	78 30w
Mosquero, U.S.A.	71	35 45N	103 59w
Mosquitos, G. of, Pan.	78	9 15N	81 10w
Moss, Norway	23	59 27N	10 40E
Moss Vale, N.S.W.	43	34 32s	150 25E
Mossaka, Congo (Fr.)	54	1 20s	16 44E
Mossâmedes, Angola	55	15 7s	12 11E
Mossbank, Canada	65	50 0N	106 0w
Mossburn, New Zealand	47	45 41s	168 15E
Mosselbaai, C. Prov.	57	34 11s	22 8E
Mossendjo, Congo (Fr.)	54	2 52s	12 46E
Mossgiel, N.S.W.	43	33 16s	144 32E
Mossman, Queensland	42	16 23s	145 24E
Mossoro, Brazil	79	5 15s	37 20w
Mossuril, Mozambique	55	14 55s	40 41E
Mossy R., Canada	65	54 10N	103 20w
Most, Czechoslovakia	16	50 31N	13 38E
Mostaganem, Algeria	50	35 51N	0 7E
Mostar, Yugoslavia	21	43 22N	17 50E
Mostardas, Brazil	77	31 0N	51 0w
Mostrim, Ireland	11	53 42N	7 38w
Mosun, China	39	23 37N	109 47E
Mosul, Iraq	30	36 20N	43 5E
Mota, Ethiopia	54	11 2N	27 50E
Motacucito, Bolivia	78	17 32s	61 32w
Motagua R., Guatemala	74	15 30N	88 40w
Motala, Sweden	23	58 32N	15 1E
Motatan, Venezuela	78	9 25N	70 40w
Motherwell, Scotland	10	55 48N	4 0w
Motihari, India	33	26 37N	85 1E
Motiti Island, N.Z.	46	37 38s	176 29E
Motozintla, Mexico	74	15 21N	92 14w
Motril, Spain	17	36 44N	3 37w
Mott, U.S.A.	70	46 27N	102 24w
Motu River, N.Z.	46	38 5s	177 43E
Motueka, New Zealand	47	41 7s	173 1E
Motuhora, New Zealand	46	38 16s	177 33E
Motul, Mexico	74	21 0N	89 20w
Moûdhros, Greece	21	39 53N	25 19E
Moudjeria, Mauritania	50	17 50N	12 15w
Moudon, Switzerland	15	46 40N	6 49E
Mouiamé, Cameroon	52	5 4N	12 1E
Mouila, Gabon	54	1 50s	11 0E
Mouka, Congo (Fr.)	54	7 20N	21 45E
Moulamein, N.S.W.	43	35 3s	144 1E
Moulamein, R., N.S.W.	43	35 6s	145 0E
Moulapamok, Cambodia	34	14 21N	105 47E
Moulins, France	12	46 35N	3 19E
Moulmein, Burma	33	16 30N	97 40E
Moulton, U.S.A.	71	29 36N	97 8w
Moultrie, U.S.A.	69	31 5N	84 0w
Mound City, Miss., U.S.A.	70	40 2N	95 15w
Mound City, S.D., U.S.A.	70	45 45N	100 3w
Moundou, Chad	54	8 40N	16 10E
Moundsville, U.S.A.	69	39 53N	80 43w
Mount Abu, India	32	24 30N	73 40E
Mount Airy, U.S.A.	69	36 31N	80 37w
Mount Angel, U.S.A.	72	45 3N	122 48w
Mount Ayliff, C. Prov.	57	30 48s	29 22E
Mount Barker, S. Australia	43	35 5s	138 52E
Mount Bellew Bridge, Ireland	11	53 28N	8 3w
Mount Brown, N.S.W.	43	29 49s	141 41E
Mount Carmel, Ill., U.S.A.	68	38 20N	88 0w
Mount Carmel, Pa., U.S.A.	68	40 46N	76 23w
Mount Cenis Pass, Fr.	20	45 15N	7 0E
Mount Clemens, U.S.A.	68	42 35N	82 50w
Mount Cuthbert, Queensland	42	19 59s	139 50E
Mount Desert I., U.S.A.	69	44 25N	68 25w
Mount Dora, U.S.A.	69	28 49N	81 32w
Mount Drysdale, N.S.W.	43	31 10s	145 50E
Mount Edgecumbe, Alas.	59	57 0N	135 25w
Mount Fletcher, C. Prov.	52	30 40s	28 31E
Mount Forest, Canada	62	43 59N	80 43w
Mount Frere, C. Prov.	57	30 51s	29 0E
Mount Gambier, S. Australia	43	37 38s	140 44E
Mount Garnet, Queens.	42	17 37s	145 6E
Mount Goldsworthy, W. Australia	44	20 25s	119 35E
Mount Hope, N.S.W.	43	32 49s	145 40w
Mount Hope, S. Australia	45	34 7s	135 23E
Mount Hope, U.S.A.	68	37 52N	81 9w
Mount Horeb, U.S.A.	70	43 0N	89 45w
Mount Hotham, Victoria	43	37 2s	146 52E
Mount Howitt, Queens.	43	26 29s	142 19E
Mount Hubert, W. Australia	44	22 33s	115 59E
Mount Ida, W. Austral.	44	29 1s	120 26E
Mount Isa, Queensland	42	20 42s	139 26E
Mount Magnet, W. Australia	44	28 2s	117 47E
Mount Margaret, W. Australia	45	28 45s	122 10E
Mount Maunganui, N.Z.	46	37 40s	176 14E
Mount McConnel, Queensland	42	20 50s	147 0E
Mount Molloy, Queens.	42	16 32s	145 20E
Mount Morgan, Queens.	42	23 40s	150 25E
Mount Morris, N.Y., U.S.A.	68	42 43N	77 50w
Mount Mulligan, Queensland	42	16 45s	144 47E
Mount Perry, Queens.	43	25 13s	151 42E
Mount Pleasant, S. Australia	43	34 43s	139 0E
Mount Pleasant, Iowa, U.S.A.	70	40 56N	91 32w
Mount Pleasant, Mich., U.S.A.	68	43 38N	84 46w
Mount Pleasant, S.C., U.S.A.	69	32 48N	79 54w
Mount Pleasant, Tenn., U.S.A.	69	35 32N	87 11w
Mount Pleasant, Texas, U.S.A.	71	33 5N	95 0w
Mount Pleasant, Utah, U.S.A.	73	39 36N	111 29w
Mount Revelstoke Nat. Park, Canada	64	51 20N	117 50w
Mount Robson, Canada	64	53 0N	119 5w
Mount Roskill, N.Z.	46	36 55s	174 42E
Mount St. Michel, France	12	48 40N	1 35w
Mount Shasta, U.S.A.	72	41 20N	122 20w
Mount Silinda, Rhod.	56	20 26s	32 32E
Mount Sir Samuel, W. Australia	44	27 32s	120 30E
Mount Sterling, U.S.A.	68	38 0N	84 0w
Mount Sterling, U.S.A.	70	39 58N	90 38w
Mount Surprise, Queens.	42	18 10s	144 17E
Mount Vernon, Ill., U.S.A.	70	38 20N	88 52w
Mount Vernon, N.Y., U.S.A.	68	40 57N	73 49w
Mount Vernon, Ohio, U.S.A.	68	40 20N	82 30w
Mount Vernon, Wash., U.S.A.	64	48 27N	122 18w
Mount Wellington, N.Z.	46	36 55s	174 51E
Mountain City, Nev., U.S.A.	72	41 52N	116 0w
Mountain City, Tenn., U.S.A.	69	36 30N	81 50w
Mountain Grove, U.S.A.	71	37 6N	92 25w
Mountain Home, Ark., U.S.A.	71	36 25N	92 29w
Mountain Home, Idaho, U.S.A.	72	43 11N	115 40w
Mountain Iron, U.S.A.	70	47 30N	92 34w
Mountain Park, Canada	64	52 50N	117 15w
Mountain View, Canada	71	35 51N	92 8w
Mountain View, Hawaiian Is.	52	19 32N	155 0w
Mountain View, U.S.A.	73	37 28N	127 16w
Mountain Village, Alas.	59	62 9N	163 49w
Mountainair, U.S.A.	73	34 32N	106 13w
Mountmellick, Ireland	11	53 7N	7 20w
Mountrath, Ireland	11	53 0N	7 30w
Mounts Bay, England	10	50 3N	5 27w
Mountshannon, Ireland	11	52 56N	8 26w
Moura, Brazil	78	1 25s	61 45w
Moura, Portugal	17	38 7N	7 30w
Mourão, Portugal	17	38 22N	7 22w
Mourdhia, Mali	50	14 35N	7 25w
Mouri, Ghana	52	5 3N	1 9w
Mourne Mts., N. Ireland	11	54 10N	6 0w
Mourne R., N. Ireland	11	54 45N	7 25w
Mouscron, Belgium	13	50 45N	3 12E
Moussoro, Chad	51	13 50N	16 35E
Moutier, Switzerland	15	47 16N	7 21E
Moutiers, France	12	45 29N	6 31E
Mouzia, Niger	52	14 25N	5 27E
Moville, Ireland	11	55 11N	7 3w
Mowbullan Mt., Queens.	43	26 47s	151 31E
Mowming, China	39	21 50N	110 32E
Mowping, China	38	37 26N	121 33E
Moy, N. Ireland	11	54 27N	6 40w
Moy R., Ireland	11	54 5N	8 50w
Moyale, Kenya	54	3 30N	39 0E
Moyen Congo, prov., Zaire	54	1 10N	20 15E
Moyie, Canada	64	49 17N	115 50w
Moynalty, Ireland	11	53 48N	6 52w
Moyo, Uganda	53	3 38N	31 43E
Moyobamba, Peru	78	6 0s	77 0w
Moyowosi, R., Tan.	53	4 0s	31 15E
Moza, Israel	29	31 48N	35 8E
Mozambique, Port. Col. Africa	55	23 30s	32 30E
Mozambique Channel, Africa	49	25 0s	40 0E
Mozdok, U.S.S.R.	25	43 45N	44 48E
Mozhaisk, U.S.S.R.	25	55 30N	36 2E
Mozyr, U.S.S.R.	25	52 0N	29 15E
Mpanda, Tanzania	53	6 22s	30 40E
Mpangwe, Zambia	56	14 8s	32 10E
Mphoengs, Rhod.	56	21 10s	27 51E
Mpigi, Uganda	63	0 14N	32 19E
Mpika, Zambia	56	11 47s	31 29E
Mporokoso, Zambia	56	9 25s	30 5E
Mpraeso, Ghana	52	6 50N	0 50w
Mpui, Tanzania	53	8 20s	31 50E
Mpwapwa, Mt., Tan.	53	6 30s	36 30E
Mqanduli, C. Prov.	57	31 48s	28 47E
Mragowo, Poland	16	53 53N	21 17E
Mrewa, Rhodesia	56	17 35s	31 45E
Mrijo, Tanzania	53	6 13s	36 30E
Msagali, Tanzania	53	6 28s	36 22E
Msaken, Tunisia	51	35 45N	10 33E
M'salu, R., Mozam.	55	12 30s	38 0E
Msambansovu, mt., Rhodesia	56	15 50s	30 0E
Msata, Tanzania	53	6 20s	38 23E
Mseni, Tanzania	53	5 2s	38 7E
Msoro, Zambia	56	13 35s	31 50E
Msta R., U.S.S.R.	25	58 30N	33 30E
Mstislavl, U.S.S.R.	25	54 0N	31 50E
Mtama, Tanzania	53	10 17s	39 22E
Mtilikwe R., Rhod.	56	21 0s	31 25E
Mtito Andei, Kenya	53	2 41s	38 12E
Mtoko, Rhodesia	56	17 25s	32 28E
Mtondo, Tanzania	53	9 33s	35 50E
Mtsensk, U.S.S.R.	25	53 25N	36 30E
Mtubatuba, Natal	52	28 23s	32 12E
Mtwalume, Natal	57	30 30s	30 38E
Mtwara, Tanzania	53	10 15s	40 15E
Mtwara, prov., Tan.	53	9 45s	38 30E
Muaná, Brazil	79	1 25s	49 15w
Muar (Bandar Maharani), Malaya	34	2 3N	102 34E
Muar, R., Malaya	34	2 15N	102 48E
Muara, Brunei	35	5 0N	115 5E
Muara, Indonesia	34	0 30s	101 0E
Muara-Antjolung, Indonesia	35	0 25N	116 45E
Muaraaman, Indonesia	34	3 10s	102 15E
Muaraenim, Indonesia	34	3 40s	103 50E
Muarasabak, Indon.	34	1 5s	103 55E
Muaratebo, Indonesia	34	1 25s	102 30E
Muaratewe, Indonesia	35	0 50s	115 0E
Mubairik, Saudi Arabia	30	23 22N	39 8E
Mubende, Uganda	53	0 30N	31 25E
Mubi, Nigeria	52	10 15N	13 12E
Mucajai R., Brazil	78	2 20N	61 30w
Muchinga Esc., mts., Zambia	56	12 30s	31 0E
Muckadilla, Queensland	43	26 32s	148 36E
Mucomaze, Mozam.	57	12 5s	40 30E
Mucuri, Brazil	79	18 0s	40 0w
Muddo Gashi, Kenya	53	0 45N	39 30E
Muddy, R., U.S.A.	73	38 35N	111 0w
Mudgee, N.S.W.	43	32 32s	149 31E
Mudhnib, Saudi Arabia	30	25 5N	44 18E
Mueda, Mozambique	53	11 40s	39 31E
Muembe, Mozambique	56	13 5s	35 39E
Mufulira, Zambia	56	12 30s	28 0E
Mufumbiro Ra., Uganda	53	1 35s	29 30E
Mugila Mts., Zaire	53	7 0s	28 50E
Mugla, Turkey	30	37 15N	28 28E
Muglad, Sudan	51	11 10N	27 35E
Mugu, Nepal	33	29 45N	82 30E
Muhammad Qol, Sudan	51	21 0N	37 9E
Muhammadabad, Iran	31	37 30N	59 0E
Muharraq, Bahrain I.	31	26 15N	50 40E
Muharraqa. *See* Sa'ad.	29		
Muhesi R., Tanzania	53	6 50s	35 0E
Muheza, Tanzania	53	5 9s	38 48E
Muhinga, Burundi	53	2 48s	30 21E
Mühldorf, Germany	14	48 15N	12 32E
Mühlhausen, Germany	14	51 12N	10 29E
Muhutwe, Tanzania	53	1 34s	31 43E
Muhuwesi R., Tan.	53	10 55s	37 0E
Mui Ca Mau, Viet Nam	34	8 40N	104 45E
Mui Nay, C., Viet Nam	34	12 50N	109 37E
Mui Ron Ma, C., Viet Nam	34	18 5N	106 28E
Muidumbe, Mozam.	53	11 49s	39 51E
Muine Bheag, Ireland	11	52 42N	6 59w
Mukah, Sarawak	35	2 55N	112 5E
Mukasa, S.W. Africa	56	17 51s	24 31E
Mukdahan, Thailand	34	16 31N	104 43E
Mukden, China	37	41 50N	123 30E
Mukebo, Zaire	56	6 49s	28 2E
Mukinge, Zambia	56	13 35s	25 56E
Muko-Muko, Indon.	34	2 20s	101 10E
Mukombwe, Zambia	56	15 43s	26 30E
Mukomwenze, Zaire	56	6 40s	27 12E
Muktinath, Nepal	33	28 45N	83 56E
Muktsar, India	32	30 30N	74 30E
Mukur, Afghanistan	31	32 56N	67 48E
Mukutawa R., Canada	65	53 10N	97 10w
Mukuy, Zaire	56	7 28s	28 37E
Mukwela, Zambia	53	17 2s	26 40E
Muladdah, 'Oman	31	23 40N	57 31E
Mulanda, Angola	56	14 58s	22 25E
Mulandi, Zambia	56	13 4s	24 33E
Mulatas, Arch de las, Panama	75	6 51N	78 31w
Mulchén, Chile	71	37 45s	72 20w
Mulde R., Germany	14	50 55N	12 42E
Muleba, Tanzania	53	1 48s	31 41E
Mule Creek, U.S.A.	70	43 19N	104 8w
Muleshoe, U.S.A.	71	34 13N	102 43w
Mulgrave, Canada	63	45 38N	61 31w
Mulgrave I., Queens.	42	10 5s	142 0E
Mulhacen Mt., Spain	17	37 4N	3 20w
Mülheim, W. Germany	14	51 26N	6 53E
Muliansolo, Zambia	56	10 1s	32 18E
Mulipa, Rhodesia	56	14 45s	31 44E
Mull I., Scotland	10	56 27N	6 0w
Mullaittivu, Sri Lanka	32	9 15N	80 55E
Mullen, U.S.A.	70	42 0N	101 0w
Mullens, U.S.A.	68	37 34N	81 22w
Muller Mts., Indonesia	35	0 30N	113 30E
Muller Ra., N. Guin.	42	5 30s	143 0E
Mullet Pen., Ireland	11	54 10N	10 2w
Mullewa, W. Australia	44	28 29s	115 30E
Mulligan R., Queens.	42	25 45s	138 45E
Mullin, U.S.A.	71	31 32N	98 34w
Mullinahone, Ireland	11	52 30N	7 31w
Mullinavat, Ireland	11	52 23N	7 10w
Mulline, W. Australia	44	29 47s	120 28E
Mullingar, Ireland	11	53 31N	7 20w
Mullins, U.S.A.	69	34 12N	79 15w
Mullumbimby, N.S.W.	43	28 30s	153 30E
Mulobezi, Zambia	56	16 49s	25 2E
Mulongo, Zaire	56	7 47s	27 0E
Multai, India	32	21 39N	78 15E
Multan, Pakistan	32	30 15N	71 30E
Multan, Terr., W. Pak.	32	30 0N	71 0E
Mulug, India	32	18 0N	79 55E
Mulumbe Mts., Zaire	56	8 30s	28 0E
Mulungushi Dam, Zambia	56	14 45s	28 45E
Mulvane, U.S.A.	71	37 30N	97 15w
Mulwarrie, W. Australia	44	29 59s	120 30E
Mumbotut Falls, Zambia	56	12 20s	29 9E
Mumbwa, Zambia	56	16 0s	27 2E
Mumpanda, Zambia	56	14 13s	25 12E
Mun, R., Siam	34	12 40N	102 30E
Muna I., Indonesia	35	5 0s	122 30E
Munabao, India	32	25 45N	70 15E
Munankwan Pass, China	67	22 0N	106 42E
Munburra, Queensland	42	14 40s	145 1E
München (Munich), Germany	14	48 8N	11 35E
Munchen Gladbach, Germany	14	51 12N	6 23E
Munchon, N. Korea	36	39 11N	127 19E
Muncie, U.S.A.	68	40 10N	85 20w
Mundandamu, Zambia	56	13 5s	23 23E
Mundare, Canada	64	53 35N	112 30w
Munday, U.S.A.	71	33 56N	99 34w

	MAP		
Munde, Mt., Tan.	53	7 33 s	31 27 E
Munden, W. Germany	14	51 25 N	9 39 E
Mundijong, W. Austral.	44	32 16 s	115 55 E
Mundo Novo, Brazil	79	11 50 s	40 29 w
Mundubbera, Queens.	43	25 35 s	151 19 E
Mungallala, Queens.	43	26 28 s	147 33 E
Mungana, Queensland	42	17 8 s	144 27 E
Mungari, Mozambique	56	17 12 s	33 42 E
Mungaroona Ra., W. Australia	44	21 40 s	118 30 E
Mungau, Angola	56	13 55 s	21 48 E
Mungbere, Zaire	53	2 32 N	28 28 E
Mungindi, Queensland	43	28 58 s	149 1 E
Munich. *See* München	14		
Munising, U.S.A.	68	46 25 N	86 39 w
Munkfors, Sweden	23	59 50 N	13 35 E
Munku Sarbyk Mt., U.S.S.R.	27	52 10 N	101 0 E
Munroe L., Canada	65	59 0 N	98 40 w
Münsingen, Switz.	15	46 53 N	7 34 E
Münster, Germany	14	51 58 N	7 37 E
Munster, prov., Ireland	11	52 20 N	8 40 w
Muntok, Indonesia	34	2 5 s	105 10 E
Mununzi, Zaire	53	0 48 N	29 8 E
Muong Hou, Laos	34	22 15 N	101 47 E
Muonio, Finland	22	67 57 N	23 40 E
Muonio R., Sweden	22	68 0 N	23 30 E
Mupa, Angola	55	16 5 s	15 50 E
Muqainama, Si. Arabia	30	22 9 N	48 51 E
Mur, R., Austria	14	47 5 N	14 0 E
Murallon Mt., Chile	77	49 55 s	73 30 w
Muranda, Rwanda	53	1 52 s	29 22 E
Muranga, Kenya	53	0 40 s	37 2 E
Murashi, U.S.S.R.	24	59 30 N	49 0 E
Murat, France	12	45 7 N	2 53 E
Murban, Trucial Oman	31	24 0 N	53 49 E
Murchison, N.Z.	47	41 49 s	172 21 E
Murchison, Falls, Ugan.	53	2 25 N	31 30 E
Murchison Mts., N.Z.	47	45 13 s	167 23 E
Murchison Rapids, Malawi	56	15 40 s	34 50 E
Murchison R., W. Australia	44	27 30 s	115 0 E
Murcia, Spain	17	38 2 N	1 10 w
Murcia, old prov., Spain	17	38 35 N	1 50 w
Murdo, U.S.A.	70	43 58 N	100 40 w
Murdoch Pt., Queens.	42	14 10 s	144 59 E
Mures R., Rumania	21	46 0 N	22 0 E
Muret, France	12	43 30 N	1 20 E
Murfreesboro, U.S.A.	69	35 50 N	86 30 w
Murgon, Queensland	43	26 15 s	151 54 E
Murgoo, W. Australia	44	27 24 s	116 18 E
Muri, Switzerland	15	47 16 N	8 21 E
Murias, Spain	17	42 52 N	6 19 w
Muriel Mine, Rhodesia	56	17 10 s	30 33 E
Muritz L., Germany	14	53 25 N	12 40 E
Murjo Mt., Indonesia	34	6 36 s	110 53 E
Murmansk, U.S.S.R.	22	68 57 N	33 10 E
Murom, U.S.S.R.	25	55 35 N	42 3 E
Muroran, Japan	36	42 25 N	141 0 E
Muros, Spain	17	42 45 N	9 5 w
Muroto C., Japan	36	33 15 N	134 10 E
Murphy, U.S.A.	72	43 13 N	46 33 w
Murphysboro, U.S.A.	71	37 46 N	89 49 w
Murray Br., S. Australia	43	35 6 s	139 14 E
Murray, Ky., U.S.A.	71	36 40 N	88 20 w
Murray, Utah, U.S.A.	70	40 41 N	111 56 w
Murray Harb., Canada	63	46 0 N	62 28 w
Murray L., U.S.A.	69	34 8 N	81 30 w
Murray Downs, N. Terr.	45	21 3 s	134 42 E
Murray Mallee, dist., S. Australia	43	34 45 s	140 15 E
Murray R., Australia	43	35 50 s	147 40 E
Murray R., Canada	64	54 40 N	121 10 w
Murray R. Basin, Vic.	43	35 0 s	142 30 E
Murraysburg, C. Prov.	57	31 58 s	23 47 E
Murrayville, Victoria	43	35 20 s	140 16 E
Murree, Pakistan	32	33 56 N	73 28 E
Mürren, Switzerland	15	46 33 N	7 45 E
Murrin Murrin, W. Australia	44	28 50 s	121 45 E
Murrumbidgee R., New South Wales	43	34 30 s	145 30 E
Murrumburrah, N.S.W.	43	34 30 s	148 15 E
Murrurundi, N.S.W.	43	31 42 s	150 51 E
Murtazapur, India	32	20 40 N	77 25 E
Murten, Switzerland	15	46 56 N	7 7 E
Murtle L., Canada	64	52 15 N	119 40 w
Murtoa, Victoria	43	36 29 s	142 29 E
Murtosa, Portugal	17	40 44 N	8 40 w
Murungu, Tanzania	53	4 7 s	31 2 E
Murwara, India	32	23 46 N	80 28 E
Murwillumbah, N.S.W.	43	28 18 s	153 27 E
Murzuq, Libya	51	25 50 N	14 10 E
Mürzzuschlag, Austria	14	47 36 N	15 41 E
Mus, Turkey	30	38 45 N	41 30 E
Musa Khel Bazar, W. Pakistan	31	30 55 N	69 50 E
Musa Khel, W. Pak.	32	30 53 N	69 52 E
Musa Qala, Afghan.	31	32 20 N	64 45 E
Musaffargarh, Pakistan	32	30 10 N	71 10 E
Musaia, Sierra Leone	52	9 45 N	11 33 w
Musala, Mt., Bulgaria	21	42 13 N	23 34 E
Musan, Korea	36	42 10 N	129 10 E
Musandam, Ras, 'Oman	31	26 26 N	56 30 E
Musangu, Zaire	56	10 31 s	23 57 E
Musasa, Tanzania	53	3 25 s	31 35 E
Muscat. *See* Masqat	31		
Muscat and 'Oman, sultanate, Arabia	31	23 0 N	58 0 E
Muscatine, U.S.A.	70	41 25 N	91 4 w
Musetula, Zambia	56	14 22 s	24 4 E
Musgrave, Queensland	42	14 55 s	143 32 E
Musgrave, Ra., S. Australia	45	26 15 s	131 0 E
Mushalagan L., Canada	63	51 20 N	69 7 w
Mushalagan R., Canada	63	52 20 N	69 0 w
Mushandyke Dam, Rhodesia	56	20 15 s	30 17 E
Mushanth, Zambia	56	15 57 s	24 0 E
Mushie, Zaire	54	2 56 s	17 4 E
Mushima, Zambia	56	14 2 s	25 0 E
Muskeg R., Canada	64	60 30 N	122 40 w
Muskegon, U.S.A.	68	43 15 N	86 17 w
Muskegon R., U.S.A.	68	43 25 N	85 50 w
Muskegon Heights, U.S.A.	68	43 12 N	86 17 w
Muskogee, U.S.A.	71	35 50 N	95 25 w
Muskwa R., Canada	64	58 20 N	123 40 w
Musmar, Sudan	51	18 6 N	35 40 E
Musofu, Zambia	56	13 30 s	29 7 E
Musokantanda, Zaire	56	10 56 s	25 7 E
Musola, Zambia	56	12 55 s	30 22 E
Musoma, Tanzania	53	1 30 s	33 48 E
Musombe, Tanzania	53	7 18 s	34 29 E
Musoshi, Zaire	56	11 54 s	27 45 E
Musquaro L., Canada	63	50 40 N	61 20 w
Musquodoboit Harbour, Canada	63	44 50 N	63 9 w
Musselshell R., U.S.A.	72	46 30 N	108 15 w
Mussooree, India	32	30 27 N	78 6 E
Mussuma, Angola	56	14 13 s	21 57 E
Mustafa Kemalpasa, Turkey	30	40 3 N	28 25 E
Mustajida, Si. Arabia	30	26 30 N	41 50 E
Mustang, Nepal	33	29 10 N	83 55 E
Musters L., Argentina	77	45 20 s	69 25 w
Mustique I., Windward Islands	75		Inset
Muswellbrook, N.S.W.	43	32 16 s	150 56 E
Mût, Egypt	51	25 58 N	28 58 E
Mut, Turkey	30	36 40 N	33 28 E
Mutana, Angola	55	16 40 s	15 1 E
Mutanda, Mozambique	56	20 59 s	33 34 E
Mutanda, Zambia	56	12 18 s	26 2 E
Mutankiang, China	36	43 50 N	129 30 E
Mutarai, U.S.S.R.	27	61 25 N	100 55 E
Mutarara, Mozambique	56	17 30 s	35 6 E
Mutha, Kenya	53	1 47 s	38 26 E
Muthill, Scotland	10	56 20 N	3 50 w
Mutiko, Zaire	53	1 40 s	28 11 E
Mutshatsha, Zaire	56	10 35 s	24 20 E
Mutsu B., Japan	36	41 0 N	141 0 E
Muttaburra, Queensland	42	22 38 s	144 29 E
Mutton Bay, Canada	63	50 50 N	59 2 w
Mutum Biyu, Nigeria	52	8 40 N	10 50 E
Muwaih, Si. Arabia	30	22 35 N	41 32 E
Muxima, Angola	55	9 25 s	13 52 E
Muyaga, Burundi	53	3 14 s	30 34 E
Muyombe, Zambia	56	10 31 s	33 29 E
Muyumba, Zaire	56	7 12 s	27 3 E
Muzaffarabad, Kashmir	32	34 25 N	73 30 E
Muzaffargarh, Pak.	32	30 10 N	71 10 E
Muzaffarnagar, India	32	29 26 N	77 40 E
Muzaffarpur, India	33	26 7 N	85 32 E
Muzeiri'a, Israel	29	32 3 N	34 53 E
Muzhi, U.S.S.R.	26	65 25 N	64 40 E
Muzoka, Zambia	56	16 37 s	27 20 E
Muztagh, mt., China	37	36 30 N	87 22 E
Mvomero, Tanzania	53	6 20 s	37 26 E
Mvuha, Tanzania	53	7 15 s	37 57 E
Mwamba Fs., Zambia	56	16 28 s	23 20 E
Mwanza, Kenya	56	1 38 s	38 13 E
Mwanza, Tanzania	56	2 30 s	33 0 E
Mwanza, prov., Tan.	56	2 30 s	33 0 E
Mwaya, Tanzania	53	9 32 s	33 55 E
Mweelrea, mt., Ireland	11	53 37 N	9 48 w
Mweka, Zaire	54	4 50 s	21 40 E
Mwenga, Zaire	53	3 7 s	28 27 E
Mwengwa, Zambia	56	15 15 s	26 7 E
Mwepe, Zambia	56	15 0 s	26 13 E
Mwepo, Zaire	56	11 50 s	26 22 E
Mweru L., Zaire	56	9 0 s	29 0 E
Mweru Swamp, Zambia	56	9 0 s	29 0 E
Mweza Ra., Rhod.	56	21 0 s	30 0 E
Mwgambwa, Zambia	56	15 28 s	26 31 E
Mwimbi, Tanzania	53	8 38 s	31 39 E
Mwinilunga, Zambia	56	11 45 N	24 25 E
Mwirasandu, Uganda	53	0 59 s	30 22 E
Mwitikira, Tanzania	53	6 29 s	35 40 E
Mymensingh. *See* Nasirabad, Bangladesh	33		
Mwomadi, Zambia	56	15 7 s	25 58 E
My Tho, Viet Nam	34	10 29 s	106 23 E
Myadhi, Gabon	54	1 10 N	13 5 E
Myanaung, Burma	33	18 25 N	95 10 E
Myaungmya, Burma	33	16 30 N	95 0 E
Mycenae, site, Greece	21	37 47 N	22 50 E
Myera, Malawi	56	14 47 s	35 13 E
Myers Chuck, Alaska	64	55 55 N	132 25 w
Myingyan, Burma	33	21 30 N	95 30 E
Myitkyina, Burma	33	25 30 N	97 26 E
Mynfontein, C. Prov.	57	30 55 s	23 57 E
Myrbals Jok, Mts., Ice.	22	63 40 N	19 0 w
Myrria, Niger	52	13 44 N	9 8 E
Myrtle Beach, U.S.A.	69	33 43 N	78 50 w
Myrtle Creek, U.S.A.	72	43 1 N	123 20 w
Myrtle Point, U.S.A.	72	43 1 N	124 7 w
Mysen, Norway	23	59 37 N	11 20 E
Mysliborz, Poland	16	52 55 N	14 50 E
Mysore, India	32	12 17 N	76 41 E
Mysore, st., India	32	13 15 N	77 0 E
Mytishchi, U.S.S.R.	25	57 50 N	37 50 E
Myton, U.S.A.	72	40 10 N	110 2 w
Myvatn L., Iceland	22	65 35 N	16 55 w
Mzenga, Tanzania	53	7 1 s	38 46 E
Mziha, Tanzania	53	5 55 s	37 46 E
Mzimba, Malawi	56	11 55 s	33 38 E
Mzuzu, Malawi	56	11 20 s	33 57 E

N

Naab, R., Germany	14	49 7 N	12 0 E
Naalehu, Hawaiian Is.	59	19 4 N	155 36 w
Naam Okora, Uganda	53	3 18 N	33 20 E
Na'an, Israel	29	31 53 N	34 52 E
Naantali, Finland	23	60 32 N	21 50 E
Naarden, Netherlands	13	52 17 N	5 10 E
Naas, Ireland	11	53 12 N	6 40 w
Nababiep, C. Prov.	57	29 36 s	17 46 E
Nabadwip, India	33	23 34 N	88 20 E
Naberera, Tanzania	53	4 15 s	36 55 E
Nabeul, Tunisia	51	36 30 N	10 40 E
Nabi Rubin, Israel	29	31 56 N	34 44 E
Nabisipi R., Canada	63	51 0 N	62 28 w
Nabiswera, Uganda	53	1 29 N	32 18 E
Nablus, Jordan	29	32 14 N	35 15 E
Naboomspruit, Trans.	57	24 32 s	28 40 E
Nabulgu, Togoland	52	10 2 N	0 58 E
Naches, U.S.A.	72	46 48 N	120 42 w
Nachi, China	39	28 50 N	105 25 E
Nachingwea, Tan.	53	10 15 s	38 55 E
Nacka, Sweden	23	59 17 N	18 12 E
Naco, U.S.A.	73	31 24 N	109 58 w
Nacogdeches, U.S.A.	71	31 33 N	94 42 w
Nacozari, Mexico	74	30 30 N	109 50 w
Nadiad, India	32	22 41 N	72 56 E
Nadlac, Rumania	21	46 10 N	20 50 E
Nærbö, Norway	23	58 40 N	5 39 E
Naestved, Denmark	23	55 13 N	11 44 E
Nafada, Nigeria	52	11 8 N	11 20 E
Näfels, Switzerland	15	47 6 N	9 3 E
Naft-i-Shāh, Iraq	30	33 35 N	45 20 E
Naft-i-Shāh, Iran	30	34 10 N	45 30 E
Naga, Philippines	35	13 38 N	123 15 E
Nagaga, Tanzania	53	10 55 s	39 7 E
Nagagami R., Canada	56	49 40 N	84 40 w
Nagaland, st., India	33	26 0 N	94 30 E
Nagalle, Ethiopia	54	5 25 N	39 30 E
Nagano, Japan	36	36 40 N	138 10 E
Nagano, pref., Japan	36	36 15 N	138 0 E
Nagaoka, Japan	36	37 30 N	138 50 E
Nagapattinam, India	32	10 46 N	79 51 E
Nagar Parkar, Pakistan	32	24 20 N	70 40 E
Nagasaki, Japan	36	32 47 N	129 50 E
Nagasaki, pref., Japan	36	32 50 N	129 40 E
Nagaur, India	32	27 15 N	73 45 E
Nagercoil, India	32	8 12 N	77 33 E
Nagina, India	32	29 30 N	78 30 E
Nagineh, Iran	31	34 27 N	57 11 E
Nagorny, U.S.S.R.	27	55 50 N	124 45 E
Nagorum, Kenya	53	4 1 N	34 31 E
Nagoya, Japan	36	35 10 N	136 50 E
Nagpur, India	32	21 8 N	79 10 E
Nagykanizsa, Hungary	16	46 27 N	17 0 E
Nagykörös, Hungary	16	47 2 N	19 48 E
Nahalal, Israel	29	32 41 N	35 12 E
Nahariyya, Israel	29	33 1 N	35 5 E
Nahāvand, Iran	30	34 16 N	48 26 E
Nahf, Israel	29	32 56 N	35 18 E
Nahlin, Canada	64	58 55 N	131 40 w
Nahuel Huapi L., Arg.	77	41 0 s	71 30 w
Naicam, Canada	65	52 30 N	104 30 w
Naik, Afghanistan	31	34 45 N	66 50 E
Na in, Persia	31	32 54 N	53 0 E
Nainpur, India	32	22 28 N	80 5 E
Nairn, and Co., Scot.	10	57 35 N	3 54 w
Nairobi, Kenya	53	1 20 s	36 50 E
Najera, Spain	17	42 26 N	2 48 w
Najibabad, India	32	29 40 N	78 20 E
Najin, Korea	36	42 12 N	130 15 E
Nakajo, Japan	36	38 0 N	139 20 E
Nakalagba, Zaire	53	2 47 N	28 2 E
Nakamura, Japan	36	33 0 N	133 0 E
Nakano Shima, Japan	36	29 50 N	130 0 E
Nakatsu, Japan	36	33 30 N	131 15 E
Nakhichevan, U.S.S.R.	24	39 14 N	45 24 E
Nakhl Mubarak, Saudi Arabia	30	24 15 N	38 15 E
Nakhon Ratchasima, Thailand	34	14 59 N	102 12 E
Nakhon Sawan, Thailand	34	15 42 N	100 4 E
Nakhon Si Thammarat, Thailand	34	8 29 N	100 0 E
Nakina, B.C., Canada	64	59 15 N	132 45 w
Nakina, Ont., Canada	62	50 10 N	86 40 w
Nako, Volta	52	10 39 N	3 4 w
Nakonde, Zambia	56	9 8 s	32 47 E
Nakop, S.W. Africa	57	28 5 s	19 57 E
Nakpali, Ghana	52	9 12 N	0 48 E
Nakskov, Denmark	23	54 50 N	11 8 E
Naktong R., Korea	36	35 30 N	128 35 E
Nakuru, Kenya	53	0 15 s	36 5 E
Nakusp, Canada	64	50 20 N	117 45 w
Nal R., Pakistan	32	27 0 N	65 50 E
Nalchik, U.S.S.R.	25	43 30 N	43 33 E
Nalerigu, Ghana	52	10 35 N	0 25 w
Nalgonda, India	32	17 6 N	79 15 E
Nallamalai Hills, India	32	15 30 N	78 50 E
Nalola, Zambia	56	15 32 s	23 2 E
Nalut, Libya	51	31 54 N	11 0 E
Nam Dinh, N. Viet Nam	34	20 25 N	106 5 E
Nam Tso, Mt., China	37	30 40 N	90 30 E
Nama, China	67	23 42 N	108 3 E
Nama, Nigeria	52	7 0 N	0 48 E
Namachire, Angola	56	11 25 s	23 38 E
Namacurra, Mozam.	55	17 30 s	36 50 E
Namakan L., N. Amer.	65	48 30 N	93 0 w
Namakzār-e Shahdād, Iran	31	30 45 N	58 30 E
Naman, China	39	25 0 N	118 30 E
Namanga, Tanzania	53	2 33 s	36 47 E
Namangan, U.S.S.R.	26	41 30 N	71 30 E
Namanyere, & Mt., Tanzania	53	7 32 s	31 8 E
Namapa, Mozambique	55	13 42 s	39 50 E
Namaqualand, C. Prov.	57	30 0 s	18 0 E
Namasagali, Uganda	53	1 0 N	33 5 E
Nambiri, Ghana	52	9 56 N	0 20 E
Namboull, Dahomey	52	10 53 N	0 58 E
Nambour, Queensland	43	26 38 s	152 49 E
Namcha Barwa, mt., China	31	29 30 N	95 10 E
Namew L., Canada	65	54 20 N	102 0 w
Namib Desert, South West Africa	55	21 0 s	14 0 E
Namja Pass, Nepal	33	30 0 N	82 25 E
Namlea, Indonesia	35	3 10 s	127 5 E
Namoa & I., China	39	23 30 N	117 0 E
Namoi R., N.S.W.	43	30 16 s	149 15 E
Nampa, U.S.A.	72	43 34 N	116 39 E
Nampo, N. Korea	38	38 45 N	125 15 E
Nampula, Mozambique	55	15 15 s	39 26 E
Namsen R., Norway	22	64 40 N	13 0 E
Namsos, Norway	22	64 28 N	11 35 E
Namtu, Burma	33	23 5 N	97 28 E
Namtumbo, Tan.	53	10 30 s	36 4 E
Namu, Canada	64	51 45 N	127 50 w
Namur, Belgium	13	50 27 N	4 52 E
Namuruputh, Kenya	53	4 35 N	35 52 E
Namutoni, S.W. Africa	55	18 49 s	16 55 E
Namwala, Zambia	56	15 50 s	26 12 E
Namwon, S. Korea	36	35 25 N	127 21 E
Namyangdong, N. Korea	36	41 30 N	128 53 E
Namyslów, Poland	16	51 6 N	17 42 E
Namyung, China	39	25 15 N	114 5 E
Nan, Thailand	34	18 52 N	100 42 E
Nan, R., Thailand	34	14 0 N	100 20 E
Nanklang, China	39	31 45 N	106 50 E
Nan Shan, mt. ra., China	37	38 0 N	98 0 E
Nana Candundo, Angola	56	12 28 s	23 0 E
Nanaimo, Canada	64	49 10 N	124 0 w
Nanam, Korea	36	41 35 N	129 35 E
Nanango, Queensland	43	26 40 s	152 0 E
Nanao, Japan	36	37 0 N	137 0 E
Nanarayim, Israel	29	32 40 N	35 35 E
Nanchang, Hupeh, China	39	31 50 N	111 50 E
Nanchang, Kiangsi, China	39	38 34 N	115 48 E
Nancheng, Kiangsi, China	39	27 30 N	116 28 E
Nancheng, Shensi, China	39	32 45 N	106 20 E
Nanchung, China	39	31 44 N	106 0 E
Nanchwan, China	39	29 10 N	107 15 E
Nancy, France	12	48 42 N	6 12 E
Nanda Devi, Mt., India	32	30 30 N	80 30 E
Nander, India	32	19 10 N	77 20 E
Nandurbar, India	32	21 20 N	74 15 E
Nandyal, India	32	15 30 N	78 30 E
Nanfeng, China	39	27 11 N	116 29 E
Nanga Eboko, Cameroon	52	4 40 N	12 26 E
Nanga Parbat, mt., Kashmir	32	35 10 N	74 35 E
Nangabadau, Indonesia	35	0 50 N	112 5 E
Nangade, Mozambique	53	11 1 s	39 38 E
Nangapinoh, Indonesia	35	0 30 s	111 50 E
Nangeya, Mts., Uganda	53	3 30 N	33 30 E
Nangodi, Ghana	52	10 57 N	0 38 w
Nangolet, Sudan	53	4 59 N	33 52 E
Nangoma, Zambia	56	15 35 s	28 1 E
Nanguruwe, Tan.	53	10 29 s	40 4 E
Nangwe, Tanzania	53	12 50 s	31 58 E
Nanjirinji, Tanzania	53	9 41 s	39 5 E
Nankang, China	39	25 42 N	114 35 E
Nankiang, China	39	32 15 N	107 1 E
Nanking, China	39	32 10 N	118 50 E
Nanjeko, Zambia	56	15 30 s	23 32 E
Nannine, W. Australia	44	26 51 s	118 18 E
Nanning, China	39	22 50 N	108 5 E
Nannup, W. Australia	44	33 59 s	115 48 E
Nanpi, China	38	38 41 N	116 41 E
Nanping, China	38	26 45 N	118 5 E
Nanping, China	38	33 0 N	104 15 E
Nansen Sd., Canada	58	81 0 N	91 0 w
Nanshan I., S. China Sea	35	10 45 N	115 55 E

	MAP		
Nansio, Tanzania	53	2 7S	33 4E
Nanson, W. Australia	44	28 28S	114 45E
Nantan, China	39	25 12N	107 40E
Nantes, France	12	47 12N	1 33W
Nanticoke, U.S.A.	68	41 12N	76 1W
Nantou, Chile	39	23 59N	120 35E
Nantua, France	12	46 10N	5 35E
Nantucket I., U.S.A.	69	41 1N	70 0W
Nantucket Sd., U.S.A.	69	41 20N	70 35W
Nantung, China	39	32 0N	120 50E
Nanutarra, W. Australia	44	22 30S	115 28E
Nanyang, China	38	33 4N	112 55E
Nanyuki, Kenya	53	0 1N	37 3E
Náo C., Spain	17	38 42N	0 17W
Naococane, L., Canada	63	53 0N	70 35W
Naoetsu, Japan	36	37 12N	138 10E
Naousa, Greece	21	40 42N	22 9E
Napa, U.S.A.	73	38 20N	122 25W
Napainiut, Alaska	59	61 31N	158 45W
Napanee, Canada	62	44 20N	77 0W
Napier, New Zealand	46	39 30S	176 56E
Napinka, Canada	65	49 20N	101 0W
Naples (Napoli), Italy	20	40 40N	14 5E
Naples, U.S.A.	69	42 35N	77 25W
Napo R., Peru	78	3 5S	73 0W
Napoleon, N.D., U.S.A.	70	46 34N	99 47W
Napoleon, Ohio, U.S.A.	68	41 20N	84 6W
Napoli. *See* Naples.	20		
Napopo, Zaire	53	4 10N	28 5E
Nara, Mali	50	15 25N	7 20W
Nara, Japan	36	34 40N	135 59E
Nara, pref., Japan	36	34 30N	136 0E
Nara Visa, U.S.A.	71	35 34N	103 7W
Naracoopa, Tasmania	42	39 38S	144 2E
Naracootre, S. Australia	42	36 50S	140 44E
Naradhan, N.S.W.	43	33 34S	146 17E
Naranjas Pt., Panama	78	7 10N	81 0W
Narasapur, India	33	16 26N	81 50E
Narasaraopet, India	32	16 14N	80 4E
Narayanganj, Bangladesh	33	23 31N	90 33E
Narayanpet, India	32	16 45N	77 30E
Narbada (Narmada) R., India	32	22 40N	77 30E
Narbonne, France	12	43 11N	3 0E
Nardo, Italy	21	40 10N	18 0E
Nare, Argentina	77	31 0S	60 30W
Narembeen, W. Austral.	44	32 7S	118 17E
Nares Str., Can.-Green	58	81 10N	65 0W
Naretha, W. Australia	45	31 0S	124 45E
Narew R., Poland	16	53 10N	21 50E
Naricual, Venezuela	78	10 0N	64 25W
Narmada (Narbada) R., India	32	22 40N	73 30E
Narnaul, India	32	28 5N	76 11E
Narngulu, W. Australia	44	28 46S	114 34E
Narni, Italy	20	42 30N	12 30E
Naro, Ghana	52	10 22N	2 27W
Narok, Kenya	53	1 10S	35 50E
Narooma, N.S.W.	43	36 14S	150 4E
Narrabri, N.S.W.	43	30 19S	149 46E
Narrandera, N.S.W.	43	34 42S	146 31E
Narrikup, W. Australia	44	34 44S	117 37E
Narrogin, W. Australia	44	32 58S	117 14E
Narromine, N.S.W.	43	32 12S	148 12E
Narsinghpur, India	32	22 54N	79 14E
Narubis, S.W. Africa	57	26 50S	18 56E
Naruto, Japan	36	34 18N	134 40E
Narva, U.S.S.R.	23	59 10N	28 5E
Narva B. and R., U.S.S.R.	23	59 30N	27 30E
Narvik, Norway	22	68 28N	17 35E
Naryan-Mar, U.S.S.R.	24	68 0N	53 0E
Narym, U.S.S.R.	26	59 0N	81 58E
Narymskoye, U.S.S.R.	26	49 10N	84 15E
Naryn, U.S.S.R.	26	41 30N	76 10E
Nasa, mt., Norway-Sweden	22	66 30N	15 30E
Nasarao, Nigeria	52	8 40N	12 19E
Nasarawa, Nigeria	52	8 32N	7 41E
Năsăud, Rumania	21	47 19N	24 29E
Naseby, New Zealand	47	45 1S	170 10E
Nashua, N.H., U.S.A.	68	42 40N	71 25W
Nashua, Iowa, U.S.A.	70	42 55N	92 34W
Nashua, Mont., U.S.A.	72	48 8N	106 18W
Nashville, Ark., U.S.A.	71	33 57N	93 50W
Nashville, Ind., U.S.A.	69	39 12N	86 10W
Nashville, Tenn., U.S.A.	69	36 12N	86 50W
Našice, Yugoslavia	21	45 32N	18 4E
Nasik, India	32	20 2N	73 50E
Nasir, Sudan	51	8 35N	33 5E
Nasirabad, India	32	26 15N	74 45E
Nasirabad (Mymensingh), Bangladesh	33	24 49N	90 26E
Naskaupi R., Canada	63	54 0N	61 33W
Nasandoye, Zaire	56	10 12S	25 3E
Nass R., Canada	64	55 5N	129 30W
Nasser City, (Kôm Ombo), Egypt	51	24 30N	32 57E
Nassau, Bahamas	75	25 0N	77 30W
Nassau G., Chile	77	55 20S	68 0W
Nässjö, Sweden	23	57 38N	14 45E
Nastapoka R., Canada	62	56 40N	76 0W
Nat Kyizin, Burma	33	14 57N	97 59E
Nata, Saudi Arabia	30	27 15N	48 35E
Nata R., Rhodesia	56	19 58S	27 10E
Natagaima, Colombia	78	3 45N	75 10W
Natal, Amaz., Brazil	78	6 55S	60 25W

	MAP		
Natal, Rio Grande do Norte, Brazil	79	5 50S	35 10W
Natal, Canada	64	49 45N	114 50W
Natal, Indonesia	34	0 35N	99 0E
Natal, prov., Rep. of South Africa	57	28 30S	30 30E
Natal Downs, Queens.	42	21 4S	146 10E
Natanz, Iran	31	33 30N	51 55E
Natashquan, Canada	63	50 14N	61 46W
Natashquan Pt., Canada	63	50 7N	61 42W
Natashquan, R., Canada	63	51 30N	62 0W
Natchez, U.S.A.	71	31 35N	91 20W
Natchitoches, U.S.A.	71	31 40N	93 3W
Nathdwara, India	32	24 55N	73 50E
Nathtigal, Cameroon	52	11 8N	6 57E
Natimuk, Victoria	43	36 35S	141 59E
Nation R., B.C., Canada	64	55 20N	123 50W
National City, U.S.A.	73	32 43N	117 5W
National Mills, Canada	65	52 52N	101 40W
National Park, N.Z.	46	39 15S	175 40E
Natitingou, Dahomey	52	10 20N	1 26E
Natividade, Brazil	79	11 30S	47 57W
Natoma, U.S.A.	70	39 14N	98 59W
Natron L., Tanzania	53	2 20S	36 0E
Naugatajap, Indonesia	34	1 20S	110 55E
Naukot, Bangladesh	31	24 50N	69 20E
Naumburg, Germany	14	51 10N	11 48E
Nauru I., Pacific Ocean	5	9 25S	166 0E
Naushahra, Bangladesh	31	34 0N	72 0E
Naushahro Firoz, W. Pakistan	39	26 51N	68 11E
Nauta, Peru	78	4 20S	73 35W
Nautanwa, India	33	27 26N	83 25E
Nautla, Mexico	74	20 20N	96 50W
Nava, Spain	17	41 22N	5 6W
Navalcarnero, Spain	17	40 17N	4 5W
Navalmoral, Spain	17	39 52N	5 16W
Navan (An Uaimh), Ire.	11	53 39N	6 40W
Navarra, old prov., Spain	17	42 40N	1 40W
Navasota, U.S.A.	71	30 25N	96 0W
Navassa I., W. Indies	75	18 30N	75 0W
Navia, Spain	17	43 24N	6 42W
Navlakhi, India	32	22 56N	70 30E
Navlya, U.S.S.R.	25	52 53N	34 15E
Návpaktos, Greece	21	38 23N	21 42E
Návplion, Greece	21	37 33N	22 50E
Navsari, India	32	20 57N	72 59E
Nawabshah, Pakistan	32	26 15N	68 25E
Nawada, India	33	24 50N	85 35E
Nawakot, Nepal	33	28 0N	85 10E
Nawalgarh, India	32	27 50N	75 15E
Náxos, Greece	21	37 8N	25 25E
Náxos I., Greece	21	37 5N	25 30E
Nāy Band, Iran	31	27 22N	52 36E
Nāy Band, Iran	31	32 27N	57 29E
Nayakhan, U.S.S.R.	27	62 10N	159 0E
Nayarit, st., Mexico	74	22 0N	105 0W
Nazamet, Niger	52	10 40N	16 0E
Nazaré, Brazil	79	13 0S	39 0W
Nazaré, Portugal	17	39 36N	9 4W
Nazaré-da-Mata, Brazil	79	7 40S	35 10W
Nazareth, Israel	29	32 42N	35 17E
Nazas, Mexico	74	25 10N	104 0W
Nazas R., Mexico	74	25 20N	104 4W
Nazir Hat, Bangladesh	33	22 35N	91 55E
Nazko, Canada	64	52 50N	123 25W
Nchanga, Zambia	56	12 45S	27 40E
Ncheu, Malawi	56	14 47S	34 35E
Nchira, Ghana	52	8 2N	1 59W
Ndabala, Zambia	56	13 18S	29 46E
N'Dali, Dahomey	52	9 55N	2 38E
Ndareda, Tanzania	56	4 15S	35 35E
Ndélé, Central African Republic	54	8 25N	20 36E
Ndikinimeki, Cameroon	52	4 46N	10 50E
Ndingoun, Cameroon	52	5 2N	11 22E
N'Djolé, Gabon	54	0 10S	10 45E
Ndola, Zambia	56	12 58S	28 40E
Ndoto Mts., Kenya	53	1 47N	37 15E
Ndoua, Cameroon	52	6 35N	13 12E
Ndoumbi, Cameroon	52	6 8N	13 30E
Ndungu, Tanzania	53	4 25S	38 4E
Neagh, Lough, N. Ire.	11	54 35N	6 25W
Neah Bay, U.S.A.	72	48 27N	124 42W
Neales R., The, S. Australia	41	28 0S	136 0E
Neapolis, Lakonia, Greece	21	36 27N	23 8E
Neapolis, Makedhonia, Greece	21	40 20N	21 24E
Near Is., Aleutian Is.	54	53 0N	172 0E
Nebine Cr., Queensland	43	28 30S	146 45E
Nebo, Queensland	42	21 43S	148 45E
Nebolchi, U.S.S.R.	25	59 12N	32 58E
Nebraska, st., U.S.A.	66	41 30N	100 0W
Nebraska R., U.S.A.	66	41 0N	98 0W
Nebraska City, U.S.A.	70	40 50N	96 0W
Nebrodi Mts., Italy	20	37 53N	14 45E
Necedah, U.S.A.	70	44 1N	90 5W
Nechako R., Canada	64	53 30N	125 0W
Neches R., U.S.A.	71	31 0N	94 20W
Nechi, Colombia	75	8 5N	74 50W
Nechi Cauca R., Colom.	75	7 0N	74 40W
Neckar R., Germany	14	48 43N	9 15E
Necochea, Argentina	77	38 30S	58 50W
Neder Kalix, Sweden	22	65 50N	23 15E
Neeb, Canada	65	53 55N	107 50W

	MAP		
Needles, U.S.A.	73	34 50N	114 35W
Needles Pt., N.Z.	46	36 3S	175 24E
Neemuch (Nimach), India	32	24 30N	74 50E
Neenah, U.S.A.	70	44 10N	88 30W
Neepawa, Canada	65	50 20N	99 30W
Nefta, Tunisia	50	33 46N	7 43E
Neftegorsk, U.S.S.R.	25	44 25N	39 45E
Nega Nega, Zambia	56	15 50S	28 3E
Négrais, Dahomey	52	10 34N	3 50E
Negaunee, U.S.A.	68	46 30N	87 36W
Negba, Israel	29	31 40N	34 41E
Negoiu, mt., Rumania	21	45 33N	24 26E
Negomano, Mozam.	53	11 26S	38 30E
Negombo, Sri Lanka	32	7 12N	79 50E
Negotin, Macedonia, Yugoslavia	21	41 29N	22 9E
Negotino, Yugoslavia	21	41 29N	22 7E
Negrais C., Burma	33	16 0N	94 30E
Negri Sembilan, Malaya	34	2 50N	102 10E
Negrillos, Bolivia	74	18 45S	68 45W
Negritos, Peru	78	4 55S	81 5W
Negro R., Argentine	77	40 0S	64 0W
Negro R., Brazil	78	0 25S	64 0W
Negro R., Uruguay	77	32 30S	55 30W
Negros I., Philippines	35	10 0N	123 0E
Neh, Iran	31	31 35N	60 5E
Nehbandān, Iran	31	31 39N	60 3E
Neidpath, Canada	65	50 12N	107 20W
Neihart, U.S.A.	72	47 0N	110 45W
Neikiang, China	37	29 35N	105 10E
Neilton, U.S.A.	72	47 27N	123 59W
Neisse, tn., Poland	16	50 30N	17 25E
Neisse, R., Germany-Poland	16	51 51N	14 37E
Neiva, Colombia	78	3 1N	75 19W
Nejafabad, Iran	31	32 40N	51 0E
Nejanilini L., Canada	65	59 30N	97 30W
Nejd, King., Saudi Arabia	30	26 30N	42 0E
Nekati, Botswana	56	20 8S	26 3E
Nekemte, Ethiopia	54	9 4N	36 30E
Neksö, Denmark	23	55 4N	15 8E
Nelia, Queensland	42	20 39S	142 12E
Neligh, U.S.A.	70	42 11N	98 2W
Nelkan, U.S.S.R.	27	57 50N	136 16E
Nellore, India	32	14 27N	79 59E
Nelma, U.S.S.R.	27	47 30N	139 0E
Nelson, Canada	64	49 30N	117 20W
Nelson, New Zealand	47	41 18S	173 16E
Nelson, dist., N.Z.	47	42 11S	172 15E
Nelson, Ariz., U.S.A.	73	35 31N	113 17W
Nelson, Nev., U.S.A.	73	35 44N	114 51W
Nelson, C., Victoria	43	38 14S	141 33E
Nelson I., Alaska	59	60 40N	164 40W
Nelson L., Canada	65	55 55N	90 0W
Nelson R., Canada	65	55 30N	96 50W
Nelson Forks, Canada	64	59 30N	124 0W
Nelson House, Canada	65	55 50N	90 0W
Nelson Strait, Chile	77	51 30S	75 0W
Nelspoort, C. Province	57	32 8S	22 59E
Nelspruit, Transvaal	57	25 29S	30 59E
Néma, Mauritania	50	16 30N	7 20W
Neman, R., Lithuania	23	55 3N	22 50E
Nemegos, Canada	62	47 40N	83 15W
Nemeiben L., Canada	65	55 30N	106 0W
Nemiscau and L., Can.	62	51 20N	77 1W
Nemours, France	12	48 16N	2 40E
Nemui, U.S.S.R.	27	55 40N	135 55E
Nemuro, Japan	36	43 20N	145 35E
Nemuro Str., Japan	36	44 0N	145 30E
Nenagh, Ireland	11	52 52N	8 11W
Nenana, Alaska	59	64 30N	149 12W
Nene R., England	10	52 38N	0 7E
Neno, Malawi	56	15 25S	34 40E
Nenusa I., Indonesia	35	4 45N	127 1E
Neodesha, U.S.A.	71	37 30N	95 44W
Neosho R., U.S.A.	71	36 20N	95 0W
Neosho, U.S.A.	71	36 56N	94 28W
Nepal, King., Asia	33	28 0N	84 30E
Nepalganj, Nepal	33	28 0N	81 40E
Nephi, U.S.A.	73	39 43N	111 52W
Nephin, mt., Ireland	11	54 1N	9 21W
Nepoko R., Zaire	53	2 20N	28 10E
Nérac, France	12	44 9N	0 20E
Nerchinsk, U.S.S.R.	27	52 0N	116 39E
Nerchinski Zavod, U.S.S.R.	27	51 10N	119 30E
Néret L., Canada	63	54 40N	71 0W
Neretva R., Yugoslavia	21	43 30N	17 50E
Nerja, Spain	17	36 43N	3 55W
Nerl R., U.S.S.R.	25	56 30N	40 30E
Nerva, Spain	17	37 42N	6 30W
Nes, Iceland	22	65 53N	17 16W
Nes, Norway	23	60 36N	9 35E
Neskaupstadur, Iceland	22	65 10N	13 43W
Ness, Loch, Scotland	10	57 15N	4 30W
Nesseby, Norway	23	70 9N	28 56E
Nesttun, Norway	23	60 17N	5 24E
Netanya, Israel	29	32 20N	34 51E
Nete, R. *See* Nethe, R., Belgium	13		
Nethe (Nete) R., Belg.	13	51 15N	5 0E
Netherdale, Queensland	42	21 10S	148 33E
Netherlands, King., Europe	13	52 0N	5 30E
Netherlands Guiana, col., S. America	79	4 0N	56 0W

	MAP		
Nethou, Pic de, mt., Spain	17	42 35N	0 40E
Neto R., Italy	20	39 10N	16 58E
Nettilling L., Canada	61	66 30N	71 0W
Netze, R., Poland	16	52 55N	16 25E
Neubrandenburg, Ger.	14	53 33N	13 17E
Neuchâtel, Switzerland	15	46 53N	6 50E
Neuchâtel, canton, Switz.	15	47 0N	64 0E
Neuchâtel, Lac de, Switzerland	15	46 53N	6 50E
Neufchâteau, Belgium	13	49 50N	5 25E
Neufchâtel, France	15	49 43N	1 30E
Neuchâtel, Lac de, Switzerland	15	46 52N	6 45E
Neu Heusis, S. W. Afr.	57	22 33S	16 48E
Neumünster, Germany	14	54 4N	9 58E
Neunkirchen, Germany	14	49 23N	7 6E
Neuquén, Argentina	77	38 0S	68 0E
Neuquén R., Argentina	77	37 20S	70 0W
Neuruppin, Germany	14	52 56N	12 48E
Neuse R., U.S.A.	69	35 5N	77 40W
Neustadt, Germany	14	49 21N	8 10E
Neustralitz, Germany	14	53 22N	13 4E
Neu Ulm, W. Germany	14	48 30N	10 1E
Neuwied, Germany	14	50 24N	7 29E
Neva R., U.S.S.R.	24	59 50N	30 30E
Nevada, U.S.A.	71	42 0N	93 25W
Nevada, st., U.S.A.	73	39 0N	117 0W
Nevada City, U.S.A.	72	39 16N	120 59W
Nevado de Colima, mt., Mexico	74	19 35N	103 45W
Nevallet, Israel	29	31 59N	34 57E
Nevanka, U.S.S.R.	27	56 45N	98 55E
Nevel, U.S.S.R.	25	56 0N	29 55E
Nevelski Mt., U.S.S.R.	27	50 0N	143 30E
Nevers, France	12	47 0N	3 9E
Nevertire, N.S.W.	43	31 50S	147 44E
Neville, Canada	65	49 58N	107 39W
Nevinnomyssk, U.S.S.R.	25	44 40N	42 0E
Nevis I., W. Indies	75	17 0N	62 30W
Nevsehir, Turkey	30	38 33N	34 40E
Nevyansk, U.S.S.R.	24	57 30N	60 0E
New R., Guyana	79	2 50N	57 50W
New Albany, U.S.A.	71	38 20N	85 50W
New Amsterdam, Guyana	79	6 15N	57 30W
New Bedford, U.S.A.	69	41 40N	70 52W
New Bern, U.S.A.	69	35 38N	77 3W
New Bethesda, C. Prov.	57	31 51S	24 34E
New Boston, U.S.A.	71	33 27N	94 26W
New Braunfels, U.S.A.	71	29 50N	98 0W
New Brighton, N.Z.	47	43 29S	172 43E
New Britain, U.S.A.	68	41 41N	72 47W
New Britain I., Bismarck Archipelago	42	6 0S	151 0E
New Brunswick, N.J., U.S.A.	68	40 30N	74 28W
New Brunswick, prov., Canada	63	46 50N	66 30W
New Caledonia Arch., Pacific Ocean	5	21 0S	165 0E
New Castile, prov., Spain	17	39 45N	3 20W
New Castle, Ind., U.S.A.	68	39 55N	85 30W
New Castle, Pa., U.S.A.	68	41 0N	80 20W
New Cristobal, Panama Canal Zone	74	9 25N	79 40W
New Denver, Canada	64	50 0N	117 25W
New England, U.S.A.	70	46 37N	102 53W
New England Ra., New South Wales	43	29 30S	152 0E
New Forest, dist., Eng.	10	50 53N	1 40W
New Glasgow, Canada	63	45 35N	62 36W
New Guinea I., Australasia	7	4 0S	136 0E
New Guinea, Terr. of	42	4 0S	136 0E
New Hampshire, st., U.S.A.	69	43 40N	71 40W
New Hampton, U.S.A.	70	43 2N	92 10W
New Hanover, Natal	57	29 22S	30 31E
New Hanover, I., Terr. of New Guinea	42	2 40S	150 5E
New Hazelton, Canada	64	55 20N	127 30W
New Hebrides Is., Pacific Ocean	5	15 0S	168 0E
New Iberia, U.S.A.	71	29 45N	91 55W
New Ireland I., Bismarck Archipelago	42	3 0S	151 30E
New Jersey, st., U.S.A.	68	39 50N	74 10W
New Kensington, U.S.A.	68	40 36N	79 43W
New Lexington, U.S.A.	68	39 40N	82 15W
New Liskeard, Canada	62	47 31N	79 41W
New London, Mo., U.S.A.	68	39 28N	92 0W
New London, Wis., U.S.A.	70	44 23N	88 41W
New London, U.S.A.	70	45 18N	94 58W
New Madrid, U.S.A.	71	36 38N	89 30W
New Meadows, U.S.A.	72	45 0N	116 19W
New Mexico, st., U.S.A.	71	34 30N	106 0W
New Norcia, W. Austral.	44	30 59S	116 8E
New Norfolk, Tas.	43	42 45S	147 0E
New Orleans, U.S.A.	71	30 0N	90 0W
New Philadelphia, U.S.A.	68	40 29N	81 25W
New Plymouth, N.Z.	46	39 4S	174 5E
New Plymouth, U.S.A.	72	43 59N	116 50W

	MAP		
New Providence I., Bahamas	75	25 0N	77 30W
New Quay, Wales	10	52 13N	4 21W
New Richmond, U.S.A.	70	45 6N	92 32W
New Roads, U.S.A.	71	30 42N	91 30W
New Rockford, U.S.A.	70	47 45N	99 0W
New Ross, Ireland	11	52 24N	6 58W
New Salem, U.S.A.	70	46 53N	101 27W
New Siberia, I., U.S.S.R.	27	75 0N	150 0E
New Siberian Is., U.S.S.R.	27	75 0N	140 0E
New Smyrna Beach, U.S.A.	69	29 0N	80 50W
New South Wales, st., Australia	43	33 0S	146 0E
New Ulm, U.S.A.	70	44 21N	94 30W
New Virginia, O.F.S.	57	28 8S	26 55E
New Waterford, Canada	63	46 13N	60 4W
New Westminster, Can.	64	49 10N	122 52W
New York, st., U.S.A.	68	42 40N	76 0W
New York City, U.S.A.	68	40 45N	74 0W
New Zealand, st., British Commonwealth	46-47	41 0S	175 0E
Newala, Tanzania	53	10 58S	39 10E
Newark, Del., U.S.A.	68	39 41N	75 47W
Newark, N.J., U.S.A.	68	40 41N	74 12W
Newark, N.Y., U.S.A.	68	43 2N	77 10W
Newark, Ohio, U.S.A.	68	40 5N	82 30W
Newaygo, U.S.A.	68	43 23N	85 50W
Newberg, U.S.A.	72	45 20N	123 0W
Newberry, Mich., U.S.A.	68	46 20N	85 32W
Newberry, S.C., U.S.A.	69	34 10N	81 10W
Newbliss, Ireland	11	54 10N	7 8W
Newbrook, Canada	64	54 24N	112 57W
Newburgh, Canada	68	44 17N	76 59W
Newbury, England	10	51 24N	1 19W
Newburyport, U.S.A.	69	42 48N	70 50W
Newcastle, Canada	63	47 1N	65 38W
Newcastle, England	10	54 58N	1 37W
Newcastle, Ireland	11	52 27N	9 4W
Newcastle, Natal	57	27 45S	29 58E
Newcastle, N.S.W.	43	32 52S	151 49E
Newcastle, Wyo., U.S.A.	70	43 52N	104 13W
Newcastle, Utah, U.S.A.	73	37 40N	113 35W
Newcastle B., Queens.	42	10 45S	142 30E
Newcastle-under-Lyme, England	8	53 2N	2 15W
Newcastle Waters, N. Terr., Australia	40	17 30S	133 28E
Newcastle West, Ireland	11	52 27N	9 4W
Newdegate, W. Austral.	44	33 17S	118 58E
Newell, U.S.A.	70	44 49N	103 27W
Newenham, C., Alaska	59	58 35N	162 0W
Newfoundland, prov., Canada	63	48 28N	56 0W
Newhaven, England	10	50 47N	0 4E
Newkirk, U.S.A.	71	36 51N	97 2W
Newland Ra., Western Australia	45	27 46S	124 0E
Newman, U.S.A.	73	37 24N	121 2W
Newmarket, England	10	52 15N	0 23E
Newmarket, Ireland	11	52 13N	9 0W
Newmarket, Jamaica	75		Inset
Newmarket-on-Fergus, Ireland	11	52 46N	8 54W
Newnan, U.S.A.	69	33 30N	84 40W
Newnes, N.S.W.	43	33 10S	150 10E
Newport, Mon., Eng.	10	51 34N	2 59W
Newport, Mayo, Ireland	11	53 54N	9 34W
Newport, Tipp., Ireland	11	52 43N	8 25W
Newport, Ky., U.S.A.	68	39 3N	84 20W
Newport, N.H., U.S.A.	69	43 23N	72 8W
Newport, Ore., U.S.A.	72	44 40N	124 2W
Newport, R.I., U.S.A.	68	41 30N	71 19W
Newport, Tenn., U.S.A.	69	35 58N	83 15W
Newport, Vt., U.S.A.	69	44 57N	72 17W
Newport, Wash., U.S.A.	72	48 11N	117 1W
Newport Beach, U.S.A.	73	33 37N	117 57W
Newport News, U.S.A.	68	37 0N	76 25W
Newquay, England	10	50 24N	5 6W
Newry, N. Ireland	11	54 10N	6 20W
Newton, Ill., U.S.A.	70	39 0N	88 10W
Newton, Iowa, U.S.A.	70	41 38N	93 2W
Newton, Kan., U.S.A.	71	38 1N	97 30W
Newton, Mass., U.S.A.	69	42 23N	70 59W
Newton, Miss., U.S.A.	71	32 20N	89 10W
Newton, N.C., U.S.A.	69	35 40N	81 14W
Newton, N.J., U.S.A.	68	41 3N	74 45W
Newton, Texas, U.S.A.	71	30 50N	93 45W
Newton Abbot, England	10	50 32N	3 37W
Newton Stewart, Scot.	10	54 57N	4 30W
Newtown, Ghana	52	5 2N	3 5W
Newtown, Victoria	43	37 38S	143 40E
Newtown, Wales	10	52 31N	3 19W
Newtown, Ireland	11	53 30N	8 34W
Newtown Butler, N. Ire.	11	54 12N	7 22W
Newtown Mt. Kennedy, Ireland	11	53 5N	6 7W
Newtown Stewart, Northern Ireland	11	54 43N	7 22W
Newtownards, N. Ireland	11	54 37N	5 40W
Newtownforbes, Ireland	11	53 46N	7 50W
Neyriz, Iran	31	29 18N	54 18E
Neyshabur, Iran	31	36 13N	58 47E
Nezhin, U.S.S.R.	25	51 5N	31 55E
Nezperce, U.S.A.	72	46 15N	116 20W

	MAP		
Ngabang, Indonesia	34	0 30N	109 55E
Ngadda, R., Nigeria	52	11 40N	13 20E
Ngala, Nigeria	52	12 21N	14 7E
Ngambé, Cameroon	52	5 48N	11 29E
Ngami, Former L., Botswana	56	20 37S	22 30E
Ngamo, Rhodesia	56	19 3S	27 25E
Ngangala, Sudan	53	4 46N	31 54E
Ngaoundere, Cameroon	52	7 15N	13 35E
Ngapara, New Zealand	47	44 57S	170 46E
Ngarambi, Tanzania	53	2 28S	38 38E
Ngaru, Tanzania	53	7 45S	38 56E
Ngaruawahia, N.Z.	46	37 42S	175 11E
Ngaruroro, R., N.Z.	46	39 25S	176 22E
Ngasamo, Tanzania	53	2 29S	33 52E
Ngatapa, New Zealand	46	38 34S	177 48E
Ngauruhoe, mt., N.Z.	46	39 13S	175 45E
Ngawi, Indonesia	34	7 24S	111 26E
Ngelebok, Cameroon	52	4 12N	14 0E
Ngerengere, Tanzania	53	6 47S	38 10E
Ngetera, Nigeria	52	12 28N	12 36E
Ngoap, Cameroon	52	4 3N	12 48E
Ngoboli, Sudan	53	4 59N	32 35E
Ngoma, S.W. Africa	56	17 49S	24 40E
Ngomahura, Rhod.	56	20 28S	30 46E
Ngong, Kenya	53	1 21S	36 39E
Ngongotaha, N.Z.	46	38 5S	176 13E
Ngoring Nor, L., China	37	34 45N	98 0E
Ngorongoro & Crater, Tanzania	53	3 10S	35 34E
Ngosa, Zambia	56	12 15S	27 18E
Ngozi, Burundi	53	2 54S	29 52E
Ngudu, Tanzania	53	2 50S	33 4E
Nguila, Cameroon	52	4 44N	11 42E
Ngulu Atoll, Pac. Oc.	35	8 20N	137 30E
Ngunga, Tanzania	53	3 39S	33 30E
Nguru, Nigeria	52	12 56N	10 29E
Nguru Mts., Tanzania	53	6 0S	37 45E
Ngusa, Zaire	53	3 18S	28 30E
Ngusi, Malawi	56	14 0S	34 55E
Nhachengue, Mozam.	56	22 35S	34 4E
Nhamapaza, R., Mozambique	56	18 0S	34 0E
Nhamefumbe, Mozam.	56	18 30S	35 11E
Nhamuai, Mozambique	56	30 34S	15 2E
Nhanvoo, L., Mozam.	56	22 22S	35 10E
Nha Trang, S. Viet Nam	34	12 15N	109 10E
Nhill, Victoria	43	36 18S	141 40E
Niafounké, Mali	50	16 0N	4 5W
Niagara, U.S.A.	70	45 45N	88 0W
Niagara Falls, N. Amer.	62	43 5N	79 5W
Niamey, Niger	52	13 27N	2 6E
Nianforando, Guinea	52	9 34N	10 42W
Niangara, Zaire	54	3 50N	27 50E
Nias I., Indonesia	34	1 0N	97 40E
Niassa, dist., Mozam.	56	13 30S	35 30E
Nibong, Tebal, Malaya	34	5 10N	100 29E
Nicaragua, rep., Central America	78	11 40N	85 30W
Nicaragua L., Central America	78	12 50N	85 30W
Nicastro, Italy	20	39 0N	16 18E
Nice, France	12	43 42N	7 14E
Niceville, U.S.A.	69	30 30N	86 30W
Nichinan, Japan	36	31 28N	131 26E
Nicholas Chan., West Indies	75	23 30N	80 30W
Nicholasville, U.S.A.	68	37 50N	84 35W
Nicholson, Canada	62	47 58N	83 47W
Nicholson L., Canada	65	62 30N	103 0W
Nicholson, Ra., W. Australia	44	27 12S	116 40E
Nicholson R., Queens.	42	17 59S	138 35E
Nickerie R., Surinam	79	5 30N	56 50W
Nicobar Is., India	28	7 18N	93 41E
Nicola, Canada	64	50 8N	120 40W
Nicolet, Canada	63	46 17N	72 35W
Nicosia, Cyprus	30	35 10N	33 25E
Nicotera, Italy	20	38 33N	15 57E
Nicoya, Costa Rica	78	10 9N	85 28W
Nicoya, G. of, Costa Rica	78	10 0N	85 0W
Nicoya Pen., Costa Rica	78	9 45N	85 40W
Nidzica, Poland	16	53 22N	20 27E
Nickershoop, C. Prov.	57	29 16S	22 52E
Niemba, Zaire	53	5 56S	28 32E
Nienburg, Germany	14	52 38N	9 15E
Nieuw Nickerie, Surinam	79	6 0N	57 10W
Nieuwoudtville, Cape Province	57	31 22N	19 6E
Nieuwpoort, Belgium	13	51 8N	2 45E
Nifale, Zambia	56	15 46S	23 16E
Nigde, Turkey	30	38 0N	34 38E
Nigel, Transvaal	57	26 27S	28 25E
Niger, rep., Africa	50	15 30N	10 0E
Niger R., W. Africa	50	13 35N	7 0W
Niger delta, Nigeria	52	5 0N	6 20E
Nigeria, Federation of, W. Africa	52	8 30N	8 0E
Nightcaps, New Zealand	47	45 57S	168 14E
Nii Shima, I., Japan	36	34 24N	139 10E
Niigata, Japan	36	37 58N	139 0E
Niigata, pref., Japan	36	37 15N	138 45E
Niihama, Japan	36	33 55N	133 10E
Niihan, I., Hawaiian Is.	59	21 50N	160 11W
Nijar, Spain	17	36 53N	2 15W
Nijerk, Netherlands	13	52 13N	5 30E

	MAP		
Nijmegen, Netherlands	13	51 50N	5 52E
Nijverdal, Neth.	13	52 24N	6 27E
Nike, Nigeria	52	6 28N	7 28E
Nikel, U.S.S.R.	22	69 24N	30 1E
Nikiniki, Indonesia	35	9 40S	124 30E
Nikki, Dahomey	52	9 58N	3 31E
Nikko, Japan	36	36 45N	139 35E
Nikolayev, U.S.S.R.	25	46 58N	32 7E
Nikolayevka, U.S.S.R.	27	45 50N	131 5E
Nikolayevski, U.S.S.R.	25	50 10N	45 35E
Nikolôyevsk, U.S.S.R.	27	53 30N	140 50E
Nikopol, U.S.S.R.	25	47 35N	34 25E
Nikshahr, Iran	31	26 10N	60 4E
Nikšić, Yugoslavia	21	42 50N	18 57E
Nila I., Indonesia	35	6 50S	129 30E
Niland, U.S.A.	73	33 16N	115 31W
Nile R., N.E. Africa	51	27 30N	30 30E
Nile Blue R. *See* Blue Nile	51		
Nile, White R. *See* White Nile	51		
Niles, U.S.A.	68	41 12N	80 47W
Nilgiri Hills, India	32	11 30N	76 30E
Nimach (Neemach), India	32	24 30N	74 50E
Nîmes, France	12	43 50N	4 23E
Nim Ka Thana, India	32	27 42N	75 50E
Nimmitabel, N.S.W.	43	36 29S	149 15E
Nimrin Wadi, Jordan	29	31 54N	35 35E
Nimule, Uganda	53	3 32N	32 3E
Nindigully, Queensland	43	28 21S	148 54E
Ninemile, Alaska	64	56 0N	130 7W
Ninety Mile Beach, North I., N.Z.	46	34 45S	172 55E
Nineveh, anc. city, Iraq	30	36 25N	43 10E
Ninghsien, China	38	35 31N	108 0E
Ningi, Nigeria	52	10 59N	9 24E
Ningkiang, China	38	32 40N	106 28E
Ningming, China	39	22 13N	106 38E
Ningpo, China	39	29 50N	121 30E
Ningshen, China	38	33 41N	108 36E
Ningsia Hui, A.R., China	38	37 15N	106 0E
Ningsiang, China	39	28 20N	112 20E
Ningteh, China	37	26 45N	120 0E
Ningtsinhsien, China	38	37 40N	115 0E
Ningtu, China	39	26 25N	115 45E
Ninguta, China	37	44 30N	129 50E
Ningwu, China	38	39 2N	112 15E
Ningyuanhsien, China	39	25 45N	111 45E
Ninh Binh, N. Viet Nam	34	20 15N	105 55E
Ninove, Belgium	13	50 51N	4 2E
Niobrara, U.S.A.	70	42 47N	98 0W
Niobrara, R., U.S.A.	70	42 50N	99 30W
Nioka, Zaire	53	2 10N	30 40E
Nioro, Mali	50	15 30N	9 30W
Nioro du Rif, Senegal	52	13 42N	15 50W
Niort, France	12	46 19N	0 29W
Nipani, India	32	16 20N	74 25E
Nipawin, Canada	65	53 20N	104 0W
Nipawin Prov. Park, Canada	65	53 50N	104 30W
Nipigon, Canada	52	49 0N	81 17W
Nipigon L., Ont., Can.	62	49 40N	88 30W
Nipin, R., Canada	65	55 30N	109 25W
Nipishish L., Canada	63	54 0N	60 55W
Nipissing L., Canada	62	46 20N	79 40W
Nipissis, R., Canada	63	51 0N	66 0W
Nipisso L., Canada	63	50 52N	65 51W
Nipomo, U.S.A.	73	35 1N	120 30W
Nirim, Israel	29	31 14N	34 21E
Nirmal, India	32	19 3N	78 20E
Nirmali, India	33	26 20N	86 35E
Nis, Yugoslavia	21	43 19N	21 58E
Nisa, Portugal	17	39 30N	7 41W
Niscemi, Sicily, Italy	20	37 8N	14 21E
Nishmi Kolimsk, U.S.S.R.	29	68 40N	161 0E
Nisiros I., Ægean Sea	21	36 35N	27 10E
Niskibi, R., Canada	65	56 16N	88 0W
Nisko, Poland	16	50 35N	22 7E
Nissan, I., Terr. of New Guinea	42	4 30S	154 10E
Nisutlin R., Canada	64	60 40N	132 40W
Nitchequon, Canada	63	53 10N	70 58W
Niteroi, Brazil	79	22 52S	43 0W
Nith R., Scotland	10	55 20N	3 5W
Nitra, Czechoslovakia	16	48 19N	18 4E
Nitra R., C. Slov.	16	48 30N	18 7E
Niut Mt., Indonesia	34	0 55N	109 30E
Nivelles, Belgium	13	50 35N	4 20E
Nivernais, prov. France	12	47 0N	3 40E
Nixon, Nev., U.S.A.	72	39 50N	119 21W
Nixon, Texas, U.S.A.	71	29 16N	97 46W
Nizamabad, India	32	18 45N	78 7E
Nizamghat, India	33	28 20N	95 45E
Nizh Lomov, U.S.S.R.	25	53 40N	43 35E
Nizhne Angarsk, U.S.S.R.	27	56 0N	109 30E
Nizhne Kamenka, U.S.S.R.	27	52 20N	136 30E
Nizhe Kolymsk, U.S.S.R.	27	68 40N	161 0E
Nizhne Toyma, U.S.S.R.	24	62 15N	44 10E
Nizhneudinsk, U.S.S.R.	27	55 0N	99 20E
Nizhni Baskunchak, U.S.S.R.	25	48 16N	46 52E

	MAP		
Nizhni Novgorod, U.S.S.R.	25	56 20N	44 0E
Nizhniy Tagil, U.S.S.R.	24	57 45N	60 0E
Nizip, Turkey	30	37 1N	37 46E
Njakwa, Malawi	56	11 2S	33 52E
Njinjo, Tan.	53	8 34S	38 44E
Njoko, R., Zambia	56	16 40S	24 10E
Njombe R., Tanzania	53	7 15S	34 30E
Nkonko, Tanzania	53	6 26S	34 58E
Nkala, Zambia	56	15 55S	26 0E
Nkambe, W. Cameroon	52	6 36N	10 37E
Nkana, Zambia	56	12 50S	28 11E
Nkandla, Natal	57	28 38S	31 8E
Nkata Bay, Malawi	56	11 33S	34 16E
Nkawkaw, Ghana	52	6 36N	0 49W
Nkeyema, Zambia	56	14 58S	25 18E
Nko, Cameroon	52	2 50N	13 2E
Nkongsomba, Cameroon	52	4 55N	9 55E
Nkunka, Zambia	56	14 48S	25 47E
Nkwalini, Natal	57	28 45S	31 33E
Nkwanta, Ghana	52	6 10N	2 10W
Nmai or Lawng Pit, R., Burma	33	25 30N	98 0E
Nnewi, Nigeria	52	6 0N	7 3E
Noakhali. *See* Maijdi, Pakistan	33		
Noanamó, Colombia	78	4 45N	77 0W
Noasanabis, S.W. Africa	57	23 26S	18 46E
Noatak, Alaska	59	67 35N	163 12W
Noatak, R., Alaska	59	67 58N	161 0W
Nobeoka, Japan	36	32 35N	131 45E
Noblesville, U.S.A.	68	40 0N	86 0W
Noccundra, Queensland	43	27 44S	142 31E
Nocera, Italy	20	39 1N	14 37E
Nocona, U.S.A.	71	33 47N	97 46W
Noda, Japan	36	36 5N	139 48E
Noda, U.S.S.R.	27	47 30N	142 5E
Noel, U.S.A.	71	36 34N	94 30W
Nogaisk, U.S.S.R.	25	46 50N	36 28E
Nogales, Mexico	73	31 15N	110 55W
Nogales, U.S.A.	73	31 17N	110 55W
Nogat, R., Poland	23	54 5N	19 5E
Nogata, Japan	36	33 48N	130 54E
Nogent le Rotrou, Fr.	12	48 20N	0 50E
Noginsk, U.S.S.R.	25	55 50N	38 25E
Noginski, U.S.S.R.	27	64 30N	90 50E
Nogoa R., Queensland	42	24 12S	147 30E
Noguora Ribagorzana R., Spain	17	42 0N	0 40E
Noires, Mts., France	12	48 11N	3 40W
Noirmoutier, I. de, Fr.	12	46 58N	2 10W
Nok Kundi, Pakistan	32	28 50N	62 45E
Nokhtuisk, U.S.S.R.	27	60 0N	117 45E
Nokomis, Canada	65	51 35N	105 0W
Nokomis, U.S.A.	70	39 20N	89 20W
Nokomis L., Canada	65	57 0N	103 10W
Nola, Cen. Afr. Rep.	54	3 35N	16 10E
Nola, Italy	20	40 54N	14 29E
Noman L., Canada	65	62 0N	109 0W
Nombre de Dios, Mex.	74	23 50N	104 10W
Nome, Alaska	59	64 35N	165 40W
Nonacho L., Canada	65	61 40N	109 30W
Nonda, Queensland	52	20 40S	142 28E
Nondwa, Tanzania	53	6 26S	35 22E
Nong Khai, Thailand	34	17 50N	102 46E
Nongoma, Natal	57	27 53S	31 42E
Nonoava, Mexico	74	27 30N	106 41W
Nontron, France	12	45 31N	0 40E
Nookawarra, Western Australia	44	26 10S	116 58E
Noonan, U.S.A.	70	48 54N	103 0W
Noongal, W. Australia	44	28 9S	116 44E
Noordost Polder, Neth.	13	52 45N	5 45E
Noorvik, Alaska	59	66 50N	161 14W
Nootka, Canada	64	49 30N	125 35W
Nootka I., Canada	64	49 40N	126 50W
Nootka Sd., Canada	64	49 30N	126 40W
Noqui, Angola	54	5 55S	13 30E
Noranda, Canada	62	48 20N	79 0W
Norbotten, prov., Sweden	22	66 58N	20 0E
Nord Katanga, prov., Zaire	54	8 0S	27 0E
Nord Kivu, prov. Zaire	54	1 0S	29 0E
Nordegg, Canada	64	52 29N	116 5W
Nordeney I., Germany	14	53 35N	7 10E
Nordhausen, Germany	14	51 29N	10 47E
Nordland, prov., Norway	22	67 0N	15 0E
Nordvik, U.S.S.R.	27	73 40N	110 57E
Nore R., Ireland	11	52 26N	7 20W
Norfolk, Nebr., U.S.A.	70	42 0N	97 20W
Norfolk, Va., U.S.A.	68	36 53N	76 17W
Norfolk I., Pacific Ocean	5	28 58S	168 3E
Norfolk Res., U.S.A.	71	36 50N	92 30W
Norheimsund, Norway	23	60 22N	6 9E
Normal, U.S.A.	70	40 30N	88 59W
Norman, U.S.A.	71	35 10N	97 35W
Norman R., Queensland	42	19 15S	142 10E
Norman Wells, Canada	60	65 40N	127 35W
Normanby, New Zealand	46	39 32S	174 18E
Normanby, R., Queens.	42	15 0S	144 16E
Normandie, prov., Fr.	12	49 0N	0 0
Normandin, Canada	63	48 49N	72 3W
Normandy, I., Papua	42	10 0S	151 0E
Normanhurst, mt., W. Australia	45	25 13S	122 30E
Normanton, Queens.	42	17 40S	141 10E

Name	Map	Lat.	Long.
Nornalup, W. Australia	44	34 57 S	116 40 E
Norquay, Canada	65	51 52 N	102 0 W
Norquin, Argentina	77	37 45 S	70 50 W
Norquinco, Argentina	77	42 0 S	71 0 W
Nörresundby, Denmark	23	57 5 N	9 52 E
Norris, U.S.A.	72	45 36 N	111 44 W
Norristown, U.S.A.	68	40 9 N	75 20 W
Norrköping, Sweden	23	58 35 N	16 10 E
Norrland, dist., Sweden	23	64 25 N	18 0 E
Norrsundet, Sweden	23	60 57 N	17 10 E
Norrtalje, Sweden	23	59 44 N	18 46 E
Norseman, W. Australia	44	32 8 S	121 43 E
Norsewood, N.Z.	46	40 4 S	176 15 E
Norsk, U.S.S.R.	27	52 30 N	130 0 E
North C., Canada	63	47 2 N	60 20 W
North C., New Zealand	46	34 25 S	173 5 E
North I., Kenya	53	4 3 N	36 0 E
North I., New Zealand	46	38 0 S	175 0 E
North Adams, U.S.A.	69	42 42 N	73 6 W
North America, cont.	58	10 to 80 N	20 to 120 W
North Battleford, Can.	65	52 50 N	108 10 W
North Bay, Canada	62	46 20 N	79 30 W
North Bend, Canada	64	49 50 N	121 35 W
North Bend, U.S.A.	72	43 20 N	124 10 W
North Borneo. *See* Sabah	35		
North Brabant, prov., Netherland	13	51 37 N	5 0 E
North Branch R., N.Z.	47	43 30 S	171 30 E
North Bunguran I., Indonesia	34	4 45 N	108 0 E
North Canadian R., U.S.A.	71	36 20 N	99 0 W
North Caribou, L., Can.	62	52 50 N	90 50 W
North Carolina, st., U.S.A.	69	35 30 N	79 0 W
North Central, dist., Vic.	43	37 10 S	145 0 E
North Central Plain, Div., N.S.W.	43	29 46 S	149 31 E
North Channel, Brit. Is.	11	55 0 N	5 30 W
North Channel, N. America	62	46 0 N	83 0 W
North Chicago, U.S.A.	70	42 19 N	87 50 W
North Coast, dist., N.S.W.	43	30 0 S	152 50 E
North Dakota, st., U.S.A.	70	47 0 N	100 0 W
North Downs, England	10	51 17 N	0 30 W
North East New Guinea, Australian Trusteeship Territory	42	5 30 S	144 30 E
North East Frontier Agency, Assam, India	33	28 0 N	95 0 E
North Eastern, dist., Vic.	43	37 0 S	146 30 E
North Eastern, prov., Kenya	53	1 30 N	40 10 E
North Eastern Region, China	37	45 0 N	115 0 E
North Esk, R., Scotland	10	56 45 N	2 30 W
North Foreland, Eng.	10	51 22 N	1 28 E
North Fork R., U.S.A.	70	39 40 N	100 15 W
North Frisian Is., Ger.	14	54 50 N	8 20 E
North Henik L., Can.	65	62 0 N	97 20 W
North Horr, Kenya	53	3 21 N	37 1 E
North Kamloops, Can.	64	50 40 N	120 25 W
North Knife, L., Can.	65	58 0 N	97 0 W
North Knife, R., Can.	65	58 35 N	96 0 W
North Lakhimpur, India	33	27 15 N	94 10 E
North Las Vegas, U.S.A.	73	36 15 N	115 9 W
North Little Rock, U.S.A.	71	34 47 N	92 17 W
North Loup, R., U.S.A.	70	42 30 N	101 0 W
North Mavora L., N.Z.	47	45 13 S	168 11 E
North Minch, chan., Scotland	10	58 10 N	5 40 W
North Moscos (Heinze) Is., Burma	33	14 0 N	97 30 E
North Nahanni R., Can.	64	62 30 N	125 0 W
North Ossetian, A.S.S.R., U.S.S.R.	26	43 30 N	44 30 E
North Pagai I., Indon.	34	2 50 S	100 0 E
North Palisade, mt., U.S.A.	73	37 2 N	118 32 W
North Platte, U.S.A.	70	41 10 N	100 50 W
North Platte, R., U.S.A.	72	42 50 N	106 50 W
North Pole	80	90 N	
North Powder, U.S.A.	72	45 2 N	117 59 W
North Rhineland, Westphalia, Germany	14	52 0 N	8 0 E
North Ronaldsay I., Scotland	10	59 20 N	2 30 W
North Saskatchewan R., Can.	65	53 50 N	113 0 W
North Sea, N.W. Europe	8	55 0 N	4 9 E
North Sydney, Canada	63	46 12 N	60 21 W
North Taranaki Bight, N.Z.	46	38 45 S	174 20 E
North Tonawanda, U.S.A.	68	43 5 N	78 50 W
North Trondelag, co., Norway	23	64 20 N	12 0 E
North Truchas Pk., U.S.A.	71	36 0 N	105 30 W
North Twin I., Canada	62	53 20 N	80 0 W
North Uist I., Scotland	10	57 40 N	7 15 W
North Vancouver, Can.	64	49 25 N	123 20 W
North Vermilion, Can.	64	58 25 N	116 0 W
North Vernon, U.S.A.	68	39 0 N	85 40 W
North Village, Bermuda	75	32 15 N	64 45 W
North Wabiskaw L., Canada	64	56 0 N	114 0 W
North West Basin, W. Australia	44	25 45 S	115 0 E
North West C., Western Australia	44	21 45 S	114 9 E
North-West River, Can.	63	52 30 N	60 10 W
North West Terr., Can.	60	65 0 N	100 0 W
North Western, prov., Zambia	46	13 0 S	25 30 E
North Western Division, Queensland	42	19 30 S	140 14 E
North Western Division, W. Australia	44	24 16 S	115 30 E
North Western Region, China	37	37 0 N	90 0 E
North Western Region, Tasmania	43	41 6 S	145 3 E
North Western Slope, dist., N.S.W.	43	30 45 S	150 40 E
Northallerton, England	10	54 20 N	1 26 W
Northam, Transvaal	57	24 55 S	27 15 E
Northam, W. Australia	44	31 35 S	116 42 W
Northampton, England	10	52 14 N	0 54 W
Northampton, U.S.A.	69	42 22 N	73 31 W
Northampton, Western Australia	44	28 21 S	114 33 E
Northcliffe, W. Austral.	44	34 38 S	116 0 E
Northeast Providence Chan., West Indies	75	26 0 N	76 0 W
Northern, prov., Zambia	56	10 30 S	31 0 E
Northern, dist., Malawi	56	11 0 S	33 30 E
Northern, prov., Sudan	51	18 0 N	34 0 E
Northern, prov., Tan.	53	4 0 S	31 10 E
Northern, prov., Ugan.	53	3 0 N	32 30 E
Northern, dist., Victoria	43	36 10 S	145 0 E
Northern Agricultural Div., W. Australia	44	30 15 S	116 30 E
Northern Circars, India	33	17 30 N	82 30 E
Northern Goldfields Div., W. Australia	45	25 17 S	125 20 E
Northern Indian L., Can.	65	57 20 N	97 40 W
Northern Ireland, Ire.	11	54 45 N	7 0 W
Northern Lights, L., Canada	62	49 15 N	90 45 W
Northern Prov., S. Leone	52	Inset	
Northern Region, China	38	37 0 N	115 0 E
Northern Region, Ghana	52	9 45 N	2 0 W
Northern Region, Tas.	43	41 8 S	147 11 E
Northern Rhodesia (Zambia), Afr.	56	14 0 S	29 0 E
Northern Tableland, dist., N.S.W.	43	30 0 S	151 30 E
Northern Territory, Australia	40-41	16 0 S	133 0 E
Northfield, U.S.A.	70	44 28 N	93 9 W
Northgate, Canada	65	49 2 N	102 18 W
Northome, U.S.A.	70	47 54 N	94 15 W
Northport, Ala., U.S.A.	69	33 14 N	87 33 W
Northport, Mich., U.S.A.	68	45 5 N	85 38 W
Northport, Wash., U.S.A.	72	48 57 N	117 46 W
Northumberland, C., S. Australia	43	37 51 S	140 30 E
Northumberland Is., Queensland	42	21 45 S	150 20 E
Northumberland Str., Canada	63	46 20 N	64 0 W
Northway, Alaska	59	62 58 N	142 0 W
Northwest Providence Chan., West Indies	75	26 0 N	78 0 W
Northwood, Iowa U.S.A.	70	43 30 N	93 14 W
Northwood, N.D., U.S.A.	70	47 45 N	97 30 W
Norton, U.S.A.	70	39 50 N	100 0 W
Norton, Rhodesia	65	17 52 S	30 40 E
Norton B., Alaska	59	64 48 N	161 30 W
Norton Sd., Alaska	59	63 50 N	164 0 W
Norwalk, U.S.A.	68	41 9 N	73 25 W
Norway, King., Europe	22-23	67 0 N	11 0 E
Norway, U.S.A.	70	45 40 N	87 58 W
Norway House, Canada	65	53 55 N	98 50 W
Norwegian Sea, North Atlantic Ocean	5	66 0 N	1 0 E
Norwich, England	10	52 38 N	1 17 E
Norwich, U.S.A.	68	42 32 N	75 30 W
Noshiro, Japan	36	40 15 N	140 0 E
Noshiro R., Japan	36	40 15 N	140 15 E
Nosok, U.S.S.R.	26	70 10 N	82 20 E
Nosovka, U.S.S.R.	25	50 50 N	31 30 E
Nosratābād, Iran	31	30 2 N	59 57 E
Nossob, R., S.W. Afr.	57	23 30 S	18 30 E
Nota, R., U.S.S.R.	22	68 20 N	30 0 E
Noteć R., Poland	16	53 5 N	17 20 E
Notikewin, R., Canada	64	56 55 N	117 50 W
Noto, Italy	20	36 52 N	15 4 E
Notodden, Norway	23	59 35 N	9 14 E
Notre Dame, Canada	63	46 18 N	64 46 W
Notre Dame, B., Can.	63	49 45 N	55 30 W
Nottaway R., Canada	62	50 50 N	78 20 W
Nottingham, England	10	52 57 N	1 10 W
Nottoway R., U.S.A.	68	37 1 N	77 50 W
Notwani R., Botswana	57	24 15 S	26 27 E
Nouakchott, Mauritania	50	18 20 N	15 50 W
Noupoort, Cape Prov.	57	31 10 S	24 57 E
Nova Chaves, Angola	55	10 50 S	21 15 E
Nova Cruz, Brazil	79	6 40 S	35 25 W
Nova Freixo, Mozam.	55	14 50 S	36 31 E
Nova Friburgo, Brazil	79	22 10 S	42 30 W
Nova Gaia, Angola	55	10 10 S	17 35 E
Nova Granada, Brazil	79	20 30 S	49 20 W
Nova Hamburgo, Brazil	77	29 40 S	51 8 W
Nova Lima, Brazil	79	20 5 S	44 0 W
Nova Lisboa, Angola	55	12 42 S	15 54 E
Nova Lusitânia, Mozam.	56	19 55 S	34 30 E
Nova Mambone, Mozambique	56	20 57 S	35 1 E
Nova Sagres, Port., Timor	35	8 25 S	127 15 E
Nova Scotia, prov., Can.	63	45 10 N	63 0 W
Nova Sofala, Mozam.	55	20 8 S	34 48 E
Nova Zagora, Bulgaria	21	42 32 N	25 59 E
Novalorque, Brazil	79	7 0 S	44 5 W
Novara, Italy	40	45 27 N	8 36 E
Novaya Kazanka, U.S.S.R.	25	49 3 N	49 28 E
Novaya Lyalya, U.S.S.R.	26	58 50 N	60 35 E
Novaya Zemlya, Is., U.S.S.R.	26	75 0 N	56 0 E
Nové Zamky, C.Slov.	16	48 2 N	18 8 E
Novelda, Spain	17	38 24 N	0 46 W
Novgorod, U.S.S.R.	25	58 30 N	31 25 E
Novgorod Severski, U.S.S.R.	25	52 2 N	33 10 E
Novi Ligure, Italy	20	44 45 N	8 47 E
Novi-Pazar, Bulgaria	21	43 25 N	27 15 E
Novi Sad, Yugoslavia	21	45 18 N	19 52 E
Novi Vinod, Y.slav.	20	45 9 N	14 50 E
Novigrad, Yugoslavia	20	45 19 N	13 33 E
Novo Redondo, Angola	55	11 11 S	13 54 E
Novo Ukrainka, U.S.S.R.	25	46 25 N	31 30 E
Novocherkassk, U.S.S.R.	25	47 27 N	40 5 E
Novogrudok, U.S.S.R.	23	53 40 N	25 50 E
Novokazalinsk, U.S.S.R.	26	45 40 N	61 40 E
Novokuznetsk, U.S.S.R.	26	55 0 N	83 5 E
Novokhopersk, U.S.S.R.	25	51 5 N	41 50 E
Novomoskovsk, R.S.F.S.R., U.S.S.R.	25	54 10 N	38 25 E
Novomoskovsk, Ukraine, U.S.S.R.	25	48 39 N	35 10 E
Novorossiysk, U.S.S.R.	25	44 43 N	37 52 E
Novorzhev, U.S.S.R.	25	57 3 N	29 25 E
Novosibirsk, U.S.S.R.	26	55 0 N	83 5 E
Novosokolniki, U.S.S.R.	25	56 33 N	28 42 E
Novouzensk, U.S.S.R.	25	50 32 N	48 17 E
Novozybkov, U.S.S.R.	25	52 30 N	32 0 E
Novska, Yugoslavia	20	45 19 N	17 0 E
Novy Oskol, U.S.S.R.	25	50 44 N	37 55 E
Novy Port, U.S.S.R.	26	67 40 N	72 30 E
Now Shahr, Iran	31	36 42 N	51 32 E
Nowa Huta, Poland	16	50 4 N	20 6 E
Nowa Ruda, Poland	16	50 35 N	16 29 E
Nowemiasto, Bydgoszcz, Poland	16	53 30 N	19 38 E
Nowemiasto, Lódz, Poland	16	51 37 N	20 38 E
Nowgong, India	33	26 20 N	92 50 E
Nowra, N.S.W.	43	34 53 S	150 35 E
Nowshera, Pakistan	32	34 0 N	71 55 E
Nowy Dwór, Poland	16	53 40 N	23 0 E
Nowy Sacz, Poland	16	49 40 N	20 41 E
Nowy Targ, Poland	16	49 30 N	20 2 E
Nowy Tomysl, Poland	16	52 19 N	16 10 E
Noxon, U.S.A.	72	48 0 N	115 45 W
Noya, Spain	17	42 48 N	8 53 W
Noyes I., Alaska	64	55 30 N	133 40 W
Noyon, France	12	49 34 N	3 0 E
Npologu, Nigeria	52	6 48 N	7 13 E
Nqutu, Natal	57	28 13 S	30 41 E
N'riquinha, Angola	55	16 0 S	21 25 E
Nsawam, Ghana	52	5 50 N	0 24 W
Nsombo, Zambia	56	10 45 S	29 59 E
Nsukka, Nigeria	52	7 0 N	7 50 E
Ntui, Cameroon	52	4 12 N	11 50 E
Ntumba, Tanzania	53	8 21 S	32 7 E
Nuala, Zambia	56	13 27 S	28 16 E
Nuanetsi, Rhodesia	56	21 15 S	30 48 E
Nuanetsi R., Rhodesia	56	21 30 S	31 0 E
Nuatja, Togoland	52	6 55 N	1 2 E
Nubian Desert, Sudan	51	21 30 N	33 30 E
Nudo Coropuna, Peru	78	15 30 S	72 30 W
Nudo del Paramillo, mt., Colombia	75	7 8 N	76 10 W
Nudushan, Iran	31	32 2 N	53 20 E
Nueces R., U.S.A.	71	28 18 N	98 39 W
Nu'eima R., Jordan	29	31 53 N	35 30 E
Nueltin L., Canada	65	60 0 N	100 0 W
Nuéve de Julio, Arg.	77	35 30 S	61 0 W
Nuevitas, Cuba	75	21 30 N	77 20 W
Nueva Gerona, I., de Pinos, Cuba	75	21 53 N	82 49 W
Nueva Rosita, Mexico	74	28 0 N	101 20 W
Nuevo G., Argentina	77	43 0 S	64 30 W
Nuevo Laredo, Mexico	74	27 30 N	99 40 W
Nuevo Rocafuerte, Ec.	78	46 27 S	169 50 E
Nugget Pt., N.Z.	47	0 55 S	76 50 W
Nuhaka, New Zealand	46	39 3 S	177 45 E
Nukha, U.S.S.R.	24	41 10 N	47 5 E
Nukhayb, Iraq	30	32 2 N	42 15 E
Nukheila, Sudan	51	19 10 N	26 0 E
Nulato, Alaska	59	64 45 N	158 15 W
Nullagine, W. Australia	44	21 50 S	120 7 E
Nullarbor Plains, Australia	45	30 50 S	129 0 E
Nulloocha, Queensland	42	22 15 S	142 40 E
Numan, Nigeria	52	9 29 N	12 3 E
Numata, Japan	36	36 40 N	139 0 E
Numazu, Japan	36	35 15 N	139 5 E
Numbera, Queensland	42	18 59 S	140 32 E
Numurkah, Victoria	43	36 0 S	145 26 E
Nun Kiang, R., China	37	48 0 N	124 0 E
Nunaksaluk I., Canada	63	55 40 N	60 12 W
Nundle, N.S.W.	43	31 24 S	151 5 E
Nundu, Congo	53	3 49 S	29 4 E
Nuneaton, England	10	52 32 N	1 29 W
Nungan, China	38	44 25 N	125 10 E
Nunkiang, China	37	49 10 N	125 20 E
Nunspeet, Netherlands	13	52 21 N	5 45 E
Nuntherungie, N.S.W.	43	30 56 S	142 36 E
Nuoro, Italy	20	40 20 N	9 20 E
Nurgarin, W. Australia	44	31 10 S	118 2 E
Nuriootpa, S. Australia	43	34 27 S	139 0 E
Nurmes, Finland	23	63 37 N	29 10 E
Nürnberg (Nuremburg), Germany	14	49 26 N	11 5 E
Nurri, Sardinia, Italy	20	39 43 N	9 13 E
Nusa Barung I., Indon.	34	8 26 S	113 30 E
Nusa Kambangan C., Indonesia	34	7 47 S	109 0 E
Nushki, Pakistan	32	29 35 N	65 55 E
Nuwakot, Nepal	33	28 10 N	83 55 E
Nuwara Eliya, Sri Lanka	37	6 58 N	80 55 E
Nuwefontein, C. Prov.	57	30 58 S	17 50 E
Nuwerus, C. Prov.	57	31 8 S	18 24 E
Nuweveldberge, Cape Province	57	32 10 S	21 45 E
Nuyts Arch, S. Austral.	45	32 25 S	133 25 E
Nuyts Point, Western Australia	40	35 4 S	116 31 E
Nyabessan, Cameroon	52	2 30 N	10 35 E
Nyahanga, Tanzania	43	2 20 S	33 35 E
Nyahua, Tanzania	53	5 29 S	33 21 E
Nyahwest, Victoria	43	35 8 S	143 26 E
Nyakabindi, Tanzania	53	3 39 S	34 0 E
Nyakanazi, Tanzania	53	3 1 S	31 16 E
Nyakasu, Burundi	53	3 54 S	30 7 E
Nyakrom, Ghana	52	5 33 N	1 48 W
Nyala, Sudan	51	12 2 N	24 58 E
Nyamandhlovu, Rhod.	56	19 50 S	28 15 E
Nyambiti, Tanzania	53	2 49 S	33 19 E
Nyamlell, Sudan	54	9 7 N	26 59 E
Nyamtumbo, Tanzania	56	10 30 S	36 4 E
Nyamwaga, Tanzania	53	1 24 S	34 35 E
Nyamwage, Tanzania	53	8 10 S	39 0 E
Nyandekwa, Tanzania	53	4 0 S	32 32 E
Nyang Chu R., China	33	29 0 N	89 30 E
Nyanguge, Tanzania	53	2 31 S	33 13 E
Nyangwena, Zambia	56	15 16 S	28 45 E
Nyanje, Zambia	56	14 25 S	31 46 E
Nyankpala, Ghana	52	9 20 N	1 10 W
Nyanza, Rwanda	53	2 25 S	29 35 E
Nyanza, Burundi	53	4 20 S	29 41 E
Nyanza, prov., Kenya	53	0 30 S	34 30 E
Nyarling R., Canada	64	60 40 N	113 40 W
Nyasaland (Malawi), rep., East Africa	56	13 0 S	34 0 E
Nyasi, Cameroon	52	4 14 N	13 51 E
Nyavikungu, Zaire	56	11 26 S	25 56 E
Nyazwidzi, R., Rhod.	56	19 30 S	31 50 E
Nybro, Sweden	23	55 20 N	10 49 E
Nyenchen Tanglha Ra., China	37	30 0 N	86 0 E
Nyengo Swamp, Zambia	56	14 40 S	22 10 E
Nyeri, Kenya	54	0 34 S	37 0 E
Nyika Plat., Malawi	56	10 40 S	34 0 E
Nyilumba, Tanzania	56	10 26 S	40 21 E
Nyimba, Zambia	56	14 33 S	30 49 E
Nyinahin, Ghana	52	6 43 N	2 3 W
Nyiregyháza, Hungary	16	48 0 N	21 47 E
Nyiro Uaso, R., Kenya	53	1 0 N	38 40 E
Nyiru, Mt., Kenya	53	2 11 N	36 49 E
Nyköbing, Denmark	23	54 46 N	11 52 E
Nyköping, Sweden	23	58 45 N	17 0 E
Nylstroom, Transvaal	57	24 42 S	28 22 E
Nymagee, N.S.W.	43	32 5 S	146 16 E
Nyngan, N.S.W.	43	31 30 S	147 8 E
Nyoko R., Zambia	56	16 30 S	24 15 E
Nyon, Switzerland	15	46 23 N	6 14 E
Nyong, R., Cameroon	52	3 52 N	12 32 E
Nyonga, and Mt., Tan.	53	6 43 S	32 2 E
Nyons, France	13	44 22 N	5 10 E
Nyssa, U.S.A.	72	43 54 N	117 1 W
Nyunzu, Zaire	53	5 55 S	28 0 E
Nzega, Tanzania	53	4 4 S	32 3 E
Nzérékoré, Guinea	50	7 49 N	8 48 W
N'zilo Dam, Zaire	56	10 30 S	25 30 E
Nzilo Falls, Zaire	56	10 27 S	25 25 E
Nzubuka, Tanzania	53	4 45 S	32 50 E

O

Name	Map	Lat.	Long.
O Shima, I., Japan	36	34 50 N	139 25 E

	MAP		
Oacama, U.S.A.	70	43 52N	99 27W
Oahe, U.S.A.	70	44 34N	100 30W
Oahe Reservoir, U.S.A.	70	45 20N	100 0W
Oahu I., Hawaiian Is.	59	21 30N	158 0W
Oak Harbour, U.S.A.	72	48 19N	122 37W
Oak Lake, Canada	65	49 45N	100 45W
Oak Park, U.S.A.	70	41 55N	87 48W
Oak Ridge, Tenn., U.S.A.	69	36 1N	84 5W
Oakdale, Calif., U.S.A.	73	37 47N	120 50W
Oakdale, La., U.S.A.	71	30 49N	92 35W
Oakes, U.S.A.	70	46 14N	98 2W
Oakesdale, U.S.A.	72	47 8N	117 13W
Oakey, Queensland	43	27 25S	151 43E
Oakhill, U.S.A.	68	38 0N	81 7W
Oakland, Calif., U.S.A.	73	37 50N	122 10W
Oakland, Ore., U.S.A.	72	43 28N	123 20W
Oakland City, U.S.A.	68	38 20N	87 20W
Oakley, U.S.A.	72	42 12N	113 58W
Oakridge, U.S.A.	72	43 48N	122 31W
Oakville, Man., Canada	65	49 56N	98 0W
Oakwood, U.S.A.	71	31 32N	95 47W
Oamaru, New Zealand	47	45 5S	170 59E
Oates Land, Antarctica	80	69 0S	160 0E
Oatlands, Tasmania	43	42 14S	147 18E
Oatman, U.S.A.	73	35 1N	114 21W
Oaxaca, Mexico	74	17 2N	96 40W
Oaxaca, st., Mexico	74	17 0N	97 0W
Oba, Canada	62	49 4N	84 7W
Obala, Cameroon	52	4 1N	11 52E
Obama, Japan	36	35 36N	135 42E
Oban, Canada	63	52 9N	108 9W
Oban, New Zealand	47	46 55S	168 10E
Oban, Nigeria	52	5 20N	8 33E
Oban, Scotland	10	56 25N	5 30W
Obatogamau L., Can.	62	49 34N	74 26W
Obbia, Somali Rep.	49	5 25N	48 30E
Obed, Canada	64	53 30N	117 10W
Obeh, Afghanistan	31	34 28N	63 10E
Ober Drauberg, Austria	14	46 44N	12 58E
Oberhausen, Germany	14	51 30N	6 50E
Oberland, dist., Switz.	15	46 25N	7 20E
Oberlin, Kan., U.S.A.	70	39 15N	100 30W
Oberlin, La., U.S.A.	71	30 37N	92 45W
Obi, Nigeria	52	8 25N	8 42E
Obi, I., Indonesia	35	1 30S	127 45E
Obi Is., Indonesia	35	1 40S	127 40E
Obiaruku, Nigeria	52	5 40N	6 8E
Obidos, Brazil	79	1 50S	55 30W
Obidos, Portugal	17	39 19N	9 10W
Obihiro, Japan	36	42 44N	143 10E
Obluche, U.S.S.R.	27	49 10N	130 50E
Obo, Cen. Afr. Rep.	54	5 35N	26 35E
Oboa, mt., Uganda	53	1 45N	34 44E
Obobogorap, Botswana	57	27 10S	20 2E
Obock, T.A.I. (Fr.)	49	12 0N	43 20E
Oborniki, Poland	16	52 39N	16 59E
Obosum, R., Ghana	52	7 4N	0 2W
Obot, Ethiopia	53	4 26N	37 17E
Oboyan, U.S.S.R.	25	51 20N	36 28E
Obozerskaya, U.S.S.R.	24	63 20N	40 15E
Observatory Inlet, Can.	64	55 30N	129 35W
Obuasi, Ghana	52	6 17N	1 40W
Obubra, Nigeria	52	6 8N	8 20E
Obudu, Nigeria	52	6 38N	9 6E
Ocala, U.S.A.	69	29 5N	82 5W
Ocampo, Mexico	74	24 55N	101 50W
Ocaña, Colombia	78	8 0N	73 30W
Ocaña, Spain	17	39 55N	3 30W
Ocanomowoc, U.S.A.	70	43 7N	88 30W
Ocate, U.S.A.	71	36 19N	104 59W
Ocean City, U.S.A.	68	39 18N	74 34W
Ocean Falls, Canada	64	52 25N	127 40W
Ocean Park, U.S.A.	72	46 29N	124 2W
Oceanlake, U.S.A.	72	44 58N	124 1W
Oceanside, U.S.A.	73	33 16N	117 27W
Ochakov, U.S.S.R.	25	46 35N	31 30E
Ochre River, Canada	65	51 10N	99 50W
Ocilla, U.S.A.	69	31 35N	83 16W
Ocmulgee, R., U.S.A.	69	32 0N	83 19W
Ocnele Mari, Rumania	21	45 8N	24 18E
Oconee, R., U.S.A.	69	32 30N	82 55W
Oconto, U.S.A.	68	44 52N	87 53W
Oconto Falls, U.S.A.	68	44 52N	88 10W
Ocotal, Honduras	75	13 41N	86 41W
Ocotián, Mexico	74	20 21N	102 42W
Octave, U.S.A.	73	34 9N	112 40W
Ocumare, Venezuela	78	10 5N	66 50W
Ocussi, Ambino, Port Timor	35	9 20S	124 30E
Oda, Ghana	52	5 50N	1 5W
Odadahraun, reg., Ice.	22	65 5N	17 0W
Odate, Japan	36	40 20N	140 30E
Odawara, Japan	36	35 20N	139 6E
Odda, Norway	23	60 3N	6 35E
Odemira, Portugal	17	37 35N	8 40W
Odemis, Turkey	30	38 15N	28 0E
Odendaalsrus, O.F.S.	57	27 48S	26 43E
Odense, Denmark	23	55 26N	10 26E
Oderzo, Italy	20	43 47N	12 29E
Odessa, Tex., U.S.A	71	31 51N	102 23W
Odessa, Wash., U.S.A.	72	47 22N	118 37W
Odessa, U.S.S.R.	25	41 30N	30 45E
Odienné, Ivory Coast	50	9 30N	7 34W
Odolanów, Poland	16	51 32N	17 40E
O'Donnell, U.S.A.	71	32 58N	101 49W
Odorhei, Rumania	21	46 12N	25 21E

	MAP		
Odra (Oder), R., Eur.	14	53 0N	14 12E
Odžak, Yugoslavia	21	45 3N	18 18E
Odzceh, Mexico	75	21 14N	87 50W
Odzi, Rhodesia	56	19 0S	32 20E
Odzi, R., Rhodesia	56	18 57S	32 14E
Oeiras, Brazil	79	7 0S	42 5W
Oelrichs, U.S.A.	70	43 1N	103 15W
Oelwein, U.S.A.	70	42 37N	91 56W
Ofanto R., Italy	20	41 8N	15 50E
Ofen P., Switzerland	15	46 39N	10 18E
Offa, Nigeria	52	8 13N	4 42E
Offaly, co., Ireland	11	53 15N	7 30W
Offenbach, Germany	14	50 6N	8 46E
Ofot Fd., Norway	22	68 27N	17 0E
Ofuasi, Ghana	52	6 12N	1 14W
Oga C., Japan	36	40 3N	139 30E
Ogahalla, Canada	62	50 6N	85 51W
Ogaki, Japan	36	35 25N	136 35E
Ogallala, U.S.A.	70	41 11N	101 42W
Ogbomosho, Nigeria	52	8 1N	3 29E
Ogden, Iowa, U.S.A.	70	42 3N	94 0W
Ogden, Utah, U.S.A.	72	41 13N	112 1W
Ogden, Mt., N. America	64	58 26N	133 31W
Ogdensburg, U.S.A.	68	44 40N	75 27W
Oglio R., Italy	20	45 15N	10 15E
Ogoja, Nigeria	52	6 38N	8 39E
Ogoki L., Canada	62	50 55N	87 10W
Ogoki R., Canada	62	50 40N	88 0W
Ogoki Res., Canada	62	50 45N	88 15W
Ogooue, R., Gabon	54	1 20S	9 0E
Ogulin, Yugoslavia	20	45 16N	15 16E
Oguta, Nigeria	52	5 44N	6 44E
Ogwashi-Uku, Nigeria	52	6 11N	6 28E
Ogwe, Nigeria	52	5 0N	7 7E
Ohakune, New Zealand	46	39 26S	171 25E
Ohanet, Algeria	50	28 20N	8 35E
Ohaupo, New Zealand	46	37 56S	175 20E
Ohio, st., U.S.A.	68	40 20N	83 0W
Ohio R., U.S.A.	68	39 50N	80 50W
Ohiwa Harbour, New Zealand	46	37 59S	177 10E
Ohre, R., C. Slov.	16	50 20N	13 10E
Ohrid, Yugoslavia	21	41 8N	20 52E
Ohridsko L., Y.slav	21	41 0N	20 50E
Ohrigstad, Transvaal	57	24 41S	30 36E
Ohura, New Zealand	46	38 51S	174 59E
Oiapoque R., Brazil	79	3 20N	52 0W
Oil City, Pa., U.S.A.	68	41 26N	79 40W
Oimyakon, U.S.S.R.	27	63 25N	143 10E
Oirot Tura, U.S.S.R.	26	51 50N	86 5E
Oise R., France	12	49 53N	3 50E
Oita, Japan	36	33 15N	131 36E
Oita, pref., Japan	36	22 0N	131 30E
Ojai, U.S.A.	73	34 30N	119 16W
Ojinaga, Mexico	74	29 30N	104 40W
Ojocaliente, Mexico	74	30 25N	106 30W
Ojos del Salado, mt., Argentina	77	27 0S	68 40W
Oju, Nigeria	52	7 0N	8 19E
Oka R., U.S.S.R.	25	54 50N	38 0E
Okahandja, S.W. Africa	57	22 0S	16 52E
Okahukura, New Zealand	46	38 48N	175 14E
Okaihau, New Zealand	46	35 19S	173 36E
Okanagan L., Canada	64	50 0N	119 30W
Okanogan, U.S.A.	72	48 25N	119 33W
Okanogan R., U.S.A.	72	48 30N	119 30W
Okanogan Ra., mts., N. America	64	49 0N	120 0W
Okara, Pakistan	32	30 50N	73 25E
Okarito, New Zealand	47	43 15S	170 9E
Okato, New Zealand	46	39 12S	173 53E
Okavango (Cubango), R., Angola	55	17 30S	18 30E
Okavango Swamp, Botswana	56	19 30S	23 0E
Okaya, Japan	36	36 5N	138 4E
Okayama, Japan	36	34 40N	133 44E
Okayama, pref., Japan	36	35 0N	133 50E
Okazaki, Japan	36	35 0N	137 8E
Okeechobee, U.S.A.	69	27 16N	80 46W
Okeechobee L., U.S.A.	60	27 0N	80 50W
Okeefenokee Swamp, U.S.A.	69	30 50N	82 15W
Okehampton, England	10	50 44N	4 1W
Oke-Iho, Nigeria	52	8 1N	3 17E
Okene, Nigeria	52	7 32N	6 11E
Okha, India	32	22 20N	69 0E
Okha, U.S.S.R.	27	53 40N	143 0E
Okhotsk, U.S.S.R.	27	59 20N	143 10E
Okhotsk, Sea of, N.E. Asia	36	55 0N	154 0E
Okhotski Perevoz, U.S.S.R.	27	61 58N	135 10E
Okiep, Cape Province	57	29 39S	17 53E
Okigwi, Nigeria	52	5 52N	7 20E
Okija, Nigeria	52	5 54N	6 55E
Okinawa I., Ryukyu Is. Japan	37	27 10N	128 0E
Okitipupa, Nigeria	52	6 31N	4 50E
Oklahoma, st., U.S.A.	71	35 40N	97 0W
Oklahoma City, U.S.A.	71	35 25N	97 30W
Okmulgee, U.S.A.	71	35 50N	96 0W
Okolo, Uganda	53	2 44N	31 41E
Okolona, U.S.A.	69	34 1N	88 47W
Okombahe, S.W. Africa	57	21 23S	15 22E
Okondja, Gabon	54	0 35S	13 45E

	MAP		
Okrika, Nigeria	52	4 37N	7 36E
Okulovski, U.S.S.R.	24	66 10N	44 0E
Okuru, New Zealand	47	43 55S	168 55E
Okushiri I., Japan	36	42 15N	139 30E
Okuta, Nigeria	52	9 14N	3 12E
Okwa, R., Botswana	56	22 20S	23 0E
Okwoga, Nigeria	52	7 3N	7 42E
Ola, U.S.A.	71	35 0N	93 11W
Olafsfjördur, Iceland	22	66 5N	18 20W
Olafsvellir, Iceland	22	64 1N	20 30W
Olafsvik, Iceland	22	64 53N	23 43W
Olancha, U.S.A.	73	66 20N	118 0W
Oland I., Sweden	23	56 45N	16 50E
Olary, S. Australia	43	32 15S	140 16E
Olathe, U.S.A.	70	38 48N	94 47W
Olavarria, Argentina	77	36 55S	60 20W
Olbia, (Terranova,) Sardinia	20	40 55N	9 30E
Old Bahama Chan., W. Indies	75	22 10N	77 30W
Old Castile, prov. Spain	17	41 55N	4 0W
Old Factory, and R., Canada	62	53 36N	78 43W
Old Fort, R., Canada	65	57 40N	110 0W
Old Harbor, Alaska	59	57 13N	153 22W
Old Head of Kinsale, Ireland	11	51 40N	8 35W
Old Serenje, Zambia	56	13 12S	30 49E
Old Shinyanga, Tanzania	53	3 34S	33 24E
Old Tati, Botswana	56	21 22S	27 46E
Old Town, U.S.A.	69	45 0N	68 50W
Oldcastle, Ireland	11	53 46N	7 10W
Oldeani, Tanzania	53	3 20S	35 32E
Olden, Norway	23	61 50N	6 50E
Oldenburg, Germany	14	53 10N	8 10E
Oldenzaal, Netherlands	13	52 19N	6 53E
Oldham, England	10	53 33N	2 8W
Oldman R., Canada	64	49 40N	113 40W
Oldoinyo Crok, mt., Kenya	53	2 32S	36 30E
Olds, Canada	64	51 50N	114 10W
Olean, U.S.A.	68	42 8N	78 25W
Olekma R., U.S.S.R.	27	58 0N	121 30E
Olekminsk, U.S.S.R.	27	60 40N	120 30E
Olenek, U.S.S.R.	27	68 20N	112 30E
Olenek, R., U.S.S.R.	27	71 0N	123 50E
Olenino, U.S.S.R.	25	56 15N	33 20E
Olenya, U.S.S.R.	24	68 20N	33 40E
Olesnica, Poland	16	51 13N	17 22E
Olga, U.S.S.R.	27	43 50N	135 0E
Olga L., Canada	62	49 45N	77 30W
Olhao, Portugal	17	37 3N	7 48W
Olib. I., Yugoslavia	20	44 23N	14 44E
Olifants R., Transvaal	57	24 5S	31 20E
Olifantshoek, Cape Province	57	27 57S	22 42E
Olifantskloof, Botswana	57	22 11S	20 5E
Olimpo, Brazil	79	21 10S	58 10W
Olio, Queensland	42	22 5S	143 11E
Oliva, Spain	17	38 58N	0 10W
Oliveira, Brazil	79	20 50S	44 50W
Olivenca, Mozambique	53	11 47S	35 13E
Olivenza, Spain	17	38 41N	7 9W
Oliver, Canada	64	49 20N	119 30W
Oliver L., Canada	65	57 15N	103 25W
Olivine Ra., N.Z.	47	44 15S	168 30E
Ollague, Chile	78	21 15S	68 10W
Olmedo, Spain	17	41 20N	4 43W
Olney, Ill., U.S.A.	68	38 40N	88 0W
Olney, Texas, U.S.A.	71	33 24N	98 48W
Oloi, R., U.S.S.R.	27	66 10N	162 0E
Oloma, Cameroon	52	3 29N	11 19E
Olomane R., Canada	63	51 10N	60 55W
Olomouc, C. Slov.	16	49 38N	17 12E
Olonets, U.S.S.R.	24	61 10N	33 0E
Oloron, France	12	43 11N	0 38W
Olot, Spain	17	42 11N	2 30E
Olovyannaya, U.S.S.R.	27	50 50N	115 10E
Olshany, U.S.S.R.	23	56 12N	25 50E
Olsztyn, Poland	16	53 45N	20 30E
Olt R., Rumania	12	43 50N	24 40E
Olten, Switzerland	15	47 21N	7 53E
Oltenita, Rumania	21	44 7N	26 42E
Olton, U.S.A.	71	34 14N	102 6W
Oltu, Turkey	30	40 35N	41 50E
Olutinsk, U.S.S.R.	24	63 7N	39 15E
Olvera, Spain	17	36 55N	5 18W
Olympia, ruins, Greece	21	37 39N	21 39E
Olympia, U.S.A.	72	47 0N	122 45W
Olympic Mts., U.S.A.	72	48 0N	124 0W
Olympus, Mt., Greece	21	40 6N	22 23E
Olympus, Mt., U.S.A.	72	47 50N	123 45W
Olympus, Mt., U.S.A.	64	46 52N	123 40W
Om R., U.S.S.R.	26	55 40N	76 30E
Omachi, Japan	36	36 30N	137 50E
Omagh, N. Ireland	11	54 36N	7 20W
Omaha, U.S.A.	70	41 15N	96 0W
Omak, U.S.A.	72	48 24N	119 30W
Oman, G. of, S.W. Asia	31	2430N	58 30E
Omapere, New Zealand	46	35 37S	173 25E
Omaruru, S.W. Africa	55	21 26S	16 0E
Omaruru, R., S.W. Africa	57	21 40S	14 40E
Omate, Peru	78	16 45S	71 0W

	MAP		
Ombai Strait, Indonesia	35	8 30S	124 50E
Omboué, Gabon	54	1 35S	9 15E
Ombrone R., Italy	20	42 48N	11 15E
Omdurman, Sudan	51	15 40N	32 28E
Omegna, Italy	20	45 52N	8 23E
Omeo, Victoria	43	37 1S	147 30E
Ometepec, Mexico	74	16 39N	98 23W
Omezs, Israel	29	32 22N	35 0E
Ominato, Japan	36	41 15N	141 10E
Omineca R., Canada	64	55 50N	125 0W
Omitara, S.W. Africa	57	22 18S	18 1E
Omiya, Japan	36	36 0N	139 32E
Ommaney, C., Alaska	64	56 10N	134 40W
Ommen, Netherlands	13	52 32N	6 26E
Omo R., Ethiopia	54	6 25N	36 10E
Omoko, Nigeria	52	5 19N	6 40E
Omolon R., U.S.S.R.	27	64 30N	161 0E2
Omono R., Japan	36	39 50N	140 45E
Omoto, Japan	36	39 50N	141 58E
Omsk, U.S.S.R.	26	55 0N	73 38E
Omu, U.S.S.R.	28	67 40N	146 0E
Omul Mt., Rumania	21	45 27N	25 30E
Omuramba Omatako R., S.W. Africa	55	21 0S	17 30E
Omuta, Japan	36	33 0N	130 26E
Oña, Spain	17	42 43N	3 25W
Onaga, U.S.A.	70	39 32N	96 14W
Onalaska, U.S.A.	70	43 51N	91 15W
Onamia, U.S.A.	70	46 3N	93 34W
Onancock, U.S.A.	68	37 42N	75 49W
Onaping L., Canada	62	47 3N	81 30W
Onawa, U.S.A.	70	42 2N	96 2W
Onaway, U.S.A.	68	45 21N	84 11W
Onda, Spain	17	39 55N	0 17W
Ondangua, S.W. Africa	55	17 57S	16 4E
Onderstedorings, C. Prov.	57	30 11S	20 35E
Ondo, Nigeria	52	7 4N	4 47E
Ondar Han, Mongolia	37	47 20N	110 35E
Öndverdarnes, C., Ice.	22	64 55N	24 2W
Onega, U.S.S.R.	24	64 0N	38 10E
Onega, G. of, U.S.S.R.	24	64 30N	37 0E
Onega, L., U.S.S.R.	24	62 0N	35 30E
Onega R., U.S.S.R.	24	63 0N	39 0E
Onehunga, N.Z.	46	36 55N	174 50E
Oneida, Ky., U.S.A.	68	37 20N	83 40W
Oneida L., U.S.A.	68	43 12N	76 0W
O'Neill, U.S.A.	70	42 30N	98 37W
Oneonta, Ala., U.S.A.	68	33 58N	86 29W
Oneonta, N.Y., U.S.A.	69	42 26N	75 5W
Onerahi, New Zealand	46	35 45S	174 22E
Ongarue, New Zealand	46	38 42S	175 19E
Ongers, R., C. Prov.	57	30 20S	23 20E
Ongerup, W. Australia	44	33 49S	118 33E
Ongin Gol, R., Mong.	38	46 0N	104 0E
Ongjin, N. Korea	37	37 53N	125 15E
Ongole, India	32	15 33N	80 2E
Onguren, U.S.S.R.	27	54 0N	108 0E
Onida, U.S.A.	70	44 42N	100 2W
Onitsha, Nigeria	52	6 6N	6 42E
Onoda, Japan	36	34 2N	131 10E
Onoke Lake, N.Z.	46	41 24S	175 9E
Onomichi, Japan	36	34 25N	133 3E
Onslow, W. Australia	44	21 40S	115 0E
Onslow B., U.S.A.	69	34 10N	77 0W
Onstwedde, Neth.	13	52 2N	7 4E
Ontake Mt., Japan	36	35 50N	137 15E
Ontario, prov., Can.	60–61	52 0N	88 10W
Ontario, Calif., U.S.A.	73	34 2N	117 40W
Ontario, Oreg., U.S.A.	72	44 1N	117 0W
Ontario L., Can.-U.S.A.	62	43 40N	78 0W
Ontonagon, U.S.A.	68	46 58N	89 12W
Onundarfjördur, Ice.	22	66 5N	23 30W
Ookala, Hawaiian Is.	59	20 0N	155 16W
Ooldea, S. Australia	45	30 27S	131 50E
Oontoo, Queensland	43	27 42S	141 0E
Oorindi, Queensland	42	20 40S	141 1E
Oostende (Ostend), Belgium	13	51 14N	2 55E
Oosterhout, Netherlands	13	51 38N	4 51E
Ootacamund, India	32	11 30N	76 44E
Ootsa L., Canada	64	53 40N	126 20W
Opala, Zaire	54	1 11S	24 45E
Opala, U.S.S.R.	27	52 15N	156 15E
Opalton, Queensland	42	23 9S	142 48E
Opanake, Sri Lanka	32	6 35N	80 40E
Opapa, New Zealand	46	39 47S	176 42E
Opasatika, Canada	62	49 30N	82 50W
Opatow, Poland	16	50 50N	21 27E
Opava, Czechoslovakia	16	49 57N	17 58E
Opelousas, U.S.A.	71	30 35N	92 0W
Opemisca L., Canada	62	50 0N	75 0W
Open Bay Is., N.Z.	47	43 51S	168 51E
Opheim, U.S.A.	72	48 53N	106 28W
Ophir, Alaska	59	63 16N	156 20W
Ophthalmia Ra., W. Australia	44	23 15S	119 30E
Opi, Nigeria	52	6 36N	7 28E
Opihi R., New Zealand	47	44 13S	171 5E
Opinaca L., Canada	62	52 32N	76 31W
Opinaca R., Canada	62	52 40N	77 10W
Opiscoteo L., Canada	63	53 20N	68 0W
Opiskotish L., Canada	63	53 0N	67 51W
Opland, prov., Norway	23	61 15N	9 30E
Opobo Town, Nigeria	52	4 36N	7 38E
Opole, Poland	16	50 42N	17 58E
Opole Lubelskie, Poland	16	51 3N	22 0E
Oporto, Portugal	17	41 8N	8 40W

Place	Map	Lat.	Long.
Opotiki, New Zealand	46	38 1 S	177 19 E
Opp, U.S.A.	69	31 19 N	86 13 W
Opua, New Zealand	46	35 19 S	174 9 E
Opunake, New Zealand	46	39 26 S	173 52 E
Or, Côte d', France	12	47 0 N	4 40 E
Ora Banda, W. Australia	44	30 20 S	121 0 E
Oracle, U.S.A.	73	32 37 N	110 43 W
Oradea, Rumania	21	47 2 N	21 58 E
Oræfajökull, mt., Ice.	22	64 2 N	16 35 W
Orahovica, Yugoslavia	21	45 35 N	17 52 E
Orai, India	32	25 58 N	79 30 E
Orallo, Queensland	43	26 15 S	148 36 E
Oran, Algeria	50	36 45 N	0 39 W
Oran, Argentina	77	23 10 S	64 20 W
Orange, France	12	44 8 N	4 47 E
Orange, N.S.W.	43	33 15 S	149 7 E
Orange, Tex., U.S.A.	71	30 0 N	93 50 W
Orange, Va., U.S.A.	68	38 17 N	78 5 W
Orange C., Brazil	77	4 20 N	51 30 W
Orange R., S. Africa	57	29 50 S	24 45 E
Orange Free State, prov., Rep. of S. Africa	57	28 30 S	27 0 E
Orange Grove, U.S.A.	71	27 58 N	97 58 W
Orangeburg, U.S.A.	69	33 27 N	80 53 W
Orangemouth, S.W. Africa	57	28 30 S	16 30 E
Orangerie B., Papua	42	10 25 S	149 50 E
Orangeville, Canada	62	43 55 N	80 5 W
Oranienburg, Germany	14	52 45 N	13 15 E
Orangefontein, Trans.	57	23 28 S	27 42 E
Oranmore, Ireland	11	53 16 N	8 57 W
Orari R., New Zealand	47	43 54 S	171 11 E
Orastie, Rumania	21	45 50 N	23 10 E
Oravita, Rumania	21	45 6 N	21 43 E
Orbetello, Italy	20	42 26 N	11 11 E
Orbigo R., Spain	17	42 40 N	5 45 W
Orbost, Victoria	43	37 40 S	148 29 E
Ordenes, Spain	17	43 5 N	8 29 W
Orderville, U.S.A.	73	37 20 N	112 37 W
Ordos, des., China	38	39 25 N	108 45 E
Ordu, Turkey	30	40 55 N	37 53 E
Ordway, U.S.A.	70	38 15 N	103 45 W
Ordzhonikidze, U.S.S.R.	24	43 0 N	44 30 E
Ore, Zaire	53	3 17 N	29 30 E
Ore Mts. (Erz Gebirge), E. Germany–C.Slov.	14	50 40 N	13 0 E
Orebrö, Sweden	23	59 20 N	15 18 E
Orebrö. co., Sweden	23	59 27 N	15 0 E
Oregon, U.S.A.	70	42 0 N	89 27 W
Oregon. st., U.S.A.	72	44 0 N	120 0 W
Oregon City, U.S.A.	72	45 10 N	122 35 W
Öregrund, Sweden	23	60 21 N	18 30 E
Orekhono-Zuyevo, U.S.S.R.	25	55 50 N	38 55 E
Orel, U.S.S.R.	25	52 57 N	36 3 E
Orel R., U.S.S.R.	25	49 5 N	55 25 E
Orellana, Peru	78	6 50 S	75 10 W
Orellana, Spain	17	39 3 N	5 30 W
Orenburg (Chkalov), U.S.S.R.	24	52 0 N	55 5 E
Orense, Spain	17	42 19 N	7 55 W
Orepuki Pahia Pt.. N.Z.	47	46 19 S	167 43 E
Oreti R., New Zealand	47	45 39 S	168 14 E
Orford Bay, Canada	64	50 30 N	124 50 W
Orient Bay, Canada	62	49 20 S	88 10 W
Orihuela, Spain	17	38 7 N	0 55 W
Orillia, Canada	62	44 40 N	79 30 W
Orinoco R., Venezuela	78	8 0 N	65 30 W
Orissa, st., India	33	21 0 N	85 0 E
Oristano, Italy	20	39 54 N	8 35 E
Oristano. Gulf of, Italy	20	39 50 N	8 22 E
Orivesi, L., Finland	23	62 15 N	29 30 E
Orizaba, Mexico	74	18 50 N	97 10 W
Orjiva, Spain	17	36 53 N	3 24 W
Orkanger, Norway	23	63 16 N	9 57 E
Orkhon R., Mongolia	65	49 0 N	104 30 E
Orkla R., Norway	23	62 55 N	9 50 E
Orkney, Transvaal	57	26 42 S	26 40 E
Orkney Islands, Scot.	10	59 0 N	3 0 W
Orland, U.S.A.	72	39 47 N	122 14 W
Orlando, Fla., U.S.A.	69	28 30 N	81 25 W
Orléans, France	12	47 54 N	1 52 E
Orléanais, reg., France	12	47 55 N	1 0 E
Orlov Gai, U.S.S.R.	25	51 4 N	48 19 E
Orlu, Nigeria	52	5 48 N	7 0 E
Ormara, Pakistan	32	25 16 N	64 33 E
Ormoc, Philippines	35	11 2 N	124 30 E
Ormond, New Zealand	69	38 33 S	177 56 E
Ormondville, N.Z.	46	40 5 S	176 19 E
Orne, R., France	12	48 12 N	0 12 E
Ornsköldvik, Sweden	23	63 17 N	18 50 E
Oro-Agor, Nigeria	52	8 12 N	5 12 E
Orocué, Colombia	78	5 55 N	71 20 W
Orodo, Nigeria	52	5 34 N	7 4 E
Orogrande, U.S.A.	73	32 22 N	106 7 W
Oron, Nigeria	52	4 48 N	8 14 E
Oropesa, Toledo, Spain	17	39 57 N	5 10 W
Oropesa, Valencia, Sp.	17	40 6 N	0 7 E
Oros, Brazil	19	6 15 S	39 0 W
Oros, Mt., Greece	21	38 15 N	23 45 E
Orosei, Italy	20	40 22 N	9 40 E
Orosháza, Hungary	16	46 32 N	20 42 E
Oroville, Calif., U.S.A.	72	39 30 N	121 30 W
Oroville, Wash., U.S.A.	72	48 57 N	119 28 W
Orroroo, S. Australia	43	32 41 S	138 31 E
Orsha, U.S.S.R.	25	54 30 N	30 25 E
Orsières, Switzerland	15	46 1 N	7 8 E
Orsk, U.S.S.R.	24	51 20 N	58 34 E
Örsova, Rumania	21	44 41 N	22 25 E
Orte, Italy	20	42 28 N	12 23 E
Ortegal C., Spain	17	43 43 N	7 52 W
Orthello, U.S.A.	72	46 51 N	119 9 W
Orthez, France	12	43 29 N	0 48 W
Ortles, Mt., Italy	20	46 31 N	10 33 E
Orton R., Bolivia	78	10 50 S	67 0 W
Ortona, Italy	20	42 21 N	14 24 E
Oruro, Bolivia	78	18 0 S	67 19 W
Orvieto, Italy	20	42 43 N	12 8 E
Osa, Pen., Costa Rica	75	8 0 N	84 0 W
Osage, Iowa, U.S.A.	70	43 15 N	92 50 W
Osage, Wyo., U.S.A.	70	44 0 N	109 27 W
Osage City, U.S.A.	70	38 37 N	95 52 W
Osaka, Japan	36	34 40 N	135 30 E
Osaka, pref., Japan	36	34 35 N	135 30 E
Osawatomie, U.S.A.	70	38 29 N	94 58 W
Osborne, U.S.A.	70	39 30 N	98 44 W
Osby, Sweden	23	55 15 N	9 38 E
Osceola, Ark., U.S.A.	71	35 44 N	89 59 W
Osceola, Iowa, U.S.A.	70	41 0 N	93 45 W
Oscoda, U.S.A.	68	44 27 N	83 20 W
Osenovka, U.S.S.R.	27	70 40 N	120 50 E
Osh, U.S.S.R.	26	40 40 N	72 55 E
Oshawa, Canada	62	43 50 N	78 45 W
Oshikago, Angola	54	17 9 S	16 10 E
Oshikango, Angola	55	17 27 S	15 33 E
Oshima, Japan	36	34 45 N	139 25 E
Oshima, I., Japan	36	34 50 N	139 25 E
Oshkosh, Nebr., U.S.A.	70	41 28 N	102 23 W
Oshkosh, Wis., U.S.A.	70	44 3 N	88 35 W
Oshogbo, Nigeria	52	7 48 N	4 37 E
Oshun R., Nigeria	52	7 37 N	4 25 E
Oshwe, Zaire	54	3 11 S	19 38 E
Osi, Nigeria	52	8 2 N	5 15 E
Osijek, Yugoslavia	21	45 34 N	18 41 E
Osimo, Italy	20	43 30 N	13 30 E
Osinino, U S.S.R.	27	70 55 N	148 50 E
Osipovichi, U.S.S.R.	25	53 25 N	28 33 E
Oskaloosa, U.S.A.	70	41 18 N	92 40 W
Oskarshamn, Sweden	23	57 15 N	16 25 E
Oskalaneo, Canada	62	48 5 N	75 15 E
Oskol R., U.S.S.R.	25	50 20 N	38 0 E
Oslo, Norway	23	59 53 N	10 52 E
Oslo Fd., Norway	23	58 30 N	10 0 E
Osmanabad, India	32	18 5 N	76 10 E
Osmaniye, Turkey	30	37 5 N	36 10 E
Osnabrück, Germany	14	52 16 N	8 2 E
Osona, S.W. Africa	57	22 1 S	16 56 E
Osorio, Brazil	77	29 53 S	50 17 W
Osorno, Chile	77	40 25 S	73 0 W
Osorno Mt., Chile	77	41 0 N	72 30 W
Osoyoos, Canada	64	49 0 N	119 30 W
Ospika R., Canada	64	56 25 N	123 50 W
Osprey Reef, Queens.	41	13 55 S	146 35 E
Oss, Netherlands	13	51 46 N	5 32 E
Ossa, Mt., Greece	21	39 47 N	22 40 E
Ossa, Mt., Tasmania	42	41 40 S	146 0 E
Ossabaw I. U.S.A.	69	31 45 N	81 8 W
Osse R., Nigeria	52	6 50 N	5 45 E
Ossining, U.S.A.	68	41 9 N	73 50 W
Ossokmanuan L., Can.	63	53 25 N	65 0 W
Ostend. *See* Oostende	13		
Oster Götland, co., Sweden	23	58 30 N	15 30 E
Oster-dal R., Sweden	23	61 30 N	13 40 E
Osteröy, I., Norway	23	61 28 N	5 30 E
Östersund, Sweden	23	63 10 N	14 45 E
Ostfold, co., Norway	23	59 25 N	11 25 E
Östhammar, Sweden	23	60 15 N	18 25 E
Ostia, Italy	20	41 47 N	12 18 E
Ostrava, C.Slov.	16	49 51 N	18 18 E
Oströda, Poland	23	53 42 N	19 58 E
Ostrogozhsk, U.S.S.R.	25	50 55 N	39 7 E
Ostroleka, Poland	23	53 4 N	21 38 E
Ostrov, Bulgaria	21	43 40 N	24 9 E
Ostrov, U.S.S.R.	25	57 25 N	28 20 E
Ostrov Stantu Gheorghe, Rumania	21	45 7 N	29 30 E
Ostrów Mazowiecka, Poland	16	52 50 N	21 51 E
Ostrów, Poland	16	51 36 N	17 44 E
Ostrowiec, Poland	16	50 55 N	21 22 E
Ostrzeszow, Poland	16	51 25 N	17 52 E
Ostuni, Italy	21	40 44 N	17 34 E
Osumi Chan, Japan	36	30 55 N	131 0 E
Osumi Group, Japan	36	30 30 N	130 45 E
Osuna, Spain	17	37 14 N	5 8 W
Oswego, N.Y., U.S.A.	68	43 29 N	76 30 W
Ota, Japan	36	36 30 N	140 30 E
Otago Harb., N.Z.	47	45 47 S	170 42 E
Otago Pen., N.Z.	47	45 48 S	170 45 E
Otaki, New Zealand	46	40 45 S	175 10 E
Otahuhu, New Zealand	46	36 56 S	174 51 E
Otane, New Zealand	46	39 54 S	176 39 E
Otaru, Japan	36	43 15 N	141 0 E
Otautau, New Zealand	47	46 9 S	168 1 E
Otavalo, Ecuador	78	0 20 N	78 20 W
Otavi, S.W. Africa	55	19 40 S	17 24 E
Otelnuk L., Canada	63	56 0 N	67 30 W
Oti R., Togo	52	8 45 N	0 8 E
Otira, New Zealand	47	42 49 S	171 35 E
Otira Gorge, N.Z.	47	42 53 S	171 33 E
Otis, U.S.A.	70	40 10 N	102 58 W
Otjiwarongo, S.W.Africa	55	20 25 S	16 45 E
Otjimbingue, S.W. Africa	57	22 19 S	16 10 E
Otočac, Yugoslavia	20	44 53 N	15 12 E
Otoineppu, Japan	36	44 45 N	142 15 E
Otokpotu, Nigeria	52	4 51 N	6 10 E
Otorohanga, N.Z.	46	38 12 S	175 14 E
Otpor, U.S.S.R.	27	49 40 N	117 10 E
Otranto, Italy	21	40 9 N	18 28 E
Otranto C., Italy	21	40 7 N	18 30 E
Otranto, Str. of, Adriatic Sea	21	40 15 N	18 40 E
Otsu, Japan	36	42 35 N	143 40 E
Otta, Norway	23	61 46 N	9 32 E
Ottawa, Canada	62	45 27 N	75 42 W
Ottawa, U.S.A.	70	41 21 N	88 59 W
Ottawa, Kan., U.S.A.	70	38 40 N	95 10 W
Ottawa, Ohio, U.S.A.	68	41 0 N	84 0 W
Ottawa Is., Canada	61	59 50 N	80 0 W
Ottawa R., Canada	62	47 45 N	78 35 W
Ottélé, Cameroon	52	3 12 N	11 12 E
Otto Beit Bridge, Zambia	56	15 59 S	28 56 E
Ottosdal, Transvaal	57	26 46 S	25 59 E
Ottoshoop, Transvaal	57	25 45 S	26 58 E
Ottumwa, U.S.A.	70	41 0 N	92 25 W
Otu, Nigeria	52	8 13 N	3 18 E
Otukpa (Ai Owuno), Nigeria	52	7 4 N	7 41 E
Oturkpo, Nigeria	52	7 10 N	8 15 E
Otway B., Chile	77	53 30 S	74 0 W
Otwock, Poland	16	52 5 N	21 20 E
Otzal Alpen, mts., Austria	14	46 58 N	11 0 E
Ouacha, Niger	52	13 27 N	9 14 E
Ouachita Mts., U.S.A.	71	34 50 N	94 30 W
Ouachita R., U.S.A.	71	33 0 N	92 15 W
Ouadane, Mauritania	50	20 50 N	11 40 W
Ouadda, Cen. Afr. Republic	54	8 15 N	22 20 E
Ouagadougou, Volta	50	12 25 N	1 30 W
Ouahigouya, Volta	50	13 40 N	2 25 W
Oualata, Mauritania	50	17 20 N	6 55 W
Ouallene, Algeria	50	24 30 N	1 20 E
Ouanda Djalé, Cent. African Rep.	54	8 55 N	22 53 E
Ouango, Cen. Afr. Repub.	54	4 19 N	22 30 E
Ouargla, Algeria	50	31 50 N	5 30 E
Ouassa, Volta	52	2 40 W	11 21 N
Oubangi, R. Zaire	54	5 0 N	20 0 E
Ouddorp, Netherlands	13	51 50 N	35 7 E
Oude Rijn R., Neth.	13	52 7 N	4 40 E
Oudenaarde (Audenarde), Belg.	13	50 50 N	3 37 E
Oudtshoorn, S. Africa	57	33 35 S	22 14 E
Ouémé, R., Dahomey	52	8 10 N	2 25 E
Ouesso, Congo	54	1 40 N	16 10 E
Ouezzane, Morocco	50	34 52 N	5 35 W
Oughterard, Ireland	11	53 26 N	9 20 W
Ouidah, Dahomey	52	6 25 N	2 0 E
Ouimet, Canada	62	48 43 N	88 35 W
Oujda, Morocco	50	34 45 N	2 0 W
Oulainen, Finland	22	64 17 N	24 50 E
Ouled Djellel, Algeria	50	34 20 N	6 30 E
Oulu (Uleåborg), Finland	22	64 58 N	25 40 E
Oulu L., Finland	22	64 25 N	27 30 E
Oulu, R., Finland	22	64 50 N	26 20 E
Oulun Lääni, Finland	22	65 0 N	27 0 E
Oum Chalouba, Chad	51	15 45 N	20 35 E
Oum Hadjer, Chad	51	13 25 N	19 35 E
Ounas R., Finland	22	67 30 N	25 0 E
Ounianga Serir, Chad	51	18 55 N	20 50 E
Ounlivou, Togo	52	7 13 N	1 29 E
Ouray, U.S.A.	73	38 3 N	107 40 W
Ouricuri, Brazil	79	7 50 S	40 5 W
Ourofan, Niger	52	14 8 N	8 11 E
Ouro-Mali, Cameroon	52	8 25 N	12 35 E
Ouro Preto, Brazil	79	20 20 S	43 30 W
Ourthe R., Belgium	13	50 3 N	5 35 E
Ouse, or Great Ouse, R. Eng.	10	52 37 N	0 22 E
Outardes, aux R., Can.	63	50 0 N	69 4 W
Outer Hebrides Islands, Scotland	10	57 30 N	7 40 W
Outer I., Canada	63	51 10 N	58 35 W
Outjo, S.W. Africa	55	20 8 S	16 8 E
Outlook, Canada	65	51 30 N	107 0 W
Outlook, U.S.A.	70	48 56 N	104 45 W
Ouyen, Victoria	43	35 1 S	142 22 E
Ovalle, Chile	77	30 33 S	71 18 W
Ovamboland, dist., S.W. Africa	55	17 20 S	16 30 E
Ovar, Portugal	17	40 51 N	8 40 W
Over Flakkee, Neth.	13	51 45 N	4 5 E
Over Tornea, Sweden	22	66 25 N	23 47 E
Överkalix, Sweden	22	66 19 N	22 50 E
Overpelt, Belgium	13	51 15 N	5 26 E
Overton, U.S.A.	73	36 31 N	114 28 W
Overwinning, Transvaal	57	23 0 S	29 47 E
Ovid, U.S.A.	70	41 1 N	102 27 W
Ovidiopol, U.S.S.R.	25	46 15 N	30 30 E
Oviedo, Spain	17	43 25 N	5 50 W
Ovoro, Nigeria	52	5 26 N	7 16 E
Ovruch, U.S.S.R.	25	51 25 N	28 45 E
Owaka, New Zealand	47	46 27 S	169 40 E
Owase, Japan	36	34 0 N	135 5 E
Owatonna, U.S.A.	70	44 3 N	93 17 W
Owego, U.S.A.	68	42 6 N	76 17 W
Owen Falls, Uganda	53	0 32 N	33 3 E
Owen Sound, Canada	62	44 40 N	80 55 W
Owen Stanley Ra., Papua	42	9 30 S	148 10 E
Owen's Creek, Queensland	42	21 5 S	148 42 E
Owensboro, U.S.A.	68	37 40 N	87 5 W
Owerri, Nigeria	52	5 29 N	7 0 E
Owhango, N.Z.	46	39 0 S	175 23 E
Owl R., Canada	65	57 40 N	93 40 W
Owo, Nigeria	52	7 18 N	5 30 E
Owosso, U.S.A.	68	43 0 N	84 10 W
Owyhee, U.S.A.	72	41 58 N	116 5 W
Owyhee, R., U.S.A.	73	43 10 N	117 37 W
Owyhee Res., U.S.A.	72	43 28 N	117 30 W
Ox Mts., Ireland	11	54 9 N	9 0 W
Oxelösund, Sweden	23	58 43 N	17 15 E
Oxford, England	10	51 45 N	1 15 W
Oxford, New Zealand	47	43 18 S	172 11 E
Oxford, Miss., U.S.A.	71	34 25 N	89 30 W
Oxford, N.Y., U.S.A.	69	42 30 N	75 37 W
Oxford, Ohio, U.S.A.	68	39 30 N	84 40 W
Oxford L., Canada	65	54 50 N	96 0 W
Oxford House, Canada	65	54 55 N	95 40 W
Oxley, N.S.W.	43	34 12 S	144 6 E
Oxnard, U.S.A.	73	34 12 N	119 14 W
Oxus. *See* Amu Darya, R., & Pyandzh R., Afghanistan–U.S.S.R.	31		
Oya, Sarawak	35	2 55 N	111 55 E
Oyem, Gabon	54	1 45 N	11 30 E
Oyen, Canada	65	51 30 N	111 30 W
Oyinische, U.S.S.R.	23	58 25 N	37 0 E
Oyjord, Norway	22	68 29 N	17 33 E
Oyo, Nigeria	52	7 46 N	3 56 E
Oyonnax, France	12	46 16 N	5 40 E
Oyster B., Tasmania	43	42 15 S	148 5 E
Oyun Kyuel, U.S.S.R.	27	69 30 N	140 50 E
Ozamis, Philippines	35	8 15 N	123 50 E
Ozark, Ark., U.S.A.	71	35 30 N	93 49 W
Ozark, Mo., U.S.A.	71	37 0 N	93 15 W
Ozark Plateau, U.S.A.	71	37 20 N	91 40 W
Ozarks, L. of the, U.S.A.	71	38 15 N	93 30 W
Ozhogin, U.S.S.R.	28	69 0 N	148 0 E
Ozieri, Italy	20	40 35 N	9 0 E
Ozona, U.S.A.	71	30 39 N	101 13 W
Ozorków, Poland	16	52 0 N	19 17 E
Ozuluama, Mexico	74	21 40 N	97 50 W

P

Place	Map	Lat.	Long.
Pa Sak, R., Thailand	34	15 30 N	101 0 E
Pa-an, Burma	33	16 45 N	97 40 E
Paan (Batang), China	37	30 0 N	99 3 E
Paarl, Cape Province	57	33 45 S	18 56 E
Paatsi R., U.S.S.R.	22	68 55 N	29 0 E
Paauilo, Hawiian Is.	59	20 5 N	155 21 W
Pab Hills, Pakistan	32	26 30 N	66 45 E
Pabna, Bangladesh	33	24 1 N	89 18 E
Pabo, Uganda	53	3 1 N	32 10 E
Pacaju R., Brazil	79	3 0 S	50 30 W
Pacaraima, Sierra, Guyana	78	5 30 N	60 0 W
Pacasmayo, Peru	78	7 20 S	79 35 W
Pachaiping, China	39	27 33 N	105 21 E
Pachbhadra (Pachpadra), India	32	25 55 N	72 10 E
Pachino, Italy	20	36 43 N	15 4 E
Pachitea R., Peru	78	9 15 S	75 0 W
Pachpadra (Pachbhadra), India	32	25 55 N	72 10 E
Pachuca, Mexico	74	20 10 N	98 40 W
Pachnar, India	33	24 36 N	77 43 E
Pachung, China	39	31 58 N	106 40 E
Pacific, Canada	64	54 45 N	128 20 W
Pacific Grove, U.S.A.	73	36 39 N	121 58 E
Pacific Ocean	5	45 0 S to 60 0 N	120 0 E to 70 0 W
Padang, Indonesia	34	1 0 S	100 20 E
Padang Pandjang, Indonesia	34	0 30 S	100 20 E
Padang Sidimpuan, Indonesia	34	1 30 N	99 15 E
Paddockwood, Canada	65	53 30 N	105 30 W
Paderborn, Germany	14	51 42 N	8 44 E
Padibe, Uganda	53	3 29 N	32 51 E
Padlei, Canada	60	62 10 N	97 5 W
Padova, Padua, Italy	20	45 24 N	11 52 E
Padre I., U.S.A.	71	27 0 N	97 20 W
Padrón, Spain	17	42 41 N	8 39 W
Padstow, England	10	50 33 N	4 57 W
Padua (Padova), Italy	20	45 24 N	11 52 E
Paducah, Ky., U.S.A.	67	37 0 N	88 40 W
Paducah, Texas, U.S.A.	71	34 0 N	100 14 W
Paekakariki, N.Z.	46	40 59 S	174 58 E
Paengaroa, N.Z.	46	37 49 S	176 29 E
Paeroa, New Zealand	46	37 23 S	175 41 E
Pafuri, Mozambique	56	22 27 S	31 30 E
Pag I., Yugoslavia	20	44 50 N	15 0 E
Pagadian, Philippines	35	7 55 N	123 30 E
Pagai I., Indonesia	34	3 0 S	100 15 E

	MAP		
Paganica, Italy	25	42 20N	13 28 E
Page, U.S.A.	70	47 14N	97 32W
Paghman, Afghanistan	31	34 39N	69 0 E
Pagosa Springs, U.S.A.	73	37 20N	107 2W
Pagwa River, Canada	62	50 2N	85 14W
Pahala, Hawaiian Is.	59	19 12N	155 28W
Pahang, st., Malaya	34	3 30N	103 9 E
Pahang R., Malaya	34	3 30N	103 9 E
Pahia Pt., N.Z.	47	46 20s	167 43 E
Pahiatua, N.Z.	46	40 27s	175 50 E
Pahoa, Hawaiian Is.	59	19 29N	154 56W
Pahokee, U.S.A.	69	26 50N	80 30W
Pahrump, U.S.A.	73	36 14N	116 0W
Pahseien, China	38	39 10N	116 20 E
Pai, Nigeria	52	9 30N	10 33 E
Paia, Hawaiian Is.	59	20 55N	156 22W
Paicheng, China	38	46 40N	122 47 E
Päijänne L., Finland	23	61 30N	25 30 E
Pailolo Chan., Hawaiian Is.	59	21 0N	156 45W
Paimbœuf, France	12	47 17N	2 0W
Paimpol, France	12	48 48N	3 4W
Painan, Indonesia	34	1 15s	100 40 E
Painesville, U.S.A.	68	41 42N	81 18W
Painted Desert, U.S.A.	73	36 40N	112 0W
Painter, Mt., S. Austral.	42	30 16s	139 19 E
Paintsville, U.S.A.	68	37 50N	82 50W
Paisley, Scotland	10	55 51N	4 27W
Paisley, U.S.A.	72	42 40N	120 30W
Paita, Peru	78	5 5s	81 0W
Paiting Ho, China	38	39 0N	104 0 E
Paiyin, China	38	36 40N	104 15 E
Paiyu Shan, China	38	37 20N	108 0 E
Paiyunopo, China	38	41 45N	109 50 E
Pajala, Sweden	22	67 13N	23 30 E
Pajares P., Spain	17	43 3N	5 45W
Pak Lay, Laos	34	18 15N	101 27 E
Pak Sane, Laos	34	18 15N	102 30 E
Pakala, India	32	13 29N	79 8 E
Pakanbaru, Indonesia	34	0 30N	101 15 E
Pakaur, India	33	24 35N	87 55 E
Pakhoi, China	39	21 30N	109 10 E
Pakhuis, Cape Province	57	32 8s	19 0 E
Pakington, W. Australia	44	28 10s	114 15 E
Pakokku, Burma	34	21 30N	95 0 E
Pakongchow, China	39	23 50N	113 0 E
Paks, Hungary	16	46 38N	18 55 E
Pakse, Laos	34	15 5N	105 52 E
Pakwach, Uganda	53	3 20N	31 50 E
Pala, Chad	51	9 25N	15 5 E
Pala, Zaire	53	6 50s	29 30 E
Pala Camp, Botswana	57	23 52s	26 58 E
Palabek, Uganda	53	3 30N	32 30 E
Palabuhan Ratu, Java, Indon.	34	7 5s	106 20 E
Palacios, U.S.A.	71	28 45N	96 15W
Palagruža, Yugoslavia	20	42 20N	16 20 E
Palaidkastron, Crete	20	35 12N	26 18 E
Palaiokhora, Greece	20	35 16N	23 39 E
Palakhino, U.S.S.R.	27	67 45N	86 5 E
Palam, India	32	19 0N	77 0 E
Palamcottah (Palayancottai), India	32	8 42N	77 46 E
Palamos, Spain	17	41 50N	3 10 E
Palampur, India	32	32 10N	76 30 E
Palana, U.S.S.R.	27	59 10N	160 10 E
Palanan B., Philippines	35	17 10N	122 30 E
Palanpur, India	32	24 10N	72 25 E
Palapo, Indonesia	35	3 0s	120 5 E
Palapye, Botswana	57	22 30s	27 7 E
Palaron, Philippines	35	17 0N	122 20 E
Palatka, U.S.A.	69	29 40N	81 40W
Palau I., Pacific Ocean	35	7 30N	134 35 E
Palauz, U.S.S.R.	24	60 50N	50 20 E
Palaw, Burma	33	13 0N	98 50 E
Palawan, I., Philippines	35	10 0N	119 0 E
Palawan Is., S. China Sea	35	10 0N	115 0 E
Palayancottai (Palamcottah), India	32	8 45N	77 45 E
Paldiski, U.S.S.R.	23	59 23N	24 9 E
Palelee, Indonesia	35	1 0N	121 50 E
Paleleh, Indonesia	35	1 10N	121 50 E
Palembang, Indonesia	34	3 0s	104 50 E
Palena, Italy	20	42 0N	14 8 E
Palencia, Spain	17	42 1N	4 34W
Palermo, Italy	20	38 8N	13 20 E
Palermo, U.S.A.	72	39 27N	121 33W
Palestine. *See* Israel and Jordan	29		
Palestine, U.S.A.	71	31 44N	95 32W
Palestine Potash Co. (North), Jordan	29	31 48N	35 31 E
Paletwa, Burma	34	21 30N	92 50 E
Palghat, India	32	10 46N	76 42 E
Palgrave, mt., W. Australia	44	23 13s	116 1 E
Pali, India	32	25 50N	73 20 E
Palime, Togo	52	6 57N	0 37 E
Palingmiao, Mongolia	38	41 45N	110 28 E
Palisade, U.S.A.	70	40 27N	101 5W
Palit, C., Albania	21	41 23N	19 23N
Palitana, India	32	21 32N	71 49 E
Palitana, India	17	20 31N	71 53 E
Palizada, Mexico	74	18 18N	92 8W
Palk Bay, Sri Lanka	32	9 30N	79 30 E
Palk Strait, India	32	10 0N	80 0 E
Palla Rd., Botswana	57	23 27s	26 38 E

	MAP		
Pallaskenry, Ireland	11	52 39N	8 53W
Pallisa, Uganda	53	1 11N	33 43 E
Palliser Bay, N.Z.	46	41 26s	175 5 E
Palm Beach, U.S.A.	69	26 46N	80 0W
Palm I., Queensland	42	18 45s	146 35 E
Palm Springs, U.S.A.	73	33 51N	116 32W
Palma, Balearic Is., Spain	17	39 33N	2 39 E
Palma, Italy	20	37 10N	13 44 E
Palma, Mozambique	55	10 50s	40 25 E
Palma B., Spain	17	39 30N	2 40 E
Palma R., Brazil	79	12 50s	46 0W
Palmasola, Venezuela	78	10 40N	68 35W
Palma Soriano, Cuba	75	20 15N	76 0W
Palmares, Pernambuco Brazil	79	8 35s	35 30W
Palmares, R. Gde. do Sul, Brazil	77	30 15s	50 30W
Palmas, C., Liberia	50	4 27N	7 46W
Palmas, G. of Italy	20	39 0N	8 30 E
Palmdale, U.S.A.	73	34 36N	118 6W
Palmeira, Brazil	77	27 50s	53 0W
Palmeira dos Indios, Brazil	79	9 25s	36 30W
Palmeirinhas, Pta. das, Angola	55	9 2s	12 57 E
Palmela, Portugal	17	38 32N	8 57W
Palmer, Alaska	59	61 48N	149 7W
Palmer Lake, U.S.A.	70	39 11N	104 53W
Palmer Land, Ant.	80	73 0s	65 0W
Palmer R., Queensland	42	15 46s	143 30 E
Palmerston, N.Z.	47	45 29s	170 43 E
Palmerston C., Queens.	42	21 32s	149 30 E
Palmerston N., N.Z.	46	40 21s	175 39 E
Palmerville, Queens.	42	16 0s	144 5 E
Palmetto, U.S.A.	69	27 33N	82 33W
Palmi, Italy	20	38 21N	15 51 E
Palmira, Colombia	78	3 50N	76 20W
Palmito del Verde I., Mexico	74	22 10N	106 0W
Palmyra (Tadmor), Syria	30	34 30N	37 55 E
Palmyra, U.S.A.	70	39 46N	91 31W
Palmyra I., Pacific Oc.	5	5 52N	162 6W
Palni, India	32	10 30N	77 30 E
Palni Hill, India	32	10 14N	77 33 E
Palo Alto, U.S.A.	73	37 25N	122 20W
Palo Seco, Trinidad	74		Inset
Palo Seco, Bay of, Panama Canal Zone	74		Inset
Paloe I., Indonesia	35	8 15s	121 40 E
Palos, C. de, Spain	17	37 38N	0 40W
Palouse, U.S.A.	72	46 54N	117 7W
Palparara, Queensland	42	24 47s	141 22 E
Palu, Turkey	30	38 45N	40 0 E
Palu, Indonesia	35	1 0s	119 59 E
Palwal, India	32	28 8N	77 19 E
Palyu Shan, China	38	37 25N	108 0 E
Pama, Volta	52	11 19N	0 44 E
Pamanukan, Indonesia	34	6 16s	107 49 E
Pamekasan, Indonesia	34	7 10s	113 29 E
Pameungpeuk, Ind.	34	7 38s	107 44 E
Paniencheng, China	38	43 20N	124 10 E
Pamiers, France	12	43 7N	1 39 E
Pamir R., Afghanistan–U.S.S.R.	31	37 20N	73 0 E
Pamirs, France	31	43 7N	1 39 E
Pamirs, mts., Central Asia	26	37 40N	73 0 E
Pamlico Sound, U.S.A.	69	35 20N	76 0W
Pampa, U.S.A.	71	35 35N	101 0W
Pampas, pls., Arg. and Urug.	78	34 0s	64 0W
Pamplona, Colombia	78	7 30N	72 30W
Pamplona, Spain	17	42 48N	1 38W
Pampoenpoort, Cape Province	57	31 3s	22 40 E
Pana, U.S.A.	70	39 25N	89 0W
Panaca, U.S.A.	73	37 50N	114 27W
Panaitan I., Indonesia	34	6 35s	105 10 E
Panama, Panama Rep.	78	9 0N	79 25W
Panama, rep., Cent. Amer.	78	9 0N	79 35W
Panama Canal, Cent. America	74		Inset
Panama Canal Zone, Central America	74		Inset
Panama City, U.S.A.	69	30 10N	85 41W
Panama, G. of, Panama	78	8 0N	78 0W
Panamint Mts., U.S.A.	73	36 15N	117 20W
Pañao, Peru	78	9 55s	75 55W
Panaria I., Italy	20	38 38N	15 3 E
Panay, I., Philippines	35	11 0N	122 30 E
Pancake Ra., U.S.A.	73	38 30N	115 55W
Pancevo, Yugoslavia	21	44 54N	20 43 E
Pandan, Philippines	35	11 45N	122 10 E
Pandassan, Sabah	35	6 32N	116 32 E
Pandharpur, India	32	17 41N	75 20 E
Pando, Uruguay	77	34 30s	56 0W
Panevežys, U.S.S.R.	23	55 42N	24 25 E
Panfilov, U.S.S.R.	26	44 30N	80 0 E
Panfilovo, U.S.S.R.	25	50 25N	42 46 E
Pangkal Pinang, Indon.	34	2 10s	106 5 E
Pangani, Tanzania	54	5 25s	39 1 E
Pangani R., Tanzania	53	4 0s	37 30 E
Pangani Rapids, Tan.	53	7 46s	38 0 E
Pangi, Zaire	54	3 18s	26 42 E

	MAP		
Pangkalanbrandan, Indonesia	34	4 1N	98 20 E
Pangkiang (Mingan), Mongolia	38	42 50N	112 52 E
Pangola R., Transvaal	56	23 40s	27 43 E
Pangong L., Tibet	32	33 50N	79 0 E
Pangrango Mt., Indon.	34	6 46s	107 1 E
Panguitch, U.S.A.	73	37 52N	112 30W
Pangutaran Grp., Philippines	35	6 18N	120 34 E
Panhandle, U.S.A.	71	35 24N	101 19W
Panipat, India	32	29 25N	77 2 E
Panipus R., Netherlands	13	52 22N	5 0 E
Panjao, Afghanistan	31	34 25N	67 0 E
Panjgur, Pakistan	32	27 0N	64 5 E
Panjim, India	32	15 25N	73 50 E
Pankshin, Nigeria	52	9 25N	9 25 E
Panmunjom, Korea	36	38 0N	126 45 E
Panna, India	32	24 40N	80 15 E
Panruti, India	32	11 49N	79 31 E
Panshan, China	38	41 15N	122 0 E
Panshih, China	38	42 58N	125 49 E
Pantar I., Indonesia	35	8 28s	124 10 E
Pantano, U.S.A.	73	32 0N	110 32W
Pantelleria I., Italy	20	36 52N	12 0 E
Pantha, Burma	33	23 50N	94 35 E
Panuco, Mexico	74	22 0N	98 25W
Panuco R., Mexico	74	22 0N	98 30W
Panyam, Nigeria	52	9 27N	9 8 E
Paochang, China	38	41 46N	115 30 E
Paocheng, China	38	33 10N	106 55 E
Paokang, China	39	31 50N	111 25 E
Paoki, China	38	34 25N	107 15 E
Paola, Italy	20	39 21N	16 2 E
Paola, U.S.A.	70	38 34N	94 55W
Paonia, U.S.A.	73	38 49N	107 32W
Paoshan, China	37	31 30N	121 25 E
Paoteh, China	38	39 0N	110 45 E
Paoting, China	38	38 50N	115 30 E
Paotow, China	38	40 45N	110 0 E
Paotsing, China	39	28 35N	109 35 E
Paoua, Chad	54	7 25N	16 30 E
Paoying, China	38	33 10N	119 20 E
Pápa, Hungary	16	47 22N	17 30 E
Papa Stour I., Scotland	10	60 20N	1 40W
Papagayo Gulf, Costa Rica	75	10 4N	85 50W
Papai, Neth. Guiana	79	2 28N	56 21W
Papaikou, Hawaiian I.	59	19 45N	155 06W
Papakura, N.Z.	46	37 4s	174 59 E
Papantla, Mexico	74	20 30N	97 20W
Papantla de Olarte, Mexico	74	20 30N	97 21 E
Papar, Sabah	35	5 45N	116 0 E
Paparoa, New Zealand	46	36 6s	174 16 E
Paparoa Range, N.Z.	47	42 5s	171 35 E
Papatoetoe, N.Z.	46	36 59s	174 51 E
Papenburg, Germany	14	53 7N	7 25 E
Papua, Gulf of, Papua	42	9 0s	144 50 E
Papua, Terr. of, New Guinea	42	8 0s	145 0 E
Papudo, Chile	77	32 29s	71 27W
Papun, Burma	33	18 0N	97 30 E
Pará. *See* Belem	79		
Pará R., Brazil	79	0 40s	48 30W
Paracatú, Brazil	79	17 10s	46 50W
Paracel I., S. China Sea	35	17 0N	112 20 E
Parachilna, S. Australia	43	31 10s	138 21 E
Parachinar, Pakistan	32	34 0N	70 5 E
Paradise, U.S.A.	72	47 27N	114 49W
Paradise Valley, U.S.A.	72	41 30N	117 33W
Paragould, U.S.A.	71	36 5N	90 30W
Paraguá R., Bolivia	78	14 30s	61 30W
Paragua R., Venezuela	79	6 0N	63 30W
Paraguai, R., Brazil	79	16 0s	57 52W
Paraguana Pen., Ven.	75	12 0N	70 0W
Paraguari, Paraguay	77	25 36s	57 0W
Paraguay, rep., S. America	77	21 to 27 30s	54 15 to 61 20W
Paraguay R., Paraguay	77	24 30s	58 20W
Paraiba *See* João Pessóa	79		
Paraiba, st. Brazil	79	7 0s	37 0W
Paraiba R., Brazil	79	21 50s	43 0W
Paraiba R., Brazil	79	7 10s	35 30W
Parainen, Finland	23	60 21N	22 11 E
Paraiso, Mexico	74	18 20N	93 10W
Parakou, Dahomey	52	9 25N	2 40 E
Paramaribo, Surinam	79	5 50N	55 10W
Paramithia, Greece	21	39 30N	20 35 E
Paraná, Argentina	77	32 0s	60 30W
Parana, Brazil	79	12 20s	47 40W
Paraná, st., Brazil	77	24 30s	51 0W
Paraná R., S. America	79	22 30s	55 0W
Paranaguá, Brazil	77	25 30s	48 30W
Paranaiba, Brazil	79	19 45s	51 15W
Paranaiba R., Brazil	79	18 20s	49 15W
Paranam, Surinam	79	5 45N	55 10W
Paranapanema R., Braz.	77	22 40s	51 0W
Paranapiacaba, Serra, Brazil	77	24 0s	48 0W
Paraparaumo, N.Z.	46	40 57s	175 0 E
Paraopeba, Brazil	79	18 48s	45 10W
Parapeti R., Bolivia	78	19 45s	62 50W
Paray le Monial, France	12	46 27N	4 7 E
Parbatsar, India	32	26 52N	75 45 E

	MAP		
Parbhani, India	32	19 8N	76 52 E
Parchim, Germany	14	53 25N	11 50 E
Pardes Hanna, Israel	29	32 28N	34 57 E
Pardo R., Baia, Brazil	79	15 20s	40 25W
Pardo R., Mato Grosso, Brazil	79	21 0s	53 25W
Pardo R., Sao Paulo, Brazil	79	20 45s	48 0W
Pardubice, reg., C.Slov.	16	49 57N	15 55 E
Pare Pare, Indonesia	35	4 0s	119 40 E
Parecis, Serra dos, Brazil	78	13 0s	60 0W
Paren, U.S.S.R.	27	62 45N	163 0 E
Parengarenga, Harb., N.Z.	46	34 31s	173 0 E
Parent, Canada	62	47 55N	74 35W
Parent, Lac, Canada	62	48 31N	77 1W
Paria, G. of, Venezuela	75	10 10N	62 0W
Paria Pen, Venezuela	75	10 50N	62 30W
Pariaguán, Venezuela	75	8 52N	64 34W
Parigi, Celebes, Indon.	35	0 50s	120 5 E
Parika, Guyana	78	6 50N	58 20W
Parikkala, Finland	23	61 35N	29 30 E
Parima, Serra, Brazil	78	3 0N	64 0W
Parinari, Peru	78	4 35s	74 25W
Parintins, Brazil	79	2 40s	56 50W
Paris, Canada	62	43 20N	80 25W
Paris, France	12	48 50N	2 20 E
Paris, Idaho, U.S.A.	72	42 13N	111 30W
Paris, Tenn., U.S.A.	69	36 30N	88 20W
Paris, Tex., U.S.A.	71	33 40N	95 30W
Pariti, Indonesia	35	0 55s	123 30 E
Park City, U.S.A.	72	40 20N	111 31W
Park Falls, U.S.A.	70	45 59N	90 27W
Park Rapids, U.S.A.	70	46 57N	45 2W
Park River, U.S.A.	70	48 25N	97 43W
Park View, U.S.A.	73	36 45N	106 33W
Parker, Ariz., U.S.A.	73	34 9N	114 19W
Parker, S.D., U.S.A.	70	43 28N	97 5W
Parker Dam, U.S.A.	73	34 15N	114 5W
Parkersburg, U.S.A.	68	39 18N	81 31W
Parkerview, Canada	65	51 28N	103 18W
Parkes, N.S.W.	43	33 9s	148 11 E
Parkmore, N. Ireland	11	55 2N	6 5W
Parknasilla, Ireland	11	51 49N	9 50W
Parkstone, U.S.A.	70	43 29N	97 58W
Parkview, U.S.A.	73	36 45N	106 35W
Parlakimidi, Indian U.	33	18 45N	84 5 E
Parma, Italy	20	44 50N	10 20 E
Parma, U.S.A.	72	43 50N	116 59W
Parma, R., Italy	20	44 27N	10 3 E
Parnaguá, Brazil	79	10 10s	44 10W
Parnaiba, Brazil	79	3 0s	41 40W
Parnaiba, R., Brazil	79	3 35s	43 0W
Parnassos Mt., Greece	21	38 32N	22 41 E
Pärnu, U.S.S.R.	23	58 27N	24 31 E
Paro Dzong, Bhutan	33	27 25N	89 30 E
Paro Pamisus Range, Afghanistan	31	34 45N	63 0 E
Paroo Chan., N.S.W.	43	30 50s	143 35 E
Paroo R., N.S.W.	43	30 0s	144 5 E
Páros, Greece	21	37 5N	25 9 E
Páros I., Greece	21	37 5N	25 12 E
Parowan, U.S.A.	73	37 51N	112 51W
Parral, Chile	77	36 10s	72 0W
Parramatta, N.S.W.	43	33 48s	151 1 E
Parras, Mexico	74	25 30N	102 20W
Parris I., U.S.A.	69	32 20N	80 30W
Parrsboro, Canada	63	45 30N	64 10W
Parry, Canada	65	49 47N	104 41W
Parry Is., N.W. Terrs. Canada	58	77 0N	110 0W
Parry Sound, Ontario, Canada	62	45 20N	80 0W
Parshall, U.S.A.	70	47 58N	102 13W
Parsnip R., Canada	64	55 30N	123 10W
Parsons, Kans., U.S.A.	71	37 26N	95 16W
Partanna, Italy	20	37 43N	12 51 E
Parthenay, France	12	46 38N	0 16W
Partinico, Italy	20	38 3N	13 6 E
Paru R., Brazil	79	0 20s	53 30W
Paruro, Peru	78	13 45s	71 50W
Parvatipuram, India	33	18 50N	83 25 E
Parwan, prov., Afg.	32	35 0N	69 0 E
Parys, Orange Free State	57	26 52s	27 29 E
Pasadena, Calif., U.S.A.	73	34 5N	118 0W
Pasadena, Tex., U.S.A.	71	29 43N	95 15W
Pasangkaju, Indonesia	35	1 10s	119 30 E
Pasarwadjo, Indonesia	35	5 40s	122 45 E
Pascagoula, U.S.A.	69	30 30N	88 30W
Pascagoula R., U.S.A.	69	30 40N	88 35W
Pasco, U.S.A.	72	46 10N	119 0W
Pasco, Cerro de, Peru	78	11 0s	76 30W
Pasewalk, Germany	14	53 30N	14 0 E
Pasfield L., Canada	65	58 0N	105 20W
Pasir Mas, Malaya	34	6 2N	102 8 E
Pasir Puteh, Malaya	34	5 50N	102 24 E
Pasirian, Indonesia	34	8 13s	113 8 E
Paslek, Poland	16	54 4N	19 39 E
Pasley, C., W. Austral.	45	33 53s	123 30 E
Pasmler, Turkey	30	40 0N	42 0 E
Pasni, Pakistan	32	25 15N	63 27 E
Paso de los Indios, Argentina	77	43 55s	69 0W
Paso Robles, U.S.A.	73	35 37N	120 44W
Passage East, Ireland	11	52 15N	7 0W
Passage West, Ireland	11	51 52N	8 20W

	MAP		
Passau, Germany	14	48 34N	13 27 E
Passchendale, Belgium	13	50 53N	3 1 E
Pássero, C., Italy	20	36 42N	15 8 E
Passo Fundo, Brazil	77	28 10 S	52 30W
Passos, Brazil	79	20 45 S	46 29W
Pastaza R., Peru	78	2 45 S	76 50W
Pasto, Colombia	78	1 11N	77 30W
Pastrana, Spain	17	40 27N	2 53W
Pasuruan, Indonesia	34	7 40 S	112 53 E
Pasvik R., U.S.S.R.	22	68 48N	29 30 E
Patagonia, U.S.A.	73	31 36N	110 47W
Patan, Gujerat, India	32	23 54N	72 14 E
Patan, Maharashtra, India	32	17 22N	73 48 E
Patani, Indonesia	35	0 15N	128 45 E
Patchewollock, Victoria	43	35 20 S	142 0 E
Patchogue, U.S.A.	68	40 46N	72 1W
Patea, New Zealand	46	39 45 S	174 30 E
Pategi, Nigeria	52	8 50N	5 45 E
Patensie, Cape Prov.	57	33 46 S	24 49 E
Pater, Mt., W. Austral.	45	27 39 S	122 50 E
Paternò, Italy	20	37 34N	14 53 E
Pateros, U.S.A.	72	48 4N	119 55W
Paterson, N.J., U.S.A.	68	40 55N	74 10W
Paterson Inlet, N.Z.	47	46 56 S	168 12 E
Paterson Ra., W. Australia	44	21 45 S	122 15 E
Pathankot, India	32	32 18N	75 45 E
Pathfinder Res., U.S.A.	72	42 0N	107 0W
Pathiu, Thailand	34	14 3N	100 29 E
Pati, Indonesia	34	6 45 S	111 3 E
Patia R., Colombia	78	2 0N	78 0W
Patiala, India	32	30 23N	76 26 E
Patjitan, Indonesia	34	8 12 S	111 8 E
Patkai Bum, mts., India	33	27 0N	95 30 E
Patmos, I., Greece	21	37 21N	26 36 E
Patna, Bihar, India	33	25 35N	85 18 E
Patonga, Uganda	53	2 47N	33 20 E
Patos de Minas, Brazil	79	18 25 S	46 30W
Patos, Para, Brazil	79	3 20 S	49 20W
Patos, Pernambuco, Brazil	79	7 5 S	37 5W
Patos, Lagôa dos, Brazil	77	31 20 S	51 0 E
Patquia, Argentina	77	30 0 S	66 55W
Patrai, Greece	21	38 14N	21 47 E
Patrai, G. of, Greece	21	38 16N	21 38 E
Patreksfjördur, B., Ice.	22	65 28N	24 0W
Pâtrocinio, Brazil	79	19 0 S	47 0W
Pattad & I., Kenya	53	2 0 S	41 10 E
Pattani, Thailand	34	6 48N	101 15 E
Patten, U.S.A.	69	45 59N	68 28W
Patterson, Calif., U.S.A.	73	37 30N	121 6W
Patterson, La., U.S.A.	71	29 44N	91 19W
Patti, Italy	20	38 9N	14 58 E
Pattukkottai, India	32	10 25N	79 20 E
Patuakhali, Bangladesh	33	22 20N	90 25 E
Patuca, Pta., Honduras	75	15 50N	84 10W
Patuca, R., Honduras	75	15 20N	84 40W
Patung, China	39	31 0N	110 30 E
Patutahi, New Zealand	46	38 38 S	177 55 E
Patzcuaro, Mexico	74	19 30N	101 40W
Pau, France	12	43 19N	0 25W
Pau d'Alho, Brazil	79	7 50 S	35 10W
Pauillac, France	12	45 11N	0 46W
Pauini R., Brazil	78	7 40 S	68 10W
Pauk, Burma	33	21 55N	94 30 E
Paulistana, Brazil	79	8 0 S	41 15W
Paullina, U.S.A.	70	42 58N	95 36W
Paulpietersburg, Natal	57	27 23 S	30 50 E
Paulsbo, U.S.A.	72	47 45N	122 40W
Paul's Valley, U.S.A.	71	34 40N	97 15W
Pauri, India	32	30 10N	78 50 E
Pavia, Italy	30	45 10N	9 10 E
Pavlodar, U.S.S.R.	26	52 33N	77 0 E
Pavlof I., Alaska	59	55 0N	161 0W
Pavlograd, U.S.S.R.	25	48 30N	35 52 E
Pavlovo, Gorki Oblast, U.S.S.R.	25	55 58N	43 5 E
Pavlovo, Yakut A.S.S.R., U.S.S.R.	27	63 5N	115 25 E
Pavlovsk, Leningrad, U.S.S.R.	25	59 40N	30 28 E
Pavlovsk, Voronezh Oblast, U.S.S.R.	25	50 26N	40 5 E
Pavlovskaya, U.S.S.R.	25	46 17N	39 47 E
Pawhuska, U.S.A.	71	36 40N	96 25W
Pawnee, U.S.A.	71	36 25N	96 49W
Pawnee City, U.S.A.	70	40 7N	96 5W
Pawtucket, U.S.A	68	41 51N	71 22W
Paxoi I., Greece	21	39 14N	20 12 E
Paxton, Ill., U.S.A.	68	40 25N	88 0W
Paxton, Neb., U.S.A.	70	41 12N	101 25W
Paya Bakri, Malaya	34	2 0N	102 40 E
Payas, Turkey	30	36 45N	36 12 E
Payerne, Switzerland	15	46 49N	6 56 E
Payette, U.S.A.	72	44 0N	117 0W
Payne L., Canada	61	59 30N	74 30W
Payne R., Canada	61	60 0N	70 0W
Paynesville, W. Austral.	44	28 1 S	118 29 E
Paynesville, U.S.A.	70	45 24N	94 44W
Paysan, U.S.A.	73	34 16N	111 18W
Paysandu, Uruguay	77	32 19 S	58 8W
Paz R., Central Amer.	74	13 57N	90 3W
Pazar, Turkey	30	41 10N	40 50 E
Pazardžik, Bulgaria	21	42 12N	24 20 E
Pe Ell, U.S.A.	72	46 32N	123 20W
Peace R., Canada	64	59 30N	111 30W
Peach Springs, U.S.A.	73	35 32N	113 29W
Peak, The, mt., England	10	53 24N	1 53W
Peak Hill, N.S.W.	43	32 39 S	148 11 E
Peak Hill, W. Australia	44	25 35 S	118 43 E
Peak Range, Queens.	42	22 50 S	148 20 E
Peake Cr., S. Australia	45	28 5 S	135 30 E
Peale, Mt., U.S.A.	73	38 26N	109 15W
Pearce, U.S.A.	73	31 56N	109 50W
Pearl Harbor, Hawaiian Is.	59	21 22N	158 0W
Pearl R., U.S.A.	71	30 50N	89 40W
Pearsall, U.S.A.	71	28 55N	99 3W
Pearse I., Alaska	64	54 9N	130 4W
Pearston, Cape Prov.	57	32 33 S	25 7 E
Pease R., U.S.A.	71	34 16N	100 15W
Pebane, Mozambique	55	17 5 S	38 5 E
Pebas, Peru	78	3 10 S	71 55W
Peč, Yugoslavia	21	42 40N	20 17 E
Pechenga (Petsamó), U.S.S.R.	22	69 30N	31 25 E
Pechora G., U.S.S.R.	24	68 40N	54 0 E
Pechora R., U.S.S.R.	24	62 30N	56 30 E
Pecica, Rumania	21	46 10N	21 3 E
Pecos, U.S.A.	71	31 25N	103 35W
Pecos R., U.S.A	71	31 0N	102 10W
Pécs, Hungary	16	46 5N	18 15 E
Peddie, Cape Province	57	33 10 S	27 9 E
Pedjantan I., Indonesia	34	0 5 S	106 15 E
Pedregal, Panama	78	8 22N	82 26W
Pedreiras, Brazil	79	4 40 S	44 25W
Pedro Afonso, Brazil	79	9 0 S	48 10W
Pedro Cays Is., Caribbean Sea	75	17 25N	77 35W
Pedro Luro, Argentina	77	39 25 S	62 50W
Pedro Miguel, Pan Can. Zone	74		Inset
Pedro Miguel Locks, Pan. Can. Zone	74	9 1N	79 36W
Pedro, R. Fernandez, Argentina	77	29 50 S	58 50W
Peebinga, S. Australia	43	34 52 S	140 57 E
Peebles, Scotland	10	55 40N	3 12W
Peekskill, U.S.A.	68	41 18N	73 57W
Peel, Isle of Man, Br. Isles	10	54 14N	4 40W
Peel R., Canada	60	66 0N	134 0W
Peel R., N.S.W.	43	30 53 S	150 40 E
Peera Peera Poolanna L., S. Australia	43	26 30 S	138 0 E
Peers, Canada	64	53 40N	116 0W
Pegasus Bay, N.Z.	47	43 20 S	173 10 E
Pegu, Burma	33	17 20N	96 29 E
Pegu Yoma Mts., Burma	33	19 0N	96 0 E
Peh K., China	39	24 20N	113 10 E
Pehan, China	37	48 17N	126 23 E
Pehcevo, Yugoslavia	21	41 41N	23 3 E
Pehpei, China	39	29 50N	106 23 E
Pethaiho, China	38	39 50N	119 30 E
Pehuajo, Argentina	77	36 0 S	62 0W
Peixe, Brazil	77	12 0 S	48 40W
Peixe, R., Brazil	77	22 0 S	51 0W
Pekalongan, Indonesia	34	6 53 S	109 40 E
Pekan, Malaya	34	3 30N	103 25 E
Pekin, U.S.A.	70	40 35N	89 40W
Peking, China	38	39 50N	116 20 E
Pelagos I., Greece	21	39 17N	24 4 E
Pelaihari, Indonesia	35	3 55 S	114 45 E
Peleaga, mt., Rumania	21	45 22N	22 55 E
Pelee I., Canada	62	41 40N	82 40W
Pelée Mt., Martinique I.	75	14 40N	61 0W
Pelee, Pt., Canada	62	41 55N	82 30W
Pelekech, mt., Kenya	53	3 48N	35 5 E
Peleng I., Indonesia	35	1 20 S	123 30 E
Pelham, U.S.A.	69	31 5N	84 6W
Pelican L., Canada	65	52 30N	100 20W
Pelican Narrows, Can.	65	55 12N	102 55W
Pelican Portage, Can.	64	55 51N	113 0W
Pelican Rapids, Canada	65	52 38N	100 42W
Pelibre Dam, Haiti	75	19 1N	71 58W
Pella, Cape Province	57	29 1 S	19 6 E
Pella, U.S.A.	70	41 25N	93 0W
Pellinge, Finland	23	60 10N	25 0 E
Pello, Finland	22	66 48N	24 13 E
Pellston, U.S.A.	68	45 34N	84 47W
Pelly, Canada	65	51 50N	102 0W
Pelly L., Canada	22	66 0N	102 0W
Pelly R., Canada	64	62 0N	132 30W
Peloponnese, Greece	21	37 10N	22 0 E
Peloro, C., Italy	20	38 15N	15 40 E
Pelorous River, N.Z.	47	41 17 S	173 5 E
Pelorous Sound, N.Z.	47	40 59 S	173 59 E
Pelotas, Brazil	77	31 42 S	52 23W
Pelotas R., Brazil	77	28 0 S	50 50W
Pelvoux, Massif du, mts., France	12	44 52N	6 20 E
Pelym, U.S.S.R.	24	59 25N	63 0 E
Pemalang, Indonesia	34	6 53 S	109 23 E
Pematang I., Indonesia	34	2 50N	96 55 E
Pemba, Zambia	56	16 28 S	27 20 E
Pemba Chan., Tanzania	53	5 0 S	39 27 E
Pemba I., Tanzania	53	5 20 S	39 40 E
Pemberton, Canada	64	50 25N	122 50W
Pemberton, W. Austral.	44	34 30 S	116 0 E
Pemberton, Queensland	43	24 56 S	152 28 E
Pembina R., Alberta, Canada	64	53 10N	115 40W
Pembina R., Man., Can.	65	49 20N	99 0W
Pembine, U.S.A.	68	45 38N	87 59W
Pembino, U.S.A.	70	49 1N	97 14W
Pembridge, England	10	52 14N	2 53W
Pembroke, Canada	62	45 50N	77 15W
Pembroke, U.S.A.	69	32 5N	81 32W
Peña, C. de, Spain	17	43 42N	5 52W
Peñafiel, Spain	17	41 35N	4 7W
Penang I., Malaya	34	5 25N	100 15 E
Peñapolis, Brazil	79	21 30 S	50 0W
Peñaranda, Spain	17	40 53N	5 13W
Peñas, G. of, Chile	78	47 0 S	75 0W
Peñas, Pta., Venezuela	75	10 50N	61 53W
Peñas de Europa, mt., Spain	17	43 15N	4 51W
Pend Oreille, L., U.S.A.	72	48 0N	116 30W
Pend Oreille, R., U.S.A.	72	48 30N	117 15W
Pendembu, Sierra Leone	52	8 7N	10 48W
Pendjari R., Dahomey	52	11 10N	1 25 E
Pendleton, U.S.A.	72	45 35N	118 50W
Pene Lunanga, Zaire	53	4 17 S	28 20 E
Penedo, Brazil	79	10 15 S	36 40W
Penetanguishene, Can.	62	44 50N	79 55W
Pengan, China	39	31 2N	106 16 E
Pengchia Yu (Agincourt) I., Taiwan	39	25 40N	120 7N
Penge, Zaire	53	4 22 S	28 26 E
Penghu (Pescadores) Is. China	39	23 40N	119 20 E
Penglai, China	38	36 48N	120 46 E
Pengpu, China	38	33 0N	117 25 E
Pengshui, China	39	29 20N	108 15 E
Penguin, Tasmania	43	41 8 S	146 6 E
Penhalonga, Rhod.	56	18 52 S	32 40 E
Peniche, Portugal	17	39 19N	9 22W
Penida I., Indonesia	35	8 45 S	115 30 E
Peninsula, div., Queens.	42	14 34 S	143 16 E
Penitentes, Sa. do., Brazil	79	8 5 S	46 0W
Penju I., Indonesia	35	5 30 S	127 45 E
Penki, China	38	41 20N	123 50 E
Penn Yan. U.S.A.	68	42 39N	77 7W
Pennant, Canada	65	50 35N	108 5W
Penner R., India	32	14 50N	78 20 E
Pennine Alpi, Alps, Eur.	15	46 10N	7 40 E
Pennine Ra., England	10	54 40N	2 20W
Pennington R., Nigeria	52	4 45N	5 30 E
Pennsylvania, st., U.S.A.	68	40 50N	78 0W
Penny, Canada	64	53 58N	121 1W
Peno, U.S.S.R.	25	57 2N	32 33 E
Penobscot B., U.S.A.	69	44 0N	69 0W
Penobscot R.. U.S.A.	69	45 0N	70 0W
Penola, S. Australia	43	37 12 S	140 50 E
Penong, S. Australia	45	31 59 S	133 5 E
Penonomé, Panama	75	8 37N	80 25W
Penrith, N.S.W.	43	33 43 S	150 38 E
Pensacola, U.S.A.	69	30 30N	87 10W
Pense, Canada	65	50 25N	105 0W
Penticton, Canada	64	49 30N	119 30W
Pentland, Queensland	42	20 32 S	145 25 E
Pentland Firth, Scot.	10	58 43N	3 10W
Penuh Mt., Indonesia	34	2 10 S	102 50 E
Penukonda, India	32	14 10N	77 32 E
Penylan L., Canada	65	61 50N	106 20W
Penza, U.S.S.R.	25	53 15N	45 5 E
Penzance, England	10	50 7N	5 32W
Penzhina G., U.S.S.R.	27	61 30N	163 0 E
Penzhino, U.S.S.R.	27	63 50N	167 58 E
Peoria, Ariz., U.S.A.	73	33 40N	112 15W
Peoria, U.S.A.	70	40 40N	89 40W
Pepa, Congo	53	7 42 S	29 46 E
Pepani, R. Cape Prov.	57	26 0 S	23 0 E
Pepel, Sierra Leone	52	8 35N	13 7W
Pepperwood, U.S.A.	72	40 26N	124 2W
Pequ'in, Israel	29	32 58N	35 20 E
Pequiri R., Brazil	77	17 35 S	56 0W
Pequiri R., Brazil	79	24 0 S	53 30W
Pera Hd., Queensland	42	12 57 S	141 30 E
Perak, st., Malaya	34	5 0N	101 0 E
Perak R., Malaya	34	5 10N	101 4 E
Perche, Collines du, France	12	48 32N	0 30 E
Percival Lakes, W. Australia	45	21 30 S	124 45 E
Percy Is., Queensland	42	21 39 S	150 16 E
Percyville, Queensland	42	19 2 S	143 45 E
Perdito, Mt., Spain	17	42 45N	0 3W
Perdu Mt., Spain. *See* Perdido, Mte	17		
Pereira, Colombia	78	4 50N	75 40W
Perekop, U.S.S.R.	25	46 10N	33 42 E
Perekop, Isth. of U.S.S.R.	26	46 10N	33 42 E
Perenjori, W. Australia	44	29 25 S	116 43 E
Perené R., Peru	78	11 0 S	74 35W
Pérere, Dahomey	52	9 50N	3 2 E
Pereyaslav-Khmeinitski, U.S.S.R.	25	50 3N	31 28 E
Pergamino, Argentina	77	33 52 S	60 30W
Perham, U.S.A.	70	46 37N	95 33W
Periam, Rumania	21	46 2N	20 59 E
Peribonca L., Canada	63	50 1N	71 10W
Peribonca R., Canada	63	50 0N	71 3W
Pericos, Mexico	74	25 10N	107 50W
Périgueux, France	12	45 10N	0 42 E
Perija, Sierra de, mts., Venezuela	75	10 0N	73 0W
Perim I., Red Sea	49	12 38N	43 25 E
Periperi, Serra do, Brazil	79	14 50 S	40 40W
Perito Moreno, Arg.	77	46 25 S	71 5W
Periyakulam, India	32	10 5N	77 30 E
Perkovič, Yugoslavia	20	43 41N	16 10 E
Perlas, Arch. de las, Panama	75	8 41N	79 7W
Perlas, Pta de, Nic.	75	11 30N	83 30W
Perlis, st. Malaya	34	6 30N	100 15 E
Perm (Molotov), U.S.S.R.	24	58 0N	56 10 E
Përmet, Albania	21	40 15N	20 21 E
Pernambuco. *See* Recife.	79		
Pernambuco, st., Brazil	79	8 30 S	38 0W
Peron, C., W. Australia	44	25 30 S	113 30 E
Peron Pen., W. Austral.	44	26 0 S	113 10 E
Péronne, France	12	49 55N	2 57 E
Perovo, U.S.S.R.	25	55 45N	37 35 E
Perow, Canada	64	54 35N	126 10W
Perpignan, France	12	42 42N	2 53 E
Perry, Iowa, U.S.A.	70	41 48N	94 5W
Perry, N.Y., U.S.A.	69	42 44N	77 59W
Perry, Okla, U.S.A.	71	36 16N	97 18W
Perryton, U.S.A.	71	36 27N	100 45W
Perryville, Alaska	59	55 55N	159 11W
Perryville, U.S.A.	71	37 43N	89 51W
Persepolis (ancient), Iran	31	29 55N	52 50 E
Persian Gulf, Asia	30	27 0N	50 0 E
Perth, W. Australia	44	31 57 S	115 52 E
Perth, Canada	62	44 55N	76 20W
Perth, Scotland	10	56 24N	3 27W
Perth, U.S.A.	68	40 33N	74 36W
Peru, Ill., U.S.A.	70	41 17N	89 15W
Peru, Ind., U.S.A.	68	40 42N	86 0W
Peru, N.Y., U.S.A.	68	44 34N	73 32W
Peru, rep., S. America	78	2 30 S to 18 0 S	69 0W to 81 15W
Perugia, Italy	20	43 6N	12 24 E
Peruibe, Brazil	77	24 20 S	47 0W
Pervomaisk, U.S.S.R.	25	48 5N	30 55 E
Pervouralsk, U.S.S.R.	24	56 55N	60 0 E
Perwell, Queensland	43	27 25 S	148 22 E
Pesaro, Italy	20	43 54N	12 53 E
Pescadores Is., China. *See* Penghu	39	23 40N	119 30 E
Pescara, Italy	20	42 28N	14 13 E
Peshawar, Pakistan	32	34 2N	71 37 E
Peshawar, Terr., W. Pakistan	32	34 30N	72 0 E
Peshtigo, U.S.A.	68	45 4N	87 46W
Pesqueira, Mexico	74	29 22N	110 58W
Pestravka, U.S.S.R.	25	52 28N	49 57 E
Petah Tiqwa, Israel	79	32 6N	34 53 E
Petaling Jaya, Malaya	34	3 4N	101 42W
Petaluma, U.S.A.	73	38 16N	122 40W
Petange, Luxembourg	14	49 33N	5 55 E
Petatlán, Mexico	73	17 31N	101 16W
Petauke, Zambia	56	14 14 S	31 12 E
Petawawa, Canada	62	45 54N	77 17W
Petén Itza L., Guat.	74	17 0N	89 41W
Peter Ist I., S. Ocean	80	69 0 S	91 0W
Peter Pond L., Canada	65	56 0N	109 0W
Peterbell, Canada	62	48 36N	83 21W
Peterborough, Canada	62	44 20N	78 20W
Peterborough, England	10	52 35N	0 14W
Peterborough, S. Austral.	43	33 0 S	138 45 E
Peterhead, Scotland	10	57 30N	1 49W
Petermann Pk., Green.	58	73 30N	27 0W
Petersburg, Alaska	59	56 50N	133 0W
Petersburg, Cape Prov.	57	32 17 S	24 58 E
Petersburg, Ill., U.S.A.	68	40 0N	89 59W
Petersburg, Ind., U.S.A.	68	38 30N	87 15W
Petersburg, Va., U.S.A.	68	37 17N	77 26W
Petit Batanga, Cameroon	52	3 10N	9 58 E
Petit Bois I., U.S.A.	69	30 16N	88 25W
Petit Cap, Canada	63	48 58N	63 58W
Petit Goâve, Haiti	75	18 27N	72 51W
Petit François, French Guiana	79	3 10N	52 20W
Petit Marigot, Leeward Is.	75		Inset
Petitcodiac, Canada	63	45 57N	65 11W
Petite Saguenay, Can.	63	47 59N	70 1W
Petitot R., Canada	64	59 45N	121 30W
Petitskiapau L., Can.	63	54 40N	66 30W
Petlad, India	32	22 30N	72 45 E
Peto, Mexico	74	20 10N	89 0W
Petone, New Zealand	46	41 13 S	174 53 E
Petoskey, U.S.A.	68	45 21N	84 55W
Petrich, Bulgaria	21	41 25N	23 12 E
Petrinja, Yugoslavia	20	45 28N	16 18 E
Petrokrepost, U.S.S.R.	25	59 53N	31 3 E
Petrolandia, Brazil	79	9 0 S	38 20W
Petrolia, Canada	62	42 54N	82 9W
Petrolina, Brazil	79	9 10 S	40 40W
Petropavlovsk, U.S.S.R.	27	53 16N	159 0 E
Petropavlovsk, U.S.S.R.	26	55 0N	69 0 E
Petropavlovsk, U.S.S.R.	25	48 27N	46 7 E
Petrópolis, Brazil	79	22 33 S	43 9W
Petroseni, Rumania	21	45 28N	23 20 E
Petrovaradin, Y.slav.	21	45 16N	19 55 E
Petrovgrad (Zrenjanin) Yugoslavia	21	45 22N	20 23 E
Petrovsk, Chita, U.S.S.R.	27	51 26N	108 30 E

	MAP		
Petrovsk, Saratov, U.S.S.R.	25	52 22N	45 19E
Petrovsk Uralsk, U.S.S.R.	24	60 10N	59 20E
Petrovskoye, U.S.S.R.	25	45 25N	42 28E
Petrozavodsk, U.S.S.R.	24	61 41N	34 20E
Petrusburg, Orange Free State	57	29 4S	25 26E
Petrusville, Cape Prov.	57	30 5S	24 41E
Petsamo. *See* Pechenga	24		
Pettigoe, Ireland	11	54 32N	7 49W
Pevek, U.S.S.R.	27	69 35N	171 0E
Pézénas, France	12	43 28N	3 24E
Pfaffikon, Switzerland	15	47 21N	8 48E
Pforzheim, Germany	14	48 53N	8 43E
Pha Rho, L., S. Korea	36	38 7N	127 48E
Phagwara, India	32	31 15N	75 45E
Phalodi, India	32	27 12N	72 24E
Phaltan, India	32	18 1N	74 31E
Phan Rang, S. Viet Nam	34	11 40N	109 9E
Phan Thiet, S. Viet Nam	34	11 1N	108 9E
Phangnga, Thailand	34	8 28N	98 30E
Phanom Dong Rahek, mts. Thailand	34	14 40N	104 0E
Pharo Dzong, China	37	27 44N	89 9E
Phatthalung, Thailand	34	7 38N	100 5E
Phayao, Thailand	34	19 10N	99 55E
Phelps, U.S.A.	68	46 2N	89 2W
Phenix City, U.S.A.	69	32 30N	85 0W
Phet Buri, Thailand	34	31 1N	99 55E
Philadelphia, Miss., U.S.A.	71	32 46N	89 4W
Philadelphia, N.Y., U.S.A.	68	44 9N	75 40W
Philadelphia, Pa., U.S.A.	69	40 0N	75 10W
Philip, U.S.A.	70	44 6N	101 37W
Philippeville, Belgium	13	50 12N	4 33E
Philippi (Wickamunna) L., Queensland	42	24 20S	138 55E
Philippine Is., rep., Asia	35	12 0N	123 0E
Philippolis, Orange Free State	91	30 15S	25 16E
Philipsburg, U.S.A.	72	46 21N	113 19W
Philipstown, Cape Prov.	57	30 28S	24 30E
Phillip I., Victoria	43	38 20S	145 15E
Phillips, Me., U.S.A.	69	44 50N	70 10W
Phillips, Texas, U.S.A.	71	35 45N	101 30W
Phillips, Wis., U.S.A.	70	45 41N	90 25W
Phillipsburg, U.S.A.	70	39 46N	99 24W
Philomath, U.S.A.	72	44 32N	123 26W
Phitsanulok, Thailand	34	16 50N	100 15E
Phœnix, U.S.A.	73	33 30N	112 10W
Phœnix Is., Pacific Oc.	7	3 30S	172 0W
Phnom Penh, Cambodia	34	11 33N	104 55E
Phong Saly, Laos	37	21 40N	102 6E
Phra Phutthabat, Thai.	34	14 44N	100 36E
Phrae, Thailand	34	18 12N	100 12E
Phu Quoc I., S. Viet Nam	34	10 15N	104 0E
Phuket, Thailand	34	8 0N	98 28E
Phulchari, Bangladesh	33	25 15N	89 40E
Pi Ho, China	39	31 50N	116 35E
Piacenza, region, Italy	20	45 3N	9 41E
Piako River, N.Z.	46	37 24S	175 32E
Pialba, Queensland	43	25 12S	152 45E
Pian Cr., N.S.W.	43	29 52S	148 30E
Pian Mwanga, Zaire	56	7 40S	28 5E
Pianosa I., Italy	20	42 12N	15 44E
Piapot, Canada	65	49 59N	109 8W
Piatra Neamt, Rumania	21	46 56N	26 21E
Piaui R., Brazil	79	7 0S	42 30W
Piau, Sa. do, Brazil	79	9 0S	43 50W
Piave R., Italy	20	45 50N	13 9E
Piazza Armerina, Italy	20	37 21N	14 20E
Pibor Post, Sudan	54	6 52N	33 0E
Pica, Chile	78	20 35S	69 25W
Picaninyemba, Rhod.	56	17 25S	28 28E
Picardie, prov., Fr.	12	50 0N	2 15E
Picayune, U.S.A.	71	30 31N	89 40W
Piccadilly, Zambia	56	13 56S	29 24E
Pichanal, Argentina	77	23 15S	64 10W
Pichieh, China	39	27 25N	105 0E
Pichilemu, Chile	77	34 22S	72 9W
Pichincha, vol., Ecuador	78	0 10S	78 30W
Pickerel L., Canada	62	48 40N	91 25W
Pickle Crow, Canada	62	51 30N	90 0W
Pico da Bandeira, mt., Brazil	79	21 0S	42 0W
Pico Truncado, Arg.	77	46 40S	68 10W
Picos, Brazil	79	7 5S	41 24W
Picton, Canada	62	44 1N	77 9W
Picton, N.S.W.	43	34 12S	150 34E
Picton, New Zealand	47	41 18S	174 3E
Pictou, Canada	63	45 41N	62 42W
Picture Butte, Canada	64	49 55N	112 45W
Picún-Leufú, Argentina	77	39 30S	69 5W
Pidurutalagala, mt., Sri Lanka	32	7 10N	80 50E
Piedimonte di Elise, Italy	20	41 22N	14 22E
Piedmont, reg., Italy	20	45 0N	7 50E
Piedmont, U.S.A.	69	33 55N	85 39W
Piedmont Plat., U.S.A.	69	34 0N	81 30W
Piedra Negra, C., Mexico	74	15 40N	96 40W
Piedra Sola, Uruguay	77	32 0S	56 10W
Piedrahita, Spain	17	40 28N	5 23W

	MAP		
Piedras R., Peru	78	11 40S	70 50W
Piedras Blancas Pt., U.S.A.	73	35 41N	121 15W
Piedras Negras, Mex	74	28 35N	100 35W
Piedras Punta, Arg.	77	35 30S	57 0W
Pienaars R., Transvaal	57	25 10S	28 0E
Pier Hd., Queensland	42	22 0S	150 10E
Pierce, U.S.A.	72	46 30N	115 17W
Pierre, U.S.A.	70	44 27N	100 18W
Piet Retief, Transvaal	57	27 1S	30 50E
Pietermaritzburg, Natal	57	29 35S	30 25E
Pietersburg, Transvaal	57	23 54S	29 25E
Pietrasanta, Italy	20	43 57N	10 12E
Pietrosul Mt., Rumania	21	47 35N	24 43E
Pieve di Cadore, Italy	20	46 25N	12 22E
Pigawasi, Tanzania	53	4 54S	33 7E
Pigeon, U.S.A.	68	43 50N	83 17E
Pigeon River, Canada	62	48 1N	89 42W
Piggot, U.S.A.	71	36 28N	90 13W
Piggs Peak, Swaziland	57	25 58S	31 15E
Pihyon, N. Korea	36	40 2N	124 25E
Pikangikum, Canada	65	51 50N	94 0W
Pike, Canada	64	59 25N	133 35W
Pikes Peak, U.S.A.	70	38 50N	105 10W
Piketberg, Cape Prov.	57	32 54N	18 42E
Pikeville, U.S.A.	68	37 30N	82 30W
Pikwitonei, Canada	65	55 35N	97 11W
Pila, Poland	16	53 10N	16 48E
Pilanesberg, Transvaal	57	25 14S	27 4E
Pilar, Brazil	79	9 35S	36 17W
Pilar, Paraguay	77	26 50S	58 10W
Pilatus, mt., Switz.	15	46 59N	8 16E
Pilaya R., Bolivia	78	21 0S	64 20W
Pilbara, W. Australia	44	21 14S	118 19E
Pilcomayo R., S. Amer.	77	19 30S	64 35W
Pilgrim's Rest, Trans.	57	24 53S	30 46E
Pilibhit, India	32	28 40N	79 50E
Pilion, mt., Greece	21	39 27N	23 7E
Pillar C., Tasmania	43	43 10S	147 55E
Pilliga, N.S.W.	43	30 22S	148 55E
Pillinger, Tasmania	43	42 20S	145 31E
Pilos, Greece	21	36 55N	21 42E
Pilot Mound, Canada	65	49 15N	99 0W
Pilot Point, U.S.A.	71	33 27N	97 0W
Pilot Rock, U.S.A.	72	45 29N	118 54W
Piltown, Ireland	11	51 59N	7 49W
Pima, U.S.A.	73	32 58N	109 54W
Pimba, S. Australia	43	31 18S	136 46E
Pimenta Bueno, Brazil	78	11 35S	61 10W
Pincher Creek, Canada	64	49 30N	113 35W
Pinchi, L., Canada	64	54 30N	124 20W
Pinckneyville, U.S.A.	71	38 3N	89 24W
Pindar, W. Australia	44	28 22S	115 45E
Pindiga, Nigeria	52	9 58N	10 53E
Pindus Mts., Greece	21	40 0N	21 0E
Pine, U.S.A.	73	34 27N	111 29W
Pine, R., Canada	65	58 30N	106 30W
Pine Bluff, U.S.A.	71	34 10N	92 0W
Pine City, U.S.A.	70	45 48N	92 59W
Pine Creek, Canada	40	13 51S	131 52W
Pine C., Canada	63	46 38N	53 35W
Pine Falls, Canada	65	50 51N	96 11W
Pine Hill, Queensland	42	23 42S	147 0E
Pine P., Canada	64	55 30N	122 35W
Pine Pt., Canada	64	60 50N	114 30W
Pine Ridge, U.S.A.	70	43 2N	102 34W
Pine R., Canada	65	58 40N	106 18W
Pine River, Canada	65	51 45N	100 30W
Pine River, U.S.A.	70	46 41N	94 20W
Pinedale, U.S.A.	73	34 51N	111 17W
Pinega, U.S.S.R.	24	64 45N	43 40E
Pinega R., U.S.S.R.	24	64 20N	43 0E
Pinerolo, Italy	20	44 47N	7 21E
Pinetop, U.S.A.	73	34 11N	109 53W
Pinetown, Natal	57	29 48S	30 54E
Pinetree, U.S.A.	72	43 44N	105 48W
Pineville, Ky., U.S.A.	69	36 42N	83 42W
Pineville, La., U.S.A.	71	31 25N	92 27W
Piney, Canada	65	49 5N	96 10W
Ping R., Thailand	39	16 40N	90 30E
Pinga, Zaire	53	0 58S	28 42E
Pingelly, W. Australia	44	32 29S	116 59E
Pingeyri, Iceland	22	65 52N	23 5W
Pinghuo, China	39	24 19N	117 3E
Pingkiang, China	39	28 45N	113 30E
Pingliang, China	38	35 20N	106 40E
Pinglo, China	39	24 30N	110 45E
Pinglo, China	38	39 1N	106 27E
Pingnam, China	39	23 32N	110 31E
Pingrup, W. Australia	44	33 31S	118 31E
Pingsiang, China	39	27 43N	113 50E
Pingsiang, China	39	22 13N	106 16E
Pingting, China	38	37 50N	113 32E
Pingtingshan, China	38	33 45N	113 28E
Pingtu, China	38	36 50N	119 50E
Pingtung, China	39	22 40N	120 30E
Pingwu, China	38	32 29N	104 31E
Pingyang, China	39	27 45N	120 25E
Pingyao, China	38	37 15N	112 10E
Pingyuan, China	38	36 12N	106 30E
Pinhel, Portugal	17	40 48N	7 0W
Pinhsien, China	38	37 28N	117 58E
Pinhsien, China	38	35 10N	108 10E
Pini I., Indonesia	34	0 10N	98 40E
Pinos, Pt., U.S.A.	73	36 40N	121 58W
Pinios R., Greece	21	39 35N	22 10E
Pinjarra, W. Australia	44	32 37S	115 52E
Pinlebu, Burma	33	24 5N	95 25E

	MAP		
Pinnacle, Queensland	42	21 11S	148 45E
Pinnaroo, S. Australia	43	35 13S	140 56E
Pinos, Mexico	74	22 20N	101 40W
Pinos, I. de, Cuba	75	21 40N	82 40W
Pintados, Chile	78	20 35S	69 40W
Pintharuka, W. Austral.	44	29 2S	115 59E
Pinyang, China	38	23 20N	109 47E
Pinyug, U.S.S.R.	24	60 5N	48 0E
Pinzgau, R., Austria	14	47 10N	12 20E
Pioche, U.S.A.	73	37 56N	114 38W
Piombino, Italy	20	42 54N	10 30E
Pioneer R., Queensland	42	21 10S	149 0E
Pioner I., U.S.S.R.	27	79 50N	92 0E
Piotrków, Poland	16	51 23N	19 43E
Pip, Iran	31	26 45N	60 10E
Pipestone, U.S.A.	70	44 0N	96 17W
Pipiriki, New Zealand	46	39 28S	175 5E
Pipmuacan L., Canada	63	49 40N	70 25W
Pippingarra, W. Australia	44	20 20S	118 9E
Piqua, U.S.A.	68	40 10N	84 10W
Pira, Dahomey	52	8 30N	1 46E
Piracicaba, Brazil	77	22 40S	47 30W
Piracuruca, Brazil	79	3 50S	41 50W
Piraievs, Greece	21	37 57N	23 42E
Pirámide Mt., Chile	77	49 0S	73 30W
Pirané, Argentina	77	25 25S	59 30W
Piranhas R., Brazil	79	6 10S	37 10W
Pirapora, Brazil	79	17 20S	45 0W
Piray, Argentina	77	26 45S	54 45W
Pirenopolis, Brazil	79	15 50S	49 0W
Pirgos, Greece	21	27 40N	21 27E
Piripaua, C., N.Z.	47	42 33S	173 30E
Piriápolis, Uruguay	77	34 50S	55 10W
Pirin Planina, Bulgaria	21	41 40N	23 30E
Piripiri, Brazil	79	4 25S	42 0W
Pirmasens, Germany	14	49 12N	7 30E
Pirot, Yugoslavia	21	43 9N	22 39E
Pirtleville, U.S.A.	73	31 27N	109 36W
Piru, Indonesia	35	3 2S	128 15E
Piryatin, U.S.S.R.	25	50 15N	32 25E
Pisa, Italy	20	43 43N	10 23E
Pisa Ra., New Zealand	47	44 52S	169 12E
Pisagua, Chile	78	40S	70 15W
Pisciotta, Italy	20	40 7N	15 12E
Pisco, Peru	78	13 50S	76 5W
Pisek, Czechoslovakia	16	49 19N	14 10E
Pishin, Iran	31	36 1N	63 38E
Pisticci, Italy	20	40 24N	16 33E
Pistilfjördur, Iceland	22	66 18N	15 30W
Pistoia, Italy	20	43 57N	10 53E
Pistol B., Canada	65	62 15N	93 5W
Pisz, Poland	23	53 38N	21 49E
Pita, Guinea	50	11 5N	12 15W
Pitcairn I., Pacific Oc.	5	25 5S	130 5W
Pite R., Sweden	22	65 22N	21 15W
Pitea, Sweden	22	65 55N	21 25E
Pitesti, Rumania	21	44 52N	24 54E
Pithapuram, India	33	17 10N	82 15E
Pithara, W. Australia	44	30 20S	116 35E
Pithiviers, France	12	48 10N	2 13E
Pitigliano, Italy	20	42 38N	11 40E
Pitt I., Canada	64	53 30N	129 50W
Pittsburg, Calif., U.S.A.	73	38 2N	121 55W
Pittsburg, Kan., U.S.A.	71	37 21N	94 43W
Pittsburg, Tex., U.S.A.	71	33 0N	94 59W
Pittsburgh, U.S.A.	68	40 25N	80 0W
Pittsfield, Ill., U.S.A.	69	39 35N	90 46W
Pittsfield, Mass., U.S.A.	69	42 28N	73 17W
Pittston, U.S.A.	68	41 19N	75 50W
Pittsworth, Queensland	43	27 41S	151 37E
Pituri R., Queensland	42	22 20S	138 15E
Piura, Peru	78	5 5S	80 45W
Piura R., Peru	78	5 20S	79 50W
Piurini L., Brazil	78	3 25S	62 45W
Piuthan, Nepal	33	28 10N	82 50E
Piyang, China	38	32 50N	113 30E
Pizzo, Italy	20	38 44N	16 10E
Placentia, Canada	63	47 20N	54 0W
Placentia B., Canada	63	47 0N	54 40W
Placentia Junc., Can.	63	47 27N	53 43W
Placerville, U.S.A.	73	38 45N	120 50W
Placetas, Cuba	75	22 15N	79 44W
Plain Dealing, U.S.A.	71	32 58N	93 44W
Plainfield, N.J., U.S.A.	68	40 37N	74 28W
Plains, Kan., U.S.A.	71	37 17N	100 32W
Plains, Mont., U.S.A.	72	47 29N	114 51W
Plains, Tex., U.S.A.	71	33 6N	102 47W
Plainview, Nebr., U.S.A.	70	42 25N	97 47W
Plainview, Tex., U.S.A.	71	34 10N	101 40W
Plainville, U.S.A.	70	39 15N	99 16W
Plainwell, U.S.A.	68	42 28N	85 40W
Pláka, C., Greece	21	36 45N	24 26E
Planaltina, Brazil	79	15 30S	47 45W
Plankinton, U.S.A.	70	43 47N	98 27W
Plano, U.S.A.	71	33 0N	96 46W
Plant City, U.S.A.	69	28 0N	82 15W
Plaquemine, U.S.A.	71	30 10N	91 10W
Plasencia, Spain	17	40 3N	6 8W
Plaster Rock, Canada	63	46 53N	67 22W
Plata, Rio de la, Arg.	77	36 0S	53 0W
Platani R., Italy	20	37 28N	13 23E
Plateau, prov., Nigeria	52	9 15N	9 0E
Plateau du Tademait, Algeria	50	28 30N	2 30E
Plati, Italy	21	38 14N	16 2E
Platinum, Alaska	59	59 1N	161 40W
Plato, Colombia	75	9 54N	74 46W

	MAP		
Platte, U.S.A.	70	43 27N	98 47W
Platte R., U.S.A.	70	41 0N	98 0W
Platteville, U.S.A.	70	40 21N	104 47W
Plattsburgh, U.S.A.	68	44 41N	73 30W
Plattsmouth, U.S.A.	70	41 0N	96 0W
Plauen, Germany	14	50 29N	12 9E
Plavinas, U.S.S.R.	23	56 32N	25 52E
Plaxton, U.S.A.	70	40 27N	88 2W
Playgreen L., Canada	65	53 20N	98 0W
Pleasant Pt., N.Z.	47	44 16S	171 9E
Pleasant Bay, Canada	63	46 51N	60 43W
Pleasant Hill, U.S.A.	70	38 45N	94 14W
Pleasantville, U.S.A.	68	39 25N	74 30W
Pleiades, mt., W. Australia	44	23 25S	114 55E
Pleiku, Viet Nam	34	13 40N	107 40E
Plenty, Bay of, N.Z.	46	37 45S	177 0E
Plesetsk, U.S.S.R.	24	62 40N	40 10E
Plessisville, Canada	63	46 14N	71 46W
Pleszew, Poland	16	51 53N	17 47E
Pletipi L., Canada	63	51 45N	70 12W
Pleven, Bulgaria	21	43 26N	24 37E
Plevlja, Yugoslavia	21	43 21N	19 21E
Plock, Poland	16	52 32N	19 40E
Ploërmel, France	12	47 55N	2 26W
Ploesti, Rumania	21	44 57N	26 5E
Plombières, France	12	47 59N	62 7E
Plonsk, Poland	16	52 37N	20 21E
Plovdic, Bulgaria	21	42 8N	24 44E
Plowce, Poland	21	52 40N	18 40E
Plummer, U.S.A.	72	47 22N	116 57W
Plumtree, Rhodesia	56	20 27S	27 55E
Pluto Mt., Queensland	43	25 23S	147 0E
Plymouth, England	10	50 23N	4 9W
Plymouth, Montserrat	75	16 44N	62 14W
Plymouth, Ind., U.S.A.	68	41 20N	86 19W
Plymouth, Wis., U.S.A.	68	43 42N	87 58W
Plzen (Pilsen), C.Slov.	16	49 45N	13 22E
Pnom Penh (Phnom Penh), Cambodia	34	11 33N	104 55E
Po, Volta	52	11 14N	1 5W
Po, R., Italy	20	45 0N	10 45E
Po Hai, Gulf, China	38	38 30N	119 0E
Pobe, Dahomey	52	7 0N	2 38E
Pocahontas, Ark., U.S.A.	71	36 17N	91 0W
Pocahontes, U.S.A.	70	40 44N	94 43W
Pocatello, U.S.A	72	42 50N	112 25W
Pocomoke City, U.S.A.	68	38 7N	75 34W
Pocos de Caidas, Brazil	77	21 50S	46 45W
Podgorica (Titograd) Yugoslavia	21	42 28N	19 17E
Podkamennaya Tunguska, U.S.S.R.	27	61 50N	90 26E
Podolsk, U.S.S.R.	25	55 30N	37 30E
Podor, Senegal	50	16 40N	14 50W
Podul-Ilóaie, Rumania	21	47 12N	27 22E
Pofadder, Cape Prov.	57	29 10S	19 22E
Pogamasing, Canada	62	46 55N	81 50W
Pogradec, Albania	21	40 57N	20 48E
Pohang, S. Korea	36	36 3N	129 26E
Pohjois Karjalan Laani, Finland	23	61 45N	29 0E
Pohsien, China	38	33 49N	115 38E
Point Calimere, India	32	10 20N	79 50E
Point Danger, Queens.	43	28 11S	153 15E
Point Edward, Canada	62	43 10N	82 30W
Point Hope (Tigara), Alaska	59	68 30N	166 35W
Point Lay, Alaska	59	69 45N	163 10W
Point Pedro, Sri Lanka	32	9 50N	80 15E
Point Rock, U.S.A.	71	31 30N	99 58W
Pointe à-Gravois, Haiti	75	18 0N	73 40W
Pointe-à-la-Hache, U.S.A.	71	29 35N	89 35W
Pointe à Pitre, Guad.	75	16 10N	61 30W
Pointe Noire, Cam.	54	4 48S	12 0E
Poitiers, France	12	46 35N	0 20W
Poitou, Plaine du, France	12	46 30N	0 1W
Pojoaque, U.S.A.	73	35 52N	106 0W
Pokaran, India	32	26 55N	71 55E
Pokataroo, N.S.W.	43	29 30S	148 34E
Pokhara, Nepal	33	28 14N	83 59E
Poko, Zaire	54	3 20N	26 40E
Pokotu, China	37	48 45N	121 58E
Pokpakh, China	39	22 20N	109 45E
Pokrov, U.S.S.R.	25	55 58N	39 10E
Pola (Pula) Y.slav.	20	44 52N	13 52E
Polacca, U.S.A.	73	35 50N	110 27W
Polan, Iran	31	25 30N	61 10E
Poland, st., Europe	16	52 0N	20 0E
Polar Sub-Glacial Basin, Ant.	80	82 0S	115 0E
Polati, Turkey	30	39 36N	32 9E
Polcura, Chile	77	37 10S	71 50W
Polessk, U.S.S.R.	23	54 50N	21 8E
Poli, Cameroon	52	8 34N	12 54E
Poliaigos I., Greece	21	36 45N	24 38E
Policarpo, Argentina	77	54 45S	65 50W
Poligny, France	12	46 50N	5 42E
Polillo I., Philippines	35	14 56N	122 0E
Poliyiros, Greece	21	40 23N	23 25E
Pollachi, India	32	10 35N	77 0E
Pollaphuca Res., Ire.	11	53 8N	6 37W
Pollensa, Spain	17	39 54N	3 2E
Pollock, U.S.A.	70	45 58N	100 9W

	MAP		
Polnovat, U.S.S.R.	26	63 50N	66 5 E
Polo, U.S.A.	68	42 0N	89 38W
Polotsk, U.S.S.R.	25	55 30N	28 50 E
Polson, U.S.A.	72	47 43N	114 13W
Poltava, Ukraine, U.S.S.R.	25	49 35N	34 35 E
Polyarney, U.S.S.R.	22	69 8N	33 20 E
Pombal, Brazil	79	6 55 S	37 50W
Pombal, Portugal	17	39 55N	8 40W
Pombetsu, Japan	36	43 5N	143 35 E
Pomene, Mozambique	56	22 45 S	35 20 E
Pomeroy, N. Ireland	11	54 37N	6 55W
Pomeroy, Ohio, U.S.A.	68	39 0N	82 0W
Pomeroy, Wash., U.S.A.	72	46 29N	117 32W
Pomona, Queensland	43	26 20 S	152 51 E
Pomona, U.S.A.	73	34 3N	117 48W
Pomona, S.W. Africa	57	27 9 S	15 18 E
Pompano, U.S.A.	69	26 12N	80 6W
Pompeys Pillar, U.S.A.	72	46 0N	107 59W
Pompora, Zambia	56	12 31 S	24 57 E
Ponas, C., N. Guinea	42	4 10 S	151 30 E
Ponask L., Canada	62	54 0N	92 30W
Ponass L., Canada	65	52 10N	104 0W
Ponca, U.S.A.	70	42 37N	98 41W
Ponca City, U.S.A.	71	36 40N	97 5W
Ponce, Puerto. Rico	75	18 0N	66 50W
Ponchatoula, U.S.A.	71	30 28N	90 28W
Pond Inlet, Canada	61	72 30N	75 0W
Pondicherry, India	32	11 59N	79 50 E
Ponds, I. of, Canada	63	53 27N	55 52W
Ponferrada, Spain	17	42 32N	6 35W
Pong Tamale, Ghana	52	9 40N	0 46W
Pongamo, U.S.S.R.	24	65 20N	34 30 E
Pongola & R., Natal	57	27 27 S	32 0 E
Ponnani, India	32	10 45N	79 59 E
Ponnyadaung Range, mts. Burma	33	22 0N	94 10 E
Ponoi, U.S.S.R.	24	67 0N	41 0 E
Ponoi R., U.S.S.R.	24	67 10N	39 0 E
Ponoka, Canada	64	52 35N	113 40W
Ponorogo, Indonesia	34	7 52 S	111 29 E
Pons, France	12	45 35N	0 34W
Pont-à-Mousson, France	12	48 54N	6 1 E
Pont l'Abbé, France	12	47 52N	4 15W
Pont Lafrance, Canada	63	47 40N	64 58W
Pont St. Esprit, France	12	44 16N	4 40 E
Ponta Grossa, Brazil	77	25 0 S	50 10W
Ponta Pora, Brazil	77	22 20 S	55 35W
Pontarlier, France	12	46 54N	6 20 E
Pontchartrain L., U.S.A.	71	30 12N	90 0W
Ponte do Púngüe, Mozambique	56	19 29 S	34 35 E
Ponte Nova, Brazil	79	20 25 S	42 54W
Pontebba, Italy	20	46 30N	13 17 E
Pontecorvo, Italy	20	41 28N	13 40 E
Pontedera, Italy	20	43 40N	10 37 E
Ponteix, Canada	65	49 46N	107 29W
Pontevedra, Spain	17	42 26N	8 40W
Pontiac, Ill., U.S.A.	68	40 50N	88 40W
Pontiac, Mich., U.S.A.	68	42 40N	83 20W
Pontian Kechil, Malaya	34	1 29N	103 23 E
Pontianak, Indonesia	35	0 3 S	109 15 E
Pontin Mts., Turkey	30	40 30N	40 0 E
Pontine Is., Italy	20	40 55N	13 0 E
Pontivy, France	12	48 5N	3 0W
Pontoise, Seine-et-Oise, France	12	49 3N	2 5 E
Pontremoli, Italy	20	44 22N	9 52 E
Ponza I., Italy	20	40 55N	12 57 E
Poole, England	10	50 42N	2 2W
Poona, India	32	18 29N	73 57 E
Pooncarie, N.S.W.	43	33 22 S	143 31 E
Poopalloe L., N.S.W.	43	31 30 S	144 0 E
Poopó L., Bolivia	78	18 30 S	67 35W
Poor Knights Is., N.Z.	46	35 30 S	174 45 E
Poorman, Alaska	59	64 6N	155 48W
Popanyinning, W. Australia	44	32 40 S	117 2 E
Popayán, Colombia	78	2 23N	76 47W
Poperinge, Belgium	13	50 51N	2 42 E
Popigai, U.S.S.R.	27	72 50N	106 0 E
Popilta L., N.S.W.	43	33 5 S	141 41 E
Poplar, U.S.A.	70	48 7N	105 4W
Poplar Bluff, U.S.A.	71	36 45N	90 22W
Poplar Park, Canada	65	50 20N	96 25W
Poplar R., Canada	65	52 45N	97 0W
Poplarville, U.S.A.	71	30 50N	89 31W
Popocatepetl, vol., Mexico	74	19 10N	98 40W
Popokabaka, Zaire	54	5 49 S	16 40 E
Popovo, Bulgaria	21	43 22N	26 14 E
Porali, R., W. Pakistan	31	25 50N	66 27 E
Porangahau, N.Z.	46	40 17 S	176 37 E
Porcher I., Canada	64	53 50N	130 30W
Porcuna, Spain	17	37 53N	4 13W
Porcupine, R., Alaska	65	67 0N	143 0W
Pórdarhyrna, mt., Ice.	22	64 15N	17 32W
Pordenone, Italy	20	45 58N	12 40 E
Porec, Yugoslavia	20	45 14N	13 36 E
Pori (Bjorneborg), Finland	23	61 27N	21 50 E
Porisvatn, L., Iceland	22	64 15N	18 52W
Porjus, Sweden	22	66 57N	19 50 E
Porkkala, Finland	23	60 15N	24 30 E
Porlamar, Venezuela	75	10 50N	63 50W
Porlell, W. Australia	44	26 57 S	118 31 E
Pornic, France	12	47 7N	2 5W
Poronaisk, U.S.S.R.	27	49 20N	143 0 E
Póros I., Greece	21	37 30N	23 30 E
Poroto Mts., Tan.	53	9 0 S	33 20 E
Porrentruy, Switzerland	12	47 24N	7 3 E
Porreta, P., Italy	20	44 2N	10 56 E
Porsangen, Norway	22	70 30N	25 35 E
Porsgrunn, Norway	23	59 10N	9 40 E
Pórshöfn, Iceland	22	66 15N	15 10W
Port Adelaide, S. Australia	43	34 46 S	138 30 E
Port Alberni, Canada	64	49 15N	124 50W
Port Albert, Victoria	43	38 42 S	146 42 E
Port Albert Victor, India	32	21 0N	71 30 E
Port Alexander, Alaska	59	56 13N	134 40W
Port Alfred, Canada	63	48 18N	70 53W
Port Alfred, Cape Prov.	57	33 36 S	26 55 E
Port Allegheny, U.S.A.	68	41 49N	78 17W
Port Allen, U.S.A.	71	30 29N	91 14W
Port Alma, Queensland	42	23 38 S	150 53 E
Port Althorp, Alaska	59	58 10N	136 30W
Port Angeles, U.S.A.	72	48 0N	123 30W
Port Antonio, Jamaica	75	18 10N	76 30W
Port Aransas, U.S.A.	71	27 49N	97 5W
Port Armstrong, Alaska	64	56 10N	134 40W
Port Arthur, Canada	62	48 25N	89 10W
Port Arthur (Lushun), China	38	38 50N	121 15 E
Port Arthur, U.S.A.	71	30 0N	94 0W
Port Augusta, S. Australia	43	32 30 S	137 45 E
Port au Port B., Can.	63	48 40N	58 50W
Port au Prince, Haiti	75	18 40N	72 20W
Port Austin, U.S.A.	68	44 3N	82 59W
Port aux Basques, Can.	63	47 32N	59 8W
Port Baker, Alaska	59	56 15N	133 15W
Port Beaufort, Cape Province	57	34 23 S	20 51 E
Port Bell, Uganda	53	0 20N	32 40 E
Port Blandford, Canada	63	48 30N	53 50W
Port Bolivar, U.S.A.	71	29 19N	94 45W
Port Bradshaw, N. Territory	41	12 20 S	136 52 E
Port Broughton, S. Australia	43	33 36 S	137 54 E
Port Burwell, Canada	62	42 40N	80 40W
Port Canning, India	33	22 17N	88 48 E
Port Cartier, Canada	63	50 5N	66 52W
Port Chalmers, N.Z.	47	45 49 S	170 38 E
Port Charles, N.Z.	46	36 33 S	175 30 E
Port Chester, U.S.A.	68	41 0N	73 41W
Port Clements, Canada	64	53 40N	132 10W
Port Clinton, Queens.	42	22 30 S	150 46 E
Port Clinton, U.S.A.	68	41 30N	83 0W
Port Colborne, Canada	62	42 50N	79 10W
Port Coquitlam, Can.	64	49 20N	122 45W
Port Cornwallis, Andaman Is., India	33	13 30N	93 0 E
Port Davey B., Tasmania	43	43 16 S	145 55 E
Port de Bouc, France	12	43 25N	4 58 E
Port de Paix, Haiti	75	19 50N	72 50W
Port Denison (Bowen), Queensland	42	20 2 S	148 12 E
Port Dickson, Malaya	34	2 30N	101 49 E
Port Elgin, Canada	62	44 25N	81 25W
Port Elizabeth, Cape Province	57	33 58 S	25 40 E
Port Elliot, S. Australia	43	35 27 S	138 46 E
Port Essington, Canada	64	54 10N	129 55W
Port Etienne, Maur.	50	21 0N	17 0W
Port Fairy, Victoria	43	38 13 S	142 14 E
Port Fitzroy, N.Z.	46	36 9 S	175 22 E
Port Francqui, Zaire	54	4 17 S	20 47 E
Port Gentil, Gabon	54	0 47 S	8 40 E
Port Germein, S. Australia	43	33 0 S	137 58 E
Port Gibson, U.S.A.	71	31 58N	91 0W
Port Hamilton, Korea	36	33 45N	127 30 E
Port Harcourt, Nigeria	52	4 40N	7 10 E
Port Hardy, Canada	64	50 41N	127 30W
Port Heiden, Alaska	59	57 0N	158 40W
Port Henry, U.S.A.	68	44 0N	73 30W
Port Herald, Malawi	56	16 55 S	35 12 E
Port Hood, Canada	63	46 0N	61 32W
Port Hope, Canada	62	44 0N	78 20W
Port Hunter, N.S.W.	43	32 52 S	152 15 E
Port Huron, U.S.A.	68	42 59N	82 23W
Port Isabel, U.S.A.	71	26 14N	97 10W
Port Jackson, N.S.W.	43	33 53 S	151 12 E
Port Kembla, N.S.W.	43	34 29 S	150 56 E
Port Laoise, Ireland	11	53 2N	7 20W
Port Lavaca, U.S.A.	71	28 39N	96 37W
Port Lincoln, S. Austral.	45	34 42 S	135 52 E
Port Loko, Sierra Leone	52		Inset
Port Louis, France	12	47 42N	3 22W
Port MacDonnell, S. Australia	43	37 55 S	140 39 E
Port Macquarie, N.S.W.	43	31 25 S	152 54 E
Port Maria, Jamaica	75	18 30N	76 50W
Port Mellon, Canada	64	49 32N	123 31W
Port Menier, Canada	63	49 51N	64 15W
Port Moller, Alaska	59	55 58N	161 0W
Port Morant, Jamaica	75	17 50N	76 30W
Port Moresby, Papua	42	9 24 S	147 8 E
Port Mouton, Canada	63	43 58N	64 50W
Port Musgrave, Queens.	42	11 55 S	141 50 E
Port Nelson, Canada	65	57 5N	92 56W
Port Nicholson, N.Z.	46	41 20 S	174 52 E
Port Nolloth, Cape Prov.	57	29 17 S	16 52 E
Port O'Connor, U.S.A.	71	28 30N	96 28W
Port of Spain, Trinidad	75	10 40N	61 20W
Port Orchard, U.S.A.	72	47 31N	122 44W
Port Orford, U.S.A.	72	42 48N	124 30W
Port Pegasus, N.Z.	47	47 12 S	167 41 E
Port Perry, Canada	62	44 6N	78 56W
Port Phillip B., Victoria	43	38 0 S	145 0 E
Port Pirie, S. Australia	43	33 10 S	137 58 E
Port Pleasant, U.S.A.	68	40 5N	74 4W
Port Radium, Canada	60	66 10N	117 40W
Port Renfrew Canada	64	48 30N	124 20W
Port Rowan, Canada	62	42 40N	80 30W
Port Royal, Jamaica	75	18 0N	76 52W
Port Said (Bur Sa'id), Egypt	51	31 16N	32 18 E
Port St. Joe, U.S.A.	69	29 49N	85 20W
Port St. Johns, Cape Province	57	31 38 S	29 33 E
Port St. Louis, France	12	43 23N	4 50 E
Port St. Servain, Canada	63	51 21N	58 0W
Port Saunders, Canada	63	50 40N	57 18W
Port Shepstone, Natal	57	30 44 S	30 28 E
Port Simpson, Canada	64	54 30N	130 20W
Port Stanley, Canada	62	42 40N	81 10W
Port Stephens B., N.S.W.	43	32 38 S	152 12 E
Port Sudan, Sudan	51	19 32N	37 9 E
Port Swettenham, Malaya	34	3 0N	101 23 E
Port Talbot, Canada	62	42 40N	81 22W
Port Townsend, U.S.A.	72	48 0N	122 50W
Port Vendres, France	12	42 32N	3 8 E
Port Wakefield, S. Australia	43	34 8 S	138 5 E
Port Washington, U.S.A.	70	43 25N	87 52W
Port Weld, Malaya	34	4 50N	100 38 E
Portachuelo, Bolivia	78	17 10 S	63 20W
Portadown, N. Ireland	11	54 27N	6 26W
Portaferry, N. Ireland	11	54 23N	5 32W
Portage, Canada	63	46 40N	65 4W
Portage, U.S.A.	70	43 31N	89 25W
Portage la Prairie, Canada	65	49 58N	98 18W
Portageville, U.S.A.	71	36 28N	89 11W
Portalegre, Portugal	17	39 19N	7 25W
Portales, U.S.A.	71	34 74	103 26W
Portarlington, Ireland	11	53 10N	7 10W
Porter L., Canada	65	61 30N	108 0W
Porterville, Cape Prov.	57	33 0 S	18 57 E
Porterville, U.S.A.	73	36 5N	119 0W
Porthill, U.S.A.	72	49 0N	116 30W
Portei Mouth, Rumania	21	44 40N	29 0 E
Portland, Canada	64	44 42N	76 11W
Portland, Me., U.S.A.	69	43 40N	70 15W
Portland, Mich., U.S.A.	68	42 52N	84 58W
Portland, N.S.W.	43	33 22 S	150 0 E
Portland, Oreg., U.S.A.	72	45 25N	122 40W
Portland B., Victoria	43	38 15 S	141 45 E
Portland, Bill of, Eng.	10	50 31N	2 27W
Portland C., Tasmania	43	40 45 S	148 0 E
Portland I., N.Z.	46	39 15 S	177 54 E
Portland Prom, Canada	61	59 0N	78 0W
Portland Pt., Jamaica	75		Inset
Portneuf, Canada	63	46 43N	71 55W
Porto. *See* Oporto, Portugal	17		
Porto Alegre, Rio Grande do Sul, Braz.	77	30 5 S	51 3W
Porto Alegre, Mato Grosso, Brazil	79	21 40 S	53 30W
Porto Alexandre, Angola	55	15 55 S	11 55 E
Porto Amboim, Angola	55	10 50 S	13 50 E
Porto Amelia, Mozam.	55	30 0 S	40 42 E
Porto Artur, Brazil	79	13 0 S	54 40W
Porto 15 de Novembro, Brazil	77	21 45 S	52 20W
Porto de Coimbra, Bolivia	79	20 0 S	58 0W
Porto de Moz, Brazil	79	1 40 S	52 10W
Porto Empédocle, Sicily	79	37 18N	13 30 E
Porto Franco, Brazil	79	9 45 S	47 0W
Porto Grande, Brazil	79	0 40N	51 30W
Porto Guassú, Brazil	77	22 0 S	54 30W
Porto Murtinho, Brazil	79	21 45 S	57 55W
Porto Nacional, Brazil	79	10 40 S	48 30W
Porto Novo, Dahomey	52	6 28N	2 42 E
Porto Recanati, Italy	20	43 26N	13 40 E
Porto Santo I., Madeira Is.	50	33 45 S	16 25W
Porto Seguro, Brazil	79	16 20 S	39 0W
Porto Tibirica, Brazil	77	21 50 S	52 20W
Porto Tolle, Italy	20	44 57N	12 20 E
Porto Torres, Italy	20	40 50N	8 23 E
Porto Uniao, Brazil	77	26 10 S	51 10W
Porto Válter, Brazil	78	8 5 S	72 45W
Porto-Vecchio, Corsica	12	41 37N	9 19 E
Porto Velho, Brazil	78	8 50 S	63 55W
Porto Xavier, Brazil	77	23 20 S	53 50W
Portobello, Panama	78	9 39N	79 40W
Portoferraio, Italy	20	45 50N	10 20 E
Portola, U.S.A.	72	39 46N	120 29W
Portomaggiore, Italy	20	44 41N	11 47 E
Portoscuso, Italy	20	39 12N	8 22 E
Portoviejo, Ecuador	78	1 0 S	80 20W
Portpatrick, Scotland	10	54 50N	5 7W
Portree, Scotland	10	57 25N	6 11W
Portrush, N. Ireland	11	55 13N	6 40W
Portsmouth, Dominica, Leeward Is.	75		Inset
Portsmouth, England	10	50 48N	1 6W
Portsmouth, Ohio, U.S.A.	68	38 45N	83 0W
Portsmouth, Va., U.S.A.	68	36 50N	76 20W
Portstewart, N. Ireland	11	55 12N	6 43W
Portugal, Europe	17	40 0N	7 0W
Portugalete, Spain	17	43 19N	3 4W
Portugalia, Angola	54	7 20 S	21 10 E
Portuguesa R., Ven.	78	9 0N	68 20W
Portuguese Timor, E. Indies	35	8 0 S	126 30 E
Portuma, Ireland	11	53 5N	8 12W
Porvenir, Chile	77	53 10 S	70 30W
Posadas, Spain	17	37 47N	5 11W
Posados, Argentina	77	27 30 S	56 0W
Poschiavo, Switzerland	15	46 19N	10 4 E
Poseh, China	39	23 50N	106 0 E
Posht Kuh, dist., Iran	30	33 0N	47 30 E
Poso, Indonesia	35	1 20 S	120 55 E
Posse, Brazil	79	14 8 S	46 25W
Possum Kingdom Res., U.S.A.	71	32 55N	98 30W
Post, U.S.A.	71	33 9N	101 24W
Post Falls, U.S.A.	72	47 44N	116 58W
Poste Maurice Cortier, Algeria	50	22 20N	1 15 E
Postiljon I., Indonesia	35	6 30 S	118 50 E
Postmasburg, Cape Province	57	28 18 S	23 5 E
Postojna, Yugoslavia	20	45 46N	14 12 E
Potalla Cr., Queensland	42	15 8 S	142 58 E
Potapovo, U.S.S.R.	26	68 55N	86 5 E
Potchefstroom, Trans.	57	26 41 S	27 7 E
Poteau, U.S.A.	71	35 3N	94 36W
Poteet, U.S.A.	71	29 2N	98 33W
Potenza, Italy	20	40 40N	15 50 E
Potes, Spain	17	43 15N	4 42W
Potgietersrus, Transvaal	57	24 10 S	29 3 E
Poti, Afghanistan	31	31 55N	65 53 E
Poti, U.S.S.R.	24	42 10N	41 38 E
Potimao, Portugal	17	37 10N	8 31W
Potiskum, Nigeria	52	11 40N	11 3 E
Potomac R., U.S.A.	68	39 40N	78 25W
Potosi, Bolivia	78	19 38 S	65 50W
Potow, China	38	38 15N	116 31 E
Potrerillos, Mt., Chile	77	26 20 S	69 30W
Potsdam, Germany	14	52 23N	13 4 E
Potsdam, U.S.A.	68	44 40N	74 59W
Potter, U.S.A.	70	41 16N	103 17W
Pottstown, U.S.A.	68	40 17N	75 40W
Pottsville, U.S.A.	68	40 39N	76 12W
Pottuvil, Sri Lanka	32	6 50N	81 50 E
Pouce Coupé, Canada	64	55 40N	120 10W
Poughkeepsie, U.S.A.	68	41 40N	73 57W
Pouso Alegre, Brazil	79	11 55 S	57 0W
Povenets, U.S.S.R.	24	62 50N	34 50 E
Poverty Bay, N.Z.	46	38 43 S	178 2 E
Povóa de Varzim, Portugal	17	41 25N	8 46W
Povorino, U.S.S.R.	25	51 12N	42 28 E
Powassan, Canada	62	46 5N	79 25W
Powder R., U.S.A.	70	46 20N	105 10W
Powell, U.S.A.	72	44 45N	108 45W
Powell's Creek, N. Terr., Australia	41	18 6 S	133 46 E
Powers, Mich., U.S.A.	70	45 40N	87 32W
Powers, Oreg., U.S.A.	72	42 53N	124 3W
Powers Lake, U.S.A.	70	48 35N	102 35W
Poyang, China	39	29 1N	116 33 E
Poyang Ho L., China	39	29 0N	116 8 E
Požarevac, Yugoslavia	21	44 35N	21 18 E
Pozega, Yugoslavia	21	45 21N	17 41 E
Poznán, Poland	16	52 25N	17 0 E
Pozo Almonte, Chile	78	20 10 S	69 50W
Pozoblanco, Spain	17	38 24N	4 51W
Pra R., Ghana	52	5 30N	1 38W
Prachin Buri, Thailand	34	14 5N	161 23 E
Prachuap Khiri Kham, Thailand	34	11 50N	99 49 E
Prades, France	12	42 38N	2 23 E
Prado, Brazil	79	17 20 S	39 20W
Prague, Czechoslovakia	16	50 5N	14 22 E
Praha. *See* Prague	16		
Prahova R., Rumania	21	44 50N	25 50 E
Prahovo, Yugoslavia	21	44 18N	22 39 E
Praid, Rumania	21	46 32N	25 10 E
Prainha, Amazonas, Brazil	78	7 10 S	60 30W
Prainha, Para, Brazil	78	1 45 S	53 30W
Prairie, Queensland	42	20 50 S	144 35 E
Prairie City, U.S.A.	72	44 58N	118 42W
Prairie du Chien, U.S.A.	70	43 0N	91 6W
Prámanda, Greece	21	39 32N	21 8 E
Prampram, Ghana	52	5 39N	0 7 E
Prang, Ghana	52	8 1N	0 56W
Pranhita R., India	32	19 0N	80 0 E
Prata, Minas Gerais, Brazil	79	19 25 S	49 0W
Prata, Para, Brazil	79	1 10 S	47 35W
Pratigau Valley, Switz.	15	46 55N	9 45 E
Prato, Italy	20	43 53N	11 5 E
Pratt, U.S.A.	71	37 40N	99 0W

	MAP		
Pratteln, Switz.	15	47 32N	7 42 E
Prattville, U.S.A.	69	32 30N	36 28W
Pravia, Spain	17	43 30N	6 12W
Preeceville, Canada	65	52 0N	102 50W
Prelate, Canada	65	50 50N	109 25W
Premier Downs, W. Australia	45	30 32 S	127 0 E
Premont, U.S.A.	71	27 19N	98 8W
Prentice, U.S.A.	70	45 30N	90 16W
Prenzlau, Germany	14	53 19N	13 51 E
Preparis Chan., N. & S., India	33	15 0N	94 0 E
Preparis I., India	33	15 0N	93 30 E
Přerov, Czechoslovakia	16	49 28N	17 27 E
Prescott, Canada	62	44 45N	75 30W
Prescott, Ariz., U.S.A.	73	34 30N	112 30W
Prescott, Ark., U.S.A.	71	33 47N	93 27W
Preservation Inlet, N.Z.	47	46 8 S	166 35 E
Presho, U.S.A.	70	43 58N	99 55W
Presidente de la Plaza, Argentina	77	27 0 S	60 0W
Presidente Epitacio, Brazil	79	21 50 S	52 20W
Presidente Hermes, Brazil	78	11 0 S	61 55W
Presidente Murtinho, Brazil	79	15 45 S	51 25W
Presidente Prudente, Brazil	77	22 5 S	51 25W
Pres. R. Peña, Arg.	77	26 48 S	60 20W
Presidio, U.S.A.	71	29 30N	104 20W
Preslav, Bulgaria	21	43 10N	26 52 E
Prešov, Czechoslovakia	16	48 58N	21 15 E
Prespa, L., Yugoslavia	21	40 50N	21 0 E
Prestbakki, Iceland	22	63 50N	18 2W
Prestea, Ghana	52	5 22N	2 7W
Preston, England	10	53 46N	2 42W
Preston, Idaho, U.S.A.	72	42 0N	112 0W
Preston, Minn., U.S.A.	70	43 39N	92 1W
Preston, Nev., U.S.A.	73	38 58N	115 2W
Preston, C., Western Australia	44	20 50 S	116 20 E
Prestwick, Scotland	10	55 30N	4 38W
Pretoria, Transvaal	57	25 44 S	28 12 E
Préveza, Greece	21	38 57N	20 47 E
Prey Veng., Cambodia	34	11 35N	105 29 E
Pribilov Is., Bering Sea	5	56 0N	170 0W
Příbram, C.Slov.	16	49 41N	14 2 E
Priboj, Yugoslavia	21	43 35N	19 32 E
Price, U.S.A.	73	39 30N	110 40W
Price I., Canada	64	52 25N	128 40W
Prichalnaya, U.S.S.R.	25	48 57N	44 33 E
Prieska, Cape Prov.	57	29 40 S	22 42 E
Priest, L., U.S.A.	72	48 33N	116 58W
Priest River. U.S.A.	72	48 11N	116 58W
Prijedor, Yugoslavia	20	44 58N	16 41 E
Prilep, Yugoslavia	21	41 21N	21 37 E
Priluki, U.S.S.R.	25	50 30N	32 15 E
Primorsk, U.S.S.R.	23	60 25N	28 45 E
Primorsko-Akhtarskaya, U.S.S.R.	25	46 2N	38 10 E
Primrose L., Canada	65	54 55N	109 40W
Prince Albert, Canada	65	53 15N	105 50W
Prince Albert, Cape Province	57	33 12 S	22 2 E
Prince Albert National Park, Canada	65	54 0N	106 10W
Prince Albert Pen., Can.	60	72 0N	116 0W
Prince Albert Sd., Can.	60	70 30N	114 0W
Prince Charles I., Can.	61	68 0N	76 0W
Prince Edward I., Can.	63	46 20N	63 0W
Prince Edward Is., Rep. of South Africa	5	46 25 S	37 30 E
Prince George, Canada	64	53 50N	122 50W
Prince of Wales C., Alaska	60	65 40N	168 0W
Prince of Wales I., Alas.	59	55 30N	132 30W
Prince of Wales I., Can.	60	73 0N	99 0W
Prince of Wales I., Queensland	42	10 35 S	142 0 E
Prince Patrick I., Can.	58	77 0N	120 0W
Prince Rupert, Canada	64	54 20N	130 20W
Prince William Sound, Alaska	59	60 30N	143 30W
Princes Town, Trinidad	75		Inset
Princess Ra., W. Austral.	44	26 10 S	121 45 E
Princess Charlotte B., Queensland	42	14 15 S	144 0 E
Princess Martha Coast, Ant.	80	72 0 S	5 0W
Princess May Ra., W. Australia	44	15 30 S	125 30 E
Princess Royal I., Can.	64	53 0N	128 40W
Princeton, Canada	64	49 27N	120 30W
Princeton, Ill., U.S.A.	70	41 20N	89 28W
Princeton, Ind., U.S.A.	68	38 20N	87 35W
Princeton, Ky., U.S.A.	68	37 6N	87 55W
Princeton, N.J., U.S.A.	68	40 18N	74 40W
Princeton, W., Va., U.S.A.	68	37 21N	81 8W
Princhester, Queens.	42	22 59 S	150 1 E
Principe Chan., Canada	64	53 20N	130 0W
Principe da Beira, Brazil	78	12 20 S	64 30W
Prineville, U.S.A.	72	44 20N	120 56W
Priozersk, U.S.S.R.	23	61 8N	30 10 E
Pripyat, R., U.S.S.R.	25	51 30N	30 0 E
Pripyat Marshes, U.S.S.R.	25	52 0N	28 30 E

	MAP		
Priština, Yugoslavia	21	42 40N	21 13 E
Pritchard, U.S.A.	69	30 47N	88 5W
Pritzwalk, Germany	14	53 10N	12 10 E
Privas, France	12	44 45N	4 37 E
Privolzhye, U.S.S.R.	25	52 52N	48 33 E
Priyutnoye, U.S.S.R.	25	47 12N	43 30 E
Prizren, Yugoslavia	21	42 13N	20 45 E
Probolinggo, Indonesia	34	7 46 S	113 13 E
Proddatur, India	32	14 45N	78 30 E
Progreso, Mexico	74	21 20N	89 40W
Prokhladny, U.S.S.R.	25	43 50N	44 2 E
Prokopyevsk, U.S.S.R.	26	54 0N	87 3 E
Prokuplje, Yugoslavia	21	43 16N	21 36 E
Proletarskaya, U.S.S.R.	25	46 42N	41 50 E
Prome, Burma	34	18 45N	95 30 E
Prophet R., Canada	64	58 0N	123 0W
Propriá, Brazil	79	10 15 S	37 0W
Propriano, Corsica	12	41 41N	8 52 E
Proserpine, Queensland	42	20 21 S	148 36 E
Prosser, U.S.A.	72	46 13N	119 48W
Prostějov, C.Slov.	16	49 30N	17 9 E
Proston, Queensland	43	26 14 S	151 32 E
Protection, U.S.A.	71	37 12N	99 28W
Protem, Cape Province	57	34 15 S	20 4 E
Provence, prov., France	12	43 40N	4 46 E
Providence, Ky., U.S.A.	68	37 25N	87 46W
Providence, R.I., U.S.A.	68	41 41N	71 15W
Providence Bay, Can.	62	45 41N	82 15W
Providence C., N.Z.	47	45 59 S	166 29 E
Providence Mts., U.S.A.	73	34 50N	115 30W
Province Wellesley, Malaya	34	5 15N	100 20 E
Provincetown, U.S.A.	69	42 5N	70 11W
Provincial Cannery, Canada	64	51 53N	127 35W
Provins, France	12	48 33N	3 15 E
Provo, U.S.A.	72	40 10N	111 45W
Provost, Canada	65	52 25N	110 20W
Prudhomme, Canada	65	52 20N	105 55W
Prudnik, Poland	16	50 20N	17 38 E
Prut, R., Rumania–U.S.S.R.	21	46 3N	28 10 E
Prydz Bay, Antarctica	80	68 0 S	75 0 E
Pryor, U.S.A.	71	36 17N	95 26W
Przemyśl, Poland	16	49 48N	22 48 E
Przeworsk, Poland	16	50 4N	22 30 E
Przhevalsk, U.S.S.R.	26	42 30N	78 20 E
Psarà I., Greece	21	38 37N	25 38 E
Psel R., U.S.S.R.	25	49 25N	33 50 E
Pskov, U.S.S.R.	23	57 50N	28 25 E
Ptich, U.S.S.R.	25	52 30N	28 45 E
Ptuj, Yugoslavia	20	46 28N	15 50 E
Puan, Argentina	77	37 30 S	63 0W
Puan, China	39	25 45N	105 1 E
Pubnico, Canada	63	43 47N	65 50W
Pucalpa, Peru	78	8 25 S	74 30W
Pucheng, China	39	28 0N	118 30 E
Puchi, China	39	29 45N	113 50 E
Puding C., Indonesia	35	3 35 S	112 0 E
Pudukkotai, India	32	10 28N	78 47 E
Puebla, Mexico	74	19 0N	98 10W
Puebla, Spain	17	42 21N	7 16W
Puebla, st., Mexico	74	18 30N	98 0W
Pueblo, U.S.A.	70	38 20N	104 40W
Pueblo Bonito, U.S.A.	73	36 7N	107 54W
Pueblo Hundido, Chile	77	26 20 S	69 30W
Pueblnouevo, Spain	17	38 18N	5 18W
Puelches, Argentina	77	38 5 S	66 0W
Puente Àlto, Chile	77	33 35 S	70 50W
Puerto Cabello, Ven.	78	10 28N	68 1W
Puente Genil, Spain	17	37 22N	4 47W
Puentearas, Spain	17	42 10N	8 28W
Puerco R., U.S.A.	73	35 20N	109 40W
Puerh, China	37	23 0N	100 50 E
Puerte de Cabras, Canary Is.	50	28 50N	13 45W
Puerto Aisen, Chile	77	45 10 S	73 0W
Puerto Armuelles, Pan.	75	8 20N	83 10W
Puerto Asis, Colombia	78	0 30N	76 30W
Puerto Ayacucho, Ven.	78	5 35N	67 30W
Puerto Barrios, Guat.	74	15 40N	88 40W
Puerto Bermudez, Peru	78	10 20 S	75 0W
Puerto Berrio, Colombia	78	6 30N	74 30W
Puerto Bolivar, Ecuador	78	3 10 S	79 55W
Puerto Cabello, Ven.	75	10 30N	68 0W
Puerto Cabezas, Nic.	75	14 0N	83 30W
Puerto Carreño, Col.	78	6 0N	67 30W
Puerto Casado, Par.	79	22 19 S	57 56W
Puerto Castilla, Hond.	75	16 0N	86 0W
Puerto Chala, Peru	78	15 56N	74 4W
Puerto Chicama, Peru	78	7 45 S	79 20W
Puetro Coig, Argentina	77	50 55 S	69 15W
Puerto Colombia, Col.	78	11 0N	75 0W
Puerto Córdoba, Col.	78	1 15 S	69 50W
Puerto Cortés, Costa Rica	75	8 20N	82 20W
Puerto Córtes, Hond.	74	15 51N	88 0W
Puerto Cumarebo, Ven.	78	11 29N	69 21W
Puerto de Hierro, Ven.	78	10 38N	62 5W
Puerto de la Cruz, Ven.	78	10 13N	64 38W
Puerto de Morelos, Mexico	74	20 49N	86 52W
Puerto de Sta. Maria, Spain	17	36 35N	6 15W
Puerto Eten, Peru	78	7 0 S	79 50W
Puerto Heath, Bolivia	78	12 25 S	68 45W
Puerto la Cruz, Ven.	75	10 15N	64 25W
Puerto Liberdad, Mex.	74	29 55N	112 41W

	MAP		
Puerto Madryn, Arg.	77	42 48 S	65 4W
Puerto Maldonado, Peru	78	12 30 S	69 10W
Puerto Montt, Chile	77	41 20 S	73 0W
Puerto Natales, Chile	77	51 50 S	72 30W
Puerto Padre, Cuba	75	21 13N	76 35W
Puerto Paez, Ven.	78	6 14N	67 26W
Puerto Peñasco, Mexico	74	31 20N	113 40W
Puerto Pinasco, Par.	77	22 30 S	57 50W
Puerto Piramide, Arg.	77	42 35 S	64 20W
Puerto Piritu, Ven.	78	10 5N	65 0W
Puerto Plata, Dom. Rep.	75	19 40N	70 40W
Puerto Princesa, Philippines	35	9 55N	118 55 E
Puerto Quellon, Chile	77	43 10 S	74 0W
Puerto Quepas, Costa Rica	75	9 29N	84 6W
Puerto Quijarro, Brazil	79	17 48 S	58 0W
Puerto Real, Spain	17	36 33N	6 12W
Puerto Rico, W. Indies	75	18 10N	66 30W
Puerto Saavedra, Chile	77	38 40 S	73 30W
Puerto Sastre, Par.	79	22 25 S	57 55W
Puerto Suarez, Bolivia	79	18 58 S	57 52W
Puerto Vallarta, Mexico	74	20 20N	105 15W
Puerto Varas, Chile	77	41 10 S	73 0W
Puerto Villamizar, Col.	78	8 25N	72 30W
Puerto Wilches, Col.	78	7 25N	73 50W
Puertollano, Spain	17	38 43N	4 7W
Pueyrredón L., Arg.	77	47 20 S	72 0W
Pugachev, U.S.S.R.	25	52 0N	48 55 E
Puge, Tanzania	53	4 44 S	33 20 E
Puger Kulon, Indonesia	34	8 20 S	113 27 E
Puget Sd., U.S.A.	72	47 15N	123 30W
Puget Théniers, France	12	43 58N	6 53 E
Pugu, Tanzania	53	6 55 S	39 4 E
Puha, New Zealand	46	38 27 S	177 51 E
Puigcerda, Spain	17	42 24N	1 50 E
Pujehun, Sierra Leone	52	7 19N	11 48W
Pujon Res., N. Korea	36	40 43N	127 34 E
Pukaki, New Zealand	47	44 5 S	170 11 E
Pukaki L., New Zealand	47	44 5 S	170 1 E
Pukatawagan, Canada	65	55 45N	101 20W
Pukchin, N. Korea	36	40 17N	125 32 E
Pukchong, N. Korea	36	40 16N	128 20 E
Pukë, Albania	21	42 2N	19 53 E
Pukearuhe, N.Z.	46	38 55 S	174 31 E
Pukekohe, N.Z.	46	37 12 S	174 55 E
Puketeraki Ra., N.Z.	47	42 58 S	172 13 E
Puketoi Range, N.Z.	46	40 30 S	176 8 E
Pukow, China	39	32 15N	118 45 E
Pula (Pola), Yugoslavia	20	44 54N	13 57 E
Pulantien, China	38	39 25N	122 0 E
Pulaski, N.Y., U.S.A.	68	43 32N	76 9W
Pulaski, Tenn., U.S.A.	69	35 10N	87 0W
Pulaski, Va., U.S.A.	68	37 4N	80 49W
Pulau Tioman, Malaya	34	2 50N	104 10 E
Pulawy, Poland	16	51 23N	21 59 E
Pulgaon, India	32	20 44N	78 21 E
Pul-i-Khumri, Afghan.	31	35 53N	68 47 E
Pulicat L., India	32	13 40N	80 15 E
Pullman, U.S.A.	72	46 45N	117 10W
Pulmakong, Ghana	52	11 5N	0 0
Pulo Anna I., Pac. Oc.	35	3 47N	132 2 E
Pultusk, Poland	16	52 43N	21 6 E
Puluntohai (Bulun Tokhai), China	37	47 4N	87 20 E
Puna I., Ecuador	78	2 55 S	80 5W
Puna de Atacama, Arg.	77	25 0 S	67 0W
Punakha, India	33	27 30N	90 0 E
Punata, Bolivia	78	17 25 S	65 50W
Punch, Kashmir	32	33 48N	74 4 E
Punda Maria, Transvaal	57	22 40 S	31 5 E
Pundahar, Mozambique	53	10 55 S	40 8 E
Pungsan, N. Korea	36	40 50N	128 14 E
Púngüè R., Mozambique	56	18 45 S	33 50 E
Punjab, st., India	32	31 0N	75 0 E
Punk I., Canada	65	51 15N	96 40W
Puno, Peru	78	15 55 S	70 3W
Punta Alta, Argentina	77	38 50 S	61 58W
Punta Arenas, Chile	77	53 0 S	71 0W
Punta de Diaz, Chile	77	28 0 S	70 45W
Punta Gorda British Honduras	74	16 10N	88 45W
Punta Gorda, U.S.A.	69	26 55N	82 0W
Puntarenas, Costa Rica	78	10 0N	84 50W
Punxsutawney, U.S.A.	68	40 56N	79 0W
Punyü, China	39	22 58N	113 17 E
Puquios, Chile	78	18 0 S	69 50W
Pur R., U.S.S.R.	26	65 30N	77 40 E
Purace, vol., Colombia	78	2 20N	76 20W
Purari, R., Papua	42	7 0 S	145 0 E
Purcel, U.S.A.	71	35 0N	97 28W
Purdy, Is., N. Guinea	42	2 58 S	146 0 E
Puri, India	33	19 50N	85 58 E
Purificacion, Mexico	74	19 40N	104 50W
Purisima, Mexico	74	26 10N	112 10W
Purli, India	32	18 50N	76 35 E
Purmerend, Neth.	13	52 30N	4 58 E
Purnamoota, N.S.W.	43	31 36 S	141 26 E
Purnea, India	33	25 45N	87 31 E
Pursat, Cambodia	34	12 34N	103 50 E
Puruktjau, Indonesia	35	0 35 S	114 35 E
Purulia, India	33	23 17N	86 33 E
Purus, R., Brazil	78	5 25 S	64 0W
Purvomai, Bulgaria	21	42 8N	25 17 E
Purwakarta, Java, Indonesia	34	6 33 S	107 27 E
Purwodadi, Java, Indonesia	34	7 7 S	110 55 E

	MAP		
Purwodadi, Java, Indonesia	34	7 51 S	110 0 E
Purworedjo, Java, Indonesia	34	7 46 S	110 0 E
Pusad, India	32	19 56N	77 36 E
Pusan, Korea	36	35 5N	129 0 E
Pushchino, U.S.S.R	27	54 20N	158 10 E
Pushkin, U.S.S.R.	25	59 45N	30 25 E
Pushkino, U.S.S.R.	25	51 19N	46 55 E
Puskitamika L., Can.	62	49 20N	76 30W
Putao (Fort Hertz), Burma	33	27 28N	97 30 E
Putahow, L., Canada	65	59 52N	101 28W
Putaruru, New Zealand	46	38 3 S	175 46 E
Putien, China	39	25 28N	119 0 E
Putignano, Italy	20	40 50N	17 5 E
Putorino, New Zealand	46	39 4 S	177 9 E
Putsonderwater, Cape Province	57	29 9 S	21 51 E
Puttalam, Sri Lanka	32	8 4N	79 55 E
Putten, Netherlands	13	52 16N	53 37 E
Putumayo R., Colombia	78	2 20 S	70 30W
Putussibau, Mt., Indon.	35	0 45N	113 50 E
Puwokerto, Indonesia	34	7 25 S	109 15 E
Puy-de-Dôme, France	12	45 46N	2 57 E
Puyallup, U.S.A.	72	47 10N	122 22W
Puyang, China	38	35 40N	114 58 E
Puysegur Pt., N.Z.	47	46 10 S	166 39 E
Pweto, Zaire	54	8 30 S	28 59 E
Pwllheli, Wales	10	52 54N	4 26W
Pya L., U.S.S.R.	22	66 8N	31 22 E
Pyandzh (Oxus) R., Afghanistan	31	38 30N	71 0 E
Pyapon, Burma	33	16 5N	95 50 E
Pyasina R., U.S.S.R.	27	72 30N	90 30 E
Pyatigorsk, U.S.S.R.	25	44 2N	43 0 E
Pyinmana, Burma	34	19 45N	96 20 E
Pykkvibaer, Iceland	22	63 50N	20 40W
Pyongan North, Prov., N. Korea	36	40 0N	125 15 E
Pyongan South, Prov., N. Korea	36	39 25N	126 10 E
Pyongyang City, Prov., N. Korea	36	39 1N	125 44 E
Pyongyang, Korea	36	39 0N	125 30 E
Pyote, U.S.A.	71	31 31N	103 3W
Pyramid L., U.S.A.	72	40 0N	119 30W
Pyrenees, mts., France–Spain	12	42 45N	1 0 E
Pyrton, mt., Western Australia	44	21 47 S	117 18 E
Pyrzyce, Poland	16	53 10N	14 55 E
Pytalovo, U.S.S.R.	25	57 5N	27 55 E
Pyu, Burma	33	18 30N	96 35 E

Q

	MAP		
Qabalan, Jordan	29	32 8N	35 17 E
Qabatiya, Jordan	29	32 25N	35 16 E
Qacha's Nek, Basuto.	57	30 8 S	28 41 E
Qadam, Afghanistan	31	33 2N	66 47 E
Qadhima, Saudi Arabia	30	22 20N	39 13 E
Qai'iya, Si. Arabia	30	26 38N	45 47 E
Qain, Iran	31	33 44N	59 6 E
Qal'at al Mu'azzam, Saudi Arabia	30	27 43N	37 37 E
Qal at Dizah, Iraq	30	36 11N	45 7 E
Qal' at Salih, Iraq	30	31 37N	47 18 E
Qala-i-Kirta, Afghan.	31	32 13N	62 57 E
Qala Nau, Afghanistan	31	35 5N	63 0 E
Qal'at Sura, Saudi Arabia	30	26 0N	38 40 E
Qalqiliya, Jordan	29	32 12N	34 58 E
Qamata, Cape Province	57	31 58 S	27 30 E
Qamruddin Karez, Pakistan	32	31 45N	68 20 E
Qana, Lebanon	29	33 12N	35 17 E
Qandahar, prov., Afg.	32	31 30N	66 30 E
Qara, Egypt	51	29 38N	26 30 E
Qara Tepe, Iraq	30	34 25N	45 0 E
Qārah, Saudi Arabia	30	29 57N	40 7 E
Qareh, R., Iran	30	39 0N	47 30 E
Qasr-e Qand, Iran	31	26 11N	60 43 E
Qarn R., Israel	29	33 3N	35 9 E
Qasr Farafirah, Egypt	51	27 0N	28 1 E
Quataghan, prov., Afg.	32	36 0N	68 45 E
Qatar, Persian Gulf	31	25 30N	51 15 E
Qatif, Saudi Arabia	31	26 30N	50 0 E
Qattara Depression, Egypt	51	29 30N	27 30 E
Qāyen, Iran	31	33 53N	59 5 E
Qazvin, Iran	30	36 18N	49 57 E
Qeshm, Iran	31	27 0N	56 15 E
Qeshm, I., Iran	31	26 50N	55 45 E
Qeisari, Israel	29	32 30N	34 53 E
Qezel Owzen, Iran	30	37 20N	48 40 E
Qila Safed, Pakistan	32	29 0N	61 30 E
Qila Saifullah, W. Pak.	32	30 42N	68 30 E
Qilt R., Jordan	29	31 51N	35 30 E
Qina, Egypt	51	26 10N	32 43 E
Qir Yam, Israel	29	32 49N	35 4 E
Qiryat 'Anavim, Israel	29	31 49N	35 7 E
Qiryat Shemona, Israel	29	33 13N	35 33 E
Qolleh-ye Damāvand, Mt., Iran	31	36 0N	52 0 E
Quairading, W. Austral.	44	32 0 S	117 21 E

	MAP		
Quambone, N.S.W.	43	30 57 s	147 53 E
Quan Long (Ca Mau), Viet Nam	34	9 7N	105 8 E
Quanah, U.S.A.	71	34 20N	99 40W
Quang Nam, Viet Nam	34	15 55N	108 14 E
Quang Ngai, Viet Nam	34	15 13N	108 58 E
Quang Tri, Viet Nam	34	16 46N	107 12 E
Quang Yen, Viet Nam	39	21 3N	106 52 E
Qu'Appelle R., Canada	65	50 40N	103 30W
Quarai, Brazil	77	30 15 s	56 20W
Quartzsite, U.S.A.	73	33 43N	114 17W
Quatre Bras, Belgium	13	50 35N	4 30 E
Quatsino, Canada	64	50 30N	127 40W
Quatsino Sd., Canada	64	50 42N	127 58W
Qubab. *See* Mishmar Ayyalon	29		
Quchan, Iran	31	37 10N	58 27 E
Que Que, Rhodesia	56	18 58 s	29 48 E
Queanbeyan, N.S.W.	43	35 17 s	149 14 E
Quebec, Canada	63	46 52N	71 13W
Quebec, prov., Can.	62–63	45 0N to 62 30N	57 0W to 80 0W
Quebrachos, Argentina	77	29 10 s	63 50W
Queen Adelaide Arch., Chile	77	52 20 s	74 0W
Queen Bess, Mt., Can.	64	51 13N	124 35W
Queen Charlotte, Can.	64	53 28N	132 2W
Queen Charlotte Is., Canada	64	53 10N	132 0W
Queen Charlotte Sd., N.Z.	47	41 10 s	174 15 E
Queen Charlotte Str., Canada	64	51 0N	128 0W
Queen Elizabeth Is.	58	77 0N	95 0W
Queen Elizabeth Nat. Park, Uganda	53	0 0	29 58 E
Queen Mary Coast, Ant.	80	70 0 s	95 0 E
Queen Maud G., Can.	60	68 15N	102 0W
Queen Victoria Spring, W. Australia	45	30 18 s	123 25 E
Queenscliff, Victoria	43	38 8 s	144 37 E
Queensland, Australia	42–43	10 40 s to 29 0 s	138 E to 153 30 E
Queenstown, Guyana	78	7 20N	58 30W
Queenstown, Cape Prov.	57	31 52 s	26 52 E
Queenstown, N.Z.	47	45 1 s	168 40 E
Queenstown, Tasmania	43	42 4 s	145 35 E
Queimadas, Brazil	79	11 0 s	39 16W
Quela, Angola	55	9 10 s	16 56 E
Quelimane, Mozam.	55	17 53 s	36 58 E
Quellón, Chile	77	43 0 s	73 50W
Quemado, Tex., U.S.A.	71	28 58N	100 32W
Quemado, N.M U.S.A.	73	34 22N	108 59W
Quemoy. *See* Kinmen, I., China	39		
Quequen, Argentina	77	38 30 s	58 30W
Queretaro, Mexico	74	20 40N	100 23W
Queretaro, st., Mexico	74	21 0N	100 0W
Quesnel, Canada	64	53 5N	122 30W
Quesnel L., Canada	64	52 30N	121 20W
Quesnel R., Canada	64	52 40N	122 0W
Questa, U.S.A.	71	36 41N	105 30W
Quetico, Canada	62	48 45N	90 55W
Quetta, Pakistan	32	30 15N	66 55 E
Quetta, Terr., W. Pak.	32	29 30N	66 0 E
Quezon City, Philippines	35	14 50N	121 0 E
Qui Nhon, Viet Nam	34	13 40N	109 13 E
Quibaxi, Angola	55	8 24 s	14 28 E
Quibdo, Colombia	78	5 41N	76 55W
Quiberon, France	12	47 29N	3 9W
Quick, Canada	64	54 35N	126 10W
Quiet L., Canada	64	61 0N	132 40W
Qui' iya, Si. Arabia	30	24 22N	43 35 E
Quilan, C., Chile	77	43 15 s	74 30W
Quilca, Peru	78	16 50 s	72 29W
Quilengues, Angola	55	14 12 s	14 12 E
Quillabamba, Peru	78	12 50 s	72 50W
Quillagua, Chile	78	21 40 s	69 40W
Quillota, Chile	77	33 2 s	71 45W
Quilon, India	32	8 50N	76 38 E
Quilpie, Queensland	43	26 35 s	144 11 E
Quimili, Argentina	77	27 40 s	63 30W
Quimper, France	12	48 0N	4 9W
Quimperlé, France	12	47 53N	3 33W
Quin, Ireland	11	52 50N	8 52W
Quincy, Calif., U.S.A.	72	39 58N	121 0W
Quincy, Fla., U.S.A.	69	30 34N	84 35W
Quincy, Ill., U.S.A.	70	39 55N	91 20W
Quincy, Mass., U.S.A.	69	42 14N	70 57W
Quincy, Wash., U.S.A.	72	47 14N	119 54W
Quines, Argentina	77	32 10 s	65 50W
Quinga, Mozambique	55	15 45 s	40 15 E
Quintana Roo, st., Mexico	74	19 0N	88 0W
Quintanar, Spain	17	39 36N	3 5W
Quintero, Chile	77	32 45 s	71 30W
Quionga, Mozambique	53	10 37 s	40 31 E
Quipungo, Angola	55	14 50 s	14 32 E
Quirindi, N.S.W.	43	31 28 s	150 40 E
Quirpon I., Canada	63	51 32N	55 28W
Quissanga, Mozam.	55	12 25 s	40 35 E
Quiterajo, Mozam.	53	11 55 s	40 30 E
Quitman, Ga., U.S.A.	69	30 49N	83 35W
Quitman, Tex., U.S.A.	71	32 47N	95 28W
Quito, Ecuador	78	0 15 s	78 35W

	MAP		
Quixadá, Brazil	79	4 55 s	39 0W
Qum, Iran	31	34 45N	50 57 E
Qumbu, Cape Province	57	31 9 s	28 53 E
Qunduz, Afghanistan	31	36 50N	69 0 E
Quoin Pt., Cape Prov.	57	34 46 s	19 37 E
Quorn, Canada	62	49 25N	90 55W
Quorn, S. Australia	43	32 25 s	138 0 E
Qurug-Tagh, mts., China	37	41 40N	90 0 E
Qus, Egypt	51	25 55N	32 50 E
Qusra, Jordan	29	32 5N	35 20 E
Quthing, Lesotho	57	30 25 s	27 43 E

R

	MAP		
Raahe, Finland	23	64 40N	24 35 E
Ra'ananna, Israel	29	32 12N	34 52 E
Raasay I., Scotland	10	57 25N	6 4W
Rabah, Mt., Nigeria	52	13 5N	5 30 E
Rabai, Kenya	53	3 55 s	39 30 E
Rabat, Morocco	50	33 9N	6 53W
Rabaul, New Guinea	42	4 4 s	152 18 E
Rabbit R., Canada	64	59 20N	126 40W
Rabbitskin R., Canada	64	61 48N	120 0W
Rābigh, Saudi Arabia	30	22 52N	39 5 E
Race C., Canada	63	46 40N	53 18W
Rachid, Mauritania	50	18 45N	11 35W
Racibórz, Poland	16	50 7N	18 18 E
Racine, U.S.A.	70	42 41N	87 51W
Radauti, Rumania	21	47 50N	25 59 E
Radford, U.S.A.	69	37 8N	80 32W
Radisson, Canada	65	52 30N	107 20W
Radium Hill, S. Australia	43	32 30 s	140 42 E
Radium Hot Springs, Canada	64	50 48N	116 12W
Radomosko, Poland	16	51 5N	19 28 E
Radom, Poland	16	51 23N	21 12 E
Radomir, Bulgaria	21	42 37N	23 4 E
Radomyshl, U.S.S.R.	25	50 30N	29 12 E
Radovič, Yugoslavia	21	41 38N	22 28 E
Radville, Canada	65	49 30N	104 15W
Radzymin, Poland	16	52 25N	21 10 E
Rae, Canada	64	62 45N	115 50W
Rae Bareli, India	33	26 18N	81 20 E
Rae Isthmus, Canada	61	66 40N	87 30W
Raeren, Belgium	13	50 42N	6 7 E
Raeside, L., Australia	44	29 20 s	122 0 E
Raetihi, N.Z.	46	39 27 s	175 17 E
Rafaela, Argentina	77	31 10 s	61 30W
Rafiah, Israel	29	31 18N	34 15 E
Rafha, Si. Arabia	30	29 43N	43 33 E
Rafsanjān, Iran	31	30 33N	56 2 E
Raga, Sudan	51	8 28N	25 47 E
Ragama, Sri Lanka	32	7 0N	79 55 E
Raghunathpali, India	33	22 15N	84 50 E
Raglan, New Zealand	46	37 55 s	174 55 E
Raglan Harb., N.Z.	46	37 58 s	174 52 E
Ragueneau, Canada	63	49 11N	68 18W
Ragusa, Sicily	20	36 56N	14 42 E
Raha, Indonesia	35	8 20 s	118 40 E
Raha, Nigeria	52	12 6N	4 4 E
Rahad el Berdi, Sudan	51	11 20N	23 40 E
Rahimyar Khan, Pak.	32	28 30N	70 25 E
Rahotu, New Zealand	46	39 20 s	173 49 E
Raichur, India	32	16 10N	77 20 E
Raigarh, India	33	21 56N	83 25 E
Raiis, Saudi Arabia	30	23 33N	38 43 E
Rainier, U.S.A.	72	46 5N	122 58W
Rainier, Mt., U.S.A.	72	46 50N	121 0W
Rainy L., N. America	65	48 30N	92 30W
Rainy River, Canada	70	48 50N	94 30W
Raipur, India	33	21 17N	81 45 E
Raith, Canada	62	48 50N	90 0W
Raj Nandgaon, India	32	21 10N	81 5 E
Rajahmundry, India	32	17 1N	81 48 E
Rajampet, India	32	14 11N	79 9 E
Rajang, Sarawak	35	2 3N	112 25 E
Rajapalaiyarn, India	32	9 25N	77 35 E
Rajapur, India	32	16 33N	73 26 E
Rajasthan, st., India	32	26 45N	73 30 E
Rajasthan Canal, India	32	28 0N	71 0 E
Rajgarh, India	32	28 40N	75 25 E
Rajgarh, India	32	24 2N	76 45 E
Rajgir, India	33	25 0N	85 25 E
Rajkot, India	32	22 15N	70 56 E
Rajkot, India	32	22 13N	70 53N
Rajpur, India	32	21 58N	75 9 E
Rajshahi, Bangladesh	33	24 22N	88 39 E
Rajshahi Div., Ban.	33	25 4N	89 0 E
Rajula, India	32	21 0N	71 25 E
Rajur, India	32	19 58N	78 58 E
Rakaia, New Zealand	47	43 45 s	172 1 E
Rakaia R., N.Z.	47	43 26 s	171 47 E
Rakaposhi, Mt, Kashmir	32	36 9N	74 40 E
Rakba, Saudi Arabia	30	22 20N	41 30 E
Rakops, Thailand	57	21 7 s	24 23 E
Rakvere, U.S.S.R.	25	59 15N	26 28 E
Raleigh, U.S.A.	67	35 50N	76 0W
Raleigh B., U.S.A.	67	35 50N	78 39W
Raley, Canada	64	49 20N	113 10W
Ralls, U.S.A.	71	33 36N	101 16W
Ram R., Canada	64	61 35N	123 50W
Rama, Israel	29	32 56N	35 21 E
Ramakhna, India	32	21 10N	78 49 E
Ramanathapuram, India	32	9 25N	78 55 E
Ramat Gan, Israel	29	32 4N	34 48 E

	MAP		
Ramatayim, Israel	29	32 9N	34 54 E
Ramathlabama, Botswana	57	52 37 s	25 33 E
Rambouillet, France	12	48 40N	1 48 E
Rambutyo, I., N. Guin.	42	2 30 s	147 55 E
Ramea, Canada	63	47 32N	57 22W
Ramechhap, Nepal	33	27 25N	86 10 E
Ramelton, Ireland	11	55 3N	7 35W
Ramgarh, India	32	27 25N	70 25 E
Ramgarh, India	33	23 40N	85 35 E
Ramla, Israel	29	31 55N	34 52 E
Rammun, Jordan	29	31 55N	35 17 E
Râmnicu-Sarat, Rumania	21	45 26N	27 3 E
Ramnicu Vilcea, Rumania	21	45 9N	24 21 E
Ramon, U.S.S.R.	25	52 8N	39 21 E
Ramona, U.S.A.	73	33 2N	116 52W
Ramore, Canada	62	48 30N	80 25W
Ramos, R., Nigeria	52	5 8N	5 22 E
Ramos, R., Mexico	74	25 20N	105 8W
Ramos Arizpe, Mexico	74	23 35N	100 59W
Ramotsaodi, Bot.	56	19 48 s	22 15 E
Ramoutsa, Botswana	57	24 50 s	25 52 E
Rampart, Alaska	59	65 35N	150 25W
Rampur, Ut.P., India	32	28 50N	79 5 E
Rampur Hat, India	33	24 10N	87 50 E
Ramree I., Burma	33	19 0N	94 0 E
Ramsey, Canada	62	47 25N	82 20W
Ramsey L., Canada	62	47 15N	82 20W
Ramsele, Sweden	23	63 31N	16 31 E
Ramsgate, England	10	51 20N	1 25 E
Ramtek, India	32	21 29N	79 26 E
Ramu R., New Guinea	42	5 51 s	144 45 E
Ranaghat, India	33	23 15N	88 35 E
Rancagua, Chile	77	34 10 s	70 50W
Rancheria, R., Canada	64	60 10N	130 12W
Ranchester, U.S.A.	72	44 57N	107 14W
Ranchi, India	33	23 19N	85 27 E
Ranco L., Chile	77	40 15 s	72 30W
Rand, New South Wales	43	35 33 s	146 32 E
Randalstown, N. Ireland	11	54 45N	6 20W
Randers, Denmark	23	56 29N	10 1 E
Randfontein, Transvaal	57	26 8 s	27 45 E
Randolph, N.Y., U.S.A.	68	42 10N	78 59W
Randolph, Vt., U.S.A.	69	43 55N	72 39W
Randolph, Utah, U.S.A.	72	41 43N	111 10W
Randsburg, U.S.A.	73	35 33N	117 44W
Råne, R., Sweden	22	66 15N	21 30 E
Råneå, Sweden	22	65 53N	22 30 E
Ranfurly, New Zealand	47	45 7 s	170 6 E
Rangamati, Bangladesh	33	22 38N	92 15 E
Rangataua, N.Z.	46	39 26 s	175 28 E
Rangaunu B., N.Z.	46	34 51 s	173 15 E
Rangely, Colo., U.S.A.	73	40 5N	108 46W
Rangeley, Me., U.S.A.	69	44 58N	70 33W
Ranger, U.S.A.	71	32 30N	98 42W
Rangia, India	33	26 15N	91 20 E
Rangiora, N.Z.	47	43 19 s	172 36 E
Rangitaiki R., N.Z.	46	38 25 s	176 45 E
Rangitata R., N.Z.	47	43 45 s	171 15 E
Rangitikei R., N.Z.	46	40 17 s	175 15 E
Rangitoto Ra., N.Z.	46	38 25 s	175 35 E
Rangkasbitung, Indon.	34	6 22 s	106 16 E
Rangoon, Burma	34	16 45N	96 20 E
Rangoon, R., Burma	33	16 22N	96 30 E
Rangpur, Bangladesh	33	24 42N	89 22 E
Rangwe, Kenya	53	0 37 s	34 37 E
Raniganj, India	33	23 40N	87 15 E
Raniwara, India	32	24 45N	72 10 E
Rankin, U.S.A.	71	31 14N	101 58W
Rankin's Springs, N.S.W.	43	33 49 s	146 14 E
Rann of Kutch, India	32	24 0N	70 0 E
Rannes, Queensland	45	24 6 s	150 11 E
Rannoch, Scotland	10	56 40N	4 32W
Ranong, Thailand	34	9 56N	98 40 E
Rantekombola Mt., Indonesia	35	3 20 s	120 0 E
Rantis, Jordan	29	32 4N	35 3 E
Rantoul, U.S.A.	70	40 18N	88 10W
Ranwanlendu, Botswana	56	19 40 s	22 30 E
Rapa Nui (Easter I.), Pacific Ocean	5	27 0 s	109 0W
Rapallo, Italy	20	44 21N	9 12 E
Rapch, Iran	31	25 35N	59 12 E
Raphoe, Ireland	11	54 52N	7 36W
Rapid Bay, S. Australia	43	35 30 s	138 2 E
Rapid City, Canada	65	50 10N	100 0W
Rapid City, U.S.A.	70	44 5N	103 14W
Rapid River, Canada	64	59 0N	129 0W
Rapid River, U.S.A.	68	45 55N	87 0W
Rapides des Joachims, Canada	62	46 13N	77 43W
Rapla, U.S.S.R.	23	59 5N	24 52 E
Rapperswil, Switzerland	15	47 13N	8 49 E
Rappville, N.S.W.	42	29 9 s	152 40 E
Raquena, Peru	78	5 0 s	74 0W
Ras Abu Madd, Saudi Arabia	30	25 0N	37 15 E
Ra's Abu Shagra, Sudan	51	21 0N	37 10 E
Ras al Hadd, Oman	31	22 30N	59 48 E
Ras al Khaima, C., Trucial Oman	31	25 25N	55 40 E

	MAP		
Ras al Mish'ab, C., Saudi Arabia	30	28 8N	48 40 E
Ras at Tannura, C., Saudi Arabia	30	26 40N	49 30 E
Ra's Baridi, C., Saudi Arabia	30	24 15N	37 30 E
Ras Dashan, Mt., Ethiopia	54	13 8N	37 45 E
Ra's-e Meydani, Iran	31	26 11N	51 10 E
Ra's-e Tang, Iran	31	25 0N	58 30 E
Ras el Melh, Libya	51	32 10N	25 0 E
Ras en Naqura, Israel	29	33 5N	35 5 E
Ras Habarba, C., Sudan	51	22 4N	36 31 E
Ras Hatiba, C., Saudi Arabia	30	22 10N	39 0 E
Ras Jiwani, W. Pak.	31	25 1N	61 47 E
Ras Kanzi, C., Tan.	53	7 5 s	39 27 E
Ras Kigomasha, Egypt	53	4 52 s	39 40 E
Ras Mkumbi, C., Tan.	53	7 32 s	39 58 E
Ras Ngomeni, Kenya	53	3 0 s	40 4 E
Ras Rakan, Qatar	31	26 11N	51 10 E
Rasa, Punta, Argentina	77	40 50 s	62 15W
Rashad, Sudan	54	11 55N	31 0 E
Rashīd (Rosetta), Egypt	31	21 20N	30 17 E
Rasht, Iran	30	37 20N	49 40 E
Rasipuram, India	32	11 28N	78 13 E
Raška, Yugoslavia	21	43 19N	20 39 E
Raso C., Brazil	79	1 50N	50 0W
Rason, L., W. Australia	40	28 45 s	124 25 E
Rasskazovo, U.S.S.R.	25	52 35N	41 50 E
Rat Is., Aleutian Is.	59	51 48N	178 5 E
Rat R., Canada	65	56 0N	99 30W
Ratangarh, India	32	28 5N	74 35 E
Rateng, Indonesia	35	8 30 s	120 30 E
Rath Luire, Ireland	11	52 21N	8 40W
Ratha, W., Iran	31	22 17N	59 0 E
Rathangan, Ireland	11	53 13N	7 0W
Rathcormack, Ireland	11	52 5N	8 19W
Rathdowney, Queens.	43	28 15 s	152 42 E
Rathdrum, Ireland	11	52 57N	6 13W
Rathdrum, U.S.A.	72	47 50N	116 55W
Rathenow, Germany	14	52 38N	12 23 E
Rathfriland, Ireland	11	54 14N	6 10W
Rathkeale, Ireland	11	52 32N	8 57W
Rathlin I., N. Ireland	11	55 18N	6 14W
Rathlin O'Birne I., Ireland	11	54 40N	8 50W
Rathmullan, Ireland	11	55 6N	7 32W
Rathnew, Ireland	11	53 0N	6 5W
Rathowen, Ireland	11	53 40N	7 30W
Ratlam, India	32	23 20N	75 0 E
Ratnagiri, India	32	16 57N	73 18 E
Ratnapura, Sri Lanka	32	6 40N	80 20 E
Raton, U.S.A.	71	37 0N	104 30W
Ratz, Mt., Canada	64	57 22N	132 20W
Raub, Malaya	34	3 47N	101 52 E
Raufarhöfn, Iceland	22	66 30N	15 49W
Raukumara, Ra., N.Z.	46	38 5 s	177 55 E
Rauma (Raumo), Finland	23	61 10N	21 30 E
Raumo. *See* Rauma	23		
Raung Mt., Indonesia	34	8 8 s	114 4 E
Ravar, Iran	31	31 20N	56 51 E
Ravenna, Italy	20	44 28N	12 15 E
Ravenna, U.S.A.	70	41 4N	98 25W
Ravensburg, Germany	14	47 48N	9 38 E
Ravenswood, U.S.A.	68	38 58N	81 47W
Ravenshoe, Queensland	42	17 43 s	145 33 E
Ravensthorpe, W. Australia	44	33 33 s	120 1 E
Ravensthorpe Ra., W. Australia	44	33 25 s	119 30 E
Ravenswood, Queens.	42	20 5 s	146 55 E
Raventazón, Peru	78	6 10 s	81 0W
Ravi R., Pakistan	32	31 0N	73 0 E
Rawalpindi, Pakistan	32	33 38N	73 8 E
Rawalpindi, Terr., W. Pakistan	32	33 0N	73 0 E
Rawānduz, Iraq	30	36 37N	44 31 E
Rawang, Malaya	34	3 20N	101 34 E
Rawdon, Canada	62	46 3N	73 40W
Rawene, New Zealand	46	35 25 s	173 32 E
Rawicz, Poland	16	51 36N	16 52 E
Rawlinna, W. Australia	45	30 58 s	125 28 E
Rawlins, U.S.A.	72	41 50N	107 30W
Rawson, Argentina	77	43 15 s	65 0W
Rawuya, Nigeria	52	12 10N	6 50 E
Ray, U.S.A.	70	48 17N	103 7W
Ray, C., Canada	63	47 33N	59 15W
Ray Mts., Alaska	59	65 40N	152 0W
Rayadrug, India	32	14 40N	76 50 E
Rayagada, India	33	19 15N	83 20 E
Raymond, Canada	64	49 30N	112 35W
Raymond, U.S.A.	72	46 40N	123 46W
Raymondville, U.S.A.	71	26 32N	97 45W
Raymore, Canada	65	51 25N	104 30W
Rayong, Thailand	34	12 38N	101 17 E
Rayville, U.S.A.	71	32 30N	91 45W
Rayne, U.S.A.	71	30 15N	92 15W
Razgrad, Bulgaria	21	43 33N	26 34 E
Razmak, Pakistan	62	32 45N	69 50 E
Razor Back, Mt., Can.	64	51 32N	125 0W
Razorback, mt., S. Australia	43	33 28 s	138 59 E
Ré, or Rhe, I., France	12	46 12N	1 30W
Reading, England	10	51 27N	0 57W
Reading, U.S.A.	69	40 20N	75 63W
Rebiana, Libya	51	24 12N	22 10 E

	MAP		
Reboly, U.S.S.R.	22	63 57N	30 40 E
Rebun I., Japan	36	45 28N	141 0 E
Recalde, Argentina	77	36 40s	61 0w
Rechitsa, U.S.S.R.	25	52 28N	30 15 E
Recherche, Arch. of the, W. Australia	45	34 0s	124 30 E
Recife (Pernambuco), Brazil	79	8 0s	35 0w
Reconquista, Argentina	77	29 10s	59 45w
Recreo, Argentina	77	29 25s	65 10w
Redang, Malaya	34	5 47N	103 1 E
Red Bay, Canada	63	44 47N	81 17w
Red Bluff, U.S.A.	72	40 14N	122 15w
Red Bluff, L., U.S.A.	71	31 59N	103 55w
Red R., Queensland	42	16 40s	142 15 E
Red R., La., U.S.A.	71	31 45N	93 0w
Red R., Minn., U.S.A.	70	48 10N	97 0w
Red, R., Vietnam	37	22 0N	104 0 E
Red Lake, Canada	65	51 10N	93 45w
Red Lake, U.S.A.	67	51 1N	94 1w
Red Lake Falls, U.S.A.	70	48 0N	96 5w
Red Sea, Arabia-Africa	48	25 0N	36 0 E
Red Cliffs, Australia	43	34 16s	142 10 E
Red Cloud, U.S.A.	70	40 6N	98 30w
Red Deer, Canada	64	52 20N	113 50w
Red Deer L., Canada	65	52 55N	101 30w
Red Deer R., Alberta, Canada	64	51 40N	114 50w
Red Deer R., Sask. Can.	65	52 45N	102 30w
Red Hill, S. Australia	43	33 30s	138 10 E
Red Indian L., Newf.	63	48 35N	57 0w
Red Lodge, U.S.A.	72	45 10N	109 10w
Red Oak, U.S.A.	70	41 0N	95 10w
Red Rock, Canada	62	49 0N	88 30w
Red Sucker L., Canada	62	54 0N	93 40w
Red Tank, Pan. Can. Zone	74		Inset
Red Tower P., Rumania	21	45 30N	24 18 E
Red Wing, U.S.A.	70	44 32N	92 33w
Redcap, Queensland	42	17 5s	144 27 E
Redcliff, Canada	65	50 10N	110 50w
Reddersburgh, O.F.S.	57	29 41s	26 10 E
Redding, U.S.A.	72	40 30N	122 25w
Redempção, Brazil	79	10 30s	55 50w
Redfield, U.S.A.	70	45 0N	98 30w
Redlands, U.S.A.	73	34 0N	117 0w
Redmond, U.S.A.	72	44 15N	121 14w
Redon, France	12	47 40N	2 6w
Redonda I., Canada	64	50 20N	125 0w
Redondela, Spain	17	42 15N	8 38w
Redondo, Portugal	17	38 39N	7 37w
Redondo Beach, U.S.A.	73	33 50N	118 22w
Redpa, Tasmania	43	40 48s	144 49 E
Redrock Pt., Canada	64	62 25N	114 11w
Redvers, Canada	65	49 35N	101 40w
Redwater, Canada	64	53 55N	113 0w
Redwood City, U.S.A.	73	37 30N	122 15w
Redwood Falls, U.S.A.	70	44 30N	95 3w
Ree, Lough, Ireland	11	53 35N	8 0w
Reed City, U.S.A.	68	43 52N	85 30w
Reed L., Canada	68	43 52N	85 30w
Reeder, U.S.A.	70	46 9N	102 58w
Reedley, U.S.A.	73	36 39N	119 28w
Reedsburg, U.S.A.	70	43 32N	90 2w
Reedsport, U.S.A.	72	43 44N	124 10w
Reefton, New Zealand	47	42 6s	171 51 E
Reese, R., U.S.A.	66	40 15N	117 10w
Refugio, U.S.A.	71	28 21N	97 16w
Regavim, Israel	29	32 32N	35 2 E
Regensburg, Germany	14	49 1N	12 7 E
Reggio (di Calabria), Italy	20	38 7N	15 38 E
Reggio (nell' Emilia), Italy	20	44 42N	10 38 E
Reghin, Rumania	21	46 46N	24 41 E
Regina, Canada	65	50 30N	104 35w
Registan, Afghanistan	31	30 15N	65 0 E
Registro do Araguaia, Brazil	79	15 40s	52 0w
Rehoboth, S.W. Africa	55	17 55s	15 5 E
Rehoboth, S.W. Africa	57	23 12s	17 1 E
Rei, R., Cameroon	52	8 42N	14 12 E
Rei Bouba, Cameroon	52	8 40N	14 15 E
Reichenbach, Germany	14	50 36N	12 19 E
Reid, W. Australia	45	30 49s	128 26 E
Reidsville, U.S.A.	69	36 21N	79 40w
Reigate, England	10	51 14N	0 11w
Reims, France	12	49 15N	4 0 E
Reina, Israel	29	32 43N	35 18 E
Reinbeck, U.S.A.	70	42 17N	92 35w
Reindeer I., Canada	65	52 30N	98 0w
Reindeer L., Canada	65	57 20N	102 20w
Reindeer R., Canada	65	55 50N	103 10w
Reinga, C., N.Z.	46	34 26s	172 41 E
Reinosa, Mexico	74	26 5N	98 18w
Reisui, Korea	36	34 25N	127 25 E
Reitz, Orange Free State	57	27 48s	28 29 E
Reivilo, Cape Province	57	27 34s	24 11 E
Rejowiec, Poland	16	51 5N	23 11 E
Rekinniki, U.S.S.R.	27	60 50N	163 30 E
Remanso, Brazil	78	7 35s	65 45w
Remarkables, mts., New Zealand	47	45 10s	168 51 E
Rembang, Indonesia	34	6 42s	111 21 E
Remeshk, Iran	31	26 54N	58 43 E
Remiremont, France	12	48 0N	6 36 E
Remontnoye, U.S.S.R.	25	47 44N	43 37 E
Remscheid, Germany	14	51 11N	7 12 E
Renco, Rhodesia	56	20 30s	31 11 E
Rendsburg, Germany	14	54 18N	9 41 E
Rene, U.S.S.R.	27	66 4N	176 0w
Renfrew, Canada	62	45 30N	76 40w
Rengat, Indonesia	34	0 30s	102 45 E
Renk, Sudan	54	11 47N	32 53 E
Renkum, Netherlands	13	51 58N	5 43 E
Renmark, S. Australia	43	34 5s	140 46 E
Rennell Sd., Canada	64	53 32N	133 28w
Rennes, France	12	48 7N	1 41w
Reno, U.S.A.	72	39 30N	119 50w
Reno, R., Italy	20	44 27N	12 15 E
Renovo, U.S.A.	68	41 20N	77 47w
Rensselaer, U.S.A.	68	41 0N	87 10w
Renton, U.S.A.	72	47 30N	122 10w
Renwicktown, N.Z.	47	41 29s	173 51 E
Reo, Indonesia	35	8 15s	120 30 E
Republic, Mich., U.S.A.	70	46 25N	87 59w
Republic, Wash., U.S.A.	72	48 39N	118 45w
Republican City, U.S.A.	70	40 8N	99 16w
Republican R., U.S.A.	70	40 0N	98 30w
Repulse B., Queensland	42	20 30s	148 46 E
Requena, Spain	17	39 30N	1 4w
Resen, Yugoslavia	21	41 5N	21 0 E
Reserve, U.S.A.	73	33 50N	108 54w
Resistencia, Argentina	77	27 30s	59 0w
Resita, Rumania	21	45 18N	21 53 E
Resolution I., Canada	61	61 30N	65 0w
Resolution I., N.Z.	47	45 40s	166 40 E
Reston, Canada	65	49 33N	101 5w
Retalhuleu, Guatemala	74	14 33N	91 46w
Retenue, Lac de, Zaire	56	11 0s	27 5 E
Rethel, France	12	49 30N	4 20 E
Rethimnon, Crete	20	35 23N	24 28 E
Réunion I., Indian Oc.	5	22 0s	56 0 E
Réus, Spain	17	41 10N	1 5 E
Reutlingen, Germany	14	48 28N	9 13 E
Reuss, R., Switzerland	14	47 15N	8 26 E
Reutte, Austria	14	47 29N	10 42 E
Revda, U.S.S.R.	24	57 0N	62 0 E
Revel, France	12	43 28N	2 0 E
Revelstoke, Canada	64	51 0N	118 0w
Revilla Gigedo I., Alaska	6	55 50N	131 20w
Rewa, India	33	24 33N	81 25 E
Rex, Alaska	59	64 10N	149 20 E
Rewari, India	32	28 15N	76 40 E
Rexburg, U.S.A.	72	43 45N	111 50w
Rexford, U.S.A.	72	48 55N	115 15w
Reydarfjördur B., Ice.	22	65 0N	14 0w
Reykjafjord, Iceland	22	65 58N	21 45w
Reykjalia, Iceland	22	65 44N	16 53w
Reykjanæs, C., Iceland	22	63 48N	22 40w
Reykjavik, Iceland	22	64 10N	22 0w
Reynolds, Canada	65	49 30N	96 0w
Reynosa, Spain	17	43 2N	4 15w
Rezekne, U.S.S.R.	23	56 30N	27 17 E
Rgotina, Yugoslavia	21	44 1N	22 18 E
Rhayader, Wales	10	52 19N	3 30w
Rheden, Netherlands	13	52 0N	6 3 E
Rhein, Canada	65	51 25N	102 15w
Rheine, Germany	14	52 17N	7 25 E
Rheinfelden, Switzerland	15	47 33N	7 47 E
Rhine, R., Germany, etc.	14	51 0N	7 0 E
Rhineland-Palatinate, land, Germany	14	50 0N	7 0 E
Rhinelander, U.S.A.	70	45 38N	89 29w
Rhino Camp, Uganda	53	2 55N	31 20 E
Rho, Italy	20	45 31N	9 2 E
Rhode Island, st., U.S.A.	68	41 38N	71 37w
Rhodes (Rhodos) Is., Greece	6	36 26N	28 18 E
Rhodes Tomb, Rhod.	56	20 30s	28 30 E
Rhodesia (Southern Rhodesia), Afr.	56	19 0s	29 0 E
Rhodope Mts., Bulgaria	21	41 40N	24 20 E
Rhône R., France	12	43 28N	4 42 E
Rhonegletscher, Switz.	15	46 45N	8 24 E
Rhum I., Scotland	10	57 0N	6 20w
Rhyl, Wales	10	53 19N	3 29w
Riachão, Brazil	79	7 20s	46 45w
Riasi, Kashmir	32	33 10N	74 50 E
Riau Archipelago, Indonesia	34	0 45N	104 5 E
Riaza, Spain	17	41 19N	3 29w
Ribadéo, Spain	17	43 35N	7 5w
Ribadesella, Spain	17	43 30N	5 7w
Ribadu, Nigeria	52	9 16N	12 39 E
Ribao, Cameroon	52	6 31N	11 28 E
Ribas do Rio Pardo	79	20 25s	54 0w
Ribat, Afghanistan	31	29 49N	61 0 E
Ribat, Pakistan	32	29 45N	60 55 E
Ribatejo, Portugal	17	39 10N	8 30 E
Ribe, Denmark	23	55 19N	8 44 E
Ribeira, R., Brazil	77	24 30s	48 0w
Ribeirão Preto, Brazil	79	21 10s	47 50w
Ribérac, France	12	45 15N	0 20 E
Rica, Mt., W. Austral.	44	21 59s	116 25 E
Riccarton, N.Z.	47	43 32s	172 37 E
Rice Lake, U.S.A.	70	45 30N	91 44w
Rich Hill, U.S.A.	71	38 3N	94 26w
Richards B., Natal	57	28 48s	32 6 E
Richardson L.S., U.S.A.	69	45 0N	70 45w
Richardson Mts., N.Z.	47	44 49s	168 34 E
Richardson R., Canada	65	58 10N	111 0w
Richardton, U.S.A.	70	46 57N	102 21w
Riche, C., W. Australia	44	34 35s	118 41 E
Richey, U.S.A.	70	47 41N	105 2w
Richfield, Idaho, U.S.A.	72	43 4N	114 14w
Richfield, Utah, U.S.A.	73	38 50N	112 0w
Richibucto, Canada	63	46 42N	64 54w
Richland, Ga., U.S.A.	68	32 4N	84 39w
Richland, Oreg., U.S.A.	72	44 48N	117 14w
Richland, Wash., U.S.A.	72	46 17N	119 17w
Richland Center, U.S.A.	70	43 19N	90 25w
Richlands, U.S.A.	68	37 7N	81 49w
Richmond, London, England	10	51 28N	0 18w
Richmond, Natal	57	29 51s	30 18 E
Richmond, N.S.W.	43	33 35s	150 42 E
Richmond, N.Z.	47	41 21s	173 12 E
Richmond, Queensland	42	20 43s	143 8 E
Richmond, Calif. U.S.A.	73	38 0N	122 30w
Richmond, Ind., U.S.A.	68	39 50N	84 50w
Richmond, Ky., U.S.A.	68	37 40N	84 20w
Richmond, Mo., U.S.A.	70	39 15N	93 58w
Richmond, Tex., U.S.A.	71	29 33N	95 46w
Richmond, Utah, U.S.A.	72	41 56N	111 51w
Richmond, Va., U.S.A.	68	37 33N	77 27w
Richmond, Mt., N.Z.	47	41 32s	173 22 E
Richmond Gulf, tn., Canada	62	56 0N	76 25w
Richmond Ra., N.Z.	47	41 30s	173 20 E
Richmond Gulf, Canada	62	56 20N	76 48w
Richton, U.S.A.	69	31 23N	88 58w
Richwood, U.S.A.	68	38 17N	80 32w
Ridgedale, Canada	65	53 0N	104 10w
Ridgeland, U.S.A.	69	32 30N	80 58w
Ridgelands, Queens.	42	23 16s	150 17 E
Ridgetown, Canada	62	42 26N	81 52w
Ridgway, U.S.A.	68	41 25N	78 43w
Riding Mountain Nat. Park, Canada	65	50 50N	100 0w
Ridley Mt., W. Austral.	45	33 12s	122 7 E
Riebeek, E., Cape Prov.	57	33 13s	26 12 E
Ried, Tyrol, Austria	14	47 18N	11 53 E
Ried, Upper Austria	14	48 14N	13 30 E
Riesen G. (Giant Mts.), Czechoslovakia	16	50 50N	16 0 E
Riesi, Italy	20	37 16N	14 4 E
Riet, R., O.F.S.	57	29 20	25 0 E
Rietbron, Cape Prov.	57	32 50s	23 8 E
Rietfontein, Cape Prov.	57	26 44s	20 1 E
Rietfontein, S.W. Africa	57	21 58s	20 58 E
Rieti, Italy	20	42 23N	12 50 E
Rifle, U.S.A.	73	39 35N	107 46w
Rift Valley, prov., Kenya	53	1 0N	36 0 E
Rig Rig, Chad	51	14 13N	14 25 E
Riga, U.S.S.R.	23	56 58N	24 12 E
Riga, G. of, U.S.S.R.	23	57 40N	23 45 E
Rigachikun, Nigeria	52	10 40N	7 26 E
Rigby, U.S.A.	72	43 39N	111 58w
Riggins, U.S.A.	72	45 28N	116 28w
Rigo, Papua	42	9 41s	147 31 E
Rigolet, Canada	63	54 10N	58 23w
Rihand Dam, India	33	24 5N	82 50 E
Riihimaki, Finland	23	60 45N	24 45 E
Riishiri, Japan	36	45 10N	140 17 E
Rijau, Nigeria	52	11 8N	5 17 E
Rijeka, Yugoslavia	20	45 20N	14 21 E
Rijssen, Netherlands	13	52 19N	6 30 E
Rijswijk, Netherlands	13	52 4N	4 22 E
Rikita, Zaire	53	5 5N	28 29 E
Rila Planina, Bulgaria	21	42 10N	23 30 E
Rima, W. ar., Saudi Arabia	31	26 0N	42 0 E
Rimbey, Canada	64	42 35N	114 15w
Rimi, Nigeria	52	12 58N	7 43 E
Rimini, Italy	20	44 3N	12 33 E
Rimouski, Canada	63	48 27N	68 30w
Rimutaka Ra., N.Z.	46	41 8s	175 13 E
Rinconada, Argentina	77	22 25s	66 10w
Rindjam Mt., Indon.	35	8 20s	116 30 E
Ringel Spitz, Mt., Switz.	15	46 54N	9 22 E
Ringim, Nigeria	52	12 13N	9 10 E
Ringköbing, Denmark	23	56 5N	8 15 E
Ringköbing Fd., Denmark	14	55 56N	8 18 E
Ringling, U.S.A.	72	46 18N	110 50w
Ringus, India	32	27 25N	75 30 E
Ringvassöy I., Norway	22	69 53N	19 25 E
Ringville, Ireland	11	52 3N	7 37w
Rinia, I., Greece	21	37 23N	25 13 E
Rio Branco, Acre Terr., Brazil	79	9 55s	67 55w
Rio Branco, Pernambuco, Brazil	79	8 20s	37 0w
Rio Branco, Uruguay	77	32 40s	53 40w
Rio Brava del Norte, R. Mexico	74	30 45N	105 0w
Rio Caribe, Venezuela	75	10 43N	63 6w
Rio Claro, Brazil	78	22 25s	47 35w
Rio Claro, Trinidad	75		Inset
Rio Claro, Sa. do, Brazil	79	16 30s	50 30w
Rio Colorado, Arg.	77	39 0s	64 0w
Rio Cuarto, Argentina	77	33 10s	64 25w
Rio de Janeiro, Brazil	79	23 0s	43 12w
Rio de Janeiro, Federal dist. Brazil	79	22 50s	43 0w
Rio das Pedras, Mozambique	56	23 75N	35 21w
Rio del Rey, R., Cam.	52	10 42N	8 37 E
Rio do Sul, Brazil	77	27 12s	49 50w
Rio Gallegos, Arg.	77	51 45s	69 20w
Rio Grande, Argentina	77	53 45s	67 46w
Rio Grande, Brazil	77	32 0s	52 20w
Rio Grande R., U.S.A.	73	35 45N	106 20w
Rio Grande de Santiago, Mexico	74	20 40N	103 20w
Rio Grande del Norte, N. America	66	20 0N	97 0w
Rio Grande do Norte, st., Brazil	79	5 40s	36 30w
Rio Grande do Sul, st., Brazil	77	29 10s	53 0w
Rio Hondo, Argentina	77	27 30s	64 55w
Rio Largo, Brazil	79	9 28s	36 0w
Rio Maior, Portugal	17	39 19N	8 57w
Rio Muerto, Argentina	77	26 15s	61 40w
Rio Mulatos, Bolivia	78	19 40s	66 50w
Rio Muni, E. G.	54	1 30N	10 0 E
Rio Negro, Brazil	77	26 0s	50 0w
Rio Seco. *See* Villa de Maria, Argentina	77		
Rio Tinto, Portugal	17	41 13N	8 32w
Rio Turbio Mines, Arg.	77	51 30s	72 40w
Rio Verde, Brazil	79	17 50s	51 0w
Rio Verde, Chile	77	52 36s	71 29w
Rio Verde, Mexico	74	21 50N	100 0w
Rio Vista, U.S.A.	73	38 12N	121 43w
Riobamba, Ecuador	78	1 50s	78 45w
Riohacha, Colombia	78	11 31N	73 0w
Rioja, Spain	17	42 28N	2 30w
Riom, France	12	45 54N	3 7 E
Rionero, Italy	20	40 55N	15 40 E
Riosucio, Colombia	78	5 30N	75 40w
Riosucio, Colombia	78	7 35N	77 0w
Riou L., Canada	65	59 0N	105 40w
Ripartimento, Brazil	78	2 10N	62 25w
Ripley, N.Y., U.S.A.	71	42 16N	79 44w
Ripley, Tenn., U.S.A.	71	35 43N	89 32w
Ripoll, Spain	17	42 15N	2 13 E
Ripon, England	10	54 8N	1 31w
Ripon, U.S.A.	70	43 51N	88 50w
Riq'ai, Saudi Arabia	31	29 1N	46 35 E
Riscom, Rhodesia	56	19 1s	29 46 E
Rishiri I., Japan	36	45 10N	141 10 E
Rishon le Zion, Israel	29	31 58N	34 48 E
Rishpon, Israel	29	32 12N	34 49 E
Rison, U.S.A.	71	33 58N	92 13w
Risör, Norway	23	58 43N	9 10 E
Riti, Nigeria	52	7 57N	9 41 E
Ritzville, U.S.A.	72	47 10N	118 24w
Riva, Italy	20	45 53N	10 50 E
Rivadavia, Argentina	77	24 5s	63 0w
Rivadavia, Chile	77	29 50s	70 35w
Rivarolo, Italy	20	45 20N	7 42 E
Rivas, Nicaragua	75	11 30N	85 50w
River Cess, Liberia	50	5 30N	9 25w
Rivera, Argentina	77	27 10s	63 10w
Rivera, Uruguay	77	31 0s	55 50w
Riverhead, U.S.A.	68	40 53N	72 40w
Riverhurst, Canada	65	50 55N	106 50w
Riverina, dist., N.S.W.	43	35 0s	145 0 E
Rivers, Canada	65	50 0N	100 25w
Rivers Inlet, Canada	64	51 40N	127 20w
Rivers, L. of, Canada	65	49 40N	105 45w
Riversdale, Cape Prov.	57	34 7s	21 15 E
Riversdale, N.Z.	47	45 45s	168 45 E
Riverside, Calif., U.S.A.	73	34 0N	117 15w
Riverside, Wyo., U.S.A.	72	41 13N	106 57w
Riverton, Canada	65	51 5N	97 0w
Riverton, N.Z.	47	46 21s	168 0 E
Riverton, S. Australia	43	34 7s	138 39 E
Riverton, U.S.A.	72	43 2N	108 26w
Rivesaltes, France	12	42 47N	2 50 E
Riviera di Levante, Italy	20	44 23N	9 15 E
Riviera di Ponente, Italy	20	43 50N	7 58 E
Rivière à Pierre, Canada	63	46 57N	72 12w
Riviere au Renard, Can.	63	49 0N	64 31w
Rivière Bleue, Canada	63	47 26N	69 2w
Rivière du Loup, Canada	63	47 50N	69 30w
Rivière Pentecôte, Canada	63	49 48N	67 20w
Rivière Pilote, Martinique	75	14 29N	60 54w
Riwaka, New Zealand	47	41 5s	172 59 E
Riyadh (Ar Riyād), Saudi Arabia	30	24 41N	46 42 E
Rizaiyeh (Urmia), Persia	30	37 40N	45 5 E
Rize, Turkey	30	41 0N	40 30 E
Rizzuto, C., Italy	20	38 54N	17 5 E
Rjukan, Norway	23	59 54N	8 33 E
Roa, Spain	17	41 41N	3 56w
Roag, L., Scotland	10	58 20N	6 55w
Roan Antelope, Zambia	56	13 2s	28 20 E
Roanne, France	12	46 3N	4 4 E
Roanoke, Ala., U.S.A.	69	33 9N	85 23w
Roanoke, Va., U.S.A.	68	37 19N	79 55w
Roanoke I., U.S.A.	69	35 55N	75 40w
Roanoke Rapids, U.S.A.	69	36 36N	77 42w
Roanoke R., U.S.A.	69	37 7N	79 7w
Robbins I., Tasmania	43	40 42s	145 0 E
Robe, S. Australia	43	37 1s	139 45 E
Robe, R., W. Australia	44	21 20s	115 41 E
Robe R., Ireland	11	53 39N	9 10w
Robert, Martinique	75	14 41N	60 41w
Robert Pt., W. Australia	44	32 34s	115 40 E

	MAP		
Robert Lee, U.S.A.	71	31 52N	100 28W
Roberts, U.S.A.	72	43 43N	112 9W
Robertsganj, India	33	24 44N	83 12E
Robertson, Cape Prov.	57	33 46S	19 50E
Robertson Ra., W. Australia	44	23 15S	121 0E
Robertsport, Liberia	50	6 45N	11 26W
Robertstown, S. Australia	43	33 57S	139 2E
Roberval, Canada	63	48 32N	72 15W
Robinson, Ont., Canada	62	50 20N	91 20W
Robinson, Yukon, Can.	64	60 24N	134 58W
Robinson Ra., W. Australia	44	25 40S	118 30E
Roblin, Canada	65	51 20N	101 30W
Roboré, Bolivia	78	18 10S	59 45W
Robson Mt., Canada	64	53 10N	119 10W
Robstown, U.S.A.	71	27 47N	97 40W
Roca, C. da, Portugal	17	38 40N	9 31W
Rocamadour, France	12	44 49N	1 33E
Rocha, Uruguay	77	34 30S	54 25W
Rochdale, England	10	53 36N	2 10W
Rochechouart, France	12	45 50N	0 49E
Rochedale, Queensland	42	21 18S	139 1E
Rochefort, France	12	45 56N	0 57W
Rochelle, U.S.A.	70	41 55N	89 5W
Rocher River, Canada	64	61 12N	114 0W
Rochester, Canada	64	54 22N	113 18W
Rochester, Ind., U.S.A.	68	41 5N	86 15W
Rochester, Michigan, U.S.A.	68	42 41N	83 8W
Rochester, Minnesota, U.S.A.	70	44 1N	92 28W
Rochester, N.H., U.S.A.	69	43 19N	71 0W
Rock, R., Canada	64	60 35N	127 0W
Rock Hill, U.S.A.	69	34 55N	81 2W
Rock Island, Canada	63	45 2N	72 5W
Rock Island, U.S.A.	70	41 30N	90 35W
Rock Lake, U.S.A.	70	48 47N	99 7W
Rock Rapids, U.S.A.	70	43 28N	96 8W
Rock River, U.S.A.	72	41 48N	106 0W
Rock Springs, Arizona, U.S.A.	73	34 2N	112 11W
Rock Springs, Montana, U.S.A.	70	46 55N	106 11W
Rock Springs, Wyo., U.S.A.	72	41 40N	109 10W
Rock Valley, U.S.A.	70	43 10N	96 17W
Rockdale, U.S.A.	71	30 37N	97 0W
Rockford, U.S.A.	68	42 20N	89 0W
Rockglen, Canada	65	49 10N	105 40W
Rockhampton, Queens.	42	23 22S	150 32E
Rockhampton Div., Queensland	42	23 28S	149 46E
Rockingham, W. Australia	44	32 15S	115 38E
Rockingham B., Queens.	42	18 5S	146 10E
Rockland, Idaho, U.S.A.	72	42 35N	112 57W
Rockland, Me., U.S.A.	67	44 7N	69 0W
Rockland, Mich., U.S.A.	70	46 44N	89 12W
Rockmart, U.S.A.	69	34 1N	85 2W
Rockport, Mo., U.S.A.	70	40 27N	95 30W
Rockport, Texas, U.S.A.	71	28 0N	97 3W
Rockville, U.S.A.	68	39 7N	77 10W
Rockwall, U.S.A.	71	32 56N	96 30W
Rockwell City, U.S.A.	70	42 23N	94 35W
Rockwood, U.S.A.	69	45 39N	69 48W
Rocky Ford, U.S.A.	66	38 7N	103 45W
Rocky Mount, U.S.A.	69	35 55N	77 48W
Rocky Mountain House, Canada	64	52 25N	115 0W
Rocky Mts., N. America	58	64 0N	140 0W
to		32 0N	107 0W
Rocky Pt., W. Australia	45	33 30S	123 57E
Rockyford, Canada	64	51 20N	113 10W
Rocroi, France	12	49 55N	4 30E
Rod., Pakistan	32	28 10N	63 5E
Roda, Spain	17	37 10N	4 47W
Rodez, France	12	44 21N	2 33E
Rodholivos, Greece	21	40 55N	24 0E
Rodhos (Rhodes) I., Greece	21	36 15N	28 10E
Rodna, Rumania	21	47 27N	24 52E
Rodney C., N.Z.	46	36 16S	174 50E
Rodonit, C., Albania	21	41 34N	19 26E
Roe, R., N. Ireland	11	55 0N	6 56W
Roebourne, W. Australia	44	20 44S	117 9E
Roermond, Netherlands	13	51 12N	6 0E
Roes Welcome Sd., Can.	61	65 0N	87 0W
Roeselare (Roulers), Belgium	13	50 57N	3 7E
Rogachev, U.S.S.R.	25	53 8N	30 5E
Rogagua L., Bolivia	78	14 0S	66 50W
Rogaland, co., Norway	23	59 0N	6 30E
Rogers, U.S.A.	71	36 20N	94 0W
Rogers City, U.S.A.	68	45 25N	83 49W
Rogerson, U.S.A.	72	42 13N	114 37W
Rogersville, U.S.A.	69	36 27N	83 1W
Roggan L., Canada	62	54 0N	77 40W
Roggan R., Canada	62	54 30N	78 30W
Roggan River, Canada	62	54 24N	78 5W
Roggeveldberg, Cape Province	57	32 10S	20 10E
Rogliano, France	12	42 57N	9 30E
Rogliano, Italy	20	39 11N	16 20E
Rognan, Norway	22	67 7N	15 25E
Rogoaguado L., Bol.	78	13 0S	65 30W
Rogue R., U.S.A.	66	42 30N	124 10W
Rohri, Pakistan	32	27 45N	68 51E
Rohtak, India	32	28 55N	76 43E
Roi Et, Thailand	34	16 5N	103 38E
Rojo C., Mexico	74	21 30N	97 30W
Rokel R. (or Seli R.), Sierra Leone	52	8 43N	12 30W
Rokhmoiva, mt., U.S.S.R.	22	66 50N	29 11E
Rokugo, C., Japan	36	37 30N	137 20E
Rolandia, Brazil	77	23 5S	52 0W
Rolette, U.S.A.	70	48 37N	99 50W
Rolla, Kansas, U.S.A.	71	37 7N	101 44W
Rolla, Mo., U.S.A.	71	38 0N	91 42W
Rolla, N.D., U.S.A.	70	48 50N	99 31W
Rolle, Switzerland	15	46 27N	6 10E
Rolleston, N.Z.	47	43 35S	172 24E
Rolleston, Queensland	42	24 25S	148 39E
Roma, Sweden	23	57 32N	18 28E
Roma I., Indonesia	35	7 30S	127 25E
Roma, Queensland	43	26 32S	148 49E
Roma Div., Queensland	43	27 14S	148 18E
Romagna, reg., Italy	20	44 22N	11 0E
Romaine R., Canada	63	51 40N	63 40W
Roman, Rumania	21	46 57N	26 55E
Roman, U.S.S.R.	27	60 20N	112 10E
Romans, France	12	45 3N	5 3E
Romanshorn, Switz.	15	47 33N	9 22E
Romanzof C., Alaska	59	61 40N	166 5W
Rome, Italy	20	41 54N	12 30E
Rome, Ga., U.S.A.	69	34 20N	85 0W
Rome, N.Y., U.S.A.	68	43 14N	75 29W
Romilly, France	12	48 31N	3 44E
Romney, U.S.A.	68	39 21N	78 45W
Romny, U.S.S.R.	25	50 48N	33 28E
Romodanovo, U.S.S.R.	25	54 26N	45 23E
Romorantin, France	12	47 20N	1 44E
Romsdal, Norway	23	62 30N	8 0E
Ron, N. Vietnam	34	17 54N	106 28E
Rona, Zaire	53	2 22N	30 42E
Ronan, U.S.A.	72	47 32N	114 8W
Ronçador Cay, Caribbean Sea	75	13 30N	80 0W
Roncador, Serra do, Brazil	79	12 0S	52 30W
Roncesvalles, Spain	17	43 0N	1 19W
Ronceverte, U.S.A.	68	37 45N	80 28W
Rondane R., Norway	23	62 0N	10 0E
Ronde I., Windward Is.	75	Inset	
Rondônia, st., Brazil	78	11 0S	63 0W
Rongotea, N.Z.	46	40 19S	175 25E
Rönne, Denmark	23	55 6N	14 44E
Ronse, Belgium	13	50 45N	3 35E
Roof Butte, U.S.A.	66	36 60N	108 30W
Roorkee, India	32	29 52N	77 59E
Roosevelt, F. D., L., U.S.A.	72	48 28N	118 14W
Roosevelt, Minn., U.S.A.	70	48 53N	95 0W
Roosevelt, Utah, U.S.A.	72	40 20N	110 1W
Roosevelt I., Antarctica	80	79 0S	161 0W
Roosevelt Mt., Canada	64	58 20N	125 20W
Roosevelt Res, U.S.A.	73	33 45N	111 10W
Roosendaal, Neth.	13	51 32N	4 29E
Root R., Canada	64	50 40N	91 50W
Roper R., N. Terr., Australia	40	14 30S	134 20E
Roosevelt Res., U.S.A.	73	33 45N	111 10W
Ropesville, U.S.A.	71	33 26N	102 7W
Roquefort, France	12	44 2N	0 20W
Roraima, Brazil	78	2 0N	61 30W
Roraima Mt., Guyana	78	5 10N	60 40W
Rorketon, Canada	65	51 24N	99 35W
Rorschach, Switzerland	15	47 28N	9 30E
Rörvik, Norway	22	64 54N	11 15E
Rosa, Zambia	56	9 30S	21 20E
Rosa, Monte, Alps, Switz.–It.	20	45 57N	7 53E
Rosalia, U.S.A.	72	47 15N	117 21W
Rosario, Argentina	77	33 0S	60 50W
Rosario, Maranhao, Brazil	79	3 0S	44 15W
Rosario, Rio Grande do Sul, Brazil	77	30 15S	55 0W
Rosario, Durango, Mex.	74	26 40N	105 30W
Rosario, Lower Calif., Mexico	74	30 0N	116 0W
Rosario, Sinaloa, Mex.	74	23 0N	106 0W
Rosario, Uruguay	77	34 20S	57 20W
Rosario de la Frontera, Argentina	77	25 50S	65 0W
Rosas, Spain	17	42 19N	3 10E
Roscoff, France	12	48 44N	4 0W
Roscommon, Ireland	11	53 38N	8 11W
Roscommon, co., Ire.	11	53 49N	8 20W
Roscommon, U.S.A.	68	44 27N	84 35W
Roscrea, Ireland	11	52 58N	7 50W
Rose Pt., Canada	64	54 20N	131 40W
Rose Blanche, Canada	63	47 38N	58 45W
Rose Harbour, Canada	64	52 15N	131 10W
Rose Lynn, Canada	64	51 26N	111 40W
Rose Valley, Canada	65	52 19N	103 49W
Roseau, Dominica	75	15 20N	61 30W
Roseau, U.S.A.	70	48 58N	95 45W
Roseberry, Tasmania	43	41 45S	145 33E
Rosebud, U.S.A.	71	31 2N	97 0W
Roseburg, U.S.A.	72	43 10N	123 10W
Rosecoe, U.S.A.	70	45 30N	99 18W
Rosedale, Queensland	42	24 38S	151 53E
Rosedale, U.S.A.	71	33 52N	91 0W
Rosehearty, Scotland	10	57 42N	2 8W
Rosenberg, U.S.A.	71	29 32N	95 45W
Rosendaal, Neth.	13	52 0N	5 59E
Rosenheim, Germany	14	47 51N	12 9E
Rosetown, Canada	65	51 35N	108 3W
Rosetta (Rashid), Egypt	51	31 20N	30 17E
Roseville, U.S.A.	73	38 47N	121 19W
Rosewood, Queensland	43	27 39S	152 36E
Rosh Ha Ayin, Israel	29	32 7N	34 56E
Rosh Pinna, Israel	29	32 58N	35 32E
Rosh Ze'ira, Israel	29	31 14N	35 15E
Rosignano, Marittimo, Italy	20	43 23N	10 28E
Rosignol, Guyana	79	6 15N	57 30W
Rosiorii-de-Vede, Rumania	21	44 9N	25 0E
Roskilde, Denmark	23	55 38N	12 3E
Roslavl, U.S.S.R.	25	53 57N	32 55E
Rosmead, Cape Prov.	57	31 29S	25 8E
Ross, New Zealand	47	42 53S	170 49E
Ross Ice Shelf, Ant.	80	80 0S	180 0W
Ross, I., Antarctica	80	77 30S	168 0E
Ross River, Canada	64	62 2N	132 28W
Ross Sea, Southern Oc.	80	74 0S	178 0E
Ross Ice Shelf, Ant.	80	80 0S	180 0W
Rossan Pt., Ireland	11	54 42N	8 47W
Rossano, Italy	20	39 36N	16 39E
Rossburn, Canada	65	50 45N	100 55W
Rossel, I., Papua	42	11 30S	154 30E
Rossignel, L., N.S., Canada	63	44 12N	65 0W
Rossignol, L., Que., Canada	62	52 43N	74 0W
Rossing, S.W. Africa	57	22 25S	14 54E
Rossland, Canada	64	49 6N	117 50W
Rosslare, Ireland	11	52 17N	6 23W
Rosslare Harb., Ireland	11	52 16N	6 20W
Rosso, Mauritania	50	16 40N	15 45W
Rossosh, U.S.S.R.	25	50 15N	39 20E
Rossport, Canada	62	48 50N	87 30W
Rosthern, Canada	65	52 40N	106 20W
Rostock, Germany	14	54 4N	12 9E
Rostov, R.S.F.S.R., U.S.S.R.	25	57 14N	39 15E
Rostov, Ukraine S.S.R. U.S.S.R.	25	47 15N	39 45E
Rösuatn, L., Norway	22	65 45N	14 0E
Roswell, U.S.A.	71	33 26N	104 32W
Rosyth, Scotland	10	56 2N	3 26W
Rotan, U.S.A.	71	32 50N	100 28W
Rothaar Geb., Germany	14	51 5N	8 12E
Rothenburg, Germany	14	49 21N	10 11E
Rother, R., England	10	50 59N	0 40W
Rotherham, England	10	53 26N	1 21W
Rothesay, Canada	63	45 23N	66 0W
Rothesay, Scotland	10	55 50N	5 3W
Rothorn Mt., Switz.	15	46 48N	8 2E
Roti I., Indonesia	35	10 50S	123 0E
Roto, New South Wales	43	33 0S	145 30E
Roto Aira L., N.Z.	46	39 3S	175 55E
Rotoehu L., N.Z.	46	38 2S	176 35E
Rotoiti L., N.Z.	46	38 3S	176 25E
Rotoma L., N.Z.	46	38 3S	176 38E
Rotorua L., N.Z.	46	38 5S	176 30E
Rotoiti L., N.Z.	47	41 51S	172 49E
Rotorua, New Zealand	46	38 9S	176 16E
Rotoroa Lake, N.Z.	47	41 55S	172 39E
Rotterdam, Neth.	13	51 55N	4 30E
Rottnest I., W. Australia	44	32 0S	115 27E
Rottweil, Germany	14	48 9N	8 38E
Rotummeroog I., Neth.	13	53 33N	6 33E
Roubaix, France	12	50 40N	3 10E
Rouen, France	12	49 27N	1 4E
Rough Ridge, N.Z.	47	45 10S	169 53E
Rouleau, Canada	65	50 10N	104 50W
Round Mountain, U.S.A.	72	38 42N	117 9W
Roundstone, Ireland	11	53 24N	9 55W
Roundup, U.S.A.	72	46 25N	108 35W
Rouxville, O.F.S.	57	30 11S	26 50E
Rouyn, Canada	62	48 20N	79 0W
Rovereto, Italy	20	45 53N	11 3E
Rovigo, Italy	20	45 4N	11 48E
Rovinj, Yugoslavia	20	45 18N	13 40E
Rovno, U.S.S.R.	24	50 40N	26 10E
Rowood, U.S.A.	73	32 52N	112 52W
Roxas, Philippines	35	11 30N	122 45E
Roxboro, U.S.A.	69	36 24N	78 59W
Roxburgh, N.Z.	47	45 33S	169 19E
Roy, U.S.A.	71	35 50N	104 6W
Roy Hill, W. Australia	44	22 30S	120 0E
Royal Oak, U.S.A.	68	42 30N	83 5W
Royan, France	12	45 37N	1 2W
Ruahine Ra., N.Z.	46	39 55S	176 2E
Ruamahanga R., N.Z.	46	41 24S	175 8E
Ruanda, Tanzania	53	10 33S	34 57E
Ruapehu, N.Z.	46	39 17S	175 35E
Ruapuke I., N.Z.	47	46 46S	168 31E
Ruasa Kikumba, Zaire	53	1 22S	29 10E
Ruatoria, New Zealand	46	37 54S	178 22E
Ruawai, New Zealand	46	36 8S	174 2E
Rub 'al Khali, Saudi Arabia	48	21 0N	51 0E
Rubbervale, Transvaal	57	23 51S	30 40E
Rubeho Mts., Tanzania	53	6 45S	36 35E
Rubezhnoye, U.S.S.R.	25	49 6N	38 25E
Rubio, Venezuela	78	7 50N	72 20W
Rubona, Uganda	53	0 29N	30 9E
Rubondo Is., Tanzania	53	2 20S	31 50E
Rubtsovsk, U.S.S.R.	26	51 30N	80 50E
Ruby, Alaska	59	64 45N	155 35W
Ruby L., U.S.A.	72	40 10N	115 30W
Ruby, Mts., U.S.A.	72	40 20N	115 30W
Ruchi, U.S.S.R.	22	67 0N	32 10E
Rudall R., W. Austral.	44	22 30S	122 17E
Rudewa, Tanzania	53	10 7S	34 47E
Rudnichny, U.S.S.R.	24	59 40N	52 20E
Rudok, China	37	33 30N	79 40E
Rudolf, I., U.S.S.R.	26	81 20N	58 0E
Rudolf L., Kenya	53	3 40N	30 20E
Rudolstadt, Germany	14	50 44N	11 20E
Rudyard, U.S.A.	68	46 14N	84 35E
Ruenya R., Mozam.	56	17 0S	33 10E
Ruffec, France	12	46 2N	0 12E
Rufiji R., Tanzania	53	7 50S	38 15E
Rufunsa, Zambia	56	15 15S	30 0E
Rufisque, Senegal	50	14 40N	17 13W
Rufino, Argentina	77	34 20S	62 50W
Rugby, England	10	52 23N	1 16W
Rugby, U.S.A.	70	48 26N	100 0W
Rügen I., Germany	14	54 22N	13 25E
Rugezi, Tanzania	53	2 7S	33 12E
Ruhama, Israel	29	31 31N	34 43E
Ruhea, Bangladesh	33	26 15N	88 30E
Ruhengeri, Rwanda	53	1 30S	29 39E
Ruhnu I., U.S.S.R.	23	57 30N	23 20E
Ruhr, R., Germany	14	51 25N	7 15E
Ruhuhu, R., Tanzania	53	10 10S	34 50E
Ruidosa, U.S.A.	71	29 58N	104 37W
Ruidoso, U.S.A.	73	33 21N	105 37W
Ruki R., Zaire	54	0 10S	18 40E
Rukori, Rhodesia	56	16 39S	32 20E
Rukungiri, Uganda	53	0 49S	29 57E
Rukwa L., Tanzania	53	8 20S	32 30E
Rum Cay I., Bahamas	75	23 40N	74 45W
Rum Jungle, N. Terr., Australia	40	13 20S	131 4E
Ruma, Yugoslavia	21	45 8N	19 50E
Rumāh, Saudi Arabia	30	25 38N	47 8E
Rumania, st. Europe	21	46 0N	25 0E
Rumbalara, N. Terr.	45	25 22S	134 30E
Rumbek, Sudan	54	6 54N	29 37E
Rumford, U.S.A.	69	44 30N	70 30W
Rumoi, Japan	36	43 55N	141 40E
Rumonge, Burundi	53	3 55S	29 26E
Rumpi, Malawi	56	11 1S	33 52E
Rumsey, Canada	64	51 51N	112 48W
Rumula, Queensland	42	16 28S	145 20E
Rumuruti, Kenya	53	0 15N	36 30E
Runanga, New Zealand	47	42 25S	171 15E
Runaway C., N.Z.	46	37 32S	178 1E
Runere, Tanzania	53	3 6S	33 18E
Rungwa, Tanzania	53	6 57S	33 22E
Rungwa, Tanzania	53	7 19S	31 40E
Rungwa R., Tanzania	53	7 0S	33 0E
Rungwe & Mt., Tan.	53	9 9S	33 43E
Runka, Nigeria	52	12 28N	7 20E
Runton Ra., W. Austral.	45	23 35S	123 15E
Rupá, India	33	27 15N	92 30E
Rupert, U.S.A.	66	42 40N	113 40W
Rupert B., Canada	62	51 50N	79 12W
Rupert R., Canada	62	51 20N	77 30W
Rupert House, Canada	62	51 30N	78 40W
Ruponda, Tanzania	53	10 10S	38 38E
Rupununi R., Guyana	78	3 30N	59 30W
Rurgwe, Rhodesia	56	20 1S	31 20E
Rurrenabaque, Bolivia	78	14 25S	67 45W
Rusambo, Rhodesia	56	16 35S	32 12E
Rusape, Rhodesia	56	18 35S	32 8E
Ruschuk (Ruse), Bulg.	21	43 48N	25 59E
Ruse (Ruschuk), Bulg.	21	43 48N	25 59E
Rush, Ireland	11	53 31N	6 7W
Rushford, U.S.A.	70	43 50N	91 18W
Rushville, Ill., U.S.A.	70	40 7N	90 31W
Rushville, Ind., U.S.A.	68	39 38N	85 22W
Rushville, Neb., U.S.A.	70	42 45N	102 22W
Rushworth, Victoria	43	36 32S	145 1E
Russas, Brazil	79	4 49S	37 48W
Russell, Canada	65	50 50N	101 20W
Russell, New Zealand	46	35 16S	174 10E
Russell, U.S.A.	70	38 55N	98 52W
Russell, L., Man., Can.	65	56 12N	101 25W
Russell L., N.W. Terr., Canada	64	62 50N	115 40W
Russell Ra., W. Austral.	45	33 10S	123 15E
Russellkonda, India	33	19 57N	84 42E
Russellville, Ala., U.S.A.	69	34 30N	87 44W
Russellville, Ark., U.S.A.	71	35 15N	93 0W
Russellville, Ky., U.S.A.	69	36 50N	86 50W
Russian Mission, Alaska	59	61 45N	161 25W
Russian Soviet Federal Socialist Republic	26–27	43 0N to 80 0N	28 0E to 180 0E
Russkaya Polyana, U.S.S.R.	26	53 55N	74 0E
Rustavi, U.S.S.R.	24	40 45N	44 30E
Rustenburg, Transvaal	57	25 41S	27 14E
Ruston, U.S.A.	71	32 30N	92 40W
Ruswil, Switz.	15	47 05N	8 8E

	MAP		
Rutana, Burundi	53	3 55 s	30 0 E
Rute, Spain	17	37 19N	4 29W
Ruth, U.S.A.	70	39 17N	115 2W
Rüti, Switzerland	15	47 15N	8 48 E
Rutland, U.S.A.	69	43 38N	73 0W
Rutlands Plains, Queens.	42	15 35 s	141 45 E
Rutledge L., & R., Can.	65	61 58N	110 58W
Rutshuru, Zaire	53	1 0s	29 25 E
Ruurlo, Netherlands	13	52 5N	6 24 E
Ruvo, Italy	20	41 7N	16 27 E
Ruvu, Tanzania	53	6 50 s	38 38 E
Ruvu R., Tanzania	53	7 0s	38 30 E
Ruvuma, prov., Tan.	53	10 45N	36 10 E
Ruvuma R., Tanzania	53	11 30 s	36 0 E
Ruwaidha, Si. Arabia	30	23 43N	44 42 E
Ruwenzori Mts., Uganda and Zaire	53	0 30N	29 5 E
Ruya, R., Rhodesia	56	17 0s	31 0 E
Ruyigi, Burundi	53	3 29 s	30 14 E
Ruza, U.S.S.R.	25	55 40N	36 18 E
Ruzayevka, U.S.S.R.	25	54 10N	45 0 E
Ruzizi R., Zaire	53	2 55 s	29 10 E
Ruzomberok, C.Slov.	16	49 3N	19 17 E
Rwanda, st., Africa	53	2 30 s	30 0 E
Rwashamaire, Uganda	53	0 53 s	30 7 E
Ryazan, U.S.S.R.	25	54 40N	39 40 E
Ryazhsk, U.S.S.R.	25	53 45N	40 3 E
Rybache, U.S.S.R.	26	46 40N	81 20 E
Rybachiy Pen., U.S.S.R.	22	69 43N	32 0 E
Rybinsk (Shcherbakov)	25	58 0N	38 50 E
Rybinsk Res., U.S.S.R.	25	58 30N	38 0 E
Rye, England	10	50 57N	0 46 E
Rye Pabch, Res., U.S.A.	72	40 40N	118 15W
Ryegate, U.S.A.	72	46 21N	109 20W
Rylstone, N.S.W.	43	32 46 s	149 58 E
Rypin, Poland	16	53 3N	19 32 E
Ryu-kyu Is., Japan	5	26 0N	127 0 E
Rzeszów, Poland	16	50 5N	21 58 E
Rzhev, U.S.S.R.	25	56 20N	34 20 E

S

Sa Dec, S Viet Nam	34	10 20N	105 46 E
Sa'ad, Israel	29	31 28N	34 33 E
Sa'ādatābād, Iran	31	30 16N	53 2 E
Saale R., Germany	14	51 25N	11 56 E
Saanen, Switzerland	15	46 29N	7 15 E
Saar, land, Germany	14	49 25N	7 0 E
Saar, R., W. Germany	14	48 46N	6 40 E
Saarbrücken, Germany	14	49 15N	6 58 E
Saaremaa I., U.S.S.R.	23	58 30N	22 10 E
Saari Selkä, mts., Fin.	22	68 25N	28 0 E
Saba I., Leeward Is.	75	17 30N	63 10W
Sabac, Yugoslavia	21	44 48N	19 42 E
Sabadell, Spain	17	41 28N	2 7 E
Sabah (N. Borneo), Malaysia	35	5 0N	117 0 E
Sabana, Dom. Repub.	75	19 7N	69 40W
Sabanalarga, Columbia	78	10 40N	74 55W
Sabang, Indonesia	34	5 50N	95 18 E
Sabará, Brazil	79	19 55 s	43 55W
Sabastya, Jordan	29	32 17N	35 12 E
Sabaudia, Italy	20	41 17N	13 2 E
Sabaya, Bolivia	78	19 5 s	68 25W
Sabha, W., Saudi Arabia	30	23 45N	50 0 E
Sabha, Libya	51	27 0N	14 40 E
Sabi R., Rhodesia	56	18 50 s	31 48 E
Sabie, Transvaal	57	25 4 s	30 48 E
Sabinal, Mexico	74	30 50N	107 25W
Sabinal, U.S.A.	71	29 34N	99 26W
Sabinas, Mexico	74	27 50N	101 10W
Sabinas Hidalgo, Mex.	74	26 40N	100 10W
Sabine, Monti, Italy	20	42 15N	12 50 E
Sabine, U.S.A.	71	29 41N	93 51W
Sabine L., U.S.A.	71	29 47N	93 50W
Sabine R., U.S.A.	71	31 30N	93 35W
Sablé, France	12	47 50N	0 21W
Sable C., Canada	63	43 29N	65 38W
Sable C., U.S.A.	69	25 5N	81 0W
Sable I., Canada	63	44 0N	60 0W
Sabon Kafi, Niger	52	14 38N	8 47 E
Sabongari, Niger	52	12 21N	3 23 E
Sabor R., Portugal	17	41 16N	7 10W
Sabzawar. *See* Shin Dand, Afghanistan	31		
Sabzawar, Iran	31	36 16N	57 35 E
Sabzvāran, Iran	31	28 43N	57 42 E
Sac City, U.S.A.	70	42 26N	95 2W
Sacaolo, Angola	56	12 50 s	22 20 E
Sacedón, Spain	17	40 29N	2 41W
Sachigo L., Canada	62	53 50N	92 12W
Saco, U.S.A.	72	48 28N	107 19W
Sacramento, U.S.A.	66	38 30N	121 30 E
Sacramento Mts., U.S.A.	73	33 0N	105 45W
Sacramento, R., U.S.A.	66	39 30N	122 0W
Sadaba, Spain	17	2 19N	1 12W
Sa'dani, Tanzania	53	5 58 s	38 35 E
Sadasivpet, India	32	19 38N	77 50 E
Sade, Nigeria	52	11 22N	10 45 E
Sadiba, Botswana	56	18 53 s	23 1 E
Sadimi, Zaire	56	9 25 s	23 25 E
Sado, I., Japan	36	38 15N	138 30 E
Sado R., Portugal	17	38 10N	8 22W
Sadon, Burma	33	25 28N	98 0 E
Sadovoya, U.S.S.R.	25	47 49N	44 45 E
Sadulgarh, India	32	29 35N	74 15 E
Saeki, Japan	36	32 58N	131 57 E
Safaha, des., Saudi Arabia	30	26 25N	39 0 E
Safaniya, Saudi Arabia	30	28 5N	49 12 E
Safed Koh, Afghanistan	31	34 15N	64 0 E
Säffle, Sweden	23	59 8N	12 55 E
Safford, U.S.A.	73	32 51N	109 42W
Saffron Walden, Eng.	10	52 2N	0 15 E
Safi, Morocco	50	32 20N	9 20W
Safiah, Israel	29	31 27N	34 46 E
Safid, Iran	30	37 0N	49 33 E
Safiriya, Israel	29	31 59N	34 51 E
Safonovo, U.S.S.R.	24	65 40N	47 50 E
Safvar, Sweden	23	63 55N	20 38 E
Saga, Japan	36	33 15N	130 20 E
Saga, pref., Japan	36	33 15N	130 0 E
Saga, Indonesia	35	2 40 s	132 55 E
Sagaba, Angola	56	11 16 s	23 9 E
Sagaing, Burma	33	22 0N	96 0 E
Sagar, Madhya Pradesh, India	32	23 50N	78 50 E
Sagar, Mysore, India	32	14 7N	75 0 E
Sagara, L., Tanzania	53	5 20 s	31 20 E
Saginaw, U.S.A.	68	43 26N	83 55W
Saginaw B., U.S.A.	68	43 50N	83 40W
Sagiz, U.S.S.R.	24	48 0N	55 40 E
Sagli, Mongolia	37	50 20N	91 40 E
Sagres, Portugal	17	37 0N	8 58W
Sagua la Grande, Cuba	75	22 50N	80 10W
Saguache, U.S.A.	73	38 7N	106 4W
Saguenay, R., Canada	63	48 22N	70 30W
Sagunto, Spain	17	39 42N	0 18W
Sahagún, Colombia	75	8 50N	75 35W
Sahágun, Spain	17	42 18N	5 2W
Sahara Desert, Afr.	50–51	23 0N	5 0W
Saharan Atlas, Algeria	50	33 0N	0 2 E
Sahaswan, India	32	28 5N	78 45 E
Sahl Arraba, Jordan	29	37 26N	35 12 E
Sahra al Hijārah, Iraq	30	30 20N	44 0 E
Sahuaripa, Mexico	74	29 30N	109 0W
Sahuarita, U.S.A.	73	31 59N	111 0W
Saida, Algeria	50	34 50N	0 11 E
Saidabad, Iran	31	29 32N	55 38 E
Saidpur, India	33	25 35N	83 15 E
Saidu, Pakistan	32	34 50N	72 15 E
Saighan, Afghanistan	31	35 16N	67 49 E
Saignelegier, Switz.	15	47 16N	7 1 E
Saigon, South Viet Nam	34	10 58N	106 40 E
Saijo, Japan	36	34 0N	133 5 E
Saikhoa Ghat, India	33	27 50N	95 40 E
Saimaa L., Finland	23	61 33N	29 35 E
Sain Shanda, Mongolia	38	44 40N	110 20 E
St. Affrique, France	12	43 58N	2 52 E
St. Albans, Canada	63	47 51N	55 50W
St. Albans, England	10	51 44N	0 19W
St. Albans, Queensland	42	24 43 s	139 56 E
St. Alban's, Vt., U.S.A.	69	44 49N	73 0W
St. Albans, W. Va., U.S.A.	68	38 21N	81 50 E
St. Amand Mont-Rond, Fr.	12	46 43N	2 28 E
St. André des Alpes, France	12	43 58N	6 30 E
St. Andrews, N.B., Can.	63	45 8N	67 4W
St. Andrews, N.Z.	47	44 33 s	171 10 E
St. Andrews, Scotland	10	56 20N	2 48W
St. Ann B., Canada	63	46 22N	60 25W
St. Ann's Bay, Jamaica	75	18 30N	77 20W
St. Anthony, Canada	63	51 24N	55 39W
St. Anthony, U.S.A.	72	44 0N	111 40W
St. Arnaud, Victoria	43	36 33 s	143 14 E
St. Arnaud Ra, N.Z.	47	42 1 s	172 53 E
St. Arthur, Canada	63	47 32N	67 28W
St. Augustin, Canada	63	51 19N	58 48W
St. Augustin R., Canada	63	51 30N	58 30W
St. Augustine, U.S.A.	69	30 0N	81 20W
St. Barbe Is. *See* Horse Island	63		
St. Barthelémy I., Leeward Islands	75	17 50N	62 50W
St. Bathans, N.Z.	47	44 53 s	170 0 E
St. Bees Head, England	10	54 30N	3 38W
St. Bernardino Pass, Switzerland	15	46 31N	9 13 E
St. Boniface, Man., Can.	65	49 50N	97 10W
St. Bride's, Canada	63	46 56N	54 10W
St. Brieuc, France	12	48 31N	2 48W
St Calais, France	12	47 56N	0 45W
St. Catherines, Canada	62	43 20N	79 10W
St. Catherine's I., U.S.A.	69	31 35N	81 10W
St. Catherine's Pt., Eng.	10	50 34N	1 18W
St. Cére, France	12	44 52N	1 53 E
St. Cergue, Switz.	15	46 27N	6 10 E
St. Charles, Ill., U.S.A.	70	41 55N	88 20W
St. Charles, Mo., U.S.A.	70	38 46N	90 30W
St. Clair, U.S.A.	68	42 47N	82 27W
St. Clair, L., Canada–U.S.A.	62	42 30N	82 40W
St. Claude, Canada	65	49 40N	98 20W
St. Claude, France	12	46 22N	5 52 E
St. Cloud, U.S.A.	70	45 36N	94 11W
St. Cœur de Marie, Can.	63	48 39N	71 43W
St. Cristopher (St. Kitts), I., Leeward Is.	75	17 20N	62 40W
St. Croix I., W. Indies	75	17 30N	64 40W
St. Croix, R., U.S.A.	70	45 15N	92 50W
St. Croix Falls, U.S.A.	70	45 24N	92 35W
St. David's I., Bermuda	75		Inset
St. Denis, France	12	48 57N	2 20 E
St. Dié, France	12	48 18N	6 56 E
St. Dizier, France	12	48 40N	5 8 E
St. Elias, Mt., Alaska	59	60 24N	141 5W
St. Elias Mts., Canada	59	60 0N	138 0W
St. Emilion, France	12	44 54N	4 30 E
St. Étienne, Basses Pyrénées, France	12	43 10N	1 20W
St. Étienne, Loire, France	12	45 27N	4 22 E
St. Eustatius I., Leeward Is.	75	17 20N	63 0W
St. Félicien, Canada	63	48 40N	72 25W
St. Fintan's, Canada	63	48 10N	58 50W
St. Florent, Corsica, France	12	42 40N	9 20 E
St. Flour, France	12	45 3N	3 7 E
St. Francis, Cape Prov.	57	34 12 s	24 55 E
St. Francis, U.S.A.	70	39 48N	101 46W
St. Francis R., U.S.A.	71	35 20N	90 35W
St. Francisville, U.S.A.	71	30 46N	91 27W
St. Gabriel de Brandon, Canada	62	46 17N	73 24W
St. Gallen, Switz.	15	47 25N	9 22 E
St. Gallen, can., Switz.	15	47 13N	9 15 E
St. Gaudens, France	12	43 7N	0 44 E
St. George, Bermuda	75		Inset
St. George, Canada	63	45 11N	66 57W
St. George, Queensland	43	28 1 s	148 41 E
St. George, S.C., U.S.A.	69	33 12N	80 34W
St. George, Utah, U.S.A.	73	37 10N	113 35W
St. George C., Canada	63	48 30N	59 16W
St. George C., U.S.A.	69	29 30N	85 0W
St. George West, Can.	65	50 33N	96 0W
St. George's, Canada	63	48 26N	58 31W
St. Georges, Canada	63	46 8N	70 40W
St George's, Grenada, West Indies	75	12 45N	61 50W
St. Georges, French Guiana	79	4 0N	52 0W
St. George's, Windward Islands	78		Inset
St. George's B., Canada	63	48 0N	58 12W
St. George's Chan., British Isles	10	52 0N	6 0W
St. George's Channel, New Guinea	42	4 0 s	152 20 E
St. George's I., Bermuda	75		Inset
St. Germain, France	12	48 48N	2 5 E
St. Gheorghe I., Rumania	54	45 8N	29 20 E
St. Gheorghe's Mouth, Rumania	21	45 0N	29 30 E
St. Gilles, France	12	46 42N	1 56W
St. Girons, France	12	42 58N	1 7 E
St. Gotthard P., Switz.	15	46 33N	8 33 E
St. Helena I., Atlantic Ocean	49	15 55 s	5 44W
St. Helena, U.S.A.	73	38 30N	122 28W
St. Helena B., Cape Province	57	32 40 s	18 10 E
St. Helena, U.S.A.	73	38 30N	122 28W
St. Helens, Eng.	10	53 28N	2 43W
St. Helens, Queensland	42	20 55 s	148 48 E
St. Helens, U.S.A.	72	45 55N	122 50W
St. Helier, Jersey	12	49 11N	2 6W
St. Hippolyte, France	12	47 20N	6 50 E
St. Hubert, Belgium	13	50 2N	5 23 E
St. Hyacinthe, Canada	62	45 40N	72 58W
St. Ignace, U.S.A.	68	45 53N	84 43W
St. Ignace I., Canada	62	48 45N	88 0W
St. Ignatius, U.S.A.	72	47 20N	114 5W
St. Imier, Switzerland	15	47 9N	6 58 E
St. Ives, Eng.	10	50 13N	5 29W
St. James, U.S.A.	70	43 59N	94 34W
St. James C., Canada	64	51 55N	131 0W
St. Jean, Canada	62	45 20N	73 50W
St. Jean, France	12	45 14N	6 30 E
St. Jean C., E. G.	54	1 10N	11 15 E
St. Jean R., Canada	63	50 45N	64 0W
St. Jean Baptiste, Can.	65	49 15N	97 20W
St Jean de Luz, France	12	43 24N	1 39W
St Jean Pied de Port, France	12	43 10N	1 14W
St. Jean-Port-Joli, Can.	63	47 15N	70 13W
St. Jérome, Lake St. John, Quebec, Canada	63	48 26N	71 53W
St. Jerome, Terrebonne, Quebec, Canada	62	45 45N	74 0W
St. John, Canada	63	45 20N	66 8W
St. John C., Canada	63	50 0N	55 30W
St. John, Kan., U.S.A.	71	37 59N	98 45W
St. John, N.D., U.S.A.	71	48 59N	99 36W
St. John L., Canada	63	48 40N	72 0W
St. John R., Canada	63	46 30N	67 40W
St. John's, Antigua	75	16 50N	62 0W
St. John's, Newf.	63	47 35N	52 40W
St. Johns, Ariz., U.S.A.	73	34 30N	109 53W
St. Johns, Mich., U.S.A.	68	43 0N	84 38W
St. John's R., U.S.A.	69	30 20N	81 30W
St. Johnsbury, U.S.A.	69	44 25N	72 1W
St. Joseph, La., U.S.A.	71	31 56N	91 17W
St. Joseph, Mich., U.S.A.	68	42 5N	86 30W
St. Joseph, Miss., U.S.A.	70	39 45N	94 45W
St. Joseph I., Canada	62	46 12N	83 58W
St. Joseph L., Canada	62	51 10N	90 50W
St. Joseph R., U.S.A.	68	42 5N	85 20W
St. Joseph d'Alma, Can.	63	48 35N	71 40W
St. Jovite, Canada	62	46 8N	74 38W
St. Junien, France	12	45 53N	0 52 E
St. Kilda, New Zealand	47	45 53 s	170 31 E
St. Kitts *See* St. Christopher	75		
St. Laurent, Canada	65	50 25N	97 58W
St. Laurent, Surinam	79	5 29N	54 3W
St. Lawrence, Canada	63	46 54N	55 23W
St. Lawrence, Queens.	42	22 16 s	149 31 E
St. Lawrence, Gulf of, Canada	63	48 25N	62 0W
St. Lawrence I., Alaska	59	63 0N	170 0W
St. Lawrence R., Canada	63	44 55N	75 2W
St. Leonard, Canada	63	47 12N	67 58W
St. Lewis, R., Canada	63	52 15N	56 30W
St. Lin, Canada	62	45 44N	73 46W
St. Lô, France	12	49 8N	1 6W
St. Louis, Senegal	50	16 8N	16 27W
St. Louis, Mich., U.S.A.	68	43 24N	84 35W
St. Louis, Mo., U.S.A.	70	38 40N	90 20W
St. Louis, R., U.S.A.	70	47 15N	92 50W
St. Lucia B., Indonesia	35	3 55N	117 50 E
St. Lucia L., Natal	57	28 5 s	32 30 E
St. Lucia Chan., W. Ind.	75	14 15N	61 0W
St. Lucia I., W. Ind.	75	14 0N	60 50W
St Lucia Lake, Natal	57	28 5 s	32 30 E
St. Luis, U.S.A.	71	37 14N	105 27W
St. Maarten I., Leeward Islands	75	18 0N	63 5W
St. Maixent, France	12	46 25N	0 12W
St. Malo, France	12	48 40N	2 0W
St. Marc, Haiti	75	19 10N	72 50W
St. Maries, U.S.A.	72	47 16N	116 35W
St. Martin, France	12	44 4N	7 15 E
St. Martin I., Leeward Islands	75	18 0N	63 0W
St. Martin, L., Canada	65	51 40N	98 30W
St. Martins, Canada	63	45 22N	65 38W
St. Martinville, U.S.A.	71	30 7N	91 49W
St. Mary B., Canada	63	46 50N	53 50W
St. Mary, C., Gambia	52	13 24N	13 10 E
St. Mary's, Canada	63	46 56N	53 34W
St. Mary's, Tasmania	43	41 32 s	148 11 E
St. Mary's, Ohio, U.S.A.	68	40 33N	84 20W
St. Marys, Pa., U.S.A.	68	41 30N	78 33W
St. Mary's B., Canada	63	46 56N	53 45W
St. Mary's C., Canada	63	46 50N	54 12W
St. Mary's Pk., S. Australia	43	31 28 s	138 30 E
St. Matthew's I., Burma	33	10 0N	98 25 E
St. Maur, France	12	48 49N	2 30 E
St. Maurice, Switz.	15	46 13N	7 0 E
St. Maurice R., Canada	62	47 20N	72 50W
St. Michael, Alaska	59	63 30N	162 10W
St. Michaels, U.S.A.	73	35 42N	109 4W
St. Moritz, Switzerland	15	46 30N	9 50 E
St. Nazaire, France	12	47 18N	2 11W
St. Nicholas R., Nigeria	52	4 20N	6 25 E
St. Niklaas, Belgium	13	51 10N	4 9 E
St. Niklaus, Switzerland	15	46 10N	7 48 E
St. Omer, France	12	50 45N	2 13 E
St. Pacôme, Canada	63	47 24N	69 58W
St. Pamphilé, Canada	63	46 58N	69 48W
St. Pascal, Canada	63	47 32N	69 48W
St. Paul, Canada	64	54 0N	111 18W
St. Paul, France	12	42 50N	2 28 E
St. Paul, Minn., U.S.A.	70	44 54N	93 5W
St. Paul, Neb., U.S.A.	70	41 16N	98 29W
St. Paul, I., Atlantic Oc.	5	0 50N	31 40W
St. Paul I., Canada	63	47 12N	60 9W
St. Paul R., Canada	63	51 30N	57 40W
St. Paul, R., Liberia	52		Inset
St. Paul's B., Canada	63	49 48N	57 58W
St. Peter, U.S.A.	70	44 16N	93 57W
St. Peter Port, Channel Islands	12	49 27N	2 31W
St. Peters, N.S., Canada	63	45 40N	60 53W
St. Peter's, P.E.I., Can.	63	46 20N	62 25W
St. Petersburg, U.S.A.	69	27 45N	82 40W
St. Pierre, France	12	48 23N	4 32W
St.-Pierre and Miquelon, Fr. Overseas Terr., N. Amer.	63	47 10N	56 50W
St. Pol, France	12	50 21N	2 20 E
St. Pölten, Austria	14	48 12N	15 38 E
St. Quentin, France	12	50 17N	1 35 E
St. Raphael, France	12	43 25N	6 47 E
St. Regis, U.S.A.	72	47 19N	115 2W
St. Rémy, France	12	43 48N	4 51 E
St. Servan, France	12	48 39N	2 0W
St. Sever, France	12	43 46N	0 35W
St. Simeon, Canada	63	47 51N	69 54W
St Stephen, Canada	63	45 16N	67 17W
St. Terese, Alaska	64	53 10N	134 45W
St. Thomas, Canada	62	42 45N	81 10W
St. Tite, Canada	62	46 45N	72 40W
St. Trond, Belgium	13	50 48N	5 10 E
St. Tropez, France	12	43 17N	6 38 E
St. Valéry en Caux, Fr.	12	49 50N	0 42 E
St. Valery-sur-Somme, France	12	50 10N	1 38 E

Name	Map	Lat.	Long.
St. Vallier, France	12	45 11N	4 50E
St. Veit, Austria	14	46 54N	14 22E
St. Vincent, C., Portugal	17	37 0N	9 0W
St. Vincent G., S. Australia	43	35 0S	138 0E
St. Vincent I., W. Indies	75	13 10N	61 10W
St. Vincent Pass, Windward Islands	75	Inset	
St. Vith, Belgium	13	50 17N	6 5E
St. Walburg, Canada	65	53 40N	109 5W
St. Yrieix, France	12	45 30N	1 12E
Ste. Agathe, Canada	62	46 2N	74 20W
Ste. Anne, Guadeloupe	75	Inset	
Ste. Anne, Martinique	75	Inset	
Ste. Anne de Beaupré, Canada	62	47 2N	70 58W
Ste. Anne de Portneuf, Canada	62	48 55N	69 0W
Ste. Anne des Chênes, Canada	65	49 40N	96 40W
Ste. Cecile, Canada	63	47 56N	64 34W
Ste. Marie, Canada	63	46 28N	71 2W
Ste. Marie, Martinique	75	14 48N	61 1W
Ste. Rose, Guadeloupe	75	16 20N	61 45W
Ste. Rose du lac, Canada	65	51 10N	99 30W
Saintes, France	12	45 45N	0 40W
Saintes, I. des, Leeward Islands	75	Inset	
Saintonge, prov., France	12	45 40N	0 50W
Sairang, India	33	23 50N	92 45E
Saitama, Pref., Japan	36	36 10N	139 15E
Sajama, Mt., Bolivia	78	18 0S	68 55W
Sajo, R., Hungary	16	48 20N	20 35E
Sak, R., Cape Province	57	30 54S	20 28E
Sak River, Cape Prov.	57	30 57S	20 20E
Saka, Kenya	53	0 11S	39 30E
Saka Kalat, W. Pakistan	32	27 10N	65 5E
Sakaba, Nigeria	52	11 5N	5 30E
Sakaiminato, Japan	36	34 30N	133 19E
Sakākah, Saudi Arabia	30	30 0N	40 8E
Sakamachi, Japan	36	35 30N	133 20E
Sakami L. & R., Canada	62	53 10N	77 0W
Sakania, Zaire	55	12 48S	28 35E
Sakar, I., New Guinea	42	5 25S	148 0E
Sakarya, R., Turkey	30	40 0N	31 0E
Sakata, Japan	36	38 55N	139 56E
Sake, Zaire	53	1 32S	29 1E
Sakete, Dahomey	52	6 40N	2 32E
Sakha, Saudi Arabia	30	30 5N	40 6E
Sakhalin I., U.S.S.R.	27	51 0N	143 0E
Sakhnin, Israel	29	32 52N	35 12E
Sakrand, Pakistan	32	26 10N	68 15E
Säkylä, Finland	23	61 4N	22 20E
Sal R., U.S.S.R.	25	47 25N	42 20E
Sala, Kenya	53	0 41N	49 9E
Sala, Sweden	23	59 58N	16 35E
Salabangka I., Indon.	35	3 0S	122 30E
Salacgriva, U.S.S.R.	23	57 43N	24 28E
Saladillo, Argentina	77	35 40S	59 55W
Saladillo R., Argentina	77	28 40S	64 0W
Salado R., Argentina	77	27 0S	63 40W
Salado R., Argentina	77	35 40S	58 10W
Salaga, Ghana	52	8 31N	0 31W
Salajar & I., Indonesia	35	6 15S	120 30E
Salala, Liberia	52	6 24N	10 7W
Salamanca, Chile	77	32 0S	71 25W
Salamanca, Spain	17	40 57N	5 40W
Salamanca, U.S.A.	68	42 10N	78 42W
Salamaua, Terr. of N. Guin.	42	7 10S	147 0E
Salamis, Greece	21	37 56N	23 30E
Salar de Atacama, Chile	77	23 30S	68 25W
Salar de Coipasa, Bol.	78	19 0S	68 0W
Salar de Uyura, Bolivia	78	20 30S	68 0W
Salatiga, Java, Indon.	34	7 23S	110 30E
Salaverry, Peru	78	8 15S	79 0W
Salawe, Tanzania	53	3 19S	32 52E
Salbris, France	12	47 25N	2 3E
Saldaña, Spain	17	42 32N	4 48W
Saldanha, Cape Prov.	57	33 0S	17 58E
Saldanha B., Cape Province	57	33 6S	18 0E
Saldus, U.S.S.R.	23	56 45N	22 37E
Sale, Morocco	50	33 29N	6 47W
Sale, Victoria	43	38 7S	147 0E
Sālehābād, Iran	31	35 44N	61 3E
Salekhard, U.S.S.R.	24	66 30N	66 25E
Salem, India	32	11 39N	78 12E
Salem, Ind., U.S.A.	68	38 38N	86 5W
Salem, Mass., U.S.A.	69	42 29N	70 53W
Salem, Mo., U.S.A.	71	37 42N	91 32W
Salem, N.J., U.S.A.	68	39 34N	75 29W
Salem, Ohio, U.S.A.	68	40 52N	80 50W
Salem, Oreg., U.S.A.	72	45 0N	123 0W
Salem, S.D., U.S.A.	70	43 50N	97 25W
Salem, Va., U.S.A.	68	37 19N	80 8W
Salembu I., Indonesia	35	5 35S	114 30E
Salemi, Italy	20	37 49N	12 47E
Salen, Scotland	10	56 42N	5 48W
Salerno, Italy	20	40 40N	14 44E
Salfit, Jordan	29	32 5N	35 11E
Sali R., Argentina	77	26 20S	65 5W
Salida, U.S.A.	66	38 33N	106 1W
Salihli, Turkey	30	38 29N	28 9E
Salima, Malawi	56	13 47S	34 28E
Salina, U.S.A.	70	38 50N	97 40W
Salina I., Italy	20	38 35N	14 50E

	Map		
Salina Cruz, Mexico	74	16 10N	95 10W
Salina Grande, Arg.	77	42 50S	64 0W
Salinas, Brazil	78	16 20S	42 10W
Salinas, Ecuador	79	2 10S	80 50W
Salinas, Mexico	74	22 40N	101 42W
Salinas, U.S.A.	73	36 40N	121 50W
Salinas R., U.S.A.	73	36 10N	121 20W
Salinas Lucia, Ra., U.S.A.	73	36 0N	121 20W
Saline Pte, Windward Is.	75	Inset	
Saline, R., Ark., U.S.A.	71	34 15N	92 30W
Saline, R., Kan., U.S.A.	70	39 10N	99 0W
Salinópolis, Brazil	79	0 40S	47 20W
Salins, France	12	46 58N	5 52E
Salisbury, England	10	51 4N	1 48W
Salisbury, Rhodesia	56	17 50S	31 2E
Salisbury, Md., U.S.A.	69	38 20N	75 38W
Salisbury, Mo., U.S.A.	68	39 25N	92 45W
Saliste, Rumania	21	45 45N	23 56E
Salka, Nigeria	52	10 20N	4 58E
Sallisaw, U.S.A.	71	35 28N	94 46W
Sallyana, Nepal	33	28 24N	82 25E
Salmo, Canada	64	49 10N	117 20W
Salmon, U.S.A.	72	45 10N	114 0W
Salmon R., Canada	64	54 40N	123 50W
Salmon R., U.S.A.	72	46 0N	116 30W
Salmon Arm, Canada	64	50 40N	119 15W
Salmon Gums, W. Australia	44	32 45S	121 30E
Salmon River Mts., U.S.A.	72	44 30N	113 25W
Salo, Finland	23	60 22N	23 3E
Salome, U.S.A.	73	33 48N	113 38W
Salon, France	12	43 39N	5 6E
Salonta, Rumania	21	46 49N	21 42E
Saloum R., Senegal	52	Inset	
Salsette I., India	32	19 5N	72 50E
Salsk, U.S.S.R.	25	46 28N	41 30E
Salso R., Sicily	20	37 6N	13 55E
Salsomaggiore, Italy	20	44 48N	9 59E
Salt Fd., Norway	22	67 15N	14 5E
Salt L., W. Australia	44	24 9S	113 47E
Salt Lakes, W. Austral.	44	24 40S	121 45E
Salt Lakes, W. Austral.	44	28 30S	119 30E
Salt Ra., Mts., W. Pak.	31	32 45N	72 40E
Salt R., Canada	64	59 40N	112 0W
Salt R., U.S.A.	73	33 50N	110 27W
Salt, R., Cape Province	57	32 40S	22 50E
Salt Fork R., Okla., U.S.A.	71	37 25N	98 45W
Salt Fork R., Tex., U.S.A.	66	33 25N	100 50W
Salt Lake City, U.S.A.	72	40 45N	112 0W
Salta, prov., Argentina	77	25 0S	65 30W
Saltillo, Mexico	74	25 30N	100 57W
Salto, Uruguay	77	31 20S	57 59W
Salto Augusto, Brazil	78	8 30S	58 0W
Salto R., Italy	20	42 15N	13 0E
Salton Sea, U.S.A.	73	33 20N	116 0W
Saltpond, Ghana	52	5 15N	1 3W
Saltspring, Canada	64	48 54N	123 37W
Saltville, U.S.A.	69	36 52N	81 48W
Salula, R., U.S.A.	69	34 12N	81 45W
Salûm, Egypt	51	31 30N	25 1E
Salûm, G. of, Egypt	51	31 31N	25 9E
Salur, India	33	18 27N	83 18E
Saluzzo, Italy	20	44 39N	7 29E
Salvador (Bahia), Brazil	79	13 0S	38 30W
Salvador, Canada	65	52 20N	109 25W
Salvador, rep., Central America	74	13 50N	89 0W
Salvador, L., U.S.A.	71	29 45N	90 15W
Salwa, Qatar	31	24 45N	50 51E
Salween R., Burma, etc.	33	20 0N	98 0E
Salyany, U.S.S.R.	24	39 40N	49 0E
Salzbrunn, S.W. Africa	57	24 33S	18 0E
Salzburg, Austria	14	47 48N	13 2E
Salzburg, prov., Austria	14	47 30N	13 0E
Salzgitter, W. Germany	14	52 12N	10 22E
Salzwedel, Germany	14	52 50N	11 11E
Sam Neua, Laos	34	20 29N	104 0E
Sama, U.S.S.R.	24	60 10N	60 15E
Samale, Indonesia	35	1 5S	130 55E
Samana Cay, I., Bah.	75	23 0N	73 40W
Samanco, Peru	78	9 10S	78 30W
Samandag, Turkey	30	36 2N	36 0E
Samanga, Tanzania	53	8 27S	39 18E
Samar, I., Philippines	35	12 0N	125 0E
Samara R., Ukraine, U.S.S.R.	25	48 45N	35 30E
Samara R., U.S.S.R.	24	52 30N	53 0E
Samarai, Papua	42	10 32S	150 35E
Samaria, dist., Jordan	29	32 44N	35 15E
Samaria (site), Jordan	29	32 15N	35 13E
Samarinda, Indonesia	35	0 28S	117 16E
Samarkand, U.S.S.R.	26	39 40N	67 0E
Samarra, Iraq	30	34 16N	43 55E
Samaso, Somali Rep.	53	3 23N	41 55E
Samassi (Mannu), R., Italy	20	39 25N	8 56E
Samastipur, India	33	25 50N	85 50E
Sambalpur, India	33	21 28N	83 58E
Sambar Tg., C., Indon.	35	3 0S	110 10E
Sambas, Indonesia	35	1 20N	109 20E
Sambawizi, Zambia	56	18 21S	26 16E
Sambhal, India	32	28 35N	78 37E

	Map		
Sambhar, India	32	26 52N	75 45E
Sambiase, Italy	20	38 57N	16 16E
Sambre R., Belgium–France	13	50 2N	4 15E
Samchök, Korea	36	37 30N	129 0E
Samdüng, Korea	36	39 30N	126 15E
Same, Tanzania	53	4 5S	37 43E
Samfya, Zambia	56	11 17S	29 44E
Samgaltai, U.S.S.R.	27	50 45N	95 0E
Samho, N. Korea	36	39 59N	127 55E
Samoa Is., Pacific Oc.	5	14 0S	171 0W
Samos I., Greece	21	37 45N	26 50E
Samothraki & I., Greece	21	40 28N	25 38E
Sampa, Ghana	52	8 0N	2 36W
Sampacho, Argentina	77	33 20S	64 50W
Sampang, Indonesia	34	7 11S	113 13E
Sampit, Indonesia	35	2 20S	113 0E
Sampit B., Indonesia	35	3 10S	113 10E
Samra, Saudi Arabia	30	25 38N	40 56E
Samreboi, Ghana	52	5 34N	7 28E
Samri, Nigeria	52	11 50N	6 44E
Samshui, China	39	23 7N	112 58E
Samsö I., Denmark	14	55 50N	10 35E
Samson, mt., W. Australia	44	22 42S	117 38E
Samsun, Turkey	30	41 15N	36 15E
Samu', Jordan	29	31 24N	35 4E
Samusole, Zaire	56	10 2S	24 3E
San, Mali	50	13 15N	4 45W
San R., Poland	16	50 25N	22 20E
San Agustin C., Phil.	35	6 30N	126 30E
San Ambrosio I., Chile	5	25 35S	79 30W
San Andreas, U.S.A.	73	38 16N	120 36W
San Andrés, mts., U.S.A.	73	33 0N	106 45W
San Andrés Tuxtla, Mexico	74	18 30N	95 20W
San Angelo, U.S.A.	71	31 30N	100 30W
San Antonio, Chile	77	33 40S	71 40W
San Antonio, N. Mexico, U.S.A.	73	33 56N	106 52W
San Antonio, Texas, U.S.A.	71	29 30N	98 20W
San Antonio C., Arg.	77	36 15S	56 40W
San Antonio C., Cuba	75	22 0N	85 0W
San Antonio R., U.S.A.	71	28 30N	97 14W
San Antonio de los Baños, Cuba	75	22 54N	82 31W
San Antonio de los Cobres, Argentina	77	24 8S	66 20W
San Antonio do Zaire, Zaire	54	6 10S	12 15E
San Antonio Oeste, Arg.	77	40 40S	65 0W
San Augustine, U.S.A.	71	31 32N	94 4W
San Bartolomeu, Port.	17	37 15N	8 17W
San Benedetto, Italy	20	45 2N	10 57E
San Benito, U.S.A.	71	26 5N	97 32W
San Bernardino, U.S.A.	73	34 0N	117 10W
San Bernardo, Chile	77	33 40S	70 50W
San Bernardo Is., Col.	78	9 50N	75 50W
San Blas, Mexico	74	26 10N	108 40W
San Blas, C., U.S.A	69	29 40N	85 25W
San Blas, Cord de, mts., Pan.	75	9 15N	78 30W
San Blas, Pta., Panama	78	9 30N	79 0W
San Borja, Bolivia	78	14 58S	67 25W
San Carlos, Argentina	77	33 50S	69 0W
San Carlos, Chile	77	36 25S	72 0W
San Carlos, Fernando Pòo	52	3 29N	8 33E
San Carlos, Mexico	74	24 30N	99 0W
San Carlos, U.S.A.	73	33 10N	110 30W
San Carlos, Venezuela	78	2 0N	67 0W
San Carlos, Venezuela	78	9 50N	68 30W
San Carlos, Venezuela	78	9 1N	71 40W
San Carlos de Bariloche, Argentina	77	41 10S	71 25W
San Carlos de la Rapita, Spain	17	40 37N	0 36E
San Carlos L., U.S.A.	73	33 15N	110 15W
San Clemente, U.S.A.	73	33 31N	117 42W
San Clemente I., U.S.A.	73	33 0N	118 30W
San Cristobal, Arg.	77	30 20S	61 10W
San Cristóbal, Dom. Rep.	75	16 50N	70 3W
San Cristóbal, Mexico	74	16 50N	92 33W
San Cristóbal, Ven.	78	7 35N	72 24W
San Diego, Calif., U.S.A.	73	32 50N	117 9W
San Diego, Texas, U.S.A.	71	27 45N	98 15W
San Diego de Cabrutica, Venezuela	78	8 30N	64 50W
San Domingo, Mexico	74	30 40N	116 0W
San Esteban, Spain	17	41 36N	3 11W
San Felipe, Chile	77	32 43S	70 50W
San Felipe, Mexico	74	21 30N	101 20W
San Felipe, Venezuela	78	10 20N	68 45W
San Feliu, Spain	17	41 45N	3 1E
San Fernando, Chile	77	34 30S	71 0W
San Fernando, Lower California, Mexico	74	30 0N	115 10W
San Fernando, Tamaulipas, Mexico	74	24 50N	98 10W
San Fernando, Phil.	35	15 5N	120 37E
San Fernando, Phil.	35	16 40N	120 23E
San Fernando, Spain	17	36 22N	6 17W
San Fernando, Trinidad	78	10 20N	61 30W

	Map		
San Fernando, U.S.A.	73	34 17N	118 29W
San Fernando de Apure, Venezuela	78	7 54N	67 28W
San Fernando de Atabapo, Venezuela	78	4 0N	67 40W
San Francisco, Arg.	77	31 30S	62 5W
San Francisco, Arg.	77	32 45S	66 10W
San Francisco, U.S.A.	73	37 45N	122 30W
San Francisco de Macoris, Dom. Rep.	75	19 19N	70 15W
San Francisco de Oro, Mexico	74	26 52N	105 50W
San Francisco Pass, Argentina–Chile	77	27 0S	68 20W
San Francisco Pk., U.S.A.	66	35 40N	112 0W
San Francisco, R., U.S.A.	73	33 30N	109 0W
San Gil, Colombia	78	6 30N	73 5W
San Giorgio, Giulia, It.	53	45 50N	13 13E
San Giovanni, Italy	20	39 16N	16 24E
San Ignacio, Paraguay	77	27 0S	57 0W
San Ignacio, L., Mexico	74	26 30N	113 0W
San Javier, Argentina	77	30 30S	60 10W
San Joaquin R., U.S.A.	73	37 0N	120 30W
San Jorge B., Mexico	74	31 20N	113 20W
San Jorge, G. of, Arg.	77	46 0S	66 0W
San Jorge, G. of, Spain	17	40 50N	0 55E
San Jorge R., Colombia	78	8 10N	75 35W
San Jose, Bolivia	78	17 45S	60 50W
San José, Colombia	78	2 40N	72 0W
San José, Costa Rica	78	10 0N	84 2W
San José, Philippines	35	15 45N	120 55E
San José, Philippines	35	10 50N	122 5E
San Jose, U.S.A.	73	37 10N	121 57W
San José, Uruguay	77	34 0S	56 50W
San José de Ocune, Col.	78	4 10N	70 5W
San José del Cabo, Mexico	74	23 0N	109 50W
San José del Guaviare, Colombia	78	2 30N	72 55W
San José do Rio Preto, Brazil	79	21 0S	49 30W
San José G., Argentina	77	42 0S	64 0W
San José I., Mexico	74	25 0N	110 50W
San Juan, Argentina	77	31 30S	68 30W
San Juan, Bolivia	78	18 0S	60 0W
San Juan, Mexico	74	23 50N	106 20W
San Juan, Jalisco, Mex.	74	21 20N	102 50W
San Juan, Queretaro, Mexico	74	20 25N	100 0W
San Juan, Puerto Rico	75	18 29N	66 6W
San Juan Capistrano, U.S.A.	73	33 32N	117 42W
San Juan Mts., U.S.A.	73	37 20N	107 0W
San Juan R., Mexico	74	21 30N	98 50W
San Juan R., U.S.A.	73	37 20N	110 15W
San Juan de Guia, C. de, Col.	78	11 10N	74 10W
San Juan de los Morros, Venezuela	78	9 55N	67 21W
San Juan del Norte, Nicaragua	78	10 50N	83 40W
San Juan del Norte Bay, Nicaragua	95	11 30N	83 40W
San Juan del Sur, Nic.	78	11 20N	86 0W
San Julian, Argentina	77	49 15S	68 0W
San Justo, Argentina	77	30 55S	60 30W
San Láraro, C., Mexico	74	24 49N	112 21W
San Leandro, U.S.A.	73	37 43N	122 6W
San Lorenzo, Ecuador	78	1 15N	78 50W
San Lorenzo, I., Mexico	74	28 30N	112 40W
San Lorenzo, Mt., Arg.	77	47 40S	72 20W
San Lucas, Bolivia	78	20 5S	65 0W
San Lucas, Mexico	74	27 14N	112 15W
San Lucas C., Mexico	74	22 50N	110 0W
San Luis del Palmar, Argentina	77	27 30S	58 30W
San Luis I., Mexico	74	30 0N	114 30W
San Luis Obispo, U.S.A.	73	35 10N	120 50W
San Luis Potosi, Mexico	74	22 10N	101 0W
San Luis Potosi, st., Mexico	74	22 30N	100 30W
San Marco, Italy	20	39 34N	15 27E
San Marcos, U.S.A.	71	29 53N	98 0W
San Marcos, I., Mexico	74	27 0N	112 25W
San Marino, rep., Italy	20	43 56N	12 25E
San Martin, Bolivia	78	14 50S	61 45W
San Martin L., Arg.	77	48 50S	72 50W
San Martin Tuxtla, vol., Mex.	74	18 29N	95 14W
San Mateo, U.S.A.	73	37 30N	122 20W
San Matias, Bolivia	78	16 25S	58 20W
San Matias, G. of, Arg.	77	41 30S	64 0W
San Miguel, Mexico	74	26 40N	107 40W
San Miguel, Salvador	60	13 30N	88 12W
San Miguel, U.S.A.	73	35 46N	120 44W
San Miguel, G. of, Pan.	78	8 10N	78 20W
San Miguel Is., Philippines	35	7 45N	118 30E
San Miguel R., Bolivia	78	16 0S	62 45W
San Miniato, Italy	20	43 40N	10 50E
San Nicolas, Argentina	77	33 17S	60 10W
San Nicolas, I., U.S.A.	73	33 15N	119 30W
San Pablo, Philippines	35	14 5N	121 10E
San Pedro, Dominican Rep.	75	18 30N	69 18W
San Pedro, Ivory Coast	50	4 50N	6 33W

	MAP		
San Pedro, Chihuahua, Mexico	74	30 40N	107 40W
San Pedro, Coahuila, Mexico	74	25 40N	103 10W
San Pedro, Paraguay	77	24 0S	57 0W
San Pedro R., Mexico	74	28 20N	106 10W
San Pedro de las Colonias, Mexico	74	24 50N	102 59W
San Pedro de Lloc, Peru	78	7 25S	79 30W
San Pedro del Parana, Paraguay	77	26 45S	55 3W
San Pedro del Pinatar, Spain	17	37 50N	0 50W
San Pietro I., Italy	20	39 9N	8 17E
San Rafael, Argentina	77	34 40S	68 30W
San Rafael, Calif., U.S.A.	73	38 0N	122 40W
San Rafael, Colombia	78	6 2N	69 52W
San Rafael, N. Mexico, U.S.A.	73	35 5N	107 56W
San Remo, Italy	20	43 48N	7 47E
San Román C., Ven.	78	12 10N	70 0W
San Roque, Spain	17	36 17N	5 21W
San Rosendo, Chile	77	37 10S	72 50W
San Saba, U.S.A.	71	31 9N	98 44W
San Salvador (Watlings) Island, Bahamas	75	24 0N	74 40W
San Salvador de Jujuy, Argentina	77	24 7S	65 30W
San Sebastian, Arg.	77	53 10S	68 30W
San Sebastian, Mexico	74	20 50N	104 50W
San Sebastian, Spain	17	43 17N	1 58W
San Severo, Italy	20	41 41N	15 23E
San Simon, U.S.A.	73	32 17N	109 16W
San Valentin Mt., Chile	77	46 30S	73 30W
San Vicente de la Barquera, Spain	17	43 30N	4 29W
San Yenacio, U.S.A.	71	27 4N	99 21W
San Ysidro, U.S.A.	73	32 32N	117 4W
Sanà, Yemen	49	15 27N	44 12E
Sana R., Yugoslavia	20	44 40N	16 43E
Sanaga, R., Cameroon	52	4 55N	12 40E
Sanana, Indonesia	35	2 5S	125 50E
Sanandaj, Iran	30	35 22N	47 7E
Sanar R., Israel	29	31 49N	34 49E
Sancha Ho., China	39	26 20N	106 10E
Sancti Spiritus, Cuba	75	21 52N	79 33W
Sanctuary, Canada	65	51 2N	108 7W
Sand L., Canada	62	51 20N	76 50W
Sand Springs, U.S.A.	71	36 12N	96 9W
Sandakan, Sabah	35	5 53N	118 10E
Sandane, Norway	23	61 47N	6 14E
Sandanski, Bulgaria	21	41 17N	23 16E
Sanday I., Orkneys, Scotland	10	59 15N	2 30W
Sandbult, Transvaal	57	23 42S	27 19E
Sanders, U.S.A.	73	35 14N	109 19W
Sanderson, U.S.A.	71	30 7N	102 26W
Sandfell, Iceland	22	63 57N	16 48W
Sandgate, Queensland	43	27 19S	152 53E
Sandia, Peru	78	14 10S	69 30W
Sandikli, Turkey	30	38 30N	30 20E
Sandilands, Canada	65	49 20N	96 16W
Sandiman, mt., W. Australia	44	24 21S	115 20E
Sandnes, Norway	23	58 50N	5 45E
Sandoa, Zaire	55	9 48S	23 0E
Sandomierz, Poland	16	50 40N	21 43E
Sandoway, Burma	33	18 20N	94 30E
Sandpoint, U.S.A.	72	48 20N	116 40W
Sandringham, Queens.	42	24 3S	139 0E
Sandspit, Canada	64	53 20N	131 40W
Sandstone, W. Australia	44	28 0S	119 15E
Sandusky, U.S.A.	68	41 25N	82 40W
Sandwich B., Canada	63	53 40N	57 15W
Sandwich C., Queens.	42	18 26S	146 22E
Sandwich Is., South, Falkland Islands	80	57 0S	27 0W
Sandwip Channel, Bangladesh	33	22 35N	91 35E
Sandy Bight, W. Australia	45	33 50S	123 20E
Sandy C., Queensland	42	23 41S	153 8E
Sandy Desert, Pakistan	32	28 0N	65 0E
Sandy Lake, & L., Can.	62	53 0N	93 0W
Sandy Narrows, Canada	65	55 4N	103 1W
Sandy R., Canada	63	54 50N	67 58W
Sanford, Fla., U.S.A.	69	28 45N	81 20W
Sanford, Me., U.S.A.	69	43 28N	70 47W
Sanford Mt., Alaska	60	62 30N	143 0W
Sanford R., W. Austral.	44	24 20S	116 30E
Sanga (Macaloge), Mozambique	56	12 22S	35 21E
Sanga, Volta	52	11 11N	0 13E
Sanga R., Congo (Fr.)	54	1 0N	16 30E
Sangame, Mozambique	56	17 40S	34 59E
Sangamner, India	32	19 30N	74 15E
Sangarea B., Guinea	52	Inset	
Sangareddipet, India	32	17 35N	78 5E
Sangatolon, U.S.S.R.	27	61 50N	149 40E
Sangchih, China	39	29 18N	110 5E
Sange, Zaire	53	3 10S	29 5E
Sange, Zaire	53	7 0S	28 10E
Sanger, U.S.A.	73	36 43N	119 31W
Sanggau, Indonesia	34	0 5N	110 30E
Sangihe, I., Indonesia	35	3 45N	125 30E
Sangihe Is., Celebes	35	3 0N	126 0E
Sangju, S. Korea	36	36 20N	128 7E
Sangkan Ho., China	38	39 40N	113 0E
Sangkulirang, Indonesia	35	1 0N	118 0E
Sangli, India	32	16 55N	74 33E
Sangmélima, Cameroon	52	2 57N	12 1E
Sangmelina, Cameroon	54	2 57N	12 1E
Sangonera R., Spain	17	37 39N	2 0W
Sangre, Pta, Fernando Póo	52	3 20N	8 20E
Sangre de Cristo Mts., U.S.A.	71	37 30N	105 50W
Sangre Grande, Trinidad	78	10 35N	61 8W
Sangro R., Italy	20	42 10N	14 30E
Sangsang, China	37	29 25N	86 41N
Sangue R., Brazil	79	12 10S	58 50W
Sangüesa, Spain	17	42 37N	1 17W
Sañicó, Argentina	77	40 15S	70 30W
Sanish, U.S.A.	70	48 0N	102 31W
Sanje, Uganda	53	0 47S	31 32E
Sanjo, Japan	36	37 48N	139 1E
Sankiang, China	39	25 43N	109 23E
Sankuru, prov., Zaire	54	3 30S	23 20E
Sankuru R., Zaire	54	4 0S	21 0E
Sanlucar de Barrameda, Spain	17	36 43N	6 23W
Sanlucar la Mayor, Sp.	17	37 25N	6 12W
Sanmen Gorge, China	38	35 0N	111 30E
Sanmenhsia, China	38	34 50N	111 28E
Sanmen Wan, China	39	29 10N	121 45E
Sannaspos, O.F.S.	57	29 6S	26 34E
Sannicandro, Italy	20	41 50N	15 34E
Sânnicolaul-Maré, Rumania	21	46 5N	20 39E
Sannieshof, Transvaal	57	26 30S	25 47E
Sano, Osaka, Japan	36	34 30N	135 20E
Sano, Tochigi, Japan	36	36 27N	139 36E
Sanok, Poland	16	49 35N	22 10E
Sanquhar, Scotland	10	55 21N	3 56W
Sansanné-Mango, Togo	52	10 20N	0 30E
Sansepolcro, Italy	20	43 34N	12 8E
Sant Antioco I., Italy	20	39 3N	8 30E
Santa R., Peru	78	9 10S	78 0W
Santa Ana, Bolivia	78	13 50S	65 40W
Santa Ana, Ecuador	78	1 10S	80 20W
Santa Ana, Mexico	74	30 31N	111 8W
Santa Ana, U.S.A.	73	33 45N	117 50W
Santa Barbara, Mato Grosso, Brazil	78	16 0S	59 0W
Santa Barbara, Minas Gerais, Brazil	78	20 0S	43 20W
Santa Barbara, Mexico	74	26 48N	105 50W
Santa Barbara, U.S.A.	73	34 25N	119 40W
Santa Barbara I., U.S.A.	73	33 40N	119 40W
Santa Catalina, Arg.	77	22 0S	66 0W
Santa Catalina, U.S.A.	66	33 20N	118 30W
Santa Catalina, G. of, U.S.A.	73	33 0N	118 0W
Santa Catalina, I., Mex.	74	25 50N	110 50W
Santa Catalina I., U.S.A.	73	33 30N	118 30W
Santa Catarina, st., Brazil	77	27 25S	48 30W
Santa Catarina, Brazil	77	27 30S	48 40S
Santa Clara, Cuba	75	22 20N	80 0W
Santa Clara, Calif., U.S.A.	73	37 10N	122 0W
Santa Clara, Utah, U.S.A.	73	37 9N	113 39W
Santa Clotilde, Peru	78	2 25S	73 45W
Santa Coloma, Spain	17	41 50N	2 39E
Santa Cruz, Angola	56	16 13S	21 57E
Santa Cruz, Argentina	77	50 0S	68 50W
Santa Cruz, Bolivia	78	17 43S	63 10W
Santa Cruz, Brazil	78	9 25S	60 30W
Santa Cruz, Canary Is.	50	28 29N	16 26W
Santa Cruz, Cuba	75	20 50N	78 10W
Santa Cruz, U.S.A.	73	36 55N	122 10W
Santa Cruz I., U.S.A.	73	34 0N	119 45W
Santa Cruz R., Arg.	77	50 10S	70 0W
Santa Cruz, U.S.A.	73	35 58N	106 1W
Santa Cruz do Sul, Brazil	77	29 45S	52 30W
Santa Dorotea, Pan.	78	7 25N	78 0W
Santa Elena, Ecuador	78	2 10S	80 50W
Santa Elena, C. de, Costa Rica	75	10 54N	85 56W
Santa Fé, U.S.A.	73	35 40N	106 0W
Santa Fé, prov., Arg.	77	31 50S	60 55W
Santa Filomena, Brazil	79	9 0S	45 50W
Santa Inés I., Chile	77	54 0S	73 0W
Santa Isabel, Argentina	77	36 10S	67 0W
Sta. Isabel, Brazil	79	14 30S	50 52W
Santa Isabel, Fernando Póo	52	3 45N	8 50E
Santa Isabel Pk., Fernando Póo	52	4 43N	8 49E
Santa Margarita, Mex.	74	24 30N	112 0W
Santa Maria, Argentina	77	26 40S	66 0W
Santa Maria, Brazil	77	29 40S	53 40W
Santa Maria, Campania, Italy	20	41 3N	14 29E
Santa Maria, Peru	78	2 35S	74 50W
Santa Maria, Switz.	15	46 34N	8 48E
Santa Maria, Zambia	56	11 2S	29 57E
Santa Maria, U.S.A.	73	34 58N	120 29W
Santa Maria B., Mexico	74	25 10N	108 40W
Santa Maria R., Mexico	74	29 50N	107 40W
Santa Maria da Vitória, Brazil	79	13 30S	44 20W
Santa Maria di Leuca, C., Italy	21	39 48N	18 20E
Santa Marta, Colombia	78	11 10N	74 10W
Santa Maura I. *see* Levkás			
Santa Monica, U.S.A.	73	34 0N	118 30W
Santa Paula, U.S.A.	73	34 27N	119 3W
Santa Rita, Brazil	79	7 25S	35 28W
Santa Rita, U.S.A.	73	32 50N	108 0W
Santa Rita, U.S.A.	75	32 50N	108 0W
Santa Rosa, Argentina	77	32 20S	65 10W
Santa Rosa, Argentina	77	36 40S	64 30W
Santa Rosa, Bolivia	78	10 25S	67 20W
Santa Rosa, Brazil	77	28 0S	54 50W
Santa Rosa, U.S.A.	71	34 57N	104 35N
Santa Rosa, U.S.A.	73	38 20N	122 50W
Santa Rosa I. Calif., U.S.A.	73	34 0N	120 15W
Santa Rosa I., Fla., U.S.A.	69	30 23N	87 0W
Santa Rosa, Mts., U.S.A.	72	41 40N	117 30W
Santa Rosalia, Mexico	74	27 20N	112 30W
Santa Teresa R., Brazil	79	13 0S	49 15W
Santa Vitoria do Palmar, Brazil	77	33 30S	53 25W
Santafe, Spain	17	37 12N	3 45W
Santahar, Bangladesh	33	24 50N	89 0E
Santai, China	39	30 58N	105 0E
Santander, Spain	17	43 27N	3 51W
Santander Jiménez, Mexico	74	24 11N	98 29W
Santañy, Spain	17	39 20N	3 5E
Santaquin, U.S.A.	73	40 0N	111 52W
Santarém, Brazil	79	2 25S	54 42W
Santarem, Portugal	17	39 12N	8 42W
Santaren Chan., Bahamas	75	23 0N	79 30W
Santee Res., U.S.A.	69	33 30N	80 15W
Santemiao, China	38	41 15N	106 20E
Santi Quaranta. *See* Sarande, Albania	21		
Santiago, Brazil	77	29 5S	54 55W
Santiago, Chile	77	23 24S	70 50W
Santiago, Dom. Rep.	75	19 30N	70 40W
Santiago, Panama	78	8 0N	81 0W
Santiago, Pta de, Fernando Póo	52	3 12N	8 43E
Santiago de Cao, Peru	78	8 0S	79 10W
Santiago de Compostela, Spain	17	42 52N	8 37W
Santiago de Cuba, Cuba	75	20 0N	75 49W
Santiago del Estero, Argentina	77	27 50S	64 20W
Santiago Ixcuintla, Mex.	74	21 50N	105 11W
Santiago Papasquiaro, Mexico	74	25 0N	105 20W
Santiaguillo, L. de, Mex.	74	24 55N	104 57W
Santis, Mt., Switz.	15	47 15N	9 21E
Santisteban, Spain	17	38 17N	3 15W
Santo Angelo, Brazil	77	28 15S	54 15W
Santo Antonio, Guaporé, Brazil	78	12 30S	63 40W
Santo Antonio, Mato Grosso, Brazil	79	15 50S	56 0W
Santo Antonio do Icá, Brazil	78	2 55S	67 50W
Santo Corazon, Bolivia	78	18 0S	58 45W
Santo Domingo, Dominican Rep.	75	18 30N	69 58W
Santo Domingo, Spain	17	42 24N	3 0W
Santo Domingo Cay, I., Cuba	75	22 0N	75 52W
Santo Tomas, Peru	78	14 31S	72 32W
Santo Tomé, Argentina	77	28 40S	56 5W
Santoña, Spain	17	43 29N	3 20W
Santos, Brazil	77	24 0S	46 20W
Santu, China	39	25 52N	113 4E
Santuaho, China	39	26 40N	119 40E
Sanur, Jordan	29	32 22N	35 15E
Sanvic, France	12	49 31N	0 7E
Sanyati R., Rhodesia	17	17 15S	29 15E
Sanyuan, China	38	34 32N	108 48E
Sanza Pombo, Angola	54	7 20S	16 0E
São Borja, Brazil	77	28 45S	56 0W
São Carlos, Brazil	77	22 0S	47 50W
São Cristovão, Brazil	79	11 0S	37 15W
São Domingos, Goias, Brazil	79	13 25S	46 10W
Sao Dumont, Brazil	79	21 35S	44 0W
São Felipe, Brazil	78	0 30N	67 25W
São Francisco, Minas Gerais, Brazil	79	16 0S	44 50W
São Francisco, Santa Catarina, Brazil	77	26 15S	48 36W
São Francisco R., Brazil	79	9 0S	39 0W
São Francişco, Brazil	77	26 20S	48 45W
Sao Hill, Tanzania	53	8 19S	35 11E
São João, Parà, Brazil	79	5 20S	48 50W
São João, Rio Grande Sul, Brazil	77	31 ps	52 0W
São João, Sao Paulo, Brazil	77	22 0S	46 50W
São João da Barra, Brazil	79	21 45S	41 0W
Sao João del Rei, Brazil	79	21 25S	44 25W
São João do Piaui, Brazil	79	8 10S	42 15W
São José do Norte, Brazil	77	32 0S	52 0W
São José do Tocantins, Brazil	79	14 30S	48 30W
São Lourenço, Brazil	79	16 30S	55 5W
São Lourenço, R., Brazil	79	16 40S	56 0W
São Luis (Maranhão), Brazil	79	2 39S	44 15W
São Manuel. *See* Teles Pires, R., Brazil	79		
São Marcos B., Brazil	79	2 0S	44 0W
São Marcos R., Brazil	79	17 0S	47 30W
São Martinho, Portugal	17	39 30N	9 8W
São Mateus, Brazil	79	18 50S	39 50W
São Paulo, Brazil	77	23 40S	46 50W
São Paulo, st., Brazil	77	22 0S	49 0W
São Paulo de Olivença, Brazil	78	3 30S	69 0W
São Raimundo Nonato, Brazil	79	19 2S	43 0W
São Romão, Brazil	78	5 45S	68 0W
São Roque C., Brazil	79	5 30S	35 10W
São Sebastião I., Brazil	77	24 0S	45 30W
Saona I., Dom. Rep.	75	18 0N	68 40W
Saône R., France	12	46 25N	4 50E
Saparua I., Indonesia	35	3 33S	128 40E
Sapele, Nigeria	52	5 50N	5 40E
Sapelo I., U.S.A.	69	31 28N	81 15W
Sapientza, Greece	21	36 33N	21 43E
Sapindji, Congo	56	9 39S	23 12E
Sapoba, Nigeria	52	6 4N	5 53E
Saposoa, Peru	78	6 55S	76 30W
Sapphire Mts., U.S.A.	72	46 30N	113 50W
Sapporo, Japan	36	43 0N	141 15E
Sapri, Italy	20	40 5N	15 37E
Sapulpa, U.S.A.	71	36 0N	96 8W
Sapure, Congo	56	10 55S	28 14E
Saqota, Ethiopia	54	12 42N	39 2E
Sar Eskand Khan, Iran	30	37 34N	47 0E
Saqqez, Iran	30	36 15N	46 20E
Sar Planina Mts., Y.slav.	21	42 10N	21 0E
Sarab, Iran	30	38 0N	47 30E
Sarajevo, Yugoslavia	21	43 52N	18 26E
Saraktash, U.S.S.R.	24	51 55N	56 20E
Saranac, U.S.A.	68	44 38N	73 45W
Saranac Lake, U.S.A.	68	44 20N	74 10W
Saranac Is., U.S.A.	68	44 17N	74 22W
Saranda, Tanzania	53	5 40S	35 0E
Sarande (Santi Quaranta), Albania	21	39 53N	20 10E
Sarangani Is., Philippines	35	5 50N	125 10E
Sarandi del Yi, Urug.	77	33 25S	55 48W
Sarangarh, India	33	21 40N	83 10E
Saransk, U.S.S.R.	25	54 10N	45 10E
Sarapul, U.S.S.R.	24	56 35N	53 40E
Sarasota, U.S.A.	69	27 10N	82 30W
Saratoga, U.S.A.	72	41 29N	106 56W
Saratoga Springs, U.S.A.	68	43 5N	73 47W
Sarau, Germany	25	53 46N	10 42E
Saravane, Laos	34	15 42N	106 3E
Sarawak, st., Malaysia	35	2 0N	113 0E
Sarbaz, Iran	31	26 38N	61 19E
Sarbisheh, Iran	31	32 30N	59 40E
Sárbogárd, Hungary	16	46 55N	18 40E
Sarda R., India	32	28 15N	80 45E
Sardalas, Libya	51	25 50N	10 30E
Sardarshahr, India	32	28 30N	74 30E
Sardinia, I., reg., Italy	20	40 0N	9 0E
Sarektjåkko, mt., Swed.	22	67 69N	17 40E
Sargans, Switzerland	15	47 3N	9 27E
Sargent, U.S.A.	70	41 41N	99 26W
Sargodha, Pakistan	32	32 10N	72 40E
Sargodha, Terr., W. Pakistan	32	31 40N	72 0E
Sari, Iran	31	36 30N	53 11E
Sarida R., Jordan	29	32 4N	35 3E
Sarikamis, Turkey	30	40 22N	42 35E
Sarina, Queensland	42	21 22S	149 13E
Sarine R., Switzerland	15	46 45N	7 5E
Sar-i-Pul, Afghanistan	31	36 10N	65 50E
Sarita, U.S.A.	71	27 13N	97 47W
Sariwon, N. Korea	36	38 35N	125 50E
Sariz, Iran	31	31 0N	55 58E
Sark I., Channel Islands	12	49 25N	2 20W
Sarlat, France	12	44 54N	1 13E
Sarles, U.S.A.	70	49 0N	98 57W
Sarmento, Angola	55	8 11S	20 43E
Sarmiento, Argentina	77	45 45S	69 10W
Sarnen, Switzerland	15	46 53N	8 13E
Sarnia, Ont., Canada	62	43 0N	82 30W
Sarno, Italy	20	40 48N	14 35E
Sarny, U.S.S.R.	24	51 17N	26 40E
Sarobi, Afghanistan	31	34 30N	69 50E
Sarpsborg, Norway	23	59 16N	11 12E
Sarreguemines, France	12	49 6N	7 4E
Sarro, Mali	50	13 40N	5 5W
Sartène, Corsica, France	12	41 38N	9 0E
Sarthe R., France	12	48 8N	0 10E
Sartynya, U.S.S.R.	24	63 30N	62 50E
Sarur, 'Oman	31	23 17N	58 4E
Sarveston, Iran	31	29 20N	53 7E
Sary Tash, U.S.S.R.	26	39 45N	73 40E
Sarych C., U.S.S.R.	25	44 25N	33 25E

	MAP		
Sarykomey, U.S.S.R.	26	45 20N	74 45 E
Sarzeau, France	12	47 31N	2 48W
Sasa, Israel	29	33 2N	35 23 E
Sasaram, India	33	24 57N	84 5 E
Sasebo, Japan	36	33 15N	129 50 E
Saser Mt., Kashmir	32	34 50N	77 50 E
Saskatchewan, prov., Canada	65	54 40N	106 0W
Saskatchewan R., Can.	65	53 40N	103 30W
Saskatoon, Canada	65	52 10N	106 45W
Saskylakh, U.S.S.R.	27	71 50N	114 20 E
Sasolburg, O.F.S.	57	26 46 S	27 49 E
Sasovo, U.S.S.R.	25	54 25N	41 55 E
Sassandra, Ivory Coast	50	5 0N	6 8W
Sassandra R., Ivory Coast	50	5 30N	6 30W
Sassari, Italy	20	40 44N	8 33 E
Sassnitz, Germany	14	54 29N	13 39 E
Sassuolo, Italy	20	44 31N	10 47 E
Sasumua Dam, Kenya	53	0 54 S	36 46 E
Satadougou, Mali	50	12 40N	11 25W
Satanta, U.S.A.	71	37 30N	101 0W
Satara, India	32	17 42N	74 2 E
Satilla R., U.S.A.	69	31 15N	81 50W
Satmala Hills, India	32	20 15N	74 40 E
Satna, India	32	24 35N	80 50 E
Sátoraljaujhely, Hung.	16	48 25N	21 41 E
Satpura Ra., India	32	21 40N	75 0 E
Satu-Mare, Rumania	20	47 46N	22 55 E
Saturnina, R., Brazil	78	12 30 S	58 12W
Saturnina (Papagoia), R., Brazil	78	12 30 S	61 30W
Sauceda, Mexico	74	25 40N	101 20W
Saucillo, Mexico	74	28 0N	105 18W
Saudi Arabia, king., Asia	30	26 0N	44 0 E
Saugerties, U.S.A.	68	42 4N	73 58W
Saugor (Sagao), Madhya Pradesh, India	32	23 50N	78 50 E
Saujbulagh, Iran	30	36 45N	45 40 E
Sauk Center, U.S.A.	70	45 44N	94 59W
Sauk Rapids, U.S.A.	70	45 36N	94 5W
Sauldre, R., France	12	47 32N	2 10 E
Saulieu, France	12	47 17N	4 14 E
Sault Ste. Marie, Can.	62	46 30N	84 20W
Sault Ste. Marie, U.S.A.	68	46 27N	84 22W
Saumlak, Indonesia	35	7 55 S	131 20 E
Saumur, France	12	47 15N	0 5W
Saunders, Canada	64	52 58N	115 40W
Saunders C., N.Z.	47	45 53 S	170 45 E
Saurbær, Iceland	22	64 24N	21 35W
Saurbær, Iceland	22	65 23N	18 15W
Saúte, Mozambique	56	22 23 S	32 55 E
Sava R., Yugoslavia	20	44 40N	16 50 E
Savage, U.S.A.	70	47 30N	104 22W
Savalou, Dahomey	52	7 57N	2 4 E
Savare, Mozambique	56	19 20 S	35 9 E
Savanna, U.S.A.	70	42 6N	90 1W
Savanna la Mar, Jamaica	75	18 10N	78 10W
Savannah, Ga., U.S.A.	69	32 0N	81 0W
Savannah, U.S.A.	70	39 55N	94 48W
Savannah, Tenn., U.S.A.	69	35 12N	88 15W
Savannah R., U.S.A.	69	33 30N	82 0W
Savannakhet, Laos	34	16 30N	104 49 E
Savant L., Canada	62	50 40N	90 30W
Savant Lake, Canada	62	50 20N	90 40W
Savantvadi, India	32	15 55N	73 54 E
Savanur, India	32	14 59N	75 28 E
Savé, Dahomey	52	8 2N	2 17 E
Save R., Mozambique	55	21 16 S	34 0 E
Saveh, Persia	30	35 2N	50 20 E
Savelugu, Ghana	52	9 38N	0 54W
Saverne, France	12	48 44N	7 20 E
Savigliano, Italy	20	44 39N	7 40 E
Savona, Italy	29	44 19N	8 29 E
Savonlinna, Finland	23	61 55N	28 55 E
Savsjö, Sweden	23	57 23N	14 43 E
Sawah Lunto, Sumatra, Indonesia	34	0 52 S	100 52 E
Sawai, Indonesia	35	3 0 S	129 5 E
Sawai Madhopur, India	32	26 0N	76 25 E
Sawara, Japan	36	35 55N	140 30 E
Sawatch Mts., U.S.A.	73	39 0N	106 30W
Sawel Mt., N. Ireland	11	54 48N	7 5W
Sawhaj, Egypt	51	26 27N	31 43 E
Sawknah, Libya	51	29 10N	15 40 E
Sawla, Ghana	52	9 15N	2 17W
Sawmills, Rhodesia	56	19 30 S	28 2 E
Sawu I., Indonesia	35	10 35 S	121 50 E
Sawu Sea, Indonesia	35	9 30 S	121 50 E
Saxby R., Queensland	42	19 35 S	141 17 E
Say Ngaoure, Nigeria	52	13 9N	2 24 E
Saya, Nigeria	52	9 30N	3 18 E
Sayabec, Canada	63	48 35N	67 41W
Sayan, Peru	78	11 0 S	77 25W
Sayda, Lebanon	30	33 38N	35 28 E
Sazin, W. Pakistan	31	35 35N	73 31 E
Sayre, U.S.A.	68	42 0N	76 30W
Sayre, U.S.A.	71	35 17N	99 35W
Sayula, Mexico	74	19 50N	103 40W
Sazan, I., Albania	21	40 30N	19 20 E
Sázava R., C.Slov.	16	49 50N	15 0 E
Sazin, Pakistan	32	35 35N	73 29 E
Sca Fell, mt., England	10	54 27N	3 15W
Scammon Bay, Alaska	59	61 50N	165 35W
Scandia, Canada	64	50 20N	112 0W

	MAP		
Scapa, Canada	64	51 55N	112 0W
Scapa Flow, Scotland	10	58 52N	3 0W
Scarborough, England	10	54 17N	0 24W
Scarborough, Tobago	75	11 11N	60 42W
Scarborough Shoal, S. China Sea	35	15 10N	117 50 E
Scargill, New Zealand	47	42 56 S	172 58 E
Scarrbury, Queensland	42	22 55 S	144 39 E
Scarriff, Ireland	11	52 55N	8 32W
Scarth, Canada	65	49 45N	101 0W
Sceales Bay, S. Australia	45	33 2 S	134 11 E
Scenio, U.S.A.	70	43 49N	102 33W
Schaf Burg, Austria	14	47 47N	13 26 E
Schaffhausen, Switz.	14	47 42N	8 36 E
Schaffhausen, canton, Switzerland	15	47 40N	8 40 E
Schagen, Netherlands	13	52 49N	4 48 E
Schefferville, Canada	63	54 52N	66 50W
Schelde (Scheldt), R., Belgium	13	51 10N	4 20 E
Schenectady, U.S.A.	68	42 50N	73 58W
Schiermonnikoog I., Netherlands	13	53 30N	6 15 E
Schio, Italy	20	45 42N	11 21 E
Schleswig, Germany	14	54 32N	9 34 E
Schober P., Austria	14	47 28N	14 40 E
Schofield, Wis., U.S.A.	68	44 54N	89 39W
Schouten Is., Indonesia	35	1 0 S	136 0 E
Schouwen I., Neth.	13	51 43N	3 45 E
Schreiber, Canada	62	48 45N	87 20W
Schuler, Canada	65	50 22N	110 5W
Schull, Ireland	11	51 32N	9 40W
Schumacher, Canada	62	48 30N	81 16W
Schurz, U.S.A.	73	38 59N	118 51W
Schuyler, U.S.A.	70	41 31N	97 4W
Schwabisch Gmund, Germany	14	48 48N	9 47 E
Schwaner Mts., Indon.	35	1 0 S	122 30 E
Schwangcheng, China	38	45 27N	126 15 E
Schwarzenburg, Switz.	15	46 49N	7 21 E
Schwarzrand, S.W. Afr.	57	26 0 S	17 0 E
Schweinfurt, Germany	14	50 3N	10 12 E
Schweinsberg, Germany	42	50 47N	8 58 E
Schweizer Reneke, Transvaal	57	27 11 S	25 18 E
Schwerin, Germany	14	53 37N	11 22 E
Schwyz, Switzerland	15	47 2N	8 39 E
Schwyz, cant., Switz.	15	47 5N	8 40 E
Scidlei, Somali, Rep.	49	1 8 S	41 52 E
Scilly Is., Brit. Is.	10	49 57N	6 20W
Scioto R., U.S.A.	68	40 10N	83 10W
Scobey, U.S.A.	70	48 49N	105 25W
Scone, N.S.W.	43	32 0 S	150 52 E
Scoresby Ld., Green.	58	72 0W	24 0N
Scotia, U.S.A.	72	40 30N	124 5W
Scotland, Br. Isles	10	57 0N	4 0W
Scotland, U.S.A.	70	43 9N	97 43W
Scotland Neck, U.S.A.	69	36 6N	77 24W
Scotsville, Ky., U.S.A.	69	36 48N	86 10W
Scott City, U.S.A.	70	38 32N	100 54W
Scott Inlet, Canada	61	71 0N	71 30W
Scott Is., Canada	64	50 40N	128 50W
Scott L., Canada	65	60 0N	106 0W
Scotts Head, Dominica	75	Inset	
Scottsbluff, U.S.A.	70	41 56N	103 41W
Scottsboro, U.S.A.	69	34 40N	86 0W
Scottsburg, U.S.A.	68	38 40N	85 46W
Scottburgh, Natal	57	30 15 S	30 47 E
Scottsdale, Tasmania	43	41 10 S	147 32 E
Scottville, U.S.A.	68	43 57N	86 18W
Scranton, U.S.A.	68	41 22N	75 41W
Scunthorpe, England	10	53 35N	0 38W
Scuol, Switzerland	15	46 43N	10 18 E
Se la Pass, India	33	27 30N	92 15 E
Sea Lake, Victoria	43	35 28 S	142 55 E
Seabra, Brazil	78	8 25 S	70 50W
Seabrook, L., W. Australia	44	30 55 S	119 32 E
Seabrook, Mt., W. Australia	44	25 23 S	117 40 E
Seaford, U.S.A.	68	38 37N	75 36W
Seaforth, Canada	62	43 35N	81 30W
Seaforth L., Scotland	10	57 52N	6 36W
Seagraves, U.S.A.	71	32 56N	102 31W
Seal Cove, Canada	63	49 57N	56 22W
Seal L., Canada	63	54 25N	61 43W
Seal R., Canada	65	58 50N	97 30W
Sealy, U.S.A.	71	29 46N	96 13W
Searchlight, U.S.A.	73	35 30N	114 58W
Searcy, U.S.A.	71	35 14N	91 46W
Searles, L., U.S.A.	73	35 45N	117 20W
Seaside, U.S.A.	72	46 0N	123 58W
Seattle, U.S.A.	72	47 36N	122 20W
Seaview Ra., Queens.	42	19 0 S	146 10 E
Seaward Kaikouras, mts., N.Z.	47	42 10 S	173 44 E
Seba, Indonesia	35	10 30 S	121 55 E
Sebastián Vizcairo Bay, Mexico	74	28 0N	114 30W
Sebastopol, U.S.A.	73	38 28N	122 40W
Sebei, dist., Uganda	53	3 0N	34 50 E
Sebes, Rumania	21	45 56N	23 40 E
Sebewaing, U.S.A.	68	43 45N	83 27W
Sebina, Botswana	56	20 55 S	27 17 E
Sebinkarahisar, Turkey	30	0 20N	38 35 E
Sebou R., Morocco	50	34 30N	5 30W

	MAP		
Sebring, U.S.A.	69	27 30N	81 47W
Sebuku I., Indonesia	35	3 30 S	116 25 E
Secchia, R., Italy	20	44 30N	10 40 E
Sechelt, Canada	64	49 25N	123 42W
Sechura B., Peru	78	5 40 S	81 0W
Sechura Des., Peru	78	6 0 S	80 30W
Secretary I., N.Z.	47	45 15 S	166 56 E
Secunderabad, India	32	17 28N	78 30 E
Sedalia, U.S.A.	70	38 40N	93 18W
Sedan, France	12	49 43N	4 57 E
Sedan, U.S.A.	71	37 7N	96 15W
Sedano, Spain	17	42 43N	3 49W
Seddon, New Zealand	47	41 40 S	174 7 E
Seddonville, N.Z.	47	41 33 S	172 1 E
Sede Ya'aqov, Israel	29	32 43N	35 7 E
Sedgewick, Canada	64	52 48N	111 41W
Sedhiou, Senegal	50	12 50N	15 30W
Sedley, Canada	65	50 10N	104 0W
Sedov Pk., U.S.S.R.	26	73 20N	55 10 E
Sedro Woolley, U.S.A.	72	48 30N	122 20W
Seeheim, S.W. Africa	57	26 48 S	17 45 E
Seeis, S.W. Africa	57	22 29 S	17 39 E
Seekoe, R., C. Prov.	57	31 0 S	24 35 E
Sefadau, Sierra Leone	52	Inset	
Sefton, NewZealand	47	43 15 S	172 41 E
Sefton Mt., N.Z.	47	43 40 S	170 5 E
Sefwi Bekwai, Ghana	52	6 10N	2 25W
Segamat, Malaya	34	2 30N	102 50 E
Segara, Botswana	56	20 10 S	25 18 E
Segbana, Dahomey	52	10 56N	3 42 E
Segbwema, Sierra Leone	52	8 0N	11 0W
Sege, Indonesia	35	2 10 S	132 5 E
Segesta, ruins, Italy	20	37 56N	12 49 E
Segin, U.S.A.	71	29 34N	97 59W
Segorbe, Spain	17	39 50N	0 30W
Segou, Mali	50	13 30N	6 10W
Segovia, Spain	17	40 57N	4 10W
Segre R., Spain	17	41 30N	0 25 E
Seguam I., Aleu. Is.	59	52 20N	172 30W
Seguam Passage, Aleutian Is.	59	52 0N	173 0W
Séguéla, Ivory Coast	50	7 55N	6 40W
Segula, I., Aleutian Is.	59	52 0N	178 8W
Segundo, U.S.A.	71	37 10N	104 47W
Segura R., Spain	17	38 9N	0 40W
Sehitwa, Botswana	56	20 22 S	22 35 E
Sehore, India	32	23 10N	77 5 E
Seibo, Dom. Republic	75	18 40N	69 2W
Seiland I., Norway	22	70 23N	23 15 E
Seiling, U.S.A.	71	36 6N	99 1W
Seim R., U.S.S.R.	25	51 45N	35 0 E
Seimchan, U.S.S.R.	27	62 40N	152 30 E
Seinajoki, Finland	23	62 47N	22 58 E
Seine R., France	12	49 28N	0 15 E
Seishin, Korea	36	41 45N	129 50 E
Seistan, dist., Iran	31	30 50N	61 0 E
Sekadau, Indonesia	34	0 5 S	110 55 E
Sekaju, Indonesia	34	2 58 S	103 58 E
Seke, Tanzania	53	3 20 S	33 31 E
Sekenke, Tanzania	53	4 15 S	34 10 E
Seki, Japan	36	35 40N	137 1 E
Sekiu, U.S.A.	72	48 17N	124 23W
Sekondi, Ghana	52	5 2N	1 48W
Sekuma, Botswana	57	24 41 S	23 50 E
Selah, U.S.A.	72	66 43N	120 31W
Selama, Malaya	34	5 12N	100 42 E
Selangor, st., Malaya	34	3 20N	101 30 E
Selaru I., Indonesia	35	8 18 S	131 0 E
Selatan, Tg., C., Indon.	35	4 10 S	114 40 E
Sclawik, Alaska	59	66 35N	160 10W
Selby, England	10	53 47N	1 5W
Selby, U.S.A.	70	45 4N	99 58W
Selden, U.S.A.	70	39 33N	100 36W
Selemdzha R., U.S.S.R.	27	52 40N	131 30 E
Selenga R., Mongolia	37	49 20N	101 0 E
Sélestat, France	12	48 15N	7 27 E
Selfridge, U.S.A.	70	46 4N	100 57W
Seli, or Rokel, R., Sierra Leone	52	Inset	
Selibaby, Mauritania	50	15 20N	12 15W
Seliger L., U.S.S.R.	25	57 15N	33 0 E
Seligman, U.S.A.	73	35 19N	112 52W
Selima O., Sudan	51	21 28N	29 31 E
Selinda Spillway, Botswana	56	13 38 S	23 0 E
Selinunte, ruins, Italy	20	37 35N	12 48 E
Selitrennoye, U.S.S.R.	25	47 10N	47 30 E
Selizharovo, U.S.S.R.	25	57 1N	33 17 E
Selkirk I., Canada	65	53 15N	99 0W
Selkirk Mts., Canada	64	51 0N	117 10W
Sellheim, Queensland	42	20 2 S	146 25 E
Sells, U.S.A.	73	31 58N	111 58W
Selma, Ala., U.S.A.	69	32 30N	87 0W
Selma, Calif., U.S.A.	73	36 36N	119 36W
Selma, N.C., U.S.A.	69	35 32N	78 18W
Selmer, U.S.A.	71	35 9N	88 36W
Selsey, England	10	50 44N	0 47W
Selukwe, Rhodesia	56	19 40 S	30 0 E
Selva, Argentina	77	29 50 S	62 0W
Selvas, reg., Brazil	78	6 30 S	67 0W
Selwyn, Queensland	42	21 30 S	140 29 E
Selwyn L., Canada	65	60 0N	104 30W
Selwyn Ra., Queens.	42	21 25 S	141 45 E
Seman R., Albania	21	40 45N	19 50 E
Semarang, Indonesia	34	7 0 S	110 26 E
Sembabule, Uganda	53	0 3 S	31 29 E
Semeru Mt., Indonesia	34	8 4 S	113 3 E

	MAP		
Semichi Is., Aleutian Is.	59	52 58N	174 0 E
Semidi Is., Alaska	59	56 0N	156 50W
Semilau, Sarawak	35	0 30N	112 5 E
Seminoe Res., U.S.A.	72	42 0N	106 55W
Seminole, Texas, U.S.A.	71	32 40N	102 34W
Seminole, Okla. U.S.A.	71	35 13N	96 44W
Semiozerny, U.S.S.R.	26	52 35N	64 0 E
Semipalatinsk, U.S.S.R.	26	50 30N	80 10 E
Semisopochnoi, I., Aleutian Is.	59	52 0N	179 40 E
Semiyarsk, U.S.S.R.	26	50 55N	78 30 E
Semliki R., Uganda	53	1 0N	30 10 E
Semmering P., Austria	14	47 38N	15 50 E
Semnan, Iran	31	35 40N	53 22 E
Semo, Indonesia	35	0 10 S	127 40 E
Sena Madureira, Brazil	78	9 5 S	68 45W
Senador Pompeu, Brazil	79	5 40 S	39 20W
Senai, Malaya	34	1 38N	103 38 E
Senane, Mozambique	56	22 46 S	34 1 E
Senanga, Zambia	56	16 12 S	23 32 E
Senatobia, U.S.A.	71	34 35N	90 0W
Sendai, Kagoshima, Japan	36	31 50N	130 20 E
Sendai, Miyagi, Japan	36	38 15N	141 0 E
Sendeling's Drift, S.W. Africa	57	28 12 S	16 53 E
Sene R., Ghana	52	7 35N	0 20W
Seneca, S.C., U.S.A.	69	34 43N	82 59W
Seneca, Oreg., U.S.A.	72	44 8N	119 1W
Seneca Falls, U.S.A.	68	42 55N	76 50W
Seneca L., U.S.A.	68	42 40N	76 58W
Senegal, Rep., Africa	50	14 30N	14 30W
Senegal, R., Senegal	50	16 30N	15 30W
Senekal, O.F.S.	57	28 18 S	27 36 E
Senga Hill, Zambia	56	9 24 S	31 13 E
Sengana R., Nigeria	52	4 22N	5 58 E
Sengilev, U.S.S.R.	25	53 57N	48 45 E
Sengwa R., Rhodesia	56	18 12 S	28 30 E
Senhor-do-Bonfim, Braz.	79	10 30 S	40 10W
Senigallia, Italy	20	43 42N	13 12 E
Senj, Yugoslavia	20	45 0N	14 58 E
Senja I., Norway	22	69 15N	17 30 E
Seniis, France	12	49 13N	2 35 E
Sennar, Sudan	51	13 30N	33 35 E
Sennaya, U.S.S.R.	25	45 13N	37 11 E
Senne R., Belgium	13	50 47N	4 17 E
Senneterre, Canada	62	48 25N	77 15W
Seno de Otway, Chile	77	53 0 S	72 0W
Seno de Skyring, Chile	77	52 20 S	72 0W
Sens, France	12	48 11N	3 15 E
Senta, Yugoslavia	21	45 55N	20 3 E
Sentinel, U.S.A.	73	32 51N	113 18W
Senya Beraku, Ghana	52	5 28N	0 31W
Séo de Urgel, Spain	17	42 22N	1 23 E
Seoni, India	32	22 5N	79 30 E
Seoul, tn. & S. City, prov., Korea	36	37 40N	127 0 E
Separation Point, Can.	63	53 40N	57 16W
Separation Point, N.Z.	47	40 47 S	173 1 E
Sepik R., Terr. of New Guinea	42	4 5 S	134 0 E
Sepolno, Poland	16	53 25N	17 35 E
Sepopa, Bechuanaland	56	18 50 S	22 8 E
Sept Iles, Canada	63	50 13N	66 22W
Sequim, U.S.A.	72	48 4N	123 2W
Sequoia National Park, U.S.A.	66	36 30N	118 40W
Serafimovich, U.S.S.R.	25	49 30N	42 50 E
Serampore, India	33	22 44N	88 30 E
Serandi, Uruguay	77	33 18N	55 38W
Serang, Indonesia	34	6 8 S	106 10 E
Serbia (Srbija), Y.slav.	21	43 30N	21 0 E
Serdobsk, U.S.S.R.	25	52 28N	44 10 E
Seredka, U.S.S.R.	25	58 12N	28 3 E
Seremban, Malaya	34	2 43N	101 53 E
Serengeti Plain, Tan.	53	2 30 S	35 0 E
Serenje, Zambia	56	13 14 S	30 15 E
Sergach, U.S.S.R.	25	55 30N	45 30 E
Sergipe, st., Brazil	79	10 30 S	37 20W
Seria, Brunei	35	4 37N	114 30 E
Serifos & I., Greece	21	37 9N	24 30 E
Sérigny R., Canada	63	55 40N	69 25W
Sericho, Kenya	53	1 8N	39 7 E
Serle Mt., S. Australia	42	30 25 S	138 57 E
Sermata I., Indonesia	35	8 15 S	128 50 E
Serna I., Indonesia	35	6 20 S	130 0 E
Serny Zavod, U.S.S.R.	26	40 0N	59 15 E
Serov, U.S.S.R.	24	59 40N	60 20 E
Serowe, Botswana	57	22 18 S	26 58 E
Serpa, Portugal	17	37 57N	7 38 E
Serpa Pinto, Angola	55	14 48 S	17 52 E
Serpentine, W. Austral.	44	32 30 S	116 30 E
Serpent's Mouth, S. America	78	8 0N	61 0W
Serpukhov, U.S.S.R.	25	54 55N	37 28 E
Serra da Bandeira, Angola	55	14 50 S	13 40 E
Serra da Estrela, Port.	23	40 10N	7 45W
Serra de Baturite, Braz.	79	4 25 S	39 0W
Serra d' Araripe, Braz.	79	7 20 S	39 40W
Serra do Malhao, Port.	17	37 23N	8 10W
Serra do Navio, Brazil	79	1 0N	53 0W
Serra Guardunha, Port.	17	40 7N	7 35W
Sérrai, Greece	21	41 5N	23 37 E
Serrania de Cuenca, Spain	17	40 10N	1 50W
Serres, France	12	44 26N	5 43 E
Serrezuela, Argentina	77	30 40 S	65 20W

	MAP		
Serrinha, Bahia, Brazil	79	11 30 s	39 0w
Sertânia, Brazil	79	8 0 s	37 20w
Sertâo, reg., Brazil	79	10 0 s	40 0w
Serti, Nigeria	52	5 24N	11 5 E
Serui, Indonesia	35	1 45 s	136 10 E
Seruli, Botswana	57	21 52 s	27 32 E
Sérvia, Greece	21	40 9N	21 58 E
Sese Is., Uganda	53	0 28 s	32 15 E
Sesfontein, S.W. Africa	55	19 7 s	13 39 E
Sesheke, Zambia	56	17 21 s	24 20 E
Sessa Aurunca, Italy	20	41 14N	13 56 E
Sestao, Spain	17	43 18N	3 0w
Sesto, Italy	20	46 42N	12 22 E
Sestri Levante, Italy	20	44 17N	9 22 E
Setana, Japan	36	42 30N	140 0 E
Setateng, Botswana	56	20 10 s	22 15 E
Sète, France	12	43 25N	3 42 E
Sete Lagôas, Brazil	79	19 20 s	44 16w
Sete Quedas Fs., Par.	77	24 5 s	54 10w
Sete Quedas I., Brazil	77	23 50 s	54 0w
Setif, Algeria	50	36 16N	5 26 E
Settat, Morocco	50	33 0N	7 40w
Sette Cama, Gabon	54	2 32 s	9 57 E
Setting L., Canada	65	55 0N	98 40w
Settlers, Transvaal	57	24 55 s	28 36 E
Setúbal, Portugal	17	38 30N	8 58w
Setubal, B. of, Portugal	17	38 24N	8 57w
Sevastopol, U.S.S.R.	25	44 35N	33 30 E
Sévérac, France	12	44 20N	3 5 E
Severn L., Canada	62	53 59N	91 0w
Severn R., Canada	62	44 52N	79 30w
Severn, R., England	10	52 15N	2 13w
Severnaya Zemlya Is., U.S.S.R.	27	79 0N	100 0 E
Sevier, U.S.A.	73	38 38N	112 14w
Sevier L., U.S.A.	73	39 0N	113 10w
Sevier R., U.S.A.	73	39 10N	112 30w
Seville, Spain	17	37 23N	6 0w
Seville, prov., Spain	17	37 0N	6 0w
Sevlievo, Bulgaria	21	43 3N	25 8 E
Sewa R., Sierra Leone	52		Inset
Seward, Alaska	59	60 0N	149 30w
Seward, U.S.A.	70	40 59N	97 4w
Seward Pen., Alaska	59	65 30N	164 0w
Sewell, Chile	77	34 10 s	70 45w
Sexsmith, Canada	64	55 20N	118 50w
Seychelles Is. Ind. Oc.	5	5 0 s	56 0 E
Seyches, France	12	44 34N	0 19 E
Seydhisfjördhur, Iceland	22	65 12N	13 52w
Seymour, Cape Prov.	57	32 32 s	26 50 E
Seymour, Ind., U.S.A.	68	39 0N	85 50w
Seymour, Wis., U.S.A.	70	44 30N	88 20w
Seymour, Texas, U.S.A.	71	33 32N	99 15w
Seymour, Victoria	43	36 58 s	145 10 E
Sézanne, France	12	48 40N	3 40 E
Sfântu Gheorghe, Rumania	21	54 52N	25 48 E
Sfax, Tunisia	51	34 49N	10 40 E
's Gravenhage, Neth. *See* Hague, The	13		
Shabani, Rhodesia	56	20 17 s	30 2 E
Shabogama L., Canada	63	48 40N	77 0w
Shabunda, Zaire	54	2 45 s	27 15 E
Shacheng, China	38	40 29N	115 31 E
Shackleton, Ant.	80	78 40 s	35 0w
Shaffa, Nigeria	52	10 30N	12 6 E
Shafter, Texas, U.S.A.	71	29 48N	104 17w
Shafter, Calif., U.S.A.	73	35 31N	119 16w
Shaftesbury, England	85	1 0N	2 12w
Shagamu, Nigeria	52	6 51N	3 39 E
Shāhābād, Iran	31	37 41N	56 47 E
Shahabad, Iran	30	34 10N	46 30 E
Shahada, India	32	21 33N	74 30 E
Shahjahanpur, India	32	27 50N	79 58 E
Shahdād, Iran	31	30 28N	57 35 E
Shahdadkot, Pakistan	32	27 50N	67 55 E
Shahadpur (Shahdadpur), Pakistan	32	25 66N	68 35 E
Shahdol, India	33	23 20N	81 25 E
Shahgarh, India	32	27 10N	69 55 E
Shahhat (Cyrene), Libya	51	32 40N	21 35 E
Shahi, Persia	31	36 29N	52 48 E
Shāhin Dezh, Iran	30	32 42N	46 38 E
Shaho, China	39	28 29N	112 52 E
Shahpur, Iran	30	38 12N	44 45 E
Shahr-e-Babak, Iran	31	30 10N	55 16 E
Shahr Kord, Iran	31	32 19N	50 49 E
Shahrig, Pakistan	32	30 15N	67 40 E
Shahrezā, Iran	31	32 0N	51 50 E
Shahrud, Iran	31	36 30N	55 0 E
Shahsavār, Iran	31	36 30N	51 5 E
Shahsien, China	39	26 25N	117 50 E
Shaikhabad, Afghan.	31	34 9N	68 41 E
Shaikh Shu'aib I., Iran	31	26 50N	53 20 E
Shajapur, India	32	23 20N	76 15 E
Shakhrizyabz, U.S.S.R.	31	39 0N	66 45 E
Shakhty, U.S.S.R.	25	47 40N	40 10 E
Shakhunya, U.S.S.R.	24	57 40N	47 0 E
Shaki, Nigeria	52	8 41N	3 21 E
Shakopee, U.S.A.	70	44 45N	93 30w
Shaktolik, Alaska	59	64 20N	161 10w
Shala Lake, Ethiopia	54	7 30N	38 30 E
Shalu, China	39	24 15N	120 30 E
Shama, Ghana	52	5 3N	1 35w
Shamaoma, Zambia	56	15 3 s	27 29 E
Shamattawa R., Canada	62	54 30N	85 50w
Shamil, Iran	31	27 33N	56 49 E
Shamo (Gobi) Desert, Mon.	37	43 40N	109 0 E
Shamokin, Pa., U.S.A.	68	40 47N	76 33w
Shamrock, U.S.A.	71	35 14N	100 15w
Shamva, Rhodesia	56	17 20 s	31 32 E
Shan State, Burma	33	21 30N	98 30 E
Shanga, Nigeria	52	9 1N	5 2 E
Shangalowe, Zaire	56	10 48 s	26 35 E
Shangani, Rhodesia	56	19 0 s	28 54 E
Shangani R., Rhod.	56	18 45 s	28 0 E
Shangcheng, China	39	31 55N	115 30 E
Shangchwan Shan, China	39	21 40N	112 45 E
Shanghai, China	39	31 15N	121 30 E
Shanghsien, China	38	33 30N	109 58 E
Shangjao, China	39	28 25N	117 50 E
Shangkao, China	39	28 17N	114 47 E
Shangkiu, China	38	34 28N	115 42 E
Shangpancheng, China	38	40 55N	118 5 E
Shangsze, China	39	22 13N	108 0 E
Shangyu, China	39	26 59N	114 32 E
Shani, Nigeria	52	10 14N	12 2 E
Shaniko, U.S.A.	72	45 1N	120 47w
Shanna, Saudi Arabia	30	19 0N	51 0 E
Shannon, New Zealand	46	40 33 s	175 25 E
Shannon Airport, Ire.	11	52 40N	9 0w
Shannon R., Ireland	11	53 10N	8 10w
Shannonbridge, Ireland	11	53 17N	8 2w
Shantar, I., U.S.S.R.	27	55 0N	137 40 E
Shanwa, Tanzania	53	2 12 s	33 40 E
Shaohing, China	39	30 0N	120 32 E
Shaowu, China	39	27 25N	117 30 E
Shaoyang, China	39	27 2N	111 25 E
Shaqra, Saudi Arabia	30	25 15N	45 16 E
Sharon Springs, U.S.A.	70	38 56N	101 47w
Shari, Saudi Arabia	30	27 21N	43 37 E
Shari B., Japan	36	44 0N	144 30 E
Shari'a R., Israel	29	31 24N	34 40 E
Sharifkhaneh, Iran	30	38 15N	45 25 E
Sharja, 'Oman	31	25 23N	55 26 E
Shark B., W. Australia	44	25 15 s	133 20 E
Sharkh, 'Oman	31	21 20N	59 0 E
Sharon, Israel	29	32 20N	34 56 E
Sharon, U.S.A.	68	41 18N	80 30w
Sharpe L., Canada	62	54 10N	93 21w
Sharukh, Iran	31	33 47N	60 10 E
Sharya, U.S.S.R.	24	58 12N	45 40 E
Shashi, Botswana	57	21 23 s	27 27 E
Shashi R., Rhodesia	57	21 37 s	28 30 E
Shasi, China	39	30 16N	112 20 E
Shasta, Mt., U.S.A.	72	41 20N	122 0w
Shasta Res., U.S.A.	72	40 45N	122 15w
Shatsk, U.S.S.R.	25	54 0N	41 45 E
Shatt al Arab, R., Iraq	30	30 0N	48 31 E
Shattuck, U.S.A.	71	36 14N	99 41w
Shaunavon, Canada	65	49 35N	108 40w
Shaw R., W. Australia	44	20 30 s	119 15 E
Shaw River, W. Australia	44	20 40 s	119 15 E
Shawan, China	37	44 34N	85 50 E
Shawano, U.S.A.	68	44 45N	88 38w
Shawhee, U.S.A.	67	35 15N	97 0w
Shawinigan Falls, Can.	62	46 35N	72 50w
Shawnee, Okla., U.S.A.	71	35 15N	97 0w
Shawneetown, U.S.A.	68	37 40N	88 10w
Shaybārā I., Si. Arabia	30	25 24N	36 50 E
Shcherbakov. *See* Rybinsk	25		
Shchigri, U.S.S.R.	25	51 55N	36 58 E
Sheboygan, Wis., U.S.A.	70	43 46N	87 45w
Shebshi, Mts., Nigeria	52	8 15N	12 0 E
Shediac, Canada	63	46 14N	64 32w
Sheelin, Ireland	11	53 48N	7 20w
Sheep Haven, Ireland	11	55 12N	7 55w
Sheerness, England	10	51 26N	0 47 E
Sheet Harbour, Canada	63	44 56N	62 31w
Shefar'am, Israel	29	32 48N	35 10 E
Sheffield, England	10	53 23N	1 28w
Sheffield, New Zealand	47	43 24 s	172 12 E
Sheffield, Tasmania	43	41 22 s	146 21 E
Sheffield Ala., U.S.A.	69	34 50N	87 50w
Sheffield, Texas, U.S.A.	71	30 41N	101 46w
Sheho, Canada	65	51 35N	103 10w
Shekhupura, W. Pak.	32	31 42N	73 58 E
Shekichen, China	38	33 10N	113 0 E
Shekki, China	39	22 30N	113 19 E
Sheklung, China	39	23 5N	113 55 E
Sheksna R., U.S.S.R.	25	59 30N	38 30 E
Shelburne, N.S., Can.	63	43 47N	65 20w
Shelburne, Ont., Can.	62	44 5N	85 13w
Shelburne B., Queens.	42	11 50 s	143 0 E
Shelby, Mich, U.S.A.	68	43 34N	86 27w
Shelby, Mont., U.S.A.	72	48 30N	111 59w
Shelby, N.C., U.S.A.	69	35 16N	81 34w
Shelbyville, Ill., U.S.A.	70	39 25N	88 45w
Shelbyville, Ind., U.S.A.	68	39 30N	85 42w
Shelbyville, Tenn., U.S.A.	69	35 30N	86 25w
Sheldon, U.S.A.	70	43 8N	95 49w
Sheldons Point, Alaska	59	62 30N	165 0w
Sheldrake, Canada	63	50 20N	64 51w
Shelekhov G., U.S.S.R.	27	59 30N	157 0 E
Shelikof Str., Alaska	59	57 0N	154 0w
Shell Creek Ra., U.S.A.	73	39 0N	114 30w
Shell Lake, U.S.A.	65	45 43N	91 52w
Shellborough, W. Australia	44	20 0 s	119 25 E
Shellbrook, Canada	65	53 20N	106 25w
Shellharbour, N.S.W.	43	34 31 s	150 51 E
Shelon R., U.S.S.R.	25	58 10N	30 30 E
Shelter Bay, Canada	63	50 3N	66 50w
Shelton, U.S.A.	72	47 14N	123 5w
Shemakha, U.S.S.R.	24	40 50N	48 28 E
Shemordan, U.S.S.R.	25	56 10N	50 50 E
Shenandoah, Iowa U.S.A.	70	40 48N	95 22w
Shenandoah, Pa., U.S.A.	68	40 50N	76 13w
Shenandoah, Va., U.S.A.	68	38 30N	78 38w
Shenandoah R., U.S.A.	68	38 50N	78 22w
Shenandoah National Park, U.S.A.	69	38 30N	78 28w
Shenchih, China	38	39 15N	112 10 E
Shendam, Nigeria	52	9 10N	9 30 E
Shendi, Sudan	51	16 46N	33 33 E
Shengjin, Albania	21	41 48N	19 34 E
Shenkursk, U.S.S.R.	24	62 15N	43 10 E
Shenmu, China	38	39 0N	110 0 E
Shentsa, China	37	30 56N	88 40 E
Sheo, India	32	26 10N	71 15 E
Sheopur Kalan, India	32	25 45N	76 45 E
Shepetovka, U.S.S.R.	24	50 10N	27 0 E
Shephelah, dist., Israel	29	31 30N	34 43 E
Shepparton, Victoria	43	36 18 s	145 25 E
Sher Qila, Kashmir	32	36 5N	74 3 E
Sherbro I., Sierra Leone	52	7 30N	12 40w
Sherbro R., Sierra Leone	52	7 43N	12 45w
Sherbrooke, N.S., Can.	63	45 10N	61 58w
Sherbrooke, Que., Can.	63	45 24N	71 57w
Shercock, Ireland	11	54 0N	6 54w
Shergarh, India	32	26 20N	72 20 E
Sheridan, Ark., U.S.A.	71	34 19N	92 27w
Sheridan, Colorado, U.S.A.	70	39 43N	105 2w
Sheridan, Wyo., U.S.A.	72	44 50N	107 0w
Sherman, U.S.A.	71	33 40N	96 35w
Sherridon, Canada	65	55 10N	101 5w
Sherwood, U.S.A.	71	31 15N	100 45w
Sheslay & R., Canada	64	58 25N	131 45w
Shestakova, U.S.S.R.	27	68 20N	147 15 E
Shethnanei L., Canada	65	58 40N	98 10w
Shetland Is., Scotland	10	60 30N	1 30w
Sheyenne, U.S.A.	70	47 51N	99 5w
Sheyenne R., U.S.A.	70	47 40N	98 15w
Shibam, South Arabia	30	16 0N	48 36 E
Shibarghan, Afghanistan	31	36 40N	65 30 E
Shibata, Japan	36	37 59N	139 15 E
Shibetsu, Japan	36	44 0N	142 30 E
Shibogama L., Canada	62	58 30N	88 40w
Shibushi, Japan	36	31 18N	131 5 E
Shichi-to Is., Japan	36	29 50N	129 0 E
Shigaib, Sudan	51	15 5N	23 35 E
Shigatse, China	37	29 10N	89 0 E
Shih Ho, China	39	31 45N	116 0 E
Shihchüan, China	38	33 5N	108 30 E
Shiheiwei, China	39	32 18N	119 3 E
Shihkiachwang, China	38	37 55N	114 30 E
Shihkwaikow, Mon.	38	41 1N	110 5 E
Shihlu, China	39	19 26N	108 55 E
Shihlung, China	39	23 57N	109 43 E
Shihpu, China	39	29 13N	121 51 E
Shihtai, China	39	30 30N	118 0 E
Shihtao, China	38	36 55N	122 25 E
Shihtsien, China	39	27 28N	108 3 E
Shihtsuishan, China	39	27 31N	108 20 E
Shikarpur, W. Pak.	32	27 58N	68 42 E
Shikiu, Japan	36	42 30N	141 17 E
Shikoku I., Japan	36	33 30N	133 30 E
Shilka, U.S.S.R.	27	52 0N	115 55 E
Shillelagh, Ireland	11	52 46N	6 32w
Shillong, India	33	25 30N	92 0 E
Shiloh (site), Jordan	29	32 4N	35 18 E
Shilovo, U.S.S.R.	25	54 25N	41 0 E
Shimabara, Japan	36	32 45N	130 30 E
Shimane, pref., Japan	36	35 0N	132 30 E
Shimanovsk, U.S.S.R.	27	52 15N	127 30 E
Shimizu, Japan	36	35 0N	138 30 E
Shimoga, India	32	13 57N	75 32 E
Shimoni, Kenya	53	4 38 s	39 25 E
Shimonoseki, Japan	36	33 58N	131 0 E
Shimpek, U.S.S.R.	26	44 50N	74 10 E
Shimsk, U.S.S.R.	25	58 15N	30 50 E
Shin Dand (Sabzawar), Afghanistan	31	33 15N	62 0 E
Shin L., Scotland	10	58 7N	4 30w
Shingu, Japan	36	33 40N	135 45 E
Shingwedzi, Transvaal	56	22 18 s	31 27 E
Shinjo, Japan	36	38 45N	140 15 E
Shinkafe, Nigeria	52	13 0N	6 28 E
Shinkolobwe (Chinkolobwe), Zaire	56	11 10 s	26 40 E
Shinyanga, Tanzania	53	3 35 s	33 20 E
Shinyanga, prov., Tan.	53	3 30 s	33 0 E
Shiogama, Japan	36	38 20N	141 0 E
Shiono C., Japan	36	33 25N	135 45 E
Ship I., U.S.A.	69	30 16N	88 55w
Shipka P., Bulgaria	21	42 43N	25 22 E
Shipki La., Ind.–China	32	31 50N	78 50 E
Shippensburg, U.S.A.	68	40 4N	77 32w
Shippigan, Canada	63	47 45N	64 43w
Shiprock, U.S.A.	73	36 18N	108 43w
Shipshaw, R., Canada	63	49 0N	71 20w
Shir Kuh, Mt., Iran	31	31 35N	54 0 E
Shirakawa, Japan	36	37 18N	140 11 E
Shiraoi, Japan	36	42 30N	141 17 E
Shirati, Tanzania	53	1 6 s	34 3 E
Shiraz, Iran	31	29 42N	52 30 E
Shire R., Malawi	56	15 30 s	35 0 E
Shire Higlands, Malawi	56	15 15 s	35 14 E
Shiretoko C., Japan	36	44 25N	145 20 E
Shiriya C., Japan	36	41 25N	141 30 E
Shirvan, Iran	31	37 30N	57 50 E
Shirwa L., Malawi	56	15 15 s	35 40 E
Shisar, Saudi Arabia	30	18 20N	53 25 E
Shishmaref, Alaska	59	66 15N	166 11w
Shitata, Sudan	53	4 40N	30 16 E
Shiukwan, China	39	24 45N	113 33 E
Shivpuri, India	32	25 18N	77 42 E
Shiwa Ngandu, Zambia	56	11 14 s	31 44 E
Shiwele Ferry, Zambia	56	11 28 s	28 30 E
Shizuoka, Japan	36	35 0N	138 30 E
Shizuoka, pref., Japan	36	35 15N	138 40 E
Shkodër, Albania	21	42 6N	19 29 E
Shkumbin R., Albania	21	41 5N	19 50 E
Shmidt I., U.S.S.R.	27	81 0N	91 0 E
Shoal C., W. Australia	44	33 50 s	121 8 E
Shoal Lake, Canada	65	50 30N	100 35w
Shoalhaven R., N.S.W.	43	34 55 s	150 5 E
Shoeburyness, England	10	51 31N	0 49 E
Shohsien, China	38	39 30N	112 25 E
Sholapur, India	32	17 43N	75 56 E
Sholl Ra., W. Australia	44	26 55 s	121 20 E
Shomera, Israel	29	33 4N	35 17 E
Shomo L., Ethiopia	54	5 45N	37 30 E
Shongopovi, U.S.A.	73	35 47N	110 35w
Shosanbetsu, Japan	36	40 37N	141 45 E
Shoshone, U.S.A.	72	43 0N	114 20w
Shoshone, L., U.S.A.	72	44 28N	111 0w
Shoshong, Botswana	57	22 59 s	26 30 E
Shoshoni, U.S.A.	72	43 16N	108 4w
Shotover R., N.Z.	47	44 49 s	168 44 E
Show Low, U.S.A.	73	34 16N	110 1w
Showa, Antarctica	80	68 30 s	40 30 E
Showyang, China	38	38 0N	113 15 E
Shreveport, U.S.A.	71	32 30N	93 50w
Shrewsbury, England	10	52 42N	2 45w
Shrule, Ireland	11	53 32N	9 7w
Shuaib, I., Iran	31	26 50N	53 15 E
Shucheng, China	39	31 25N	117 0 E
Shugozero, U.S.S.R.	25	59 57N	34 3 E
Shuguli Falls, Tan.	53	8 35 s	37 30 E
Shuicheng, China	39	26 45N	104 52 E
Shuifeng Dam, Korea–China	38	40 15N	125 10 E
Shuikiaho, China	39	32 18N	117 7 E
Shumagin Is., Alaska	59	55 0N	161 0w
Shumen (Kolarovgrad), Bulgaria	21	43 16N	26 55 E
Shumerlya, U.S.S.R.	25	55 30N	46 10 E
Shumikha, U.S.S.R.	26	55 15N	63 30 E
Shunan, China	39	29 40N	119 0 E
Shunat Nimrin, Jordan	29	31 55N	35 36 E
Shunchang, China	39	26 50N	117 55 E
Shungnak, Alaska	59	67 5N	156 45w
Shuntak, China	39	22 53N	113 10 E
Shuqra, South Arabia	30	13 22N	45 34 E
Shuqra, South Arabia	49	13 22N	45 47 E
Shur R., Iran	31	28 20N	55 0 E
Shur R., Iran	30	37 0N	48 9 E
Shur R., Iran	31	31 0N	57 35 E
Shusf, Iran	31	31 52N	60 0 E
Shutur Khun Kotal, Afghanistan	31	34 28N	65 0 E
Shuswap L., Canada	64	51 0N	119 0w
Shuweika, Jordan	29	32 20N	35 1 E
Shuya, U.S.S.R.	25	56 50N	41 28 E
Shuyak, I., Alaska	59	58 56N	153 0w
Shuyang, China	38	34 10N	118 45 E
Shwebo, Burma	33	22 30N	95 45 E
Shwegu, Burma	33	24 15N	96 50 E
Shweli R., Burma	33	23 45N	96 45 E
Shyaulyai, U S.S.R.	24	56 0N	23 7 E
Shyok, Kashmir	32	34 15N	78 5 E
Shyok R., Kashmir	32	34 30N	78 15 E
Si Kiang, China	39	22 35N	113 15 E
Siahan Range, Mts., Pakistan	32	27 30N	64 40 E
Siakiang, China	39	27 35N	115 10 E
Siakwan, China	37	25 33N	100 9 E
Sialkot, Pakistan	32	32 32N	74 30 E
Siam (Thailand), king., Asia	34	16 0N	102 0 E
Siam, G. of, Thailand	34	10 0N	102 30 E
Sian, China	38	34 2N	109 0 E
Siang K., R., China	39	27 10N	112 45 E
Siangcheng, China	38	33 15N	115 5 E
Siangfan, China	39	32 6N	112 0 E
Siangning, China	38	36 0N	110 50 E
Siangsiang, China	39	27 50N	112 30 E
Siangtan, China	39	28 0N	112 55 E
Siangyang, China	39	32 18N	111 0 E
Siangyin, China	39	28 42N	112 48 E
Siantur, Indonesia	34	3 0N	99 0 E
Siaokan, China	39	31 0N	114 0 E
Siapa R., Venezuela	78	1 55N	65 30w
Siapu, China	39	26 58N	120 0 E
Siargo I., Philippines	35	10 0N	126 3 E
Siāreh, Iran	31	28 50N	60 15 E
Siátista, Greece	21	40 15N	21 33 E
Siau I., Indonesia	35	2 50N	125 25 E

	MAP		
Sibasa, Transvaal	57	22 53 S	30 25 E
Sibayi, L., Natal	57	27 20 S	32 45 E
Sibbald, Canada	65	51 24N	110 10W
Sibenik, Yugoslavia	20	43 48N	15 54 E
Siberia, reg., N. Asia	5	65 0N	100 0 E
Siberut I., Indonesia	34	1 30 S	99 0 E
Sibi, Pakistan	32	29 30N	67 48 E
Sibiti, Congo	54	3 38 S	13 9 E
Sibiu, Rumania	21	45 45N	24 9 E
Sibley, Iowa, U.S.A.	70	43 21N	95 4W
Sibley, La., U.S.A.	71	32 32N	93 18W
Siboa, Indonesia	35	0 35N	120 0 E
Sibolga, Sumatra, Indonesia	34	1 50N	98 45 E
Sibsagar, India	33	27 0N	94 45 E
Sibu, Sarawak	35	2 20N	111 57 E
Sibutu I., Philippines	35	4 45N	119 30 E
Sicamous, Canada	64	50 49N	119 0W
Sicasico, Bolivia	78	17 20 S	67 45W
Siccus R., S. Australia	43	31 45 S	139 18 E
Sichang, China	37	27 55N	102 28 E
Sichwan, China	38	33 10N	111 30 E
Sicily I., Italy	20	37 30N	14 0 E
Sicuani, Peru	78	14 10 S	71 10W
Siddipet, India	32	18 0N	79 0 E
Sidhi, India	33	24 20N	81 55 E
Sidhirokastron, Greece	21	37 20N	21 46 E
Sidi Barrani, Egypt	51	31 32N	25 58 E
Sidi Bel Abbès, Algeria	50	35 13N	0 45W
Sidmouth C., Queens.	42	13 27 S	143 33 E
Sidney, Canada	64	48 40N	123 30W
Sidney, Mont., U.S.A.	70	47 41N	104 11W
Sidney, N.Y., U.S.A.	68	42 18N	75 20W
Sidney, Ohio, U.S.A.	68	40 18N	84 6W
Sidra, G. of, Libya	51	31 0N	19 30 E
Siedlce, Poland	16	52 10N	22 20 E
Sieg, R., Germany	14	50 48N	7 45 E
Siegen, Germany	14	50 52N	8 2 E
Siemiatycze, Poland	16	52 28N	22 50 E
Siena, Italy	20	43 20N	11 20 E
Sienfeng, China	39	29 45N	109 10 E
Sienkü, China	39	28 55N	120 45 E
Sienyang, China	38	34 25N	108 40 E
Sieradz, Poland	16	51 37N	18 41 E
Siero, Spain	17	43 25N	5 40W
Sierpc, Poland	16	52 55N	19 43 E
Sierra Blanca, U.S.A.	73	31 0N	105 15W
Sierra Blanca Mt., U.S.A.	73	33 15N	106 0W
Sierra City, U.S.A.	72	39 33N	120 39W
Sierra de Alcaraz, Spain	17	38 40N	2 20W
Sierra de Aracena, Spain	17	37 55N	6 50W
Sierra de Espuna, Spain	17	37 52N	1 40W
Sierra de Gata, Spain	17	40 20N	6 20W
Sierra de Gredos, Spain	17	40 20N	5 0W
Sierra de Guadalupe, Spain	17	39 28N	5 30W
Sierra de Guadarrama, Spain	17	41 0N	4 0W
Sierra de Gudar, Spain	17	40 30N	0 45W
Sierra de Monchique, Portugal	17	37 21N	8 34W
Sierra de la Culebra, Spain	17	41 55N	6 20W
Sierra de la Demanda, Spain	17	42 15N	3 0W
Sierra de la Giganta, Mexico	74	25 0N	111 0W
Sierra de las Minas, Guatemala	74	15 10N	89 39W
Sierra de los Alamitos, Mexico	74	26 40N	102 15W
Sierra de los Filabres, Spain	17	37 12N	2 20W
Sierra de Nayarit, Mex.	74	22 50N	104 30W
Sierra de San Lazaro, Mexico	74	23 30N	110 0W
Sierra de San Pedro, Spain	17	39 18N	6 40W
Sierra de Tamaulipas, Mexico	74	23 30N	108 20W
Sierra de Tolox, Spain	17	36 40N	5 0W
Sierra Gorda, Chile	77	23 0 S	69 15W
Sierra Grillemona, Spain	17	38 20N	1 40W
Sierra Imataca, Ven.	75	8 0N	61 30W
Sierra Juarez, Mexico	74	32 0N	115 40W
Sierra Leone, st., W. Afr.	52	9 0N	12 0W
Sierra Madre del Sur, Mexico	74	17 30N	100 0W
Sierra Madre Occidental, Mexico	74	24 0N	105 0W
Sierra Maestra, Cuba	75	20 0N	76 50W
Sierra Martés, Spain	17	39 20N	1 0W
Sierra Mojada, Mexico	74	27 19N	103 42W
Sierra Morena, Spain	17	38 20N	4 0W
Sierra Nevada, Spain	17	37 3N	3 15W
Sierra Nevada, U.S.A.	73	38 0N	120 0W
Sierra Nevada de Santa Marta, Colombia	75	10 55N	73 50W
Sierra San Pedro Martir, Mexico	74	31 0N	115 15W
Sierra Vizcaino, Mexico	74	27 20N	114 0W
Sierre, Switzerland	15	46 17N	7 31 E
Sifnos, I., Greece	21	37 0N	24 45 E
Sifton, Canada	65	51 25N	100 10W
Sifton P., Canada	64	57 57N	126 17W
Sigerfjord, Norway	22	68 40N	15 33 E

	MAP		
Sighet, Rumania	21	47 57N	23 52 E
Sighisoara, Rumania	21	46 12N	24 50 E
Sigli, Indonesia	34	5 25N	96 0 E
Siglufjördur, Iceland	22	66 12N	18 55W
Sigmaringen, Germany	14	48 5N	9 13 E
Sigsig, Ecuador	78	3 0 S	78 50W
Sigtuna, Sweden	23	59 36N	17 44 E
Siguenza, Spain	17	41 3N	2 40W
Siguia, R., Nicaragua	75	12 15N	84 40 E
Siguiri, Guinea	50	11 31N	9 10W
Sigulda, U.S.S.R.	23	57 10N	24 55 E
Sigura, U.S.A.	73	38 53N	112 1W
Sihoal, China	38	34 0N	105 5 E
Sihsien, China	38	36 40N	110 45 E
Sihsien, China	37	29 53N	118 27 E
Sihwashan, China	39	25 26N	114 12 E
Si'ir, Jordan	29	31 35N	35 9 E
Siirt, Turkey	30	37 57N	41 55 E
Sijarira Ra, mts., Rhodesia	56	17 36 S	27 45 E
Sikalongo, Zambia	56	16 54 S	27 12 E
Sikar, India	32	27 39N	75 10 E
Sikasso, Mali	50	11 7N	5 35W
Sikeston, U.S.A.	71	36 56N	89 32W
Sikhote Alin Ra., U.S.S.R.	27	46 0N	136 0 E
Sikinos & I., Greece	21	36 40N	25 8 E
Sikkani Chief R., Can.	64	57 30N	122 40W
Sikkim, st., N.E. India	33	27 50N	88 50 E
Sikonge, Tanzania	53	5 35 S	32 45 E
Siku, China	38	33 40N	104 20 E
Sikwangshan, China	38	28 0N	111 20 E
Sil R., Spain	17	42 23N	7 30W
Silamulun Ho, R., China	38	43 15N	118 30 E
Silat edh Dhahr, Jordan	29	32 19N	35 11 E
Silchar, India	33	24 45N	93 0 E
Siler City, U.S.A.	69	35 44N	79 30W
Silghat, India	33	26 35N	93 0 E
Siliao Ho, R., China	38	43 45N	122 40 E
Silifke, Turkey	30	36 22N	33 58 E
Siliguri, India	33	26 45N	88 25 E
Silin, China	39	24 28N	105 33 E
Silinhot, China	38	43 15N	116 0 E
Silistra, Bulgaria	21	44 6N	27 19 E
Siljan L., Sweden	23	60 55N	14 45 E
Siljan, mt., Sweden	23	60 55N	14 44 E
Silkeborg, Denmark	23	56 10N	9 32 E
Sillajhuay, mt., Chile	78	19 40 S	68 40W
Siloam Springs, U.S.A.	71	36 12N	94 31W
Sils, Switzerland	15	46 25N	9 45 E
Silsbee, U.S.A.	71	30 18N	94 8W
Siluko, Nigeria	52	6 31N	5 8 E
Silute, U.S.S.R.	23	55 20N	21 27 E
Silva Porto, Angola	55	12 22 S	16 55 E
Silver City, Pan. Can. Zone	74	9 21N	79 53W
Silver City, U.S.A.	73	32 50N	108 10W
Silver Creek, U.S.A.	68	42 33N	79 9W
Silver Lake, U.S.A.	72	43 10N	121 5W
Silver Streams, Cape Province	57	28 20 S	23 33 E
Silverton, N.S.W.	43	31 52 S	141 10 E
Silverton, Texas, U.S.A.	71	34 29N	101 15W
Silverton, Colo., U.S.A.	73	37 50N	107 40W
Silves, Portugal	17	37 14N	8 26W
Silvies, R., U.S.A.	72	43 58N	119 0W
Silwan, Jordan	29	31 59N	35 15 E
Simakumba, Zambia	56	14 18 S	23 35 E
Simalugui, Inda	33	26 55N	94 45 E
Simanggang, Sarawak	35	1 10N	111 45 E
Simard L., Canada	62	47 40N	78 40W
Simba, Kenya	53	2 11 S	37 35 E
Simba, Tanzania	53	1 44 S	34 13 E
Simbo, Tanzania	53	4 38 S	33 3 E
Simbo, Tanzania	53	4 57 S	29 43 E
Simcoe, Canada	62	42 50N	80 20W
Simcoe L., Canada	62	44 30N	79 30W
Simenga, U.S.S.R.	27	62 50N	107 55 E
Simeulue I., Indonesia	34	2 45N	95 45 E
Simferopol, U.S.S.R.	25	44 55N	34 3 E
Simi I., Greece	21	36 35N	27 50 E
Simikot, Nepal	33	30 0N	81 50 E
Simiti, Colombia	75	7 57N	73 57W
Simla, India	32	31 2N	77 15 E
Simleul-Silvaniei, Rum.	21	47 17N	22 50 E
Simme R., Switzerland	15	46 38N	7 30 E
Simo, L., Finland	22	66 5N	27 20 E
Simo, R., Finland	22	66 0N	26 0 E
Simonette, R., Canada	64	54 30N	118 0W
Simonstown, Cape Prov.	57	34 12 S	18 26 E
Simoya, Zambia	56	13 52 S	23 11 E
Simplon P., Switzerland	15	46 15N	8 0 E
Simplon Tunnel, Switzerland–Italy	15	46 17N	8 7 E
Simpson Hill, W. Australia	45	26 30 S	126 20 E
Sin Cowe I.	35	9 50N	114 45 E
Sinabang, Indonesia	34	2 30N	46 30 E
Sinai, pen., Egypt	51	29 0N	34 0 E
Sinaia, Rumania	21	45 21N	25 38 E
Sinaloa, Mexico	74	25 50N	108 20W
Sinaloa, st., Mexico	74	25 0N	107 30W
Sincé, Colombia	75	9 14N	75 8W
Sincelejo, Colombia	75	9 17N	75 23W
Sinchang-ni, Hamgyong S., N. Korea	36	40 12N	128 35 E

	MAP		
Sinchang-ni, Pyongan, S., N. Korea	36	39 19N	126 9 E
Sincheng, China	38	45 45N	124 20 E
Sincheng, Kwangsi, China	39	24 10N	108 47 E
Sincheng, Honan, China	38	34 30N	113 55 E
Sinclair, U.S.A.	72	41 48N	107 7W
Sinclair Mills, Canada	64	54 5N	121 40W
Sind Sagar Doab, Pak.	32	32 0N	71 30 E
Sindangbarang, Indon.	34	7 27 S	107 9 E
Sinde, Zambia	56	17 32 S	25 51 E
Sinde, Zambia	56	14 10 S	31 45 E
Sinelnikovo, U.S.S.R.	25	48 25N	35 30 E
Sinendé, Dahomey	52	10 19N	2 27 E
Sines, Portugal	17	37 56N	8 51W
Sinfeng, Kiangsi, China	39	25 25N	114 57 E
Sinfeng, Kiangsi, China	39	27 5N	106 38 E
Sing Buri, Siam	34	14 46N	100 21 E
Singa, Sudan	51	13 10N	33 57 E
Singapore, st., Asia	34	1 17N	103 51 E
Singapore, Str. of, S.E. Asia	34	1 10N	103 40 E
Singaradja, Indonesia	35	8 15 S	115 10 E
Singida, Tanzania	53	4 48 S	34 42 E
Singida, prov., Tan.	53	6 45 S	34 30 E
Singitkós, G., Greece	21	40 15N	24 0 E
Singkaling Hkamti, Burma	33	26 0N	95 45 E
Singkawang, Indonesia	34	1 0N	109 5 E
Singkep I., Indonesia	34	0 30 S	104 20 E
Singkil, Indonesia	34	2 20N	97 50 E
Singleton, N.S.W.	43	32 30 S	151 6 E
Singleton, Mt., W. Australia	44	29 27 S	117 15 E
Singtze, China	39	29 25N	116 6 E
Sinhailien, China	38	34 35N	119 20 E
Sinhwa, China	39	27 38N	111 5 E
Sining, China	37	36 50N	102 10 E
Sinj, Yugoslavia	20	43 42N	16 39 E
Sinjär, Iraq	30	36 19N	41 52 E
Sinjil, Jordan	29	32 3N	35 15 E
Sinkan, China	39	27 45N	115 28 E
Sinkat, Sudan	51	18 55N	36 49 E
Sinkiang, China	38	35 35N	111 25 E
Sinkiang-Uigur, aut. reg., China	37	42 0N	88 0 E
Sinkin, China	38	39 30N	122 27 E
Sinlo, China	38	38 25N	114 50 E
Sinnamary, Fr. Guiana	79	5 15N	52 55W
Sinni R., Italy	20	40 6N	16 15 E
Sinmin, China	38	42 2N	122 45 E
Sinning, China	39	26 17N	110 48 E
Sinnûris, Egypt	51	29 26N	30 31 E
Sinoia, Rhodesia	56	17 20 S	30 8 E
Sinop, Turkey	30	42 1N	35 11 E
Sinpin, China	38	41 50N	125 0 E
Sinsiang, China	38	35 30N	113 55 E
Sinsien, China	38	38 30N	112 45 E
Sintang, Indonesia	35	0 5N	111 35 E
Sintai, China	38	37 1N	114 29 E
Sinton, U.S.A.	77	28 0N	97 30W
Sintra, Portugal	19	38 47N	9 25W
Sintu, China	31	30 57N	104 12 E
Sinu, R., Colombia	78	8 50N	76 5W
Sinuiji, Korea	38	39 40N	124 28 E
Sinyang, China	39	32 10N	114 0 E
Sioma, Zambia	56	16 38 S	23 37 E
Sion, Switzerland	15	46 14N	7 20 E
Sioux City, U.S.A.	70	42 32N	96 25W
Sioux Falls, U.S.A.	70	43 35N	96 40W
Sioux Lookout, Canada	62	50 10N	91 50W
Sipia, China	38	33 36N	118 55 E
Siparia, Trinidad	78	10 15N	61 30W
Siping, China	38	33 25N	114 1 E
Sipiwesk L., Canada	65	55 0N	97 40W
Sipolilo, Rhodesia	56	16 37 S	30 42 E
Sipora I., Indonesia	34	2 10 S	99 45 E
Sipul, N. Guinea	42	5 57 S	148 50 E
Siquirres, Costa Rica	78	10 5N	83 30W
Sir Wilfred Laurier, mt., Canada	64	52 48N	119 49W
Sira, India	32	13 41N	76 49 E
Siracusa, Italy	20	37 4N	15 17 E
Sirajganj, Bangladesh	33	24 25N	89 47 E
Sirake, Papua	42	9 2 S	141 2 E
Sire, Ethiopia	54	9 2N	36 52 E
Siret R., Rumania	21	47 58N	26 5 E
Sirna I., Greece	21	36 22N	26 42 E
Sirohi, India	32	24 52N	72 53 E
Sironj, India	32	24 5N	77 45 E
Siros. I., Greece	21	37 28N	24 57 E
Sirsa, India	32	29 33N	75 4 E
Sirsiri (Lopeja), Sudan	53	4 22N	31 58 E
Sirte. *See* Surt, Libya	51		
Sisak, Yugoslavia	20	45 30N	16 21 E
Sisaket, Siam	34	15 8N	104 18 E
Sishen, S.W. Africa	57	27 55 S	22 59 E
Sisiang, China	38	32 43N	107 50 E
Sisianghsien, China	38	33 0N	107 40 E
Sisipuk L., Cànada	65	55 40N	120 0W
Sisophon, Cambodia	34	13 31N	102 59 E
Sissach, Switzerland	15	47 28N	7 48 E
Sisseton, U.S.A.	70	45 46N	97 1W
Sisteron, France	12	44 12N	5 57 E
Sisters, U.S.A.	72	44 18N	121 31W
Sitachwe, Botswana	57	24 24 S	20 39 E
Sitalike, Tanzania	53	6 37 S	31 7 E
Sitapur, India	32	27 38N	80 45 E

	MAP		
Sitges, Spain	17	41 17N	1 47 E
Sitia, Crete	20	35 13N	26 6 E
Sitka, Alaska	59	57 5N	135 20W
Sittang, R., Burma	33	18 30N	96 40 E
Situbondo, Indonesia	34	7 45 S	114 0 E
Siu Shui, China	39	29 10N	115 0 E
Siuan, China	39	29 30N	118 42 E
Siuwu, China	38	35 10N	113 30 E
Siuyen, China	38	40 20N	123 15 E
Sivand, Iran	31	30 11N	52 51 E
Sivas, Turkey	30	39 43N	36 58 E
Siverek, Turkey	30	37 44N	39 22 E
Sivrihisar, Turkey	30	39 30N	31 35 E
Siwa, Egypt	51	29 10N	25 30 E
Siwalik Range, Nepal	32	28 0N	83 0 E
Siwan, India	33	26 13N	84 27 E
Sixth Cataract, Sudan	51	16 20N	32 40 E
Siying, China	38	21 14N	110 16 E
Sjaelland I., Denmark	23	55 30N	11 30 E
Sjönsta, Norway	22	67 10N	16 3 E
Sjövegan, Norway	22	68 45N	17 58 E
Skadarsko, L., Y.slav.–Albania	21	42 15N	19 20 E
Skadovsk, U.S.S.R.	25	46 17N	32 52 E
Skafta, R., Iceland	22	63 56N	18 30 E
Skaftaros, B., Iceland	22	63 40N	17 43 E
Skagarfjördur, Iceland	22	65 50N	19 30W
Skagastölstindane, mt., Norway	23	61 28N	7 53 E
Skagaströnd, Iceland	22	65 50N	20 12W
Skagen, Denmark	23	57 45N	10 35 E
Skagerrak, str., Den.–Norway	23	57 50N	9 0 E
Skagway, Alaska	59	59 30N	135 20W
Skalar, Iceland	22	66 20N	14 43W
Skálfandafljót R., Iceland	22	65 30N	17 30W
Skara, Sweden	23	58 25N	13 30 E
Skardu, Kashmir	32	35 20N	75 35 E
Skeena Mts., Canada	64	56 40N	128 0W
Skeena R., Canada	64	54 20N	129 20W
Skegness, England	10	53 9N	0 20 E
Skeldon, Guyana	79	6 0N	57 20W
Skellefte, R., Sweden	22	64 30N	19 30 E
Skellefteå, Sweden	22	64 45N	20 59 E
Skelleftstrand, Sweden	22	64 45N	21 15 E
Skellig Rocks, Ireland	11	51 47N	10 30W
Skelton, Antarctica	80	79 0 S	161 0W
Skene, Sweden	23	57 30N	12 35 E
Skerries, Is., N. Ireland	11	55 14N	6 40W
Skhiza I., Greece	21	36 41N	21 47 E
Skiathos I., Greece	21	39 12N	23 30 E
Skibbereen, Ireland	11	51 33N	9 16W
Skiddaw, mt., England	10	54 39N	3 9W
Skidegate, Canada	64	53 20N	132 0W
Skidegate Inlet, Canada	22	53 20N	132 0W
Skien, Norway	23	59 12N	9 35 E
Skihist Mt., Canada	64	50 10N	121 50W
Skikda (Philippeville), Algeria	50	36 50N	6 49 E
Skipness, Scotland	10	55 46N	5 20W
Skiros & I., Greece	21	38 55N	24 34 E
Skire, Denmark	23	56 33N	9 2 E
Skjalfandi, B., Iceland	22	66 5N	17 30W
Skjern, Denmark	23	55 57N	8 30 E
Skópelos I., Greece	21	39 9N	23 47 E
Skopin, U.S.S.R.	25	53 55N	39 32 E
Skoplje, Yugoslavia	21	42 1N	21 32 E
Skövde, Sweden	23	58 24N	13 52 E
Skovorodino, U.S.S.R.	27	53 50N	124 0 E
Showhegan, U.S.A.	69	44 49N	69 40W
Skowman, Canada	65	51 58N	99 35W
Skudeneshavn, Norway	23	59 10N	5 10 E
Skukuza, Transvaal	57	24 52 S	31 35 E
Skunk R., U.S.A.	70	41 15N	91 45W
Skwierzyna, Poland	16	52 35N	15 30 E
Skye, I., Scotland	10	57 15N	6 10W
Skykomish, U.S.A.	64	47 43N	121 29W
Slagelse, Denmark	23	55 23N	11 19 E
Slamet Mt., Indonesia	34	7 12 S	109 15 E
Slane, Ireland	11	53 42N	6 32W
Slaney R., Ireland	11	52 52N	6 45W
Slangberge, Mt., Cape Province	57	31 32 S	20 48 E
Slănic, Rumania,	21	45 14N	25 58 E
Slantsy, U.S.S.R.	21	59 7N	27 57 E
Slate Is., Canada	62	48 40N	87 0W
Slatina, Rumania	25	44 28N	24 22 E
Slaton, U.S.A.	71	33 26N	101 35W
Slave Coast, reg., W. Africa	52	6 0N	2 30 E
Slave Lake, Canada	64	55 25N	114 50W
Slave Pt., Canada	64	61 15N	116 0W
Slave R., Canada	64	60 40N	112 50W
Slavgorod, R.S.F.S.R., U.S.S.R.	26	53 10N	78 50 E
Slavgorod, White Russ., U.S.S.R.	25	53 30N	31 3 E
Slavkov (Austerlitz), Czechoslovakia	16	49 10N	16 52 E
Slavonski, Yugoslavia	21	45 20N	17 40 E
Slavyansk, R.S.F.S.R., U.S.S.R.	25	45 15N	38 11 E
Slavyanskaya, Ukraine, U.S.S.R.	25	48 55N	37 30 E
Sleaford, England	10	53 0N	0 22W
Sleepers, Is , Canada	61	56 50N	80 30W
Sleepy Eye, U.S.A.	70	44 15N	94 44W

	MAP		
Slesvig, dist., Denmark	14	55 10N	9 0 E
Slidell, U.S.A.	71	30 17N	89 47W
Slieve Auchty, mt., Ireland	11	53 4N	8 30W
Slieve Bloom, mt., Ireland	11	53 4N	7 40W
Slieve Donard, mt., N. Ireland	11	54 10N	5 57W
Slieve Mish, mt., Ireland	11	52 12N	9 50W
Slievenamon Mt., Ireland	11	52 25N	7 37W
Sligo, Ireland	11	54 17N	8 28W
Sligo, co., Ireland	11	54 10N	8 35W
Sligo B., Ireland	11	54 20N	8 40W
Slim River, Malaya	34	3 50N	101 29 E
Slite, Sweden	23	57 42N	18 45 E
Sliven, Bulgaria	21	42 42N	26 19 E
Slocan, Canada	64	49 40N	117 30W
Sloka, U.S.S.R.	23	56 57N	23 40 E
Slonim, U.S.S.R.	23	53 4N	25 19 E
Slovakia, dist., C.Slov.	16	48 30N	19 0 E
Slovakian Ore Mts., C.Slov.	16	48 30N	19 20 E
Slovenia, fed. unit, Yugoslavia	20	46 10N	14 40 E
Sluis, Netherlands	13	51 18N	3 23 E
Slupca, Poland	16	52 15N	17 52 E
Slupsk, Poland	16	54 30N	17 3 E
Slurry, Cape Province	57	25 49 S	25 52 E
Slyne Hd., Ireland	11	53 25N	10 10W
Slyudyanka, U.S.S.R.	27	51 40N	103 30 E
Smalltree L., Canada	65	61 0N	105 0W
Smara, Spanish Sahara	50	26 48N	11 20W
Smeaton, Canada	65	53 30N	104 50W
Smederevo, Yugoslavia	21	44 40N	20 57 E
Smederevska Palanka, Yugoslavia	21	44 23N	21 0 E
Smela, U.S.S.R.	25	49 30N	32 0 E
Smiley, Canada	65	51 38N	109 27W
Smith, Canada	64	55 10N	114 0W
Smith, R., Canada	64	59 40N	126 35W
Smith Arm, Canada	60	66 30N	123 0W
Smith Center, U.S.A.	70	39 50N	98 50W
Smithburne R., Queens.	42	17 5 S	141 15 E
Smithers, Canada	64	54 45N	127 10W
Smithfield, O.F.S.	57	30 13 S	26 32 E
Smithfield, U.S.A.	72	41 50N	111 51W
Smith's Falls, Canada	62	44 55N	76 0W
Smithton, Tasmania	43	40 53 S	145 6 E
Smithville, U.S.A.	71	30 0N	97 12W
Smjorfjöll, mt., Iceland	22	65 35N	14 40W
Smoky Bay, S. Austral.	45	32 22 S	134 3 E
Smoky C., N.S.W.	43	30 50 S	153 2 E
Smoky Falls, Canada	62	50 10N	82 10W
Smoky Hill, R., U.S.A.	70	38 45N	98 0W
Smoky R., Canada	64	55 35N	117 50W
Smoky Lake, Canada	64	54 8N	112 16W
Smöla, I., Norway	23	63 23N	8 3 E
Smolensk, U.S.S.R.	25	54 45N	32 0 E
Smólikas Mt., Greece	21	40 9N	20 58 E
Smolyan, Bulgaria	21	41 36N	24 38 E
Smooth Rock Falls, Can.	62	49 17N	81 37W
Smoothstone L., Canada	65	54 35N	107 0W
Snaefell, mt., Iceland	22	64 47N	15 30W
Snaefell, mt., I. of Man	10	54 18N	4 26W
Snaefellsjökull, mt., Ice.	22	64 45N	23 25W
Snake L., Canada	65	55 25N	106 0W
Snake R., U.S.A.	72	45 10N	116 45W
Snake Ra., U.S.A.	73	39 0N	114 20W
Snake River, U.S.A.	72	44 12N	110 40W
Snake River Plain, U.S.A.	72	43 30N	113 0W
Snåsa, Norway	22	64 15N	12 23 E
Sneek, Netherlands	13	53 2N	5 40 E
Sneeuberge, mts., Cape Province	57	32 0 S	24 40 E
Sněžka, mt., Poland–Czechoslovakia	16	50 40N	15 55 E
Sniardwy, L., Poland	16	55 40N	21 40 E
Snöhetta, mt., Norway	23	62 19N	9 16 E
Snohomish, U.S.A.	64	47 53N	122 9W
Snoksdalur, Iceland	22	64 58N	21 44W
Snow Hill, U.S.A.	68	38 10N	75 21W
Snowbird L., Canada	65	60 45N	103 0W
Snowdon, mt., Wales	10	53 4N	4 8W
Snowdrift, & R., Can.	65	62 10N	110 0W
Snowflake, U.S.A.	73	34 30N	110 7W
Snowshoe, Canada	64	53 43N	121 0W
Snowtown, S. Australia	43	33 47 S	138 8 E
Snowville, U.S.A.	72	41 59N	112 46W
Snowy R., N.S.W.	43	36 13 S	148 30 E
Snyder, Okla., U.S.A.	71	34 40N	98 58W
Snyder, Tex., U.S.A.	71	32 44N	100 55W
Soaker, Mt., N.Z.	47	45 22 S	167 15 E
Soalala, Madagascar	55	16 3 S	45 30 E
Soap Lake, U.S.A.	72	47 28N	120 24W
Soba, Nigeria	52	11 0N	8 2 E
Sobaek Sanmaek, S. Korea	36	36 0N	128 0 E
Sobat R., Sudan	51	8 32N	32 40 E
Sobrado, Brazil	79	5 35 S	53 0W
Sobral, Brazil	79	3 50 S	40 30W
Sochi, U.S.S.R.	25	43 35N	39 48 E
Society Is., Pacific Oc.	5	17 0 S	151 0W
Socompa, Chile	77	24 25 S	68 45W
Socorro, Colombia	78	6 25N	73 25W
Socorro, U.S.A.	73	34 0N	106 54W
Socotra I., E. Africa	5	12 30N	54 0 E

	MAP		
Soda Creek, Canada	64	52 25N	122 10W
Soda, L., U.S.A.	73	35 10N	116 0W
Soda Plains, Kashmir	32	35 30N	79 0 E
Soda Springs, U.S.A.	72	42 38N	111 34W
Sodankylä, Finland	22	67 29N	26 40 E
Soddu, Ethiopia	54	7 0N	37 57 E
Söderhamn, Sweden	23	61 18N	17 10 E
Söderköping, Sweden	23	58 31N	16 35 E
Södermanland, co., Sweden	23	59 10N	16 30 E
Sodiri, Sudan	51	14 25N	29 0 E
Sodium, Cape Province	57	30 15 S	23 15 E
Soekmekaar, Transvaal	57	23 30 S	29 57 E
Soest, Netherlands	13	52 9N	5 19 E
Sofala, Mozambique	56	20 8 S	34 42 E
Sofia, Bulgaria	21	42 45N	23 20 E
Sofiski, U.S.S.R.	27	52 20N	133 50 E
Sogakofe, Ghana	52	6 1N	0 33 E
Sogamoso, Colombia	78	5 50N	72 50W
Sogn and Fjordane, prov., Norway	23	61 40N	6 0 E
Sogndal, Norway	23	58 20N	6 15 E
Sogndalsfjöra, Norway	23	61 15N	7 4 E
Sogne Fjord, Norway	23	61 10N	6 0 E
Soignies, Belgium	13	50 35N	4 5 E
Soissons, France	12	49 25N	3 19 E
Sok R., U.S.S.R.	25	53 30N	50 30 E
Sókhós, Greece	21	40 48N	23 22 E
Sokobo, Central Afr. Republic	54	6 45N	24 59 E
Sokodé, Dahomey	52	9 0N	1 11 E
Sokol, U.S.S.R.	25	59 30N	40 5 E
Sokolka, Poland	16	53 25N	23 30 E
Sokolo, Mali	50	14 50N	6 18W
Sokoto, Nigeria	52	13 2N	5 16 E
Sokoto R., Nigeria	52	12 30N	6 10 E
Sol Iletsk, U.S.S.R.	24	51 20N	54 50 E
Solai, Kenya	53	0 3N	36 8 E
Solander I., N.Z.	47	46 36 S	166 58 E
Solano, Philippines	35	16 25N	121 15 E
Soledad, Colombia	78	10 45N	74 50W
Soledad, U.S.A.	73	36 29N	121 22W
Soledad, Venezuela	78	8 15N	63 55W
Solenzara, Corsica	12	41 53N	9 23 E
Solfonn, mt., Norway	23	60 2N	65 7 E
Soligalich, U.S.S.R.	25	59 5N	42 10 E
Solikamsk, U.S.S.R.	28	59 38N	56 50 E
Solimões R., Brazil	78	2 15 S	66 30W
Solingen, Germany	14	51 10N	7 4 E
Sollefteå, Sweden	23	63 12N	17 20 E
Soller, Spain	17	39 43N	2 45 E
Solnechnogorsk, U.S.S.R.	25	56 10N	36 57 E
Solnhofen, Germany	14	48 54N	11 0 E
Sologne, dist., France	12	47 40N	2 0 E
Solok, Indonesia	34	0 55 S	100 40 E
Solomon, R., S. Fork, U.S.A.	70	39 25N	99 10W
Solomon, R., N. Fork, U.S.A.	70	39 45N	99 0W
Solomon Is., Pacific Oc.	5	8 0 S	160 0 E
Solomon's Pool, Jordan	29	31 42N	35 7 E
Solon Springs, U.S.A.	70	46 20N	91 47W
Solothurn, Switzerland	15	47 13N	7 32 E
Solothurn, can., Switz.	15	47 18N	7 40 E
Solsty, U.S.S.R.	25	58 10N	30 10 E
Solta, Yugoslavia	20	43 24N	16 15 E
Solun, Inner Mongolia	38	46 40N	120 40 E
Solun, China	37	46 40N	120 40 E
Solunska, Mt., Y.slav.	21	41 44N	21 31 E
Solvay, U.S.A.	68	43 5N	76 17W
Sölvesborg, Sweden	23	56 5N	14 35 E
Solway, Firth, Irish Sea	10	54 40N	3 30W
Solwesi, Zambia	56	12 10 S	26 16 E
Somabula, Rhodesia	56	10 40 S	29 38 E
Somali, Rep. st., E. Africa	40	5 0N	47 0 E
Somaliland, Fr., N.E. Africa	49	12 0N	43 0 E
Sombor, Yugoslavia	21	45 46N	19 17 E
Sombrerete, Mexico	74	23 40N	103 40W
Sombrero I., Leeward Islands	75	18 30N	63 30W
Somers, U.S.A.	64	48 4N	114 18W
Somerset, Bermuda	75	Inset	
Somerset, Canada	65	49 26N	98 39W
Somerset, Colo., U.S.A.	73	38 57N	107 27W
Somerset, Ky., U.S.A.	68	37 5N	84 40W
Somerset I., Bermuda	75	Inset	
Somerset East, Cape Province	57	32 42 S	25 35 E
Somerset West, Cape Province	57	34 8 S	18 50 E
Somersworth, U.S.A.	69	43 15N	70 51W
Somerton, U.S.A.	73	32 39N	114 43W
Somes, R., Rumania	21	47 15N	23 45 E
Somme R., France	12	50 12N	1 30 E
Sommières, France	12	43 47N	4 6 E
Somosierra, Pto. de, Spain	17	41 9N	3 39W
Somovit, Bulgaria	21	43 39N	24 44 E
Son La, N. Viet Nam	34	21 20N	103 55 E
Sonchon, Korea	36	39 45N	125 0 E
Sönderborg, Denmark	23	54 55N	9 49 E
Sondrio, Italy	20	46 10N	9 53 E
Sone, Mozambique	56	17 17 S	34 52 E
Sonepat, India	32	29 0N	77 5 E

	MAP		
Sonepur, India	33	20 55N	83 50 E
Song, Nigeria	52	9 48N	12 33 E
Songea, mt., Tanzania	53	10 40 S	35 40 E
Songkhla, Siam	34	7 13N	100 37 E
Songkoi, R., Viet Nam	39	20 20N	26 20 E
Songo, Sudan	51	9 59N	24 20 E
Songwe, Zaire	56	12 10 S	29 57 E
Songwe, Malawi	56	9 42 S	33 47 E
Sonkovo, U.S.S.R.	25	57 50N	37 5 E
Sonmiani, Pakistan	32	25 25N	66 40 E
Sono, R. Brazil,	79	9 30 S	48 0W
Sonora, Calif., U.S.A.	73	37 59N	120 26W
Sonora, st., Mexico	74	28 0N	111 0W
Sonora, Texas, U.S.A.	71	30 31N	100 32W
Sonsorol Is., Pacific Oc.	35	4 20N	132 14 E
Soo Junction, U.S.A.	68	46 20N	85 14W
Soochow, China	39	31 18N	120 41 E
Sopot, Poland	16	54 27N	20 30 E
Sopron, Hungary	16	47 41N	16 37 E
Sop's Arm, Canada	63	49 46N	56 56W
Sör Tröndelag, prov., Norway	23	63 0N	11 0 E
Sora, Italy	16	41 45N	13 36 E
Söraker, Sweden	23	62 30N	17 32 E
Sorata, Bolivia	78	15 50 S	68 50W
Sorel, Canada	62	46 0N	73 10W
Sorell, Tasmania	43	42 44 S	147 30 E
Sorell, C., Tasmania	43	42 12 S	145 11 E
Sörfold, Norway	22	67 5N	14 20W
Sorgono, Italy	20	40 0N	9 7 E
Soria, Spain	17	41 43N	2 32W
Sorocaba, Brazil	77	23 31 S	47 35W
Sorong, Indonesia	35	0 55 S	131 15 E
Soroti, Uganda	53	1 42N	33 38 E
Söröya I., Norway	22	70 35N	22 45 E
Söröya Sd., Norway	22	70 25N	23 0 E
Sorrento, Italy	20	40 38N	14 23 E
Sorrento, Victoria	43	38 22 S	144 43 E
Sorris Sorris, S.W. Afr.	57	20 57 S	14 50 E
Sorsele, Sweden	22	65 31N	17 30 E
Sorsogon, Philippines	35	13 0N	124 0 E
Sortavala, U.S.S.R.	23	61 46N	30 48 E
Sosa, S. Korea	36	37 38N	126 57 E
Sosan, S. Korea	36	36 40N	126 35 E
Soscumica L., Canada	62	50 20N	77 30W
Sosna R., U.S.S.R.	25	52 30N	38 0 E
Sosnovka, U.S.S.R.	27	54 15N	110 0 E
Sosnowiec, Poland	16	50 20N	19 10 E
Sosva, U.S.S.R.	24	59 10N	61 30 E
Sosva R., U.S.S.R.	24	63 10N	63 30 E
Sosvovka, U.S.S.R.	25	53 10N	41 25 E
So-to Is., Korea	36	34 0N	127 15 E
Sotkamo, Finland	22	64 9N	28 25 E
Soto la Marina, Mexico	74	23 30N	97 50W
Soto la Marina, lag., Mexico	74	23 40N	97 40W
Sotra I., Norway	23	60 15N	5 0 E
Sotuta, Mexico	74	20 30N	89 20W
Souanke, Congo	54	2 10N	14 10 E
Soudhas B., Crete	20	35 50N	24 22 E
Souflion, Greece	21	41 12N	26 18 E
Soufrière, vol., Guad.	75	16 20N	61 40W
Soufrière, vol., St. Vincent	75	13 10N	61 10W
Sources, Mt., aux., Lesotho	57	28 40 S	28 54 E
Soure, Brazil	79	0 35 S	48 30W
Souris, Canada	65	49 40N	100 20W
Souris, R., U.S.A.	70	48 35N	101 29W
Sousa, Brazil	79	7 0 S	38 10W
Sousse, Tunisia	51	35 50N	10 45 E
Soustons, France	12	43 45N	1 19W
South, C., (Ka Lae), Hawaiian Is.	59	8 58N	155 40W
South I., Kenya	53	2 40N	36 35 E
South I., New Zealand	47	43 0 S	170 0 E
South Pt., Canada	63	49 6N	62 11W
South Africa, Republic, of, st., Africa	57	30 0 S	25 0 E
South America, cont.	76	12 30N to 55 30 S	35 0W to 81 0W
South Australia, st., Australia	40–41	32 0 S	139 0 E
South Baldy, Mt., U.S.A.	73	34 7N	107 20W
South Bend, Ind., U.S.A.	68	41 38N	86 20W
South Bend, Wash., U.S.A.	72	46 39N	123 56W
South Boston, U.S.A.	69	36 42N	78 58W
South Branch, N.Z.	47	43 34 S	171 10 E
South Bunguran Is., Indonesia	34	2 30N	108 55 E
South Carolina, st., U.S.A.	67	33 40N	80 30W
South Charleston, U.S.A.	68	38 20N	81 40W
South China Sea, Pacific Ocean	39	20 0N	115 0 E
South Coast, dist., N.S.W.	43	36 0 S	149 45 E
South Daja I., Indonesia	35	7 55 S	130 15 E
South Dakota, st., U.S.A.	70	44 40N	101 0W
South Downs, England	10	50 53N	0 10W
South East Province, Sierra Leone	52	Inset	
South East Cape, Tas.	43	43 38 S	146 48 E

	MAP		
South East Is., W. Australia	45	34 17 S	123 30 E
South Eastern Dist., S. Australia	43	37 0 S	140 30 E
South Eastern Region, Tasmania	43	42 34 S	147 32 E
South Esk Tableland, W. Australia	45	20 0 S	127 0 E
South Fork, R., Kansas, U.S.A.	70	39 15N	100 30W
South Fork, R., Mont., U.S.A.	72	47 40N	113 15W
South Fork, R., S.D., U.S.A.	70	43 20N	101 0W
South Gamboa, Pan. Can. Zone	74	9 4N	79 40W
South Georgia, Falkland Is. Dep., Ant.	5	54 30 S	37 0W
South Henik L., Canada	65	61 30N	98 0W
South Horr, Kenya	53	2 20N	36 48 E
South Invercargill, N.Z.	47	46 26 S	168 23 E
South Knife, R., Canada	65	55 30N	96 0W
South Loup, R., U.S.A.	70	41 10N	99 40W
South Milwaukee, U.S.A.	68	42 50N	87 52W
South Moscos (Laungglon Bok), Burma	33	13 53N	97 56 E
South Nahanni, Canada	64	61 5N	123 30W
South Nahanni R., Can.	60	62 30N	127 0W
South Orkney Is., Falkland Is. Dep., Ant.	6	63 0 S	45 0W
South Pines, U.S.A.	69	35 10N	79 25W
South Pittsburg, U.S.A.	69	35 3N	85 44W
South Platte R., U.S.A.	70	40 50N	102 45W
South Pole, Antarctica	80		
South Porcupine, Can.	62	48 30N	81 12W
South Portland, U.S.A.	69	43 45N	70 15W
South Ronaldsay I., Scotland	10	58 46N	2 58W
South River, Canada	62	45 52N	79 21W
South Sandwich Is., Falkland Is. Dep. Ant.	5	57 0 S	27 0W
South Saskatchewan R., Canada	65	51 0N	109 0W
South Shetland Is., Br. Antarctic Territory	5	62 0 S	59 0W
South Shields, England	10	54 59N	1 26W
South Sioux City, U.S.A.	70	42 32N	96 25W
South Tableland, dist., N.S.W.	43	35 45 S	149 15 E
South Tarakani Bight, New Zealand	46	39 40 S	174 5 E
South Tröndelag, Nor.	23	63 10N	11 0 E
South Twin, I., Canada	62	53 0N	79 50W
South Uist I., Scotland	10	57 10N	7 10W
South West Africa, mandate of Republic of South Africa	57	23 0 S	17 30 E
South West Cape, N.Z.	47	47 16 S	167 31 E
South Western Div., Queensland	43	26 54 S	144 11 E
South Western Div., W. Australia	44	33 10 S	117 44 E
South Western Region, China	37	35 0N	95 0 E
South Western Slope, dist., N.S.W.	43	35 0 S	148 0 E
South Yemen, Asia	28	12 50N	45 0 E
Southampton, Canada	62	44 30N	81 25W
Southampton, England	10	50 54N	1 23W
Southampton, U.S.A.	68	40 54N	72 22W
Southampton I., Canada	61	64 30N	84 0W
Southbridge, N.Z.	47	43 48 S	172 16 E
Southend, Canada	65	56 28N	103 14W
Southend, England	10	51 32N	0 43 E
Southern Prov., Kenya	53	1 45 S	37 0 E
Southern Prov., Zambia	56	16 15 S	26 30 E
Southern Prov., Malawi	56	15 0 S	35 0 E
Southern Prov., Tan.	53	10 20 S	37 30 E
Southern Alps, N.Z.	47	43 41 S	170 11 E
Southern Cross, W. Australia	44	31 12 S	119 15 E
Southern Indian L., Can.	65	57 0N	99 0W
Southern Ocean	80	62 0 S	160 0W
Southern Region, Tas.	42	43 0 S	146 21 E
Southern Rhodesia (Rhodesia), Afr.	56	19 0 S	29 0 E
Southland, New Zealand	47	45 51 S	168 13 E
Southport, England	10	53 38N	3 1W
Southport, Queensland	43	28 0 S	153 25 E
Southport, U.S.A.	69	33 55N	78 0W
Southwest Pt., Canada	63	49 23N	63 31W
Soutpansberge, Mts., Transvaal	57	22 55 S	29 30 E
Sovetsk, U.S.S.R.	25	57 38N	48 53 E
Sovetskaya Gavan (Soviet Harbour), U.S.S.R.	27	48 50N	140 0 E
Sovietskaya, Antarctica	80	78 7 S	78 0 E
Soya, Japan	36	45 30N	141 50 E
Soya C., Japan	36	45 30N	142 0 E
Sozh R., U.S.S.R.	25	53 50N	31 30 E
Spain, rep., Europe	17	40 0N	5 0W
Spalding, England	10	52 47N	0 9W
Spalding, S. Australia	43	33 29 S	138 31 E
Spalding, U.S.A.	70	41 44N	98 25W
Spandau, Germany	14	52 32N	13 13 E

	MAP		
Spangler, U.S.A.	69	40 39N	78 48W
Spaniard's Bay, Canada	63	47 38N	53 20W
Spanish, Canada	62	46 12N	82 20W
Spanish Fork, U.S.A.	72	40 0N	111 50W
Spanish Sahara, terr., N.W. Afr.	50	25 0N	13 0W
Spanish Town, Jamaica	75	18 0N	77 20W
Sparks, U.S.A.	72	39 30N	119 45W
Sparti, Greece	21	37 7N	22 23E
Sparta, Ga., U.S.A.	69	33 17N	82 58W
Sparta, Tenn., U.S.A.	69	35 55N	85 29W
Sparta, Wis., U.S.A.	70	43 53N	90 46W
Spartanburg, U.S.A.	69	35 0N	82 0W
Spartivento C., Italy	20	37 56N	16 4E
Spartivento C., Sardinia	20	38 52N	8 50E
Spassk, U.S.S.R.	24	59 15N	47 0E
Spassk Dalni, U.S.S.R.	27	44 40N	132 40E
Spassk-Ryazanski, U.S.S.R.	25	54 30N	40 25E
Spearfish, U.S.A.	70	44 32N	103 51N
Spearman, U.S.A.	71	36 13N	101 14W
Speers, Canada	65	52 43N	107 32W
Speightstown, Barbados	75	13 15N	59 39W
Speke Gulf, Tan.	53	2 15S	33 30E
Spenard, Alaska	59	61 0N	149 50W
Spencer, Idaho, U.S.A.	72	44 20N	112 13W
Spencer, Iowa, U.S.A.	70	43 9N	95 6W
Spencer, Neb., U.S.A.	70	42 54N	98 43W
Spencer, W. Va., U.S.A.	68	38 47N	81 24W
Spencer B., S.W. Africa	57	25 40S	14 50E
Spences Bridge, Canada	64	50 25N	121 20W
Spencer Gulf, S. Austral.	43	34 30S	137 0E
Spenser Mts., N.Z.	47	42 15S	172 45E
Sperrin Mts., N. Ireland	11	54 50N	7 0W
Spessart Mts., Germany	14	50 0N	9 25E
Spey, R., Scotland	10	57 10N	3 50W
Speyer, Germany	14	49 19N	8 26E
Spiddle, Ireland	11	53 14N	9 19W
Spiez, Switzerland	15	46 40N	7 40E
Spili, Crete	20	35 13N	24 31E
Spillimacheen, Canada	64	51 6N	117 0W
Spinazzola, Italy	20	40 58N	16 5E
Spinifex Ra., Australia	45	26 1S	125 58E
Spioenberg, Mt., Cape Province	57	31 18S	21 38E
Spioenberg Mt., Cape Province	57	31 0S	19 47E
Spirit Lake, U.S.A.	72	47 59N	116 56W
Spirit River, Canada	64	55 45N	119 0W
Spiritwood, Canada	65	53 24N	107 33W
Spitzbergen (Svalbard), Norway	80	78 0N	17 0E
Split, Yugoslavia	20	43 31N	16 26E
Split L., Canada	65	56 15N	96 0W
Splügen Pass, Switz.	15	46 30N	9 20E
Spofford, U.S.A.	71	29 9N	100 19W
Spokane, U.S.A.	72	47 35N	117 30W
Spoleto, Italy	20	42 45N	12 42E
Spooner, U.S.A.	70	45 50N	91 52W
Spory Navolok C., U.S.S.R.	26	75 50N	68 40E
Spotted Is., Canada	63	53 30N	55 44W
Spragge, Canada	62	46 15N	82 40W
Sprague, U.S.A.	72	47 19N	117 59W
Sprague River, U.S.A.	72	42 58N	121 31W
Spratley I., S. China Sea	35	8 38N	111 57E
Spray, U.S.A.	72	44 50N	119 45W
Spree R., Germany	14	52 23N	13 52E
Spremberg, Germany	14	51 33N	14 21E
Spring City, U.S.A.	73	39 30N	111 30W
Spring Mts., U.S.A.	73	36 29N	115 45W
Spring Valley, U.S.A.	70	43 40N	92 29W
Springbok, Cape Prov.	57	29 42S	17 54E
Springdale, Canada	63	49 30N	56 6W
Springdale, Ark., U.S.A.	71	36 12N	94 5W
Springdale, Wash., U.S.A.	72	48 2N	117 44W
Springerville, U.S.A.	73	34 9N	109 16W
Springfield, Colo., U.S.A.	71	37 26N	102 42W
Springfield, Canada	68	42 52N	80 57W
Springfield, N.Z.	47	43 19S	171 56E
Springfield, Ill., U.S.A.	70	39 50N	89 40W
Springfield, Mass., U.S.A.	69	42 8N	72 37W
Springfield, Mo., U.S.A.	71	37 15N	93 20W
Springfield, Ohio, U.S.A.	68	39 50N	83 48W
Springfield, Oreg., U.S.A.	72	44 3N	123 1W
Springfield, Tenn., U.S.A.	69	36 35N	86 55W
Springfield, Vt., U.S.A.	69	43 20N	72 30W
Springfontein, O.F.S.	57	30 15S	25 40E
Springhill, Canada	63	45 40N	64 4W
Springhouse, Canada	64	51 56N	122 7W
Springs, Transvaal	57	26 13S	28 25E
Springsure, Queensland	42	24 8S	148 6E
Springvale, Queensland	42	23 32S	140 38E
Springville, N.Y., U.S.A.	68	42 31N	78 41W
Springville, Utah, U.S.A.	72	40 11N	111 45W
Springwater, Canada	65	51 58N	108 23W
Spungbera, Mozam.	56	20 28S	32 47E
Spur, U.S.A.	71	33 28N	100 47W
Spurn Hd., England	10	53 34N	0 8W
Spuzzum, Canada	64	49 45N	121 20W
Squamish, Canada	64	49 45N	123 10W
Square Island, Canada	63	52 47N	55 47W
Squillace, Italy	20	38 47N	16 31E
Squires, Mt., W. Australia	45	26 14S	127 46E
Srbija (Serbia), Prov., Yugoslavia	21	43 30N	21 0E
Srebrnica, Yugoslavia	21	44 10N	19 18E
Sredinny Ra., U.S.S.R.	27	57 0N	160 0E
Sredna Gora Mts., Bulgaria	21	42 40N	25 0E
Sredne Kolymsk, U.S.S.R.	27	67 20N	154 40E
Sredne Vilyuisk, U.S.S.R.	27	63 50N	123 5E
Sredwe Tambovskoye, U.S.S.R.	27	50 55N	137 45E
Srem, Poland	16	52 6N	17 2E
Sremska Mitrovica, Yugoslavia	21	44 55N	19 39E
Srepok, R., Cambodia	34	14 0N	107 0E
Sretensk, U.S.S.R.	27	52 10N	117 40E
Sri Lanka, Asia	32	7 30N	80 50E
Srikakulam, India	33	18 14N	84 4E
Srikolayatji (Kolayat), India	32	27 56N	73 2E
Srinagar, Kashmir	32	34 12N	74 50E
Srnetica, Yugoslavia	20	44 28N	16 38E
Sroda, Poland	16	52 15N	17 19E
Staaten R., Queensland	42	16 30S	142 25E
Stadarhdskirja, Iceland	22	65 23N	21 50W
Standlandet, I., Norway	23	62 10N	5 5E
Stafafell, Iceland	22	64 24N	14 46W
Staffa, I., Scotland	10	56 26N	6 21W
Stafford, England	10	52 49N	2 9W
Stafford, U.S.A.	71	37 58N	98 32W
Stalać, Yugoslavia	21	43 43N	21 28E
Stalden, Switz.	15	46 14N	7 53E
Stalin Mt., Canada	64	58 10N	124 45W
Stalinabad (Dushanbe), U.S.S.R.	26	38 40N	68 50E
Stalinstadt (Eisenhüttenstadt), E. Germany	16	52 9N	14 41E
Stalowawola, Poland	16	50 35N	22 0E
Stamford, Conn., U.S.A.	68	41 5N	73 30W
Stamford, Queensland	42	21 15S	143 46E
Stamford, Tex., U.S.A.	71	32 58N	99 47W
Stamprietfontein, S.W. Africa	57	24 20S	18 28E
Stamps, U.S.A.	71	33 20N	93 30W
Stanberry, U.S.A.	70	40 9N	94 0W
Standerton, Transvaal	57	26 55S	29 13E
Standish, U.S.A.	68	43 58N	83 57W
Stanford, Cape Prov.	57	34 29S	19 28E
Stanford, U.S.A.	72	47 7N	110 10W
Stanislav (Ivano Frankovsk), U.S.S.R.	24	49 0N	24 40E
Stanke Dimitrov, Bulg.	21	42 15N	23 6E
Stanley, N.B., Canada	63	46 20N	66 50W
Stanley, Sask., Canada	65	55 30N	104 40W
Stanley, Tasmania	43	40 46S	145 19E
Stanley, Idaho, U.S.A.	72	44 15N	114 57W
Stanley, N.D., U.S.A.	65	48 20N	102 23W
Stanley, Wis., U.S.A.	70	44 56N	91 0W
Stanmore Ra. W. Australia	45	21 30S	128 35E
Stanovoi Ra., U.S.S.R.	27	55 0N	130 0E
Stanthorpe, Queensland	43	28 36S	151 59E
Stanton, Canada	60	69 40N	128 40W
Stanton, U.S.A.	71	32 4N	101 46W
Stanwell, Queensland	42	23 30S	150 18E
Staples, U.S.A.	70	46 21N	94 44W
Stapleton, U.S.A.	70	41 30N	100 31W
Star City, Canada	65	52 55N	104 20W
Stara Plainina (Balkan Mts.), Bulgaria	21	43 15N	23 0E
Stara Zagora, Bulgaria	21	42 26N	25 39E
Staraya Russa, U.S.S.R.	25	57 58N	31 10E
Stargard, Poland	16	53 20N	15 0E
Staritsa, U.S.S.R.	25	56 33N	35 0E
Starke, U.S.A.	69	30 0N	82 10W
Starkville, Miss., U.S.A.	69	33 27N	88 50W
Starkville, Colo., U.S.A.	71	37 5N	104 30W
Starnes, Canada	65	57 14N	94 0W
Starobelsk, U.S.S.R.	25	49 27N	39 0E
Starodub, U.S.S.R.	25	52 30N	32 50E
Starogard, Poland	15	53 55N	18 30E
Stary Kheidzhan, U.S.S.R.	27	60 0N	144 50E
Stary Oskol, U.S.S.R.	25	51 12N	37 55E
Staszow, Poland	16	50 34N	21 9E
State College, U.S.A.	68	40 47N	77 49W
Staten I. (I. de los Estados), Argentina	77	54 40S	64 0W
Statesboro, U.S.A.	69	32 26N	81 46W
Statesville, U.S.A.	69	35 48N	80 51W
Staunton, Ill., U.S.A.	70	39 0N	89 47W
Staunton, Va., U.S.A.	69	38 7N	79 4W
Stav Fd., Norway	23	61 28N	5 15E
Stavanger, Norway	23	58 57N	5 40E
Stavern, Norway	23	59 0N	10 1E
Stavoren, Netherlands	13	52 53N	5 21E
Stavropol, U.S.S.R.	25	45 5N	42 0E
Stawell, Victoria	43	36 58S	142 47E
Stawell R., Queensland	42	20 17S	143 30E
Steamboat Springs, U.S.A.	72	40 30N	106 50W
Stebark, Poland	16	53 30N	20 10E
Steele, U.S.A.	70	46 55N	99 55W
Steelpoort, Transvaal	57	24 41S	30 14E
Steelton, U.S.A.	68	40 17N	76 50W
Steep Rock, Man., Can.	65	51 30N	98 40W
Steep Rock, Ont., Can.	62	48 50N	91 50W
Stegi, Swaziland	57	26 30S	32 0E
Steinbach, Canada	65	49 32N	96 40W
Steinhausen, S.W. Africa	57	21 49S	18 20E
Steinkjer, Norway	23	63 59N	11 40E
Steinkopf, C. Prov.	57	29 15S	17 48E
Stella, Botswana	57	26 42S	24 45E
Stellaland, Cape Prov.	57	26 45S	24 50E
Stellarton, Canada	63	45 34N	62 40W
Stellenbosch, Cape Prov.	57	33 58S	18 50E
Stelvio, P. di, Italy	20	46 32N	10 28E
Stenay, France	12	49 29N	5 12E
Stendal, Germany	14	52 36N	11 50E
Stensele, Sweden	22	65 3N	17 20E
Stepanakert, U.S.S.R.	24	40 0N	46 25E
Stephen, U.S.A.	70	48 30N	96 49W
Stephens, C., N.Z.	47	40 43S	173 59E
Stephens I., Canada	64	54 0N	131 0W
Stephens I., N.Z.	47	40 40S	174 1E
Stephens Pass, str., Alaska	64	57 40N	133 50W
Stephenville, Canada	63	48 31N	58 30W
Stephenville, U.S.A.	71	32 12N	98 14W
Stepnoi (Elista), U.S.S.R.	25	46 25N	44 17E
Stepnyak, U.S.S.R.	26	53 0N	70 30E
Sterkaar, Cape Prov.	57	31 4S	23 43E
Sterkstroom, Cape Prov.	57	31 32S	26 32E
Sterkwater, Transvaal	57	24 0S	28 47E
Sterling, Colo., U.S.A.	70	40 40N	103 0W
Sterling, Ill., U.S.A.	70	41 46N	89 45W
Sterling, Kan., U.S.A.	71	38 14N	98 12W
Sterling City, U.S.A.	71	31 47N	100 58W
Sterlitamak, U.S.S.R.	24	53 40N	56 0E
Stettin (Szczecin), Poland	14	53 27N	14 27E
Stettler, Canada	64	52 25N	112 40W
Steubenville, U.S.A.	68	40 21N	80 39W
Stevens Pt., U.S.A.	68	44 32N	89 34W
Stevenson L., Canada	65	54 0N	96 10W
Stewart, Canada	64	63 20N	139 50W
Stewart I., Chile	77	54 50S	71 30W
Stewart I., New Zealand	47	46 58S	167 54E
Stewart Sd., India	33	13 0N	92 45E
Stewartstown, N. Ire.	11	54 35N	6 40W
Stewiacke, Canada	63	45 9N	63 22W
Steynsburg, Cape Prov.	57	31 15S	25 49E
Steyr, Austria	14	48 3N	14 25E
Steytlerville, Cape Prov.	57	33 17S	24 19E
Stigler, U.S.A.	71	35 15N	95 12W
Stikine R., Canada	64	58 0N	131 0W
Still Bay, Cape Province	57	34 22S	21 27E
Stillwater, Minn., U.S.A.	70	45 3N	92 47W
Stillwater, Okla., U.S.A.	71	36 4N	97 2W
Stillwater, N.Y., U.S.A.	67	42 55N	73 41W
Stillwater Mts., U.S.A.	72	39 45N	118 10W
Stilwell, U.S.A.	71	35 48N	94 37W
Stimson, Canada	62	48 58N	80 30W
Stip, Yugoslavia	21	41 42N	22 10E
Stirling, Canada	64	49 30N	112 30W
Stirling, New Zealand	47	46 14S	169 49E
Stirling, Scotland	10	56 17N	3 57W
Stirling, co., Scotland	10	56 3N	4 10W
Stirling Ra., W. Austral.	44	34 0S	118 0E
Stjördalshalsen, Norway	23	63 29N	10 51E
Stockerau, Austria	14	48 24N	16 12E
Stockett, U.S.A.	72	47 22N	111 7W
Stockholm, Sweden	23	59 17N	18 3E
Stockholm, co., Sweden	23	59 40N	18 45E
Stockport, England	10	53 25N	2 11W
Stockton, Calif., U.S.A.	73	38 0N	121 20W
Stockton, Kan., U.S.A.	70	39 30N	99 16W
Stockton, Mo., U.S.A.	71	37 43N	93 49W
Stockton-on-Tees, Eng.	10	54 34N	1 20W
Stoffberg, Transvaal	57	25 27S	29 49E
Stoke, New Zealand	47	41 20S	173 16E
Stoke-on-Trent, Eng.	10	53 1N	2 11W
Stokes Bay, Canada	62	45 0N	81 22W
Stokes Pt., Tasmania	43	40 5S	144 0E
Stokkseyri, Iceland	22	63 50N	20 52W
Stokksnes C., Iceland	22	64 17N	14 45W
Stoiac, Yugoslavia	21	43 8N	17 59E
Stolbovoi I., U.S.S.R.	27	74 10N	135 40E
Stolbovaya, U.S.S.R.	27	64 50N	153 50E
Stonecliffe, Canada	62	46 13N	77 56W
Stonehaven, Scotland	10	56 58N	2 11W
Stonehenge, Queensland	42	24 21S	143 15E
Stonewall, Canada	65	50 10N	97 20W
Stony L., Canada	65	58 50N	98 20W
Stony Pt., Victoria	43	38 15S	145 11E
Stony R., Alaska	59	61 40N	157 20W
Stony Crossing, N.S.W.	43	35 1S	143 34E
Stony Rapids, Canada	65	59 15N	105 55W
Stony Tunguska R., U.S.S.R.	27	60 30N	98 0E
Stora Lulevatten, L., Sweden	22	67 20N	19 0E
Stora Sjöfallet, mt., Sweden	22	67 30N	18 0E
Storavan, L., Sweden	22	65 45N	18 10E
Store Baelt, str., Denmark	23	55 28N	11 0E
Stören, Norway	23	63 0N	10 20E
Storm B., Tasmania	43	43 10S	147 30E
Storm Lake, U.S.A.	70	42 37N	95 10W
Stormberg, C. Prov.	57	31 16S	26 17E
Stormberge, Mts., C. Prov.	57	31 26S	26 32E
Storms River, C. Prov.	57	33 59S	23 52E
Stornoway, Scotland	10	58 12N	6 23W
Storolfshvall, Iceland	22	63 48N	20 15W
Storsjön, Sweden	23	62 50N	13 10E
Storuman, L., Sweden	22	65 5N	17 10E
Stoughton, Canada	65	49 40N	103 0W
Stour R., Eng.	10	52 25N	2 13W
Stout L., Canada	65	52 0N	94 40W
Stowmarket, England	10	52 11N	1 0E
Stow-on-the-Wold, Eng.	9	51 55N	1 42W
Strabane, N. Ireland	11	54 50N	7 28W
Stradbally, Ireland	11	53 2N	7 10W
Stradbroke I., Queens.	43	27 40S	153 12E
Strahan, Tasmania	43	42 8S	145 24E
Stralsund, Germany	14	54 17N	13 5E
Strand, Cape Province	57	34 9S	18 48E
Strangford, N. Ireland	11	54 23N	5 34W
Strangford, L., N. Ire.	11	54 30N	5 37W
Strangeways Springs, S. Australia	45	29 8S	136 33E
Stranorlar, Ireland	11	54 48N	7 47W
Stranraer, Scotland	10	54 54N	5 0W
Strasbourg, Canada	65	51 10N	104 55W
Strasbourg, France	12	48 35N	7 42E
Strasburg, U.S.A.	70	46 10N	100 11W
Stratford, Canada	62	43 23N	81 0W
Stratford, N.Z.	46	39 20S	174 19E
Stratford, Calif., U.S.A.	73	36 10N	119 51W
Stratford, Tex., U.S.A.	71	36 17N	102 2W
Stratford-on-Avon, Eng.	10	52 12N	1 42W
Strathalbyn, S. Australia	43	35 13S	138 53E
Strathcona Prov. Pk., Canada	64	49 40N	125 40W
Strathmore, Canada	64	51 5N	113 25W
Strathmore, Queens.	42	20 31S	147 33E
Strathnaver, Canada	64	53 20N	122 30W
Strathroy, Canada	64	42 58N	81 38W
Stratton, U.S.A.	70	39 2N	102 35W
Straumnes, C., Iceland	22	66 26N	23 7W
Strawn, U.S.A.	71	32 37N	98 30W
Streaky B., S. Australia	45	32 51S	134 18E
Streator, U.S.A.	68	41 9N	88 52W
Streeter, U.S.A.	70	46 41N	99 20W
Strelka, U.S.S.R.	27	58 5N	93 10E
Strickland R., Papua	42	7 0S	141 45E
Strokestown, Ireland	11	53 47N	8 6W
Stromboli I., Italy	20	38 48N	15 12E
Ströms, L., Sweden	22	64 0N	15 30E
Stromsburg, U.S.A.	70	41 9N	97 35W
Stromstad, Sweden	23	58 55N	11 15E
Strömsund, Sweden	23	63 51N	15 35E
Stronsay I., Scotland	10	59 8N	2 38W
Stuart Bluff Ra., N. Territory	45	22 43S	132 30E
Struer, Denmark	23	56 30N	8 35E
Struga, Yugoslavia	21	41 13N	20 44E
Struma R., Bulgaria	21	41 50N	23 18E
Strumica, Yugoslavia	21	41 28N	22 41E
Struthers, U.S.A.	68	41 6N	80 38W
Strydenburg, Cape Prov.	57	29 58S	23 40E
Strzelecki Cr., Queens.	43	28 23S	140 18E
Stuart, Neb., U.S.A.	70	42 40N	99 7W
Stuart, Va., U.S.A.	69	36 39N	80 20W
Stuart, I., Alaska	59	63 36N	162 30W
Stuart L., Canada	64	54 40N	124 40W
Stuart Mts., N. Z.	47	45 2S	167 39E
Stuart R., Canada	64	54 20N	123 50W
Stuart's Ra., Australia	41	29 10S	135 0E
Studholme Junc., N.Z.	47	44 42S	171 9E
Stull L., Canada	62	54 26N	92 20W
Stung Treng, Cambodia	34	13 26N	106 0E
Stupart R., Canada	65	55 45N	93 50W
Sturgeon B., Canada	65	52 0N	98 0W
Sturgeon L., Canada	62	49 50N	90 0W
Sturgeon L., Canada	64	44 30N	78 45W
Sturgeon Bay, U.S.A.	68	44 52N	87 20W
Sturgeon Falls, Canada	62	46 25N	79 50W
Sturgis, Mich., U.S.A.	68	41 50N	85 25W
Sturgis, S.D., U.S.A.	70	44 27N	103 30W
Stuttgart, Germany	14	48 46N	9 18E
Stuttgart, U.S.A.	71	34 31N	91 32W
Stykkisholmur, Iceland	22	65 2N	22 40W
Styr R., U.S.S.R.	24	51 4N	25 20E
Styria, dist., Austria	14	47 26N	15 0E
Styx, Queensland	42	22 31S	149 37E
Suakin, Sudan	51	19 0N	37 20E
Suancheng, China	39	31 0N	118 43E
Süanen, China	39	30 0N	109 30E
Suanhan, China	39	31 27N	107 39E
Suanhwa, China	38	40 35N	115 0E
Suao, Formosa	39	24 32N	121 42E
Subansiri R., India	33	28 0N	94 0E
Subarnarekha R., India	33	22 30N	86 45E
Subiaco, Italy	20	41 56N	13 5E
Subotica, Yugoslavia	21	46 6N	19 29E

Place	MAP	Lat.	Long.
Success, Canada	65	50 28N	108 6W
Suceava, Rumania	21	47 38N	26 16 E
Suchitoto, Salvador	74	13 56N	89 0W
Suchow, China	38	34 10N	117 20 E
Süchowola, Poland	16	53 33N	23 3 E
Suckling, Mt., Papua	42	9 50 S	148 58 E
Sucre, Bolivia	78	19 0 S	65 15W
Sucunduri, R., Brazil	78	6 25 S	58 50W
Sucurai R., Brazil	79	19 0 S	52 45W
Sud Katanga, prov., Zaire	55	10 0 S	23 40 E
Suda R., U.S.S.R.	25	59 40N	36 30 E
Sudair, reg., Si. Arabia	30	25 50N	45 0 E
Sudan, st., Africa	51	15 0N	30 0 E
Sudan, U.S.A.	71	34 3N	102 30W
Sudavik, Iceland	22	66 2N	22 59W
Sudbury, Canada	62	46 30N	81 0W
Sudereyri, Iceland	22	66 9N	23 45W
Sudeten Highlands, Czechoslovakia	16	50 20N	16 45 E
Sudi, Tanzania	53	10 8 S	39 58 E
Sueca, Spain	17	39 12N	0 21W
Suemez I., U.S.A.	64	55 15N	133 20W
Suez (As Suways), Egypt	51	31 0N	32 20 E
Suez, G. of, Egypt	51	28 40N	33 0 E
Sufaina, Saudi Arabia	30	23 6N	40 44 E
Suffield, Canada	64	50 13N	111 11W
Suffolk, U.S.A.	69	36 47N	76 33W
Sufuk Wells, Trucial Oman	31	23 53N	51 48 E
Sugar City, U.S.A.	70	38 17N	103 41W
Sugarloaf Pt., N.S.W.	43	32 22 S	152 30 E
Suguti, Tanzania	53	1 46 S	33 40 E
Suhe Bator, Mongolia	37	50 10N	106 14 E
Suhl, Germany	14	50 35N	10 40 E
Suhsien, China	38	33 38N	117 0 E
Suhum, Ghana	52	6 0N	0 27W
Suichung, China	38	40 20N	120 15 E
Suichwan, China	39	26 29N	114 28 E
Suihsien, China	39	31 58N	113 20 E
Suihwa, China	37	46 40N	126 57 E
Suikhai, China	39	21 29N	110 13 E
Suining, Hunan, China	39	26 25N	109 45 E
Suining, Szechwan, China	39	30 30N	105 30 E
Suiping, China	38	33 10N	114 0 E
Suir, R., Ireland	11	52 22N	7 40W
Suita, Japan	36	34 56N	135 38 E
Suiteh, China	38	37 35N	110 0 E
Sukabumi, Indonesia	34	6 56 S	106 57 E
Sukadana, Indonesia	35	1 10 S	110 0 E
Sukhinichi, U.S.S.R.	25	54 8N	35 10 E
Sukhona R., U.S.S.R.	24	60 30N	45 0 E
Sukhumi, U.S.S.R.	24	43 0N	41 0 E
Sukkertoppen, Green.	61	65 40N	53 0W
Sukkur, Pakistan	32	27 50N	68 46 E
Sukses, S.W. Africa	57	21 01 S	16 52 E
Sukunka R., Canada	64	55 30N	122 0W
Sukuta, Gambia	52	13 13N	15 12W
Sula Is., Indonesia	35	1 45 S	125 0 E
Sulaco R., Cent. Amer.	75	14 50N	87 15W
Sulaiman Ra., Pakistan	32	30 30N	69 50 E
Sulaimiya, Si. Arabia	30	24 3N	47 30 E
Sulam Tsor, Israel	29	33 4N	35 6 E
Sulawesi (Celebes), Indonesia	35	2 0 S	120 0 E
Sulina, Rumania	21	45 10N	29 40 E
Sulina Mouth, Rum.	21	45 10N	29 35 E
Sulitjelma, Norway	22	67 10N	16 5 E
Sulitjelma, mt., Sweden	22	67 17N	17 28 E
Sullana, Peru	78	5 0 S	80 45W
Sullivan, Ill., U.S.A.	68	39 40N	88 40W
Sullivan, Ind., U.S.A.	68	39 5N	87 26W
Sullivan, Mo., U.S.A.	71	38 12N	91 10W
Sullivan Bay, Canada	64	50 55N	126 50W
Sullivan I., Burma	33	10 50N	98 20 E
Sullivan Lake, Canada	64	52 20N	112 0W
Sully, France	12	47 45N	2 20 E
Sulmona, Italy	20	42 3N	13 55 E
Sulphur, La., U.S.A.	71	30 15N	93 20W
Sulphur, Okla., U.S.A.	71	34 32N	96 50W
Sulphur Pt., Canada	64	60 50N	114 50W
Sulphur Springs, U.S.A.	71	33 0N	95 30W
Sulphur Springs Creek, U.S.A.	71	32 41N	102 0W
Sultan, Canada	62	47 36N	82 47W
Sultan Hamud, Kenya	53	2 1 S	37 21 E
Sultanabad, Iraq	31	29 55N	49 50 E
Sultaniyeh, Iran	30	36 28N	48 52 E
Sultanpur, India	33	26 18N	82 10 E
Sulu Arch., Philippines	35	6 0N	121 0 E
Sulu Sea, Philippines	35	8 0N	120 0 E
Suluq, Libya	51	31 44N	20 14 E
Sumatra, U.S.A.	72	46 37N	107 30W
Sumatra I., Indonesia	34	0 40N	100 20 E
Sumba I., Indonesia	35	9 45 S	119 35 E
Sumba, Zambia	56	8 32 S	30 30 E
Sumbawa I., Indonesia	35	8 34 S	117 17 E
Sumbawabesar, Indon.	35	8 30 S	117 25 E
Sumbawanga, Tanzania	53	8 0 S	31 33 E
Sumbing Mt., Indonesia	34	7 19 S	110 3 E
Sumbur, Mongolia	38	46 30N	108 30 E
Sumgait, U.S.S.R.	24	40 37N	49 43 E
Sumiswald, Switz.	15	47 2N	7 45 E
Summer L., U.S.A.	72	42 50N	120 50W
Summerhill, Ireland	11	53 30N	6 44W
Summerside, Canada	63	46 29N	63 41W

Place	MAP	Lat.	Long.
Summerville, Ga., U.S.A.	69	34 29N	85 21W
Summerville, S.C., U.S.A.	69	33 2N	80 11W
Summit, Alaska	59	63 27N	148 59W
Summit, Canada	62	47 50N	72 20W
Summit, U.S.A.	74	44 54N	71 52W
Summit Lake, Canada	64	54 15N	123 0W
Summit Peak, U.S.A.	73	37 19N	106 40W
Sumner, New Zealand	47	43 35 S	172 48 E
Sumner, U.S.A.	70	42 47N	92 5W
Sumner L., N.Z.	47	42 42 S	172 15 E
Sumperk, Czechoslov.	16	49 59N	17 0 E
Sumter, U.S.A.	69	34 0N	80 10W
Sumy, U.S.S.R.	25	50 57N	34 50 E
Sun Kosi, Nepal	33	27 30N	86 0 E
Suna, Tanzania	53	5 28 S	34 43 E
Sunburst, U.S.A.	72	48 57N	111 57W
Sunbury, U.S.A.	68	40 50N	76 46W
Sunbury, Victoria	43	37 30 S	144 40 E
Sunchon, S. Korea	36	34 55N	127 35 E
Sunda Sea, Indonesia	35	6 30 S	118 0 E
Sunda Str., Indonesia	34	6 20 S	105 30 E
Sundarbans, The, India and Bangladesh	33	22 0N	89 0 E
Sundargarh, India	33	22 3N	84 5 E
Sundarnagar, India	32	31 35N	76 55 E
Sundance, U.S.A.	70	44 30N	104 27W
Sunday, Str., W Australia	44	16 20 S	123 10 E
Sundays R., Cape Prov.	57	32 10 S	24 40 E
Sunderland, England	10	54 54N	1 22W
Sundre, Canada	64	51 49N	114 46W
Sundridge, Canada	62	45 45N	79 25W
Sundsvall, Sweden	23	62 23N	17 25 E
Sungai, Indonesia	34	2 10 S	101 30 E
Sungari R., China	38	45 0N	125 10 E
Sungei Lembing, Malaya	34	2 53N	103 4 E
Sungei Patani, Malaya	34	5 38N	100 29 E
Sungei Siput, Malaya	34	4 51N	101 6 E
Sunghsien, China	38	34 10N	112 10 E
Sungkiang, China	39	31 0N	121 20 E
Sungpan, China	37	32 50N	103 20 E
Sungtao, China	39	28 10N	109 0 E
Sungtze, China	39	30 25N	111 50 E
Sungüé, Mozambique	56	21 18 S	32 25 E
Sungurlu, Turkey	30	40 12N	34 21 E
Sunyang, China	39	28 30N	119 25 E
Sunndalsöra, Norway	23	62 39N	8 37 E
Sunnyside, Wash., U.S.A.	72	46 28N	120 5W
Sunnyside, Utah, U.S.A.	73	39 35N	110 52W
Sunray, U.S.A.	71	36 0N	101 45W
Sunson, Ghana	52	9 35N	0 0
Suntai, Nigeria	52	7 57N	10 16 E
Suntar, U.S.S.R.	27	62 15N	117 30 E
Sunyani, Ghana	52	7 21N	2 22W
Suo Sea, Japan	36	33 45N	131 45 E
Suolahti, Finland	23	62 38N	25 59 E
Suomussalmi, Finland	22	64 52N	29 13 E
Suonenjoki, Finland	23	62 37N	27 20 E
Supai, U.S.A.	73	36 16N	112 41W
Supaul, India	33	26 10N	86 40 E
Superior, Ariz., U.S.A.	73	33 19N	110 10W
Superior, Mont., U.S.A.	72	47 10N	114 51W
Superior, Neb., U.S.A.	70	40 0N	98 0W
Superior, Wis., U.S.A.	70	46 45N	92 0W
Superior, L., Canada–U.S.A.	70	47 40N	87 0W
Suphan dag, Mts., Turkey	30	30 0N	42 30 E
Supiori I., Indonesia	35	10 30 S	135 30 E
Supu, China	39	27 43N	110 29 E
Supung Dam, N. Korea	36	40 45N	125 0 E
Suq ash Shuyukh, Iraq	30	31 48N	46 36 E
Sur. *See* Tyre.	30		
Sur, Muscat & Oman	31	22 38N	59 28 E
Sur, Pt., U.S.A.	73	36 15N	121 50W
Sura, U.S.S.R.	24	63 40N	45 30 E
Sura R., U.S.S.R.	25	55 30N	46 20 E
Surabaja, Indonesia	34	7 17 S	112 45 E
Surag, Iran	31	25 40N	58 48 E
Surakarta, Indonesia	34	7 35 S	110 48 E
Surat, India	32	21 12N	72 55 E
Surat, Queensland	43	27 10 S	149 6 E
Surat Thani, Thailand	34	9 3N	99 28 E
Suratgarh, India	32	29 18N	73 55 E
Surazh, U.S.S.R.	25	53 5N	32 27 E
Surbiton, Queensland	42	23 12 S	146 40 E
Sûre R., Luxembourg	13	49 5N	5 50 E
Surendranagar, India	32	22 45N	71 40 E
Suretka, Costa Rica	78	9 40N	83 0W
Surf Inlet, Canada	64	53 8N	128 50W
Surgurlu, Turkey	30	40 14N	34 25 E
Surgut, U.S.S.R.	26	61 20N	73 28 E
Suri, India	33	23 50N	87 34 E
Suriapet, India	32	17 10N	79 40 E
Surif, Jordan	29	31 40N	35 4 E
Suriname Guyana	79	4 0N	56 0W
Suriname, R., Guyana	79	4 30N	55 30W
Surprise L., Canada	64	59 40N	133 11W
Sursee, Switzerland	15	47 11N	8 6 E
Surt, Libya	51	31 20N	16 20 E
Suruga B., Japan	36	34 45N	138 30 E
Susa, Italy	20	45 8N	7 3 E

Place	MAP	Lat.	Long.
Susa, Iran	30	32 10N	48 20 E
Sušac I., Yugoslavia	20	42 46N	16 30 E
Susak, Yugoslavia	20	45 19N	14 25 E
Susangerd, Iran	30	31 38N	48 13 E
Susanino, U.S.S.R.	27	52 50N	140 14 E
Susanville, U.S.A.	72	40 26N	120 43W
Susquehanna, R., U.S.A.	68	41 50N	76 20W
Susques, Argentina	77	23 35 S	66 25W
Sussex, Canada	63	45 45N	65 37W
Susten, P., Switzerland	15	46 44N	8 27 E
Sustut R., Canada	64	56 20N	127 20W
Sutherland, Canada	65	52 15N	106 40W
Sutherland, Cape Prov.	57	32 33 S	20 40 E
Sutherland, U.S.A.	70	41 13N	101 8W
Sutherland Ra., W. Australia	45	25 42 S	125 21 E
Sutherland Sd., N.Z.	47	44 43 S	167 34 E
Sutherlin, U.S.A.	72	43 26N	123 20W
Sutlej R., Pakistan	32	30 0N	73 0 E
Sutsien, China	38	33 58N	118 30 E
Sutton, New Zealand	47	45 34 S	170 8 E
Sutton, U.S.A.	70	40 40N	97 53W
Sutwik I., Alaska	59	56 30N	157 10W
Suurberg Mts., Cape Prov.	57	33 15 S	25 30 E
Suva Planina, Y.slav.	21	43 10N	22 5 E
Suwa, Japan	36	36 3N	138 6 E
Suwa L., Japan	36	36 12N	137 50 E
Suwada, Saudi Arabia	30	22 40N	44 30 E
Suwalki, Poland	23	54 8N	22 59 E
Suwannee, R., U.S.A.	69	30 0N	83 10W
Suweima, Jordan	29	31 46N	35 35 E
Suwen, China	39	20 27N	110 2 E
Süwon, Korea	36	37 25N	126 55 E
Suyung, China	39	28 20N	105 20 E
Svanvik, U.S.S.R.	22	68 44N	30 0 E
Svartisen, mt., Norway	22	66 40N	14 16 E
Svatovo, U.S.S.R.	25	49 35N	38 5 E
Svealand, dist., Sweden	23	60 0N	15 0 E
Sveg, Sweden	23	62 2N	14 27 E
Svendborg, Denmark	23	55 14N	10 35 E
Sverdlovsk, U.S.S.R.	24	56 50N	60 30 E
Sverdrup Is., Canada	58	79 0N	97 0W
Svilengrad, Bulgaria	21	41 49N	26 12 E
Svisloch R., U.S.S.R.	25	53 45N	28 10 E
Svishtov, Bulgaria	21	43 36N	25 22 E
Svobodny, U.S.S.R.	27	51 20N	128 0 E
Svolvær, Norway	22	68 15N	14 40 E
Swabian Jura, Germany	14	48 30N	9 40 E
Swain Reefs, Queens.	42	21 45 S	152 20W
Swainsboro, U.S.A.	69	32 38N	82 22W
Swakop, R., S.W. Africa	57	22 36 S	16 0 E
Swakopmund, S.W. Afr.	57	22 37 S	14 30 E
Swale R., England	10	54 18N	1 30W
Swalinbar, Ireland	11	54 12N	7 42W
Swamihalli, India	32	14 55N	76 35 E
Swan Is., Caribbean Sea	75	17 22N	83 57W
Swan L., Canada	65	52 30N	100 50W
Swan R., W. Australia	44	31 35 S	116 0 E
Swan R., Alb., Canada	64	55 0N	115 40W
Swan R., Sask., Canada	65	52 0N	102 12W
Swan Hill, Victoria	43	35 15 S	143 31 E
Swan River, Canada	65	52 10N	101 25W
Swansea, Wales	10	51 37N	3 57W
Swartberg, Cape Prov.	57	30 15 S	29 23 E
Swartmodder, Cape Province	57	34 0 S	20 39 E
Swartruggens, Transvaal	57	25 39 S	26 42 E
Swastika, Canada	62	48 7N	80 6W
Swat, dist., Pakistan	32	35 0N	72 20 E
Swatow, China	39	23 25N	116 40 E
Swaziland, Botswana S. Africa	57	26 35 S	31 30 E
Sweden, King., Europe	22–23	67 0N	15 0 E
Swedru, Ghana	52	5 32N	0 41W
Sweet Home, U.S.A.	72	44 24N	122 45W
Sweetwater, U.S.A.	71	32 30N	100 30W
Sweetwater R., U.S.A.	72	42 20N	107 30W
Swellendam, Cape Prov.	57	34 2 S	20 29 E
Swidnica, Poland	16	50 50N	16 30 E
Swiebodzin, Poland	16	52 15N	15 37 E
Swiecie, Poland	16	53 25N	18 30 E
Swift Current, Canada	65	50 20N	107 45W
Swilly L., Ireland	11	55 12N	7 35W
Swindon, England	10	51 33N	1 47W
Swindle I., Canada	64	52 30N	128 35W
Swinford, Ireland	11	53 57N	8 57W
Swinoujscie, Poland	16	53 55N	14 18 E
Switzerland, Rep., Eur.	15	46 30N	8 0 E
Sword Ra., Queensland	42	21 35 S	141 25 E
Swords, Ireland	11	53 27N	6 15W
Sychevka, U.S.S.R.	25	55 45N	34 10 E
Sydney, Canada	63	46 7N	60 7W
Sydney, N.S.W.	43	33 53 S	151 10 E
Sydney Mines, Canada	63	46 18N	60 15W
Sydpröven, Greenland	61	60 30N	45 20W
Syktyvkar, U.S.S.R.	24	61 45N	50 40 E
Sylacauga, U.S.A.	69	33 10N	86 15W
Sylarna, mt., Sweden	23	63 2N	12 20 E
Sylhet, Bangladesh	33	24 43N	91 55 E
Sylt I., Germany	14	54 50N	8 20 E
Sylvan Lake, Canada	64	52 20N	114 10W
Sylvania, U.S.A.	69	32 45N	81 37W
Sylvester, U.S.A.	69	31 31N	83 50W
Sym, U.S.S.R.	26	60 20N	87 50 E
Syr Darya R., U.S.S.R.	26	45 0N	65 0 E

Place	MAP	Lat.	Long.
Syracuse, Kan., U.S.A.	71	37 59N	101 45W
Syracuse, U.S.A.	68	43 4N	76 11W
Syria, Rep., Asia	30	35 0N	38 0 E
Syriam, Burma	34	16 45N	96 17 E
Syrian Des., Si. Arabia	30	31 30N	40 0 E
Syuldzhyukar, U.S.S.R.	27	63 25N	113 40 E
Syzran, U.S.S.R.	25	53 12N	48 30 E
Szamotuly, Poland	16	52 35N	16 34 E
Szczecin (Stettin), Poland	14	53 27N	14 27 E
Szczecin, prov., Poland	16	53 25N	14 32 E
Szczecinĕk, Poland	16	53 43N	16 41 E
Szczytno, Poland	16	53 33N	21 0 E
Szechwan, prov., China	37	30 10N	106 0 E
Szeged, Hungary	16	46 16N	20 10 E
Székesfehérvár, Hung.	16	47 15N	13 25 E
Szekszárd, Hungary	16	46 22N	18 42 E
Szemao, China	37	22 50N	101 0 E
Szenan, China	39	27 50N	108 25 E
Szengen, China	39	23 20N	108 5 E
Szengen, China	39	24 56N	108 23 E
Szentes, Hungary	16	46 39N	20 21 E
Szeping, China	38	43 10N	124 18 E
Szeshui, China	38	34 50N	113 20 E
Szewui, China	39	23 30N	112 35 E
Szolnok, Hungary	16	47 10N	20 15 E
Szombathely, Hungary	16	47 14N	16 38 E
Szubin, Poland	16	53 0N	17 35 E
Szydlowiec, Poland	16	51 15N	20 51 E

T

Place	MAP	Lat.	Long.
T.A.I. (Fr.)	49	11 30N	42 15 E
Ta Liang Shan, China	37	28 0N	103 0N
Taas, U.S.A.	73	36 27N	105 33W
Taba, Saudi Arabia	30	26 53N	42 30 E
Tabagé, Pta., Brazil	79	2 55 S	40 0W
Tabarka, Tunisia	51	36 55N	8 55 E
Tabas, Iran	31	33 32N	56 55 E
Tabas, Iran	31	32 48N	60 12 E
Tabasará, Serrania de, mts., Panama	75	8 35N	81 40W
Tabasco, st., Mexico	74	17 45N	93 30W
Tabatinga, Brazil	78	4 10 S	69 58W
Tabatinga, Sa. de, Braz.	79	11 0 S	44 0W
Tabéla, Niger	52	13 37N	4 10 E
Taber, Canada	64	49 45N	112 10W
Tabernas, Spain	17	37 4N	2 24W
Taberñes de Valldigna, Spain	17	39 40N	0 16 E
Tabigha (site), Israel	29	32 53N	35 33 E
Table B., Canada	63	53 40N	56 15W
Table B., Cape Prov.	57	33 35 S	18 25 E
Table Mt., Cape Prov.	57	34 0 S	18 22 E
Tabletop Mt., Queens.	42	25 0 S	148 30 E
Tábor, Czechoslovakia	16	49 25N	14 39 E
Tabor Mt., Israel	29	32 40N	35 21 E
Tabora, Tanzania	53	5 2 S	32 45 E
Tabora, prov., Tan.	53	6 0 S	32 0 E
Taboria, Guinea	52	Inset	
Tabou, Ivory Coast	50	4 30N	7 20W
Tabriz, Iran	30	38 7N	46 20 E
Tabuk, Si. Arabia	30	28 28N	36 30 E
Tacatu R., Brazil	78	3 45N	60 0W
Tachintala, China	38	45 13N	121 38 E
Táchira, Venezuela	78	8 10N	72 10W
Tachu, China	39	30 50N	107 20 E
Tacloban, Philippines	35	11 1N	125 0 E
Tacna, Peru	78	18 0 S	70 20W
Taco Pozo, Argentina	77	25 25 S	63 45W
Tacoma, U.S.A.	72	47 15N	122 30W
Tacora Vol., Peru	78	17 40 S	70 0W
Tacuarembo, Uruguay	77	31 45 S	56 0W
Tadmor, New Zealand	47	41 27 S	172 45 E
Tadmor. *See* Palmyra	30		
Tadoussac, Canada	63	48 11N	69 42W
Tadpatri, India	32	14 50N	78 0 E
Tadzhik S.S.R., U.S.S.R.	26	35 30N	70 0 E
Taebaek Sanmaek, mt., S. Korea	36	37 30N	128 40 E
Taegu, Korea	36	35 50N	128 25 E
Taejon, Korea	37	35 30N	127 22 E
Tafo, Ghana	52	6 15N	0 20W
Taft, Ala., U.S.A.	73	35 8N	119 29W
Taft, Tex., U.S.A.	71	27 58N	97 27W
Taga Dzong, Bhutan	33	27 5N	90 0 E
Taganrog, U.S.S.R.	25	47 12N	38 50 E
Taganrog G., U.S.S.R.	25	47 0N	38 30 E
Tagawa, Japan	36	33 43N	130 56 E
Tagbilacao, Philippines	25	9 45N	124 0 E
Tagish, Canada	64	60 20N	134 10W
Tagish L., Canada	64	60 0N	134 10W
Tagliamento R., Italy	20	45 38N	13 5 E
Taguatinga, Brazil	79	12 26 S	45 50W
Tagula I., Papua	42	11 40 S	153 15 E
Tagus R., Spain-Port.	17	39 44N	5 50W
Tahakopa, N.Z.	47	46 30 S	169 23 E
Tahat Mt., Algeria	50	23 5N	5 45 E
Tahcheng, China	37	46 42N	83 0 E
Tāheri, Iran	31	27 31N	52 22 E
Tahiti I., Society Is.	5	17 45 S	149 30W
Tahlat, R., W. Pakistan	31	28 40N	62 0 E
Tahoe, U.S.A.	72	39 8N	119 50W
Tahoe, L., U.S.A.	73	39 6N	120 0W
Tahoka, U.S.A.	71	33 9N	101 45W
Tahora, New Zealand	46	39 2 S	174 49 E
Tahoua, Niger	52	14 57N	5 19 E

	MAP		
Tahrud, Iran	31	29 29N	57 45 E
Tahsien, China	39	31 12N	108 13 E
Tahta, Egypt	51	26 44N	31 32 E
Tahtsa L., Canada	64	53 40N	127 12W
Tahuamanu R., Bolivia	78	11 10S	68 45W
Tai, Ivory Coast	50	5 55N	7 30W
Tai Hu, China	39	31 10N	120 0 E
Taian, China	38	36 20N	117 0 E
Taiihow, China	38	32 30N	119 50 E
Taiihow Wen, China	39	28 55N	121 10 E
Taiiri R., New Zealand	47	45 12S	170 12 E
Taif, Saudi Arabia	30	21 5N	40 27 E
Taihan Shan, China	38	36 30N	114 0 E
Taihape, New Zealand	46	39 41S	175 48 E
Taiho, China	39	26 47N	114 52 E
Taihsien, China	38	39 2N	112 57 E
Taihu, China	39	30 30N	116 14 E
Taikang, China	38	34 6N	114 50 E
Taikang, China	39	26 31N	108 19 E
Tailai, China	38	46 27N	123 15 E
Tailakovy, U.S.S.R.	26	59 15N	74 0 E
Tailem Bend, Australia	43	35 12S	139 29 E
Taimyr B., U.S.S.R.	28	76 0N	100 0 E
Taimyr L., U.S.S.R.	27	74 50N	102 0 E
Taimyr Pen, U.S.S.R.	28	75 0N	100 0 E
Tain, Scotland	10	57 49N	4 4W
Tainan, China	39	23 0N	120 15 E
Taining, China	39	26 56N	117 5 E
Taipeh, China	39	25 0N	121 30 E
Taiping, Malaya	34	4 50N	100 43 E
Taipugenuku, R., New Zealand	47	42 3S	173 55 E
Taira, Japan	36	37 0N	140 55 E
Taishan, China	39	27 32N	119 32 E
Taishan, I., China	39	30 20N	122 25 E
Taishan, Mt., China	38	36 30N	117 25 E
Taishet, U.S.S.R.	27	55 58N	97 25 E
Taitao Pen., Chile	77	46 30S	75 0W
Taitung, China	39	22 40N	121 5 E
Taiwan (Formosa), I., China	39	23 30N	121 0 E
Taiyetos Mts., Greece	21	37 0N	22 23 E
Taiyiba, Israel	29	32 16N	35 0 E
Taiyiba, Israel	29	32 36N	35 27 E
Taiyiba, Jordan	29	31 55N	35 17 E
Taiyibe R., Jordan	29	32 32N	35 37 E
Taiyüan, China	38	38 0N	112 30 E
Tajima, Fukushima, Japan	36	37 12N	139 45 E
Tajimi, Gifu, Japan	36	35 26N	137 12 E
Tajumulco, Volcan de Guatemala	74	15 20N	91 50W
Tajura, Libya	51	32 52N	13 27 E
Tak (Rahaeng), Thai.	34	17 0N	99 10 E
Takabba, Kenya	53	3 27N	40 14 E
Takada, New Zealand	47	40 51N	172 50 E
Takalar, Indonesia	35	5 30S	119 30 E
Takamatsu, Japan	36	34 20N	134 5 E
Takaoka, Japan	36	36 40N	137 0 E
Takapau, New Zealand	46	40 2S	176 21 E
Takapuna, New Zealand	46	36 47S	174 47 E
Takásaki, Japan	36	36 20N	139 0 E
Takata, Japan	36	37 51N	137 38 E
Takaungu, Kenya	53	3 35S	39 45 E
Takayama, Japan	36	36 17N	137 9 E
Takefu, Japan	36	35 50N	136 10 E
Takeo, Cambodia	34	11 3N	104 50 E
Täkestän, Iran	30	36 2N	49 40 E
Takhia Tash, U.S.S.R.	26	42 0N	59 59 E
Tahking, China	39	23 10N	111 45 E
Takingeun, Indonesia	34	4 45N	96 50 E
Takla L., Canada	64	55 20N	126 30W
Takla Landing, Canada	64	55 30N	125 50W
Takla Makan, desert, China	37	39 40N	85 0 E
Takoradi, Ghana	52	4 58N	1 55W
Taksang, India	33	27 59N	92 50 E
Taku, Canada	64	59 40N	133 55W
Taku R., Canada	64	58 40N	133 30W
Takum, Nigeria	52	7 18N	9 56 E
Tala, U.S.S.R.	27	72 40N	113 50 E
Talamanca, Cord. de, Central America	75	9 20N	83 20W
Talara, Peru	78	4 30S	81 10 E
Talasea, Indonesia	42	5 14S	150 5 E
Talass, U.S.S.R.	26	42 40N	72 0 E
Talata Mafara, Nigeria	52	12 38N	6 4 E
Talaud Is., Indonesia	35	4 30N	127 10 E
Talavera, Spain	17	39 55N	4 45W
Talca, Chile	77	35 20S	71 46W
Talcahuano, Chile	77	36 40S	73 10W
Talcher, India	33	21 0N	85 10 E
Talachin, China	38	36 40N	105 5 E
Taldy Kurgan, U.S.S.R.	26	45 10N	78 45 E
Talfit, Jordan	29	32 5N	35 17 E
Talgan, Afghanistan	31	36 59N	69 33 E
Talguppa, India	32	14 10N	74 55 E
Tali, Shensi, China	38	34 48N	109 48 E
Tali, Yunnan, China	37	25 50N	100 0 E
Tali Post, Sudan	54	5 55N	30 44 E
Talia, S. Australia	45	33 23S	134 58 E
Taliabu I., Indonesia	35	1 45S	125 0 E
Talien. *See* Dairen.	38		
Talihina, U.S.A.	71	34 42N	95 2W
Talisayan, Philippines	35	8 55N	123 50 E
Talish Mts., Iran	30	38 30N	48 30 E
Talkeetna, Alaska	59	62 30N	150 5W
Talkeetna Mts., Alaska	59	62 30N	149 0W
Tall Afar, Araq	30	36 22N	42 27 E
Talladega, U.S.A.	69	33 30N	86 0W
Tallahassee, U.S.A.	69	30 20N	84 15W
Tallangatta, Victoria	43	36 10S	147 14 E
Tallinn, U.S.S.R.	23	59 29N	24 58 E
Tallulah, U.S.A.	71	32 28N	91 10W
Talluza, Jordan	29	32 17N	35 18 E
Talmaciu, Rumania	21	45 38N	24 19 E
Talmage, Canada	65	49 46N	103 40W
Talnoye, U.S.S.R.	25	48 57N	30 35 E
Talodi, Sudan	51	10 35N	30 22 E
Talovaya, U.S.S.R.	25	51 13N	40 38 E
Taltal, Chile	77	25 23S	70 40W
Taltson R., Canada	64	61 24N	112 40W
Taluk, Indonesia	34	0 30S	101 45 E
Talyawalka Cr., N.S.W.	43	32 12S	143 0 E
Tama, U.S.A.	70	41 57N	92 36W
Tamale, Ghana	52	9 22N	0 50W
Tamale Port (Yapei), Ghana	52	9 9N	1 7W
Tamano, Japan	36	34 35N	133 59 E
Tamanrasset (Ft. Laperrine), Alg.	50	22 56N	5 30 E
Tamar R., England	10	50 33N	4 15W
Tamar R., Tasmania	42	41 15S	147 0 E
Tamási, Hungary	16	46 40N	18 18 E
Tamaské, Niger	52	14 55N	5 55 E
Tamatave, Madagasgar	55	18 2S	49 25 E
Tamaulipas, st., Mexico	74	24 0N	99 0W
Tamazula, Mexico	74	24 55N	106 58W
Tambach, Kenya	53	0 41N	35 43 E
Tambacounda, Senegal	50	13 55N	13 45W
Tambalan, Indonesia	35	3 10N	115 35 E
Tambara, Moz. *See* Inhacora	56		
Tambaqui L., Brazil	78	3 5S	63 50W
Tambelan Is., Indonesia	35	1 0N	107 30 E
Tambellup, W. Australia	44	34 4S	117 37 E
Tambo, Queensland	42	24 54S	146 14 E
Tambo de Mora, Peru	78	13 30S	76 20W
Tambov, U.S.S.R.	25	52 45N	41 20 E
Tambura, Sudan	54	5 40N	27 25 E
Tamchakett, Mauritania	50	17 25N	10 40W
Tamega R., Portugal	17	41 12N	8 5W
Tamel Aike, Argentina	77	48 10S	71 0W
Tamenglong, India	33	25 0N	93 35 E
Tamgak Mts., Niger	50	19 12N	8 35 E
Tamil Nadu, St. India	32	11 0N	77 0 E
Taming, China	38	36 20N	115 10 E
Tamins, Switzerland	15	46 50N	9 24 E
Tammin, W. Australia	44	31 38S	117 29 E
Tammisaari, Finland	23	60 0N	23 21 E
Tammun', Jordan	29	32 18N	35 23 E
Tampa, U.S.A.	69	28 0N	82 25W
Tampa B., U.S.A.	69	27 30N	82 40W
Tampere (Tammerfors), Finland	23	61 30N	23 50 E
Tampico, Mexico	74	22 20N	97 50W
Tampin, Malaya	34	2 28N	102 13 E
Tamsag Bulak, Mon.	37	47 10N	117 21 E
Tamsagout, Mauritania	50	24 5N	6 35W
Tamshiyacu, Peru	78	4 0S	73 0W
Tamsui, China	39	25 10N	121 28 E
Tamu, Burma	33	24 13N	94 12 E
Tamworth, N.S.W.	43	31 0S	150 58 E
Tana, Norway	22	70 23N	28 13 E
Tana Fd., Norway	22	70 35N	28 30 E
Tana, L., Ethiopia	54	13 5N	37 30 E
Tana R., Kenya	53	1 0S	39 40 E
Tana R., Norway	22	69 50N	26 0 E
Tanacross, Alaska	60	63 40N	143 30W
Tanaga, I., Aleutian Is.	59	51 50N	178 0W
Tanahbala I., Indonesia	34	0 30S	98 30 E
Tanahdjampea I., Indon.	35	7 20S	120 35 E
Tanahgcogot, Indonesia	35	1 55S	116 15 E
Tanahmasa I., Indonesia	34	0 5S	98 20 E
Tanami, N. Terr. Austral.	45	20 02S	129 43 E
Tanana, Alaska	59	65 15N	152 10W
Tanana R., Alaska	59	64 25N	145 30W
Tananarive, Madag.	55	18 55S	47 35 E
Tanaro R., Italy	20	44 9N	7 50 E
Tanchai, China	39	26 3N	107 44 E
Tanchon, Korea	36	40 30N	129 0 E
Tanchow, China	39	25 18N	109 18 E
Tanda, India	33	26 33N	82 35 E
Tandaai, Rhodesia	56	19 36S	32 48 E
Tandag, Philippines	35	9 10N	126 0 E
Tandala, Tanzania	53	9 27S	34 13 E
Tăndarei, Rumania	21	44 39N	27 40 E
Tandaragee, N. Ireland	11	54 22N	6 23W
Tandil, Argentina	77	37 15S	59 6W
Tandil, Sa. del, Arg.	77	38 0S	58 0W
Tandjung, Indonesia	35	2 10S	115 25 E
Tandjungbali, Indon.	34	2 59N	99 45 E
Tandjung Pandan, Indonesia	34	2 50S	107 45 E
Tandjung Selor, Indon.	35	2 55N	117 25 E
Tandjungpinang, Indon.	34	1 5N	104 30 E
Tandjungperiuk, Java	34	6 8S	106 55 E
Tando Adam, Pakistan	32	25 45N	68 40 E
Tando Muhammad Khan, Pakistan	32	25 0N	68 40 E
Tandou L., N.S.W.	43	32 40S	142 0 E
Tandur, India	32	19 11N	79 30 E
Taneatua, New Zealand	46	38 4S	177 1 E
Tanega Shima, Japan	36	30 30N	131 0 E
Taneycomo, L., U.S.A.	71	36 40N	93 45W
Tanezrouft, reg., Alg.	50	22 40N	1 0 E
Tanga, Tanzania	53	5 5S	39 8 E
Tangail, Bangladesh	33	24 15N	90 0 E
Tanganyika, L., E. Afr.	53	8 30S	31 0 E
Tangata, Mozambique	56	17 13S	34 17 E
Tangerang, Java, Indon.	34	6 12S	106 34 E
Tangho, China	38	32 40N	112 51 E
Tangi, Pakistan	32	34 20N	71 35 E
Tangier, Morocco	50	35 50N	5 49W
Tangkak, Malaya	34	2 18N	102 32 E
Tangku, China	38	39 0N	117 40 E
Tanghla Ra., China	37	33 0N	90 0 E
Tangorin, Queensland	42	21 45S	144 9 E
Tangshan, China	38	39 40N	118 10 E
Tangtu, China	39	31 37N	118 29 E
Tanguieta, Dahomey	52	10 40N	1 21 E
Tangyang, China	39	30 49N	111 36 E
Tanhsien, China	38	36 3N	115 31 E
Tanhsien, China	39	19 37N	109 18 E
Tanimbar Is., Indonesia	35	7 30S	131 30 E
Tanjay, Philippines	35	9 30N	123 5 E
Tanjore (Thanjavur), India	32	10 48N	79 12 E
Tank, W. Pakistan	32	32 14N	70 25 E
Tannin, Canada	62	49 40N	91 0W
Tano R., Ghana	52	6 0N	2 30W
Tanout, Niger	52	14 50N	8 55 E
Tansing, Nepal	33	27 55N	83 30 E
Tanta, Egypt	51	30 45N	30 57 E
Tantoyuca, Mexico	74	21 21N	98 10W
Tantura *See* Dor	29		
Tanur, India	32	11 1N	75 46 E
Tanzania Republic	53	5 0S	38 30 E
Tanzilla R., Canada	64	58 25N	130 0W
Taohsien, China	39	25 37N	111 31 E
Taokow, China	38	35 30N	114 30 E
Taolaichao, China	38	44 45N	125 50 E
Taonan, China	38	45 30N	122 20 E
Taormina, Italy	20	37 52N	15 16 E
Taoudenni, Mali	50	22 40N	3 55W
Taourirt, Morocco	50	34 20N	3 0W
Taoyuan, Hunan, China	39	28 52N	111 20 E
Taoyuan, Taiwan, China	39	25 0N	121 14 E
Tapa, U.S.S.R.	23	59 15N	26 0 E
Tapa Shan, China	39	32 0N	109 0 E
Tapachula, Mexico	74	14 58N	92 22W
Tapah, Malaya	34	4 12N	101 15 E
Tapajós R., Brazil	79	4 30S	56 10W
Tapaktuan, Indonesia	34	3 30N	97 10 E
Tapanahoni R., Surinam	79	3 30N	55 30W
Tapanshang, China	38	43 30N	118 20 E
Tapanui, New Zealand	47	45 56S	169 18 E
Tapauá, Brazil	78	5 40S	64 20W
Tapauá R., Brazil	78	6 0S	65 40W
Tapiche R., Peru	78	6 0S	74 0W
Tapirapeco, Sa., Venezuela–Brazil	78	1 0N	65 0W
Tappahannock, U.S.A.	68	37 55N	76 51W
Tappita, Liberia	50	6 36N	8 52W
Tappo, Ghana	52	10 10N	2 35W
Tapiti R., India	32	21 25N	75 30 E
Tapurucuara, Brazil	78	0 23S	65 1W
Taquari R., Brazil	78	18 10S	56 0W
Tara, Zambia	56	16 58S	26 45 E
Tara, Queensland	43	27 17S	150 31 E
Tara, U.S.S.R.	26	56 55N	74 30 E
Tara Hill, Ireland	11	53 35N	6 36W
Tara R., U.S.S.R.	26	56 30N	76 30 E
Tara R., Yugoslavia	21	43 10N	19 20 E
Taraba R., Nigeria	52	7 50N	11 15 E
Tarabulus (Tripoli), Leb.	30	34 26N	35 51 E
Taracón, Spain	17	40 1N	2 59W
Taradale, N.Z.	46	39 33S	176 53 E
Tarakan, Indonesia	35	3 20N	117 35 E
Tarakit, Mt., Kenya	53	2 1N	35 9 E
Taralga, N.S.W.	43	34 26S	149 52 E
Taramakau R., N.Z.	47	42 43S	171 15 E
Taranaki, dist., N.Z.	46	39 5S	174 51 E
Taranga Hill, India	32	24 0N	72 40 E
Taransay I., Scotland	10	57 54N	7 0W
Taranto, Italy	20	40 30N	17 11 E
Taranto G., Italy	20	40 0N	17 15 E
Tarapaca, Colombia	78	2 45S	69 45W
Tarapoto, Peru	78	6 20S	76 20W
Tarare, France	12	45 54N	4 26 E
Tararua Range, N.Z.	46	40 45S	175 25 E
Tarascon, France	12	43 48N	4 39 E
Tarat, Algeria	50	26 4N	9 7 E
Tarata, Peru	78	17 20S	70 0W
Tarauacá, Brazil	78	8 6S	70 45W
Tarauacá, R., Brazil	78	7 57S	70 45W
Tarawera, N.Z.	46	39 2S	176 36 E
Tarawera Lake, N.Z.	46	38 13S	176 27 E
Tarawera Mt., N.Z.	46	38 14S	176 32 E
Tarazona, Spain	17	41 55N	1 43W
Tarbagatai Ra., U.S.S.R.	26	47 20N	82 30 E
Tarbela Dam, W. Pak.	33	34 7N	73 30 E
Tarbes, France	12	43 15N	0 3 E
Tarboro, U.S.A.	69	35 55N	77 3W
Tarbrax, Queensland	42	21 3S	142 26 E
Tarcoola, S. Australia	40	30 44S	134 36 E
Tardin, China	37	37 17N	92 58 E
Taree, New South Wales	43	31 50S	152 30 E
Tarfaya, Morocco	50	27 55N	12 55W
Târgoviste, Rumania	21	44 55N	25 33 E
Târgu-Frumos, Rum.	21	47 12N	27 2 E
Târgu Neamt, Rum.	21	47 12N	26 25 E
Târgu Ocna, Rumania	21	46 18N	26 39 E
Tarifa, Spain	17	36 1N	5 36W
Tarija, Bolivia	78	21 30S	64 30W
Tarim R., China	37	40 40N	85 20 E
Tarka, Niger	52	14 35N	7 58 E
Tarka, R., Cape Prov	57	34 50S	26 10 E
Tarkastad, Cape Prov.	57	32 0S	26 16 E
Tarkhankut C., U.S.S.R.	25	45 25N	32 30 E
Tarko Sale, U.S.S.R.	26	64 55N	77 50 E
Tarkwa, Ghana	52	5 20N	2 0W
Tarlac, Philippines	35	15 30N	120 25 E
Tarma, Peru	78	11 25S	75 45W
Tärna, Sweden	22	65 45N	15 10 E
Tarnak Rud, R., Afghan.	31	32 0N	66 40 E
Tarnobrzeg, Poland	16	50 30N	21 45 E
Tarnów, Poland	16	50 3N	21 0 E
Tarnowskie Góry, Pol.	16	50 27N	18 54 E
Tarõm, Iran	31	28 10N	55 42 E
Taroom, Queensland	43	25 36S	149 48 E
Taroudant, Morocco	50	30 35N	9 0W
Tarpon Springs, U.S.A.	69	28 5N	82 45W
Tarqumiya, Jordan	29	31 35N	35 1 E
Tarragona, Spain	17	41 5N	1 17 E
Tarraleah, Tasmania	43	42 9S	146 14 E
Tarrasa, Spain	17	41 26N	2 1 E
Tarrega, Spain	17	41 40N	1 7 E
Tarreteurken, Niger	52	15 6N	5 58 E
Tarri Mashen, Somali. Rep.	49	0 48N	41 30 E
Tarshiha, Israel	29	33 1N	35 15 E
Tarsus, Turkey	30	36 58N	34 55 E
Tartagal, Argentina	77	22 30S	63 50W
Tartary Str., U.S.S.R.	27	54 0N	141 0 E
Tartu, U.S.S.R.	23	58 25N	26 58 E
Tartus, Syria	30	34 59N	35 57 E
Taruntung, Indonesia	34	2 0N	99 0 E
Tasawah, Libya	51	25 50N	14 0 E
Taschereau, Canada	62	48 40N	78 40W
Taseko Mt., Canada	64	51 12N	123 7W
Taseko, R., Canada	64	51 30N	123 20W
Tasgaon, India	32	17 2N	74 39 E
Tashauz, U.S.S.R.	26	42 0N	59 20 E
Tashigong, China	37	32 31N	79 33 E
Tashihkao, China	38	40 32N	122 30 E
Tashkent, U.S.S.R.	26	41 20N	69 10 E
Tashkepri, U.S.S.R.	26	36 25N	62 53 E
Tashkumyr, U.S.S.R.	26	41 40N	72 10 E
Tashkurghan, Afghan.	31	36 49N	67 37 E
Tasikmalaja, Indonesia	34	7 18S	108 12 E
Tasin (Yangli), China	39	22 50N	107 28 E
Tasjön L., Sweden	22	64 15N	15 45 E
Taskan, U.S.S.R.	27	63 10N	150 0 E
Tasman Bay, N.Z.	47	40 59S	173 25 E
Tasman Mount, N.Z.	47	43 34S	170 12 E
Tasman Mts., N.Z.	47	41 3S	172 25 E
Tasman R., N.Z.	47	45 52S	170 9 E
Tasman Sea, N.Z.	5	42 30S	168 0 E
Tasmania, I., st., Australia	43	49 0S	146 30 E
Tatai, Japan	36	34 45N	133 45 E
Tatar A.S.S.R., U.S.S.R.	24	55 30N	51 30 E
Tatarsk, U.S.S.R.	26	55 20N	75 50 E
Tate, Queensland	42	17 27S	144 18 E
Tateyama, Japan	36	35 0N	139 50 E
Tathlina L., Canada	64	60 30N	117 30W
Tatien, China	39	25 45N	118 0 E
Tating, China	39	27 0N	105 35 E
Tatinnai L., Canada	65	60 50N	97 50W
Tatla Lake, Canada	64	51 55N	124 40W
Tatlayoka Lake, Can.	64	51 35N	124 24W
Tatnam C., Canada	65	57 20N	91 0W
Tatsaitan, China	37	37 44N	95 08 E
Tatsu, China	37	29 40N	105 45 E
Tatta, Pakistan	32	24 48N	67 55 E
Tatui, Brazil	77	23 22S	47 53W
Tatum, U.S.A.	71	33 15N	103 16W
Tatung, Anhwei, China	39	30 50N	117 45 E
Tatung, Shansi, China	38	40 10N	113 10 E
Tatungkow, China	38	39 55N	124 10 E
Tatvan, Turkey	30	38 30N	42 12 E
Tauapecacu, Brazil	78	2 35S	61 0W
Taubate, Brazil	77	23 5S	45 30W
Taumarunui, N.Z.	46	38 53S	175 15 E
Taumaturgo, Brazil	78	9 0S	73 0W
Taung, Cape Province	57	27 33S	24 47 E
Taungdwingyi, Burma	33	20 1N	95 40 E
Taunggyi, Burma	33	20 50N	97 0 E
Taungup, Burma	33	18 48N	94 20 E
Taungup Pass, Burma	33	18 20N	93 40 E
Taunsa Barr, W. Pak.	31	30 40N	70 45 E
Taunton, England	10	51 1N	3 7W
Taunton, Mass., U.S.A.	69	41 55N	71 6W
Taunus, mts., W. Ger.	14	50 15N	8 20 E
Taupo, and L., N.Z.	46	38 41S	176 7 E
Taurage, U.S.S.R.	23	55 17N	22 18 E
Tauranga, N.Z.	46	37 35S	176 11 E
Tauranga Harb., N.Z.	46	37 30S	176 5 E
Taureau, Lac, Canada	62	46 50N	73 40W
Taurianova, Italy	20	38 22N	16 1 E
Taurus, Mts., Turkey	30	37 0N	33 0 E
Táuste, Spain	17	41 58N	1 18W
Tavani, Canada	60	62 10N	93 30W
Tavannes, Switzerland	15	47 13N	7 13 E
Tavas, Turkey	30	37 35N	29 8 E
Tavda, U.S.S.R.	26	58 7N	65 8 E
Tavda R., U.S.S.R.	24	59 30N	63 0 E
Taveta, Kenya	53	3 20S	37 40 E
Tavira, Portugal	17	37 8N	7 40W

	MAP		
Tavolzhanka, U.S.S.R.	25	51 40N	42 56 E
Tavong, Burma	33	14 7N	98 18 E
Tavoy, I., Burma	33	13 0N	98 20 E
Taw R., England	10	50 58N	3 58W
Tawang, India	33	27 37N	91 50 E
Tawas City, U.S.A.	68	44 18N	83 28W
Tawau, Sabah	35	4 12N	117 58 E
Taweisha, Sudan	51	12 20N	26 30 E
Tawitawi I., Philippines	35	5 10N	120 0 E
Tay, Firth of, Scotland	10	56 25N	3 8W
Tay L., Scotland	10	56 30N	4 10W
Tay R., Scotland	10	56 37N	3 58W
Taya Wan (Bias Bay), China	39	22 30N	114 45 E
Tayabamba, Peru	78	8 15S	77 10W
Tayen, China	39	30 10N	115 0 E
Taylor, U.S.A.	71	30 30N	97 30W
Taylor, Arizona, U.S.A.	73	34 58N	110 7W
Taylor, Neb., U.S.A.	70	41 50N	99 25W
Taylor Mt., U.S.A.	73	35 30N	107 34W
Taylorville, U.S.A.	68	39 32N	89 20W
Tayma, Saudi Arabia	30	27 35N	38 30 E
Taytay, Philippines	35	10 45N	119 30 E
Tayu, China	39	25 38N	114 9 E
Tayulehsze, China	37	29 8N	95 9 E
Tayung, China	39	29 2N	110 21 E
Taz R., U.S.S.R.	26	65 40N	82 0 E
Taza, Morocco	50	34 15N	4 0W
Tazin L., Canada	65	59 40N	109 0W
Tazin R., Canada	65	59 50N	109 0W
Tbilisi (Tiflis), U.S.S.R.	24	41 50N	44 50 E
Tchad, Rep., Africa	51	12 0N	17 0 E
Tchad L., Chad	51	13 30N	14 0 E
Tchaourou, Dahomey	52	9 0N	2 23 E
Tchetti, Dahomey	52	7 38N	1 40 E
Tchibanga, Gabon	54	2 45S	11 12 E
Tchimazazaré, Niger	52	14 45N	7 30 E
Tchingaraguen, Niger	52	15 30N	7 55 E
Tchpao (Tienpao), China	39	23 29N	106 43 E
Tczew, Poland	16	54 8N	18 50 E
Te Anau, tn. & L., N.Z.	47	45 15S	167 45 E
Te Araroa, N.Z.	46	37 39S	178 25 E
To Aroha, N.Z.	46	37 32S	175 44 E
Te Awamutu, N.Z.	46	38 1S	175 20 E
Te Kaha, N.Z.	46	37 44S	177 44 E
Te Karaka, N.Z.	46	38 26S	177 53 E
Te Kauwhata, N.Z.	46	37 25S	175 9 E
Te Kinga, N.Z.	47	42 38S	171 30 E
Te Kopuru, N.Z.	46	36 2S	173 56 E
Te Kuiti, N.Z.	46	38 20S	175 11 E
Te Puke, N.Z.	46	37 46S	176 22 E
Te Teko, N.Z.	46	38 2S	176 46 E
Te Waewae B., N.Z.	47	46 13S	167 33 E
Teague, U.S.A.	71	31 37N	96 23W
Teague, L., W. Austral.	44	25 45S	120 45 E
Teano Ra., W. Australia	44	24 20S	118 0 E
Teapa, Mexico	74	17 35N	92 56W
Tebessa, Algeria	50	35 28N	8 9 E
Tebicuary, R., Paraguay	77	26 30S	57 30W
Techiman, Ghana	50	7 35N	1 58W
Tecuci, Rumania	21	45 51N	27 27 E
Tecumseh, U.S.A.	68	42 4N	83 57W
Tees, R., England	10	54 36N	1 58W
Tefé, Brazil	78	3 25S	64 50W
Tefé, R., Brazil	78	4 50S	65 55W
Tegal, Indonesia	34	6 52S	109 8 E
Tegelen, Netherlands	13	51 20N	6 9 E
Teggiano, Italy	20	40 24N	15 32 E
Tegina, Nigeria	52	10 5N	6 11 E
Tego, Queensland	43	28 50S	146 45 E
Tegucigalpa, Honduras	75	14 10N	87 0W
Teguema, Niger	52	15 35N	9 10 E
Tehachapi, U.S.A.	73	35 9N	18 29W
Tehachapi Mts., U.S.A.	73	34 58N	119 0W
Teharu, Indonesia	35	3 20S	129 30 E
Tehchow, China	38	37 29N	116 15 E
Tehping, China	38	37 29N	116 58 E
Tehran, Persia	31	35 44N	51 30 E
Tehtsin (Aluntze), China	37	28 28N	98 48 E
Tehuacan, Mexico	74	18 20N	97 30W
Tehuantepec, Mexico	74	16 10N	95 19W
Tehuantepec, isth., Mex.	74	17 0N	94 30W
Tehuantepec, G. of, Mex	74	16 0N	95 0W
Teifi R., Wales	10	52 4N	4 14W
Teikovo, U.S.S.R.	25	56 55N	40 30 E
Teita Hills, Kenya	53	3 20S	38 20 E
Tejo R., Portugal	17	39 15N	8 35W
Tekamah, U.S.A.	70	41 46N	96 9W
Tekapo, New Zealand	47	43 59S	170 31 E
Takapo L., N.Z.	47	43 53S	170 33 E
Tekeli, U.S.S.R.	26	44 50N	79 0 E
Tekkali, India	33	18 35N	85 30 E
Tekoa, U.S.A.	72	42 16N	117 3W
Tel Adashim, Israel	29	32 39N	35 17 E
Tel Aviv-Jaffa (Yafo), Israel	29	32 4N	34 45 E
Tel Hanan, Israel	29	32 47N	35 3 E
Tel Malhata, Israel	29	31 13N	35 2 E
Tela, Honduras	74	15 40N	87 28W
Telanaipura, Sumatra	34	1 40S	103 35 E
Telap R., New Zealand	47	44 19S	170 15 E
Telavi, U.S.S.R.	24	42 0N	45 30 E
Telegraph Cr., Canada	64	58 0N	131 10W
Telemark, co., Norway	23	59 30N	8 30 E
Teles Pires (São Manuel), R., Brazil	79	9 0S	57 0W
Telescope Pk., U.S.A.	73	36 6N	117 10W
Telisze, China	38	39 50N	122 0 E
Telkwa, Canada	64	54 40N	127 0W
Tell, Jordan	29	32 12N	35 12 E
Tell Asur Mt., Jordan	29	31 59N	35 17 E
Tell City, U.S.A.	68	38 0N	86 44W
Tell Mond, Israel	29	32 15N	34 56 E
Teller, Alaska	59	65 12N	167 0W
Tellicherry, India	32	11 45N	75 30 E
Telluride, U.S.A.	73	37 58N	107 50W
Telok Anson, Malaya	34	4 0N	101 0 E
Telok Betong, Indon.	34	5 20S	105 15 E
Telom R., Malaya	34	4 20N	101 46 E
Telsen, Argentina	77	42 30S	66 50W
Teluk Pelabuhan Ratu, Java, Indonesia	34	7 0S	106 28 E
Telukdalam, Indonesia	34	0 45N	97 50 E
Tema, Ghana	52	5 41N	0 0
Temagani L., Canada	62	47 0N	80 10W
Temax, Mexico	74	21 10N	88 50W
Tembe, Congo	53	0 27S	28 25 E
Tembeling R., Malaya	34	4 20N	102 23 E
Temecula, U.S.A.	73	33 30N	117 7W
Temerloh, Malaya	35	3 27N	102 25 E
Temir, U.S.S.R.	24	49 0N	57 10 E
Temir Tau, U.S.S.R.	26	53 10N	87 20 E
Temiscamie, R., Can.	62–63	51 30N	72 0W
Temiskaming, Canada	62	46 44N	79 5W
Temora, N.S.W.	42	34 30S	147 30 E
Temosachic, Mexico	74	28 58N	107 50W
Tempe, U.S.A.	73	33 28N	112 0W
Tempio Pausania, Italy	20	40 53N	9 6 E
Temple, U.S.A.	71	31 5N	97 28W
Temple B., Queensland	42	12 15S	143 3 E
Templemore, Ireland	11	52 48N	7 50W
Temuco, Chile	77	38 50S	72 50W
Temuka, N.Z.	47	44 14S	171 17 E
Tenabo, Mexico	74	20 2N	90 12W
Tenacingo, Mexico	74	18 58N	99 33W
Tenakee, Alaska	59	57 50N	135 15W
Tenakee Springs, Alaska	64	57 50N	135 15W
Tenali, India	32	16 15N	80 35 E
Tenango, Mexico	74	19 0N	99 40W
Tenasserim, div., Burma	34	14 0N	98 30 E
Tendo, Japan	36	38 25N	140 25 E
Tendou, Dahomey	52	9 5N	2 38 E
Tendre, Mt., Switz.	15	46 36N	6 19 E
Tenerife, I., Canary Is.	50	28 20N	16 40W
Tengchowfu. *See* Penglai	38		
Tengchung, China	37	24 58N	98 30 E
Tenggarong, Indonesia	35	0 25S	116 55 E
Tenggol I., Malaya	34	4 48N	103 39 E
Tenghsien, Honan, China	38	32 40N	112 5 E
Tenghsien, Shantung, China	38	35 12N	117 2 E
Tengiz L., U.S.S.R.	26	50 30N	69 0 E
Tengkow, China	38	39 45N	106 40 E
Tengyun, China	39	23 20N	111 0 E
Tenille, U.S.A.	69	32 58N	82 50W
Tenindewa, W. Austral.	44	28 30S	115 20 E
Tenkasi, India	32	8 55N	77 20 E
Tenke, Congo	56	11 24S	26 53 E
Tenke, Congo	56	10 30S	26 10 E
Tenkodogo, Volta	50	12 0N	0 10W
Tennessee, st., U.S.A.	71	35 20N	89 0W
Tennessee R., U.S.A.	69	35 10N	85 10W
Tenosique, Mexico	74	17 30N	91 24W
Tenryu R., Japan	36	35 30N	137 45 E
Tent L., Canada	65	62 25N	108 0W
Tenterfield, N.S.W.	43	29 0S	152 0 E
Teófilo-Otoni, Brazil	79	17 50S	41 30W
Teotepec, Mexico	74	16 5N	97 2W
Tepa, Ghana	52	6 57N	20 3W
Tepalcatepec, R., Mex.	74	18 50N	102 30W
Tepelenë, Albania	21	40 19N	20 1 E
Tepic, Mexico	74	21 30N	105 0W
Teplice, Czechoslovakia	16	50 39N	13 43 E
Tepoca, C., Mexico	74	30 16N	112 50W
Tequila, Mexico	74	20 50N	103 50W
Ter Apel, Netherlands	13	52 53N	7 5 E
Tera, Niger	50	14 0N	0 57 E
Teramo, Italy	20	42 40N	13 40 E
Terang, Victoria	43	38 3S	142 59 E
Terawhiti, C., N.Z.	46	41 16S	174 38 E
Tercan, Turkey	30	39 50N	40 30 E
Tercero, R., Argentina	77	33 0S	64 0W
Terek R., U.S.S.R.	25	43 45N	45 20 E
Terempa I., China Sea	34	3 5N	106 20 E
Teresa Cristina, Brazil	77	24 45S	51 3W
Teresina, Brazil	77	24 40S	51 10W
Teresina, Piaui, Brazil	79	52 0S	42 45W
Terewah L., N.S.W.	43	29 42S	147 20 E
Terhazza, Mali	50	23 45N	4 55W
Terkezi, Chad	51	18 27N	21 40 E
Terlizzi, Italy	20	41 8N	16 32 E
Termez, U.S.S.R.	26	37 0N	67 15 E
Termini, Italy	20	37 59N	13 51 E
Termoli, Italy	20	42 0N	15 0 E
Ternate I., Indonesia	35	0 45N	127 25 E
Terneuzen, Netherlands	13	51 20N	3 50 E
Terni, Italy	20	42 34N	12 38 E
Ternopol, U.S.S.R.	24	49 30N	25 40 E
Terrace, Canada	64	54 30N	128 35W
Terracina, Italy	20	41 17N	13 12 E
Terralba, Italy	20	39 42N	8 38 E
Terre Haute, U.S.A.	68	39 26N	87 20W
Terrebonne B., U.S.A.	71	29 12N	90 30W
Terrell, U.S.A.	71	32 44N	96 19W
Terrenceville, Canada	63	47 41N	54 44W
Terry, U.S.A.	70	46 46N	105 17W
Terschelling I., Neth.	13	53 25N	5 20 E
Teruel, Spain	17	40 22N	1 8W
Tervola, Finland	22	66 6N	24 59 E
Tesachirire, Mozam.	56	15 30S	33 10 E
Tešanj, Yugoslavia	21	44 38N	17 59 E
Teshi, R., Nigeria	52	9 15N	4 20 E
Teshio R., Japan	36	44 45N	142 0 E
Teslin, Canada	64	60 20N	132 45W
Teslin L., Canada	64	60 10N	132 40W
Teslin R., Canada	64	60 20N	133 0W
Teso, dist., Uganda	53	1 40N	33 30 E
Tess R., Mongolia	37	50 40N	93 20 E
Tessalit, Mali	50	20 20N	0 55 E
Tessaoua, Niger	52	13 47N	7 56 E
Tessier, Canada	65	51 48N	107 26W
Test R., England	10	51 7N	1 30W
Tetachuck L., Canada	64	53 15N	126 0W
Tetas, Pta., Chile	77	23 50S	70 45W
Tete, Mozambique	56	16 10S	33 30 E
Teterev R., U.S.S.R.	25	50 30N	29 30 E
Teteven, Bulgaria	21	42 58N	24 17 E
Tetlin, Alaska	59	63 5N	142 32W
Teton R., U.S.A.	72	47 58N	111 10W
Tetovo, Yugoslavia	21	42 1N	21 2 E
Tetuan, Morocco	50	35 30N	5 25W
Teturi, Congo	53	0 1N	28 55 E
Tetyukhe, U.S.S.R.	27	44 45N	135 40 E
Teuco R., Argentina	77	25 30S	60 25W
Teufen, Switz.	15	47 23N	9 28 E
Teulon, Canada	65	50 30N	97 20W
Teun I., Indonesia	35	7 10S	129 10 E
Teutoburger Forest, Ger.	14	52 10N	8 0 E
Texada I., Canada	64	49 38N	64 45W
Texarkana, Ark., U.S.A.	71	33 55N	94 1W
Texarkana, Tex., U.S.A.	71	33 55N	94 2W
Texas, Queensland	43	28 49S	151 15 E
Texas, st., U.S.A.	71	31 40N	98 30W
Texas City, U.S.A.	71	29 20N	95 15W
Texel I., Netherlands	13	53 5N	4 50 E
Texhoma, U.S.A.	71	36 30N	101 45W
Texline, U.S.A.	71	36 24N	103 0W
Texoma L., U.S.A.	71	34 0N	96 37W
Teyateyaneng, Lesotho	57	29 9S	27 45 E
Teyr Zebna, Lebanon	29	33 14N	35 23 E
Teziutlán, Mexico	74	19 50N	97 30W
Tezpur, India	33	26 40N	92 45 E
Tha-anne R., Canada	65	60 25N	96 0W
Thaba N'chu, O.F.S.	57	29 10S	26 52 E
Thaba Putsua Mt.,	57	29 45S	27 58 E
Thabana Ntlenyana Mt., Lesotho	57	29 12S	29 22 E
Thabazimbi, Transvaal	57	24 40S	26 4 E
Thaddeus I., U.S.S.R.	28	75 0N	144 0 E
Thadiq, Si. Arabia	30	25 16N	45 59 E
Thai Nguyen, N. Viet Nam	39	21 35N	105 46 E
Thakhek, Laos	34	17 25N	104 45 E
Thal, Pakistan	32	33 28N	70 33 E
Thal Desert, Pakistan	32	31 0N	71 30 E
Thala Pass, Burma	33	28 25N	97 23 E
Thale Luang L., Siam	34	7 35N	100 15 E
Thallon, Queensland	43	28 30S	148 57 E
Thalwil, Switz.	15	47 17N	8 33 E
Thames, New Zealand	46	37 7S	175 34 E
Thames, Firth of, N.Z.	46	37 0S	175 25 E
Thames R., Canada	62	42 25N	82 15W
Thames R., England	10	51 24N	0 24W
Thana, India	32	19 12N	72 59 E
Thangool, Queensland	42	24 36S	150 42 E
Thanhhoa, N. Viet Nam	37	19 35N	105 40 E
Thanjavur (Tanjore), India	32	10 45N	79 17 E
Thann, France	12	47 48N	7 5 E
Thano Bula Khan, Pak.	32	25 20N	67 45 E
Thar (Great Indian) Desert, India	32	28 35N	72 0 E
Tharad, India	32	24 30N	71 30 E
Tharawaddy, Burma	33	17 30N	96 0 E
Thargomindah, Queens.	43	27 58S	143 46 E
Thásos, Greece	21	40 50N	24 50 E
Thásos I., Greece	21	40 40N	24 40 E
Thatcher, Ariz., U.S.A.	73	32 51N	109 44W
Thatcher, Colo., U.S.A.	71	37 32N	104 9W
Thatòn, Burma	34	17 0N	97 39 E
Thaungdut, Burma	33	24 30N	94 40 E
Thayar, U.S.A.	71	36 32N	91 33N
Thayetmyo, Burma	33	19 20N	95 18 E
Thazi, Burma	33	21 0N	96 5 E
The Dalles, U.S.A.	72	45 30N	121 10W
The Flatts, Bermuda	75		Inset
The Great Divide, Australia	41	25 0S	148 0 E
The Great Wall, China	38	38 0N	109 0 E
The Grenadines, Is., West Indies	75	12 30N	61 0W
The Hague, Neth.	13	52 5N	4 19 E
The Naze, England	10	51 53N	1 17 E
The Pas, Canada	65	53 45N	101 15W
The Peak, N.S.W.	43	31 31S	145 51 E
The Range, Rhodesia	56	19 0S	31 2 E
The Rock, N.S.W.	43	35 15S	147 2 E
The Sound, Den.–Swed.	23	56 0N	12 42 E
The Thumbs, mt., N.Z.	47	43 35S	170 40 E
The Wash, England	10	53 0N	0 25 E
The Weald, England	10	51 10N	0 1N
Thedford, U.S.A.	70	42 0N	100 30W
Thekulthili L., Canada	65	61 3N	110 0W
Thelon R., Canada	65	62 35N	104 3W
Themaïkos Kólpos. *See* Thessaloniki, G. of Greece	21		
Theodore, Queensland	42	24 55S	150 3 E
Theodore Roosevelt R., Braz.	78	9 30S	60 30W
Theresa R., Queensland	42	36 23N	25 20 E
Thermopolis, U.S.A.	72	43 39N	108 15W
Thermopylæ, P. of Greece	21	38 48N	22 45 E
Thessalon, Canada	62	46 20N	83 30W
Thessaloniki (Salonika), Greece	21	40 38N	23 0 E
Thessaloniki, G. of (Thermaïkos Kólpos), Greece	21	40 15N	22 45 E
Thessaly, div., Greece	21	39 30N	22 0 E
Thetford, England	10	52 25N	0 44 E
Thetford Mines, Can.	63	46 8N	71 18W
Theunissen, O.F.S.	57	28 26S	26 43 E
Thevenard, S. Australia	45	32 10S	133 44 E
Thibodaux, U.S.A.	71	29 49N	90 47W
Thicket Portage, Canada	65	55 25N	97 45W
Thief R. Falls, U.S.A.	70	48 15N	96 0W
Thielsen Mt., U.S.A.	72	43 10N	122 0W
Thiene, Italy	20	45 42N	11 29 E
Thiers, France	12	45 52N	3 33 E
Thiès, Senegal	50	14 50N	16 51W
Thika, Kenya	53	1 0S	37 8 E
Thionville, France	12	49 20N	6 10 E
Thira, Greece	21	36 23N	25 27 E
Thirasia I., Greece	21	36 26N	25 21 E
Third Cataract, Nile, Sudan	51	19 50N	30 20 E
Thivai, Greece	21	38 19N	23 19 E
Thiviers, France	12	45 25N	0 54 E
Thjorsa R., Iceland	22	64 25N	19 0W
Thlewiaza R., Canada	65	60 20N	98 0W
Thoa, R., Canada	65	61 0N	107 50W
Thomas, U.S.A.	71	35 45N	98 47W
Thomaston, U.S.A.	69	41 40N	73 8W
Thomastown, Ireland	11	52 32N	7 10W
Thomasville, Alabama, U.S.A.	69	31 55N	87 42W
Thomasville, Fla., U.S.A.	69	30 50N	84 0W
Thomasville, N.C., U.S.A.	69	35 5N	80 4W
Thompson R., Queens.	42	23 50S	143 20 E
Thompson R., U.S.A.	70	40 20N	93 40W
Thompson Falls, U.S.A.	72	47 5N	115 20W
Thompson Landing, Canada	65	62 45N	111 7W
Thompson Sd., N.Z.	47	45 9S	166 59 E
Thompsons, U.S.A.	73	38 58N	109 41W
Thomson's Falls, Kenya	53	0 2N	36 27 E
Thonon, France	12	46 22N	6 29 E
Thori, Nepal	33	27 20N	84 40 E
Thornborough, Queens.	42	16 54S	145 2 E
Thornbury, N.Z.	47	46 17S	168 9 E
Thouin, C., Australia	44	20 19S	118 13 E
Thowa, seasonal r., Kenya	53	1 25S	39 45 E
Thrace, div., Greece	21	41 10N	26 0 E
Three Forks, U.S.A.	72	45 54N	111 32W
Three Hills, Canada	64	51 43N	113 15W
Three Hummock I., Tasmania	43	40 30S	144 59 E
Three Lakes, U.S.A.	70	45 46N	89 11W
Three Points, C., Ghana	52	4 43N	6 57 E
Three Rivers, U.S.A.	71	28 30N	98 10W
Throssell, L., Australia	45	27 31S	121 45 E
Throssell Ra., Australia	44	22 0S	121 45 E
Thubun Lakes, Canada	65	61 30N	111 0W
Thuin, Belgium	13	50 20N	4 17 E
Thule, Greenland	58	76 0N	68 0W
Thun, Switzerland	15	46 45N	7 38 E
Thunder B., U.S.A.	68	45 0N	83 22W
Thunder River, Canada	64	52 13N	119 20W
Thuner See L., Switz.	15	46 42N	7 42W
Thunkar, Bhutan	33	27 55N	91 0 E
Thur R., Switzerland	15	47 32N	9 10 E
Thurgau, can., Switz.	15	47 34N	9 10 E
Thuringian Forest, Ger.	14	50 35N	11 0 E
Thurles, Ireland	11	52 40N	7 49W
Thurles, Queensland	43	26 28S	146 51 E
Thursday I., Queensland	42	10 30S	142 3 E
Thurso, Canada	62	45 36N	75 15W
Thurso, Scotland	10	58 34N	3 31W
Thusis, Switzerland	15	46 42N	9 26 E
Thutade L., Canada	64	57 0N	127 0W
Thylungra, Queensland	43	26 3S	143 26 E
Thysville, Congo	54	5 12S	14 53 E
Tian Head, Canada	64	53 55N	133 50W
Tiaret, Algeria	50	35 28N	1 12 E
Tiaro, Queensland	43	25 44S	152 32 E
Tiassale, Ivory Coast	50	5 58N	4 57W
Tiati, Mt., Kenya	53	1 16N	35 55 E
Tibati, Cameroon	52	6 22N	12 30 E
Tiber R., Italy	20	42 30N	12 20 E
Tiberias, L., Israel	29	32 47N	35 32 E
Tiberias, Israel	29	32 49N	35 36 E
Tibesti, dist., Sahara	51	20 55N	17 0 E
Tibet, Auto. Reg., China	37	32 30N	86 0 E

	MAP		
Tibnin, Lebanon	29	33 12N	35 24 E
Tiboku, Falls, Guyana	78	5 50N	59 30W
Tibooburra, N.S.W.	43	29 23S	142 0 E
Tiburon I., Mexico	74	29 0N	112 30W
Tichit, Mauritania	50	18 35N	9 20W
Ticino, can., Switzerland	15	46 20N	8 45 E
Ticino R., Italy	20	45 23N	8 47 E
Ticino R., Switzerland	15	46 20N	8 56 E
Tickhill, England	75	3 26N	1 6W
Ticonderoga, U.S.A.	68	43 50N	73 28W
Ticul, Mexico	74	20 20N	89 50W
Tiddim, Burma	33	23 20N	93 45 E
Tidjikja, Mauritania	50	18 4S	11 35W
Tiefencastel, Switz.	15	46 41N	9 34 E
Tiel, Netherlands	13	51 54N	5 5 E
Tien Shan, U.S.S.R.–China	37	43 0N	86 0 E
Tienchen, China	38	40 27N	114 9 E
Tienen, Belgium	13	50 48N	4 57 E
Tienho, China	39	24 54N	108 47 E
Tienkiang, China	39	30 25N	107 30 E
Tienpao. *See* Tchpao, China	39		
Tienshui, China	38	34 30N	105 34 E
Tientsin, China	38	39 10N	117 0 E
Tientu, China	39	18 13N	109 29 E
Tientung, China	39	23 45N	107 1 E
Tierp, Sweden	23	60 20N	17 30 E
Tierra Amarilla, U.S.A.	73	36 42N	106 33W
Tierra del Fuego, S. America	77	54 0S	69 0W
Tietar, Spain	17	39 55N	5 50W
Tieté R., Brazil	79	21 10S	49 50W
Tiffin, U.S.A.	68	41 5N	83 10W
Tifrah, Israel	29	31 19N	34 42 E
Tifton, U.S.A.	69	31 28N	83 32W
Tigara (Point Hope), Alaska	59	68 20N	166 50W
Tighnabruaich, Scotland	10	55 55N	5 13W
Tignish, Canada	63	46 58N	63 57W
Tigre R., Peru	78	3 30S	74 35W
Tigre R, Venezuela	78	9 10N	63 30W
Tigris, R., Iraq	30	37 0N	42 30 E
Tigyaing, Burma	33	23 45N	96 10 E
Tihama, plain, S. Arabia	30	23 0N	39 0 E
Tijoca, Brazil	79	1 0S	46 35W
Tijuana, Mexico	74	32 30N	117 10W
Tikamgarh, India	32	24 44N	78 57 E
Tikan, New Guinea	42	5 57S	149 7 E
Tikang, China	39	31 13N	118 0 E
Tikau, Nigeria	52	11 27N	11 5 E
Tikhoretsk, U.S.S.R.	25	45 56N	40 5 E
Tikhvin, U S.S.R.	25	59 35N	33 30 E
Tiko, W. Cameroon	52	4 4N	9 20 E
Tikrit, Iraq	30	34 35N	43 37 E
Tiksi, U.S.S.R.	27	71 50N	129 0 E
Tikwiri, Rhodesia	56	18 38S	32 10 E
Tilamuta, Indonesia	35	0 40N	122 15 E
Tilburg, Netherlands	13	51 31N	5 6 E
Tilbury, Canada	62	42 17N	84 33W
Tilbury, England	10	51 27N	0 24 E
Tilden, U.S.A.	70	42 3N	97 46W
Tilder, U.S.A.	71	28 29N	98 30W
Tilhar, India	32	28 0N	79 45 E
Tillabéry, Niger	50	14 15N	1 40 E
Tillamook, U.S.A.	72	45 27N	123 56W
Tilley, Canada	64	50 28N	111 38W
Tillsonburg, Canada	62	42 53N	80 55W
Tilo, Greece	21	36 29N	27 21 E
Tilos, I., Greece	21	37 27N	27 27 E
Timaru, New Zealand	47	44 23S	171 14 E
Timashevskaya, U.S.S.R.	25	45 35N	39 0 E
Timau, Kenya	53	0 5N	37 15 E
Timber Lake, U.S.A.	70	45 29N	101 2W
Timbedra, Mauritania	50	16 10N	8 15W
Timboon, Victoria	43	38 31S	143 0 E
Timboulaga, Niger	52	15 55N	7 50 E
Timbuktu. *See* Tombouctou	50		
Timinoun, Algeria	50	29 30N	0 20 E
Timiris C., Mauritania	50	19 20N	16 30W
Timisoara, Rumania	21	45 43N	21 15 E
Timmins, Canada	62	48 28N	81 25W
Timok R., Yugoslavia	21	44 10N	22 40 E
Timoleague, Ireland	11	51 40N	8 51W
Timon, Brazil	79	5 8S	42 52W
Timor I., E. Indies	35	9 0S	125 0 E
Timor Sea, Indonesia	35	10 0S	127 0 E
Timote, Argentina	77	35 20S	62 20W
Timotes, Venezuela	75	9 0N	70 47W
Tin R., Jordan	29	32 16N	35 5 E
Tina R., Cape Province	57	31 5S	28 55 E
Tinacca Point, Philippines	35	5 30N	125 25 E
Tinahely, Ireland	11	52 48N	6 30W
Tindivunam, India	32	12 15N	79 35 E
Tindouf, Algeria	50	27 40N	8 15W
Tineo, Spain	17	43 21N	6 27W
Tingha, N.S.W.	43	29 57S	151 9 E
Tinghai, China	39	30 0N	122 10 E
Tinghsien, China	38	38 30N	115 0 E
Tingo Mariá, Peru	78	9 10S	76 0W
Tingnan, China	39	24 40N	114 59 E
Tingpien, China	38	37 31N	107 5 E
Tingsi, China	38	36 30N	104 31 E
TingtseWan Bay, China	38	36 33N	120 49 E

	MAP		
Tinguéré, Cameroon	52	7 30N	12 40 E
Tingvoll, Norway	23	62 56N	8 13 E
Tinjoub, Algeria	50	29 20N	5 40W
Tinnoset, Norway	23	59 45N	9 3 E
Tinogasta, Argentina	77	28 0S	67 40W
Tinombo, Indonesia	35	0 30N	120 20 E
Tinos, & I., Greece	21	37 33N	25 8 E
Tinpahar, India	33	25 0N	87 45 E
Tinpak, China	39	21 40N	111 15 E
Tinquiririca, mt., Chile	77	34 47S	70 22W
Tinto, W. Cameroon	52	5 33N	9 35 E
Tinui, New Zealand	46	40 52S	176 5 E
Tinwald, New Zealand	47	43 55S	171 43 E
Tionaga, Canada	62	48 0N	82 0W
Tiou Mousgou, Niger	52	15 8N	7 35 E
Tipongpani, India	33	27 20N	95 55 E
Tipperary, Ireland	11	52 28N	8 10W
Tipperary, co., Ireland	11	52 37N	7 55W
Tipton, Calif., U.S.A.	73	36 3N	119 19W
Tipton, Ind., U.S.A.	68	40 18N	86 0W
Tipton, Iowa, U.S.A.	70	41 46N	91 13W
Tiptonville, U.S.A.	71	36 22N	89 30W
Tira, Israel	29	32 14N	34 56 E
Tirān, Iran	31	32 52N	50 59 E
Tiranë (Stalin), Albania	21	41 18N	19 49 E
Tiraspol, U.S.S.R.	25	46 55N	29 35 E
Tirat Karmal, Israel	29	32 46N	34 58 E
Tirat Tsevi, Israel	29	32 26N	35 31 E
Tirat Yehuda, Israel	29	32 1N	34 56 E
Tirau, New Zealand	46	37 59S	175 50 E
Tire, Turkey	30	38 5N	27 50 E
Tirebolu, Turkey	30	40 58N	38 45 E
Tiree, I., Scotland	10	56 31N	6 49W
Tirich Mir, Mt., Pak.	32	36 15N	72 0 E
Tirgu Jiu, Rumania	21	45 0N	23 16 E
Tirgu Mures, Rumania	21	46 31N	24 38 E
Tirnava, Rumania	21	44 10N	23 31 E
Tirnăveni, Rumania	21	46 20N	24 20 E
Tirnavos, Greece	21	39 45N	22 18 E
Tirodi, India	32	21 40N	79 40 E
Tiros, Brazil	79	19 0S	46 0W
Tirso R., Italy	20	40 33N	9 12 E
Tirua Point, N.Z.	46	38 23S	174 40 E
Tiruchirappali (Tiruchchirappalli), India	32	10 30N	76 18 E
Tirunelveli, India	32	8 45N	77 45 E
Tirupati, India	32	13 45N	79 30 E
Tiruppattur, India	32	12 30N	78 30 E
Tiruppur, India	32	11 12N	77 22 E
Tiruvalur, India	32	10 45N	79 40 E
Tiruvannamalai, India	32	12 10N	79 12 E
Tisdale, Canada	65	52 50N	104 0W
Tishomingo, U.S.A.	71	34 8N	96 35W
Tisted, Denmark	23	56 58N	8 40 E
Tisza R., Hungary	16	47 38N	20 44 E
Tiszafüred, Hungary	16	47 38N	20 50 E
Tit Ary, U.S.S.R.	27	71 50N	126 50 E
Titahi, B., N.Z.	46	41 6S	174 51 E
Titicaca, L , Bolivia–Peru	78	15 30S	69 30W
Tititira Pt., N.Z.	47	43 39S	169 23 E
Titiwa, Nigeria	52	12 0N	12 40 E
Titlagarh, India	33	20 15N	83 5 E
Titograd (Podgorica), Yugoslavia	21	42 30N	19 19 E
Tito Veles, Yugoslavia	21	41 46N	21 47 E
Titovo Užice, Yugoslavia	21	43 55N	19 50 E
Titu, Kenya	53	2 51N	38 55 E
Titule, Zaire	54	3 14N	25 32 E
Titusville, Fla., U.S.A.	69	28 37N	80 50W
Titusville, Pa., U.S.A.	68	41 35N	79 39W
Tiva R., Kenya	53	2 25S	38 30 E
Tiverton, England	10	50 54N	3 30W
Tivoli, Italy	20	41 58N	12 45 E
Tiwi, 'Oman	31	22 45N	59 12 E
Tizi-Ouzou, Algeria	50	36 45N	4 0 E
Tizimin, Mexico	74	21 0N	88 1W
Tjalong, Indonesia	34	4 30N	95 43 E
Tjareme Mt., Indonesia	34	6 55S	108 27 E
Tjeggelvas, L., Sweden	22	66 30N	18 0 E
Tjiamis, Indonesia	34	7 18S	108 21 E
Tjibatu, Indonesia	34	7 8S	107 59 E
Tjidjulang, Indonesia	34	7 42S	108 27 E
Tjilatjap, Indonesia	34	7 43S	109 0 E
Tjipatudja, Indonesia	34	7 42S	108 2 E
Tjirebon, Indonesia	34	6 45S	108 32 E
Tjolotjo, Rhodesia	56	19 46S	27 46 E
Tjornes, C., Iceland	22	66 13N	17 7W
Tlala Mabeli, Botswana	56	11 18S	26 22 E
Tlaxcala, st., Mexico	74	19 30N	98 20W
Tlaxiaco, Mexico	74	17 10N	97 40W
Tlemcen, Algeria	50	34 52N	1 20W
Tlhapin, Botswana	57	23 19S	21 47 E
Tmassah, Libya	51	56 10N	15 40 E
Toad R., Canada	64	28 40N	125 0W
Toay, Argentina	77	36 50S	64 30W
Toba, Japan	36	34 30N	136 45 E
Toba L., Indonesia	34	2 40N	98 50 E
Toba Kakar Hills, Pak.	32	31 30N	69 0 E
Toba Tek Singh, Pak.	32	30 55N	72 25 E
Tobago I., W. Indies	75	11 10N	60 30W
Tobercurry, Ireland	11	54 3N	8 43W
Tobermory, Canada	62	45 12N	81 40W
Tobermory, Scotland	10	56 37N	6 4W
Tobi I., Carolines	35	2 55N	131 50 E
Tobin, L., W. Australia	45	21 46S	125 40 E

	MAP		
Toboali, Indonesia	35	3 0S	106 25 E
Tobre, Dahomey	52	10 8N	2 0 E
Tobruk (Tubruq), Libya	51	32 3N	23 50 E
Tocal, Queensland	42	23 52S	143 32 E
Tocantinópolis, Brazil	79	6 20S	47 25W
Tocantins R., Brazil	78	14 30S	49 0W
Toccoa, U.S.A.	69	34 34N	83 21W
Tochigi, Japan	36	36 30N	139 40 E
Tochigi, pref., Japan	36	36 45N	139 45 E
Toco, Chile	77	22 0S	69 40W
Tocopilla, Chile	77	22 5S	70 10W
Tocumwal, N.S.W.	43	35 45S	145 31 E
Tocuyo R., Venezuela	75	11 0N	69 20W
Todenyang, Kenya	53	4 32N	35 55 E
Todgarh, India	32	25 45N	73 55 E
Todi, Italy	20	42 47N	12 24 E
Todjo, Indonesia	35	1 20S	121 15 E
Todos, G. de, Brazil	79	13 5S	38 45W
Todos Santos, Mexico	74	23 30N	110 20W
Todro, Zaire	53	3 10N	30 12 E
Toetoes B., New Zealand	47	46 42S	168 41 E
Tofield, Canada	64	53 25N	112 50W
Toggenburg, Switzerland	15	47 20N	9 4 E
Toghral Ombo, China	37	35 10N	81 40 E
Togian Is., Indonesia	35	0 20S	121 50 E
Togliatti, U.S.S.R.	25	53 30N	49 15 E
Togo I., Japan	36	36 15N	133 25 E
Togo, rep., W. Africa	52	6 15N	1 35 E
Toijala, Finland	23	61 15N	23 50 E
Toinya, Sudan	54	6 17N	29 46 E
Tokaanu, New Zealand	46	38 58S	175 46 E
Tokaj, Hungary	16	48 8N	21 27 E
Tokanui, New Zealand	47	46 34S	168 56 E
Tokar, Sudan	51	18 19N	37 47 E
Tokara Str., Japan	36	30 0N	130 0 E
Tokarahi, New Zealand	47	44 56S	170 39 E
Tokaroa, New Zealand	46	38 20S	175 50 E
Tokat, Turkey	30	40 22N	36 35 E
Tokelau Is., Pacific Oc.	5	9 0S	172 0W
Tokomaru B., N.Z.	46	38 8S	178 22 E
Tokombere, Nigeria	52	11 8N	3 20 E
Tokushima, Japan	36	34 0N	134 45 E
Tokushima, pref., Japan	36	35 50N	134 30 E
Tokuyama, Japan	36	34 8N	131 57 E
Tokyo, Japan	36	35 45N	139 45 E
Tokyo, pref., Japan	36	35 40N	139 30 E
Tolaga Bay, N.Z.	46	38 21S	178 20 E
Tolbukhin, Bulgaria	21	43 37N	27 49 E
Toledo, Spain	17	39 50N	4 2W
Toledo, Ohio, U.S.A.	68	41 40N	83 40W
Toledo, Oreg., U.S.A.	72	44 38N	123 59W
Toledo, Wash., U.S.A.	72	46 27N	122 55W
Toledo, Montes de, mts., Spain	17	39 32N	4 30W
Tolfino, Canada	64	49 6N	125 54W
Tolga, Algeria	50	34 46N	5 22 E
Tolga, Queensland	42	17 16S	145 30 E
Tolima, Mt., Colombia	78	4 50N	75 15W
Tolitoli, Indonesia	35	1 5N	120 50 E
Tolleson, U.S.A.	73	33 30N	112 19W
Tolo, Zaire	54	2 56S	18 51 E
Tolo, G. of, Indonesia	35	2 20S	122 10 E
Tolokiwa, I., N. Guin.	42	5 18S	147 40 E
Tolon, Ghana	52	9 26N	1 3W
Tolosa, Spain	17	43 8N	2 5W
Tolsta Hd., Scotland	10	58 20N	6 10W
Toluca, Mexico	74	19 20N	99 50W
Tolun, China	38	42 22N	116 30 E
Tom Burke, Transvaal	56	23 5S	28 0 E
Tomah, U.S.A.	70	43 58N	90 30W
Tomahawk, U.S.A.	68	45 25N	89 40W
Tomakomai, Japan	36	42 42N	141 35 E
Tomamai, Japan	36	44 15N	141 40 E
Tomaszów Mazowiecki, Poland	16	51 30N	19 57 E
Tombador, Sa. do, Brazil	79	11 0S	41 0W
Tombel, Cameroon	52	4 42N	9 37 E
Tombigbee R., U.S.A.	71	33 45N	88 35W
Tombouctou (Timbuktu), Mali	50	16 50N	3 0W
Tombstone, U.S.A.	73	31 40N	110 0W
Tomelloso, Spain	17	39 10N	3 2W
Tomini, Indonesia	35	0 30N	120 30 E
Tomini, G. of, Indonesia	35	0 10S	122 0 E
Tommot, U.S.S.R.	27	58 50N	126 20 E
Tomo R., Colombia	78	5 30N	69 40W
Tomorrit, Mt., Albania	21	40 38N	20 0 E
Tomsk, U.S.S.R.	26	56 30N	85 12 E
Tonalá, Mexico	74	16 8N	93 41W
Tonalea, U.S.A.	73	36 22N	110 56W
Tonantins, Brazil	78	2 45S	67 45W
Tonasket, U.S.A.	72	48 42N	119 28W
Tonawanda, U.S.A.	68	43 10N	78 49W
Tone R., Japan	36	36 15N	139 30 E
Tonga Is., Pacific Oc.	5	21 0S	175 0W
Tongaat, Natal	57	29 33S	31 9 E
Tongariro, mt., N.Z.	46	39 7S	175 50 E
Tonghing, China	39	21 34N	108 0 E
Tongo, Chile	77	30 16S	71 31W
Tongsa Dzong, Bhutan	33	27 35N	90 35 E
Tongue R., U.S.A.	66	48 50N	106 0W
Tonj, Sudan	54	7 20N	28 44 E
Tonj R., Sudan	54	5 50N	20 20 E
Tonk, India	32	26 6N	75 54 E
Tonkawa, U.S.A.	71	36 41N	97 35W
Tonkin, G. of, S. China Sea	34	20 0N	108 0 E

	MAP		
Tonlé Sap, L., Cambodia	34	13 0N	104 0 E
Tonneins, France	12	44 42N	0 20 E
Tonnerre, France	12	47 50N	4 0 E
Tönning, Germany	14	54 18N	8 57 E
Tonopah, U.S.A.	73	38 0N	117 16W
Tönsberg, Norway	23	59 19N	11 3 E
Tonto Basin, U.S.A.	73	33 58N	111 19W
Toodyay, W. Australia	44	31 37S	116 35 E
Tooele, U.S.A.	72	40 30N	112 15W
Toogoolawah, Queens.	43	27 5S	152 21 E
Tooloombah, Queens.	42	22 43S	149 32 E
Toompine, Queensland	43	27 12S	144 20 E
Toowong, Queensland	43	27 30S	152 58 E
Toowoomba, Queens.	43	27 32S	151 56 E
Top L., U.S.S.R.	22	65 35N	32 0 E
Topeka, U.S.A.	70	39 0N	95 45W
Topki, U.S.S.R.	26	55 25N	85 20 E
Topley, Canada	64	54 32N	126 5W
Toplita, Rumania	21	46 55N	25 27 E
Topock, U.S.A.	73	34 45N	114 30W
Topolobampo, Mexico	74	25 40N	109 10W
Toppenish, U.S.A.	72	46 23N	120 19W
Tor B., W. Australia	40	35 8S	117 33 E
Torbat-e-Heydariyeh, Iran	31	35 22N	59 8 E
Torbat-e Jam, Iran	31	35 16N	60 34 E
Torbay, Canada	63	47 40N	52 42W
Tordesillas, Spain	17	41 30N	5 0W
Töre, Sweden	22	65 55N	22 40 E
Torei, U.S.S.R.	27	50 45N	104 40 E
Torfajokull, mts., Ice.	22	63 55N	19 15W
Torgau, Germany	14	51 32N	13 0 E
Torhout, Belgium	13	51 5N	3 7 E
Torin, Mexico	74	27 33N	110 5W
Torino (Turin), Italy	20	45 4N	7 40 E
Torit, Sudan	53	4 20N	32 55 E
Tormes R., Spain	17	41 7N	6 0W
Tornado Mt., Canada	64	49 55N	114 40W
Torne Träsk, L., Nor.	22	68 20N	19 25 E
Torneå. *See* Tornio, Fin.	22		
Tornio (Torneä), Finland	22	65 57N	24 12 E
Tornio, R., Finland	22	67 0N	23 50 E
Tornquist, Argentina	77	38 0S	62 15W
Toro, Niger	52	15 0N	5 32 E
Toro, King. of, Uganda	53	0 30N	30 40 E
Toro, Spain	17	41 33N	5 24W
Toro, Cerro del, mt., Chile	77	29 0S	69 50W
Toro, Pta., Pan. Can. Zone	74	9 22N	79 57W
Toronaíos, G. of, Greece	21	40 5N	23 40 E
Toronto, Canada	62	43 39N	79 20W
Toronto, N.S.W.	43	33 0S	151 30 E
Toronto, U.S.A.	68	40 27N	80 38W
Toronto L., Mexico	74	27 40N	105 30W
Toropets, U.S.S.R.	25	56 30N	31 40 E
Tororo, Uganda	53	0 43N	34 13 E
Torquay, Canada	65	49 9N	103 31W
Torquay, England	10	50 27N	3 31W
Torre Annunziata, Italy	20	40 45N	14 26 E
Torre de Moncorve, Portugal	17	41 12N	7 8W
Torredonjimeno, Spain	17	37 48N	4 2W
Torrelaguna, Spain	17	40 50N	3 38W
Torrelavega, Spain	17	43 20N	4 5W
Torremolinos, Spain	17	36 40N	4 30W
Torrens, L., S. Australia	43	31 0S	137 45 E
Torrens R., Queensland	42	22 10S	145 8 E
Torrente, Spain	17	39 26N	0 28W
Torreon, Mexico	74	25 33N	103 25W
Tôrres, Brazil	77	29 20S	49 43W
Torres, Mexico	74	28 50N	110 50W
Torres Novas, Portugal	17	39 27N	8 33W
Torres Strait, Queens.	42	10 20S	142 0 E
Torres Vedras, Port.	17	39 5N	9 15W
Torrevieja, Spain	17	37 59N	0 42W
Torrey, U.S.A.	73	38 18N	111 24W
Torricelli Mts. N. Guin.	42	3 20S	142 15 E
Torridon L., Scotland	10	57 35N	5 50W
Torrington, Conn., U.S.A.	68	41 50N	73 9W
Torrington, Wyoming., U.S.A.	70	42 5N	104 9W
Torrowangee, N.S.W.	43	31 22S	141 30 E
Torsby, Sweden	23	60 7N	13 0 E
Tortola, I., Virgin Is.	75	18 28N	64 40W
Tortona, Italy	20	44 53N	8 54 E
Tortosa C., Spain	17	40 41N	0 52 E
Tortue, I. de la, Haiti Republic.	75	20 5N	72 57W
Tortuga I., Haiti Rep.	75	20 10N	72 40W
Tortuga I., Venezuela	78	10 58N	65 20W
Torud, Iran	31	35 25N	55 0 E
Torugart Pass, China	65	40 35N	75 0 E
Toruń, Poland	16	53 0N	18 39 E
Tory I., Ireland	11	55 17N	8 12W
Torzhok, U.S.S.R.	25	57 5N	34 55 E
Tosa B., Japan	36	33 15N	133 30 E
Töss, Switz.	15	47 30N	8 43 E
Tostado, Argentina	77	29 15S	61 50W
Tosya, Turkey	30	41 0N	34 0 E
Totana, Spain	17	37 45N	1 30W
Toteng, Botswana	56	20 20S	23 0 E
Totma, U.S.S.R.	24	60 0N	42 40 E
Toto, Nigeria	52	8 25N	7 4 E
Totonicapan, Guat.	74	14 50N	91 20W
Tottenham, N.S.W.	43	32 15S	147 15 E

Place	Map	Lat.	Long.
Tottori, Japan	36	35 30N	134 15E
Touba, Guinea	50	8 15N	7 40W
Toubkal, Djebel, mt., Morocco	50	31 0N	7 30W
Tougan, Volta	50	13 20N	3 5W
Touggourt, Algeria	50	33 10N	6 0E
Tougué, Guinea	50	11 25N	11 50W
Toul, France	12	48 40N	5 53E
Toulnustouc R., Canada	63	50 30N	60 8W
Toulon, France	12	43 10N	5 55E
Toulouse, France	12	43 37N	1 28E
Toungo, Nigeria	52	8 20N	12 3E
Toungoo, Burma	33	19 0N	96 30E
Touraine, prov., France	12	47 20N	0 30E
Tourane, Viet Nam. *See* Da Nang	34		
Tourcoing, France	12	50 42N	3 10E
Tournai, Belgium	13	50 35N	3 25E
Tournon, France	12	45 5N	4 50E
Tournus, France	12	46 35N	4 54E
Tours, France	12	47 22N	0 40E
Touws River, Cape Prov.	57	33 20S	20 0E
Towada L., Japan	36	40 30N	141 0E
Towanda, U.S.A.	68	41 46N	76 30W
Tower, U.S.A.	70	47 50N	92 15W
Toweranna, Australia	44	20 57S	117 50E
Towner, U.S.A.	70	48 25N	100 27W
Townsend, U.S.A.	72	46 21N	111 32W
Townshend C., Queens.	42	22 15S	150 31E
Townshend I., Queens.	42	22 16S	150 31E
Townsville, Queensland	42	19 15S	146 45E
Townsville Div., Queens.	42	20 26S	146 41E
Towshan, China	39	22 5N	112 50E
Towson, U.S.A.	68	39 26N	76 37W
Towyn, Wales	10	52 37N	4 8W
Toyah, U.S.A.	71	31 17N	103 17W
Toyahvale, U.S.A.	71	30 55N	103 45W
Toyama, Japan	36	36 40N	137 15E
Toyama, pref., Japan	36	36 45N	137 30E
Toyama B., Japan	36	37 0N	137 30E
Toyohashi, Japan	36	34 45N	137 25E
Toyooka, Tottori, Japan	36	35 46N	134 58E
Tozeur, Tunisia	50	34 1N	8 10E
Trabzon, Turkey	30	41 0N	39 45E
Tracadie, Canada	63	47 30N	64 55W
Tracy, Calif., U.S.A.	73	37 45N	121 25W
Tracy, Minn., U.S.A.	70	44 11N	95 33W
Tradom, China	37	29 40N	84 20E
Trafalgar, C., Spain	17	36 10N	6 2W
Traiguen, Chile	77	38 10S	72 50W
Trail, Canada	64	49 5N	117 40W
Trainor, L., Canada	64	60 23N	120 18W
Trajan's Gate, Bulg.	21	42 20N	23 57E
Trajan's Wall, Rumania	21	44 12N	28 30E
Tralee, Ireland	11	52 16N	9 42W
Tralee B., Ireland	11	52 17N	9 55W
Tramelan, Switz.	15	47 13N	7 7E
Tramore, Ireland	11	52 10N	7 10W
Tranås, Sweden	23	58 3N	15 0E
Trancas, Argentina	77	26 10S	65 20W
Trang, China	34	7 33N	99 38E
Trangan I., Indonesia	35	6 40S	134 20E
Trangie, N.S.W.	43	32 4S	148 0E
Trani, Italy	20	41 17N	16 24E
Transcona, Canada	65	49 50N	97 0W
Transkei, Bantu Area, Rep. of S. Africa	57	32 15S	28 15E
Transvaal, prov., Rep. of S. Africa	57	25 0S	29 0E
Transylvania, dist., Rumania	21	46 19N	25 0E
Transylvanian Alps, Rumania	21	45 30N	25 0E
Trapani, Italy	20	38 1N	12 30E
Trapper Pk., U.S.A.	72	46 0N	114 28W
Traralgon, Victoria	43	38 6S	146 31E
Traryd, Sweden	23	56 35N	13 45E
Tras os Montes e Alto Douro, prov., Port.	17	41 30N	7 30E
Trasimento L., Italy	20	43 10N	12 5E
Travellers L., N.S.W.	43	33 17S	141 59E
Travemünde, Germany	14	53 58N	10 52E
Travers, Mt., N.Z.	47	42 1S	172 45E
Traverse City, U.S.A.	68	44 45N	85 39W
Travnik, Yugoslavia	21	44 17N	17 39E
Trayning, W. Australia	44	31 8S	117 42E
Traynor, Canada	65	52 20N	103 32W
Trébbia R., Italy	20	44 52N	9 30E
Třebíč, Czechoslovakia	16	49 17N	15 50E
Trebinje, Yugoslavia	21	42 44N	18 22E
Třeboň, Czechoslovakia	16	48 59N	14 48E
Treherne, Canada	65	49 39N	98 41W
Treinta y Tres, Urug.	77	33 10S	54 50W
Trekalano Mine, Queensland	42	21 30S	139 55E
Trelawney, Rhodesia	56	17 30S	30 17E
Trelew, Argentina	77	43 10S	65 20W
Trelleborg, Sweden	23	55 20N	13 5E
Tremedal, Brazil	79	15 15S	42 40W
Trementina, U.S.A.	71	35 28N	104 30W
Tremiti Is., Italy	20	42 8N	15 30E
Tremonton, U.S.A.	72	41 45N	112 13W
Tremp, Spain	17	42 10N	0 52E
Trenary, U.S.A.	68	46 10N	87 0W
Trenche R., Canada	62	48 10N	73 0W
Trenčín, Czechoslovakia	16	48 52N	18 4E
Trengganu, st., Malaya	34	4 55N	103 0E
Trenque Lauquen, Arg.	77	36 0S	62 45W
Trent, R., England	10	53 33N	0 44W
Trentino-Alto Adige, reg., Italy	20	46 5N	11 0E
Trento, Italy	20	46 5N	11 8E
Trenton, Canada	62	44 10N	77 40W
Trenton, Mo., U.S.A.	70	40 4N	93 34W
Trenton, Nebr., U.S.A.	70	40 12N	101 2W
Trenton, N.J., U.S.A.	68	40 15N	74 41W
Trenton, Tenn., U.S.A.	68	35 58N	88 55W
Trepassey, Canada	63	46 43N	53 25W
Tres Arboles, Uruguay	77	32 15S	56 30W
Tres Arroyos, Argentina	77	38 20S	60 20W
Tres Coraçoes, Brazil	79	21 30S	45 30W
Tres Esquinas, Col.	78	0 45N	75 8W
Três Lagôas, Brazil	79	20 50S	51 50W
Tres Montes Pen., Chile	77	47 0S	75 35W
Tres Puentes, Chile	77	27 50S	70 15W
Tres Puntas C., Arg.	77	47 0S	66 0W
Tres Rios, Brazil	79	22 20S	43 30W
Treskavika Planina, Y.slav.	21	43 40N	18 20E
Treuer, Ra., N. Terr.	45	22 14S	131 10E
Tréveray, France	35	48 38N	5 24E
Treviglio, Italy	20	45 31N	9 35E
Treviso, Italy	20	45 40N	12 15E
Trévoux, France	12	45 57N	4 47E
Triang, Malaya	34	3 13N	102 27E
Tribune, U.S.A.	70	38 0N	101 45W
Trichur, India	32	10 30N	76 18E
Trida, N.S.W.	43	33 2S	144 57E
Trier, Germany	14	49 55N	6 37E
Trieste, Italy	20	45 39N	13 45E
Triglav Mt., Yugoslavia	20	46 30N	13 45E
Trigno R., Italy	20	42 5N	14 50F
Trikkala, Greece	21	39 34N	21 47E
Trim, Ireland	11	53 34N	6 48W
Trincomalee, Sri Lanka	32	8 38N	81 15E
Tring, Canada	63	46 17N	71 0W
Trinidad, Bolivia	78	14 54S	64 50W
Trinidad, Cuba	75	21 40N	80 0W
Trinidad, U.S.A.	71	37 15N	104 30W
Trinidad, I., Arg.	77	39 10S	62 0W
Trinidad I., W. Indies	75	10 30N	61 20W
Trinité, Martinique	75	Inset	
Trinity, U.S.A.	71	31 0N	95 40W
Trinity B., Canada	63	48 0N	53 35W
Trinity Mts., U.S.A.	72	40 10N	118 45W
Trinity R., Texas, U.S.A.	71	32 10N	96 15W
Trinity R., Calif., U.S.A.	72	40 50N	122 50W
Trins, Austria	17	47 4N	11 22E
Trion, U.S.A.	69	34 35N	85 15W
Tripoli (Tarabulus), Libya	51	32 49N	13 15E
Tripoli (Tarabulus), Lebanon	30	34 26N	35 51E
Tripolis, Greece	21	37 31N	22 25E
Tripolitania, reg., Libya	51	30 56N	13 30E
Tripp, U.S.A.	70	43 15N	97 58W
Tripura, st., India	53	24 0N	92 0E
Tristan da Cunha I., Atlantic Oc.	5	37 6S	12 20W
Triste G., Venezuela	75	11 0N	68 0W
Triumpho, Brazil	29	7 0S	50 50W
Trivandrum, India	52	8 31N	77 0E
Trnava, Czechoslovakia	16	48 23N	17 35E
Trochu, Canada	64	51 50N	113 20W
Trodley I., Canada	62	52 20N	79 20W
Troglav, Mt., Y.slav.	20	43 56N	16 36E
Troia, Italy	20	41 22N	15 19E
Trois Pistoles, Canada	63	48 5N	69 10W
Trois Rivières, Canada	62	46 25N	72 40W
Troitsk, R.S.F.S.R., U.S.S.R.	26	54 10N	61 35E
Troitsko-Pechorsk, U.S.S.R.	24	62 40N	56 10E
Trolladyngja, mt., Ice.	22	64 50N	17 27W
Trollhättan, Sweden	23	58 17N	12 20E
Trombetas R, Brazil	79	0 30S	57 35W
Trompsburg, O.F.S.	57	30 2S	25 50E
Troms, prov., Norway	22	69 10N	19 0E
Tromsö, Norway	22	69 40N	19 0E
Tronador, vol., Arg.	77	41 53S	71 0W
Trondheim, Norway	23	63 25N	10 25E
Trondheims Fd., Nor.	23	63 40N	10 45E
Troodos Mt., Cyprus	30	34 58N	32 55E
Tropic, U.S.A.	73	37 40N	112 7W
Trostan Mt., N. Ireland	11	55 4N	6 10W
Troup, U.S.A.	71	32 9N	95 5W
Trout L., N.W. Terr., Canada	64	60 40N	121 40W
Trout L., Ont., Canada	65	51 20N	93 15W
Trout Pk., U.S.A.	72	44 31N	109 28W
Trout R., N.W. Terr., Canada	64	61 0N	120 40W
Trout River, Canada	63	49 29N	58 8W
Trouville, France	12	49 21N	0 5E
Trowutta, Tasmania	43	41 8S	145 1E
Troy, anc. cy., Turkey	30	39 50N	26 14E
Troy, Ala., U.S.A.	69	31 50N	86 0W
Troy, Mont., U.S.A.	72	48 25N	116 3W
Troy, Kan., U.S.A.	70	39 46N	95 4W
Troy, N.Y., U.S.A.	68	42 45N	73 39W
Troy, Ohio, U.S.A.	68	40 0N	84 10W
Troyan, Bulgaria	21	42 57N	24 43E
Troyes, France	12	48 19N	4 3E
Trubchevsk, U.S.S.R.	25	52 33N	33 47E
Trucial 'Oman, st., Arabia	31	24 0N	54 30E
Truckee, U.S.A.	72	39 23N	120 10W
Trujillo, Honduras	78	16 0N	86 0W
Trujillo, Peru	78	8 0S	79 0W
Trujillo, Spain	17	39 28N	5 55W
Trujillo, U.S.A.	71	35 31N	104 45W
Truman, U.S.A.	71	35 40N	90 31W
Trumbull, Mt., U.S.A.	73	36 25N	113 40W
Trundle, N.S.W.	43	32 52S	147 35E
Truro, Canada	63	45 21N	63 14E
Truro, England	10	50 17N	5 2W
Truth or Consequences, U.S.A.	73	33 10N	107 16W
Trutnov, Czechoslovakia	16	50 37N	15 54E
Tryon, U.S.A.	69	35 15N	82 16W
Tsabong, Botswana	57	26 12S	22 12E
Tsaidam Swamp, China	37	37 0N	95 0E
Tsane, Botswana	57	24 5S	21 54E
Tsanghsien, China	38	38 19N	116 54E
Tsangki, China	39	31 45N	106 0E
Tsangpo R., China	37	29 20N	90 0E
Tsaohsien, China	38	34 50N	115 45E
Tsaring Nor, China	37	35 0N	97 0E
Tsau, Botswana	56	20 4S	22 27E
Tsavo, Kenya	53	3 0S	38 28E
Tsavo R., Kenya	53	3 7S	38 15E
Tselinograd, U.S.S.R.	26	51 10N	71 40E
Tsemah, Israel	29	32 43N	35 36E
Tsessebe, Botswana	36	20 43S	27 32E
Tsetserleg, China	37	47 26N	101 22E
Tsha, Zaire	53	2 0N	30 3E
Tshela, Zaire	54	5 4S	13 0E
Tshetsheng, Botswana	56	23 42S	23 10E
Tshibeke, Zaire	53	3 0S	28 40E
Tshibinda, Zaire	53	2 38S	28 37E
Tshikapa, Zaire	54	6 17S	21 0E
Tshindjamba, Zaire	56	10 50S	22 50E
Tshinsenda, Zaire	56	12 15S	28 0E
Tshofa, Zaire	54	5 8S	25 8E
Tshongola, Zaire	56	12 14S	29 47E
Tshuapa R., Zaire	54	1 20S	23 40E
Tshwane, Botswana	56	22 30S	21 38E
Tsian, China	37	41 12N	126 5E
Tsian, China	38	34 42N	105 50E
Tsiaotso, China	38	35 15N	113 30E
Tsienshan, China	39	30 35N	116 30E
Tsigara, Botswana	56	20 18S	25 50E
Tsimlyansk, U.S.S.R.	25	47 45N	42 0E
Tsimo, China	38	36 30N	120 30E
Tsinan, China	38	36 45N	116 55E
Tsingcheng, China	38	37 10N	117 40E
Tsinghai, prov., China	37	36 0N	9 50E
Tsinghai, China	38	38 56N	116 52E
Tsinghwachen, China	38	35 10N	113 0E
Tsinging, China	38	37 59N	114 58E
Tsingkiang, China	39	27 50N	115 38E
Tsingliu, China	39	26 13N	116 50E
Tsinglo, China	38	38 40N	112 0E
Tsingning, China	38	35 25N	105 50E
Tsingshih, China	39	29 30N	111 47E
Tsingshuiho, China	38	40 5N	111 40E
Tsingsi (Kweishun), China	37	23 10N	106 32E
Tsingsien, China	39	26 30N	109 30E
Tsingtao, China	38	36 0N	120 25E
Tsingtung Res., China	38	38 10N	106 30E
Tsingyuan, China	38	36 36N	104 35E
Tsingyun, China	39	23 45N	112 55E
Tsining, China	38	35 30N	116 35E
Tsinling Shan, Mts., China	38	34 0N	107 30E
Tsinyang, China	38	35 7N	112 51E
Tsippori, Israel	29	32 46N	35 16E
Tsitsihar, China	37	47 20N	124 0E
Tsivory, Madagascar	55	24 2S	46 0E
Tsolo, Cape Province	57	31 18S	28 46E
Tsomo, Cape Province	57	32 2S	27 51E
Tsowhsien, China	38	35 25N	117 0E
Tsu, Japan	36	34 45N	136 25E
Tsuchiura, Japan	36	36 12N	140 10E
Tsugaru, Str., Japan	36	41 30N	140 30E
Tsuge, Japan	36	32 15N	130 40E
Tsumeb, S.W. Africa	55	19 12S	17 50E
Tsumis, S.W. Africa	57	23 50S	17 6E
Tsungfa, China	39	23 35N	113 35E
Tsungming Tao, I., China	39	32 0N	122 0E
Tsungsin, China	38	35 5N	107 0E
Tsungso, China	39	22 26N	107 29E
Tsunhwa, China	38	40 15N	117 55E
Tsunyi, China	39	27 40N	107 0E
Tsuruga, Japan	36	35 35N	136 0E
Tsuruoko, Japan	36	38 45N	139 45E
Tsushima, Is., Japan	36	34 30N	129 20E
Tsuyama, Japan	36	35 0N	134 0E
Tsyurupinsk, U.S.S.R.	25	46 42N	32 46E
Tuaheni Point, N.Z.	46	38 42S	178 5E
Tuai, New Zealand	46	38 50S	177 10E
Tuakau, New Zealand	46	37 16S	174 59E
Tual, Indonesia	35	5 30S	132 50E
Tuam, Ireland	11	53 30N	8 50W
Tuamarina, N.Z.	47	41 25S	173 59E
Tuamgraney, Ireland	11	52 54N	8 32W
Tuamotu Arch., Pac. Oc.	5	17 0S	144 0W
Tuan, China	39	24 5N	108 10E
Tuapse, U.S.S.R.	25	44 5N	39 10E
Tuatapere, N.Z.	47	46 7S	167 43E
Tuba City, U.S.A.	73	36 8N	111 16W
Tubac, U.S.A.	73	31 41N	111 4W
Tubani, Botswana	57	24 46S	24 18E
Tubarão, Brazil	77	28 30S	49 0W
Tubas, Jordan	29	32 20N	35 22E
Tubayq, J. at, Jordan	30	29 40N	37 30E
Tubbataha Reefs, Philippines	35	8 55N	120 0E
Tübingen, Germany	14	48 31N	9 4E
Tubo R., Nigeria	52	10 30N	7 10E
Tubuai Is. (Austral Is.)	5	23 30S	150 0W
Tubruq (Tobruk), Libya	51	41 10N	75 15W
Tucabaca, Bolivia	78	18 30S	58 55W
Tucacas, Venezuela	78	10 50N	68 25W
Tuchang, China	39	29 15N	116 15E
Tuchodi R., Canada	64	58 0N	124 30W
Tuchola, Poland	16	53 33N	17 52E
Tuckanarra, W. Austral.	44	27 8S	118 1E
Tucker's Town, Bermuda	75	32 19N	64 43W
Tucson, U.S.A.	73	32 10N	111 0W
Tucumán, Argentina	77	26 50S	65 20W
Tucumari, U.S.A.	71	35 12N	103 45W
Tucupita, Venezuela	78	9 10N	62 0W
Tucurui, Brazil	79	3 45S	49 48W
Tudela, Navarra, Spain	17	42 4N	1 39W
Tudela, Valladolid, Spain	17	41 37N	4 39W
Tudor, Lac, Canada	63	55 50N	65 0W
Tudos Santos B., Mex.	74	32 0N	117 0W
Tuella R., Portugal	17	41 50N	7 10W
Tuen, Queensland	43	28 33S	145 37E
Tufi, Papua	42	9 3S	149 16E
Tugela R., Natal	57	28 44S	31 0E
Tugidak, I., Alaska	59	56 30N	154 40W
Tuguegarao, Philippines	35	17 35N	121 42E
Tugur, U.S.S.R.	27	53 50N	136 45E
Tuhshan, China	39	25 40N	107 30E
Tuitu I., S. China Sea	35	10 55N	114 20E
Tukang Besi Is., Indon.	35	6 0S	124 0E
Tukarak I., Canada	62	56 15N	78 10W
Tukituki R., N.Z.	46	39 45S	176 55E
Tukobo, Ghana	52	5 3N	2 23W
Tukrah, Egypt	51	32 20N	20 10E
Tukuyu, Tanzania	53	9 12S	33 35E
Tula, Hidalgo, Mexico	74	20 0N	99 20W
Tula, Tamaulipas, Mex.	74	23 0N	99 40W
Tula, Nigeria	52	9 57N	11 12E
Tula, U.S.S.R.	25	54 13N	37 32E
Tulak, Afghanistan	31	54 5N	63 40E
Tulan, China	37	36 18N	98 29E
Tulancingo, Mexico	74	20 0N	98 30W
Tulare, U.S.A.	73	36 20N	119 20W
Tulare, L., U.S.A.	73	36 0N	119 15W
Tularosa, U.S.A.	73	33 3N	106 2W
Tulbagh, Cape Province	57	33 16S	19 6E
Tulcan, Ecuador	78	0 50N	77 50W
Tulcea, Rumania	21	45 13N	28 46E
Tulear, Madagascar	55	23 20S	43 45E
Tulemalu L., Canada	65	62 50N	100 0W
Tuli, Rhodesia	56	21 58S	29 13E
Tuli R., Rhodesia	56	21 30S	29 0E
Tulkarm, Jordan	29	32 19N	35 10E
Tulla, Ireland	11	52 53N	8 45W
Tulla, U.S.A.	71	34 31N	101 46W
Tullahoma, U.S.A.	69	35 23N	86 12W
Tullamore, Ireland	11	53 17N	7 30W
Tulle, France	12	45 16N	1 47E
Tullins, France	12	45 18N	5 29E
Tullow, Ireland	11	52 48N	6 45W
Tully, Queensland	42	17 49S	146 0E
Tulmaythah, Egypt	51	32 30N	20 50E
Tulnustuk R., Canada	63	49 50N	68 13W
Tuloma R., U.S.S.R.	22	68 30N	32 0E
Tulsa, U.S.A.	71	36 10N	96 0W
Tulsequah, Canada	64	58 39N	133 35W
Tuluá, Colombia	78	4 20N	76 6W
Tulum, Mexico	74	20 10N	87 40W
Tulun, U.S.S.R.	27	54 40N	100 10E
Tulungagung, Indonesia	34	8 5S	111 54E
Tumaco, Colombia	78	1 50N	78 45W
Tumatumari, Guyana	78	5 20N	58 55W
Tumba L., Zaire	54	0 50S	18 0E
Tumbarumba, N.S.W	43	35 44S	148 0E
Tumbes, Peru	78	3 30S	80 20W
Tumbur, Sudan	53	4 18N	31 37E
Tumbwé, Zaire	56	11 26S	27 19E
Tumby B., S. Australia	45	34 21S	136 8E
Tumen, N. Korea	36	42 56N	129 47E
Tumeremo, Venezuela	78	7 20N	61 30W
Tumkur, India	32	13 18N	77 12E
Tummo, Libya	51	22 30N	14 25E
Tump, Pakistan	32	26 7N	62 16E
Tumpat, Malaya	34	6 11N	102 10E
Tumu, Ghana	52	10 55N	1 59W
Tumucumaque, Serra, Brazil	79	2 30N	55 0W
Tumut, N.S.W.	43	35 16S	148 13E
Tumwater, U.S.A.	72	47 0N	122 58W
Tunapuna, Trinidad	75	10 38N	61 23W
Tunas de Zaza, Cuba	75	21 39N	79 34W
Tunbridge Wells, Eng.	10	51 7N	0 16E
Tuncurry, N.S.W.	43	32 9S	152 29E
Tunduma, Zambia	56	9 20S	32 48E
Tunduru, Tanzania	53	11 0S	37 25E
Tundhza, R., Bulgaria	21	42 0N	26 35E

	MAP		
Tung Ting L., China	39	29 15N	112 30 E
Tunga P., India	33	29 0N	94 14 E
Tungabhadra R., India	32	15 30N	77 0 E
Tungaru, Sudan	51	10 20N	30 50 E
Tungchan, China	38	35 7N	109 0 E
Tungchang. *See* Liaocheng, China	38	36 30N	116 0 E
Tungcheng, China	39	31 5N	117 0 E
Tungchow, China	38	34 48N	109 48 E
Tungjen, China	39	27 40N	109 10 E
Tunkang, China	39	22 29N	120 26 E
Tungkiang, Szechwan, China	39	31 55N	107 30 E
Tungkiang, Heilung Kiang, China	37	47 39N	132 32 E
Tungkiang, Taiwan, China	37	22 20N	120 30 E
Tungkun, China	39	23 0N	113 45 E
Tungkwang, China	38	34 30N	110 10 E
Tungkwanshan, China	39	31 0N	112 45 E
Tunglan, China	39	24 30N	107 0 E
Tungliao, China	38	43 45N	122 15 E
Tungliu, China	39	30 20N	116 56 E
Tunglu, China	39	29 50N	119 35 E
Tungnafellsjökull, mt., Iceland	22	64 40N	18 15W
Tungnahryggsjökull, mt., Iceland	22	65 43N	18 47W
Tungping, China	38	35 50N	116 20 E
Tungsha Tao (Pratas) I., China	39	20 45N	116 43 E
Tungshan, China	39	31 10N	120 30 E
Tungshan I., China	39	23 45N	117 30 E
Tungshek, China	39	18 46N	109 17 E
Tungshen, China	39	39 57N	109 59 E
Tungsten, U.S.A.	72	40 47N	118 14W
Tungtai, China	38	32 56N	120 10 E
Tungtao, China	39	26 15N	109 25 E
Tungtze, China	39	28 0N	106 55 E
Tunguska, Lower, R., U.S.S.R.	27	64 0N	95 0 E
Tunguska, Stony, R., U.S.S.R.	27	61 0N	98 0 E
Tungyang, China	39	29 15N	120 10 E
Tunhwa, China	37	43 24N	128 14 E
Tunhwang, China	37	40 5N	94 45 E
Tuni, India	33	17 22N	82 43 E
Tunica, U.S.A.	71	34 41N	90 27W
Tunis, Tunisia	51	36 42N	10 6 E
Tunisia, King., Africa	50–51	33 30N	9 10 E
Tunja, Colombia	78	5 40N	73 25W
Tunki, China	39	29 55N	118 19 E
Tunliu, China	38	36 15N	112 51 E
Tunnsjöen L., Norway	22	64 45N	13 25 E
Tuntatuliag, Alaska	59	60 20N	162 44W
Tunuyán R., Argentina	77	33 30S	68 0W
Tuolumne, U.S.A.	73	37 59N	120 16W
Tupelo, Miss., U.S.A.	69	34 25N	88 52W
Tupelo, Okla., U.S.A.	67	34 36N	96 26W
Tupinambaranas I., Brazil	78	3 0S	58 0W
Tupiza, Bolivia	78	21 30S	65 40W
Tupper, Canada	68	55 30N	120 1W
Tupper L., U.S.A.	68	44 12N	74 30W
Tupungato, Mt., Arg.	77	33 15S	69 50W
Tuquerres, Colombia	78	1 15N	77 40W
Tur, Jordan	29	31 47N	35 14 E
Tura, India	33	25 30N	90 16 E
Tura, U.S.S.R.	27	64 20N	99 30 E
Tura R., U.S.S.R.	24	58 30N	63 0 E
Turakina, New Zealand	46	40 3S	175 16 E
Turakina, R., N.Z.	46	39 40S	175 32 E
Turakirae, Hd., N.Z.	46	41 26S	174 56 E
Turama, R., Papua	42	7 10S	143 30 E
Tūrān, Iran	31	35 45N	56 45 E
Turayf, Saudi Arabia	30	31 44N	38 28 E
Turbaco, Colombia	78	10 20N	75 23W
Turbat, Pakistan	32	26 0N	63 0 E
Turbi, Kenya	53	2 20N	38 34 E
Turbo, Colombia	78	8 5N	76 50W
Turda, Rumania	21	46 35N	23 48 E
Turek, Poland	16	52 3N	18 30 E
Turfan, China	37	43 6N	89 24 E
Turfan Depression, China	37	43 6N	88 49 E
Tŭrgovishte, Bulgaria	21	43 17N	26 38 E
Turgutlu, Turkey	30	38 30N	27 48 E
Turgwe R., Rhodesia	56	20 15S	31 50 E
Turi, Pta., Brazil	79	1 25S	44 50W
Turia R., Spain	17	39 40N	1 0W
Turiassu, Brazil	79	1 40S	45 19W
Turiessu R., Brazil	79	3 0S	46 30W
Turin, Canada	64	49 59N	112 35W
Turin (Torino), Italy	20	45 3N	7 40 E
Turkestan, U.S.S.R.	26	43 10N	68 10 E
Turkey, Rep., Asia	30	39 0N	36 0 E
Turki, U.S.S.R.	25	52 0N	43 15 E
Turkmenistan, U.S.S.R.	26	39 0N	59 0 E
Turks and Caicos Is., West Indies	75	21 20N	71 20W
Turks I. Passage, West Indies	75	21 30N	71 20W
Turku (Åbo), Finland	23	60 27N	22 14 E
Turkwell R., Kenya	53	3 0N	35 25 E
Turlock, U.S.A.	73	37 31N	120 50W
Turnagain, C., N.Z.	46	40 28S	176 39 E
Turnagain, R., Canada	64	59 0N	128 10W

	MAP		
Turnberry, Canada	65	53 25N	101 45W
Turner, U.S.A.	72	48 55N	108 28W
Turner L., Canada	65	56 20N	108 10W
Turner Valley, Canada	64	50 40N	114 30W
Turnhout, Belgium	13	51 19N	4 57 E
Türnor L., Canada	65	56 35N	108 50W
Tûrnovo, Bulgaria	21	43 5N	25 41 E
Turnu Măgurele, Rum.	21	43 46N	24 56 E
Turnu Severin, Rum.	21	44 39N	22 41 E
Turon, U.S.A.	71	37 47N	98 28W
Turriff, Canada	62	44 57N	77 13W
Turriff, Scotland	10	57 32N	2 28W
Tursi, Italy	20	40 15N	16 27 E
Turtle Hd., I., Queens.	42	10 50S	142 37 E
Turtle Is., Sierra Leone	52	7 40N	13 3W
Turtle L., Canada	65	53 40N	108 35W
Turtle Lake, N.D., U.S.A.	70	47 32N	100 57W
Turtle Lake, Wis., U.S.A.	70	45 19N	92 6W
Turtleford, Canada	65	53 30N	108 50W
Turua, New Zealand	46	37 14S	175 35 E
Turubah, Si. Arabia	30	28 25N	43 12 E
Turukhansk, U.S.S.R.	26	65 50N	87 50 E
Turun ja Porin Lääni, Finland	23	62 10N	22 0 E
Turutka, U.S.S.R.	27	61 10N	114 50 E
Turya, U.S.S.R.	24	62 50N	50 15 E
Tuscaloosa, U.S.A.	69	33 9N	87 31W
Tuscany, reg., Italy	20	43 28N	11 15 E
Tuscarora, U.S.A.	72	41 22N	116 15W
Tuscola, Ill., U.S.A.	68	39 48N	88 20W
Tuscola, Mich., U.S.A.	70	43 20N	83 40W
Tuscola, Texas, U.S.A.	71	32 13N	99 46W
Tuscumbia, U.S.A.	69	38 15N	92 30W
Tushikow, China	38	41 25N	115 55 E
Tuskar Rock, Ireland	11	52 13N	6 11W
Tutayev, U.S.S.R.	25	57 55N	39 30 E
Tuticorin, India	32	8 50N	78 12 E
Tutóia, Brazil	79	2 45S	42 20W
Tutrakan, Bulgaria	21	44 2N	26 40 E
Tutshi L., Canada	64	60 8N	134 50W
Tuttle, U.S.A.	70	47 9N	100 1W
Tuttlingen, Germany	14	47 59N	8 50 E
Tutuko, mt., N.Z.	47	44 35S	168 1 E
Tuva, A.S.S.R., U.S.S.R.	27	52 0N	95 0 E
Tuwaiq, J., Saudi Arabia	30	22 0N	46 0 E
Tuxpan, Mexico	74	20 50N	97 30W
Tuxtla, Gutierrez, Mexico	74	16 50N	93 10W
Tuy, Spain	17	42 3N	8 39W
Tuy, R., Venezuela	78	10 20N	66 30W
Tuya L., Canada	64	59 5N	130 40W
Tuyen Quang, Viet Nam	34	21 48N	105 18 E
Tuymaza, U.S.S.R.	24	54 50N	53 20 E
Tuyun, China	39	26 5N	107 20 E
Tuz Gülu, L., Turkey	30	38 45N	33 30 E
Tūz Khurmatu, Iraq	30	34 52N	44 41 E
Tuzla, Yugoslavia	21	44 34N	18 41 E
Tvedestrand, Norway	23	58 38N	8 58 E
Tveitsund, Norway	23	59 2N	8 31 E
Twante, Burma	33	16 35N	96 0 E
Tweed R., Scotland	10	55 42N	2 10W
Tweed Heads, Queens.	43	28 0S	153 34 E
Tweedsmuir Prov. Park., Can.	64	53 10N	126 20W
Tweeling, O.F.S.	57	27 38S	28 30 E
Twelve Foot Roads, U.S.S.R.	25	44 58N	47 42 E
Twelve Pins, Mts.,Ire.	11	53 31N	9 50W
Twentynine Palms, U.S.A.	73	34 11N	116 4W
Twillingate, Canada	63	49 42S	54 45W
Twin Bridges, U.S.A.	72	45 32N	112 18W
Twin Falls, U.S.A.	72	42 30N	114 30W
Twin Peaks, U.S.A.	72	44 40N	114 30W
Twin Valley, U.S.A.	70	47 20N	96 15W
Twisp, U.S.A.	72	48 23N	120 10W
Two Harbors, U.S.A.	70	47 10N	91 39W
Two Hills, Canada	64	53 43N	111 52W
Two Rivers, U.S.A.	68	44 10N	87 35W
Two Thumb Ra., N.Z.	47	43 45S	170 44 E
Twofold B., N.S.W.	43	37 8S	149 59 E
Tyler, Minn., U.S.A.	70	44 16N	96 13W
Tyler, Texas, U.S.A.	71	32 20N	95 15W
Tyndall, Mt., N.Z.	47	43 16S	170 41 E
Tyne, R., England	10	54 58N	1 56W
Tynemouth, England	10	55 1N	1 27W
Tynset, Norway	23	62 17N	10 47 E
Tyre (Sur), Lebanon	30	33 15N	35 14 E
Tyri Fd., Norway	23	60 2N	10 3 E
Tyrol, prov., Austria	14	46 50N	11 20 E
Tyrone, co., N. Ireland	11	54 40N	7 15W
Tyrrell L., Victoria	43	35 20S	142 55 E
Tyrrhenian Sea, Europe	20	40 0N	12 30 E
Tys Fd., Norway	22	68 5N	16 28 E
Tyub Karagan C., U.S.S.R.	24	44 40N	50 10 E
Tyumen, U.S.S.R.	26	57 0N	65 18 E
Tzaneen, Transvaal	56	23 47S	30 9 E
Tzechung, China	39	29 47N	104 51 E
Tzeki, China	39	47 46N	117 3 E
Tzekung, China	39	29 25N	104 30 E
Tzekwei, China	39	31 0N	110 46 E
Tzepo, China	38	36 30N	117 45 E

	MAP		
Tzeyang, Shantung, China	38	35 39N	116 38 E
Tzeyang, Szechwan, China	38	30 6N	104 36 E

U

	MAP		
Uanda, Queensland	42	21 38S	144 51 E
Uatuma, R., Brazil	78	2 30S	58 0W
Uaupés, Brazil	78	0 0	67 20W
Uaupés R., Brazil	78	0 10N	68 20W
Uba, Brazil	79	21 8S	42 59W
Uba, Nigeria	52	10 29N	13 9 E
Ubangi, prov., Zaire	54	4 0N	19 30 E
Ubauro, Pakistan	32	28 15N	69 45 E
Ubayyid, Wadi al, Iraq	30	32 10N	42 00 E
Ubeda, Spain	17	38 3N	3 23W
Uberaba, Brazil	79	19 0S	48 20W
Uberlandia, Brazil	79	19 50S	48 0W
Ubiaja, Nigeria	52	6 41N	6 22 E
Ubiña Pk., mt. Spain,	17	43 3N	6 12W
Ubombo, Natal	57	27 31S	32 4 E
Ubon, Thailand	34	15 15N	104 50 E
Ubort R., U.S.S.R.	25	51 45N	28 30 E
Ubsa Nor, Mongolia	37	50 20N	92 30 E
Ubu an Na'm, Saudi Arabia	30	25 17N	38 54 E
Ubundi, Zaire	54	0 18S	25 28 E
Ucayali, R., Peru	78	6 0S	75 0W
Uchigo, Japan	36	41 33N	137 0 E
Uchinya, U.S.S.R.	26	60 5N	65 15 E
Uchivra B., Japan	36	42 30N	141 0 E
Uchur R., U.S.S.R.	27	58 0N	131 0 E
Ucluelet, Canada	64	48 57N	125 32W
Udaipur, India	32	24 36N	73 44 E
Udaipur Garhi, Nepal	33	27 0N	86 35 E
Udamalpet, India	32	10 35N	77 15 E
Uddajaur L., Sweden	22	65 55N	17 50 E
Uddevalla, Sweden	23	58 21N	11 55 E
Udgir, India	32	18 25N	77 5 E
Udhampur, Kashmir	32	33 0N	75 5 E
Udi, Nigeria	52	6 23N	7 21 E
Udine, Italy	20	46 5N	13 10 E
Udipi, India	32	13 25N	74 42 E
Udmurt, A.S.S.R., U.S.S.R.	26	57 30N	52 30 E
Udon Thani, Thailand	34	17 29N	102 46 E
Udubo, Nigeria	52	11 52N	10 35 E
Udzungwa Ra., Tan.	53	8 20S	35 50 E
Uebonti, Indonesia	35	0 55S	121 30 E
Ueda, Japan	36	36 30N	138 10 E
Uele, prov., Zaire	54	3 0N	26 0 E
Uele R., Zaire	54	3 35N	25 0 E
Uelen, U.S.S.R.	27	66 4N	170 0W
Uelzen, Germany	14	53 0N	10 33 E
Uere R., Zaire	54	3 50N	24 40 E
Ufa, U.S.S.R.	24	54 45N	55 55 E
Ufa R., U.S.S.R.	24	56 30N	58 10 E
Ugab R., S.W. Africa	55	20 55S	14 30 E
Ugalla R., Tanzania	53	6 0S	32 0 E
Ugamas, S.W. Africa	57	28 0S	19 41 E
Uganda, st., E. Africa	53	2 0N	32 0 E
Ugep, Nigeria	52	5 57N	8 2 E
Ughelli, Nigeria	52	5 27N	5 55 E
Ugie, Cape Province	57	31 10S	28 13 E
Ugijar, Spain	17	36 58N	3 7W
Uglegorsk, U.S.S.R.	27	49 10N	142 5 E
Uglich, U.S.S.R.	25	57 33N	38 13 E
Uglovka, U.S.S.R.	25	58 16N	33 22 E
Ugra R., U.S.S.R.	25	54 45N	35 30 E
Ugulyat, U.S.S.R.	27	64 50N	120 20 E
Uhi, Nigeria	52	5 30N	5 50 E
Uhiro, Tanzania	53	2 26S	34 0 E
Uhrichsville, U.S.A.	68	40 23N	81 22W
Uianari, Brazil	78	1 0N	64 55W
Uigé, Angola	54	7 45S	15 10 E
Uiju, Korea	36	40 15N	124 35 E
Uil, U.S.S.R.	24	49 20N	54 40 E
Uinta Mts., U.S.A.	72	40 50N	110 30W
Uis, S.W. Africa	57	21 8S	14 49 E
Uitenhage, Cape Prov.	57	33 40S	25 28 E
Uithuizen, Netherlands	13	53 24N	6 41 E
Ujiji, Tanzania	53	4 50S	29 45 E
Ujjain, India	32	23 9N	75 43 E
Ujiyamada, Japan	36	34 30N	136 47 E
Ujpest, Hungary	16	47 36N	19 8 E
Uka, U.S.S.R.	27	57 50N	162 0 E
Ukara I., Tanzania	53	1 44S	33 0 E
Ukehe, Nigeria	52	6 40N	7 24 E
Ukerewe, Is., Tanzania	53	2 9S	32 52 E
Ukhrul, India	33	25 10N	94 25 E
Ukiah, U.S.A.	72	39 0N	123 16W
Ukraine S.S.R., U.S.S.R.	24	48 0N	35 0 E
Ukwi, Botswana	57	23 22S	20 30 E
Ulak, I., Aleutian Is.	59	51 54N	178 59W
Ulan Bator, Mongolia	37	48 0N	107 0 E
Ulan Gom, Mongolia	37	49 59N	92 0 E
Ulan Nur, Mongolia	38	44 30N	104 0 E
Ulan Ude, U.S.S.R.	27	52 0N	107 30 E
Ulanhot, China	38	46 3N	122 0 E
Ulaya, Tanzania	53	7 8S	36 53 E
Ulaya, Tanzania	53	4 23S	33 25 E
Ulcinj, Yugoslavia	21	41 58N	19 10 E
Ulco, Cape Province	57	28 21S	24 15 E
Uleåborg. *See* Oulu.	23		
Ulee Lheue, Indonesia	34	5 30N	95 20 E

	MAP		
Ulgi-Hid, Mongolia	38	43 40N	108 7 E
Ulladulla, N.S.W.	43	35 21S	150 29 E
Ullapool, Scotland	10	57 54N	5 10W
Ullung Do, Korea	36	37 30N	130 30 E
Ulm, Germany	14	48 23N	10 0 E
Ulmarra, N.S.W.	43	29 31S	153 6 E
Ulricehamn, Sweden	23	56 47N	13 26 E
Ulster, prov., Ireland	11	54 45N	6 30W
Ultima, Victoria	43	35 22S	143 18 E
Uluguru Mts., Tanzania	53	7 0S	37 30 E
Ulutau, U.S.S.R.	26	48 50N	67 5 E
Ulva I., Scotland	10	56 30N	6 12W
Ulverstone, Australia	42	41 11S	146 11 E
Ulyanovsk, U.S.S.R.	25	54 25N	48 25 E
Ulyasutay, Mong.	37	47 50N	96 50 E
Ulysses, U.S.A.	71	37 37N	101 27W
Umaisha, Nigeria	52	8 2N	7 11 E
Umala, Bolivia	78	17 25S	68 5W
Uman, U.S.S.R.	25	48 40N	30 12 E
Umaria, India	32	23 35N	80 45 E
Umarkot, Pakistan	32	25 15N	69 40 E
Umatilla, U.S.A.	72	45 58N	119 37W
Umboi, I., Terr. of New Guinea	42	5 42S	148 0 E
Umbrella Mts., N.Z.	47	45 35S	169 5 E
Umbria, U.S.A.	66	41 18N	114 0W
Umbria, reg., Italy	20	45 53N	12 30 E
Umei R., Sweden	22	64 45N	18 30 E
Umeå, Sweden	23	63 45N	20 20 E
Umfolozi R., Natal	57	28 25S	32 15 E
Umfuli R., Rhodesia	56	17 45S	29 45 E
Umgusa, Rhodesia	56	19 25S	27 51 E
Umgwasema, Rhodesia	56	15 50S	29 0 E
Umiat, Alaska	59	69 20N	151 58W
Umkomaas, Natal	57	30 13S	30 48 E
Umkomaas, R., Natal	57	30 3S	30 30 E
Umm al Qaiwain, Trucial Oman	31	25 30N	55 34 E
Umm az Zamul, Saudi Arabia	31	22 35N	55 18 E
Umm Bel, Sudan	51	13 35N	28 0 E
Umm Birka, Mt., Saudi Arabia	30	27 28N	36 58 E
Umm Dam, Sudan	51	13 50N	31 0 E
Umm el Fahm, Israel	29	32 31N	35 9 E
Umm Harb, Si. Arabia	30	26 38N	36 42 E
Umm Lajj, Saudi Arabia	30	25 0N	37 23 E
Umm Ruwaba, Sudan	51	12 50N	31 10 E
Umm Said, Qatar	31	25 0N	51 40 E
Ummadau, Nigeria	52	12 37N	7 18 E
Ummaz Zamul, S.W. Asia	66	22 30N	55 20 E
Umnak, I., Aleutian Is.	59	53 20N	168 20W
Umniati R., Rhodesia	56	8 0S	29 0 E
Umpqua R., U.S.A.	72	43 30N	123 0W
Umtali, Rhodesia	56	18 58S	32 38 E
Umtata, Cape Province	57	31 36S	28 49 E
Umuahia-Ibeku, Nigeria	52	5 31N	7 26 E
Umvukwe Ra., Rhodesia	56	17 20S	30 40 E
Umvuma, Rhodesia	56	19 16S	30 30 E
Umzimkulu, R., Natal	57	30 45S	30 30 E
Umzimvubu R., Cape Province	57	31 30S	29 30 E
Umzingwane R., Rhodesia	56	21 30S	29 40 E
Umzinto, Natal	57	30 22S	30 40 E
Una, Mt., New Zealand	47	42 13S	172 36 E
Una R., Yugoslavia	20	44 50N	16 15 E
Unagaidya, U.S.S.R.	27	59 10N	142 0 E
União, Brazil	79	4 42S	42 58W
Unalakleet, Alaska	59	63 58N	160 45W
Unalaska, I., Aleutian Is.	59	53 40N	166 40W
Unango, Mozambique	56	12 51S	35 23 E
Unare R., Venezuela	75	9 0N	65 0W
Uncia, Bolivia	78	18 25S	66 40W
Uncocua, Angola	55	16 30S	13 40 E
Uncompahgre Pk., U.S.	73	38 5N	107 3W
Underberg, Natal	57	29 48S	29 32 E
Unecha, U.S.S.R.	25	52 50N	32 37 E
Ungarie, N.S.W.	43	33 38S	146 56 E
Ungava Bay, Canada	61	59 30N	67 0W
Unggi, Korea	36	42 20N	130 25 E
União do Vitoria, Brazil	77	26 5S	51 0W
Unimak I., Alaska	59	54 30N	164 0W
Unini, R., Brazil	78	1 50S	63 0W
Union, Argentina	77	35 5S	65 52W
Union, Mo., U.S.A.	70	38 26N	90 59W
Union, Miss., U.S.A.	71	32 33N	89 4W
Union, N.Y., U.S.A.	69	42 5N	76 5W
Union, S.C., U.S.A.	67	34 40N	81 35W
Union City, Pa., U.S.A.	68	41 54N	79 53W
Union City, Tenn., U.S.A.	69	36 25N	89 0W
Union Gap, U.S.A.	72	46 32N	120 30W
Union of Soviet Socialist Republics	26–27	35 0N to 70 0N	20 0 E to 180 0 E
Union Springs, U.S.A.	69	32 9N	85 44W
Uniondale, Cape Prov.	57	33 39S	23 7 E
Uniontown, U.S.A.	68	39 54N	79 45W
Unionville, Mich., U.S.A.	69	43 39N	83 30W
Unionville, Mo., U.S.A.	70	40 28N	92 59W
United Kasaienne, prov., Zaire	54	6 0S	21 20 E
United Kingdom	10	50 0N to 61 0N	8 0W to 2 0 E

	MAP		
United States of America, rep.	66-67	25 0N to 49 0N	67 0W to 125 0W
Unity, Canada	65	52 30N	109 5W
Unnao, India	32	26 35N	80 30E
Uno, Canada	65	50 17N	101 3W
Unst., I., Scotland	10	60 50N	0 55W
Unter Walden, Switz.	15	46 50N	8 15E
Unuk R., Alaska	64	56 10N	131 0W
Unye, Turkey	30	41 5N	37 15E
Unzha, U.S.S.R.	24	57 40N	44 8E
Unzha R., U.S.S.R.	25	58 0N	43 40E
Upata, Venezuela	75	8 2N	62 25W
Upemba, L., Congo	55	10 40S	26 56E
Upernavik, Greenland	58	72 45N	56 0W
Upington, Cape Prov.	57	28 25S	21 15E
Upleta, India	32	21 46N	70 16E
Upolu, Pt., Hawaiian Is.	59	20 16N	155 52W
Upper Arrow L., Canada	64	50 30N	117 50W
Upper Austria	14	48 15N	14 0E
Upper Erne, L., Ireland	11	54 15N	7 35W
Upper Foster L., Canada	65	56 50N	105 30W
Upper Hutt, N.Z.	46	41 8S	175 5E
Upper Klamath, L., U.S.A.	72	42 20N	123 50W
Upper Laberge, Canada	64	61 0N	135 5W
Upper Lake, U.S.A.	72	39 11N	122 55W
Upper Musquodoboit, Canada	63	45 10N	62 58W
Upper Nile, prov., Sudan	54	8 50N	29 55E
Upper North, S. Austral.	43	32 0S	138 30E
Upper Red, L., U.S.A.	70	48 7N	95 0W
Upper Region, Ghana	52	11 0N	2 0W
Upper Sandusky, U.S.A.	68	40 50N	83 20W
Upper Taimyr, R., U.S.S.R.	27	73 40N	96 0E
Upper Volta (Volta) Republic, Africa	50	12 0N	0 30W
Uppsala, Sweden	23	59 53N	17 42E
Uppsala, prov., Sweden	23	60 0N	17 30E
Upton, U.S.A.	70	44 8N	104 35W
Ur, Iraq	30	30 58N	46 6E
Uracará, Brazil	78	2 20S	57 50W
Urakawa, Japan	36	42 10N	142 45E
Ural Mts., U.S.S.R.	24	60 0N	59 0E
Ural, R., U.S.S.R.	24	49 0N	52 0W
Uralla, N.S.W.	43	30 37S	151 29E
Uralsk, U.S.S.R.	24	51 20N	51 20E
Urambo, Tanzania	53	5 1S	32 5E
Urandangi, Queensland	42	21 31S	138 16E
Urangan, Queensland	43	25 17S	152 47E
Uranium City, Canada	65	59 28N	108 40W
Uraricoera R., Brazil	78	3 30N	62 30W
Urawa, Japan	36	35 50N	139 40E
Urbana, Ill., U.S.A.	68	40 5N	88 10W
Urbana, Ohio, U.S.A.	68	40 5N	83 40W
Urbino, Italy	20	43 43N	12 38E
Urcos, Peru	78	13 30S	71 30W
Urda, U.S.S.R.	25	48 52N	47 23E
Urema, Mozambique	56	18 59S	34 33E
Uren, U.S.S.R.	25	57 35N	45 55E
Ures, Mexico	74	29 30N	110 30W
Urfa, Turkey	30	37 12N	38 50E
Urfahr, Austria	14	48 19N	14 17E
Urgench, U.S.S.R.	26	41 40N	60 30E
Urgun, Afghanistan	31	32 55N	69 12E
Uri, can., Switzerland	15	46 43N	8 35E
Uribia, Colombia	78	11 40N	72 20W
Urim, Israel	29	31 18N	34 32E
Urimbin, Queensland	43	28 16S	143 50E
Urique, R., Mexico	74	27 30N	107 30W
Urk, Netherlands	13	52 39N	5 36E
Urkerland, Netherlands	13	52 40N	5 35E
Urla, Turkey	30	38 18N	26 46E
Urmia. *See* Rizaiyeh	30		
Urmia, L., Iran	30	37 30N	45 30E
Urošovac, Yugoslavia	21	42 23N	21 10E
Uruaçu, Brazil	79	14 50S	49 20W
Uruapan, Mexico	74	19 30N	102 0W
Urubamba, Peru	78	13 5S	72 10W
Urubamba R., Peru	78	11 0S	73 0W
Uruçui, Brazil	79	7 20S	44 28W
Uruguai R., Brazil	77	27 20S	53 30W
Uruguaiana, Brazil	77	29 50S	57 0W
Uruguay, rep., S. Amer.	77	30 0S to 35 0S	53 0W to 58 0W
Uruguay R., S. America	77	28 0S	56 0W
Urumchi, China	37	43 40N	87 50E
Urunga, N.S.W.	43	30 28S	153 0E
Urungu R., China	37	46 30N	88 50E
Uruwira, Tanzania	53	6 25S	31 20E
Uruzgan, Afg.	32	32 0N	66 40E
Uruzgan, prov., Afg.	32	33 30N	66 0E
Uryupinsk, U.S.S.R.	25	50 45N	42 3E
Urzhum, U.S.S.R.	25	57 10N	49 56E
Urziceni, Rumania	21	44 46N	26 42E
Usa R., U.S.S.R.	24	66 20N	56 0E
Usak, Turkey	30	38 43N	29 28E
Usakos, S.W. Africa	57	21 58S	15 30E
Usambara, mts., Tan.	53	4 55S	38 20E
Usedom, I., Germany	23	53 50N	13 55E
Usfan, Saudi Arabia	30	21 58N	39 27E
Ushetu, Tanzania	53	4 10S	32 16E
Ushuaia, Argentina	77	54 50S	68 23E
Usk R., England	10	51 37N	2 56W
Usküdar, Turkey	30	41 0N	29 5E
Usman, U.S.S.R.	25	52 5N	39 48E
Usoro, Nigeria	52	5 27N	6 5E

	MAP		
Uspallata P., Argentina	77	33 0S	69 40W
Uspenski, U.S.S.R.	26	48 50N	72 55E
Ussel, France	12	45 32N	2 18E
Ussurysk, U.S.S.R.	27	43 40N	131 50E
Ust Aldan, U.S.S.R.	27	63 30N	129 15E
Ust Amginskoye, U.S.S.R.	27	62 50N	13450E
Ust Bolsheretsk, U.S.S.R.	27	52 40N	156 30E
Ust Chaun, U.S.S.R.	27	68 30N	171 0E
Ust Ilga, U.S.S.R.	27	55 5N	104 55E
Ust Ilimpeya, U.S.S.R.	27	63 20N	105 0E
Ust Ishim, U.S.S.R.	26	57 45N	71 10E
Ust Izhma, U.S.S.R.	24	65 15N	53 0E
Ust Kamchatsk, U.S.S.R.	27	56 10N	162 0E
Ust Kamenogorsk, U.S.S.R.	26	50 0N	82 20E
Ust Karengi, U.S.S.R.	27	54 40N	116 45E
Ust Khairyuzovo, U.S.S.R.	27	57 15N	156 55E
Ust Kozhva, U.S.S.R.	24	65 0N	57 0E
Ust Kut, U.S.S.R.	27	56 50N	105 10E
Ust Labinskaya, U.S.S.R.	25	45 15N	39 50E
Ust Maya, U.S.S.R.	27	60 30N	134 20E
Ust Mil, U.S.S.R.	27	59 50N	133 0E
Ust Nyuhzha, U.S.S.R.	27	56 45N	121 5E
Ust Olenek, U.S.S.R.	27	73 0N	120 10E
Ust Port, U.S.S.R.	26	70 0N	84 10E
Ust Shchugor, U.S.S.R.	24	64 15N	57 20E
Ust Tigil, U.S.S.R.	27	58 0N	158 10E
Ust Tsilma, U.S.S.R.	24	65 25N	52 0E
Ust Tungir, U.S.S.R.	27	55 25N	120 15E
Ust Ukhta, U.S.S.R.	24	63 55N	54 0E
Ust Usa, U.S.S.R.	24	66 0N	56 30E
Ust Vaga (Ust Vazhsk,) U.S.S.R.	24	62 50N	42 50E
Ust Vorkuta, U.S.S.R.	26	67 7N	63 35E
Ustye, U.S.S.R.	27	57 40N	94 50E
Uster, Switzerland	15	47 21N	8 44E
Usti, Czechoslovakia	16	50 40N	14 7E
Ustica I., Italy	20	38 42N	13 10E
Ustka, Poland	16	54 35N	16 55E
Ustyansk, U.S.S.R.	28	71 0N	136 0E
Usuki, Japan	36	33 10N	131 50E
Usulutan, Salvador	74	13 25N	88 28W
Usumacinata, R., Mex.	74	17 0N	41 0W
Usumbura (Bujumbura), Burundi	53	3 16S	29 18E
Usutu, R., Swaziland	57	26 45S	32 10E
Utah, st., U.S.A.	73	39 35N	111 30W
Utah, L., U.S.A.	72	40 10N	111 50W
Ute Creek, R., U.S.A.	71	36 0N	103 45W
Utegi, Tanzania	53	1 19S	34 15E
Utengule, Tanzania	53	8 45S	33 52E
Utete, Tanzania	53	8 0S	38 45E
Uthal, Pakistan	32	25 50N	66 35E
Uthmaniya, Si. Arabia	30	25 5N	49 6E
Utica, U.S.A.	69	43 5N	75 18W
Utiel, Spain	17	39 37N	1 11W
Utik L., Canada	65	55 20N	96 5W
Utikuma L., Canada	64	55 50N	115 30W
Utrecht, Natal	57	27 38S	30 20E
Utrecht, Netherlands	13	52 3N	5 8E
Utrera, Spain	17	37 12N	5 48W
Utsunomiya, Japan	36	36 30N	139 50E
Uttar Pradesh, st., India	32	27 0N	80 0E
Uttaradit, Siam	34	17 36N	100 5E
Uudenmaan Lääni, Finland	23	60 30N	25 0E
Uusikaarlepyy, Finland	23	63 33N	22 35E
Uusikaupunki, Finland	23	60 47N	21 28E
Uvalde, U.S.A.	71	29 20N	100 0W
Uvat, U.S.S.R.	26	59 5N	68 50E
Uvinza, Tanzania	53	5 0S	30 25E
Uvira, Zaire	53	3 17S	29 2E
Uwajima, Japan	36	33 10N	132 35E
Uwainid, Si. Arabia	30	24 55N	45 58E
Uyak, Alaska	59	57 30N	154 0W
Uyo, Nigeria	52	5 1N	7 53E
Uyun, Saudi Arabia	30	26 34N	43 50E
Uyuni, Bolivia	78	20 35S	66 55W
Uza R., U.S.S.R.	25	52 45N	45 45E
Uzbek S.S.R., U.S.S.R.	26	41 0N	63 0E
Uzerche, France	12	45 25N	1 35E
Uzès, France	12	44 1N	4 26E
Uzh R., U.S.S.R.	25	51 15N	29 45E

V

Vaal, R., S. Africa	57	27 40S	25 30E
Vaaldam, res., O.F.S.	57	27 0S	28 15E
Vaals, Netherlands	13	50 46N	6 1E
Vaalwater, Transvaal	57	24 15S	28 8E
Vaasan Lääni, Finland	23	63 10N	21 35E
Vác, Hungary	16	47 49N	19 10E
Vacaville, U.S.A.	73	38 27N	122 0W
Vache, I.à, Haiti	75	18 2N	73 35W
Vadsö, Norway	22	70 3N	29 50E
Vaduz, Liechtenstein	15	47 8N	9 31E
Værōy, I., Norway	22	67 40N	12 40E
Vàh, R., Czechoslovakia	16	49 10N	18 20E
Vahsel B., Antarctica	80	75 0S	35 0W
Vaigach, U.S.S.R.	26	70 10N	59 0E
Vaigach I., U.S.S.R.	26	70 0N	60 0E
Val d'or, Canada	62	48 7N	77 97W

	MAP		
Val Marie, Canada	65	49 15N	107 45W
Valadares, Portugal	17	41 4N	8 38W
Valais, can., Switz.	16	46 8N	7 40E
Valcheta, Argentina	77	40 40S	66 20W
Valdepeñas, Spain	17	38 43N	3 25W
Valderaduey, R., Spain	17	42 0N	5 22W
Valdes Pen., Argentina	77	42 30S	63 45W
Valdivia, Chile	77	39 50S	73 14W
Valdosta, U.S.A.	69	30 50N	83 20W
Valença, Bahia, Brazil	79	13 20S	39 15W
Valença do Piaùi, Brazil	79	6 20S	41 55W
Valença, Portugal	17	42 1N	8 34W
Valence, France	12	44 57N	4 54E
Valencia, Càceres, Spain	17	39 25N	7 18W
Valencia, Valencia, Spain	17	39 27N	0 23W
Valencia, old prov., Spain	17	39 20N	0 40W
Valencia, Venezuela	15	10 15N	68 0W
Valencia, G. of, Spain	15	39 30N	0 20E
Valencia, Albufera de	17	39 21N	0 23W
Valencia Lagune, Venezuela	75	10 15N	67 45W
Valenciennes, France	12	50 20N	3 34E
Valentia I., Ireland	11	51 54N	10 22W
Valentin, Sa. do, Brazil	79	6 40S	43 30W
Valentine, Neb., U.S.A.	70	42 52N	100 31W
Valentine, Texas, U.S.A.	71	30 32N	104 30W
Valenza, Italy	20	45 19N	8 39E
Valera, Venezuela	75	9 0N	70 38W
Valetta, Malta	18	35 54N	14 30E
Valga, U.S.S.R.	23	57 45N	26 0E
Valguarnera, Italy	20	37 30N	14 22E
Valier, U.S.A.	72	48 21N	112 17W
Valinco, G., France	20	41 40N	8 52E
Valjevo, Yugoslavia	21	44 18N	19 53E
Valka, U.S.S.R.	23	57 43N	25 59E
Valkenswaard, Neth.	13	51 21N	5 29E
Vall de Uxo, Spain	17	39 51N	0 13W
Valladolid, Spain	17	41 38N	4 43W
Valladolid, Mexico	74	20 30N	88 20W
Valle, Norway	23	59 13N	7 33E
Valle d'Aosta, reg., Italy	20	45 45N	7 22E
Valle de la Pascua, Ven.	75	9 15N	66 0E
Valle de Santiago, Mex.	74	20 25N	101 15W
Vallecas, Spain	17	40 23N	3 41W
Vallejo, U.S.A.	73	38 10N	122 15W
Vallenar, Chile	77	28 30S	70 50W
Valles, Mexico	74	22 0N	99 10W
Valley City. U.S.A.	70	46 50N	98 20W
Valley Falls, U.S.A.	72	42 32N	120 15W
Valleyfield, Canada	62	45 15N	74 8W
Valleyview, Canada	64	55 5N	117 25W
Vallorbe, Switzerland	15	46 42N	6 20E
Valmiera, U.S.S.R.	23	57 37N	25 38E
Valognes, France	12	49 30N	1 28W
Valona (Vlonë), Albania	21	40 29N	19 29E
Valparaiso, Chile	77	33 2S	17 40W
Valparaiso, Mexico	74	22 50N	103 32W
Valparaiso, U.S.A.	68	41 28N	87 4W
Vals R., O.F.S.	57	27 43S	27 30E
Valtimo, Finland	22	63 39N	28 50E
Valuiki, U.S.S.R.	25	50 10N	38 5E
Valverde, Spain	17	37 35N	6 47W
Vammala, Finland	23	61 20N	22 55E
Van, Turkey	30	38 30N	43 20E
Van Alstyne, U.S.A.	71	33 27N	96 34W
Van Bruyssel, Canada	63	47 58N	72 10W
Van Buren, Ark., U.S.A.	71	35 30N	94 20W
Van Buren, Me., U.S.A.	69	47 10N	68 1W
Van Buren, Mo., U.S.A.	71	37 0N	91 0W
Van Diemen C., Queens.	42	16 30S	139 46E
Van Diemen G., N. Terr.	40	12 0S	132 0E
Van gölu, L., Turkey	30	38 30N	43 0E
Van Reenen P., Natal	57	28 22S	29 27E
Van Tassell, U.S.A.	70	42 41N	104 3W
Van Wert, U.S.A.	68	40 55N	84 30W
Vancouver, Canada	64	49 20N	123 10W
Vancouver, U.S.A.	72	45 40N	122 35W
Vancouver, C., W. Australia	43	35 0S	118 8E
Vancouver I., Canada	64	49 50N	126 30W
Vandalia, Ill., U.S.A.	68	38 57N	89 4W
Vandalia, Mo., U.S.A.	70	39 16N	91 30W
Vanderbijlpark, Trans.	57	26 42S	27 54E
Vandergrift, U.S.A.	68	40 36N	79 33W
Vanderhoof, Canada	64	54 0N	124 0W
Vanduzi, Mozambique	56	18 58S	33 15E
Vänern L., Sweden	23	58 47N	13 50E
Vanersborg, Sweden	23	58 26N	12 27E
Vanga, Kenya	53	4 33S	39 5E
Vanguard, Canada	65	49 55N	107 20W
Vanimo, New Guinea	42	2 50S	141 25E
Vankaner, India	32	22 39N	70 59E
Vankleek Hill, Canada	62	45 32N	74 40W
Vännäs, Sweden	23	63 58N	19 48E
Vannes, France	12	47 40N	2 47W
Vannöy, I., Norway	22	70 6N	19 50E
Vanrook, Queensland	42	16 53S	141 57E
Vanrhynsdorp, Cape Province	57	31 36S	18 44E
Vansbrö, Sweden	23	60 32N	14 15E
Vanwyksvlei, Cape Province	57	30 18S	21 49E
Varanasi (Banaras), India	33	25 22N	83 8E
Varanger Fd., Norway	22	69 50N	31 0E

	MAP		
Varano, L., dj, Italy	20	41 50N	15 45E
Varazdin, Yugoslavia	20	46 20N	16 20E
Varberg, Sweden	23	57 17N	12 20E
Vardar R., Yugoslavia	21	41 25N	22 20E
Varde, Denmark	23	55 38N	8 29E
Vardo I., Norway	22	70 20N	31 17E
Varena, U.S.S.R.	23	54 17N	24 30E
Varennes, France	12	49 13N	5 3E
Varennes-sur-Allier, France	12	46 19N	3 24E
Vareš, Yugoslavia	21	44 12N	18 23E
Varese, Italy	20	45 49N	8 50E
Varkaus, Finland	23	62 20N	27 50E
Värmland, co., Sweden	23	59 45N	13 0E
Varna, Bulgaria	21	43 13N	27 56E
Värnamo, Sweden	23	57 10N	14 3E
Varzeneh, Iran	31	32 25N	52 40E
Vasa Barris, R., Brazil	79	0 10S	37 30W
Vasht (Khāsh), Iran	31	28 20N	61 6E
Vasilevka, U.S.S.R.	27	58 0N	125 10E
Vaslui, Rumania	21	46 38N	27 42E
Vassar, Canada	65	49 10N	95 55W
Vassar, U.S.A.	68	43 23N	83 33W
Västerås, Sweden	23	59 37N	16 38E
Västerbotten, co., Swed.	23	64 58N	18 0E
Väster Dal R., Sweden	23	60 30N	14 0E
Västernorrland, co., Sweden	23	63 15N	18 0E
Västervik, Sweden	23	57 43N	16 43E
Västmanland, co., Swed.	23	89 45N	16 20E
Vasto, Italy	20	42 8N	14 40E
Vathi, Greece	21	37 46N	27 1E
Vatnajökull Mountains, Iceland	22	64 30N	16 30W
Vatneyri, Iceland	22	65 42N	23 57W
Vatra-Dornei, Rum.	21	47 22N	25 22E
Vättern L., Sweden	23	58 25N	14 30E
Vattudal L., Sweden	23	64 0N	15 0E
Vaud, can., Switzerland	15	46 35N	6 30E
Vaughn, Mont., U.S.A.	72	47 33N	111 33W
Vaughn, N.M., U.S.A.	71	34 35N	105 10W
Vaupés, R., Colombia	78	1 5N	71 50W
Vauxhall, Canada	64	50 5N	112 9W
Vav, India	32	24 25N	71 30E
Vavuniya, Sri Lanka	32	8 50N	80 28E
Vaxjö, Sweden	23	56 52N	14 50E
Vecht R., Netherlands	13	52 31N	6 25E
Vedea R., Rumania	21	44 0N	25 20E
Vedenskoye, U.S.S.R.	27	69 50N	94 0E
Veendam, Netherlands	13	53 5N	6 52E
Veenendaal, Neth.	13	52 2N	5 34E
Vefsna, R., Norway	22	65 51N	13 10E
Vega I. & Fd., Norway	22	65 37N	12 0E
Vega, U.S.A.	71	35 15N	102 27W
Veghel, Netherlands	13	51 37N	5 32E
Vegreville, Canada	64	53 30N	112 5W
Veinticinco de Mayo, Buenos Aires, Arg.	77	35 27S	60 10W
Veinticinco de Mayo, La Pampa, Argentina	77	37 30S	67 44W
Vejer, Spain	17	36 15N	5 59W
Vejle, Denmark	23	55 47N	9 30E
Velarde, U.S.A.	73	36 14N	106 1W
Velas C., Costa Rica	75	10 22N	85 53W
Velasco, U.S.A.	71	29 0N	95 23W
Velddrif, Cape Province	57	32 42S	18 11E
Velebit Planina, Mts., Yugoslavia	20	44 50N	15 20E
Vélez, Colombia	78	6 3N	73 55W
Velez Malaga, Spain	17	36 48N	4 5W
Velez Rubio, Spain	17	37 41N	2 5W
Velhas R., Brazil	79	17 45S	44 30W
Valikaya R., U.S.S.R.	23	56 40N	28 40E
Veliki Ustyug, U.S.S.R.	25	60 47N	46 20E
Velikie Luki, U.S.S.R.	25	56 25N	30 32E
Velikonda Range, India	32	14 45N	79 10E
Velizh, U.S.S.R.	25	55 30N	31 11E
Velletri, Italy	20	41 43N	12 43E
Vellore, India	32	12 57N	79 10E
Velsk, U.S.S.R.	24	61 10N	42 5E
Velsen, Netherlands	13	52 27N	4 40E
Velva, U.S.A.	70	48 4N	100 58W
Venado, Mexico	74	22 50N	101 10W
Venado Tuerto, Arg.	77	33 50S	62 0W
Vendas Novas, Portugal	17	38 39N	8 27W
Vendôme, France	12	47 47N	1 3E
Vendrell, Spain	17	41 10N	1 30E
Veneto, reg., Italy	20	45 30N	12 0E
Venezia (Venice), Italy	20	45 27N	12 20E
Venezuela, rep., S. America	78	8 0N	65 0W
Venezuela, G. of, Ven.	78	11 30N	71 0W
Vengurla, India	32	15 53N	73 45E
Venice (Venezia), Italy	20	45 27N	12 20E
Venice, Gulf of, Italy	20	45 20N	13 0E
Venkatagiri, India	32	14 0N	79 35E
Venkatapuram, India	32	18 20N	80 30E
Venlo, Netherlands	13	51 22N	6 11E
Venraij, Netherlands	13	51 31N	6 0E
Ventana, Pta. de la, Mexico	74	24 4N	109 48W
Ventana, Sa. de la, Arg.	77	38 0S	62 30W
Ventersburg, O.F.S.	57	28 7S	27 9E
Venterstad, C. Prov.	57	30 57S	25 48E
Ventimiglia, Italy	20	43 50N	7 39E
Ventotene I., Italy	20	40 48N	13 25E
Ventspils, U.S.S.R.	23	57 25N	21 32E
Ventuari R., Venezuela	78	5 20N	66 0W

	Map	Lat.	Long.
Ventura, U.S.A.	73	34 48N	119 22W
Vera, Argentina	77	29 30S	60 20W
Vera, Spain	17	37 16N	1 52W
Vera Cruz, Mexico	74	19 10N	96 10W
Vera Cruz, st., Mexico	74	19 0N	96 15W
Veravel, India	32	20 53N	70 27E
Vercelli, Italy	20	45 19N	8 25E
Verdalsöra, Norway	23	3 47N	11 30E
Verde R., Argentina	77	41 55S	66 0W
Verde R., Brazil	79	19 0S	53 0W
Verde R., Chih., Mex.	74	27 0N	107 20W
Verde R., Jalisco, Mex.	74	21 10N	102 30W
Verde R., U.S.A.	66	34 0N	111 40W
Verden, Germany	14	52 56N	9 15E
Verdigre, U.S.A.	70	42 41N	98 0W
Verdon R., France	12	44 4N	6 35E
Verdun, France	12	49 12N	5 24E
Vereeniging, Transvaal	57	26 38S	27 57E
Verga C., Guinea	50	10 13N	14 30W
Vergara, Spain	17	43 9N	2 28W
Vergemont, Queensland	42	23 32S	143 0E
Verin, Spain	17	41 57N	7 27W
Verkhne Kolymsk, U.S.S.R.	27	65 50N	150 30E
Verkhne-Tolmak, U.S.S.R.	25	47 15N	36 28E
Verkhneuralsk, U.S.S.R.	24	53 52N	59 12E
Verkhoture, U.S.S.R.	24	58 48N	60 47E
Verkhoyansk, U.S.S.R.	27	67 50N	133 50E
Verkhoyansk Ra., U.S.S.R.	27	66 0N	129 0E
Verkhoye, U.S.S.R.	25	52 55N	37 15E
Verlo, Canada	65	50 25N	108 35W
Vermeulle, L., Canada	63	54 45N	69 50W
Vermilion, Canada	62	47 40N	73 5W
Vermilion Bay, Canada	65	49 50N	93 20W
Vermilion Bay, U.S.A.	71	29 45N	92 0W
Vermilion Chutes, Can.	64	58 20N	115 0W
Vermilion, L., U.S.A.	70	47 52N	92 30W
Vermilion R., Canada	62	46 18N	81 30W
Vermillion, U.S.A.	70	42 45N	98 55W
Vermont, st., U.S.A.	69	43 40N	72 50W
Vernal, U.S.A.	72	40 28N	109 37W
Verner, Canada	62	46 25N	80 8W
Verneukpan, Cape Prov.	57	30 0S	21 0E
Vernon, Canada	64	50 20N	119 15W
Vernon, U.S.A.	71	34 8N	99 15W
Vero Beach, U.S.A.	69	27 39N	80 23W
Veroia, Greece	21	40 34N	22 18E
Veroli, Italy	20	41 43N	13 24E
Verona, Italy	20	45 27N	11 0E
Veropol, U.S.S.R.	27	65 30N	168 50E
Versailles, France	12	48 48N	2 8E
Versoix, Switzerland	15	46 17N	6 10E
Vert C., Senegal	50	14 45N	17 30W
Verulam, Natal	57	29 38S	31 2E
Verviers, Belgium	13	50 37N	5 52E
Verwood, Canada	65	49 30N	105 40W
Vesegonsk, U.S.S.R.	25	58 42N	37 13E
Vesoul, France	12	47 38N	6 11E
Vest-Agder, co., Nor.	23	58 30N	7 0E
Vest Fjorden, Norway	22	68 0N	15 0E
Vesta, Costa Rica	78	9 50N	83 0W
Vesterälen Is., Norway	22	69 0N	15 30E
Vestfold, co., Norway	23	59 15N	10 0E
Vestmannaeyjar, Iceland	22	63 27N	20 15W
Vestnes, Norway	23	62 39N	7 5E
Vestvagoy I., Norway	22	68 18N	15 20E
Vesuvius, Mt., Italy	20	40 50N	14 22E
Veszprem, Hungary	16	47 8N	17 57E
Vetlanda, Sweden	23	57 24N	15 3E
Vetluga, U.S.S.R.	25	57 53N	45 45E
Vetluga R., U.S.S.R.	24	57 0N	45 30E
Vetluzhki, U.S.S.R.	25	57 17N	45 12E
Vettore, Mte., Italy	20	42 50N	13 15E
Veurne, Belgium	13	51 5N	2 40E
Vevey, Switzerland	15	46 28N	6 51E
Veys, Iran	30	31 38N	48 55E
Vezen Mt., Bulgaria	21	42 50N	24 20E
Viacha, Bolivia	78	16 30S	68 5W
Viana, Brazil	79	3 0S	44 40W
Viana, Portugal	17	38 20N	7 59W
Viana, Spain	17	42 10N	7 10W
Viana do Castelo, Port.	17	41 43N	8 49W
Vianopolis, Brazil	79	16 40S	48 35W
Viareggio, Italy	20	43 52N	10 13E
Vibank, Canada	65	50 25N	104 0W
Vibo Valentia, Italy	20	38 40N	16 5E
Viborg, Denmark	23	56 27N	9 23E
Vic en Bigorre, France	12	43 24N	0 3E
Vicenza, Italy	20	45 32N	11 31E
Vich, Spain	17	41 58N	2 19E
Vichada, R., Colombia	78	4 50N	69 30W
Vichuga, U.S.S.R.	25	57 25N	41 55E
Vichy, France	12	46 9N	3 26E
Vicksburg, U.S.A.	68	32 25N	91 0W
Vico, Italy	20	45 30N	7 45E
Vicosa, Brazil	79	9 28S	36 25W
Victor, U.S.A.	70	38 45N	105 7W
Victor Harb., S. Austral.	43	35 30S	138 37E
Victoria, W. Cam.	52	4 1N	9 10E
Victoria, Canada	64	48 30N	123 25W
Victoria, Chile	77	38 22S	72 29W
Victoria, Guinea	50	10 50N	14 39W
Victoria, Hong Kong	39	22 25N	114 15E
Victoria, Sabah	35	5 20N	115 20E
Victoria, Texas, U.S.A.	71	28 50N	97 0W
Victoria, Va., U.S.A.	70	38 53N	99 4W
Victoria, st., Australia	43	37 0S	144 0E
Victoria, L., E. Africa	53	1 0S	33 0E
Victoria, L., N.S.W.	43	34 0S	141 15E
Victoria L., N.S.W.	43	32 27S	143 23E
Victoria Mt., Burma	33	21 15N	93 55E
Victoria, Mt., Papua	42	8 54S	147 40E
Victoria Pk., Canada	64	50 10N	126 0W
Victoria Ra., N.Z.	47	42 12S	172 7E
Victoria R., N. Terr.	40	15 30S	131 0E
Victoria Beach, Canada	65	50 45N	96 32W
Victoria de las Tunas, Cuba	75	20 58N	76 59W
Victoria de Santo Antao, Brazil	79	8 20S	35 23W
Victoria Falls, Rhodesia	56	17 58S	25 45E
Victoria Harb., Canada	62	44 45N	79 45W
Victoria Land, Ant.	80	75 0S	160 0E
Victoria Nile R., Ugan.	53	1 30N	32 30E
Victoria River Downs, N. Terr	40	16 30S	131 20E
Victoria West, Cape Province	57	31 25S	23 4E
Victoriaville, Canada	63	46 4N	71 56W
Victorica, Argentina	77	36 20S	65 30W
Victorville, U.S.A.	73	34 33N	116 23W
Vicuña, Chile	77	30 0S	70 50W
Vidalia, U.S.A.	69	32 13N	82 25W
Vidin, Bulgaria	21	43 59N	22 57E
Viedma, Argentina	77	40 50S	63 0W
Viedma L., Argentina	77	49 30S	72 30W
Viella, Spain	17	42 43N	0 44E
Vienna (Wien), Austria	14	48 12N	16 22E
Vienna, U.S.A.	68	37 26N	88 50W
Vienne, France	12	45 31N	4 53E
Vienne, R., France	12	47 5N	0 10E
Vientiane, Laos	34	18 7N	102 35E
Vierwaldstättersee, Switzerland	15	47 0N	8 30E
Vierzon, France	12	47 13N	2 5E
Vieste, Italy	20	41 52N	16 10E
Viet Nam, st., Asia	34	15 30N	109 0E
Vieux Fort, St. Lucia	75	13 46N	60 58W
Vigan, Philippines	35	17 35N	120 28E
Vigia, Brazil	29	0 50S	48 5W
Vigo, Spain	17	42 12N	8 41W
Vigors, mt., W. Austral.	44	22 29S	118 15E
Vijayawada (Vijayavada), India	52	16 31N	80 39E
Vijosë, R., Albania	21	40 35N	19 30E
Vik, Iceland	22	63 25N	19 0W
Vikarabad, India	32	17 20N	77 55E
Viking, Canada	64	53 7N	111 50W
Vikna, I., Norway	22	64 55N	10 55E
Vikulovo, U.S.S.R.	26	56 50N	70 40E
Vila Armindo Monteiro, Port. Timor	35	9 0S	125 20E
Vilà Arriaga, Angola	55	14 35S	13 30E
Vilà Bittencourt, Brazil	78	1 20S	69 20W
Vila Cabral, Mozam.	56	13 8S	35 30E
Vila Caldas Xavier, Mozambique	56	14 26S	33 0E
Vila Coutinho, Mozam.	56	14 38S	34 20E
Vila da Maganja, Mozambique	55	17 15S	37 25E
Vila da Ponte, Angola	55	14 35S	16 40E
Vila de Cangamba, Ang.	55	13 25S	19 40E
Vila de Sena, Mozam.	56	17 23S	34 40E
Vila Fontes, Mozam.	56	17 50S	35 12E
Vila Gamito, Mozam.	56	14 11S	32 59E
Vila General Machado, Angola	55	11 58S	17 22E
Vila Gouveia, Mozam.	56	18 3S	33 11E
Vila Henrique de Carvalho, Angola	55	9 40S	20 12E
Vila Luiza, Mozam.	57	25 44S	32 40E
Vila Luso, Angola	55	11 53S	19 55E
Vila Machado, Mozam.	56	19 18S	34 11E
Vila Mariano Machado, Angola	55	13 3S	14 35E
Vila Mouzinho, Mozam.	56	14.45S	34 20E
Vila Murtinho, Brazil	78	10 20S	65 20W
Vila Novo de Gaia, Portugal	17	41 4N	8 40W
Vila Nova de Malaca, Timor	35	8 25S	127 0E
Vila Novo do Seles, Angola	55	11 35S	14 22E
Vila Paiva de Andrada, Mozam.	56	18 44S	34 3E
Vila Pereira d'Eça, Ang.	55	16 48S	15 50E
Vila Pery, Mozam.	56	19 4S	33 29E
Vila Real, Portugal	17	41 17N	7 48W
Vila Real de Santo Antonio, Portugal	17	37 10N	7 28W
Vila Robert Williams, Angola	55	12 37S	15 40E
Vila Salazar, Angola	55	9 12S	14 48E
Vila Teixeira da Silva, Angola	55	12 10S	15 50E
Vila Vasco da Gama, Mozam.	56	14 55S	32 17E
Vila Verissimo, Sarmento, Angola	54	8 15S	20 50E
Vila Viçosa, Portugal	17	38 45N	7 27W
Vilaine R., France	12	47 35N	2 10W
Vilanculos, Mozam.	56	22 0S	35 15E
Vilacanota, Nudo de, Mt., Peru	78	15 0S	70 30W
Vileika, U.S.S.R.	23	54 30N	27 0E
Vilhelmina, Sweden	22	64 35N	16 50E
Vilhena, Brazil	78	12 30S	60 0W
Viliya, R., U.S.S.R.	23	54 57N	24 35E
Viljandi, U.S.S.R.	23	58 23N	25 38E
Villa Ahumada, Mexico	74	30 40N	106 40W
Villa Angela, Arg.	77	27 34S	60 45W
Villa Bella, Bolivia	78	10 25S	65 30W
Villa Brana, Arg.	77	27 25S	62 48W
Villa Cisneros, Spanish Sahara	50	23 50N	15 43W
Villa Cisneros, terr., Sp. Sahara	50	25 0N	13 30W
Villa de Cura, Ven.	75	10 0N	67 30W
Villa de Maria (Rio Seco), Argentina	77	29 55S	63 50W
Villa Federal, Argentina	77	31 0S	58 50W
Villa Hayes, Paraguay	77	25 0S	57 20W
Villa Huidobro, Arg.	77	34 50S	64 43W
Villa Julia Molina, Dominican Rep.	75	19 15N	69 50W
Villa Madero, Mexico	74	23 25N	104 10W
Villa Maria, Argentina	77	32 20S	63 10W
Villa Maza, Argentina	77	36 40S	63 25W
Villa Mercedes, Arg.	77	33 40S	65 24W
Villa Montes, Bolivia	78	21 10S	63 30W
Villa Nora, Transvaal	56	23 34S	28 1E
Villa Orestes Pereyro, Mexico	74	23 0N	105 52W
Villa Teixeira de Sousa, Angola	56	11 4S	22 5E
Villa Viscarra, Bolivia	78	17 59S	65 40W
Villacarrillo, Spain	17	38 7N	3 3W
Villach, Austria	14	46 37N	13 51E
Villafranca, Italy	20	44 49N	7 30E
Villafranca, Badajoz, Spain	17	38 35N	6 18W
Villafranca, Barcelona, Spain	17	41 21N	1 40E
Villafranca, Leon, Spain	17	42 38N	6 50W
Villagarcia, Spain	17	42 34N	8 46W
Villaguay, Argentina	77	32 0S	58 45W
Villagrán, Mexico	74	24 31N	99 22W
Villahermosa, Mexico	74	17 45N	92 50W
Villajoyosa, Spain	17	38 30N	0 12W
Villalon, Spain	17	42 5N	5 4W
Villanueva, Spain	17	38 10N	3 0W
Villanueva, Spain	17	38 25N	5 0W
Villanueva, U.S.A.	73	35 20N	105 23W
Villanueva de la Serena, Spain	17	38 59N	5 50W
Villanueva y Geltru, Spain	17	41 13N	1 40E
Villaputzu, Italy	20	39 28N	9 33E
Villarego, Spain	17	40 13N	3 18W
Villarica, Chile	77	39 16S	72 20W
Villarreal, Spain	17	39 55N	0 3W
Villarrica, Paraguay	77	25 40S	56 30W
Villarrobledo, Spain	17	39 18N	2 36W
Villavicencio, Colombia	78	4 20N	73 35W
Villaviciosa, Spain	17	43 32N	5 27W
Villazon, Bolivia	77	22 0S	65 35W
Ville Marie, Canada	62	47 21N	79 26W
Ville Platte, U.S.A.	71	30 43N	92 16W
Villena, Spain	17	38 39N	0 52W
Villefranche, Alpes Maritimes, France	12	43 42N	7 18E
Villefranche, Aveyron, France	12	44 21N	2 2E
Villeneuve, France	12	44 24N	0 42E
Villeurbanne, France	12	45 46N	4 55E
Villiers, O.F.S.	57	27 2S	28 36E
Villisca, U.S.A.	70	40 56N	95 0W
Villupuram, India	32	11 59N	79 31E
Vilna, Canada	64	54 6N	111 59W
Vilnius, U.S.S.R.	23	54 38N	25 25E
Vilvoorde, Belgium	13	50 56N	4 26E
Vilyui R., U.S.S.R.	27	63 58N	125 0E
Vilyuisk, U.S.S.R.	27	63 40N	121 20E
Vimmerby, Sweden	23	57 40N	15 55E
Vina R., Cameroon	52	6 50N	13 18E
Viña del Mar, Chile	77	33 0S	71 30W
Vinalhaven I., U.S.A.	69	49 5N	68 55W
Vinaroz, Spain	17	40 30N	0 37E
Vincennes, U.S.A.	68	88 40N	87 30W
Vindel R., Sweden	22	64 50N	19 0E
Vindhya Ra., India	32	22 50N	77 0E
Vineland, U.S.A.	68	39 30N	75 0W
Vinh, Viet Nam	34	18 45N	105 38E
Vinh Yen, Viet Nam	39	21 18N	105 36E
Vinho, Mozambique	56	16 10S	32 30E
Vinita, U.S.A.	71	36 40N	95 12W
Vinkovci, Yugoslavia	21	45 19N	18 48E
Vinnitsa, U.S.S.R.	25	49 15N	28 30E
Vinton, La., U.S.A.	71	30 14N	93 32W
Vinton, Iowa	70	42 6N	92 0W
Vipiteno, Italy	20	46 55N	11 25E
Virac, Philippines	35	13 30N	124 20E
Virago Sd., Canada	64	54 0N	132 0W
Virajpet, India	32	12 15N	75 50E
Viramgam, India	32	23 5N	72 0E
Viransehir, Turkey	30	37 10N	39 38E
Virden, Canada	65	49 50N	101 0W
Vire, France	12	48 50N	0 53W
Virgenes, C., Arg.	77	52 20S	68 25W
Virgin Is., W. Indies	75	18 40N	64 30W
Virgin, R., Canada	65	57 15N	108 0W
Virgin R., U.S.A.	73	36 45N	114 15W
Virgin Gorda, I., Virgin Is.	75	18 45N	64 26W
Virginia, Ireland	11	53 50N	7 5W
Virginia, U.S.A.	70	47 40N	92 40W
Virginia, st., U.S.A.	68	37 40N	78 10W
Virginia Ra., Australia	45	28 0S	123 45E
Virginia Beach, U.S.A.	68	36 51N	75 59W
Virginia City, Mont., U.S.A.	72	45 21N	111 57W
Virginia City, Nev., U.S.A.	72	39 17N	119 42W
Virginia Fs., Canada	64	61 50N	125 50W
Virginiatown, Canada	62	48 9N	79 36W
Virihaure, Sweden	22	67 28N	17 27E
Viroqua, U.S.A.	70	43 31N	90 57W
Virovitica, Yugoslavia	20	45 51N	17 21E
Virton, Belgium	13	49 35N	5 32E
Virtsu, U.S.S.R.	23	58 32N	23 33E
Viru, Peru	78	8 35S	78 50W
Virudunagar, India	32	9 30N	78 0E
Vis, I., Yugoslavia	20	43 0N	16 10E
Visalia, U.S.A.	73	36 30N	119 20W
Visby, Sweden	23	57 37N	18 25E
Viscount Melville Sd., Canada	58	78 0N	108 0W
Višegrad, Yugoslavia	21	43 47N	19 17E
Viseu, Brazil	79	1 10S	46 20W
Viseul de Sus, Rumania	21	47 40N	23 24E
Vishakhapatnam, India	33	17 45N	83 20E
Vishera, U.S.S.R.	24	62 20N	52 30E
Viso, Mte., Italy	20	44 40N	7 3E
Visoko, Yugoslavia	21	43 58N	18 10E
Visp, Switzerland	15	46 17N	7 52E
Vista Alegre, Brazil	78	1 50N	61 5W
Vistula (Wisla) R., Pol	16	52 30N	19 40E
Vita, Canada	65	49 10N	96 40W
Vitebsk, U.S.S.R.	25	55 10N	30 15E
Viterbo, Italy	20	42 25N	12 8E
Vitiaz Str., N. Guinea	42	5 30S	146 50E
Vitigudino, Spain	17	41 1N	6 35W
Vitim, U.S.S.R.	27	59 45N	112 25E
Vitim R., Siberia	27	58 40N	112 50E
Vitoria, Spain	17	42 50N	2 41W
Vitoria da Conquista, Brazil	79	15 0S	42 0W
Vitorinho, Mozam.	56	17 25S	36 0E
Vitré, France	12	48 8N	1 12W
Vitry-le-Francois, France	12	48 43N	4 33E
Vitshumbi, Zaire	53	0 41S	29 21E
Vittangi, Sweden	22	67 41N	21 40E
Vittoria, Italy	20	36 58N	14 30E
Vittorio Veneto, Italy	20	45 59N	12 18E
Vitu Is., Terr. of New Guinea	42	4 50S	149 11E
Vitznau, Switzerland	15	47 1N	8 30E
Vivero, Spain	17	43 39N	7 38W
Vivien, W. Australia	44	27 57S	120 32E
Viviers, France	12	44 30N	4 40E
Vizcaino Desert, Mexico	74	27 40N	113 50W
Vizeu, Portugal	17	40 41N	7 59W
Vizianagaram, India	33	18 10N	83 25E
Vizzini, Italy	20	37 9N	14 43E
Vlaardingen, Neth.	13	51 55N	4 19E
Vladimir, U.S.S.R.	25	56 8N	40 20E
Vladivostok, U.S.S.R.	27	43 10N	131 53E
Vleesfontein, Transvaal	57	24 47S	26 18E
Vlieland I., Netherlands	13	53 30N	4 55E
Vlissingen (Flushing), Netherlands	13	51 26N	3 34E
Vlonë (Valona), Albania	21	40 32N	19 28E
Vltava R., C.Slov.	16	49 35N	14 10E
Voeröy I., Norway	22	67 36N	12 40E
Vogel, C., Papua	42	9 48S	150 0E
Vogelkop, Indonesia	35	1 25S	133 0E
Vogel Peak, Nigeria	52	8 30N	11 35E
Vogelsberg, Germany	20	50 33N	9 12E
Voghera, Italy	41	44 59N	9 1E
Vohemar, Madagascar	55	13 25S	50 0E
Voi, Kenya	53	3 29S	38 32E
Voi R., Kenya	53	3 30S	39 40E
Voiniama, Liberia	52	8 15N	10 15E
Voiron, France	12	45 22N	5 35E
Vojmsjön, L., Sweden	22	64 55N	16 40E
Volborg, U.S.A.	70	45 50N	105 43W
Volchansk, U.S.S.R.	25	50 17N	36 58E
Volda, Norway	23	62 9N	6 5E
Volga, U.S.S.R.	25	57 58N	38 16E
Volga Res., U.S.S.R.	25	56 40N	36 30E
Volga R., U.S.S.R.	25	48 30N	45 30E
Volgograd, U.S.S.R.	25	48 43N	44 25E
Volkhov, U.S.S.R.	25	59 55N	32 25E
Volkhov R., U.S.S.R.	25	59 30N	32 0E
Volkovysk, U.S.S.R.	25	53 9N	24 30E
Volksrust, Transvaal	57	27 24S	29 53E
Volla, Italy	20	40 19N	15 12E
Vollenhove, Neth.	13	52 40N	5 58E
Volnovakha, U.S.S.R.	25	47 35N	37 30E
Volochanka, U.S.S.R.	27	71 5N	94 10E
Volodarsk, U.S.S.R.	25	58 30N	39 5E
Vologda, U.S.S.R.	25	59 25N	40 0E
Volokolamsk, U.S.S.R.	25	56 5N	36 0E
Vólos, Greece	21	39 24N	22 59E
Vólos, G. of, Greece	21	39 10N	23 0E
Volosovo, U.S.S.R.	23	59 27N	29 32E
Volovhayevka, U.S.S.R.	27	48 40N	134 30E
Volovo, U.S.S.R.	25	53 30N	38 2E

	MAP		
Volsk, U.S.S.R.	25	52 5N	47 28 E
Volta, L., Ghana	52	6 0N	0 0
Volta R., Ghana	52	6 0N	0 30W
Volta Redonda, Brazil	77	22 30S	43 0W
Voltaire, C., W. Australia	44	14 18S	125 35 E
Volterra, Italy	20	43 24N	10 50 E
Voltri, Italy	20	44 25N	8 43 E
Volturno R., Italy	20	41 18N	14 20 E
Volzhskiy, U.S.S.R.	25	48 53N	44 55 E
Von Treuer T'land, W. Australia	45	26 40S	122 45 E
Voorburg, Netherlands	13	52 5N	4 24 E
Vopnafjördur, Iceland	22	65 45N	14 45W
Vopnafjördur, B., Ice.	22	65 50N	14 30W
Vorarlberg, prov., Austria	14	47 20N	10 0 E
Vorderrhein R., Switz.	15	46 40N	9 0 E
Vordingborg, Denmark	23	55 0N	11 54 E
Vorkuta, U.S.S.R.	24	67 48N	64 20 E
Vorona R., U.S.S.R.	25	52 0N	42 20 E
Voronezh, U.S.S.R.	25	51 40N	39 10 E
Voronezh R., U.S.S.R.	25	52 30N	39 30 E
Voronya R., U.S.S.R.	22	68 35N	35 30 E
Voroshilovgrad (Lugansk), U.S.S.R.	25	48 33N	39 15 E
Vorovskoye, U.S.S.R.	27	54 30N	155 50 E
Vosburg, Cape Province	57	30 33S	22 52 E
Voss, Norway	23	60 38N	6 26 E
Votkinsk, U.S.S.R.	24	57 0N	53 55 E
Vouchaba, Cameroon	52	5 8N	12 50 E
Vouga R., Portugal	17	40 46N	8 10W
Vouma R., Cameroon	52	4 0N	13 30 E
Vouziers, France	12	49 22N	4 40 E
Voves, France	12	48 15N	1 38 E
Voznesene, U.S.S.R.	24	61 1N	35 40 E
Voznesensk, U.S.S.R.	25	47 35N	31 15 E
Voznesenskaya, U.S.S.R.	27	55 15N	94 50 E
Vranje, Yugoslavia	21	42 34N	21 54 E
Vratsa, Bulgaria	21	43 13N	23 30 E
Vrbas R., Yugoslavia	20	44 30N	17 10 E
Vrede, O.F.S.	57	27 24S	29 6 E
Vredefort, O.F.S.	57	27 0S	26 58 E
Vredenburg, Cape Prov.	57	32 51S	18 0 E
Vredendal, Cape Prov.	57	31 41S	18 35 E
Vrindaban, India	32	27 37N	77 40 E
Vršac, Yugoslavia	21	45 8N	21 18 E
Vryburg, Botswana	57	26 55S	24 45 E
Vryheid, Natal	57	27 54S	30 47 E
Vught, Netherlands	13	51 38N	5 20 E
Vukovar, Yugoslavia	21	45 21N	18 59 E
Vulcan, Canada	64	50 25N	113 15W
Vulcan, U.S.A.	68	45 46N	87 51W
Vulcan Mt., Rumania	21	46 17N	22 59 E
Vulcan or Shag Pt., N.Z.	47	45 29S	170 50 E
Vulcano I., Italy	20	38 25N	14 58 E
Vunduzi R., Mozam.	56	18 0S	33 45 E
Vung Tau, Vietnam	34	10 28N	107 12 E
Vurra, Uganda	53	2 53N	30 53 E
Vuti, Rhodesia	56	16 36S	29 27 E
Vyatka R., U.S.S.R.	25	56 30N	51 0 E
Vyazma, U.S.S.R.	25	55 10N	34 15 E
Vyazniki, U.S.S.R.	25	56 10N	42 10 E
Vychegda R., U.S.S.R.	24	61 50N	52 30 E
Vyshni Volochek, U.S.S.R.	25	57 30N	34 30 E

W

	MAP		
Wa, Ghana	52	10 7N	2 25W
Waal R., Netherlands	13	51 54N	5 35 E
Wabasca, Canada	64	55 57N	113 45W
Wabash, U.S.A.	68	40 48N	85 45W
Wabash R., U.S.A.	68	40 42N	45 20W
Wabeno, U.S.A.	68	45 25N	88 40W
Wabigoon L., Canada	65	49 44N	92 34W
Wabiskaw R., Canada	64	57 40N	115 30W
Wabowden, Canada	65	54 55N	98 35W
Wabrzezno, Poland	16	53 16N	19 0 E
Wabuk Pt., Canada	62	55 30N	85 30W
Wabush City, Canada	63	52 45N	66 58W
Wabuska, U.S.A.	73	39 10N	119 13W
Wacker, Alaska	64	55 30N	131 40W
Waco, U.S.A.	71	31 30N	97 0W
Waconichi L., Canada	62	50 0N	74 0W
Wad Banda, Sudan	51	13 10N	27 50 E
Wad Hamid, Sudan	51	16 30N	32 45 E
Wad Medani, Sudan	51	14 28N	33 30 E
Waddamana, Tasmania	43	41 59S	146 34 E
Waddington Mt., Can.	64	51 10N	125 20W
Wadena, Canada	65	52 0N	103 50W
Wadena, U.S.A.	70	46 28N	95 4W
Wädenswil, Switzerland	15	47 14N	8 30 E
Wadesboro, U.S.A.	69	35 2N	80 2W
Wadhams, Canada	64	51 30N	127 30W
Wadi, India	33	17 0N	77 0 E
Wadi, Nigeria	52	9 44N	13 5 E
Wadi Aswad, Muscat and Oman	31	23 0N	56 0 E
Wadi al Birk, Si. Arabia	30	22 20N	46 30 E
Wadi ar Rima, Si. Arabia	30	26 0N	42 0 E
Wadi Hawran, Iraq	30	33 20N	41 0 E
Wadi Jarir, Si. Arabia	30	24 46N	42 0 E
Wadi Sabha, Si. Arabia	30	23 50N	48 30 E
Wadi Sirra, Si. Arabia	30	22 25N	44 20 E
Wadi Tharthar Depression, Iraq	30	34 0N	43 0 E
Wadowice, Poland	16	49 52N	19 30 E
Wadsworth, U.S.A.	72	39 11N	119 21W
Wafra, Neutral Zone, Arabia	30	28 33N	48 3 E
Wageningen, Neth.	13	51 58N	5 40 E
Wager Bay, Canada	61	66 0N	91 0W
Wagga Wagga, N.S.W.	43	35 7S	147 24 E
Wagin, Nigeria	52	12 42N	7 10 E
Wagin, W. Australia	44	33 17S	117 25 E
Wagon Mound, U.S.A.	71	36 0N	104 44W
Wagoner, U.S.A.	71	35 59N	95 27W
Wagrowiec, Poland	16	52 48N	17 19 E
Wahai, Indonesia	35	2 48S	129 35 E
Waharoa, New Zealand	46	37 46S	175 48 E
Wahiawa, Hawaiian Is.	59	21 30N	158 2W
Wahpeton, U.S.A.	70	46 20N	96 45W
Wahoo, U.S.A.	70	41 16N	96 35W
Wai, India	32	17 56N	73 57 E
Waiai R., N.Z.	47	45 36S	167 45 E
Waiau, New Zealand	47	42 39S	173 5 E
Waibeem, Indonesia	35	0 30S	132 50 E
Waigeo Island, Indon.	35	0 5S	130 30 E
Waiha, New Zealand	47	44 45S	170 51 E
Waihao R., N.Z.	47	44 46S	171 10 E
Waiheke Island, N.Z.	46	36 48S	175 6 E
Waihi, New Zealand	46	37 23S	175 52 E
Waihola, New Zealand	47	46 1S	170 8 E
Waihola L., N.Z.	47	45 59S	170 8 E
Waihou, R., N.Z.	46	37 15S	175 40 E
Waikabubak, Indonesia	35	9 45S	119 25 E
Waikaka, N.Z.	47	45 55S	169 1 E
Waikare Iti, L., N.Z.	46	38 42S	177 11 E
Waikare Lake, N.Z.	46	37 26S	175 13 E
Waikaremoana, N.Z.	46	38 42S	177 12 E
Waikaremoana L., N.Z.	46	38 49S	177 9 E
Waikari, N.Z.	47	42 58S	172 41 E
Waikato R., N.Z.	46	37 32S	174 45 E
Waikerie, S., Australia	43	34 9S	140 0 E
Waikiekie, N.Z.	46	35 57S	174 16 E
Waikiwi, N.Z.	47	46 21S	168 21 E
Waikokopu, N.Z.	46	39 3S	177 52 E
Waikouaiti, N.Z	47	45 36S	170 41 E
Waikouaiti Downs, N.Z.	47	45 30S	170 25 E
Wailuku, Hawaiian Is.	59	20 54N	156 30W
Waimakariri R., N.Z.	47	43 17S	171 59 E
Waimangaroa, N.Z.	47	41 43S	171 46 E
Waimate, N.Z.	47	44 43S	171 3 E
Waimea Plain, N.Z.	47	45 55S	168 35 E
Wainganga R., India	32	21 0N	79 45 E
Waingapu, Indonesia	35	9 35S	120 11 E
Waini R., Guyana	78	7 50N	59 5W
Wainiha, Hawaiian Is.	59	22 12N	159 32W
Wainwright, Canada	65	52 50N	110 50W
Wainwright, Alaska	59	70 39N	160 10W
Waiotapu, N.Z.	46	38 21S	176 25 E
Waiouru, N.Z.	46	39 28S	175 41 E
Waipa River, N.Z.	46	38 14S	175 17 E
Waipahi, N.Z.	47	46 6S	169 15 E
Waipahu, Hawaiian Is.	59	21 21N	159 1W
Waipapa Pt., N.Z.	47	46 40S	169 51 E
Waipara, New Zealand	47	43 3S	172 46 E
Waipawa, New Zealand	46	39 56S	176 38 E
Waipiro, N.Z.	46	38 2S	178 22 E
Waipu, New Zealand	46	35 59S	174 29 E
Waipukurau, N.Z.	46	40 1S	176 33 E
Wairarapa L., N.Z.	46	41 14S	175 15 E
Wairau River, N.Z.	47	41 38S	173 15 E
Wairio, New Zealand	47	45 49S	168 3 E
Wairoa, New Zealand	46	39 3S	177 25 E
Wairoa R., Gisborne, N.Z.	46	38 50S	177 32 E
Waitaki R., N.Z.	47	44 23S	169 55 E
Waitara, N.Z.	46	38 59S	174 15 E
Waitara River, N.Z.	46	39 7S	174 23 E
Waitoa, New Zealand	46	37 37S	175 40 E
Waitotara, N.Z.	46	39 49S	174 44 E
Waitotara R., N.Z.	46	39 35S	174 50 E
Waitsburg, U.S.A.	72	46 18N	118 8W
Waiuku, New Zealand	46	37 15S	174 45 E
Waiyeung, China	39	23 12N	114 32 E
Wajima, Japan	36	37 30N	137 0 E
Wajir, Kenya	53	1 42N	40 20 E
Wakabinu, L., Canada	62	50 48N	89 40W
Wakaia, New Zealand	47	45 44S	168 51 E
Wakamatsu, Fukuoka, Japan	36	33 50N	130 45 E
Wakamatsu, Fukushima, Japan	36	37 30N	139 57 E
Wakasa B., Japan	36	35 45N	135 30 E
Wakatipu, L., N.Z.	47	45 5S	168 33 E
Wakaw, Canada	65	52 40N	105 45W
Wakayama, Japan	36	34 15N	135 15 E
Wakayama, pref., Japan	36	33 50N	135 30 E
Wake Forest, U.S.A.	69	35 58N	78 30W
Wake I., Pacific Ocean	5	19 0N	167 0 E
Wakefield, England	10	53 41N	1 31W
Wakefield, N.Z.	47	41 24S	173 5 E
Wakefield, Mich., U.S.A.	70	46 39N	89 27W
Wakefield, Va., U.S.A.	68	36 59N	77 0W
Wakeham Bay, Canada	61	61 30N	72 0W
Wakhan Mt., Afghan.	31	37 0N	73 0 E
Wakkanai, Japan	36	45 28N	141 25 E
Wakkerstroom, Transvaal	57	27 24S	30 10 E
Wako, Canada	62	49 50N	91 22W
Wakool R., N.S.W.	43	35 25S	144 15 E
Wakre, Indonesia	35	0 30S	131 5 E
Walamba, Zambia	56	13 28S	28 42 E
Walbrzych, Poland	16	50 45N	16 18 E
Walcha, N.S.W.	43	30 55S	151 31 E
Walcheren I., Neth.	13	51 30N	3 35 E
Walcott, U.S.A.	72	41 48N	106 54W
Walcz, Poland	16	53 17N	16 27 E
Wald, Switzerland	15	47 17N	8 56 E
Walden, U.S.A.	72	40 45N	106 17W
Walden Zee, Neth.	13	53 10N	5 5 E
Waldport, U.S.A.	72	44 26N	124 4W
Waldron, Canada	65	50 53N	102 35W
Waldron, U.S.A.	71	34 50N	94 5W
Walembele, Ghana	52	10 27N	2 0W
Walensee, L., Switz.	15	47 7N	9 18 E
Walenstadt, Switz.	15	47 6N	9 20 E
Wales, Gt. Britain	10	52 30N	3 30W
Wales, Alaska	59	65 38N	168 9W
Walewale, Ghana	52	10 20N	0 47W
Walgett, N.S.W.	43	30 0S	148 5 E
Walhalla, Victoria	43	37 50S	146 25 E
Walikale, Zaire	53	1 29S	28 5 E
Walkaway, W. Austral.	44	28 56S	114 48 E
Walker, Ariz., U.S.A.	73	34 30N	112 52W
Walker, Minn., U.S.A.	70	47 6N	94 33W
Walker L., Canada	63	50 20N	67 11W
Walker L., U.S.A.	73	38 40N	118 40W
Walkerston, Queens.	42	21 11S	149 8 E
Walkerton, Canada	62	44 10N	81 10W
Wall, U.S.A.	70	44 0N	102 15W
Walla Walla, U.S.A.	72	46 0N	118 25W
Wallace, Idaho, U.S.A.	72	47 40N	116 0W
Wallace, Neb., U.S.A.	70	40 54N	101 40W
Wallace, N.C., U.S.A.	69	34 42N	78 0W
Wallaceburg, Canada	62	42 40N	82 30W
Wallacetown, N.Z.	47	46 21S	168 19 E
Wallachia, reg., Rum.	21	44 40N	24 0 E
Wallal, Queensland	43	26 32S	146 7 E
Wallal Downs, W. Australia	44	19 42S	121 0 E
Wallangarra, Queens.	43	28 56S	151 58 E
Wallaroo, S. Australia	43	33 55S	137 33 E
Wallowa, U.S.A.	72	45 32N	117 31W
Wallowa Mts., U.S.A.	72	45 15N	117 30W
Walmsley L., Canada	65	63 25N	109 0W
Wallsend, N.S.W.	43	35 55S	151 40 E
Wallula, U.S.A.	72	46 4N	118 58W
Wallumbilla, Queens.	43	26 33S	149 9 E
Walmer, Cape Province	57	33 58S	25 35 E
Walnut Ridge, U.S.A.	71	36 7N	91 0W
Walong, India	33	28 3N	97 0 E
Walsall, England	10	52 36N	1 59W
Walsenburg, U.S.A.	71	37 42N	104 45W
Walsh, Queensland	42	16 40S	144 0 E
Walsh, U.S.A.	71	37 28N	102 15W
Walsh R., Queensland	42	16 50S	144 3 E
Walterboro, U.S.A.	69	32 53N	80 40W
Walters, U.S.A.	71	34 18N	98 24W
Waltham, Canada	62	45 57N	76 57W
Waltman, U.S.A.	72	43 5N	107 16W
Walvis Bay, Cape Prov.	57	23 0S	14 28 E
Wamala L., Uganda	53	0 20N	31 50 E
Wamba, Zaire	54	2 10N	28 5 E
Wamba, Nigeria	52	8 58N	8 34 E
Wamba, Tanzania	53	5 50S	34 14 E
Wamego, U.S.A.	70	39 14N	96 19W
Wami R., Tanzania	53	6 10S	38 30 E
Wamlana, Indonesia	35	3 10S	126 30 E
Wana, Pakistan	32	32 20N	69 32 E
Wanaaring, N.S.W.	43	29 36S	144 8 E
Wanaka, New Zealand	47	44 42S	169 10 E
Wanaka L., N.Z.	47	44 33S	169 7 E
Wanan, China	39	26 25N	114 44 E
Wanapiri, Indonesia	35	4 30S	135 50 E
Wanapitei, Canada	62	46 30N	80 45W
Wanapitei L., Canada	62	46 45N	80 40W
Wanbi, S. Australia	43	34 46S	140 21 E
Wanchuan, China	38	40 55N	114 40 E
Wanda, Peru	78	8 15S	78 10W
Wanderer, Rhodesia	56	19 38S	29 58 E
Wando, S. Korea	38	34 50N	126 50 E
Wandoan, Queensland	43	26 5S	149 55 E
Wanga, Zaire	53	2 59N	29 14 E
Wangaehu R, N.Z.	46	39 45S	175 25 E
Wanganui, N.Z.	46	39 55S	175 3 E
Wangerooge, I., Ger.	14	53 47N	7 52 E
Wangunui R., N.I., N.Z.	46	39 25S	175 4 E
Wanganui R., S.I., N.Z.	47	43 3S	170 26 E
Wangaratta, Victoria	43	36 20S	146 7 E
Wangi, Kenya	53	2 0S	41 0 E
Wangianna, S. Australia	43	29 37S	137 35 E
Wangiwangi I., Indon.	35	5 22S	123 37 E
Wangkiang, China	39	30 10N	116 40 E
Wangtu, China	38	38 45N	115 8 E
Wanhsien, China	39	30 50N	108 30 E
Wanhsien, China	38	36 45N	107 24 E
Wankie, Rhodesia	56	18 18S	26 30 E
Wanka R., *See* Coco R.	75		
Wanless, Canada	65	54 11N	101 25 E
Wanstead, New Zealand	46	40 8S	176 30W
Wantsai, China	39	28 10N	114 10W
Wanyang Shan, China	39	26 30N	113 45 E
Wanyuan, China	39	31 48N	108 1 E
Wapakoneta, U.S.A.	68	40 35N	84 10W
Wapato, U.S.A.	72	46 29N	120 26W
Wapikopo L., Canada	62	52 50N	88 10W
Wapiti, Canada	62	49 50N	84 17W
Wapiti R., Canada	64	55 5N	119 0W
Wappau L., Canada	64	55 30N	112 0W
Wapsipinicon, R., U.S.A.	70	42 15N	91 30W
War, Uganda	53	2 36N	30 53 E
War Gudud, Kenya	53	3 8N	40 31 E
Warangal, India	32	17 58N	79 45 E
Waratah, Tasmania	43	41 30S	145 30 E
Warburton, Victoria	43	37 41S	145 42 E
Warburton Ra., Austral.	45	25 55S	126 28 E
Warburton, The R., S. Australia	44	27 30S	138 30 E
Ward, New Zealand	47	41 49S	174 11 E
Ward Cove, Alaska	64	55 25N	132 10W
Ward Hunt, C., Papua	42	8 4S	148 5 E
Warden, O.F.S.	57	27 50S	29 0 E
Wardha, India	32	20 45N	78 39 E
Wardha, R., India	32	20 43N	78 45 E
Wardlow, Canada	64	50 56N	111 31W
Ware, Canada	64	57 26N	125 41W
Warialda, N.S.W.	43	29 29S	150 33 E
Wariap, Indonesia	35	1 30S	134 5 E
Warkworth, N.Z.	46	36 24S	174 41 E
Warm Springs, Mont., U.S.A.	72	46 12N	112 50W
Warm Springs, Nev., U.S.A.	73	38 20N	116 34W
Warman, Canada	65	52 25N	106 30W
Warmbad, S.W. Africa	57	28 25S	18 42 E
Warmbad, Transvaal	57	24 51S	28 19 E
Warnemünde, Ger.	14	54 9N	12 5 E
Warner, Canada	64	49 20N	112 10W
Warner Range, U.S.A.	72	41 30N	120 20W
Warner Robins, U.S.A.	64	32 41N	83 16W
Warra, Queensland	43	26 55S	150 51 E
Warracknabeal, Victoria	43	36 9S	142 26 E
Warragul, Victoria	43	38 1S	145 57 E
Warrawagine, Australia	44	20 47S	120 40 E
Warrego Ra., Queens.	42	24 50S	145 40 E
Warrego R., Queens.	43	28 30S	145 35 E
Warren, Ark., U.S.A.	71	33 35N	92 4W
Warren, N.S.W.	43	31 42S	147 51 E
Warren, Ohio, U.S.A.	68	41 18N	80 52W
Warren, Pa., U.S.A.	69	41 52N	79 10W
Warren Cr., N.S.W.	43	31 15S	147 55 E
Warren I., Alaska	64	55 53N	133 55W
Warren R., Australia	44	34 12S	116 15 E
Warrenpoint, N. Ireland	11	54 7N	6 15W
Warrensburg, U.S.A.	70	38 43N	93 44W
Warrens Landing, Can.	65	53 40N	98 0W
Warrenton, Cape Prov.	57	28 9S	24 47 E
Warrenton, U.S.A.	72	46 10N	128 58W
Warri, Nigeria	52	5 30N	5 41 E
Warri Warri, N.S.W.	43	29 1S	141 55 E
Warriedar, mt., W. Australia	44	29 2S	117 2 E
Warrina, S. Australia	45	28 11S	135 50 E
Warrington, England	10	53 25N	2 38W
Warrington, N.Z.	47	45 43S	170 35 E
Warrington, U.S.A.	69	30 22N	87 16W
Warrnambool, Victoria	43	38 12S	142 31 E
Warroad, U.S.A.	70	49 0N	95 21W
Warsaw (Warszawa), Poland	16	52 13N	21 0 E
Warsaw, Ind., U.S.A.	68	41 18N	85 50W
Warta R., Poland	16	52 40N	16 10 E
Waru, Indonesia	35	3 30S	130 36 E
Warud, India	32	21 30N	78 16 E
Warwick, England	10	52 17N	1 36W
Warwick, Queensland	43	28 10S	152 1 E
Warwick, U.S.A.	68	41 43N	71 25W
Wasa, Canada	64	49 45N	115 50W
Wasbank, Natal	57	28 15S	30 9 E
Wasco, Calif., U.S.A.	73	35 39N	119 20W
Wasco, Oreg., U.S.A.	72	45 34N	120 44W
Wase, Nigeria	52	8 40N	9 50 E
Waseca, U.S.A.	70	44 2N	93 30W
Wasekamio L., Canada	65	56 50N	108 40W
Washburn, N.D., U.S.A.	70	47 25N	101 0W
Washburn, Wis., U.S.A.	70	46 41N	90 52W
Washington, D.C., U.S.A.	68	38 50N	77 0W
Washington, Ga., U.S.A.	69	33 43N	82 46W
Washington, Indiana	68	38 40N	87 10W
Washington, Iowa, U.S.A.	70	41 17N	91 42W
Washington, Mo., U.S.A.	70	38 30N	91 0W
Washington, N. C., U.S.A.	69	35 35N	77 0W
Washington Ohio, U.S.A.	68	39 34N	83 25W
Washington, Pa., U.S.A.	68	40 10N	80 17W
Washington, Utah, U.S.A.	73	37 8N	113 29W
Washington, st., U.S.A.	72	47 20N	120 0W
Washington I., U.S.A.	68	45 22N	86 55W
Waskaiowaka L., Can.	65	56 35N	96 40W
Waskesiu Lake, Canada	65	53 50N	106 0W
Wassenaar, Netherlands	13	52 8N	4 24 E

Place	Map	Latitude	Longitude
Wassy, France	12	48 30N	4 58 E
Watansoppeng, Indon.	35	4 30 S	119 50 E
Watapu, R., N.Z.	46	37 55N	178 15 E
Wataroa, New Zealand	47	43 18 S	170 24 E
Wataroa R., N.Z.	47	43 7 S	170 16 E
Water Valley, U.S.A.	71	34 10N	89 30W
Waterberg, S.W. Africa	55	20 30 S	17 18 E
Waterbury, U.S.A.	69	41 32N	73 0W
Waterbury L., Canada	65	58 0N	104 20W
Waterfall, Alaska	64	55 25N	133 0W
Waterford, Ireland	11	52 16N	7 8W
Waterford, co., Ireland	11	52 10N	7 40W
Waterford Harb., Ire.	11	52 10N	6 58W
Waterhen L., Canada	65	52 10N	99 40W
Waterloo, Belgium	13	50 43N	4 25 E
Waterloo, Canada	62	43 30N	80 32W
Waterloo, Sierra Leone	52	8 26N	13 8W
Waterloo, Ill., U.S.A.	70	38 20N	90 10W
Waterloo, Iowa, U.S.A.	70	42 34N	92 20W
Watersmeet, U.S.A.	70	46 15N	89 12W
Waterton, R., Canada	64	49 15N	114 50W
Waterton Lakes Nat. Pk., Can.	64	49 10N	114 0W
Watertown, S.D., U.S.A.	70	45 0N	97 0W
Watertown, N.Y. U.S.A.	68	43 58N	75 57W
Watertown, Wis., U.S.A.	70	43 10N	88 46W
Waterval-Bo., Transvaal	57	25 40 S	30 18 E
Waterville, Ireland	11	51 49N	10 10W
Waterville, Me., U.S.A.	69	44 35N	69 40W
Waterville, Wash., U.S.A.	72	47 41N	120 2W
Watervliet, U.S.A.	68	42 46N	73 43W
Waterways, Canada	64	56 55N	111 20W
Watford, England	10	51 38N	0 23W
Watford City, U.S.A.	70	47 50N	103 37W
Wathaman R., Canada	65	56 50N	104 30W
Watheroo, W. Australia	44	30 15 S	116 0W
Watino, Canada	64	55 41N	117 40W
Watkins Glen, U.S.A.	68	42 25N	76 55W
Watlam, China	39	22 41N	110 10 E
Watlings I. *See* San Salvador I.	75		
Watonga, U.S.A.	71	35 49N	98 27W
Watrous, Canada	65	51 40N	105 25W
Watrous, U.S.A.	71	35 46N	104 51W
Watsa, Zaire	53	3 0N	29 30 E
Watson, Canada	65	52 10N	104 30W
Watsonville, U.S.A.	73	36 54N	121 48W
Watseka, U.S.A.	70	40 44N	87 43W
Watson Lake, Canada	64	60 7N	128 48W
Watten, Queensland	42	21 1 S	144 1 E
Wattwil, Switzerland	15	47 18N	9 6 E
Watubella Is., Indon.	35	4 28 S	131 54 E
Wau, Sudan	54	7 45N	28 1 E
Wau, Terr. of N. Guin.	42	7 25 S	146 42 E
Waubay, U.S.A.	70	45 25N	97 16W
Wauchula, U.S.A.	69	27 35N	81 50W
Waugh, Canada	65	49 40N	95 20W
Waukarlycarly, L., W. Australia	44	21 18 S	121 46 E
Waukegan, U.S.A.	70	42 20N	87 50W
Waukesha, U.S.A.	70	42 59N	88 17W
Waukon, U.S.A.	70	43 13N	91 34W
Wauneta, U.S.A.	70	40 28N	101 24W
Waupaca, U.S.A.	70	44 22N	89 8W
Waupun, U.S.A.	70	43 38N	88 44W
Waurika, U.S.A.	71	34 9N	98 0W
Wausau, U.S.A.	70	44 59N	89 35W
Wautoma, U.S.A.	70	44 6N	89 19W
Wauwatosa, U.S.A.	70	43 0N	88 0W
Wave Hill, N. Terr., Australia	40	17 32N	131 0 E
Waveney R., England	10	52 24N	1 20 E
Waverley, Canada	63	44 47N	63 32W
Waverley, New Zealand	46	39 46 S	174 37 E
Waverly, Iowa, U.S.A.	70	42 40N	92 30W
Waverly, N.Y., U.S.A.	69	42 0N	76 33W
Wavre, Belgium	13	50 43N	4 38 E
Wawanesa, Canada	65	49 30N	99 40W
Wawoi R., Papua	42	7 50 S	143 0 E
Waxahachie, U.S.A.	71	32 25N	97 0W
Way, L., W. Australia	44	26 45 S	120 16 E
Waycross, U.S.A.	69	31 14N	82 24W
Wayne, U.S.A.	70	42 15N	97 0W
Wayne W., Va., U.S.A.	68	38 13N	82 25W
Waynesbore, Ga., U.S.A.	69	33 4N	82 1W
Waynesbore, Miss., U.S.A.	69	31 40N	88 40W
Waynesboro, Pa., U.S.A.	68	39 45N	77 35W
Waynesboro, Va., U.S.A.	68	38 4N	78 58W
Waynesburg, U.S.A.	69	39 54N	80 12W
Waynoka, U.S.A.	71	36 36N	98 55W
Wazirabad (Balkh), Afghanistan	31	36 44N	66 47 E
Weatherford, Texas, U.S.A.	71	32 50N	97 50W
Weatherford, Okla., U.S.A.	71	35 32N	98 45W
Webb City, U.S.A.	71	37 6N	94 31W
Weber, New Zealand	46	40 24 S	176 20 E
Webster, S.D., U.S.A.	70	45 25N	97 44W
Webster, Wis., U.S.A.	70	45 54N	92 23W
Webster City, U.S.A.	70	42 33N	93 49W
Webster Green, U.S.A.	70	38 35N	90 16W
Webster Springs, U.S.A.	68	38 30N	80 25W
Weda, Indonesia	35	0 30N	127 50 E
Weddell Sea, Ant.	80	72 30 S	40 0W
Wedderburn, Victoria	43	36 20 S	143 33 E
Wedgeport, Canada	63	43 44N	66 0W
Wedza, Rhodesia	56	18 40 S	31 33 E
Wee Waa, N.S.W.	43	30 11 S	149 26 E
Weed, U.S.A.	72	41 27N	122 25W
Weenen, Natal	57	28 48 S	30 7 E
Weert, Netherlands	13	51 15N	5 43 E
Weesen, Switzerland	15	47 8N	9 6 E
Wegrow, Poland	16	52 24N	22 0 E
Wei Ho, R., Honan, China	38	35 45N	114 30 E
Wei Ho, R., Shensi, China	38	34 15N	107 45 E
Weichow Tao, I , China	39	21 3N	109 8 E
Weifang, China	38	36 45N	119 5 E
Weihai, China	38	37 30N	122 10 E
Weihwei. *See* Chihsien, China	38		
Weimar, Germany	14	51 0N	11 20 E
Weinan, China	38	34 30N	109 30 E
Weinfelden, Switz.	15	47 34N	9 7 E
Weinheim, Germany	14	49 33N	8 40 E
Weipa, Queensland	42	12 24 S	142 0 E
Weir R , Queensland	45	28 20 S	149 45 E
Weir R., Canada	65	56 0N	93 45W
Weiser, U.S.A.	72	44 10N	117 0W
Weiyüan, Kansu, China	38	35 10N	104 20 E
Weiyuan, Szechwan, China	39	29 35N	104 30 E
Wejherowo, Poland	16	54 35N	18 12 E
Wekusko, Canada	65	54 45N	99 45W
Wekusko L., Canada	65	54 40N	99 50W
Welby, Canada	65	50 43N	101 29W
Welch, U.S.A.	68	37 28N	81 38W
Welcome, Queensland	42	15 20 S	144 40 E
Weld Ra., W. Austral.	44	26 53 S	117 30 E
Welford, Queensland	43	25 9 S	143 42 E
Welkom, O.F.S.	57	28 0 S	26 50 E
Welland, Canada	62	42 59N	79 14W
Welland, R., England	10	52 43N	0 10W
Wellawaya, Sri Lanka	32	6 40N	81 10 E
Wellesley Is., Queens.	42	17 20 S	139 30 E
Wellin, Belgium	13	50 5N	5 6 E
Wellington, Canada	62	43 57N	77 20W
Wellington, Cape Prov.	57	33 38 S	18 57 E
Wellington, N.S.W.	43	32 30 S	149 0 E
Wellington, N.Z.	46	41 19 S	174 46 E
Wellington, dist., N.Z.	46	40 8 S	175 36 E
Wellington, S. Australia	43	35 16 S	139 21 E
Wellington, U.S.A.	71	37 10N	97 25W
Wellington, Colorado, U.S.A.	70	40 44N	105 0W
Wellington, Nev., U.S.A.	73	38 46N	119 23W
Wellington, Texas, U.S.A.	71	34 50N	100 14W
Wellington I., Chile	77	49 30 S	75 0W
Wellington L., Victoria	43	38 5 S	147 22 E
Wellington Ra., W. Australia	44	26 30 S	122 0 E
Wells, Minn., U.S.A.	70	43 43N	93 45W
Wells, Nev., U.S.A.	72	41 9N	115 0W
Wells L., W. Australia	45	26 44 S	123 15 E
Wells Gray Prov. Park	64	52 30N	120 0W
Wellsboro, U.S.A.	68	41 46N	77 20W
Wellsford, N.Z.	46	36 16 S	174 32 E
Wellsville, Mo., U.S.A.	70	39 0N	91 30W
Wellsville, N.Y., U.S.A.	68	42 9N	77 53W
Wellsville, Utah, U.S.A.	72	41 37N	111 58W
Wellton, U.S.A.	73	32 41N	114 6W
Wels, Austria	14	48 9N	14 1 E
Welshpool, Wales	10	52 40N	3 9W
Welwyn, Canada	65	50 20N	101 30W
Wembere R., Tanzania	53	4 40 S	34 0 E
Wenatchee, U.S.A.	72	47 25N	120 20W
Wenchi, Ghana	52	7 46N	2 8W
Wenchow, China	39	28 0N	120 35 E
Wendell, U.S.A.	72	42 46N	114 45W
Wendover, U.S.A.	72	40 46N	114 1W
Wengnui, China	38	43 0N	118 45 E
Wengteng, China	38	37 15N	122 0 E
Wenhsien, China	38	32 55N	104 35 E
Wenlock R., Queens.	42	12 15 S	142 0 E
Wensi, China	38	35 25N	111 7 E
Wensiang, China	38	34 35N	110 40 E
Wentworth, N.S.W.	43	34 2 S	141 54 E
Weott, U.S.A.	72	40 19N	123 55W
Wepener, O.F.S.	57	29 42 S	27 3 E
Weri, Indonesia	35	3 10 S	132 30 E
Werris Creek, N.S.W.	43	31 18 S	150 38 E
Wersar, Indonesia	35	1 30 S	131 55 E
Wesel, Germany	14	51 39N	6 34 E
Weser R., Germany	14	53 33N	8 30 E
Weslaco, U.S.A.	71	26 9N	97 59W
Wesleyville, U.S.A.	63	42 9N	80 1W
Wessington, U.S.A.	70	44 30N	98 37W
Wessington Springs, U.S.A.	70	44 8N	98 32W
West, U.S.A.	71	31 48N	97 3W
West B., U.S.A.	71	29 5N	89 30W
West Bay, Sierra Leone	52	Inset	
West Bend, U.S.A.	70	43 27N	88 10W
West Bengal, prov., India	33	25 0N	90 0 E
West Beskids, C.Slov.	16	49 30N	19 20 E
West Branch, U.S.A.	68	44 17N	84 15W
West Bromwich, Eng.	10	52 32N	2 1W
West Camerooon	52	5 50N	9 20 E
West C., New Zealand	47	45 55 S	166 29 E
West Chester, U.S.A.	68	39 58N	75 36W
West Columbia, U.S.A.	71	29 10N	95 41W
West Daja I., Indonesia	35	7 25 S	127 10 E
West Des Moines, U.S.A.	70	41 32N	93 46W
West Dvina R., U.S.S.R.	24	55 40N	28 0 E
West Fork, R., U.S.A.	71	33 25N	98 0W
West Frankfort, U.S.A.	70	37 56N	89 0W
West Germany, rep., Europe	14	47 0N to 55 0N	6 0E to 11 0E
West Harbour, N.Z.	47	45 51 S	170 33 E
West Hartlepool, Eng.	10	54 42N	1 11W
West Helena, U.S.A.	71	34 32N	90 37W
West Indies, arch.	75	10 0 to 23 30N	59 0 to 85 0W
West Irian, Indonesia	35	4 0 S	135 0 E
West Java, Indonesia	34	6 35 S	106 42 E
West Lake, prov., Tang.	53	2 0 S	32 0 E
West Leichhardt, Queensland	42	20 34 S	139 43 E
West Lunga R., Zambia	56	12 30 S	24 28 E
West Magpie R., Can.	63	51 15N	65 0W
West Memphis, U.S.A.	71	35 4N	90 3W
West Monroe, U.S.A.	71	32 31N	92 6W
West Nicholson, Rhodesia	56	21 2 S	29 20 E
West Nile, dist., Ugan.	53	3 0N	31 15 E
West Pakistan, Province, Pakistan	32	26 35N	65 50 E
West Palm Beach, U.S.A.	69	26 50N	80 0W
West Plains, U.S.A.	71	36 43N	91 55W
West Point, Canada	63	49 55N	64 30W
West Point, Ga., U.S.A.	69	32 54N	85 10W
West Point, Miss., U.S.A.	71	33 40N	88 40W
West Point, Nebr., U.S.A.	70	41 50N	96 36W
West Point, Va., U.S.A.	68	37 34N	76 49W
West Road, R., Canada	64	53 10N	124 0W
West Samoa I., Pac. Oc.	7	14 0 S	172 0W
West Schelde, Neth.	13	51 23N	3 50 E
West Siberian Plain, U.S.S.R.	26	62 0N	75 0 E
West Virginia, st., U.S.A.	68	38 45N	81 0W
West Wyalong, N.S.W.	43	33 56 S	147 10 E
West Yellowstone, U.S.A.	72	44 40N	111 2W
West York I., S. China Sea	35	11 10N	115 15 E
Westbank, Canada	64	49 50N	119 25W
Westbrook, Me., U.S.A.	69	43 40N	70 22W
Westbrook, Texas U.S.A.	71	32 21N	100 58W
Westbury, Tasmania	43	41 30 S	146 51 E
Westby, N.S.W.	43	35 30 S	147 24 E
Westby, U.S.A.	70	48 55N	104 2W
Western, prov., Ghana	52	5 40N	1 40W
Western, div., N.S.W.	43	31 48 S	144 7 E
Western, prov., Nigeria	52	7 0N	5 0 E
Western, prov., Zambia	56	13 0 S	28 0 E
Western, dist., S. Australia	45	32 0 S	133 30 E
Western, prov., Ugan.	53	0 40N	30 30 E
Western, dist., Victoria	43	37 45 S	142 30 E
Western Australia, st., Commonwealth of Australia	40	13 45 S to 35 0 S	13 0 E to 129 20 E
Western Bay, Canada	63	46 40N	52 30W
Western Ghats, Mts., India	32	15 30N	74 30 E
Western Port, U.S.A.	68	30 30N	79 5W
Western, prov., Kenya	53	0 30N	34 30 E
Western Region, Tasmania	43	42 4 S	145 35 E
Western Sayan, U.S.S.R.	27	52 30N	94 0 E
Western Shaw, Australia	44	21 48 S	119 9 E
Westerwald Mts., Ger.	14	50 39N	8 0 E
Westfield, Canada	63	45 27N	66 20W
Westhope, U.S.A.	70	48 57N	101 0W
Westland, dist., N.Z.	47	43 33 S	169 59 E
Westland Bight, N.Z.	47	42 55 S	170 5 E
Westlock, Canada	64	54 20N	113 55W
Westmeath, co., Ireland	11	53 40N	7 30W
Westminster, Md., U.S.A.	68	39 36N	77 1W
Westmorland, U.S.A.	73	33 2N	115 39W
Weston, Sabah	35	5 10N	115 35 E
Weston, Oreg., U.S.A.	72	45 51N	118 29W
Weston, W. Va., U.S.A.	68	39 0N	80 29W
Weston I., Canada	62	52 30N	79 50W
Weston-super-Mare, England	10	51 20N	2 59W
Westonia, Australia	44	31 12 S	118 38 E
Westport, Ireland	11	53 44N	9 31W
Westport, New Zealand	47	41 46 S	171 37 E
Westport, U.S.A.	72	46 55N	124 2W
Westray, Canada	65	53 30N	101 24W
Westray I., Scotland	10	59 18N	3 0W
Westree, Canada	62	47 26N	81 34W
Westview, Canada	64	49 50N	124 31W
Westville, Ill., U.S.A.	68	40 0N	87 40W
Westville, Okla., U.S.A.	71	36 0N	94 33W
Westwood, Queensland	42	23 38 S	150 8 E
Westwood, U.S.A.	72	40 20N	120 20W
Weta, Ghana	52	1 0N	0 58 E
Wetar, Indonesia	35	7 50 S	126 30 E
Wetaskiwin, Canada	64	52 55N	113 24W
Wete, I., Tanzania	53	5 3 S	39 41 E
Wetteren, Belgium	13	51 0N	3 53 E
Wettingen, Switz.	15	47 28N	8 20 E
Wetzikon, Switz.	15	47 19N	8 48 E
Wetzlar, Germany	14	50 33N	8 30 E
Wewak, Terr. of New Guinea	42	3 29 S	143 28 E
Wewoka, U.S.A.	71	35 11N	96 30W
Wexford, Ireland	11	52 20N	6 28W
Wexford, co., Ireland	11	52 20N	6 25W
Wexford Harb., Ireland	11	52 20N	6 25W
Weyburn, Canada	65	49 40N	103 50W
Weymont, Canada	62	47 50N	73 50W
Weymouth, Canada	63	44 30N	66 1W
Weymouth, England	10	50 36N	2 28W
Weymouth C., Queens.	42	12 35 S	143 27 E
Whakamaru, N.Z.	46	38 28 S	175 49 E
Whakatane, N.Z.	46	37 57 S	177 1 E
Whakatane R., N.Z.	46	38 15 S	177 1 E
Whales, B. of, Ant.	80	78 0 S	165 0W
Whampoa, China	39	23 8N	113 28 E
Whangamata, N.Z.	46	37 13 S	175 52 E
Whangamomona, N.Z.	46	39 8 S	174 44 E
Whangarei, N.Z.	46	35 43 S	174 21 E
Whangarei Harb., N.Z.	46	35 46 S	174 29 E
Whangaroa, N.Z.	46	35 4 S	173 46 E
Whangaroa Harb., N.Z.	46	35 4 S	173 46 E
Whangaruru Harb., N.Z.	46	35 22 S	174 22 E
Wharanui, N.Z.	47	41 55 S	174 6 E
Wharfedale, England	20	54 7N	2 4W
Wharton, U.S.A.	71	29 19N	96 7W
Wheatland, U.S.A.	70	42 5N	104 58W
Wheatley, Canada	63	42 7N	82 29W
Wheatley, England	16	51 44N	1 8W
Wheaton, U.S.A.	70	45 48N	96 29W
Wheeler, Oreg., U.S.A.	72	45 42N	123 56W
Wheeler, Texas, U.S.A.	71	35 28N	100 14W
Wheeler, R., Que., Can.	63	56 0N	67 0W
Wheeler, R., Sask., Can.	65	57 30N	106 0W
Wheeler Peak, U.S.A.	73	39 0N	115 0W
Wheeling, U.S.A.	68	40 2N	80 41W
Whisky Gap, Canada	64	49 0N	113 3W
Whiskyjack L., Canada	65	58 0N	102 0W
Whistler, U.S.A.	69	30 50N	88 10W
Whitby, England	10	54 29N	0 37W
Whitby. Queensland	42	16 10 S	145 26 E
Whitcombe, Mt., N.Z.	47	43 10 S	170 54 E
Whitcombe P., N.Z.	47	43 12 S	171 0 E
White B., Canada	63	50 0N	56 35W
White I., N.Z.	46	37 30 S	177 13 E
White Mts., C.Slov.	16	49 0N	17 50 E
White Mts., U.S.A.	73	37 30N	118 30W
White R., Ark., U.S.A.	71	36 5N	92 6W
White R., Colo., U.S.A.	73	40 10N	108 50W
White R., Ind., U.S.A.	68	38 40N	87 20W
White R., S.D., U.S.A.	70	43 45N	100 0W
White Sea, U.S.S.R.	24	66 0N	38 0 E
White City, U.S.A.	70	38 50N	96 44W
White Cliffs, N.S.W.	43	30 50 S	143 10 E
White Cliffs, N.Z.	47	43 26 S	171 55 E
White Deer, U.S.A.	71	35 29N	101 5W
White Drin R., Y.slav.	21	42 30N	20 35 E
White Gull Lakes, Can.	63	55 30N	64 40W
White Hall, U.S.A.	70	39 25N	90 23W
White Hope, W. Austral.	44	31 0 S	121 38 E
White, L., U.S.A.	71	29 46N	92 30W
White Nile R., Sudan	51	9 30N	31 40 E
White Otter L., Canada	65	49 5N	91 55W
White Pass, Canada	64	59 40N	135 3W
White River, Canada	62	48 35N	85 20W
White River (Whitrivier), Transvaal	57	25 20 S	31 0 E
White River, U.S.A.	70	43 39N	100 42W
White Russia S.S.R., U.S.S.R.	24	53 30N	27 0 E
White Sulphur Springs, W. Va., U.S.A.	68	37 50N	80 16W
White Sulphur Springs, Mont., U.S.A.	72	46 32N	110 57W
White Volta R., Ghana	52	9 0N	1 14W
Whitebird, U.S.A.	72	45 48N	116 21W
Whitecourt, Canada	64	54 10N	115 45W
Whiteface, U.S.A.	71	33 32N	102 36W
Whitefish, U.S.A.	72	48 25N	114 25W
Whitefish L., Canada	65	62 35N	107 20W
Whitefish Pt., U.S.A.	68	46 5N	85 0W
Whitehall, Ireland	11	52 42N	7 2W
Whitehall, Michigan., U.S.A.	68	43 22N	86 20W
Whitehall, Montana., U.S.A.	72	45 53N	112 6W
Whitehall, Wis., U.S.A.	70	44 18N	91 18W
Whitehaven, England	10	54 33N	3 35W
Whitehead, N. Ireland	11	54 45N	5 42W
Whitehorse, Canada	64	60 40N	135 5W
Whiteman, Ra., New Guinea	42	5 50 S	149 50 E

	MAP		
Whitemud R., Canada	64	56 30N	118 0W
Whitemouth, Canada	65	50 0N	96 10W
Whitemouth L., Canada	65	49 15N	95 50W
Whitesail L., Canada	64	53 35N	127 45W
Whitesand R., Canada	64	54 30N	116 0W
Whitesboro, U.S.A.	71	33 37N	96 58W
Whiteshell Prov. Park, Canada	65	50 0N	95 30W
Whitetail, U.S.A.	70	48 55N	105 13W
Whitewater, U.S.A.	70	42 48N	88 45W
Whitewater L., Canada	62	50 50N	89 10W
Whitewater Baldy, mt., U.S.A.	73	33 20N	108 40W
Whitewood, Canada	65	50 20N	102 20W
Whiteville, U.S.A.	69	34 20N	78 40W
Whitfield, Victoria	43	36 42S	146 24E
Whitmire, U.S.A.	69	34 33N	81 40W
Whitney, Canada	62	45 31N	78 14W
Whitney, mt., U.S.A.	73	36 30N	118 20W
Whitrivier (White River), Transvaal	57	25 20S	31 0E
Whitsunday I., Queens.	42	20 15S	149 4E
Whittle, C., Canada	63	50 11N	60 8W
Whittlesea, Victoria	43	37 27S	145 9E
Whittlesea, Cape Prov.	57	32 11S	26 50E
Whitton, N.S.W.	43	34 30S	146 6E
Whitwell, U.S.A.	69	35 11N	85 31W
Wholdaia L., Canada	65	60 40N	104 20W
Whyalla, S. Australia	43	33 2S	137 30E
Wiaga, Ghana	52	10 42N	1 16W
Wiarton, Canada	62	44 50N	81 10W
Wichita, U.S.A.	71	37 40N	97 20W
Wichita Falls, U.S.A.	71	38 55N	98 30W
Wick, Scotland	10	58 26N	3 5W
Wickamunna L. *See* Philippi L.	42		
Wickenburg, U.S.A.	73	33 58N	112 46W
Wickepin, W. Austral.	44	32 42S	117 33E
Wickett, U.S.A.	71	31 32N	102 58W
Wicklow, Ireland	11	53 0N	6 2W
Wicklow, co., Ireland	11	52 59N	6 25W
Wicklow Hd., Ireland	11	52 59N	6 3W
Wicklow Mts., Ireland	11	53 0N	6 30W
Wide Bay, Terr. of New Guinea	42	4 52S	152 0E
Widgemooltha, Austral.	44	31 29S	121 30E
Wielun, Poland	16	51 15N	18 40E
Wien. *See* Vienna.	14		
Wiener Neustadt, Austria	14	47 49N	16 15E
Wierden, Netherlands	13	52 22N	6 35E
Wierzbnik, Poland	16	51 2N	21 10E
Wiesbaden, Germany	14	50 7N	8 17E
Wigan, England	10	53 33N	2 38W
Wiggins, Colo., U.S.A.	70	40 16N	104 3W
Wiggins, Minn., U.S.A.	71	30 51N	89 7W
Wigtown, Scotland	10	54 52N	4 27W
Wil, Switzerland	15	47 28N	9 3E
Wilber, U.S.A.	70	40 32N	97 0W
Wilburton, U.S.A.	71	34 50N	95 17W
Wilcannia, N.S.W.	43	31 30S	143 26E
Wilderness, Cape Prov.	57	34 0S	22 33E
Wildhorn, mt., Switz.	15	46 22N	7 22E
Wildrose, U.S.A.	70	48 36N	103 17W
Wildwood, U.S.A.	68	39 0N	74 50W
Wilge R., O.F.S.	57	27 0S	28 15E
Wilgena, S. Australia	45	30 53S	134 53E
Wilhelm, Mt., New Guinea	42	5 55S	145 0E
Wilhelmina Mt., Guyana	79	3 50N	56 30W
Wilhelmshaven, Ger.	14	53 30N	8 9E
Wilhelmstal, S.W. Africa	57	21 54S	16 19E
Wilkes, Antarctica	80	65 0S	111 0E
Wilkes Land, Ant.	80	69 0S	120 0E
Wilkes Sub-Glacial Basin, Ant.	80	85 0S	136 0E
Wilkes-Barre, U.S.A.	68	41 15N	75 52W
Wilkesboro, U.S.A.	69	36 9N	81 10W
Wilkie, Canada	65	52 27N	108 42W
Willamina, U.S.A.	72	45 3N	123 30W
Willandra Billabong R., N.S.W.	43	33 10S	144 30E
Willapa, B., U.S.A.	72	46 40N	124 0W
Willara, U.S.A.	73	34 38N	106 2W
Willard, U.S.A.	72	41 28N	112 3W
Willaumez, Pen., New Guinea	42	5 1S	150 5E
Willcox, U.S.A.	73	32 17N	109 55W
Willemstad, Curaçao	75	12 5N	69 0W
William Creek, S. Australia	45	28 52S	136 10E
William Mt., Victoria	43	37 11S	142 33E
William, Mt., W. Australia	44	33 8S	116 10E
William R., Canada	65	58 30N	109 20W
William II Coast, Ant.	80	67 0S	90 0E
Williams, U.S.A.	73	35 16N	112 11W
Williams Lake, Canada	64	52 20N	122 10W
Williamsburg, Ky., U.S.A.	68	36 54N	84 10W
Williamsburg, Va., U.S.A.	69	37 18N	76 42W
Williamson, W., Va., U.S.A.	68	37 40N	82 19W
Williamsport, U.S.A.	68	41 18N	77 1W

	MAP		
Williamston, U.S.A.	69	35 50N	77 5W
Williamstown, Victoria	43	37 46S	144 58E
Williamsville, U.S.A.	71	37 2N	90 32W
Willisau, Switzerland	15	47 7N	7 59E
Williston, Cape Prov.	57	31 20S	20 53E
Williston, Fla., U.S.A.	69	29 25N	82 28W
Williston, N.D., U.S.A.	70	48 10N	103 35W
Willits, U.S.A.	72	39 28N	123 27W
Willmar, U.S.A.	70	45 10N	95 8W
Willoughby C., S. Australia	43	35 45S	138 2E
Willowbunch, Canada	65	49 20N	105 35W
Willow L., Canada	64	62 0N	119 0W
Willow R., Canada	64	53 15N	122 10W
Willow Lake, U.S.A.	70	44 40N	97 39W
Willow River, Canada	64	44 40N	97 40W
Willow Springs, U.S.A.	71	37 0N	92 0W
Willowlake, R., Canada	64	62 20N	121 30W
Willowmore, Cape Prov.	57	33 15S	23 30E
Willows, U.S.A.	72	39 30N	122 13W
Willowvale, Cape Prov.	57	32 15S	28 31E
Wills Cr., Queensland	42	22 0S	139 45E
Wills Point, U.S.A.	71	32 41N	95 59W
Willunga, S. Australia	43	35 15S	138 30E
Wilmette, U.S.A.	70	42 5N	87 45W
Wilmington, S. Austral.	43	32 37S	138 0E
Wilmington, Del., U.S.A.	68	39 45N	75 33W
Wilmington, Ill., U.S.A.	70	41 20N	88 10W
Wilmington, N.C., U.S.A.	69	34 18N	68 55W
Wilmington, Ohio, U.S.A.	68	39 26N	83 48W
Wilpena Cr., S. Australia	43	31 15S	139 30E
Wilsall, U.S.A.	72	46 0N	110 39W
Wilson, U.S.A.	69	35 40N	77 50W
Wilson, mt., U.S.A.	73	37 52N	108 11W
Wilson R., Queensland	43	27 20S	142 45E
Wilson, R., W. Austral.	44	16 40S	128 0E
Wilton, U.S.A.	70	47 9N	100 47W
Wiltz, Luxembourg	13	49 57N	5 55E
Wiluna, W. Australia	43	26 40S	120 25E
Wimborne, Canada	64	52 0N	113 40W
Wimmera, dist., Vic.	43	36 30S	142 0E
Wimmera R., Victoria	43	36 48S	142 50E
Winburg, O.F.S.	57	28 30S	27 2E
Winchester, England	10	51 4N	1 19W
Winchester, N.Z.	47	44 11S	171 17E
Winchester, Idaho, U.S.A.	72	46 14N	116 35W
Winchester, Ind., U.S.A.	68	40 10N	85 0W
Winchester, Ky., U.S.A.	68	38 1N	84 0W
Winchester, Va., U.S.A.	68	39 15N	78 9W
Winconsin R., U.S.A.	70	43 20N	90 15W
Wind R., U.S.A.	72	43 30N	109 20W
Wind R., Ra., U.S.A.	72	43 0N	109 30W
Windber, U.S.A.	68	40 12N	78 50W
Windelisi, Indonesia	35	2 30S	134 10E
Winder, U.S.A.	69	34 0N	83 40W
Windera, Queensland	43	26 17S	151 51E
Windermere, England	10	54 24N	2 56W
Windflower L., Canada	64	63 30N	118 30W
Windham, Alaska	64	57 40N	133 20W
Windhoek, S.W. Africa	57	22 30S	17 2E
Windom, U.S.A.	70	43 50N	95 5W
Windorah, Queensland	43	25 24S	142 36E
Window Rock, U.S.A.	73	35 44N	109 2W
Windsor, N.S., Canada	63	44 59N	64 5W
Windsor, Ont., Canada	62	42 25N	83 0W
Windsor, England	9	51 28N	0 36W
Windsor, New Zealand	47	44 59S	170 49E
Windsor, Colo., U.S.A.	70	40 34N	104 55W
Windsor, Mo., U.S.A.	70	38 30N	93 30W
Windsor, Vt., U.S.A.	69	43 30N	72 25W
Windsorton, Cape Prov.	57	28 16S	24 44E
Windward Is., W. Indies	75	13 0N	63 0W
Windward Pass., Carib.	75	20 0N	74 0W
Winefred L., Canada	65	55 30N	110 30W
Winfield, Canada	64	52 58N	114 23W
Winfield, U.S.A.	71	37 10N	97 0W
Wingham, Canada	62	43 55N	81 25W
Wingham, N.S.W.	43	31 48S	152 22E
Winifred, U.S.A.	72	47 32N	109 25W
Winifreda, Argentina	77	36 10S	64 20W
Winisk L., Canada	62	52 55N	87 40W
Winisk R., Canada	62	54 40N	87 0W
Wink, U.S.A.	71	31 47N	103 7W
Winkler, Canada	65	49 15N	98 0W
Winlock, U.S.A.	72	46 28N	123 0W
Winneba, Ghana	52	5 25N	0 36W
Winnebago, U.S.A.	70	43 45N	94 10W
Winnebago L., U.S.A.	70	44 0N	88 15W
Winnemucca, U.S.A.	72	41 0N	117 44W
Winnenucca, L., U.S.A.	72	40 15N	119 15W
Winner, U.S.A.	70	43 25N	99 51W
Winnetka, U.S.A.	70	42 5N	87 50W
Winnett, U.S.A.	72	47 2N	108 28W
Winnfield, U.S.A.	71	31 57N	92 38W
Winnibigoshish, L., U.S.A.	70	47 31N	93 58W
Winning Pool, W. Australia	44	23 9S	114 30E
Winnipeg, Canada	65	49 50N	97 15W
Winnipeg, L., Canada	65	52 30N	98 0W
Winnipeg R., Canada	65	50 35N	95 30W
Winnipeg Beach, Can.	65	50 30N	96 58W

	MAP		
Winnipegosis, and L., Canada	65	52 40N	100 0W
Winnsboro, La., U.S.A.	71	32 10N	91 44W
Winnsboro, S.C., U.S.A.	69	34 23N	81 5W
Winnsboro, Tex., U.S.A.	71	32 58N	95 17W
Winena, Minn., U.S.A.	70	44 4N	91 45W
Winona, Miss., U.S.A.	71	33 29N	89 44W
Winooski, U.S.A.	69	44 28N	73 10W
Winschoten, Neth.	13	53 9N	7 3E
Winslow, U.S.A.	73	35 0N	110 40W
Winston-Salem, U.S.A.	69	36 6N	80 18W
Winter Garden, U.S.A.	69	28 33N	31 85W
Winter Haven, U.S.A.	69	28 0N	81 42W
Winter Park, U.S.A.	69	28 34N	81 19W
Winters, U.S.A.	71	31 58N	99 58W
Winterset, U.S.A.	70	41 19N	94 0W
Winterswijk, Neth.	13	51 58N	6 43E
Winterthur, Switz.	15	47 30N	8 44E
Winthrop, Minn., U.S.A.	70	44 31N	94 27W
Winthrop, Wash., U.S.A.	72	48 30N	120 12W
Winton, N.Z.	47	46 8S	168 20E
Winton, Queensland	42	22 21S	143 0E
Winton, U.S.A.	69	36 24N	76 59W
Wirraminna, S. Austral.	45	31 10S	136 8E
Wirrappa, S. Australia	43	31 27S	136 58E
Wirrulla, S. Australia	45	32 25S	134 37E
Wisbech, England	10	52 39N	0 10E
Wisconsin, st., U.S.A.	70	44 40N	89 40W
Wisconsin R., U.S.A.	70	43 14N	90 30W
Wisconsin Dells, U.S.A.	70	43 37N	89 46W
Wisconsin Rapids, U.S.A.	70	44 22N	89 47W
Wisdom, U.S.A.	72	45 39N	113 28W
Wiseman, Alaska	59	67 50N	150 0W
Wishek, U.S.A.	70	46 20N	99 32W
Wisla (Vistula), R., Poland	16	52 30N	19 40E
Wismar, Germany	14	53 53N	11 23E
Wisner, U.S.A.	70	42 0N	96 47W
Wissembourg, France	12	49 2N	7 57E
Witbank, Transvaal	57	25 51S	29 14E
Witham, England	10	51 48N	0 39E
Withersfield, Queens.	42	23 36S	147 36E
Wittenberg, Germany	14	51 51N	12 39E
Wittenberge, Germany	14	53 0N	11 44E
Wittstock, Germany	14	53 10N	12 30E
Witu, Kenya	53	2 20S	40 20E
Witvlei, S.W. Africa	57	22 23S	18 32E
Wkara, R., Poland	16	52 40N	20 35E
Wloclawek, Poland	16	52 39N	19 11E
Wlodawa, Poland	16	51 33N	23 31E
Wloszczowa, Poland	15	50 51N	19 58E
Wodgina, W. Australia	44	21 15S	118 34E
Wodonga, Victoria	43	36 5S	146 50E
Wokam I., Indonesia	35	5 45S	134 28E
Woking, Canada	64	55 35N	118 50W
Wolf L., Canada	64	60 30N	131 0W
Wolf R., Canada	64	60 30N	132 0W
Wolf Creek, U.S.A.	72	47 2N	112 3W
Wolfe I., Canada	62	44 7N	76 27W
Wolfenden, Canada	64	52 0N	119 25W
Wolfram, Queensland	42	17 6S	145 0E
Wolhusen, Switzerland	15	47 4N	8 4E
Wollaston Is., Chile	77	55 40S	67 30W
Wollaston L., Canada	65	58 20N	103 30W
Wollaston Pen., Can.	60	69 30N	113 0W
Wollogorang, Queens.	42	17 13S	138 0E
Wollongong, N.S.W.	43	34 25S	150 54E
Wolmaransstad, Trans.	57	27 12S	26 13E
Wolomin, Poland	16	52 19N	21 15E
Wolseley, Canada	65	50 25N	103 15W
Wolseley, Cape Prov.	57	33 26S	19 7E
Wolseley, S. Australia	43	36 14S	140 58E
Wolvega, Netherlands	13	52 54N	6 1E
Wolverhampton, Eng.	10	52 35N	2 6W
Wondai, Queensland	43	26 20S	151 49E
Wonder Gorge, Zambia	56	14 35S	29 7E
Wongan, W. Australia	44	30 51S	116 37E
Wonju, S. Korea	36	37 28N	127 59E
Wonosari, Indonesia	34	7 58S	110 36E
Wönsan, Korea	36	39 20N	127 25E
Wonthaggi, Victoria	43	38 29S	145 31E
Woocalla, S. Australia	43	31 42S	137 8E
Wood L., Canada	65	55 30N	103 20W
Wood Buffalo Pk., Can.	64	59 30N	113 0W
Wood Lake, U.S.A.	70	42 9N	100 14W
Woodanilling, W. Australia	44	33 31S	117 24E
Woodarra, W. Austral.	44	27 51S	121 15E
Woodbine, Queensland	42	23 40S	147 30E
Woodburn, N.S.W.	43	29 1S	153 21E
Woodburn, Queensland	43	28 44S	142 14E
Woodchopper, Alaska	59	65 20N	143 32W
Woodford, Ireland	11	53 3N	8 23W
Woodland, U.S.A.	73	38 40N	121 50W
Woodlands, Queens.	42	23 16S	148 50E
Woodlark, I., Papua	42	9 2S	152 40E
Woodpecker, Canada	64	53 30N	122 40W
Woodridge, Canada	65	49 20N	96 20W
Woodruff, Ariz., U.S.A.	73	34 48N	110 2W
Woodruff, Utah, U.S.A.	72	41 31N	111 3W
Woodside, Victoria	43	38 28S	146 53E
Woods, L., N. Territory	40	17 50S	133 30E
Woods L., Canada	63	54 30N	65 0W

	MAP		
Woods, L. of the, Can.	65	49 30N	94 30W
Woodstock, N.B., Can.	63	46 11N	67 37W
Woodstock, Ont., Can.	62	43 10N	80 45W
Woodstock, England	9	51 51N	1 20W
Woodstock, Queensland	42	19 25S	142 45E
Woodstock, U.S.A.	70	42 16N	88 30W
Woodsville, U.S.A.	69	44 10S	72 0W
Woodville, N.Z.	46	40 20S	175 53E
Woodville, U.S.A.	71	30 42N	94 27W
Woodward, U.S.A.	71	36 25N	99 30W
Woolgar, Queensland	42	19 47S	143 27E
Wooloomber, L., W. Australia	45	22 0S	123 55E
Woombye, Queensland	43	26 40S	152 55E
Woomera, S. Australia	43	31 9S	136 56E
Woondoola, Queensland	42	18 34S	140 52E
Woonsocket, R.I., U.S.A.	68	42 0N	71 30W
Woonsocket, S.D., U.S.A.	70	44 5N	98 16W
Wooramel R , Australia	44	25 30S	114 30E
Wooroorooka, Queens.	43	29 0S	145 41E
Wooster, U.S.A.	68	40 38N	81 55W
Wootton Bassett Eng.	95	1 32N	135W
Worcester, Cape Prov.	57	33 39S	19 27E
Worcester, England	10	52 12N	2 12W
Worcester, U.S.A.	69	42 14N	71 49W
Worfield, England	20	52 34N	2 22W
Wörgl, Austria	14	47 29N	12 3E
Worikambo, Ghana	52	10 43N	0 11W
Workum, Netherlands	13	52 59N	5 26E
Worland, U.S.A.	72	44 2N	107 59W
Worms, Germany	14	49 37N	8 21E
Wortham, U.S.A.	71	31 46N	96 30W
Worthing, England	10	50 49N	0 21W
Worthington, U.S.A.	70	43 36N	95 30W
Wota, Ethiopia	54	7 4N	35 51E
Wour, Chad	51	21 30N	15 50E
Wowoni I., Indonesia	35	4 5S	123 5E
Wrangel, I., U.S.S.R.	27	71 10N	180 0E
Wrangell & I., Alaska	59	56 30N	132 25W
Wrangell Mts., Alaska	59	61 40N	143 30W
Wrath, C., Scotland	10	58 38N	5 0W
Wray, U.S.A.	70	40 8N	102 17W
Wrens, U.S.A.	69	33 13N	82 23W
Wrentham, England	9	52 24N	1 39E
Wrentham, Canada	64	49 34N	112 11W
Wright, Canada	64	51 45N	121 30E
Wrightson, Mt., U.S.A.	73	31 47N	110 58W
Wrigley, Canada	60	63 0N	123 30W
Wroclaw (Breslau), Pol.	16	51 5N	17 5E
Wu Kiang R., China	39	27 35N	108 0E
Wubin, W. Australia	44	30 8S	116 30E
Wuchen, China	38	41 30N	108 30E
Wuchia, China	38	39 10N	111 45E
Wuchih Shan, Mt., China	39	18 59N	109 45E
Wuching, China	38	38 9N	106 12E
Wuchow, China	39	23 26N	111 19E
Wuchwan, China	39	28 30N	108 10E
Wudhan, Muscat & Oman	31	23 48N	57 32E
Wudinna, S. Australia	45	33 4S	135 30E
Wuhan, China	39	30 45N	114 15E
Wuhu, China	39	31 21N	118 30E
Wukangchekiang, China	39	30 35N	119 50E
Wukang, Hunan, China	39	26 39N	110 33E
Wukari, Nigeria	52	7 57N	9 42E
Wuki (Taning), China	39	31 26N	109 30E
Wukung Shan, China	39	27 20N	113 40E
Wum, W. Cameroon	52	6 40N	10 2E
Wümme R., Germany	14	53 5N	9 15E
Wuneba, Sudan	53	4 49N	30 22E
Wuning, China	39	29 20N	115 0E
Wunnummin L., Canada	62	52 50N	89 20W
Wuntho, Burma	33	23 55N	95 45E
Wuping, China	39	25 5N	116 20E
Wuppertal, Germany	14	51 15N	7 8E
Wuppertal, Cape Prov.	57	32 13S	19 12E
Würzburg, Germany	14	49 46N	9 55E
Wurzen, Germany	14	51 21N	12 45E
Wushan, China	39	31 10N	109 55E
Wushenchi, China	38	39 31N	108 40E
Wushishi, Nigeria	52	9 42N	6 0E
Wusih, China	39	31 40N	120 30E
Wusu, China	37	44 21N	84 41E
Wutai, China	38	41 25N	114 8E
Wutai Shan, China	38	39 0N	113 10E
Wuting. *See* Hweimin, China	38		
Wuting, Yunnan, China	71	25 30N	102 25E
Wuting Ho, R., China	38	37 30N	110 15E
Wutu, China	38	33 27N	104 37E
Wuwei, China	37	38 0N	102 30E
Wuwei, Anhwei, China	37	31 21N	117 50E
Wuwei, Kansu, China	37	38 0N	102 54E
Wuyi, Chekiang, China	39	28 50N	119 45E
Wuyi, Hopeh, China	38	37 59N	116 0E
Wuyi Shan, China	39	26 30N	116 30E
Wuyo, Nigeria	52	10 23N	11 50E
Wuyun, China	37	49 15N	129 39E
Wyalkatchem, Australia	44	31 8S	117 22E
Wyandotte, U.S.A.	68	42 18N	83 10W
Wyandra, Queensland	43	27 12S	145 56E
Wyangala Res., N.S.W.	43	34 6S	149 22E
Wyara L., Queensland	43	28 42S	144 15E
Wye, R , Wales & Eng.	10	52 0N	2 36W

	MAP		
Wyemandoo, mt., Australia	44	28 28 S	118 29 E
Wymore, U.S.A.	70	40 10N	96 38W
Wynberg, Cape Prov.	57	34 2S	18 28 E
Wynbring, S. Australia	45	30 38 S	133 33 E
Wyndham, W. Austral.	44	15 33 S	128 3 E
Wyndham, N.Z.	47	46 20 S	168 51 E
Wyndham, Ra., W. Australia	44	16 40 S	124 0 E
Wyndmere, U.S.A.	70	46 54N	97 8W
Wynne, U.S.A.	71	35 15N	90 45W
Wynnum, Queensland	43	27 29 S	152 58 E
Wynyard, Canada	65	51 45N	104 10W
Wynyard, Tasmania	43	40 59 S	145 45 E
Wyoming, st., U.S.A.	72	42 48N	109 0W
Wyong, N.S.W.	43	33 14 S	151 24 E
Wytheville, U.S.A.	69	37 0N	81 3W

X

Xánthi, Greece	21	41 7N	24 56 E
Xapuri, Brazil	78	10 35 S	68 35W
Xavantes, Serra dos, Brazil	79	12 0 S	49 30W
Xenia, Ohio, U.S.A.	68	39 40N	83 52W
Xieng Khouang, Laos	34	19 21N	103 23 E
Ximana, Mozambique	56	19 20 S	34 0 E
Xingu R., Brazil	79	2 25 S	52 35W
Xique-Xique, Brazil	79	10 40 S	42 40W

Y

Yaamba, Queensland	42	23 7 S	150 25 E
Yaan, China	37	20 0N	103 2 E
Yaapeet, Victoria	43	35 38 S	142 0 E
Ya'bad, Jordan	29	32 27N	35 10 E
Yaballo, Ethiopia	53	4 57N	37 45 E
Yabassi, Cameroon	52	4 30N	9 57 E
Yablonovy Mts., Siberia	27	53 0N	114 0 E
Yacamunda, Queensland	42	21 20 S	147 8 E
Yacuiba, Bolivia	77	22 0 S	63 25W
Yadgir, India	32	16 45N	77 5 E
Yadkin R., U.S.A.	69	36 14N	81 10W
Yagaba, Ghana	52	10 14N	1 20W
Yagur, Israel	29	32 45N	35 4 E
Yahatahama, Japan	36	33 25N	132 29 E
Yahk, Canada	64	49 15N	116 10W
Yahuma, Zaire	54	1 10N	23 5 E
Yaizu, Japan	36	34 45N	138 10 E
Yajua, Nigeria	52	11 27N	12 49 E
Yakataga, Alaska	59	60 6N	142 32W
Yakima, U.S.A.	72	46 30N	120 30W
Yakima R., U.S.A.	72	47 0N	120 30W
Yako, Ivory Coast	50	12 58N	2 11W
Yakobi I., Alaska	64	58 0N	136 40W
Yakoma, Zaire	54	4 0N	22 17 E
Yakrigourou, Dahomey	52	10 42N	1 50 E
Yaku Shima, I., Japan	36	30 20N	130 30 E
Yakuluku, Congo	53	4 16N	28 52 E
Yakut A.S.S.R., U.S.S.R.	27	62 0N	130 0 E
Yakutat, Alaska	59	59 38N	139 40W
Yakutsk, U.S.S.R.	27	62 5N	129 40 E
Yalabusha, R., U.S.A.	71	33 46N	90 0W
Yale, U.S.A.	68	43 9N	82 47W
Yalgoo, W. Australia	44	28 16 S	116 39 E
Yalkubul, Pta., Mexico	74	21 32N	88 37W
Yalleroi, Queensland	42	24 3 S	145 42 E
Yallourn, Victoria	43	38 10 S	146 18 E
Yalpunga, N.S.W.	43	29 2 S	142 2 E
Yalta, U.S.S.R.	25	44 30N	34 10 E
Yalu R., Korea	36	41 30N	126 30 E
Yalung, R., China	37	32 0N	100 0 E
Yalutorovsk, U.S.S.R.	26	56 30N	65 40 E
Yamagata, Japan	36	38 15N	140 15 E
Yamagata, pref., Japan	36	38 30N	140 0 E
Yamaguchi, Japan	36	34 10N	131 32 E
Yamaguchi, pref., Japan	36	34 20N	131 40 E
Yamal Pen., U.S.S.R.	26	71 0N	70 0 E
Yamama, Si. Arabia	30	24 8N	47 29 F
Yaman Tau, Mt., U.S.S.R.	24	54 20N	57 40 E
Yamanashi, pref., Japan	36	35 40N	138 40 E
Yambio, Sudan	53	4 35N	28 16 E
Yambol, Bulgaria	21	42 30N	26 36 E
Yamdrok Tso, China	37	29 0N	90 40 E
Yamèthin, Burma	33	20 30N	96 15 E
Yamhsien, China	39	22 0N	108 32 E
Y'Ami, Philippines	35	21 5N	122 5 E
Yamil, Nigeria	52	12 53N	8 4 E
Yamma Yamma L., Queensland	43	26 16 S	141 20 E
Yampi Sound, W. Australia	44	15 15 S	123 30 E
Yamrat, Nigeria	52	10 11N	9 55 E
Yamun, Jordan	29	32 29N	35 14 E
Yan, Nigeria	52	10 5N	12 11 E
Yanac, Victoria	43	36 0 S	141 15 E
Yanaoca, Peru	78	14 10 S	71 10W
Yanaul, U.S.S.R.	24	56 25N	55 0 E
Yanco, N.S.W.	43	34 38 S	146 27 E
Yanda R., N.S.W.	43	31 0 S	145 48 E
Yanda, Nigeria	52	11 32N	10 48 E
Yandabome, N. Guinea	42	7 2 S	145 50 E

	MAP		
Yandanooka, W. Australia	44	29 18 S	115 29 E
Yandaran, Queensland	42	24 10 S	152 8 E
Yandé Millimou, Guinea	52		Inset
Yandoon, Burma	33	17 1N	95 38 E
Yandunburra, Queens.	43	21 2 S	144 14 E
Yangambi, Zaire	54	0 47N	24 20 E
Yangarakata, Zaire	53	2 53N	30 25 E
Yangchow, China	38	32 25N	119 25 E
Yangchuan, China	38	37 52N	113 29 E
Yanggang, Prov., N. Korea	36	41 5N	128 0 E
Yangkao, China	38	40 20N	113 40 E
Yangso, China	39	24 40N	110 15 E
Yangtse R., China	37	30 30N	109 0 E
Yangtse Gorges, China	39	30 50N	109 30 E
Yangtsun, China	38	39 25N	117 0 E
Yangwol, Korea	36	37 15N	128 15 E
Yankton, U.S.A.	70	43 0N	97 25W
Yanping, China	39	22 25N	112 0 E
Yantabulla, N.S.W.	43	29 20 S	145 0 E
Yao, Chad	51	12 56N	17 33 E
Yaomen, China	38	44 30N	125 45 E
Yaoundé, Cameroon	52	3 50N	11 35 E
Yapei (Tamale Port), Ghana	52	9 10N	1 10W
Yappar R., Queensland	42	18 43 S	142 15 E
Yaqui, R., Mexico	74	28 28N	109 30W
Yar, U.S.S.R.	24	58 5N	52 0 E
Yaracuy R., Venezuela	78	10 25N	68 40W
Yaraka, Queensland	42	24 53 S	144 3 E
Yarboutenda, Senegal	52	13 20N	13 50W
Yarda, Chad	51	18 35N	19 0 E
Yare R., England	10	52 36N	1 28 E
Yarensk, U.S.S.R.	24	62 10N	49 8 E
Yari R., Colombia	78	1 0N	73 40W
Yaritagua, Venezuela	75	10 5N	69 7W
Yarkand, China	37	38 24N	77 20 E
Yarkhun R., Pakistan	32	36 30N	72 45 E
Yarm, England	7	54 31N	1 21W
Yarmouth, Canada	63	43 53N	65 45W
Yarmouth, England	10	50 42N	1 29W
Yarmuk R., Syria	29	32 43N	35 40 E
Yaroslavl, U.S.S.R.	24	57 35N	39 55 E
Yarra Yarra L., W. Australia	44	29 12 S	115 45 E
Yarraden, Queensland	42	14 28 S	143 15 E
Yarraman Cr., Queens.	43	26 46 S	152 1 E
Yarrawonga, Victoria	43	36 0 S	146 0 E
Yarrow, Scotland	10	55 32N	3 0W
Yartsevo, U.S.S.R.	27	60 20N	90 0 E
Yartsevo, U.S.S.R.	25	55 5N	32 40 E
Yarumal, Colombia	78	7 0N	75 20W
Yas, I., Trucial Oman	31	24 15N	52 32 E
Yashi, Nigeria	52	12 23N	7 54 E
Yashikera, Nigeria	52	9 49N	3 25 E
Yasinski L., Canada	62	53 10N	77 0W
Yass, N.S.W.	43	34 50 S	149 0 E
Yas'ur, Israel	29	32 54N	35 10 E
Yat, Bolivia	78	19 10 S	62 10W
Yata, R., Bolivia	78	10 30 S	65 40W
Yates Pt., N.Z.	47	44 29 S	167 49 E
Yates R., Canada	64	59 50N	116 30W
Yates Center, U.S.A.	71	37 52N	95 46W
Yathkyed L., Canada	65	63 0N	98 0W
Yatsushiro, Japan	36	32 35N	130 51 E
Yatta, Jordan	29	31 27N	35 6 E
Yatta Plat, Kenya	53	2 28 S	38 0 E
Yatton, Queensland	42	22 31 S	149 5 E
Yaupi, Ecuador	78	2 55 S	78 0W
Yauri, Peru	78	14 50 S	71 25W
Yauyos, Peru	78	12 10 S	75 50W
Yavari R., Peru	78	4 50 S	72 0W
Yavne, Israel	29	31 52N	34 45 E
Yavneel, Israel	29	32 43N	35 34 E
Yawata, Japan	36	33 50N	130 45 E
Yawri B., Sierra Leone	52	8 22N	13 0W
Yazd (Yezd), Iran	31	31 56N	54 21 E
Yazd-e Khyast, Iran	31	31 38N	52 4 E
Yazdan, Afghanistan	31	33 36N	60 57 E
Yazoo, R., U.S.A.	71	32 40N	90 30W
Yazoo City, U.S.A.	71	33 0N	90 20W
Yding Skovhöj, hill, Denmark	23	56 0N	9 49 E
Ye, Burma	33	15 15N	97 50 E
Yea, Victoria	43	37 8 S	145 26 E
Yebyn, Burma	33	14 13N	98 9 E
Yecla, Spain	17	38 35N	1 5W
Yedseram, R., Nigeria	52	10 40N	13 10 E
Yeeda River, tn., W. Australia	44	17 39 S	123 39 E
Yeelanna, S. Australia	45	34 6 S	135 50 E
Yefremov, U.S.S.R.	25	53 15N	38 3 E
Yegorlyk, R., U.S.S.R.	25	46 15N	41 30 E
Yegoryevsk, U.S.S.R.	25	55 27N	38 55 E
Yegros, Paraguay	77	26 20 S	56 25W
Yehsien, China	38	37 12N	119 58 E
Yehud, Israel	29	32 3N	34 53 E
Yei, Sudan	53	4 3N	30 40 E
Yeisk (Yeysk), U.S.S.R.	25	46 40N	38 12 E
Yeji, Ghana	52	8 11N	0 41W
Yelanskoye, U.S.S.R.	27	61 25N	128 0 E
Yelarbon, Queensland	43	28 33 S	150 49 E
Yelets, U.S.S.R.	25	52 40N	38 30 E
Yell I., Scotland	10	60 35N	1 5W
Yellandu, India	33	14 59N	74 46 E
Yellow Sea, China	37	36 30N	124 0 E

	MAP		
Yellow R. *See* Hwang Ho, China	38		
Yellowhead P., Canada	64	53 0N	118 30W
Yellowknife, Canada	64	62 30N	114 10W
Yellowknife R., Canada	64	63 30N	113 30W
Yellowstone L., U.S.A.	72	44 25N	110 20W
Yellowstone R., U.S.A.	70	46 40N	105 45W
Yellowstone Nat. Park, U.S.A.	72	44 40N	110 30W
Yelnya, U.S.S.R.	25	54 35N	33 15 E
Yelsk, U.S.S.R.	25	51 50N	29 3 E
Yelvertoft, Queensland	42	20 5 S	138 43 E
Yelwa, Nigeria	52	10 49N	8 41 E
Yemen, st., Arabia	49	15 0N	44 0 E
Yenagoa, Nigeria	52	4 55N	6 4 E
Yenakiye, U.S.S.R.	25	48 15N	38 5 E
Yenan, China	38	36 55N	109 20 E
Yenangyat, Burma	34	21 2N	94 49 E
Yenanma, Burma	34	19 47N	94 49 E
Yenangyaung, Burma	35	20 30N	95 0 E
Yenbo', Saudi Arabia	30	24 0N	38 5 E
Yenchang, Shensi, China	38	36 40N	110 10 E
Yencheng, Honan, China	38	33 35N	113 58 E
Yencheng, Kiangsu, China	38	33 20N	120 10 E
Yenchih, China	38	37 52N	107 15 E
Yenchwan, China	38	36 58N	110 0 E
Yendi, Togo	52	9 29N	0 1W
Yeni, Niger	52	13 28N	3 0 E
Yenisei G., U.S.S.R.	26	72 20N	81 0 E
Yenisei, R., Siberia	26	68 0N	86 30 E
Yeniseisk, U.S.S.R.	27	58 39N	92 4 E
Yenki, China	37	43 12N	129 30 E
Yenking, China	37	40 30N	116 0 E
Yenotavevka, U.S.S.R.	25	47 15N	47 0 E
Yenshih, China	38	34 50N	113 0 E
Yentai. *See* Chefoo, China	38		
Yenting, China	39	31 10N	105 26 E
Yenyuka, U.S.S.R.	27	58 20N	121 20 E
Yeo L. W., Australia	45	28 0 S	124 30 E
Yeola, India	32	20 0N	74 30 E
Yeotmal, India	32	20 20N	78 15 E
Yeovil, England	10	50 57N	2 38W
Yeppoon, Queensland	42	23 5 S	150 47 E
Yerba Buena, Chile	77	28 0 S	70 25W
Yerbent, U.S.S.R.	26	39 30N	58 50 E
Yezd. *See* Yazd, Iran	31		
Yerevan, U.S.S.R.	34	40 10N	44 20 E
Yerilla, W. Australia	44	29 24 S	121 47 E
Yerington, U.S.A.	73	39 0N	119 14W
Yerköy, Turkey	30	39 38N	34 29 E
Yermakovo, U.S.S.R.	27	52 35N	126 20 E
Yermo, U.S.A.	73	34 54N	116 43W
Yerofei Paulovich, U.S.S.R.	27	54 0N	122 0 E
Yershov, U.S.S.R.	25	51 15N	48 27 E
Yerwa, Nigeria	52	11 55N	13 10 E
Yesil R., Turkey	30	41 0N	36 40 E
Yeso, U.S.A.	71	34 25N	104 36W
Yessei, U.S.S.R.	27	68 25N	102 10 E
Yetman, N.S.W.	43	28 55 S	150 52 E
Ye-u, Burma	33	22 45N	95 27 E
Yeu, I. d', France	12	46 4N	2 20W
Yeulba, Queensland	43	26 3 S	149 20 E
Yeungchun, China	39	22 15N	111 40 E
Yeungkong, China	39	1 55N	112 0 E
Yeungshan, China	39	24 19N	112 32 E
Yevpatoriya, U.S.S.R.	25	4 15N	33 20 E
Yevseyeva, U.S.S.R.	27	67 10N	153 5 E
Yeya R., U.S.S.R.	25	46 40N	39 0 E
Yeysk (Yeisk), U.S.S.R.	25	46 40N	38 12 E
Yezelovo, U.S.S.R.	26	67 20N	74 5 E
Yianisadhes, I., Crete	20	35 20N	26 10 E
Yiannitsa, Greece	21	40 46N	22 24W
Yicheng, China	38	35 35N	111 45 E
Yihhsien, China	38	34 40N	117 33 E
Yilan, China	39	24 44N	121 39 E
Yin Shan, China	38	41 30N	111 0 E
Yinchwan, China	38	38 30N	106 20 E
Yindarlgooda, L., W. Australia	44	30 40 S	121 52 E
Yingcheng, China	38	31 0N	113 30 E
Yingchow. *See* Fowyang	38		
Yinghsien, China	38	39 36N	113 27 E
Yingkow, China	38	40 45N	122 9 E
Yingshang, China	38	32 33N	116 10 E
Yingshanhsien, China	39	30 50N	115 45 E
Yingtak, China	39	24 10N	113 5 E
Yingtan, China	39	28 13N	116 54 E
Yinkanie, S. Australia	43	34 22 S	140 25 E
Yinkiang, China	39	28 10N	108 40 E
Yinmabin, Burma	33	22 10N	94 55 E
Yinnie Tharra, W. Australia	44	24 36 S	116 7 E
Yioúra, I., Greece	21	37 35N	24 43 E
Yioúra, I., Greece	21	39 23N	24 10 E
Yirol, Sudan	54	6 20N	30 45 E
Yithion, Greece	21	36 46N	22 34 E
Yitu, China	38	36 40N	118 25 E
Yiyang, China	39	28 31N	112 3 E
Yizre'el, Israel	29	32 34N	35 19 E
Ylikitka L., Finland	22	66 10N	29 20 E
Ylitornio, Finland	22	66 10N	23 57 E
Ylivieska, Finland	22	64 5N	24 47 E
Ymir, Canada	64	49 20N	117 20W

	MAP		
Yoakum, U.S.A.	71	29 10N	97 0W
Yog Pt., Philippines	35	13 55N	124 20 E
Yoho National Park, Canada	64	51 30N	116 30W
Yokadouma, Cameroon	54	3 35N	14 50 E
Yokkaichi, Japan	36	35 0N	136 30 E
Yoko, Cameroon	52	5 50N	12 20 E
Yokohama, Japan	36	35 30N	139 32 E
Yokosuka, Japan	36	35 20N	139 40 E
Yola, Nigeria	52	9 10N	12 29 E
Yolaina, Cord. de, mts., Nicaragua	75	11 30N	84 0W
Yonago, Japan	36	35 25N	133 30 E
Yonaguni, I., Japan	39	24 29N	123 0 E
Yonezawa, Japan	36	37 50N	140 5 E
Yongama, Zaire	54	0 1 S	24 25 E
Yongdok, S. Korea	36	36 53N	129 30 E
Yongdungpo, S. Korea	36	37 35N	126 55 E
Yonibana, S. Leone	52		Inset
Yonker, Canada	65	52 40N	109 40W
Yonkers, U.S.A.	68	40 57N	73 51W
Yonov, Nigeria	52	7 33N	8 42 E
Yoqne'am, Israel	29	32 40N	35 6 E
York, England	10	53 58N	1 7W
York, Pa., U.S.A.	68	39 58N	76 46W
York, Neb., U.S.A.	70	40 56N	97 35W
York, W. Australia	44	31 52 S	116 47 E
York, C., Queensland	42	10 35 S	142 30 E
York Factory, Canada	65	57 0N	92 30W
Yorke Pen., S. Austral.	43	34 30 S	137 35 E
Yorketown, S. Australia	43	35 0 S	137 33 E
Yorkrakine, Australia	44	31 22 S	117 18 E
Yorkton, Canada	65	51 11N	102 28W
Yorktown, U.S.A.	71	29 0N	97 30W
Yosemite Nat. Pk., U.S.A.	73	37 40N	119 40W
Yoshida, Japan	36	35 40N	138 50 E
Yoshiwara, Japan	36	35 18N	138 41 E
Yösu, Korea	36	34 40N	127 35 E
Yotsing, China	39	28 10N	120 55 E
Youanmi, W. Australia	44	28 34 S	118 48 E
Youbou, Canada	64	48 52N	124 12W
Youghal, Ireland	11	51 58N	7 51W
Youghal Bay, Ireland	11	51 55N	7 50W
Young, Canada	65	51 45N	105 45W
Young, N.S.W.	43	34 19 S	148 18 E
Young, U.S.A.	73	34 10N	110 56W
Young Ra., N.Z.	47	44 12 S	169 20 E
Younghusband Pen., S. Australia	43	35 45 S	139 15 E
Youngstown, Canada	64	51 35N	111 10W
Youngstown, U.S.A.	68	41 7N	80 41W
Yoyang, China	39	29 28N	113 0 E
Yozgat, Turkey	30	39 51N	34 47 E
Ypres, Belgium	13	50 50N	2 52 E
Ypsilanti, U.S.A.	68	42 14N	83 39W
Yreka, U.S.A.	72	41 43N	122 38W
Ysleta, U.S.A.	73	31 43N	106 17W
Yssingeaux, France	12	45 9N	4 8 E
Ystad, Sweden	23	55 26N	13 50 E
Ytyryk, U.S.S.R.	27	66 25N	151 0 E
Yu Shan, mt., Formosa	39	23 30N	121 0 E
Yuan Kiang, R., China	39	20 9N	111 25 E
Yuanling, China	39	28 30N	110 5 E
Yuanyang, China	37	23 13N	102 49 E
Yuba City, U.S.A.	72	39 14N	122 0W
Yubetsu, Japan	36	44 15N	143 40 E
Yucatan, st., Mexico	74	21 30N	86 30W
Yucatan Chan., W. I.	74	22 0N	86 30W
Yucca, U.S.A.	73	34 54N	114 9W
Yuchen, China	39	36 55N	116 40 E
Yudino, U.S.S.R.	26	55 10N	67 55 E
Yuganskie, U.S.S.R.	26	66 0N	71 40 E
Yugoslavia, rep., Eur.	21	44 0N	20 0 E
Yuhsien, Honan, China	38	34 4N	113 40 E
Yuhsien, Hopeh, China	38	39 42N	114 45 E
Yuhwan, China	39	28 10N	121 15 E
Yükan, China	39	28 53N	116 35 E
Yukikow, China	39	31 31N	118 7 E
Yukon, terr., Canada	64	60 40N	145 0W
Yukon R., Alaska	59	62 0N	162 0W
Yule R., W. Australia	44	21 0 S	118 0 E
Yuli, Nigeria	52	9 44N	10 12 E
Yülin, Shensi, China	38	38 20N	109 15 E
Yuma, Arizona, U.S.A.	73	32 40N	114 40W
Yuma, Colo., U.S.A.	70	40 9N	102 45W
Yuma B., Dom. Rep.	75	18 0N	68 45W
Yumbe, Uganda	53	3 28N	31 15 E
Yumen, China	37	40 19N	97 12 E
Yumuna (Jumna), R., India	32	26 0N	80 20 E
Yuna, W. Australia	44	28 17 S	115 2 E
Yunaska, I., Aleutian Is.	59	52 40N	170 40W
Yundamindera, W. Australia	44	29 4 S	122 3 E
Yungan, China	39	25 50N	117 25 E
Yungchun, China	39	25 20N	118 15 E
Yungchung Shan, China	38	38 50N	112 25 E
Yungera, Victoria	43	34 42 S	143 3 E
Yungfeng, China	39	27 20N	115 20 E
Yungfu, China	39	25 1N	109 58 E
Yunghing, China	39	26 3N	112 43 E
Yunghwo, China	38	36 48N	110 32 E
Yungshun, China	39	29 3N	109 50 E
Yungsin, China	39	26 55N	114 10 E
Yungsui, China	39	29 7N	115 37 E
Yungtsi, China	38	34 50N	110 25 E

Name	MAP	Lat	Long
Yungyun, China	39	24 30N	113 47 E
Yünhsien, China	38	32 30N	111 0 E
Yünhwo, China	39	28 5N	119 30 E
Yunlin, China	39	23 44N	120 31 E
Yünnan, prov., China	37	25 0N	102 30 E
Yunndaga, W. Australia	44	29 45s	121 0 E
Yunsiao, China	39	24 0N	117 20 E
Yunta, S. Australia	43	32 32s	139 30 E
Yunta, Cr., S. Australia	43	32 50s	139 50 E
Yuribei, U.S.S.R.	26	71 20N	76 30 E
Yuryevets, U.S.S.R.	25	57 25N	43 2 E
Yut I., Indonesia	35	5 30s	133 0 E
Yushu, China	37	33 6N	96 48 E
Yutu, China	37	26 1N	115 17 E
Yutze, China	38	37 44N	112 42 E
Yuyang, China	39	28 45N	108 35 E
Yüyao, China	39	30 0N	121 20 E
Yuyu, China	38	40 20N	112 30 E
Yüyüan, China	39	24 44N	112 13 E
Yuzha, U.S.S.R.	25	56 40N	42 10 E
Yverdon, Switzerland	15	46 47N	6 39 E
Yvetot, France	12	49 37N	0 44 E

Z

Name	MAP	Lat	Long
Zaandam, Netherlands	13	52 26N	4 49 E
Zabéré, Volta	52	11 12N	0 22w
Zābol, Iran	31	31 7N	61 27 E
Zāboli, Iran	31	27 9N	61 37 E
Zabrze, Poland	16	50 24N	18 50 E
Zabzugu, Ghana	52	9 20N	0 27 E
Zacatecas, Mexico	74	22 49N	102 34w
Zacatecas, st., Mexico	74	23 30N	103 0w
Zacoalco, Mexico	74	20 10N	103 40w
Zadar, Yugoslavia	20	44 8N	15 8 E
Zadawa, Nigeria	52	11 25N	10 12 E
Zafora, I., Greece	21	36 5N	26 24 E
Zafra, Spain	17	38 26N	6 30w
Zafriyya, Israel	29	31 59N	34 50 E
Zagan, Poland	16	51 39N	15 22 E
Zagnanago, Dahomey	52	7 18N	2 28 E
Zagorsk, U.S.S.R.	25	56 20N	38 10 E
Zagreb, Yugoslavia	20	45 50N	16 0 E
Zagros Mts., Iran	30	33 45N	47 0 E
Zagubica, Yugoslavia	21	44 15N	21 47 E
Zāhedān (Duzdab), Iran	31	29 33N	60 48 E
Zahlah, Lebanon	30	33 54N	35 49 E
Zahle, Lebanon	30	33 52N	35 50 E
Zaindeh R., Iran	31	32 30N	51 0 E
Zaire, Africa	54	2 0s	16 0 E
Zaire R., Zaire	54	2 0N	23 0 E
Zaisan L., U.S.S.R.	26	48 0N	84 0 E
Zaječar, Yugoslavia	21	43 53N	22 18 E
Zaka, Rhodesia	56	20 20s	31 28 E
Zakbayeme, Cameroon	52	4 0N	10 32 E
Zākhu, Iraq	30	37 10N	42 25 E
Zakinthos, Greece	21	37 48N	20 57 E
Zakinthos I., Greece	21	37 50N	20 50 E
Zaklilow, Poland	16	50 45N	22 10 E
Zalaegerszeg, Hungary	16	46 53N	16 47 E
Zalanga, Nigeria	52	10 23N	10 8 E
Zalau, Nigeria	52	10 23N	8 58 E
Zălău, Rumania	21	47 12N	23 5 E
Zalew Wislany, U.S.S.R. & Pol.	23	54 20N	19 50 E
Zalingei, Sudan	51	13 5N	23 10 E

Name	MAP	Lat	Long
Zambesi Delta, Mozam.	56	18 55s	36 4 E
Zambezi (Zambese) R., S.E. Africa	55	16 30s	32 30 E
Zambezia, dist., Mozam.	56	16 50s	36 0 E
Zambia (N. Rhodesia), rep., Afr.	55	14 0s	29 0 E
Zamboanga, Philippines	35	6 59N	122 3 E
Zamfara R., Nigeria	52	12 8N	5 0 E
Zamora, Mexico	74	20 0N	102 21w
Zamora, Spain	17	41 30N	5 45w
Zamora R., Ecuador	78	3 40s	78 0w
Zamość, Poland	16	50 50N	23 22 E
Zan, Ghana	52	9 26N	0 17w
Zanaga, Congo	54	2 40s	13 40 E
Zancara R., Spain	17	39 20N	3 0w
Zandvoort, Netherlands	13	52 21N	4 36 E
Zanesville, U.S.A.	68	39 56N	82 2w
Zangue R., Mozam.	56	18 5s	35 5 E
Zanguébé, Niger	52	14 59N	6 5 E
Zanjan, Iran	30	36 43N	48 30 E
Zanjon R., Argentina	77	30 30s	68 30w
Zanthus, W. Australia	45	30 55s	123 29 E
Zanzibar, Tanzania	53	6 2s	39 20 E
Zanzibar Chan., E. Afr.	53	6 10s	38 55 E
Zanzibar I., E. Africa	53	6 2s	39 20 E
Zaouiat Reggane, Alg.	50	26 45N	0 5 E
Zapata, U.S.A.	71	26 55N	99 14w
Zaporozhye, U.S.S.R.	25	47 50N	35 10 E
Zara, Turkey	30	39 58N	37 43 E
Zaragoza, Coahuila, Mexico	74	28 30N	101 0w
Zaragoza, Durango, Mexico	74	26 0N	103 40w
Zarand, Iran	31	30 46N	56 34 E
Zaranda, Nigeria	52	10 12N	9 35 E
Zaraza, Venezuela	78	9 25N	65 20w
Zard Kuh, Mt., Iran	30	32 0N	50 26 E
Zarembo I., Alaska	64	56 20N	132 50w
Zari, Nigeria	52	13 8N	12 37 E
Zaria, Nigeria	52	11 0N	7 40 E
Zarnuqa, Israel	29	31 53N	34 47 E
Zarqa R., Jordan	29	32 10N	35 37 E
Zaruma, Ecuador	78	3 40s	79 30w
Zary, Poland	16	51 37N	15 10 E
Zashiversk, U.S.S.R.	27	67 25N	142 40 E
Zaskar Mountains, Kashmir	32	33 15N	77 30 E
Zastron, O.F.S.	57	30 18s	27 7 E
Zatishe, U.S.S.R.	27	66 5N	158 55 E
Zavareh, Iran	31	33 35N	52 28 E
Zavetnoye, U.S.S.R.	25	47 13N	43 50 E
Zavitinsk, U.S.S.R.	27	50 10N	129 20 E
Zawada, Poland	16	50 52N	23 10 E
Zawi, Rhodesia	56	17 0s	30 10 E
Zawichost, Poland	16	50 50N	21 56 E
Zawiercie, Poland	16	50 30N	19 13 E
Zduńska Wola, Poland	16	51 37N	18 59 E
Zeballos, Canada	64	49 57N	126 10w
Zebediela, Transvaal	57	24 25s	29 25 E
Zebila, Ghana	52	11 1N	0 26w
Zeebrugge, Belgium	13	51 19N	3 12 E
Zeehan, Tasmania	43	41 52s	145 25 E
Zeeland, prov., Neth.	13	51 30N	3 50 E
Zeerust, Transvaal	57	25 31s	26 4 E
Zefat, Israel	29	32 58N	35 29 E

Name	MAP	Lat	Long
Zeila, Somali Rep.	49	11 15N	43 30 E
Zeimar R., Jordan	29	32 17N	35 9 E
Zeist, Netherlands	13	52 5N	5 15 E
Zeita, Jordan	29	32 23N	35 2 E
Zeita R., Israel	29	31 38N	34 51 E
Zeitz, Germany	14	51 3N	12 9 E
Zelechów, Poland	16	51 47N	21 52 E
Zelenodolsk, U.S.S.R.	25	55 55N	48 30 E
Zelenogorsk, U.S.S.R.	23	60 23N	29 45 E
Zelenogradsk, U.S.S.R.	23	54 53N	20 29 E
Zelzate, Belgium	13	51 13N	3 47 E
Zemio, Cent. Afr. Rep.	54	5 2N	25 5 E
Zemlya George, U.S.S.R.	26	80 30N	45 0 E
Zemun, Yugoslavia	21	44 52N	20 30 E
Zengbé, Cameroon	52	5 55N	12 40 E
Zenica, Yugoslavia	21	44 10N	17 57 E
Zenzontepec, Mexico	74	16 31N	97 31w
Zepče, Yugoslavia	21	44 28N	18 2 E
Zerbst, Germany	14	51 59N	12 8 E
Zerinogolovskoye, U.S.S.R.	26	54 25N	65 0 E
Zermatt, Switzerland	15	46 2N	7 46 E
Zernez, Switzerland	15	46 42N	10 7 E
Zeya, U.S.S.R.	27	54 2N	127 20 E
Zeya R., U.S.S.R.	27	52 30N	127 0 E
Zezenere R., Portugal	17	39 55N	8 0w
Zhadanov (Mariupol), U.S.S.R.	25	47 5N	37 31 E
Zhigansk, U.S.S.R.	27	66 35N	124 10 E
Zhitomir, U.S.S.R.	25	50 20N	28 40 E
Zhlobin, U.S.S.R.	25	52 55N	30 0 E
Zhob R., Pakistan	32	31 5N	69 10 E
Zhokhov, I., U.S.S.R.	27	76 4N	153 0 E
Zhukovka, U.S.S.R.	25	53 35N	33 50 E
Zib, Israel	29	33 3N	35 5 E
Zielona Góra, Poland	16	51 57N	15 31 E
Zierikzee, Netherlands	13	51 40N	3 55 E
Zigon, Burma	33	18 25N	95 35 E
Ziguei, Chad	51	14 50N	15 50 E
Ziguinchor, Senegal	50	12 25N	16 20w
Zikhron Ya'Aqov, Israel	29	32 34N	34 56 E
Zile, Turkey	30	40 15N	36 0 E
Zilfi, Saudi Arabia	30	26 12N	44 52 E
Zilina, Czechoslovakia	16	49 14N	18 40 E
Zillah, Libya	51	28 0N	17 45 E
Zilling Tso, L., China	37	31 40N	39 0 E
Zima, U.S.S.R.	27	54 0N	102 5 E
Zimane, Mozambique	56	22 9s	33 25 E
Zimapan, Mexico	74	20 40N	99 20w
Zimba, Zambia	56	17 20s	26 25 E
Zimbabwe Ruins, Rhodesia	56	20 16s	31 0 E
Zimi, Sierra Leone	52	7 25N	11 22w
Zimnicea, Rumania	21	43 39N	25 26 E
Zimovniki, U.S.S.R.	25	47 10N	42 25 E
Zinder, Niger	52	13 48N	9 0 E
Zinga, Tanzania	53	9 16s	38 41 E
Zingst, Germany	14	54 24N	12 45 E
Zipaquira, Colombia	78	5 0N	74 0w
Zira, Iran	31	28 12N	51 29 E
Zirje, I., Yugoslavia	20	43 40N	15 40 E
Zirko, I., Trucial Oman	31	24 55N	53 4 E
Zitacuaro, Mexico	74	19 20N	100 30w
Zittau, Germany	16	50 54N	14 47 E
Ziyyoria, Israel	29	31 56N	34 47 E
Zlatitsa, Bulgaria	21	42 41N	24 7 E

Name	MAP	Lat	Long
Zlatograd, Bulgaria	21	41 22N	25 7 E
Zlatoust, U.S.S.R.	24	55 10N	59 30 E
Zliten, Libya	51	32 25N	14 35 E
Zmiev, U.S.S.R.	25	49 45N	36 27 E
Znamenka, U.S.S.R.	25	48 45N	32 30 E
Znamensk, U.S.S.R.	23	54 37N	21 17 E
Znojmo, Cz.	16	48 50N	16 2 E
Zoar, Cape Province	57	33 30s	21 26 E
Zóbuè, Mozambique	56	15 39s	34 29 E
Zofe, Ghana	52	6 15N	0 48 E
Zofingen, Switzerland	15	47 17N	7 57 E
Zogno, Italy	54	45 49N	9 41 E
Zolotonosha, U.S.S.R.	25	49 45N	32 5 E
Zomba, Malawi	56	15 25s	35 16 E
Zombi, Zaire	53	3 31N	29 11 E
Zonguldak, Turkey	30	41 28N	31 50 E
Zongwe. Zaire	56	7 1s	30 10 E
Zorra, I., Pan. Can. Zone	74	9 18N	79 52w
Zorritos, Peru	78	3 50s	80 40w
Zouar, Chad	51	20 30N	16 25 E
Zoutkamp., Neth.	13	53 20N	6 18 E
Zrenjanin (Petrovgrad) Yugoslavia	21	45 22N	20 23 E
Zseelim, Israel	29	31 3N	34 32 E
Zuarunga, Ghana	52	10 49N	0 52w
Zuba, Nigeria	52	9 11N	7 12 E
Zug, Switzerland	15	47 10N	8 31 E
Zug, can., Switzerland	15	47 9N	8 35 E
Zugdidi, U.S.S.R.	24	42 30N	41 48 E
Zuger See, Switzerland	15	47 7N	8 35 E
Zuid Holland, prov., Netherlands	13	52 0N	4 35 E
Zuidhorn, Netherlands	13	53 15N	6 23 E
Zuie, Liberia. Inset.	52		
Zulia, Uganda	53	4 11N	34 1 E
Zulia R., Venezuela	75	8 40N	72 15w
Zululand, prov., Natal	57	28 0s	32 0 E
Zûmbo, Mozambique	56	15 35s	30 28 E
Zummo, Nigeria	52	9 51N	12 59 E
Zune, Mozambique	56	18 59s	35 18 E
Zungeru, Nigeria	52	9 49N	6 9 E
Zungu, Nigeria	52	10 4N	9 49 E
Zuni, U.S.A.	73	35 4N	108 51w
Zupanovo, U.S.S.R.	27	53 50N	159 40 E
Zürich, Switzerland	51	47 22N	8 32 E
Zürich, can., Switz.	15	47 26N	8 40 E
Zürich See, Switzerland	15	47 18N	8 40 E
Zuru, Nigeria	52	11 27N	5 4 E
Zutphen, Netherlands	13	52 9N	6 12 E
Zuwarah, Libya	51	32 50N	12 10 E
Zverovo, U.S.S.R.	26	71 40N	83 20 E
Zvolen, Czechoslovakia	16	48 33N	19 10 E
Zvornik, Yugoslavia	21	44 26N	19 7 E
Zwai L., Ethiopia	54	8 0N	38 50 E
Zweibrücken, Germany	14	49 15N	7 20 E
Zweisimmen, Switz.	15	46 33N	7 22 E
Zwettl, Austria	14	48 35N	15 9 E
Zwickau, Germany	14	50 43N	12 30 E
Zwolle, Netherlands	13	52 31N	6 6 E
Zwolle, U.S.A.	71	31 39N	93 41w
Zyatya, U.S.S.R.	27	57 50N	102 45 E
Zymoetz R., Canada	64	54 30N	128 0w
Zyrardów, Poland	16	52 3N	20 35 E
Zyryn, Poland	16	51 30N	22 5 E
Zywiec, Poland	16	49 42N	19 12 E

GAZETTEER

A dictionary of up-to-date information including geographical, historical and political facts about the major divisions and natural features of the world.

NOTE: All U.S. cities with 35,000 population or over are included.

USING THE GAZETTEER

- **Bold** type indicates an entry with pronunciation shown; commas separate alternate spellings.
- - denotes breaks between syllables.
- ′ denotes accented syllables.
- *Italic* type indicates geographical (or political) categories of the entry.

PRONUNCIATION KEY

The following are always pronounced as shown, except where noted in parentheses following the entry.

a as in at	ay as in bay	i as in ill	oi as in oil	ū as in ūse	g as in get
ā as in āte	e as′in end	ī as in īce	oo as in good	û as in ûrn	gu as in Guam
ȧ as in ȧ kin′	ē as in hē	î as in sîr	ōō as in tōō	y as in yet	j as in jet
â as in bâre	ė as in ė·vent′	o as in odd	ou as in out	ẏ as in mẏth	qu as in quit
ä as in cär	ê as in hêr	ō as in ōld	ow as in owl	ȳ as in trȳ	s as in set
ă as in ăll	ēe as in sēen	ö as in wön	oy as in boy	c as in cat	
ai as in aid	ew as in new	ô as in ôr	u as in up	ch as in chat	

Abbreviations

*   Capital or County seat
=   same as

A

ab.	about
Ala.	Alabama
Alas.	Alaska
Amer.	American
anc.	ancient
Ariz.	Arizona
Ark.	Arkansas
A.S.S.R.	Autonomous Soviet Socialist Republic

B

(B)	Brazzaville
bel.	belongs (to)
Belg.	Belgian
bet.	between
Bib.	Biblical
Brit.	British

C

Cal., Calif.	California
cen.	center
Colo.	Colorado
Conn.	Connecticut

D

D.C.	District of Columbia
Dan.	Danish .
Del.	Delaware
dept.	department
dist.	district
div.	divided
Dut.	Dutch

E

E	east, eastern
emp.	empire
Eng.	English
esp.	especially
estab.	established
Eur.	Europe

F

Fed.	Federation
Fla.	Florida
Fr.	French
ft.	feet

G

Ga.	Georgia
Ger.	German
Gk.	Greek

H

Haw.	Hawaii
hist.	historical, historically

I

I.	island
Ida.	Idaho
Ill.	Illinois
imp.	important
incl.	includes, including
Ind.	Indiana
Is.	Islands
It.	Italian

J

Jap.	Japanese

K

Kan.	Kansas
Ky.	Kentucky

L

(L)	Leopoldville
L.	Lake
La.	Louisiana
lat.	latitude
Lat.	Latin
long.	longitude

M

m.	miles
Mass.	Massachusetts
max.	maximum
Me.	Maine
Md.	Maryland
Medit.	Mediterranean
Mich.	Michigan
Minn.	Minnesota
Miss.	Mississippi
Mo.	Missouri
mod.	modern
Mont.	Montana
Mt.	mountain
Mts.	mountains

N

N	north, northern
N.C.	North Carolina
N.D.	North Dakota
N.H.	New Hampshire
N.J.	New Jersey
N.M.	New Mexico
N.Y.	New York
Neb.	Nebraska
Neth.	Netherlands
Nev.	Nevada
nr.	near

O

O.	ocean
Okla.	Oklahoma
Ore.	Oregon

P

Pa.	Pennsylvania
penin.	peninsula
Phil.	Philippine
pop.	population
Port.	Portuguese
prov.	province

R

R.	river
reg.	region
Rep.	Republic
R.I.	Rhode Island
R.S.F.S.R.	Russian Soviet Federated Socialist Republic
Russ.	Russian

S

S	south, southern
S.	sea
S.C.	South Carolina
S.D.	South Dakota
Span.	Spanish
sq.	square
S.S.R.	Soviet Socialist Republic
surr.	surrounded by

T

Tenn.	Tennessee
terr.	territory

U

U.	university
U.S.	United States (of America
U.S.S.R.	Union of Soviet Socialist Republics

V

Va.	Virginia
Vt.	Vermont

W

W	west, western
Wash.	Washington
Wisc.	Wisconsin
W.Va.	West Virginia
WW I	World War I
WW II	World War II
Wyo.	Wyoming

A

Äa'chen (kĕn) or **Aix-lä-chä-pelle'** (eks-läshȧ) *City* NW West Germany; trade, manufacturing

Äal'bôrg *County* and *City* NE Denmark

Äar'gau (gou) *Canton* N cen. Switzerland; * **Äar'au** (ou) on **Äa'rė R.**; textiles, instruments

Äar'hūs *County, City,* port on *Bay* E cen. Denmark

Ab'ȧ-cō: Great Ab'ȧ-cō, Little Ab'ȧ-cō *Islands* of the Bahamas

Ä-bä-dän' *Town* on *Island* W Iran; oil refineries

Ä-be-ō'ku-tä (koo) *Town,* * of *Province* SW Nigeria; trade

Ab-êr-dēen' *Burgh* * of *County* NE Scotland; agriculture, fisheries, quarries, cattle. 2. *Lake,* Northwest Terrs., Canada

Ab-i-djän' *Town* * of Ivory Coast Spart

Ab'i-lēne *City* NW cen. Texas, U.S.; pop. 89,653; dairy, food products

Ab-khä'zi-ȧn A.S.S.R. *Republic* NW Georgia, U.S.S.R.; agriculture, forests, minerals

Ä'brȧ *Province* Luzon, Phil. Is.; corn, rice, timber

Ä-brūz'zi e Mô'li-sė *Compartimento* cen. Italy; agriculture, livestock

Ȧ-bȳ'dös 1. *Anc. town* Asia Minor. 2. *Anc. town* anc. Egypt

Ab-ẏs-sĭn'i-ȧ *Kingdom* E Africa, now ETHIOPIA

Ȧ-cä'di-ȧ 1. Original name of NOVA SCOTIA. 2. *National Park,* Me. coast, U.S.

Ä-cä-pul'cō (pool') *Town* W Mexico; port

Ä-cä-tĕ-nän'gō *Volcano* 12,980 ft., Guatemala

Ac'crȧ *City* * of Ghana, SE part; pop. 491,-000; port

Ȧ-chae'ȧ and **Ē'lis** (kē') *Department* NW Peloponnesus, Greece

Ä-ci-re-ä'le (chē-râ) *City* E Sicily; port, resort

Ac-ön-cä'guȧ 1. *Mountain* 23,081 ft., W Argentina; highest peak of Western Hemisphere. 2. *River, Province* cen. Chile

Ä'crė 1. *River* 330 m., W cen. South America. 2. *Territory* W Brazil; rubber. 3. *City* on *Bay* NW Israel; port

Ac'tön *Municipal borough* SE England; part of greater London

Ä'dak *Island,* Aleutian Is., SW Alas., U.S.

Ä-dä-nä' *City* S Turkey, Asia; rail, commercial cen.

Ad'dis Ab'ȧ-bȧ *City* * of Ethiopia, cen. part; pop. 600,000

Ad'ė-lāide *City* * of South Australia, SE Australia; trade, educational cen.

Ä'dėn *Protectorate* Brit. crown colony and *City* its * on *Gulf,* SW Arabia; pop. ab. 600,000

Äd'di-ge (dē-jâ) *River* 220 m., NE Italy

Ad-i-ron'dack *Mountains* *Mountain chain* NE N.Y., U.S.; resorts

Ȧ-dri-at'ic Sea Arm of Mediterranean S. E of Italy

Ȧ-dẏ-gei' *Autonomous Region* (gä'i) *Region* of S R.S.F.S.R., U.S.S.R., Eur.; agriculture, oil

Ȧ-dzhar' A.S.S.R. (jär') *Republic* SW Georgia, U.S.S.R., Eur.

Ȧe-gē'ȧn Islands (ȧ-jē') *Islands* of **Aegean Sea** bet. Asia Minor & Greece; incl. the Cyclades, Sporades, Dodecanese, etc.

Ae-tō'li-ȧ and **Ac-ȧr-nä'ni-ȧ** *Department* W cen. Greece

Ä'fars and Issas (E'sus) *Fr. Terr.* NE Africa; formerly **Fr. Somaliland,** 9,000 sq. mi.; pop. 125,000

Af-ghan'i-stan, Kingdom of *Country,* C Asia; 250,000 sq. m.; pop. 17,099,000; * Kabul; 28 provinces each headed by governor; *Main cities:* Kandahar, Herat, Mazar-i-Sharif; *Main rivers:* Hari Rud, Helmand, Kunduz, Lora; *Geog.:* towering ranges, arid desert, small fertile valley; *Climate:* cold winter, hot, dry summer, scant rain.

Flag: black, red, green vertical stripes, center bearing open mosque between 2 flags in 2 sprays of wheat tinted by scroll inscribed Afghanistan, above it 1308 in Persian.

Ethnic comp.: Pathans — 60%, Tadjiks—31%, Uzbeks—5%, Hazaras — 3%; *Language:* Dari (official), Pushtu, Farsi, Uzbek, Turkoman, Kirghiz; *Religion:* Islam (state), Sunni Moslem.

Products: sheep, cereals, cotton, sugar, beef, fruit, nuts, salt, silver, copper, coal, iron, rubies, lapis lazuli, silk, wool textiles, carpets; *Minerals:* natural gas, coal, iron ore, chromite, beryl, lapis lazuli; *Major exports:* primary and processed agricultural products, pelts; *Major imports:* capital goods, petroleum products, sugar; *Industries:* mining, agriculture, handicrafts. *Currency:* Afghani. *Head of Government:* King; *Legislature:* bicemal parliament; *Judiciary:* Moslem religious law.

Af'ri-cȧ *Continent* world's second largest ab. 11,730,000 sq. m.

Ä-gä'nä *Town* W Guam, its * on *Bay*

Ag'in-cōurt (aj') *Village* N France; battle scene 1415

Ä'grȧ 1. *City* * of *Division, District* cen. India. 2. *Former province* of Brit. India, now part of **United Provinces of Agra and Oudh**

Ä-gri-gen'tō (jen') *Commune* * of *Province,* Sicily, Italy

Ä-guä-dil'lä (dē'yä) *Municipality* NW Puerto Rico; port

Ä-guäs-cä-lien'tes *City* * of *State* cen. Mexico; climate

Ä-gui-lär' *Commune* S Spain; olives, grapes

Ȧ-gul'hȧs, Cape Southern point of Africa

Ä-gu'sän (goo') *Province* Mindanao, Phil. Is.; agriculture

Äh-mȧd-ä-bäd' *City* W cen. India

Äh-mȧd-nä'gȧr *City* * of *District,* Bombay prov., W India

Ä-huä-chä-pän' *Town* * of *Department* SW El Salvador; trade

Ah'vė-nan-mäa or **A'land Islands** (ō') *Archipelago, Department* of Finland bet. Sweden and Finland

Äh-wäz' *Town* SW Iran; oil, commerce

Ai-chi (ī-chē) *Prefecture* Honshu, Japan

Ai-gun' (ī-goon') *City* N Manchuria; port

Ain (an) *Department* E France

A-ir' (ēr') or **Az-bine'** (bēn') Mountainous area of the Sahara

Aisne (ân) *Department, River* 175 m., N France; WWI battles

Aix (āks) *City* SE France

Aix-lä-Chä-pelle' (shå) see AACHEN

Ä-jac'cio (yät'chô) *Commune* on *Gulf* * of Corsica on W coast; port, fisheries

Åj-mēr' *City* NW India; salt trade, cotton cloth

Ä-jus'cō (hōōs') *Mountain*, volcano, 13,612 ft. Mexico

Ä-kä-shi *City* Honshu, Japan; industrial

Ak-där', Je'bel (ja'bal) *Mountain* range Oman, Arabia

Ä-ki-tä *City* * of *Prefecture* Honshu, Japan; silk, lumber

Å-kō'lä *City* cen. India; cotton trade

Ak'rön *City* NE Ohio, U.S.; pop. 275,425; rubber goods, aircraft

Ä'kûr-ey-ri (ā) *Town* N Iceland; Iceland's 2nd city

Ak-yab' *Town* * of *District* Lower Burma; port

Al-å-bam'å *State*, named from Muskogean Indian tribe of same name; 51,609 sq. m.; *pop.:* 3,444,165 (*rank:* 21st); SE U.S.; *Boundaries:* Mississippi, Georgia, Florida, Tennessee, Gulf of Mexico; *Major cities:* Birmingham, Mobile, * Montgomery; *Major rivers:* Mobile, Alabama, Tombigbee; *Major lakes:* Wheeler, Guntersville, Wilson, Martin; 67 counties.

Nickname: Cotton State, Yellowhammer State; *Motto:* "Audemus jura nostra defendere" (We dare defend our rights); *Flag:* red cross of St. Andrew on white field; *Flower:* camellia; *Bird:* yellowhammer; *Fish:* tarpon; *Tree:* southern (longleaf) pine; *Song:* Alabama.

Industry: cotton, primary metals, tex-tiles, wood & wood products; *Natural resources:* bituminous coal, iron ore; *Major sources of income:* manufacturing.

Admitted to Union: 1819 (22nd state).

Places of interest: Mound State Park, Russel Cave Ntl. Monument, DeSoto State Park.

A-là-gō'ås *State* E

Ä-lä-jue'lä (hwä') *Province, Town* cen. Costa Rica; sugar, cattle, coffee

Al-å-mē'da *City* W Calif., U.S.; pop. 70,968; shipping, manufacturing, canning

Al'å-mō, The *Fort* San Antonio, Texas, U.S.

Å-las'kå *State*, named from Aleutian word meaning "Great Land"; 586,400 sq. m.; *pop.:* 302,173 (*rank:* 50th); NW-N America; *Boundaries:* British Columbia, Pacific Ocean, Bering Sea, Arctic Ocean; *Major cities:* * Juneau, Anchorage, Fairbanks; *Major Rivers:* Yukon, Tanana, Koyukuk, Kuskowin; *Major lakes:* Iliamna; 32 counties, 10 boroughs.

Nickname: Land of the Midnight Sun, The Great Land, Last Frontier; *Motto:* "North to the future"; *Flag:* blue field with 7 gold stars, representing Big Dipper; 8th star represents North Star; *Flower:* forget-me-not; *Bird:* willow ptarmigan; *Fish:* king salmon; *Tree:* Sitka spruce; *Song:* Alaska's Flag.

Industry: seafood, timber, pulp, oil, gas, petro-chemicals; *Natural resources:* gold, copper, coal, platinum, oil, natural gas, petroleum; *Major source of income:* Fed-eral defense installations.

Admitted to Union: 1959 (49th state).

Places of interest: Mt. McKinley Ntl. Park, Glacier Bay Ntl. Monument.

Å-las'kå Range *Mountain range* S Alas. U.S.; highest — MT. McKINLEY

Äl-bä-ce'te (sä'tå) *Commune*, * of *Province* SE Spain; cutlery

Al-bä'ni-å, People's Republic of *Country*, Europe; 11,100 sq. m.; pop. 2,255,000; * Tirana; 27 districts; *Main cities:* Durrës, Korfë, Shkodër, Vlonë; *Main rivers:* Drin, Mat, Shkumbi, Vjose; *Geog.:* hills, mts. frequently covered with scrub forest, flat-to-rolling coastal plains; *Climate:* coast — mild wet winters, Jan. low 42°F, dry hot summers, July high 83°F, interior—cooler.

Flag: black, 2 headed eagle centered on red field — surmounted by red star outlined in yellow.

Ethnic comp.: Gheg, Tosk language groups; *Language:* Gheg (North); Tosk (South) (official); *Religion:* Moslem 70%, Christian 18%, Catholic 12%.

Products: cereals, tobacco, timber, oil, chrome ore, lignite, copper, textiles, cement; *Minerals:* oil, coal, copper, iron, nickel; *Major exports:* oil, copper, coal, iron, nickel, petroleum, bitumen, tobacco; *Major imports:* machinery, equipment, rolled steel, wheat; *Industries:* food processing plants, chemical refineries, oil refineries, production construction materials, mining.

Currency: lek.

Head of Government: Chairman of Praesidium; *Legislature:* People's Assembly; *Judiciary:* Supreme Court, People's Tribune of Prefecture, People's Tribune of Sub-Prefecture.

Äl'bå-nẏ 1. *City,* * of N.Y., U.S.; pop. 114,873; industrial cen. 2. *City* SW Ga. U.S.; pop. 72,623; pecans. 3. *River* 610 m. Ontario, Canada

Äl-bay' (bī') *Province* Luzon, Phil. Is.; hemp, sugar, coconuts

Al-bêr'gå *River* 350 m. N South Australia

Al'bêrt, Lake *Lake* Uganda-Congo (L)

Al-bêr'tå *Province* W Canada; 248,800 sq. m.; pop. 1,553,000; * Edmonton; wheat, cattle, fish, coal, timber

Al'bu-quer-que (kêr-kē) *City* cen. N.M., U.S.; pop. 243,751; commerce, canning, oil

Al'cå-traz *Island* San Francisco Bay, Calif., U.S.; former penitentiary site.

Äl-coy' *Commune* SE Spain; paper manufacture

Ål-dan' *River* 1500 m., U.S.S.R., Asia

Äl'dêr-ney (ni) *Island* of The Channel Is.; agriculture, cattle

Å-len-côn (län-sôn') *City* NW France; lace

Å-lep'pō or **A-lep'** *City* NW Syria

A-les' *City* S France; raw silk trade

Ä-les-sän'dri-ä *Commune*, * of *Province* NW Italy; rail, trade cen.

Ȧ′lė-sund (soon) *City* W Norway; port, fisheries

Ȧ-leū′tian Islands (shȧn) *Island chain, District* W Alas., bet. Bering S. and N Pacific O.; fish, furs

Al-ex-an′dêr Archipelago *Island group* SE Alas., U.S.

Al-ex-an′dri-ȧ 1. *City* N Va., U.S.; pop. 110,938; commerce, manufacturing. 2. *City* cen. La., U.S.; pop. 41,557; manufacturing. 3. *Governorate* and *City* Lower Egypt; commercial port

A-ley′ (lā′) *Town,* summer * of Lebanon

Al-gė-ci′rȧs (jė-sē′) *City* SW Spain; port

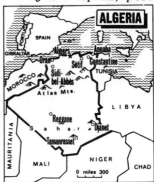

Al-gē′ri-ȧ, Democratic and Popular Republic of *Country* NW Africa; 952,200 sq. m.; pop. 14,392,000; * Algiers; 15 regional administrative entities (Wilayas) subdivided in 676 communes; *Main cities:* Oran, Constantine, Annaba, Sidibel — Abbés, Sétif; *Main river:* Chéliff; *Geog.:* flat to rolling coastal plains. 2 Atlas **Mt.** chains cross country laterally. To S lies Sahara; *Climate:* irregular. Winter, rain in N in Oct. Summer, hot, little rainfall.

Flag: red star, red crescent superimposed on background of green (left half), white (right half).

Ethnic comp.: Arabs, Berbers, Touareg; *Language:* Arabic, French (official), Ber-

ber dialects; *Religion:* Sunni Moslem (state); Roman Catholic, Protestant, Jewish.

Products: cereals, wine, citrus fruit, dates, oil, natural gas, iron ore, phosphates, salt, heavy engineering, construction materials, textiles; *Minerals:* petroleum, natural gas, coal, iron ore, phosphate, lead zinc, antimony, copper, tungsten; *Major exports:* oil, wine; *Major imports:* foodstuffs, manufactured goods, transportation equipment; *Industries:* heavy engineering, construction materials, textiles.

Currency: dinar.

Head of Government: President of National Revolutionary Council; *Legislature:* National Revolutionary Council, Council of Ministers, *Judiciary:* Supreme Court at apex (in process of transition from French system).

Al-giers′ (jẽrz′) 1. *City* on *Bay* * of Algeria; port. 2. Former name of ALGERIA

Al-ham′brȧ *City* SW Calif., U.S.; pop. 62,125; residential

Ä-li-cän′te *City* * of *Province* SE Spain; port, wine, textiles

A′li-gärh *City* * of *District* N India; trade

Alk′mäar *Commune* W Netherlands; cheese, butter, grain

Al Ku-wāit′ (koo) *Town* * of Kuwait principality; port

Al′läh-ȧ-bad′ 1. *District* of *Division* N India. 2. *City* N cen. India; imp. trade cen.

Al-lė-ghe′nẏ (gā′) 1. *River* 325 m., W Pa., U.S. 2. *Mountain ranges* of Appalachian system, E cen. U.S.

Al′len Pärk *City* SE Mich. U.S.; pop. 40,-747

Al′lėn-town *City* E Pa., U.S.; pop. 109,527; commerce, industry

Al-lep′pi *Town* S India; port

Al-lier′ (yā′) *Department, River* (250 m.), cen. France

Äl′mä-Ä-tä′ *City* * of *Region,* R.S.F.S.R., U.S.S.R., Asia

Äl-mä-den′ (dän′) *Commune* S cen. Spain; quicksilver

Äl-me-ri′ä (rē′) *City* * of *Province* SE Spain; harbor

Ä′lôr *Island* of *Group* Lesser Sunda Is., Indonesia

Alpes′ - Ma-ri-times′ (alp′ma-rē-tēm′) *Department* SE France

Alps *Mountain system* S cen. Europe extending ab 660 m.; in France, Italy, Switzerland, Austria, Yugoslavia; scenery, lakes, glaciers

Al′sace (sas) *Former province* Germany and France, now in NE France

Al′sace-Lör-rāine′ *Region* bet. France, Germany, Belgium and Switzerland (now French)

Al′sek *River* 260 m. SW Yukon and SE Alas., U.S.

Al′tai 1. *Mountain system* W China. 2. *Territory* R.S.F.S.R., U.S.S.R., Asia; agriculture, minerals

Ält′dôrf *Commune* cen. Switzerland; of William Tell fame

Äl′tėn-burg (boork) *City* cen. East Germany; manufacturing; grain, livestock

Äl′ton *City* SW Ill., U.S.; pop. 39,700; shipping

Äl′tō-nä *City* N West Germany; manufacturing

Al-tōō′nȧ *City* S cen. Pa., U.S.; pop. 62,-900; industrial

Äl′wȧr *City* * of *State* NW India

Ä-mä-gä-sä-ki *City* Honshu, Japan; chemicals, iron-steel

A′ma-gêr *Island* part

of Copenhagen, Denmark

Ä-mä-ku-sä (koo) *Island group* off W Kyushu, Japan

Ä-mäl′fi *Town* S Italy; mountain drive

Ä-mä-mi or **Ō-shi-mä** (shē) *Island group* S Japan [Brazil

A-mȧ-pa′ *Territory* N

Am-ȧ-ril′lō *City* NW Texas, U.S.; pop. 127,010; industry, commerce

Am′ȧ′zon *River* 4000 m., South America: worlds′ largest river

Ȧm-bä′lä *City* * of *Division* and *District* East Punjab, India

Am-boi′nȧ *Town* * of *Division* and of *Island* E Indonesia; spices, fruits

Ȧ-mer′i-cȧ — Name often used for U.S.; pl. **The Americas** incl. all lands of W Hemisphere

Ämes City *City,* Iowa, U.S.; pop. 39.505; education cen.

A-miens′ (myan′) *City* N France; textiles

Am-man′ *Town* * of Jordan, NW part; pop. 450,000; Bib. — **Am′mön;** Anc. — **Phil-ȧ-del′phi-ȧ** (fil, fi)

Ä-moy′ *City* on *Island* SE China; port

Am-rao′ti (rou′) *Town* * of *District* cen. India; cotton cen.

Am-rit′sȧr *City* * of *District* N India; manufacturing

Am′stêr-dam 1. *City* * of Netherlands, W part; pop. 804,000; commerce, manufacturing, bridges, canals. 2. *Island* (Fr.) S Indian O.

A-mu′ Dar-yä′ (mōō′) *River* 1500 m., U.S.S.R., W Asia

Ä′mund-sėn Gulf Body of water bet. N Northwest Terrs. Canada and Banks and Victoria Is.

Ȧ-mur′ (mōōr′) *River* 2800 m. NE Asia, Manchuria-U.S.S.R.

Ä-nȧ-dẏr′ *River* 450

m. to *Gulf*, U.S.S.R., Asia

An'a-heĭm *City* SW Calif., U.S.; pop. 166,701; citrus fruits

An-a-tō'liä *Area* of Turkey from Asia Minor to Black S.

An'chŏr-ȧge (ij) *City* in *District* S cen. Alas., U.S.; pop. 48,-029; port

Än-co-hu'mä (ōō') *Peak* of Mt. Sorata, Bolivia; 21,490 ft; see ILLAMPU

An-cō'nä *City* * of *Province* cen. Italy; Adriatic port

An-dȧ-lu'sia (lōō'zhȧ) *Region* S Spain; minerals, grain, fruit

An'dȧ-mȧn and Nic'o-bär Islands *Island groups, Province*, Bay of Bengal, India

Än'dêr-lecht (lekt) *Commune* cen. Belgium; weaving

An'dêr-sön 1. *City* cen. Ind., U.S.; pop. 70,787; automobiles. 2. *City* NW S.C., U.S.; shipping

An'dēs *Mountain system* W South America extending 4500 m.

Än'dhrȧ   Prȧ-desh' (däsh') *State* S India on Bay of Bengal

An-di-jhan' *City*, R.S.F.S.R., U.S.S.R., Asia; cotton cen.

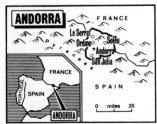

An-dôr'ra, Valleys of *Country* Pyrenees Mountains between France & Spain; 180 sq. m.; pop. 18,000; 6 districts, each with an elected parish council; *Main cities:* * Andorra la Vella, Les Escaldes, San Julian de Loria; *Main river:* Valira; *Geog.:* mt., green pastures on mt. sides; *Climate:* cool summers, wettest May through Oct. Abundant winter snowfall.

Flag: vertical bands of blue, yellow, red with national coat of arms in center.

Ethnic comp.: Andorrans, Spanish, French; *Language:* Catalan (official), French, Spanish; *Religion:* Roman Catholic (state).

Products: timber, cereals, potatoes, tobacco, iron, stone, slate, alum, lead, jasper, tourism; *Minerals:* iron ore, lead; *Major exports:* timber, cattle, lumber products; *Major imports:* fuel, perfumes, clothing, radios, t.v.; *Industry:* tourism, agriculture, lumbering, livestock raising.

Currency: French franc, Spanish peseta.

Head of Government: Veguers (designated representatives) of President of France and Bishop of Lerida (Spain); *Legislature:* general council; *Judiciary:* battles (court prosecuters) represent France, Spain.

Än-dre-ä'nŏf Islands *Island group* of Aleutian Is., Alas., U.S.

Än'dri-ä *Commune* SE Italy; trade cen.

An'drös 1. *Island*, largest of the Bahamas. 2. *Island* and *Town* N Cyclades

A-ne'to, Pi'co de (pē'kō, ä-nā'tō) *Peak* 11,169 ft. NE Spain

Ȧn-gȧ-ra' *River* 1100 m. U.S.S.R., Asia

Ān'gel Falls (jĕl) *Waterfall* 3200 ft. high, SE Venezuela

Ang'êr-mȧn (ông') *River* 279 m., cen. Sweden

Än-gers' (zhä') *City* W France; slate, liqueurs, shoes, rope

An'gle-sey (g'l-si) *Island* NW Wales; pastureland

An-glō-Ē-gẏp'tiȧn Sū-dan' (jip'shȧn) see SUDAN

An-gō'lȧ or **Portuguese West Africa** *Colony*

(Port.) SW Africa; 481,350 sq. m.; pop. 5,362,000; * Luanda; agriculture, diamonds; wax

Än-gō'rȧ see ANKARA

Än-gos-tu'rä (tōō') now CIUDAD BOLIVAR

Än-gou-lême (gōō-lâm') *City* W France; manufacturing, esp. paper

Angus *County* E Scotland; agriculture, livestock

Änhält *Former state* cen. Germany

Än'hwei' (hwä') *Province* E China; agriculture

An-jou' (zhōō') *Historical region* NW France

An'kȧ-rȧ *City* on *River* (115 m.), * of *Vilayet* and * of Turkey in W cen. Turkey, Asia; pop. 288,000; imp. trade cen.

Ȧn-nam' *Region* cen. Vietnam on S China S.; rice

Ȧn-nap'ö-lis *City* * of Md., U.S.; pop. 29,-592; U.S. Naval Academy site

An-nȧ-pûr'nȧ *Mountain range* of Himalayas, Nepal

Ann Ȧr'bŏr *City* SE Mich., U.S.; pop. 99,797

An-ne-cy' (an-sē') *City* E France; textiles

Än'shän' *Town* S Manchuria; steel

Än-tä-kyä', anc. **An'ti-och** (ok) *City* S Turkey, Asia

Än-täl-yä' or **Ä-dä-li-ä'** *Vilayet, Town, Gulf* SW Turkey, Asia

Ant-ärc'tĭc *Region, Ocean* incl. waters of Atlantic, Pacific and Indian Oceans

Ant-ärc'ti-cä *Continent* at South Pole; ab. 5,000,000 sq. m.; mountains 10,000 to 15,000 ft.; mostly unexplored

An-tibes' (tēb') *City* SE France; port

An-tie'tȧm *Village* N Md., U.S.; 1862 battle site

An-ti'guȧ (tē'gȧ) *Island* Brit. West Indies, E cen. Leeward Is.; *

St. Johns; harbors, sugar, cotton

Än-ti'guä (tē') *City* S cen. Guatemala, its former *

An-til'lēs *Island groups* of West Indies: **Greater Antilles** incl. Cuba, Haiti, Dominican Rep., Puerto Rica, Jamaica; **Lesser Antilles** incl. Virgin, Windward, Leeward Is.

An'ti-och (ok) See ANTAKYA

An-tip'o-dēs 1. *Island group* of New Zealand. 2. *Name* for Australia and New Zealand

Än-ti'que (tē'kâ) *Province* Panay, Phil. Is.; fishing, sugar cane

Än-to-fä-gäs'tä *City* * of *Province* N Chile; exports minerals

Än-to-fäl'lä (fä'yä) *Volcano* 21,129 ft. NW Argentina

An'trim *County* NE Northern Ireland; basalt, oats, flax, peat

Än'tung' (doong') *Province* S Manchuria; trade

Ant'wêrp *City* * of *Province* N Belgium; harbor; trade, manufacturing

Ȧ - nu - rä'dhȧ - pu - rȧ (noo, poo) *Town* Ceylon; sacred to Buddhists

Ȧ-nyui' (nyōō'i) *River* 420 m. U.S.S.R., Asia

Ȧn-zhe'rö Sud-zhensk' *Town* R.S.F.S.R., U.S.S.R., Asia

Än-zin' (zan') *Commune* N France; coal area

An'zi-ō *City* W Italy; port; Allied landing site, WW II

A-ō-mō-ri *City* * of *Prefecture* Honshu, Japan; harbor

Ä'pä-pä *Town* SW Nigeria; port

Ä-pä-pō'ris *River* 500 m. S Colombia

A'pil-dōorn *Commune* cen. Netherlands; paper

Ap'en-nīnes *Mountain range* 800 m. long, cen. Italy; agriculture, trees, pasturage

Ä'pō, Mount *Moun-*

lain 9690 ft., highest of Phil. Is.

Á-pos′tle Islands (pos′ ′l) *Islands* Lake Superior, U.S.

Ap-på-lăch′i-å *Region* SE U.S. incl. ranges of Appalachian Mts.

Ap-på-lăch′i-ån Mountains *Mountain system* E North America: Quebec, Canada-N Ala., U.S.

Ap′pén-zell *Canton, Commune* NW Switzerland; sheep, embroidery, agriculture

Ap′ple-tön *City* E Wisc., U.S.; pop. 57,143; manufacturing

Ap-po-mat′töx *Town* SE cen. Va., U.S.; Confederate surrender, 1865

Ä-puä′niä *Commune,* * of *Province* cen. Italy

Á-pū′li-å *Compartimento* SE Italy; "heel" of Italian "boot"; agriculture, livestock, salt

Ä-pu′re (pōō′rå) *State* and *River* 420 m. W Venezuela

Ä-pu-ri′mäc (pōō-rē′) *River* 500 m. Peru

A′qa-bå anc. **Ē′lath** *Town* at *Gulf,* SW Jordan; port

Äq′sū′ *Town, Oasis* W China; trade cen.

Aq′ui-lå (wi) *Commune* * of *Province,* cen. Italy; linen, paper, leather

Aq-ui-tā′ni-å (wi) Historical division of SW France, later **Aq′ui-tāine** (wi)

Á-rä′bi-å *Peninsula* SW Asia; 1,000,000 sq. m.; fertile coast areas; incl. Saudi Arabia, Qatar, Trucial Oman, Oman, Aden, Yemen

Á-rä′bi-ån Des′ért *Desert* E Egypt, E of Nile R. along Gulf of Suez and Red S.

Á-rä′bi-ån Sea Part of Indian O. India-Arabia

Ar′å-by poetic name for ARABIA

A-rå-cä-ju′ (zhōō′) *City* E Brazil

Ä-räd′ *City* W Romania; commerce, industry

Ä-rä-fu′rä Sea (fōō′) *Sea* Indonesia-Australia

Ar′å-gon *Region, anc. kingdom* NE Spain; manufacturing, mining, agriculture

A-rå-guai′å (gwī′) *River* 1100 m., cen. Brazil

Á-raks′ *River* 635 m., E U.S.S.R.

Ar′ål, Lake *Inland sea* U.S.S.R., Asia

Ār′åm *Anc. country* SW Asia, Lebanon Mts-Euphrates

Ar′å - rat *Mountain* 16,916 ft., E Turkey

Är-cä′di-å 1. *City* SW Calif., U.S.; pop. 42,-868. 2. *Department* cen. Peloponnesus, Greece

Ärc′tic Archipelago *Island group* in Arctic O., incl. Baffin, Victoria, Banks, Devon, etc.

Ärc′tic Red *River* 230 m. Northwest Terrs., Canada

Ärc′tic Regions incl. **Arctic O.** and lands in and adjacent to it

Ärc′tic Ocean *Ocean* N of Continental land masses at **Arctic Circle;** 5,441,000 sq. m.

Ar-dė-bil′ (bēl′) *City* NW Iran; trade

Ar-deche′ (desh′) *Department* SE France

Är-dennes′ (den′) 1. *Region* incl. parts of SE Belgium, Luxembourg, France; battles WW I, II. 2. *Department* NE France

Ä-re-ci′bō (sē′) *Municipality, Town,* N Puerto Rico

Ä-re-qui′på (kē′) *City* * of *Department,* S Peru; industrial, educational cen.

Ä-rez′zō (rät′) *Commune* * of *Province,* cen. Italy; manufacturing

Ar - gen - teuil′ (zhän-tu′y′) *Commune* N France; g r a p e s, chemicals

Är-gėn-ti′nå (jėn-tē′), Republic *Country,* S S America; 1,072,163 sq. m.; pop. 25,040,-000; 22 provinces, Federal capital dis-

ARGENTINA

trict, National Territory of Tierra del Fuego; *Main cities:* * Buenos Aires, Córdoba, Rosario, La Plata; *Main rivers:* Paraná, Negro, Salado, Colorado, Chubut; *Geog.:* subtropical lowlands, Andean Mts., Patagonian Steppe, Tierra del Fuego, heartland is rich temperate plains known as Pampa; *Climate:* hot subtropical to rainy to temperate.

Flag: horizontal blue (top, bottom), white (center) bands. Center is "Sun of May" commemorating freedom from Spain.

Ethnic comp.: Caucasian (Europeans), Indian, mestizos, Arab descent; *Language:* Spanish (official), Italian, French, German; *Religion:* Roman Catholic (state); Protestant, Jewish.

Products: meat, cereals, wool, cotton, edible oils, oil, coal, iron ore, cement, steel, pig-iron, beer; *Minerals:* silver, beryl, coal, copper, iron ore, natural gas, manganese, salt, petroleum, lead, sulfur, tin, uranium, tungsten, zinc; *Major exports:* agriculture — livestock products, grains, meat, wool, vegetable oil, hides — skin; *Major imports:* machinery — electrical equipment, wood — lumber, newsprint, crude oil, automotive equip-

ment — parts, iron — steel products, chemicals; *Industries:* agriculture, manufacture of cars, electricity, steel, cement, petroleum, livestock products.

Currency: peso.

Head of Government: President; *Legislature:* National Congress — Senate, House of Deputies *Judiciary:* Supreme Court at apex — separate branch of gov't.

Är-gônne′ *Plateau* NE France; battles WW I and II.

Är′gös *City* NE Peloponnesus, Greece

Är′gun′ (gōōn′) *River* 450 m. Manchuria-U.S.S.R.

Ä-ri′cå (rē′) *City* N Chile; port

Ar-i-zō′nå *State,* named from Papago Indian word "arizonac" meaning "a small, everflowing stream"; 113,909 sq. m.; *pop.:* 1,772,482 (*rank:* 33rd); SW U.S.; *Boundaries:* Mexico, California, Nevada, Utah, New Mexico; *Major cities:* * Phoenix, Tucson, Flagstaff; *Major rivers:* Colorado, Little Colorado; *Major lakes:* Mohave, Theodore Roosevelt, Mead Reservoir; 14 counties.

Nickname: Grand Canyon State, Sunset State, Apache State; *Motto:* "Ditat Deus" (God Enriches); *Flag:* copper-colored star centered on radiating red, & yellow stripes, horizontal blue bar; *Flower:* Saguaro cactus; *Bird:* cactus wren. *Tree:* Paloverde; *Song:* Arizona.

Industry: transportation equipment, electrical & other machinery, metals, food; *Natural resources:*

copper, uranium, lead, zinc, gold, silver; *Major sources of income:* government, manufacturing.

Admitted to Union: 1912 (48th state).

Places of interest: Grand Canyon, Petrified Forest Ntl. Park.

Ȧr'kȧn-sas (sǎ) *State,* name is corruption of name of Indian tribe Quapaw which lived in region at time of discovery by DeSoto; 53,104 sq. m.; *pop.:* 1,923,295 (*rank:* 32nd); SC U.S.; *Boundaries:* Texas, Oklahoma, Missouri, Tennessee, Mississippi, Louisiana, Mississippi River; *Major cities:* * Little Rock, North Little Rock, Fort Smith; *Major rivers:* Arkansas, Mississippi, Ouachita, White; *Major lakes:* Bull Shoals, Ouachita, Beaver, Norfolk; 75 counties.

Nickname: Land of Opportunity; *Motto:* "Regnat populus" (The people rule); *Flag:* star studded blue & white diamond on red field, diamond shape represents Arkansas, the only diamond producing state; *Flower:* apple blossom; *Bird:* mockingbird; *Tree:* shortleaf pine; *Song:* Arkansas.

Industry: cotton, chemicals, food, furniture, wood, paper, apparel, machinery; *Natural resources:* bauxite, forests, diamond mines, oil, natural gas; *Major source of income:* manufacturing.

Admitted to Union: 1836 (25th state).

Places of interest: Hot Springs Ntl. Park.

Ȧr-khan'gȧlsk *City* * *of Region* N

R.S.F.S.R., U.S.S.R., Eur.; timber port

Ärl'bêrg *Pass* Alpine valley, W Austria

Ärles (ärl) *City* SE France; medieval kingdom

Är'ling-tön 1. *Town* NE Mass., U.S.; pop. 53,524; residential. 2. *City* N Texas, U.S.; pop. 90,643. 3. *County* N Va., U.S.; Tomb of Unknown Soldier, grave of John F. Kennedy

Är'ling-tön Heïghts *Village* NE Ill., U.S.; pop. 64,884; residential

Är-mägh' (mä') *County* S Northern Ireland; agriculture, livestock

Ȧr-mȧ-vir' (vyēr') *City* S R. S. F. S. R., U.S.S.R.; Eur.; agriculture

Är-mē'ni-ȧ *Anc. country* W Asia, now parts in U.S.S.R., Turkey, Iran

Är-mē'ni-ȧn S.S.R. *Republic* of U.S.S.R., S Eur.; * Yerevan; agriculture, lumbering, livestock

Är-men-tieres' (tērz') *Commune* N France; industrial cen.

Ärn'hem *Commune* E Netherlands; precision instruments

Är'nö *River* 140 m. cen. Italy; WW II crossing [dia

Är'rȧh *Town* NE India

Ar'rȧs *City* N France; grain market

Är'tȧ *Department* NW Greece

Ȧr-te'mövsk (tye') *City* Ukraine, U.S.S.R.; salt, coal

Är-tois' (twä') *Historical region* N cen. France

Ä-ru'bä (rōō') *Islands* (Neth.) off NW Venezuela; oil refineries

Är-vȧ'dȧ *City* C Colo., U.S.; pop. 46,814; food processing agriculture

Ashe'ville *City* W N.C., U.S.; pop. 57,681; resort, manufacturing

Ä-shi-kä-gä *City* Honshu, Japan; weaving

Ashkh'ȧ-bad *City* * of Turkmen S.S.R., U.S.S.R., Asia

Ā'sia (zhȧ) *Continent,* world's largest: ⅓ of world's land area ab. 16,500,000 sq. m.; over ½ world's pop. ab. 1,164,000; Eastern hemisphere

Ā'sia Mī'nör *Peninsula* W Asia bounded by Black, Mediterranean, Aegean Seas; forms large part of Turkey

As-mä'rȧ *Town* Eritrea, N Ethiopia

As-nieres' (ȧ-nyâr') *Commune* N France; boating, dyes, perfume

Ä-sō *Volcano* Kyushu, Japan; five peaks, world's largest crater

As-sam' *State* NE India; tea

Ȧs-sin'i-boine *River* 450 m. S Canada

Ȧs-si'si (sē') *Commune* cen. Italy

Ȧs-syr'i-ȧ *Anc. empire* W Asia

Ä'sti *Commune* * of *Province* NW Italy; sparkling wine

As'trȧ-khan *City* * of *Region,* R.S.F.S.R., U.S.S.R., Eur.

Ä-sun-ciôn' (s ō ō n-syôn') *City,* * and chief port of Paraguay, S cen. part; pop. 360,000; commerce, industry

As-wan' *City* * of *Province* Upper Egypt; dam

As-yut' (yōōt') *City* * of *Province,* Upper Egypt; pottery, ivory

Ä-tä-cä'mä *Province, Desert* N cen. Chile; borax lakes

Ät'bä-rä *River* 500 m., NE Africa

Ȧ - tchaf - ȧ - lay'ȧ (lī') *River* 225 m. S La., U.S.

Ath-ȧ-bas'kȧ *River* 765 m., and *Lake* 2842 sq. m. W cen. Canada

Ath'ẽns *City* * of Greece, S cen. part; pop. ab. 2,000,000; commercial, manufacturing, cultural cen.

Ath'ẽns *City* NE Ga., U.S.; pop. 44,342; manufacturing, education cen.

Ath'ös *Mountain* 6670 ft. NE Greece; "Holy Mountain"

At'kȧ *Island* of Aleutian Is. SW Alas., U.S.

At-lan'tȧ *City,* * and largest city of Ga., U.S., NW cen part; pop. 496,973; commercial, rail, education cen.

Ȧt-lan'tic City *City* SE N.J., U.S.; pop. 47,859; resort

Ȧt-lan'tic Ocean Body of water separating North and South America from Europe and Africa; ab. 31,500,000 sq. m.

At'lȧs Mountains *Mountain system* 1500 m. long N Africa

Ä-trä'tö *River* 350 m. NW Colombia

Ä-trek' *River* 300 m. NE Iran

At-tȧ-wȧ-pis'kȧt *River* 465 m. Ontario, Canada

At'ti-cȧ and Boe-ō'tia (bi-ō'shȧ) *Department* E cen. Greece

At'tu (tōō) *Island* westernmost of Aleutian Is.

Ä-tuel' (twel') *River* 300 m. W Argentina

Aube (ōb) *Department* NE France

Au-ber-vil-liers' (ō-bêr-vē-lyä') *Commune* N France; chemicals, glass, perfume, rubber

Au-bus-sôn' (ō) *Commune* cen. France; carpets, tapestries

Ăuck'lȧnd *City* * of *District* N New Zealand; port

Aude (ōd) *Department* S France

Augs'bûrg (ouks') *City* S West Germany; textiles

Ău-gus'tȧ 1. *City* E Ga., U.S.; pop. 59,864; cotton, lumber. 2. *City* * of Me., U.S.; pop. 21,680; lumber, shoes, textiles, paper

Au - gus'tä (ou-gōōs') *Commune* SE Sicily;

salt, oil, wine, fish

Ău-rō′rà 1. *City* cen. Colo., U.S.; pop. 74,-974; 2. *City* NE Ill., U.S.; pop. 74,182; industry

Ausch′wits (oush′vitz) *Commune* S Poland; concentration camp WW II

Ăus′têr-litz *Commune* W cen. Czechoslavakia

Ăus′tin *City* * of Texas cen. part, U.S.; pop. 251,808; political, educational, commercial cen.

Ăus-trā′lia, Commonwealth of *Country,* Indian Ocean, S of Indonesia; 2,974,581 sq. m.; pop. 12,690,-000; 6 federated states each with elected legislature headed by Premier; *Main cities:* * Canberra, Sydney, Melbourne, Brisbane, Adelaide, Perth, Hobart; *Main rivers:* Murray, Darling, Murrumbidgee, Clarence, Tweed; *Geog.:* smallest continent, low irregular plateau, Great Barrier Reef off coast to E; *Climate:* wide variation, less subject to extremes.

Flag: blue with Union Jack in top left corner, large white star beneath symbolizes freedom, right half carries 5 smaller white stars representing Southern Cross.

Ethnic comp.: British origin, Anglo Saxon, Aborigines; *Language:* English (official); *Religion:* Anglican, Roman Catholic, Methodist, Baptist, Presbyterian.

Products: wool, wheat, meat, dairy products, sugar cane, hides — skins, iron — steel, motor vehicles, chemicals, oil, natural gas, coal, lead, copper, gold, iron ore, bauxite; *Minerals:* asbestos, silver, bauxite, gold, coal, copper, iron ore, gypsum, lignite, mica, manganese, salt, petroleum, opals, lead, sulfur, pyrites, antimony, tin, titanium, uranium, tungsten, zinc; *Major exports:* wool, wheat, meat, sugar, dairy products, fruits; *Major imports:* machinery — transportation equipment, manufactured goods, chemicals, mineral fuels, crude materials, food, beverages; *Industries:* mining, refining, agriculture, manufacturing.

Currency: pound/dollar (Australian).

Head of Government: Queen Elizabeth II represented by Governor General, Prime Minister; *Legislature:* Federal Parliament — Senate, House of Representatives; *Judiciary:* High Court of Australia, federal, state courts.

Ăus′tri-à, Republic of *Country,* C Europe; 32,374 sq. m.; pop. 7,496,000; 9 provinces each administered by provincial government chosen by provincial legislature; *Main cities:* * Vienna, Graz, Linz, Salzburg, Innsbruck;

Main rivers: Danube, Inn, Mur; *Geog.:* mt. with Alps, approaches dominating W, S provinces, E, Vienna in Danube River Basin; *Climate:* Jan. national average 9°F, July 68°F, rainfall 27″–69″.

Flag: red, white, red horizontal stripes with national coat of arms centered on white stripe.

Ethnic comp.: S Germanic stock with Slavic admixtures, Slovenes; *Language:* German (official), Slovenian, Croatian, Hungarian; *Religion:* Roman Catholic, Protestant.

Products: timber, cereals, sugar, potatoes, graphite, lignite, steel, iron ore, pig iron, plastics, pharmaceuticals, fertilizers, paper pulp, machinery, transportation equipment; *Minerals:* iron ore, petroleum, magnesite, rock salt; *Major exports:* machinery, iron, steel, textiles, chemicals, wood, paper; *Major imports:* machinery, transportation equipment, textiles, minerals, fuels, chemicals; *Industries:* oil refining, tourism, food — beverages, chemicals, textiles, ceramics, stone — glass, metal goods.

Currency: schilling.

Head of Government: President, *Legislature:* bicameral parliament — Bundesrat, Nationalrat; *Judiciary:* Constitutional Court. Keeps justice separate from legislature, administrative authorities. No distinction between civil, criminal cases.

Ăus′tri-à-Hun′gà-rẏ *Former monarchy* cen. Eur. incl. Hungary,

Austria, Czechoslovakia, parts of Italy, Poland, Yugoslavia, Romania

À-vei′ro (vā′i-rōō) *City* on *Lagoon,* * of *District* NW Portugal; salt, mercury

Ä-ver′sä *Commune* S Italy; white wine

À-vi-gnôn′ (vē-nyôn′) *City* SE France; commerce, manufacturing

Ä′vi-lä *City* * of *Province* cen. Spain

Ā′von *River* 96 m. cen. England; Shakespeare fame

Ä-wä-ji *Island* of Japan, S of Honshu

Ax′min-stêr *Town* SW England; carpets

Ay-din′ (ī) *Town* * of *Vilayet* SW Turkey, Asia; trade

Āyles′bûr-ẏ *Municipal borough* SE cen. England; lace

Āyr or **Āyr′shîre** *County, Burgh* SW Scotland; port, manufacturing

Ay-sen′ (ī-sān′) *Province, Commune* S Chile

Ä-zêr-baï-dzhän′ S.S.R. *Republic* of U.S.S.R., Eur.; * Baku; minerals, oil wells

Ä-zêr-baï-jän′ *Province* NW Iran; fertile area

Ā′zōres *Island group* (Port.) N Atlantic O.; fruit, wine, grain

B

Bā′àl-bek, anc. Hē-li-op′ö-lis *Village* E Lebanon [bylon

Bā′bèl *City,* anc. Ba-**Ba′bush-kin** (b o o s h) *City* R.S.F.S.R., U.S.S.R., Eur.

Bab′ẏ-lon *Anc. city,* * of **Bab-ẏ-lō′ni-à,** mod. S Iraq

Back River *River* 605 m. N Canada

Bä-cô′lôd *City,* Negros, Phil. Is.; sugar cen.

Bä-dä-jôz′ (hôth′) *City* * of *Province,* SW Spain; trade cen.

Bä-dä-lō′nà *Commune* NE Spain; port

Bä′dèn *Former state* SW Germany, now

part of **Bä'děn-Wûrt'těm-bêrg**, *State* West Germany

Bad Lands *Region* SW S.D., U.S.; barren area

Baf'fin Bay *Inlet* of Atlantic O. Greenland-Baffin I.

Baf'fin Island *Island*, largest of Canadian Arctic Arch.

Bagh'dad *City* * of *Province* and * of Iraq, E cen. part; pop. 500,000; imp. since anc. times

Bä'ghel-khånd *Former agency* E cen. India

Bä'gō *Municipality* Negros, Phil. Is.

Bä'guiō (gyō) *City* Luzon; summer * of Phil. Is.

Bå-hä'må Islands *Islands* (Brit.) SE of Fla., U.S.; * Nassau on New Providence I.; agriculture, fish, resort

Bå-hä'wål-pur (poor) *Town* * of *State*, Punjab, W Pakistan

Bä-hi'ä Blånc'ä ('ē') *City* E Argentina; port

Båh-raich' (rīk') *Town* * of *District* N India; trade cen.

Båh-raīn' Islands *Archipelago* W Persian Gulf; pearls, oil

Bahr el Ghä-zal' *River* ab 500 m., Sudan

Bå-i'ä (ē') *State* E Brazil

Baja California *State* NW Mexico

Baī-kal', **Lake** *Lake*, Siberia, U.S.S.R., Asia

Bä-kår-gånj' *District* East Pakistan

Bä'kêr Island *Island* (U.S.) cen. Pacific O.

Bä'kêrs-fiĕld *City* S Cal., U.S.; pop. 69,-515; oil industry

Bä-ku' (kōō') *City* * of Azerbaidzhan Rep., U.S.S.R.; oil

Bal-å-klä'vå *Village* SW Crimea, U.S.S.R. Eur.; port

Bal-bō'å *District* SE Canal Zone

Båld'win Pärk *City* S Cal., U.S., pop. 47,-285

Bal-ė-ar'ic Islands *Islands*, *Province* E Spain; incl. Majorca, Minorca, etc.

Bä'li *Island* E of Java, Indonesia

Bä-li-ke-sir' (sēr') *City* * of *Vilayet* NW Turkey, Asia

Bä-lik-pä'pän *Town* on *Bay* SE Borneo, Indonesia; oil

Bǎl'kån Peninsula *Peninsula* SE Eur., bounded by Adriatic, Ionian, Mediterranean, Aegean and Black Seas; incl. Yugoslavia, Bulgaria, Romania, Greece, Albania, Turkey in Eur. called **Bǎl'kån States**

Bäl-khäsh', **Lake** *Lake* Kazakh, U.S.S.R.

Bal'lå-rat *City* SE Australia; gold

Bǎl'tic Sea *Arm* of Atlantic O., N Eur.

Bǎl'tic States *Republics* of U.S.S.R.: Latvia, Estonia, Lithuania

Bǎl'ti-môre *City* Md., U.S.; pop. 905,759; imp. port

Bå-lū-chi-stän' *Region* W Pakistan

Ba-ma-ko' *Town* * of Mali, S part; pop. 175,000

Bam'bêrg *City* S cen. West Germany; textiles, breweries

Bä-nät' *Region* N Yugoslavia, formerly div. bet. Romania and Hungary

Bän-dä'mä *River* 370 m. Ivory Coast

Bän-djêr-mä'sin *Town* S Borneo, Indonesia; trade cen.

Bän'doeng (doong) *City* J a v a , Indonesia; manufacturing

Bän'drå *Town* W India; resort

Banff (bamf) 1. *Town* and *National Park*, SW Alberta, Canada. 2. *County* NE Scotland

Banff'shire *County* SE Scotland; quarries, fish, cattle

Ban'gå-lôre *City* * of *District*, Mysore, S India; trade cen.

Bang'kå *Island* off SE Sumatra, Indonesia

Bang'kok *City* * of Thailand, S part; pop. 2,800,000; port

Bang-la-desh', *Country*, Formerly E Pakistan, S Asia; 55,130 sq. m.; pop. 62,944,000; *Main cities:* * Dacca, Chittagong; *Main rivers:* Ganges, Brahmaputra; *Geog.:* subtropical alluvial plain; *Climate:* averages 85″ rainfall, temperature averages 84°F.

Ethnic comp.: Bengalis Assamese; *Language:* English, Bengali; *Religion:* Moslem, Hinduism, Christian, Buddhist.

Products: jute, sugar cane, wheat, grain, tea, timber, fish; *Mineral:* natural gas; *Major export:* jute; *Industries:* textile, paper mills, shipbuilding.

Bän-gui' (gē') *Town* * of Central African Republic; pop. 150,-000

Bang - wē - ū'lū Lake *Lake* N Zambia

Banks Island *Island* Northwest Territories, Canada

Bän'ku-rä (koo) *Town* and *District*, NE India

Bän'nu (noo) *Town* and *District*, N West Pakistan

Bäns-wä'rå *State* and *Town*, NW India

Bär-bā'dōs *Country*, E Caribbean; 166 sq. m.; pop. 250,000; 11 parishes, Bridgetown City. *Main city:* * Bridgetown; *Geog.:* coral origin, relatively flat rising gent-

ly from W coast in series of terraces to ridge in center; *Climate:* tropical, pleasant. Average temperature 77°F.

Flag: 3 equal sized vertical bands, outer 2 ultramarine, center gold, broken black staff of Neptune centered on gold band.

Ethnic comp.: African, White (mainly British); *Language:* English (official); *Religion:* Anglican, Methodist, Moravian, Roman Catholic.

Products: sugar, molasses, rum, margarine, lard, mangoes, plastics, electronics; *Major exports:* sugar, rum, molasses; *Major imports:* food, machinery, transportation equipment, chemicals, petroleum products; *Industry:* tourism, fishing, animal husbandry.

Currency: E Caribbean dollar.

Head of Government: Queen Elizabeth II represented by governor general; *Legislature:* bicameral Parliament — House of Assembly, Senate; *Judiciary:* Supreme Court highest court.

Bär'bå-rẏ *Region* N African Coast, Egypt to Atlantic O.; **Bär' bå-rẏ States:** Morocco, Algiers, Tunis, Tripoli

Bär-cė-lō'nå (sė) *City* * of *Province* NE Spain; chief port, manufacturing cen.

Bär-cōō' River 600 m., Australia

Ba-reil'ly̆ (rāl') City * of Division and District, N India

Bar'ents Sea Area of Arctic O. N of Norway and U.S.S.R.

Bä'ri City * of Province SE Italy; port, manufacturing

Bä'ri-à State W India

Bä-ri-sän' Mountains Mountain system W Sumatra

Bä-ri'tō (rē') River 550 m. SE Borneo

Bär'king Urban district SE England

Bar-le-Dūc' Commune NE France; manufacturing

Bär-let'tà City SE Italy; port

Bar-nà-ūl' (ber) Town, R.S.F.S.R., U.S.S.R., Asia; mines, factories

Bà-rō'dà City * of State and Division, W India; jewelry

Bà-rot'se-land Former Region of Northern Rhodesia, now part of Zambia

Bär-qui-si-me'tō (kē-sē-mā') City NW Venezuela; export cen.

Bär-rän-quil'lä (kē'yä) City N Colombia; port

Bar'rōw 1. Town nr. Point N Alas., U.S. 2. County Borough NW England; industry. 3. Island off W Australia

Bär-thol'ö-mew Bay'ou mū bī'ōō) River 275 m. Ark.-La., U.S.

Bär'wön Upper course of Darling R., SE Australia

Bä'sil or Bäsle (bäl) City * of Canton NW Switzerland; manufacturing

Bash'kir A.S.S.R. Republic, R.S.F.S.R., U.S.S.R. Eur.; forestry, agriculture, minerals, horses

Bä-si'län (sē') Island of Group, Phil. Is.; wood, fish

Basque Provinces (bask) Region N Spain; forests, vineyards, mines

Bäs'rä City * of Prov-

ince, S Iraq; port

Bäs-Rhin' (bä-ran') Department NE France

Bàs-sein' (sān') City * of District, Lower Burma; rice

Basses - Alpes' (bäs - zalp') Department SE France

Basses - Py - re - nees' (bäs-pē-rā-nā') Department SW France

Bass Islands Islands (3) W Lake Erie, U.S.

Bä-sti'à (stē') City NE Corsica; commerce

Bas-togne' (t ô n ' y ') Town SE Belgium; WW II battle

Bà-su'tō-land (sōō') Brit. Colony now LESOTHO, republic South Africa; * Maseru; livestock

Bä'tä Town * of Spanish Guinea; pop. 3500; port

Bà-täan' Province and Peninsula L u z o n , Phil. Is.; WW II battles

Bà-tan'gàs Municipality on Bay, * of Province, Luzon, Phil. Is.; sugar, lumber, coconuts

Bà-tä'vi-à City now DJAKARTA, on Bay; * of former Neth. Indies

Bath City and County borough SW England; resort

Bath'ûrst Town * of Gambia; pop. 28,000; seaport

Bāt'ön Rouge (rōōzh) City * of La., U.S.; pop. 165,963; chemicals, petroleum

Bat'tle (t'l) River ab. 340 m. W Canada

Bat'tle Crēēk City S Mich., U.S.; pop. 38,-931; breakfast foods

Bà-tūm' City * of Adzhar A.S.S.R., U.S.S.R.; port

Baut'zen (bou') City SE East Germany; manufacturing

Bà-var'i-a State S West Germany; * Munich; agriculture, manufacturing

Bà-var'i-àn Alps Range of Alps bet. Austria and Germany

Bāy City City E Mich.

U.S.; pop. 49,449; lumber, coal, fish

Bay'kal, Lake (bī) see BAIKAL

Bāy-önne' City NE N.J., U.S.; pop. 72,-743; petroleum industry

Bay - reuth' (bī - roit') City SW West Germany; industrial

Bāy'town City SE Texas, U.S.; pop. 43,980

Bear River ab. 350 m. Ida. and Utah, U.S.

Bē'äs River ab 300 m. N India

Beau'fört Sea (bō') Part of Arctic O. N of Alaska and Canada

Beau'mont (bō') City SE Texas, U.S.; pop. 115,919; oil port

Bech-ū-ä'nà-land now BOTSWANA

Bed'förd Municipal borough SE cen. England; farm tools

Bed'förd-shire County SE cen. England; agriculture, lace

Bed'lōe's Island Island N. Y. Bay, N. Y., U.S.; site of Statue of Liberty

Bēer-shē'bà Town and Subdistrict, S Israel

Bēes'tön and Stä'ple-förd (p'l) Urban district N cen. England

Bei-rūt' (bā) City * of Lebanon, N part; pop. 700,000; port

Be'là-yà River ab. 700 m., U.S.S.R., Eur.

Bè-lem' City N Brazil; seaport

Bel'fast County borough * of Northern Ireland; shipbuilding, seaport, linen

Bel - fort' (fôr') Commune E France, manufacturing

Bel-fôrt', Ter-ri-toire' dê (twar') Department E France

Bel-gaum' (goum') Town * of District W India; weaving

Bel'gian Con'gō (jàn) see ZAIRE

Bel'gium (jum), Kingdom of Country, NW Europe; 11,780 sq. m.; pop. 10,000,000; 9 provinces, 2,586 communes; Main cit-

ies: * Brussels, Antwerp, Ghent, Liege, Charleroi, Mons; Main rivers: Scheldt, Meuse; Geog.: flat, increasingly hilly, forested terrain toward SE; Climate: cool, temperate, rainy, average summer temperature, 60°F.

Flag: vertical bands — black, yellow, red left to right.

Ethnic comp.: Flemings — Walloons; Language: French — Flemish (official), German; Religion: Roman Catholic, Protestant, Jewish.

Products: coke, coal, steel, iron, machinery, transportation equipment, textiles, chemicals, pharmaceuticals, sugar, oil, glass; Minerals: coal, iron, lead, zinc, copper, manganese, phosphates; Major exports: machinery, cars, glass, nonferrous metals, chemicals, textiles, diamonds, iron — steel products; Major imports: grains, ores, petroleum, chemicals, machinery, electrical equipment, cars; Industry: steel — metal manufacturing, diamond cutting, chemical production, oil refining, glass making, textile mills.

Currency: franc.

Head of Government: Monarch; Legislature: bicameral Parliament — Senate, Chamber of Representatives; Judiciary:

modeled on French system, based on Napoleonic Code. Trial by jury only in criminal, political cases.

Bel'grāde City * of Yugoslavia and of Serbia Republic; pop. 697,000; industrial and communication cen.

Bė-lize' (lēz') City * of District E Brit. Honduras; port

Bel'leau Wood (lō) Wood N France; WW I battle site

Bėl-lēek' Parish and Village Northern Ireland; china

Belle' Fourche' (fōōsh') River ab. 350 m. Wyo., U.S.

Belle'ville City SW Ill., U.S.; pop. 41,699; coal area

Belle'vūe City Va. U.S.; pop. 61,102

Bell'flow-êr City Calif., U.S.; pop. 51,454

Bel'ling ham City Va., U.S.; pop. 39,375

Bel - lu'nō (bāl - lōō') Commune * of Province NE Italy; trade

Bė-loit' City S Wisc., U.S.; pop. 35,729; manufacturing, dairy farms

Bel-yan'dō River ab. 250 m. NE Australia

Bė-nä'rės City * of Division N India; ancient holy city

Ben'ė-lux = countries of Belgium, Netherlands and Luxembourg

Be-ne-ven'tō (bâ-nâ) Commune * of Province S Italy

Ben'gàl Former Province NE Brit. India, * Calcutta; 1947 div. into **East Ben'gàl**, Pakistan and **West Ben'gàl**, India

Ben'gàl, Bay of Arm of Indian O. bet. India and Burma

Ben-gä'zi City * of Province, co-* of Libya N part; port

Be'ni (bâ) River 1000 m. Bolivia

Be'ni Su-ef' (bâ'ni-soo-wāf') City * of Province, Upper Egypt

Bė-nō'ni Town NE Republic of South Africa; gold mining

Be'nue (bā'nwā) River ab 870 m. W Africa

Bep'pu (pōō) City on Bay Kyushu, Japan

Be-rär' (bā) Division of **Central Provinces and Berar**, cen. India

Bêr'bė-rà City N Somalia; seaport

Bêr-bice' (bēs') County and River 300 m. E

Bêr'chėm (kėm) Commune N Belgium

Bêrch-tės-gä'dėn (bêrk) Town Bavarian Alps, West Germany

Bêr-di'chev (dyē'chéf) City Ukraine, U.S.S.R.; trade cen.

Be-re'zi-nà (bye-ryā'zyi) River 350 m. White Russia, U.S.S.R.

Bė-rez'ni-ki (byi-ryôs') City R.S.F.S.R., U.S.S.R., Eur.; industry

Bêr'gä-mō Commune * of Province N Italy; commercial cen.

Bêr'gėn City NW Norway; manufacturing, seaport

Be'ring Sea Area of N Pacific O., bet. Alas. and Siberia

Be'ring Strait Strait bet. Arctic O. and Bering S.

Bêrke'ley (bêrk'li) City W Cal., U.S.; pop. 116,716; residential, industrial

Bêrk'shire 1. County S England; agriculture, livestock. 2. **Hills** or **Bêrk'shires** Mountain range W Mass., U.S.

Bêr'lin City E Germany, former * of Germany; div. 1949: **West Berlin**, part of West German Federal Republic, pop. 2,200,600; **East Berlin**, * of East German Democratic Republic; pop. ab. 1,083,800

Ber-me'jō (hō) River 1000 m. N Argentina

Bêr - mū'dà Islands (Brit. Colony), ab. 360 islands, W At-

lantic O., E of U.S.; * Hamilton on **Bermuda I.**

Bêrn City * of Canton and * of Switzerland; pop. 166,200; manufacturing, cultural cen.

Bêr'nėse Alps Mountain range S cen. Switzerland

Ber'wick (ik) County SE Scotland; agriculture, fish, livestock

Bêr'wỳn City NE Ill., U.S.; pop. 52,502; residential

Bė-sän-côn' (zän-sôn') City E France; manufacturing, trade

Bes-sà-rā'bi-à 1. Area SE Europe from Danube R. to Black S. 2. Former province E Romania, now part of Moldavian S.S.R.; agriculture

Beth'el Town anc. Palestine, N of Jerusalem

Bė-thes'dà (thez') District and Suburb cen. Md., U.S.; pop. 71,621

Beth'lė-hem 1. Town nr. Jerusalem, Jordan; City of David, birthplace of Jesus. 2. City E Pa., U.S.; pop. 72,686; iron, steel, cigars, hosiery

Bet'wä (bāt') River 360 m. cen. India

Bev'êr-lỳ City NE Mass., U.S.; pop. 38,348; shoe machinery

Bex'ley (li) Urban district SE England; hardware

Bey-ō-glu' (be-ē-ō-lōō') City, division of Istanbul, Turkey

Be'zhi-tsà (byā) Town R.S.F.S.R., U.S.S.R., Eur.; locomotives

Be-ziers' (bā-zyā') City S France; commerce, industry

Bez-wä'dà (bāz) Town SE India; rail, trade cen.

Bhad'gaon (bud'goun) Town cen. Nepal

Bhä'gàl-pur (poor) City * of Division NE India; trade cen.

Bhà-mō' Town * of District Upper Burma; trade cen.

Bhà'ràt (bu'rut) = INDIA, its anc. and official name

Bhà'ràt-pur (poor) City * of State NW India

Bhät'pä-rà City W Bengal India; industrial

Bhav-nà'gàr (bou-nug') Town * of State W India; port

Bhi'mä (bē') River ab. 400 m. S India

Bhō-päl' City * of State cen. India; agriculture

Bhū-tan', Kingdom of Country, E Himalayas, C Asia; 16,000 sq. m.; pop. 1,000,000; 4 regions each headed by governor appointed by King; Main cities: * Thimphu (Thimbu), Punakhu, Paro, Bunthang; Main rivers: Dangme Chu, Amo Chu, Tongsa Chu, Lhobrak; Geog.: landlocked Himalayan Kingdom, N boundary with Tibet, inaccessible snow capped peaks, inner region fertile valleys, forests in S plains; Climate: varies with altitude. Valley of C Bhutan temperate, S plains subtropical.

Flag: divided diagonally with orange to left, red to right, white dragon centered.

Ethnic comp.: Bhote, Nepalese, Lepcha, Santal; Language: Bhutanese (official), Tibetan dialects; Religion: Mahayana Buddhist, Hindu.

Products: rice, wax, timber, wheat, cloth, mush, elephants, po-

nies, yaks, limestone, gypsum; *Major exports:* timber, fruit; *Major imports:* textiles, light equipment; *Industry:* mining, lumber.

Currency: Indian rupee.

Head of Government: King; *Legislature:* National Assembly (Tsongdu).

Biä-lÿ'stôk *City* NE Poland; textiles

Biar-ritz' *Commune* SW France; resort

Biel (bēl) *Commune* nr. *Lake* NW Switzerland; manufacturing

Bie'lė-feld (bē') *City* West Germany; manufacturing

Big Black *River* 330 m. W cen. Miss., U.S.

Big Blūe *River* 300 m. Neb. and Kan., U.S.

Big'hôrn *River* 336 m. Wyo.-Mont., U.S.

Big Sioux (sōō) *River* ab. 300 m. S.D. and Iowa, U.S.

Bi-här' 1. *Town* in *Division* and *State* NE India; agriculture, mining. 2. **and O-ris'sà** former province of Brit. India

Bi-kä-nėr' *City* * of *State* NW India; livestock, carpets

Bi-ki'ni (kē') *Atoll* of Marshall Is.

Bil-bä'ō *City* N Spain; trade, manufacturing

Bi-li'rän (bē-lē') *Island* cen. Phil. Is.

Bil'lings *City* S cen. Mont., U.S.; pop. 61,581; shipping cen.

Bil-li'ton (lē') *Island* Java Sea, Indonesia

Bi-lox'i *City* SE Miss., U.S.; pop. 48,486; fisheries

Bin-gêr-ville' *Town* Ivory Coast

Bing'hàm-tön (àm) *City* S N.Y., U.S.; pop- 64,123; manufactur.

Binh Dinh *Town* E South Vietnam

Bi'ō-Bi'ō (bē') *River* 238 m. S cen. Chile

Bir'kėn-head (h e d) *County borough* NW England; shipping

Bir'ming-ham 1. *City*

N cen. Ala., U.S.; pop. 300,910; industrial cen. 2. *City* and *county borough* W cen. England; rail and metal cen.

Bi'rö-bi-dzhän' *Town* * of *Region* (Jewish Autonomous Region) SE R. S. F. S. R., U.S.S.R., Asia

Bis'cāy or **Viz-cä'yä** *Province* N Spain

Bis'cāy, Bay of *Inlet* of Atlantic O., W France and N Spain

Bis'cäyne Bay *Inlet* of Atlantic O., SE Fla., U.S.

Bisk (byēsk) *T o w n* R.S.F.S.R., U.S.S.R., Asia

Bis'märck (biz') 1. *City* * of N.D., U.S.; pop. 34,703; trade cen., flour. 2. **Archipelago** *Island group* (ab. 200) W Pacific O., Terr. of New Guinea; incl. New Britain, Admiralty Is., New Ireland, etc. 3. **Sea** W Pacific O.; site of WW II battle

Bis-sau' (sou') *Town* * of P o r t u g u e s e Guinea; port

Bit'têr-rōōt Mountains *Range* of Rocky Mts., Idaho-Mont., U.S.

Bi'yà (bē') *River* ab. 350 m. U.S.S.R., Asia

Bi-zêrte' *City* N Tunisia; seaport

Black'bûrn *County borough* NW England; textiles

Black Forest *Region* S West Germany; resort area

Black Hills *Mountains* South Dakota-Wyo., U.S.; minerals

Black River 1. *River* 280 m. Mo.-Ark., U.S. 2. *River* 200 m. Wisc., U.S.

Black'pōōl *County borough* NW England; resort

Black Sea *Sea* bet. Europe and Asia; 168,000 sq. m.

Blanc', Mont (môn blänk') *Mountain* 15,781 ft.; highest of the Alps, SE France at Italian border

Blär'ney (ni) *Town* SW Eire

Blen'heim (im) *Village* S West Germany

Block Island *Island* Atlantic O., R.I., U.S.; fishing cen.

Bloem - fôn - tein' (blōōm-fôn-tān') *City* Orange Free State E Republic of South Africa; trade cen.

Blōōm'fiēld *City* NE N.J., U.S.; pop. 52,-029; manufacturing

Blōōm'ing-tön 1. *City* cen. Ill., U.S.; pop. 39,992; commerce, manufacturing. 2. *City* SE Minn., U.S.; pop. 81,970. 3. *City* SC Ind., U.S.; pop. 42,890; education cen.

Blue'grass (blōō') *Region* cen. Ky., U.S.

Blue Ridge Mountains *Range* of Appalachian Mts., W.Va. into Ga., U.S. [SE Asia

Bō *River* ab. 500 m.

Bö - bruisk' (brōō'isk) *City* * of *Region* White Russia, U.S.S.R.

Bō'cà Rà-tōn' *Town* SE Fla., U.S.

Bō'chum (koom) *City* W cen. West Germany; iron, coal, steel

Boë - ō'tià (bē - ō'shà) *Anc. republic* E cen. Greece, now part of mod. dept. of **Attica and Boeotia**

Boe'roe (bōō'rōō) *Island* Malay Arch., Indonesia

Boe'toeng (bōō'toong) *Island* off SE Celebes, Indonesia

Bō'gôr *City* Java, Indonesia

Bō-gö-tä' *City* * of Colombia, W cen. part; pop. 2,500,000; cultural cen.

Bō-hē'mi-à *Province* W Czechoslovakia; mining, agriculture, manufacturing

Bō - hôl' *Island* and *Province* S cen. Phil. Is.; agriculture, weaving

Boi'se (zi) *City* * of Ida., U.S., SW part; pop. 74,481; foodstuffs, quarries

Boks'bûrg *Town* NE

Republic of South Africa; gold cen.

Bō'li-vär 1. *Department* N Colombia. 2. *Province* W cen. Equador. 3. *State* SE Venezuela, * **Cuidad Bolivar,** port

Bō-liv'i-a, Republic of *Country;* S America; 424,200 sq. m.; pop. 5,062,000; 9 departments each headed by prefect, subdivided into 98 provinces; *Main cities:* * La Paz, Cochabamba, Santa Cruz, Sucre; *Main rivers:* Beni, Guaiporé, Maimoré, Pilcomayo, Paraguay; *Geog.:* high plateau region, altiplano, semitropical rain forests, Ilanos, Amazon, Chaco lowlands; *Climate:* varies with area.

Flag: horizontal red, yellow, green bands top to bottom, coat of arms on yellow band.

Ethnic comp.: Amerindian, European, Cholo, Japanese, Okinawan; *Language:* Spanish (official), Indian dialects — Quechua, Aymara; *Religion:* Roman Catholic.

Products: coffee, tin, oil, natural gas, silver, lead, copper, bauxite; *Minerals:* tin, lead, zinc, silver, copper, tungsten, bismuth, antimony, gold, sulphur, oil; *Major exports:* tin, petroleum, tungsten, silver, antimony, lead, zinc, coffee; *Major imports:* ma-

chinery, iron — steel, vehicles, food staples; *Industries:* food processing, mining, textile mills, leather goods, cement, glass, ceramics.

Currency: pesos.

Head of Government: President; *Legislature:* government rules by decree; *Judiciary:* Supreme Court at Sucre, departmental, lower courts.

Bōl′tŏn *County borough* NW England; woolens

Bōl-zä′nō *Commune* * of *Province* NE Italy; trade cen.

Bom-bāy′ *City* * of *Province* on *Island* W cen. India; port, cotton cen.

Bō′mu (mōō) *River* ab. 500 m. cen. Africa

Bōne *Commune* NE Algeria; seaport, manufacturing

Bonn *City* * of West German Federal Republic, W cen. part; pop. 299,400; manufacturing, educational cen.

Bōō′thi-ā, Gulf of *Gulf* SW of Baffin I. Northwest Terrs., Canada

Bōō′tle (t′l) *County borough* NW England; seaport

Bôr-deaux′ (dō′) *City* SW France; port, industrial cen.

Bôr′gêr-hout *Commune* N Belgium

Bö-ri′slăv (ryē′) *City* Ukraine, U.S.S.R.; oil, natural gas

Bō-ri-sö-glebsk′ *City* R.S.F.S.R., U.S.S.R., Eur.; grain

Bôr′nē-ō *Island* of Malay Arch., world's 3rd largest; divided: N part = part of Malaysia (formerly Brit. colony of Sarawak); S part = unit of Indonesia; good harbors; agriculture, minerals

Bôrn′hŏlm *Island, County* of Denmark, Baltic S.

Bos′ni-a (boz′) *Region* cen. Yugoslavia, now part of **Bosnia and Her-zė-gö-vi′nà** (vē′) Federated Republic

Bos′pö-rus *Strait* bet. Turkey in Asia and Turkey in Eur.

Bōs′siêr City *City* NW La., U.S.; pop. 41,595

Bôs′tŏn *City* * of Mass. U.S.; pop. 641,071; financial, commercial, industrial cen.; fish, wool

Bot′à-nỳ Bay *Inlet* of South Pacific O. SE Australia

Both′ni-à *Arm* of Baltic S. bet. Finland and Sweden

Bot-swä′na, Republic of *Country;* formerly Republic of Bechuanaland; S Africa; 222,000 sq. m.; pop. 675,000; 9 districts, 3 town councils; *Main cities:* * Gaberones, Kanye, Serowe, Molepolole, Francistown, Lobatse; *Main rivers:* Okavango, Choba, Limpopo; *Geog.:* vast tableland, mean altitude of 3,300 ft. Natural habitat for most species of African fauna; *Climate:* generally subtropical, varies with latitude, altitude, average rainfall 18″.

Flag: blue field divided by black horizontal band, narrow white stripe on either side.

Ethnic comp.: Bantus, Bushmen, Europeans, Asians, Hottentots; *Language:* English (official), Tswana, Kholsan,

Afrikaans; *Religions:* Christian, tribal.

Products: meat, carcasses, cattle, hides — skins, asbestos, dairy products, manganese; *Major exports:* livestock, hides — skins, canned meats, beans, sorghum, manganese, motor vehicles; *Major imports:* cereals, petroleum products, textiles, sugar; *Industries:* meat processing, mining, cattle industry, tourism.

Currency: S African rand.

Head of Government: President; *Legislature:* unicameral Parliament — National Assembly; *Judiciary:* High Court presided over by chief justice. Constitution contains code of fundamental human rights, enforced by High Court.

Bôt′trôp *City* W West Germany; coal

Bouches - du - Rhône′ (bōōsh-d′rōn′) *Department* SE France

Bou′gain-ville (bōō′gàn) *Island,* largest of Solomon Is.; fertile soil

Boul′dêr (bōl′) 1. *City* N cen. Colo., U.S.; pop. 66,870; mining area. 2. *Dam* = HOOVER DAM

Bou-logne′ (bōō-lôn′y′) *City* N France; port

Bour-bŏn-nais′ (boorbŏn-ā′) *Hist. region* of cen. France

Bourges (boorzh) *Commune* cen. France

Bōw *River* 315 m. Alberta, Canada

Bo′wie (bōō) *Town* SC Md., U.S.; pop. 35,028; dairy, poultry, truck farms

Bōwl′ing Grēen *City* SW Ky., U.S.; pop. 36,253; manufacturing, education cen.

Bō′zėn see BOLZANO

Brà-bant′ *Province* (former *Duchy*) cen. Belgium

Brad′förd *County bor-*

ough N England; worsted cen.

Bräh-mà-pu′trà (pōō′) *River* 1800 m. Tibet and India

Brà-i′lä (ē′) *City* E Romania; shipping

Brain′trēe *Town* E Mass., U.S.; pop. 35,050; manufacturing, shipbuilding

Bran′cō, Ri′ō (rē′) *River* ab. 350 m. N Brazil

Bran′dėn-bûrg *City* cen. East Germany; manufacturing

Brant′förd *City* Ontario, Canada; manufacturing

Brà-sil′ià (zēl′) *City* * of Brazil, cen. part; pop. 44,000

Brä-sôv′ (shôv′), Germ. **Krōn′städt** *City* cen. Romania; manufacturing

Bra′ti-sla-va *City* E cen. Czechoslovakia; shipping

Braun′schweig (broun′shvīk) or **Bruns′wick** *City* E West Germany; trade, manufacturing

Brà-zil′, Federative Republic of *Country,* E-C S America; 3,287,200 sq. m.; pop. 92,240,000; 22 states, 4 territories, Federal district; *Main cities:* * Brasilia, São Paulo, Rio de Janeiro, Belo Horizonte, Recife, Salvador, Porto Alegre; *Main rivers:* Amazon, São Francisco, Paraná, Uruguay, Paraguay; *Geog.:* N — densely forested lowlands, Amazon River Basin, NE — semiarid scrubland, CW, S — hills, mts., rolling plains, narrow coastal

belt; *Climate:* warm, humid, moderate to heavy rainfall, tropics.

Flag: yellow diamond on green field, blue glove with 23 white stars & band with "Ordeme Progresso" centered on diamond.

Ethnic comp.: Portuguese, African, American, Indian, Italian, German, Japanese; *Language:* Portuguese (official), Italian, German, Japanese; *Religion:* Roman Catholic, Protestant, Jewish.

Products: coffee, cotton, sugar, pinewood, cocoa, meat, rice, fruit, sisal, oil, iron ore, manganese, quartz, beryl, motor vehicles, plastics, petro-chemicals, cement, aquamarine, topaz, steel; *Minerals:* iron, manganese, bauxite, nickel, lead, asbestos, chrome ore, gold, tungsten, copper; *Major exports:* coffee, beans, raw cotton, iron ore, cane sugar, pinewood, corn, cocoa beans; *Major imports:* wheat, crude petroleum, machinery, chemicals, metals, vehicles; *Industries:* mining, agriculture, forestry, food processing, chemicals, textiles, metallurgical products, vehicles, electrical — communications equipment.

Head of Government: President; *Legislature:* bicameral National Congress — Senate, Chamber of Deputies; *Judiciary:* Supreme Court (11 justices) at apex.

Braz'ös *River* 870 m. cen. Texas, U.S.

Braz'zà-ville *City* * of Congo Republic (B), SE part; pop. 133,000; port

Breck'nŏck-shire *County* SE Wales; farming, mining, livestock

Bre-da' (brä) *Commune* S Netherlands; carpets, cloth

Bre'mėn (brä') *City* * of *State* NW West Germany; commerce

Brem'êr-hä-vėn *City* NW West Germany; seaport

Brem'êr-tön *City* Va., U.S.; pop. 35,307

Bren'nêr Pass *Pass* bet. Austria and Italy, Alps

Brent'förd and Ches'wick (chez'ik) *Urban district* SE England

Bre'scia (brä'shä) *Commune* * of *Province* N Italy; manufacturing

Brest 1. *Commune* NW France; naval station, manufacturing. 2. *Region* White Russia U.S.S.R.; * **Brest Li-tôvsk'**, trade cen.

Bridge'pôrt (brij') *City* SW Conn., U.S.; pop. 156,542; industrial

Bridge'town (toun) *Town* * of Barbados on Barbados I.; port

Brigh'tön (brī) *County borough* S England; resort

Brin'di-si (zi) *Commune* * of *Province* SE Italy; trade cen.

Bris'bāne (briz') *City* * of Queensland, Australia; port

Bris'töl 1. *City* N Conn., U.S.; pop. 55,487; manufacturing. 2. *City, county borough* SW cen. England; shipping. 3. **Bay** Arm of Bering S., SW Alas.; salmon. 4. **Channel** Arm of Atlantic O. bet. Wales and England

Brit'ain ('n) Term referring to Great Britain; Lat. **Bri-tan'ni-à**

Brit'ish Ant-ärc'ti-cà *Territories* incl. Falkland Is., South Sandwich Is., Antarctic Terr., Graham's Land

Brit'ish Cö - lum'bi - à *Province* W Canada; * Victoria; harbors, forests, minerals, agriculture

Brit'ish Com'mön-wealth of Nations Association of Na-

tions under the United Kindgom of Great Britain and Northern Ireland including dominions, dependencies and colonies; mod. term for **Brit'ish Em'pīre**; * London, England

Brit'ish East Africa former terrs. now KENYA, UGANDA, TANZANIA

Brit'ish Gui-a'nà = GUYANA

Brit'ish Hon-dū'ràs *Colony* (Brit.) Central America; * Belize; forest products, fruits

Brit'ish In'di-à Parts of India under Brit. rule before 1947; * New Delhi

Brit'ish Isles (īlz) *Island group* W Europe incl. Great Britain, Ireland and nearby islands

Brit'ish South Africa *Territories* (Brit.) outside Rep. of South Africa; incl. Basutoland, Botswana, Swaziland

Brit'ish West In'diès (dēz) *Islands* (Brit.) of West Indies incl. Bahama, Leeward, and Windward Is., Barbados, Trinidad and Tobago, and Jamaica; see WEST INDIES FEDERATION (former 1958)

Brit'tà-nÿ *Hist. region* NW France

Br'nô (bûr') or **Brunn** *City* cen. Czechoslovakia; manufacturing

Broad (brôd) *River* ab. 220 m. W N.C., U.S.

Brock'tön *City* SE Mass. U.S.; pop. 89,040

Brom'ley (li) *Municipal borough* SE England

Bronx *Borough* of N.Y. City (N) also *County* of N.Y. State, U.S.; residential, industrial

Brook'līne *Town* E Mass., U.S.; pop. 58,886; residential

Brook'lÿn *Borough* of N.Y. City (E), U.S.; same area also Kings County, N.Y.; residential

Brook'lÿn Cen'têr *City* SE Minn., U.S.; pop. 35,173; residential

Browns'ville *City* S Texas, U.S.; pop. 52,522; port

Bruges (brōōzh), **Brug'gė** *Commune* NW Belgium; commerce, canals, bridges

Bru'nei (brōō') *City* on *Bay*, formerly Brit., NW Borneo; port, oil

Bruns'wick 1. *City* SE Ga., U.S.; shrimp, shipbuilding. 2. *City* cen. Germany; see BRAUNSCHWEIG

Brus'sėls, Bru-xelles' (bruk-sel') *City* * of Belgium, cen. part; pop. 1,500,000; manufacturing

Brÿ-ansk' *City* * of *Re-*

gion SW R.S.F.S.R., U.S.S.R., Eur.; trade, manufacturing

Bu-cär-rä-män'gä (bōō) *City* N cen. Colombia; agricultural cen.

Bū'cha-rest (kȧ) *City* * of Romania, SE part; pop. 1,500,000; trade, industrial cen.

Bu'chen-wäld (bōō'kėn) *Village* cen. Germany; WW II concentration camp

Buck'ing - hȧm - shire *County* SE cen. England; livestock, agriculture

Bū-cö-vi'nȧ (vē') *Region* E cen. Europe, formerly all Romanian; N part now in Ukranian S.S.R.

Bū'dȧ-pest *City* * of Hungary, cen. part; pop. 2,017,000; trade, manufacturing, political cen.

Bue'nȧ Pärk (bwä') *City* Cal., U.S.; pop.63,646

Bue-nä-ven-tū'rä (bwä) *City* W Colombia; imp. port

Bue'nös Air'ēs (bwä', âr') 1. *Province* and *City* * of Argentina, E part; pop. 5,900,- 000; port. 2. *Lake* SE Chile

Buf'fȧ-lō *City* NW N.Y. U.S.; pop. 462,768; industrial, trade cen.

Bug (boog) *River* 450 m. U.S.S.R.-Poland

Bui'tėn-zôrg (boi') = BOGOR

Bu - jum - bu'rȧ (boo') *Town* * of Burundi; pop. 75,000

Bu'kȧ (bōō') *Island* of Solomon Is., Terr. of New Guinea

Bu-khä'rȧ (bōō) *City* Uzbek, U.S.S.R.; Islam holy place

Bu-läk' (bōō) *Port* of Cairo, Egypt

Bu-lȧ-wä'yō (bōō) *Town* Rhodesia; trade cen.

Bul-gar'i-ȧ, Peoples' Republic of *Country,* Balkan Peninsula; 42,820 sq. m.; pop. 8,467,000; 27 provinces, 1 city (Sofia); *Main cities:* * Sofia, Plovdiv, Varna, Russe, Burgas; *Main rivers:* Danube, Mu-

ritsa, Islcur, Tundzha; *Geog.:* Danubian tableland — N, Stara Planina Mts. in C, Thracian Plain, Rodope Mountains in S, SW; *Climate:* on fringe of zone of humid continental climate, considerable variation.

Flag: horizontal stripes of white, green, red with state emblem — lion framed by wheat stalks located oṅ top (white) stripe near hoist

Ethnic comp.: Bulgarians, Turks, Macedonians, Armenians, Gypsies, Greeks; *Language:* Bulgarian (official), Turkish, Greek, Armenian; *Religion:* Bulgarian Orthodox Church, Roman Catholic, Protestant, Jewish.

Products: wheat, maize, barley, sugar, beer, tomatoes, grapes, oil, lead, zinc, copper, chemicals, machines; *Minerals:* lead, zinc, copper, iron ore, coal; *Major exports:* fuels, raw materials, minerals, foodstuffs, machines — equipment, dairy products; *Major imports:* machines — equipment, fuels, minerals, raw materials, metals, animal — vegetable products; *Industries:* oil refining, tourism, food processing, metallurgy, textiles, chemicals, rubber, mining.

Currency: lev.

Head of Government: Chairman, Council of State; *Legislature:* National Assembly; *Judiciary:* Supreme Court — "supreme judicial supervision" oveṙ all courts and Chief Prosecutor.

Bull Run (bool) *Stream* NE Va., U.S.; Civil War battle site

Bu'nȧ (bōō') *Village* NE New Guinea; WW II base

Bun'kêr Hill *Site* of battle 1775, Boston, Mass., U.S.

Bûr'bank *City* SW Cal., U.S.; pop. 88,871

Bûr'di-kin *River* 425 m. Queensland, Australia

Bûr-dwän' *Town* * of *Division* Bengal, NE India

Bu-re'yȧ (rä') *River* 480 m. U.S.S.R., Asia

Bur'gôs (bōōr') *City* * of *Province* N cen. Spain; manufacturing

Bûr'gun-dẏ *Region,* former kindgom, France and Switzerland

Bur-hän'pur (boor, poor) *Town* cen. India; silk, brocade

Bûr'ling-tön 1. *City* NW Vt., U.S.; pop. 38,633; port. 2. *City* NC N.C., U.S.; pop. 35,930; manufacturing

Bûr'mȧ, Union of *Country* SE Asia; 261,760 sq. m.; pop. 27,580,- 000; Burma Proper, 4 constituent states, Chin special division; *Main cities:* * Rangoon, Mandalay, Moulmeen, Bassein; *Main rivers:* Irrawaddy, Salween, Sittang, Mekong; *Geog.:*

rimmed on N, E, W by mts.

Flag: 6 white stars on blue rectangular field in upper left corner; rest is red.

Ethnic comp.: Burmans, Karens, Indians, Pakistanis; *Language:* Burmese (official), Shan, Karen, Chin, English; *Religion:* Buddhist, Hinduism, Christian, Islam.

Products: rice, timber (teak), rubber, cotton, coconuts, silver, lead, zinc, copper, iron, sapphires, rubies, jade, oil, petroleum products; *Minerals:* petroleum, tin, tungsten, lead, zinc, silver, nickel cobalt, precious stones — sapphires, rubies, jade; *Major exports:* rice, teak; *Major imports:* textiles, machinery, transport equip., foodstuffs; *Industries:* agriculture, forestry, fisheries, rice milling, petroleum refining, textiles, mining.

Currency: kyat.

Head of Government: Union Revolutionary Council; *Legislature:* Council of Ministers; *Judiciary:* chief court of 6 judges serves as final court of appeals except cases tried by special crimes court.

Bûr'mȧ Rōad *Highway* 2100 m. Rangoon-Chungking

Bûrn'ley (li) *County borough* NW England; textiles, iron

Bur-sä' (boor) *City* * of *Vilayet* NW Turkey, Asia; carpets, silk

Bûr'tön on Trent *County borough* W cen. England; breweries

Bu-run'di (bōō-rōōn'), Republic of *Country,* C Africa; 10,750 sq. m.; pop. 3,702,000; 8 provinces each with government appointed governor; *Main*

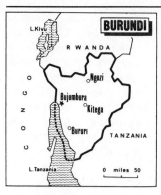

cities: * Bujumbura, Kitega; *Main rivers:* Kagera, Ruvuva, Malagarasi, Ruzizi, Akanyaru; *Geog.:* grassy uplands, rugged hills with tortured relief. Located 2° S of Equator; *Climate:* average 24 hr. temp. 73.4° with marked drops in upland interior. Average rainfall 31.2".

Flag: white diagonal saltire, center broken to form circle containing 3 stars in pyramid arrangement — panels at top-bottom of cross are red, sides green.

Ethnic comp.: Bahuta or Hutu, Tutsi, Twa or Batwa; *Language:* Rundi, French (official), Swahili; *Religions:* Roman Catholic, Moslem, animist.

Products: coffee, cotton, livestock, hides — skins, kaolin; *Major exports:* coffee, cotton, hides, minerals; *Major imports:* textiles, leather, vehicles, machinery — spare parts, food products, petroleum; *Industries:* agriculture, food processing, mining.

Currency: Burundi franc.

Head of Government: President; *Legislature:* Political Bureau; *Judiciary:* Supreme Court at apex, judges appointed by president.

Bur-yat' - Mon'göl A.S.S.R. (boor) *Republic* of R.S.F.S.R.,

Siberia, U.S.S.R.; forests, furs, fish

Bū-shire' (shēr') *City* SW Iran; port

Bū'stô Är-si'ziō (sē') *Commune* N Italy; cotton, wine

Būte'shire *County* SW Scotland; agriculture, fish

Būtte *City* SW Mont., U.S.; pop. 23,368; world's largest mineral deposits

Bẏd'goszcz (gôshch), **Brôm'bêrg** *City* N Poland; industrial

Bye-lö-rus'sian S.S.R. (rush'ȧn) = WHITE RUSSIAN S.S.R.

Bȳ'lot Island *Island* W of Baffin Bay, Canada

Bẏ'tôm *City* SW Poland; industrial

Bẏ'zȧn - tine Em'pīre (tin) *Empire* S and SE Eur. and W Asia, 4th-15th centuries

Bẏ-zan'ti-um *Anc. city* site of mod. Istanbul

C

Cä-bä-nä-tuän' *Municipality* Luzon, Phil. Is.; trade cen.

Cȧ-bin'dȧ *Town* W Angola; seaport

Cab'öt Strait *Channel* bet. Gulf of St. Lawrence and Atlantic O.

Cä'ce-res (sâ-râs) *Commune* * of *Province* W Spain; factories

Cache (cash) *River* ab. 230 m. NE Ark., U.S.

Cȧ-diz' 1. *City,* * of *Province* on *Bay* (inlet of *Gulf*) SW Spain; port. 2. *Municipality,* Negros, Phil. Is.

Caen (kän) *City* NW France; commerce, manufacturing

Caer - när'vön - shire (cär) *County* NW Wales; slate, minerals

Caer-phil'lẏ (cär-fil') *Urban district* SE Wales; cheese

Cae-sa-rē'ȧ (sē-zȧ) *Anc. city,* Palestine; port; now QISARYA

Cä-gä-yän' *River* 220 m. Luzon, Phil. Is.

Cä'gliä-ri (lyä) *Commune* on *Gulf* * of *Province* S Sardinia, Italy

Cä'guäs *Municipality* E cen. Puerto Rico; tobacco

Cȧ-ha'bȧ *River* 200 m. cen. Ala., U.S.

Caï'rō (kī') *Governorate* and *City,* * of Egypt and of the United Arab Republic; pop. 4,219,800; educational, industrial cen.

Cāith'ness *County* N Scotland; fish, agriculture

Cȧ-jon' Pass (hōn') *Pass* S Cal., U.S.

Cä-lä'bri-ä *Compartimento* S Italy; "toe" of It. "boot"; quarries, agriculture, livestock

Cä'läh *Anc.* * of Assyria; mod. **Nimrud**

Ca'lais (lä) *City* N France; manufacturing port

Cä-lä-trä'vä *Municipality* Negros, Phil. Is.

Cal'cȧ-sieu (shōō) *River* ab. 200 m. La., U.S.

Cal-cut'tȧ *City* NE India; former seat of government; seaport, educational cen.

Cal'ė-dön *River* 230 m. SE Africa

Cal'gȧ-rẏ *City* S Alberta, Canada; trade

Cä'li *City* W Colombia; trade cen.

Cal'i-cut *City* S India; port, calico

Cal-i-fôr'niȧ *State,* named from book by Ordonez de Montalvo; 158,693 sq. m.; *pop.:* 19,953,134 (*rank:* 1st); W U.S.; *Boundaries:* Mexico, Arizona, Nevada, Oregon, Pacific Ocean; *Major cities:* * Sacramento, Los Angeles, San Francisco, Oakland, San Diego; *Major rivers:* Sacramento, San Joaquin, Klamath; *Major lakes:* Salton Sea, Tahoe, Goose; 58 counties.

Nickname: Golden State; *Motto:* "Eureka" (I have found it); *Flag:* bear and red star on white field with red horizontal bar at bottom;

Flower: golden poppy; *Bird:* California valley quail; *Mineral:* gold; *Rock:* serpentine; *Tree:* California redwood; *Song: I love you, California.*

Industry: fabricated metals, printing, publishing, transportation equipment, food processing, aerospace, tourism; *Natural resources:* timber, petroleum, boron, other minerals; *Major source of income:* manufacturing, trade.

Admitted to Union: 1850 (31st state).

Places of Interest: Sierra Nevada Mt. Range, Squaw Valley, Lake Tahoe, Yosemite Ntl. Park, Sequoia Park.

Cäl-lä'ō (cä-yä'ō) *City* on *Bay,* * of *Province* W Peru; port

Cal-tȧ-nis-set'tȧ *Commune* * of *Province* cen. Sicily, Italy

Cal'ū-met *Industrial area* NE Ill. and NW Ind., U.S.; incl. several cities nr. Chicago

Cal-va-dôs' *Department* NW France

Cal'vȧ-rẏ *Site* of Jesus' crucifixion nr. anc. Jerusalem

Cä-mä-guey' (g w ä') *City* * of *Province* E cen. Cuba; trade cen.

Cä - m ä- ri'nes (rē'), **Nôr'te** and **Sur** (sōōr) *Provinces,* Luzon, Phil. Is.

Cam-bāy' *Town* at *Gulf,* * of *State,* W cen. India

Cam'bêr-well *City* SE Australia

Cam-bō'di-ȧ Khmer

Republic — Kingdom of *Country*, SE Asia; 71,000 sq. m.; pop. 7,054,000; 20 provinces, 4 autonomous municipalities; *Main cities*: * Phnom Penh, Battambang, Kompong, Cham, Kampot; *Main river*: Mekong; *Geog.*: alluvial plain drained by Mekong River; *Climate*: tropical; monsoon belt.

Flag: 2 blue stripes, wider red center band with representation in white of great temple of Angkor Wat.

Ethnic comp.: Cambodians, Vietnamese, Chinese, Chams; *Language*: Cambodian or Khmer (official), French; *Religions*: Hinayana Buddhism (state), Roman Catholic.

Products: rice, rubber, maize, livestock, timber, fish, oil; *Major exports*: rice, rubber; *Major imports*: metals — metal products, mineral products, food products, machinery; *Industries*: oil refining, agriculture.

Currency: riel.

Head of Government: Premier (Constitutional monarchy overthrown 1970); *Legislature*: bicameral National Assembly, Council of Kingdom; *Judiciary*: High Court of Justice at apex, supervised by Council of Magistry under direction of Minister of Justice.

Cam-brāi' *City* N France; linen, cotton, lace

Cam'bri-à = Lat. name for WALES

Cam'bridge (brij) 1. *City* NE Mass., U.S.; pop. 100,361; commercial, manufacturing, educational cen. 2. *County* and *Municipal borough* E

England; university

Cam'dèn *City* SW N.J., U.S.; pop. 102,551; port

Cam'è-lot Legendary site of King Arthur's court, England or Wales

Ca-mè-rōōn' *Peak* 13,-350 ft. Nigeria

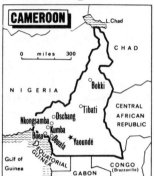

Ca-me-rōōn', Federal Republic of *Country*; WC Africa; 183,360 sq. m.; pop. 5,933,-000; 2 states each has premier & local assembly; *Main cities*: * Yaoundé, Douala, Buea, Nkongsamba, Kumba; *Main rivers*: Sanaga, Nyong; *Geog.*: S — low coastal plain with equatorial rain forests, C — transitional plateau, W — mountainous forests, N — low rolling savannah gardens; *Climate*: varied.

Flag: vertical stripes from left to right — green, red, yellow, 2 yellow stars on upper half of green stripe.

Ethnic comp.: Bantu, pygmies, semi Bantu; *Language*: French, English (official), 24 major African languages also spoken; *Religion*: Christian, Moslem, animist.

Products: cocoa, cotton, coffee, timber, bananas, aluminum, gold, uranium; *Major exports*: coffee, cocoa beans, aluminum, wood, cotton, rubber, peanuts, palm oil; *Major imports*: vehicles, transportation equipment, machinery, food, beverages, tobacco; *Industries*: agriculture, manufac-

turing, processing plants, forestry.

Currency: CFA franc.

Head of Government: President; *Legislature*: unicameral Federal National Assembly; *Judiciary*: Federal Court of Justice at apex.

Cam'êr-ōōns, Ca-mè-roun' (rōōn') = *Former protectorate* (variously Germ., Brit., Fr.) W Africa now CAMEROON

Cä-mi-guin' (mē-gēn') *Island* off N Mindanao, Phil. Is.

Cä-mō'tes *Island group* and *Sea*, Phil. Is.

Cäm-pä'niä *Compartimento* S Italy; fertile mountainous area

Cam-pē'chē *City* * of *State* SE Mexico; woods, hides, sisal

Cam - pi'nà Gran'dè (pē') *City* E Brazil

Cam-pi'nàs (pē') *City* SE Brazil; coffee area

Cäm-pö-bäs'sō *Commune* * of *Province* cen. Italy

Cam-pō-bel'lō *Island* New Brunswick, Canada; F.D.R. summer home

Cam'pos (pōōs) *City* SE Brazil; trade cen.

Cā'naan (nàn) *Area* of Palestine bet. Jordan R. and Mediterranean S.

Ca'nà-dà *Country*, N America; 3,851,800 sq. m.; pop. 21,897,-000; 10 provinces, 2 large N territories; *Main cities*: * Ottawa, Montreal, Toronto, Vancouver, Winnepeg, Edmonton, London, Windsor, Quebec; *Main rivers*: Machenzie, Yukon,

St. Lawrence, Nelson, Columbia, Churchill; *Geog.*: the Shield, a rugged area of pre-Cambrian rock covers most of E, C Canada, N is arctic archipelago, W is vast prairie region stretching to Rocky Mts.; *Climate*: varies, arctic — mild.

Flag: vertical bands, wide white center band with narrower red bands each side, red maple leaf in center.

Ethnic comp.: British, French, other Europeans; *Language*: English, French (official), German, Ukrainian, Italian; *Religions*: Roman Catholic, United Church of Canada, Anglican.

Products: cereals, livestock, paper, lumber, dairy products, pulp, fish, furs, petroleum, copper, iron ore, nickel, zinc, steel, motor manufactures, industrial materials; *Minerals*: petroleum, nickel, copper, iron ore, zinc, natural gas, asbestos, lead; *Major exports*: wheat, lumber, crude petroleum, vehicles & parts, newsprint, nickel, copper, aluminum, wood pulp; *Major imports*: textiles, chemicals, communications, electrical — scientific equipment, non-farm equipment, steel, aircraft — parts; *Industries*: tourism, mining, motor vehicles, meat processing, oil refining, forestry, fishing, trapping, smelting — refining.

Currency: Canadian dollar.

Head of Government: British Monarch, Prime Minister, Governor General represents Monarch; *Legislature*: Parliament

— Senate, House of Commons; *Judiciary:* based largely on British law.

Cả-nā'di-ản *River* 906 m. N.M.-Texas-Okla., U.S.

Cả-nal' Zōne *Territory* leased to U.S. for Panama Canal, cen. America

Cả-nâr'ý Islands *Island group* (Sp.) off NW Africa; agriculture

Cả-nav'êr-ål *Peninsula* E Fla., U.S.; site of Cape KENNEDY

Can'bêr-rả *City* * of Australia, SE part; pop. 124,500; farm area

Can'di-ả *City* N Crete; island's largest city

Cả-nē'ả *City* * of *Department* and * of *Crete*, N coast; port

Cannes (kan) *Commune* SE France; resort, port

Can'nŏck *Urban district* W cen. England; coal

Cän-tal' *Department* S cen. France

Can'têr-bur-ý (bêr) 1. *City* SE Australia. 2. *City* and county borough SE England; ecclesiastical cen.

Can'tŏn *City* NE Ohio, U.S.; pop. 110,053; manufacturing

Can-ton', Kwäng'chow' (jō') *City* SE China; imp. port

Cả-pän'nö-ri *Commune* cen. Italy = group of villages

Cāpe Bret'ŏn *Cape* on *Island* Nova Scotia, E Canada; coal

Cāpe Cod *Peninsula* enclosing *Bay* SE Mass., U.S.

Cāpe Fear (fēr) *River* ab. 200 m. N.C., U.S.

Cāpe Hat'têr-ås *Point* on island, E N.C., U.S.

Cāpe of Good Hōpe *Cape* and *Province* S Rep. of South Africa

Cāpe Town *City* SW Rep. of South Africa; seaport

Cāpe Vêrde Islands (vêrd) *Island group* (P o r t.) off **Cāpe Vêrde,** W Africa

Cả'piz (pēs) *Municipality* * of *Province*

Panay I., Phil. Is.

Cä'pri (prē) *Island* in Bay of Naples SE Italy

Cap'u-ả *Commune* S Italy; WW II fighting

Cả-rac'ås *City* * of Venezuela, N part; pop. 2,175,400

Car'dả-mön Hills *Range* S India

Cär'de-näs *City* on *Bay* W cen. Cuba; seaport

Cär'diff *County borough* SE Wales; industrial port

Cär'di-gản-shîre *County* W Wales; livestock, lead mines

Car-ib-bē'ản Sea *Arm* of Atlantic O. bet. N and S America

Car'i-bōō Mountains *Range* of Rocky Mts., Brit. Columbia, Canada

Car'i-bou Mountains (bōō) *Range* W Alberta, Canada

Cär'lisle (līl) *City* and county borough NW England; rail cen.

Cär'lŏw *County* SE Eire

Cärls'bad 1. *City* SE N.M., U.S.; potash mines, caverns. 2. *City*, Austria, see KARLOVY VARY

Cär - mär'then - shîre *County* S Wales; farming, mining, quarrying

Cär-nä'rō *Former province* Italy; now in Croatia, Yugoslavia

Car'ō-lïne Islands *Archipelago* (U.S. Trust Terr.) E of Phil. Is., W Pacific O.; incl. Yap, Truk, Easter I., Palau Is.

Cả-rō-ni' (nē') *River* 550 m. E Venezuela

Cär-pā'thi-ản Mountains *Mountain system* bet. Czechoslovakia and Poland

Cär-pā'thi-ản Rū-thē'ni-ả *Former province* E Czechoslovakia, part of Hungary, now in Ukraine, U.S.S.R.

Cär-pên-târ'i-ả, Gulf of *Gulf* NE Australia

Cả-rä'rả *Former commune,* now part of APUANIA, Italy

Car'röt *River* ab. 220 m. Saskatchewan,

Canada

Cår-shal'tŏn *Urban district* S England

Cär'sŏn City Cal., U.S.; pop. 71,150

Cär'sŏn City *City* * of Nevada W part; pop. 15,468; farming, lumbering, mining

Cär-tả-gē'nả (jē') 1. *City* NW Colombia; seaport. 2. *City* SE Spain; port

Cär'thage (thij) *Anc. city* and *State,* N Africa nr. mod. Tunis

Cas-ả-blan'cả *City* W Morocco; seaport

Cas-cāde' Mountains *Range* NW U.S.

Cas'cō Bay *Inlet* of Atlantic O., SW Me., U.S.

Cas'pêr *City* cen. Wyo., U.S.; pop. 39,361; oil industry

Cas'pi-ản Sea *Lake* bet. Eur. and Asia; world's largest inland body of water; 169,-380 sq. m.

Cäs'sėl see KASSEL

Cås-si'nō (sē') *Commune* cen. Italy; WW II battle site

Cä - stel' Gän - dôl'fō *Commune* cen. Italy; papal palace

Cä-stel-läm-mä're di Stä'biả *Commune* S Italy; seaport

Cäs-tel-lon' de lä Plä'nä (tâ-yôn') *City* * of *Province* E Spain

Cas-tile' (tēl') *Region* and *Anc. kingdom* cen. Spain

Cas'tle-förd (cas''l) *Urban district* N England; manufacturing

Cas'tle Här'böur *Gulf* off NE Bermuda I.

Cas'tôr 1. *Peak* 13,879 ft., E peak of ZWILLINGE (Twins). 2. *Peak* 10,800 ft. NW Wyo., U.S.

Cäs'trïes *Town* * of Saint Lucia, Brit. Windward Is.

Cä'strôp - Rau'xėl (rouk') *City* W West Germany; coal, manufacturing

Cat-ả-lō'ni-ả *Hist. region* NE Spain

Cat-ả-mär'cả *Town* * of *Province* NW Ar-

gentina; f a r m i n g, mining

Cả-tän-duä'nes *Island* off SE Luzon, Phil. Is.; agriculture

Cả-tä'niä *Commune* on *Gulf,* * of *Province* E Sicily, Italy; manufacturing

Cả-tän-zä'rō *City* * of *Province* S Italy

Cả-tăw'bả *River* ab. 250 m. N.C., U.S.

Cả-thāy' = old name for China during Middle Ages

Cats'kill Mountains *Range* of Appalachians SE N.Y., U.S.

Cau'cä (cou') *River* 600 m. W Colombia

Cău-cā'sia (zhả) *Region* bet. Black S. and Caspian S., U.S.S.R.; incl. **Cău'cả-sus Mts.,** boundary bet. Eur. and Asia

Cău'field *City* SE Australia, suburb of Melbourne

Cau'rä (cou') *River* 450 m. cen. Venezuela

Cău'vê-rý *River* 475 m. S India

Cả-val'lý *River* 300 m. W Africa

Cav'ản *County* N Eire; agriculture

Cä-vi'te (vē'tâ) *City* * of *Province* Luzon, Phil. Is.; WW II battles

Căwn'pōre *City* N India; industrial cen.

Cay-enne' (kī) *City* on *Island,* * of French Guiana

Cāy'mản Islands *Island group* of Brit. West Indies

Ce-a-ra' (sā-ả-ra') *State* NE Brazil

Ce-bu' (sā-bōō') *City* * of *Province* on *Island,* E cen. Phil. Is.; harbor

Cē'dả (sē') *River* 329 m. Minn.-Iowa, U.S.

Cē'dả Rapids (sē') *City* E Iowa, U.S.; pop. 110,642; rail cen., manufacturing

Ceg'led (tseg'lād) *City* cen. Hungary

Cel'ė-bēs (sel') *Island* S of *Sea,* Malay Arch., Indonesia; forest products

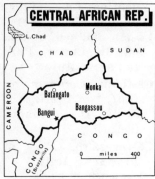

Cen'tral Af'ri-can Republic *Country*, almost exact center of Africa; 234,000 sq. mi.; pop. 1,645,000; 14 Prefectures; *Main cities:* * Bangui, Bangassou, Bambari; *Main rivers:* Shari, Ubangi; *Geog.:* high well-watered plateau, drained by 2 major river systems; *Climate:* rainy season May–Oct., average monthly temperature at Bangui 70°–90°.

Flag: horizontal bars of blue, white, green, yellow bisected by vertical red bar — yellow bar appears on blue band at upper left.

Ethnic comp.: Hamitic, Bantu; *Language:* French (official), Sangho; *Religions:* animist, Christian, Moslem.

Products: timber, cotton, coffee, groundnuts, maize, millet, sorghum, diamonds; *Minerals:* manganese ore; diamonds, gold, uranium, iron ore, copper, zinc, tin; *Major exports:* diamonds, cotton, coffee, wood; *Major imports:* machinery, electrical equipment, transportation materials — equipment, textiles; *Industries:* light industries, mining, forestry.

Currency: franc.

Head of Government: President; *Legislature:* rules by decree; *Judiciary:* Supreme Court with justices appointed by President.

Cen'tral A-mer'i-ca (sen') *Area* bet. Mexico, N America and Colombia, S America; incl. Guatemala, Honduras, Brit. Honduras, El Salvador, Nicaragua, C o s t a Rica, Panama

Cen'tral Greece and Eu-boe'a (sen'grēs) *Division* cen. Greece

Cen'tral In'di-a (sen') Group of states of Brit., India; * Indore

Cen'tral Pro'vince (sen') *Province* S cen. Ceylon; * Kandy; tea

Cen'tral Pro'vin-ces and Be-rär' *Former province* cen. India; n o w MA'DHYA PRADESH

Ceph-a-lō'ni-a (sef) *Island*, Ionian Is. W Greece

Ce'räm (sä') *Island* and *Sea*, cen. Moluccas, Indonesia

Ce'ri-gō (châ') *Island*, S Ionian Is. Greece

Cer'rô de Päl-pä-när' (ser') *Mountain* 19,-830 ft. N Chile

Cer'rô de Päs'cō (ser') *Mountain* 15,000 ft. cen. Peru

Ce-se'nä (châ-zä') *Commune* N Italy; wine, sulphur, silk

Ces'ke Bu'de-jo-vi-ce (ches'kâ boo'dye-yô-vi-tse) *City* W Czechoslovakia; breweries, manufacturing

Ceu'tä (sä'oo) *City* NW Sp. North Africa

Cey-lon' (sē) *Island*, see SRI LANKA

Cha-blis' (shä-blē') *Commune* NE cen. France; wine

Chä-chä'ni *Peak* 20,000 ft. S Peru

Chä'cō *Region* S cen. South America incl. parts of Bolivia, Paraguay, Argentina; swamp area

Chad, Republic of *Country*, NC Africa; 487,920 sq. m.; pop. 3,700,000; 14 prefectures, 50 sub-prefectures, 26 administrative districts; *Main cities:* * Fort Lamy,

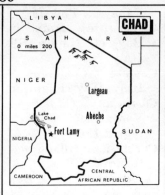

Faya-Largeau, Fort Archambault, Moundou; *Main river:* Chari; *Geog.:* Sahara desert — N, savannah — C, tropical — S; *Climate:* N mostly dry, heavy rainy season April – mid-Oct. in S, June–Sept. — C.

Flag: vertical stripes of blue, yellow, gold.

Ethnic comp.: Moslem, Bantu, some Europeans; *Language:* French (official), tribal languages, Arabic dialects; *Religions:* Moslem, Christian, animist.

Products: cotton, cattle, meat, fish, skins, leather; *Minerals:* natron (sodium carbonate), shale oil, tungsten; *Major exports:* cotton, cattle; *Major imports:* mineral products, foodstuffs, beverages, electrical machinery & parts, textiles, transportation equipment; *Industries:* fishing, food processing, mining.

Currency: CFA franc.

Head of Government: President; *Legislature:* National Assembly; *Judiciary:* highest court is Supreme Court.

Chad, Lake *Lake* W Chad; 10,000 sq. m.

Chal'ce-don (kal'sė) *Anc. city*, n o w KADIKOY

Chal-cid'i-ce (kal-sid'i-sē) *Peninsula* and *Department*, NE Greece

Chal'cis (kal'sis) *City* cen. Greece

Chal-dē'a (kal) *Anc. region* on Persian Gulf, S Babylonia

Chä-lôns' - sur - Marne' (sha) *Commune* NE France; manufacturing

Chä-mär-tin' de lä Rô'-sä (tēn') *Commune* cen. Spain

Chăm'bä *State* NW India; mountainous

Chăm'bäl *River* 650 m. cen. India

Cham-be-ry' (shän-bā-rē') *City* E France; commerce

Cha-mô-nix' (sha-mô-nē') *Valley* E France; winter sports

Cham-pagne' (shäm-pan'y') *Region*, former prov., NE France; wines

Cham - paign' (sham - pān') *City* E Ill., U.S.; pop. 56,532; commerce, industry

Cham-pläin', Lake (sham) *Lake* Vt.-N.Y., U.S., into Canada

Chăb-dêr-nä-gôr' *Settlement* E India, formerly French

Chăn'di-gärh *City* N India

Chäng'än' now SIAN

Chäng'chow' (jō') now LUNGKI

Chäng'chun' (choon') or **Hsin'king'** (shin' jing') *City* S Manchuria; soybean trade

Chäng'shä' *City* SE cen. China; port; brass, linen, silk

Chäng'teh' (du') *City* SE cen. China; cen. of "rice bowl".

Chäng'tse' *Peak* 24,730 ft. Mt. Everest group S Tibet

Chan'nel Islands *Islands* (Brit.) in English Channel; incl. Alderney, Guernsey, Jersey, Sark; cattle, agriculture

Chan - til - ly' (shän-tē-yē') *Commune* N France; lace

Chao'än' (chou') *City* SE China; river trade

Chao Phrä-yä (chou p'hrä) *River* 750 m. Thailand

Chao'tung' (jou'toong') *City* S China; commerce, mining

Chä-pa'ĕvsk *T o w n* U.S.S.R., Eur.

Chä'prä *Town* NE India; commerce

Chä-pul-te-pec' (pool) *Fortress* nr. Mexico City, Mexico

Chär-dzhou' (jō'oo) *Town* U.S.S.R., Asia; cotton trade

Cha-rente' (sha-ränt') *River* 225 m., and *Department* W France

Cha-rente'-Ma-ri-time' (sha-ränt', tēm') *Department* W France

Cha-ri' (sha-re') *River* 1400 m. into Lake Chad

Char'i-tön (shar') *River* 280 m. Iowa-Mo., U.S.

Chár-khä'ri *State* N cen. India

Chärles'tön 1. *City* SE S.C., U.S.; pop. 66,-945; port. 2. *City* * of W.Va. W cen. part, U.S.; pop. 71,505; industrial cen.

Chär'lötte (shär') *City* S N.C., U.S.; pop. 241,178; commerce, cotton industry

Chär'lötte   À-mä'lie (shär', mäl'yĕ) *City* * of St. Thomas I. and * of U.S. Virgin Is., West Indies; port

Chär'löttes-ville *City* C Va., U.S.; pop. 38,-880; ed. cen.

Chär'lötte-town (sh, toun) *City* * of Prince Edward I., Canada

Chär'tres (tr') *City* N cen. France; cathedral, manufacturing

Cha - teau'   Thier - ry' (shä-tō' tye-rē') *Commune* N France; battles 1814, 1870, 1918

Chat'hàm *Municipal borough* SE England; naval cen.

Chat-tà-hōō'chēe *River* 410 m. Ga.-Ala.-Fla., U.S.

Chat-tà-nōō'gà *City* SE Tenn., U.S.; pop. 119,082; industrial port

Chau-mont' (shō-môn') *Commune* NE France; manufacturing

Chĕ-chen' - In-gush'

A.S.S.R. (g ō ō s h') *Former republic* of U.S.S.R., Eur.

Che'fōō' (ju') *City* NE China; commercial port

Chĕ'jū *Town* on *Island* S Korea

Che'ki-äng' (ju'ji) *Province* E China coast

Che-liff' (shä-lēf') *River* 430 m. Algeria

Chelms'förd *Municipal borough* SE England; trade cen.

Chel'sea (si) *Borough* of London, England

Chel'tĕn-hàm ('am) *Municipal borough* SW England; spas

Chĕ-lya'binsk *City* * of *Region* R.S.F.S.R., Asia; industrial

Chem'nitz (kem') *City* SE East Germany; manufacturing

Che-näb' *River* 590 m. W Pakistan

Cheng'tu' (chung'dōō') *City* S cen. China; anc. city, fertile area

Cher'bourg (shâr'boorg) *City* NW France; port

Cher'chen' (ju-ur'-chung') *River* ab. 420 m. W China

Chĕ-rem'khö-vö *Town* U.S.S.R. Asia; coal

Cher (shâr) *Department* cen. France

Cher-i-bon' *Town* * of *Residency* Java, Indonesia; rice port

Cher-kas'sў *City* cen. Ukraine U.S.S.R.; refineries

Cher-kessk' *Town* * of **Cher-kess'** Autonomous Reg., U.S.S.R. Eur.

Chĕr-ni'göv (nyē') *City* * of *Region* Ukraine, U.S.S.R.; shoes, flour

Cher-ni'kövsk (nya') *City* U.S.S.R., Eur.; manufacturing

Cher-nôv'tsў *City* * of *Region* Ukraine, U.S.S.R.; cultural cen.

Ches'à-pēake *City* SE Va., U.S.; pop. 89,-580; residential

Ches'à-pēake Bāy *Bay*, inlet of Atlantic O., Md.-Va., U.S.

Chesh'ire *County* NW England; dairying, mining

Ches'têr 1. *City* SE Pa., U.S.; pop. 56,331; industrial port. 2. *City* and *County borough*, NW England; port, rail cen.

Ches'têr-fiĕld *Municipal borough* N cen. England; coal, iron

Chev'i-öt Hills *Hills*, English-Scottish border

Chey-enne' (shī) 1. *City* * of Wyo. (W cen.), U.S.; pop. 40,-914. 2. *River* 290 m. S.D., U.S.

Chhá'tar-pur (chu', poor) *State* cen. India

Chi-äng' Maī' *City* * of *Province* NW Thailand; trade cen.

Chi-an'ti Mountains (ki) *Range* cen. Italy; wines

Chiä'päs *State* SE Mexico

Chi'bà (chē') *City* * of *Prefecture* Honshu, Japan; trade

Chi-cä'gō (shi) *City* NE Ill., U.S.; pop. 3,366,-957; port; world's leading grain and livestock market

Chi-cä'gō Heights *City* NE Ill., U.S.; pop. 40,900; manufacturing, residential

Chi-ca'pà (shi) *River* 310 m. S Africa

Chic'ö-pēe *City* SW Mass., U.S.; pop. 66,-676; rubber products

Chie'ti (kyâ') *Province* cen. Italy; textiles

Chi-huä'huä (wä'wä) *City* * of *State* N Mexico; silver mines

Chil'ē, Republic of *Country*, SW coast of S America, bordered by Peru, Argentina, Bolivia, Drake Passage, Pacific Ocean; 292,260 sq. m.; pop.

10,151,000; 25 provinces; *Main cities:* * Santiago, Valparaiso, Concepcion, Antofagasta; *Main rivers:* Loa, Maule, Bio-Bio, Valdiva; *Geog.:* N — desert, C — agricultural, S — forest; *Climate:* C zone — mild Mediterranean climate, S — cool, damp.

Flag: white horizontal stripe over longer red stripe, blue square in upper left corner containing five pointed white star.

Ethnic comp.: Europeans, Amerindians; *Language:* Spanish (official), *Religion:* Roman Catholic.

Products: fishmeal, wool, fruit, pulp, paper petroleum products; *Minerals:* copper, iron ore, nitrates, oil, molybdenum, iron, steel; *Major exports:* copper, copper goods, iron ore, pulp, paper, fishmeal, wool, fruit; *Major imports:* machinery, equipment, agricultural products, transport equipment; *Industries:* paper, paper products, chemical, petrochemical production, forestry, fishing, mining.

Currency: escudo.

Head of Government: President; *Legislature:* bicameral National Congress–Senate, Chamber of Deputies; *Judiciary:* tribunals judge civil, criminal cases.

Chil-lan' (che-yän') *City* S cen. Chile; trade

Chi-lo-e' (chē-lō-ā') *Island, Province* SW Chile; coal

Chim-bō-rä'zō *Peak* 20,702 ft. W cen. Ecuador

Chim-kent' *Town* Kazakh U.S.S.R.

Chĩ'nà, People's Republic of *Country*, Asia; 4,300,000 sq. m.; pop. 771,527,000;

CHINA

21 provinces; *Main cities:* *Peking, Shanghai, Shichcia-chuang, Tientsin, Harbin, Nanking, Shenyang, Wuhan, Chunking, Kwang-chow, Changchun; Main rivers:* Yangtze, Yellow, Amur, Yu; *Geog.:* mts., fertile plains, deltas; *Climate:* temperate.

Flag: red field, gold star, arc of 4 smaller stars to left in upper left.

Ethnic comp.: Han, Tibetan, Manchu, Mongolian, tribal; *Language:* Chinese (official), N: Mandarian dialects, S: Wu, Cantonese, Hakka; *Religion:* atheist (state), Confucian, Buddhist, Muslim, Taoist, Christian.

Products: rice, sugar, wheat, peas, soybeans, groundnuts, tobacco, cotton, tea, silk, hemp, jute, flax, livestock, lumber; *Minerals:* coal, iron ore, tin, antimony, tungsten, iron, steel; *Major exports:* agriculture — food products, metals, textiles; *Major imports:* wheat, chemical fertilizers, iron and steel, machinery, transportation equipment, raw materials; *Industries:* electricity, cement, chemicals, fertilizers, ma-

chine tools, woolen — silk textiles.

Currency: yuan.

Head of Government: Premier; *Political Leader:* Chairman of central committee of communist party; *Legislature:* National People's Congress; *Judiciary:* 2 gov't. organs — Supreme People's Court, Supreme People's Procuratorate.

Chĭ'nȧ Sea Part of Pacific O. bet. Japan and Malay Penin.; div. into **East** and **South China S.**

Chin'dwin' *River* 550 m. W Upper Burma

Ching'förd *Urban district* SE England

Chin'hsien' (jin'shyen') *Town* Manchuria; cattle trade

Chin'kiang' (jin'ji-äng') *City* E China; port

Chin-näm-pō *City* W North Korea; port

Chin'wäng'tao' (dou') *Town* NE China; port

Chiog'gia (kyôd'jä) *City* NE Italy; fishing

Chĭ'os (kĭ') *Island, Department* and *City* of Greece, Aegean S.

Chi-ta' *City* on *River* * of *Region,* U.S.S.R., Asia; minerals, timber

Chi-träl' *River* 300 m. India-Afghanistan

Chit'ta-gông *Town* * of *Division* E Pakistan; trade cen.

Chka'löv *City* * of *Region,* U.S.S.R., Eur.; trade cen.

Choi-seul' (shwa-zûl') *Island* of Solomon Is.

Chô'lôn' *City* S Vietnam; industrial

Chô'mô Lhä'ri *Peak* 23,930 ft. bet. Tibet and Bhutan

Chöng-jin *City* NE Korea; port

Chō-pi-côl'qui (kē) *Peak* 22,000 ft. Peru

Cho'rzow (ko'zhōōf) *City* SW Poland; nitrate, iron, coal

Chō-sen 1. Jap. for KOREA. 2. *Strait* connecting S. of Japan and Yellow S.

Chō-shi *Town* Honshu, Japan; port, fishing

Chow'tsun' (jō') *Town* NE China; port, silk industry

Christ'chûrch (krīst') *City* South I. New Zealand; grain cen.

Chris-ti-ä'nȧ (kr) *Town* E Rep. of South Africa; diamonds

Christ'mȧs Island (kris') 1. *Island* (Brit.) Indian O. 2. *Island* (Brit.) Line Is. cen. Pacific O.

Chu (chōō) *River* 600 m. U.S.S.R., Asia

Chu-but' (choo-vōōt') *Territory* S Argentina

Chu-kôt' National District (choo) *District* U.S.S.R., Asia; incl. **Chu-kôt'ski Penin.**

Chū'lä Vis'tȧ *City* SW Calif., U.S.; pop. 67,-901; fruit

Chu-lȳm' (choo) *River* 700 m. Siberia U.S.S.R., Asia

Chung'hsien' (joong' shyen') *City* S cen. China; river port

Chung'king' (choong') or **Päh'hsien'** (shyen') *City* S China; trade port; * of China 1937-46.

Chûrch'ill *River* 1000 m. cen. Canada

Chûrch'ill Downs *Race track* Louisville Ky., U.S.

Chū' Sän' *Archipelago* East China S.; trade

Chu-sö-va'yȧ (choo) *River* 430 m. U.S.S.R. Asia

Chu'vash A.S.S.R. (chōō') *Republic* E cen. R.S.F.S.R.,

U.S.S.R., Eur.; lumber

Cic'êr-ō (sis') *City* NE Ill., U.S.; pop. 67,-058; engines

Cien-fue'gōs (s y â n fwä') *Municipality* on *Bay* W cen. Cuba; sugar processing

Ci-li'ci-ȧ (si-lish'i-ȧ) *Anc. country* SE Asia Minor

Cim'ȧr-rōn (sim') *River* 600 m. N.M., U.S.

Ci-nä-rū'cō (sē) *River* 280 m. Colombia-Venezuela

Cin-cin-nat'i (sin-si) *City* SW Ohio, U.S.; pop. 452,524; trade, manufacturing

Cis-cău-cā'sia (sis, zhȧ) *Region* N of Caucasus Mts. U.S.S.R.

Ci-tläl-te'petl (sē, tä') *Peak* 18,700 ft. cen. Mexico

Ciu - däd' Bō - li'vär (syōō, lē') *City* SE Venezuela; port

Ciu-däd' Juä'rez (syōō, wä') *City* N Mexico

Ciu-däd' Re-al' (syōō) *Commune* * of *Province* S cen. Spain

Ciu - däd' Tru - jil'lo (syōō, trōō - hē'yō) *City* former name of * of Dominican Rep., now SANTO DOMINGO

Ciu - däd' Vic - tō'ri - ä (syōō) *Town* cen. Mexico; sugar cen.

Ci-vi-ta-vec'chia (chē-vē-tä-vek'kiä) *City* cen. Italy; port

Clack - man'nȧn - shire *County* cen. Scotland

Clȧre *County* W Eire

Clärk Fôrk *River* 300 m. Mont.-Ida., U.S.

Clēar' wătêr *City* WC Fla., U.S.; pop. 52,-074; business, resort

Cler-mont' - Fer-rand' (môn', rän') *City* S cen. France

Cleve or **Cleves** (klāv) *City* E West Germany; manufacturing

Clēve'lȧnd *City* N Ohio, U.S.; pop. 750,903; industrial port

Clēve'lȧnd Heights (hītz) *City* N Ohio; pop. 60,767; residential

Cli-chy' (klē-shē') *Com-*

mune N France; chemicals, rubber

Clif′tön *City* N.J., U.S.; pop. 82,437; factories

Cluj (klōōzh), **Klau′sèn-bûrg** (klou′) *City* cen. Romania; industry

Clȳde *River* S Scotland into **Fîrth of Clȳde**

Clȳde′bank *Burgh* W cen. Scotland; ship-building

Cō-ä-hui′lä (wē′) *State* NE Mexico

Cōast Range *Mountains* W North America

Cōat′bridge (brij) *Burgh* S cen. Scotland; coal, iron

Cō′blenz see **KOBLENZ**

Cō′bûrg 1. *City* SE Australia. 2. *City* E West Germany; manufacturing

Co-cà-nä′dà *City* E India; exports

Cō-chä-bäm′bä *City* * of *Department* cen. Bolivia; trade cen.

Cō′chin *Town* in *Region*, former *State*, SW India

Cō′chin Chī′nà *Area* of S Vietnam, formerly of Fr. Indo-China

Coi or **Sông′ koī′** (**Red River**) *River* 500 m. SE Asia

Coim′bà-tōre′ *City* S India; mills, factories

Cō-im′brà *City* * of *District* cen. Portugal; earthenware

Cōl′ches-têr *Municipal borough* SE England; oysters, farming

Cō-li′mä (lē′) *Volcano* 12,790 ft. W cen. Mexico

Cōl′mär *Commune* NE France; textiles

Cö-logne′ (lōn′) *City* W West Germany; imp. industrial port

Cô-lômbes′ (lōmb′) *Commune* N France; Paris suburb

Cö-löm′bi-à, Republic of *Country* NW South America, bordered by Caribbean Sea, Venezuela, Brazil, Peru, Ecuador, Pacific Ocean, Panama; 439,530 sq. m.; pop. 21,265,000; 22 departments, 4 inten-

dencias, 4 comisarias, special district of Bogota; *Main cities:* * Bogota, Barranquilla, Cartagena; *Main rivers:* Magdalena, Cauca, Amazon; *Geog.:* E plains, C highlands, Coast mountains, flat; *Climate:* tropical on coast to cool springlike, frequent rain in highlands.

Flag: Top half yellow; bottom half blue, red stripe of equal width.

Ethnic comp.: Mestizos, Europeans, Mulattoes, Negroes, Amerindians; *Language:* Spanish (official), Indian languages; *Religion:* Roman Catholic (state).

Products: coffee, meat, bananas, cotton, tobacco, sugar; *Minerals:* oil, emeralds, gold, coal, platinum, salt, limestone; *Major exports:* textiles, emeralds, coffee, crude petroleum, agricultural products; *Major imports:* metals, metal products, machinery, electronic equipment, chemicals, transport vehicles; *Industries:* industrial talc, petrochemicals, pharmaceuticals, consumer goods.

Currency: pesos

Head of Government: President; *Legislature:* Congress — Senate, Chamber of Representatives; *Judiciary:* Supreme Court, subordinate courts.

Cö-löm′bō *City* * of Sri Lanka; pop. 551,200; port

Cö-lōn′ *City* * of *Province* N cen. Panama; port

Col-ö-rä′dō *State*, named from Spanish word meaning "red"; 104,247 sq. m.; *pop.:* 2,207,259 (*rank:* 30th); SW U.S.; *Boundaries:* Utah, New Mexico, Oklahoma, Kansas, Nebraska, Wyoming; *Major cities:* * Denver, Pueblo, Colorado Springs, Boulder; *Major rivers:* Colorado, Arkansas, South Platte, Rio Grande; *Major lakes:* Blue Messa, John Martin, Granby; 63 counties.

Nickname: Centennial State; *Motto:* "Nil sine numine" (Nothing without providence); *Flag:* red letter C encloses gold ball & rests against blue, white & blue bars; *Flower:* Rocky Mt. columbine; *Bird:* lark bunting; *Animal:* big horn sheep; *Tree:* Colorado blue spruce; *Song:* Where the Columbines Grow.

Industry: electrical equipment, printing, publishing, machinery, lumber, chemicals, fabricated metals, food processing, oil & mineral refining, agriculture, mining, tourism; *Natural resources:* oil, molybdenum, coal, uranium, vanadium; *Major source of income:* government, trade.

Admitted to Union: 1876 (38th state).

Places of interest: Rocky Mt. Natl. Park, Mesa Verde Ntl. Park.

Col-ö-rä′dō Springs *City* E cen. Col., U.S.; pop. 135,060; site of

U.S. Air Force Academy

Cö-lum′bi-à 1. *River* 1270 m. W Canada and U.S. 2. *City* * of S.C. (W cen.), U.S.; pop. 113,542; manufacturing. 3. *City* cen. Mo., U.S.; pop. 58,804; farm area

Cö-lum′bus 1. *City* W Ga., U.S.; pop. 154,168; cotton mills. 2. *City* * of Ohio (cen.) U.S.; pop. 539,677; trade, manufacturing

Col′ville *River* 320 m. Alas., U.S.

Cöm-man′dêr Islands = KOMANDORSKIE

Com′mū-nist Peak *Peak* 24,590 ft. U.S.S.R., Asia; was Stalin Peak

Cō′mō *Province* and *Commune* at *Lake* N Italy; resort area

Com′ö-rō Islands *Islands* (Fr.) bet. Mozambique and Madagascar

Comp′tön *City* SW Cal. U.S.; pop. 78,611; glass, steel

Con′à-krȳ *Town* * of Guinea; pop. 172,500; port

Côn-cep-cion′ (s e p-syôn′) *City* * of *Province* cen. Chile

Côn′chös *River* 300 m. N Mexico

Con′cörd 1. *City* * of N.H., U.S.; pop. 30,022; manufacturing, granite. 2. *Town* NE Mass., U.S. 3. *City* W Cal., U.S.; pop. 85,164; diversified retailing

Côn-côr′diä *City* E Argentina

Cō′ney Island (ni) *Resort* Brooklyn, N.Y., U.S.

Con′gō *River* ab. 3000 m. W Africa now ZAIRE

Con′gō, Peoples Republic of (**Braz′zà-ville**,) *Country*; W-C Africa, 129,960 sq. m.; pop. 901,200; 9 regions, capital district; *Main cities:* * Brazzaville; Pointe Noire, Dolisie; *Main rivers:* Congo, Oubangue, Ogooué; *Geog.:* coast-

al plain, Niari Valley — SC, C Batéké Plateau, Congo River Basin; *Climate:* tropical.

Flag: red field, in upper left-hand corner is 5-pointed star above crossed yellow hammer, hoe, surrounded by green palm branches.

Ethnic comp.: Bantu; *Language:* French (official), tribal languages; *Religion:* animist, Roman Catholic.

Products: timber, groundnuts, tobacco, petroleum, copper, iron ore, lead, gold, manganese, diamonds; *Minerals:* petroleum, copper, iron ore, lead, gold, manganese, diamonds, potash; *Major exports:* wood, industrial diamonds; *Major imports:* machinery, electrical equipment, vehicles, parts, chemicals, mineral products, textiles, clothing; *Industries:* agriculture, forestry, fishing, mining, sugar refining, brewing, flour milling.

Currency: CFA franc.

Head of Government: President; *Legislature:* none, political power concentrated in Central Committee of Congolese labor party, Council of State; *Judiciary:* Supreme Court. Judges appointed by President.

Con'gō, **Democratic**

Rep. of the *Republic see* ZAIRE

Con'nacht (ut) *Province* NW Eire

Con-nect'i-cut (net') 1. *River* 400 m. NE U.S. 2. *State* E U.S.; * Hartford; 4,820 sq. m.; pop. 3,032,217; 8 counties; insurance, manufacturing

Con-nect'i-cut (net') *State,* named from Indian word meaning "long river"; 5009 sq. m.; *pop.:* 3,032,217 (*rank:* 24th); NE U.S.; *Boundaries:* Rhode Island, Massachusetts, New York, Atlantic Ocean; *Major cities:* * Hartford, Bridgeport, New Haven, Waterbury; *Major rivers:* Connecticut River, Housatonic; *Major lakes:* Candlewood; 8 counties.

Nickname: Constitution State, Land of Steady Habits; *Motto:* "Qui transtulit sustinet" (He who transplanted, sustains); *Flag:* state seal on blue field; *Flower:* mountain laurel; *Bird:* American robin; *Tree:* white oak.

Industry: chemicals, instruments, trade, transportation equipment, machinery, manufacture of aircraft engines & propellers, firearms, submarines, vacation & recreation, tourism, insurance; *Natural resources:* mica, stone in small amounts; *Major source of income:* manufacturing.

Admitted to Union: Jan. 9, 1788 (5th state).

Places of interest: Whitfield House, Mark Twain's Home, Mystic Seaport, Peabody Museum of Natural History.

Con'stance = KONSTANZ

Côn-stän'tä (tsä) *City*

SE Romania; petroleum export

Côns - tán - tine' (tēn') *City* * of *Department* NE Algeria

Con-stan-ti-nō'ple (p'l) = ISTANBUL

Con-ti-nen'tál Di-vîde' *Watershed* of North America: N.M.-Colo.-Wyo. - Ida. - Mont. - Canada; drainage to east or to west

Cooch Be-här' *State* NE India; rice, tobacco

Cook, Mount *Mountain* 13,700 ft. SE Alas., U.S.

Cook Inlet *Inlet* of Pacific O. S Alas., U.S.

Cook Islands *Island group* S Pacific O.; bel. to New Zealand

Cōō'lidge Dam (lij) *Dam* of Gila R., Ariz., U.S.

Coo'pêrs-town (toun) *Village* cen. N.Y., U.S.; site of Baseball Hall of Fame

Cōō'sà *River* 285 m. Ala., U.S.

Cō-pèn-hä'gèn *City* * of Denmark (E coast) pop. 875,000

Cop'pêr *River* 300 m. S Alas., U.S.

Cor'àl Sea Area of Pacific O. bet. Australia and New Hebrides

Cor'àl Gābles *City* S Fla., U.S.; pop. 42,-494; residential, ed. center

Côr'cö-ràn, Mount *Peak* 14,040 ft. SE cen. Cal., U.S.

Côr'dö-bä 1. *City* * of *Province* N cen. Argentina; industrial cen. 2. or **Côr'dö-vä** *City* * of *Province* S Spain; gold, silver

Côr-fū' *City* on *Island* within *Department* Ionian Is. off NW Greece; olives, fruits

Cor'inth *City, Gulf, Subdivision* S Greece

Côrk *City* * of *County* SW Eire; port

Côr-niche' (nēsh') *Road* (3 parallel highways) along Riviera, S Eur.

Côr'ning *City* S N.Y., U.S.; glassware

Côrn'wàll *County* SW England

Cor-ö-man'del Coast

Coast SE India

Cō-rö-nä'dä Bay *Inlet* of Pacific O. W Costa Rica

Cō-rō-nel' *City* S cen. Chile; coal cen., port

Côr'pus Chris'ti (kris') *City* on *Bay,* S Texas, U.S.; pop. 204,525

Cör-reg'i-dôr *Island* Manila Bay, Phil. Is.; WW II battle

Côr-reze' (râz') *Department* S cen. France

Côr-rien'tes (ryän'tâs) *City* * of *Province* NE Argentina

Côrse *Department* SE France = CORSICA

Côr'si-cà *Island* (Fr.) Mediterranean S. off SE France; wine, olives, citrus fruits

Côr-val'lis *City* W Ore., U.S.; pop. 35,153; ed. center

Cö-sen'zä *Commune* * of *Province* S Italy

Cos'tà Me'sà (mä') *City* Cal., U.S.; pop. 72,-660

Cos'tà Ri'cà, Republic of *Country,* S C America, 19,650 sq. m.; pop. 1,890,000; 7 provinces; *Main cities:* * San José, Alajuela, Puntarenas, Cartago, Limon; *Main rivers:* Rio Grande, San Carlos; *Geog.:* high rugged mountains, hills drained by streams, rivers. Forests cover ⅔ area; *Climate:* influenced by tropical location, adjacent warm ocean waters.

Flag: 2 blue horizontal stripes (top, bottom), 2 white inner stripes, wide red center band with country's coat of arms.

Ethnic comp.: Euro-

pean descent (primarily Spanish), Indian, Negro; *Language:* Spanish (official), Jamacian dialect of English; *Religion:* Roman Catholic.

Products: bananas, coffee, cocoa, meat, sugar, cotton, bauxite, sulphur, pharmaceuticals, plastics; *Minerals:* bauxite, gold, copper, sulphur, manganese, iron ore; *Major exports:* coffee, bananas, meat, sugar, cocoa, fertilizers; *Major imports:* manufactured goods, machinery — transport equipment, chemicals, foodstuffs, fuel, mineral oils; *Industries:* agriculture, forestry, fishing, textile industry, mining.

Currency: colone.

Head of Government: President; *Legislature:* unicameral Legislative Assembly; *Judiciary:* Supreme Court, subsidiary courts.

Cō-tä-bä'tō *Province* Mindanao Phil. Is.

Côte d'A-zūr' French coast of Mediterranean S. [E France

Côte-d'Ôr' *Department*

Côtes-du-Nord' (kōt-du-nôr') *Department* NW France

Cō-tö-pax'i *Volcano* 19,-500 ft. cen. Ecuador

Cott'bus *City* East Germany; cloth, rail cen.

Coun'cil Bluffs (sil) *City* SW Iowa, U.S.; pop. 60,348; grain trade, nurseries

Cour'àn-tȳne (cōr') *River* ab. 300 m. N South America

Cöv'èn-trẏ *City* and *county borough* cen. England; machinery

Cöv'ing-tön *City* N Ky., U.S.; pop. 52,535

Crä-iô'vä *City* S Romania; industrial cen.

Cran'stön *City* N R.I., U.S.; pop. 73,037

Crä'têr Lake *Lake* S Ore., U.S.; National

Park

Crēe *Lake* Saskatchewan, Canada

Cre-mō'nà *Commune* * of *Province* N Italy; manufacturing

Crēte or **Can'di-à** *Island, Division* of Greece, E Mediterranean S.; fruits

Creuse (krûz) *Department* cen. France

Crewe (krōō) *Municipal borough* NW England; rail cen.

Crī-mē'à *Peninsula, Former republic* S U.S.S.R., Eur.; agriculture

Cris-tō'bàl *Town* in *District,* NW Canal Zone [SE Europe

Crō-ā'tia, Peoples Republic of (shà) *Republic* NW Yugoslavia; * Zagreb

Crôss *River* 300 m. Nigeria-Cameroons

Croy'dön (kroi') *County borough* S England; manufacturing

Crô-zet' Islands (ze') *Islands* (Fr.) S Indian O. [cen. Angola

Cuän'zà *River* 500 m.

Gulf of Mexico — U.S.A. — BAHAMAS — Marianao — Havana — Santa Clara — Sancti Spiritus — Camagüey — Holguin — HAITI — 0 miles 200 — Caribbean Sea — HONDURAS — NICARAGUA — JAMAICA — **CUBA**

Cū'bà, Republic of *Country,* N boundary of Caribbean Sea; 44,210 sq. m.; pop. 8,900,000; 6 provinces subdivided into 55 regions; *Main cities:* * Havana, Marianao, Holguin, Camagüey, Santiago de Cuba, Guantánamo, Santa Clara; *Main river:* Cauto; *Geog.:* ⅗ flat — rolling with wide, fertile valleys, plains. Remainder mts., hilly; *Climate:* semitropical.

Flag: red equilateral triangle at staff side; centered on triangle

is white star; backgound 3 blue horizontal stripes separated by 2 white stripes.

Ethnic comp.: European (mainly Spanish), mulatto, Negro, Oriental; *Language:* Spanish (official); *Religion:* Roman Catholic.

Products: sugar, tobacco, rice, maize, iron ore, nickel, copper, chromite, nitrates; *Minerals:* nickel, copper, cobalt, chromite, iron ore, manganese, nitrates; *Major exports:* sugar, nickel, tobacco, shrimps, lobster, beef; *Major imports:* petroleum, equipment — machinery, food; *Industries:* sugar refining, cigarettes — cigar making, rum, textiles, fishing, oil refining, nickel processing, cement — fertilizer production, food processing.

Currency: peso at par with dollar.

Head of Government: Prime Minister, rules by decree; *Legislature:* Council of Ministers (nominal power); *Judiciary:* mixture of Spanish-American law, communist legal theory.

Cu'cu-tä (cōō'cōō) *City* N Colombia

Cud'dà-lōre *Town* SE India; port

Cuen'cä (cwäng') 1. *City* S Ecuador; panama hats. 2. *Commune* * of *Province* E cen. Spain

Cuer-nä-vä'cä *Town* S cen. Mexico; caverns

Cu-ià-ba' (cōō) *River* 300 m. SW Brazil

Cui'tō (cwē') *River* 400 m. Angola, SW Africa

Cū-mä-nä' *City* N Venezuela; port

Cum'bêr-lànd 1. *River* 687 m. Ky.-Tenn., U.S. 2. *County* NW England; coal, iron

Cu-ne'ni (cōō-nä') *River* 700 m. Angola

Cu'ne-ō (cōō'nâ) *Commune* * of *Province* NW Italy

Cu-rà-cao' (coor-à-sou') *Island* of Netherlands Antilles

Cu-rä-ray' (cōō-rä-rī') *River* 490 m. Ecuador-Peru

Cu-ri-ti'bà (cōō-ri-tē') *City* S Brazil

Cur'rènt *River* 250 m. Mo.-Ark., U.S.

Cûr'zön Line *Boundary* U.S.S.R.-Poland

Cutch *State* and *Peninsula* W India; salt

Cut'tàck *City* E India; silver work

Cuy-à-hōg'à Fàlls (cà' hōg') *City* NE Ohio, U.S.; pop. 49,678; rubber items

Cu-yū'ni (cōō) *River* 300 m. N South America

Cuz'cō (cōōs') *Peak* 17,800 ft. SW Bolivia

Cẏc'là-dēs (sic') *Department Island group* (ab. 220) of Greece; S Aegean S.

CYPRUS — TURKEY — 0 miles 50 — Kyrenia — Nicosia — Famagusta — Paphos — Larnaca — Limassol — Mediterranean Sea

Cy'prus (sī'), Republic of *Country,* Mediterranean Sea; 3,570 sq. m.; pop. 647,000; 6 districts; *Main cities:* * Nicosia, Limassol, Famagusta, Larnaca, Paphos, *Main river:* Pedieos; *Geog.:* island, SW is Troodos Mountains, on N coast is Kyrenia range. The C plain lies between 2 ranges; *Climate:* typical Mediterranean.

Flag: outline map of island in gold above crossed green olive branches on white field.

Ethnic comp.: Greek,

Turk, Armenian, Maronite, other minorities; *Language:* Greek, Turkish (official), English; *Religion:* Eastern Orthodox, Moslem.

Products: citrus fruit, potatoes, olives, grapes, copper, iron pyrites, wine; *Minerals:* copper, asbestos, iron pyrites, chromites, terra umbra, yellow ocher; *Major exports:* fruits — vegetables, copper — concentrates, iron pyrites, wine, asbestos; *Major imports:* machinery — transportation equipment, manufactures; *Industries:* tourism, mining, agriculture.

Currency: Cyprus pound at par with sterling.

Head of Government: Greek Cypriot President, Turkish Cypriot Vice President; *Legislature:* unicameral House of Representatives; *Judiciary:* based on English common law — Supreme Court at apex.

Czech-ö-slö-vä'ki-à, Socialist Republic *Country,* C Europe; 49,360 sq. m.; pop. 15,499,000; Czech Republic, Solvak Republic; *Main cities:* * Prague, Brno, Bratislava, Ostrava, Pilsen, Kosice; *Main rivers:* Labe, Vltava, Danube, Morava, Váh, Nitra, Hron; *Geog.:* regions: Bohemia — plateau surrounded by mts., Moravia — C region

somewhat hillier than Bohemia; Slovakia — rugged mts., lowlands; *Climate:* temperate.

Flag: blue triangle extending length of staff with apex toward center, white band on upper half on remaining space, red band on lower half.

Ethnic comp.: Czech, Slovak, Magyar, German, Polish, Ukrainian; *Language:* Czech, Slovak (official), German, Hungarian; *Religion:* Roman Catholic, C z e c h o s l o v a k Church, Protestant.

Products: timber, hops, cereal, coal, iron ore, graphite, garnets, silver, lead, lignite, pitchblende, steel, textiles, beer, glass, leather; *Minerals:* coal, antimony, magnesite, iron ore, graphite, garnets, silver, lead, lignite; *Major exports.* machinery, motor vehicles, iron — steel, chemicals; *Major imports:* machinery, industrial raw materials, food, live animals, manufactured goods; *Industries:* iron — steel refining, brewing, leather products, textiles, mining.

Currency: koruna.

Head of Government: President; *Legislature:* bicameral Czechoslovak Federal Assembly—Chamber of Deputies, Chamber of People; *Judiciary:* Supreme Court, lower courts — no trial by jury.

Cze-stô-cho'wa (chenstô-kô'vä) *City* S cen. Poland; manufacturing

D

Dac'cà *City* * Bangladesh; muslin, jewelry

Dä'chau (kou) *Town* S West Germany; WW II concentration camp

Dag'èn-hàm (àm) *Urban district* SE England; automobiles

Dag-ès-tan' A.S.S.R. *Republic* R.S.F.S.R., U.S.S.R., Eur.; cattle

Dä-gū'pän *Municipality* Luzon, Phil. Is.; port

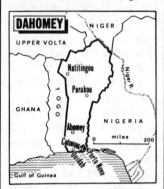

Dà-hō'mey (mi), Republic of *Country,* W Africa; 44,910 sq. m.; pop. 2,800,000; 6 departments; *Main cities:* * Porto Novo, Cotonou, Abomey, Parakou; *Main rivers:* Niger, Oveme, Mono, Couffo; *Geog.:* N of C lagoons country flat, generally covered with dense vegetation; *Climate:* hot, humid much of year, tempered by sea breeze.

Flag: vertical green stripe on staff side, upper horizontal yellow stripe, lower horizontal green stripe.

Ethnic comp.: Fon, Yoruba, Adja, Bariba, Peul, Somba; *Language:* French (official), African dialects — Fon, Mina, Yoruba, Dendi; *Religions:* animist, Moslem, Roman Catholic, Protestant.

Products: palm kernels, palm oil, groundnuts, cotton, coffee, tobacco, coconuts, livestock, gold, iron, chrome, furniture; *Minerals:* oil, gold, iron, limestone; *Major exports:* palm kernel oil, kapok, cotton, peanuts, coffee;

Major imports: food products, textiles, machinery, vehicles, iron — steel products; *Industries:* processing palm oil products, textiles, beverages, mining, light industry.

Currency: CFA franc.

Head of Government: President; *Legislature:* none in operation though provided for in constitution; *Judiciary:* Supreme Court highest court plus courts of 1st instance and appeal. Each department has own tribunal.

Daï'ren' (dĭ') or **Ta'lien'** (dä') *City* E China; Yellow S. port

Dà-kär' *City* * of Senegal, W part; seaport

Dà-kō'tà or **James** *River* 710 m. N.D. and S.D., U.S.

Däl *River* 250 m. S cen. Sweden

Dal-hou'sie (zi) *Town* N e w Brunswick, Canada; resort

Dal'làs *City* NE Texas, U.S.; pop. 844,401; oil and insurance cen. cotton trade, manufacturing

Dal-mā'ti-à (shà) *Coastal area* of Yugoslavia

Dä'lỳ *River* 300 m. N Australia

Dä'lỳ City *City* W Calif. U.S.; pop. 66,922

Dà-mas'cus *City* * of Syria, SW part; pop. 800,000; anc. city

Dam-i-et'tà *City* N Egypt; port

Dä'mö-där *River* 350 m. NE India

Dà Nang *U.S. base* South Vietnam

Dan'bûrỳ *City* SW Conn., U.S.; pop. 50,781; manufacturing

Dan'übe *River* 1725 m. cen. Eur.

Dan'ville 1. *City* E Ill., U.S.; pop. 42,570; trade cen. 2. *City* S Va., U.S.; pop. 46,391; tobacco market

Dan'zig, Gdänsk *City* on *Gulf* N Poland

Dàr-bhàn'gà *City* NE

India; trade cen.

Där-dà-nelles' (nelz'), *anc.* **Hel'lès-pont** *Strait* W Turkey, separates Eur.-Asia

Där-di-stän' *Region* N India and Pakistan

Där' es Sà-läam' *District* and *City* E Tanganyika

Dä-rien' (ryān') 1. Early name of PANAMA. 2. Gulf of *Inlet* of Caribbean S. Panama-Colombia

Där-jēe'ling *District* and *Town* NE India

Där'ling 1. *River* 1160 m. SE Australia. 2. *Range* SW Western Australia

Där'ling-tön *County borough* N England; rail cen., iron, steel

Därm'städt (shtät) *City* S cen. West Germany; manufacturing; former * of Hesse

Därt'moor *Tableland* SW England

Där'win, formerly **Pôrt Där'win** and **Pälm'êr-stön** *City* * of Northern Terr., Australia

Dasht'-i-Ka-vir' (vēr') = **Great Salt Desert** N cen. Iran

Dāte Līne hypothetical N-S line ab. 180° from Greenwich, England; place where each day begins

Dà'ti-à *State* N cen. India

Dau'gàv-pils (dou') or **Dvinsk** *City* E Latvia, U.S.S.R.; trade

Dau-phi-ne' (dō-fē-nā') *Alps* in *Hist. region* and *Former province* SE France

Dä'vao (vou) *City* on *Gulf,* * of *Province* Mindanao, Phil. Is.; volcanic soil; hemp

Dav'èn-pōrt *City* E Iowa, U.S.; pop. 98,469; trade, industrial cen., cereals

Dā'vis Strait *Strait* bet. Baffin I.-Greenland

Dà-wa' *River* 370 m. S Ethiopia

Dăw'sön 1. *City* Yukon Terr. N Canada; gold rush 1898. 2. *River* 380 m. E Australia

Dāy'tön *City* SW Ohio, U.S.; pop. 243,601

Dāy-tō'nà Beach *City* E Fla., U.S.; pop. 45,327; winter resort

Dead Sea (ded) *Lake* bet. Israel and Jordan

Dēar'bôrn *City* SE Mich., U.S.; pop. 104,199; automobiles

Dēar'bôrn Heights *City* SE Mich., U.S.; pop. 80,069

Death Valley (deth) *Valley* Cal., U.S.; lowest point in U.S.

De'bre-cèn (tsen) *City* E Hungary

De-cätûr 1. *City* cen. Ill., U.S.; pop. 90,397; corn, iron area. 2. *City* N Ala., U.S.; pop. 38,044; diversified manufacturing

Dec'càn name given to penin. of India and former states S of Narbada R.

Dēe *River* 90 m. NE Scotland; salmon

Dēep Crēek Lake *Lake*, artificial, Md., U.S.

Deh'rà Dun (dā', dōōn) *Town* N India

Del'à-wāre *State*, named in honor of Lord De La Warr; 2,057 sq. m.; *pop.:* 548,104 (*rank:* 46th); Ə U.S.; *Boundaries:* Maryland, Pennsylvania, New Jersey, Delaware River, Atlantic Ocean; *Major cities:* * Dover, Wilmington; *Major rivers:* Delaware, Nanticoke, Christina; 3 counties. *Nickname:* Diamond State, Blue Hen State; *Motto:* "Liberty and Independence;" *Flag:* state seal in buff diamond on blue field with date Delaware ratified constitution; *Flower:* peach blossom; *Bird:* blue hen chicken; *Tree:* American holly; *Song:* Our Delaware.

Industry: apparel, textile mill items, chemical manufacturing, oil refining, manufacture of transportation equipment, chicken; *Natural re-*

sources: fish, shellfish, small quantities stone & gravel; *Major source of income:* manufacturing.

Admitted to Union: Dec. 7, 1789 (1st state).

Places of interest: New Castle, one of the best preserved colonial towns.

Del'à-wāre Wà'têr Gap *Gorge* Pa.-N.J., U.S.

Delft *Commune* SW Netherlands; pottery

Del'hi (i) *City* now NEW DELHI

Del'mèn-hôrst *Commune* N cen. West Germany; manufacturing

Dē'los *Island*, smallest of the Cyclades S Aegean S.

Del'phī (fī), **Del-phoi'** (fē') *Town* S Greece

Dem'à-vend *Mountain* 18,550 ft. N Iran

De-mē'tri-às *Anc. city* NE Greece

Den'bigh-shire (bi) *County* N Wales

Den'märk, Kingdom of *Country*, mouth of Baltic Sea — NW Europe; 16,630 sq. m.; pop. 4,952,000; 17 provinces; *Main cities:* * Copenhagen, Aarhus, Odense, Aalborg; *Main rivers:* Stora, Skjern A, Varde A, Gudena; *Geog.:* low elevation, flat or undulating landscape; *Climate:* temperate.

Flag: white cross, red field.

Ethnic comp.: Scandinavian, German; *Language:* Danish (official); *Religions:*

Lutheran (state), Roman Catholic.

Products: livestock, meat, dairy products, fish, ships, machinery, electrical equipment, beer, transport equipment; *Minerals:* peat, lignite, cryolite, coal; *Major exports:* machinery — equipment, textiles, agricultural products; *Major imports:* machinery — fittings, fuels, chemicals, explosives, iron — steel; *Industries:* shipbuilding, food processing, manufacture machinery — chemicals, agriculture, fishing, mining, brewing, tourism.

Currency: krone.

Head of Government: King; *Legislature:* unicameral Folketing; *Judiciary:* 100 local courts, 2 high courts, several special courts, Supreme Court.

Den'tön *City* NE Texas, U.S.; pop. 39,874; ed. center

Den'vêr *City* * of Colo., NE cen. Colo., U.S.; pop. 514,678

Der'bẏ (där') *County borough* * of **Der'bẏ-shire** county, N cen. England

Des-chutes' (dà-shōōt') *River* 250 m. Ore., U.S.

De-se-à'dō (dā) *River* 300 m. S Argentina

De-shi-mä *Island* (artificial) Nagasaki harbor, Japan

Des Moines' (dè moin') 1. *City* * of Iowa S cen. part, U.S.; pop. 200,587; corn, coal area. 2. *River* 327 m. Iowa-uo., U.S.

Des-nä' *River* 550 m. U.S.S.R., Eur.

Dès Plaines (dè) *City* NE Ill., U.S.; pop. 57,239; residential

Des'sau (sou) *City* cen. East Germany

Dè-troit' *City* SE Mich. U.S.; pop. 1,511,482

Deur'nè (dûr') *Commune* N Belgium

Deut'sches Reich' (doi', rīk') **Deutsch'länd** (doich') = GERMANY

Deux-Sevres' (du-sā'-vr') *Department* W France

Dev'il's Island *Island* off N Fr. Guiana

De'vèn-têr (dā') *Commune* E Netherlands

De'vön Island *Island* Northwest Terrs., Canada

Dev'ön-shire *County* SW England; farming, mining, livestock, textiles

De-wäs' *Two states* cen. India

Dews'bur-ẏ (dūz'bêr) *County borough* N England; iron, wool

Dhär *State* cen. India

Dhá'rám-pur (p o o r) *State* W India

Dhär-wär' *Town* W India; cotton

Dhau'là-gi'ri, Mount (dou') *Peak* 26,800 ft. N India

Dhen-kä'näl (dän) *State* NE India

Dhōl'pur (poor) *State* NW India

Dhrän'gà-dhrä *State* W India

Dī-à-mán-ti'nà (tē') *River* 470 m. E Australia

Dī'à-mönd Head *Cape* Honolulu harbor Hawaii, U.S.

Die'gō - Suä'rez (dyā') *Town* N Madagascar; one of world's best harbors

Di-eppe' (ep') *City* N France; port, ivory

Di'göel (dē'gool) *River* 400 m. SE Irian

Di-jon' (dē-zhôn') *City* E France; trade, manufacturing

Di-näj'pur (poor) *Former district* Brit. India; now div.: Pakistan and India

Di-nar'ic Alps *Range*, Yugoslavia, parallel to Adriatic

Din'di-gul *Town* S India; tobacco cen.

Din'gle Bay (g'l) *Inlet* of Atlantic O. SW Eire

Dī'ö-mēde Islands *Islands* (2) B e r i n g

Strait; one Russ.; one Amer.

Dis'kō *Island* W Greenland; coal

Dis'trict of Cö-lum'bi-à, Washington; *Federal district,* * of U.S.; E U.S.; 69 sq. m.; *pop.:* 756,510; *Boundaries:* Maryland, Virginia, Potomac River.

Motto: "Justitia omnibus" (Justice to all); *Flower:* American beauty rose.

Industry: scientific research, manufacture of scientific equipment, real estate, tourism; *Major source of income:* federal government.

Places of interest: Capitol, White House, Supreme Court, Smithsonian Institution, Ntl. Archives, Library of Congress.

Dix'ie (dik'si) refers to S States of U.S.

Di-ya'la *River* 300 m. E Iraq

Di-yär-be-kir' (kēr') *City* SE Turkey, Asia; trade cen.

Djà-kär'tà formerly **Bà-tā'vi-à** *City* N Java, * of Indonesia; pop. 4,774,000; imp. port

Djäm'bi *Town* Sumatra, Indonesia; oil

Djer'bà *Island* cen. Mediterranean S.; fruit

Dji-bou'ti (boō') *City* * Fr. Terr. of Afars and Issas; port

Djok - jà - kär'tà = JOGJAKARTA

Dmi'tri - ev (di - mē') *Town* U.S.S.R., Eur.

Dne - prö-dzêr - zhinsk' (nep-rö-dêr) *City* Ukraine, U.S.S.R.

Dne - prö - pè - trôvsk' (nep-rö) *City* * of *R e g i o n* Ukraine, U. S. S. R.; wheat trade, manufacturing

Dne-prö-stroi' (nep-rö) *Dam* across Dnieper R. Ukraine; hydroelectric plant

Dnie'pêr (nē') *River*

1400 m. R.S.F.S.R., U.S.S.R., Eur.

Dnies'têr (nês') *River* 850 m. U.S.S.R., Eur.

Dō'ce (sè) *River* 360 m. E Brazil

Dō-dec'à-nēse *Island group* (Gk.) SE Aegean S.

Dō'hà *Town* * of Qatar

Dol'ö-mītes (m ī t s) *Range* of Alps NE Italy

Dö-lō'rès *River* 230 m. SW Colo., U.S.

Dōm *Peak* 14,940 ft. SW cen. Switzerland

Dom-i-ni'cà (nē') *Island, Brit. colony,* Brit. West Indies; * Roseau; forests

DOMINICAN REPUBLIC

Santiago
HAITI *San Juan* *La Vega*
Hispaniola *Santo Domingo*
San Cristóbal
0 miles 100

U. S. A.
CENTRAL AMERICA *Atlantic Ocean*
Caribbean Sea
SOUTH AMERICA

Dö-min'i-càn Republic *Country,* W Indies; 18,820 sq. m.; pop. 4,540,000; 26 provinces; *Main cities:* * Santo Domingo, Santiago, La Vega, San Francisco, San Juan; *Main rivers:* Yague, del Norte, Jaina, Ozama, Yague del Sur; *Geog.:* 4 E-W mt. ranges, large valley (Cibao) upper C part; *Climate:* tropical maritime.

Flag: divided by white cross into 4 rectangular sections — upper left, lower right dark blue, other 2 red — coat of arms in C cross.

Ethnic comp.: mulatto, European (mainly Spanish), Negro; *Language:* Spanish (official), *Religion:* Roman Catholic (state).

Products: sugar, coffee, cocoa, tobacco, bananas, bauxite, iron ore, cement,

beer, glass, textiles, peanut oil, textiles, soft drinks, flour; *Minerals:* bauxite, nickel, iron, petroleum (potential unknown); *Major exports:* sugar, coffee, chocolate, tobacco, bauxite, molasses; *Major imports:* wheat, vegetable oils, cars, tractors, pharmaceutical products; *Industries:* sugar refining, food processing, manufacture chemicals, beverages, tobacco.

Currency: peso at par with dollar.

Head of Government: President; *Legislature:* National Congress (bicameral) Chamber of Deputies, Senate; *Judiciary:* Supreme Court of Justice sole jurisdiction over President, members of Congress — hears appeals from lower courts.

Dôn *River* 1200 m. U.S.S.R. Eur.

Don'bas or **Dö-nets' Bä'sin** *Region* E Ukraine, U.S.S.R.

Don'càs-têr *County borough* N England; coal

Don Cos'sàcks Territory *Region* of Don R., U.S.S.R.

Don'è-gàl *County* N Eire; fish, farming, livestock

Dö-nets' *River* 670 m. U.S.S.R., Eur.; also see DONBAS

Don'nẏ-brook *Suburb* of Dublin, Eire

Dôr-dogne' (dôn'y') *Department* and *River* 300 m. SW France

Dôr'drecht (drekt) or **Dôrt** *Commune* SW Neth.; trade, shipping cen.

Dôr'set-shire *County* S England; farming, sheep, fish, quarries

Dôrt see DORDRECHT

Dôrt'mund (moont) *City* N cen. West Germany; mining, industrial, trade cen.

Dō′thăn *City* SE Ala., U.S.; pop. 36,733; manufacturing

Dou-ai′ (dōō-ā′) *City* N France; manufacturing, educational cen.

Dou-ä′là (dōō) *Town* Cameroon; port

Doubs (dōō) *Department* and *River* 270 m. E France

Dou′ro (dō′rōō), **Due′rō** (dwā′) *River* 485 m. Spain-Portugal

Dŏ′vêr 1. *City* * of Del., U.S.; pop. 17,488. 2. *Municipal borough* SE England

Dŏ′vêr, Strait of *Channel* SE England-N France

Down *County* SE Northern Ireland; farming, livestock, granite

Down′ey (i) *City* SW Cal., U.S.; pop. 88,-445 [England

Downs, The *Hills* S

Drāke Passage *Strait* bet. Cape Horn and S Shetland Is., S America

Drä-mä *City* * of *Department* N Greece

Dräm′mėn *City* S Norway; port, mills

Drän-cy′ (sē′) *Commune* N France

Drä′vä, Drau (drou) *River* 450 m. Austria-Yugoslavia

Dres′dėn (drez′) *City* SE East Germany; cultural, manufacturing cen.

Drö-gö-bẏch′ *City* in *Region* Ukraine, U.S.S.R.; trade cen.

Drôme *Department* SE France

Drum′mönd Island *Island* Lake Huron, U.S.

Du-băwnt′ (dōō) *River* 580 m. and *Lake*, N cen. Canada

Dub′lin *City* on *Bay*, * of *County* and * of Rep. of Ireland (Eire), E part; pop. 569,000; shipbuilding, glass, iron, breweries

Du-buque′ (būk′) *City* E Iowa, U.S.; pop. 62,309; Miss. R. port

Dud′ley (li) *County borough* W cen. England;

---

coal, bricks, brass, iron

Duis′bûrg (dooz′) *City* W West Germany; imp. Rhine port

Du-lä′wän (dōō) *Municipality* Mindanao Phil. Is.

Dul′ce (dōōl′sà) *River* 360 m. N Argentina

Du-luth′ (lōōth′) *City* NE Minn., U.S.; pop. 100,578; lake port, industrial cen.

Dum′bär-tŏn Oaks (ōks) *Mansion* Washington, D.C., U.S.; site of UN planning meeting 1944

Dum′ Dum *Town* NE India; ammunition

Dum-fries′shîre (frēs′) *County* S Scotland; farming, livestock

Dū-nà-gi′ri *Mountain* 23,180 ft. Himalayas N India

Dū′näv-skä *Former county* NE Yugoslavia

Dun-bär′tŏn-shîre *County* W cen. Scotland; livestock, coal, textiles, ships

Dun′dălk Bay *Inlet* of Irish S. NE Eire

Dun-dēe′ *Burgh* E Scotland; port, manufacturing

Dun-ē′din *City* South I. New Zealand; port

Dun-fêrm′ling (lin) *Burgh* E Scotland; manufacturing

Dun′gàr-pur (doong′, poor) *State* NW India

Dun-kêrque′ (kêrk′), **Dun′kìrk** *City* N France; port; WW II site

Dun Laogha′rẹ (lâ′), **Dun-lēa′rẏ** *City borough* E Eire; cattle port, fisheries

Du-ran′gō *City* * of *State* NW cen. Mexico; farm, mine, lumber cen.

Dûr′bàn *City* E Natal, Rep. of South Africa; port

Dûr′hàm (àm) 1. *City* NE cen. N.C., U.S.; pop. 95,438; cotton, tobacco market. 2. *County* N England; coal, iron, steel

Dus′sėl-dôrf (dōō′) *City* and *District* NW

West Germany; Rhine port

Dutch East Indies = INDONESIA

Dutch Gui-a′na (gi-an′à) = SURINAM

Dutch Här′bör *Village* E Aleutian Is., U.S.; port, naval base

Dutch New Gui′nea (gi′ni) = IRIAN

Dutch West Indies = NETHERLANDS ANTILLES

Dvi-nä′ 1. *River* 630 m. U.S.S.R. N Eur. 2. *Gulf* N U.S.S.R., Eur.

Dvinsk = DAUGAVPILS

Dwär′kä *City* W India; sacred city, port

Dẏkh′ Tau (tou) *Mountain* 17,080 ft. U.S.S.R., Eur.

Dzau-dzhi′kau (dzou-jē′kou) *City* R.S.F.S.R., U.S.S.R., Eur.; industry, trade

Dzer-zhinsk′ (dyer) *City* R.S.F.S.R., U.S.S.R., Eur.

Dzham-bul′ (bōōl′) *Town* * of *Region* U.S.S.R., Asia

Dzhir-gä-län-tu′ (tōō′) *Town* W Outer Mongolia; imp. trade cen.

E

Ea′ling *Municipal borough* SE England

East, the = Countries of Asia, the Orient

East An′gli-à *Kingdom* of Anglo-Saxon England; mod. Norfolk and Suffolk

East Ben′gàl *Region* E Pakistan; former prov. of Brit. India

East′bourne (bōrn) *County borough* S England; resort

East Chi-cä′gō (shi) *City* NW Ind., U.S.; pop. 46,982; manufacturing

East Clēve′lànd *City* N Ohio, U.S.; pop. 39,-600; electrical products

East Dè-troit′ *City* SE Mich., U.S.; pop. 45,920

Eas′têr Island *Island* (Chile) S Pacific O.

Eas′têrn Hem′i-sphēre (sfēr) = E half of

---

earth incl. Eur., Asia, Africa, Australia

Eas′têrn Range (rānj) = KAMCHATKA MTS.

Eas′têrn States 1. *States* (6) of New England, NE U.S. 2. *States* of U.S. along Atlantic O. 3. *States* of India (NE) former agency

East Flan′dêrs *Province* NW cen. Belgium; wheat, flax

East Gêr′mà-nẏ (jêr′) = GERMAN DEMOCRATIC REP.

East Ham *County borough* SE England; docks

East Härt′förd *Town* N Conn., U.S.; pop. 57,583; manufacturing, residential

East In′dies refers to INDOCHINA; sometimes incl. all SE Asia

East Lan′sing *City* S Mich., U.S.; pop. 47,540; educational cen.

East Lön′dön *City* S Rep. of South Africa

East Lŏ′thi-àn *County* SE Scotland

East′māin *River* 375 m. E Canada

East Or′ange (inj) *City* NE N.J., U.S.; pop. 75,471

East-phal′i-à (fāl′) E part of anc. Saxony, Germany

East Point *City* NW cen. Ga., U.S.; pop. 39,315

East Prov′i-dence *City* R.I., U.S.; pop. 48,-151; industrial

East River *Strait* Manhattan - Brooklyn - Queens, N.Y. City, U.S.

East Sāint Lou′is (lōō′) *City* SW Ill., U.S.; pop. 69,996; manufacturing, livestock

Eau Clâire′ (ō) *City* W Wisc., U.S.; pop. 44,-987; lumber cen.

E′brō (ā′) *River* 480 m. NE Spain

Ec′cles (′lz) *Municipal borough* W England

Ech′ō Can′yŏn (ek′) *Ravine* NE Utah, U.S.

Ec′uà-dôr, Republic of *Country*, S America;

106,510 sq. m.; pop. 6,510,000; 19 provinces each headed by elected governor, appointed prefect; *Main cities:* * Quitto, Guayaquil; *Main rivers:* Guayas, Esmeraldas; *Geog.:* Costa (C plain), Sierra (highlands), Oriente (E jungle), Archipelago de Colón (Galapagos Islands in Pacific); *Climate:* varying.

Flag: yellow, blue, red stripe — coat of arms in center.

Ethnic comp.: Indian, mestizo, European (chiefly Spanish), Negro; *Language:* Spanish (official), Quechua; *Religions:* Roman Catholic, Protestant.

Products: bananas, coffee, cocoa, sugar, fish, balsa wood, oil, copper, silver, textiles, cement, quinine; *Minerals:* petroleum, calcium carbonate, copper, gold, silver; *Major exports:* bananas, coffee, cocoa; *Major imports:* machinery, transportation equipment, chemicals, paper products; *Industries:* agriculture, forestry, fishing, food processing, oil refining, textiles.

Currency: sucre.

Head of Government: President; *Legislature:* bicameral National Congress — Senate, Chamber of Deputies; *Judiciary:* highest court is Supreme Court.

Ē'dam *Commune* W Netherlands

E'dē (ā') 1. *Commune* E Netherlands. 2. *City* W Nigeria

E-dī'na *Village* E Minn., U.S.; pop. 44,046; residential

Ed'in-burgh (bur-ö) *City* and *Burgh* * of Scotland, SE part; pop. 468,000; printing, publishing cen.

E-dir'nė *City* * of *Vilayet* NW Turkey, Eur.; trade, manufacturing

Ed'mön-tön 1. *City* * of Alberta, NW Canada; rail, air cen.; fur trade. 2. *Municipal borough* SE England

Ē'döm *Anc. country* S of Dead S.

Ed'ward, Lake *Lake* E cen. Africa

E-fä'te *Island* New Hebrides Is. administrative cen.

Ē'gẏpt (jipt), United Arab Republic, NE Africa, 364,140 sq. m.; pop. 35,065,000; 25 provinces (including Sinai); *Main cities:* * Cairo, Alexandria, Giza, Port Said; *Main river:* Nile; *Geog.:* 96% desert with Nile Valley, delta, few oases under cultivation; *Climate:* warm, arid.

Flag: red, white, black horizontal stripes — 2 5-pointed green stars on white stripe.

Ethnic comp.: Hamitic origin, minorities of Nubians, Bedouins; *Language:* Arabic (official); *Religions:* Sunni Moslem, Islam (state), Coptic Church.

Products: cotton, rice, sugar, cereals, oil, iron ore, salt, phosphate rock, sulphur, gypsum, olivine, steel, textiles, fertilizers; *Minerals:* petroleum, phosphate, iron ore, salt, manganese, limestone, sulphur, gypsum; *Major exports:* cotton — cotton goods, rice, crude oil — oil products; *Major imports:* wheat, petroleum, industrial machinery, vehicle parts, edible oils; *Industries:* food processing, textiles, oil refining, steel manufacturing, motor assembly, tourism.

Currency: Egyptian pound.

Head of Government: President; *Legislature:* unicameral People's Assembly; *Judiciary:* based on French. Highest court is Court of Cassation.

E-hi-me *Prefecture,* Shikoku, Japan

Eind'hō-vėn (īnt') *Commune* S Netherlands; electrical equipment

Ei'rė (ā')=IRELAND, REPUBLIC OF

Ei'sė-näck (ī'zė-näk) *City* SW East Germany; manufacturing

Eis'le-bėn (īs'lā) *City* W cen. East Germany

El Al-a-mein' (mān') *Village* N Egypt

Ē'lath now 'AQABA

El'ba *Island* W cen. Italy; iron-ore

El'bė *River* 720 m. Czechoslovakia - Germany

El'bêrt, Mount *Peak* 14,431 ft. Colo., U.S.

El'blag (blông), **El'bing** *City* N Poland, formerly Germany; port

El-bö-rus' (rōōz'), **El-brus'** (brōōz') *Mountain* 18,480 ft.; Europe's highest; Caucasus Mts., U.S.S.R.

El-burz' Mts. *Range* N Iran

El Ca-jōn (hōn') *City* S

Cal., U.S.; pop. 52,273; residential

El'che (châ) *City* SE Spain; dates, manufacturing

El'ė-phant (fànt) *River* 250 m. South-West Africa

El-ė-phan-tī'ne (fan) *Island* Nile R. Egypt

El Faï-yum' (yōōm') *Town* Upper Egypt

El Fer-rôl' *City* NW Spain; harbor

El'gin (jin) *City* NE Ill., U.S.; pop. 55,691; butter, watches

El'gon, Mount *Peak* 14,175 ft. E cen. Africa

E-lis'à-beth-ville (liz') *Town* * of *Province* (now KATANGA) SE Rep. of Congo (L)

E-liz'à-beth *City* NE N.J., U.S.; pop. 112,654; manufacturing

Elk'härt *City* N Ind., U.S.; pop. 43,152

Elk'tön *Town* NE Md., U.S.; marriage mill until 1938

Elles'mēre Island (elz') *Island* NE Northwest Terrs., Canada

El'lice Islands (lis) *Island group* (Brit.) see GILBERT and ELLICE IS.

El'lis Island *Island* N.Y. Bay, U.S.; immigration cen. til 1954

El-lōre' *City* E India

El Man-su'rà (soor') *City* Lower Egypt

Elm'hûrst *City* NE Ill., U.S.; pop. 50,547

El Min'yà *City* Upper Egypt

El-mī'rà *City* S N.Y., U.S.; pop. 39,945

El Mis'ti *Volcano* 19,110 ft. S Peru

El Mon'tė *City* S Cal., U.S.; pop. 69,837; manufacturing, residential

El Oued' (wed'), **El Wad'** *Town, Oasis,* NE Algeria

El Pas'ō *City* W Texas, U.S.; pop. 322,261; trade, manufacturing

El Sal'và-dôr, Republic of El Salvador *Country,* C America; 7,720 sq. m.; pop. 3,774,000; 14 departments;

Main cities: * San Salvador, Santa Ana, San Miguel; *Main rivers:* Lempa, San Miguel; *Geog.:* mt. ranges running E–W divide country into narrow Pacific coastal belt (S) subtropical C region of valleys, plateaus, mts.

Flag: horizontal stripes — blue, white, blue with National coat of arms in center white stripe.

Ethnic comp.: Mestizos, Amerindians, Europeans; *Language:* Spanish (official), Nahuati; *Religion:* Roman Catholic.

Products: coffee, cotton, sugar, maize, sisal, sesame, indigo, balsam, rice, shrimp, gold, silver, salt, cement, fertilizers; *Minerals:* quartz, diatomaceous earth, kaolin, gypsum, limestone, pumice; *Major exports:* coffee, cotton, shrimp, sugar, cottonseed cakes, cotton fabric; *Major imports:* transport equipment, chemical products, fuels, lubricants, raw materials, industrial machinery, consumer goods; *Industries:* tourism, food processing, manufacture of textiles, shoes, chemicals.

Currency: colone.

Head of Government: President; *Legislature:* unicameral legislature; *Judiciary:* Supreme Court at apex, 2 courts of appeal, departmental, municipal courts.

El'si-nōre = HELSINGOR

Ē'lẏ, Isle of *County* E England

E-lẏr'i-à *City* N Ohio, U.S.; pop. 53,427

Em-ba' *River* 350 m. U.S.S.R., Asia

Em'dėn *City* N West Germany; port

Em'êr-ȧld Isle = IRELAND, the island

E-mi'liä (mē') *Compartimento* N Italy

E-min-ö-nū' *District* of Istanbul, Turkey

Em'mėn *Commune* NE Netherlands

Em'press Ău-gus'tȧ Bay *Inlet* Bougainville NW Solomon Is.

Ems *River* 205 m. NW Germany

En'dêr-bẏ Land *Projection* (Brit.) of Antarctica

En'fiĕld 1. *Urban District* SE England; rifles 2. *Town* N Conn., U.S.; pop. 46,189

E n g ' ė l s *Town* R.S.F.S.R., U.S.S.R., Eur.; agriculture

Eng'lȧnd (ing') *Country* S and E Great Britain island; division of United Kingdom; 51,355 sq. m.; pop. 54,022,000; * London; 45 counties; iron, steel, coal, manufacturing

Eng'lish Channel (ing') *Strait* S England-N France

Ē'nid *City* N Okla., U.S.; pop. 44,008; grain, oil, meat industries

E-ni-wē'tok *Atoll* Marshall Is. W Pacific O.

En'nȧ *Province* Sicily, Italy

En-sche-de' (skė-dā') *Commune* E Netherlands; industry

En-teb'bė *Town* Uganda; on equator

En-ze-li' (lē') now PAHLEVI

E-per-nāẏ' (ä) *Commune* NE France; champagne

Eph'ė-sus (ef') *Ruins* of anc. city W Asia Minor

E-pi'rus 1. *Anc. country* NW Greece. 2. *Division* E Greece

Ep'söm and Ew'ėll (ū') *Municipal borough* SE England; site of **Ep'söm Downs** racecourse

Ē-quã'tör = imaginary circle on earth's surface equidistant from N and S poles

EQUATORIAL GUINEA

E-quȧ-tōr'i-ȧl Gui'nea (gi'ni), Republic of *Country,* W Africa; 10,830 sq. m.; pop. 320,000; 2 provinces: Fernando Po, Rio Muni; *Main cities:* * Santa Isabel, Bata; *Main rivers:* Benito, Muni, Campo; *Geog.:* 2 large volcanic formations separated by valley which crosses island E-W; *Climate:* tropical.

Flag: horizontal green, white, red stripes joined by blue triangle on staff side. Centered is coat of arms.

Ethnic comp.: Bantu; *Language:* Spanish (official), Arabic, Pidgin English; *Religions:* animist, Roman Catholic, Protestant.

Products: cocoa, coffee, timber, sugar, cotton, tobacco, groundnuts, indigo, fish; *Minerals:* uranium, iron ore, possible petroleum; *Major exports:* cocoa, wood, coffee; *Major imports:* foodstuffs, building materials, petroleum products, pharmaceutical products, textiles, motor vehicles; *Industries:* forestry, fishing.

Currency: peseta.

Head of Government: President; *Legislature:* National Assembly (unicameral); *Judiciary:* apex is Supreme Court.

E-rä'klēi-ön = HERAKLEION

Er'ė-bus, Mt. *Peak* 13,200 ft. Ross I. Ant-

arctica

E-rė-pe-cu-ru' (kōōrōō') *River* 250 m. N Brazil

E-rē'tri-à *City* anc. Greece, S Euboea I.

E-re-vän' = YEREVAN

Er'fûrt *City* * of *District* SW East Germany

Erg, El *Regions* of sand dunes, Sahara Desert

Ē'rie (ri) *City* NW Pa., U.S.; pop. 129,231

Ē'rie, Lake (ri) *Lake* NE U.S.; one of 5 Great Lakes

Ē'rie Canal (ri) *Canal* Buffalo-Albany N.Y., U.S.　　[poetic name

Er'in = IRELAND, a

Er'ith *Urban district* SE England; yachting

Er-i-trē'a *Area* of NE Ethiopia on Red S., former It. colony

Es'bjerg (byark) *City* SW Jutland, Denmark; meats, fish, dairy products

Es-cä-län'te *Municipality* Negros, Phil. Is.

Es-con-di'dō (dē') *City* S Cal., U.S.; pop. 36,792; business

Ē'shêr *Urban district* S England

E'skil-stu-na (ä'shilstōō) *City* SE Sweden; steel, cutlery

Es-ki-se-hir' (she) *City* * of *Vilayet* W Turkey, Asia; meerschaum　　　[SPAIN

Es - pä'nä (n y ä) =

Es-pi'ri-tū Sän'tō *Island* largest of New Hebrides, SW Pacific O.

Es'sėn *City* NW West Germany; Krupp works: arms, locomotives　[Australia

Es'sėn-dön *City* SE

Es-sė-qui'bō (kwē') *River* 600 m. W Guyana

Es'sex *County* SE England; farming, fish, manufacturing

Ess'ling-ėn *City* SW West Germany

Es-tō'ni-à or **Es-tō'ni-ȧn S.S.R.** *Republic* of U.S.S.R., N Eur.; * Tallin; agriculture, livestock; independent 1918-40

E-tä′wȧh *Town* N India; cotton mills

Ē-thi-ō′pi-ȧ, Empire of *Country,* E Africa; 395,000 sq. m.; pop. 25,452,000; 14 provinces; *Main cities:* * Addis, Asmara, Diredawa, Dessie; *Main rivers:* Shibeli, Abbai, Ganale Dorya, Awash, Omo; *Geog.:* C of country high, partly mt. plateau, cut by numerous rivers — terrain gradually slopes to lowlands, plains; *Climate:* plateau — temperate, lowlands — hot.

Flag: green, yellow, red horizontal stripes, C, in orange is crowned lion bearing in right forepaw crossstaff with national banner.

Ethnic comp.: Gallas (Hamitic), Amharas — Tigres (mainly Semitic), Nilotic, others; *Language:* Amharic (official), English, Gallinya, Somali, Tigrinya; *Religions:* Ethiopian Orthodox, Muslim, animist.

Products: coffee, pulses, oil seeds, cereals, hides — skins, tobacco, sugar, salt; *Minerals:* gold, platinum, iron, manganese ore, potash, copper, nickel, asbestos; *Major exports:* coffee, hides — skins, oil seed — pulses; *Major imports:* machinery — transportation equipment, textiles, yarns — fabrics, foodstuffs, building materials, petroleum

products; *Industries:* textiles, food processing, building materials, printing, leather, chemicals.

Currency: dollar.

Head of Government: Emperor; *Legislature:* Parliament; *Judiciary:* apex is Supreme Imperial Court.

Et′nà, Aet′nà *Volcano* 10,740 ft. NE Sicily

E-trur′i-ȧ (troor′) *Anc. country* cen. Italy

Et′têr-beek (bāk) *Commune* cen. Belgium

Eu-boe′ȧ (ū-bē′) *Island* largest of Greece, Aegean S.; with CENTRAL GREECE, a division

Eū′clid *City* N Ohio, U.S.; pop. 71,552; grapes, machinery

Eū-gēne′ (jēn′) *City* W Ore., U.S.; pop. 76,-346; gold, silver

Eū-phrā′tēs (frā′) *River* 1700 m. SW Asia

Eūr-ā′sia (z h ȧ) = world's largest land mass: Europe and Asia

Eure (ûr) 1. *Department* N France. 2. -et-Loir′ (ā-lwar′) *Department* N cen. France

Eū′rōpe *Continent,* E hemisphere; 3,800,-000 sq. m.; div. into many countries

Ev′ȧns-tön *City* NE Ill., U.S.; pop. 79,-808; education cen.

Ev′ȧns-ville *City* SW Ind., U.S.; pop. 138,-764; machinery

E-ven′kẏ *National district* N cen. Siberia, U.S.S.R.

Ev′êr-est, M o u n t *Mountain,* world's highest, 29,028 ft., Nepal-Tibet, Himalayas

Ev′êr-ett 1. *City* NE Mass., U.S.; pop. 42,-485; iron, paints. 2. *City* NW cen. Wash., U.S.; pop. 53,622; port, lumber, fish

Ev′êr-glādes *Marshland* S Fla., U.S.

E′we-land (ā′wä) *Region* W African coast;

former slave coast

Ex′ė-têr *City* and *county borough* SW England; rail, farming, shipping cen.

Ex-ū′mȧ *Island group* Bahama Is.

Eyre (âr) *Peninsula* and *Lake* S Australia

F

Fä-en′zä *Commune* N Italy; pottery

Fāer′ōes (fär′ōz) *Island group* (Dan.) N of Brit. Isles, Atlantic O.

Fair′banks *Town* cen. Alas., U.S.; pop. 14,-771; port, gold, lumber

Fair′fiēld 1. *City* SW Conn., U.S.; pop. 56,-487; port 2. *City* NWC Cal., U.S.; pop. 44,146

Fāir Lȧwn *City* NE N.J., U.S.; pop. 37,-975; cement, textiles

Fair′weath-êr, Mount (weth) *Peak* 15,315 ft. Alas., U.S.-Brit. Columbia, Canada

Faīz′ȧ-bad 1. *Town* NE Afghanistan. 2. see FYZABAD, India

Fȧl′kîrk *Burgh* cen. Scotland; flour, iron, coal, chemicals

Fȧlk′lȧnd Islands *Brit. colony* S Atlantic O.; * Stanley; whaling, sealing, sheep

Fȧll Ri′vêr *City* SE Mass., U.S.; pop. 96,-898.

Fal′stêr *Island* of Denmark, Baltic S.

Fä-mȧ-gu′stȧ (gōō′) *City* on *Bay,* * of *District* E Cyprus; port

Fä′nō *Commune* E cen. Italy; manufacturing

Fär East = Countries and Islands of E Asia

Fär Eas′têrn Region or Republic former area of E Siberia, U.S.S.R.

Fāre′hȧm *Urban district* S England

Fär′gō *City* E N.D., U.S.; pop. 53,365; manufacturing, trade

Fȧ-rid′kōt (rēd′) *State* NW India

Fȧ-rid′pur (rēd′poor) *District* E Pakistan; formerly Brit. India

Fȧr′ōe Islands see FAEROES

Fȧr-rukh′ä-bäd (rook′) *City* * of *District* N India

Fär West = area of U.S. west of Great Plains

Fä-tih′ (tē′) *District* of Istanbul, Turkey

Fät′shän′ *City* SE China; commerce, industry

Fāy′ette-ville (ėt-vil) *City* S cen. N.C., U.S.; pop. 53,510; manufacturing

Fed′êr-ȧl District = capital area of a country

Federated M a l a y States, Federation of Malaya = Former states, S Malay Penin; now part of MALAYSIA

Felt′hȧm *Urban district* SE England

Fen (fun) *River* 300 m. NE China

Fengh′kieh′ (fung′ji-e′) *City* S cen. China

Feng′tien′ (fung′ti-en′) now MUKDEN

Feng′tu′ (fung′dōō′) *City* S cen. China

Fen′nö-scan′di-ȧ = Geological term for Scandinavia

Fē-ö-dō′si-yȧ (s h i) *T o w n* R.S.F.S.R., U.S.S.R., Eur.; port

Fêr-man′ȧgh (ȧ) *County* Northern Ireland; farming, livestock

Fêr-nän′dō Pō′ö *Island Province* Equatorial Guinea (Sp.)

Fė-rōze′pōre *City* * of *District* NW India; grain, cotton trade

Fêr-rä′rȧ *Commune* * of *Province* N Italy

Fez *City* N Morocco; sacred city

Fez-zan′ *Desert, Oasis, Region,* SW Libya

Fie′sö-le (fyâ′) *Commune* cen. Italy; ruins, resort

Fīfe *County* E Scotland; farming, limestone

Fi′ji (fē′jē) (Independent nation within British Commonwealth) *Country,* SW Pacific; 7,060 sq. m.; pop. 546,000; 4 administrative divi-

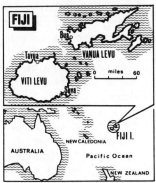

sions; *Main islands:* Viti Levu, Vanua, Levu, Taveuni, Kandavu; *Main cities:* * Suva, Lautoka; *Main rivers:* Rewa, Dreketi; *Geog.:* larger islands of volcanic origin, mountainous, surrounded by coral reefs. Windward sides covered with dense tropical forests, leeward sides contain grassy plains; *Climate:* tropical oceanic type, tempered by prevalent SE winds which control it. Average temperature 78°F.

Flag: blue field with Union Jack upper left, shield of Fiji coat of arms centered on right.

Ethnic comp.: Indians, Fijians, Europeans, Rotumans, Polynesians, others; *Language:* English (official), Indian, local; *Religions:* Methodist (state), Hindu, Roman Catholic, Muslim.

Products: sugar, coconuts, coconut oil, molasses, lumber, rice, fruit; *Minerals:* gold, copper, bauxite, manganese; *Major exports:* sugar, gold, molasses, lumber, coconut oil; *Major imports:* machinery, fuels, clothing, cotton fabrics, food; *Industries:* dairy, timber, fishing, mining, tourism.

Currency: dollar.

Head of State: British Monarch; *Head of Government:* Prime

Minister; *Legislature:* Parliament; *Judiciary:* Court of Appeal, Supreme Court.

Finch'ley (li) *Urban district* SE England; residential

Find'lay (li) *City* NW Ohio, U.S.; pop. 35,800; manufacturing

Fin'ger Lakes *Lakes* W N.Y., U.S. (Seneca, Cayuga, Keuka, Canandaigua, Owasco, Skaneateles)

Fin-is-tere' (târ') *Department* NW France

Finke *River* 400 m. cen. Australia

Fin'land, Republic of *Country,* N Europe; 130,160 sq. m.; pop. 4,819,000; 12 provinces; *Main cities:* * Helsinki, Tampere, Turku, Lahti, Oulu; *Main rivers:* Kemi, Oulu, Tornio; *Geog.:* lakes, forests, swamps; *Climate:* extends in frigid zone, moderated by influence of Gulf Stream.

Flag: extended blue cross on white field.

Ethnic comp.: Finns, Swedish, Russians, Lapps; *Language:* Finnish (official), Swedish, Russian, Lapp; *Religions:* Evangelical Lutheran (state), Greek Orthodox.

Products: timber, dairy products, transport equipment, machinery, mineral production, plastics, ceramics, textiles, engineering, chemicals, rubbers, paper, pulp, glass, plywood; *Minerals:* iron, copper, nickel, zinc, titanium, cobalt; *Major ex-

ports:* paper products, machinery, transport equipment, chemicals, textiles, clothing; *Major imports:* raw materials, fuels, lubricants, machinery, automobiles, aircrafts, foodstuffs, textiles; *Industries:* forestry, mining, paper manufacturing, manufacture of transportation equipment — machinery.

Currency: markka.

Head of Government: President; *Legislature:* unicameral Parliament; *Judiciary:* local courts, appellate courts, Supreme Court.

Fin'land, Gulf of Arm of Baltic S.

Fin'lay (li) *River* 250 m. Brit. Columbia, Canada

Finsch'hä-fen *Village* SE New Guinea

Fin-stêr-äar'hôrn *Peak* 14,025 ft. Switzerland

Fīre Island *Island* N.Y., U.S.; lighthouse

Fi-ren'ze (tsâ) 1. *City* = FLORENCE. 2. *Province* cen. Italy

Fitch'bûrg *City* cen. Mass., U.S.; pop. 43,343; industrial cen.

Fitz'roy *River* 300 m. W Australia

Fiū'me (mâ) It. name of RIEKA

Flan'dêrs, East and **West** *Provinces* N Belgium

Flat'bush (boosh) *District* of Brooklyn, N.Y. City, U.S.

Flens'bûrg *City* N West Germany

Flin'dêrs *River* 500 m. NE Australia

Flint 1. *River* 265 m. W Ga., U.S. 2. *City* SE cen. Mich., U.S.; pop. 193,317

Flint'shire *County* NE Wales

Flor'ence, It. **Fi-ren'ze** *Commune* cen. Italy

Flō'res *Island* of Lesser Sundas, Indonesia

Flō-ri-à-nop'ö-lis *City* S Brazil; harbor

Flor'i-dà *State,* named from Spanish word

meaning "feast of flowers;" 58,560 sq. m.; *pop.:* 6,789,443 (*rank:* 9th); SE U.S.; *Boundaries:* Georgia, Alabama, Gulf of Mexico, Atlantic Ocean; *Major cities:* Miami, Tampa, Jacksonville, * Tallahassee; *Major rivers:* St. Johns, Apalachicola, Suwannee; *Major lakes:* Lake Okechobee, Lake George, Kissimmee; 67 counties.

Nickname: Sunshine State, Everglade State, Peninsula State; *Motto:* "In God We Trust;" *Flag:* state seal on white field crossed by diagonal red bars; *Flower:* orange blossom, *Bird:* mockingbird; *Tree:* Sabal palm; *Song:* Suwannee River.

Industry: oranges, fresh vegetables, tourism, food processing, chemical manufacturing, electronics; *Natural resources:* phosphate rock, zircon, limestone, peat, forests (mostly pine), fish, shellfish; *Major source of income:* wholesale & retail trade.

Admitted to Union: 1845 (27th state).

Places of interest: Cape Kennedy, Everglades Ntl. Park, Florida Caverns State Park, Mayakka State Park, Cypress Gardens.

Flor'i-dà Keys (kēz) *Islands* S Fla., U.S.

Flô'ri-nä (rē) *Department* N Greece

Flô-ris'sànt *City* E Mo., U.S.; pop. 65,908

Flush'ing *Site* Long I. Queens, N.Y. City, U.S.; site of Worlds' Fairs 1939, 1964

Flȳ *River* 650 m. SE New Guinea

Fond' Du Lac *City* SEC Wisc., U.S.; pop.

35,515; manufacturing

Fog'gia (fôd'jä) *Commune* * of *Province* SE Italy

Fô-li'gnô (lē') *Commune* cen. Italy

Fŏlke'stŏne (stun) *Municipal borough* SE England; port

Fon'taine - bleau (ten-blō) *Commune* N France; chateau

Fōō'chow' see MINHOW

Foots'crāy *City* SE Australia; quarries, manufacturing

For'à-kêr, Mount *Mountain* 17,000 ft. S cen. Alas., U.S.

Fôr-bid'dèn *City* = LHASA

For'est Hills *Community* Queens, N.Y. City, U.S.; site of tennis tournaments

Fôr'fàr-shîre now ANGUS

Fŏr-li' (lē') *Commune* * of *Province* N Italy; manufacturing

Fôr-mō'sà or **Taī-wän** *Island* off SE China; pop. 14,700,000; * Taipei; agricultural, forest products, mining; seat of Chinese Nationalist Government since 1949

Fôr-mō'sà 1. *Territory* N Argentina. 2. *Bay* of Indian O., SE Kenya. 3. *Strait* SE China-Formosa I.

Fôrst *City* East Germany; textiles

Fôrt Ben'ning *Infantry post* W Ga., U.S.

Fôrt Col'lins *City* N Col., U.S.; pop 43,-337; ed. center

Fôrt-dè-Frånce' *City* * of Martinique, Fr. West Indies

Fôr-tè-le'zà (là') *City* NE Brazil; port

Fôr'tès-cūe *River* 350 m. W Australia

Fôrt George (jôrj) *River* 520 m. Quebec, Canada

Fôrth *River* into **Firth of Fôrth,** arm of North S.

Fôrt Knox (nox) *Military reservation* N cen. Ky., U.S.; U.S. gold depository

Fort - La - my' (fôr-la-mē') *Town* * of Chad NW part; pop. 150,-000

Fôrt Lău'dêr-dāle *City* SE Fla., U.S.; pop. 139,590; resort

Fôrt Leav'èn - wörth (lev') *Military reservation* E Kan., U.S.; federal penitentiary

Fôrt Mc-Hen'rẏ *National monument* Md., U.S.; site of writing of national anthem

Fôrt Nel'sön *River* 260 m. Brit. Columbia, Canada

Fôrt Smith *City* W Ark., U.S.; pop. 62,-802; trade, industry

Fôrt Sum'têr *Fort* Charleston S. C., U.S.; site of attack starting Civil War

Fôrt Wayne (wān) *City* SE Ind., U.S.; pop. 177,671; rail, manufacturing cen.

Fôrt Wil'liam (yàm) *City* Ontario, Canada; imp. port

Fôrt Wörth *City* N Texas, U.S.; pop. 393,476; trade, transportation cen.

Fou-geres' (fōō-zhâr') *City* NW France; quarries, manufacturing

Four Côr'nêrs (fôr) *Site* only place in U.S. where four states meet: Colo., N.M., Ariz., Utah

Fow'liang' (fōō'li-äng') *Town* SE China; porcelain

Fox Islands 1. *Islands* (2) Lake Mich., U.S. 2. *Island group* of Aleutian Is., Alas., U.S.

Frā'ming-ham *Town* NE Mass., U.S.; pop. 64,048; manufacturing

France, French Republic *Country,* W Europe; 212,920 sq. m.; pop. 51,300,000; 95 departments; *Main cities:* * Paris, Lyon, Marseille, Lille, Bordeaux, Toulouse, Nantes, Nice, Strasbourg, Saint Etienne, Le Harve, Rennes; *Main rivers:*

Rhone, Durance, Loire, Garonne, Rhine, Seine; *Geog.:* ⅔ flat, N-W primarily broad plain, rest mts. S — Pyrenese, E — Alps; *Climate:* varied; S — Mediterranean, W-N — cool winters, mild summers.

Flag: vertical stripes — blue, white, red.

Ethnic comp.: French, Italians, Spaniards, Algerians, Portuguese; *Language:* French (official), Breton, Flemish, Spanish, Catalan, Basque; *Religions:* Roman Catholic, Protestant, Jewish.

Products: wheat, barley, fruit, wine, cider, livestock, timber, iron ore, coal, oil, natural gas, bauxite, lead, silver, antimony, salt, iron, steel, metals, aircraft, chemicals, textiles, watches, jewelery, woodwork, pottery, glass, paper, carpets; *Minerals:* iron ore, potash, bauxite, coal, natural gas, sulphur, zinc, lead, pyrites, phosphates, uranium, oil, silver, antimony; *Major exports:* chemical products, iron — steel, silk — cotton textiles, motor cars,

wine, food, soap, perfume, glass; *Major imports:* wool, cotton, chemicals, coke, oil, oleaginous fruits — seeds, machinery, skins, timber, rubber, copper, coffee; *Industries:* aluminum industry, electrical industry, tourism, mining, metal working, clothing manufacturing, machinery, chemicals, metallurgical industries.

Currency: new franc.

Head of Government: President; *Legislature:* bicameral Parliament — Senate, National Assembly; *Judiciary:* 2 parts — regular court system and system that deals with administration and relation to French citizen.

Frän-cō'ni-à 1. *Former division* S cen. Germany. 2. *Mountain range* of White Mts. N.H., U.S.

Frank'fört *City* * of Ky. N cen. Ky., U.S.; pop. 21,356

Fränk'fûrt on the Main (mīn) *City* W cen. West Germany; commerce, manufacturing

Fränk'fûrt on the Ō'dêr *City* E cen. East Germany; manufacturing

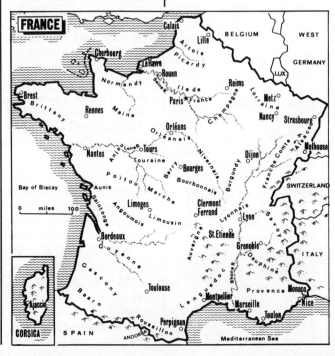

Franz Jō′sėf Land *Archipelago* Arctic O., U.S.S.R.

Frā′ser (zhêr) *River* 700 m. Brit. Columbia, Canada

Fred′ėr-ic-tŏn *City* * of New Brunswick, SE Canada; lumber trade

Fred′ėr-iks-bêrg *City* E Denmark; Copenhagen suburb

Frēe′pôrt *Village* SE N.Y., U.S.; pop. 40,-374; residential

Frēē′town *Town* * of Sierra Leone; pop. 110,000; fine harbor

Freī′bêrg 1. *City* S East Germany; manufacturing, silver mines. 2. *City* S West Germany

Freī′tȧl *City* S East Germany

Frē-man′tle *Municipality* SW Australia

Frē′mont *City* W Calif., U.S.; pop. 100,869

French Ant-ärc′ti-cȧ *Territory* (Fr.) incl. islands in Indian O. and area of mainland

French Cŏm-mū′ni-tẏ *Federation* of France, its territories, overseas depts. and republics; replaced French Union 1958

French E-quȧ-tô′ri-ȧl Af′ri-cȧ *Former Fr. terr.* now div: CHAD, CONGO (b), GABON

French Gui-ä′nȧ (gi) *Department*, Fr.; NE coast of South America; * Cayenne; agriculture, woods

French Guin′ea (gin′i) *Former Fr. terr.* now GUINEA

French In′di-ȧ *Former Fr. terr.* E India

French In′dō-chī′nȧ *Former Fr. colonies*, E Indochina; now CAMBODIA, LAOS, VIETNAM

French O-ce-an′i-ȧ (she) = Fr. islands of Pacific O.

French Pol-ẏ-nē′sia (zhȧ) *Territory* (Fr.) S Pacific O.; incl. Society, Marquesa, Gambier, Austral Is., Tuamotu Arch.; * Papeete on Tahiti, Society Is.

French Sö-mä′li-land *Territory* (Fr.) E Africa; * Djibouti; salt

French Sū-dan′ *Former Fr. terr.* now SUDAN

French West Africa *Former Fr. terrs.* now DAHOMEY, GUINEA, IVORY COAST, MAURITANIA, NIGER, SENEGAL, SUDAN, UPPER VOLTA

French Union now FRENCH COMMUNITY

French West In′dies *Islands* (Fr.) of West Indies: Martinique, Guadeloupe, etc.

Fres′nō (frez′) *City* S cen. Calif., U.S.; pop. 165,972; fruit

Fri′bourg (frē′boor) *Commune* * of *Canton* W cen. Switzerland; manufacturing

Friē - drichs - hä′fėn (driks) *City* S West Germany; imp. port

Friend′lẏ Islands (frend′) or TONGA ISLANDS

Friēs′lȧnd (frēz′) *Province* N Netherlands; dairying

Fri′sian Islands (frizh′ȧn) *Island chain* North S.; **West** bel. to Netherlands, **East** to Germany, **North** to Germany and Denmark [Italy

Fri′ū-li *Province* NE

Frŏ′bish-êr Bay *Inlet* SE Baffin I., N Canada

Frŏn′tiēr Il-lä′qas (kȧz) *Districts* NW Kashmir, N India

Frŏ-si-nō′ne (nä) *Province* cen. Italy

Frūn′zė *City* * of Kirgiz S. S. R., U.S.S.R., Asia

Fu′ji, Fu-ji-yä′mä (fōō) *Mountain* 12,388 ft. Honshu, J a p a n, sacred

Fū-kä-e *Island* off Kyushu, Japan

Fū′kien′ *Province* SE China; agriculture, forestry

Fu-ku-i (foo-koo) *City* * of *Prefecture* Honshu, Japan; textiles

Fu-ku-ō-kä (foo-koo) *City* * of *Prefecture*

Kyushu, Japan; manufacturing

Fu-ku-shi-mä (foo-koo) *City* * of *Prefecture* Honshu, Japan; trade

Fu-ku-yä-mä (foo-koo) *City* Honshu, Japan

Ful′dȧ (fool′) *City* on *River* cen. W Germany; manufacturing

Ful′lêr-tŏn *City* SW Calif., U.S.; pop. 85,826; oil [Is.

Fū-nȧ-fū′ti *Atoll* Ellice

Fun-chal′ (fōōn-shäl′) *Commune* Madeira Is. Portugal; resort

Fun′dẏ, Bay of *Inlet* of Atlantic O. SE Canada

Furth (fûrt) *City* SE West Germany; manufacturing

Fu-sän (foo) or **Pu-sän** (poo) *City* S Korea

Fu′shun′ (fōō′shoon′) *Town* S Manchuria; coal

Fū-tū′nȧ Islands see WALLIS and FUTUNA IS.

Fu-yu′ (fōō′) *Town* cen. Manchuria

Fyn (foon) *Island* cen. Denmark

Fȳz′ȧ-bad *City* N India; rail cen., sugar refining

G

Gä-bė-rō′nes *Town* * of Bechuanaland now Botswana

Gä′bes *Town* on *Gulf* SE Tunisia; port

Ga-bôn′ Republic *Country*, W coast of Africa; 102,320 sq. m.; pop. 475,000; 9 prefectures divided into 28 districts; *Main cities*: * Liberville, Port Gentil, Lambaréné; *Main*

rivers: Ogooue, Ngounie, Abanga; *Geog.:* nearly all dense equatorial rain forest; *Climate:* hot, humid.

Flag: horizontal bands — green, yellow, blue top — bottom.

Ethnic comp.: Bantu, at least 40 tribal groups, Frenchmen; *Language:* French (official), Fang, Bantu tongues; *Religions:* Roman Catholic, Moslem.

Products: timber, cocoa, coffee, oil, natural gas, manganese, uranium, gold; *Minerals:* oil, manganese, uranium, gold, lead, zinc, phosphate, diamonds; *Major exports:* wood, petroleum, manganese; *Major imports:* tobacco, refined petroleum products — industrial chemicals; machinery — parts, transportation equipment, metal products; *Industries:* forestry, mining, mineral processing.

Currency: CFA franc.

Head of Government: President; *Legislature:* unicameral National Assembly; *Judiciary:* headed by Supreme Court. Also courts of first instance or justices of peace.

Gȧ′dȧg *Town* W India;

Gads′dėn 1. *City* NE Ala., U.S.; pop. 53,-928; mineral, lumber area. 2. **Pûr′chȧse** *Land area* SW U.S. (Ariz., N.M.); purchased from Mexico 1853

Gaines′ville *City* N Fla., U.S.; pop. 64,-510; ed. center

Gâird′nêr *Lake* S Australia

Gȧ-lä′pȧ-gös Islands *Island group* of Ecuador, Pacific O.; * San Cristobal; wild life

Gȧ-lā′tia (shȧ) *Anc.*

country cen. Asia Minor

Gä′lätz *City* E Romania; port

Gāles′bûrg *City* W Ill., U.S.; pop. 36,290

Gȧ-li′cia (shȧ) 1. *Region* E cen. Eur. now part of U.S.S.R. 2. *Region, Anc. Kingdom,* NW Spain

Gal′i-lēe 1. *District* N Israel; scene of Jesus' ministry. 2. **Sea of** *Lake* N Israel

Gal′lȧ-tin   R a n g e *Mountains* S Mont., U.S.   [port

Gälle   *Town* Ceylon;

Gal-li′näs, Point (gä-yē′) N point of South America, Colombia

Gȧl-lip′ö-li 1. *Commune* SE Italy; port. 2. *Peninsula* NW Turkey, Eur.

Gal′vės-tön   *City* SE Texas, U.S.; pop. 61,809; imp. port

Gȧl′way   *County* and *Municipal borough* on **Bay,** W Eire

Gam′bi-ȧ *River* 460 m. W Africa

Gam′bi-ȧ, The Gambia, Republic of *Country,* W Africa; 4,000 sq. m.; pop. 381,000; 6 rural areas, Bathurst; *Main city:* * Bathurst; *Main river:* Gambia; *Geog.:* low lying area, thick mangrove swamps — river flats behind. Sand hills, rolling plateaus behind flats; *Climate:* subtropical.

Flag: horizontal stripes — red, blue, green — blue center band bordered by 2 narrow white stripes.

Ethnic comp.: Madingos, Fulas, Woloffs, Jolas, Sarahulis; *Lan-*

guage: English (official), Malinke, Wolof; *Religions:* Moslem, Christian, animist.

Products: groudnuts, groundnut oil — cake, dried — smoked fish, palm kernels, rice, millet; *Major exports:* peanuts, palm kernels, hides, dried mollusks, beeswax; *Major imports:* food, textiles, clothing, machinery — transport equipment; *Industries:* agriculture, peanut oil refining, cotton weaving, garment making, soft drink bottling, fishing.

Currency: Gambia pound.

Head of Government: President; *Legislature:* unicameral House of Representatives; *Judiciary:* Supreme   Court, Court of Appeals, subordinate courts. Judges appointed by central government.

Gam′bier Islands *Island group* (Fr.) S Pacific O.

Gam-tōōs′   *River* 300 m. Rep. of South Africa

Gȧn′dȧk *River* 400 m. Nepal-N India

Gan′ges (jēz)   *River* 1550 m. NE India; sacred to Hindus

Gȧng′pur (poor) *Indian state* NE India

Gȧng′tok *Town* * of Sikkim   [S France

Gard (gar) *Department*

Gär-dē′nȧ   *City* SW Cal., U.S.; pop. 41,021; manufacturing, residential

Gär′dėn City *City* SE Mich., U.S.; pop. 41,864

Gär′dėn Grōve *City* SW Calif., U.S.; pop. 122,524; residential

Gär′dėn of the Gods *Region* ab. 500 acres, Colo., U.S.

Gär′dėn Rēach *Suburb* of Calcutta NE India

Gär′field Heights (hīts) *City* N Ohio, U.S.;

pop. 41,417; manufacturing

Gar - ian′ (gur - yan′) *Town* NW Libya

Gär′lȧnd *City* NE Texas, U.S.; pop. 81,437

Gȧ-ronne′ *River* 355 m. SW France

Gar′rẏ, Lake   *Lake* Northwest   Terrs., Canada

Gâr′ẏ *City* NW Ind., U.S.; pop. 175,415

Gas-cön-āde′ *River* 250 m. S cen. Mo., U.S.

Gas′cö-nẏ 1. *Hist. region* SW France. 2. *Gulf* SE part of Bay of Biscay

Gas′coyne (coin) *River* 400 m. W Australia

Gȧ′shêr-brum (broom) *Peak* 26,470 ft. N India

Gas′pe (pā) *Peninsula, Cape, Bay* SE Quebec Canada;   hunting, fishing

Gas-tō′ni-ȧ   *City* SW N.C., U.S.; pop. 47,-142; industry

Gātes′head (gāts′hed) *County borough* N England; manufacturing, mines, quarries

Gat′i-neau (nō) *River* 240 m. SW Quebec, Canada

Gȧ-tōō′mȧ   *T o w n* Rhodesia; gold

Gȧul, Gȧulle, Gal′li-ȧ *Anc. country* W Eur. incl. most of mod. France

Gau′ri Sȧn′kȧr (gou′) *Peak* 23,440 ft. N Nepal

Gav′lė (yâv′)   *City⁻* E Sweden; port

Gȧ-yä′ *City* NE India; sacred to Buddhists

Gä′zȧ *City* * of *District* SW Israel; port

Gä-zi-än-tep′   *Town* * of *Vilayet* S Turkey Asia; educational cen.

Gdänsk see DANZIG

Gdẏ′ni-ȧ   *City* N Poland; port

Gee-lông′ (je) *Port* SE Australia; wool

Ge-hen′nȧ = New Testament   word   for "hell"; see HINNOM

Ge′lä (jä′) *Commune* S Sicily; ruins

Gel-sėn-kir′chėn (kėn) *City* N cen. West Ger-

many; industry, coal

Gė-nē′vȧ (jė), **Ge-neve′** (zhe-nâv′)   *City* on *Lake,* * of *Canton* SW Switzerland; tourist, cultural cen.; manufacturing

Gen′ö-ȧ (jen′), **Ge′nö-vä** (jä′) *City* on *Gulf* in *Province* NW Italy; imp. port

Gent see GHENT

Gen′töf-tė *City* E Denmark   [rea; port

Gen-zän *City* NE Ko-

George (jôrj) *River* 365 m. Quebec, Canada

George, Cape (jôrj) *Cape* Nova Scotia, Canada

George, Lake (jôrj) *Lake* E N.Y., U.S.; resort area

George′town (jôrj′) 1. *Section* of Washington, D.C., U.S. 2. *City* * and chief port of Guyana

George′ Town (jôrj′) or **Pė-nang′** *City* Penang I.   Malaysia; port

Geor′gia (jôr′jä) *State,* named in honor of King George II of England; 58,876 sq. m.; *pop.:* 4,589,575 *(rank:* 15th); S U.S.; *Boundaries:* S Carolina,   N   Carolina, Tennessee, Alabama, Florida,   Atlantic Ocean; *Major cities:* * Atlanta, Savannah, Columbus; *Major rivers:* Altamaha, Chattahoochee,   Savannah; *Major lakes:* Lanier,   Allatoona, Seminole; 159 counties.

Nickname: Empire State of the South, Peach State, Cracker State; *Motto:* "Wisdom, Justice, Moderation;" *Flag:* state seal on vertical blue bar, Confederate flag to   right;   *Flower:* Cherokee rose; *Bird:* brown thrasher; *Tree:* live oak; *Song:* Georgia.

Industry: textile mill items, lumber, pulp & paper products, food processing, man-

ufacture of transportation equipment, chemicals; *Natural resources:* kaolin, marble, limestone, ochre, granite, slate, iron ore, mica, bauxite, talc, forests; *Major source of income:* industry, manufacturing.

Admitted to Union: Jan. 2, 1788 (4th state).

Places of interest: Okefenokee Swamp Park, Warm Springs, Andersonville Prison Park, Chickamauga-Chattanooga Ntl. Park.

Geor-gi'na (jôr-jē') *River* 400 m. N cen. Australia

Ge'rä (gā') *City* SW East Germany; industry

Ger'man East Africa (jêr') *Ger. Terrs.* prior to WW I

Ger-ma'ni-a (jêr) *Anc. region* cen. Eur., larger than mod. Germany

Ger'man Vol'ga Republic (jêr') *Former republic* U.S.S.R., Eur.

Ger'ma-ny (East), German Democratic Republic *Country*, NC Europe; 41,800 sq. m.; pop. 17,684,000; 14 administrative areas; *Main cities:* * East Berlin, Leipzig, Dresden, Karl Marx Stat, Magdeburg; *Main rivers:* Elbe, Oder, Saale, Havel, Spree; *Geog.:* N — low hills, lakes, C — partly mountainous, S — sandy arid section, fertile plain, heavily forested; *Cli-*

mate: summer 65°F, winter 30°F.

Flag: black, red, gold horizontal stripes — national coat of arms in center.

Ethnic comp.: Germans with small group of Sorbs; *Language:* German (official); *Religions:* Protestant, Roman Catholic.

Products: cereal, live stock, lignite, coal, potash, copper ore, iron ore, steel, precision instruments, chemicals, fertilizers, synthetic rubber — fibers, drugs, plastics, vehicles; *Minerals:* lignite, copper, iron; *Major exports:* machinery, railway rolling stock, chemicals, fertilizers, clothing, textiles, fuel oil; *Major imports:* mineral ores, coal, rolled steel, fertilizer, crude oil, wood, cotton — wool, paper, pulp, foodstuff, forage — feeds, raw skins; *Industries:* chemical — electrical industries, steel refining, mining.

Currency: ostmark.

Head of Government: Chairman of State Council; *Legislature:* unicameral People's Chamber; *Judiciary:* 3 levels — district courts (courts of the first instance), area courts, Supreme Court.

Ger'ma-ny (West), Federal Republic of Germany, *Country*, NC Europe; 97,970 sq. m.; pop. 61,194,-000; 10 Laender (states); *Main cities:* * Bonn, West Berlin, Hamburg, Munich, Cologne, Essen, Dusseldorf, Frankfurt-am-Main, Dortmund, Stuttgart, Bremen; *Main rivers:* Rhine, Danube, Ems, Weser, Elbe; *Geog.:* flat in N, hilly in C-W areas, rising in S to Black

Forest, Bavarian Alps; *Climate:* summer 65°, winter 30°, dropping to 0° and below. Lowlands, rainfall 20″, 74″ in Alps.

Flag: horizontal bands — black, red, gold top — bottom.

Ethnic comp.: German, small Danish population, Italian, Greek, Turk, Spanish, Yugoslav; *Language:* German (official; *Religions:* Protestant, Roman Catholic, Jewish.

Products: cereal, fruit, wine, beer, timber, livestock, coal, lignite, iron ore, metal ore, potash, oil, iron, steel, machinery, machine tools, textiles, chemicals, motor vehicles, shipbuilding, electricity, building materials, petrochemicals; *Minerals:* coal, iron ore, lead, zinc, potash, salt, fluorspar, barites, pyrites, graphites, basalt, petroleum, natural gas; *Major exports:* mechanical engineering products, motor vehicles, chemicals, electrical engineering products, iron, steel, wine, machine tools; *Major imports:* foodstuffs, nonferrous metals,

semifinished products, chemical products, iron, steel, textiles, industrial raw materials; *Industries:* breweries, automobile manufacturing, wine making, textile mills, forestry, mining, food industry, chemical — steel production, machinery, trade, shipbuilding, tourism.

Currency: Deutschemark.

Head of Government: President; *Legislature:* bicameral Parliament — Bundestag, Bundesrat; *Judiciary:* independent; highest court is Federal Constitutional Court. Others — Federal High Court of Justice, other federal courts.

Ger'mis-tön (jêr') *City* NE Rep. of South Africa; gold

Gers (zhâr) *Department* SW France

Get'tys-bûrg *Borough* S Pa., U.S.; Civil War battle site

Ghä'na, Republic of *Country*, W Africa; 92,100 sq. m.; pop. 8,767,000; 8 regions, 47 districts; *Main cities:* * Accra, Kumasi, Sekondi-Takoradi, Tamale, Cape Coast; *Main rivers:* Volta, Pra, Tano, Ofin; *Geog.:* coastline

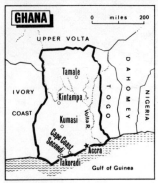

GHANA

largely low sandy shore, backed by plains — intersected by rivers — streams. N from shore is tropical rain forests broken by densely forested hills, rivers. To N is savannah, grassland plains; *Climate:* similar to equatorial countries.

Flag: horizontal stripes of red, gold, green with black star in center of gold stripe.

Ethnic comp.: Akan, Ashanti, Ewe; *Language:* English (official), tribal languages; *Religions:* Christian, Moslem, animist.

Products: cocoa, groundnuts, timber, rubber, tobacco, yams, gold, diamond, manganese, bauxite, aluminum; *Minerals:* gold, diamonds, manganese, bauxite, iron ore, beryl, limonite, nickel, graphite, chromite; *Major exports:* cocoa, cocoa butter, gold, diamonds, aluminum, timber; *Major imports:* machinery — transportation equipment, cereals, alumina, petroleum, textiles; *Industries:* agriculture, fisheries, food processing, mining.

Currency: cedi.

Head of Government: President; *Legislature:* unicameral National Assembly; *Judiciary:* apex is supreme court which has powers of judicial review, may rule

on constitutionality of any legislative or executive action.

Ghăts, Eastern and **Western** *Mountain ranges* S India

Ghent, Gent *City* NW cen. Belgium; commerce, manufacturing

Ghôr, the *Region*, valley of the Dead Sea

Gi-brăl'têr (ji) *Town* on **Rock of Gibraltar,** a peninsula and Brit. colony, S Spain

Gi-brăl'têr, Strait of (ji) *Passage* Spain-Africa

Gib'sŏn Desert *Desert* W Australia; salt lakes

Gies'sĕn (gēs') *City* cen. West Germany; manufacturing

Gi-fu (foo) *City* * of *Prefecture* Honshu, Japan; paper goods

Gi - hulng'än (h ē - hōōlng') *Municipality* Negros, Phil. Is.

Gi-jon' (hē-hôn') *City* NW Spain; port

Gi'lå (hē') *River* 630 m. SW U.S.

Gil'bêrt *River* 250 m. NE Australia

Gil'bêrt and El'lice Islands (lis) *Brit. colony* W Pacific O. incl. Gilbert Is., Ellice Is., Phoenix Is. and Line Is., Christmas I., Fanning I., Washington I.; * Tarawa; copra, phosphates

Gil'e-åd *Region* anc. Palestine, mod. NW Jordan

Gil'ling-håm (jil') *Municipal borough* SE England; fruit, cement

Gi-rônde' (zhē) *Department* SW France

Giu'bä (jōō') *River* 1000 m. Somalia

Gi'zå, El Gi'zĕh (gē') *City* * of *Province,* Upper Egypt, 5 m. from pyramids

Glä'cier National Park (shēr) *Park* glaciers, mountains, N W Mont., U.S.

Gläd'bäch - Rheydt' (bäk-rīt') *City* NW West Germany; textiles

Gläd'beck *City* W West Germany; coal

Glå - môr'găn - shire *County* SE Wales; coal, iron, steel

Glas'gōw *Burgh* W cen. Scotland; port, manufacturing

Glei'witz (glī'vits) see GLIWICE

Glen'dāle 1. *City* SW Calif., U.S.; pop. 132,752; manufacturing 2. *City* S Ariz., U.S.; pop. 36,228

Glen-elg' *River* 280 m. SE Australia

Glen-gar'rẏ *Valley* NW Scotland; lake

Gli-wi'ce (vē'tse) *City* SW Poland; manufacturing

Glôm'mä *River* 375 m. E Norway

Glouces'têr (glos') *County borough* of **Glouces'têr - shire** county, SW cen. England; iron, textiles

Gō'å *City*, former terr. of Port. India, W India; port

Gōat Island *Island* Niagara R. N.Y., U.S.

Gō'bi, the *Desert* 500,-000 sq. m. cen. Asia

Gō-dä'vå-ri *River* 900 m. cen. India

God'hävn *Town* W Greenland; scientific station

Gôdt'haab (hôp) *Town* * of Greenland, SW coast

God'win Ăus'tĕn *Peak* 28,250 ft. N Kashmir

Gog'rå *River* 570 m. N India

Gōld Cōast 1. former Brit. colony, now GHANA. 2. *Coast* of Gulf of Guinea; gold

Gōl'dĕn Gāte *Strait* Pacific O.-San Francisco Bay, Calif., U.S.

Gōl'dĕn Thrōne *Peak* 23,600 ft. N Kashmir

Gō'mĕl *City* * of *Region* W h i t e Russia U.S.S.R., Eur.; trade

Go-me'rä (mä') *Island* of Canary Is.

Gö-môr'räh see SODOM

Gō'nå *Settlement* New Guinea; WW II site

Gōn'dål *State, Town* W India

Good Hōpe, Cape of

Cape S tip of Africa, Rep. of South Africa

Gōōse Bay = U.S.-Canada Air base Labrador, Newfoundland

Göp'ping-ĕn *City* S West Germany; manufacturing

Gō'råkh-pur (poor) *City* * of *Division* N India

Gô'ri *Town* Georgia S cen. U.S.S.R.

Go-ri'ziä (rē') *Commune* * of *Province* NE Italy; resort, manufacturing

Gôr'ki *City* * of *Region* E cen. R.S.F.S.R., U.S.S.R.; imp. industrial city

Gôr'litz *City* SE East Germany; manufacturing

Gör-lôv'kå *City* Ukraine SW U.S.S.R.

Gô'rẏn *River* 485 m. E U.S.S.R.

Gôr'zow (zōōf), Ger. **Länds'bêrg** *City* W Poland; industry

Gō'sain-than' (sīn-tän') *Peak* 26,290 ft. S Tibet

Gos'pōrt *Municipal borough* S England; naval barracks

Go'tå (yu') *River* and *Canal* S Sweden; 360 m., 58 locks

Go'tå-land (yu') S *Division* of Sweden; incl. 12 provs.

Go-tė-bôrg' (yu), **Goth' ĕn-bûrg** *City* S Sweden; industrial port

Gō'tha (tä) *City* SW East Germany; manufacturing

Go'thåm = New York City, U.S.; humorous reference

Got'land *Island Province* SE Sweden; fish, agriculture, sheep

Göt'ting-ĕn *City* W cen. West Germany

Gôtt'wald-ôv (val-dôf), formerly **Zlin** (zlēn) *Town* cen. Czechoslovakia; shoes

Gou'då *Commune* SW Netherlands; cheese

Goul'bûrn (gōl') *River* 280 m. SE Australia

Göv'êr-nörs Island *Island* New York Bay, U.S.

Grä'håms-town *Town*

S Rep. of South Africa; educ. cen.

Gra-ja-u' (ōō') *River* 450 m. NE Brazil

Gram'pi-an Hills *Mountains* cen. Scotland

Gram'pi-ans *Mountains* SE Australia

Gra-na'da 1. *City* * of *Department* SW Nicaragua; sugar, coffee, hides. 2. *City* * of *Province* S Spain

Grand *Rivers* of U.S.: 1. 260 m. SW Mich. 2. 300 m. NW Mo. 3. 200 m. N S.D.

Grand Bank *Banks* E and S of Newfoundland, Atlantic O.; cod

Grand Ca-nal' 1. *Canal*, main thoroughfare of Venice, Italy. 2. *Inland waterway* NE China

Grand Can'yon *Gorge* of Colo. R. in *National Park:* 280 m. long, mile deep; NW Ariz., U.S.

Grand Com-bin' (bän') *Peak* 14,160 ft. S Switzerland

Grand Cou'lee *Valley* cen. Wash., U.S.; dam

Grande', Ri'o (rē') see RIO GRANDE (U.S.)

Gran'de, Ri'o (rē'ōō) *Rivers:* 1. 250 m. W Africa. 2. 300 m. E Brazil 3. 680 m. E Brazil

Grand Forks *City* E N.D., U.S.; pop. 39,-008; business

Grand Prair'ie *City* N Texas, U.S.; pop. 50,904

Grand Rap'ids *City* W Mich., U.S.; pop. 197,649

Grand Te'ton *Peak* 13,765 ft. NW Wyo., U.S.; *National Park*

Grand Turk *Island* dependency of Jamaica

Gran'ite City *City* SW Ill., U.S.; pop. 40,-440; steel, granite

Gran Pa-ra-di'so (dē'-zō) *Peak* 13,325 ft. NW Italy

Gran'ville Lake *Lake* Manitoba Canada

Gras', Lac de (grä') *Lake* Northwest

Terrs. Canada

Grasse *Commune* SE France; perfumes

Gratz See GRAZ

Graves'end *Municipal borough* SE England

Grays Peak *Mountain* 14,275 ft. cen. Colo., U.S.

Graz, earlier **Gratz** *City* SE Austria

Great Au-stra'li-an Bight (bīt) *Bay* S Australia

Great Bar'ri-er Reef *Coral reef* off NE Australia, 1250 m.

Great Ba'sin *Elevated area* of U.S.: parts of Nev., Utah, Calif., Ida., Wyo., Ore.

Great Bear Lake *Lake* 12,200 sq. m. Northwest Terrs. Canada

Great Brit'ain ("n), The United Kingdom of Great Britain and Northern Ireland, *Country*, off the NW coast of Europe; 94,220 sq. m.; pop. 55,700,000; England, Wales, Scotland, N Ireland each divided into separate administrative units; *Main cities:* * London, Birmingham, Glasgow, Liverpool, Manchester, Sheffield, Leeds, Edinburgh, Bristol, Teesside, Belfast; *Main rivers:* Severn, Thames, Trent, Aire, Great Ouse, Wye, Tay, Nene, Clyde, Spey, Tweed, Tyne; *Geog.:* generally rolling land. NW — SW hilly. E — SE undulating downs, low lying plains; *Climate:* temperate, equable.

Flag: red, white, blue Union Jack combines Patron Saints of England, Scotland, Ireland.

Ethnic comp.: English, Scotch, Welsh, Irish; *Language:* English (official), Celtic languages — Gaelic, Welsh, Manx, French; *Religions:* Church of England, Church of Scotland (state), Roman Cath-

olic, Presbyterian, Methodist, Baptist, other minorities.

Products: livestock, milk eggs, barley, wheat, beer, whiskey, vegetables, potatoes, poultry, fish, coal, copper, lead, tin, iron, steel, machinery, non-ferrous metals, motor cars, aircraft, ships, precision instruments, woolen — cotton textiles, chemicals, plastics, petroleum products, clothing, paper, woodwork; *Minerals:* coal, iron, limestone, tin, gravel, oil shale, natural gas; *Major exports:* machinery, cars, aircraft, chemicals, cotton — fabrics, iron — steel, metals, petroleum products, fruits, vegetables, meat, meat preparations, whiskey; *Major imports:* petroleum, machinery, non-ferrous metals, meat, fruit, mineral manufacturers, scrap metal, cereals, wool, cotton, rubber; *Industries:* steel industry, coal mining, shipping, finance, fishing, oil refining, tourism, insurance, engineering, food processing, mining, automobile manufacturing.

Currency: pound.

Head of Government: Monarch; *Legislature:* Parliament; *Judiciary:* independent of legislature, executive branches. Cannot review constitutionality of legislation.

Great Di-vide' = CONTINENTAL DIVIDE

Great Di-vi'ding Range or **Eastern Highlands** *Mountain ranges* E Australia

Great Falls *City* cen. Mont., U.S.; pop. 60,091; copper works, mineral deposits

Great Lakes *Lakes*,

chain of 5: Superior, Michigan, Huron, Erie and Ontario, cen. North America

Great Plains *Plains*, cen. North America (U.S. and Canada)

Great Salt Desert See DASHT-I-KAVIR

Great Salt Lake *Lake* N Utah, U.S.; 2360 sq. m.

Great San'dy Desert *Desert* W Australia

Great Slave Lake *Lake* Northwest Terrs. Canada

Great Smo'ky Mountains *Range* of Appalachian Mts., N.C.-Tenn., U.S.

Great Vic-to'ri-a Desert *Desert* W and S Australia

Great Wall of Chi'na *Wall* for defense, built 205 B.C., 2000 m. bet. Mongolia and China

Great Whale *River* 365 m. Quebec, Canada

Greece (grēs), Kingdom of *Country;* SE Europe; 51,000 sq. m.; (islands 9,850 sq. m.); pop. 9,051,000; 52 provinces; *Main cities:* * Athens, Salonika, Patias, Volos, Heraklion (Crete); *Main rivers:* Aliakmon, Peneus, Warder, Achelous; *Geog.:* predominantly mt. Much dry, rocky land, about 25% arable; *Climate:* mild wet winters, hot dry summers, rarely extreme.

Flag: white cross superimposed on blue background in upper left corner. Remainder of flag 5 blue, 4 white horizontal stripes.

Ethnic comp.: Greeks Turks, Macedonian Slavs, Albanians, Armenians, Bulgarians; *Language:* Greek (official), Turkish, Albanian, Armenian; *Religions:* Greek Orthodox Church (state), Moslem.

Products: tobacco, cereals, fruit, olives, rice, cheese, cotton, iron ore, iron pyrites, bauxite, manganese, chrome, chemicals, textiles; *Minerals:* lignite, bauxite, iron, nickeliferous iron ore, chromite, barite, magnesite; *Major exports:* tobacco, currants, cotton, unprocessed aluminum, iron, nickel, citrus fruits; *Major imports:* machinery, iron — steel, crude oil, meat, passenger cars, trucks; *Industries:* tourism, shipbuilding, oil refining, mining, food processing, textile industry, aluminum, nickel — chemical refineries.

Currency: drachma.

Head of Government: Regent (Monarch); *Legislature:* Parliament dissolved by junta; *Judiciary:* Council of state highest court. Military courts under government control play key role.

Grēe'ley *City* N Col., U.S.; pop. 38,902; business, ed. center
Grēen *Rivers* of U.S.: 1. 360 m. Ky.-Ohio. 2. 730 m. Wyo.-Utah-Colo.
Grēen Bay *City* on *Inlet* E Wisc., U.S.; pop. 87,809; river, lake port, factories
Grēen'land 1. *Island* 839,800 sq. m.; pop. 40,000; world's largest, N America, bel. to Denmark; * Godthaab; hunting, fishing. 2. *Sea* part of Arctic O. NE of Greenland

Grēen Mountains *Range* of Appalachians, Canada-Mass., U.S.
Grēen'öck *Burgh* SW Scotland; port
Grēens'bö-rö *City* N cen. N.C., U.S.; pop. 144,076
Grēen'ville 1. *City* W Miss., U.S.; pop. 39,648; cotton. 2. *City* NW S.C., U.S.; pop. 61,208; textiles
Green'wich (gren'ij) *Borough,* London, England; Greenwich meridian is basis for standard time
Green'wich (gren'ich) 1. *Town* SW Conn., U.S.; pop. 59,755. 2. *Village* artist and student section of N.Y. City, U.S.
Greïfs'wäld *City* N East Germany
Greiz (grīts) *City* S East Germany
Grė-nä'dä *Island* Brit. Colony, Windward Is. Brit. West Indies; * St. George's
Gren'à-dines (dēnz) *Islands* ab. 600 of Windward Is., Brit. West Indies
Grė-nō'ble (b'l) *City* SE France; manufacturing, esp. gloves
Gret'nà Grēen *Village* S Scotland; famous as elopement site
Gri-jal'vä (häl') *River* 350 m. SE Mexico
Grims'by *County borough* E England; harbor
Gri-quà-land East (grē') *Territory* S Rep. of South Africa; agriculture, sheep
Gri'quà-land West (grē') *Region* S cen. Rep. of South Africa
Griz'zly Mountain *Peaks* 1. 13,800 ft. cen. Colo., U.S. 2. 14,000 W cen. Colo., U.S.
Griz'zly Pēak *Peaks* 1. 13,740 ft. SW Colo., U.S. 2. 13,700 ft. SW Colo., U.S.
Grôd'nô (or **Gär-di'näs**) *City* * of *Region* White Russia, W cen. U.S.S.R.
Grō'ning-ėn *City* * of

Province NE Netherlands; commerce
Grōōt-fôn-tein' (tān') *Town* N South-West Africa; mines
Grōs-se'tō (sā') *Province* cen. Italy
Gro'tön *Town* Conn., U.S.; pop. 38,523
Grôz'ný *City* * of *Region* nr. Caspian S. S U.S.S.R., Eur.; oil
Grü'dziadz (jônts), Ger. **Grau'denz** (grou') *City* N cen. Poland; agricultural cen.
Gru-yere' (yâr') *District* W cen. Switzerland; cheese
Guä-dä-lä-jä'rä (hä') *City* W cen. Mexico; industrial, agricultural, mining cen.
Guä-dàl-cà-nal' *Island,* Brit. Solomon Is.; WW II site
Guăl-dàl-quiv'ir *River* 374 m. S Spain
Gua-dà-lupe' (lōōp') 1. *River* 300 m. SE Texas, U.S. 2. *Island* off NW Mexico
Guä-dà-lū'pe Hi-däl'gō, Gūs-tä'vō A Mä-de'rō (dā') *City* cen. Mexico; pilgrimage site
Gua-dė-loupe' (lōōp') *Islands,* part of *Department* of France, E West Indies
Guä-diä'nä *River* 515 m. Spain-Portugal
Guä-ji'rä (hē') *Peninsula* N Columbia
Guäm = *Island* (U.S. possession) of Mariana Is., W Pacific O. * Agana
Guä-nä-juä'tō (hwä') *City* * of *State* cen. Mexico
Guän-tä'nä-mō *Municipality* and *Town* on *Bay* E Cuba; sugar cen., U.S. naval base
Gua - po - re' (pōō-râ') *River* 950 m. W cen. South America
Guar'di-àn, the (gär') *Peak* 13,625 ft. SW Colo., U.S.
Guä-tė-mä'là, Republic of *Country,* C America; 42,040 sq. m.; pop. 5,400,000; 23 departments; *Main cities:* * Guate-

mala City, Quezaltinango, Escuintla, Barrios; *Main rivers:* Motagua, Usumacinta, Polochic; *Geog.:* central highland region, Pacific plain, lowlands of fertile river valleys; *Climate:* 2 seasons, wet — (May–Oct.), dry (Nov.–May).

Flag: vertical blue, white, blue stripes — coat of arms on white.

Ethnic comp.: Maya Indians, mixed Spanish — Indian; *Language:* Spanish (official), Maya — Quiché Indian dialects; *Religion:* Roman Catholic.

Products: coffee, cotton, bananas, chicle, sugar, essential oils, cereals, zinc, lead, nickel, sulphur, tires, plastics, pharmaceuticals, tobacco, textiles, furniture, paper products; *Minerals:* nickel, zinc, silver, lead, limestone; *Major exports:* coffee, cotton, bananas, meat; *Major imports:* industrial machinery, textiles, chemical — pharmaceutical products, construction materials; *Industries:* food processing, oil refining, nickel extraction, beverages, shoe making, commerce — finance, lumber industry, machinery — metal products.

Currency: quetzal at par with dollar.

Head of Government: President; *Legisla-*

ture: unicameral Congress; *Judiciary:* Supreme Court is highest court.

Guä-viä're (râ) *River* 450 m. SW cen. Colombia

Guä-yä-quil' (kēl') *City* SW Ecuador; port

Guern'sey (gêrn'zi) *Island* of Channel Is.; cattle [S Mexico

Guer-re'rō (ger) *State*

Gui-ä'nä (gi) *Region* N South America incl. Guyana, Fr. Guiana, Surinam, N Brazil, S and E Venezuela

Gui-enne' (gē) or **Aqui-tä'niä** *Hist. region* SW France

Guild'förd (gīl') *Municipal borough* S England

Guin'ea (gin'i), Republic of *Country,* on "bulge" of W Africa; 96,860 sq. m.; pop. 4,175,000; 4 regions, 29 administrative districts; *Main cities:* * Conakry, Kankan, Kindia; *Main rivers:* Niger, Bating, Konkouré; *Geog.:* narrow coastal belt, pastoral Foutah Djallon, upper Guinea, SE forest region; *Climate:* 2 zones — tropical, sudanic.

Flag: equal sized vertical bands, red, yellow, green.

Ethnic comp.: Peuls, Malinké, Soussou, Foulbe; *Language:* French, tribal languages; *Religions:* Moslem, animist, Christian.

Products: rice, bananas, palm products, coffee, millet, pineapples, ground-

nuts; *Minerals:* bauxite, iron ore, diamonds, gold; *Major exports:* alumina, bananas, iron ore; *Major imports:* cotton textiles, rice, vehicles, cement, machinery, petroleum products, sugar; *Industries:* mining, hydroelectric plants, aluminum smelting, bauxite refining.

Currency: Guinea franc at par with CFA franc.

Head of Government: President; *Legislature:* National Assembly; *Judiciary:* at apex is high court.

Guin'ea, Gulf of (gin'i) *Inlet* of Atlantic O. W cen. Africa

Gu-jä-rät' (goo) *State* W India

Guj-rän-wä'lä (gooj) *Town* * of *District* West Pakistan

Guj'rät (gooj') *Town* West Pakistan; crafts

Gul'bär-gä (gool') *Town* S cen. India; cotton, flour, paint

Gulf'pôrt *City* S Miss., U.S.; pop. 40,791; business

Gulf States = States of U.S. bordering Gulf of Mexico

Gulf Strēam *Ocean current* (warm) from Gulf of Mexico to N Atlantic O.

Gu-mäl' Pass *Mountain pass* W India frontier

Gum-mä (goom) *Prefecture* Honshu, Japan

Gum'ti (goom') *River* 500 m. N India

Gun-tur' (goon-tōōr') *City* E India; tobacco, cotton trade

Gun-zän (goon) *Port* SW Korea; rice

Gur'lä **Män-dhä'tä** (goor') *Peak* 25,355 ft. SW Tibet

Gu-ru-pi' (gōō-rōō-pē') *River* 350 m. NE Brazil

Gu'ryėv or **Gu'rėv** (gōō) *Town* * of *Region* Kazakh, on Caspian S. U.S.S.R. SW Asia

Guy-ä'nä (gi), Republic of *Country,* NE coast of S America; 83,000 sq. m.; pop. 740,000; 9 administrative districts; *Main cities:* * Georgetown, Mackenzie, New Amsterdam, Linden; *Main rivers:* Essequibo, Courantyne, Berbice, Mazaruni, Cuyuni; *Geog.:* low-lying coastal region, heavily forested interior, region of mountains — savannahs in S-W; *Climate:* tropical; average rainfall: 80–102".

Flag: green background, red triangle edged with black on yellow triangle edged with white.

Ethnic comp.: Negroes, mulattoes, Indians, Amerindians; *Language:* English (official); *Religions:* Christian, Hindu, Moslem.

Products: rice, bananas, palm products, coffee, millet, pineapples, groundnuts, sugar; *Minerals:* bauxite, iron ore, diamonds, gold; *Major exports:* bauxite, aluminum, sugar, rice, timber, shrimp, gold, diamonds; *Major imports:* foodstuffs, manufactured goods, petroleum products, beverages, tobacco; *Industries:* consumer goods, sugar processing, aluminum smelting, wood — pulp.

Currency: dollar.

Head of Government: Governor - General;

Executive leader: Prime Minister; *Legislature:* Parliamentary democracy; *Judiciary:* Court of Appeals, High Court are highest judiciary bodies.

Gwä'li-ôr *Town* and former *State* N cen. India

Gwÿ'dir *River* 450 m. SE Australia

Gyäng'tse' *Town* SE Tibet; woolens

Györ (dyur), Ger. **Rääb** *City* NW Hungary

Gy' - Pa-rä-na' (zhē') *River* 500 m. W cen. Brazil

H

Häar'lem *City* W Netherlands; tulips

Habs'bûrg (haps') *Hamlet* N cen. Switzerland

Hä-chi-nō-he *Town* Honshu, Japan

Hä-chi-ō-ji *City* Honshu, Japan; weaving

Hack'ėn-sack *City* on *River* NE N.J., U.S.; pop. 35,911

Hadd, Cape *Cape* E Oman

Hä-de'ji-ä (dä') *River* 375 m. N Nigeria

Hä-dhrä-maut' (mōōt') *Coast region,* E Aden

Ha-fun', Cape (fōōn') *Cape* E point of Africa

Hä'gėn *City* cen. West Germany; industry

Hä'gêrs-town *City* N Md., U.S.; pop. 35,-862; factories

Hague, The (häg) *City* SW Netherlands; site of International court

Haï'fä *City* * of *District* NW Israel; imp. port

Haï'lär' *River* 240 m. Manchuria [China

Haï'nän' *Island* off SE

Hai'phong' (fông') *Port* N Vietnam

Häi'ti, Republic of *Country,* W Indies; 10,710 sq. m.; pop. 5,059,000; 20 prefectures; *Main cities:* * Port-au-Prince, Cap Haïtien, Gonaives, Port de Paix, Les Cayes, Jérémie; *Main rivers:* Artibonite, Guayamouc; *Geog.:*

⅔ of country mts.; *Climate:* semiarid because mts. prevent moist trade winds from reaching Haiti.

Flag: black — red halved vertically, white rectangular panel with coat of arms in center.

Ethnic comp.: African, mulatto, some European — Levantine; *Language:* French (official), Creole; *Religion:* Roman Catholic (state).

Products: coffee, sisal, sugar, rum, essential oils, bananas, cocoa, cotton, bauxite, copper, textiles; *Minerals:* bauxite, copper, gold, silver, antimony, tin, sulphur, coal, nickel, gypsum; *Major exports:* softballs, baseballs, sisal, shellfish, fruits, handicrafts, bauxite, coffee, sugar, essential oils; *Major imports:* vehicles, petroleum, machinery, electrical equipment, wheat, fish, fats — oils, paper, cotton fabrics, raw materials, foodstuffs; *Industries:* tourism, coffee processing, sugarcane, sisal — edible oils, manufacture of textiles, soup, cement; transformation industries, mining.

Currency: gourde.

Head of Government: President; *Legislature:* unicameral legislative Chamber; *Judiciary:* highest court is Court of Cassation. Judges appointed by President

for 10 year term — may rule on constitutionality of laws, actions of lower courts.

Hä-kä-tä Bay *Inlet* of S. of Japan; Fukuoka harbor

Hä-ko-dä-te *City* Hokkaido, Japan; port

Häl'bêr-städt *City* W cen. East Germany; manufacturing

Hä-le-ä-kä-la' *Mountain* and crater, Hawaii, U.S.

Ha'leb See ALEPPO

Hal'i-fax 1. **Bay** *inlet* of Pacific O., E Australia. 2. *City* * of Nova Scotia, E Canada; harbor, factories. 3. *County borough* N England

Häl'lè *City* S cen. East Germany; trade, industry

Hal-mà-he'rà *Island,* largest of the Moluccas, Indonesia

Halm'städ *City* SW Sweden; port

Hal'sing-bôrg (hel') *City* SW Sweden; port

Ha'ma *City* W Syria

Ha-mad', El W part of Syrian Desert

Ham'à-dan *City* * of *Province* W Iran; commerce

Hä-mä-mä-tsu (tsoo) *City* Honshu, Japan; industry

Häm-bôrn' now part of DUISBURG - HAMBORN

Häm'bûrg *City* * of *State* NW West Germany; imp. port

Ham'dèn *Town* S Conn., U.S.; pop. 49,357

Hä'mèln, **Ham'è-lin** *City* cen. West Germany; factories

Häm-hung (hoong) = KANKO

Ham'il-tön 1. *City* * of Bermuda Is. on Bermuda I. 2. *City* SW Ohio, U.S.; pop. 67,865; industry. 3. *City* SE Ontario, Canada; transportation cen. 4. *River* 600 m. Labrador, Canada. 5. *Burgh* S cen. Scotland; coal, iron

Hämm *City* N cen.

West Germany; machinery

Ham'mönd *City* NW Ind., U.S.; pop. 107,790; industry

Hamp'shîre, officially **South-amp'tön** *County* S England

Hamp'stead (sted) *Borough* London, England

Hamp'tön 1. *City* SE Va., U.S.; pop. 120,779; fisheries. 2. **Bay** *Inlet* of Atlantic O., E Long I. N.Y., U.S.

Hamp'tön Rōads *Channel,* Port Va., U.S.

Hän *River* 900 m. E cen. China

Hang'chow *City* on Bay E China; port, silks

Han'kow *City* E cen. China, now part of Wuhan; port

Hän-nō'vêr *City* NE West Germany; commerce, industry

Hä-noi' *City* * of North Vietnam; pop. 1,000,000

Han'ō-vêr Island *Island* off SW Chile

Hän'yäng' *City* E cen. China, now part of Wuhan

Hà'rà-muk (mook) *Peak* 16,015 ft. Kashmir [coffee trade

Hä'ràr *City* E Ethiopia;

Här'bin or **Pin'kiang'** (bin'ji-äng') *City* cen. Manchuria; trade

Här'bûrg - Wil'helms-bûrg (vil') *City* NE West Germany now part of Hamburg

Här-däng'êr **Fjord** (fyôrd) *Inlet* SW Norway

Hàr'dwär *Town* N India; pilgrimage site

Hä'ri, was **Djäm'bi** *River* 450 m. Sumatra

Hä'ri Rūd' *River* 650 m. Afghanistan-Turkmen S.S.R.

Här'lèm 1. *District* of Manhattan borough, N.Y. City, U.S. 2. *River channel* bet. Hudson and East Rivers, N.Y., U.S.

Här'pêrs Fer'rẏ *Town* NE W.Va., U.S.; J. Brown's raid 1859

Har-ri-can'äw *River* 250 m. Quebec, Canada

Har'ris-bûrg *City* * of Pa., U.S.; pop. 68,061; rail, manufacturing cen.

Har'ro-gāte *Municipal borough* N England; resort

Har'rōw *Urban district* London, England; boys' school

Härt'förd *City* * of Conn., U.S.; pop. 158,017; insurance

Här'vàrd, Mount *Peak* 14,400 ft. Colo., U.S.

Härz (härtz) *Mountains* W cen. West Germany; mines

Häs'tings *County borough* S England; battle 1066.

Hä'ti-à *Island group* in Ganges R. E Pakistan

Hat'têr-às, Cape *Cape* E N.C., U.S.

Hat'ties-bûrg *City* SE Miss., U.S.; pop. 38,277; diversified manufacturing

Haute- (ōt) *Departments,* France: **Haute-Ga-rônne',** S; **Haute-Loire'** (lwär'), S cen.; **Haute-Marne',** NE; **Hautes-Alpes'** (ōt-zalp'), SE; **Haute-Saône',** E; **Haute-Sa-voie'** (vwa'), E; **Hautes - Py-re-nees'** (ōt-pē-rā-nā') SW; **Haute-Vienne',** W cen.; **Haut-Rhin'** (ō-ran'), NE

Hà-van'à *City* * of Cuba, NW part; pop. ab. 1,000,000; sugar tobacco, port

Ha'vêr-hill (il) *City* NE Mass., U.S.; pop. 46,120; shoes

Hä'vrè = LE HAVRE

Hà-waï'i *Island (County)* largest of *Chain*

Hà-waï'i (wī'ē) *State,* named for Hawaiki, legendary homeland of Polynesians; 6,424 sq. m.; *pop.:* 769,913 (*rank:* 40th); Pacific Ocean; *Boundary:* Pacific Ocean; *Major cities:* * Honolulu, Hilo; 132 islands, 4 counties.

Nickname: Aloha State; *Motto:* "Ua mau ke ea o ka aina i ka pono" (The life of

the land is perpetuated in righteousness); *Flag:* 8 alternating white, red, blue bars, representing main islands of state, Union Jack in upper left; *Flower:* red hibiscus; *Bird:* Nene or Hawaiian goose; *Tree:* Kukui or candlenut; *Song:* Hawaii Ponoi, (*Hawaii's Own*) (unofficial).

Industry: sugar, pineapples, lumber, fabricating metals, glass, tourism, food, printing, publishing; *Natural resources:* bauxite deposits — undeveloped; *Major source of income:* government.

Admitted to Union: 1959 (50th state).

Places of interest: Waikiki, Diamond Head, Hawaiian Volcanoes Ntl. Park, Na Pali Wilderness Area.

Hä'wàsh *River* 500 m. E Ethiopia

Hăwkes'bûr-ỳ *River* 340 m. SE Australia

Hăw'thôrne *City* S Cal., U.S.; pop. 53,-304; manufacturing, residential

Hāy *River* 320 m. NW Canada

Hāyes *River* 300 m. W cen. Canada

Hāyes, Mount *Peak* 13,740 ft. E Alas., U.S.

Hāyes and Här'ling-tön *Urban District*, London, SE England

Hāy'wàrd *City* W Calif. U.S.; pop. 93,058

Ha-zär', Kuh'i (kōō'hi) *Peak* 14,500 ft. SE Iran [Pakistan

Hà-zä'rà *Area* NW

Heard Island (hêrd) *Island* (Brit.) S Indian O.

Heart (härt) *River* 200 m. N.D., U.S.

Heb'ri-dēs 1. *Islands* (**Outer** and **Inner**) Atlantic O., W Scotland. 2. **Sea** or **Gulf** Body of water off NW Scotland

Hec'à-tē Strait *Channel* bet. W Canada and Queen Charlotte Is.

Heer'lèn (här') *Commune* SE Netherlands; industrial cen.

Heï'dèl-bêrg *City* SW West Germany

Heï'dèn-heïm *City* S West Germany

Hei-jō (hä) see PYONG-YANG

Heil-bronn' (hīl) *City* S West Germany

He-jaz' *Kingdom*, W Saudi Arabia; * Mecca

Hel'è-nà *City* * of Mont., U.S.; pop. 22,730

Hel'gō-land, Hel'-i-gō-land *Island* North S. W Germany

Hē-li-op'ō-lis Anc. holy city, Lower Egypt

Hel'lès-pont see DARDANELLES

Hell Gāte Narrow part of East R., New York City, U.S.

Hel'mànd *River* 650 m. SW Afghanistan

Hel-sing-ör', El'si-nōre *City* E Denmark; port; scene of Hamlet

Hel'sin-ki *City* * of Finland; pop. 534,-000

Hel-vē'tia (shà) Lat. for SWITZERLAND

Hemp'stead (sted) *Village* SE N.Y., U.S.; pop. 39,411; business, residential, ed. cen.

Hen'dön *Urban district* SE England; textiles

Heng'è-lō *Commune* E Netherlands

Hen-zà-dä' *Town* * of *District* Lower Burma; rice, tobacco cen.

He-rät' *City* of *Province* NW Afghanistan; palaces

Her'è-förd-shïre *County* W England

Her'förd *City* N cen. West Germany; manufacturing

Her'nè *City* W West Germany; coal, factories

Hert'förd-shïre *County* SE England; farms

Her'tō - gèn - bôsch, Bois-lê-Duc' (bwä) *Commune* S Netherlands

Hêr'vey Bay (vi) *Inlet*

of Pacific O., E Australia

Hêr-zè-gō-vi'nà (vē') *Region* NW Balkan Penin.; now part of BOSNIA and HERZEGOVINA

Hesse 1. *State* SW West Germany; * Wiesbaden. 2. *State* (former) SW Germany; * Darmstadt

Hes'tön and I'sle-wörth (z'l) *Municipal borough* SE England

Hī-à-lē'àh *City* SE Fla. U.S.; pop. 102,297

Hī-bêr'ni-à Lat. = IRELAND

Hi-dal'gō *State* cen. Mexico

Hier'rô (yer') *Island* W Canary Is.

High'lànd Pärk (hī') *City* SE Mich., U.S.; pop. 35,444; cars

High'lànds (hī') *Area* N of Grampians, Scotland

High Point (hī') *City* N cen. N.C., U.S.; pop. 63,204; furniture

Hi-kō-ne (hē) *Town* Honshu, Japan

Hil'dès-heïm (hīm) *City* NE West Germany; manufacturing

Hīl'là *Town* and *Province* cen. Iraq

Hi'lō (hē') *City* on *Bay* E Hawaii I.; harbor

Hil'vêr-sum *Commune* W Netherlands

Hi-mä'chàl Prà-desh' (däsh') *Territory* of India, NW India; * Simla

Hi - mà - lā'yàs, The *Mountain system* S Asia, 1500 m.; highest peak Mt. Everest

Hi-me-ji *City* Honshu, Japan; industrial cen.

Hin'dèn-bûrg *City* formerly Germ. now Polish = ZABRZE

Hin'dū Kush' (koosh') *Mountain range* cen. Asia

Hin-du-stan' = "place of the Hindus"-INDIA

Hin'nöm *Valley* nr. anc. Jerusalem = GEHENNA (Gk.)

Hi-rä-tsu-kà *City* Honshu, Japan

Hi-ro-sä-kà *City* Hon-

shu, Japan; silk, fruit, lacquer

Hi-rō-shi'mà (shē') *City* * of *Prefecture* Honshu, Japan; target of first atomic bomb used in warfare, Aug. 1945

His-pàn-iō'là *Island* cen. West Indies inc. Haiti and Dominican Rep.

Hi-tä-chi *City* Honshu, Japan; industrial cen.

Hi'và O'à (hē') *Island* Fr. Oceania; Gaugin's burial place

Hjor'ring (yûr') *City* and *County* Jutland, Denmark; shipping

Hō'bärt *City* * of Tasmania, Australia; harbor, factories

Hō-bō'kèn *City* NE N.J., U.S.; pop. 45,-380; rail cen., port, factories

Hō-dei'dà (dā') *City* Yemen; industrial port

Hōd'me-zō-vä'sär-hely (shär-hä) *City* SE Hungary

Hōf *City* E West Germany; factories

Hö'fei' (fä'), formerly **Lū'chow'** (jō') *City* E China

Ho-füf' *Oasis* and *Town* S Saudi-Arabia

Hō-hèn-zôl'lêrn *Province*, *Hist. region* S Germany

Hö'kiäng' (ji - äng') *Province* Manchuria NE China

Hok-kai'dō *Island* and *Prefecture* N Japan; fish, timber, coal

Hol'lànd = NETHERLANDS

Hol-lan'di-à *Division* and *Town* NE Irian, New Guinea, Indonesia

Hol'lỳ-wood 1. *City* SE Fla., U.S.; pop. 106,-873; resorts. 2. *District* Los Angeles, Calif., U.S.; movie industry

Hōl'steïn *Region* N West Germany

Hōl'yöke *City* SW Mass., U.S.; pop. 50,-112; fine papers

Hō'lỳ Rō'màn Em'pīre *Empire* cen. Eur. 800-1800

Hom′bûrg or **Bäd Hom′bûrg** *City* cen. West Germany; resort

Hôms *City* W Syria; silks

Hō′nän′ *Province* E cen. China; agriculture, coal, cotton, silk

Hon-dū′rås, Republic of *Country,* C America, 43,280 sq. m.; pop. 2,900,000; 18 departments; *Main cities:* * Tegucigalpa, San Pedro, Sula, La Ceiba, Puerto Cortes; *Main rivers:* Guayapo, Patuca, Aguan, Uluá; *Geog.:* 2 major mt. ranges bisect Honduras NW–SE with tropical lowlands along coastal areas; fertile valleys, plateaus lie between mt. branches; *Climate:* temperate in interior to tropical in lowlands.

Flag: 2 blue horizontal bands separated by white stripe holding cluster of 5 blue stars.

Ethnic comp.: Mestizo, Indian, Negro, European; *Language:* Spanish (official), English; *Religion:* Roman Catholic.

Products: bananas, coffee, timber, cattle, tobacco, beans, maize, rice, fish, silver, gold, lead, zinc, iron ore; *Minerals:* coal, bauxite, iron ore, lignite; *Major exports:* bananas, coffee, lumber, silver, meat, cotton, tobacco; *Major imports:* petroleum products, consumer durables, transportation equip-

ment, machinery, chemicals, fertilizer; *Industries:* food processing, oil refining, forestry, mining, meat packing.

Currency: lempira.

Head of Government: President; *Legislature:* unicameral Congress; *Judiciary:* Supreme Court of Justice, Courts of Appeal, other courts established by law. Supreme Court divided into 3 chambers covering criminal matters, civil matters, labor — administrative appeals.

Hon-dū′ras, Brit. see BRIT. HONDURAS

Hong′ Kong *Colony* (Brit.) SE China; 390 sq. m.; pop. 3,927,-000; * Victoria; commercial cen.

Hō-ni-ä′rå *Town* Guadalcanal, * of Brit. Solomon Is.

Hon-ō-lū′lū *City* Oahu I. Hawaii, U.S.; * of Hawaii; pop. 324,-871; imp. port

Hon′shū or **Hon′dō** *Island* largest, considered mainland of Japan

Hōōgh′lÿ *Channel,* most imp. of Ganges R. NE India

Hook′êr Island *Island* Arctic O., U.S.S.R.; meteorological station

Hōō′vêr, Bōul′dêr Dam *Dam* of Colorado R., Nev. and Ariz., U.S.

Hōpe, Point *Cape* NW Alas., U.S.; whaling

Hō′peh′, Hō′pei′ (pä′) *Province* NE China; coal, trade

Hōpe′town *Town* S Rep. of South Africa; diamonds

Hôrn, Cape *Cape* S tip of South America on **Hôrn I.**

Hôrn′chûrch *Urban district* SE England

Hor′sėns *City* Jutland Denmark; dairy port

Hôrse′shoe Fall (shōō) see N I A G A R A FALLS

Hôs-pi-tä-lėt′ *City* NE

Spain; textiles

Hô-tin′ (tēn′) 1. *Former department* Romania. 2. *Town.* = KHOTIN

Hot Springs *City* W cen. Ark., U.S.; pop. 35,631; resort

Hoūs′tön *City* SE Tex., U.S.; pop. 1,232,802 port, petroleum products

Hōve *Municipal borough* S England

Howe, Cape SE tip of Australia

How′lånd Island *Island* of U.S. cen. Pacific O. nr. equator

How′råh *City* NE India; rail, industrial cen.　[CHIKU

Hsin-chu = SHIN-

Hsing′än′ *Region, Province* NW Manchuria

Hsin′king′ (jing′) = CHANGCHUN

Hual-cän′ *Peak* 21,000 ft. W Hawaii I., U.S.

Huäl-lä′gä (wä-yä′) *River* 700 m. N and W Peru

Huäl-lä-ti′ri (wä-yä-tē′) *Peak* 19,800 ft. Bolivia-Chile

Huäs - cä - rän′ (wäs) *Peak* 22,200 ft. W Peru

Hub′bård, Mount *Peak* 14,950 ft. Alas. U.S.-Yukon Canada

Hub′li (hoob′) *Town* W India; rail cen.

Hud′dêrs-fiêld *County borough* N England; woolens, iron

Hud′sön *River* 306 m. E N.Y., U.S.

Hud′sön Bay *Inland sea* 850 m. x 600 m. E NW Terrs. Canada; joined to Atlantic O. by **Hud′sön Strait**

Hue′ (hū-ā′) *City* N South Vietnam; rice

Hue - hue - tė - nän′gō (wā-wä) *Town, Department* W Guatemala; mining

Huel′vä *Commune* * of *Province* SW Spain; mines, fisheries

Hues′cä (wäs′) *Commune* * of *Province* NE Spain; factories

Hui′lä (wē′) *Volcano* 18,700 ft. W cen. Colombia

Hū′kow *Town* SE [China

Hull 1. *City, County* SW Quebec Canada; commerce. 2. *County borough* N England; imp. port

Hum′bêr *Estuary* E England

Hum′böldt 1. *River* 290 m. N Nev., U.S. 2. *Bay* Pacific O. inlet NW Calif., U.S. 3. *Peak* 14,000 ft. S cen. Colo., U.S.

Hump, the *Air route* India-China, E Himalayas

Hun (hoon) 1. *River* 300 m. NE China. 2. *River* 240 m. S Manchuria

Hū′nän′ *Province* SE cen. China

Hun′gå-rÿ, Hungarian People's Republic *Country,* EC Europe; 35,900 sq. m.; pop. 10,345,000; 19 counties; *Main cities:* * Budapest, Miskolc, Debrecen, Pecs; *Main rivers:* Danube, Tisza, Drava, Rába; *Geog.:* most a flat plain with exception of low mt. ranges in NC–NE and S of Lake Balaton in W; *Climate:* well balanced. Jan. — 31°F, July — 71°F. Annual precipitation 25″.

Flag: red, white, green bands from top — bottom.

Ethnic comp.: Hungarians or Magyars, other Europeans, (Germans, Slovaks, Croats, etc.); *Language:* Hungarian; *Religions:* Roman Catholic, Protestant, Eastern Orthodox Jewish.

Major exports: transport equipment, medicine, machinery, shoes; *Major imports:* crude oil, raw cotton, cars, trucks, rolled steel; *Industries:* mining, chemical refining, metallurgy, food processing.

Currency: pound.

Head of Government: Presidential Council; *Legislature:* unicameral National Assembly; *Judiciary:* highest court is Supreme Court responsible to National Assembly. No trial by jury.

Hung-nam *Town* E North Korea

Hung'shui' (shwā') *River* 700 m. S China

Hun'têr *River* 300 m. SE Australia

Hun'ting - dön - shire *County* E cen. England

Hun'ting-tön *City* W W.Va., U.S. pop. 74,-315; tobacco, apples, coal, gas

Hun'ting-tön Beach *City* SW Cal., U.S.; pop. 115,960

Hunts'ville *City* N Ala., U.S.; pop. 137,802; factories, natural gas

Hū'on Gulf *Inlet* of Solomon S. New Guinea

Hū'peh' (pā') *Province* E cen. China

Hū'ron, Lake *Lake* of The Great Lakes, NE cen. U.S.

Hûrst'ville *City* SE Australia

Hutch'in-sön *City* cen. Kans., U.S.; pop. 36,885; grain, salt, oil

Huy'tön with Rō'bẏ (hī') *Urban district* NW England

Hwaī *River* 350 m. E China　　　[China

Hwaī'ning' *City* E

Hwäng' Haī', Yellow Sea *Sea* bet. China and Korea

Hwäng' Hō', Yel'lōw River *River* 2700 m. N cen. and E China

Hwei (hwā) *River* 200 m. N China

Hȳ-an'nis Pôrt *Town* S Mass., U.S.; sum-

mer resort

Hȳde Pärk 1. *Village* SE N.Y., U.S.; birthplace of F. D. Roosevelt. 2. *Park* London, England

Hȳ'dêr-à-bad 1. *City* (and former state) S cen. India; factories. 2. *City* SW Pakistan; rail cen., handicrafts

Hyō-gō *Prefecture* Honshu, Japan

I

I'ao (ē'ou) *Canyon* Maui I. Haw., U.S.

Iä'si *City* NE Romania, early *　　　[geria

I-bä'dän *City* W Ni-

I-ba-que' (ē-vä-gä') *City* W cen. Colombia

I-bä-rä-ke *Prefecture* Honshu, Japan

Ī-bē'ri-à 1. *Anc. region,* now Soviet Rep. of GEORGIA. 2. *Peninsula* SW Europe incl. Spain and Portugal

I-bi-cui' (ē-vē-kwē') *River* 400 m. S Brazil

I-cel' (ē-chel') *City* * of *Vilayet* S Turkey

Īce'länd, Republic of *Country,* N Atlantic; 39,760 sq. m.; pop. 211,400; 18 counties or provinces, 10 boroughs; *Main cities:* * Reykjavík, Kopavogur, Akvreyri, Hafnarfjordur, Akranes; *Main rivers:* Thjórsá, Skjalfandafljót, Jökulsa; *Geog.:* volcanic origin. 75% consists of glaciers, lakes, mountainous lava desert, other wasteland, rest cultivated or used for grazing land; *Climate:* moderating influence of Gulf Stream, damp cool summers, mild, windy winters.

Flag: red cross edged in white on blue field.

Ethnic comp.: Icelanders, Danes, Americans, Germans, Norwēgians; *Language:* Icelandic (Old Norse) (official); *Religion:* Evangelical Lutheran Church (state).

Products: fish, fish oils, whales, mutton, wood, sheepskin, hay, seaweed, aluminum, diatomite, fertilizers, cement, scrap metals; *Minerals:* few minerals but great source of hydroelectric power; *Major exports:* fish, fish products, aluminum ingots, agricultural products; *Major imports:* ships and food grains, machinery, textiles, petroleum products, metals, metal products; *Industries:* fishing — fish processing, manufacture of electric motors, fertilizer.

Currency: knonur.

Head of Government: President; *Legislature:* bicameral Parliament (Althing); *Judiciary:* Supreme Court, District Courts, special courts. Constitution protects judiciary from infringement by other 2 branches of gov.

I'chäng (ē') *City* E cen. China

I-chi-nö-mi-yä *Town* Honshu, Japan

Ī'dà 1. *Mountain* NW Asia Minor, site of anc. Troy. 2. *Mountain,* highest in Crete

Ī'dà-hō *State,* named from Shoshoni Indian word meaning "sunup;" 83,557 sq. m.; pop.: 713,008 (*rank:* 42nd); W. U.S.; *Boundaries:* Washington, Montana, Wyoming, Utah, Nevada, Oregon, Canada; *Major city:* * Boise; *Major rivers:* Salmon, Snake, Clearwater; *Major*

lakes: Coeur d'Alene, Pend Oreille, Priest; 44 counties.

Nickname: Gem State; *Motto:* "Esto perpetua" (May you exist forever); *Flag:* state seal centered on a blue field; *Flower:* syringa; *Bird:* mountain bluebird; *Tree:* western white pine; *Song: Here We Have Idaho.*

Industry: chemicals, printing, publishing, stone, clay & glass items, lumbering, agriculture; *Natural resources:* forests, silver, lead, zinc, phosphate; *Major source of income:* manufacturing, agriculture.

Admitted to Union: 1890 (43rd state).

Places of interest: Sun Valley, Idaho primitive area; Selway-Bitterroot Wilderness, Hell's Canyon.

I'dà-hō Fălls *City* E Ida., U.S.; pop. 35,-776; business

I'dle-wīld (d'l) former name of John F. Kennedy International Airport N.Y., U.S.

I'dèn-bûrg (ē') *Peak* 15,748 ft. New Guinea

Ie'pêr (yä') = YPRES

I-guäs-sū' *River* 380 m. S Brazil

Ijs'sèl (ī') *River* E Netherlands to **Ijs'-sèl-meer** (mär), former Zuider Zee

Ī-kar'i-à *Island* of Aegean Is.

I-ki *Island* NW Kyushu, Japan

I'län' (ē') *Town* E Manchuria; port, furs

Ile'-dê-Fränce (ēl') 1. *Historical Region* N cen. France. 2. = MAURITIUS

Ile' dê la Ci-te' (sē-tā') *Island* Seine R., Paris, France; Cathedral of Notre Dame

I-lek' (lyek') *River* 300 m. E U.S.S.R., Eur.

Il'förd *Municipal borough* SE England;

paper [W China
I'li' (ē'lē') *River* 800 m.
I-li-ni'zä (ē-lē-nē') *Peak*
17,390 ft. Ecuador
Il-lam'pū (ē-yäm') *Peak*
of Mt. Sorata, W Bo-
livia; 21,276 ft.
Ille-et-Vi-laine' (ēl-ā-
vē-len') *Department*
NW France
Il-li-mä'ni (ē-yē) *Peak*
21,180 ft. W Bolivia
Il-li-nois' (noi') *State*,
named from Indian
word and French suf-
fix meaning "tribe of
superior men;" 56,-
400 sq. m.; *pop.:*
11,113,976 (*rank:*
5th); Mid-W U.S.;
Boundaries: Wiscon-
sin, Iowa, Missouri,
Kentucky, Indiana,
Lake Michigan; *Ma-
jor cities:* Chicago,
Rockford, Peoria,
* Springfield; *Major
rivers:* Mississippi,
Ohio, Wabash, Illi-
nois, Rock, Kaskas-
kia; *Major lakes:*
Crab Orchard Lake;
113 counties.

Nickname: Prairie
State, Land of Lin-
coln; *Motto:* "State
Sovereignty, Nation-
al Union;" *Flag:*
adaptation of state
seal centered on
white field; *Flower:*
violet; *Bird:* cardi-
nal; *Tree:* oak; *Song:*
Illinois.

Industry: fabricated
metal products,
printing & publish-
ing, agricultural &
electrical machinery,
meat packing; *Natu-
ral resources:* coal,
petroleum, fluorspar,
sand & gravel, forest;
*Major source of in-
come:* manufacturing.

Admitted to Union:
1818 (21st state).

Places of interest: Lin-
coln Log Cabin State
Park, New Salem
State Park, Illinois
Beach.

Il-lyr'i-à *Anc. country*
E Adriatic coast
Il'mėn *Lake* 300-700
sq. m. NW U.S.S.R.
I-lō'cos Nôr'te (tâ),

I-lō'cos Sūr *Prov-
inces* Luzon, Phil. Is.
I-lō-i'lō (ē') *City* * of
Province Panay I.
Phil. Is.; commerce
I-lō-rin' (rēn') *Town* *
of *Province* W Nigeria
I-mä-bä-ri *Town* Shi-
koku, Japan; port
I - man'drà *L a k e*
U.S.S.R., Eur.
Im-bä-bū'rä *Volcano*
15,028 ft. N Ecuador
Im-pe'riä (pâ') *Prov-
ince* and *Port* NW
Italy
Imp'hàl *City* NE India
In'cà, Pä'sō del *Pass*
15,620 ft. Argentina-
Chile
In-cä-huä'si *Peak* 21,-
720 ft. NW Argentina
In'chon' or **Jin-sin** *City*
Seoul's port, South
Korea [Sweden
In'däl *River* 260 m. N
In-dē-pen'dènce 1. *City*
W Mo., U.S.; pop.
111,662; Harry S Tru-
man library. 2. *Fjord*
N Greenland
In-dė-ra-gi'ri *District*
and *River* 225 m.
Sumatra, Indonesia
In'di-à, Republic of
Country, SC Asia;
1,261,820 sq. m.; pop.
573,380,000; 18
states, 9 union terri-
tories; *Main cities:*
* New Delhi, Bom-
bay, Calcutta, Mad-
ras, Ahmedabad, Hy-
derabad, Bangalore,
Kanpur, Nagpur,
Poona; *Main rivers:*

Ganges, Brahmapu-
tra, Godavari, Krish-
na; *Geog.:* 3 regions
— Himalaya Mts.,
Gangetic plain —
well watered, fertile,
peninsula; *Climate:*
tropical in S, tem-
perate in N.

Flag: horizontal
bands of saffron,
white, green, with
blue spoked wheel in
center of white stripe.

Ethnic comp.: Indo-
Aryans, Aryo-Dra-
vidians, Scytho-Dra-
vidians, Dravidians,
Mongolo-Dravidians;
Language: Hindi,
English (official), Ori-
ya, Punjabi, Tamil,
Kashmiri, Malaya-
lam, Telegu, Assa-
mese, Bengali, Gu-
jarari, Kannada,
Marathe, Urdu; *Reli-
gions:* Hindu, Mos-
lem, Christian, Sikh,
Jain, others,

Products: rice, wheat,
dal (pulses), tea, cot-
ton, jute, jowar,
maize, bajra, oil
seeds, sugar, ground-
nuts, fruit, timber,
tobacco, coal, iron
ore, manganese, gyp-
sum, bauxite, cotton
textiles, iron, steel,
machinery, transport
equipment, jute tex-
tiles, chemicals, pa-
per, rubber; *Miner-
als:* coal, iron, mica,

manganese, alumin-
ium, limite, oil, gyp-
sum, bauxite; *Major
exports:* tea, jute tex-
tiles, cotton textiles,
iron ore, iron, steel,
leather, fruit, nuts,
tobacco, sugar; *Ma-
jor imports:* wheat,
other foodstuffs, raw
cotton, chemicals,
electricals, transport
equipment, machin-
ery, rice, copper; *In-
dustries:* mining,
manufacture of iron,
steel, textiles, chem-
icals, cement, indus-
trial machinery,
equipment, agricul-
ture.

Currency: rupee.

Head of Government:
President; *Legisla-
ture:* union parlia-
ment — Council of
States, Lok Jabha
(People's Council);
Judiciary: independ-
ent judicial system
resembling that of
Anglo-Saxon coun-
tries, Supreme Court
at apex.

In-di-an'à *State,* name
means "land of In-
dians;" 36,291 sq.
m.; *pop.:* 5,193,669
(*rank:* 11th); Mid-W
U.S.; *Boundaries:*
Michigan, Ohio, Ken-
tucky, Missouri,
Iowa, Lake Michi-
gan; *Major cities:* *
Indianapolis, Gary,
Hammond, Fort
Wayne; *Major rivers:*
Wabash, Maumee,
St. Joseph, Kanka-
kee; *Major lakes:*
Monroe Reservoir,
Mississippi Reser-
voir; 93 counties.

Nickname: Hoosier
State; *Motto:* "The
cross-roads of Ameri-
ca;" *Flag:* gold torch,
19 stars on blue field;
Flower: peony; *Bird:*
cardinal; *Tree:* tulip
tree; *Song: On the
Banks of the Wabash.*

Industry: basic steel,
machinery, chemi-
cals, primary metals,
motor vehicles, pe-
troleum products;
Natural resources:

coal, petroleum, building stone, limestone, clay; *Major source of income:* manufacturing.

Admitted to Union: 1816 (19th state).

Places of interest: Indiana Dunes State Park, Brown County State Park, Wyandotte Cave.

In-di-ȧn-ap′ö-lis *City* * of Ind., U.S.; pop. 744,624

In′di-ȧn or **Thär Desert** *Region* NW India; 100,000 sq. m.

In′di-ȧn Em′pīre parts of India penin. under Brit. rule until 1947

In′di-ȧn Ocean *Ocean* surr. by Africa, Asia, Australia, Antarctica; ab. 28,375,000 sq. m.

In′di-ȧn River *Inlet* of Atlantic O. E Fla., U.S.

In′di-ȧn States *Areas* ruled by natives or Brit. India, now within Rep. of INDIA

In-di-gir′kȧ *River* 850 m. U.S.S.R., Asia

In-dō-chǐ′nȧ *Peninsula* SE Asia, incl. Burma, Thailand, Laos, Cambodia, Vietnam, parts of Malaysia

In-dō-nē′sia (zhȧ), Republic of *Country,* SE Asia; 575,450 sq. m.; pop. 118,609,000; 26 provinces subdivided into 281 regencies; *Main cities:* * Djakarta, Palembang, Medan, Macassar, Surabaya, Bandung; *Main rivers:* Kapuas, Digul, Barito, Mahakam, Kajan, Hari; *Geog.:* large islands, C mt. range rising from fairly extensive

lowlands, coastal plains. Many islands have volcanoes active & dormant; *Climate:* tropical. Upland areas on main island provide temp. contrast to constant heat of lowlands.

Flag: horizontal bands — red at top, white at bottom.

Ethnic comp.: Java, Sumatra, Sulawesi, Bali, Lombok, Borneo, Moluccas, Chinese; *Language:* Bahasa Indonesia (official), English; *Religions:* Moslem, Christian.

Products: rubber, rice, maize, copra, palm products, sugar, tobacco, tea, coffee, vegetables, meat, dairy produce, oil, tin, bauxite, coal, textiles, paper, glass, cement; *Minerals:* tin, rubber, oil, bauxite, nickel, copper, low grade coal, manganese; *Major exports:* oil, rubber, petroleum products, tin ore, copra, coffee, tobacco; *Major imports:* textiles, machinery, transportation equipment, rice, fertilizer, chemicals; *Industries:* mining, oil refining, hydroelectric plants, shipbuilding, light manufacturing for domestic market, food processing.

Currency: rupiah.

Head of Government: President; *Legislature:* Parliament, People's Consultative Assembly; *Judiciary:* Supreme Court at apex.

In-dōre′ *City* cen. India, * of former *State;* cotton [m. S India

In-drä′vȧ-ti *River* 330

In′drė (an′) *Department* cen. France

In′drė - et - Loire′ (an′-drä-lwar′) *Department* NW cen. France

In′dus *River* W Paki-

stan; 1700-1900 m.

In′gle-wood (g′l) *City* SW Calif., U.S.; pop. 89,985; chinchilla, planes

In′go-dȧ *River* 360 m. U.S.S.R., Asia

In′göl-städt *City* SE West Germany

In-gu-lets′ (lyets′) *River* 300 m. Ukraine U.S.S.R.

In-hȧm-ba′nė *Port* on *Bay* SE Mozambique

In-ish-mōre′ *Island* Galway Bay, W Ireland

Ink′stêr *City* SE Mich., U.S.; pop. 38,595

In′lȧnd Sea *Waterway* Honshu-Shikoku-Kyushu, Japan

In′lȧnd Wȧ′têr-wāy *System* of rivers, bays and canals: 1. U.S. Atlantic coast, Mass.-Fla.; U.S. 2. Gulf coast Fla.-Tex. U.S.

Inn *River* 320 m. Switzerland, Austria, Germany

In′nes-fāil = poetic IRELAND

Inns′bruck (brook) *City* W Austria

I-nö-nu′ *Village* NW Turkey Asia

In′têr-lä-kėn *Commune* SE Switzerland

International Dȧte Line see DATE LINE

In-vêr-ness′ *Burgh* * of -shire, *County* NW Scotland

Iô-än′ni-nä (yô) *City* * of *Department* NW Greece

Ī-ō′ni-ȧ *Anc. district* W Asia Minor

Ī-ō′ni-ȧn Islands *Island group* in **Ī-ō′ni-ȧn Sea** bet. Italy and Greece; bel. to Greece

Iô′niô *Province* SE Italy

Ī′ō-wȧ *State,* named probably from an Indian word meaning "this is the place" or from Ioways meaning "sleepy ones;" 56,290 sq. m.; *pop.:* 2,825,041 (*rank:* 25th); Mid-W U.S.; *Boundaries:* Minnesota, Wisconsin, Illinois, Missouri, Nebraska, South Dakota, North Dakota, Canada; *Major cities:*

* Des Moines, Cedar Rapids, Sioux City; *Major rivers:* Mississippi, Missouri, Des Moines, Big Sioux; *Major lakes:* Spirit Lake, Clear, Storm Red Rock; 99 counties.

Nickname: Hawkeye State; *Motto:* "Our liberties we prize and our rights we will maintain;" *Flag:* vertical blue, white, red bars, flying eagle carrying state motto; *Flower:* wild rose; *Bird:* eastern goldfinch; *Tree:* oak; *Song: The Song of Iowa.*

Industry: corn, hogs, chemicals, stone, clay & glass items, agriculture, food processing, manufacture of farm equipment; *Natural resources:* cement, stone, sand, gravel, gypsum; *Major source of income:* manufacturing.

Admitted to Union: 1846 (29th state).

Place of interest: Effigy Mounds Ntl. Monument.

Ī′ō-wȧ City *City* E Iowa, U.S.; pop. 46,-850; ed. center

I′pin′ (ē′), was **Su′chow′** (jō′) *City* S cen. China; exports

I′pōh (ē′) *City* Penang, Malaysia; commerce

Ips′wich *County borough* E England; port

I-qui′que (ē-kē′kâ) *City* N Chile; nitrate

I-ran′, *Country,* SW Asia; 627,000 sq. m.; pop. 27,781,000; 14 provinces, 6 independent governorates;

Main cities: * Teheran, Isfahan, Meshed, Tabriz, Abadan, Shiraz, Ahwaz; *Main rivers:* Karun, Safid, Karkheh, Zayandeh; *Geog.:* semiarid plateau, high mt. ranges, barren desert; *Climate:* semiarid, semitropical.

Flag: horizontal bands — green, white, red from top to bottom, with sun rising over lion brandishing sword on white band.

Ethnic comp.: Persians, Turks, Baluchis, Arabs, Kurds, Lurs, Armenians, Georgians; *Language:* Persian, Farasi (official), French, English; *Religions:* Shia Moslem, Sunni Moslem, Zoroastrian, Christian, Jewish.

Products: wool, cotton, skins, silk, cereals, fruit, livestock, opium, oil, natural gas, coal, lead, iron ore, copper, zinc, petrochemicals, metallurgy, steel, motor vehicles, carpets, textiles, leather, caviar, rubber, pharmaceuticals; *Minerals:* oil, natural gas, iron, chrome, copper, lead, zinc, coal, gypsum, limestone, barite, salt; *Major exports:* oil, carpets, cotton, fruit; *Major imports:* machinery, iron, steel, chemicals, drugs; *Industries:* sugar refining, oil refining, food processing.

Currency: rial.

Head of Government: Shah; *Legislature:* bicameral Senate and Majlis; *Judiciary:* under guidance of Minister for Justice. *Courts:* civil, criminal, appeal.

Ī′ran 1. **Plateau of** *Highland* W Asia; 1,000,000 sq. m.; salt deserts. 2. **Mountains**

Sarawak-Borneo
I-rä-puä′tō *City* cen. Mexico; farming

I-raq′, Republic of *Country,* SW Asia, 169,240 sq. m.; pop. 9,529,000; 16 provinces; *Main cities:* * Baghdad, Basra, Mosul, Kirkuk; *Main rivers:* Tigris, Euphrates; *Geog.:* NE highland region, Syrian Desert, fertile lowland region; *Climate:* temperatures range from more than 120°F in July and Aug. to below freezing in Jan.

Flag: horizontal stripes, red, white, black with 3 green stars on center.

Ethnic comp.: Arabs, Kurds, Turks, Persians, Assyrians; *Language:* Arabic (official), English, Kurdish; *Religions:* Sunni Moslem, Shia Moslem, Druze.

Products: building materials, textiles, cement, cereals, dates, wool, cotton, rice, tobacco, oil, petrochemicals; *Major exports:* oil, agricultural products, livestock, cement; *Major imports:* machinery, iron, steel, cars, tea, sugar, clothing, pharmaceuticals; *Industries:* oil refining, flour milling, processing of agricultural products.

Currency: dinar.

Head of Government: President; *Legislature:* Revolutionary Command Council; *Judiciary:* based on

French. Courts: civil, religious, special (cases of national security).

I-rä-zū′ *Volcano* 11,200 ft. cen. Costa Rica

Īre′länd (or Eire) *Country,* Atlantic Ocean, on second largest of British Isles; 26,600 sq. m.; pop. 2,966,000; 32 counties; *Main cities:* * Dublin, Cork, Limerick, Dun, Laoghaire, Waterford; *Main rivers:* Shannon, Liffey, Suir, Boyne, Nore, Barrow; *Geog.:* C plateau, surrounded by isolated groups of mts. & hills, dotted with peat bogs — shallow lakes; *Climate:* relatively mild — free from extremes, average temperature 40°F winter, 60°F summer. Rain, dampness common features.

Flag: vertical bands — green, white, orange.

Ethnic comp.: Irish, Anglo-Irish; *Language:* Irish, English (official); *Religions:* Roman Catholic, Protestant, Episcopal, Presbyterian.

Products: dairy produce, tobacco, cereal, livestock, beer, whiskey, silver, metals, chemicals, sugar, chocolate, zinc, lead; *Minerals:* lead, zinc, copper, silver; *Major exports:* dairy products, metal ores, meat, livestock, textiles; *Major imports:* machinery, transportation equipment,

chemicals, grains, foodstuffs, textiles, metals, metal products, petroleum; *Industries:* metal manufacture, vehicle assembly, tourism, brewing, textile mills.

Currency: Irish pound at par with sterling.

Head of Government: President; *Legislature:* bicameral Parliament — Senate, House of Representatives (Dáil); *Judiciary:* closely resembles British.

Ir′i-ȧn *Area* W half of New Guinea, part of Indonesia; formerly **Neth. New Guinea**

I-ri-ri′ *River* 570 m. N Brazil

Ī′rish Free State *Dominion* of Brit. Commonwealth 1922-37, now REP. OF IRELAND

Ī′rish Sea *Sea* bet. England and Ireland

Ir-kutsk′ *City* * of *Region* S R.S.F.S.R., U.S.S.R., Asia; furs, minerals, factories

Ir-rȧ-wäd′dẏ *River* 1350 m. cen. Burma

Ir-tẏsh′ *River* 2200 m. U.S.S.R., cen. Asia

Îr′ving *City* NE Tex., U.S.; pop. 97,260

Îr′ving-tön *Town* NE N.J., U.S.; pop. 59,743; factories

I-sȧ-be′lȧ 1. *Cape, Port* N Dominican Rep. 2. *Province* Luzon, Phil. Is. 3. *Municipality* Negros, Phil. Is. 4. or **Al-bė-märle** *Island,* largest of Galapagos

Is′chi-ȧ (ki) *Town* on *Island* Tyrrhenian S., S Italy

I-sē *Old province* Honshu, Japan; shrines

I-sere′ (ē-zâr′) *Department* SE France

Is′fȧ-han *City* * of *Province,* former * of Persia, W cen. Iran; metalwork, brocades

I-she-kä-ri *River* 275 m. Hokkaido, Japan

I-shi-kä-wä *Prefecture* Honshu, Japan

I-shim′ *River* 1330 m. U.S.S.R., cen. Asia

I-shi-nō-mä-ki *Town* Honshu, Japan; port
Ī'sis name for upper Thames R., England
Is - ken - dè - ron' (ēs, rōōn'), **Al-ex-an-dret'tà** *City* S Turkey, Asia; port
Is'kêr *River* 249 m. cen. Bulgaria
Isle of Man, Wight, etc. see MAN, ISLE OF
Is-ma-i-li'à (lē') *Town* NE Egypt
Is-pär-tä' *Town* * of *Vilayet* SW Turkey, Asia

Is'rà-èl (iz'), State of *Country,* Middle E; 17,500 sq. m.; pop. 2,999,000; 6 districts; *Main cities:* * Jerusalem, Tel Aviv, Haifa, Ramat Gan; *Main rivers:* Jordan, Kishon; *Geog.:* 4 regions — coastal plain, C mts., Jordan Rift Valley (Lake Tiberias, Jordan River, Dead Sea), Negev Desert; *Climate:* equable in N, C mts., to very hot in Negev.

Flag: white field centered blue outline of 6-pointed star of David bordered above and below by blue horizontal stripes.

Ethnic comp.: Jews, Arabs; *Language:* Israeli (Hebrew) (official), Arabic; *Religions:* Jewish (state), Moslem, Greek Orthodox.

Products: fruit, cereals, olives, vegetables, dairy products, tobacco, cotton, potash, oil, salt, copper, phosphates, textiles, wines, polished diamonds, plastics, electricals; *Minerals:*

potash, phosphate, bromine, phosphate rock, copper, iron, ceramic clays, glass sand, gypsum; *Major exports:* diamonds, citrus fruits, textiles, clothes, food products, chemicals, fertilizers, mining products; *Major imports:* rough diamonds, machinery, transportation equipment, nonmetallic mineral manufacture, food, live animals, raw materials, chemicals; *Industries:* light industries, mining, engineering, food processing, wine making, textile mills, mining, quarrying.

Currency: Israeli pound.

Head of Government: President; *Legislature:* unicameral Knesset; *Judiciary:* secular, religious courts independent of legislature. No right of review of Knesset's acts.

Is'sỳk-Kul *Lake* Kirgiz U.S.S.R., Asia
Is-tan-bul' (bōōl'), formerly **Con-stan-ti-nō'ple,** anc. **Bỳ-zan'-ti-um** *City* * of *Vilayet,* former * of Turkey, NW Turkey, Eur.; pop. 2,000,000
Is'tri-à *Peninsula* NE Adriatic coast, formerly It. now Yugoslavian
I-tal'iàn East Africa former It. colonies: ERITREA, ETHIOPIA, SOMALIA
It'à-lỳ, Italian Republic, *Country,* S Europe; 116,280 sq. m.; pop. 54,418,000; 93 provinces; *Main cities:* * Rome, Milan, Naples, Turin, Genoa, Palermo, Bologna, Florence, Catania, Venice; *Main rivers:* Po, Tiber, Arno; *Geog.:* rugged & mountainous except for Po Valley, heel of "the boot" in S and small coastal area;

Climate: generally mild, Mediterranean with wide variations.

Flag: vertical bands — green, white, red.

Ethnic comp.: Italians, some German speaking people around Bolzano Province, Solvenes; *Language:* Italian (official), German; *Religions:* Roman Catholic, Protestant, Jewish.

Products: wine, olive oil, fruit, olives, cereals, sugar, vegetables, oil, sulphur, iron pyrites, iron ore, zinc, bauxite, cotton, silk textiles, motor vehicles, domestic appliances, machine tools, iron, steel, chemicals; *Minerals:* mercury, iron ore, lignite, pyrites, coal, sulphur; *Major exports:* wine, fruit, olives, olive oil, vegetables, fabrics, clothing, shoes, iron, steel, machinery, motor cars, plastics, petroleum products; *Major imports:* iron, steel, mechanical, electrical equipment, motor cars, oil, coal, copper, raw oils, meat, paper; *Industries:* tourism, oil refining, mining, shipping, food processing,

wine making, textile manufacturing.

Currency: lire.

Head of Government: President; *Legislature:* bicameral Parliament — Senate, Chamber of Deputies; *Judiciary:* essentially based on Roman law as modified in Napoleonic code.

I-tà-pe-cu-ru' (pā-kōō-rōō') *River* 450 m. NE Brazil
I-tà-pi-cu-ru' (pē) *River* 350 m. E Brazil
I-tas'cà, Lake *Lake* N Minn., U.S.; source of Miss. R.
Ith'à-cà 1. *City* S cen. N.Y., U.S.; pop. 26,226. 2. *Island* of Ionian Is. Greece
I-và-i' (ē') *River* 300 m. S Brazil
I-va'nö-vö *City* * of *Region* R.S.F.S'R., U.S.S.R., Eur.; heavy industry
Ī'vö-rỳ Cōast, Republic of *Country,* W Africa; 189,030 sq. m.; pop. 4,482,000; 24 departments; *Main cities:* * Abidjan, Bouaké, Gagnoa; *Main rivers:* Bandama, Sassandra, Comoé, Cavally; *Geog.:* 40% rain forest, remainder wooded, grassy savannah with NW mountainous area; *Climate:*

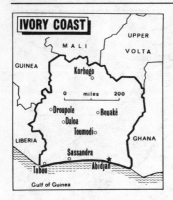

tropical climate zone.

Flag: vertical bands — orange, white, green (left to right).

Ethnic comp.: Agnis-Ashantis, Krousmen, Mandé, Baoulé; *Language:* French (official), tribal languages; *Religions:* animist, Moslem, Roman Catholic.

Products: coffee, cocoa, timber, bananas, yams, cotton, palm oil, fruit preserves, diamonds, manganese, pineapples; *Minerals:* diamonds, manganese, iron ore; *Major exports:* coffee, timber, cocoa, bananas, pineapples; *Major imports:* machinery, electrical, transportation equipment, petroleum products; *Industries:* forestry, fishing, agriculture, agricultural processing, tuna packing, truck & bus assembly, oil refining, textile, clothing manufacturing.

Currency: CFA franc.

Head of Government: President; *Legislature:* unicameral National Assembly; *Judiciary:* 4 chambers: constitutional, judicial, administrative, auditing; also High Court of Justice to try government officials for high crimes, Supreme Court at apex.

I-wä-te *Prefecture* Honshu, Japan

I'wö (ē') *City* W Nigeria

I'wö Ji'mà (ē', jē') *Island* of Volcano Is. S

---

of Tokyo, Japan; WW II battle

Ix-elles' (ek-sel') *Commune* Brussels suburb cen. Belgium

I'zhèvsk (ē') *Town* R.S.F.S.R., U.S.S.R., Eur.; steel

Iz'mä-il *City* * of *Region* Ukraine U.S.S.R.

Iz-mir', formerly **Smỳr'nà** *City* * of *Vilayet*, on *Gulf* W Turkey, Asia; imp. port

Iz-täc-ci'huätl (ēs-täk-sē') *Mountain* 16,880 ft. SE Mexico

J

Jà'bàl-pur = JUBBULPORE

Jä'bôr *Port* Jaluit I. * of Marshall Is.

Jack'sön 1. *City* * of Miss., U.S.; pop. 153,968; cotton, textiles, rail cen. 2. *City* S Mich., U.S.; pop. 45,484; machinery. 3. *City* W Tenn., U.S.; pop. 39,996; manufacturing. 4. **Mount** *Peak* 13,685 ft. cen. Colo., U.S.

Jack'sön-ville *City* NE Fla., U.S.; pop. 528,865; port

Jà-ciu' (kwē') *River* 300 m. S Brazil

Ja-en' (hä-än') *Commune* * of *Province* S Spain

Jaf'fà, anc. **Jop'pà** *City* W cen. Israel; port; part of Tel Aviv

Jäff'nà *Town* on *Peninsula* N Ceylon; port

Jag'gèd Mountain *Peak* 13,835 ft. SW Colo., U.S.

Ja-guà-ri'bè (rē') *River* 350 m. NE Brazil

Jaï'pur (poor) *City* (and former state) NW India; trade, industry

Jaï'sàl-mer *State* NW India; mostly desert

Jà-kär'tä = DJAKARTA

Jà-lal'à-bad *Town* E Afghanistan

Jä-lä'pä (hä) 1. *Town* * of *Department* SE Guatemala. 2. *City* E Mexico; coffee

Jä-les'cö (hä-lēs') *State* W cen. Mexico

Jäl'nà *Town* S cen. India

Jàl-paï-gu'ri (goo') 1. *Town* NE India. 2. *Former district* now div. bet. India and E Pakistan

Jal'u-it *Island* largest of Marshall Is.

Jà-mäi'cà (member British Commonwealth of Nations) *Country*, Caribbean — W Indies; 4,410 sq. m.; pop. 2,022,000; 14 parishes; *Main cities:* * Kingston, Montego Bay, Spanish Town; *Main rivers:* Black, Minho; *Geog.:* mountainous island; *Climate:* tropical, humid.

Flag: cross with 4 triangles in juxtaposition, diagonal cross gold, top and bottom triangles emerald green, hoist and fly triangles black.

Ethnic comp.: Negroes, Mulattoes, Europeans, Chinese, East Indians, Syrians; *Language:* English (official), Jamaican Creole; *Religions:* Anglican, Baptist, Roman Catholic, Methodist, Moslem, Hindu, Jewish.

Products: sugar, rum, molasses, bananas, alumina, cocoa, bauxite; *Minerals:* bauxite, gypsum, silica, marble, ceramic clays; *Major exports:* bauxite, alumina, sugar, rum, molasses, bananas; *Major imports:* foodstuffs, manufactured goods, machinery, transportation equipment; *Industries:* manufac-

---

turing (rum, beer, clothing, furniture), tourism, sugar processing, forestry, fishing, mining, refining.

Currency: Jamaican dollar.

Head of Government: British Monarch represented by Governor General; *Legislature:* bicameral parliament — Senate, House of Representatives; *Judiciary:* Supreme Court at apex.

Jāmes 1. *Bay* S of Hudson Bay bet. Ontario and Quebec, E Canada. 2. *River* 340 m. cen. Va., U.S. 3. *Peak* 13,260 ft. Colo., U.S.

Jāmes'town 1. *City* SW N.Y., U.S.; pop. 39,795; manufacturing. 2. *Island* E Va., U.S.; 1st permanent Eng. settlement in America. 3. *Town* * of St. Helena I.

Jàm'mū *Town* and *Region* S Kashmir

Jäm-nà'gàr *City* W India

Jäm'shed-pur *City* NE India; metalwork

Jānes'ville *City* S Wisc. U.S.; pop. 46,426; industry [W India

Jàn'ji-rà *Island*, *State*

Jan May'èn Island (yän mī') *Island* (Norway) Arctic O.

Jao'rä (jou') *Town* * of *State* W cen. India

Jä-pan', *Country* off E coast of Asia; 142,730 sq. m.; pop. 104,649,000; 46 prefectures; *Main cities:* * Tokyo, Osaka, Nagoya, Yokohama, Kyoto, Kóbe, Kitakyushu, Kawasaki, Sapporo, Fukooka; *Main rivers:* Tone, Shinano, Ishikari, Kitakami; *Geog.: Main islands:* Honshu, Kyushu, Hokkaido, Shikoku, about ⅘ of country covered with hills and mountains, many volcanoes — active & dormant, numerous earthquakes due to unstable geological

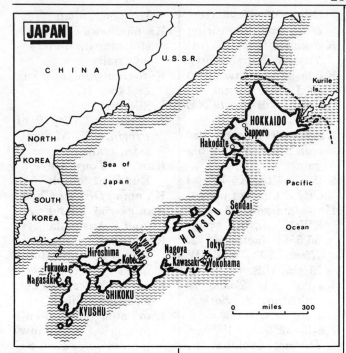

position; *Climate:* ranges from subtropical on Kyushu to cool on Hokkaido.

Flag: red sun on white field.

Ethnic comp.: Japanese, Korean, Ainus, Chinese, American; *Language:* Japanese (official); *Religions:* Shinto, Buddhist, Christian minority.

Products: rice, fish, fruit, sweet potatoes, cereals, tea, timber, oil, non-ferrous metals, motor vehicles, textiles, synthetic rubber, electronics, machinery, precision instruments, chemicals, fertilizers, ceramics, wood products, metals; *Minerals:* coal, copper, zinc, aliminum, lead, nickel; *Major exports:* iron, steel products, ships, cars, cotton, fabrics, sewing machines, china, rubber, electronic equipment, cameras, toys; *Major imports:* crude oil, petroleum products, raw cotton, coal, wood, iron ore, scrap iron, wheat, sugar; *Industries:* fisheries, tourism, forestry, manufacture of transportation equipment, iron, steel, chemicals,

Emperor; *Legislature:* Diet — House of Representatives, House of Counselors; *Judiciary:* Supreme Court, courts established by law including district courts, high courts (courts of appeal).

Ja-pan', Sea of *Sea* W of Japan

Ja-pu-ra' *River* 1750 m. NW South America

Ja-ri' (rē') *River* 360 m. NE Brazil

Jär'vis Island *Island* of Line Is.; air field

Jash'pur *State* NE India

Jath (jut) *Town* * of *State* W India

Jä'va 1. *Island* Malay Arch., Indonesia; agriculture. 2. **Sea** *Area* of Pacific O. N of Java

Ja-va-ri' (rē') *River* 650 m. NW cen. South America

Ja-whär' *State* W India

Jef'fer-son *River* 250 m. SW Mont., U.S.

Jef'fer-son City *City* * of Mo., U.S.; pop. 32,407; agriculture, mining

Je-hōl' *City* * of *Region, Province* NE China

Je-le'nia Go'rä (ye-le', gōō'), Ger. **Hirsch'berg** *City* SW Poland

Je'lep-lä' *Pass* 14,390 ft. Sikkim

Je'nä (yā') *City* S cen.

East Germany; glass

Je-qui-ti-nhō'nha (kē-tē-nyō'nya) *River* 500 m. E Brazil

Je-rez' (hâ-rāz') *City* SW Spain; trade cen.

Jer'i-chō (kō) *Village* cen. Jordan; imp. anc. city

Jêr'sey (zi) *Island* of Channel Is. * St. Helier; resort

Jêr'sey City (zi) *City* NE N.J., U.S.; pop. 260,545; port, manufactures

Je-rū'sa-lem *City* formerly of S cen. Palestine; Holy city of Moslems, Christians, Jews; was div.: Old City part of Jordan; New City, (W part) = * of Israel; pop. 66,000 (in total); 1967 united under Israel

Jêr'vis Bay *Inlet* of S Pacific O. SE Australia

Jes'sel-tön *Town* * of Brit. North Borneo

Jes-sōre' *District* formerly NE Brit. India, now div. bet. E Pakistan and India

Jew'ish Au-ton'ö-mous Region = BIRO-BIDZHAN

Jha'bu-a *City* * of *State* SW cen. India

Jha'la-wär *State* NW India

Jhang' - Ma-ghi-ä'nä *Town* * of **Jhang** dist. N Pakistan

Jhän'si *City* * of Division N India

Jhe'lum (jā') 1. *River* 450 m. Kashmir. 2. *Town* * of *District* W Pakistan

Jid'da *Port* Hejaz, W Saudi Arabia [India

Jind *Town, State* NW

Jin-sen = INCHON

Joao Pes-sō'a (zhwoun) *City* E Brazil

Jodh'pur *City* * of *State* NW India; camels, wheat, metalware

Jōg-ja-kär'ta *City, Sultanate* S Java, former * of Indonesia

Jō-han'nes-bûrg *City* NE Rep. of South Africa; gold, produce, manufactures

John Day *River* 281 m. N Ore., U.S.

Johns'town *City* SW cen. Pa., U.S.; pop. 42,476; iron, coal cen.

Jo-hōre' *State* and *Strait* Malaysia, S Malay Penin.

Jō'li-et *City* NE Ill., U.S.; pop. 8,378; industrial cen.

Jō-lō' (hō) *Island* Sulu Arch. Phil. Is.

Jon'kö-ping (yûn'chû) *City* * of *Province* S Sweden; matches

Jop'lin *City* SW Mo., U.S.; pop. 39,256

Jôr'dan *River* 200 m. Syria-Israel

Jôr'dan, Hashemite Kingdom of *Country,* SW Asia; 35,570 sq. m.; (37,730 sq. m.; in 1967); pop. 2,339,-000; 8 governorates; *Main cities:* * Amman, Zerqa, Irbid, (Jerusalem, Nablus part of Israel since 1967); *Main rivers:* Jordan, Yarmuk; *Geog.:* E desert, Jordan River valley divides land into small rocky W Bank and large E Bank; *Climate:* summers hot & dry, winters cold except for Jordan River Valley, gulf of Agaba.

Flag: horizontal stripes — black, white, green from top to bottom, joined at hoist.

Ethnic comp.: Arabs with minorities of Armenians, Circassians; *Language:* Arabic (official); *Religions:* Sunni Moslem (state), Christian.

Products: cereals,

fruits, phosphates; *Minerals:* phosphate, potash, marble manganese, iron, sulphur, copper; *Major exports:* phosphates, tomatoes, fruits, vegetables, cement, marble; *Major imports:* foodstuffs, machinery, vehicles, crude petroleum, textiles; *Industries:* tourism, oil refining, phosphate mining, tanning. *Currency:* dinar. *Head of Government:* Monarch; *Legislature:* bicameral National Assembly — Senate, Chamber of Deputies; *Judiciary:* civil, religious, special courts provided for in constitution.

Juä'rez (h w ä') = CIUDAD JUAREZ

Jū'bà *River* 1000 m. E Africa

Jū'bà-land *Region* S Somalia, one - time colony

Jub'bul-pōre *City* * of *Division* cen. India

Jou'cär (hōō) *River* 300 m. E Spain

Jū'dah *Kingdom,* anc. S Palestine, later **Jū-dē'à**

Jū-gō-slä'vi-à = YUGOSLAVIA

Juiz' dè Fô'rà (zhwēzh') *City* E Brazil; manufacturing

Jūl'iàn Alps *Mts.* NW Yugoslavia

Jū-li-an'à Top *Peak* 15,420 ft. W New Guinea

Jul'lun-dur *City* * of *Division* NW India

Jum'nà *River* 860 m. N cen. India

Ju-nä'gàrh *Town* * of *State* W India

Jun-cäl' (hōōn) *Peak* 19,880 ft. Chile-Argentina

Junc'tion Peak *Mt.* 13,625 ft. S cen. Calif. U.S.

Jū'neau (nō) *City* SE Alas., U.S.; * of Alas.; pop. 6,050; harbor, fisheries

Jung'frau (yoong'frou) *Peak* 13,670 ft. SW cen. Switzerland

Jū'pi-têr Peak *Mt.* 13,-835 ft. SW Colo., U.S.

Jur (joor) *River* 300 m. SW Sudan

Ju'rà (joor') 1. *Department* E France. 2. *Mts.* bet. France and Switzerland

Jū-rua' (rwa') *River* 1200 m. NW cen. South America

Jū-rue'nà (rwā') *River* 600 m. W cen. Brazil

Jū-tà-i' (ē') *River* 400 m. NW Brazil

Jut'lànd *Peninsula* N Eur. incl. Danish mainland and N West Germany

K

Kab-àr-di'nō - Bal-kar'-i-àn A.S.S.R. *Republic* SE R.S.F.S.R., U.S.S.R., Eur.

Kä'bul 1. *City* * of Afghanistan; pop. 292,000. 2. *River* 360 m. Afghanistan-India

Kä-dhi-maīn' *City* cen. Iraq; holy city

Kä-di-koy' anc. **Chal'-cè-don** (kal'sè) *City* Turkey, Asia

Kà-di'yèv-kà (dyē') *T o w n* Ukraine U.S.S.R.

Kae'sông' (ka'ï), **Kaī-jō** *City* W North Korea; 1951 truce site

Ka'fä *Region* SW Ethiopia; coffee said to originate here

Kä-fū'e *River* 500 m. N Rhodesia

Kä-gä-wä *Prefecture* Shikoku, Japan

Kä-ge'rä (gā') *River* 429 m. E Africa

Kä-gi *City* W cen. Taiwan

Kä-go-shi-mä *City* on Bay, * of *Prefecture* Kyushu, Japan

Kaī'fing' *City* E cen. China; one-time *

Kaī Islands *Island group* Malay Arch. Indonesia

Kaī-jō = KAESONG

Kaī-läs' *Mt. range* SW Tibet

Kaī-lū'ä *Village* W Hawaii I , Haw., U.S.

Kaīr-ouän', **Kaīr-wän'** *City* NE Tunisia; Moslem holy city

Kaī-sêrs-lau'têrn (lou')

City SW West Ger; many; manufacturing

Kaī-shū, Hae-jū (hī) *Town* W North Korea

Kà-là-dan' *River* 300 m. Lower Burma

Kä-lä-hàn'di *State* NE India

Kä-lä-hä'ri Desert *Plateau* South Africa; big game

Kal-à-mä'tà, Kä-lä'mài *City* S Greece; port

Kal-à-mà-zōō' 1. *City* SW Mich., U.S.; pop. 85,555; factories. 2. *River* 200 m. SW Mich., U.S.

Kà-lät' 1. *Town* W Pakistan. 2. *Former state* Brit. India

Kä-lä-wä'ō *Village, District* Molokai I., Haw., U.S.; leper settlement [CHUAN

Kāl'gän now WAN-

Kà-li'nin (lē') *City* * of *Region* R.S.F.S.R., U.S.S.R., Eur.

Kà-li'nin-grad (lē'), Ger. **Kö'nigs-bêrg** *City* * of **Kà-li'nin-gradsk** *Region* W R.S.F.S.R., U.S.S.R.

Kä'lisz (lēsh), Ger. **Kä'-lisch** *Commune* cen. Poland

Kä'lix *River* 267 m. N Sweden; many rapids

Kal'mär *City* * of *Province* SE Sweden; port

Kal'mỳk A.S.S.R. *Former republic* U.S.S.R., Eur., now div.

Kà-lū'gà *City* * of *Region* cen. R.S.F.S.R., U.S.S.R., Eur.

Kä'mà *River* 1200 m. E R.S.F.S.R., U.S.S.R., Eur.

Kä-mä-ku-rä *Town* Honshu, Japan

Kam-chat'kà *Peninsula* site of *River* 350 m. and *Mountains,* NE R.S.F.S.R., U.S.S.R., Asia; fish, furs

Kà-mè-nets' Pö-dôl'ski *City* and *Region* Ukraine U.S.S.R.

Kà'met *Peak* 25,445 ft. N India

Käm-pä'lä *Town* * of Uganda; pop. 331,900

Kän *River* 350 m. SE China

Kän or Hän *River* 220 m. cen. Korea

Kä-nä-gä-wä *Prefecture*

Honshu, Japan

Kä-nä-zä-wä *City* Honshu, Japan; imp. industrially

Kàn-chèn-jun'gà *Peak* 28,145 ft. Nepal-Sikkim

Kan'dà-här *City* * of *Province* SE Afghanis.an; trade cen.

Kan'dỳ *Town* Ceylon; Buddhist temple

Kä'nem *District* Chad

Kan'gà-rōō Island *Island* S Australia

Käng'e-än *Island* of *Group* Java S. Indonesia

Käng'to' *Peak* 23,260 ft. Assam-Tibet

Kan'hsien' (gän'shi-en') formerly **Kan'chow'** (gän'jō') *Town* SE China

Kan-ià-pis'kau (kou) *River* 445 m. N Quebec, Canada

Ka'nin Peninsula *Peninsula* into Barents S., U.S.S.R., Eur.

Kan-kà-kēe' *River* 225 m. Ind.-Ill., U.S.

Kän-kō or **Häm-hung** (hoong) *City* N Korea

Kä'nō *City* * of *Province* N Nigeria; trade

Kän'pur *City* N cen. India; industrial cen.

Kan'sàs *State,* named from Sioux word meaning "people of the south wind;" 82,264 sq. m.; *pop.:* 2,249,071 (*rank:* 29th); Mid-W U.S.; *Boundaries:* Nebraska, Missouri, Oklahoma, Colorado; *Major cities:* Wichita, Kansas City, * Topeka; *Major rivers:* Arkansas, Kansas, *Major lakes:* Tottle Creek, Cedar Bluff, Cheney, Perry; 105 counties.

Nickname: Sunflower State, Jay-Hawker State; *Motto:* "Ad astra per aspera" (to the stars through difficulties); *Flag:* blue field with wreath & yellow sunflower over state seal; *Flower:* sunflower; *Bird:* western meadow lark; *Tree:* cotton-

wood; *Song: Home on the Range.*
Industry: wheat, food processing, chemicals, non-electrical machinery production; *Natural resources:* petroleum, natural gas, coal, helium, zinc, lead; *Major source of income:* wholesale & retail trade.
Places of interest: Abilene; Dodge City.
Kan'sȧs City 1. *City* NE Kan., U.S.; pop. 168,213; industrial cen. 2. *City* W Mo., U.S.; pop. 507,087; industry, commerce
Kan'sū' *Province* N cen. China; agriculture, cattle, minerals
Kä'poe-äs (poo) *River* 450 m. Borneo, Indonesia [Korea
Kap-san *City* N North
Kȧ-pur'thȧ-lȧ *State* NW India
Kä'rä *Strait* connecting Sea with Barents S., U.S.S.R., Eur.
Kȧ-rȧ-cha'ĕv **Region** *Former autonomous region* R.S.F.S.R., U.S.S.R., Eur.
Kȧ-rä'chi *City* W Pakistan, former *; port, trade cen.
Kä-rä'fu-tō Jap. name of SAKHALIN
Kä-rä-gän-dä' *City* * of *Region* Kazakh, U.S.S.R., Asia; coal
Kä - rä - Käl - päk' **A.S.S.R.** *Area* Uzbek U.S.S.R.
Kar-ȧ-kō'rȧm 1. *Mt. range* N Kashmir. 2. *Pass* 18,290 ft., main route Kashmir-China. 3. *Ruins* of anc. * of Mongolia
Kä'rä Kûl' *Lake* Tadzhik U.S.S R., Asia
Kä'rä Kum' (kōōm') *Desert* 110,000 sq. m Turkmen, U.S.S.R., Asia
Kä-rä-tsu *City* Kyushu, Japan; port
Kȧ-rau'li (rou') *State* N cen. India
Kär'bȧ-la *Town* and *Province* cen. Iraq; holy city
Kȧ-rē'lō - Finn'ish S.S.R. *Constituent*

Republic, NW U.S.S.R., Eur.; * Petrozavodsk; forests, furs, fish
Kä-ri-käl' *Town* and *Province* SE India; Fr. India before 1954
Kä-ri-mä'tä *Islands* and *Strait* W of Borneo, Indonesia
Kar-i-sim'bi *Peak* 14,-785 ft. E Congo (L)
Kar-kheh' (ka') *River* 340 m. W Iran
Kär'li *Village* W India; Buddhist caves
Kar'lô-vỷ Va'rỷ, Ger. **Kärls'bad, Cärls'bad** *Town* W Czechoslovakia; springs
Kärls-kro'na (krōō') *City* S Sweden; harbor
Kärls'rū-hė *City* S West Germany; manufacturing
Kärl'städ *City* SW Sweden; factories
Kär'näk *Village* Upper Egypt; hist. temples
Kär'pȧ-thos *Island* of Dodecanese Is.
Kȧr-rōō' *Tableland* Rep. of South Africa
Kä-rūn' *River* 450 m. W Iran
Kä-saï' 1. *River* 1200 m. SW Africa. 2. *Province* was Lusambo, Congo (L)
Kä-shän' *City* cen. Iran; carpets, melons
Kash'gär or **Shū'fū'** *Town* W China; wool, tea, cotton
Kä'shing', Chia'hsing' (ji-ä') *City* E China; eggs, poultry, rice
Kash'mir (mẽr) or **Jȧm'mū and Kash'mir** *State* N India, in dispute bet. India and Pakistan; * Srinagar; agriculture, Cashmere goats, woods
Kas-kas'ki-ȧ *River* 300 m. SW Ill., U.S.
Käs'sėl, Cäs'sėl *City* West Germany; machinery
Kas'sė-rine (rēn) *Village* and *Pass* cen. Tunisia
Kȧ-sur' (soor') *Town* W Pakistan
Kȧ-täh'din *Peak* 5268 ft., highest in Me., U.S.

Kȧ-tän'gȧ *Province* S Congo (L); * Elizabethville; minerals
Kä'thi-ȧ-wär (ti) *Peninsula* W India
Kat'maī, Mount *Volcano* S Alas., U.S.
Kät-män-dū' *City* * of Nepal
Kä-to-wi'ce (vē'tse), **Kät'to-witz** *City* S Poland; coal cen.
Kat'rine, Loch (lok) *Lake* cen. Scotland
Kä'tsi-nȧ *Town* and anc. *Kingdom* N Nigeria
Kat'tė-gat *Arm* of North S. bet Sweden and Denmark
Kȧ-tūn' *River* 400 m. U.S.S.R., Asia
Kau'näs (kou'), **Kôv'nö** *City* * of *District* cen. Lithuania; onetime *; factories
Kȧ-val'lȧ *City* * of *Department* on *Gulf* Macedonia N E Greece
Ka-vi-eng' *Town* NW New Ireland; port
Ka-vir', Dasht-i- (vēr') *Salt Desert* N cen. Iran
Kä-wä-gu-chi (goo) *City* and *Lake* Honshu, Japan
Kä-wä-sä-ki *City* Honshu, Japan; elec. equipment
Kȧ-wē'ȧh Peaks *Four Mts.* S cen. Calif., U.S.; over 13,000 ft.
Kay'ak (kī') *Island* off SE Alas., U.S.
Kay-se-ri' (kī, rē') *City* * of *Vilayet* cen. Turkey Asia
Kä-zäkh' S.S.R. *Constituent Republic* of U.S.S.R. cen. Asia; * Alma Ata; agriculture, minerals
Kȧ-zan' 1. *River* 450 m. cen. Canada. 2. *City* * of Tatar Rep. E R.S.F.S.R., U.S.S.R., Eur.; commerce, industry
Kȧz-bek' *Peak* 16,540 ft. U.S.S.R., Eur.
Kaz-vin' (vēn') *City* * of *Province* NW Iran; trade cen.
Keär'nỷ *Town* NE N.J. U.S.; pop. 37,585; factories

Kecs'ke-met (kech'ke-māt) *City* cen. Hungary; market cen.
Ke'däh (kā') *Area* S Malay Penin. Malaysia; rubber, rice
Ke-där'näth *Peak* 23,-420 ft. NE India
Ke-di'ri (dē') *City* Java, Indonesia; sugar cen.
Ke'doe, Ke'du (kā'dōō) *Residency* Java, Indonesia; agricultural
Kēele *River* 230 m. NW Terrs. Canada
Kēe'lung' (loong'), **Ki-run** (roon) *City* N Formosa (Taiwan); port, naval base
Keigh'ley (kē'li) *Municipal borough* N England; woolens
Kei-jo (kā) now SEOUL
Kė-lan'tan *Area* S Malay Penin., Malaysia [U.S.S.R.
Kem *River* 140 m.
Ke'mė-rō-vō *City* * of *Region* R.S.F.S.R., U.S.S.R., Asia; heavy industry
Ke'mi *Port* on *River* 300 m. N Finland
Kē'naī Peninsula *Peninsula* S Alas., U.S.
Ken'il - wörth *Urban district* cen. England; castle ruins
Ke-ni-tra' (kä-nē) now PORT LYAUTEY
Ken'nė-bec *River* 165 m. cen. Me., U.S.
Ken'nė-dỷ, Cape *Cape* E Fla., U.S.; rocket launching cen.
Kė-nog'ȧ-mi *River* 200 m. cen. Ontario, Canada
Kė-nō'shȧ *City* SE Wisc., U.S.; pop. 78,-805; industrial
Ken'sing-tön *Borough* of London, England
Kent *County* SE England; farming, dairying, fishing, manufacturing
Ken-tuck'ỷ *State* named from Cherokee Indian word probably meaning "dark and bloody ground;" 40,395 sq. m.; *pop.:* 3,219,311 (*rank:* 23rd); SE U.S.; *Boundaries:* Tennessee, Virginia, West Virginia, Ohio, Indiana, Illinois,

Missouri; *Major cities:* Louisville, Lexington, * Frankfort; *Major rivers:* Ohio, Tennessee, Kentucky; *Major lakes:* Kentucky — Cumberland reservoirs; 119 counties.

Nickname: Bluegrass State; *Motto:* "United we stand, divided we fall;" *Flag:* state seal on blue field; *Flower:* goldenrod; *Bird:* cardinal; *Tree:* tulip tree (yellow poplar); *Song: My Old Kentucky Home.*

Industry: tobacco, liquor, animal raising, food processing, making of machinery, chemicals, metal goods; *Natural resources:* coal, oil, natural gas; *Major source of income:* manufacturing.

Admitted to Union: 1792 (15th state).

Places of interest: Mammoth Cave Ntl. Park, Cumberland Ntl. Forest, Cumberland Gap Ntl. Historical Park.

Ken'ya, Republic of *Country,* E coast of Africa; 224,960 sq. m.; pop. 11,460,000; 40 rural districts, & Nairobi; *Main cities:* * Nairobi, Mombasa, Nakuru, Kisumu; *Main rivers:* Tana, Athi, Turkwell, Vaso Nyiro; *Geog.:* N ⅗ arid, almost waterless. Region N of Tana River rises into mts. of Ethiopia. Thornbush scrubland reaches about 175

miles inland from coast. Great Rift Valley is in C and W regions; *Climate:* except for coast and immediate interior, climate cool and invigorating due to altitude.

Flag: horizontal black, red, green stripes separated by narrow white bands, warrior's shield and crossed spears centered on flag.

Ethnic comp.: Africans (Bantu, Nilotic), Asians, Europeans, Arabs, Somalis; *Language:* English, Swahili (official), Kikuyu, Luo, other African languages; *Religions:* animist, Roman Catholic, Protestant, Moslem.

Products: coffee, tea, sisal, meat, cotton, skins, maize, fish, pyrethrum, wattle, petroleum, soda ash, salt, limestone, copper, cement, plastics, chemicals; *Minerals:* small quantities of soda ash, salt, copper, gold, silver; *Major exports:* coffee, tea, sisal, pyrethrum extract, flowers, meat, meat preparations; *Major imports:* machinery, transportation equipment, manufactured goods; lubricants, chemicals; *Industries:* oil refining, food processing, tourism, mining, quarrying, forestry, fishing.

Currency: Kenyan shilling.

Head of Government: President; *Legislature:* unicameral — National Assembly; *Judiciary:* Supreme Court at apex.

Ke-ōn'jhár *Town* * of *State* NE India

Kė-rak (rok) *Anc emirate* now in Jordan

Ke'rä-lä (kā') *State* SW India

Kêrch *City* on *Penin-*

sula E Crimea S. U.S.S.R.; metallurgy, port

Kêr'guė-lèn, Des'ö-lā-tion Island *Island* of *Arch.* of Fr. Union, S Indian O.

Kė-rin'tji (che) *Peak* 12,465 ft. Sumatra; volcanic

Kerk'ra-dė *Commune* SE Netherlands

Kêr-män' anc. **Cär-mā'na** *City* * of *Province* SE Iran; carpets

Ker-män-shäh' *City* * of *Province* W Iran

Kêrn *River* 200 m. S cen. Calif., U.S.

Ker'rẏ *County* SW Eire

Ker'u-len *River* 650 m N Ouger Mongolia

Ket *River* 500 m. S Siberia, U.S.S.R., Asia

Ketch'i-kàn *Town* SE Alas., U.S.; port; salmon, pulp

Ket'têr-ing 1. *City* SW Ohio, U.S.; pop. 69,-599; manufacturing. 2. *Urban district* cen. England

Keū'kà, Lake *Lake* W N.Y., U.S.; one of Finger lakes

Key Lär'gō (kē) *Island* largest of Fla. Keys SE U.S.

Key West *City* on *Island* SW Fla., U.S.; pop. 27,563

Khà-ba'rövsk *City* * of *Territory* R.S.F.S.R., U.S.S.R., Asia; fur, mineral cen.

Khä-bur' *River* 200 m. Turkey-Syria

Khai'rä-gärh *Town* * of *State* NE India

Khair'pur *Town* * of *State* S West Pakistan

Khà-kass' Autonomous Region *Region* R.S.F.S.R., S Siberia, U.S.S.R.

Khà'li-fàt *Peak* 11,440 ft. Pakistan

Khä - nà - qin' (kēn') *Town* E Iraq; oil

Khän'bä - lik' (lēk') *Town* (mod. PEIPING) Mongol name of Kubla Khan's * of China   [India

Khànd-pä'rà *State* NE

Khan'kà, Han'kà *Lake* 1700 sq. m. Manchuria-U.S.S.R.

Khan'tẏ-Man'si *District* W Siberia, U.S.S.R., Asia

Khà'ràg-pur *City* NE India

Khär'kôv *City* * of *Region* NE Ukraine U.S.S.R.; rail cen.

Khär'tà-phu (pōō) *Peak* 23,800 ft. Himalayas

Khär-ti-chäng'ri *Peak* 23,420 ft. Himalayas

Khär-toum', Khär-tum' (tōōm') *City* * of *Province* and * of Sudan; pop. 160,000

Khä'si *District* NE India

Khà-tan'gà *River* 800 m. U.S.S.R., Asia

Kher-sôn' *City* in *Region* S Ukraine U.S.S.R.; port

Khe'tà *River* 500 m. U.S.S.R., Asia

Khi-lôk' *River* 350 m. U.S.S.R., Asia

Khing'än' (shin g') *Mountain ranges* (2) E Asia

Khir-bät' Qum-rän' *Site* NW Jordan; Dead Sea Scrolls 1947

Khôb'dō *River* 300 m. Outer Mongolia

Khō'i (ē) *Town* NW Iran; trade cen.

Khö-per' (pyôr') *River* 560 m. R.S.F.S.R., U.S.S.R., Eur.

Khor-ram-shahr' (koor) *Town* W Iran

Khō'tän', Hō'tien' *Town, Oasis* W China; supply cen.

Khul'nä *Town* * of *District* E Pakistan

Khẏ'bêr Pass *Pass* 33 m. long bet. Afghanistan and India

Kiä'ling' (ji-ä') *River* 500 m. cen. China

Kia'mu'sze', Chia'mus' su' (ji-ä'moo'soo') *City* NE China

Ki'än' (jē'), **Lü'ling'** *Town* SE China

Kiäng'ling' (ji-äng'), **King'chow'** (jing'jō') *City* E cen. China

Kiang'si' (ji-äng'sē') *Province* SE China

Kiang'sū' (ji-äng') *Province* E China

Kiang'tu' (ji-äng'dōō'), **Yäng'chow'** (jō') *City* E China

Kiao'chow' (ji-ou'jō')

District and *Bay* NE China

Ki'bō (kē') *Peak* (highest) 19,315 ft. of Mt. Kilimanjaro

Kiēl *City* N West Germany; port

Kiēl or **Kaī'sêr Wil'helm Canal** *Canal* 61 m. long, Baltic to North S.

Kiel'ce, Kel'tsẏ *City* * of *Dept.* S Poland

Ki'ev (kē'yef) *City* * of *Province* and * of Ukraine S.S.R., U.S.S.R., Eur.; commercially, industrially, historically imp.

Ki-gä'li *Town* * of Rwanda; pop. 17,000

Kil-dare' *County* E Eire; farming, textiles, brewing

Ki-li-màn-jä'rō, Mount *Mountain* 19,315 ft. NE Tanzania; Africa's highest point

Kil-ken'nẏ *County* SE Eire; mining, brewing, quarrying

Kil-lär'ney (ni) *District, Lakes* (3) SW Eire

Kil-lēen' *City* E Texas, U.S.; pop. 35,507

Kil-mär'nöck *Burgh* SW Scotland; coal, manufactures

Kim'bêr-ley (li) *Town* Cape of Good Hope, Rep. of South Africa; world's diamond cen.

Kin (kēn) *River* 250 m. SW Korea

Kin-à-bà-täng'än *River* 350 m. N Borneo, Malaysia

Kin-à-bu-lū' *Mountain* 13,455 ft. N Borneo, Malaysia

Kin-cär'dine-shîre, formerly **The Mearns** (mûrnz) *County* E Scotland; livestock. quarrying, fishing

Ki'nesh-mà (kē') *City* R.S.F.S.R., U.S.S.R., Eur.

King'chow' now KIANGLING

King Chris'tian IX Land (kris') and **King Frederick VI Land** *Coastal regions* SE Greenland

King Island 1. *Island* Bering Strait W Alas. U.S.; walrus hunting. 2. *Island* Bass Strait

S Australia

King's Peak *Peak* 13,-495 ft. NE Utah, U.S.

Kings'tön 1. *City* SE Ontario, Canada; shipping. 2. *City* * of Jamaica; port

Kings'town 1. *City* and *Bay* St. Vincent I. West Indies. 2. now DUN LAOGHAIRE

King Wil'liam Island *Island* NW Terrs., Canada [China

Kin'hwä' (jin') *City* E

Kin-rôss' *County* E cen. Scotland; textiles

Kinshasa *City* * of *Province* and * of Zaire, SW part; pop. ab. 1,000,000; air cen.; formerly **Leopoldville**

Kin'tä Val'ley *Area* Malay Penin. W Malaysia; tin

Kir-ghiz' (gēz') early name of KAZAKH S.S.R.

Kir-giz' *Range* (gēz') *Mountains* U.S.S.R., cen. Asia

Kir-giz' S.S.R. (gēz') *Republic* of U.S.S.R., cen. Asia; livestock, grains

Ki'rin' (kē') 1. *Province* cen. Manchuria, China. 2. or **Yung'ki'** (yoong'jē') *City* E Manchuria, China; port

Kîrk-cäl'dẏ (cä') *Burgh* E Scotland; port

Kîrk-cūd'bright (kōō'brī) *County* and *Burgh* S Scotland

Kîrk-pat'rick, Mount *Peak* 14,600 ft. S Victoria Land, Antarctica

Kir-kūk' *Town* in *Province* NE cen. Iraq; oil, sheep

Ki'röv (kē') *City* * of *Region* R.S.F.S.R., U.S.S.R., Eur.; cultural, industrial cen.

Ki-rō'và-bad *City* SW U.S.S.R., Eur.; textiles, mines

Ki-rō'vō-grad *City* * of *Region* Ukraine U.S.S.R., Eur.; agriculture

Ki'rövsk (kē') *Town* R.S.F.S.R., U.S.S.R., Eur.; uranium

Ki-run (kē-roon) see KEELUNG

Kir-yū *Town* Honshu, Japan; weaving

Kish *Anc. city* now in Iraq; imp. ruins

Ki'shàn-gärh *Former state* NW India

Ki'shi-nev *City* SW U.S.S.R., Eur.; former * of Bessarabia

Kis'kà *Island* W Aleutian Is., Alas., U.S.

Kis'lö-vodsk *City* R.S.F.S.R., U.S.S.R., Eur.

Kis'tnà, formerly **Krish'nà** *River* 800 m. S India

Kit Kär'sön Peak *Peak* 14,100 ft. S Colo., U.S.

Kitch'è-nêr *City* SE Ontario, Canada

Kit'tẏ Hǎwk *Village* E N.C., U.S.; site of Wright brothers' first plane flight 1903

Kiu'kiang' (ji-ōō'ji-äng') *City* SE China; tea, pottery

Kiung'shän' (chi-oong') *City* Hainan I. SE China; port

Ki'vū (kē') *Lake* 1025 sq. m. cen. Africa (Congo-Rwanda)

Ki-zil' Ir-mäk' *River* 600 m. cen. Turkey, Asia

Klä'gin-furt (foort) *City* S Austria; factories

Klam'àth *River* 250 m. S Ore., U.S.

Klär *River* 215 m. cen. Norway-W Sweden

Klon'dīke *Region, River* Yukon, NW Canada; gold rush 1897-99

Klông or **Me-klông** *River* 300 m. W Thailand

Klū-āne' *Lake* and *River* SW Yukon, Canada

Klẏ-az'mà *River* 425 m. U.S.S.R., Eur.

Klyū-chev'skà-yà Sôp'kà *Volcano* 15,900 ft. Siberia, U. S. S. R., Asia

Knox'ville (nox') *City* E Tenn., U.S.; pop. 174,587; commerce, industry

Kō'bē *City* Honshu, Japan; port, factories

Ko-bén-havn' (kû-pén-houn') = COPEN-

HAGEN

Kō'blenz or **Cō'blenz** *City* and *District* W cen. West Germany; commerce, industry

Kō-buk' (book') *River* 275 m. NW Alas., U.S.

Kō-chi *City* * of *Prefecture* Shikoku, Japan

Kō'di-ak *Island* S Alas., U.S.; salmon, furs

Koe'päng (kōō') = KUPANG

Koe'tä-rä'djä (kōō') = KUTARAJA

Kō'fu *City* Honshu, Japan; silk market

Kog'à-ràh *City* SE Australia

Kō-hä'lä *Village* N Hawaii I., Haw. U.S.; home of 1st king

Kō-hät' *Town* * of *District* N West Pakistan

Kō - kand' *City* S U.S.S.R., Asia; trade

Kō'kö-mō *City* N cen. Ind., U.S.; pop. 44,-042; metal goods

Kō-ku-rä (koo) *City* Kyushu, Japan; port

Kō'là or **Kôl'ski Peninsula** *Peninsula* bet. White S. and Arctic O., NW U.S.S.R., Eur.; Murmansk area

Kō-lär' Gōld Fiēlds *City* S India; gold

Kōl'hà-pur (poor) *City* * of *State* W India; trade cen.

Köln = COLOGNE

Kō-lō'ä *Village, District* Kauai I., Haw., U.S.; Hawaii's 1st sugar plantation

Kô-lôb'rzeg (rhek), Ger. **Kôl'bêrg** *City* NW Poland; port

Kö-lôm'nà *City* nr. Moscow, U.S.S.R., Eur.; factories

Kö-lẏ'mà 1. *River* 1110 m. U.S.S.R., Asia. 2. *Range* E U.S.S.R.

Kö-màn-dôr'ski-è or **Cöm-man'dêr Islands** *Islands* Bering S., E U.S.S.R.

Kö-mä'ti *River* 500 m. S Africa

Kö'mi A.S.S.R. *Republic* NE R.S.F.S.R., U.S.S.R., Eur.; forests, minerals

Kō'mi-Pêrm'iak *Na-*

tional district NW Siberia, U. S. S. R., Asia

Kom-sö-môlsk' *City* R.S.F.S.R., S E U.S.S.R., Asia; steel, shipyards

Kö'nigs-bêrg = KAL-ININGRAD

Kon-stȧn-ti'növ-kȧ (te') *City* Ukraine W U.S.S.R., Eur.

Kôn'stänz, Con'stȧnce *City* S West Germany; factories

Kôn-yä' *City* * of *Vilayet* SW Turkey, Asia

Koo'tė-nāi *River* 400 m. SW Canada-NW U.S.

Kö'pė-nick, Cö'pė-nik area of East Berlin

Kō-re-ä' (rä) *State* NE India

Kō-rē'ȧ see NORTH KOREA, SOUTH KOREA.

Kō-rē'ȧ Strait *Channel* Korea-Japan, site of **Korean Arch.**

Kō-ri-yä-mä *City* Honshu, Japan; silk mills

Kôrr'ce (chė), It. **Co-riz'zä** (rēt') *Town* * of *Prefecture* SE Albania; textiles, flour

Kö-ryak' National District *District* E U.S.S.R. on Bering S.; fish

Kôs, Cos *Island* of Dodecanese, SW Turkey, Asia

Kos-ci-us'kō, Mount *Peak* 7330 ft., highest in Australia, SE part

Kosh'tän Tau' (tou') *Mountain* 16,875 ft. U.S.S.R., Eur.

Kō - shū, Kwäng - jū *Town* SW South Korea   [Nepal-India

Kō'si *River* 305 m.

Kô'si-ce (shi-tse), Ger. **Kä'schau** *City* SE Czechoslovakia; industrial

Kö-strö-ma' *River* 250 m. and *City* * of *Region* N cen. R.S.F.S.R., U.S.S.R., Eur.

Kō'tȧh *Town* * of *State* NW India; muslin, carpets

Kö'then (tėn) *City* East Germany; factories

Kot'tō *River* 400 m.

cen. Africa

K ö v - r ô v' *Town* R.S.F.S.R., U.S.S.R., Eur.

Kow'lōōn', Kau'lūn' (kow') *Town* on *Peninsula* SE China, bel. to Hong Kong; imp. commercially

Koy'u-kuk (kī') *River* 425 m. W Alas., U.S.

Krä-kȧ-tau' (tou') *Island volcano* nr. Java, Indonesia

Krä'kow (kōōf), **Krä'-kau** (kou) *City* * of *Department* S Poland; educational cen.

Krȧ-mȧ-tôrsk' *City* Ukraine, U.S.S.R.; industry

Kras'no-där *City* * of *Territory* R.S.F.S.R., S U.S.S.R., Eur.; industrial, cultural cen.

Kras'no-vodsk *Town* on *Gulf* * of *Region* U.S.S.R. cen. Asia

Kras'no-yärsk *Town* * of *Territory* W cen. Siberia, U.S.S.R.; commerce, industry, gold

Kras'nẏ Lūch' *City* Ukraine U.S.S.R.

Kre'feld (krä') *City* West Germany; textiles

Kre'mėn-chūg *City* Ukraine, U.S.S.R.

Kre-mė-nets' *City* Ukraine, U.S.S.R.

Krem'lin = a citadel, walled part of Russ. city; site of government buildings in Moscow

Krems *City* N Austria; machinery

Krish'nȧ now KISTNA

Kri-voi' Rôg' *City* Ukraine, U.S.S.R.; mines

Krōn'shtadt *Town* on *Bay*, NW U.S.S.R. Eur.

Krö-pot'kin *Town* U.S.S.R. Eur.; grain

Krū'gêr National Park *Game reserve* NE Rep. of South Africa

Krū'gêrs-dôrp *Town* NE Rep. of South Africa; gold cen.

Krung Thep (kroong t'hȧp) =BANGKOK

Kuä'lȧ Lum'pur (loom'-poor) *City* * of Malaysia, W cen. Malay Penin.; pop. 216,230

Kū-ban' *River* 510 m. U.S.S.R. Eur.

Kū'ching *City* Borneo, Malaysia; trade cen.

Ku'fow', Chu'fou' (fōō') *Town* NE China; home of Confucius

Kūh-i-Di-när' (dē) *Peak* 14,030 ft. SW Iran

Kūi'bẏ-shev, was **Sȧ-ma'rȧ** *City* * of *Region* cen. U.S.S.R., Eur.; port

Kū'kông' *City* SE China; coal cen.

Kū'lȧ Gulf *Gulf* Solomon Is.; WW II battles

Ku-ma' *River* 400 m. U.S.S.R. Eur.

Ku-mä-gä-yä *Town* Honshu, Japan

Ku-mä-mō-tō *City* * of *Prefecture*, Kyushu, Japan

Kū-mä'si *City* S cen. Ghana; mod. city

Kum-bȧ-kō'nȧm *City* S India; Brahman cen.

Kun'lun', Shän' *Mountain ranges* cen. Asia

Kun'ming', was **Yunnan'** *City* SW China; trade cen.

Kun-sän = GUNZAN

Kuô'piô *City* * of *Department* S Finland; lumber cen.

Kū'päng = KOEPANG

Ku-rä' *River* 825 m. NE Turkey to Caspian S.

Kûr-di-stän' *Region* (nonpolitical) SW Asia: Turkey, Iraq, Iran

Ku-re (koo) *City* Honshu, Japan; harbor

Kur-gan' (koor) *City* * of *Region* cen. U.S.S.R., W Asia; trade cen.

Ku-ri-hä-mä *Town* SE Honshu, Japan; Comm. Perry's landing site, 1853

Kū'ril or **Ku'rile Islands** *Islands* (ab. 32) N of Japan; bel. to Russia

Kū'ril Strait *Strait* bet. *Islands* and U.S.S.R.

Kûr-lȧnd = K U R - ZEME

Kur'rȧm *River* 200 m. NW Pakistan

Kursk (koorsk) *City* * of *Region* E cen. R.S.F.S.R., U.S.S.R., Eur.

Ku-ru-me (koo-roo) *City* Kyushu, Japan; cotton fabric

Kur'ze-me, Kûr'lȧnd *Province* W Latvia U.S.S.R.

Ku-shi-ro *City* Hokkaido, Japan; port

Kus'ko-kwim *River* 550 m. SW Alas., U.S.

Ku-stȧ-naī' *Town* * of *Region* Kazakh, U.S.S.R. cen. Asia

Ku-tä'i-si *City* Georgia, U.S.S.R.; trade, coal

Kūt'al I-mär'ȧ *Town* SE cen. Iraq

Kū'tä Rä'jä *Port* Sumatra, Indonesia

Ku-wāit', State of *Country*, NE corner of Arabian Peninsula; 9,370 sq. m.; pop. 850,000; 3 provincial governorates; *Main cities:* * Kuwait, Hawaii; *Geog.:* consists largely of sandy, riverless desert interspersed with small hills. Vegetation sparse; *Climate:* intensely hot. Rainfall less than 4".

Flag: green, white, red stripes from top to bottom joining at staff side with black trapezoid.

Ethnic comp.: Kuwaitis, other Arabs, Persians, Indians, Pakistanis, others; *Language:* Arabic (official), English; *Religions:* Sunni Moslem, Shia Moslem, Christian.

Products: crude oil, petroleum, petrochemicals, fertilizers; *Minerals:* oil, natural gas; *Major exports:* oil, petroleum products; *Major imports:*

foodstuffs, building materials, automobiles, industrial equipment, electrical products; *Industries:* banking, oil refining, entrepôt trade, fishing.

Currency: dinar.

Head of Government: Amir (selected from and by members of Mubarak lineage of Al-Sabah family); *Legislature:* National Assembly; *Judiciary:* in sheik's name by civil, religious courts.

Kuz-netsk' (kooz) *City* R.S.F.S.R., U.S.S.R., Eur.; trade cen.

Kuz-netsk' Basin *Basin* of Tom R., U.S.S.R., Asia; iron, coal

Kwä'jà-lein (lin) *Island* Marshall Is. W Pacific O.   [S Africa

Kwän'dō *River* 600 m.

Kwäng'chow' (jō') 1. official name for CANTON. 2. *Territory* SE China, formerly Fr.

Kwäng-jū = KOSHU

Kwäng'si' *Province* SE China; rice, forests

Kwäng'tung' (doong') *Province* SE China; agriculture, harbors

Kwän'tung' (doong') *Territory* S Manchuria, China

Kwei'chow' (gwä'jō') *Province* S China; agriculture, forestry

Kwei'lin' (gwä') *City* SE China

Kwei'sui' (gwä'swä') *Town* N China; trade

Kwei'yäng' or **Kwei'-chū'** (gwä') *City* S China

Kyō'gà *Lake* 1000 sq. m. S cen. Uganda

Kyông'sông = SEOUL

Kyō'tō *City* * of *Prefecture,* anc. * of Japan; Honshu, Japan

Kȳ-rē'ni-à *District* N Cyprus

Kyū'shū *Island* S Japan; fine harbors

Kẏ-zẏl' Kum' *Desert* 100,000 sq. m. U.S.S.R., cen. Asia

Kzẏl'-Ôr-dä' *Town* * of *Region* U.S.S.R., cen. Asia

L

Lab'rà-dôr 1. *Peninsula* E Canada; div. bet. Quebec and Newfoundland provs. 2. *Current* flows S along W Greenland, E Newfoundland

Là-bū'àn *Island* off NW Borneo, Malaysia

Lac'cà-dīve and A-min-di'vi Islands (dē') *Islands,* Terr. of India, Arabian S.

Läch'làn (läk') *River* 800 m. SE Australia

Là-cō'ni-à *Department* and *Anc. country* SE Greece; * Sparta

Lä Cö-rū'na (nyä) *City* * of *Province* NW Spain; port

Lä Crôsse' *City* W Wisc., U.S.; pop. 51,-153; shipping cen., manufacturing

Là-däkh' *District* and *Mountain range* E Kashmir

Lad'ō-gà *Lake* N U.S.S.R.; 7000 sq. m.; largest in Eur.

Lä'e *Town* SE New Guinea; WW II base

Lä-fày-ette' 1. *City* W cen. Ind., U.S.; pop. 44,955; commerce. 2. *City* La., U.S.; pop. 68,908; market cen.

Là-gōōn' Islands = ELLICE ISLANDS

Lä'gos *City* on *Island* * of Nigeria, SW part; pop. 700,000; port

Lä Guaī'rà *Town* N Venezuela

La-gū'nà *Province* Luzon, Phil. Is.   [VANA

Lä Hä-bä'nä = HA-

La Hä'brà *City* S Cal., U.S.; pop. 41,350

Là-hōre' 1. *City* * of West Pakistan; trade cen. 2. *Former division* NW Brit. India, now div. Pakistan-India

Läh'ti *City* S Finland

Laï'chow' (jō') now YEHSIEN

Lail-lä'hue (lī-yä'wä) *Peak* 16,995 ft. Bolivia-Peru

Läke Chärles *City* SW La., U.S.; pop. 77,998

Lake District *Region* NW England; resorts

Läke'hûrst *Borough* E N.J., U.S.; site of

Hindenburg fire 1937

Läke'land *City* cen. Fla., U.S.; pop. 41,-550; business

Lake of the Woods *Lake* N Minn., U.S.-S Canada

Lake Plac'id (plas') *Village* NE N.Y., U.S.

Lake Suc-cess' (suk-ses') *Village* SE N.Y. U.S.

Läke'wood 1. *City* N Ohio U.S.; pop. 70,-173. 2. *City* S. Cal., U.S.; pop. 82,973; residential. 3. *City* N Col., U.S.; pop. 92,-787

Lä Män'chä *Region* S cen. Spain

Là-märck', Mount *Peak* 13,300 ft. S cen. Calif. U.S.

Läm-ba-re-ne' (rä-nä') *Town* W Gabon

La Me'sa (mä') *City* S Cal., U.S.; pop. 39,-178

Lam'mêr-mūir or **Lam'-mêr-moor** *Hills Range* SE Scotland

Là-motte' *Peak* *Peak* 12,720 ft. Utah, U.S.

Läm-päng *Town* * of *Province* NW Thailand

Läm'pông *Bay* and *District* S Sumatra, Indonesia

Lan'àrk-shîre *County* S cen. Scotland; ships, textiles, mining

Lan'cà-shire, Lan'càs-têr *County* NW England; mining, shipping, manufacturing

Lan'cas-têr 1. *City* SE Pa., U.S.; pop. 57,-690; tobacco, farming, livestock cen.; factories. 2. *Municipal borough* NW England; textiles

Län'chow' (jō') = KAOLAN

Landes (länd) *Department* SW France

Lands End *Cape* SW England

Länds'hūt *City* SE West Germany; manufacturing

Läng'chung' (joong') *City* S cen. China

Lang'ley, Mount (li) *Peak* 14,040 ft. S cen. Calif., U.S.

Län-gre'o (grä') *City*

NW Spain

Lang' Son' *Town* NE North Vietnam

Lan'sing *City* * of Mich., U.S.; pop. 131,546; automobiles

Län'tsäng' = Chin. for MEKONG

Lä'nus *City* E Argentina

Lao'hō-kōw' (lou') *City* E cen. China

Laoigh'is (lä'ish), **Leix** (läx) *County* cen. Eire

Lao' Kay' (lou' kī') *Town* N Vietnam

Laos (lous), Kingdom of *Country;* SE Asia; 88,780 sq. m.; pop. 2,700,000; 16 provinces; *Main cities:* * Vientiane, Luang, Prabang, Savannakhet; *Main river:* Mekong; *Geog.:* large part of terrain, particularly in N, covered by dense jungle, rugged mountains; *Climate:* monsoonal.

Flag: 3-headed white elephant, standing on 5 steps under white parasol against red field.

Ethnic comp.: Thai, Indonesian, Chinese; *Language:* Lao (official), French; *Religion:* Theravada Buddhist, animist.

Products: rice, maize, opium, tobacco, timber, citrus fruit, tea, tin, iron ore, leather, coffee, cardamon, hides; *Minerals:* tin, some iron ore, gold, copper, manganese; *Major exports:* tin, coffee, resins, wood; *Major imports:* foodstuff, petroleum products, transportation equipment; *In-*

dustries: tin mining, forestry, agriculture.

Currency: kip.

Head of Government: King; *Legislature:* bicameral National Assembly, King's Council; *Judiciary:* independent and separate of executive, legislative powers.

Lä Päl'mä *Island* of Canary Is., Spain

Lä Päm'pä *Territory* S cen. Argentina

Là Paz' 1. *City* * of *Department* and * of Bolivia; pop. 562,000; industry, trade. 2. *Department* S El Salvador. 3. *Department, Town* SW Honduras. 4. *Town* on *Bay* NW Mexico

Lap'land *Region* above Arctic Circle: parts of Norway, Sweden, Finland and Kola Penin. of U.S.S.R.; reindeer, fish

Lä Plä'tä 1. *City* E Argentina; city plan like Wash., D.C. 2. *River* 225 m. Uraguay-Argentina. 3. *Unit* of Span. South America, 18th cent. 4. *Mountains* SW Colo., U.S. 5. *Peak* 14,340 ft. Colo., U.S.

Lap'tev Sea (tyèf) *Area* of Arctic O. U.S.S.R., Asia

La-rache' (rash') *City* NW Morocco; port, fisheries

Lar'à-mie *River* 200 m., *Mountain range* Colo. Wyo., U.S.

Lärch *River* 300 m. Quebec, Canada

Là-re'dō (rä') *City* S Tex., U.S.; pop. 69,-024; industrial port

Là-ris'sà *City* * of *Department* Thessaly, Greece

La Rô-chelle' (shel') *City* W France

L ä r s Chris'tèn-sèn Cōast (kris') *Coast* of Antarctica on Indian O. (Norway)

Läs Crū'cès *City* S N.M., U.S.; pop. 37,857

Lä Se-re'nä (rä') *City* cen. Chile

Làsh'kàr *City* N cen. India; trade

Läs Päl'mäs *City* * of *Province* Canary Is. Spain; port

Lä Spe'ziä (spä') *City* on *Gulf* * of *Province* NW Italy; harbor

Las'sèn Peak *Volcano* 10,545 ft. NE Calif., U.S.

Läs Ve'gàs (vä') *City* SE Nev., U.S.; pop. 125,787; tourists

Läs Vil'las (vē'yäs) *Province* W cen. Cuba

Lat-à-ki'à (kē') *City* * of *Territory* (coastal region) W Syria; tobacco

Lat'in À-mer'i-cà = *Area* incl. Span. America and Brazil

Là-ti'nä (tē'), formerly **Lit-tō'ri-à** *Province* cen. Italy

Lä'ti-um (shi) *Compartimento* and *Anc. country* cen. Italy

Lä Tôr-tū'gä *Island* N cen. Venezuela

La Tri-ni-te' (trē-nē-tä') *Commune* E Martinique

Lat'vi-àn S.S.R. *Republic* of U.S.S.R. N Eur.; * Riga; lumber, agriculture, livestock; Balkan republic before 1940

Laun'ces-tön *City* Tasmania, Australia; trade cen.

Lä Ū-niôn' 1. *Province* Luzon, Phil. Is.; coconuts, sugar. 2. *Town* * of *Department* E El Salvador

Lău-ren'tian Moun-tains (shàn) *Mountain range* Quebec, Canada

Lău-sanne' *Commune* W Switzerland; manufacturing

Lau-tō'kà (lou) *Town* Fiji Is.; sugar cen.

La-val' *Commune* NW France

Lä Ven'tä (vän') *Village* SE Mexico

Läw'rènce 1. *City* NE Mass., U.S.; pop. 66,915; paper, textiles, rubber products. 2. *City* E Kan., U.S.; pop. 45,698

Läw'tön *City* SW Okla.,

U.S.; pop. 74,470; cotton, factories

Lēaf 1. *River* 200 m. SE Miss., U.S. 2. *River* 295 m. Quebec, Canada

Leam'ing-tön (l e m') *Municipal borough* cen. England; resort

Leav'èn-wörth (lev') *City* NE Kan., U.S.; nearby FORT LEAVENWORTH

Leb'à-nön, Republic of *Country;* SW Asia; 3,400 sq. m.; pop. 2,788,000; 5 provinces; *Main cities:* * Beirut, Tripoli, Zahlé, Saida, Tyre; *Main rivers:* Litani, Hasbani; *Geog.:* narrow coastal plain behind which are high Lebanese mts. Farther E fertile Begaa Valley & Anti-Lebanese mts. extending to Syrian frontier; *Climate:* typically Mediterranean.

Flag: horizontal stripes — wide white band in middle, narrower red band above, below with green cedar tree centered on white.

Ethnic comp.: Arabs, Armenians, Druze, Jews, others; *Language:* Arabic (official), French, English, Armenian; *Religions:* Christian, Muslin, Druze, Jewish, others.

Products: fruit, cereals, vegetables, skins, textiles, tobacco, livestock; *Minerals:* bitumen, iron ore, lime, salt; *Major exports:* citrus, vegetables, textiles; *Ma-*

jor imports: aircraft, motor vehicles, cigarettes, household appliances, wheat, corn; *Industries:* cement, oil refining, food processing, textiles.

Currency: pound.

Head of Government: President; *Legislature:* Chamber of Deputies; *Judiciary:* based on Turkish, French models. Also religious courts.

Le Bour-get' (boor-zhä') *Commune* N France; Lindbergh's landing 1927

Lec'ce (lät'chä) *Commune* * of *Province* SE Italy; textiles

Lec'cō (läk') *Commune* N Italy; manufacturing

Lè Conte' *Peak* 13,960 ft. S cen. Calif., U.S.

Lē'dō *Town* NE India; start of Stillwell (formerly **Ledo**) Road, military highway to Burma

Lēeds *City,* county borough N England; industrial cen.

Leeu'wär-dèn (lä'vär) *Commune* N Netherlands; commerce, industry

Leeū'win, Cape *Cape* SW tip of Australia

Lēe'wàrd Islands 1. *Island china* of Lesser Antilles E West Indies; div. bet. U.S. (Virgin Is.), France, Netherlands, Britain. 2. *Island group* of Society Is. (Fr.) S Pacific O.

Le-gäs'pi *Municipality* E Phil. Is.

Leg'hôrn, It. **Li-vôr'nō** *Commune* cen. Italy; straw hats

Leg-ni'ca (nē'tsä), Ger. **Liēg'nitz** *City* SW Poland; rail cen.

Lê Hä'vrè *City* N France; commercial port

Leices'têr (les') *City,* county borough of **Leices'têr-shire** *County,* cen. England; hosiery, boots, shoes, farms

Leich'härdt (līk') *River*

220 m. Queensland, Australia

Lei'dèn or **Ley'dèn** (lī') *Commune* SW Netherlands; publishing

Leigh (lē) *Municipal borough* NW England; coal, iron, glass

Lein'stèr (len') *Province* SE Eire

Leïp'zig *City* SW East Germany; publishing

Lēith *Former burgh* SE Scotland; now part of Edinburgh

Lê Mäns' (män') *City* NW France; commerce, manufacturing

Lem'bêrg = LVOV

Lem'nôs *Island* of Greece N Aegean S.

Lê Moūs-tier' (tyä') *Cave* SW France; archaeological finds

Lē'nà *River* 3000 m. E cen. Siberia, U.S.S.R.

Len'in-à-bad *Town* * of *Region* U.S.S.R. cen. Asia

Len-in-à-kän', formerly A - le - ksan'dro - pôl *City* Armenia, U.S.S.R.; industrial

Len'in-grad *City* * of *Region* NW R.S.F.S.R., U.S.S.R., Eur.; * of Russia 1712-1917 as **St. Pē'tèrs-bûrg**, and 1914-24 as **Pet'ro-grad**; cultural, industrial

Len'in Peak *Mountain* 23,385 ft. U.S.S.R. cen. Asia

Len'insk - Kuz-nets'kiy (kooz) *Town* S cen. U.S.S.R., Asia

Len'nöx *Town* W Mass., U.S.; Tanglewood music festivals

Le-ôn' (lā) 1. *City* cen. Mexico; textiles. 2. *City* * of *Dept.* W Nicaragua; farming, commerce, industry. 3. *City* * of *Province* NW Spain; manufactures. 4. *Region* and *anc. kingdom* NW Spain

Lē'o-nīne City *Area* of Rome, Italy; incl. Vatican

Lē'o-pōld II, Lake *Lake* W Congo (L)

Lē'o-pōld-ville see KINSHASA

Le'pä-yä, Li-ba'và *City* * of *District* W Latvia; port

Le-pon'tīne Alps *Range* Italy-Switzerland

Le'ri-dä (lā') *Commune* * of *Province* NE Spain; manufactures

Lē'ros *Island* of Dodecanese Is.

Les Baux' (lā-bō') *Commune* SE France

Les'bos or **Mỳt-i-le'ne** (lē') *Island* Greek; E Aegean S.; olives

Lesotho, Kingdom of *Country;* formerly Republic of Basutoland; EC part of Republic of S Africa; 11,720 sq. m.; pop. 1,142,000; 9 administrative districts; *Main cities:* * Maseru, Leribe, Mohale's Hoek; *Main river:* Orange; *Geog.:* W lowland terrain and chief agricultural zone, the rest mountainous; *Climate:* tropical belt tempered by elevation.

Flag: 2 narrow vertical bands of green, red on left side with the rest of banner being blue. In center of blue field is white traditional Basuto, conical-shaped, straw hat.

Ethnic comp.: Bantu; *Language:* Sotho, English (official); *Religions:* Roman Catholic, Protestant, animist.

Products: wool, mohair, skins, cereals, livestock; *Mineral:* diamonds; *Major exports:* wool, dia-

monds, mohair, livestock; *Major imports:* foodstuffs, textiles, clothing, transportation equipment, chemicals; *Industries:* printing, carpet weaving, brewing, candle making, tire retreading.

Currency: South African rand.

Head of Government: King; *Legislature:* bicameral parliament; *Judiciary:* established under British rule.

Les'sêr An-til'lês *Islands* one of 3 divisions of West Indies; incl. Virgin Is., Windward and Leeward Is., and Netherlands West Indies; also Barbados, Trinidad, Tobago

Leū'kàs, It. Sän'tä Mau'rä (mou') *Island* of Ionian Is. Greece

Lê-val-lois' - Per-ret' (lwä' pe-re') *Commune* N France; port

Le-vant' *Area* E shore of Mediterranean, Greece-Egypt

Le-vant' States *Countries* of Levant area

Lê-veque', Cape *Cape* N West Australia

Le-vêr-kū'sèn (lā) *City* W West Germany; manufactures

Le-vī'à-thàn Peak *Peak* 13,535 ft. Colo., U.S.

Lew'ès (lū') *River* 338 m. S cen. Yukon, Canada

Lew'is-tön (lū') *City* SW Me., U.S.; pop. 41,779; textiles

Lew'is with Har'ris *Island* of Outer Hebrides NW Scotland

Lex'ing-tön 1. *City* NE Ky., U.S.; pop. 108,-137; tobacco, horses. 2. *Town* NE Mass., U.S.; start of Am. Revolution, 1775. 3. *Town* W cen. Va., U.S.; quarries, Natural Bridge

Ley'tē (lā') 1. *Island* E Phil. Is.; agriculture, minerals, timber. 2.

Gulf E of island; WW II battle

Ley'tön (lā') *Municipal borough* SE England

Lhä'sà *City* * of Tibet; Buddhist sacred city

Lhô'tse S *Peak* of Mt. Everest; 28,100 ft.; bauxite

Liao (li-ou') *River* 700 m. S Manchuria

Liao'ning' (li-ou'); formerly **Fèng'ti-en', Shèng'king'** (jing') *Province* S Manchuria

Liao'peh' (li-ou'bā') *Province* SW Manchuria

Liao'tung' (li-ou'doong') *Peninsula* and *Gulf* S Manchuria

Liao'yäng' (li-ou') *City* S Manchuria; cotton

Liao'yuän' (li-ou') *Town* SW Manchuria; market cen.

Li'ärd (lē') *River* 550 m. W Canada

Li'be-rec (rets) *City* W Czechoslovakia; cloth

Lĭ-bē'ri-à, Republic of *Country,* W Africa; 43,000 sq. m.; pop. 1,193,000; 9 counties; *Main city:* * Monrovia; *Main river:* Morro; *Geog.:* from a narrow strip of coastal land dotted with lagoons, creeks, marshes, country rises in series of plateaus. Low mountains occur intermittently but few above 3,000 ft.; *Climate:* tropical rain forest belt.

Flag: 11 red & white stripes with white star on blue field in upper left corner.

Ethnic comp.: Kru, Mandingo, Gola; *Language:* English (official), tribal lan-

guages; *Religions:* Protestant, Moslem, animist.

Products: rubber, coffee, cocoa, rice, sugar, palm kernels, timber, iron ore, gold, diamonds; *Minerals:* iron ore, diamonds, bauxite, manganese, columbite, tantilite; *Major exports:* iron ore, rubber, diamonds; *Major imports:* manufactured goods, machinery, transportation equipment, food; *Industries:* agriculture, forestry, fishing, mining.

Currency: Liberian dollar on par with U. S. dollar.

Head of Government: President; *Legislature:* bicameral legislature — Senate, House of Representatives; *Judiciary:* headed by Supreme Court. Subordinate courts established as necessary by act of legislature.

Li-bre-ville′ (lē-brevēl′) *Town* * of Gabon; port

Lib′y̆-à, Libyan Arab Republic, *Country,* NC coast of Africa; 810,000 sq. m.; pop. 2,053,000; 10 geographic regions; *Main cities:* * Tripoli, Benghazi, Misurata, Khoms - Cussabat; *Geog.:* 95% barren, rock strewn plains & sand, 2 small areas of hills & mts. 2% of land arable; *Climate:* rainfall irregular, scant. Ghibli, hot, dry, dust laden

southern wind, lasts from 1–4 days.

Flag: horizontal stripes, red, white, black from top to bottom, twice as long as wide.

Ethnic comp.: Arabs, Berbers, aborigines, Negroes, Italians; *Language:* Arabic (official), English, Italian; *Religion:* Sunni Moslem.

Products: olives, dates, citrus fruit, cereals, wool, livestock, fish, tobacco, oil, fabrics, leather; *Minerals:* oil, gypsum, chalk, limestone, marble, iron ore, potassium; *Major export:* crude oil; *Major imports:* oil drilling equipment & machinery, iron, steel pipes, tubes, fittings, manufactured goods — food products; *Industries:* manufacturing (food processing, textiles, soap, detergent, paper bags, wrapping paper), mining.

Currency: Libyan pound.

Head of Government: Chairman of Revolutionary Command Council; *Legislature:* Parliament dissolved in 1969; *Judiciary:* based on European civil law. Islamic law applied in matters regarding personal status of Moslems.

Li-cän-cä′bur (vōōr) *Volcano* 19,455 ft. N Chile

Lich′tèn-bêrg (lik′) *Village* E Berlin, Germany; WW II concentration camp

Lick′ing *River* 350 m. NE Ky., U.S.

Li′di-ce (se) *Village* W Czechoslovakia; 1942 Nazi massacre

Li′dō (lē′) *Island reef* outside Venice Lagoon NE Italy; resort

Liech′tèn-stein (lik′), Principality of *Country,* C Europe; 62 sq.

m.; pop. 22,500; * Vaduz; 11 districts; *Main river:* Rhine; *Geog.:* ⅓ is Rhine Valley, rest mountainous; *Climate:* typical Alpine.

Flag: 2 horizontal bands, blue over red with gold crown centered in blue field.

Ethnic comp.: Germans (Alemanni), Italians, Spaniards, Greeks, Turks; *Language:* German (official), Alemannic, French; *Religions:* Roman Catholic, Protestant.

Products: textiles, metal ware, light machinery, precision instruments, ceramics, leather, wood work, electrical equipment, cameras; *Minerals:* some quarrying; *Major exports:* machinery, tools, artificial teeth, textiles, chemicals, food; *Industries:* international banking, tourism, food processing, production of precision manufactures, textiles.

Currency: Swiss franc.

Head of Government: Monarch; *Legislature:* unicameral Diet; *Judiciary:* independent, 3 levels of regular courts, administrative court, constitutional court.

Li-ege′ (āzh′) *City* * of *Province* E Belgium; coal, manufacturing

Lieg′nitz (lig′) = LEGNICA

Li-gū′ri-à *Compartimento* NW Italy on **Li-gūr′i-àn** S.; incl. It. Riviera; fruits, machinery, resorts

Li-gūr′i-àn Alps *Range* NW Italy

Lille, formerly **Lisle** (lēl) *City* N France; commerce, industry

Li′mà *City* NW Ohio, U.S.; pop. 53,734; heavy industry

Li′mà (lē′) *City* * of *Department,* * of Peru, cen. part; pop. 2,526,000; economic, cultural, political cen.

Li-may′ (mī′) *River* 250 m. cen. Argentina

Lim′bûrg *Region* W Eur. div. bet.: *Province* SE Netherlands and *Province* NE Belgium; limburger cheese

Lim′êr-ick *City* * of *County* SW Eire; farming, fish, livestock

Li-moges′ (mōzh′) *City* W cen. France; porcelain

Li-môn′ Bāy *Inlet* of Caribbean S., Canal Zone

Lim-pō′pō *River* 1000 m. SE Africa to Indian O.

Li-nä′res *Commune* S Spain; mining

Lin′coln (kön) 1. *City* * of Neb., U.S.; pop. 149,518; commerce, shipping. 2. *City,* county borough of **Lin′cöln-shíre** E England

Lin′coln, Mount (kön) *Peak* 14,285 ft. cen. Colo., U.S.

Lin′coln Pärk (kön) *City* SE Mich., U.S.; pop. 52,984

Lin′dèn *City* NE N.J., U.S.; pop. 41,409; industry

Lin′di 1. *River* 400 m. NE Congo (L). 2. *Port* Tanzania

Line Islands *Island group,* U.S. (Kingman Reef, Palmyra I.) and Brit. (Washington, Fanning, Christmas), cen. Pacific O.

Lin-gä-yen′ *Gulf* and

Municipality N Luzon, Phil. Is.

Lin'ko-ping (chö) *City* SE Sweden; manufacturing

Linz *City* N Austria; river port; manufacturing

Li-pä' *Municipality* Luzon, Phil. Is.

Lip'ȧ-ri Islands *Island group* off N Sicily

Li'petsk (lē') *Town* R.S.F.S.R., U.S.S.R., Eur.; resort

Lip'pė *Former State* NW Germany

Lis'bön *City* * of **Lis-bō'ȧ** district and * of Portugal, W part; pop. 1,000,000; fine harbor, manufacturing

Lisle (lēl) = LILLE

Li'sū-land (lē') *Region* S China; mountains

Lith-ū-ā'ni-ȧ, Lit-va' *Baltic republic* until 1940, now **Lith-ū-ā'ni-ȧn S.S.R.** *Republic* of U.S.S.R. N Eur.; * Vilnyus; agriculture, lumber, livestock, iron

Lit'tle Ȧ-mer'i-cȧ *Settlement* of Byrd Expedition, Ross S., Antarctica

Lit'tle Beȧr Peak *Peak* 14,000 ft. Colo., U.S.

Lit'tle Big Hôrn *River* S Mont., U.S.; General Custer's defeat 1876

Lit'tle Col-o-rä'dō *River* 300 m. NE Ariz., U.S.

Lit'tle Mis-sou'ri (zoor') *River* 560 m. Wyo.-N.D., U.S.

Lit'tle Neck Bay *Inlet* W Long I. N.Y., U.S.

Lit'tle Rock *City* * of Ark., U.S.; pop. 132,-483; mineral, farm area; manufacturing

Lit'tle Sioux (sōō) *River* 235 m. Minn.-Iowa, U.S.

Lit-tō'ri-ȧ now LATINA

Liu'chow' (li-ōō'jō'), was **Mä'ping** *City* SE China

Liv'êr-môre *City* W Cal., U.S.; pop. 37,-703

Liv'êr-pōōl *City* and county borough NW

England; port, flour

Liv'ing-stöne *Town* S Zambia; former * of Northern Rhodesia

Li-vō'ni-ȧ 1. *City* SE Mich., U.S.; pop. 110,109. 2. *Former province* of Russia, now LATVIA and ESTONIA

Li-vôr'nō *Province* cen. Italy

Liz'ȧrd Point S point of Great Britain

Lju'blja-nä (yōō'blyä), **Laī'bach** (bäk) *City* NW Yugoslavia

Ljung'an (yung') *River* 234 m. E Sweden

Ljus'nän (yōōs') *River* 267 m. cen. Sweden

Llul-lail-la'cō (yōō-yi-yä') *Volcano* 22,055 ft. N Chile   [Chile

Lō'ä *River* 275 m. N

Lo-an'gė *River* 425 m. cen. Angola

Lō'bos or **Sēal Islands** *Islands* off N Peru

Lō-cär'nō *Commune* SE cen. Switzerland

Lodz (lōōj) *City* * of *Department* cen. Poland; textile cen.

Lō'fō-tėn *Island group* NW Norway; fish

Lō'gȧn, Mount *Peak* 19,850 ft. SW Yukon, Canada

Lo-grō'no *Commune* * of *Province* N Spain

Loire (lwar) 1. *River* 625 m. longest in France, SE part. 2. *Departments* of France: **Loire** SE; **Loire - In-fe-rieure'** (fä-ryêr') NW; **Loi-ret'** (lwa-re') N cen.; **Loir-et-cher'** (ä-shär')

Lol'lȧnd *Island* of Denmark, Baltic S.

Lo-mä'mi *River* 900 m. cen. Congo (L) [tina

Lō'mäs *Town* E Argen-

Löm'bȧrd *Village* NE Ill., U.S.; pop. 35,977

Lom'bȧr-dy *Compartimento* N Italy

Lom-bok' *Island* and *Strait* E of Bali, Indonesia

Lô-me' (mä') *Town* * of Togo Rep.; port

Lo-me'lȧ (mä') *River* 290 m. cen. Congo Rep. (L)

Lō'mönd, Loch (lok) *Lake* S cen. Scotland

Lön'dön 1. *City* SE Ontario, Canada; industrial. 2. *City* = **Greater London**: SE England incl. **City of London** (old city) and **County of London** (administrative unit); * of United Kingdom, * of Brit. Commonwealth; pop. 7,-880,760; world's largest city; commercial, industrial, cultural cen.

Lön'dön-der-ry 1. *County borough*, * of *County* NW Northern Ireland; harbor, trade, manufacturing. 2. *Cape* N point of W Australia

Löng Bēach *City* SW Calif., U.S.; pop. 358,633

Löng'förd *County* E cen. Eire

Löng Is'lȧnd (ī') *Island* SE N.Y., U.S. bet. **Long Island Sound** and Atlantic O.

Löngs Peak *Mountain* 14,255 ft. Colo., U.S.

Löng'view (vū) *City* NE Tex., U.S.; pop. 45,547; oil

Long'xuyen' (swē'un) *Town* S Vietnam

Look'out Peak *Peak* 13,675 ft. Colo., U.S.

Lo-pat'kȧ, Cape *Cape* into Kuril Strait, E U.S.S.R., Asia

Lo-pō'ri *River* 340 m. cen. Congo (L)

Lo-rāin' *City* N Ohio, U.S.; pop. 78,185; port

Lôr'cä *Commune* SE Spain; mines

Lō'rė-leī *Rock* at Rhine R. West Germany; famous in legend

Lô-rient' (ryän') *Commune* NW France; port

Lôr-rȧine' *Medieval kingdom*, later *Duchy* W Eur.; incl. in ALSACE-LORRAINE

Lôs Al'ȧ-mōs *Town* N.M., U.S.; nuclear test site

Lôs An'gė-lės (jė) *City* SW Calif., U.S.; pop. 2,816,061; resort, industrial city   [China

Lō'shän' *City* S cen.

Los Ne'gros (nä') *Islands* of Admiralty Is.

Los Sän'tos *Province* cen. Panama

Lôt 1. *River* 300 m. S France. 2. *Department* S cen. France

Lôt-et-Ga-rônne' (-ä-) *Department* SW France   [Scotland

Lō'thi-ȧn *Region* S

Loū-ise', Lake (ēz') *Lake* SW Alberta, Canada

Lou-i-si-an'ȧ (loo-i-zi) *State*, named in honor of King Louis XIV of France; 48,523 sq. m.; *pop.*: 3,643,180 (*rank*: 20th); SE U.S.; *Boundaries*: Mississippi, Arkansas, Texas, Gulf of Mexico; *Major cities*: New Orleans, Shreveport, * Baton Rouge; *Major river*: Mississippi; *Major lakes*: Lake Pontchartrain, Lake Borgne; 64 parishes.

Nickname: Pelican State, Bayou State; *Motto*: "Union, justice, confidence;" *Flag*: state seal & motto on blue field; *Flower*: magnolia; *Bird*: brown pelican (unofficial); *Tree*: bald cypress; *Song*: Song of Louisiana.

Industry: cotton, rice, sugar cane, dairy, cattle, soybeans, oil & natural gas refining, pulp & paper making, fish canning; *Natural resources*: petroleum, fish & shellfish, natural gas, sulphur, gas, salt; *Major source of income*: manufacturing, wholesale & retail trade.

Admitted to Union: 1812 (18th state).

Places of interest: Mardi Gras, New Orleans, Cajun Country.

Lou-i-si-an'ȧ Pûr'chȧse *Territory* of U.S.; 885,000 sq. m. from Miss. R.-Rocky Mts., Gulf of Mex.-Canada; bought from France 1803

Louis'ville (loo͞o'i) *City* N cen. Ky., U.S.; pop. 361,472; rail, market cen.

Loup (loop) *River* 300 m. E cen. Neb., U.S.

Lourdes (loord) *Commune* SW France; pilgrimage shrine

Lou-ren'co Mar-ques' (rän'sū, kash') *City* * of Mozambique, S part

Louth *County* NE Eire

Lo-vat' *River* 320 m. U.S.S.R., Eur.

Löve'land Mountain *Peak* 13,625 ft. cen. Colo., U.S.

Lo-ve'ni-à, Mount *Peak* 13,225 ft. Utah, U.S.

Low Countries *Region* N Eur. incl. Netherlands, Belgium, Luxembourg

Low'ell *City* NE Mass., U.S.; pop. 94,239; textiles, literary cen.

Low'er Aus'tri-à *Province* NE Austria

Low'er Bûr'mà *Coast region* of Burma

Low'er Cä-li-fôr'niä *Peninsula* NW Mexico bet. Pacific O. and Gulf of Calif.; incl. a *State* and *Territory*

Low'er E'gýpt (jipt) *Region* Nile Delta, N Egypt

Low'er Sax'ö-nÿ *State* N West Germany

Lowes'tôft *Municipal borough* E England; china

Low'lands, the *Area* S of Grampians, Scotland

Loy'ál-tÿ Islands *Island group* (Fr.) SW Pacific O.

Lo'yäng' or **Ho'nan'** *City* E cen. China

Lô-zere' (zār') *Department* S France

Lū-à-lä'bà *River* 400 m. cen. Africa

Lū-an'dà *City* * of District, * of Angola; port

Luäng'prä-bäng' *Town,* State N Laos; residential *

Lū-äng'wä *River* 400 m. E Zambia

Lū-à-pū'là *River* Zambia-Congo (L)

Lub'böck *City* NW Tex., U.S.; pop. 149,-101; cotton-seed oil, meats

Lū'beck *City,* * of District on *Bay* N East Germany; imp. port

Lū'blin (blēn) *City* * of *Department* E Poland; leather, textiles

Lū-cä'ni-ä 1. *Compartimento* S Italy. 2. *Peak* 17,150 ft. Yukon, Canada

Lūc'cä *Commune* * of *Province* cen. Italy; silk

Lu-cerne' (sêrn'), **Luzêrn'** *Lake, Commune* * of *Canton* cen. Switzerland; tourism

Lū'chow' (jō') = HOFEI, LUHSIEN

Luck'now (nou) *City* N India; rail cen., paper, metal

Lû'dén-scheid (shīt) *City* W cen. Germany; resort, factories

Lu-dhi-ä'nà (loo) *Town* NW India; wool, grain cen.

Lūd'wigs-bûrg (viks) *City* SW West Germany; factories

Lūd-wigs-hä'fén (viks) *City* W West Germany; commercial port

Lū-em'be (bä) *River* 300 m. Angola

Lū-gä'nö *Commune* on *Lake* SE cen. Switzerland; resort

Lu-gansk', Vö-ro-shi'-löv-grad (shē') *City* * of *Region;* coal, factories

Lū'go *Commune* * of *Province* NW Spain; trade cen.

Lū'hsien' (shi-en'), formerly **Lū'chow'** (jō') *City* S cen. China; salt trade

Luik (loik) = LIEGE

Lū-ke'nie (kä'nyâ) *River* 450 m. cen. Congo (L) [Sweden

Lū'lé *River* 280 m. N

Lū-lū'à *River* 600 m. S Congo (L)

Lund *City* SW Sweden; publishing

Lu'né-bûrg *City* * of *District* N West Germany; factories

Lun'ga (loong') *Village, River* NW Guadalcanal; WW II battles

Lung'ki' (kē'), formerly **Chang'chow'** (jäng'-jō') *City* SE China; commerce

Lung'kiang' (ji-äng'), **Tsi'tsi-här** *City* N Manchuria; port

Lū'rāy *Town* N Va., U.S.; caverns nearby

Lū-sä'kà *Town* E Zambia; former * of Northern Rhodesia

Lū-säm'bō = KASAI

Lū'shai Hills *Region* NE India

Lū-si-tā'ni-à = classical name of PORTUGAL

Lūt = DASHT-I-LUT

Lū'tön *Municipal borough* SE cen. England; hats

Lutsk, Luck (lootsk) *City* Ukraine, U.S.S.R.; textiles

Lux'em-burg (bûrg, boorg), **Grand Duchy** of *Country,* W Europe; 1,000 sq. m.; pop. 347,000; 3 districts; *Main cities:* * Luxembourg, Esch/Alzette, Differdange; *Main rivers:* Alzette, Sûre; *Geog.:* hilly, wooded country; *Climate:* cool, temperate, rainy.

Flag: horizontal stripes — red, white, blue from top to bottom.

Ethnic comp.: Luxemburgers; *Language:* Letzeburgesch (official), French, German, English; *Religions:* Roman Catholic, Protestant, Jewish.

Products: potatoes, barley, oats, wheat; *Minerals:* iron ore, slate; *Major exports:* steel, chemicals, plastic fibers, rubber, textiles; *Major imports:*

coal, iron ore, machinery, transportation equipment, food; *Industries:* steel, chemical industries, rubber, fertilizer, food processing.

Currency: Swiss franc.

Head of Government: Grand Duke; *Legislature:* unicameral Parliament; *Judiciary:* influenced by Napoleonic Code, highest court is cour supérieure de justice which is Supreme Court of Appeal and decides upon revisions of legal procedures.

Lux'ôr, El Uq'sor *Town* Upper Egypt; ruins

Lū-zêrn' = LUCERNE

Lū-zon' 1. *Island,* most imp. of Phil. Is.; agriculture. 2. **Strait** *passage* bet. *Island* and S Taiwan

Lvov, Lwow (là-vôf'), **Lem'bûrg** *City* and *Region* Ukraine, U.S.S.R.; formerly Polish; factories

Lwän *River* 400 m. NE China

Lya'khöv Islands *Islands* U.S.S.R., Asia; Ice Age remains

Lÿ'àll-pur (poor) *Town* West Pakistan; cotton cen.

Lÿ-cē'um *Locale* anc. Athens; Aristotle's teachings

Lyd'dà *City* in *District* W Israel

Lÿme Bay *Inlet* SW England

Lÿnch'bûrg *City* S cen. Va., U.S.; pop. 54,-083; tobacco market

Lÿnn 1. *City* NE Mass., U.S.; pop. 90,294; shoe cen. 2. *Canal,* fiord, SE Alas., U.S.; imp. gateway to Klondike

Lÿn'wood *City* S Cal., U.S.; pop. 43,353

Ly-ön-nais' (lē-ö-nä') *Hist. region* SE cen. France

Ly-ons' (lē-ôn') *City* E cen. France; silk manufacture

Lys'kämm (lēs') *Peak*

14,888 ft. Italian-Swiss border

Lỷs'và *City* W U.S.S.R., Asia

M

Maas (Dut.) = MEUSE

Maas-tricht' (trikt') *Commune* SE Netherlands; trade

Mả-cä'ō *Town* in *Port. Colony*, SE **Macao I.**, Pearl R., SE China

Mac'cles-fīeld (ėlz) *Municipal borough* NW England; silk cen.

Mac-e-dō'ni-à (mas) 1. *Region* cen. Balkan penin. site of *Anc. country*. 2. *Division* N Greece; farming. 3. *Republic* SE Yugoslavia

Ma-cei-ô' (sā) *City* E Brazil; sugar, cotton

Mä-ce-rä'tä (che) *Commune* * of *Province* cen. Italy

Mảc-ken'zie *District*, *River* 1120 m. into *Bay*, Northwest Terrs., Canada

Mack'i-nac *Island* in *Straits* Lake Huron-Lake Mich., U.S.

Mä'cön *City* cen. Ga., U.S.; pop. 122,423; commerce, industry

Mảc-quär'ie *River* 750 m. SE Australia

Mảc-tän' *Island* off E Cebu, Phil. Is.

Mad-à-gas'car, Malagasy Republic *Country*, Indian Ocean; 229,230 sq. m.; pop. 7,223,000; 6 provinces; *Main cities:* * Tananarive, Tamatave, Majunga, Fianarantsoa, Diégo Suarez; *Main rivers:* Mangoro, Tkopa, Betsiboka, Tsiribihina, Mangoky; *Geog.:* 4th largest island in world. Interior is high plateau with mt. peaks ranging to 9,450'; *Climate:* interior has temperate climate, coastal region is tropical.

Flag: equal-sized bands, white on staff side, red extending horizontally on upper half of remaining side, green on lower half.

Ethnic comp.: Hova, Betsimisáraka, Betslieo, others; *Language:* Malagasy, French (official); *Religions:* Roman Catholic, Protestant, animist.

Products: coffee, vanilla, rice, cloves, sugar, meat, ylang-ylang (oil), graphite, mica, chrome, phosphates, precious stones, metals, textiles; *Minerals:* graphite, mica, gold, industrial beryl; *Major exports:* coffee, vanilla, sugar, rice, raffia; *Major imports:* transportation machinery, textiles, chemicals, pharmaceuticals, machinery, electrical appliances; *Industries:* motor assembly, food processing, silk, cotton weaving, oil refining, mining.

Currency: Malagasy franc.

Head of Government: President; *Legislature:* bicameral — National Assembly, Senate; *Judiciary:* 2 basic jurisdictions — a supreme court, court of appeals and labor.

Mä'däng *Town* * of *District* NE New Guinea; port

Mả-dēi'rà 1. *River* 2100 m. W Brazil. 2. *Island* of *Group* (Port.) E Atlantic O.; wine

Mả'dhyả Prả-desh' (dāsh') *Province* cen. India; incl. former Central Provs., Berar, **Mả'dhyả Bhä'rät**

Ma-di-oen' (yōōn') *City* Java, Indonesia

Mad'i-sön *City* * of Wisc., U.S.; pop. 173,258

Mad'i-sön Heīghts *City* SE Mich., U.S.; pop. 38,599

Mả-doe'rà, Ma-du'rà (doo') *Island* off Java, Indonesia

Mả-dras' 1. *City* * of *State* SE India; main E coast port. 2. *States, former agency* incl. 5 states S India

Mä'dre de Diōs 1. *River* 900 m. Peru-Bolivia. 2. *Archipelago* S Pacific O. off Chile

Mả-drid' *City* * of *Province*, * of Spain, cen. part; pop. 2,500,-000; commercial, manufacturing, cultural cen.

Mad'u-rà, Mả-du'raī *City* S India

Mä-e-bä-shi *City* Honshu, Japan; silk cen.

Mäel'ström *Whirlpool* Norwegian S.

Maf'è-king *Town* former * of Bechuanaland, now Botswana; trade cen.

Mả-gả-dan' *Port* E U.S.S.R., Asia

Mag-dả-lē'nà *Department* and *River* 1060 m. Colombia

Mag'dả-lėn Islands *Islands* E Quebec, Canada

Mag'dė-bûrg *City* * of *District* N East Germany; sugar cen.

Mä-ge-läng' *City* Java, Indonesia

Mả-gel'làn, Strait of (jel') *Strait* S South America

Mag-gio're, Lake (majō'rà) *Lake* N Italy

Mag-ni'to-gôrsk (nē') *City* R.S.F.S.R., U.S.S.R., Asia; imp. iron-steel cen.

Mả-gwe' (gwā') *Town, District, Division* Mandalay, Burma

Mä-hä'käm, Koe-taī' (kōō-tī') *River* 400 m. Borneo, Indonesia

Mả-hal'là el Kū'brà *City* Lower Egypt

Mả-hä'nả-dà *River* 512 m. E India

Mả-hä'räsh'trà *State* W cen. India

Ma-he' (hä') *City* SW India; was Fr.

Mả'hi *River* 300 m. W India

Mä-hon' (ôn') *City* * of Minorca I. Spain; port

Mäid'stōne *Municipal borough* SE England

Maī-kô p' *City* S R.S.F.S.R., U.S.S.R., Eur.; mineral area

Maīn *River* 300 m. cen. West Germany

Mäine *State*, named from French province of Maine; 33,215 sq. m.; *pop.:* 993,663 (*rank:* 38th); New England U.S.; *Boundaries:* New Hampshire, Canada, Atlantic Ocean; *Major cities:* Portland, Bangor, * Augusta; *Major rivers:* St. Johns, Androscoggin, Kennebec, Penobscot, St. Croix; *Major lakes:* Moosehead Lake; 16 counties.

Nickname: Pine Tree State; *Motto:* "Dirigo" (I direct); *Flag:* state seal on blue field; *Flower:* white pine cone, tassel; *Bird:* chickadee; *Tree:* eastern white pine; *Song: State of Maine Song.*

Industry: lobsters, tourism, shipbuilding, wood products, food processing, leather goods, textiles; *Natural resources:* forests, offshore waters; *Major source of income:* wood products.

Admitted to Union: 1820 (23rd state).

Places of interest: Bar Harbor, Acadia Ntl. Park, Moosehead Lake, Baxter State Park.

Mäine'-et-Loire' (ä-lwär') *Department* W France

Mainz *City* cen. West Germany; port, factories

Maī-pū' *Peak* 17,355 ft. Chile-Argentina

Mäit'lånd *Town* SE

Australia; coal, farming

Maī-zu-ru _City_ Honshu, Japan; port

Mȧ-jôr′cȧ (yôr′) _Island_ largest of Balearic Is. Spain; fertile, mountainous

Mȧ-jung′ȧ _Town_ NW Madagascar; port

Mȧ′kȧ-lū _Peak_ 27,790 ft. Himalayas, Nepal

Mä-kä-ri-kä′ri _Salt basin_ Botswana

Mȧ-kas′sȧr 1. _City_ Celebes I., Indonesia; port. 2. _Strait_ Borneo-Celebes

Mȧ-ke′yėv-kȧ (kä′) _City_ Ukraine U.S.S.R.; imp. steel cen.

Mä-khäch-kä-lä′, formerly **Pė-trôvsk′** _City_ SE R. S. F. S. R., U.S.S.R., Eur.; fish, cotton

Mal′ȧ-bär Coast _Region_ SW India

Mȧ-lac′cȧ _Municipality_ on _Strait_ S Malay Penin., Malaysia; rubber, port

Ma′lȧ-gȧ _City_ * of _Province_ S Spain; commercial port

Mal-ȧ-gas′ÿ Republic, Mad-ȧ-gas′cȧr _Island republic_ E Africa, formerly Fr.; 230,000 sq. m.; pop. 7,000,-000; * Tananarive; agriculture

Mȧ-lāi′tȧ _Island_ of Brit. Solomon Is.

Mȧ′lȧ-kȧnd _Region_ West Pakistan

Mä-läng′ _City_ Java, Indonesia; coffee

Ma′lar-ėn _Lake_ SE Sweden

Mal-ȧ-spi′nȧ (spē′) _Glacier_ S Alas., U S

Mä-lä-tyä′ _City_ * of _Vilayet_ E Turkey, Asia

Mä-lä′wi, Republic of

Country, E Africa; 45,410 sq. m.; pop. 4,772,000; 23 districts; _Main cities:_ * Zomba, Blantyre-Limbe, Lilongwe; _Main rivers:_ Shire, Bua, Rukuru; _Geog.:_ part of Great Rift Valley traverses Malawi from N–S. Mts. E–W of Rift Valley; _Climate:_ varies with altitude, dry season May – Oct., wet Nov.–April.

Flag: horizontal stripes — black, red, green, half of red sun in center of top (black) stripe.

Ethnic comp.: Bantu, Asian — European minorities; _Language:_ English (official), Chinyanja, Chitumbukaere, Bantu; _Religions:_ Christian, Moslem, animist.

Products: tea, tobacco, groundnuts, maize, cotton, dried vegetables, coffee, tung oil, rice; _Minerals:_ limestone, bauxite, coal, constructional stone; _Major exports:_ tea, tobacco, peanuts, corn, cotton; _Major imports:_ textiles, motor vehicles, petroleum products, medical & pharmaceutical goods, food products; _Industries:_ quarrying, agriculture, food processing.

Currency: Malawi pound at par with sterling.

Head of Government: President; _Legislature:_ unicameral National Assembly; _Judiciary:_ Supreme Court of Appeal at apex.

Mȧ-lāy′ȧ, Federation of Mainland area of Malaysia

Mä′lāy Archipelago _Island group_ (world's largest) SE Asia, incl. East Indies, New Guinea, Phil. Is.

Mä′lāy Peninsula _Pen-_

insula SE Asia; incl. parts of Burma, Thailand, Malaysia; onetime **Mä′lāy States** (Brit.)

Mȧ-lāy′siȧ (zhȧ), (Malaya, Sarawak, Sabah) _Country,_ SE Asia; 128,478 sq. m.; pop. 10,500,000; 13 states; _Main cities:_ * Kuala Lumpur, Johore, Bahru, Georgetown, Kuching, Kota Kinabalu; _Main rivers:_ Perak, Pahang in Malaya, Rajang in Sarawak, Kinabatanga in Sabah; _Geog.:_ 80 % tropical jungle, 12 % mts. Separated by S China Sea; _Climate:_ 70°F – 90°F, higher elevations cooler, more variable; annual rainfall 100″.

Flag: 14 horizontal red, white stripes, yellow crescent, star on dark blue field in upper left.

Ethnic comp.: Malaya — Malays, Chinese, Indians, Pakistanis. Sarawak — Dayaks, Chinese. Sabah — tribes (esp. Kadazans), Chinese, Malays; _Language:_ Malay (official), English, Chinese — Indian dialects; _Religions:_ Islam (state), Buddhism, Confucianism, Taoism.

Products: rubber, palm oil, rice, timber, copra, tea, palm products, tin, iron ore, petroleum, pineapples, pepper, sago; _Minerals:_ tin, iron ore; _Major exports:_ rubber, tin, forest products; _Major imports:_ foodstuffs, in-

dustrial machinery, metals, electrical equipment, transportation equipment; _Industries:_ oil & sugar refining, steel plants, manufacture of fertilizers.

Currency: Malaysian dollar.

Head of Government: Paramount Ruler; _Legislature:_ bicameral Parliament — Senate, House of Representatives; _Judiciary:_ based on English common law. Highest court is Federal Court.

Mäl′dȧ _District_ E Pakistan-E India

Mäl′dėn _City_ NE Mass. U.S.; pop. 56,127

Mäl′dive Islands, Republic of Maldives, _Country,_ N Indian Ocean; 115 sq. m.; pop. 115,000; 19 atolls; _Main islands:_ King's Island, Minicoy, Gan Island; _Main atolls:_ * Male, Addu, Ihavandiffulu, Tiladummati; _Geog.:_ coral islands, vegetation varies from grass & scrub to dense woods of fruit trees, coconut palms; _Climate:_ hot, humid with little daily variation

Flag: white crescent in center of green rectangle, bordered by red field.

Ethnic comp.: Sinhalese; _Language:_ Maldivian (official); _Religion:_ Islam (state).

Products: fish, coconuts, millet, fruit, coir, rope; _Major exports:_ fish, coconuts,

copra, coir, cowrie shell, tortoise shell, local handicraft products; *Major imports:* rice, flour, kerosene, oil, sugar, textiles, drugs; *Industries:* fish processing, boat building, fishing, copra, coconut oil production.

Currency: Ceylon rupee.

Head of Government: President; *Legislature:* unicameral People's Council (Majlis); *Judiciary:* based on Islamic law.

Mä'li, Republic of *Country,* W Africa; 465,000 sq. m.; pop. 5,217,000; 6 regions; *Main cities:* * Bamako, Mopti, Ségou, Kayes, Sikasso; *Main rivers:* Niger, Senegal; *Geog.:* most of coutry in W African savannah region, N is Sahara Desert; *Climate:* S, W have short but regular rainy season.

Flag: vertical bands green, yellow, red from left to right.

Ethnic comp.: Negro-Hamitic; *Language:* French (official), tribal languages; *Religions:* Islam, Christian.

Products: groundnuts, cotton, meat, rice, millet, gum, skins, sorghum, fish, karité; *Minerals:* unexploited deposits of bauxite, uranium, oil, iron; *Major exports:* cotton, livestock, peanuts, fish; *Major*

imports: vehicles & parts, cotton cloth, iron, steel, petroleum products; *Industries:* textile making, fruit processing.

Currency: Mali franc at par with CFA franc.

Head of Government: President; *Legislature:* Military Committee on National Liberation; *Judiciary:* based on French codes. Supreme Court at apex.

Mä-lin'che (lēn') *Peak* 14,635 ft.; cen. Mexico

Mal'lēe *Region* Victoria, Australia

Mal'mö *City* SW Sweden; port

Mäl'tä *Island* of **Mäl'-tēse Is.,** Brit. Commonwealth nation, Mediterranean S.; 122 sq. m.; pop. 317,-000; * Valletta

Mäl'vêrn *City* SE Australia

Mäm-be-rä'mō *River* 500 m. W Irian

Mam'möth Cāve *Caverns* SW Ky., U.S.

Mä-mō-re' (rä') *River* 1200 m. Bolivia

Man, Isle of *Island* off NW England; * Douglas

Mä-nä'dō *City* Celebes I. Indonesia; coffee

Mä-nä'guä *City* on *Lake* * of *Department,* * of Nicaragua

Ma-na'mä *Town* * of Bahrein Is. (Brit.), Persian Gulf

Mä-nas'säs *Town* NE Va., U.S.; battles of Bull Run 1861-2

Mä-nä-tä'rä *Peak* 12,-140 ft. NW Venezuela

Mä-naus' (nous') *City* W Brazil; port

Mänche *Department* NW France

Man'ches-têr 1. *City* S N.H., U.S.; pop. 87,-754; factories. 2. *City* and *County borough* NW England; port, world's cotton cen. 3. *City* N Conn., U.S.; pop. 47,994; residential

Man-chu'ri-ä (choo')

Territory NE China; was **Man-chū'kuō** (kwō) 1932-45 under Jap.; agriculture

Mänd, Mund *River* 300 m. SW Iran

Man'dä-läy' *City* * of *District* and *Division* Upper Burma

Män'de *State* N India

Man'gä-lōre *City* S India; coffee, pepper

Man-has'set Bay *Inlet* Long I. N.Y., U.S.

Man-hat'tän *Island, Borough* of N.Y. City, N.Y., U.S.; incl. city's financial, cultural, commercial areas

Man-hat'tän Bēach *City* S Cal., U.S.; pop. 35,352

Man-i-kuä'gän *River* 310 m. Quebec, Canada

Mä-nil'ä *City* on *Bay* Luzon, Phil. Is.; former *; chief port

Mä'ni-pur (poor) *Territory* and *River* 210 m. NE India

Mä-ni-sä' *City* * of *Vilayet* W Turkey, Asia; manufacturing

Man-i-tō'bä *Lake* in *Province* cen. Canada; * Winnipeg; agriculture esp. wheat

Man-i-zä'les *City* W cen. Colombia; coffee

Manj'rä *River* 320 m. S cen. India

Man-när', Gulf of *Area* of India O. SE of India; pearl fisheries

Man'nêr-heim *Line* Fortified area (Finnish), now NW U.S.S.R.

Mann'heim *City* cen. West Germany; Rhine port

Mans'fïëld 1. *City* N cen. Ohio, U.S.; pop. 55,047; manufacturing. 2. *Municipal borough* N cen. England; coal area

Män'to-vä, Män'tu-ä *Commune* * of *Province* N Italy; manufacturing

Mä'nus *Island,* largest of Admiralty Is.

Mä-nych' *Valley* SE U S.S.R., Eur.

Mä'ping' =LIUCHOW

Mä-pue'rä (pwä') *River* 270 m. N Brazil

Mar-ä-caï'bō *Lake, City* NW Venezuela; imp. petroluem cen.

Mä-rä-cay' (kī') *City* N Venezuela

Mä - rä - non' (nyôn') *River* 800 m. Peru

Mä-räsh' *City* * of *Vilayet* S cen. Turkety, Asia

Mär'ble-head (bėl-hed) *Town* NE Mass., U.S.; yachting

Mär'chès *Compartimento* cen. Italy

Mär'cus Island *Island* (Jap.) W Pacific O.

Mär'dän *Town* N West Pakistan

Mär' del Plä'tä *City* E Argentina; resort

Mä-reb' *River* 250 m. E Africa

Märe Island *Island* W cen. Calif., U.S.; naval base

Mär-gä-ri'tä (rē') *Island* Caribbean S., Venezuela

Mär'gäte *Municipal borough* SE England

Mär-gė-län' *Town* U.S.S.R. cen. Asia

Mä'ri, A.S.S.R. *Republic* E R.S.F.S.R., U.S.S.R., Eur.

Mar - i - an'äs *Island* group (U.S.) W Pacific O.; incl. Guam, Tinian, Saipan, etc.

Mä-riä-nä'ō *Municipality* and *City* W Cuba

Mä-rī'äs *River* 250 m. NW Mont., U.S.

Mä'ri-bôr, Mär'bûrg *City* NW Yugoslavia

Mä-riė' Bÿrd Land *Area* of Antarctica E of Ross S.

Ma-riė' Ga-länte' *Island* (Fr.) E West Indies

Mä-rin-dū'que (ke) *Island, Province* cen. Phil. Is.

Mä-rin'gä *River* 270 m. S cen. Africa

Mar'i-ön 1. *City* cen. Ohio U.S.; pop. 38,-079. 2. *City* NE Ind., U.S.; pop. 39,607; manufacturing

Mar'i-tīme Alps *Range* S France-Italy

Mar'i-tīme Provinces *Provinces* of Canada: New Brunswick,

Prince Edward I., Nova Scotia

Mar'i-tīme Territory *Territory* SE U.S.S.R. Asia

Mä-ri'tsä (rē') *River* 320 m. SE Eur.

Märk'hȧm, Mount *Peak* 15,000 ft. Antarctica

Mär'mȧ-rȧ *Island* in *Sea* NW Turkey, Eur.-Asia; marble

Märne *Department, River* 325 m. NE France

Mȧ-rō'ni *River* 420 m. N South America

Mȧ-rōōn' Peak *Peak* 14,125 ft. Colo., U.S.

Mär-que'sȧs Islands (kä') *Islands* (Fr.) S Pacific O.

Mȧr-rä'kech (kesh)*City* W cen. Morocco

Mär-sä'lä *City* Sicily

Mär-seilles' (sä') *City* SE France; imp. port

Mär'shȧll Islands *Islands* of U.S. Trust Terr. W Pacific O.

Märsh Peak *Peak* 12,220 ft. E Utah, U.S.

Mär-ti-nique' (nēk') (French Overseas Department) *Country,* Caribbean Sea; 420 sq. m.; pop. 365,000; *Main city:* * Fort-de-France; *Geog.:* volcanic island, mt. terrain; *Climate:* varies from 76°F–81°F.

Flag: French flag.

Ethnic comp.: Negores, mulattoes, Caribs, French; *Language:* French (official), Creole; *Religion:* Roman Catholic.

Products: bananas, sugar, rum, pineapples, cocoa, coffee, livestock; *Major exports:* rum, bananas, sugar; *Major imports:* foodstuffs; *Industries:* distilling, food processing, tourism, fishing.

Currency: French franc.

Head of Government: Paris appointed prefect; *Legislature:* elected general council; *Judiciary:* follows French system. Represented in French Parliament by 3 deputies, 2 Senators.

Mär'trė, Lake *Lake* Northwest Terrs. Canada

Mä-rẏ', formerly **Mêrv** *Town* U.S.S.R. cen. Asia

Mȧr'y-lȧnd *State,* named in honor of Henrietta Maria (Queen of Charles I of England); 10,577 sq. m.; *pop.:* 3,922,399 (*rank:* 18th); Mid-Atlantic Coast U.S.; *Boundaries:* Delaware, District of Columbia, Pennsylvania, West Virginia, Virginia, Atlantic Coast; *Major cities:* Baltimore, * Annapolis; *Major rivers:* Chesapeake Bay, Susquehanna; *Major lakes:* Deep Creek, Pretty Boy, Loch Raven Reservoir; 23 counties.

Nickname: Old Line State, Free State; *Motto:* "Scuto bonae voluntatis tuae coronast nos" (With the shield of thy goodwill, Thou hast covered us); "Fatti maschii, parole femine" (Manly deeds, womanly words); *Flag:* geometric black & gold pattern in opposite quarters, red — white crosses in others; *Flower:* black-eyed Susan; *Bird:* Baltimore oriole; *Tree:* white oak; *Song: Maryland, My Maryland.*

Industry: primary metals, processed foods, transportation equipment, scientific research centers manufacturing; *Natural resources:* coal, seafood, lumber; *Ma-*

jor source of income: manufacturing, trade.

Admitted to Union: April 28, 1788.

Places of interest: Ft. McHenry, Harpers Ferry Ntl. Park, Assateague Ntl. Park.

Mä - sän, Mä - säm - pō *City* SE South Korea; port

Mäs-bä'te *Town* on *Island, Province* cen. Phil. Is.

Mas'ê-rū *Town* * of Basutoland Brit. South Africa

Mȧs'qat and Ō-man' *Sultanate* SE Arabia; 82,000 sq. m.; pop. 700,000; * **Mȧs'qat;** agriculture, livestock, oil

Mä'sön-Dix'ön Line = S boundary of Pa., U.S.

Mas-sȧ-chū'setts *State,* named from Algonquian name, Massadchu-es-at meaning "Great - hill - small place;" 8257 sq. m.; *pop.:* 5,689,170 (*rank:* 10th); New England U.S.; *Boundaries:* Conn., R.I., N.Y., Vermont, New Hampshire, Atlantic Ocean; *Major cities:* * Boston, Worcester, Springfield, Cambridge; *Major rivers:* Connecticut, Merrimack, Charles, Housatonic; *Major lakes:* Assawompset Pond, Quabbin, Wachusett Reservoirs; 14 counties.

Nickname: Bay State, Old Colony State, Puritan State; *Motto:* "Ense petit placidam sub libertate quietum" (By the sword we seek peace, but peace only under liberty); *Flag:* state seal on white field on one side, other side has green pine tree on blue field; *Flower:* mayflower; *Bird:* chickadee; *Tree:* American elm; *Song: Hail, Massachusetts. Industry:* electrical &

non-electrical machinery, processed food, fabricated metal products, printing, publishing, agriculture; *Natural resources:* lumber, fish & shellfish; *Major source of income:* Industry.

Admitted to Union: Feb. 6, 1788.
Places of interest: Provincetown, Boston, Cape Cod, Nantucket.

Mas-sȧ-chū'setts Bay, *State* NE U.S.; 8257 sq. m.; pop. 5,689,170; * Boston; 14 counties; shoes, paper, textiles, fish

Mas-sif' Cen-tral' (sēf', sän) *Plateau* SE cen. France

Mas'sive, Mount *Peak* 14,415 ft. Colo., U.S.

Mȧ-su-li-pȧ'tȧm, Bȧn'-dȧr *City* E cen. India; port

Mat-ȧ-mō'rōs *City* NE Mexico; hides, coffee

Mȧ-tan'zȧs *Municipality* and *City* * of *Province* W cen. Cuba; harbor

Mä-te'rä (tâ') *Commune* * of *Province* S Italy

Mȧ'thu-rä (too) = MUTTRA

Ma'tö Grōs'sō *State, Plateau* SW Brazil

Mät'sū *Island* SE China (Nationalist)

Mä-tsu-e (tsoo) *City* Honshu, Japan

Mä-tsu-mō-tō *City,* Honshu, Japan; commerce, silkworms

Mä-tsu-shi-mä *Islands* Honshu, Japan

Mä-tsu-yä-mä *City* Skikoku, Japan

Mä-tsu-zä-kä *Town* Honshu, Japan; cotton textiles

Mat-tȧ-ga'mi *River* 275 m. Ontario, Canada

Mat'têr-hôrn, Mônt Cêr-van' (sêr) *Peak* 14,780 ft., It.-Swiss border

Mat'têr-hôrn Peak *Peak* 13,585 ft. Colo., U.S.

Mau'i (mou') *Island* of Haw., U.S. (2nd

largest) S cen. part; sugar

Mau'nä Ke'ä (mou', kā') *Volcano* 13,785 ft. Hawaii I., Haw., U.S.; world's highest island mountain

Mau'nä Lō'ä (mou') *Volcano* 13,680 ft. Hawaii I., Haw., U.S.; world's largest mountain

MAURITANIA

Mău-ri-tā'ni-à, Islamic Republic of *Country*, NW Africa; 419,000 sq. m.; pop. 1,276,- 000; 8 regions, 1 district; *Main cities:* * Nouakchott, Port-Etienne, Kaédi, Rosso; *Main river:* Senegal; *Geog.:* narrow belt along Senegal River Valley, broad E–W band characterized by vast sand plains and fixed dunes held in place by sparse grass and scrub trees, large N arid region shading into Sahara Desert; *Climate:* hot and dry except for certain sections in S.

Flag: yellow star over yellow crescent on green field.

Ethnic comp.: Arabs, Negro-Hamitic; *Language:* French (official), Arabic; *Religion:* Islam (state).

Products: livestock, gum, fish, millet, dates, maize, copper, salt, leather, tobacco, iron ore; *Minerals:* iron ore, copper, gypsum; *Major exports:* iron ore, livestock, salt, dates, gum arabic; *Major imports:* petroleum products, cement, tires, tea, machinery, vehicles,

electrical equipment; *Industries:* meat & fish processing, fishing, animal husbandry, oil refining.

Currency: CFA franc.

Head of Government: President; *Legislature:* unicameral National Assembly; *Judiciary:* constitutionally independent. Supreme Court at apex.

MAURITIUS

Mău-ri'ti-us (rish'i) *Country,* Indian Ocean; 800 sq. m.; pop. 890,000; 3 administrative districts; *Main cities:* * Port Louis, Beau Bassin, Rose Hill, Curepipe; *Geog.:* volcanic in origin, almost surrounded by coral reefs; *Climate:* conditioned by SE trade winds, tropical lowlands.

Flag: horizontal stripes — red, blue, white, green top — bottom.

Ethnic comp.: Indians, Creoles, Chinese, Europeans; *Language:* English (official), French, Creole, Hindi; *Religions:* Hindu, Roman Catholic, Muslim, Protestant, Anglican.

Products: sugar, tea, tobacco, maize, aloe, timber, potatoes, fish; *Major exports:* sugar, molasses; *Major imports:* foodstuffs, manufactured goods, machinery & transportation equipment, chemicals, fertilizers; *Industries:* agriculture, sugar industry, production of sugar,

tea, tobacco, fiber, rum, cigarettes, salt, lime, bricks.

Head of Government: Prime Minister; *Legislature:* unicameral Legislative Assembly; *Judiciary:* based primarily on French. Highest court is Supreme Court.

Mä-wen'zi *Peak* 16,890 ft. Mt. Kilimanjaro

Ma'yà *River* 500 m. U.S.S.R., Asia

Mä-yä-guez' (gwāz') *Municipality* and *city* W Puerto Rico; port

Mä-yä-ri' (rē') *Municipality* E Cuba

Ma-yenne' *Department* NW France

Māy'fāir *District* W London

Māy'myō *Town* Lower Burma, summer *

Māy'ō *County* NW Eire; fishing

Mä'yō *River* 250 m. W Mexico

Mä-yôn', Mount *Volcano* 7943 ft. Luzon, Phil. Is.; perfect volcanic cone, vapor halo

Ma-zär'-i-Sha-rif' (rēf') *City* N Afghanistan

Maz-à-rū'ni *River* 270 m. Guyana

Mä-zä-tlän' *City* W Mexico; port

Mbä-bäne' (bän') *Town* * of Swaziland

McAl'lèn *City* S Texas, U.S.; pop. 37,636; business

Mc-Clin'töck Channel *Passage* bet. Victoria and Prince of Wales Is. Northwest Terrs., Canada

Mc-Kées'pôrt *City* SW Pa., U.S.; pop. 37,- 977; steel, coal, gas

Mc-Kin'ley, Mount (li) *Mountain* 20,300 ft. S cen. Alas., U.S.; highest in North America

Mēad, Lake *Reservoir* Ariz. - Nev., U.S.; world's largest artificial lake

Mēath *County* E Eire

Mec'cà *City* * of Saudi Arabia; pop. 150,000; Mohammed's birthplace

Me'chè-lèn (kè), **Ma-**

lines' (lēn') *Commune* N Belgium

Meck'lèn-bûrg *Former state* N Germany

Me-dän' *City* Sumatra Indonesia

Me-dèl-lin' (lēn') *City* NW Colombia

Med'förd *City* NE Mass., U.S.; pop. 64,397

Med'i-cine Bōw (sin) *Peak* 12,000 ft. of *Range*, Wyo., U.S.

Me-di'nà (dē') *City* Saudi Arabia; tomb of Mohammed

Med-i-tèr-rā'nè-àn Sea *Inland sea* Eur.-Africa-Asia; 966,755 sq. m.

Mè-djêr'dà *River* 230 m. N Africa

Mee'rut (mā') *City* * of *Division* N India; Sepoy Mutiny

Mee - stêr Côr-ne'lis (mā', nä') *City*, Java Indonesia

Meiggs (megs) *Peak* 15,520 ft. cen. Peru

Meīs'sèn *City* SE East Germany; china

Mè-klông = 1. *River* KLONG. 2. *City* SAMUT SONGKARAM

Mek-nes' *City* N Morocco, former *

Me-kông *River* 2600 m. SE Asia

Mel-à-nē'sia (zhà) = *Islands* of Pacific O. NE of Australia

Mel'bourne (bûrn) 1. *City* SE Australia; harbor. 2. *City* E Fla., U.S. pop. 40,236

Me-lil'la (lē'yä) *City* N Morocco

Me-li-tô'pöl *Town* Ukraine U.S.S.R., Eur.; agriculture, fish

Mē'los, Mi'lō (mē') *Island* Cyclades, Greece

Mel'ville, Lake *Lake* SE Labrador Canada

Mel'vlle, Island *Island* off N Australia

Mel'ville Sound, Vis'count (vī') *Sound* Northwest Terrs., Canada

Me'mèl (mā'), **Klaï'pe-dä** *City* * of *Territory* W Lithuania

Mem'phis (fis) 1. *City* SW Tenn., U.S.; pop.

623,530; port, commerce, industry. 2. *Anc. city* Egypt

Men-de-res' *River* 240 m. W Turkey, Asia

Men-dō'zà *City* * of *Province* W Argentina; grape, wine cen.

Mėng' Chiang' (ji-äng') *Buffer state* (Jap.) bet. Manchukuo and Outer Mongolia 1937-45

Meng'tsz' (mung' zu') *City* S China; tin, shipping

Men'lō Pärk *Village* cen. N.J., U.S.

Men-tôn' (män) *Commune* SE France; resort

Men'tôr *City* NE Ohio, U.S.; pop. 36,912

Mer-ce-dä'riō *Peak* 22,210 ft. W Argentina

Mer-ce'des (sā'dâs) 1. *Town* E Argentina. 2. *City* cen. Argentina. 3. *City* SW Uruguay; port

Mêr-gui' (gwē') *Town, District, Archipelago* Lower Burma

Me'ri-dä (mā') 1. *City* SE Mexico; sisal. 2. *Commune* SW Spain. 3. *Mountain range* W Venezuela

Mer'i-den *City* S Conn. U.S.; pop. 55,959

Me-rid'i-àn *City* E Miss., U.S.; pop. 45,083; textiles

Mer - i - on'éth - shire *County* W Wales

Me-ri-ti' (mā-rē-tē') *City* SE Brazil

Mêr'thỳr Tỳd'fil *County borough* SE Wales

Mêr'tön and Môr'dèn *Urban district* S England

Me'rū, Mount (mā') *Peak* 14,955 ft. N Tanzania

Me'sa (mā) *City* SC Ariz., U.S.; pop. 62,853; business

Mė-sä'bi Range *Mountains* NE Minn., U.S.

Me'sà Vêrde' (mā') *National park* SW Colo., U.S.

Mė-shed' *City* NE Iran; trade cen.

Mes-ö-pö-tä'mi-à *Region* Tigris-Euphrates rivers SW Asia; in mod. Iraq

Mesquite *City* NE Texas, U.S.; pop. 55,131

Mès-sē'ni-à *Department* Peloponnesus, Greece

Mes-si'nà (sē') *City* * of *Province* on *Strait* NE Sicily; port, silks

Me'tà (mā') *River* 685 m. Colombia

Mė-thū'en *Town* NE Mass., U.S.; pop. 35,456

Metz *City* NE France; metal industries, coal; German before 1918

Meûrthe- et -Mō-selle' (mûr-tā-mō-zel') *Department* NE France

Meûse, Dut. Maas 1. *River* 575 m. W Eur. 2. *Department* NE France [Mexico

Mex-i-cal'ē *Town* NW

MEXICO 0 miles 600

UNITED STATES

Ciudad Juarez

Monterrey

Gulf of Mexico

Guadalajara

Mexico City

Campeche

Puebla

BRITISH HOND.

Acapulco

Pacific Ocean

GUATEMALA EL SALVADOR HONDURAS NICARAGUA COSTA RICA

Mex'i-cō, United Mexican States *Country,* N America; 760,000 sq. m.; pop. 48,313,-000; 29 states, 1 federal district, 2 territories; *Main cities:* * Mexico City, Guadalajara, Monterrey, Cuidad Juarez, Leon, Puebla, Mexicali; *Main rivers:* Rio Grande, Lerma, Santiago, Usumacinta, Grijalva, Balsas, Panuco; *Geog.:* low desert plains, jungle-like coastal strips, high plateaus, rugged mountains; *Climate:* dry, tropical.

Flag: green, red, white vertical stripes with national coat of arms in center.

Ethnic comp.: Mestízos, Amerindians, Europeans; *Language:* Spanish (official), Indian languages; *Religions:*

Roman Catholic (state), Protestant, Jewish, others.

Products: cotton, sisal, coffee, sugar, maize, wheat, beans, rice, shrimp, timber, cattle, tequila, pulque; *Minerals:* zinc, silver, sulphur, copper, iron ore, lead, coal, tin, antimony, mercury; *Major exports:* cotton, sugar, coffee, sulphur, shrimp; *Major imports:* industrial machinery, motor vehicles & parts, chemicals, communications & transportation equipment, electric power equipment; *Industries:* cars, machinery, construction, petrochemicals, steel, cement, tourism.

Currency: peso.

Head of Government: President; *Legislature:* bicameral Congress; *Judiciary:* local, federal courts, Supreme Court at apex.

Mex'i-cō City *City* * of Mexico and Fed. Distr., cen. part; pop. 3,484,000

Mex'i-cō, Gulf of *Gulf* SE North America

Me'zin (mā') *River* 550 m. N U.S.S.R., Eur.

Mī-am'i *City* SE Fla., U.S.; pop. 334,859; winter resort

Mī-am'i Bēach *Island City* SE Fla., U.S.; pop. 87,072; resort

Mich'i-gàn *State,* named from Indian word meaning "turtle" or from Michigama meaning "great water;" 58,216 sq. m.; *pop.:* 8,875,083 (*rank:* 7th); Mid-W U.S.; *Boundaries:* Indiana, Wisconsin, Ohio, Canada; Lake Michigan, Lake Superior, Lake Huron, Lake Erie; *Major cities:* * Lansing; Detroit, Flint, Dearborn, Grand Rapids;

Major rivers: Grand, Kalamazoo, Escanaba, Saginaw; *Major lakes:* Houghton, Torch, Charlevoix, Burt; 83 counties.

Nickname: Wolverine State; *Motto:* "Si quaeris penisulam amoenam circumspice" (If you seek a pleasant peninsula, look about you); *Flag:* state seal on blue field; *Flower:* apple blossom; *Bird:* robin; *Tree:* white pine; *Song: Michigan, My Michigan.*

Industry: primary & fabricated metals, paper, food, tourism, mining, lumbering, automotive industry, machine & machine parts; *Natural resources:* copper, iron ore, lumber; *Major source of income:* manufacturing.

Admitted to Union: 1837 (26th state).

Places of interest: Isle Royale Ntl. Park, Porcupine Mt. State Park; Greenfield Village.

Mich'i-gàn City *City* N Ind., U.S.; pop. 39,369; factories, resort

Mi-chu'rinsk, formerly **Köz-lôv'** *City* W U.S.S.R., Eur.

Mī-crō-nē'sia (zhà) *Islands* of W Pacific O. E of Phil. Is., N of equator

Middle Con'gō former Fr. terr., now Rep. of Congo (B)

Middle East = indefinite area incl. countries of S, SW Asia, NE Africa

Middle Loup (loōp) *River* 220 m. cen. Neb., U.S.

Mid'dles-brough ('lz-bru) *County borough* N England; iron

Mid'dle-sex ('l) *County* SE England; residential

Mid'dle-town (toun) 1. *City* SW Ohio, U.S.; pop. 48,767; factories 2. *City* S Conn., U.S.;

pop. 36,924; manu-facturing, residential

Mid'lånd 1. *City* W Tex., U.S.; pop. 59,-463; cattle, oil. 2. *City* E Mich., U.S.; pop. 35,176; manu-facturing

Mid'lånds, The = cen. counties of England

Mid-lō'thi-ån, formerly **Ed'in-burgh** (bur-ö) *County* SE Scotland; farming, factories

Mid'wåy *Islands* (East-ern I., Sand I.) cen. Pacific O.; bel. to U.S.

Mid'west City *City* Okla., U.S.; pop. 48,-114

Mi-e (mē) *Prefecture* Honshu, Japan

Mi-län' *Commune* * of **Mi-lä'nō** prov. N It-aly; manufacturing, commerce, publishing

Mil'förd *City* S Conn., U.S.; pop. 50,858; oysters, hardware

Milk *River* 625 m. N Mont., U.S.

Mi'lō (mē') = MELOS

Mil-wău'kēe *City* SE Wisc., U.S.; pop. 717,099

Min 1. or **Min'kiang'** (ji-äng') *River* 350 m. S cen. China. 2. or **Min-kông'** *River* 250 m. SE China

Min-då-nä'ō *Island* S. of *Sea,* S Phil. Is.

Min'dèn *City* S West Germany; factories

Min-dō'rō *Island* and *Strait* cen. Phil. Is.

Min'hōw', Fōō'chow' (jō') *City* SE China; port

Min-nē-ap'ö-lis *City* SE Minn., U.S.; pop. 434,400; St. Paul's twin city; flour mills

Min-nė-sō'tå *State,* named from Sioux meaning "sky-tinted water;" 84,068 sq. m.; *pop.:* 3,805,069 *(rank:* 19th); NE U.S.; *Boundaries:* North Dakota, South Dakota, Iowa, Wis-consin, Canada, Lake Superior; *Major cit-ies:* Minneapolis, *St. Paul, Duluth; *Major rivers:* Mississippi, Red, Minnesota, Rainy, St. Croix;

Major lakes: Supe-rior, Red, Lake of the Woods; 87 counties.

Nickname: Gopher State, North Star State, Land of 10,000 Lakes; *Motto:* "L'Etoile du Nord" (The Star of the North); *Flag:* state seal & 19 gold stars on blue field; *Flower:* pink and white lady's slipper; *Bird:* loon; *Tree:* red (Norway) pine; *Song: Hail, Minnesota.*

Industry: corn, but-ter, dry milk, cheese, stone, clay, glass items, food process-ing, manufacture of machinery, pulp & paper, lumbering, printing, publishing; *Natural resources:* iron ore, taconite; *Major source of in-come:* manufacturing.

Admitted to Union: 1858 (32nd state).

Places of interest: Itasco State Park, Pipestone Ntl. Mon-ument.

Min-nė-ton'kå *City* SE Minn. U.S.; pop. 35,776

Mi-nôr'cå *Island* of Belearic Is., Spain; * Mahon

Minsk *City* * of *Region,* * of White Russia, SW U.S.S.R.

Min'tō, Lake *Lake* Quebec, Canada

Min'yå Kon'kå *Moun-tain* 24,900 ft. S China

Miq'ue-lon (mik'è) *Is-land* (Fr.) Atlantic O. off Newfoundland

Mi-råj' *States* W India

Mi-rim' (rēm') *Lake* Uruguay-Brazil

Mir'pur Khäs' (mēr') *City* S West Pakistan

Mir'zä-pur *City* N In-dia; pilgrimage cen.

Mi-sä'mis *Former prov.* Mindanao, Phil. Is.

Mish-å-wä'kå *City* N Ind., U.S.; pop. 35,-517; manufacturing, residential

Mis'kolc (mish'kôlts) *City* NE Hungary

Mis-si-naï'bi *River* 270 m. Ontario, Canada

Mis-sis-sip'pi *State,* named from Indian word meaning "the great water;" 47,716 sq. m.; *pop.:* 2,216,-912 *(rank:* 29th); SE U.S.; *Boundaries:* Louisiana, Arkansas, Tennessee, Alabama, Gulf of Mexico; *Ma-jor cities:* * Jackson, Greenville, Gulfport; *Major rivers:* Missis-sippi, Yazoo, Pearl, Big Black; *Major lakes:* Grenada, Bar-nett, Sardis, Enid; 82 counties.

Nickname: Magnolia State; "Motto Vir-tute et armis" (By valor and arms); *Flag:* horizontal red, white, blue bars with Confederate flag in upper left; *Flower:* magnolia; *Bird:* mockingbird; *Tree:* magnolia; *Song: Go, Mississippi.*

Industry: food, lum-ber, apparel, chemi-cals, transportation equipment, fishing; *Natural resources:* pe-troleum, natural gas, sand & gravel, sea-food; *Major source of income:* manufactur-ing.

Admitted to Union: 1817 (20th state).

Places of interest: Vicksburg Ntl. Mili-tary Park and Ntl. Cemetery, Tupelo Ntl. Battlefield.

Mis-sou'ri (zoor') *State,* named from Indian word probably mean-ing "muddy water;" 69,686 sq. m.; *pop.:* 4,677,399 *(rank:* 13th); S Mid-W U.S.; *Boundaries:* Iowa, Il-linois, Kentucky, Ar-kansas, Oklahoma, Kansas, Nebraska; *Major cities:* St. Louis, Kansas City, * Jefferson City; *Ma-jor rivers:* Missouri, Mississippi, Osage; *Major lakes:* Lake of the Ozarks, Table

Rock and Pomme de Terre Reservoirs; 114 counties and St. Louis.

Nickname: Show Me State, Gateway to the West; *Motto:* "Salus populi supre-ma ex esto" (Let the welfare of the people be the supreme law); *Flag:* state seal cen-tered on horizontal red, white, blue bars; *Flower:* downy haw-thorn; *Bird:* blue-bird; *Tree:* dogwood; *Song: Missouri Waltz.*

Industry: transporta-tion equipment, food, chemicals, printing, publishing, machin-ery, fabricated met-als; *Natural resources:* lead, iron ore, stone, cement; *Major source of income:* manufac-turing.

Admitted to Union: 1821 (24th state).

Places of interest: Hannibal, Lake of the Ozarks, Joplin.

Mis-tås-si'ni (sē') *Lake* Quebec, Canada

Mi-su-rä'tå *City* * of *Province* NW Libya

Mitch'åm *Municipal borough* S England

Mitch'èll *River* 300 m. NE Australia

Mi-tō (mē) *City* Hon-shu, Japan; industry, commerce

Mi-yä-gi (mē) *Prefec-ture* Honshu, Japan

Mi-yä-ji-mä (mē-yä-jē) *Island* Inland S., Ja-pan

Mi-yä-kō-nō-jō (mē) *Town* Kyushu, Japan

Mi-yä-zä-ki (mē) *City* * of *Prefecture* Kyu-shu, Japan; port

Mi-zu-sä-wä *Town* Honshu, Japan; In-ternational observa-tory

Mjo'sä (myu') *Lake* SE Norway

Mō'ab *Anc. kingdom* Syria; now in SW Jordan

Mō-bile' (bēl') *City* on *Bay* SW Ala., U.S.; pop. 190,026

Mô'dė-nä *Commune* *
of *Province* N Italy;
leather, silk, glass

Mo-de'stō *City* C Cal.,
U.S.; pop. 61,712;
business

Moe'si, Mu'si (mōō')
River 325 m. Sumatra
Indonesia

Mog-à-di-sci-ō (dish'-
i-ō) *City* * of Somali;
pop. 141,770; port

Mo'gi-lev *City* * of
Region White Russia
U.S.S.R.; industrial

Mo-ja've (hä') *Desert*
S Calif., U.S.

Mō-ji *City* Kyushu,
Japan; coal port

Môk'shà *River* 380 m.
U.S.S.R., Eur.

Mol-dä'vi-à, Ger. Mol'-
dau (dou) Former
principality; former
prov. of Romania

Mol-dä'vi-àn S.S.R. *Republic* SW U.S.S.R.,
Eur.; * Kishenev

**Mō'lėn-beek - Saint -
Jean'** (bāk-san-zhän')
Commune cen. Bel-
gium   [aly; port
Mol-fet'tà *City* SE It-
Mō-line' (lēn') *City*
NW Ill., U.S.; pop.
46,237; machinery

Mö-lô'gà *River* 340 m.
W U.S.S.R., Eur.

Mo-lö-kaī' *Island* cen.
Haw., U.S.

Mo-lō'pō *River bed* S
Africa

Mô'lö-töv = PERM

Mô'lö-töv, Mount *Peak*
23,000 ft. U.S.S.R.
cen. Asia

Mo-luc'càs or **Spīce Islands** *Islands* E In-
donesia; forests,
spices

Mom-bä'sà *Municipal-
ity, Island* S Kenya

Mon'à-cō, Principality
of *Country,* SE
France; 370 **acres,**

pop. 27,000; * Mona-
co; *Main districts:*
Monaco-ville, Monte
Carlo, La Conda-
mine; *Geog.:* 3 main
areas — La Conda-
mine (business dis-
trict), Monte Carlo,
Monaco-ville; *Cli-
mate:* mild Mediter-
ranean.

Flag: red, white hori-
zontal stripe.

Ethnic comp.: Mone-
gasques, French, Ital-
ians, Russians; *Lan-
guage:* French (offi-
cial); *Religion:* Ro-
man Catholic (state).

Major imports:
France supplies elec-
trical power and com-
munications; *Indus-
tries:* tourism, drug
manufacturers, pub-
lishing, manufacture
of precision tools.

Currency: French
franc.

Head of Government:
Prince — Monarch;
Legislature: unicam-
eral National Coun-
cil; *Judiciary:* no
death penalty, based
on French.

Mon'à-ghan (h a n)
County NE Eire
Mō'nà *Island* (Sp.) in
Passage bet. Haiti
and Puerto Rico
Monch (mûnk) *Peak*
13,465 ft. W cen.
Switzerland
Mon-gal'à *River* 400 m.
S cen. Africa
Mon-ghyr' (gir') *Town*
NE India; factories
Mon-gi-bel'lō (ji) =
Mt. ETNA
Mon-gō'lià *Territory* E
cen. Asia N of China,
incl. Tuva Region
U.S.S.R. Inner and
Outer Mongolia
Mon-gō'lia, Inner *Re-
gion* SE Mongolia,
Chinese
Mon-gō'lià, Mongolian
People's Republic
Country, NC Asia;
604,100 sq. m.; pop.
1,290,000; 18 prov-
inces, 2 independent
cities; *Main cities:* *
Ulan Bator, Dark-
han, Choibalsan;

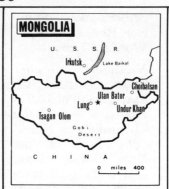

MONGOLIA

Main rivers: Selenga,
Kerulen, Orhon;
Geog.: Gobi Desert,
salt lakes, prairies;
Climate: continental.

Flag: red, blue, red
vertical stripes with
yellow symbols of
traditional national-
istic and historic sig-
nificance on left (red)
stripe.

Ethnic comp.: Khalka
Mongols, Kazakhs,
Oirat Mongols, Tur-
kic minority; *Lan-
guage:* Mongolian,
Russian; *Religion:*
Tibetan Buddhist.

Products: livestock,
wool, hides, furs, but-
ter, timber, leather,
electricity; *Minerals:*
coal, iron ore, gold,
iron, steel; *Major ex-
ports:* livestock, wool,
butter, meat prod-
ucts; *Major imports:*
consumer goods, ma-
chinery, equipment,
industrial raw mate-
rials; *Industries:* min-
ing, quarrying.

Currency: tugrik.

Head of Government:
Chairman of Praesid-
ium of Khural; *Legis-
lature:* Great Peo-
ple's Khural; *Judi-
ciary:* based on Com-
munist model.

Mon'i-tör Peak *Peak*
13,700 ft. SW Colo.,
U.S.
Mon ' mouth - shíre
(muth) *County* W
England
Mön-rōe' *City* N La.,
U.S.; pop. 56,374; in-
dustrial
Mön-rō'vi-à *City* * of
Liberia
Môns, Bêr'gėn *Com-
mune* SW Belgium

Mon-tan'à *State,*
named from Latin
meaning "mountain-
ous regions;" 147,138
sq. m.; *pop.:* 694,409
(*rank:* 43rd); NW–
Rocky Mt. U.S.;
Boundaries: Idaho,
Wyoming, South Da-
kota, North Dakota,
Canada; *Major cit-
ies:* Great Falls, Bil-
lings, Butte, * Hele-
na; *Major rivers:*
Missouri, Yellow-
stone, Kootenai; *Ma-
jor lakes:* Flathead,
Fort Peck and Can-
yon Ferry Reser-
voirs; 56 counties.

Nickname: Treasure
State; *Motto:* "Oro y
plata" (Gold and sil-
ver); *Flag:* state seal
on blue field; *Flower:*
bitterroot; *Bird:*
western meadow
lark; *Tree:* Ponderosa
pine; *Song: Montana.*

Industry: chemicals,
stone, clay & glass
items, lumber, pri-
mary metals, food,
petroleum & coal
items, printing, pub-
lishing; *Natural re-
sources:* petroleum,
sand & gravel, phos-
phate rock; *Major
source of income:* gov-
ernment.

Admitted to Union:
1889 (41st state).

Places of interest:
Glacier Ntl. Park,
Yellowstone Ntl.
Park, Custer Battle-
field.

Mont-clāir' *Town* NE
N.J., U.S.; pop. 44,-
043; residential
Mon-tė-bel'lo *City* S
Cal., U.S.; pop. 42,807
Mon'tė Cär'lō *Com-
mune* Monaco; casino
Mon-te-cris'tō *Island*
(It.) off W cen. Italy
Mon-tē'gō Bay *Seaport*
Jamaica I.; fruits
Mon-tė-nē'grō *Feder-
ated Republic* S Yugo-
slavia; former king-
dom; * Titograd
Mon-tė-rey' (rā') *City*
on *Bay* W Calif.,
U.S.; formerly * of
Span. Calif.

Mon-tė-rey' Park (rā') *City* W Cal., U.S.; pop. 49,166; residential

Mon-tėr-rey' (rā') *City* NE Mexico

Mon-tė-vi-de'ō (dā') *City* * of *Dept.*, * and chief port of Uruguay, S part

Mon-tė-zū'mȧ Peak 13,130 ft., Colo., U.S.

Mont-gŏm'êr-ẏ 1. *City* * of Ala., U.S.; pop. 133,386; commerce. 2. *Town* * of *District* West Pakistan. 3. or -shire*County* E Wales

Mon-ti-cel'lō (sel') *Residence* of T. Jefferson, Charlottesville, Va., U.S.

Môn-lu-côn' (sôn') *City* cen. France; steel

Môn-mar'trė *Area* N Paris, France

Môn-pēl'iêr *City* * of Vt., U.S.; pop. 8,609; granite, maple syrup

Môn-pēl-lier' (yā') *City* S France

Mont-rē-ăl' *City* on *Island* S Quebec, Canada; Canada's largest city; port, commerce

Môn - treuil' (tru'y') *Commune* N France; factories, fruits

Môn-treux' (trû) *Villages* W Switzerland

Mont-sėr-rat' *Island* West Indies

Môn'zä *Commune* N Italy; factories

Mōōse Lake *Lake* Manitoba, Canada

Môp'pō, Môk'pō *City* S Korea; harbor

Mō-räd'ȧ-bäd *City* N India; brasses

Mō-ran', Mount *Peak* 12,595 ft. Wyo., U.S.

Mo-rä'tu-wȧ *Town* Ceylon

Mo-rä'vi-ȧ *Former Kingdom* and *Province*, cen. Czechoslovakia; now part of **Moravia and Silesia** prov.

Mô'rav-skä O'stra-va *City* cen. Czechoslovakia; factories, coal

Mör'ay (i), **El'gin** *County* NE Scotland

Môr-bi-hän' (bē-än') *Department* N W France

Môr-dō'vi-ȧn A.S.S.R. *Republic* R.S.F.S.R.,

U.S.S.R., Eur.; agriculture

Mō-reau' (rō') *River* 250 m. S.D., U.S.

Mō-re'liä (rā') *City* SW Mexico; cattle farms

Mō-re'lōs (rā') *State* S cen. Mexico

Mo-rī'ȧh *Hill* S anc. Palestine; sacrifice of Isaac

Mō-ri-ō-kä *City* Honshu, Japan; textiles

Môr'ley (li) *Municipal borough* N England

Môr'ō *Gulf*, former *Province* Phil. Is.

Mo-roc'cō, Kingdom of *Country*, NW Africa; 166,000 sq. m.; pop. 16,312,000; 19 provinces, 2 prefectures; *Main cities:* * Rabat, Casablanca, Marrakesh, Fez, Meknes, Tangier; *Main rivers:* Oum-er-Rbia, Dra, Moulouya; *Geog.:* Atlas Mts. form barrier on one side coast, on other dry steppes merge into Sahara Desert; *Climate:* dry steppe.

Flag: green 5 pointed star centered on red field.

Ethnic comp.: Arabs, Berbers, Jews, French, Spaniards; *Language:* Arabic (official), Berber, French, Spanish; *Religions:* Islam (state), Sunni Moslem, Jewish, Roman Catholic.

Main products: cereals, fruit, wine, olives, almonds, wheat, barley, corn, sugar, livestock; *Minerals:* phosphates, iron ore, coal, manganese, pyrrhotine, lead, zinc, cop-

per; *Major exports:* phosphates, tourism, vegetables, citrus fruit, wine, canned fish; *Major imports:* wheat, sugar, industrial equipment, machinery, cotton, synthetic textile yarn, iron, steel products; *Industries:* food processing & canning, sugar refining, milling, tobacco production.

Currency: dirham.

Head of Government: King; *Legislature:* unicameral Chamber of Representatives; *Judiciary:* independent system with Supreme Court at apex.

Mō-ro-cō-cä'lä *Peak* 17,000 ft. W Bolivia

Mor'ris Jes'up, Cape *Cape* N point of Greenland

Mor'ris-town *Town* N N.J., U.S.

Mos'cow (kou), **Mös-kva'** *City* on **Moskva** R. (315 m.); * of *Region*, * and largest city of U.S.S.R., E cen. part; pop. 6,600,000; political, cultural, economic cen.

Mō-selle' (zel') *River* 320 m., *Department* NE France

Mös-qui'tō (kē') 1. *Gulf* N Panama. 2. *Peak* 13,795 ft. Colo., U.S.

Môs-ta-ga-nem' *City* NW Algeria; port

Mo-sūl' *City* in *Province* N Iraq; trade

Mo-tä'guä *River* 340 m. Guatemala

Möth'êr-well and Wish'ȧw *Burgh* S cen. Scotland; coal, iron

Moū-lins' (lan') *City* cen. France

Moūl-mein' (mān') *City* Lower Burma; port

Moū-loū'yȧ *River* 300 m. Morocco

Moun'tȧin Province *Province* Luzon, Phil. Is.

Moun'tȧin View *City* W Cal., U.S.; pop. 51,092; manufacturing, residential

Mount Ath'ôs *Department* Macedonia,

Greece

Mount Vêr'nŏn 1. *City* SE N.Y., U.S.; pop. 72,778. 2. *Estate*, burial place of George Washington NE Va., U.S.

Mō-zam-bique' (bēk') 1. *Port. colony* SE Africa; * Lourenco Marques; agriculture, food, jute. 2. *City* on *Island* in *Channel* off coast; port

Msta ('m-sta') *River* 270 m. U.S.S.R., Eur.

Mū'äng-Thai' (tī') = THAILAND

Muhl-hau'sėn (h o u') *City* SW East Germany; industry

Mūir, Mount *Peak* 14,025 ft. Calif., U.S.

Mūir Glacier *Glacier* SE Alas., U.S.

Mūir Woods *National monument* W Calif., U.S.; redwoods

Muk'den' (m ō ō k'), **Shėn'yäng'**, **Fėng'-tien'** *City* S Manchuria; trade, educational cen.

Mul-ha-cen' (mōō-lä-sän') *Peak* 11,400 ft. S Spain

Mül'heīm *City* W West Germany; commerce, industry

Mul-house' (mu-lōōz'), **Mul-hau'sėn** *Commune* NE France

Mu'ling' (mōō') *River* 260 m. E Manchuria

Mul-tän' (mool) *City* * of *Division* N West Pakistan; trade

Mun (mōōn) *River* 350 m. Thailand

Mun'chen - Gläd'bäch (kėn, bäk) *Former city* W Germany

Mun'cie (si) *City* E cen. Ind., U.S.; pop. 69,080; trade cen.

Mū'nich (nik), **Mun'-chen** (kėn) *City* * of Bavaria SE West Germany; educational cen., breweries

Mun'stėr 1. *Province* S Eire. 2. *City* W cen. West Germany; manufacturing, commerce

Mū-rä'nō *Suburb* of Venice, Italy; glass

Mûr'chi-sön *River* 400 m. W Australia

Mûr'ci-ȧ (shi) 1. *Anc.*

kingdom, *Region* SE Spain. 2. *Commune* * of *Province* SE Spain; factories

Mu'res, Mu'resh (mōō') *River* 400 m. Hungary-Romania

Murgh - äb' (moorg) *River* 450 m. Afghanistan-U.S.S.R.

Mur - mansk' (moor) *City* * of *Region* NW U.S.S.R., Eur.; ice-free port

Mu-rō-rän (moo) *City* Hokkaido, Japan; port, navy base

Mûr'ray (ri) *River* 1200 m. Australia's chief river, SE part

Mûr-rum-bidg'ēe *River* 1000 m. SE Australia

Mus'cat and Ō-man', Sultanate of *Country,* SE part Arabian Peninsula; 82,000 sq. m.; pop. 750,000; *Main city:* * Muscat; *Geog.:* tip of Musandam Peninsula, fertile, populous Batinab Plain, Muscat — Matrah Coastal area, interior mt., desert fringes; *Climate:* one of world's hottest, 3–6" rainfall.

Flag: plain red.

Ethnic comp.: Arabs, Negroes, Indians, Baluchis; *Language:* Arabic (official); *Religion:* Sunni Moslem (state), Shia Moslem.

Products: dates, sugar, dried limes, pomegranates, dried fish; frankincense, coconuts; *Mineral:* oil; *Major exports:* oil, dates, hides; *Major imports:* foodstuffs, cotton goods; *Industry:* oil refining.

Currency: Saidi riyal at par with sterling.

Head of Government:

Sultan; *Legislature:* none.

Mus-kē'gön *City* at *River* mouth, W Mich., U.S.; pop. 44,-631; port, rail cen.

Mus-kō'gēe *City* E Okla., U.S.; pop. 37,-331; oil, gas, factories

Mus-kō'kȧ *District,* Lake Ontario, Canada; resorts

Mus'sėl-shell *River* 300 m. Mont., U.S.

Mū'tän'kiäng' (ji-äng') *City* on *Mū'tän' R.* (300 m.) E Manchuria

Mut'trȧ *City* N India; cotton, paper

Mu-zȧf'fȧr-pur (poor) *Town* NE India; trade cen.

Muz-tagh' A-tä' (mōōs-tä') *Range, Peak* 24,-390 ft. W China

Myit'nge (ngâ) *River* 250 m. Upper Burma

Mȳ'men-singh *Town* * of *District* N East Pakistan

Mȳ-sôre' *City* in *State* S India; famed palace

Mȳt-i-lē'ne 1. *Island* now LESBOS. 2. *City* Lesbos I., Greece; harbor

N

Nä'bhȧ *Town* * of *State* NW India

Nab'lus, anc. **Shē'chem** (kėm) *Town* NW Jordan

Nȧ'di-ȧ *Town* in *District* N India [India

Nȧ-di-äd' *Town* W

Nä-gä-nō *City* * of *Prefecture* Honshu, Japan; silk cen.

Nä-gä-ō-kä *City* Honshu, Japan; oil cen.

Nä-gä-sä-ki *City* of *Prefecture* Kyushu, Japan; port; atomic bomb destruction WW II [of India

Nä'gêr-coil *City* S tip

Nȧ-gôr'nö-Kȧ-rȧ-bakh' *Autonomous region* Azerbaidzhan S.S.R., U.S.S.R.

Nä-gō-yä *City* Honshu, Japan; planes

Näg'pur (poor) *City* * of *Division* S cen. India

Nä-hä *City* Okinawa I., Ryukyu Is.; port

Nä-huel' Huä-pi', Lake *Lake* SW Argentina

Nairn'shîre *County* NE Scotland

Naī-rō'bi *Town* * of Kenya; pop. 477,600

Nä-kä-tsu *Town* Kyushu, Japan

Nä - khi - che - vän' *A.S.S.R.* *Republic* of Azerbaidzhan S.S.R. U.S.S.R. Asia

Nä-män-gän' *Town* U.S.S.R. cen. Asia; trade

Nȧ-mä'quȧ-land *Coast area* SW Africa; sandy plains, copper

Näm'chä Bär'wä *Peak* 25,445 ft. SE Tibet

Näm'hoi', **Fät'chän'** *City* SE China; industry, commerce

Nam'oi *River* 525 m. SE Australia

Näm' Tsô' *Salt lake* E Tiber [Thailand

Nän *River* 350 m. W

Nän'chäng' *City* SE China; commerce

Nän'cheng' (jung') *City* NE China; commerce

Nän'cȳ *City* NE France; manufacturing

Nȧn'dä De'vi (dä') *Peak* 25,645 ft. N India

Nan-dȧ-rū'ȧ *Peak* 12,-900 ft. cen. Kenya

Nȧn'gȧ Pȧr'bȧt *Peak* 26,660 ft. NW Kashmir

Nan'king' *City* E China; former * of China; cloth, paper, pottery [China

Nän'kōw' *Town* NE

Nän'ning' = YUNG-NING

Nän'sei (sä) = RYU-KYU IS.

Nän' Shän' *Mountain range* cen. China

Nän-terre' (târ') *Commune* N France

Nantes (nänt) *City* NW France; commerce

Nan-tuck'ėt *Island* at *Sound* SE Mass., U.S.; resort

Nän'tung' (toong') *City* E China; port

Nap'ȧ *City* W Cal., U.S.; pop. 35,978; residential

Nä'ples (pulz), **Nä'pö-li** *Commune* (in **Napoli** prov.) on *Bay* SW Italy; imp. port

Nä'po *River* 550 m. NW

South America

Nä-rä *City* * of *Prefecture* Honshu, Japan

Nä'rȧ *Channel* 250 m. East Pakistan

Nä-rä'yȧn-gȧnj *Town* East Pakistan

Nȧr-bȧ'dȧ *River* 800 m. cen. India

Nä'rew (ref) *River* 285 m. NE Poland

Nar-rȧ-gan'sett *Town* on *Bay* S R.I., U.S.

Nȧr'vȧ *City* NE Estonia; industrial cen.

Nash'u-ȧ *City* S N.H., U.S.; pop. 55,820

Nash'ville *City* * of Tenn., U.S.; pop. 447,877; industrial port [sacred city

Nä'sik *Town* W India;

Nas'sȧu *City* New Providence I., * of Bahamas; harbor

Nȧ-tal' 1. *City* NE Brazil; port. 2. *Province* E Rep. of South Africa

Nȧ-tash'kwȧn *River* 250 m. Quebec, Canada

National City *City* S Cal., U.S.; pop. 43,-184; residential, Armed Forces

Nat'u-rȧl Bridge *Village* W cen. Va., U.S.

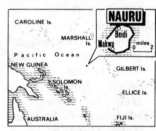

Nä-ū'rū, Republic of *Country,* C Pacific; 8 sq. m.; pop. 7,400; 14 districts; *Main cities:* * Nauru; *Geog.:* phosphatic-rock island, Buada Lagoon; *Climate:* hot, temperature 76°–93°F., average rainfall 18".

Flag: blue field halved by gold bar, white 12-pointed star lower left.

Ethnic comp.: Nauruans, Pacific islanders, Chinese, Europeans; *Language:* English (official); *Religions:* Anglican, Roman Catholic.

Main product: phosphates; *Mineral:* phosphate; *Major export:* phosphate; *Major imports:* hardware, food, vehicles, machinery, timber, furniture, fuels, medicines; *Industry:* mining.

Currency: Australian dollar.

Head of Government: President; *Legislature:* unicameral Parliament; *Judiciary:* Supreme Court established by constitution, Parliament may create other courts.

Nav'à-jō Peak (hĭ) *Peak* 13,400 ft. Colo., U.S.

Naum'bêrg (n o u m') *City* S cen. East Germany; manufactures

Nà-và-nà'gàr *State* W India [*dom* N Spain

Nà-vàrre' *Anc. king-*

Nax'ös *Island* largest of Cyclades, Greece

Nä-yä-rit' (rēt') *State* W Mexico

Naz'à-rèth *Town* NE Israel; site of Jesus's childhood

Ndō'lä *Town* N Zambia; copper cen.

Neagh, Lough (lok nä') *Lake* Northern Ireland, largest in Brit. Isles, 153 sq. m.

Nëar East = Countries of SW Asia and Balkan States

Nëar Islands *Islands* W Aleutians SW Alas., U.S.

Nè-bras'kà *State,* named from Oto Indian word meaning "flat water;" 77,227 sq. m.; *pop.:* 1,483,-791 (*rank:* 35th); Mid-W U.S.; *Boundaries:* South Dakota, Iowa, Missouri, Kansas, Colorado, Wyoming; *Major cities:* Omaha, * Lincoln; *Major rivers:* Missouri, North Platte, South Platte; *Major lakes:* Lewis and Clark, McConaughy; 93 counties.

Nickname: Cornhusker State; *Motto:* "Equality before the law;" *Flag:* state seal on blue field; *Flower:* goldenrod; *Bird:* western meadow lark; *Tree:* American elm; *Song: Beautiful Nebraska.*

Industry: primary metals, transportation equipment, food, electrical & other machinery, chemicals, fabricated metal items, printing, publishing; *Natural resources:* oil, natural gas; *Major source of income:* agriculture, wholesale & retail trade.

Admitted to Union: 1867 (37th state).

Places of interest: Scotts Bluff Ntl. Monument; Chimney Rock Ntl. Historical Site, Pioneer Village, Homestead Ntl. Monument.

Ne-chak'ō *River* 255 m. Brit. Columbia, Canada [Tex., U.S.

Nech'es *River* 280 m. E

Neck'àr *River* 245 m. SW Germany

Nëe'dle Mountain *Peak* 12,130 ft. Wyo., U.S.

Ne-fud' (fōōd') *Desert* N Saudi Arabia

Neg-à-pà'tàm *Town* S India; port [Israel

Neg'ev *Desert area* S

Ne'grō, Ri'ō (nē', nä') 1. *River* 1400 m. Colombia - Venezuela - Brazil. 2. *River* 630 m. S cen. Argentina. 3. *River* 290 m. cen. Uruguay

Ne'grôs (nä') *Island* cen. Phil. Is.

Nei'và (nä') *Peak* 12,-100 ft. Colombia

Nejd *Kingdom* and *Tableland* cen. Arabia

Nel-lōre' *Town* S India; imp. port

Nel'sön *River* 390 m. Manitoba, Canada

Ne'màn, Nie'màn (nē') *River* 500 m. U.S.S.R. E cen. Eur.

Nè-nets' National District *District* NE

U.S.S.R., Eur.; reindeer

Ne-ō'shö *River* 460 m. Kans.-Okla., U.S.

Nè-pal', Kingdom of *Country,* C Asia; 54,360 sq. m.; pop. 11,526,000; 14 zones, 75 districts; *Main cities:* * Katmandu, Biratnager, Lalitpur, Patan, Pokhara, Bhatgaon; *Main rivers:* Kali, Karnali, Gandak, Kosi; *Geog.:* 3 regions, S — flat, fertile strip, C hill country, Himalayas; *Climate:* ranges from subtropical summers, mild winters to cool summers, severe winters.

Flag: 2 red right-angled triangles bordered in blue at hoist, upper with white moon crescent, lower with white sun.

Ethnic comp.: Nepalis; *Language:* Nepali (official), English; *Religions:* Hindu (state), Buddhist, Christian.

Products: rice, maize, millet, wheat, jute, timber, oil seeds, ghee, hides, medicinal herbs; *Minerals:* coal, iron ore, copper, mica, lead, zinc, cobalt, nickel, lignite, talc, beryl, silver, semiprecious stones; *Major exports:* grain, jute, rice, ghee, oil seeds, timber, herbs; *Major imports:* textiles, vehicles & parts, foodstuffs, petroleum products, machinery & equipment; *Industries:*

jute, textiles, yarns, cigarettes, vegetable oil crushing, sugar mills.

Currency: rupee.

Head of Government: King; *Legislature:* unicameral National Panchayat; *Judiciary:* Supreme Court at apex.

Ner'chinsk *Town* E U.S.S.R., Asia; export trade

Ness, Loch (lok) *Lake* NW Scotland

Neth'êr-lànds, *Country,* NW Europe;

12,900 sq. m.; pop. 13,419,000; 11 provinces; *Main cities:* * The Hague, Amsterdam, Rotterdam, Utrecht, Eindhoven; *Main rivers:* Maas (Meuse), Tjssel, Waal; *Geog.:* country low, flat except for some hills in SE. ½ below sea level making dikes requisite for land use. Continuing reclamation of land from sea; *Climate:* temp. rarely exceeds 75°F. Winter long, dreary, damp.

Flag: horizontal bands — red, white, blue from top to bottom.

Ethnic comp.: Dutch; *Language:* Dutch (official), Frisian; *Religions:* Roman Catholic, Dutch Reformed.

Products: cattle, pigs, poultry, cereals, dairy produce, vegetables, fruit, flower bulbs, coal, petroleum, natural gas, chemicals,

steel, textiles, plastics, leather; *Minerals:* natural gas, salt, coal, crude oil; *Major exports:* eggs, meat, flower bulbs, petroleum products, chemicals, textiles, machinery, electric equipment; *Major imports:* grains, petroleum, chemicals, textiles, iron & steel products, machinery, electrical equipment, motor vehicles; *Industries:* engineering, tourism, shipbuilding, entrepôt trade.

Currency: guilder.

Head of Government: Monarch; *Legislature:* bicameral States General; *Judiciary:* Auditing court for reviewing finances, Canton courts for minor offenses, district courts for more serious cases, courts of appeal, Supreme Court at apex.

Neth'êr-lȧnds An-til'lēs (before 1949 **Cū-rȧ-cao'** (sō) or **Dut. West Indies** *Territory* in West Indies; * Willemstad on Curacao; oil refining

Neth'êr-lȧnds Indies now INDONESIA

Neth'êr-lȧnds New Gui'nėa = IRIAN

Neû - cha - tel' (shȧ) *Lake, Commune, Canton* W Switzerland

Neuil - ly' - sur - Seine' (nû - yē' - sur - sān') *Commune* N France; automotive cen.

Neu-köln' (noi) *Suburb* of Berlin; industrial

Neu-mun'stêr (noi) *City* N West Germany; manufactures

Ne-u-quen' (nȧ-ōō-kän') *River* 375 m. W cen. Argentina

Neūse (nūs) *River* 260 m. N.C., U.S.

Neuss (nois) *City* W West Germany; industry

Nė-vä'dȧ *State*, named from Spanish meaning "snow-clad;" 110,540 sq. m.; *pop.:* 488,738 (*rank:* 47th);

W — Rocky Mt. U.S.; *Boundaries:* Oregon, Idaho, Utah, Arizona, California; *Major cities:* Las Vegas, Reno, * Carson City; *Major rivers:* Humboldt, Colorado, Truckee; *Major lakes:* Pyramid, Walker, Tahoe, Mead; 16 counties.

Nickname: Sagebrush State, Silver State; *Motto:* "All for our country;" *Flag:* blue field with gold & green insignia upper left; words "Battle Born" recall that Nevada gained statehood during Civil War; *Flower:* sagebrush; *Bird:* mountain bluebird; *Tree:* single-leaf Pinon pine; *Song: Home Means Nevada.*

Industry: stone, clay, glass items, chemicals, printing, publishing, food items, lumber, electrical machinery, fabricated metals; *Natural resources:* copper, gold, sand & gravel, diatomite; *Major source of income:* services.

Admitted to Union: 1864 (36th state).

Places of interest: Las Vegas, Reno, Lake Tahoe, Virginia City.

Ne'vis *Island* of Leeward Is. (Brit.) West Indies

New (nū) *River* 255 m. Va.-W.Va., U.S.

New Ȧl'bȧ-ny *City* S Ind., U.S.; pop. 38,-402; residential

New Am'stêr-dam *City* on Manhattan I., N.Y., U.S.; became New York City

New'ȧrk (nū') 1. *City* NE N.J., U.S.; pop. 382,417; transportation, insurance cen.; manufacturing. 2. *City* cen. Ohio., U.S.; pop. 41,836; glass, tires, stoves

New Bed'förd *City* SE Mass., U.S.; pop.

101,777; manufacturing, fish

New Brit'ain ('n) 1. *City* N Conn., U.S.; pop. 83,441; manufacturing. 2. *Island* largest of Bismarck Arch.; cocoa, coconuts. 3. *District*, incl. *Island*, Terr. of New Guinea; * Rabaul

New Bruns'wick 1. *City* cen. N.J., U.S.; pop. 41,885; rail, manufacturing, market cen. 2. *Province* SE Canada; 28,354 sq. m.; pop. 626,000; * Fredericton; agriculture, forestry, fish

New Cal-ė-dō'niȧ *Island* of *Fr. Territory* SW Pacific O.; * Noumea; agriculture

New Cas-tle (cas"l) *City* W Pa., U.S.; pop. 38,559; industrial cen.

New'cas-tle ('l) 1. *City* SE Australia. 2. *Municipal borough* W cen. England; manufactures. 3. **Newcastle upon Tȳne** *City, county borough* N England; shipbuilding, chemicals, coal, iron

New'chwäng' *City* S Manchuria

New Del'hi (del'i) *City* * of Rep. of India, N part; pop. 2,344,051

New Eng'lȧnd *Section* NE U.S.; incl. Me., N.H., Vt., Mass., R.I., Conn.

New-found-land' (nū-fun) 1. *Island* off E Canada. 2. *Province* E Canada· includes Labrador; * St. John's; 154,734 sq. m.; pop. 513,000; fish

New Geor'gia (jôr'jȧ) *Island* of *Island group* Brit. Solomon Is.

New Guin'ea (gin'i) *Island* (world's 2nd largest) E Malay Arch.; div.: W = Irian, Indonesia; NE = part of Terr. of New Guinea, SE = Papua, both administered by Australia

New Hamp'shȋre *State*, named from English county of Hampshire; 9,304 sq. m.; *pop.:* 737,681 (*rank:*

41st); New England U.S.; *Boundaries:* Maine, Vermont, Massachusetts, Canada, Atlantic Ocean; *Major cities:* Manchester, * Concord; *Major rivers:* Connecticut, Merimack, Androscoggin; *Major lake:* Winnipesaukee; 10 counties.

Nickname: Granite State; *Motto:* "Live free or die;" *Flag:* state seal on blue field; *Flower:* lilac; *Bird:* purple finch; *Tree:* paper (white) birch; *Song: Old New Hampshire* and *New Hampshire, My New Hampshire.*

Industry: leather items, electrical & other machinery, printing, publishing, textile mill items, paper items, food items; *Natural resources:* sand & gravel & stone, fish; *Major source of income:* manufacturing.

Admitted to Union: June 21, 1788.

Places of interest: White Mts., The Flume, Lake Winnipesaukee.

New Hā'vėn *City* S Conn., U.S.; pop. 137,707; manufacturing, port

New Heb'ri-dēs *Island group* SW Pacific O.; a *Condominium* administered by Fr., Brit. and Australians; coconuts, coffee, cocoa, cotton

New Īre'lȧnd *Island* in *District* of Terr. of New Guinea, Bismarck Arch.; coconuts

New Jêr'sey (si) *State*, named from channel island of Jersey; 7836 sq. m.; *pop.:* 7,168,-164 (*rank:* 8th); Mid-Atlantic coast U.S.; *Boundaries:* New York, Pennsylvania, Delaware, Atlantic Ocean; *Major cities:* Newark, Jersey City,

Paterson, Elizabeth, * Trenton; *Major rivers:* Raritan, Delaware, Hudson, Passaic; *Major lakes:* Hopatcong, Budd, Culvers; 21 counties.

Nickname: Garden State; *Motto:* "Liberty and Prosperity;" *Flag:* state seal on yellow field; *Flower:* purple violet; *Bird:* eastern goldfinch; *Tree:* red oak; *Song:* New Jersey Loyalty Song (unofficial).

Industry: chemicals, drugs, machinery, food items, primary & fabricated metals, transportation equipment, apparel, fishing, tourism; *Natural resources:* forests, stone, sand, gravel, iron, zinc & clay, fishing; *Major source of income:* manufacturing.

Admitted to Union: Dec. 18, 1787.

Places of interest: Atlantic City, Fort Lee, High Point State Park, Stokes State Forest, Princeton.

New Lön'dön *City* SE Conn., U.S.; port

New Mex'i-cō *State,* named from country of Mexico; 121,666 sq. m.; *pop.:* 1,016,-000 (*rank:* 37th); SW U.S.; *Boundaries:* Arizona, Colorado, Texas, Mexico; *Major cities:* Albuquerque, * Santa Fe; *Major rivers:* Rio Grande, Pecos, Canadian; *Major lakes:* Navajo, Conchas, Elephant Butte Reservoir; 32 counties.

Nickname: Land of Enchantment; *Motto:* "Crescit eundo" (It grows as it goes); *Flag:* stylized red sun, symbol of Zia pueblo of Indians, on yellow field; *Flower:* yucca; *Bird:* road runner; *Tree:* Pinon (nut pine); *Song:* O, Fair New Mexico.

Industry: food items, petroleum & coal items, lumbering, electronics, apparel, farming, tourism, mining; *Natural resources:* petroleum, natural gas, potassium salts, copper, uranium, molybdenum, forests; *Major source of income:* government.

Admitted to Union: 1912 (47th state).

Places of interest: Tacos & Acoma pueblos, Navajo, Apache & Ute Reservations, Carlsbad Caverns Ntl. Park, Fort Union, Gran Quivira.

New Or'lé-àns *City* SE La., U.S.; pop. 593,-471; port

New Plý'mouth (muth) *Borough* New Zealand; port, dairy cen.

New'pôrt 1. *City* SE R.I., U.S.; pop. 34,-562; port, resort, naval base. 2. *County borough* W England; port, manufactures

New'pôrt Beach *City* S Cal., U.S.; pop. 49,-422; manufacturing, residential

New'pôrt News *City* SE Va., U.S.; pop. 138,-177; tobacco, coal

New Prov'i-dénce *Island* of Bahama Is.; site of Nassau, * of Bahamas

New Rō-chelle' (shel') *City* SE N.Y., U.S.; pop. 75,385; manufacturing

New Sī-bē'ri-àn Islands *Island group* Arctic O., U.S.S.R., Asia

New'tön *City* NE Mass. U.S.; pop. 91,066, incl. 14 Villages

New Wörld = term for Western Hemisphere

New Yôrk *State,* named in honor of English Duke of York; 49,-576 sq. m.; *pop.:* 18,-190,470 (*rank:* 2nd); E Coast — Mid-Atlantic U.S.; *Boundaries:* Vermont, Massachusetts, Connecticut, New Jersey, Pennsylvania, Lake

Erie, Lake Ontario, Atlantic Ocean, Delaware River, St. Lawrence River; *Major cities:* New York City, Buffalo, Rochester, Syracuse, * Albany, Niagara Falls; *Major rivers:* St. Lawrence, Hudson, Mohawk; *Major lakes:* Finger Lakes, Champlain, Erie; Ontario; 62 counties.

Nickname: Empire State; *Motto:* "Excelsior" (Ever upward); *Flag:* state coat of arms on blue field; *Flower:* rose; *Bird:* bluebird; *Tree:* sugar maple.

Industry: printing, publishing, apparel, machinery, agriculture, fishing, instruments, transportation equipment, food items; *Natural resources:* seafood, iron ore, petroleum, zinc, natural gas, gypsum, salt, titanium, talc, quarried stone, forests; *Major source of income:* manufacturing.

Admitted to Union: July 26, 1788.

Places of interest: NYC, Niagara Falls, Genesee Gorge, Mohawk Valley — Leatherstocking Land, Lake George, Saratoga Springs, Hyde Park.

New Yôrk State Barge Canal *Canal system* 525 m. connecting Hudson R. with Lake Erie N.Y., U.S.

NEW ZEALAND

New Zēa'lànd (inde-

pendent member British Commonwealth) *Country,* S Pacific; 103,740 sq. m.; pop. 2,995,000; 111 counties; *Main cities:* * Wellington, Auckland, Christchurch, Dunedin, Hutt; *Main rivers:* Walkato, Clutha, Waihou, Rangitaiki, Mokau; *Geog.:* N part has rolling hills, low mountains — S half rises from fertile coast plains to volcanic mt. peaks in center; *Climate:* temperate.

Flag: royal blue with 4 stars of Southern Cross emblazoning banner. In top left quarter is Union Jack.

Ethnic comp.: Europeans, Maoris, Polynesians, Chinese; *Language:* English (official), Maori; *Religions:* Anglican, Presbyterian, Roman Catholic

Products: dairy produce, mutton, lamb, cereals, beef, wool, hides, skins, timber, fruit, coal, oil, natural gas, gold, iron ore, copper, lead, machinery, cloth; *Minerals:* ironsands, oil, gas, gold, aggregate, limestone, pumice, surpentine, clays, bentonite; *Major exports:* wool, butter, lamb, meat, dary products; *Major imports:* machinery, related equipment, industrial raw materials; *Industries:* meat & food preserving, machinery, motor repair, sawmilling, mining, oil refining.

Currency: New Zealand dollar.

Head of Government: British Monarch represented by Governor General; *Legislature:* Parliament — House of Representatives; *Judiciary:* independ-

ent judiciary including Court of Appeal, Supreme Court, Magistrates' Court with Privy Council as final step.

Ne'zhin (nyā') *Town* Ukraine, U.S.S.R.

Nez' Pêrce' *Peak* 11,-900 ft. Wyo., U.S.

Nī-ag'à-rà Fălls 1. *Falls* of *River*, U.S.-Canada border, incl. Canadian Falls (Horseshoe) 158 ft. high and Amer. Falls 167 ft. 2. *City* W N.Y., U.S.; pop. 85,615; resort, hydroelectric power, manufacturing. 3. *City* Ontario, Canada; hydroelectric power, manufactures

Nia-mey' (mā') *Town* * of Rep. of Niger; pop. 43,000

Ni'äs (nē') *Island* off Sumatra, Indonesia

Nic-à-rä'guà *Lake* 2972 m. S Nicaragua

Nic-à-rä'guà, Republic of *Country*, C America; 57,140 sq. m.; pop. 2,131,000; 16 departments, 1 territory; *Main cities:* * Managua, Leon, Matagalpa, Granada, Chinandega; *Main rivers:* Rio Grande, Escondido, Coco, San Juan; *Geog.:* western part coastal plain gradually rising toward rugged mts. Interior is sparsely inhabited wilderness; *Climate:* tropical.

Flag: 2 blue horizontal bands separated by central white stripe with encircled triangle.

Ethnic comp.: Mesti-

zos, Negroes, Zambos, Amerindians; *Language:* Spanish (official); *Religion:* Roman Catholic.

Products: cotton, coffee, timber, sugar, sesame, bananas, fish, tungsten, livestock, gold, silver, copper, petroleum, chemicals; *Minerals:* copper, gold, silver, tungsten, gypsum, precious stones; *Major exports:* cotton, cottonseed, coffee, meat, gold, sesame, wood; *Major imports:* chemical products, raw materials for industry, machinery, transportation equipment, manufactured goods; *Industries:* food processing, mining, manufacture of chemicals, insecticides, fertilizers.

Currency: cordob.

Head of Government: President; *Legislature:* bicameral Congress; *Judiciary:* Supreme Court at apex.

Nice (nēs) *City* SE France; port, resort

Nic'o-bär Islands *Island group* Bay of Bengal, with Andaman Is. forms prov. of India

Nic-ö-si'à (sē') *Town* * of *District*, * of Cyprus, cen. part; weaving, tanning

Ni'ger (jêr) *River* 2600 m. W Africa

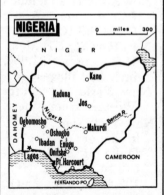

Ni'ger (jer), Republic of *Country*, WC Africa; 459,180 sq. m.; pop. 3,955,000; 7 departments; *Main*

cities: * Niamey, Zinder, Dosso, Agades; *Main river:* Niger; *Geog.:* situated S of Sahara, S is arable savannah; *Climate:* semiarid in S, desert climate in Sahara N.

Flag: horizontal bars of orange, white, green. Orange orb in center of white stripe.

Ethnic comp.: Hausa, Tuareg, Peulh, Jerma, Shanghai; *Language:* French (official), Arabic, Hausa; *Religion:* Moslem.

Products: millet, groundnuts, livestock, skins, beans, manioc, cotton, rice, gum arabic, natron, uranium, tin, salt; *Minerals:* uranium, iron ore; *Major exports:* groundnuts, peanuts, livestock; *Major imports:* cotton, textiles, motor vehicles & parts, food, drinks; *Industries:* cement, flour, vegetables, oil, metal works, plastic, processing uranium deposits.

Currency: CFA franc.

Head of Government: President; *Legislature:* unicameral National Assembly; *Judiciary:* 4 judicial bodies — Court of Justice, Supreme Court, High Court of Justice, Court of State Security.

ies: * Lagos, Ibadan, Ogbomosho, Kano, Oshogbo, Ife, Iwo; *Main rivers:* Niger, Benue, Sokoto, Yobe, Gana, Kaduna; *Geog.:* 4 regions — coastal belt hot, humid mangrove swamp, N of coast — zone of tropical rain forest & oil palm bush, C plateau high relatively dry open woodland & savannah, extreme N — semidesert; *Climate:* 2 seasons — dry, wet. Rainfall 150″ on coast and 25″ in extreme N.

Flag: 2 vertical green stripes with white center stripe.

Ethnic comp.: Yoruba, Hausa, Ibo, Fulani; *Language:* English (official), Pidgin, Ibo, tribal languages; *Religions:* Moslem, Christian, animist.

Products: palm products, cocoa, hides, skins, cotton, groundnuts, timber, cement, textiles, columbite, steel, rubber, oil, tin, coal; *Minerals:* petroleum, tin, coal, limestone; *Major exports:* raw cotton, cocoa, petroleum, peanuts, palm nuts & oil, crude rubber; *Major imports:* chemicals, food, machinery, transportation equipment, manufactured goods; *Industries:* mining, forestry, agriculture, cement, fishing, lumber & plywood mills, textile mills, petroleum refinery.

Currency: Nigerian pound.

Head of Government: (Military Rule) General; *Legislature:* Supreme Military Council Rules by Decree; *Judiciary:* Federal Supreme Court at apex. High Courts of Justice in each state.

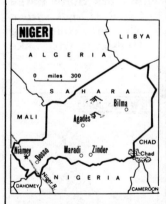

Nī-gē'ri-à (jē') Republic of *Country*, W Africa; 356,670 sq. m.; pop. 65,611,000; 12 states; *Main cit-*

Ni-i-gä-tä *City* * of Prefecture Honshu, Japan; port

Ni-i-tä-kä *Peak* 13,600 ft. cen. Formosa

Nij′me-gėn (nĭ′mä) *Commune* E Netherlands; WW II battles

Nik-kō *Village* Honshu Japan; resort, shrines

Ni-kö-la′ev (yef) *City* * of *Region* Ukraine, U.S.S.R., Eur.

Ni-kô′pöl *Town* Ukraine, U.S.S.R., Eur.; trade

Nīle *River*, world's longest 4100 m. E-NE Africa; incl. **Victoria Nile, White Nile, Blue Nile**

Nîmes (nēm) *City* S France; commerce

Nin′ė-veh *Anc. city* * of Assyria, site now Kuyunjik, Iraq

Ning′hsien′ (shi-en′), **Ning′pō′** *City* E China; port

Ning′sia′ (shi-à) *Town* * of *Province* Inner Mongolia, N China

Ni-ō-brâr′à *River* 431 m. Wyo., U.S.

Nip′i-gon *Lake* 1730 sq. m. Ontario, Canada

Nip′is-sing *Lake* 330 sq. m. Ontario, Canada

Nip-pon′ = official name of JAPAN

Nish *City* Serbia, E Yugoslavia; industry, commerce

Ni-shä-pur′ (pōōr′) *Town* NE Iran; turquoise mines

Ni-shi-nō-mi-yä *City* Honshu, Japan; sake

Ni-tė-roi′ (nē) *City* SE Brazil

Nizh′ni Nov′gö-rod = GORKIY

Nizh′ni Tå-gil′ *City* R.S.F.S.R., Asia; mineral products

Niz-wa′, Kūh-iū *Peak* 13,500 ft. N Iran

Nmai (nà-mĭ′) *River* 320 m. Upper Burma

Nō-ä′täk *River* 320 m. NW Alas., U S

Nō-be-ō′kå *City* Kyushu, Japan

Nob Hill *Hill* SW San Francisco, Calif., U.S.

No-ginsk′ *City* U.S.S.R., Eur.

Nōme *City* W Alas.,

U.S.; pop. 2,488; commercial cen.; mining

Nön′ni *River* 660 m. N Manchuria

Nord (nôr) *Department* N France

Nōrd′kẏn *Cape* NE Norway, N point of Mainland of Eur.

Nôrd′vik *Bay, Town* N cen. U.S.S.R., Asia

Nôr′folk (fuk) 1. *City* SE Va., U.S.; pop. 307,951; port, commerce, industry. 2. *County* E England

Nôr′man *City* Ohio, U.S.; pop. 52,117

Nôr′man-dẏ *Hist. region* and *Former Province* NW France

Nor′ris-town *Borough* SE Pa., U.S.; pop. 38,169; manufactures

Norr′kö-ping (chö) *City* SE Sweden; port

Nôrr′land *Division* N Sweden

Nôrth A-mer′i-cå *Continent* (3rd in size) W Hemisphere; 9,385,-000 sq. m.; incl. Greenland, Canada, U.S., Mexico, Cen. America, West Indies

Nôrth-amp′tön *County borough*, **Nôrth′amp-tön-shire** *county* cen. England; shoes

Nôrth Bôr′nē-ō *Area* of Malaysia, N Borneo I.; former Brit. colony

Nôrth Cå-nä′di-ån *River* 760 m. Okla., U.S.

Nôrth Cape *Cape* off N Norway; N point of Eur.

Nôrth Car-ō-lī′nå *State*, named in honor of King Charles I of England; 57,712 sq. m.; *pop.*: 5,082,059 (*rank:* 12th); E coast U.S.; *Boundaries:* South Carolina, Georgia, Tennessee, Virginia, Atlantic Ocean; *Major cities:* Charlotte, Winston-Salem; * Raleigh; *Major rivers:* Yadkin, Cape Fear, Neuse, Roanoke; *Major lakes:* Fontana, Mattamuskeet; 100 counties.

Nickname: Tar Heel

State, Old North State; *Motto:* "Esse quam videri" (To be, rather than to seem); *Flag:* gold scrolls & NC (separated by white star) on blue bar; red & white horizontal bar to right; *Flower:* dogwood; *Bird:* cardinal; *Tree:* pine; *Song:* The Old North State.

Industry: agriculture, fishing, bricks, textile items, tobacco items, furniture & fixtures, food items, electrical machinery, chemicals, apparel; *Natural resources:* stone, sand, gravel, feldspar, mica, clays, lithium, forests, fish; *Major source of income:* manufacturing.

Admitted to Union: Nov. 21, 1789.

Places of interest: Cape Hatteras National Seashore, Fort Raleigh Ntl. Historical Site, Blue Ridge Ntl. Parkway, Great Smoky Mts. Ntl. Park.

Nôrth Cău′cà-sus *Former region* R.S.F.S.R. U.S.S.R., Eur.

Nôrth Chan′nėl *Strait* of Atlantic O. Ireland-Scotland

Nôrth Chi-cä′gō *City* NE Ill., U.S.; pop. 47,275

Nôrth′cöte *City* SE Australia

Nôrth Då-kō′tà *State*, named from Dakota tribe meaning "united in friendly compact;" 70,665 sq. m.; *pop.*: 617,761 (*rank:* 17th); Mid-W U.S.; *Boundaries:* Montana, Minnesota, South Dakota, Canada; *Major cities:* Fargo, * Bismarck, Grand Forks; *Major rivers:* Red River of the North, Missouri, Sheyenne; *Major lakes:* Devils, Sakakawea Reservoir; 53 counties.

Nickname: Flicker-

tail State; *Motto:* "Liberty and Union, Now and Forever, One and Inseparable;" *Flag:* eagle with American shield on breast, holds sheaf of arrows left claw, olive branch right, carries in beak banner inscribed "E Pluribus Unum' — above eagle sunburst encloses 13 stars, beneath scroll inscribed "North Dakota" — on blue field with yellow fringe; *Flower:* wild prairie rose; *Bird:* western meadow lark; *Tree:* American elm; *Song:* North Dakota Hymn.

Industry: food items, printing, publishing, machinery, cattle, dairy items; *Natural resources:* petroleum, sand — gravel, natural gas, lignite coal, oil; *Major source of income:* agriculture.

Admitted to Union: 1889 (39th state).

Places of interest: International Peace Garden, Snake Creek Ntl. Wildlife Refuge, Theodore Roosevelt Ntl. Memorial Park.

Nôrth-Ēast New Gui′nēa *Area* NE New Guinea, *Division* of Terr. of New Guinea, Australia

Nôrth′êrn Dvi-nä′ *River* 1100 m. N U.S.S.R., Eur.

Nôrth′êrn High′lånds (hī′) *Region* N Scotland

Nôrth′êrn Īre′lånd *Division* of United Kingdom, NE Ireland; * Belfast

Nôrth′êrn Rhō-dē′sia (zhà) = ZAMBIA

Nôrth′êrn Terr′i-tôr-ẏ *Territory* N Australia; * Darwin

Nôrth Island *N Island* of New Zealand

Nôrth Kō-rē′à, Democratic People's Republic of Korea *Country*, NE Asia; 46,810 sq. m.; pop.

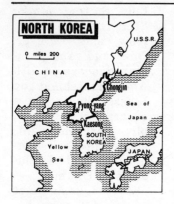

NORTH KOREA

13,900,000; 9 provinces, 4 municipalities, 1 urban special district; *Main cities:* * Pyongyang, Kaesong, Chongjin; *Main rivers:* Tumen, Yalu, Ch'ongch'on, Taedong, Nam; *Geog.:* land of mts., less than ⅕ total area cultivable; *Climate:* continental.

Flag: broad center red stripe bordered top & bottom by thin white stripe. Left of center is white disc containing 5-pointed red star.

Ethnic comp.: Koreans; *Language:* Korean (official); *Religions:* Buddhist, Confucian, Christian, Shamanism.

Products: cereals, dairy products, livestock, fish, iron ore, oil, coal, baryte, textiles, steel, cement; *Minerals:* coal, iron ore, zinc, lead, copper, gold, graphite, silver, tungsten; *Major exports:* machinery and equipment, ferrous and nonferrous metals, minerals, chemicals, fuel, oil; *Major imports:* machinery and equipment, fuel, chemicals, textiles; *Industries:* mining, manufacture of machinery & textiles.

Currency: won.

Head of Government: Chairman of the Presidium of the Supreme People's Assembly; *Legislature:*

Supreme People's Assembly; *Judiciary:* Soviet system used as model. Courts in descending order: Supreme People's Court, People's Tribunals of Provinces, Counties, Communities.

North Las Ve'gås (vā') *City* SE Nev., U.S.; pop. 36,216

North Lit'tle Rock *City* cen. Ark., U.S.; pop. 60,040; industrial

North Må-rōōn' Peak *Mountain* 14.000 ft. Colo., U.S.

North Minch *Strait* Scotland-Outer Hebrides

North Os-sē'tian A.S.S.R. (shån) *Republic* SE R.S.F.S.R., U.S.S.R., Eur.

North Platte *River* 618 m. Colo.-Neb., U.S.

North Pōle = earth's N axis, Arctic O.

North Rhīne-West-phā'liå *State* of West Germany

North Sea *Sea* arm of Atlantic O. bet. N Eur. continent and Great Britain

North Ton-å-wän'då *City* W N.Y., U.S.; pop. 36,012

North-um'bêr-lånd 1. *County* N England; coal, shipping. 2. *Strait* Prince Edward I. - SE Canada. 3. *Cape* SE Australia

North-um'bri-å *Early kingdom* of Britain, NE England

North Vi-et'nam', *Country*, SE Asia; 63,340 sq. m.; pop. 23,178,000; 4 provinces; *Main cities:* * Hanoi, Haiphong, Vinh; *Main rivers:* Red, Black, Lo, Ca; *Geog.:* country mostly mountainous or hilly particularly in N & NW. Lowlands heavily populated & cultivated; *Climate:* monsoonal.

Flag: yellow star centered on red field.

Ethnic comp.: Viet-

namese, Tays, Muongs, Thais, Nungs, Mees, Chinese; *Language:* Vietnamese (official), Chinese dialects; *Religions:* Buddhist, Taoist, Roman Catholic, Confucian.

Products: rice, sugar, maize, sweet potatoes, cotton, raw silk, fish, timber, coal, phosphates, chromite, salt, steel, textiles, cement, machinery, handicrafts, paper; *Minerals:* anthracite coal, tin, chrome, apatite, phosphate; *Major exports:* coal, wood, tea, coffee, spices; *Major imports:* machinery & transportation equipment, metals, chemicals, petroleum; *Industries:* food processing, manufacture of iron & steel, fertilizers, textiles, paper, cement.

Currency: dong.

Head of Government: President; *Legislature:* National Assembly; *Judiciary:* indepedent judiciary subordinate to other branches of government.

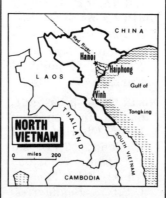

North-West Frön'tiēr Province *Former province* NW Brit. India, now part of Pakistan

North'west Pas'såge (ij) *Passage* Atlantic O.-Pacific O. N of North America

North'west Territories *Division* N Canada incl. Hudson Bay and Arctic islands, mainland N of 60° lat.

North'west Territory *Region* NW of Ohio R., U.S.; incl. Ohio, Ind., Ill., Wisc., Mich., part of Minn.; first U.S. national terr. estab. 1787

Nôr'wălk 1. *City* SW Calif., U.S.; pop. 91,-827. 2. *Town* SW Conn., U.S.; pop. 79,-113; manufacturing

NORWAY

Nôr'wāy, Kingdom of *Country*, N Europe; 125,250 sq. m.; pop. 3,866,000; 20 provinces; *Main cities:* * Oslo, Trondheim, Bergen, Stavanger; *Main river:* Glomma; *Geog.:* comprised mainly of high plateaus, rugged mountains. Highlands broken by fertile valleys, dotted with lakes; *Climate:* strongly influenced by Gulf Stream — relatively mild winters. Interior winter temp. extremely cold.

Flag: white cross with blue inner cross on red field.

Ethnic comp.: Norwegians, Lapps; *Language:* Norwegian, Lappish, Finnish; *Religion:* Evangelical Lutheran (state).

Products: fish, timber, whale oil, barley, hay, furs, iron ore, pyrites, pig iron, aluminum, copper, coal, oil, paper pulp, iron, steel, transport equipment, chemicals, hydroelectricity; *Minerals:* limestone, granite, quartz, iron ore, coal, molybdenite, copper, zinc,

lead, offshore oil; *Major exports:* nonferrous metals, paper, paper board, paper pulp, iron, steel; *Major imports:* industrial machinery, petroleum, petroleum products, textiles; *Industries:* mining, shipping, tourism, food manufacturing, printing, publishing, manufacture of metal products, paper & pulp, machinery.

Currency: kroner.

Head of Government: Monarch; *Legislature:* Storting; *Judiciary:* similar to U.S. system; special High Court of the Realm hears impeachment cases; Supreme Court and regular courts.

Nôr-wē'gian Sea (jàn) *Arm* of Arctic O., Greenland-Norway

Nôr'wich 1. *Town* SE Conn., U.S.; pop. 41,-433; textiles, cutlery, machinery. 2. *County borough* E England

Nō-shi-rō *Town* Honshu, Japan; timber

Nō'sop *River* 450 m. SW Africa

Nôs'si-Be (bā) *Island* (Fr.) off NW Madagasgar

Nô'tec (tets-y'), **Net'zè** *River* 275 m. W Poland

Not'tà-wāy *River* 400 m. Quebec, Canada

Not'ting-hàm *City, County borough,* **Not'-ting-hàm-shîre** *County* N cen. England

Nou-me'à (nōō-mā') *Town* * of New Caledonia colony, SW coast; fine harbor

Nō'và Gō'à = PANGIM

No-vä'rä *Commune* * of *Province* NW Italy

Nō'và Scō'tià (shà) *Province* SE Canada; 21,425 sq. m.; pop. 764,000; * Halifax; agriculture, fish, coal

Nô'và-yà Zèm-lya' 2 *Islands* (Arctic O.) off NE U.S.S.R., Eur.

Nov'go-rod *City* * of

Region NW U.S.S.R., Eur.; meats, mills, metallurgy

No'vi Säd' *City* NE Yugoslavia; commerce, industry, port

Nô-vö-cher-kassk' *City* S cen. U.S.S.R., Eur.

Nô-vö-rös-sisk' *City* on Black S. U.S.S.R., Eur.; port

Nô-vo-si-birsk' *City* * of *Region* S R.S.F.S.R., cen. U.S.S.R.; Asia; imp. industrial cen.

Nū'bi-àn Desert *Desert area* NE Sudan

Nū'do Au-sän-gä'tè (ou), **Ausangate Knot** *Mountain* 20,000 ft.; SE Peru

Nū-e'ces (ā'sès) *River* 338 m. Tex., U.S.

Nue'vō Lä-re'dō (nwä', rä') *City* E Mexico

Nue'vō Le-ôn' (nwä', lä) *State* NE Mexico

Nū-ku-à-lô'fà *City* * of Tonga Is.; port

Nū'ku Hi'và (hē') *Island,* largest of Marquesas (Fr.) Is.

Null-àr'bör *Plain* SW Australia; rocket cen.

Nu-mä-zu (noo, zoo) *Town* Honshu, Japan; resort

Nun-ēa'tön *Municipal borough* cen. England

Nū'ni-vak *Island* off W Alas., U.S.

Nun'kiang' (noon'ji-äng') *Province* N cen. Manchuria

Nuô'rô *Province* Sardinia, Italy

Nûrn'bêrg, **Nū'rèm-bêrg** *City* SE West Germany

Nȳ-as'à *Lake* 11,000 sq. m. SE Africa

Nȳ-as'à-land now MALAWI

Nyi'regy-hä-zä (nyē'-red-y') *City* NE Hungary; manufactures

Ny'kö-ping (nû'chû) *Town* SE Sweden

Nyông *River* 280 m. Cameroun

O

Ō-ä'hu (hōō) *Island* of Hawaiian Is., Haw., U.S.; most imp., 3rd in size

Ōak'lànd *City* W Calif.,

U.S.; pop. 361,561; industrial port

Ōak Làwn *Village* NE Ill., U.S.; pop. 60,305

Ōak Park 1. *Village* NE Ill., U.S.; pop. 62,511; residential. 2. *City* SE Mich., U.S.; pop. 36,762

Ōak Ridge (rij) *City* E Tenn., U.S.; pop. 28,-319; atomic research

Oä-xä'cä (wä-hä'cä) *City* * of *State* SE Mexico; wool, coffee

Ob *River* 2500 m. into *Gulf* at Arctic O., W U.S.S.R., Asia

Ō - bêr - äm'mêr - gau (gou) *Village* Germany

Ō'bêr - Gä'bèl-hôrn *Peak* 13,365 ft. SW cen. Switzerland

Ō'bêr-hau-sèn (hou) *City* W West Germany; industrial

Oc'ci-dent (si) = The West; refers to Western culture

Ō-ce-an'i-à (she) = islands of cen. and S Pacific O.

Ō'cean Island (shàn) *Island* of Gilbert and Ellice Is.

Oceanside *City* S Cal., U.S.; pop. 40,494; business, Armed Forces

Ō'chil Hills (kil) *Hills* cen. Scotland

Ōc-mul'gēe *River* 255 m. cen. Ga., U.S.

Ō-cō'nēe *River* 250 m. cen. Ga., U.S.

Ō-dä-wä-rä *Town* Honshu, Japan

Ō'dèn-sè *City* * of *County* Fyn I., Denmark; manufacturing

Ō'dèr *River* 560 m. cen. Eur.

Ō-des'sà 1. *City* W Tex., U.S.; pop. 78,-380; oil. 2. *City* * of *Region* on *Bay,* Ukraine U.S.S.R., Eur.; imp. port

Of'fà-lȳ *County* cen. Eire

Of'fèn-bach (bäk) *City* cen. West Germany

Ō-gä-ki *Town* Honshu, Japan

Og-bo-mō'shō *City* W Nigeria

Og'dèn *City* N Utah, U.S.; pop. 69,478

Ō-gēe'chēe *River* 250 m. E Ga., U.S.

O-gō'ki *River* 300 m. Ontario, Canada

Ō-gö-oue' (wä') *River* 700 m. Gabon

Ō-hī'ō *State,* named from Wyandot word meaning "great river;" 41,222 sq. m.; *pop.:* 10,652,017 *(rank:* 6th); N U.S.; *Boundaries:* Pennsylvania, West Virginia, Kentucky, Indiana, Michigan, Lake Erie; *Major cities:* Cleveland, Cincinnati, * Columbus, Toledo, Dayton, Youngstown; *Major rivers:* Ohio, Miami, Muskingum; *Major lakes:* Erie, Grand; 88 counties.

Nickname: Buckeye State; *Motto:* "With God all things are possible;" *Flag:* pennant shaped — white bordered red circle & white stars on blue triangle with red & white bars; *Flower:* scarlet carnation; *Bird:* cardinal; *Tree:* Ohio buckeye; *Song:* Beautiful Ohio.

Industry: transportation equipment, primary & fabricated metals, machinery, rubber & plastic items, lumbering; *Natural resources:* bituminous coal, limestone, sand & forests, gravel, salt, oil, fishing, petroleum, gypsum; *Major source of income:* manufacturing.

Admitted to Union: 1803 (17th state).

Places of interest: Fort Ancient, Octagon, Mound Builder and Serpent Mound State Parks, Fallen Timbers State Park, Ohio Caverns.

Oi'röt Autonomous Region *Region* R.S.F.S.R., U.S.S.R., Asia; cattle, timber

Oise (waz) *River* 186

m., *Department* N France

Ō-i-tä *City* * of *Prefecture* Kyushu, Japan

O'jos del Sä-lä'dō (hōz) *Peak* 22,572 ft. NW Argentina

Ō'ka 1. *River* 530 m. S R.S.F.S.R., U.S.S.R., Asia. 2. *River* 950 m. cen. R.S.F.S.R., U.S.S.R., Eur.

Ō-ka-nā'gan *River* 300 m., *Lake* Brit. Columbia, Canada

Ō-kä-yä-mä *City* * of *Prefecture* Honshu, Japan; port, cottons

Ō-kä-zä-ki *Town* Honshu, Japan

Ō-kēe-chō'bēe, Lake *Lake* SE Fla., U.S.; 2nd largest in U.S.

Ō-ke-fe-nō'kēe *Swamp* SE Ga., U.S.

O-khotsk' *Town* on coast of *Sea* E U.S.S.R., Asia

Ō-ki-nä-wä *Island* of *Island group* Ryukyu Is., incl. in *Prefecture* S Japan

Ō-kla-hō'ma *State,* named from 2 Choctaw Indian words meaning "red people;" 69,919 sq. m.; *pop.:* 2,559,253 (*rank:* 27th); S Central U.S.; *Boundaries:* Colorado, Kansas, Missouri, Arkansas, Texas, New Mexico; *Major cities:* * Oklahoma City, Tulsa; *Major rivers:* Red, Arkansas, Cimarron, Canadian; *Major lakes:* Texoma, Eufaula, Oologah Reservoir; 77 counties.

Nickname: Sooner State; *Motto:* "Labor omina vincit" (Labor conquers all things); *Flag:* symbols of war & peace on blue field; *Flower:* mistletoe; *Bird:* scissor-tailed flycatcher; *Tree:* redbud; *Song: Oklahoma.*

Industry: fabricated metals, apparel, lumbering, food, machinery, petroleum & coal items, stone, clay &

glass items, transportation equipment; *Natural resources:* petroleum, coal, natural gas & natural gas liquids, cement, sulphur, asphalt, zinc, gypsum, forests; *Major source of income:* government.

Admitted to Union: 1907 (46th state).

Places of interest: Platt Ntl. Park, Ouacheta Ntl. Forest; Durl's Den.

Ō-kla-hō'ma City *City* * of Okla., U.S.; pop. 366,481; commercial, financial, industrial

Ō-kō-vang'gō *River* 1000 m. SW cen. Africa

O'land *Island* off SE Sweden; alum

Ōld Bäld'y Peak *Mountain* 14,125 ft. S Colo., U.S.

Ōld'bur-y *Urban district* W cen. England; steel, iron, chemicals

Ōld Cas-tile' (tēl') *Provincial region* N Spain

Ōl'den-bûrg *City* and *Former state,* NW West Germany; manufacturing

Ōld Fāith'ful *Geyser* NW Wyo., U.S.

Ōld'ham (am) *County borough* NW England; cotton

O-lek'ma *River* 700 m. E U.S.S.R., Asia

O-le-nek' (nyôk') *River* 1325 m. N U.S.S.R., Asia   [SE Africa

Ol'i-fänts *River* 350 m.

Ō-li-vä'res (râs) *Peak* 20,510 ft. W Argentina

O'lives, Mount of *Ridge* E of Jerusalem, Israel

Ol-la'gue (o-yä'gwä) *Peak* 19,260 ft. N Chile

O'lô-mouc (mōtz) **Ol'-mutz** *City* cen. Czechoslovakia; industrial

Olsz'tyn (ôlsh'), **Äl'len-stein** *City* N Poland; manufactures

Ōlt, Ger. **Ält** *River* 308 m. S Romania

Ō-lym'pi-ä 1. *City* * of Wash., U.S.; pop. 23,111; lumber prod-

ucts, canneries, oysters. 2. *Plain* S Greece; religious cen.

O-lym'pic Mountains *Mountains* of *Penin.* NW Wash., U.S.

Ō-lym'pus *Mountain range* Thessaly NE Greece; home of gods in Gk. mythology

Ôm *River* 450 m. W Siberia, U.S.S.R.

O'ma-hä *City* E Neb., U.S.; pop. 347,328; stockyards, grain, manufacturing

O'ma-hä Beach *Coast area* NW France; WW II landing site June 6, 1944

Ō-man' 1. popular name of MASQAT AND OMAN. 2. *Gulf* Arm of Arabian S., Oman-Iran

Ôm-bi'lin (bē') *Village* Sumatra, Indonesia; coal cen.

Om-dûr-man' *City* NE cen. Sudan

O'mō *River* 400 m. SW Ethiopia

O-mö-loi' *River* 380 m. N U.S.S.R., Asia

Ö-mö-lôn' *River* 600 m. NE U.S.S.R., Asia

Ômsk *City* * of *Region* cen. U.S.S.R., W Asia; trade, industrial cen.

Ō-mu-rä (moo) *City* Kyushu, Japan; aircraft

Ō-mu-tä (moo) *City* Kyushu, Japan; coal

Ō-ne'ga *Lake* 3764 sq. m., Eur.'s 2nd largest; *River* 250 m. into *Bay* NW U.S.S.R., Eur.

O-nit'sha *Town* * of *Province* S cen. Nigeria

O-no-mi-chi *City* Honshu, Japan; industrial

Ō'non *River* 610 m. Outer Mongolia-U.S.S.R.

On-tä-ke *Peak* 10,050 ft. Honshu, Japan

On-târ'i-ō 1. *Province* S, cen. Canada; 412,580 sq. m.; pop. 7,425,-000; * Toronto; agriculture, minerals. 2. *Lake* 7540 sq. m. NE cen. U.S.; smallest of Great Lakes. 3. *City* SE Cal., U.S.; pop. 64,118; residential

Ōost-en'de = OSTEND

O'pa-va *City* cen. Czechoslovakia

Ō-pin'a-ka *River* 280 m. Quebec, Canada

Ô-pô'le, Ôp'peln *City* SW Poland

Ō-pōr'tō, Pōr'to (tōō) *City* NW Portugal

Ô-rä'deä (dyä) *City* NW Romania; industrial, cultural, commercial cen.

O-ran' *City* * of *Department* NW Algeria

Or'ange (inj) 1. *City* NE N.J., U.S.; pop. 32,566; pharmaceuticals, machinery. 2. *River* 1300 m. South Africa. 3. *City* S Cal., U.S.; pop. 77,374; residential

Or'ange Free State (inj) *Province* E cen. Rep. of South Africa

Ôrch'hä *State* cen. India   [Australia

Ôrd *River* 300 m. N

Ö-re-bro' (brōō') *City* * of *Province* S cen. Sweden; shoes

Or'e-gön *State,* named probably from the Shoshoni Indian word meaning "a place of plenty;" 96,981 sq. m.; *pop.:* 2,091,385 (*rank:* 31st); NW coast—Pacific Coast; *Boundaries:* Columbia River, Washington, Idaho, Snake River, Nevada, California; *Major cities:* Portland, * Salem, Eugene; *Major rivers:* Columbia, Snake, Willamette; *Major lakes:* Upper Klamath, Malheur, Crater; 36 counties.

Nickname: Beaver State; *Motto:* "The Union;" *Flag:* state seal & lettering in yellow on blue field; *Flower:* Oregon grape; *Bird:* western meadow lark; *Fish:* Chinook salmon; *Tree:* Douglas fir; *Song: Oregon, My Oregon.*

Industry: fishing, farming, lumbering, lumber & wood items, food items, pa-

per items, machinery, fabricated metals, printing, publishing; *Natural resources:* forests, fish, gold, silver, mercury, copper, lead, zinc, uranium, nickel, coal; *Major source of income:* manufacturing, wholesale & retail trade.

Admitted to Union: 1859 (33rd state).

Places of interest: Crater Lake Ntl. Park, Mt. Hood, Oregon Caves Ntl. Monument, Fort Clatsop Ntl. Memorial, McLoughlin House Ntl. Historical Site.

O-re'khō-vō - Zū'gė-vö *City* W R.S.F.S.R., U.S.S.R., W Eur.

O-rel' *City* * of *Region* U.S.S.R., cen. Eur.; market cen.

Ō'rėn - bûrg n o w CHKALOV

Ō-ren'se (rän'sā) *Commune* * of *Province* NW Spain; wine, lumber

Ō'ri-ėnt = the East; countries of E Asia, the Far East

Ō-ri-hue'lä (wā') *City* SE Spain; manufacturing, agriculture

Ō-ri-nō'cō *River* 1500 m. Venezuela

O-ris'sä *State* E India; agriculture

Ō-ri-zä'bä *City* E Mexico; agriculture

Ôr'khon *River* 450 m. N Outer Mongolia, China

Ôrk'ney Islands (ni) *Archipelago* constitutes *County* off NE Scotland; fish, agriculture, livestock

Ôr-land'ō *City* cen. Fla., U.S.; pop. 99,006; citrus fruits

Ôr-le-ans' (lä-än') *Commune* N cen. France; manufactures; site of Joan of Arc victory

Ôr'ly (li) *Commune* N France; Paris airport

Ôr-môc' *Municipality* on *Bay* Leyte, Phil. Is.; port

Ôrne *Department* NW France

Ôr'ping-tön *Urban district* SE England

Ôr-rė-fôrs *Town* SE Sweden; crystal

Ôrsk *Town* U.S.S.R., Eur.; oil refining

Ôr'tôn *River* 340 m. Peru-Bolivia

O-rū'ro *City* * of *Department* W Bolivia; trade cen.

O-sage' (sāj') *River* 500 m. Kans.-Mo., U.S.

Ō'sä-kä *City* on *Bay* * of *Prefecture*, Honshu, Japan; port, chemicals, manufactures

Osh'ä-wa *City* SE Ontario, Canada; port

Ō-shi-mä Islands *Island* largest of *Group*, N Japan

Osh'kosh *City* E Wisc., U.S.; pop. 53,221; trading cen., manufacturing [geria

O-shog'bō *City* W Ni-

Ō'si-jek (yek) *City* N Yugoslavia; shipping

O-si-pen'kō *T o w n* Ukraine W U.S.S.R., Eur.; export trade

Os'lō, formerly **Kris-ti-än'i-ä** *City* * of Norway, SE part; pop. 484,000; commerce, shipping, industry

Ôs-nä-bruck' *City* * of *District* N cen. West Germany; manufacturing

Ō'sō, Mount *Peak* 13,700 ft. Colo., U.S.

Os-sē'ti-ä (shä) *Region* U.S.S.R., SE Eur.; div. into NORTH OSSETIAN A.S.S.R. and SOUTH OSSETIAN AUTONOMOUS REGION

Os'si-ning *Village* SE N.Y., U.S.; Sing Sing state prison

Os'tend *Commune* NW Belgium; port, fish

Os'ti-ä *Village* nr. Rome, Italy; ruins

Ô'stra-va, Mô'rav-skä *City* cen. Czechoslavakia

Ö-styak'-Vö-gūl' **National District** now KHANTY-MANSI

O-tä-ru (roo) *City* on *Bay*, Hokkaido, Japan; harbor

Ō-tsu (tsoo) *City* Honshu, Japan

Ot'tä-wa 1. *City* SE Ontario, * of Canada; pop. 290,741; cultural, industrial cen. 2. *River* 685 m. Ontario-Quebec, Canada

Ot'to-mán or **Tûr'kish** **Empire** *Former empire* Eur.-Africa-Asia; * Constantinople; 13th century-1923

Ouach'i-tä (wäsh') *River* 600 m. La.-Ark., U.S.

Oua-gä-dou'gou (wä) *Town* * of Upper Volta; imp. trade cen.

Oudh *Former prov.* of Brit. India

Oudj'da (ōōj'dä) *City* NE Morocco

Ou'lu, U'le-bôrg (ōō') *City* * of *Department* N cen. Finland; port

Oum êr Rė-bi'ä (oom, bē') *River* 250 m. cen. Morocco

Ou-rāy' Peak *Peak* 14,000 ft. Colo., U.S.

Ou'trė-mônt (ōō') *City* Montreal I. Quebec, Canada

Ō'vêr-land Park *City* Kan., U.S.; pop. 76,623

O-vie'dō (vyä') *City* * of *Province* NW Spain; manufactures

Ow'ėn, Mount *Peak* 12,920 ft. Wyo., U.S.

Ow'ėns-bör-o *City* NW Ky., U.S.; pop. 50,329; tobacco market

Ow'ėn Stan'ley Range (li) *Mountains* E New Guinea

Ō-wȳ'hēe *River* 250 m. Ore., U.S.

Ox'förd *County borough* * of **Ox'förd - shire** *county*, cen. England; university

Ox'närd *City* SW Cal., U.S.; pop. 71,225; business

O-yä'hue (wâ) *Peak* 19,225 ft. SW Bolivia; volcano

Ô-ya-pôck' *River* 300 m. N South America

Ō'yō *City* * of *Province* W Nigeria

Oys'têr Bay *Inlet* and *Village* SE N.Y., U.S.; home of Theo. Roosevelt

Ō'zärk Mountains *Ta-* bleland   Mo.-Ark.-Okla., U.S.

P

Pä-biä-ni'ce (nē'tse) *Commune* cen. Poland; linen

Pä-chū'cä *City* cen. Mexico; silver

Pä-cif'i-cä *City* W Cal., U.S.; pop. 36,020

Pä-cif'ic Islands Trust Territory (sif') *Islands* of Pacific O. assigned to U.S. 1947: Caroline, Marshall, Mariana Is. (except Guam)

Pä-cif'ic Ocean (sif') *Ocean* Arctic Circle-Antarctic R e g i o n, bet. N and S America and Australia and E Asia; 70,000,000 sq. m.

Pä'däng *City* Sumatra, Indonesia; exports

Pad'ding-tön *Borough* of London, England

Pä-dêr-bôrn' *City* cen. West Germany; manufacturing

Pad'ū-ä, It. Pä'dö-vä *Commune* * of *Province* NE Italy; manufacturing, trade

Pä-gä-di'än (dē') *Municipality* Mindanao, Phil. Is.

Pä-gō'dä **Mountain** *Peak* 13,490 ft. Colo., U.S.

Pä'gō Pä'gō (or päng'ō) *Town* Tutuila I., Samoa; excellent harbor, * of American Samoa [E Malaysia

Pä-hang' *River* 285 m.

Pah-le-vi' (vē') *City* NW Iran; port

Pāint'ėd Desert *Region* N cen. Ariz., U.S.; colored rock

Pāis'ley (li) *Burgh* SW Scotland; textiles, shawls, threads

Paī'tä *Town* NW Peru; port

Pak-i-stan' (W Pakistan) *Country*, S Asia; 310,400 sq. m.; pop. 53,620,000; *Main cities:* * Islamabad, Lahore, Rawalpindi; Karachi; *Main river:* Indus; *Geog.:* Thar Desert,

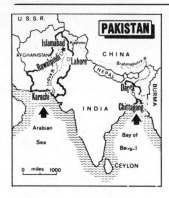

E plain extends to Toba, Rakar mt. ranges; *Climate:* hot, dry near coast, cool in NE uplands, less than 10″ annual rainfall.

Flag: green field, white vertical stripe down left side, white crescent & star on green field.

Ethnic comp.: Pathans, Sindhis, Punjabis, Baluchis; *Language:* English, Urdu, Sindhi, Punjabi, Pushtu, Baluchi; *Religions:* Moslem, Hindu, Christian, Buddhist.

Products: cereals, cotton, rice, livestock, skins, coal, limestone, hydroelectricity, oil, natural gas, textiles; *Mineral:* natural gas; *Major export:* cotton; *Industries:* cotton — textile mills.

Currency: rupee.

Head of Government: President; *Judiciary:* martial law.

Pak-se′ (sä′) *Town* S Laos   [SE India
Pä-lär′ *River* 230 m.
Pȧ-lat′i-näte *Former terr.* S Germany, ruled by counts and emperors
Pal′ȧ-tine (tin) *Hill,* one of Rome's 7
Pä-lau′ (lou′), **Pėl-lew′** (lōō′) *Island group* of Caroline Is. (U.S.)
Pä-lä′wän *Island* SW Phil. Is.; fish, agriculture, forests
Pä-lem-bäng′ *City* Sumatra, Indonesia; port, trade cen.
Pȧ-len′ci-ȧ *City* * of

Province N Spain; manufacturing
Pä-ler′mō *City* on *Bay,* * of *Province,* * of Sicily, S Italy; port, trade, fisheries
Pal′ės-tīne *Area* and *Anc. country* of SW Asia; * Jerusalem; now div. bet. Israel and Jordan
Pȧl′ghät *Town* S India
Pal - i - säde′, Middle *Peak* 14,050 ft. S cen. Calif., U.S.
Pal-i-säde′, North *Peak* 14,250 ft. S cen. Calif. U.S.   [Ceylon-India
Pȧlk Strait *Channel*
Pȧl′mä *Commune* on *Bay* * of Majorca I. and of Baleares prov. E Spain; imp. port
Päl′mäs, Cape *Cape* S Liberia
Päl′mäs, Läs see LAS PALMAS
Pälm Beach *Town* SE Fla., U.S.; resorts
Pälm′êr *Archipelago Island group* South America-Antarctica
Pälm′êr-stön n o w DARWIN, Australia
Pälm′êr-stön, North *City* North I. New Zealand
Pal′ō Al′tō *City* W Calif., U.S.; pop. 55,966; industrial
Pä-lo-mä′ni *Peak* 18,925 ft. W Bolivia
Pal′ö-mär, Mount *Peak* 6126 ft. SW Calif., U.S.; giant telescope
Pȧ-louse′ (lōōs′) *River* 220 m. Ida.-Wash., U.S.   [ft. N Chile
Päl-pä′nä *Peak* 19,815
Pȧ-mir′ *Region* of high altitude cen. Asia
Pam′li-cō Sound *Sound* E N.C., U.S.
Päm′päs *Plains* 1000 m. cen. Argentina
Päm-plō′nä *City* N Spain; manufactures
Pan′ȧ-mä Canal *Canal* across *Isthmus,* links North-South America, Atlantic-Pacific Oceans; canal and 10 m. strip = CANAL ZONE

Pan′ȧ-mä, Republic of *Country,* C America; 28,750 sq. m.; pop. 1,414,000; 9 prov-

inces; *Main cities:* * Panama City, Colón, David; *Main rivers:* Tuira, Bayano, Santa Maria; *Geog.:* bisected by Panama Canal, largely mts. & hilly with 2 main mt. ranges; *Climate:* tropical. Rainfall heavy, seasonal.

Flag: 4 rectangles — lower left blue, upper right red, upper left white with blue star in middle, lower right white with red star in middle.

Ethnic comp.: Mulattoes, Negroes, Europeans, Amerindians; *Language:* Spanish (official), English, Italian, French, Greek, East Indian, Cuna Indian; *Religions:* Roman Catholic, Protestant.

Products: rice, bananas, shrimp, maize, cocoa, sugar, coffee, cattle, coconuts, oranges, cotton, timber, petroleum, copper; *Minerals:* copper, molybdenum; *Major exports:* bananas, petroleum products, shrimp, petroleum derivatives; *Major imports:* crude oil, machinery, vehicles & parts, sugar, chemical products; *Industries:* shipping, tourism, food processing, manufacture of textiles, clothing, shoes, cement, pharmaceuticals.

Currency: balboa at par with dollar.

Head of Government:

(Provisional Junta Government) Provisional President; *Legislature:* National Assembly suspended; *Judiciary:* headed by 9 member Supreme Court.

Pä-nay′ (nī′) *Island* on *Gulf* cen. Phil. Is.
Pän de A-zu′cär (dâ-ä-sōō′) *Peak* 15,975 ft. Venezuela
Pän-gä′ni *River* 330 m. Tanzania
Pän-gä-si-nän′ *Province* Luzon, Phil. Is.
Pan-gim′ (shēn′) now GOA
Pan′han-dle handlelike projection of land
Pä-ni′zo (nē′) *Peak* 18,025 ft. SW Bolivia
Pan-mun-jön (moon) *Village* cen. Korea, site of 1953 armistice
Pan-tȧ-näl′ *Swamp region* SW Brazil
Pän-tel-le-ri′ä (tâ-lâ-rē′) *Island* (It.) Mediterranean S.
Pä′nū-cō *River* 240 m. cen. Mexico
Pä′pȧl States = Temporal lands of popes 750-1870, cen. Italy
Pao′ting′ (bou′) now TSINGYUAN
Pä-pe-e′te (pâ-ā′tâ) *Town* NW Tahiti, * of Society Is. and * of Fr. Oceania; port
Pap′u-ȧ 1. Name for New Guinea I. 2. *Gulf* S coast of New Guinea
Pa′pu-ȧ, Terr. of was Brit. New Guinea *Territory* of Australia, incl. SE New Guinea and adjacent islands; * Port Moresby
Pȧ-ra′ 1. *State* NE Brazil; * **Pȧ-ra′** or BELEM. 2. E mouth of Amazon R., Brazil
Pä-rä′guä 1. *River* 435 m. E Venezuela. 2. *River* 230 m. E Bolivia
Pa-rȧ-guȧs-su′ (sōō′) *River* 320 m. E Brazil

Par′ȧ-guay (gwī or guä), Republic of *Country,* S America; 157,050 sq. m.; pop. 2,395,000; 16 departments; *Main cities:*

* Asuncion, Concepcion, Encarnacion; *Main rivers:* Paraguay, Pilcomayo, Paraná; *Geog.:* landlocked, E Paraguay — gently rolling country with hills, tropical forests, fertile grassland; Paraguay (Chaco) low plain with marshes, dense scrub forests; *Climate:* semitropical.

Flag: individual design on each side — both sides — 3 horizontal stripes of red, white, blue from top to bottom — 1 side — national coat of arms, other side — treasury seal.

Ethnic comp.: Mestizos, Amerindians, Europeans; *Language:* Spanish (official), Guarani; *Religions:* Roman Catholic (state), Indian cults.

Products: meat, timber, cotton, coffee, sugar, tobacco, wheat, chemicals, yerbamaté, textiles; *Minerals:* limestone, salt, talc, mica, kaolin, copper; *Major exports:* meat products, quebracho extract, vegetable oils, essential oils; *Major imports:* foodstuffs, machinery, motors, transportation equipment, nonferrous metals & manufactures, iron, iron products; *Industries:* tourism, food processing, meat packing, refining of quebracho, manufacturing

of cotton, sugar, wood, vegetable oils.

Currency: guarani.

Head of Government: President; *Legislature:* bicameral Congress — Senate, Chamber of Deputies; *Judiciary:* Supreme Court at apex.

Pa-rà-i'ba (ē'và) 1. *Two rivers* = **Pa-rà-i'bà dō Nôr'tė** 240 m. E Brazil, **Pa-rà-i'bà dō Sūl** 660 m. S Brazil. 2. *State* E Brazil

Par-à-mar'i-bō *City,* * of Surinam (Dut. Guiana); port

Pä-rä-mu-shi-rō *Island* N of Kuril Is. (U.S.S.R.)

Pä-rä-nä' 1. *City* E Argentina; river port. 2. *River* 2040 m. SE cen. South America. 3. *River* 300 m. cen. Brazil. 4. *State* S Brazil

Pa-rà-nà-i'bà (ē'và) *Headstream* of Parana R. SE Brazil

Pa - rà - na - pà - ne'mà (nä') *River* 470 m. SE Brazil

Pär'bà-ti *River* 220 m. cen. India

Par'do (dōō) 1. *River* 310 m. E Brazil. 2. *River* 290 m. S Brazil. 3. *River* 230 m. SW Brazil

Par'du-bi-ce (tse) *Town* NW Czechoslovakia

Pä'riä, Gulf of *Inlet* Trinidad-Venezuela

Pä-ri'cu-tin (rē'kōō-tēn) *Volcano* (modern) 200 m. W of Mexico City, Mexico

Par'is *City* * of France, N cen. part; pop. 2,-607,600; commercial, cultural, fashion cen.

Pär'kėrs-bûrg *City* NW W. Va., U.S.; pop. 44,208; business

Pärk Ridge *City* NE Ill., U.S.; pop. 42,-466; residential

Pär'mà 1. *City* N Ohio, U.S.; pop. 100,216. 2. *Commune* * of *Province* N Italy; textiles

Par-nà-i'bà (ē'và) *River* 800 m. NE Brazil

Pär'nū *City* on *Bay* SW Estonia; imp. port

Pâr'os *Island* of Cyclades Is.; marble

Par-rà-mat'tà *Town* SE Australia

Par'ris Island *Island* S S.C., U.S.

Par'rỳ Islands *Islands* Northwest Terrs., Canada incl. Melville, Bathurst, Borden, Cornwallis, Prince Patrick

Pär'söns Peak *Mountain* 12,120 ft. cen. Calif., U.S.   [Brazil

Pà-rū' *River* 350 m. N

Pas-à-dē'nà 1. *City* SW Calif., U.S.; pop. 113,327; resort. 2. *City* SE Texas, U.S.; pop. 89,277; residential

Pä'say (sī) now RIZAL

Päs-dė-Ca-lais' (le') *Department* N France

Pàs-sā'ic *City* NE N.J., U.S.; pop. 55,124

Pas-sà-mà-quod'dỳ Bay *Inlet* bet. New Brunswick, Canada-SE Me., U.S.

Päs-tä'zä *River* 400 m. cen. Ecuador

Päs'to *Volcano* 13,990 ft., and *City* SW Colombia; gold

Pat-à-gō'nià *Barren region* Chile and Argentina, Andes Mts.-Atlantic O.

Pä-täm-bän', Cer'rô de (ser') *Peak* 12,299 SW Mexico

Pä'tän 1. *Town* W Indies; pottery, knives. 2. *Town* E cen. Nepal

Pat'êr-sön *City* N N.J., U.S.; pop. 144,824

Pà-ti-ä'là *City, District,* former *State* NW India   [Dodecanese

Pat'mös *Island* of

Pàt'nà 1. *City* * of *Division* NE India; was opium cen. 2. *State* NE India   [Brazil

Pa'tos (tōōs) *Lake* S

Pà-tras' *City* on *Gulf* Peloponnesus, Greece; port

Pä-tū'cä *River* 300 m. Honduras

Pau (pō) *Commune* SW France

Pä-vi'ä (vē') *Commune* * of *Province* N Italy

Pà-vil'iön Dōme *Peak* 11,355 ft. S Calif., U.S.

Păw-tuck'ėt *City* N R.I., U.S.; pop. 76,-984; industrial

Pä-yä-chä'tä *Peak* 20,-765 ft. N Chile

Päyne Lake *Lake* Quebec, Canada

Pay-sän-dū' (pī) *City* * of *Department* W Uruguay

Pä-yūn' *Peak* 12,070 ft. W Argentina

Pēa'bod-y *City* NE Mass., U.S.; pop. 48,080; residential, manufacturing

Peace (pēs) *River* 1065 m. W Canada

Pēale, Mount *Peak* 13,090 ft. Utah, U.S.

Pêarl (pûrl) 1. *River* 290 m. Miss., U.S. 2. *River* SE China

Pêarl Här'bör *Inlet* Honolulu's port, Oahu I. Haw., U.S.; site of Jap. attack Dec. 7, 1941

Pēa'rỳ-land *Region* N Greenland

Pė-chen'gà *Village, Territory* NW U.S.S.R., Eur.

Pė-chō'rà *River* 1125 m. into *Bay* U.S.S.R., NE Eur.

Pe'cös (pā') *River* 735 m. N.M.-Tex., U.S.

Pecs (pāch) *Municipality* S Hungary; coal

Pe'drō Mi-guel' (pā', gel') *Town, Locks* Panama Canal

Pēe'bles-shîre *County* SE Scotland

Pēe' Dēe *River* 235 m. N.C.-S.C., U.S.

Pēel 1. *River* 365 m. NW Canada. 2. *Sound* bet. Prince of Wales and Somerset Is., Canada

Pe-gu' (gōō') *Mountain range* Lower Burma

Peh, Pei (bā) *River* 220 m. SE China

Peī-hō *River* 350 m. NE China

Pei'ping' (bā'), **Pē-king** *City* * of People's Rep. of China, NE part; pop. 7,000,000; literary cen.

Peī'pus (poos) *Lake* Estonia U.S.S.R.

Pė-kä-lông'än *City* Java, Indonesia

Pē'king = PEIPING

Pel′ė-liū *Island* of Palau Is.

Pel-lew′ Islands (lōō′) *Islands* off N Australia

Pel′lȧ *Department* and *Anc. city* * of Macedonia, cen. Greece

Pel′lỷ 1. *River* 330 m. Yukon, Canada. 2. *Lake* Northwest Terrs., Canada

Pel-o-pön-nē′sus *Division* on *Peninsula* S mainland of Greece

Pė-lō′tȧs *City* S Brazil; meat industry

Pel-vou′ (vōō′) *Mountain* 12,970 ft., of group SE France

Pem′bȧ *Island* off Tanzania

P e m ′ b r o k e-s h ȋ r e (brook) *County* SW Wales; mines, farms, quarries

Pe-nang′ *City* (George Town) on *Island* off W Malay Penin., NW Malaysia

Pe′nas (pā′nyäs) *Cape, Gulf* SW Chile

Pėng′pu′ (pōō′) *Town* E China

Pėn′ki′ (chē′) *Town* S Manchuria; coal

Pėn-nell′, Mount *Peak* 11,320 ft. S Utah, U.S.

Pen′nêr *Two rivers* cen. India: **Northern** 350 m., **Southern** 245 m.

Pen′nīne Alps *Range* of Alps, Switzerland-Italy

Pen′nīne Chȧin *Range* N cen. England

Penn-sỷl-vā′niȧ *State,* named in honor of William Penn; 45,333 sq. m.; *pop.:* 11,793,-909 (*rank:* 3rd); Mid-Atlantic U.S.; *Boundaries:* New York, Delaware, Maryland, West Virginia, Ohio, Delaware River, Lake Erie; *Major cities:* Philadelphia, Pittsburgh, Erie, Scranton, Allentown, * Harrisburg; *Major rivers:* Delaware, Allegheny, Susquehanna; *Major lakes:* Erie, Wallenpaupack; Pymatuning and Bear Creek

Reservoirs; 67 counties.

Nickname: Keystone State; *Motto;* "Virtue, liberty, and independence;" *Flag:* state seal & motto supported by 2 horses on gold-bordered blue field; *Flower:* mountain laurel; *Bird:* ruffed grouse; *Tree:* hemlock.

Industry: fuels, leather & rubber goods, primary & fabricated metals (iron & steel), food items, agriculture, machinery, chemicals, apparel, coal mining, paper, printing; *Natural resources:* coal, oil, natural gas, cement, stone, sand, gravel, forests; *Major source of income:* manufacturing.

Admitted to Union: December 12, 1787.

Places of interest: Philadelphia: Betsy Ross House, Liberty Bell, Carpenters' Hall, Independence Hall — Gettysburg Ntl. Military Park, Valley Forge State Park, Hopewell Village, Washington's Crossing State Park.

Pė-nob′scŏt *Bay* S Me., U.S.

Pen-sȧ-cō′lȧ *City* on *Bay* NW Fla., U.S.; pop. 59,507; harbor, air base, fish, lumber

Pent′lȧnd Fȋrth *Channel* Orkney Is.-Scotland

Pen′zȧ *City* * of *Region* U.S.S.R., E Eur.; agriculture, manufacturing

Pen′zhi-nȧ *Town* on *River* into *Bay* NE U.S.S.R., Asia

Pē-ō′ri-ȧ *City* NW cen. Ill., U.S.; pop. 126,-963; trade, industry

Pe′räk (pā′) *State* W Malay Penin., Malaysia; tin, agriculture

Per-di′dō, Mount (dē′), **Mônt Per-dû′** *Peak*

11,000 ft. Sp.-Fr. border

Per-i-bon′kȧ *River* 280 m. Quebec, Canada

Pe-ri-gueux′ (pā-rē-gû′) *Commune* SW cen. France; manufacturing

Pêr′kins, Mount *Peak* 12,555 ft. S Calif., U.S.

Pêr′lis *State* S Malay Penin, Malaysia; rice

Pêrm was **Mô′lö-töv City** R.S.F.S.R., U.S.S.R., Asia; commerce, manufactures

Pêr-nȧm-bū′cō 1. *State* E Brazil. 2. *City* now RECIFE

Per-pi-gnan′ (pē-nyän′) *City* S France; manufacturing

Pêr′sia (zhȧ) *Kingdom* anc. and mod. (now IRAN), SW Asia; anc. * **Pêr-sep′ö-lis**

Pêr′sian Gulf (zhȧn) *Arm* of Arabian S., Arabia-Iran

Pêr′sian Gulf States (zhȧn) *States* along Persian Gulf: incl. Bahrian, Qatar, Trucial Oman, etc.; shiekdoms. Brit. management; oil, date palms

Pêrth 1. *City* * of Western Australia, SW Australia; trade cen. 2. *Burgh* * of **Pêrth′shȋre** *County* cen. Scotland; textiles

Pêrth Am′boy *City* cen. N.J., U.S.; pop. 38,-798; port, smelting and refining, manufacturing

Pė-ru′ (rōō′), Republic of *Country,* W Coast of S America; 500,000 sq. m.; pop. 13,586,-000; 24 departments; *Main cities:* * Lima, Callao, Arequipa,

Trujillo; *Main rivers:* Ucayali, Marañon; *Geog. & Climate:* 3 regions: coastal area — arid or semiarid with mild, equable temp.; Andes Mountains — climate ranges from temperate to frigid; isolated eastern lowlands — montana — humid climate.

Flag: vertical stripes — red, white, red with country's coat of arms surrounded by laurel boughs, topped by crown in center white stripe.

Ethnic comp.: Amerindians, Mestizos, Europeans; *Language:* Spanish (official), Quechua, Aymara; *Religion:* Roman Catholic.

Products: fish, fish products, sugar, cotton, coffee, wool, rice, copper, silver, coal, iron ore, zinc, lead, oil, vanadium, chemicals, steel, motor assembly, glass; *Minerals:* copper, silver, lead, zinc, iron, tungsten, bismuth, molybdenum, gold; *Major exports:* copper, fish meal, silver, iron, sugar, cotton, coffee; *Major imports:* capital goods, industrial raw materials, intermediate goods; *Industries:* mining, food processing, oil refining, manufacture of consumer goods, textiles, foodstuffs, household wares, metal products, chemicals.

Currency: sole.

Head of Government: President; *Legislature:* disbanded bicameral Congress; *Judiciary:* Supreme Court at apex.

Pe-ru′gia (rōō′jȧ) *Commune* * of *Province* cen. Italy; velvet, silk, brandy

Pe′sä-rō (pā′) *City* * of

Pe'sä-rō e Ur-bi'nō (â oor-bē') *prov.* E cen. Italy; manufacturing

Pes-cå-dō'res *Island group* (Chinese) Formosa Strait

Pe-scä'rä *City * of Province* cen. Italy; resort

Pė-shä'wår *City * of District* NW Pakistan; trade

Pest (pesht) = part of BUDAPEST since 1872

Pest'er-zse-bet (pesh₁-ter-zhä-bet) *City* suburb of Budapest, Hungary

Pë'têr-bör-ough (bör-ö) 1. *City* SE Ontario, Canada; agricultural area. 2. *Municipal borough* cen. England; trade cen.

Pe-te-rō'ä (pä-tä) *Peak* 13,420 ft. cen. Chile; volcanic

Pë'têrs-bûrg *City* SE Va., U.S.; pop. 36,-103; shipping, tobacco industry

Pet'ri-fīed Forest *National park* E Ariz., U.S.

Pet'ro-grad see LENINGRAD

Pet-rō-pav'lôvsk *City* U.S.S.R., cen. Asia; trade cen.

Pė-trop'ö-lis *City* SE Brazil

Pet-ro-zà-vodsk', Kà-li'ninsk (lē') *City* NW U.S.S.R., Eur.; guns

Pet'sà-mō *Territory* NW U.S.S.R., Eur.; formerly Finnish

Pfôrz'heīm *City* SW West Germany; manufacturing

Phal'tàn (p'hàl') *State* W India

Phä-nöm Dông Räk (p'hä) *Mountain range* Thailand-Cambodia

Phän-räng (p'hän) *Town* on *Bay* S Vietnam; agricultural cen.

Phil-à-del'phi-à (fil-a-del'fi-à) 1. *City* SE Pa., U.S.; pop. 1,-948,609; commercial, cultural, financial, industrial cen.; site of 1st and 2nd Continental Congresses,

signing of Declaration of Independence; * of U.S. 1790-1800. 2. *Anc. city* W Turkey, Asia

Phi'lippe-ville (fil') *City* NE Algeria; port

Phi'lip-pi (fil') *Anc. town* N cen. Macedonia, Greece

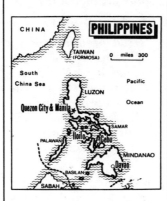

Phil'lip-pine (fil'i-pēn), Republic of the *Country,* SE Asia; 115,600 sq. m.; pop. 37,008,-000; 65 provinces; *Main cities:* * Manila, Cebu, Davao, Iloiló; *Main rivers:* Cagayan, Agno, Pampanga (on Luzon), Aguson (on Mindanas); *Geog.:* archipelago with some active volcanoes; larger islands mountanous; uplands make up 65 % of land area; most islands have narrow coastal lowlands; *Climate:* lies in tropics, astride typhoon belt.

Flag: horizontal bands — top blue, bottom red joined at staff side with white triangle.

Ethnic comp.: Filipinos, Chinese, Americans, Spaniards; *Language:* Filipino (official), English, Spanish, Chinese; *Religions:* Roman Catholic, Protestant, Moslem.

Products: rice, copra, sugar, abaca (hemp), maize, tobacco, timber, pineapples, bananas, copper, iron ore, chromite, gold, silver, nickel, ura-

nium, coal; *Minerals:* iron ore, copper, gold, manganese, chromium, nickel, zinc, molybdenum, silver; *Major exports:* abaca, canned pineapple, copra, logs, lumber, sugar, coconut oil, copper concentrates; *Major imports:* mineral fuels, lubricants, base metals, textiles, nonelectrical machinery, transportation equipment, electric machinery; *Industries:* mining, textile, other durable manufacturing, forestry, fishing, hydroelectric plants.

Currency: peso.

Head of Government: President; *Legislature:* bicameral Congress — Senate, House of Representatives; *Judiciary:* independent system. Power lodged in Supreme Court, Appeals Court, trial courts, inferior courts.

Phil'lip-pine Sea (fil'i-pēn) *Area* of W Pacific O. E of Phil. Is.

Phoe-ni'ci-a (fe-nish'à) *Anc. country* W Syria

Phoe'nix (fē') 1. *City * of Ariz., U.S., SW cen. part; pop. 581,-562. 2. *Islands* of Gilbert and Ellice group

Phryg'e-a (frij') *Anc. country* W cen. Asia Minor

Phu-ket (p'hōō) *Town* on *Island* SW Thailand; tin mines, port

Piä-cen'zä (chen') *Commune * of Province* N Italy; manufacturing

Pic'àr-dỷ *Hist. region* N France

Pi-chin'chä (pē-chēn') *Volcano* 15,710 ft. Ecuador

Pi'cō Ri-ve'rå (pē', vä') *City* S Cal., U.S.; pop. 54,170

Pi-chu'-Pi-chu' (chōō') *Peak* 18,600 ft. S Peru

Pic'tou (tōō) *Town* N

Nova Scotia, Canada; port

Pied'mont, Pie-môn'te (pyâ-môn'tà) *Compartimento'* NW Italy

Pierre (pyâr) *City * of S.D., U.S.; cen. part; pop. 9,699; shipping, saddles

Piē - têr - mar'it - bûrg *Town* former * of Nepal; tanneries, furniture

Pi'geon Peak (jun) *Peak* 13,970 ft. SW Colo., U.S.

Pīkes Peak *Mountain* 14,110 ft. E cen. Colo., U.S.

Pil-co-mä'yō (pēl) *River* 1000 m. S cen. South America

Pi'li (pē'lē) *Peak* 19,850 ft. N Chile

Pil'làr, Cape *Cape* SE Tasmania

Pī'löt Knob (nob) *Peak* 13,750 ft. SW Colo., U.S.

Pī'löt Peak *Peak* 11,740 ft. NW Wyo., U.S.

Pil'sèn = PLZEN

Pin'chot, Mount (shō) *Peak* 13,470 ft. S cen. Calif., U.S.

Pin'dus *Mountain chain* NW Greece

Pīne Bluff *City* SE Ark. U.S.; pop. 57,389; industrial, trade cen.

Pi-ne'gà *River* 500 m. U.S.S.R., Eur.

Ping, Me-ping *River* 360 m. W Thailand

Pin'kiang' (ji-äng') see HARBIN

Pinsk *City * of Region,* White Russia, U.S.S.R., Eur.; manufacturing

Piô'tr-kow (kōōf), **Pe-trö-kôv'** *Commune* cen. Poland; textiles

Pi-rà-ci-ca'bà (pē, ce) *City* SE Brazil; trade

Pī-raē'us *City* E cen. Greece; seaport for Athens

Pi-ra'nhàs (nyàs) *River* 250 m. NE Brazil

Pir'mä-sens *City* SW West Germany; leather items

Pi'sà (pē'zà) *Commune * of Province* cen. Italy; resort, tower

Pi-stō'iä *Commune * of Province* cen. Italy; manufacturing

Pit *River* 280 m. N Calif., U.S.

Pit'câirn Island *Island*, Brit. colony, cen. Pacific O.

Pitts'bûrgh *City* SW Pa., U.S.; pop. 520,-117; river port; iron, steel, educational cen.

Pitts'fiẽld *C i t y* W Mass., U.S.; pop. 57,-020; cultural, industrial cen.

Plà-cen'tia Bay (sen'-shà) *Bay* SE Newfoundland, Canada; site of Atlantic Charter 1941

Pla'cid, Lake (sĩd) *Lake* NE N.Y., U.S.

Plāin'fiẽld *City* NE N.J., U.S.; pop. 46,-862; machinery

Plä'tä-no *River* 325 m. S Mexico

Platte 1. *River* 300 m. Iowa-Mo., U.S. 2. *River* 310 m. cen. Neb., U.S.

Platts'bûrgh *City* NE N.Y., U.S.; naval battles, 1776, 1814

Plau'ẽn (plou') *City* S cen. East Germany; cotton textiles

Ple'ven *City* * of *Department* N Bulgaria; cattle, wine cen.

Plô-es'ti (yesh') *City* SE cen. Romania; oil

Plõ'mõ *Mountain* 22,-300 ft. S cen. Chile

Plôv'div *City* * of *Department* S Bulgaria; trade cen.

Plỳm'outh (u t h) 1. *Town* on *Bay* SE Mass., U.S.; site of early colony. 2. *City*, on *Sound*, SW England; port, naval base

Pl'zen (pul'), **Pil'sẻn** *City* SW Czechoslovakia; breweries, industry

Pnôm'penh' *City* * of Cambodia, SE part; pop. 394,000; trade

Põ *River* 415 m. N Italy

Põ-cà-tel'lo *City* SE Ida., U.S.; pop. 40,-036

Põ'co-no *Mountains Heights* E Pa., U.S.

Po - dolsk' *T o w n* R.S.F.S.R., U.S.S.R., Eur.; factories

Põ'dôr *Town* N Senegal

Põ Haï, Gulf of NW *Arm* of Yellow S.

Põ'hsien' (shi-en') *City* E China; commerce

Pointe-a-Pi'tre (pwan-ta-pē') *Town* E Guadeloupe

Poi-tiers' (pwa-tyā') *City* W cen. France

Põ'lànd, Polish People's Republic, *Country*, E Europe; 120,-600 sq. m.; pop. 32,-670,000; 22 provinces; *Main cities:* * Warsaw, Lódź, Krakow, Wroclaw (Breslau), Poznán, Gdansk (Danzig), Szczecin (Stettin); *Main rivers:* Vistula, Oder, Bug; *Geog.:* consists primarily of lowlands; mts. along southern borders; *Climate:* temperate with moderately severe winters, mild summers.

Flag: equal sized horizontal bands — upper white, lower red.

Ethnic comp.: Poles, Ukranians, Byelorussians; *Language:* Polish (official); *Religions:* Roman Catholic, Eastern Orthodox, Protestant, Jewish.

Products: rye, dairy products, sugar, fish, timber, coal, coke, lignite, copper, sulphur, locomotives, ships, cement, iron, steel, textiles, chemicals, electronics; *Minerals:* coal, lignite, sulphur, copper ore, salt, zinc; *Major exports:* chemicals,

foodstuffs, coal, copper, sulphur, ships, textiles, steel, cement; *Major imports:* oil, iron ore, fertilizers, wheat, leather footwear; *Industries:* mining, machine manufacture, manufacture of chemicals, power, foodstuff.

Currency: zloty.

Head of Government: Chairman of the Council of State; *Legislature:* Sejm; *Judiciary:* Supreme Court, national, local courts subordinate to party policies & directives.

Põ'làr Regions *Areas* around N and S Poles

Põle Crẽek Mountain *Peak* 13,735 ft. SW Colo., U.S.

Põ'lish Cor'ri-dör *Land strip*, various ownership; now N Poland

Pol'lux 1. *Peak* 13,430 ft. W peak of ZWILLINGE (Twins). 2. *Peak* 11,080 ft. NW Wyo., U.S.

Põ'lotsk *City* * of *Region* White Russia, U.S.S.R.

Pöl-ta'và *City* * of *Region* Ukraine, U.S.-S.R.; grain, leather

Pol-ỳ-nẽ'sia (zhà) 1. *Islands* of cen. Pacific O. 2. FRENCH POLYNESIA

Pom-êr-ā'nià 1. *Bay* NE Germany - NW Poland. 2. *Hist. region* on Baltic S. now bel. to Poland

Po-mõ'nà 1. *City* SW Calif., U.S.; pop. 87,-384; shipping. 2. *Island*, largest of Orkney Is.

Pom'pà-no Beach *City* S Fla., U.S.; pop. 37,724

Pom-pe'ii (pâ'ẻ) *Anc. city* S Italy; excavations; mod. **Pom-pe'i**

Põ'nà-pe (pā) *Island* E Caroline Is.

Pôn'ce (sâ) *City* and *Municipality* S Puerto Rico; shipping

Pon-di-cher'rỳ *Town* SE India, former * of Fr. India; textiles

Pon'do-land *Area* S Rep. of South Africa

Pön'tà Grôs'sà *City* S Brazil

Pont'chàr-trāin' *Lake* SE La., U.S.

Pôn-te-ve'drä (v ā ') *Commune* * of *Province* NW Spain

Pon'ti-àc *City* SE Mich. U.S.; pop. 85,279; automobile equipment

Pon-ti-ä'näk *City* Borneo, Indonesia; port

Pon'tine (tẽn), **Pon'zä** *Islands* of *Group* W of Naples, Italy

Pon-tỳ-põõl' *Urban district* W England; coal, factory area

Põõle *Municipal borough* S England; fish, pottery

Põõ'nà *City* * of *District* W India; mills

Põ-pä-yän' *City* SW Colombia; cultural cen.

Po-põ-cä-tẻ-petl' (pet'l) *Volcano* 17,885 ft. SE cen. Mexico

Põ'quis (kẽs) *Peak* 18,-830 ft. N Chile

Pôr-ban'dàr *Town* * of *State* W India; port

Pôr'cū-pīne 1. *River* 400 m. Yukon, Canada-NE Alas., U.S. 2. *Range* NW Mich., U.S.

Pô'ri, **Björ'nẻ-bôrg** (byûr') *City* SW Finland; port, factories

Pôrs'äng-êr Fjord *Inlet* N Norway

Pôrt Ad'ẻ-lāide *City* SE Australia; seaport

Pôrt Är'thûr 1. *City* SE Tex., U.S.; pop. 57,371; shipping. 2. *City* SW Ontario, Canada; p o r t. 3. *Town* S Manchuria. E cen. China; port

Pôrt-au-Prince' *City* * and main seaport of Haiti; pop. 300,000

Pôrt Blâir *Town* Andaman Is., Bay of Bengal, India; harbor

Pôrt E-liz'à-beth *Town* S Rep. of South Africa; imp. port, factories

Pôrt Här'côurt *City* S Nigeria; port

Pôrt Hū'ron *City* SE

Mich., U.S.; pop. 35,-794; lake port

Pôrt Jack'sön *Inlet* SE Australia; harbor

Pôrt'lånd 1. *City* SW Me., U.S.; pop. 65,-116; port. 2. *City* NW Ore., U.S.; pop. 382,-619; manufacturing, industrial, shipping

Pôrt Lou'is (lōō'ĭ) *City* * of Marituis I.; port

Pôrt Lyau-tey' (lyō-tā'), **Ke-ni-tra'** *Port* NW Morocco; WW II landing, 1942

Pôrt Mōres'bẏ *City* S Terr. of Papua, New Guinea; port

Pôr'to A-le'grė (tōō, lā') *City* S Brazil; port, commercial cen.

Pôrt of Spāin *Town* NW Trinidad, * of Trinidad and Tobago; pop. 125,000; port

Pôr'tō Nō'vō *Town* * of Dahomey, SE part; pop. 80,000; port

Pôrt Phil'lip Bay (fil') *Harbor* of Melbourne, Australia

Pôrt Saīd' *City* NE Egypt; port

Pôrts'mouth (muth) 1. *City* SE Va., U.S.; pop. 110,963; industrial port. 2. *County borough* S England; port

Pôrt Stan'ley (li) *Town* * of Falkland Is.; port

Pôrt Su-dan' (sōō) *Town* NE Sudan; port

Pôrt Tal'böt *Urban district* SE Wales; coal

Pôr'tu-gàl, Republic of *Country*, E Europe; 34,500 sq. m.; pop. 9,496,000; 18 dis-

tricts; *Main cities:* * Lisbon, Oporto, Coimbra, Vila Nova de Gaia, Setúbal; *Main rivers:* Tagus, Douro, Guadiana; *Geog. & Climate:* divided in two by Tagus R; N mountainous, receives considerable, rain, has moderate climate; S rolling plains with less rainfall, hotter climate.

Flag: approximately ⅓ is green (along the staff), remainder is red; centered on dividing line is national coat of arms.

Ethnic comp.: Portuguese, a mixture of Celtic, Arab, Berber, Phoenician, Carthaginian; *Language:* Portuguese (official); *Religion:* Roman Catholic.

Products: cereals, wine, olive oil, fruit, timber, cork, sardines, tungsten, copper, coal, textiles, chemicals, steel, pulp, electrical equipment, tools; *Minerals:* wolfram, cassiterite, beryl, copper, pyrites, coal, iron ore; *Major exports:* machinery, textiles, food, wine, cork, sardines, diamonds; *Major imports:* optical instruments, cotton, steel, wheat, corn, machinery, industrial equipment, petroleum products; *Industries:* motor assembly, tourism, engineering, mining, food precessing, shipbuilding, wine making, textile manufacture, ship repair.

Currency: escudo.

Head of Government: President; *Legislature:* bicameral parliament — National Assembly, Corporative Chamber; *Judiciary:* influenced by French model; Supreme Tribunal of Justice at apex.

Pôr'tu-guese E Africa (gēz) now MOZAM-BIQUE; **W Africa** = ANGOLA

Pôr'tu-guese Guin'ea (gēz, gin'ĭ) *Colony* W Africa, * Bissau; peanuts, oils, ivory, hides

Pôr'tu-guese India (gēz) see GOA

Pôr'tu-guese (gēs) **Ti-môr'** *Colony* E part of Timor I. Malay Arch. * Dili; agriculture

Pō'sėn = POZNAN

Pô'shän' *Town* NE China; industry

Po-ten'zä *Commune* * of *Province* S Italy

Po-tō'måc *River* 500 m. W.Va.-Va.-Md., U.S.

Pō-to-si' (sē') 1. *City* * of *Department* SW Bolivia; silver. 2. *Peak* 13,765 ft. SW Colo., U.S.

Pō'trô *Peak* 19,125 ft. NW Argentina

Pots'dam *City* cen. East Germany; factories; WW II conference 1945

Pour-ri', Mônt (pōō-rē') *Peak* 12,425 ft. E France

Pow'dêr *River* 375 m. Wyo.-Mont., U.S.

Pow'ėll, Mount *Peak* 13,535 ft. Colo , U.S.

Pō'yäng' Hū *Lake* SE China

Pôz'nän, Ger. Pō'sėn *City* * of *Department* W cen. Poland; manufacturing, cultural cen.

Prague (präg), **Pra'ha** *City* * of Czechoslovakia, W part; pop. 1,103,200; industrial, commercial cen.

Präh-ran' *City* SE Australia

Prä'tō *Commune* cen. Italy; textiles

Pres'cött *City* cen. Ariz., U.S.; mining

Pres-i-den'tial Range (shål) *Range* of White Mts., N.H., U.S. [SLAVA

Press'bûrg = BRATI-

Pres'tön *County borough* NW England; port, factories

Pre-tō'ri-å *City*, administrative * of Rep.

of South Africa, NE part; pop. 448,000

Prib'i-lôf Islands *Island group* SE Bering S. Alas., U.S.; fur seals

Prich'ård *City* SW Ala., U.S.; pop. 41,-578

Prince Al'bêrt *Peninsula, Sound,* Victoria I. Northwest Terrs., Canada

Prince Ed'wård Island *Island Province* SE Canada; pop. 110,-000; * Charlottetown; fish, forests, agriculture

Prince Ed'wård Islands *Islands* (2) S Indian O., South Africa

Prince of Wāles Island 1. *Island*, largest of Alexander Arch. SE Alas., U.S. 2. *Island* NW Terrs., Canada

Prince Pat'rick Island *Island* of Parry Is. NW Terrs., Canada

Prince Rū'pêrt *City* W Brit. Columbia, Canada; port, fisheries

Prince'tön, Mount *Peak* 14,175 ft. Colo., U.S.

Prin'ci-pe (si) *Island* (Port.) off W Africa; agriculture

Pri'pyåt (prē') *River* 5 0 0 m. through *Marshes* White Russia-Ukraine, U.S.S.R.

Prö-kô'pėvsk *City* S cen. U.S.S.R., Asia; mines

Prōme *Town* * of *District* Lower Burma; port

Prom'ön-tō-rẏ *Point* *Point* NW Utah, U.S.; Golden Spike Monument

Pros'pec-törs Mountain *Peak* 11,230 ft. Wyo., U.S.

Prô-vence' (väns') *Hist. region* SE France

Prov'i-dėnce *City* * of R.I., U.S.; pop. 179,-213; manufacturing, port

Prov'ince-town *Town* SE Mass., U.S.; 1620 landing of Pilgrims

Prō'vō *Peak* 11,055 ft.; *City* N cen. Utah, U.S.; pop. 53,131; commerce, industry

Prus'sia (prush'å) *Former state* N and cen.

Germany; div. 1945-7 Poland-U.S.S.R.

Prūt *River* 500 m. E Romania

Psel *River* 420 m. Ukraine U.S.S.R.

Pskôv *City* * of *Region* W cen. U.S.S.R., Eur.; port; rail, commercial cen.

Ptär′mi-gản Peak (tär′) *Peak* 13,735 ft. cen. Colo., U.S.

Pue′blä (pwäb′) *City* * of *State*, SE cen. Mexico; old city; textiles, pottery

Pû-eb′lō *City* SE cen. Colo., U.S.; pop. 97,-453; commerce, industry, minerals

Puer′to Plä′tä *Commune* and *City* N Dominican Rep.; port

Puer′tö Ri′cō (rē′) *Island* of West Indies (U.S.); * San Juan; agriculture

Pū′get Sound (jḙt) *Arm* of Pacific O., W Wash., U.S.

Pulj (pōōl′y′), **Pō′lä** *Town* NW Yugoslavia; port

Pu′nả-khả (poo′) *Town* winter * of Bhutan

Pun′jäb 1. *Former province* NW Brit. India; 1947 div.: **East Pun′-jäb** (*state*) NW India, **West Pun′jäb** part of West Pakistan

Pun′tä A-re′näs (pōōn′, rä′) *City* S Chile; port; world's southernmost city

Pu-pä-yäx′ (yäk′) *Peak* 19,080 ft. W Bolivia

Pu-rä-ce′ (sä′) *Volcano* 15,420 ft. SW Colombia

Pu-rä′li *River* 310 m. West Pakistan

Pu-rä′ri *River* 280 m. E cen. New Guinea

Pûr′gả-tô′rẏ Peak *Peak* 13,720 ft. S Colo., U.S.

Pu′ri (poo′), **Jả′gản-näth** *Town* E India; Hindu pilgrimage site

Pu-rūs′ (pōō) *River* 2000 m. Peru-Brazil

Pu-sän, Fu-sän (oo) *City* S Korea; port

Push′kảr (poosh′) *Lake* NW cen. India; sacred water

Push′kin (poosh′) *Town*

NW U.S.S.R., Eur.; resort

Put′-in-Bay (poot′) *Bay* of Lake Erie, Ohio, U.S.; Comm. Perry victory, 1813

Pu′tô′ Shän (pōō′) *Island* E China; sacred to Buddhists

Pu-tu-mä′yo (pōō-tōō) *River* 980 m. Colombia-Peru-Brazil

Puy-de-Dōme′ (pû-ēd-dōm′) *Department* S cen. France

Pyä′si-nả *River* 350 m. N U.S.S.R., W Asia

Pya-ti-gôrsk′ *Town* S U.S.S.R., Eur.; resort

Pȳ′los, It. **Nä-vä-ri′nō** (rē′) SW Peloponnesus, Greece; harbor

Pyöng-yäng or **Hei-jô** (hä) *City* * of North Korea; pop. 653,000

Pẏr′ả-mid Peak *Mountain:* 1. 14,000 ft. Colo., U.S. 2. 10,300 ft. NW Wyo., U.S.

Pẏr′ả-mids *Anc monuments* (3) nr. Cairo, Egypt

Pẏr′é-nēes, Pi-rḙ-ne′ōs (nä′) *Mountains* Span.-Fr. border

Pẏ-re-nees′ (rả-nä′) *Department* France

Pẏ-re-nees′ - O-rien-tale′ (rä-nä′ zô-ryän-tal′) *Department* S France

Q

Qä′tär *Arab shiekdom* on *Peninsula*, Persian Gulf; 8,000 sq. m.; pop. 80,000; * Doha; oil

Qät-tä′rä Depression *Low area* N Egypt

Qē′nả *City* * of *Province* Upper Egypt; glass jars

Qi′zel U-zun′ (oo-zoon′) *River* 450 m. NW Iran

Quän′dả-rẏ Peak *Peak* 14,256 ft. Colo., U.S.

Quän′ti-cō *Town* NE Va., U.S.; Marine Corps base

Qu′Ap-pelle′ (ka) *River* 270 m. cen. Canada

Que-bec′ 1. *Province* E Canada; 594,860 sq. m.; pop. 5,976,000; * Quebec; agriculture, fish, mining, forestry.

2. *City* its *; pop. 166,984; port, manufacturing

Quēen Al-ex-an′drả Range *Mountains*, Victoria Land, Antarctica

Q u ē e n Chär′lötte (shär′) *Islands* and *Sound* W Brit. Columbia, Canada

Quēen Mâr′ẏ Coast *Area* at Antarctic Circle, Brit.

Quēen Mẚud Gulf *Gulf* NW Terrs., Canada

Quēen Mẚud Land (Norwegian) Antarctica

Quēens *Borough* (largest of 5) of N.Y. City, U.S.; manufacturing

Quēens′land *State* NE Australia; * Brisbane; exports sugar, animal products

Que-moy′ (kē) *Island* off SE China (Nationalist)

Que-nä-mä′ri (k ä) *Mountain* 19,190 ft. SE Peru

Que-re′tä-rō (kâ-rä′) *City* * of *State* cen. Mexico

Quet′tä (kwet′) *Town* * of *District* W cen. West Pakistan; trade

Que-zäl-te-nän′gō (kâ-säl-tâ) *City* * of *Department* SW Guatemala; grain area

Que′zôn City (kä′) *City* Luzon, Phil. Is.; * of Republic of the Philippines; pop. 500,000

Quil′mes (kēl′mâs) *City* E Argentina; industry, resort

Quim-sä-chä′tä (kēm) *Peak* 19,880 ft. N Chile

Quim-sä-crūz′ (kēm) *Peak* 19,355 ft. W Bolivia

Quin′cẏ 1. *City* W Ill., U.S.; pop. 45,288; commerce, industry. 2. *City* E Mass., U.S.; pop. 87,966; shipyards; home of John, John Q. Adams

Quin′tō (kēn′) *River* 250 m. N cen. Argentina

Quir′i-nảl *Hill* one of of 7 of Rome, Italy

Qui′tō (kē′) *City* * of Ecuador, N part;

pop. 530,000; cultural cen.

Qum (koom) *City* NW cen. Iran; grain, cotton region

R

Rả-bät′ *City* * of Morocco, NW part; pop. 250,000; port

Rả-baul′ (boul′, bōōl′) *Town* New Brit. I., Terr. of New Guinea

Rä-ci′borz (tsē′boosh), **Ra′ti-bôr** *City* SW Poland, formerly German

Rả-cine′ (sēn′) *City* SE Wisc., U.S.; pop. 95,-162; industry, port

Rä′dhản-pur (poor) *Town* * of *State* W India   [E Wales

Rad′nör-shire *County*

Rä′dôm *Commune* E cen. Poland; industrial

Rä-gu′sả (gōō′) 1. *Commune* * of *Province* SE Sicily, Italy. 2. or **Dū′brov-nik** Yugoslavia port

Rä′had *River* 270 m. Ethiopia-Sudan

Raï′chur *Town* S cen. India

Raï′gärh *Town* * of *State* NE India; silk

Rai-niēr′, Mount (rả) *Peak* in *National Park* 14,400 ft. W cen. Wash., U.S.

Rāin′ẏ Lake *Lake* Canada-Minn., U.S.

Raï′pur (poor) *Town* E cen. India

Rä - jả - mun′drẏ (moon′) *City* E India; timber

Rä′jäng *River* 300 m. Sarawak, Borneo

Rä′jả-sthän *State* NW India within *Region* (also **Räj-pu-tä′nả**)

Räj′kōt *Town* * of former *State* W India

Räj-pi′plả (pē′) *Town* * of *State* W India

Räj-shä′hi *Town* * of *District* E Pakistan

Rä-kả-häng′ả *Atoll* (U.S.) cen. Pacific O.

Rả-kả-pô′shi *Peak* 25,-560 ft. N Kashmir

Rä′kos-pa-lo-ta (kosh) *City* cen. Hungary

Rä-ku-tō *River* 270 m. S Korea

Rǎ'leigh (li) *City* * of N.C., U.S.; pop. 121,-577; cotton, tobacco, educational cen.

Rà-ma'di *Town* cen. Iraq

Räm-gàn'gä *River* 370 m. N India

Räm'lèh *City*, resort of Alexandria, Egypt

Räm'pur (poor) *City* * of *State* N India; sugar, damask, pottery

Ram'sēs *Anc. city* E Egypt

Rams'gāte *Municipal borough* SE England; yachting, fishing

Rä'mu (mōō) *River* 300 m. NE New Guinea

Rän'chi *Town* NE India; health cen.

Rän'dêrs *City* Jutland, Denmark; port

Ränd-fôn-tein' (tän') *City* NE Rep. of South Africa; gold

Rand'wick *City* SE Australia

Ränge'ley (r ā n j ' l i) *Lakes* W Me., U.S.

Ran-gōōn' *City* on *River*, * of Burma, S part; pop. 740,000; imp. port

Rång'pur (poor) *Town* * of *District* E Pakistan

Rän-te-mä'ri-ō *Peak* 11,285 ft. Celebes I., Indonesia

Rä-päl'lō *Commune* NW Italy; port

Rap'id City *City* SW S.D., U.S.; pop. 43,-836; trade

Rä'pi-dō (pē) *River* cen. Italy; WW II site

Räp'ti *River* 400 m. Nepal   [Cook Is.

Rar-o-ton'gà *Island* of

Räs' Dä-shän' *Peak* 15,160 ft. N Ethiopia

Rä-shin *Port* NE North Korea

Rat Islands *Group* W Aleutians, Alas., U.S.

Rǎt-läm' *Town* cen. India

Rà-ven'nà *Commune* * of *Province* N Italy

Rä'vi *River* 450 m. N India

Rä-wal-pin'di *City* * of *Division* and former * of Pakistan, N West Pakistan; pop. 340,-200; industrial

Read'ing (red') 1. *City*

SE Pa., U.S.; pop. 87,643; industrial. 2. *County borough* S England

Rēar'guärd (gärd) *Peak* 12,350 ft. S Mont., U.S.

Rè-ci'fè (sē') *City* (was Pernambuco) E Brazil; imp. port

Reck'ling - hau - sèn (hou) *City* W West Germany; commerce

Red'cloud Peak *Peak* 14,050 ft. SW Colo., U.S.

Red Dēer *River* 385 m. Alberta, Canada

Red'lands *City* SE Cal., U.S.; pop. 36,355; residential

Red Mountain 1. *Peak* 11,930 ft. S cen. Calif. U.S. 2. *Peak* 13,500 ft. W cen. Colo., U.S.

Re-don'dō Beach *City* S Cal., U.S.; pop. 56,075; manufacturing, residential

Red Peak 1. *Mountain* 11,700 ft. cen. Calif., Calif., U.S. 2. *Mountain* 13,600 ft. S Colo., U.S.

Red River 1. *River* 1018 m. N.M.-Tex.-Okla - Ark.-La., U.S. 2. **of the Nôrth** *River* 310 m. cen. U.S.-cen. Canada

Red Sea *Inland sea* bet. Arabia-Africa

Red'wood *City* W Cal., U.S.; pop. 55,686; residential, manufacturing

Re'gèns-bûrg (rä') *City* SE West Germany

Reg'gio (räd'jō) 1. **di Cä-lä'bri-ä** *Commune* * of *Province* S Italy. 2. **nell' E-mi'liä** (näl-lä-mē') *Commune* * of *Province* N Italy; commerce, manufacturing

Rè-gi'nà (jī') *City* * of Saskatchewan prov. (S part) Canada; pop. 131,127; trade cen.

Reich (rīk) = Empire: 1st Reich = Holy Roman Emp.; 2nd Reich = Bismarck Emp.; 3rd Reich = Nazi Emp.

Reï'chèn-bêrg (rī'kèn) see LIBEREC

Reï'gāte *Municipal borough* S England

Rēims, Rhēims *City* NE France; cathedral, champagne, textiles; site of German surrender 1945

Rein'dēer Lake (rān') *Lake* cen. Canada

Reïn'steïn, Mount *Peak* 12,600 ft. S cen. Calif., U.S.

Re'mä-gèn (rä') *Town* W cen. West Germany; WW II battle

Rem'scheïd (shīt) *City* W cen. West Germany; cutlery, tools

Ren-frew' (frōō') *Burgh*, **Ren-frew'shire** *county*, SW Scotland

Rennes (ren) *City* NW France; manufacturing

Rē'nō *City* NW Nev., U.S.; pop. 72,863; commercial cen., legal gambling

Re-pub'li-càn *River* 445 m. Neb.-Kans., U.S.

Resht *City* NW Iran

Re-sis-ten'cià (tän'siä) *City* N Argentina

Res-o-lu'tion Island (lōō'shàn) *Island* off SE Baffin I., Canada

Re-ū-niôn' (rā) *Island* (Fr. *Dept.*) off Madagascar, W Indian O.

Reut'ling-èn (roit') *City* SW West Germany; manufacturing

Rè-vēre' *City* E Mass., U.S.; pop. 43,159; beach resort

Rè-vil'là-gi-gē-dō *Island* SE Alas., U.S.; site of Ketchikan

Rē'wà *Town* * of *State* E cen. India

Rey'kja-vik (rā'kyä) *Town* * of Iceland, SW coast; pop. 81,-500; port

Rhēims = REIMS

Rheïn'hau-sèn (hou) *Commune* W West Germany; port, coal

Rheïn'wäld-hôrn (vält) *Peak* 11,144 ft. SE Switzerland

Rhine, Rheïn, Rijn (rīn), **Rhin** (ran) *River* 820 m. W Eur.

Rhine'land *Area* of West Germany W of Rhine R.

Rhine'land - Pà-la't-i-

nate *State* of W Germany, W of Rhine R.

Rhōde Is'lànd (ī') *State*, named from the Greek Island of Rhodes; 1,214 sq. m.; *pop.*: 946,725 (*rank*: 39th); E Coast — New England U.S.; *Boundaries*: Massachusetts, Connecticut, New York, Atlantic Ocean; *Major cities*: * Providence, Pawtucket, Newport; *Major rivers*: Sakonnet, Backstone, Woonasquatuket, Pawtacket; *Major lakes*: Worden Pond, Scituate Reservoir; 5 counties.

Nickname: Little Rhody; *Motto*: "Hope;" *Flag*: golden anchor & 12 gold stars on white field; *Flower*: violet; *Bird*: Rhode Island red; *Tree*: maple; *Song*: Rhode Island.

Industry: plastic items, agriculture, jewelry, silverware, textiles, metal production, rubber products, electrical machinery; *Natural resources*: forests, sand, gravel, graphite, fish; *Major source of income*: manufacturing.

Admitted to Union: May 29, 1790.

Places of interest: beach resorts, Roger Williams Memorial, Samuel Slater's Mill.

Rhōdes *City* on *Island*, * of Greek Aegean Is.; 2 harbors; fruit

Rhō-dē'sia (shà), *Coun-*

try, SC Africa; 150,-330 sq. m.; pop. 5,285,000; 7 provinces; *Main cities:* * Salisbury, Bulawayo, Umtali, Gwelo; *Main rivers:* Zambezi, Nata, Limpopo, Sabi; *Geog.:* ⅔ belongs to hydrographic basin of Zambesi. Rest divided between river basins of Kalahari, Sabi, Limpopo; *Climate:* altitude has mitigating effect on climate except Zambezi and Limpopo Valleys which are hot, moist. Rain averages 28″.

Flag: equal vertical stripes of green, white, green, national coat of arms center of white stripe.

Ethnic comp.: Bantu, Europeans, Coloureds, Asians; *Language:* English (official), Afrikaans, Shona, Sindebele; *Religions:* animist, Christian.

Products: maize, tobacco, livestock, cotton, sugar, dairy products, citrus fruit, tea, fish, asbestos, copper, gold, coal, phosphates, textiles, general manufactures; *Minerals:* asbestos, chrome ore, coal, copper, gold, iron ore, limestone, lithium, nickel, phosphate, rock and tin; *Major exports:* tobacco, asbestos, copper, apparel, meats, chrome, sugar; *Major imports:* machinery — transportation equipment, textiles, petroleum products, iron — steel products, fertilizers, foodstuff; *Industries:* manufacturing, food processing, oil refining, tourism.

Currency: Rhodesian pound at par with sterling.

Head of Government: President; *Legisla-*

ture: bicameral Parliament; *Judiciary:* high court in Salisbury at apex.

Rhon′ddä *Urban district* SE Wales; coal
Rhône 1. *River* 500 m. Switzerland - France. 2. *Department* S France
Ri-äd′ = RIYADH
Ri-bei-rao′ Pre′to (vä-rou′ pra′tōō) *City* SE Brazil; coffee area
Rich′ärd-sön *City* NE Texas, U.S.; pop. 48,582
Rich′e-lieū (rish′) *River* 210 m. Quebec, Canada
Rich′fïeld *City* SE cen. Minn., U.S.; pop. 47,231
Rich′mönd 1. *City* W Calif., U.S.; pop. 79,-043; industrial port. 2. *City* E Ind., U.S.; pop. 43,999; manufacturing. 3. *County* of N.Y. and *Borough* of N.Y. City, U.S. 4. *City* * of Va., U.S.; pop. 249,621; trade cen., tobacco market, manufacturing. 5. *City* SE Australia; manufacturing. 6. *Municipal borough* S England
Rie′kä, Ri-je′kä (r′ye′), It. **Fiü′me** (mä) *City* NW Yugoslavia; port
Rie′ti (ryä′) *Commune* * of *Province* cen. Italy; livestock, agriculture
Ri′gà (rē′) *City* on *Gulf* * of Latvia; port
Ri′mi-ni *City* N Italy; port, resort
Rimp′fïsch-hôrn *Peak* 13,791 ft. SW Switzerland
Rin-côn′ *Peak* 18,350 ft. N Chile
Ri′ō Al′tō Peak (rē′) *Peak* 13,570 ft. S cen. Colo., U.S.
Ri′ō Cuär′tō *Town* N cen. Argentina; agricultural cen.
Rï′ō de Jà-nei′rō (rē′, nä′) 1. *City*, former * of Brazil, SE part; one of world's finest harbors; cultural cen. 2. *State* SE Brazil
Ri′o Gran′dè (rē′ōō) *City* S Brazil; port

Ri′ō Grande or **Ri′ō Brä′vō** (rē′) *River* 1800 m. Colo.-N.M.-Tex., U.S.-Mexico
Ri′o Gran′dè (rē′ōō) 1. *River* 250 m. W Africa (also **Co-rū-bäl′, Kom′bà**). 2. *River* 680 m. E Brazil. 3. *River* 300 m. E Brazil
Ri′ō Mu′ni (rē′, mōō′) *Province*, mainland of Equatorial Guinea, site of *
Ri′ō Ne′grō (rē′, nä′) see NEGRO, RIO
Ri′ō Pie′dräs (rē′, pyä′) *Municipality* NE Puerto Rico; industrial
Ri′tō Al′tō Peak (rē′) *Mountain* 13,570 ft. Colo., U.S.
Rit′têr, Mount *Peak* 13,155 ft. cen. Calif., U.S.
Riv′êr-sïde *City* SE Calif., U.S.; pop. 140,089; commerce, resort; fruit area
Ri-vie′rä (vyâ′) *Region* on Mediterranean S., SE France-NW Italy (Fr. = **Côte d′A-zūr′**)
Ri-yädh′ *City* * of Saudi Arabia, E cen. part; pop. ab. 185,000
Ri-zäl′ *Province* Luzon, Phil. Is.
Rōad′ Town *Town* * of Brit. Virgin Is. on Tortola I.; pop. 1500
Rō-anne′ *Commune* SE cen. France; mills
Rō′à-nōke 1. *City* W cen. Va., U.S.; pop. 92,115; rail, manufacturing cen. 2. *Island* E N.C., U.S.; 1st English settlement in N America 3. *River* 380 m. Va.-N.C., U.S.
Rob′sön, Mount *Peak* 12,970 ft. E Brit. Colombia, Canada
Rô′cà *Cape* SW point of Portugal
Roch′däle *County borough* NW England
Roch′es-têr 1. *City* SE Minn., U.S.; pop. 53,-766; Mayo Clinic. 2. *City* W N.Y., U.S.; pop. 296,233; port; manufacturing, educational cen. 3. *City* SE England
Rock *River* 300 m. Wisc.-Ill., U.S.

Rock′däle *City* SE Australia
Rock′förd *City* N Ill., U.S.; pop. 147,370; manufacturing
Rock-hamp′tön *City* E Australia; shipping
Rock Is′länd (ī′) *City* NW Ill., U.S.; pop. 50,166; port
Rock′ville *City* C Md., U.S.; pop. 41,564; residential
Rock′ẏ Mountains, Rock′ies *Mountain system* W North America; Mexico-U.S.-Canada-Arctic
Rodg′êrs Peak (roj′) *Peak* 13,055 ft. Calif., U.S.
Rōes Wel′cöme *Strait* Southampton I.-mainland, Northwest Terrs., Canada
Rōgue (rōg) *River* 220 m. Ore., U.S.
Rō′kän *River* 225 m. Sumatra, Indonesia
Ro-kel′ *River* 300 m. Sierra Leone
Roll′ing Mountain *Peak* 13,695 ft. Colo., U.S.
Rō′mä = ROME, Italy
Rō-mäine′ *River* 225 m. Quebec, Canada
Rō′màn Em′pïre *Anc. Empire* 264 B.C.-180 A.D., incl. S Eur., Britain, N Africa, Asia Minor, Egypt, Armenia, Mesopotamia, Syria, Palestine, NW Arabia

Ro-mä′nià, or Rū-mä′-nià, Socialist Republic of *Country*, SE Europe; 91,670 sq. m.; pop. 20,140,000; 39 counties and City of Bucharest; *Main cities:* * Bucharest, Cluj, Constanta, Iasi, Timisoara, Ploesti;

Main rivers: Danube, Prut, Siret, Olt, Lalomita, Jiu; *Geog.:* occupies greater part of V-shaped lower basin of Danube system and hilly eastern regions of middle Danube basin. Carpathian Mts., Transylvanian Alps separate plains in E & S from Transylvanian Plateau in NW; *Climate:* continental climate.

Flag: equal-sized vertical bands from left to right — coat of arms in center — red star atop emblem proclaims Communist State.

Ethnic comp.: Rumanians, Hungarians, Germans, Ukranians, Jews; *Language:* Rumanian (official), Hungarian, German, Ukranian, Yiddish; *Religions:* Rumanian (Eastern) Orthodox, Roman Catholic, Protestant, Jewish.

Products: maize, wheat, livestock, timber, fruit, grapes, sugar, oil, natural gas, salt, coal, iron ore, bauxite, iron, steel, cement, chemicals, engineering, electronics, machine tools; *Minerals:* petroleum, copper, lead, zinc, bauxite, manganese, bismuth, mercury, silver, iron ore, coal; *Major exports:* fuel, oil, gas, cereals, cement, wood products; *Major imports:* machinery, equipment, iron ore, coke, motor vehicles, electric motors; *Industries:* shipbuilding, tourism, forestry, mining, food processing, textile manufacturing.

Currency: lei.

Head of Government: President; *Legislature:* Grand National Assembly; *Judiciary:* function to defend the socialist order & personal rights. Supreme Court guarantees uniformity of procedure by supervising.

Rōme 1. *City* cen. N.Y., U.S.; pop. 50,148; industry. 2. *City* * of Italy, cen. part; pop. 2,731,000; cultural cen., famous ruins, site of Vatican City

Röm′förd *Urban district* SE England; iron foundries

Roo′sė-velt (rō′) 1. *Dam, Lake* S cen. Ariz., U.S. 2. *Island* Ross Dependency, Antarctica. 3. *Island* (**Thē′ö-dōre**) D.C., U.S. 4. *Lake* (**Frank′-lin D.**) N cen. Wash., ٠ U.S.

Rō′pêr *River* 325 m. N cen. Australia

Rō′sä, Môn′ta *Mountain* 15,215 ft. Swiss-Italian border

Rō′sȧ-liē Peak *Mountain* 13,575 ft. cen. Colo., U.S.

Rô-sä′rio *City* E cen. Argentina; imp. port

Rōse′mēad *City* S Cal., U.S.; pop. 40,972

Rō-set′tȧ, Rȧ-shid′ *City* Lower Egypt; Rosetta Stone found nearby

Rōse′ville *City* SE Mich., U.S.; pop. 60,529 [Denmark

Rös′kil-dė *City* E

Rôss and Crom′ȧr-tẏ *County* N Scotland; sheep, fish

Rôss Bar′riêr or **Rôss Shelf Ice** *Ice wall* and *shelf* along S Ross S., Antarctica

Rôss Dependency *Section* of Antarctica (Brit., administered by New Zealand) bet. 160° E and 150° W long. incl. **Rôss I.** and shores of **Rôss S.**

Ros′tock *City* East Germany; port, fisheries, manufactures

Rös-tôv′ *City* * of *Region* U.S.S.R., SE Eur.; cultural, industrial cen.

Roth′êr-hȧm *County*

borough N England; iron, coal area

Rô′ti *Island* nr. Timor, Indonesia

Rot′têr-dam *City* W Netherlands; manufacturing, commercial port

Rou-baix′ (rōō-be′) *City* N France; textiles, leather

Rou-en′ (rōō-än′) *City* N France; manufacturing, commerce

Rou-mā′niȧ (rōō) = ROMANIA *Republic* SE Europe; iron-steel, machinery, oil, timber, textiles, footwear, food processing

Rô-vi′gō (vē′) *Commune* * of *Province* NE Italy

Rôv′nö *Commune* W Ukraine U.S.S.R.; industrial

Row′ley Rē′gis (rou′li-rē′jis) *Urban district* W cen. England; iron, coal, pottery

Row′têr, Mount (rou′) *Peak* 13,750 ft. W cen. Colo., U.S.

Rox′burgh (b û r - ö) *County* SE Scotland

Roy′al, Mount *Height* Montreal City, Canada

Roy′ȧl Gôrge (gôrje) *Gorge* Grand Canyon, Colo., U.S.

Roy′ȧl Ōak *City* SE Mich., U.S.; pop. 85,499

Rū-ä′hä *River* 300 m. cen. Tanzania

Rū-än′dä-U-run′di (ōō-rōōn′) *Territory,* formerly Germ. East Africa, later Belg. Trust Terr.; div. 1962 RWANDA and BURUNDI

Rub′ al Khä′li (roob′), **Great San′dẏ Desert** *Desert* 3000 sq. m. S Arabia [Kenya

Rū′dolf, Lake *Lake* N

Rū-fi′ji (fē′) *River* 250 m. Tanzania

Rug′bẏ *Urban district* cen. England

Rû′gėn *Island* Baltic S.; Germany's largest island; fishing

Rūhr *Valley* of *River* 144 m. West Germany; mining area, incl. great industrial centers; imp. WW I, WW II.

Ruīs′lip Nôrth′wood *Urban district* SE England

Ruiz (rwēz) *Peak* 17,-390 ft. W cen. Colombia

Rū′ki *River* 250 m. NW Congo (L)

Rū-mā′niȧ = ROMANIA

Run′nẏ-mēde *Meadow* S England; Magna Charta signing

Rū′pêrt *River* 380 m. Quebec, Canada

Rū′pêrt's Land *Territory* N Canada, now part of NW Terrs.

Rū-pu-nū′ni *River* 250 m. Guyana

Ru′se (roo′) *City* NE Bulgaria; industry, commerce

Rush′mōre, Mount *Peak* 6040 ft. W S.D., U.S.; president's faces

Rus′sėll, Mount *Peak* 14,190 ft. E Calif., U.S.

Rus′sia (rush′ȧ) 1. *Popular name* for U.S.S.R. 2. *Former empire* E Eur., N and NW Asia; * St. Petersburg

Rus′sian Sō′vi-et Federated Sō′cial-ist Rep. (rush′ȧn, sō′-shȧl) = R.S.F.S.R. *Republic,* largest of U.S.S.R., E Eur.-N and W Asia; * Moscow; incl. many autonomous reps., terrs., regions

Rû′string-ėn *City* NW West Germany; resort, manufacturing

Ru-thē′ni-ȧ (rōō) *Region* formerly in NE Hungary, then Czechoslovakia, now incl. in Ukraine as ZAKARPATSKAYA

Rut′lȧnd-shire *County* E cen. England

Ru-vu′mȧ (rōō - vōō′) *River* 400 m. Tanzania

Ru-wėn-zō′ri (r ō ō) *Mountains* Uganda-Congo (L)

Rwän′dä, Republic of *Country,* C Africa; 10,170 sq. m.; pop. 3,783,000; 10 provinces; *Main cities:* *

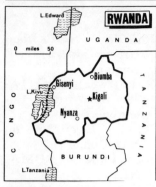

Kigali, Buture; *Main rivers:* Kagera, Nyawarongo, Akanyaru; *Geog.:* mainly grassy uplands, hills extend SE from chain of volcanoes in NW; *Climate:* temperate because of high altitude.

Flag: vertical stripes — red, yellow, green with a large black "R" centered on yellow stripe.

Ethnic comp.: Bantu, Nilotic, Pygmoids; *Language:* Rwanda (official), French (official), Kiswahili; *Religions:* Christian, animist.

Main products: coffee, cotton, hides, tea, beans, cassava, maize, quinine, pyrethrum, tin ore, iron ore, cassiterite, methane gas; *Minerals:* cassiterite, columbotantalite, wolfram, amblygonite, beryl, bismuth, phosphates, monazite, magnatite, natural gas; *Major exports:* coffee, cassiterite, wolfram; *Major imports:* textiles, iron, petroleum, vehicles; *Industries:* mining, agriculture, construction, manufacturing.

Currency: Rwanda franc.
Head of Government: President; *Legislature:* unicameral National Assembly; *Judiciary:* Supreme Court insures that Constitution is respected
Rȳ'an Peak *Mountain* 11,900 ft. Ida., U.S.

Rhȳ'binsk 1. Reservoir or Sea *Lake* NW U.S.S.R., Eur. **2.** *City* = SHCHERBAKOV
Ryȧ-zan' *City* * of *Region* cen. R.S.F.S.R., U.S.S.R., Eur.

Rȳde *City* SE Australia
Ryū'kyū Islands *Island chain* W Pacific O. bet. Taiwan-Japan; bel. to U.S except for Amami group (Jap.)
R z h e v *C i t y* N W U.S.S.R., Eur.; commerce, industry

S

Säa'lė *River* 225 m. cen. Germany
Säar'länd *Region* of **Säar R.;** *State* of West Germany, * **Säar'brûck-ėn;** coal, iron, steel
Sä-bä-dell' *Commune* NE Spain; agriculture, manufacturing
Sä'bäh *Division* of Malaysia, N Borneo; formerly Brit. North Borneo
Sȧ-bē'tȧ Peak *Peak* 13,600 ft. cen. Colo., U.S.
Sȧ-bine' (bēn') *River* 380 m. Tex.-La., U.S.
Sä'ble *Island, Cape* SW Nova Scotia, Canada; sand bar
Sac-rȧ-men'tō 1. *City* * of Calif., U.S., N cen. part; pop. 254,413; industrial cen. **2.** *River* 382 m. NW Calif., U.S.
Sad'dle Mountain *Peak* 10,680 ft. NW Wyo., U.S.
Sȧ'di-yä *Town* NE India; WW II base
Sä-dō *Island* off NW Honshu, Japan; silver, gold
Säfe'tẏ Islands *Islands* off N Fr. Guinea, incl. Devil's I.
Sa'fi *City* NW Morocco; port
Sä-gä *City* * of *Prefecture* Kyushu, Japan; fish, coal
Sȧ-gaing' (gīng') *Town* * of *Division* and *District*, Upper Burma; port

Sä-gay' (gī') Municipality Negros, Phil. Is.
Sag'i-nȧw *City* cen. Mich., U.S.; pop. 91,-849; port, rail cen., machinery
Sag-uė-nāy' *River* 400 m. (with Peribonka R.) Quebec, Canada; hydroelectricity, resorts
Sa-hand', Kuh'i (kōō') *Mountain* 12,100 ft. NW Iran
Sȧ-har'ȧ *Desert area* N Africa, div.: France, Great Britain, Italy, Spain
Sȧ-hä'rȧn-pur (poor) *City* N India
Saī'dȧ-pet *Town* S India
Saī-gon' *City* on *River*, * of South Vietnam, SE part; pop. 2,200,-000; port
St. Äl'bȧns *City, Municipal borough* SE England; shipping
St. Ȧu'gus-tine (tēn) *City* NE Fla., U.S.; pop. 12,352
St. Bri-euc' (san brē-û') *City* NW France
St. Cath'ȧ-rines (rinz) *City* SE Ontario, Canada; manufacturing
St. Chris'tö-phêr (kris'-tö-fêr) = ST. KITTS
St. Clāir, Lake *Lake* Mich., U.S.-Ontario, Canada
St. Clāir' Shores *City* SE Mich., U.S.; pop. 88,093; residential
St. Cloud' (san klōō') *Commune* N France
St. Cloud' *City* C Minn., U.S.; pop. 39,691; business
St. Croix' (sânt kroi'), **San'tȧ Crūz'** *Island* largest of U.S. Virgin Is.; sugar cane
St.-Den'is (or sand-nē') **1.** *City* * of Reunion I. (Fr.). **2.** *Commune* N France
Ste. Anne' dê Beau-pre' (bō-prä') *Village* S Quebec, Canada
St. E-lī'ȧs *Peak* 18,000 ft. of *Range* SW Yukon Terr., Canada-E Alas., U.S.
Ste. Mȧ-riē' *Cape* S tip Madagascar I.

Saint E-tienne' (san-tä) *City* SE cen. France
St. Fran'cis (sĭs) *River* 425 m. Mo.-Ark., U.S.
St. Gäl'lėn *Commune* * of *Canton* NE Switzerland; trade cen.
St. Geor'ge's (jôr'jiz) **1.** *Town* Grenada I., * of Windward Is., Brit. West Indies. **2.** *Channel* bet. Wales-Ireland
Saīnt Gilles' (san-zhēl') *Commune* cen. Belgium
St. Hė-lē'nȧ *Island* (Brit.) S Atlantic O. off W Africa; Napoleon's exile 1815-21
St. Hel'ėns *County borough* NW England
St. Hel'ier (yêr) *Town* Jersey I., * of Channel Is.
St. John' 1. *City* New Brunswick, Canada; shipping, manufacturing. **2.** *Lake* Quebec, Canada. **3.** *Peak* 11,410 ft. Wyo., U.S. **4.** *River* 450 m. NE U.S.-SE Canada
St. Johns' 1. *River* 276 m. Fla., U.S. **2.** *Town* Antigua I., * of Leeward Is., Brit. West Indies
St. John's' *City* * of Newfoundland, Canada; pop. 79,884
St. Jō'seph (zef) **1.** *City* NW Mo., U.S.; pop. 72,691; industrial, livestock cen. **2.** *Lake* SW Ontario, Canada. **3.** *River* 210 m. Mich.-Ind., U.S.
St. Kil'dȧ *City* SE Australia; residential
St. Kitts, St. Chris'töpher (fêr) *Island* of Brit. Leeward Is., E West Indies
St. Läw'rence (rėns) **1.** *River* 760 m. Quebec-Ontario, Canada, into **Gulf of St. Läw'rence** off E Canada. **2.** *Island* W Alas., U.S.; excavations. **3.** **Sēa'wāy** *Waterway* Canada-U.S., Atlantic O.-Great Lakes
Saint Lō' (san) *Commune* NW France
Saint Lou-is' (san-lwē')

City on *Island*, was * of Senegal

St. Lou′is (lōō′is) 1. *City* E Mo., U.S.; pop. 622,236; fur market, manufacturing. 2. *River* 220 m. Minn., U.S.

St. Lou′is Park (lōō′) *City* SE Minn., U.S.; pop. 48,883; residential

St. Lū′cia (shȧ) *Island* (Brit.) of Windward Is., E West Indies

Saint-Ma-lō′ (san) *Gulf* NW France

St. Mar′y's *Island* site of * of Gambia

Saint - Maur′ - des - Fos-ses′ (san-môr′ dȧ-fô-sā′) *Commune* N France; manufacturing

St. Mau′rice (mä′ris) *River* 325 m. Quebec, Canada

St. Mö-ritz′ *Commune* E Switzerland; resort

St. Na-zaire′ *Commune* NW France; manufacturing port

St. Ni-co-las′ (nē-kô-lä′), **Sint-Ni′klass** (nē′) *Commune* NW cen. Belgium; manufacturing

St. Ou-en′ (san-twan′) *Commune* N France; manufacturing

St. Pȧul 1. *City* * of Minn., E part, U.S.; pop. 309,980; twin city with Minneapolis; commercial, manufacturing cen. 2. *River* 280 m. Liberia

St. Pē′têrs-bûrg 1. *City* W cen. Fla., U.S.; pop. 216,232; port, resort. 2. *City* former * of U.S.S.R., now LENINGRAD

St. Pierre′ and Miq′ue-lon′ (-pyâr′, mē-klon′) *Territory* (Fr.); 2 islands S of Newfoundland; fish

St. Quen′tin *Commune* N France; textiles

St. Thom′ȧs (tom′) 1 *Island* of U.S. Virgin Is.; commercial cen. resort. 2. see SAO TOME

St. Vin′cent (sėnt) 1 *Island* of Windward Is., Brit. West Indies;

cotton, agriculture. 2. *Cape* SW Portugal

Saī-pan′ *Island* of U.S. Trust Terr., W Pacific O.

Saī-shū *Town* on *Island* off S Korea

Saī-tä-mä *Prefecture* Japan

Sä-jä′mä (hä′) *Peak* 21,390 ft. W Bolivia

Sä-kaī *City* Honshu, Japan; textiles

Sä-kär′yä *River* 300 m. Turkey, Asia

Sä-kä-tä *City* Honshu, Japan; rice cen.

Sa′khȧ-lin, Jap. **Kä-rä-fū-tō** *District* N part of *Island* in S. of Okhotsk; fish, oil, coal

Sä-ki-shi-mä **Islands** *Island* group of Ryukyu Is., Japan

Sä-lä′do *River* 250 m. NE Mexico

Sä-lä′do, Ri′ō (rē′) *Rivers* (3), Argentina: 1. 1120 m., N part. 2. 850 m. W part. 3. 415 m. E part

Sä-lä′jär (yär) *Island* off SW Celebes I., Indonesia

Sal-ȧ-man′cȧ *Commune* * of *Province* W Spain; manufacturing

Sal′ȧ-mis 1. *City* imp. in anc. Cyprus, E part. 2. *Island* SE Greece

Säl-cän-tay′ (tī′) *Peak* 20,550 ft. Peru

Säle (sāl) *Urban district* NW England

Sa-le′ (lä′), **Sla** *City* NW Morocco; port

Sä′lėm 1. *City* NE Mass., U.S.; pop. 40,556; port, textiles, shoes. 2. *City* * of Ore., NW part, U.S.; pop. 68,296; industrial, trade cen. 3. *City* S India; trade

Sal′én-tīne Peninsula = "heel" of Italy

Sä-ler′nō *City* on *Gulf* * of *Province* S Italy

Säl′förd *County borough* NW England

Sȧ-lī′nȧ *City* cen. Kan., U.S.; pop. 37,714

Sȧ-lī′nȧs (lē′) *City* W Cal., U.S.; pop. 58,-896; business

Sȧ-line′ (lēn′) *River* 200 m. Kan., U.S.

Sȧlis′bur-ẏ (salz′) *Town* * of Rhodesia, NE part; pop. 390,000; gold, agricultural area

Salm′ön (sam′) *River* 420 m. Ida., U.S.

Sȧ-lon′i-kȧ, Thes-sä-lô-ni′ke (nyē′) *City* on **Gulf of Salonika** NE Greece; port

Sal-sette′ *Island* off W cen. India

Sȧlt 1. *River* 200 m. Ariz., U.S. 2. *River* 200 m. Mo., U.S.

Säl′tä *City* * of *Province* N Argentina

Säl-til′lo (tē′yō) *City* NE Mexico; mines, agriculture

Sȧlt Lake 1. see GREAT SALT LAKE. 2. *Region* SW cen. Australia; lakes, gold

Sȧlt Lake City *City* * of Utah, N part, U.S.; pop. 175,885; Mormon cen.; commerce, industry

Säl′tō *City* * of *Department* NW Uruguay; port, meat industry

Sȧ-lū′dȧ *River* 200 m. S.C., U.S.

Sal′vȧ-dôr, Bȧ-hi′ȧ (ē′) *City* E Brazil; commercial port

Sal′wēen, Sal′win (wēn) *River* 1750 m. SE Asia, E Tibet-Lower Burma

Sälz′bûrg *City* * of *Province* W Austria; resort, manufacturing

Sä′mär *Island, Sea* E Phil. Is.

Sȧ-ma′rȧ *River* 360 m. U.S.S.R., Eur.

Sȧ-mâr′i-ȧ *District* of anc. Palestine, cen. part; part in mod. Israel

Sam′ȧr-kand *City, Region*, Uzbek S.S.R., U.S.S.R.; industrial

Sa-mȧr′rȧ *Town* N cen. Iraq [India

Sȧ-mō′ȧ *Island* group SW cen. Pacific O., div. into: 1. **American Samoa**, * Pago Pago on Tutuila I., fish, copra; 2. WESTERN SAMOA (New Zealand)

Sä′môs *Island, Department*, Aegean Is., Greece

Sam′ō-thrāce *Island* (Gk.) Aegean S.

Säm-sun′ (sōōn′) *City* on *Bay* * of *Vilayet*, N Turkey, Asia; port

Sä-mut Söng-khräm, formerly **Me-klông** *City* W Thailand; port [Poland

Sän *River* 280 m. SE

Sän′-a′ *City* * of Yemen; trade cen.

Sä′nȧ-gȧ *River* 430 m. Cameroun

San An′gė-lō (jė) *City* W cen. Texas, U.S.; pop. 63,884; commerce, manufacturing

San An-tō′ni-ō *City* on *River* (200 m.) S cen. Tex., U.S.; pop. 654,-153; commerce, industry

San Bêr-nȧr-di′nō (dē′) 1. *City* S Calif., U.S.; pop. 104,251; resort. 2. *Mountains* S Calif., U.S. 3. *Strait* Luzon-Samar Is., Phil. Is.

San Blas′ *Gulf, Isthmus, Mountains* N Panama

San Brū′nō *City* W Cal., U.S.; pop. 36,254

San Cär′lôs 1. *Municipality* Luzon, Phil. Is. 2. *Municipality* Negros, Phil. Is.

Sän Cle-men′te (män′-tâ) *Peak* 13,315 ft. S Argentina

San Cris-tō′bȧl 1. *City* W Venezuela. 2. *Commune* S Dominican Rep. 3. *Town* on *Island*, Galapagos Is.

Sän-dä′kän *Town* former * of North Borneo

San Di-e′gō (ā′) 1. *City* on *Bay*, SW Calif., U.S.; pop. 696,769; port, resort, fruit cen. 2. *Cape* S Argentina

San Dō-min′gō now DOMINICAN REP.

San′dring-hȧm *Village* E England; royal residence

Sand′wich Islands now HAWAIIAN IS.

Săn′dwip (dwēp) *Island* East Pakistan

San Fêr-nan′dô 1. *City* E Argentina; port. 2. *City* SW Spain; port. 3. *Municipality* cen. Luzon, Phil. Is.; sugar cen., rice

San′förd, Mount *Peak* 16,200 ft. S Alas., U.S.

San Fran-cis′cō (sĭs′) *City* on *Bay* W Calif., U.S.; pop. 715,674; shipping, financial, commercial, industrial cen.

San′gà *River* 400 m. Congo (L)

San′gà-mön *River* 225 m. Ill., U.S.

San-gän′, Kōh′-i- *Peak* 12,870 ft. Afghanistan

Săn-gay′ (gī′) *Volcano* 17,750 ft. Ecuador

Säng′i Islands *Island group* Indonesia, NE of Celebes I.

Săn′gli *Town* * of *State* W India

Sän I-si′drō (sē′) 1. *Town* E Argentina. 2. *Municipality* on *Bay* Leyte, Phil. Is.

San Jà-cin′tō (sĭn′) *River* 100 m. SE Tex., U.S.; Mexican War battle

San Joa-quin′ (wä-kēn′) 1. *River* 350 m. Calif., U.S. 2. *Mountain* 13,-500 ft. Colo., U.S.

Sän Jor′ge (hôr′hâ) *River* 250 m. N Colombia

San Jo-se′ (hō-zā′) 1. *City* W Calif., U.S.; pop. 445,779; manufacturing, fruit cen. 2. *City* * of *Province* and * of Costa Rica, cen. part; pop. 580,-000; coffee trade

San Juan′ (won′) 1. *River* 360 m. Colo.-N.M.-Utah, U.S. 2. *Mountains* Colo., U.S.

Sän Juán′ (hwän′) 1. *City* and *Municipality* * of Puerto Rico, NE part; pop. 432,377; port. 2. *Hill* E Cuba; battle, Span. Am. War, 1898

Săn′kiang′ (ji-äng′) *For-*

mer Province E Manchukuo

Sän-ku′ru (kōō′rōō) *River* 340 m. Congo (L)

San Lĕ-an′drō *City* W Calif., U.S.; pop. 68,698; dairy area

Săn Luis′ Pō-tō-si′ (lwēs′, sē′) *City* * of *State* cen. Mexico

Sän Mär′cō *Island* of Venice, Italy

Sän Mä-ri′nō (rē′), *Country,* in Apennines SW of Rimini, Italy; 24 sq. m.; pop. 20,000 (20,000 resident abroad); *Main city:* * San Marino; *Main rivers:* San Marino, Fumicello; *Geog.:* landlocked, much of country co-extensive with Mount Titano; *Climate:* temperate.

Flag: horizontal stripes of white, blue with national coat of arms in center.

Ethnic comp.: of Italian origin; *Language:* Italian (official); *Religion:* Roman Catholic.

Products: wine, cereals, cattle, cheese, olive oil, ceramics, lime, colors, paints, building stone, concrete, textiles, varnishes; *Major exports:* wine, woolens, furniture, ceramics, stamped postcards; *Major imports:* manufactured goods; *Industries:* tourism, manufacturing (paper, leather, furs, textiles), quarrying of building stone.

Currency: Italian lira.

Head of Government: State Congress has

executive power; *Legislature:* Great & General Council; *Judiciary:* in hands of Legal Commissioner.

San Mà-te′ō (tā′) *City* W Calif., U.S.; pop. 78,991; residential

Sän Mi-guel′ (gel′) *River* 475 m. E Bolivia

San Nic′o-làs Island *Island* off SW Calif., U.S.

Sän Pä′blō, City of *City* Luzon Phil. Is.

San Rà-fael′ (fel′) *City* W Cal., U.S.; pop. 38,977; residential

San Sal′và-dôr 1. *City* * of *Department* and * of El Salvador, pop. 472,000; commercial, cultural cen. 2. *Island* of Bahama Is.

San Sa-bas′tian (chàn) 1. *City* N Spain; commercial port. 2. *Municipality* NW Puerto Rico

Sän Se-ve′rō (vâ′) *Commune* SE Italy

Sànt *State* W India

San′tà An′à *City* SW Calif., U.S.; pop. 156,601; manufacturing

Sän′tà Ä′nä *City* * of *Department* NW El Salvador

San′tà Bär′bà-rà 1. *City* on *Channel* SW Calif., U.S.; pop. 70,215; resort. 2. *Island* of *Chain* off SW Calif., U.S.

San′tà Cat-à-li′nà (lē′) *Island* of Santa Barbara group SW Calif., U.S.; resort

San′tà Clar′à 1. *City* W Calif., U.S.; pop. 87,717. 2. *Municipality* and *City* W cen. Cuba; sugar, tobacco

San′tà Cruz′ (krōōz′) 1. *City* on *River* 250 m. in *Territory* S Argentina. 2. *City* * of *Department* E Bolivia. 3. **de Te-ne-ri′fe** (dâ tâ-nâ-rē′fâ) *City* * of *Province* Canary Is. Spain. 4. *Island* off SW Calif., U.S. 5. *Islands* (Brit.) SW Pacific O.

San′tà Fe′ (fā′) 1. *City* * of N.M., U.S.; pop. 41,167; tourist, art cen. 2. *Peak* 13,145 ft. Colo., U.S. 3. *Trail* W Mo.-Santa Fe-West

Săn′tä Fe′ (fā′) *City* * of *Province* E Argentina; port

San′tà Is′à-bel (ĭz′) *Town* Equatorial Guinea; former * of Span. Guinea

San′tà Mà-ri′à (rē′) 1. *City* S Brazil; manufacturing. 2. *Volcano* 12,300 ft. Guatemala

San′tà Mär′tà *City* N Colombia; port

San′tà Mon′i-cà *City* on *Bay* SW Calif., U.S.; pop. 88,289; resort, residential

Săn-tän-dêr′ *City* * of *Province* N Spain; commercial port

San′tà Rō′sà *City* NW Cal., U.S.; pop. 50,-006; business

Sän-ti-ä′gō 1. *City* * of *Province* and * of Chile, cen. part; pop. 2,314,000. 2. *Commune* and *City* N cen. Dominican Rep. 3. *Commune* NW Spain. 4. *Bay* E Cuba

Sän-tiä′gō de Cù′bä *Seaport* S Cuba

Sän-tiä′gō del Es-te′rō (tā′) *City* * of *Province* N Argentina

Sän′tō An-dre′ (drā′) *City* SE Brazil

San′tō Do-min′gō *City* * of Dominican Rep.; pop. 462,000

San′tös *City* SE Brazil; coffee export

Sän Vä-len-tin′ (tēn′) *Peak* 13,310 ft. S Chile

Sao Fran-cis′co (sou fran-sēsh′kōō) *River* 1800 m. E Brazil

Sao Lou-ren′co (sou lō-rän′sōō) *River* 340 m. SW Brazil

Sao Luiz′ (sou lwēs′) *City* NE Brazil; port

Sao Mà-nuel′ (sou, nwâl′) *River* 600 m. cen. Brazil

Sao Mi-guel′ (sou mē-gâl′) *Island* largest of Azores

Saone (sōn) 1. *River* 300 m. E France. 2.

-et-Loire' (lwär') *Department* E cen. France

Sao Pau'lo (sou pou'lōō) *City* * of *State* SE Brazil; imp. city, manufacturing, commerce

Sao To-me' (sou tōō-mâ') *Island* and *Town* its * off W Africa; part of Port. colony: **Sao To-me' e Prin'ci-pe** (ē prēn'sē)

Sä-poe'di (pōō') *Island* Malay Arch., Indonesia

Säp-pō-rō *City* Hokkaido, Japan; breweries, manufacturing

Sar-à-gos'sà *City* * of *Province* NE Spain; trade, manufacturing

Sà-raï'ke-lä *State* NE India

Sä'rä-je-vō (ye) *City* * of Bosnia and Herzegovina Rep., cen. Yugoslavia; carpets, tobacco; site of assassination precipitating WW I

Sar'à-nac Lakes *Lakes* (3) NE N.J., U.S.

Sä'rän-gärh *State* NE India

Sà-ransk' *Town* * of Mordovian Rep. R.S.F.S.R., U.S.S.R.

Sä-rä-sä'rä *Peak* 19,-500 ft. Peru

Sar-à-sō'tà *City* SW Fla., U.S.; pop. 40,-237; business, resort

Sar-à-tō'gà *Village* now Schuylerville, E N.Y. U.S.; Revolutionary war battles

Sar-à-tō'gà Springs *City* E N.Y., U.S.; resort

Sà-ra'töv *City* * of *Region* SE R.S.F.S.R., U.S.S.R., Eur.

Sa-rä'wäk *Division* of Malaysia, N Borneo

Sär'dà *River* 220 m. N India

Sär-din'i-à *Island* of *Compartimento*, SW Italy

Sàr-gō'dhà *Town* W Pakistan

Särk *Island* of Channel [Is.

Sär'ni-à *City* SE Ontario, Canada; port

Särre = SAAR

Sarthe (sart) *Department* NW France

Sä-rẏ Sū' *River* 520 m. U.S.S.R., Asia

Sä-se-bō *City* Kyushu, Japan; port

Sas - katch'i - wàn 1. *Province* W Canada; 250,000 sq. m.; pop. 961,000; * Regina; agriculture, esp. wheat. 2. *River* SW and S cen. Canada, 2 branches: **North** and **South** 1205 m. total

Sas-kà-tōōn' *City* S Saskatchewan, Canada; trade cen.

Sàs-san'drà *River* 300 m. W Ivory Coast

Säs'sä-ri *Commune* * of *Province* S India; trade, manufacturing

Sà-til'lä *River* 220 m. Ga., U.S.

Sät'pu-rà Range (poo) *Hills* W cen. India

Sä-tsu-mä (tsoo) *Old province* Kyushu, Japan; pottery

Sàt-ti'mà (tē') *Peak* 13,215 ft. cen. Kenya

Sä'tū-Mä're *City* NW Romania; commerce

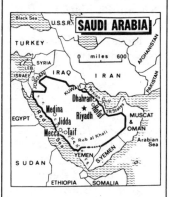

Sau'di A-rä'bi-à (sou'), Kingdom of *Country*, Near East; 927,000 sq. m.; pop. 6,000,-000; 4 provinces; *Main cities:* * Riyadh, Jidda, Mecca, Hofuf, Medina; *Geog.:* 9/10 covered by barren plateau; W — Hyaz Mts. border narrow coastal plain along Red Sea; low lying plain along Persian Gulf; *Climate:* arid, high temp., extreme humidity.

Flag: green & white — green field has Arabic script "There is no god but God, and Mohammed is His Prophet."

Ethnic comp.: Arabs, Negroes, Baluchis; *Language:* Arabic (official); *Religion:* Islam (state), Sunni Moslem.

Products: dates, wheat, barley, coffee, sheep, camels, limes, hides, wool, iron ore, copper, phosphates, silver, oil; *Minerals:* oil, gypsum, copper, manganese, silver, gold, sulphur, lead; *Major exports:* petroleum, petroleum products; *Major imports:* motor vehicles, cereals, power generating machinery, food; *Industries:* oil refining, mining, water desalting plant, tourism.

Currency: rial.

Head of Government: King; *Legislature:* Council of Ministers performs legislative functions; *Judiciary:* Shari'a law applied by courts.

Său'gör *Town* N India

Sault' Sâinte Mà-riē' (sōō', rē') *City* S Ontario, Canada; industrial

Sä'vä, Save (sav), **Sau** (zou) *River* 450 m. N Yugoslavia

Sä-vaï'i *Island*, largest of Samoa

Sa - va - län', Kūh'-i- *Peak* 15,785 ft. NW Iran

Sà-van'nàh 1. *City* SE Ga., U.S.; pop. 118,-349; cotton port. 2. *River* 315 m. E Ga., U.S.

Sä'vànt-vä'di *Town* * of *State* W India

Sa'vè, Sä'bi *River* 400 m. SE Africa

Sa-voie' (vwa') 1. *Department* E France. 2. or SAVOY

Sä-vō'nä *City* * of *Province* NW Italy; port, industry

Sà-voy' (voi') *Hist. region* SE France-NW Italy, now in France; incl. **Sa-voy' Alps**

Säv'skä *Former county* N Yugoslavia, now in Croatia

Săw'tōōth Mts. *Ranges* S cen. Ida., U.S.

Saxe = Fr. for **Saxony**, used in names of former duchies: **Saxe-Cō'bûrg**

Sax'ö-nẏ *Former duchy,* *Kingdom, State* cen. Germany; now W East Germany; minerals, manufacturing

Sä-yän' Mts. *Range* U.S.S.R., Asia

Scan - di - nä'vi - à = countries of Sweden, Denmark, Norway, Iceland

Scär'bör-ough (bûr-ö) *Municipal borough* N England; port

Schaer'beek (skar'bāk) *Commune* cen. Belgium

Schel'dė (skel'), **Scheldt** (skelt) *River* 270 m. France-Belgium

Schė-nec'tà-dẏ (skė) *City* E N.Y., U.S.; pop. 77,859; industrial, electric plants

Sche'vė-ning-ėn (skä') *Resort* SW Netherlands

Schie-däm' (ske) *Commune* SW Netherlands

Schles'wig 1. *City* NW West Germany; manufacturing. 2. *Hist. region* NW Germany, former duchy; now incl. in **Schles'wig-Hōl'steĩn**, *State*, N West Germany

Schön-brunn' (broon') *Palace* Vienna, Austria

Schö'nė-beck *City* cen. East Germany; manufactures

Schö'nė-bêrg *Section* E Berlin, East Germany

Schreck'hôrn, Grōss *Peak* 13,385 ft. SW Switzerland

Schwarz'wald (shvärts'-vält) = BLACK FOREST

Schwein'furt (shvīn') *City* S West Germany; manufacturing, port

S c h w e n'n i n g - ė n (shven') *City* S West Germany; clocks

Schwe-rin' (shvä-rēn')
City NW East Germany; manufacturing

Sci-ō'tō (sī) *River* 238
m. Ohio., U.S.

Scot'lånd *Division* of
United Kingdom of
Great Britain and
Northern Ireland, N
Great Britain; 30,400
sq. m.; pop. 5,188,-
000; * Edinburgh; 33
counties

Scots'dåle *City* cen.
Ariz., U.S.; pop. 67,-
823

Scran'tön *City* NE Pa.,
U.S.; pop. 103,564

Scun'thôrpe *Urban district* E England

Scū'tå-ri *Lake* Yugoslavia-Albania

Sēal *River* 240 m. Manitoba, Canada

Sēa'sīde *City* W Cal.,
U.S.; pop. 35,935

Sē-at'tle (t'l) *City* W
cen. Wash., U.S.;
pop. 530,831; commercial, industrial
port   [VASTOPOL

Sė-bas'tö-pôl = SE-

Se-cun'dêr-ä-bäd *Town*
S cen. India

Se-gō'viä *River* 450 m.
N Nicaragua

Sei'bo (sā'vō) *Commune*
* of *Province* E Dominican Rep.; coffee,
cacoa, sugar

Seim (säm) *River* 435
m. U.S.S.R., Eur.

Seine (sän) 1. *River* 480
m. N France. 2. *Departments* (4) N
France: **Seine'et-
Marne'** (ā märn'),
-et-Oise' (ā waz'),
-In-fe-rieure' (an-fā-
ryûr')

Sei-shin (sâ), **Chöng-jin**
City NE Korea; port

Sei-shū (sâ) *City* S
Korea

Sė-lang'ör *State* SW
Malay Penin., Malaysia; tin, rubber

Se-len-gä' *River* 750 m.
N cen. Asia

Sel'kîrk 1. *County* SE
Scotland; sheep. 2.
Mountains Brit. Columbia, Canada

Sė-mä'räng *City* Java,
Indonesia; port

Sė-me'növ (myô') *Peak*
15,350 ft. Kirgiz,
U.S.S.R.

Sė-me'roe (rōō) *Volcano* 12,000 ft. Java,
Indonesia

Se-mi-på-la'tinsk *City*
* of *Region* U.S.S.R.,
W Asia; livestock
products

Sen-daī *City* Honshu,
Japan; cultural cen.

Sen'ė-cå Lake *Lake* (of
Finger Lakes) W
N.Y., U.S.

Sen-ė-gal', Republic of
Country, bulge of W
Africa, 77,810 sq. m.;
pop. 4,154,000; 7 regions; *Main cities:* *
Dakar, Thies, Rufisque, St. Louis,
Kaolack; *Main rivers:* Senegal, Saloum,
Gambia, Casamance;
Geog.: mostly rolling
plains with savannah-type vegetation,
low altitude; SW is
marshy swamps interspersed with tropical rain forests; *Climate:* 2 well defined
dry, humid seasons.
Annual rainfall 24″
to 60″ in some areas.

Flag: green, yellow,
red vertical stripes
with green star in
middle   (yellow)
stripe.

Ethnic comp.: Wollofs, Bambaras, Mandingos etc.; *Language:* French (official), Wollof, other
African languages;
Religions: Christian,
animist, Moslem.

Products: groundnuts, groundnut oil,
millet, livestock, rice,
maize, peanuts, salt,
cement, vegetable
oils, phosphates;
Minerals: calcium,
aluminium phos-

phates, limestone, titanium, ilmenite, zincon, vistile; *Major
exports:* groundnuts,
peanuts, canned fish;
Major imports: food,
textiles, machinery,
chemical & petroleum products; *Industries:* manufacturing
(peanut oil, cement,
textiles, food processing, leather, shoes,
chemicals), phosphate mining, mining.

Currency: CFA franc.

Head of Government:
President; *Legislature:* National Assembly; *Judiciary:*
independent judiciary with Supreme
Court at apex.

Seoul (sōl), was **Kei-jō**
(kä) *City* * of South
Korea, N part; pop.
5,000,000

Se'pik (sä') *River* 600
m. North-East New
Guinea

Sė-quoi'å *National Park*
S cen. Calif., U.S.;
trees, Mt. Whitney

Se-raing' (ran') *Commune* E Belgium;
manufacturing, mining   [India

Ser'åm-pōre *Town* NE

Sêr'bi-å *Republic*, one
of 6 federated republics of Yugoslavia,
NW part; * Belgrade;
former Balkan kingdom

Ser'gö = now KADI-
YEVKA

Ser'ôv *City* R.S.F.S.R.,
U.S.S.R., Asia

Se-rōw'e *Town* E
Botswana

Sêr-pū'khôv (pōō') *City*
R.S.F.S.R., U.S.S.R.,
Eur.; textiles, grain,
timber cen.

Ser'rå dos Aī-mo-res'
(sâr', dōōz ī-mōō-râs')
Area E Brazil

Ser'rai (sâ'râ) *City* * of
Dept. N cen. Greece;
agricultural cen.

Sete, Cette *City* S
France; commercial
port

Se-tif' (sä-tēf') *Commune* NE Algeria

Sė-tit', **Bahr** (tēt') *River* 350 m. E Africa

Sė-tu'bål (tōō') *City* on
Bay SW Portugal;
port

Seûl, **Lake** *Lake* W
Ontario, Canada

Se-vän', **Gök'chä** *Lake*
Armenian S. S. R.,
U.S.S.R.

Sė-vas'to-pôl *City*, *Peninsula* on *Bay* of
Black S., S U.S.S.R.;
Eur.; port, naval base

Seven Hills *Hills* of
Rome, Italy: Palatine, Capitoline,
Quirinal, Aventine,
Caelian, Esquiline,
Viminal

Sev'êrn 1. *River* 420 m.
Ontario, Canada. 2.
River 210 m. W England

Se'vėr-nà-ya *Zėm-la'*
(syä') *Islands* Arctic
O., U.S.S.R., Asia

Sė-vier' (vēr') *River*
279 m. Utah, U.S.

Sė-ville' *City* * of Se-
vil'la (vē'yä) prov.
SW Spain; buildings

Se'vres (sâ'vr') *Commune* N France; porcelain

Sew'ård (sū') *Peninsula* W Alas., U.S.;
gold

Sey-chelles' (sâ-shelz')
Islands (Brit.) Indian
O. E of Tanzania; *
Port Victoria; coconuts, spices

Sey-hän' (sä) 1. *River*
780 m. S cen. Turkey,
Asia. 2. *City* =
ADANA

Sfax *City* E Tunisia;
port, olives

's Gra-vėn-ha'gė (kė)
= HAGUE, THE

Shäh Fu-lä-di' (dē')
Mountain 16,872 ft.
E cen. Afghanistan

Shäh-ja-hän'pur (poor)
City N India

Shāk'êr Heights (hīts)
City N Ohio; pop.
36,306; residential

Shakh'tÿ *City* SW
U.S.S.R., Eur.

Sha'lå-mär Gardens
Gardens E of Lahore
West Pakistan

Shä'mō' = Chinese
name of GOBI Desert

Shang'haï *City* E China; industrial cen.

and commercial port of China

Shan'nön *River* 240 m. N cen. - SW Eire; longest of Brit. Isles

Shän'si' *Province* NE China; coal, cereals, wool, opium [Burma

Shan States *States* E

Shan'tung' *Province* NE China; silk industry

Shao'hing' (shou'shing') *City* E China; trade

Shärk Bay *Bay* of Indian O. W Australia; pearls

Shärps'bûrg *Village* N Md., U.S.; Antietam battle site

Shä'si' (sē') *City* E cen. China; port

Shas'tà, Mt. *Peak* 14,-160 ft. N Calif., U.S.

Shà-vä'nō Peak *Peak* 14,180 ft. Colo., U.S.

Shà-win'i-gàn Falls *City* and *Falls* S Quebec, Canada; light and power plants

Shchèr-bà-kôv', was **Rÿ'binsk** *City* W U.S.S.R., Eur.; port

Shē'bà *Anc. country* S Arabia

She-boy'gàn *City* E Wisc., U.S.; pop. 48,-484; cheese, plumbing fixtures

Shef'fiēld *City, County borough* N England; cutlery cen., plating

Shek-sna' *River* 280 m. W U.S.S.R., Eur.

Shen-àn-dō'àh *Valley, River, National Park* N Va., U.S.

Shen'si' *Province* NE cen. China; cereals, coal

Shêr'brō *Island* SW Sierra Leone

Shêr'brooke *City* S Quebec, Canada; manufacturing

Sher'i-dàn, Mount *Peak* 13,700 ft. Colo., U.S.

Shêr'màn, Mount *Peak* 14,035 ft. Colo., U.S.

's Her'tō - gen - bôsch ('ser', bôs) *Commune* S Netherlands

Shêr'wood Forest *Anc. forest* cen. England

Shet'länd Islands *Archipelago* off N Scotland; fishing, sheep, ponies

Shey - enne' (shī - en') *River* 325 m. N.D., U.S.

Shi-be'li, Web'be (bä') *River* 700 m. E Africa

Shi-gä (shē) *Prefecture* Honshu, Japan

Shi-gä'tse *Town* SE Tibet; trade

Shi-kär'pur (poor) *City* W Pakistan; silks, precious stones

Shi-kō'ku *Island* of Japan, 4th in size; agriculture, minerals

Shil'kà *River* 300 m. U.S.S.R., Asia

Shil'là *Peak* 23,000 ft. Kashmir

Shi-mä-ne *Prefecture* Honshu, Japan

Shi-mi-zu (zoo) *City* Honshu, Japan; tea port

Shi-mōn-nō-se'ki *City* on *Strait* Honshu, Japan; port

Shi-nä-no *River* 225 m. Honshu, Japan

Shin-chi-ku (koo) *City* NW Taiwan

Shin-gi-shu (shōō) *City* NW Korea; lumber trade, manufacturing

Shin-shu = CHINJU

Shi-räz' *City* SW cen. Iran; industry, commerce

Shi're (shē') *River* 370 m. SE Africa

Shi-zu-ō-kä *City* * of *Prefecture* Honshu, Japan; industrial

Shkä'rä Tau (tou) *Mountain* 17,000 ft. U.S.S.R., Eur.

Shkō'dêr, Scu'tà-ri (skōō') *Town* * of *Prefecture* NW Albania; trade cen.

Shō-kä *City* W Taiwan

Shō'lä-pur (poor) *City* W India; trade, manufacturing

Shôrt'länd Islands *Island group* Brit. Solomon Is.

Shrēve'pôrt *City* NW La., U.S.; pop. 182,-064; commercial, industrial cen.

Shrews'bur-ÿ (shrōōz') *Municipal borough* W England; brewing, tanning

Shrop'shire *County* W England; agriculture, coal, china

Shun-sen (shoon) *Town* E South Korea

Shū'shàn *Anc. city,* now ruins, SW Iran

Shū'yà *Town* cen. U.S.S.R., Eur.; textiles

Shwe'li (shwä') *River* 350 m. Upper Burma

Si (shē), **Si'kiang'** (shē'-ji-äng') *River* over 1000 m. SE China into China S.

Si (sē) *River* 300 m. E Thailand

Si-äl'kōt *City* * of *District* W Pakistan

Sī-am' 1. *Kingdom,* since 1949 THAILAND. 2. **Gulf** *Inlet* of South China S., S of Thailand

Si'än' (shē'), **Chäng'än'** *City* NE cen. China; trade cen., imp. hist.

Siang, Hsiang (shi-äng') 1. *River* 350 m. SE cen. China. 2. formerly **Yū** *River* 400 m. S China

Siang'tän' (shi-äng') *City* SE cen. China; trade cen.

Sī-bē'ri-à *Area:* N Asia Ural Mts.-Pacific O., R.S.F.S.R. in Asia, U.S.S.R.; natural resources, furs

Si-biū' *City* W cen. Romania

Sic'i-lÿ (sis') *Island, Compartimento,* SW Italy; * Palermo; fruit, olives, wine, sulfur

Si'di-bel-Ab-bes' (sē') *Commune* NW Algeria

Sid'ley, Mount (li) *Peak* 12,000 ft. Antarctica

Sī'dön *City* SW Lebanon

Sid'rà, Gulf of *Inlet* of Mediterranean S. N Libya

Sie'nä (syâ') *Commune* * of *Province* cen. Italy; manufacturing, fine buildings

Si-er'ra Lē-ōne', Republic of *Country,* W Africa; 27,900 sq. m.; pop. 2,640,000; 4 provinces; *Main cities:* * Freetown, Bo, Kenema, Makeni; *Main rivers:* Rokel, Sewa, Moa, Song,

Little and Great Searcies; *Geog.:* 3 regions — coastal belt of mangrove swamps, wooded hill country, upland plateaus with mountains near E frontier; *Climate:* tropical.

Flag: horizontal bars — green, white, blue from top to bottom.

Ethnic comp.: Guineans, Creole; *Language:* English, Pidgin, tribal languages; *Religions:* animist, Moslem, Christian.

Products: cassava, rice, maize, vegetables, palm kernels, copra, cocoa, fish, coffee, ginger, timber, diamonds, iron ore, bauxite, rutile, textiles; *Minerals:* diamonds, iron ore, bauxite, rutile; *Major exports:* diamonds, iron ore, palm kernels, coffee, cocoa; *Major imports:* transportation equipment, manufactured goods, machinery, food (grains); *Industries:* oil refining, extractive industries, manufacture of soap, mineral water, furniture.

Currency: leone.

Head of Government: President; *Legislature:* unicameral House of Representatives; *Judiciary:* independent judiciary. Highest court is Court of Appeal.

Si-er'rà Mad're *Mountain ranges:* 1. S

Wyo., U.S.; part of Continental Divide. 2. SE Mexico. 3. Luzon, Phil. Is.

Si - er'rà   Nè - vad'à *Mountain range* E Calif., U.S.

Si'käng' (shē') *Province* S China

Si - ka - ram',   Mount *Peak* 15,620 ft. E Afghanistan

Si'khō-te A-lin' (sē'kō-tä ä-lēn') *Mountain range* E U.S.S.R.

Sik'kim *Monarchy,* Protectorate of India; 2745 sq. m.; pop. 187,000; * Gangtok; agriculture

Si-lē'sia (zhà) 1. *Region* E Eur., variously bel. to Poland, Germany, Czechoslovakia. 2. *Peak* 13,600 ft. Colo., U.S.

Si'lex, Mount *Peak* 13,-635 ft. Colo., U.S.

Sill, Mount *Peak* 14,-255 ft. S Calif., U.S.

Sil-laj-huay' (sē-yäk-wī') *Peak* 19,670 ft. W Bolivia

Sil'li-màn, Mount *Peak* 11,190 ft. Calif., U.S.

Sil'vêr-hēels,   Mount *Peak* 13,835 ft. Colo., U.S.

Sil'vêr Plūme Mountain *Peak* 13,500 ft. Colo., U.S.

Sil'vêr   R u n   Peak *Mountain* 12,610 ft. Mont., U.S.

Sim-birsk' now ULYANOVSK

Sim'cōe, Lake *Lake* Ontario, Canada

Sim-fêr-ô'pöl *City* S R.S.F.S.R., U.S.S.R., Eur.; industry

Simi Valley *City* SW Cal., U.S.; pop. 56,-464

Sim'là *Town* NW India; former Brit. summer *

Si'naī *Mountain* (Bib. **Mt. Horeb**) on *Peninsula* NE Egypt

Si-nä-lō'à *State* W Mexico

Sind 1. *Province,* formerly NW India, now W Pakistan. 2. *River* 240 m. cen. India

SINGAPORE   0 miles 10

MALAYA

(MALAYSIA)

Causeway Johore Bahru

Nee Soon

Bt.Timat

Singapore Town

Strait of Singapore

Sin'gà-pōre, Republic of *Country,* SE Asia; 224 sq. m.; pop. 2,193,000; *Main cities:* * Singapore & its largest suburb Jurong; *Main rivers:* Sungei, Seletar; *Geog.:* Island; low lying, originally consisted of swamp & jungle; now virtually all urban industrialized; C plateau contains a water catchment area, natural reserve; *Climate:* high temperatures, high humidity, copious rainfall.

Flag: 2 horizontal stripes red over white, with white crescent & 5 stars in upper right hand section.

Ethnic comp.: Chinese, Malays, Indians, Pakistanis, Europeans, Arabs; *Language:* Malay, English, Chinese, Tamil; *Religions:* Confucian, Taoist, Buddhist, Christian, Moslem.

Products: fish, coconut oil, textiles, chemicals, building materials; *Major exports:* crude rubber, petroleum products, electrical machinery, motor vehicles; *Major imports:* rubber, petroleum products, vehicles, woven fabrics other than cotton; *Industries:* motor assembly, shipbuilding, engineering, tourism, oil refining, entrepôt trade, quarrying, manufacturing.

Currency: Singapore dollar.

Head of Government: President; *Legislature:* unicameral Parliament; *Judiciary:* judicial power vested in High Court, Court of Appeal.

Si'ning', Hsi'ning' (shē') *City* W cen. China

Sin'kiang' (shin'ji-äng') *Province* W China

Sint-Ni'klaas (nē'), St.-Ni-co-las' (san-nē-kô-lä') *Commune* NW cen. Belgium

Sioux City (sōō) *City* W Iowa, U.S.; pop. 85,925; trade, industrial cen.

Sioux Falls (sōō) *City* SE S.D., U.S.; pop. 72,488; commerce, industry

Si'ple, Mount (p'l) *Peak* 15,000 ft. Antarctica

Si-rä-cu'sä (kōō'zä) 1. *Province* SE Sicily, Italy. 2. *City* see SYRACUSE (2.)

Sir-mur' (moor') *State* NW India

Si-rō'hi *State* NW India

Sit'kà *Town* Baranof I. SE Alas., U.S.; trade

Sit'täng *River* 350 m. E cen. Burma

Si-väs' *City* * of *Vilayet* E cen. Turkey, Asia; trade

Sjael'land (shel') *Island* of *Island group* E Denmark; site of Copenhagen   [DEN

Sjen'yang' = MUK-

Skag'êr-rak *Arm* of North S. bet. Norway and Denmark

Skag'wāy *City* SE Alas., U.S.; gold rush

Ska'nē (skō') *Section* S Sweden

Skan-e-at'e-lès *Lake* of Finger Lakes cen. N.Y., U.S.

Skēe'nà *River* 335 m. Brit. Columbia, Canada

Skel-lef'tè (shel) *River* 325 m. N Sweden

Sker'ries (riz) *Islands* S Irish S.

Skō'kie *City* NE Ill., U.S.; pop. 68,627

Skōp'lje (lye) *City* S

Yugoslavia; industry, commerce

Skunk *River* 265 m. Iowa, U.S.

Skȳe *Island* off NW Scotland; sheep, cattle, fish   [S.

Skȳ'rös *Island* Aegean

Slä'met *Peak* 11,250 ft. Java, Indonesia

Slask (shlônsk) = Polish SILESIA

Slāve *River* 265 m. W cen. Canada

Slà-vō'ni-à *Region* SE Eur., now part of Croatia, Yugoslavia

Slà-vyansk' *Town* E Ukraine U.S.S.R.; industry

Slīde Mountain *Peak* 11,095 ft. Calif., U.S.

Sli'gō *Municipal borough* and *City,* * of *County* N Eire; port

Slough (slou) *Municipal borough* SE England; motors

Slo-vä'ki-à, Slô'ven-skô *Province* E cen. Czechoslovakia; livestock, mining, farms

Slo-vē'ni-à *Federated Republic* NW Yugoslavia; * Ljubljana

Slu-bi'ce (slōō-bē'tse), **Frank'fûrt** *City* W Poland, formerly part of Frankfurt on Oder

Slupsk (slōōpsk), Ger. **Stôlp** *City* N Poland

Smeth'wick *County borough* W cen. England; factories

Smi'chov (smē'kôf) *City* W cen. Czechoslovakia

Smi'ley Mountain (li) *Peak* 11,500 ft. Ida., U.S.

Smōk'ẏ *River* 245 m. Alberta, Canada

Smō'kẏ Hill *River* 540 m. Colo.-Kans., U.S.

Smo-lensk' *City* * of *Region* R.S.F.S.R., U.S.S.R., Eur.; trade, manufacturing, cultural cen.

Smẏr'nà now IZMIR

Snāke *River* 1038 m. NW U.S.; Wyo.-Ida.-Ore.-Wash.

Snef'fèls, Mount *Peak* 14,145 ft. Colo., U.S.

Snōw'mass   Mountain *Peak* 14,080 ft. Colo., U.S.

Snōw Mountains *Range* New Guinea

So-cī'ė-tẏ (sī') **Islands** *Island group* (Fr.) S Pacific O., incl. Windward and Leeward Is.; * Papeete on Tahiti [ft. N Chile

So-cômʹpä *Peak* 19,785

Sodʹöm *Bib .City,* with GOMORRAH; known for wickedness

Soe- see SU-

Soem-bä'wȧ (sōōm) = SUMBAWA

Sō-fīʹȧ (fē') *City,* * of *Department,* * of Bulgaria in W part; pop. 868,200; manufacturing, transportation

Sō-hagʹ (hajʹ) *City* Upper Egypt

Sō-hōʹ *District* London, England; restaurants

Sōʹkō-tō *Town* * of *Province* NW Nigeria

Sō-li-mä'nä *Peak* 20,- 735 ft. S Peru

Sō'ling-ėn (zō') *City* W West Germany; industrial

Sōʹlō *River* 335 m. Java, Indonesia

Sô-logne' (lôn'y') *Area* cen. France; reclaimed for farming

Solʹö-mön Islands *Island group* (Brit.) W Pacific O., largest Guadalcanal; * Honiara; timber, copra

So-lö-vetsʹki Islands *Island group* White S., U.S.S.R., Eur.

So-mäʹlia, Sö-mäʹli, Democratic Republic of *Country,* E Coast of Africa; 246,- 000 sq. m.; pop. 2,730,000; * Mogadishu; 8 provinces; *Main cities:* Hargeisa, Kisimayu, Berbera;

Main rivers: Juba, Shebelli; *Geog.:* N hilly. C & S flat with average altitude of less than 600 feet; *Climate:* prevailing factors are monsoon winds, hot climate, scarce irregular rainfall, recurring droughts.

Flag: 5-pointed white star against azure blue background.

Ethnic comp.: Somalis, Galla, Danakil; *Language:* Arabic, Italian, English, Somali; *Religion:* Sunni Moslem.

Products: livestock, fruit, oil seeds, hides, skins, frankincense, myrrh, sugar, maize, sorghum, fish, bauxite, uranium, iron ore, leather, textiles; *Minerals:* salt, charcoal, limestone, meerschaum, uranium; *Major exports:* bananas, hides, skins, livestock, charcoal; *Major imports:* manufactured goods, cereals, food preparation, chemicals, transportation equipment; *Industries:* food processing, mining, fishing.

Currency: Somali shilling.

Head of Government: Head of Supreme Revolutionary Council; *Legislature:* National Assembly abolished, Revolutionary Council rules by decree; *Judiciary:* based on Islamic law.

Sömʹêr-set Island *Island* Northwest Terrs., Canada

Sömʹêr-set-shîre *County* SW England; fruit, cattle

Sömʹêr-ville *City* NE Mass., U.S.; pop. 88,779; industry

Sômme *Department* N France

Sōn *River* 487 m. NE cen. India

Sônʹdri-ō *Province* N Italy

Sō-ne-que'rä (kā') *Peak* 18,650 ft. SW Bolivia

Sō-nōʹrä 1. *River* 300 m. NW Mexico. 2. *Peak* 11,430 ft. E Calif., U.S.

Sönʹpur (poor) *State* NE India

Sōō'chow' (jō') now WUHSIEN

Sōpʹrōn, Ōʹdėn-bûrg *City* W Hungary

Sō-rä'tä *Mountain,* Bolivia; peaks ANCOHUMA, ILLAMPU

Sō-ro-caʹbȧ *City* SE Brazil; trade

Sōr-renʹtō *City* on *Peninsula* S Italy; fruits

Sôr-so-gônʹ *Municipality* on *Bay,* * of *Province* Luzon, Phil. Is.

Sôs-nôʹwiec (v y e t s) *City* SW Poland; coal

Sôsʹvȧ *River* 350 m. U.S.S.R., Asia

So-täʹrä *Peak* 14,550 ft. SW Colombia

Sou'ris (sōō') *River* 500 m. S Canada

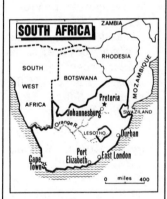

South Afʹri-cȧ, Republic of *Country,* S tip of Africa; 472,360 sq. m.; pop. 21,282,- 000; 4 provinces; *Main cities:* * Pretoria, Johannesburg, Cape Town, Durban, Port Elizabeth; *Main rivers:* Orange, Limpopo; *Geog.:* narrow coastal zone, extensive interior plateau with altitudes ranging from 3,000 to 6,000 ft.; *Climate:* generally moderate.

Flag: horizontal bands — orange, white, blue top to bottom — composite of provincial flags & Union Jack centered on middle band.

Ethnic comp.: Bantu, Europeans, Coloured, Asians; *Language:* Afrikaans, English, Tsongo, Xhosa, Zulu, Sotho, Tswana, Venda; *Religions,* Banta Churches, Dutch Reformed, Anglican, animist.

Products: cereals, groundnuts, fruit, timber, sugar, livestock, wool, cotton, gold, copper, coal, diamonds, uranium, iron ore, asbestos, manganese ore, corundum; *Minerals:* gold, copper, coal, diamonds, antimony, iron ore, copper, uranium, manganese, chrome, asbestos; *Major exports:* diamonds, wool, fruit, copper, iron, steel, gold; *Major imports:* industrial machinery, equipment, transportation equipment, precision instruments; *Industries:* mining, manufacturing (textiles, iron, steel), chemicals, fertilizer, automobile assembly, metal working, electrical & nonelectrical machinery & equipment, mining machinery.

Currency: rand.

Head of Government: President; *Legislature:* bicameral Parliament — Senate, House of Assembly; *Judiciary:* based on uncodified Roman Dutch code. Supreme Court has appelate division, provincial and local divisions.

South Ȧ-merʹi-cȧ *Continent* W hemisphere; ab. 7,000,000 sq. m.; pop. 190,038,000; 4th in size; Brazil, largest country; incl. 13 countries

South-ampʹtön *County borough* S England

South A-räʹbiȧ, Fed. of see YEMEN, PEOPLES DEM. REP. OF

South Är'gen-tine Peak (jĕn-tēn) *Mountain* 13,600 ft. Colo., U.S.

South Äus-trāl'iā *State* cen. Australia; * Adelaide

South Bend *City* N Ind., U.S.; pop. 125,-580; manufacturing

South Bûr'rō Mountain *Peak* 12,745 ft. Utah, U.S.

South Car-o-li'nä *State,* named in honor of King Charles I of England; 31,055 sq. m.; *pop.*: 2,590,516 (*rank:* 26th); E Coast, S Atlantic U.S.; *Boundaries:* North Carolina, Georgia, Atlantic Ocean, Savannah River; *Major cities:* * Columbia, Charleston, Greenville; *Major rivers:* Pee Dee, Santee, Savannah, Edisto; *Major lakes:* Marion, Moultrie, Murray; 46 counties.

Nickname: Palmetto State; *Motto:* "Dum spiro spero" (While I breathe I hope); *Flag:* white palmetto & crescent on blue field; *Flower:* Carolina (yellow) jessamine; *Bird:* Carolina wren; *Tree:* cabbage palmetto; *Song: Carolina.*

Industry: machinery, fishing, textiles, chemicals, pulp & paper, cotton, tobacco, wood products, food items; *Natural resources:* forests, clay, cement, limestone, gravel, phosphate rock manganese, fish; *Major source of income:* manufacturing.

Admitted to Union May 23, 1788.

Places of interest: Kings Mt. Ntl. Military Park, Cowpens Ntl. Battlefield, Fort Sumter.

South Chi'nä Sea *Area* of Pacific O. surr. by China, Indonesia,

Malay Penin., Phil. Is.

South Dä-kō'tä *State,* named from Dakota tribe meaning "united in friendly compact;" 77,047 sq. m.; *pop.*: 666,257 (*rank:* 44th); N mid-W U.S.; *Boundaries:* North Dakota, Montana, Wyoming, Nebraska, Iowa, Minnesota; *Major cities:* Sioux Falls, * Pierre; *Major rivers:* Missouri, James; *Major lakes:* Missouri River Basin Project — lakes and reservoirs; 67 counties.

Nickname: Coyote State, Sunshine State; *Motto:* "Under God the people rule;" *Flag:* state seal surrounded by gold circle, stylized sun & lettering in yellow on blue field; *Flower:* American pasque-flower; *Bird:* ring-necked pheasant; *Animal:* coyote; *Gem stone:* rose quartz; *Tree:* Black Hills spruce; *Song:* Hail *South Dakota.*

Industry: stone, clay, glass items, wheat, corn, flaxseed, oats, machinery, food processing, printing, publishing, making of wood products; *Natural resources:* gold, sand & gravel, stone, cement, silver; *Major source of income:* agriculture — food processing.

Admitted to Union: 1889 (40th state).

Places of interest: Black Hills Ntl. Forest, Custer Ntl. Forest, Mt. Rushmore.

South'end' on Sēa *County borough* SE England; resort

Sou'thêrn Alps (su') *Mountain r a n g e* South I. New Zealand

Southern and Antarctic Terrs. *Territories* of France, S Indian O.: incl.: Karguelan

Arch., New Amsterdam, Adelie Coast

Southern Ye'mén *Rep.* S Arabian Penn.; 112,000 sq. mi.; pop. 1,300,000.

South'field *City* SE Mich., U.S.; pop. 69,285

South'gate *Urban district* SE England

South' Gāte *City* SW Calif., U.S.; pop. 56,-909; manufacturing

South Island *Island* largest of New Zealand, cen. part

SOUTH KOREA

South Kō-rē'a, Republic of *Country,* NE Asia; 38,450 sq. m.; pop. 31,460,000; 9 provinces; *Main cities:* * Seoul, Pusan, Taegu, Inchon; *Main rivers:* Tumen, Yalu, Ch'ongch'on, Taedong, Nam; *Geog.:* mountainous peninsula. Good harbors on W & S coasts; *Climate:* hot, humid in summer, rainfall concentrated in summer months.

Flag: divided circle of red (top), blue (bottom) centered on white field — black bar design in each corner.

Ethnic comp.: Koreans, Chinese; *Language:* Korean (official), English; *Religions:* animist, Buddhist, Confucian, Christian.

Products: rice, cereals, beans, tobacco, cotton, fish, coal, tungsten, iron ore, graphite, electricals, footwear, textiles,

silk, cement, fertilizers, iron, steel, machinery, petrochemicals; *Minerals:* coal, iron ore, lead, zinc, copper, gold, graphite, silver, tungsten; *Major exports:* minerals, chemicals, fuel & oil, machinery & equipment, manufactured goods, tungsten, ferrous and nonferrous metals; *Major imports:* machinery, equipment, fuel, chemicals, textiles; *Industries:* oil refining, mining, textile manufacturing, manufacture of machinery.

Currency: won.

Head of Government: President; *Legislature:* unicameral National Assembly; *Judiciary:* Supreme Court at apex.

South Look'out Peak *Peak* 13,500 ft. Colo., U.S.

South Nä-han'ni *River* 250 m. Northwest Terrs., Canada

South Ork'ney Islands (ni) *Islands* (Brit.) S Atlantic O.

South Os-sē'tia (shä) *Autonomous region* Georgia, U.S.S.R.

South Platte *River* 424 m. Colo.-Neb., U.S.

South Pōle S end of earth's axis; surr. area = **South Pō'lär Regions**

South'pôrt *County borough* NW England

South San Fran-cis'cō (sis') *City* W calif., U.S.; pop. 46,646; industrial

South Seas *Area* incl. islands of Pacific O.

South Shiēlds *County borough* N England

South Tē'tön *Peak* 12,-500 ft. Wyo., U.S.

South Vi-et'nam, Republic of *Country,* SE Asia 66,270 sq. m.; pop. 19,300,000; 45 provinces; *Main cities:* * Saigon, Da Nang, Hué; *Main rivers:* Mekong, Don

Nal, Ba; *Geog.*: C part dominated by Annamite Mt. chain which falls to narrow, fertile coastal plains on E & to higher, less fertile plateaus on W. S Mekong R Delta; *Climate*: tropical, monsoonal.

Flag: yellow field crossed at center by 3 narrow red horizontal lines.

Ethnic comp.: Vietnamese, Bahnar, Rhade, other Highlanders, Cambodians, Chinese, Europeans; *Language*: Vietnamese (official), Chinese, French, English; *Religions*: Taoist, Buddhist, Caodaist, Roman Catholic, Hoa Hoa.

Products: rice, rubber, maize, sugar, tea, coffee, tobacco, cinnamon, bamboo, timber, charcoal, groundnuts, copra, vegetable dyes, fresh & dried fish, phosphates, textiles, cement, paper, consumer goods, oxygen, acetylene, carbonic acid; *Minerals*: coal, phosphates, salt, basalt, laterite, granite, limestone *Major exports*: rubber, shrimp, feathers, cinnamon, tea; *Major imports*: rice, machinery, chemicals, motor vehicles, iron & steel products; *Industries*: sugar refining, food processing, light machinery assembly, fishing.

Currency: piastre.

Head of Government: President; *Legislature*: bicameral National Assembly; *Judiciary*: highest court is Supreme Court, French influence on legal system.

South - West Af'ri-cà *Territory* of Rep. of South Africa, NW; * Windhoek; grazing, fish, minerals

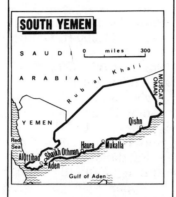

South Ye'mėn, People's Republic of *Country*; S coast of Arabian Peninsula; 112,000 sq. m.; pop. 1,500,-000; 6 provinces; *Main cities*: * Madinet al-Shaab, Aden, Shaikh Othman, Mukalla; *Geog.*: coastal area largely sandy, moving inland terrain becomes mts. interspersed with deep valleys; *Climate*: extraordinarily hot, summer temp. exceeding 130°F. Average rainfall less than 3″ annually.

Flag: red, white, black horizontally striped banner with red star on blue triangular field at staff side.

Ethnic comp.: Arabs, Indians, Baluchis, Somalis; *Language*: Arabic (official), English; *Religions*: Sunni Moslem, Hindu, Christian.

Products: cotton, sorghum, sesame, millet, cereals, coffee, hides, skins, fruit, textiles; *Major exports*: petroleum products, raw cotton, hides, skins, fuel oil; *Major imports*: rice, wheat, flour, tea, cotton & rayon piece goods, petroleum products; *Industries*: oil refining, entrepôt trade.

Currency: dinar at par with sterling.

Head of Government: Chairman of Presidential Council; *Legislature*: Supreme People's Council; *Judiciary*: based on Islamic Law. Highest court is People's Tribunal.

Sō'vetsk, Til'sit *City* R.S.F.S.R., U.S.S.R., Eur.; factories

Sō'vi-et Central Asia *Region* W Asia, incl. several reps.

Sō'vi-et Rus'sia (rush'à), **Sō'vi-et Un'ion** (yōōn'yön) refers to U.S.S.R.

Spāin, *Country*, SW Europe; 195,000 sq. m.; pop. 33,462,000; 50 provinces; *Main cities*: * Madrid, Barcelona, Valencia, Seville, Zaragoza; *Main rivers*: Ebro, Guadalquluir, Duero, Tajo, Guadiana; *Geog.*: high plateaus with mt. & river barriers; *Climate*: temperate, equable.

Flag: red horizontal bands separated by wider yellow band, national coat of arms in center.

Ethnic comp.: Spanish; *Language*: Spanish (official), regional dialects; *Religion*: Roman Catholic (state).

Products: cereals, livestock, fruit, wines & spirits, sugar, timber, fish, onions, honey, rice, cotton, vegetables; *Minerals*: coal, iron ore, pyrites, uranium, potash, lignite, oil, mercury; *Major exports*: manufactures, citrus fruit, footwear, textiles & clothing, machinery, chemicals, furniture; *Major imports*: feedgrains, machinery, transportation & electrical equipment, metals, chemicals, tobacco; *Industries*: iron, steel, textiles, oil refining, chemicals, cement, shipbuilding, cellulose, leather, paper.

Currency: peseta.

Head of Government: Dictator (Monarch exiled in 1931); *Legislature*: unicameral Cortes; *Judiciary*: laws enacted by the Cortes applied by tribunals & juzgados. Supreme Court, Territorial High Courts, Provincial High Courts.

Spä'lä-tō see SPLIT
Spän'dau (dou) *Commune* cen. East Germany
Span'ish Guin'ea (gin'i) = EQUATORIAL GUINEA
Span'ish Nôrth Af'ri-cà *Territory* of Spain N Morocco, 2 cities: Ceuta and Melilla
Span'ish Peaks *Mountains* (2): E 12,710 ft.; W 13,625 ft.; Colo., U.S.
Span'ish Sà-har'à *Colony* (Sp.) NW Africa
Spär'tà *Anc. city* Peloponnesus S Greece
Spär'tàn-bûrg *City* NW S.C., U.S.; pop. 44,-546; farming, factories, marble
Spe'ziä (spâ') = LA SPEZIA
Spīce Islands = MOLUCCAS

Spits'bêr-gèn *Archipelago* (Norway) Arctic O.; coal

Split, Ital. **Spä'lä-tō** *City* Croatia, Yugoslavia; shipping

Split Mountain *Peak* 14,050 ft. Calif., U.S.

Spō-kane' (kan') *City* E Wash., U.S.; pop. 170,516; commercial, financial, industrial

Spôr'ā-dēs *I s l a n d g r o u p s* (**Northern, Southern**) Aegean S., Greece

Spree (shprā) *River* 220 m. E cen. Germany

Spring'fïeld 1. *City* * of Ill., U.S., cen. part; pop. 91,753; manufacturing, home of A. Lincoln. 2. *City* SW Mass., U.S.; pop. 163,905; manufacturing. 3. *City* SW Mo., U.S.; pop. 120,096; industrial cen. 4. *City* W Ohio, U.S.; pop. 81,926; trade, manufacturing

Springs *City* NE Rep. of South Africa; trade

Squăw Valley *Valley* E Calif., U.S.; skiing

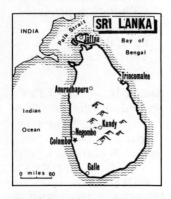

Sri Lanka (member of British Commonwealth) *Country,* formerly Ceylon, Indian Ocean; 25,330 sq. m.; pop. 13,255,000; 22 districts; *Main cities:* * Colombo, Jaffna, Kandy, Galle, Negombo; *Main river:* Mahaweli Ganga; *Geog.:* pear shaped island. N half is plain slightly above sea level, SC hilly & mountainous; *Climate:* tropical.

Flag: narrow green, orange vertical stripes on left — yellow lion carrying sword in upraised paw against red background — bordered in yellow, with yellow vertical band separating stripes from red background.

Ethnic comp.: Sinhalese, Tamils, Moors; *Language:* Sinhal (official), English, Tamil; *Religions:* Buddhist, Hindu, Christian, Muslim.

Products: tea, rubber, coconuts, rice, cinnamon; *Minerals:* graphite, sapphires, some gems; *Major exports:* tea, rubber, coconut products; *Major imports:* rice, food products, textiles, machinery, transportation equipment; *Industries:* mining, cement, paper, paper board, tobacco products, chemicals, leather goods.

Currency: rupee.

Head of Government: British Monarch represented by Governor General; *Legislature:* bicameral Parliament — Senate, House of Representatives; *Judiciary:* Supreme Court, Commissioners of Assize Criminal Court of Appeals, subordinate courts. Final judicial authority is Privy Council.

Sri-nàg'àr *City* * of Kashmir, SW part

Staf'förd-shire *County* W cen. England; * **Staf'förd;** coal, factories, pottery

Stāines *Urban district* SE England

Stä'lin see BRASON, Romania; GARMO PEAK, U.S.S.R.; VARNA, Bulgaria

Stä - lin - ā - bäd' since 1961 DYUSHAMBE

Stä'lin-grad now VOLGOGRAD

Stà-li-nir' (nyēr') since 1961 TSKHINVALI

Stal'i-nö now DONETSK

Stà-li'nö-gôrsk (lē') now BOBRIKI

Sta'linsk since 1961 NOVOKUZNETSK

Stam-boul' (bōōl') *Area* of Istanbul, Turkey; site of anc. Byzantium

Stam'förd *City* SW Conn., U.S.; pop. 108,798; manufacturing

Stan'is-laus Peak (lôs) *Peak* 11,200 ft. Calif., U.S.

Stà-ni-slav' *City* * of *Region* (incl. **Stà-nislä'wow** (vōōf) former Polish dept.) W Ukraine, U.S.S.R.

Stan'ley (li) *Town* * of Falkland Is.; port

Stan'ley Falls (li) *Falls* Upper Congo R., Congo (L)

Stan'ley-ville (li) *Town, Province* Congo (L)

Stan'tön Peak *Peak* 11,665 ft. Calif., U.S.

Stär Peak *Peak* 13,560 ft. Colo., U.S.

Stat'èn Island *Island* N.Y. Bay; forms Richmond, borough of N.Y. City, U.S.

Stä-väng'êr *City* SW Norway; port

Stav'rö-pôl *City* * of *Territory* SE R.S.F.S.R., U.S.S.R., Eur.

Stēele, Mount *Peak* 16,645 ft. Yukon, Canada

Sten'däl (shten') *City* W cen. East Germany

Steppes (steps) *Region* W cen. Asia; wide, treeless tracts

Stêr'ling Heïghts *City* Mich., U.S.; pop. 61,365

Stet-tin' (tēn'), Polish **Szcze-cin'** (che-tsēn') *City* NW Poland (formerly Ger.); commerce, industry, port

Stew'àrt (stū') 1. *River* 320 m. Yukon, Canada. 2. *Island, County* South I. New Zealand

Stew'àrt Peak (stū') *Peak* 14,030 ft. Colo., U.S.

Sti-kēne' (kēn') 1. *Mountains* Brit. Columbia, Canada. 2. *River* 335 m. Canada-S Alas., U.S.

Stîr'ling-shire *County* cen. Scotland; coal, textiles

Stock'hōlm *City* * of *Province,* * of Sweden SE part; pop. 800,-000; industrial, commercial, manufacturing port

Stock'pôrt *County borough* NW England; manufacturing

Stock'tön *City* cen. Calif., U.S.; pop. 107,644; commercial, manufacturing, port

Stock'tön on Tēes *Municipal borough* N England; shipbuilding

Stōke on Trent *City, County borough* W cen. England; pottery, coal

Stôrm Bay *Inlet* of Pacific O. Tasmania, Australia

Stôrm King Peak *Peak* 13,750 ft. Colo., U.S.

Strähl'hôrn *Peak* 13,-750 ft. Switzerland

Strāits, the *Straits* bet. Mediterranean S. and Black S.; incl. Bosporus, Dardanelles

Strāits Settlements *Former Brit. colony,* Malay Penin.; incl. Singapore and areas now in Malaysia

Stras'boûrg *City* NE France; trade, manufacturing, coal

Strat'förd 1. *Town* SW Conn., U.S.; pop. 49,-775; manufacturing. 2. *Town* Ontario, Canada

Strat'förd on A'vön *Municipal borough* cen. England; Shakespeare's home

Strath-mōre' *Valley* cen. Scotland

Stret'förd *Urban district* NW England; industry

Strick'lànd *River* 225 m. cen. New Guinea

Strïp'ed Mountain *Peak* 13,160 ft. Calif., U.S.

Strom'bo-li *Volcano* on *Island* off N Sicily

Stū'árt *Lake, River* 220 m. Brit. Columbia, Canada

Stûr'bridge (brij) *Town* cen. Mass., U.S.; colonial restoration

Stutt'gärt *City* S cen. West Germany; publishing cen., manufacturing

Stẏr *River* 300 m. Ukraine, U.S.S.R.

Sū'bo-ti-ca (tsä) *City* NE Yugoslavia; industry, commerce

Su'chow' (sōō'jō') see TUNGSHAN

Su'cre (sōō') *City*, constitutional * of Bolivia; pop. 58,400

Sū'dan *Region* N cen. Africa; deserts, plains

Sū'dan', Republic of the *Country*, NE Africa, 967,500 sq. m.; pop. 15,963,000; 9 provinces; *Main cities:* * Khartoum, Omdurman, Port Sudan, Albara, Al-Ubayd; *Main rivers:* Nile (Blue & White); *Geog.:* tropical forests, savannahs, swampland, scrubland, sandy, arid hills, desert; *Climate:* desert.

Flag: horizontal red, white, black stripes, with green triangle extending from staff to ⅓ flag's length.

Ethnic comp.: Arabs, Nubians, Nilotics, Negroes; *Language:* Arabic (official), English, tribal languages; *Religions:* Islam (state), Sunni Muslim, animist, Christian minorities.

Products: millet, sesame, groundnuts, cotton, gum arabic, livestock, timber, dates, hides, pulses; *Minerals:* gold, iron ore, manganese ore, salt, chrome ore, copper; *Major exports:* cotton, gum arabic, sesame, peanuts, oil cake & meal, sheep, goats; *Major imports:* cotton textiles, motor vehicles & parts, machinery, base metals, chemicals, petroleum products; *Industries:* food & vegetable oils.

Currency: Sudanese pound.

Head of Government: Chairman of Revolutionary Command Council (RCC); *Legislature:* none. Function carried by RCC; *Judiciary:* divided into separate systems to administer civil, criminal, tribal courts — distinct from Moslem law

Sū-dà-nēse' *Republic*, formerly **French Sūdan**, now MALI

Sud'bûr-ẏ *City* SE Ontario, Canada; nickel

Sū-de'tèn (dā') *Mountain ranges* N and NW Czechoslovakia; region seized by Germans 1938

Su-ez' (sōō) 1. *City* and *Governorate* at *Gulf*, Lower Egypt. 2. *Canal* across *Isthmus* NE Africa; 100 m. long; Suez-Port Said; completed 1869

Suf'folk (uk) *County* E England; fish, livestock

Sug'àr-lōaf (shug') = PAO DE ACUCAR

Suisse (su-ēs') Fr. for SWITZERLAND

Sui'yuan' (swā'yu-än') *Province* N China

Su'ket (soo'kāt) *State* NW India

Su-khô'nà (soo) *River* 350 m. N cen. U.S.S.R., Eur.

Su'khu-mi (soo') *Town* Georgia U.S.S.R.

Suk'kur (s o o'k o o r)

Town West Pakistan; irrigation cen.

Sū'là *River* 240 m. Ukraine, U.S.S.R.

Su - laī - män' (soo-lī) *Mountain range* NW India

Su-lāi-ma-ni'yȧ (nē') *Town* NE Iraq

Sul-tän-ä-bäd' n o w IRAQ *City*

Su'lu (sōō'lōō) *Archipelago, Province, Sea* SW Phil. Is.

Su-mä'trȧ *Island* W Indonesia; agriculture, esp. rubber, tobacco

Sum'bȧ (sōōm') *Island* S Indonesia; sandalwood; agriculture

Sum-bä'wȧ (sōōm) *Island* S Indonesia; livestock

Su'mẏ (sōō') *Town* Ukraine, U.S.S.R.; mills, factories

Sun'dȧ (sōōn') *Islands:* **Greater** and **Lesser**, Malay Arch., Indonesia

Sun'dêr-lȧnd *County borough* N England; shipping, manufacturing

Sun'gä'ri' (soon') *River* 800 m. SE Manchuria

Sung'kiang' (soong'ji-äng') 1. *Province* cen. Manchuria. 2. *Town* E China

Sun'light Peak (līt) *Peak* 14,060 ft. Colo., U.S.

Sun'nẏ-vāle *City* W Calif., U.S.; pop. 95,408

Sun'shīne Peak *Peak* 14,020 ft. Colo., U.S.

Sun Valley *Resort area* cen. Ida., U.S.

Su-pē'ri-ör, Lake *Lake* 31,820 sq. m. N U.S.; largest of 5 Great Lakes, world's largest fresh water lake

Sur-ȧ-bä'jȧ (soor) *City* on *Strait* NE Java, Indonesia; imp. port, trade cen.

Sur-ȧ-kär'tȧ (soor) *City* S cen. Java, Indonesia

Su-rat' *City* W India; brocades, carpets

Sûr'bi-tön *Municipal borough* S England; factories [NE India

Sur-gu'jȧ (gōō') *State*

Su-ri-bä'chi, Mount *Volcano* S Iwo Jima I., Volcano Is.; WW II fame

Su'ri-nam (soo') or **Dutch Gui-ä'na** (gi) *Territory* of Neth., N South America; * Paramaribo; bauxite, agriculture

Su-ri-na'mè *River* 400 m. N Surinam

Surkh-äb' (soor-käb') *River* 400 m. U.S.S.R. cen. Asia

Sur'mä (soor') *River* 560 m. NE India-Pakistan

Sûr'rey (ri) *County* S England; farming, sheep

Su-sit'nȧ (sōō) *River* 280 m. S Alas., U.S.

Sus-que-han'nȧ (kwe) *River* 444 m. N.Y.-Pa.-Md., U.S.

Sus'sèx *County* S England; fish, sheep, farming

Suth'êr-lȧnd 1. *County* N Scotland; fish, deer 2. *Falls* South I. New Zealand

Sut'lej *River* 900 m. Tibet-West Pakistan

Sut'têrs Mill *Site* nr. village of Coloma, Calif., U.S.; gold discovered 1848

Sut'tön and **Chēam** *Urban district* S England

Sut'tön in **Ash'fièld** *Urban district* N cen. England; hosiery, coal, lime

Su'vȧ (sōō') *Town* * of Fiji Is. Terr.; harbor

Su-wan'nēe (soo) *River* 240 m. Ga.-Fla., U.S.

Svä'lbärd *Territories* of Norway in Arctic O.

Sve'a-land (svä') =

Cen. Division of Sweden

Svend′bôrg *City* Fyn I. Denmark; port

Svêrd-lôvsk′ *City* * of *Region* S R.S.F.S.R., U.S.S.R., Asia; cultural, industrial, mining cen.

Sve′ri-ge (svar′yè) = SWEDEN

Svi-yä′gà *River* 250 m. U.S.S.R., E Eur.

Swän Islands *Islands* (2) W Caribbean S., U.S.

Swän′sēa *County borough* SE Wales; port

Swät *River* 400 m. West Pakistan

Swä′tow′ (tou′) *Town* SE China; harbor

Swä′zi-land, Kingdom of *Country,* S Africa; 6,700 sq. m.; pop. 447,000; 4 districts; *Main cities:* * Mbabane, Manzini, Havelock Mine; *Main rivers:* Komati, Umbuluzi, Usutu, Mhiatuze; *Geog.:* 3 regions — mountainous highveld, middleveld, Lubombo Plateau; *Climate:* ranges from humid, near-temperate to sub-tropical.

Flag: horizontal stripes from top to bottom: blue, yellow, crimson, yellow, blue — shield, 2 spears, staff centered on wide crimson band.

Ethnic comp.: Bantu, Europeans; *Language:* English, Swazi; *Religion:* Moslem, Christian, animist.

Products: sugar, timber, citrus, rice, cotton, maize, sorghum, asbestos, livestock, iron ore, tobacco, pineapples; *Minerals:* iron ore, asbestos, coal, kaolin, barites, pyrophyllite, gold, tin, silver, diaspore; *Major exports:* asbestos, iron ore, sugar, wood pulp, other wood products; *Major imports:* food, beverages, tobacco, manufactured goods, machinery, transportation equipment; *Industries:* processing agricultural products, processing wood, mining.

Currency: South African rand.

Head of Government: Monarch; *Legislature:* bicameral Parliament following British model; *Judiciary:* Court of Appeal, High Court highest courts.

Swē′dèn, Kingdom of *Country,* N Europe, 173,500 sq. m.; pop. 8,849,000; 25 districts; *Main cities:* * Stockholm, Göteborg, Malmö; *Main rivers:* Lule, Pite, Indal, Skellefte, Ume; *Geog.:* gently rolling hills in S, mts. in N. 7% of area arable. Half country forested, lakes cover 9% of area; *Climate:* Varies between N, S. In N temperature below freezing 7 months of year. 11 months cold season in N, half that in S.

Flag: yellow cross horizontally on blue field.

Ethnic comp.: Swedes, Finns, Danes, Germans, Norwegians; *Language:* Swedish (official); *Religion:* Lutheran Church (state).

Products: timber, dairy produce, fish, iron ore, lead, zinc, copper, magnetite, iron — steel, machinery, transport equipment, chemicals, petrochemicals, rubber, paper, pulp; *Major exports:* base metals, lumber, machinery, pulp, paper, iron ore; *Major imports:* machiney, chemicals, fuel products, base metals; *Industries:* tourism, mining, shipbuilding, base metal industries.

Currency: kroner.

Head of Government: Monarch; *Legislature:* bicameral Parliament (Riksdag) — Upper Chamber, Lower Chamber; *Judiciary:* includes Supreme Court, rural municipal, appellate courts, various special courts.

Swin′dön *Municipal borough* S England; locomotives

Swit′zêr-lànd, *Country,* W Europe; 15,940 sq. m.; pop. 6,428,000; 22 cantons; *Main cities:* * Bern, Zurick, Basle, Geneva, Lausanne, Win-terrhur; *Main rivers:* Rhine, Rhone, Aare, Inn; *Geog.:* Switzerland forms Great European watershed. Great Alpine Mt. chain constitutes 60% of country. Jura Mts. take up 10%; *Climate:* temperate, varies with altitude.

Flag: square shape with white cross against red field.

Ethnic comp.: Swiss, Spaniards, Austrians; *Language:* German, French, Italian (official), Romansch; *Religions:* Protestant, Roman Catholic, Jewish.

Products: diary produce, livestock, cereals, fruit, wine, timber, chocolate, salt, iron ore, magnesium ore, machinery, precision instruments, watches, textiles, chemicals; *Major exports:* machinery, watches, chemicals, textiles; *Major imports:* chemicals, crude oil, clothing, machines, motor vehicles; *Industries:* tourism, banking, wine growing, manufacture of machinery, watches, chemicals.

Currency: Swiss franc.

Head of Government: Federal Council; *Legislature:* bicameral legislature (Federal Assembly); *Judiciary:* single regular (Federal Tribunal), special military, administrative courts.

Sýd′ney (ni) *City* SE Australia; imp. port

Sýr′à-cūse 1. *City* cen. N.Y., U.S.; pop. 197,-208; trade, manufacturing cen. **2.** or It. **Si-rä-cu′sa** (cōō′zä) *City* * of *Province* SE Sicily, Italy; port

Sýr′ Dar-yä′ *River* 1500 m. U.S.S.R., Asia

Sýr′i-à, Syrian Arab Republic, *Country,*

SYRIA

Near E, 71,210 sq. m.; pop. 6,432,000; 13 provinces; *Main cities:* * Damascus, Aleppo, Homs, Hama; *Main rivers:* Euphrates, Orontes; *Geog.:* Anti-Lebanon, Alawite Mts., Euphrates River Valley, Jabal al-Druze Mts., E dotted with valley oases; *Climate:* Mediterranean type in W, extreme desert type with wide range of temp. in E.

Flag: top red stripe, white center stripe, black bottom stripe, 3 green stars on white stripe.

Ethnic comp.: Arabs, Kurds, Armenians, Druzes; *Language:* Arabic (official), French, Aramaic; *Religions:* Moslem, Christian, Jewish.

Products: wheat, barley, cotton, livestock, hides and skins, wool, silk, oil, natural gas, fruit, olives, tobacco; *Minerals:* petroleum; *Major exports:* raw cotton, cattle, sheep, lentils; *Major imports:* textiles, machinery, petroleum products, vehicles, foodstuffs; *Industries:* oil refining, tourism, food processing, manufacture of glass, textiles, apparel, soap.

Currency: Syrian pound.

Head of Government: President; *Legislature:* unicameral, Peo-

ple's Council; *Judiciary:* amalgam of Ottoman, French and Islamic laws. 3 levels of courts: Courts of First Instance, Courts of Appeal, Court of Cassation.

Sẏr′i-ȧn Desert *Desert* Arabia - Syria - Iraq - Transjordan
Sẏz′rȧn *City* U.S.S.R., Eur.; grain trade
Szcze′cin (che′tsēn) see STETTIN
Sze′chwän′ (se′) *Province* S cen. China
Sze′ged *City* S Hungary; industrial, commercial port
Sze′kes-fe-her-vär (sä′-kesh-fe-här-vär) *City* W cen. Hungary; trade
Sze′ping′kai′ (soo′) *Town* S Manchuria

T

Tȧ-bas′cō *State* SE Mexico
Tä′bläs *Island, Strait* cen. Phil. Is.
Tä′ble Mountain (b'l) *Peak* 11,100 ft. Wyo., U.S.
Tȧ-briz′ (brēz′), **Tȧu′ris** *City* NW Iran; imp. commercially
Tä-cä-nä′ *Volcano* 13,-335 ft. SW Guatemala
Tȧ-cō′mȧ *City* W cen. Wash., U.S.; pop. 154,581; port, fishing, manufacturing, lumber cen.
Tȧ-cō′rȧ *Peak* 19,520 ft. S Peru
Tä-cū-bä′yä *City* cen. Mexico, Fed. distr.
Tä-dzhik′ S.S.R. *Republic* of U.S.S.R. cen. Asia; * Dyushambe
Tae-gū (ta), **Taī-kyū** *City* SE South Korea
Tae-jôn (ta), **Taī-den** *City* W South Korea
Taf-tän′, Kūh-i- *Volcano* 13,260 ft. SE Iran
Ta′gȧn-rog *City* on *Gulf* S R.S.F.S.R., Eur.; metal items
Tä′gus *River* 565 m. Spain-Portugal

Ta-hi′ti (hē′) *Island* of Society Is. (Fr.), S Pacific O.
Tä′hōe, Lake *Lake* Nev.-Calif., U.S.; resorts
Tä′hua (wä) *Peak* 17,-455 ft. W Bolivia
Taī-än *Town* NE China; nr. **Mt. Taī** sacred mountain
Taī-chū, was **Taī-wän** *City* W cen. Taiwan
Taī-mẏr′ *National district* on *Peninsula* crossed by *River* (400 m.) through *Lake* to *Bay*, N cen. Siberia, U.S.S.R., Asia
Taī-nän *City* SW Taiwan; commercial cen.
Taī-peh (bä) *City* * of Rep. of China, Taiwan; pop. 964,000
Taī′ping′ *City* NW Malaysia

TAIWAN (FORMOSA)

Taī-wän (Nationalist China, Formosa), Republic of China *Country*, 90 miles SE of Chinese mainland; 13,880 sq. m.; pop. 14,420,000; 5 provinces; *Main cities:* * Taipei, Kaohsiung, Tainan, Taichung, Chilung; *Main islands:* Formosa, Quemoy, Matsu, Pescadores; *Main rivers:* Cho-shui, Tan-shui, Hsia-tan-shui; *Geog.:* Taiwan — ⅔ of islands rugged foothills, mt. chains. Coastal plain occupies W third; *Climate:* oceanic, subtropical.

Flag: red field, blue rectangle in upper left corner containing 12-pointed white sun.

Ethnic comp.: Chi-

nese (Han), Aborigines; *Language:* Mandarin Chinese (official), Amoy Chinese; *Religions:* Buddhism, Taoism, Moslem, Roman Catholic.

Products: rice, tea, sugar, bananas, pineapples, sweet potatoes, camphor, turmeric, fish, tobacco, timber, oil, coal, iron, aluminum, sulphur, iron and steel, petrochemicals, cement, fertilizers, textiles; *Minerals:* coal, volcanic sulphur, natural gas, petroleum; *Major exports:* textiles, chemicals, metals, machinery, plywood, sugar, bananas, canned mushrooms; *Major imports:* machinery, chemicals, transportation equipment, soybeans, raw cotton, timber, crude oil, wheat; *Industries:* oil refining, manufacture of textiles, electrical appliances, chemicals, food processing.

Currency: Taiwan dollar.

Head of Government: President; *Legislature:* unicameral National Assembly; *Judiciary:* in ascending order — district tribunals, High Court, Supreme Court. Independent Administrative Court, Commission for Disciplinary Punishment of Officials.

Tä - ju - mul′cō (hōō-mōōl′) *Volcano* 13,-815 ft. W Guatemala
Tä-kä-mä-tsu *City* Shikoku, Japan; port
Tä-kä-ō *City* SW Taiwan; port
Tä-kä-ō-kä *City* Honshu, Japan; bronze, rice cen.
Tä-kä-sä-ki *City* Honshu, Japan; silk trade
Tä′klä Mä-kän′ *Desert* W China; fertile soil
Tä-ku-tu′ (kōō - tōō′)

River 220 m. Brazil-Guyana

Täl'cä *City* * of *Province* cen. Chile; trade, manufacturing

Täl-cä-hua'nō (wä') *Port* S cen. Chile

Tal'dy̆-Kur-gan' (koor) *Town* * of *Region* Kazakh, U.S.S R., cen. Asia

Tä'li', was **Tung'chow'** (toong'jō') *Town* NE cen. China

Tä-li'say (lē'sī) *Municipality* Negros, Phil. Is.

Tal'lä-has'sēe *City* * of Fla. N part, U.S.; pop. 71,897; tobacco, lumber industries

Tal-lä-hatch'ie *River* 300 m. Miss., U.S.

Tal-lä-pōō'sä *River* 270 m. Ala., U.S.

Tal'lin *City* * of Estonian S.S.R. NW U.S.S.R., Eur.; port, manufacturing

Tä'mä *Peak* 13,125 ft. N Colombia

Tä-mau-li'päs (mou-lē') *State* E Mexico

Tåm-bôv' *City* * of *Region* cen. R.S.F.S.R., U.S.S.R., Eur.; grain

Tam'på *City* on *Bay* W cen. Fla., U.S.; pop. 277,767; resort, fishing, cigars

Tam'pe-re, Tam-mêr-fôrs' *City* SW Finland; power plants, factories

Tam-pi'cō (pē') *City* E Mexico; commercial cen., port

Tä'nå *River* 500 m. E Africa

Tä'nä, Te'nô *River* 200 m. NE Norway

Tä'nä, Tsä'nä *Lake* N Ethiopia

Tan'ä-nä *River* 475 m. cen. Alas., U.S.

Ta-na-na-rive' (rēv') *City* * of Malagasy Rep., E cen. part; pop. 321,654

Tän-ci-tä'rō (se) *Mountain* 12,665 ft. SW Mexico

Tä-ne-gä-shi-mä *Island* off Kyushu, Japan

Tan-gàn-yi'kå (yē') 1. *Lake* SE Africa. 2. *Former Terr.* (Germ., then Brit.) and *Re-*

public E Africa; now part of TANZANIA

Tan-gier' (jēr') *City* on *Bay* N Morocco; former international zone (England, France, Spain)

Täng'shän' *City* NE China; coal cen.

Tan-jōre' *City* * of *District* S India; carpets, jewelry

Tän'tä *City* Lower Egypt

Tan-zan'i-å (Tanganyika, Zanzibar, and Pemba), United Republic of *Country*, E Coast of Africa; 362,820 sq. m.; pop. 14,100,000; 20 regions; *Main cities:* * Dar-es-Salaam, Zanzibar; *Main rivers:* Ruvu, Wami, Rufiji, Great Ruaha, Mbenkuru, Ruvuma; *Geog.:* Tanganyika low lying E coastal area, high plateau in WC region, scattered mt. areas. Zanzibar low lying island coral limestone; *Climate:* governed by 2 monsoons.

Flag: diagonal black band from lower left to upper right flanked by narrower yellow band. Field of flag green (upper left), blue (lower right).

Ethnic comp.: Bantu, Hamitic, Nilo-Hamitic, Indians, Pakistanis, Arabs, Europeans; *Language:* English, Swahili (official), Arabic, tribal languages; *Religions:* Moslem, Christian, animist.

Products: sisal, cotton, coffee, cashew nuts, cloves, colve oil, timber, oil seeds, meat, hides & skins, copra, diamonds, gold, tin, lead, mica, leather, textiles; *Minerals:* diamonds, gold, salt, mica sheets, precious gems, gen tanzanite, tin; *Major exports:* sisal, cotton, coffee, diamonds, cashew nuts, petroleum products; *Major imports:* machinery & transportation equipment, manufactured goods, textiles; *Industries:* light industries, food processing.

Currency: Tanzania shilling.

Head of Government: President; *Legislature:* unicameral National Assembly; *Judiciary:* combines tribal, Islamic, British law. High Court at apex.

Tao'nän' (tou') *Town* S Manchuria

Ta-på-joz' (zhôs') *River* 500 m. N Brazil

Täp'ti *River* 435 m. India; unnavigable

Ta-quå-ri' (kwå-rē') *River* 450 m. S cen. Brazil

Tä'rän-tō *City* * of former *Province* (now *Ionio*) SE Italy; port

Tä'rä-wä *Island* atoll, * of Gilbert and Ellice Is. (Brit.)

Tarbes (tarb) *City* SW France; trade, manufacturing

Ta'rim' (dä'rēm') *River* 1250 m. W China

Tarn *River* 233 m., *Department* S France

Tarn-et-Ga-ronne' (nä-ga-rôn') *Department* S France

Tär'now (nōōf) *City* SE Poland; industry, commerce

Tar-rä-gō'nå *Commune* * of *Province* NE Spain; manufacturing, wine industry

Tär-rä'sä *Commune* NE Spain; manufacturing

Tär'tū *City* * of *Province* E Estonia, U.S.S.R.; manufacturing

Täsch'hôrn *Peak* 14,760 ft. SW Switzerland

Tä'shi Dhhō Dzông' *Town* * of Bhutan, W part

Tash-kent' *City* * of Uzbek S.S.R., R.S.F.S.R., U.S.S.R., cen. Asia; agriculture, manufacturing

Tas'mån, Mount *Peak* 11,465 ft. South I. New Zealand

Tas-mä'ni-å (taz) *Island* S Pacific O., *State* of Australia; * Hobart

Tas'mån Sea Area of South Pacific O., W New Zealand - SE Australia

Tä'tår A.S.S.R. *Republic* E R.S.F.S.R., U.S.S.R., Eur.; * Kazan; agriculture, livestock

Tä'tå-ry̆, Gulf of *Strait* N end of Sea of Japan

Tä'trå Mountains *Mountain* group of Carpathians, Czechoslovakia

Tä'tung' (dä'toong') *City* NE China; trade

Tăunt'ön *City* SE Mass., U.S.; pop. 43,756; manufacturing

Tău'rus Mountains *Mountain* chain S Turkey, Asia

Tåv-da' *River* 650 m. W Siberia, U.S.S.R.

Tāy *River* 120 m., largest in Scotland, E part

Tä-yä'bäs *Province* Luzon, Phil. Is.

Tay'lör *City* SE Mich., U.S.; pop. 70,020

Täy'lör, Mount *Peak* 11,380 ft. N.M., U.S.

Täy'lör Mountain *Peak* 13,600 ft. Colo., U.S.

Taz *River* 600 m. NW Siberia, U.S.S.R.

Tbi'li-si see TIFLIS

Tēa'neck *Township* NE N.J., U.S.; pop. 42,355

Tēe'wi - not, Mount *Peak* 12,315 ft. NW Wyo., U.S.

Tef-fe′ (tâ-fâ′) *River* 500 m. W Brazil

Te-gäl′ *Town* Java, Indonesia; port

Tè-gū-ci-gal′pà (gōō-si) *City* * of Honduras; silver, gold mines

Teh-rän′, Te-hè-ran′ *City* * of *Province* and * of Iran N part

Teh′ri (tā′rē) *State* N India

Tè-huän′tè-pec, Gulf of *Inlet* of Pacific O. SE Mexico

Tel′ A-viv′ (vēv′) *City* W Israel; modern commercial city

Tel′è-scōpe Peak *Peak* 11,050 ft. Calif., U.S.

Tem′ple, Mount (p′l) *Peak* 11,635 ft. Alberta, Canada

Te-mu′cō (mōō′) *City* S cen. Chile; trade

Ten′êr-ife (êf) *Island* largest of Canary Is.

Teng′ri Khän′ *Peak* 23,620 ft. cen. Asia

Ten-nès-sēe′ *State*, named from name of ancient capital of Cherokee tribe; 42,244 sq. m.; *pop.*: 3,924,164 (*rank*: 7th); SE U.S.; *Boundaries*: Kentucky, Virginia, North Carolina, Georgia, Alabama, Mississippi, Arkansas, Missouri; *Major cities*: Memphis, * Nashville, Chattanooga; *Major rivers*: Mississippi, Tennessee, Cunberland; *Major lakes*: Reelfoot and lakes created by TVA; 95 counties.

Nickname: Volunteer State; *Motto*: "Tennessee — America at its best;" *Flag*: 3 white stars in white-bordered blue circle on red field, narrow white & blue stripes at right; *Flower*: iris; *Bird*: mockingbird; *Tree*: tulip poplar; *Song*: *Tennessee Waltz*.

Industry: stone, clay & glass items, fabricated metals, apparel, textile items, chemicals, processed food, agriculture, lumbering; *Natural resources*: forests, coal, stone, cement, zinc, phosphate rock; *Major source of income*: manufacturing.

Admitted to Union: 1796 (16th state).

Places of interest: Great Smoky Mts. Ntl. Park, Cumberland Gap Ntl. Historical Park, Cherokee Ntl. Forest.

Ten′sas (sǎ) *River* 250 m. La., U.S.

Te′rä-mō (tâ′) *Commune* * of *Province* cen. Italy

Têr-cei′rà (sā′) *Island* cen. Azores

Te′rek (tā′) *River* 380 m. U.S.S.R., Eur.

Te-rè-si′nà (tā-rè-zē′) *City* NE Brazil

Têr-nä′te *Island* of Moluccas, Indonesia; spices

Ter′ni *Commune* * of *Province* cen. Italy; factories

Têr-nō′pöl *City* W Ukraine, U.S.S.R.

Ter′rè Haute′ (hōt′) *City* W Ind., U.S.; pop. 70,286; manufacturing, mining

Ter′rèl, Mount *Peak* 11,560 ft. Utah, U.S.

Tes′lin (tez′) *Lake* NW Canada

Tē′tön Range *Mountain range* NW Wyo., U.S.; site of **Grand Tē′tön** peak 13,766 ft. in **Grand Tē′tön** *National Park*

Te-tuän′ (twän′) *City* Spanish North Africa

Teu′co (tā′oo) *River* 350 m. N Argentina

Tex-är-kan′à *Twin cities* Tex.-Ark., U.S.

Tex′às *State*, named from Indian word meaning "friends;" 267,339 sq. m.; *pop.*: 11,196,730 (*rank*: 4th); S U.S.; *Boundaries*: New Mexico, Oklahoma, Arkansas, Louisiana, Mexico, Gulf of Mexico; *Major cities*: * Austin, Houston, Dallas, Fort Worth, San Antonio, El Paso; *Major rivers*: Pecos, Colorado, Brazos, Trinity, Red, Rio Grande; 254 counties.

Nickname: Lone Star State; *Motto*: "Friendship;" *Flag*: single star on vertical blue bar with red and white bar to right; *Flower*: bluebonnet; *Bird*: mockingbird; *Tree*: pecan; *Song*: *Texas, Our Texas*.

Industry: food items, transportation equipment, primary & fabricated metals, oil & natural gas refining, making of chemicals; *Natural resources*: petroleum, natural gas, sulphur, agriculture; *Major source of income*: wholesale & retail trade, manfacturing.

Admitted to Union: 1845 (28th state).

Places of interest: Big Bend Ntl. Park, Palo Duro Canyon, Judge Roy Bean Museum.

Tex′às City *City* SE Texas, U.S.; pop. 38,908; manufacturing

Tey′de or **Te-ne-ri′fe, Pi′co de** (pē′cō dâ tē′dâ, tā-nâ-rē′fe) *Volcano* 12,190 ft. Tenerife I.

THAILAND

Thai′land (tī′), King-dom of *Country*, SE Asia; 198,250 sq. m.; pop. 37,768,000; 71 provinces; *Main cities*: * Bangkok, Thonburi, Chiengmai, Nakorn, Sawan; *Main rivers*: Chao Phraya, Mekong; *Geog.*: C plain, NE large plateau, N mts., valleys, S rain forest; *Climate*: tropical.

Flag: 2 red stripes, top & bottom, wider center blue band.

Ethnic comp.: Thais, Chinese, Vietnamese, Americans; *Language*: Thai (official), English, Chinese; *Religions*: Hinayana Buddhism, Islam, Confucianism, Christian.

Products: rice, rubber, timber, sugar, maize, coconuts, kenaf, groundnuts, buffaloes, tobacco, tin ore, iron ore, wolfram; *Minerals*: iron, lignite, thiorite, gypsum, steel, aluminium, copper, zinc; *Major exports*: rice, rubber, corn, tin, teak, tapioca, jute, kenaf; *Major imports*: petroleum products, iron & steel, motor vehicles, textiles, mining, construction & industrial, electrical machinery; *Industries*: wood processing, textile manufacture, wearing apparel manufacture, mining.

Currency: baht.

Head of Government: Monarch; *Legislature*: bicameral Parliament — Senate, House of Representatives; *Judiciary*: highest court Supreme Court.

Thames (temz) *River* 210 m. S England

Thar (tär) or **In′di-àn Desert** *Region* W Pakistan-NW India; 100,000 sq. m.

Thēbes *Anc. city*, cen. of Egyptian civilization, Upper Egypt

Thêr-mop′y̆-laē *Mountain pass* E Greece

Thes-sà-lô-ni′kè (nyē′) 1. *Department* Mace-

donia, Greece. 2. *City* = SALONIKA

Thes′sà-lẏ *Division* of anc. and mod Greece, E penin.

Thomp′sön *River* 270 m. Brit. Columbia, Canada

Thom′sön *River* 300 m. Queensland, Australia

Thou′sànd Islands *Islands* (ab. 1500) St. Laurence R. U.S.-Canada

Thou′sànd Lake Mountain *Peak* 11,250 ft. Utah, U.S.

Thou′sànd Ōaks *City* SW Cal., U.S.; pop. 36,334

Thrāce (thrās) *Region* E Balkan Penin., SE Eur.; div: **Wes′têrn** NE Greece, **Eas′têrn** Turkey, Eur.

Thrēe Rivers *City* S Quebec, Canada; industrial port

Thu′le (tōō′) *Settlement* NW Greenland, U.S. air base

Thumb, the (thum) *Peak* 13,880 ft. Calif., U.S.

Thun′dêr Mountain *Peak* 13,575 ft. Calif., U.S.

Thû-rin′gi-à (ji) *Former state* cen. Germany; agriculture, forests

Thûrs′dày Island *Island* Queensland, Australia; pearl cen.

Ti′à Jua′nà (tē′, wä′) = TIJUANA

Tī′bêr *River* 244 m. cen. Italy

Tī-bē′ri-às *Anc. town* NE Palestine; cen. of learning

Ti-bet′ *Country*, presently *Dependency* of Communist China; 470,000 sq. m.; pop. 1,300,000; * Lhasa; agriculture

Tieh′ling′ (ti-e′) *Town* S Manchuria

Tien′ Shän′ (ti-en′) *Mountain chain* U.S.S.R.-China

Tien′shui′ (shwä′) *City* N. cen. China; trade

Tien′tsin′ *City* NE China; educational, commercial cen., port

Ti-er′rà del Fu-e′gō (fōō-ā′) *Island* of *Archipelago* off S South America; div. bet. Argentina (E)-Chile (W)

Tiê-te′ (tā′) *River* 500 m. SE Brazil

Tif′lis, Tbi′li-si *City* * of Georgian S.S.R., U.S.S.R.; trade, manufacturing

Ti′gre (tē′grâ) *River* 350 m. Ecuador-Peru

Tī′gris *River* 1150 m. Iraq-Turkey

Ti-jua′nä (wä′) *Town* NW Mexico

Til′bûrg *Commune* S Netherlands; industrial cen.

Til′sit = SOVETSK

Ti-mi-soa′rä (tē-mi-shwä′) *City* nr. **Ti′-mis R.** (tē′) 270 m. SW Romania; commerce, industry

Ti-môr′ 1. *Island* Lesser Sunda Is., S Malay Arch., div. bet. Portugal (E) and Indonesia (W); agriculture, forests 2. *Sea* bet. Timor-NW Australia

Tim-pà-nō′gös, Mount *Peak* 12,000 ft. Utah, U.S.

Ti-ni-an′ *Island* W Pacific O.; WW II site [India

Tin-nė-vel′lẏ *Town* S

Tip-pė-cà-noe′ (nōō′) *River* 200 m. Ind., U.S.

Tip-pė-rar′ẏ *County* S Eire; mining, livestock, agriculture

Tip′tön *Urban district* W cen. England; coal

Ti-rä′nė *Town* * of *Prefecture* and * of Albania, cen. part; pop. 170,000

Ti′rich Mir′ (tē′, mēr′) *Peak* 25,260 ft. NW Pakistan

Ti-rōl′, Tẏ′rōl *Region* Austria-Italy

Tis′tä *River* 300 m. NE India

Ti′sza, Theiss (tīs) *River* 800 m. U.S.S.R.-Hungary-Yugoslavia

Ti-tä′gàrh *Town* W India

Ti-tä′nō, Mount *Mountain* 2435 ft.; site of San Marino

Ti-ti-cä′cà, Lake *Lake* Peru-Bolivia; world's highest navigable lake 12,500 ft.

Ti′tō-gräd (tē′) or **Pōd′-gō-ri-ca** (rē-tsä) *Town* * of Montenegro Rep. S Yugoslavia

Ti′vö-li *Commune* cen. Italy; anc. ruins, fountains

Ti′zi-n-Tam-jurt′ *Peak* 14,760 ft. Morocco

Tläx-cä′lä *Town* * of *State* cen. Mexico

Tlem-cen′ (sen′) *City* NW Algeria; commerce

To-bä′gō *Island* West Indies; part of TRINIDAD and TOBAGO

To-bä-tä *Town* Kyushu, Japan; coal port

To-bôl′ *River* 800 m. Ural Mts. U.S.S.R.

Tō′bruk (brook) *Port* Libya; WW II fame

Tō-can-tins′ (tēns′) *River* 1700 m. E Brazil

Tō-chi-gi *Town* in *Province* Honshu, Japan; silk weaving

Tō-côr-pū′ri, Cer′rōs de (ser′ōz dâ) *Mountain* 22,160 ft. Bolivia

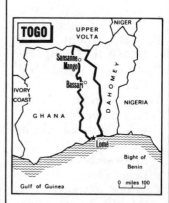

Tō′gō, *Republic* of *Country*, W Africa; 21,000 sq. m.; pop. 1,955,000; 18 districts; *Main cities:* * Lomé, Sansanne Mango, Bassari, Anécho; *Main rivers:* Oti, Mono, Haho, Anie; *Geog.:* 2 savannah plains regions separated by SW-NE range of hills; *Climate:* tropical.

Flag: 3 green, 2 yellow horizontal stripes

with white star on red square in upper left.

Ethnic comp.: Ewe, Mina, Hamitic; *Language:* French (official), Ewe, Twi, Hausa, Dagomba, Tim, Mina; *Religions:* animist, Roman Catholic, Moslem, Protestant.

Products: coffee, cocoa, palm products, maize, cotton, yams, iron ore, bauxite, manioc, limestone, cassava, phosphates; *Minerals:* phosphates, iron ore, bauxite, limestone; *Major exports:* phosphates, cocoa, coffee, palm nuts, cotton; *Major imports:* cotton textiles, machinery, motor vehicles, tobacco, petroleum products; *Industries:* mining, food processing, cement manufacture, textile mills, brewery.

Currency: CFA franc.

Head of Government: President; *Legislature:* none; *Judiciary:* highest review court Supreme Court.

Tō-kė-wän′nà *Mountain* 13,175 ft. Utah, U.S.

Tō-ku-shi-mä *City* * of *Prefecture* Shikoku, Japan; port

Tō-ku-yä-mä *Town* Honshu, Japan; port

Tō′kẏ-ō *City* on *Bay*, * of *Prefecture*, * of Japan, Honshu I.; pop. 10,863,000; manufacturing, cultural cen.

Tō-lē′dō 1. *City* NW Ohio, U.S.; pop. 383,-818; port, factories. 2. *Commune* * of *Province* cen. Spain; textiles, arms

Tō-li′mä (lē′) *Volcano* 18,435 ft. Colombia

Tol′lẏ-gunge (gunj) *Town* E India

Tō-lu′cà (lōō′) 1. *City* * of Mexico state, cen. Mexico. 2. *Vol-*

cano (**Ne-vä'dō de**) 15,025 ft. Mexico

Tom *River* 450 m. U.S.S.R., Asia

Tom-á-säk'i *Peak* 12,-270 ft. Utah, U.S.

Tô-mä'szow (shōōf or shō) *Com.iune* cen. Poland; manufactures

Tom-big'bēe *River* 410 m. Alas., U.S.

Tom'bō *Island* off Fr. Guinea; site of *

Tomb'stōne (tōōm') *Town* SE Ariz., U.S.; former mining cen.

Tō'mō *River* 260 m. Colombia

Tômsk *City* * of *Region* U.S.S.R., Asia; educational cen.

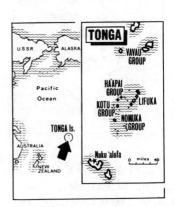

Tôn'gá, Kingdom of *Country*, S Pacific Ocean, S of Western Samoa; 270 sq. m.; pop. 123,000; *Main cities:* * Nuku'alofa, Tongatapu, Ha'apai, Vava'u; *Main rivers:* none; *Geog.:* archipelago, majority of islands have limestone base, some volcanic origin with limestone formations superimposed; *Climate:* subtropical.

Flag: red with white square canton, red cross centered in canton.

Ethnic comp.: Tongans (Polynesians), Europeans; *Language:* Tongan, English; *Religions:* Christian (especially Wesleyan).

Products: copra, bananas; *Mineral:* oil; *Major exports:* copra, bananas; *Major im-*

ports: food, textiles; *Industries:* tourism, extraction of fruit juices, tobacco factory, food processing.

Currency: Tongan dollar at par with Australian dollar.

Head of Government: Monarch; *Legislature:* unicameral legislative assembly; *Judiciary:* King-in-Council, Supreme Court, Magistrates Court, Lands Court.

Ton'gá-land *Region* SE Africa, Rep. of South Africa

Tongue (tung) *River* 245 m. Mont., U.S.

Tônk *Town* * of *State* NW India

Ton'kin' 1. *Region* of North Vietnam, former Fr. protectorate. 2. *Gulf* arm of South China S.

Ton'le Sap' (lä), **Great Lake** *Lake* W Cambodia

Töns'berg (bar) *City* NE Norway; port, Norway's oldest city

To-pē'ká *City* * of Kans., U.S.; pop. 125,011; flour, meat packing, metal works

To-ri'nō (rē') *City* (see TURIN) * of *Province* NW Italy

Tôr'nè *River* 250 m. N Sweden [cen Chile

Tö'rō *Peak* 20,930 ft.

Tö-ron'tō *City* * of Ontario (SE part), Canada; pop. 664,584; commercial, industrial port

Tôr-quay' (kē') *Municipal borough* SW England; pottery, resort

Tôr'rä *Peak* 11,661 ft. W Colombia

Tor'ránce *City* SW Calif., U.S.; pop. 134,584; industrial

Tor're An - nun - ziä'tä (rä, nōōn) *Commune* S Italy; resort

Tor're del Gre'cō (rä dâl grä'kō) *Commune* S Italy; resort

Tôr-re-ôn' *City* NE Mexico; textiles, flour

Tor'rèys Peak (riz)

Peak 14,265 ft. Colo. U.S.

Tôr'toise Islands (tis) = GALAPAGOS IS.

Tôr-tō'lá *Island* largest of Brit. Virgin Is.

Tôr-tō'sá *City* NE Spain; manufacturing

Tôr-tu'gä, Lä (tōō') *Island* off N Venezuela

Tō'run (rōōn), **Thorn** (tôrn) *City* N Poland; commerce, industry

Tot'tèn-hám *Urban district* Greater London, England

Tot-to-ri *City* * of *Prefecture* Honshu, Japan; textiles, port

Toub'kal (tōōb') *Peak* 13,660 ft. Morocco

Toug-gourt' (too-goort') *Territory*, *Town*, *Oasis* NE Algeria

Tou-lôn' (tōō) *City* SE France; port

Tou-louse' (tōō-lōōz') *City* S France; educ. cen., manufacturing

Tou-rāine' (tōō) *Hist. region* NW France

Tour - coing' (tōōr-kwan') *City* N France; manufacturing

Tour-nāi' (tōōr), **Dōor'-nik** *Commune* SW Belgium; commerce, manufacturing

Tours (tōōr) *City* NW cen. France; manufacturing, commerce

Towns'ville *City* NE Australia; port

To-yä-mä *City* * of *Prefecture* Honshu, Japan; port

To-yo-hä-shi *City* Honshu, Japan

Träb-zôn' *City* * of *Vilayet* NE Turkey; port

Trá-fal'gàr *Cape* SW Spain; Nelson's victory 1805

Trá-lēe' *Bay*, *Port*, *Urban district* SW Eire [cen. Asia

Trans A-laï' *Mt. range*

Trans-căceu-cä'sia (shá) *Region* S of Caucasus Mts.

Trans-jôr'dán now JORDAN

Trans - väal' (briefly South African Rep.)

Province NE Rep. of South Africa; minerals

Tran-sÿl-vä'niá *Region* NW cen. Romania; nr. **Transylvanian Alps** South Carpathians)

Trä'pä-ni *City* * of *Province* Sicily, Italy; port

Tra'vàn-cōre *Region*, former state, S India; rice, minerals

Treas'ûre Island (trezh') *Island* (manmade) San Francisco, Calif., U.S.

Treng-gä'nu (nōō) *State* Malaysia

Trent, Tren'tō *Commune* * of *Province* NE Italy; manufacturing

Tren'tön *City* * of N.J., U.S.; pop. 104,638; manufacturing

Tres Ar-rô'yōs (trâs) *City* E Argentina; cattle, farming

Tres Crū'ces (trâs, sâs) *Peak* 20,850 ft. N Chile

Tre-vi'sō (vē') *Commune* * of *Province* NE Italy

Trich-i-nop'ö-lÿ *City* S India; manufacturing, commerce

Tri-chur' (choor') *Town* S India; temple

Trier (trēr), **Treves** (trevz) *City* W cen. West Germany; manufacturing, mining

Tri-e'ste 1. *Area* **Free Terr.** of Trieste 1947-53; S part to Yugoslavia; N part: 2. *City* on *Gulf* NE Italy; port

Trik'ká-lá *City* * of *Department* cen. Greece

Trin'i-dad and To-bä'-gō, *Country*, Caribbean; 1,865 sq. m.; pop. 1,206,000; 8 counties, ward of Tobago; *Main cities:* * Port of Spain, San Fernando, Arima, Scarborough (Tobago); *Main river:* Ortoire on Trinidad; *Geog.:* Trinidad — 3 low mt. ranges cross E-W, tropical forests cover half island. To-

TRINIDAD & TOBAGO

bago — main ridge of volcanic origin; *Climate:* tropical. Cooler on Tobago.

Flag: black band edged with white diagonally from upper left to lower right on red field.

Ethnic comp.: Negroes, Indians, Mulattoes, Chinese, Europeans; *Language:* English (official), Hindi and other Indian languages; *Religions:* Roman Catholic, Anglican, Hindu, Christian, Moslem.

Products: sugar, rum, cocoa, coffee, copra, bananas, timber, oil, asphalt, fertilizers; *Minerals:* petroleum, lignite coal, gypsum, iron, clay, limestone, crude oil; *Major exports:* chemicals, fruits and vegetables, oil, sugar, mineral fuels, lubricants and related products; *Major imports:* crude oil, machinery & transportation equipment, foodstuffs, material, chemicals; *Industries:* oil refining, sugar manufacture, molasses, rum, fruit juices.

Currency: Trinidad & Tobago dollar.

Head of Government: Governor General representing English Monarch; *Legislature:* bicameral Parliament — Senate, House of Representatives; *Judiciary:* supreme authority High Court.

Trin'i-tỷ 1. *River* 360 m. E Tex., U.S. 2. *Peak* 13,810 ft. SW Colo., U.S.

Trip'ö-li 1. *Region,* **Trip-o-li-tan'iả,** N African coast. 2. *City* * of *Province,* * of Libya; pop. 379,900; port. 3. *Town* NW Lebanon; port

Trip'o-lis *City* S Greece; manufacturing

Tri'pu-rä *Territory* NE India; former state

Tri-sul' (sōōl') *Peak* 23,380 ft. N India

Tri-van'drum *City* SW India; port

Tr'no-vo (tûr') *City* cen. Bulgaria

Trô'itsk *City* Ural area U.S.S.R., Asia

Trōm-be'tås (bā') *River* 350 m. N Brazil

Trō'men *Volcano* 12,-795 ft. W Argentina

Trōms'ö *City* N Norway; port

Trônd'heim (hām) 1. *City* cen. Norway; commercial port. 2. *Fjord* W cen. Norway

Troy 1. *City* E N.Y., U.S.; pop. 62,918. 2. *Anc. city* NW Asia Minor. 3. *City* SE Mich., U.S.; pop. 39,419

Troyes (trwä) *City* NE France

Trū'chås Peak *Peak* 13,110 ft. N.M., U.S.

Trū'cial O-man', Trū'-cial Coast, Trū'cial States (shẳl) *Region* and *Shiekdoms* of Persian Gulf States, SE Arabia; oil

Trū-jil'lo (hē'yō) 1. *City* now SANTO DOMINGO * of Dominican Rep. 2. *City* NW Peru; commercial cen. 3. *Town* * of *State* W cen. Venezuela

Truk *Island group* Caroline Is. (U.S. Trust Terr.)

Tsäng'wū', was **Wū'-chow'** (jō') *City* SE China; port

Tshuä'pä (chwä') *River* 420 m. S cen. Africa

Tsi'nän' (jē') *City* NE China; trade

Tsing'haï', Ching'haï'

Lake in *Province* W cen. China

Tsing'tao' (dou') *City* NE China; port

Tsing'yuän' *City* NE China

Tsi'ning' (jē') *City* NE China; manufacturing

Tsin'kiảng' (jin'ji-äng') *City* SE China; port

Tsū *City* Honshu, Japan; port

Tsū-gi-tä-kä *Peak* 12,-900 ft. Formosa

Tsun'yi' (ē') *Town* S China

Tsū-rū-mi *Town* Honshu, Japan; industrial

Tsū-rū-ō-kä *City* Honshu, Japan; textiles

Tsū-shi-mä *Island* of Japan on *Strait* NW of Kyushu

Tsū-yä-mä *Town* Honshu, Japan

Tū-ä-mō-tū Archipelago *Island group* of Fr. Polynesia, S Pacific O.

Tū-bū'rän *Municipality* Cebu I. Phil. Is.; port

Tu-cu-män' (tōō-cōō) *City* * of *Province* N Argentina; sugar

Tu-ge'lả (tōō-gā') *River* 300 m. E Rep. of South Africa

Tuk-uh-nik'i-vätz, Mt. *Peak* 12,000 ft. Utah, U.S.

Tū'lả *City* * of *Region* cen. R.S.F.S.R., U.S.S.R., Eur.; metal work

Tū-lä'gi *Town* on *Island* of Solomon Is., W Pacific O.

Tul'sả *City* NE Okla., U.S.; pop. 331,638; financial, commercial cen., oil industry

Tū'mẻn' *River* 220 m. NE Korea-SE Manchuria

Tū-nä'ri *Peak* 17,000 ft. cen. Bolivia

Tung (doong) *River* 280 m. SE China

Tun-gä-bhả'drä *River* 400 m. S India

Tung'chow' (jō) now NANTUNG

Tung'hsien' (shi-en') *City* NE China

Tung'hwä' *City* S Manchuria; lumber

Tung'kiang' (ji-äng') *Town* E Manchuria

Tung'kwän' *Town* NE China   [SE China

Tung'ting' Hū' *Lake*

Tūn-gū-rä'guä *Volcano* 16,685 ft. Ecuador

Tun-gū'skả *Rivers* (3) cen. Siberia, U.S.S.R.: (1) **Lower** 2000 m. (2) **Stony** 1000 m. (3) **Upper** = lower Angara R.

Tū'nis 1. *Former Barbary State* and Fr. *Protectorate,* N Africa; now TUNISIA. 2. *City* on *Gulf* * of Tunisia; pop. 800,000

TUNISIA

Tū-ni'sia (shẳ), Republic of *Country,* Coast of Africa; 63,360 sq. m. (Sahara 18,360 sq. m.); pop. 5,147,000; 12 governorates, 82 delegations, 749 sheikdoms, 116 communes; *Main cities:* * Tunis, Sfax, Bizerta, Sousse, Kairouan; *Main river:* Medjerda; *Geog.:* N wooded fertile area. C area of coastal plains. S region borders Sahara; *Climate:* along coast is Mediterranean.

Flag: red crescent & star in white circle on red field.

Ethnic comp.: Berbers, Arabs; *Language:* Arabic (official), French; *Religions:* Islam (state), Moslem.

Products: fruit, olives, dates, wine, cereals, sheep, almonds, fish; *Minerals:* phosphate, cement deposit, oil, iron ore, lead ore, zinc ore; *Major exports:* phosphates,

olive oil, crude petroleum, wine, iron ore; *Major imports:* foodstuffs, industrial raw materials, machinery and equipment, transportation equipment; *Industries:* chemical works, textile industry, food processing, metal works, railroad repair yards, tourism.

Currency: dinar.

Head of Government: President; *Legislature:* unicameral National Assembly; *Judiciary:* 3 tiers — primary jurisdiction, appeal, High Court.

Tū-pūn-gä'tō *Peak* 22,-300 ft. Argentina-Chile
Tu-ra' *River* 400 m. U.S.S.R., Asia
Tū'rin, It. To-ri'nō (rē') *Commune* * of Torino prov. NW Italy; manufacturing, commerce
Tûr-kė-stan' *Town* R.S.F.S.R., U.S.S.R., cen. Asia

Tûr'key (ki), Republic of *Country,* Asia Minor and SE Europe; 301,300 sq. m.; pop. 36,910,000; 67 provinces; *Main cities:* * Ankara, Istanbul, Izmir, Adana, Bursa; *Main rivers:* Kizil Irmak, Yesil Irmak, Seylan, Maeander, Tigris, Euphrates; *Geog.:* fertile Agean & Mediterranean areas, C plateau, straits; *Climate:* 3 zones — temperate, transitional area, steppe type.

Flag: white crescent & white star on red field.

Ethnic comp.: Turks, Kurds, Arabs, Circassians, Greeks and Armenians; *Language:* Turkish (official), Kurdish, Arabic; *Religions:* Moslem (state), Orthodox, Gregorian, Jewish minorities.

Products: cotton, tobacco, cereals, figs, silk, olives, nuts, sultanas, sugar, hides and skins, wool, sheep, goats, timber, opium, grapes; *Minerals:* coal, lignite, oil, iron ore, copper, chrome, boracite, mercury, iron, manganese; *Major exports:* tobacco, cotton, hazelnuts, raisins, chrome, citrus fruits; *Major imports:* machinery and transportation equipment, petroleum products, iron — steel products, fertilizers and plastics; *Industries:* steel, iron, sugar — cotton refining, tires, textiles, fertilizers.

Currency: Turkish lira.

Head of Government: President; *Legislature:* bicameral Grand National Assembly; *Judiciary:* based on Italian criminal law, Swiss civil law, German commercial law. Judiciary independent.

Tûr'kish Empire = OTTOMAN EMPIRE
Tûr-ki-stan' *Region* cen. Asia: U.S.S.R.-China-Afghanistan
Tûrk'men S.S.R. *Republic* of U.S.S.R., cen. Asia; * Ashkhabad; livestock, oil
Tûrks and Cāi'cös Islands *Islands* dependency of Jamaica
Tur'ku (toor'koo) *City* SW Finland; port
Tûr'ret Peak *Peak* 13,-825 ft. Colo., U.S.

Tus-cȧ-lōō'sȧ *City* W cen. Ala., U.S.; pop. 65,773; manufacturing
Tus'cȧn Archipelago *Island group* bet. Corsica and Italy
Tus'cȧ-ny *Compartimento* cen. Italy; mining, farming, manufacturing
Tus'con (tōō'son) *City* S Ariz., U.S.; pop. 262,933; trade cen., resort
Tū-ti-cô-rin' *Town* S India; port
Tū-tu-i'lä (ē') *Island* SW Pacific O.; site of Pago Pago, * of Amer. Samoa
Tū-tū-pä'cä *Volcano* 18,960 ft. S Peru
Tū'vȧ Autonomous Region, was **Tan'nū Tū'vȧ** *Region* R.S.F.S.R., U.S.S.R., Asia; livestock
Twick'ėn-hȧm *Municipal borough* London, SE England
Tȳ'lêr *City* NE Tex., U.S.; pop. 57,770; commerce, industry
Tȳn'dȧll, Mount *Peak* 14,025 ft. Calif., U.S.
Tȳne'mouth (m u t h) *County borough* on **Tȳne R.** N England; port
Tȳre *Town* S Lebanon; anc. * of Phoenicia
Tȳ-rōl' = TIROL
Tȳ-rōne' *County* W cen. Northern Ireland
Tȳr-rhē'ni-ȧn Sea *Area* of Mediterranean S. SW of Italy
Tyū-men' *City* * of *Region* R.S.F.S.R., U.S.S.R., Asia
Tzė'liū'tsing' (jing') *City* S cen. China
Tzu, Tzė *River* 375 m. SE China

U

Ua-tū-ma' (wa) *River* 350 m. N Brazil
Uau - pes' (wow - pās') *River* 700 m. Colombia-Brazil
Ū-ban'gi *River* 700 m. cen. Africa

Ū-ban'gi-Shä'ri *Former terr.* Fr. Equatorial Africa, now CENTRAL AFRICAN REP.
U'bē (ōō') *City* Honshu, Japan; port
U-bi'nä (ōō-vē') *Peak* 16,830 ft. Bolivia
U-bi'näs (ōō-bē') *Peak* 17,390 ft. Peru
Ub'su Nur' (sōō-nōōr') *Lake* Outer Mongolia
U-cä-yä'li (ōō) *River* 1200 m. Peru
U-da' *River* 470 m. U.S.S.R., Asia
U-dai'pur (ōō-dī'poor) *City* * of *State* (also **Me-wär'**) NW India
U'di-ne (ōō'dē-nâ) *Commune* NE Italy; manufacturing
Ud'murt A.S.S.R. (ood'-moort) *Republic* R.S.F.S.R., U.S.S.R., Eur.; lumber, livestock, grain
U-e-dä (oo) *Town* Honshu, Japan
Ue'le (we') *River* 700 m. cen. Africa
U-fa' (oo) 1. *City* Ural area, U.S.S.R. Eur.; industrial, cultural cen. 2. *River* 430 m. U.S.S.R., Eur.

Ū-gan'dȧ, Republic of, *Country,* 91,130 sq. m.; pop. 9,500,000; 18 administrative districts; *Main cities:* * Kampala, Jinji, Entebbe, Masaka, Masindi; *Main rivers:* Victoria Nile, Albert Nile, Aswa, Pager, Kafu, Katonga; *Geog.:* plateau, mts.; *Climate:* tropical.

Flag: black, yellow, red, black, yellow, red horizontal stripes

with national em-
blem — crested crane,
in white circle in
center.

Ethnic comp.: Nilot-
ics, Hamitics, Bantu,
Asians, refugees from
Rwanda, Sudan,
Congo; *Language:*
English (official),
Kiswahili, tribal
languages; *Religions:*
animist, Christian,
Muslim.

Products: cotton, cof-
fee, tea, tobacco, sug-
ar, maize, ground-
nuts, timber, fish,
castor seed; *Miner-
als:* copper, tin ore,
wolfram, beryl, cas-
siterite; *Major ex-
ports:* coffee, cotton,
copper, tea, feeds;
Major imports: ma-
chinery & transpor-
tation equipment,
cotton and synthetic
fabrics, manufactures
of metals & clothing;
Industries: food
products, textiles,
cigarettes, brewing,
enamel hollow ware,
cement, wooden box-
es, soap.

Currency: Uganda
shilling.

Head of Government:
President; *Legisla-
ture:* unicameral Na-
tional Assembly; *Ju-
diciary:* Supreme
Court high court,
district, native
courts.

U-ji-yä-mä-dä *City*
Honshu, Japan; Ja-
pan's sacred city

Uj'jain (ōō'jin) *City* W
cen. India; holy city

Uj'pest (ōō'y'pesht)
City cen. Hungary

Uk'kèl *Commune* cen.
Belgium

Ū-krāi'ni-àn **S.S.R.**
Constituent republic of
U.S.S.R., SW part; *
Kièv; agriculture,
livestock

U'län Bä'tôr (ōō') *City*
* of Mongolian Rep.
N cen. part; pop.
195,300; commercial,
sacred city

U'län U-de' (ōō', ōō)

City R.S.F.S.R.,
U.S.S.R., Asia; in-
dustrial

Ulm (oolm) *City* West
Germany; commerce,
manufacturing

Ul'stêr *Former province*
N Ireland, now div.
into NORTHERN
IRELAND and Ul'-
stêr prov. N Eire

U'lugh Muz-tagh' (ōō'-
lōō mooz-tä') *Peak*
25,340 ft. W China

Ul-ya'növsk *City* * of
Region R.S.F.S.R.,
U.S.S.R., Eur.; in-
dustrial

U-man' (ōō) *City*
Ukraine U.S.S.R.

Um'bri-à *Comparti-
mento* cen. Italy;
farming

U'mè (ōō') *River* 290
m. N Sweden

Ūn-à-las'kà *Bay, Is-
land* of Aleutians SW
Alas., U.S.

Un-cöm-päh'gre *Peak*
14,305 ft. Colo., U.S.

Un-gä'và *Region* E Canada, Hudson Bay-
Labrador; minerals

Ū'ni-mak *Island* largest
of Aleutians SW Alas.
U.S.

Ūn'iön City *City* NE
N.J., U.S.; pop. 58,-
537; industrial

Ūn'iön of South Africa
= SOUTH AFRICA,
REP. of

**Ūn'iön of Sō'vi-et So-
cialist Republics,
U.S.S.R.** *Country,* N
Eurasia, 8,650,000
sq. m.; pop. 241,748,-
000; 15 republics;
Main cities: * Mos-
cow, Leningrad,
Kiev, Tashkent, Ba-
ku, Kuibyshev,
Sverdlovsk, Khar-
kov, Gorki, Novosi-
birsk; *Main rivers:*
Dnieper, Dniester,
Don, Volga, Ob,
Yenisei, Lena, Amur;
Geog.: broad plain
broken by low hills,
mt. ranges, Siberian
lowlands, deserts of
C Asia; *Climate:* long
cold winters, short
summers.

Flag: red with yellow
hammer & sickle be-

low yellow star in
upper left.

Ethnic comp.: Rus-
sians, Ukranians,
Turkmenians, Uz-
beks, Kirghiz, Tad-
jiks, Uighurs; *Lan-
guage:* Russian (offi-
cial), corresponding
to nationalities; *Reli-
gions:* Russian Ortho-
dox, Armenian, Geor-
gian, Lutheran, Ro-
man Catholic, Sunni
Muslim, Jewish,
Buddhist.

Products: food, cere-
als, vegetables, sugar,
timber, cotton, live-
stock, dairy produce,
tobacco, fruit, fish;
Minerals: oil, coal,
iron ore, manganese,
apatite, potassium,
phosphates; *Major
exports:* oil, coal, iron
ore, iron, steel, elec-
tricity, machinery,
transport equipment,
paper, cotton, vege-
table oil, clocks,
watches; *Major im-
ports:* machinery and
equipment, consumer
goods, fuel, raw ma-
terials; *Industries:*
machinery, transport
equipment, iron and
steel, oil refining
electricity, chemicals,
machine tools, preci-
sion instruments,
shipping, food proc-
essing, paper.

Currency: ruble.

Head of Government:
Chairmen of Supreme
Soviet; *Legislature:*
bicameral Supreme
Soviet; *Judiciary:*
Supreme Court high-
est.

**Ū-nī'ted A'ràb Repub-
lic** = 1. Official name
of EGYPT. 2. *Union*
of Egypt and Syria
1958-61

**Ū-nī'ted King'döm of
Greāt Bri'tain and
Nôr'thêrn Īre'lànd**
(U.K.) = *Kingdom*
incl. Great Britain
(England, Scotland,
Wales) and Northern
Ireland; 94,220 sq.
m.; pop. 56,100,000;
* London, England;
varied industries,
farming, shipping

Ū-nī'ted Nā-tions
(shuns) *International
terr.* N.Y. City, U.S.;
U.N. headquarters

Ū-nī'ted Provinces now
UTTAR PRADESH

**Ū-nī'ted Stātes of À-
mer'i-cà,** USA, *Coun-
try,* N America;
3,549,000 sq. m.; pop.
206,481,000; 50
states; *Main cities:*
* Washington, D. C.;
New York, Los An-
geles, Chicago, Phila-
delphia, Detroit, Bos-
ton, San Francisco,

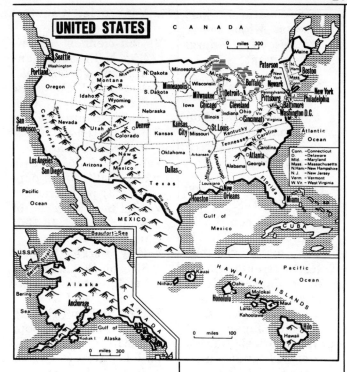

UNITED STATES

Pittsburgh, St. Louis, Cleveland, Houston, Baltimore, Dallas; *Main rivers:* Mississippi, Missouri, Rio Grande, Yukon, Arkansas, Colorado, Ohio — Allegheny, Red, Columbia; *Geog.:* 3 N-S highland belts — 2 in W, 1 in E, interior lowland between; *Climate:* subarctic in Alaska to subtropical.

Flag: 13 horizontal red, white stripes, 50 five-pointed stars on blue field in upper left.

Ethnic comp.: whites, Negroes; *Language:* English (official), *Religions:* Protestant, Roman Catholic, Jewish, Eastern Orthodox.

Products: cereals, fruit, cotton, tobacco, timber, livestock, coal, iron, copper, oil, natural gas, lead, zinc, molybdenum, gold, silver, bauxite, stone, sand and gravel, garnets, steel, aircraft, motor vehicles, electrical and non-electrical machinery, chemicals, metals, paper, cement, clothing, textiles, telecom-

munication apparatus, plastic materials, resin, firearms, ammunition; *Minerals:* oil, copper, coal, iron ore, natural gas, mica, nitrogen, molybdenum, zinc, lead, sulphur, vanadium, cadmium, uranium, bauxite, phosphate, rock, nitrates, quicksilver, potash, limestone, cement rocks, borates, gold, silver; *Major exports:* machinery, grain, food, livestock, chemicals, vehicles, aircraft, tobacco, oil seeds, cotton, coal, petroleum products, textiles, clothing, pulp, paper and products, other manufactured goods; *Major imports:* food, livestock, machinery, raw materials, petroleum, petroleum products, iron & steel, non-ferrous metals, coffee, chemicals, alcoholic drinks; *Industries:* mining, manufacture of textiles, clothing, chemicals, metals, machinery, paper, cement, plastics, firearms, vehicles, aircraft, banking, food processing, tourism.
Currency: U. S. dollar.

Head of Government: President; *Legislature:* bicameral Congress — House of Representatives, Senate; *Judiciary:* Supreme Court at apex. Principle of judicial review of constitutionality of laws cornerstone of Supreme Court's power.

Ū-ni-vêr′si-ty City *City* E Mo., U.S.; pop. 46,309

U-ni-vêr′si-ty Peak *Peak* 13,585 ft. Calif., U.S.

Un′ley (li) *City* South Australia

Un′zha (ōōn′) *River* 365 m. U.S.S.R., Eur.

U-pō′lu (ōō-pō′lōō) *Island* of Western Samoa

Up′pêr Är′ling-tön *City* Ohio, U.S.; pop. 38,-630

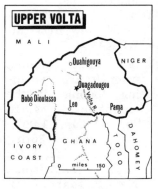

UPPER VOLTA

Up′pêr Vōl′ta, Republic of *Country,* W Africa; 105,880 sq. m.; pop. 5,346,000; 4 departments; *Main cities:* *Ouagadougou, Bobo Dioulasso, Ouahigouya; *Main rivers:* Black, White, Red Voltas, Sourou; *Geog.:* plateau. E — low hills separate White Volta & Niger R basins; *Climate:* Nov.–March comfortable, dry, — hot, dry March–May, hot, wet remainder of year.

Flag: equal-sized horizontal bands — black, white and red.

Ethnic comp.: Mossi, Samo; *Language:* French (official), Af-

rican languages (Mossi, Samo, Gourounsi, Lobi); *Religions:* animist, Moslem.

Products: livestock, millet, sorghum, maize, fish, yams, gold, rice, diamonds, copper, manganese, chrome, cotton, groundnuts; *Minerals:* none exploited, manganese, limestone; *Major exports:* livestock, cotton, peanuts; *Major imports:* textiles, clothing, motor vehicles and parts, fruit, vegetables, machinery; *Industries:* textiles, bicycle assembly, maintenance & repairing vehicles.

Currency: CFA franc.

Head of Government: President; *Legislature:* unicameral National Assembly; *Judiciary:* Supreme Court at apex.

Up′pêr Vōl′ta, Republic of *Republic* W Africa (former Fr. terr.); 95,444 sq. m.; pop. 5,300,000; * Ouagadougou; livestock

Upp′sä-la *City* * of *Province* E Sweden; machinery, publishing

Ū′ral 1. *Mountains:* range div. Eur.-Asia, U.S.S.R.; minerals, forests, heavy industry. 2. *River* (unnavigable) 1400 m. U.S.S.R. Eur.-Asia

Ū-ralsk′ *City* Kazakh U.S.S.R. cen. Asia

U-ra-ri-coe′ra (ōō, cwā′) *River* 360 m. N Brazil

U-rä′wä (ōō) *Town* Honshu, Japan

Ur-fä′ *City* * of *Vilayet* SE Turkey

Ur′gä (oor′) now ULAN BATOR   [NW Iran

Ur′mi-a (oor′) *Lake*

U-rū-bäm′bä (ōō) *River* 450 m. cen. Peru

Ū′ru-guay (gwī or gwā), Oriental Republic of *Country,* S America; 72,170 sq. m.; pop.

2,945,000; 19 departments; *Main cities:* * Montevideo, Paysandu, Salto, Mercedes; *Main rivers:* Uruguay, Negro, Rio de la Plata, Cuareim, Yaguarón, Mirim; *Geog.:* rolling, grassy plains, low hills; *Climate:* temperate.

Flag: 5 white, 4 blue horizontal stripes with yellow sun against white field in upper left corner.

Ethnic comp.: Europeans, Mestizos; *Language:* Spanish (official), *Religion:* Roman Catholic.

Products: wool, meat, dairy products, hides and skins, wheat, marble, linseed oil, textiles, fruit, wine, rice; *Minerals:* marble, building stone, gravel, small deposits of iron ore; *Major exports:* wool, meat, hides; *Major imports:* raw materials, fuels, lubricants, machinery — parts, cars, construction materials, foodstuffs; *Industries:* oil refining, mining, meat packing, textiles, building materials, beverages, chemicals.

Currency: peso.

Head of Government: President; *Legislature:* bicameral General Assembly — Senate, Chamber of Deputies; *Judiciary:* headed by Supreme Court.

U-rum'chi (ōō-rōōm') *City* W China; commercial cen.
U-run'di (ōō-rōōn') *Former terr.* (Ger.) and Mandate (Belg.) E Africa, now BURUNDI
U-sa' *River* 350 m. U.S.S.R., Eur.
U.S. Grant Peak *Peak* 13,690 ft. SW Colo., U.S.
Ush'bä *Peak* 15,400 ft. Georgia U.S.S.R.
Us-kub' = SKOPLJE
Us-ku-där', was Scū'tä-ri *Town* Turkey, Asia; manufacturing, commerce
Us-su'ri (ōō-soor') *River* 450 m. U.S.S.R. Asia
U'sti (ōō') *City* W Czechoslovakia; manufacturing
Ust Urt (ōōst oort) *Plateau* U.S.S.R. cen. Asia
U-sū-mä-cin'tä (sēn') *River* 330 m. Guatemala-Mexico
U-sum-bu'rä (ōō-soom-boor') now BUJUMBURA
Ū'täh *State,* named from Ute tribe meaning "people of the mountains;" 84,916 sq. m.; *pop.:* 1,059,273 (*rank:* 36th); W–Rocky Mt. U.S.; *Boundaries:* Arizona, Nevada, Idaho, Wyoming, Colorado; *Major cities:* * Salt Lake City, Ogden; *Major rivers:* Colorado, Green Sevier; *Major lakes:* Great Salt Lake, Utah, Sevier; 29 counties.

Nickname: Beehive State; *Motto:* "Industry;" *Flag:* state seal in gold circle on blue field; *Flower:* Sego lily; *Bird:* California gull; *Tree:* blue spruce; *Song: Utah, We Love Thee.*

Industry: processed foods & metals, stone, clay & glass items, farming, spacecraft building, printing, publishing; *Natural resources:* copper, petroleum,

iron, natural gas, forests; *Major source of income:* federal government.

Admitted to Union: 1896 (45th state).

Places of interest: Zion Canyon, Bryce Canyon, Hovenweep Ntl. Monument.

Ute Peak *Peak* 12,300 ft. Colo., U.S.
Ū'ti-cà *City* cen. N.Y., U.S.; pop. 91,611; port, manufacturing
Ū'trecht (trekt) *City* * of *Province* cen. Netherlands; commercial
U-tsu-mo-mi-ya *City* Honshu, Japan
Ut'tàr Prä-desh' (däsh') *State* N India incl. Ganges plains; grains
U-tuä'dō (ōō) *Municipality* W cen. Puerto Rico
U-wä-ji-mä *Town* Shikoku, Japan
Ux'bridge *Urban district* SE England (Greater London)
Uz'bek S.S.R. (ooz') *Constituent Republic* of U.S.S.R., cen. Asia; * Tashkent; agriculture, mining
Ūzh'go-rod *City* Ukraine, U.S.S.R.; trade cen.

V

Väal *River* 700 m. Rep. of South Africa
Vä-dūz' *Commune* * of Liechtenstein
Vai'gàch *Island* N U.S.S.R., Eur.
Väkh *River* 550 m. U.S.S.R. Asia
Väksh *River* 400 m. U.S.S.R. cen. Asia
Vàl-daï' Hills *Plateaus, hills* W U.S.S.R., Eur.; Volga R. source
Väl'dez (däz) *Peninsula* S Argentina
Va-lence' (läns') *Commune* SE France; manufacturing
Vä-len'ci-à (shi) 1. *Anc. kingdom* E Spain. 2. *Commune* * of *Province* E Spain; manufacturing. 3. *City* N

Venezuela; manufacturing, commerce
Va-len-ciennes' (sien') *City* N France; manufacturing, coal area
Val-là-do-lid' *Commune* * of *Province* N cen. Spain; manufacturing
Väl-le'cäs (bä-yä') *Commune* cen. Spain
Väl-le'jo (lä'ō) *City* cen. Calif., U.S.; pop. 66,733; port, trade
Vàl-let'tà *City* * of Malta; pop. 16,135; port, naval base
Val'ley Fôrge (li fôrj) Site of Washington's headquarters 1777-78, SE Pa., U.S.
Val'ley Strēam (li) *City* SE N.Y., U.S.; pop. 40,413
Va-lois' (lwa') *Hist. duchy* N France
Val-pà-rai'sō (rä' or rī') *City* on *Bay* * of *Province* cen. Chile; commercial port
Van *Salt lake, Vilayet* E Turkey
Van-cou'vêr (cōō') 1. *City* SW Wash., U.S.; pop. 42,493; imp. shipping, lumber cen. 2. *City* Brit. Columbia, Canada; imp. port, manufacturing cen. 3. *Mountain* 15,700 ft. Yukon, Canada. 4. *Island* off Brit. Columbia, W Canada; minerals, fish, forests
Var *Department* SE France
Vär'där *River* 200 m. Yugoslavia-Greece
Vä-re'se (rä'sâ) *Commune* * of *Province* N Italy; silk industry
Vär'nä, was Stä'lin *City* NE Bulgaria; port
Vas'quez Peak (kez) *Peak* 12,800 ft. Colo., U.S.
Vàs-têr-as' (ōs') *City* E Sweden; factories
Vat'i-càn City *State* within Rome, Italy; 109 acres; papal palaces, museums, St. Peter's Basilica
Vàt'têrn *Lake* S Sweden
Vau-cluse' (vō-clōōz') *Department* S E France
Ve-lä-de'rō (dä') *Peak*

20,735 ft. NW Argentina

Ve-län' (vå) *Peak* 12,-350 ft. It.-Swiss border

Ve-le'tä, Pi-cä'cho de (vâ-lä') *Peak* 11,380 ft. S Spain

Vė-li'kie Lu'ki (lē', lōō') *Town* * of *Region* R.S.F.S.R., U.S.S.R., Eur.

Vėl-lōre' *City* S India

Vel'sėn *Commune* W Netherlands; port

Ven-dee' (vän-dā') *Department* W France

Vend'sys-sėl-Thy' (sus, tu') *Island* N Jutland, Denmark

Ve-nē'ti-à (shi), **Ve-ne'ziä** (nâ') *Anc.* and *mod. region* NE Italy; fertile, mineral-rich area; div. into 3 compartimenti: 1. **Venezia Eu-gä'ne-ä** (a-oo-gä'). 2. **Venezia Giu'-liä** (jōō'). 3. **Venezia Tri-den-ti'nä** (dân-tē')

Ven-ė-zu-e'là, Republic of *Country,* N coast of South America; 352,140 sq. m.; pop. 11,000,000; 20 states, federal district, 2 federal territories, federal dependencies; *Main cities:* * Caracas, Maracaibo, Barquisimeto, Valencia, Maracay; *Main rivers:* Orinoco, Caroni, Caura, Apure; *Geog.:* Andes Mountains (NW), coastal zone, plains, highlands, Angel Falls; *Climate:* torrid zone, temperature varies with altitude.

Flag: yellow, blue, red horizontal bands with crest in left corner top yellow stripe, semicircle of 7 stars in middle of center (blue) stripe.

Ethnic comp.: Mestizos, Negroes, Mulattoes, Amerindians; *Language:* Spanish (official); *Religion:* Roman Catholic.

Products: coffee, cocoa, sugar, oil, iron ore, gold, diamonds, manganese, asbestos, gypsum, iron, steel; *Minerals:* oil, iron ore, salt, coal, gold, diamonds; *Major exports:* oil and petroleum products, iron ore; *Major imports:* vehicles, iron, steel, wheat, mining and constrution equipment, organic chemicals; *Industries:* mining, oil refining, manufacture of textiles, building materials, clothing, shoes, food, steel, chemicals.

Currency: bolivar.

Head of Government: President; *Legislature:* bicameral Congress — Senate, Chamber of Deputies; *Judiciary:* Supreme Court highest court.

Ven'ice (is), It. **Ve-ne'-ziä** (nä') 1. *City* on 118 islands in *Lagoon* NE Italy; canals, buildings, glass, lace. 2. **Gulf of** N area of Adriatic S.

Ven-tuä'ri *River* 350 m. S Venezuela

Ven-tūr'à (**San Buenaventura**) *City* SW Cal., U.S.; pop. 55,-797; business

Ve'rà-crūz' *City* in *State* E Mexico; port

Ver-cel'li (vâr-chel') *Commune* * of *Province* NW Italy; trade

Vêrde, Cape = VERT

Vêr'di-gris (grēs) *River* 280 m. Kans.-Okla., U.S.

Vêr-dun' 1. *City* Quebec, Canada; manu-facturing. 2. *City* NE France; battles WW I, WW II

Vêr-kho-yansk' *Mountains* U.S.S.R. Asia

Vêr-mil'iön Peak *Peak* 13,870 ft. Colo., U.S.

Vêr-mont' *State,* named from French meaning "green mountains;" 9,609 sq. m.; *pop.:* 444,732 (*rank:* 48th); NE coast — New England U.S.; *Boundaries:* New York, New Hampshire, Massachusetts, Canada; *Major cities:* Burlington, * Montpelier; *Major river:* Connecticut *Major lake:* Lake Champlain; 14 counties.

Nickname: Green Mountain State; *Motto:* "Freedom and unity;" *Flag:* state seal on blue field; *Flower:* red clover; *Bird:* hermit thrush; *Animal:* Morgan horse; *Tree:* sugar maple; *Song:* Hail, Vermont.

Industry: wood & paper items, rubber & plastic items, food products, computer components, stone items, lumbering, quarrying, dairy farming, machine making; *Natural resources:* granite, marble, asbestos, slate, forests; *Major source of income:* manufacturing.

Admitted to Union: 1791 (14th state).

Places of interest: Stowe, Bennington Battle Monument.

Ve-rō'nà *Commune* * of *Province* NE Italy; textiles

Vė-ro'ni-cà *Peak* 19,-340 ft. Peru

Vêr-sailles' (sĭ') *City* N France; imp. treaties signed at palace

Vêrt or **Vêrde** *Cape* W point of Africa

Ver-viers' (vyā') *Commune* E Belgium

Ves'tàl Peak *Peak* 13,-850 ft. Colo., U.S.

Ves'têr-ä-lėn *Islands* NW Norway

Ve-sū'vi-us *Volcano* SW Italy nr. Naples

Vet-lu'gà (lōō') *River* 500 m. U.S.S.R. Eur.

Vi'bôrg (vē') 1. *City* Jutland, Denmark. 2. *City* U.S.S.R. = VYBORG

Vi-cen'zä (vē-chen') *Commune* * of *Province* NE Italy

Vi-chä'dà *River* 335 m. Colombia

Vi'chẏ (vē') *Commune* cen. France; resort; Fr. seat of government 1940-42

Vicks'bûrg *City* W Miss., U.S.; Civil War battle site

Vic-tō'ri-à 1. *City* * of Brit. Colombia, Canada; pop. 57,453; port, commerce, manufacturing. 2. *City* * of Hong Kong; port, trade cen. 3. *River* 400 m. N cen. Australia. 4. *State* SE Australia

Vic-tō'ri-ä 1. *Island* and *Strait* Arctic Arch. Northwest Terrs. Canada. 2. *Lake* 26,830 sq. m. E cen. Africa. 3. *Peak* 13,240 ft. Papua, New Guinea. 4. *Point* S Burma. 5. *City* SE Texas, U.S.; pop. 41,349; business

Vic-tō'ri-à Falls 1. *Falls* Zambezi R. S Africa. 2. now IGUASSU

Vic-tō'ri-à Land *Area* of Antarctica, Ross Dependency

Vi-en'nà, Ger. **Wien** (vēn) *City* * of *District* and * of Austria E part; pop. 1,644,-900

Vienne (vyen) 1. *Department* W cen. France. 2. *River* 215 m. SW cen. France

Vien-tiane' *Town* administrative * of Laos; pop. 132,000

Vi-et'nam' see NORTH VIETNAM, SOUTH VIETNAM

Vi-et'nam' *Country,* former Fr. terr., SE Asia; 1954 div. at 17th parallel: 1. **Vi-et'näm', Democratic Rep. of** (North); 61,-290 sq. m.; pop. 21,-150,000; * Hanoi; rice, fish. 2. **Vi-et'näm', Rep. of** (South); 65,-900 sq. m.; pop. 18,-330,000; * Saigon

Vi'gō (vē') *City* NW Spain; port, manufacturing

Vil-kits'ki Strait *Channel* N U.S.S.R., Asia

Ville-ûr-banne' (vēl) *Commune* E cen. France; industry

Vil'nỷ-us, Vil'nà, Vil'nō, Ger. **Wil'nä** (vil') *City* * of Lithuania; trade, cultural cen.

Vi-lyui' (lū'i) *River* 1500 m. U.S.S.R., Asia

Vi'nä del Mär' (vē') *City* cen. Chile; resort

Vin - cennes' (senz') *Commune* N France

Vin'dèl *River* 225 m. N Sweden

Vīne'länd 1. *City* SW N.J., U.S.; pop. 47,-685; business cen. 2. *Coast area* N North America; visited by Norse 1000 B.C.

Vin'ni-tsà *City* * of *Region* Ukraine U.S.S.R.; factories

Vîr-gin'iä (jin') *State,* named in honor of Elizabeth, the "Virgin Queen;" 40,815 sq. m.; *pop.:* 4,648,-494 (*rank:* 14th); S-Atlantic US.; *Boundaries:* West Virginia, Maryland, North Carolina, Tennessee, Kentucky, Atlantic Ocean; *Major cities:* Norfolk, * Richmond, Portsmouth, Newport News; *Major rivers:* Potomac, Rappahannock, York, James; *Major lakes:* Smith Mountain, John H. Kerr Reservoir; 96 counties.

Nickname: Old Dominion State; *Motto:*

"Sic semper tyrannis" (Thus always to tyrants); *Flag:* state seal on blue field; *Flower:* dogwood; *Bird:* cardinal; *Song:* Carry Me Back to Old Virginia.

Industry: electrical equipment, tobacco, apparel, furniture & fixtures, agriculture, shipbuilding, chemical manufacturing, textiles, wood products; *Natural resources:* forests, coal, stone, sand, gravel, zinc; *Major source of income:* government.

Admitted to Union: June 25, 1788.

Places of interest: Yorktown, Williamsburg, Mt. Vernon, Monticello.

Vîr-gin'iä Beach *City* SE Va., U.S.; pop. 172,106; Armed Forces, residential, resort

Vîr-gin'iä City *Village,* now ghost town W Nev., U.S.; gold, silver mines 1850

Vir'gin Islands (jin) *Islands* NE West Indies div.: 1. **Amer. Virgin Is.** * Charlotte Amalie on St. Thomas. 2. **Brit. Virgin Is.** * Road Town

Vis (vēs), **Lis'sà** *Island* off Yugoslavia

Vi-sä'yàn Islands *Islands* cen. Phil. Is.; incl. Cebu, Leyte, Negros, Panay, etc.

Vis'count Mel'ville Sound (vī') *Sound* Northwest Terrs. Canada

Vi'sō, Mount (vē') *Peak* 12,600 ft. NW Italy

Vis'tū-là *River* 625 m. N Poland

Vi'tebsk (vē') *City* * of *Region* White Russia, U.S.S.R.; industrial cen.

Vi-ter'bō *Commune* * of *Province* cen. Italy; manufacturing

Vi'ti Le'vu (vē', vōō) *Island* largest of Fiji Is.

Vi-tim' (tēm') *River*

1100 m. Siberia, U.S.S.R., Asia

Vi-tō'ri-à 1. *City* N Spain; manufacturing. 2. *City* E Brazil; port

Vi-try'-sur-Seine' (trē', sân') *Commune* N France; manufacturing

Vi-zä'gà-pà'tàm *City* E India; port, textiles

Vi-zi-à-nàg'ràm *Town* E India

Vlad'i-mir *City* of *Region* R.S.F.S.R., U.S.S.R., Eur.

Vla-di-vos-tok' *City* R.S.F.S.R., U.S.S.R., Asia; imp. port

Vlõ'nä *Town* on *Bay* in *Prefecture* SW Albania; port

Vôl-cän' *Peak* 18,075 ft. cen. Chile

Vol'gà *River* 2325 m., U.S.S.R.; Eur.'s longest

Vol'go-grad, was **Stä'-lin-grad** *City* * of *Region* U.S.S.R., Eur.; imp. industrially

Vô'lög-dà *City* * of *Region* R.S.F.S.R. U.S.S.R. Eur.; trade, factories

Vō'los *City* on *Gulf* NE Greece; port

Volsk *Town* R.S.F.S.R., U.S.S.R., Eur.; port

Vol'tà 1. *River* 250 m. W Africa; formed by **Black Vol'tà** (headstream) and **White Vol'tà** 450 m. 2. *Republic* see UPPER VOLTA

Vö-lỷn' *Region* Ukraine U.S.S.R.

Vö-rô'nezh *City* * of *Region* on *River* (290 m.) R. S. F. S. R., U.S.S.R. Eur.; imp. industrial cen.

Võ-ro-shi'lov (shē') *City* R.S.F.S.R., U.S.S.R., Asia; industrial, agricultural cen.

Vō - ro - shi'löv - grad (shē') *City* * of *Region* Ukraine, U.S.S.R.; coal area; factories

Vō-ro-shi'lovsk (shē) *City* Ukraine U.S.S.R.; industrial

Vôr'sklà *River* 270 m. Ukraine, U.S.S.R.

Vosges (vōzh) *Department, Mountains* NE France

Vul'càn Crest *Peak* 13,-720 ft. S Colo., U.S.

Vyat'kà 1. *River* 800 m. U.S.S.R., Eur. 2. *City* now KIROV

Vy'bôrg (vē') *City* on *Bay* R.S.F.S.R., U.S.S.R., Eur.

Vỷ'chèg-dà *River* 700 m. U.S.S.R., Eur.

Vỷsh'ni Vö-lô'chek *City* R.S.F.S.R., U.S.S.R., Eur.; factories

W

Wäas, Mount *Peak* 12,585 ft. Wash., U.S.

Wä'bash *River* 475 m. Ind.-Ill., U.S.

Wä'cō *City* cen. Tex., U.S.; pop. 95,326; commerce, shipping

Wä-daï', Ouä-daï' *Former sultanate* now in E Chad

Wad'ding-tön, Mount *Peak* 13,260 ft. Brit. Colombia, Canada

Waī-ki-ki' (kē') *Beach* Oahu, Haw., U.S.

Waīn-gàn'gä *River* 360 m. cen. India

Wä-kä-mä-tsu 1. *City* Kyushu, Japan; coal port. 2. *City* Honshu, Japan; pottery, fabrics

Wä-kä-yä-mä *City* * of *Prefecture* Honshu, Japan; port

Wäke'fïeld *City,* county borough, N England; coal, manufacturing

Wäke Island *Island* (U.S.) N cen. Pacific O.

Wäl'brzych (bzhik), **Wäl'dèn-bûrg** *City* SW Poland

Wäl'chè-rèn (väl'kè) *Island* off SW Netherlands

Wäl'deck *Former state* W Germany

Wäles *Principality* W Great Britain, *Division* of United Kingdom; 8000 sq. m.; pop. 2,720,000; * Cardiff; 12 counties

Wäl'grēen Coast *Region* coast of Antarctica

Wäl'là-sey (si) *County borough* NW England; docks

Wal'ling-förd *Town* S Conn., U.S.; pop. 35,714

Wal'lis and Fu-tu'nà (fōō-tōō') *Island groups* (Fr.) cen. Pacific O.; * Matu-Utu

Wäl-lō'ni-à = name for Fr. speaking area of Belgium

Wălls'end *Municipal borough* N England; coal area

Wăl'nut Creek *City* W Cal., U.S.; pop. 39,-844; residential

Wăl'săll *County borough* W cen. England

Wăl'tham *City* NE Mass., U.S.; pop. 61,-582; watches

Wăl'thăm-stōw *Municipal borough* SE England; industry

Wän'chuän', was **Käl'gän'** *City* N China

Wän'hsien' (shi-en') *City* S cen. China; port

Wän'nè-Eĭck'il (vän', ĭk') *City* W West Germany; coal, beer

Wän'stead and Wood'förd (sted) *Municipal borough* SE England

Wäp-si-pĭn'i-cŏn *River* 255 m. E Iowa, U.S.

Wă'ràn-gàl *City* S cen. India

Wär'bûr-tŏn *River* 275 m. S cen. Australia

Wår'dhä *River* 290 m. cen. India

Wärm Springs *Village* W Ga., U.S.; site of health foundation estab. by F. D. Roosevelt

Wär're-gō *River* 400 m. E cen. Australia

Wär'ren 1. *City* NE Ohio, U.S.; pop. 63,-494; steel. 2. *City* SE Mich., U.S.; pop. 179,260

Wär'ring-tön *County borough* NW England; manufacturing

Wär'săw, Wär-szä'wä (vär, vä) *City* * of *Department* and * of Poland, cen. part; pop. 1,273,600; commerce, manufacturing

Wär'tà, Wär'the (vär'-

tà) *River* 445 m. W Poland

Wär'wick (ik) *City* R.I. U.S.; pop. 83,694

Wăr'wick-shìre *County* cen. England

Wä'sàtch Mountain *Peak* 13,550 ft. Colo., U.S.

Wäsh'ing-tön *City* see DISTRICT OF COLUMBIA

Wäsh'ing-tön 1. *City* * of U.S., E part; co-extensive with fed. distr.: Dist. of Columbia; 69 sq. m.; pop. 756,510; political, cultural, educational cen. 2. *State* NW U.S.; 68,192 sq. m.; pop. 3,409,169; * Olympia; 39 counties; lumber, fruit, fish, quarries. 3. *Lake* W cen. Wash., U.S.

Wäsh'ing-tön *State*, named for first President of U.S., George Washington; 68,192 sq. m.; *pop.*: 3,409,-169 (*rank:* 22nd); NW, Pacific U.S.; *Boundaries:* Oregon, Idaho, Canada, Pacific Ocean; *Major cities:* Seattle, Tacoma, * Olympia, Spokane; *Major rivers:* Columbia, Snake; *Major lakes:* Lake Chelan, F. D. Roosevelt; 39 counties.

Nickname: Evergreen State, Chinook State; *Motto:* "Al-ki" (Bye and Bye); *Flag:* state seal on green field; *Flower:* coastal rhododendron; *Bird:* willow goldfinch; *Tree:* western hemlock; *Song: Washington, My Home.*

Industry: printing, publishing, transportation equipment, machinery, metals, manufacture of aircraft, chemicals, primary metals; *Natural resources:* forest, coal, uranium, silicon, stone, fish; *Major source of income:* government, whole-

sale & retail trade, manufacturing.

Admitted to Union: 1889 (42nd state).

Places of interest: Mt. Ranier Ntl. Park, Olympia Ntl. Park.

Wäsh'i-tă *River* 500 m. Okla., U.S.   [Kenya

Wa'sō Nyi'rō *River* cen.

Wă'têr-bur-ẏ (ber) *City* S Conn., U.S.; pop. 108,033; brass. cen.

Wă'têr-förd *County* S Eire

Wă'têr-lōō 1. *City* NE Iowa, U.S.; pop. 75,-533; commerce, manufacturing. 2. *Commune* cen. Belgium; Napoleon's defeat 1815

Wă'têr-tön - Glā'cier (shêr) *International Park* Alberta, Canada-Mont., U.S.

Wă'têr-town *Town* NE Mass., U.S.; pop. 39,-307; textiles

Wät'förd *Municipal borough* SE England

Wät'lings Island was **San Sal'và-dôr** *Island* of Bahamas

Wät'sön, Mount *Peak* 11,470 ft. Utah, U.S.

Wät'tèn-scheid (shīt) *City* W West Germany; factories, coal

Wău-kē'gàn *City* NE Ill., U.S.; pop. 65,-269; wire, iron

Wău'kè-shă *City* SE Wisc., U.S.; pop. 40,258; manufacturing

Wău-wà-tō'sà *City* SE Wisc., U.S.; pop. 58,676

Wä'vêr-ley (li) *Municipality* SE Australia

Wà-zir-i-stän' *Mountain area* W Pakistan

We, Weh (wā) *Island* off Sumatra, Indonesia; imp. port

Webbe *River* 280 m. SE Ethiopia

Wed'dèll Sea *Arm* of Atlantic O., Antarctica

Wei (wā) *River* 400 m. N cen. China

Wei'hai'wei (wā'hī'-wā') *City* NE China; port

Wei'hsien' (wā'shi-en') *City* NE China; trade

Wei'mär (vī') *City* SW East Germany; Ger. Rep., called **Wei'mär, Rep.** formed here 1919

Weiss'hôrn (vīs') *Peak* 14,800 ft. Switzerland

Weiss'kū-gèl (v ī s') *Peak* 12,290 ft. Austria-Italy

Weiss'miēs (vīs') *Peak* 13,225 ft. Switzerland

Wel'lånd Ship Cà-nal' *Canal* L. Erie-L. Ontario, Canada

Wel'ling-tön *City* * of New Zealand, North I.; pop. 288,000; port

Wel'tè-vre-dèn (vel', vrä) *Section* of Batavia, Indonesia

Wem'bley (bli) *Municipal borough* SE England

Wer'rä (ver') *River* 280 m. cen. West Germany

We'sêr (vä') *River* 280 m. N cen. West Germany

We-sêr-mun'dè (vä) now BREMERHAVEN

Wes'sèx *Anc. kingdom* S Great Britain

West Al'lis *City* SE Wisc., U.S.; pop. 71,-723; manufacturing

West Ben'gàl *State* NE India incl. Calcutta

West Brom'wich (ich) *County borough* W cen. England

West Co-vi'nà (vē') *City* SW Calif., U.S.; pop. 68,034; fruit

Wes'têrn Äus-trāl'iä *State* W third of Australia; * Perth

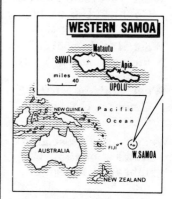

Wes'têrn Sà-mō'à, The Independent State of

Country, S Pacific Ocean; 1,100 sq. m.; pop. 199,000; * Apia; geographic districts; *Main islands:* Savai'i, Upolu, Manono, Apolima; *Geog.:* volcanic rocks, coral reefs; *Climate:* tropical.

Flag: Southern Cross top left corner on background of red.

Ethnic comp.: Samoans, Pacific Islanders, Europeans; *Language:* Samoan, English (official), *Religion:* Christian.

Products: copra, bananas, cocoa, fish, taro, coffee, bark, cloth, handicrafts; *Minerals:* none; *Major exports:* copra, bananas, cocoa, taro; *Major imports:* meat, clothing and textiles, flour, canned fish, motor vehicles, tobacco; *Industries:* tourism, handicrafts, fruit processing, furniture, clothing, soap.

Currency: W Samoan dollar (at par with New Zealand dollar).

Head of Government: scion of traditional line — after this head of state will be elected by legislature; *Legislature:* Legislative Assembly; *Judiciary:* Supreme Court highest court.

West Ham *County borough* SE England

West Hart'förd *Town* S Conn., U.S.; pop. 68,031; residential

West Här'tle-pööl *Municipal borough* N England

West Hā'ven *City* S Conn., U.S.; pop. 52,851

West In'dies Associated States *Country*, Caribbean; 1,120 sq. m.; pop. 562,000; *Main cities:* * Castries, St. Georges, Kingstown, Roseau, St. Johns, Basseterre; *Geog.:* in-

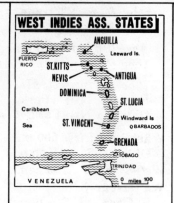

WEST INDIES ASS. STATES

ner arc volcanic rock, outer arc sandstone, limestone; *Climate:* tropical.

Ethnic comp.: Negroes, Mulattoes, Europeans, Caribs; *Language:* English (official); *Religion:* Anglican, Roman Catholic.

Products: bananas, coconut oil, cocoa, copra, nutmeg, rum, salt, vanilla, molasses, arrowroot, sweet potatoes; *Major exports:* bananas, sugar, cotton; *Major imports:* food; *Industries:* tourism, hydroelectric plants, rum distilleries, fishing, canning.

Currency: W Indian dollar.

Government: All islands self-governing internally, usually under Prime Minister. Britain responsible for defense and foreign affairs.

West I'ri-än (ē') *Division* of Indonesia, W half of New Guinea

West'land *City* SE Mich., U.S.; pop. 86,749

West Lō'thi-ån *County* SE Scotland

West'mēath *County* N cen. Eire

West'min-stêr 1. *City and Borough* cen. London England. 2. *City* S Cal., U.S.; pop. 59,865

West'môr-land *County* NW England

West New Gui'nea = WEST IRIAN

West New York *City*

NE N.J., U.S.; pop. 40,627

Wes'tön Peak *Peak* 13,500 ft. Colo., U.S.

West Or'ange (ȧnj) *City* NE N.J., U.S.; pop. 43,715

West Pälm Bēach *City* SE Fla., U.S.; pop. 57,375; resort

West-phä'liȧ (fä') *Area* (prov. of former Ger. state of Prussia) West Germany; mines

West Point U.S. Military Academy SE N.Y., U.S.

Western Sȧ-mō'ȧ, Terr. of *Islands, Terr.* of New Zealand, W Samoa Is.; copra

West Span'ish Peak *Peak* 13,620 ft. Colo., U.S.

West Vîr-gin'iȧ (jin') *State*, named in honor of Elizabeth, the "Virgin Queen;" 24,-181 sq. m.; *pop.:* 1,744,237 (*rank:* 34th); E coast — SE U.S.; *Boundaries:* Pennsylvania, Maryland, Virginia, Kentucky, Ohio; *Major cities:* * Charleston, Huntington, Wheeling; *Major rivers:* Ohio, Monongahela, Potomac, Kanawha; *Major lakes:* East Lynn Reservoir; 55 counties.

Nickname: Mountain State, Panhandle State; *Motto:* "Montani semper liberi" (Mountaineers are always free); *Flag:* state seal on blue-bordered white field; *Flower:* rhododendron (big laurel); *Bird:* cardinal; *Animal:* black bear; *Tree:* sugar maple; *Song:* The West Virginia Hills.

Industry: metals, printing, publishing, iron, processed food, coal, forestry & mining, production of chemials; *Natural resources:* coal, petroleum, natural gas, salt, forests; *Major*

source of income: manufacturing.

Admitted to Union: 1863 (35th state).

Places of interest: White Sulphur Springs, Harper's Ferry, Grave Creek Mound.

Wet'têr-hôrn (v e t') *Peak* 12,150 ft. cen. Switzerland

Wet'têr-hôrn Peak 14,020 ft. Colo., U.S.

Wex'förd *County* SE Eire

Wey'mouth (wā'muth) *City* E Mass., U.S.; pop. 54,610; shoes, granite

Whēa'tön *City* Md., U.S.; pop. 66,247

Whēe'lêr Peak 1. *Peak* 13,060 ft. E Nev., U.S. 2. *Peak* 13,150 ft. N N.M·, U.S.

Whēe'ling *City* N W.Va., U.S.; pop. 48,188; manufacturing, commerce

White 1. *River* 690 m. Ark., U.S. 2. *River* 325 m. S.D., U.S. 3. *River* 280 m. NW Tex., U.S.

White'crôss Mountain *Peak* 13,550 ft. Colo., U.S.

White Dōme *Peak* 13,-615 ft. Colo., U.S.

White'hôrse *Town* * of Yukon Terr., Canada; S part

White'house Mountain *Peak* 13,490 ft. Colo., U.S.

White Mountain *Peak* 14,240 ft. E cen. Calif., U.S.

White Mountains 1. *Mountains* Calif.-Nev., U.S. 2. *Mountains* N.H., U.S.

White Nile see NILE R.

White Peak *Peak* 13,-600 ft. Colo., U.S.

White Pīne Peak *Peak* 11,490 ft. Nev., U.S.

White Plāins *City* SE N.Y., U.S.; pop. 50,-220; residential

White Rock Mountain *Peak* 13,530 ft. Colo., U.S.

White Rus'sian or **Byelö-rus'sian** S. S. R.

(rush'ȧn) *Constituent republic* of U.S.S.R., W part; * Minsk; livestock, agriculture

Whīte Sea *Gulf* of Barents S. N U.S.S.R. Eur. [TA R.

White Vōl'tȧ see VOL-

Whit'ney, Mount (ni) *Peak* 14,495 ft. SE cen. Calif., highest in continental U.S.

Whit'tiêr *City* S Cal., U.S.; pop. 72,863; residential

Wich'i-tă 1. *City* S cen. Kans., U.S.; pop. 276,554; industry, commerce. 2. *River* 230 m. N Tex., U.S.

Wich'i-tă Fălls *City* N Tex., U.S.; pop. 97,564; oil cen.

Wick'lōw *County* E Eire

Wid'nes *Municipal borough* NW England; manufacturing

Wien (vēn)= VIENNA

Wies'bä-dėn (vēs') *City* W cen. West Germany

Wig'ȧn *County borough* NW England

Wight, Isle of (wīt) *Island County* of England, English Channel; resorts

Wig'tön *County* SW Scotland

Wild'spit-zė (vilt') *Peak* 12,380 ft. Austria

Wil-hel-mi'nȧ (m ē') *Peak* 15,585 ft. W cen. New Guinea

Wil-helms-hä'vėn (vil) *City* NW West Germany; North S. port

Wilkes'-Bar-rė *City* E Pa., U.S.; pop. 58,856; industry

Wilkes Land *Region* Indian O. coast, Antarctica

Wil'lėm-städ (vil') *City* * of Netherlands Antilles on Curacao I.; port

Willes'dėn *Municipal borough* SE England

Wil'liȧms-bûrg *City* SE Va., U.S.; colonial restoration

Wil'liȧm-sön, Mount *Peak* 14,385 ft. cen. Calif., U.S.

Wil'liȧms-pôrt *City* N cen. Pa., U.S.; pop.

37,918; manufacturing

Wil'lough-bẏ (lô) *City* SE Australia

Wil'ming-tön 1. *City* N Del., U.S.; pop. 80,386; port, commerce, industry. 2. *City* SE N.C., U.S.; pop. 46,169; commercial port

Wil'nō (vil') = VILNYUS

Wil'sön, Mount *Peak* 14,240 ft. Colo., U.S.

Wil'sön Peak 1. *Peak* 14,025 ft. Colo., U.S. 2. *Peak* 11,095 ft. Utah, U.S.

Wilt'shire *County* S England

Wim'ble-dön (b'l) *Municipal borough* S England; tennis events

Wim'mêr-ȧ *River* 230 m. SE Australia

Win'chėll, Mount *Peak* 13,750 ft. Calif., U.S.

Wind'hoek (vint'hook) *Town* * of South-West Africa; minerals, educational cen.

Win'döm Peak *Peak* 14,090 ft. Colo., U.S.

Wind'sör 1. *City* SE Ontario, Canada; industrial cen. esp. cars *Municipal borough* 2. or **New Wind'sör** S England; Windsor castle

Wind'wȧrd Islands 1. *Islands* (Brit.) S chain of Lesser Antilles, West Indies; * St. George's on Grenada I. 2. *Islands* of Society Is., Fr. Polynesia, incl. Tahiti

Wind'wȧrd Passage *Channel* E Cuba-NW Hispaniola

Win'isk *River* 400 m. Ontario, Canada

Win'ni-peg 1. *City* * of Manitoba, Canada, S part; pop. 257,005; cattle, grain market. 2. *Lake* S cen. Manitoba, Canada

Win-ni-peg-ō'sis *Lake* W Manitoba, Canada

Win'stön-Sä'lėm *City* N cen. N.C., U.S.; pop. 132,913

Win'têr-thur' (tōōr)

Commune NE cen. Switzerland

Wis-con'sin *State*, named from French corruption of Indian word meaning "gathering of the waters;" 56,154 sq. m.; *pop.*: 4,417,933 (*rank*: 16th); Lakes Region — N U.S.; *Boundaries*: Minnesota, Iowa, Illinois, Michigan, Lake Michigan, Lake Superior; *Major cities*: Milwaukee, * Madison; *Major rivers*: St. Croix, Mississippi; *Major lakes*: Winnebago, Poygan, Mendota, Pentenwell Castle Rock; 72 counties.

Nickname: Badger State, America's Dairyland; *Motto*: "Forward;" *Flag*: state seal on blue field; *Flower*: wood violet; *Bird*: robin; *Animal*: badger, *Fish*: muskellunge; *Wildlife animal*: white-tailed deer; *Tree*: sugar maple; *Song*: On Wisconsin.

Industry: beer, metals, transportation equipment, machinery, paper & pulp; *Major source of income*: manufacturing.

Admitted to Union: 1848 (30th state).

Places of interest: Chequamegon Ntl. Forest, Nicolet.

Wis'têr, Mount *Peak* 11,480 ft. NW Wyo., U.S.

Wis'mär (vis') *City* on Bay NW East Germany; port

Wit'tėn (vit') *City* W cen. West Germany

Wit'tėn-bêrg (vit') *City* N East Germany; manufacturing

Wit-tėn-bêr'gė (v i t) *City* S East Germany; port

Wō'bûrn *City* NE Mass., U.S.; pop. 37,406; residential

Wlo-cla'wek (vlô-tslä'vek) *Commune* N

Poland; manufacturing

Wō'king *Urban district* S England; resort

Wol'lȧs-tön *Lake* Saskatchewan, Canada

Wol'vêr - hamp - tön (wool') *County borough* W cen. England; iron, coal area

Wood, Mount *Peak* 15,880 ft. Yukon, Canada

Wood'bridge *Town* cen. N.J., U.S.; pop. 78,846; brick, tile

Wood Grēen *Urban district* SE England; residential

Wood Mountain *Peak* 13,640 ft. Colo., U.S.

Wōōn-sock'ėt *City* N R.I., U.S.; pop. 46,820; manufacturing

Worces'têr (woos') 1. *City* cen. Mass., U.S.; pop. 176,572; industrial cen. 2. *County borough*, * of **Worces'têr - shire** (woos') county W cen. England; manufacturing

Wörms *City* SW cen. West Germany; river port

Wör'thing *Municipal borough* S England; resort

Wran'gėl Island *Island* off N U.S.S.R. Asia, Arctic O.

Wran'gėll, Mount *Peak* 14,000 ft. of **Wran'gėll Mts.** S Alas., U.S.

Wro'claw (vrô'tsläf), Ger. **Bres'lau** (lou) *City* * of Department SW Poland; commerce, manufacturing

Wu (wōō) *River* 500 m. cen. China

Wu'chäng' (wōō') *City* E cen. China; * of Hupeh prov.

Wu'chow' (wōō'jō') now TSANGWU

Wu'hän' (wōō') = The HAN CITIES

Wu'hing' (wōō') was **Hu'chow'** (hōō'jō') *City* E China

Wu'hsien' (wōō'shi-en') was **Sōō'chow'** (jō') *City* E China; port, anc. city

Wu'hu' (wōō'hōō') *City* E China; trade cen.

Wul'stèn Peak (wool') *Peak* 13,666 ft. Colo., U.S.

Wup'pêr-tϊl (voop') *City* on **Wupper R.** W cen. West Germany industrial

Wûrt'tèm-bêrg *Former state* S Germany; n o w BADEN-WURTTEMBERG

Wûrz'bûrg *City* S cen. West Germany; manufacturing

Wu'sih' (wōō'shē') *City* E China; trade

Wu' Taï' Shän' (wōō') *Mountain* 10,000 ft. NE China; sacred to Buddhists

Wu'tsin' (wōō'jin') was **Chäng'chow'** (jō') *City* E China; trade

Wu'wei' (wōō'wā') was **Liäng'chow'** (jō') *City* N cen. China

Wȳ'àn-dotte *City* SE Mich., U.S.; pop. 41,-061; chemicals

Wȳn'bêrg *Town* S Rep. of South Africa

Wy-ō'ming *State,* named after Wyoming Valley, Pennsylvania Indian word means "alternating mountains and valleys;" 97,914 sq. m.; *pop.*: 332,416 (*rank*: 49th); Rocky Mt. U.S.; *Boundaries*: Montana, South Dakota, Nebraska, Idaho, Colorado, Utah; *Major cities*: * Cheyenne, Casper; *Major rivers*: North Platte, Bighorn, Green, Snake; *Major lakes*: Yellowstone, Jackson, Flaming Gorge Reservoir; 23 counties.

Nickname: Equality State; *Motto*: "Equal Rights;" *Flag*: state seal & buffalo on a red & white bordered blue field; *Flower*: Indian paintbrush; *Bird*: meadowlark; *Tree*: cottonwood; *Song*: *Wyoming*.

Industry: petroleum & coal items, food items, stone, clay & glass items, lumber & wood, printing, publishing; *Natural resources*: petroleum, natural gas, sodium salts, iron ore, uranium, forests; *Major source of income*: government.

Admitted to Union: 1890 (44th state).

Places of interest: Yellowstone Ntl. Park, Grand Teton Ntl. Park, Devil's Tower.

X

Xan'the (zan') *City* NE Greece

Xin-gu' (shēng-gōō') *River* 1300 m. cen. Brazil

Y

Yä'än', Yä'chow' (jō') *Town* S China

Yak'i-mä *City* S Wash., U.S.; pop. 45,588; business

Yà-kutsk' A.S.S.R. (kōōtsk') *Republic* R.S F.S.R., U.S.S.R., Asia; * **Yà-kutsk'**

Yäl'tà *Town* R.S.F.S.R. U.S.S.R., Eur.; WW II conference site

Yä'lu' (lōō') *River* 300 m. Manchuria-Korea

Yä'lung' (loong') *River* 725 m. S China

Yä-mä-gä-tä *City* * of *Prefecture* Honshu, Japan; silk cen.

Yä-ma-gu-chi (goo) *City* * of *Prefecture* Honshu, Japan

Yà-ma'lö-Ne-nets' *National district* R.S.F.S.R., U.S.S.R., Asia

Yä-mä-nä-shi *Prefecture* Honshu, Japan

Yä-mä-tō *Former province* Honshu, Japan; now NARA

Ya'nà *River* 750 m. U.S.S.R., Asia

Yäng'ku' (chu') *City* NE China

Yang'tzē' *River* 3200 m. China's chief river, S part

Ya-oun-de' (ōōn-da') *Town* * of Cameroun; pop. 130,000

Yap *Island* of *Group* W Caroline Is., U.S. Trust Terr.

Yä-qui' (kē') *River* 420 m. N.M., U.S.

Yär-kand' *River* 500 m. *Town,* Oasis W China

Yär'mouth, Greāt Yär'-mouth (muth) *County borough* E England; port, herring

Yä-rö-slavl' *City* * of *Region* R.S.F.S.R., U.S.S.R., Eur.

Yär-vi-cō'yä *Peak* 17,-390 ft. N Chile

Yä-wä-tä *City* Kyushu, Japan; iron works; port

Yè-gôr'èvsk *City* W c e n. R.S.F.S.R., U.S.S.R., Eur.

Ye'hsien' (shi-en'), was **Lu'chow'** (jō') *City* NE China

Yeisk (yä'esk) *Town* R.S.F.S.R., U.S.S.R., Eur.; port

Yè-lets' *City* R.S.F.S.R. U.S.S.R., Eur.; trade

Yel'lōw 1. *River* China, see HWANG HO. 2. *Sea* China-Korea

Yel'lōw-stōne 1. *River* 670 m. Wyo.-Mont., U.S. 2. *Lake* in *National Park* NW Wyo., U.S.

Yem'èn, Yemen Arab Republic, *Country,* Arabian Peninsula; 74,000 sq. m.; pop. 5,000,000 ±; 6 provinces; *Main cities*: * San'a, Taiz, Hodeida, Sadah; *Geog.*: hot, sandy, semi-desert strip, well-watered mt. interior; *Climate*: mt., desert.

Flag: red, white, black horizontal bands (top to bottom), green star centered on white stripe.

Ethnic comp.: Arabs (Yemenis); *Language*: Arabic (official); *Religion*: Islam (Sunni and Shia) (state).

Products: coffee, cotton, gat (narcotic), grapes, oil seeds, textiles, hides, raisins, salt; *Minerals*: none surveyed; *Major exports*: coffee, hides, skins, salt, gat; *Major imports*: textiles, sugar, glass; *Industries*: light industries, salt extraction.

Currency: rial.

Head of Government: President; *Legislature*: unicameral National Council; *Judiciary*: tribal system.

Yemen, Peoples Dem Rep. of *Country* SW Arabian penin.; SW Asia; 112,000 sq. mi.; pop. 1,280,000

Yè-nà-ki'yè-vö (kē') *City* Ukraine U.S.S.R., Eur.

Yen'än' or **Fu'shih'** (fōō') *Town* NE cen. China

Yen'bō, Yan'bu *City* W Arabia; Red S. port

Ye-ni-sei' (sä') *River* 2800 m. W Siberia U.S.S.R. Asia

Yer'bà Bue'nà Island (bwä'), was **Gōat I.** *Island* San Francisco Bay, Calif., U.S.

Ye-re-vän', E-re-vän' *City* * of Armenian S.S.R. SW U.S.S.R., Eur.

Yezd *City* * of *Province* cen. Iran; industrial

Ying'kōw', New' chwäng' (nū') *City* Manchuria, China; port

Yok-kaï-chi *City* S Honshu, Japan; port

Yō-ko-hä-mä *City* SE Honshu, Japan; imp. silk port, industry, commerce

Yō-ko-su-kä *City* SE Honshu, Japan; port

Yom *River* 300 m. NW Thailand

Yo-nä-go *Town* W Honshu, Japan; harbor

Yo-ne-zä-wä *City* N Honshu, Japan; weaving

Yon'kêrs *City* SE N.Y., U.S.; pop. 204,370; factories

Yônne *Department* NE cen. France

Yôrk 1. *City* S Pa., U.S.; pop. 50,335; industry. 2. *City, county borough* of **Yôrk'-shîre** county N England; manufacturing

Yôrk'town (toun) *Town* SE Va., U.S.; site of surrender ending Amer. Revolution 1781

Yôr'u-bà-land *Area,* former kingdom, N Nigeria

Yō-sem'i-tē *National Park* cen. Calif., U.S.; falls, cliffs

Youngs'town (yungs'-toun) *City* NE Ohio, U.S.; pop. 139,788; industrial cen.

Yp'si-lon *Peak* 13,505 ft. Colo., U.S.

Yu now SIYANG R., 400 m. S China

Yuän' *River* 500 m. SE cen. China

Yū-cä-mä'ni *Peak* 17,-860 ft. S Peru

Yū-cà-tan' *Peninsula* cen. and South America; incl. *State* SE Mexico, Brit. Honduras, N Guatemala

Yug (yōōk) *River* 330 m. U.S.S.R., Eur.

Yū-go-slä'vià, Socialist Federal Republic

of *Country,* SE Europe; 98,720 sq. m.; pop. 20,924,000; 6 republics; *Main cities:* * Belgrade, Zagreb, Skopje, Surajevo, Llubljiana; *Main rivers:* Danube & tributaries (Drava, Sava, Morava, Varder); *Geog.:* 2 sections — lowland hills, plains, rugged mts.; *Climate:* coast — hot summers, mild winters, interior — moderate.

Flag: blue, white, red horizontal bands (top to bottom) large red star edged with yellow in center.

Ethnic comp.: Serbs, Croats, Solvenes, Macedonians, Albanians, Montenegrans, Hungarians; *Language:* Serbo-Croatian, Slovenian, Macedonian (official); *Religion:* Eastern Orthodox, Roman Catholic, Moslem.

Products: maize, wheat, livestock, grapes, plums, wines, spirits, timber, sugar, fish, copper, lead, lignite, iron ore, petroleum, iron, steel; *Minerals:* coal, iron ore, petroleum, bauxite, copper, lead, zinc; *Major exports:* meat, fish, ships, machinery, tobacco, hardwood; *Major imports:* machinery and transportation equipment, iron, steel, wheat, raw materials, chemicals; *Industries:* tourism, manufacturing (metals, woodwork, chemicals, textiles), food processing, mining.

Currency: dinar.

Head of Government: President; *Legislature:* Federal Assembly; *Judiciary:* Constitutional Court — rules on disputes between Republic and Federal Government

or between Republics.

Yū'kon 1. *Territory* NW Canada; 205,346 sq. m.; pop. 15,000; * Whitehorse; forests, minerals. 2. *River* SW Yukon terr.

Yung'ki' (yoong'ji'), **Ki'rin'** (kē') *City* E Manchuria, China; imp. trade cen.

Yung'kia' (yoong'jiä'), was **Wèn'chow'** (jō') *City* E China; port

Yung'ning' (yoong'), was **Nän'ning'** *Town* SE China; port

Yung'ting' (yoong'), or **Hun** (hoon) *River* 300 m. NE China

Yun'nän' 1. *Province* S China. 2. *City* its * now KUNMING

Z

Zaan-däm' *Commune* W Netherlands; lumber

Zab, Great *River* 260 m. SE Turkey, Asia

Zab, Little *River* 230 m. Iran-Iraq

Zäb'rze (zhe), Ger. **Hin'dèn-bêrg** *City* SW Poland; industrial

Zä-cä-te'cäs (tä') *City* * of *State* cen. Mexico; mines

Zä'där, It. **Zä'rä** *City* W Yugoslavia; port

Zag'à-zig *City* Lower Egypt; trade cen.

Zà-gôrsk' *Town* R.S.F.S.R., U.S.S.R., Eur.; pilgrimage spot

Zä'greb *City* * of Croatia Rep., NW Yugoslavia; industry, commerce

Zaire, Republic of *Country;* Formerly Democratic Republic of the Congo; SC Africa; 895,350 sq. m.; pop. 22,113,000; 8 provinces, Federal District of Kinshasa; *Main cities:* * Kinshasa, Lubumbashi, Kisangani, Jadotville, Luluabourg, Matadi; *Main rivers:* Zaire (Congo), tributaries; *Geog.:* basin

shaped plateau, covered by tropical rain forest, surrounded by mt. terraces in W, plateaus merging into savannahs in S and SW, dense grasslands in NW, high mt. in E; *Climate:* hot, humid.

Flag: green with gold ball in center. Inside ball is hand-held torch of brown & red.

Ethnic comp.: Pygmies, Negroes, Hamites; *Language:* French (official), Lingala, Kingwana, Kikongo, Tshiluba, plus 200 languages, dialects; *Religions:* Roman Catholic, animist, Protestant.

Products: palm oil, rubber, coffee, timber, cotton, copper, diamonds, pitch blende, azurite, malachite; *Minerals:* copper, zinc, cobalt, diamonds, tin, columbite-tantalite, manganese, coal, oil; *Major exports:* copper, diamonds, coffee, palm oil; *Major imports:* machinery, transportation equipment, textiles, foodstuffs, manufactured goods; *Industries:* food processing, forestry, mining, clothing manufacture, textile mills.

Currency: zaire.

Head of Government: President; *Legislature:* unicameral National Assembly; *Judiciary:* independent judiciary, Supreme

Court of Justice at apex.

Zaire *River* ab. 3000 m. W. Africa; formerly **Congo**

Za - kar - pat'ska - ya Russ. for RUTHE-NIA

Zä-ko-pä'ne *Commune* S Poland; resort

Zäm-bä'les (lâs) *Mountain range, Province* Luzon, Phil. Is.

Zam-bē'zi *River* 1650 m. S Africa

Zam'bi-ä, Republic of *Country;* Formerly Republic of Northern Rhodesia; SC Africa; 290,590 sq. m.; pop. 4,608,000; 8 provinces; *Main cities:* * Lusaka, Kitwe, Ndola, Livingstone; *Main river:* Zambezi; *Geog.:* high plateau, watershed crosses N, Victoria Falls; *Climate:* subtropical — modified by altitude.

Flag: green field, 3 small vertical stripes of red, plack, orange in lower right, orange eagle above stripe.

Ethnic comp.: Bantu, Asian, European; *Language:* English (official), Bantu (Nyanja, Benba, Lozi, Luvale, Tonga); *Religion:* animist, Protestant, Roman Catholic.

Products: maize, tobacco, groundnuts, timber, manganese, zinc, cobalt, lead, livestock, vegetables, cotton; *Minerals:* copper, cobalt, lead, zinc, iron (unexploited); *Major exports:* copper, lead, zinc, cobalt, tobacco; *Major imports:* machinery, transportation equipment, chemicals, food, petroleum products, manufactured articles; *Industries:* mining, food processing, quarrying, textiles, furniture, construction materials.

Currency: kwacha.

Head of Government: President; *Legislature:* unicameral National Assembly; *Judiciary:* independent, Supreme Court at apex.

Zäm-bo-än'gä *City* * of *Province* Mindanao, Phil. Is.; trade cen.

Zānes'ville *City* SE cen. Ohio, U.S.; pop. 33,045; manufacturing

Zan'te, Zà-kyn'thös *Island Department* Ionian Is., Greece

Zan'zi-bär *City* on *Island* off E Africa, former Brit. prot. and Rep., now part of Tanzania

Zà-pä'tà *Peninsula* and *Swamp* W cen. Cuba

Zä-pö-rô'zhė *City* * of *Region* Ukraine, U.S.S.R., Eur.; industrial cen.

Zä-rä-gō'zä Span. for SARAGOSSA

Zär'dėh Kuh (kōō) *Peak* 14,920 ft. W Iran

Zēe'länd *Province* SW Netherlands

Zem - pō - äl - te - pec' (zäm) *Peak* 11,135 ft. SE Mexico

Zen-shu *Town* SW Korea

Ze-rav-shän' *River* 400 m. U.S.S.R. cen. Asia

Zet'land = SHET-LAND *County* and *Islands*

Ze'yà (zyā') *River* 765 m. U.S.S.R., Asia

Zhda'növ *City* Ukraine, U.S.S.R.; port

Zhi-tô'mir, Ji-tô'mir *City* * of *Region* Ukraine, U.S.S.R.; industrial

Zi-näl' Rōt'hôrn *Peak* 13,855 ft. SW Switzerland

Zï'ön *Hill* NE Jerusalem, Israel; site of anc. Temple

Zï'ön *National park* SW Utah, U.S.; cliffs

Ziz'kôv (zhish') *Former city,* now incl. in Prague, Czechoslovakia

Zlä-tö-ust' (ōōst') *City* R.S.F.S.R., U.S.S.R., Asia; machinery, iron

Zom'bà *City* * of Malawi; pop. 11,000

Zôn-gul-däk' *City* * of *Vilayet* NW Turkey, Asia; port

Zuï'dêr Zēe *Former inlet* and *Lake,* now reclaimed land, N Netherlands

Zu'lu - land (zōō'lōō) *Area* of Natal prov. E South Africa

Zü'pō, Piz (pēts) *Peak* 13,120 ft. It.-Swiss border

Zu'rich (zoor'ik) *City* on *Lake* * of *Canton* NE cen. Switzerland; largest Swiss city; imp. industrial cen.; resort

Zwick'au (ou) *City* S cen. East Germany; factories, mines

Zwol'le *Commune* E Netherlands; industry

Zy-rär'dow (zhi, dōōf) *Commune* cen. Poland; textiles

Zẏr'i-àn *Autonomous Area* now KOMI A.S.S.R.